# ARCHBOLD

## 2014

### THIRD SUPPLEMENT TO THE 2014 EDITION

*EDITOR*

P.J. RICHARDSON, Q.C., LL.M. (Lond.), Dip. Crim. (CANTAB.)
*of Gray's Inn and the Inner Temple, Barrister*

*SUPPLEMENT EDITORS*

WILLIAM CARTER, M.A. (OXON.)
*of Gray's Inn, Barrister*

STEPHEN SHAY, B.A. (OXON.)
*of the Middle Temple, Barrister*

SWEET & MAXWELL

 THOMSON REUTERS

Published in 2014 by Sweet & Maxwell, Friars House, 160 Blackfriars Road, London, SE1 8EZ, part of Thomson Reuters (Professional) UK Limited (Registered in England & Wales, Company No.1679046. Registered Office and address for service: 2nd floor, Aldgate House, 33 Aldgate High Street, London, EC3N 1DL).
Printed and bound in Great Britain by Ashford Colour Press, Gosport, Hants.
Typeset by Sweet & Maxwell, Friars House, 160 Blackfriars Road, London, SE1 8EZ.
For further information on our products and services, visit: http://www.sweetandmaxwell.co.uk

No natural forests were destroyed to make this product; only farmed timber was used and replanted.

A CIP catalogue record for this book is available from the British Library

ISBN MAINWORK 978-0-414-02860-9
ISBN THIRD SUPPLEMENT 978-0-414-03082-4

# SERVICE INFORMATION

## The Archbold service

*Archbold: Criminal Pleading, Evidence and Practice* consists of one main text volume (including the tables and index). This volume is re-issued annually, and is updated by cumulative supplements, the e-update service (see below) and *Archbold Review*.

## The supplement

Three cumulative supplements, containing updating material for the main volume, are published in each year as part of the service.

This is the third supplement of 2014.

New material is incorporated into this supplement using the same paragraph numbers as appear in the mainwork. All material new to this supplement is marked in the text by a ★ bold star in the margin.

After consulting the main work on any given subject, reference should always be made to the same paragraph number in the current supplement to check that there have been no new developments since the main text volume was published. The supplement will also track material which has been removed or relocated as part of the re-issue process.

The back cover contains a list of all important developments included in this supplement for the first time and where they can be found.

All references in the text to cases, statutes and statutory instruments are contained in the tables printed at the beginning of this supplement.

Please email smg.archbold@thomson.com with comments/suggestions for any of the Archbold services.

## Archbold eBook upgrade

Archbold 2014 is available as an eBook on the iPad, PC and Mac. As a purchaser of *Archbold: Criminal Pleading, Evidence and Practice* 2014, 63rd edition you are also entitled to purchase one copy of the Archbold eBook at a special upgrade price. To find more information about the Archbold eBook please visit the Archbold website www.sweetandmaxwell.co.uk/archbold or contact our customer services team on 0845 600 9355.

## Archbold e-update activation code

As a subscriber to Archbold 2014 you have free and unlimited access to the accompanying weekly e-update service and online archive. If you are a new user accessing the service for the first time then please visit www.sweetandmaxwell.co.uk/archbold where you will be asked to complete a simple short registration process, and to enter the following activation code to start receiving updates:

AB2014

If you are an existing user of the e-update then your access will automatically be updated for the new edition and there is no need to re-register.

# TABLE OF CONTENTS

## TABLE OF CONTENTS

# ABBREVIATIONS OF LEGISLATION

The following abbreviations have been adopted throughout.

| | |
|---|---|
| AFA | Armed Forces Act |
| CAA | Criminal Appeal Act |
| CDA | Crime and Disorder Act |
| CDDA | Company Directors Disqualification Act |
| CEMA | Customs and Excise Management Act |
| CJA | Criminal Justice Act |
| CJCSA | Criminal Justice and Court Services Act |
| CJIA | Criminal Justice and Immigration Act |
| CJPA | Criminal Justice and Police Act |
| CJPOA | Criminal Justice and Public Order Act |
| CLA | Criminal Law Act |
| CPIA | Criminal Procedure and Investigations Act |
| C(S)A | Crime (Sentences) Act |
| CYPA | Children and Young Persons Act |
| DTA | Drug Trafficking Act |
| DTOA | Drug Trafficking Offences Act |
| ECHR | European Convention on Human Rights |
| FSMA | Financial Services and Markets Act |
| LASPOA | Legal Aid, Sentencing and Punishment of Offenders Act |
| MCA | Magistrates' Courts Act |
| MHA | Mental Health Act |
| PACE | Police and Criminal Evidence |
| PCA | Proceeds of Crime Act |
| PCCA | Powers of Criminal Courts Act |
| PCC(S)A | Powers of Criminal Courts (Sentencing) Act |
| PJA | Police and Justice Act |
| RIPA | Regulation of Investigatory Powers Act |
| RSA | Road Safety Act |
| RSC | Rules of the Supreme Court (Revision) |
| RTA | Road Traffic Act |
| RTOA | Road Traffic Offenders Act |
| SCA | Serious Crime Act |
| SOA | Sexual Offences Act |
| SOCPA | Serious Organised Crime and Police Act |
| VCRA | Violent Crime Reduction Act |
| YJCEA | Youth Justice and Criminal Evidence Act |

# TABLE OF STATUTES

*References in bold indicate where legislation is reproduced in full*

# TABLE OF NON-UK LEGISLATION

# TABLE OF EUROPEAN AND INTERNATIONAL TREATIES AND CONVENTIONS

*References in bold indicate where legislation is reproduced in full*

# TABLE OF EUROPEAN DIRECTIVES AND REGULATIONS

# TABLE OF STATUTORY INSTRUMENTS

*References in bold indicate where legislation is reproduced in full*

# TABLE OF CASES

# TABLE OF PRACTICE DIRECTIONS

*References in bold indicate where legislation is reproduced in full*

# TABLE OF HUMAN RIGHTS CASES

CHAPTER 1

# THE INDICTMENT

## II. *NATURE OF INDICTABLE OFFENCES*

### B. CLASSIFICATION OF OFFENCES

#### (1) By mode of trial

As to the insertion of section 22A into the MCA 1980 (low-value shoplifting to be a summary offence), see *post*, § 1-108a.  ★**1-18**

## III. *SENDINGS FOR TRIAL*

### B. PRINCIPAL PROVISIONS

#### (2) Sending of cases to the Crown Court

**Crime and Disorder Act 1998, ss.50A, 51–51E**

*Notices in serious or complex fraud cases*

With effect from March 27, 2014, the Public Bodies (Merger of the Director of Public Prosecutions and the Director of Revenue and Customs Prosecutions) Order 2014 (S.I. 2014 No. 834), art. 3(3), and Sched. 2, paras 14 and 15, amended section 51B of the 1998 Act, so as to repeal subsection (9)(c). Articles 5 and 6 of the order contain saving and transitional provisions.  ★**1-27**

**S.I. 2014 No. 834, arts 5, 6**

*The abolition of the office of the DRCP: supplementary*

**5.**—(1) This order does not affect the validity of anything done (or having effect as if done) by or in relation to the DRCP before the coming into force of this order.

(2) Anything done (or having effect as if done) by or in relation to the DRCP has effect, so far as is necessary for continuing its effect after the coming into force of this order, as if done by or in relation to the DPP.

(3) Anything (including legal proceedings) which at the coming into force of this order is in the process of being done by or in relation to the DRCP may be continued by or in relation to the DPP.

(4) So far as is necessary or appropriate, after the coming into force of this order, a reference to the DRCP in an enactment, agreement (whether written or not), instrument or other document is to be treated as a reference to the DPP.

(5) In this article—
  (a) a reference to the DRCP includes a reference to the RCPO, a Revenue and Customs Prosecutor, a member of the staff of the RCPO other than a Revenue and Customs Prosecutor and a person appointed under section 38 of the CRCA 2005, and
  (b) a reference to the DPP is to be read, so far as is necessary or appropriate, as being a reference to the CPS, a Crown Prosecutor, a member of the staff of the CPS other than a Crown Prosecutor or a person appointed under section 5 of the POA 1985.

*Saving of powers to conduct proceedings*

**6.**—(1) Where the DPP has conduct of proceedings by virtue of article 5(3), the DPP is to be treated, notwithstanding the repeals and amendments made by this order—
  (a) as acting under the enactment under which the DRCP was acting at the coming into force of this order, and
  (b) as having the same powers to take steps in relation to those proceedings as the DRCP would have had.

(2) In this article—

1

(a) a reference to the DRCP includes a reference to a Revenue and Customs Prosecutor and a person appointed under section 38 of the CRCA 2005, and

(b) a reference to the DPP is to be read, so far as is necessary or appropriate, as being a reference to a Crown Prosecutor or a person appointed under section 5 of the POA 1985.

Article 2 provides that the "CRCA 2005" is the Commissioners for Revenue and Customs Act 2005, the "DPP" is the Director of Public Prosecutions, the "DRCP" is the Director of Revenue and Customs Prosecutions, the "POA 1985" is the Prosecution of Offences Act 1985, and the "RCPO" is the Revenue and Customs Prosecutions Office.

### (5) Procedure

#### (a) *In a magistrates' court*

**1-34a**    The 2013 criminal practice directions (see the main work) are now reported at [2013] 1 W.L.R. 3164.

### D. Mode of Trial for Offences Triable Either Way and Certain Summary Offences

### (2) Procedure

#### (a) *Statutory provisions*

### Procedure for indication of intention as to plea

#### Magistrates' Courts Act 1980, ss.17A–17E

*Initial procedure: accused to indicate intention as to plea*

**1-88**    The plea before venue provisions in section 17A of the 1980 Act require that a defendant be present in court throughout the procedure and that he should be informed of his rights by the court itself and not merely by an advocate acting on his behalf; the legislature, in enacting section 17A, must have intended that, where a court failed to follow the requirements of the section, it was acting without jurisdiction every bit as much as if, for instance, it had purported to try a defendant on a charge of homicide; here, where the defendant had pleaded guilty to the either-way offence with which he was charged, after his counsel had informed the court that his client intended to plead guilty, but without any of the section 17A procedure being gone through, and had then been committed to the Crown Court for sentence, the proceedings were a nullity: *R. (Rahmdezfouli) v. Wood Green Crown Court* [2014] 1 Cr.App.R. 20, DC.

#### Magistrates' Courts Act 1980, s.22A

**★1-108a**    With effect from May 13, 2014 (Anti-social Behaviour, Crime and Policing Act 2014 (Commencement No. 2, Transitional and Transitory Provisions) Order 2014 (S.I. 2014 No. 949)), a new section 22A was inserted into the 1980 Act by the Anti-social Behaviour, Crime and Policing Act 2014, s.176(1) and (3), providing for "low-value shoplifting" to be a summary offence.

*Low-value shoplifting to be a summary offence*

**22A.**—(1) Low-value shoplifting is triable only summarily.

(2) But where a person accused of low-value shoplifting is aged 18 or over, and appears or is brought before the court before the summary trial of the offence begins, the court must give the person the opportunity of electing to be tried by the Crown Court for the offence and, if the person elects to be so tried—

(a) subsection (1) does not apply, and

(b) the court must send the person to the Crown Court for trial for the offence.

(3) "Low-value shoplifting" means an offence under section 1 of the Theft Act 1968 in circumstances where—

(a) the value of the stolen goods does not exceed £200,

(b) the goods were being offered for sale in a shop or any other premises, stall, vehicle or place from which there is carried on a trade or business, and

(c) at the time of the offence, the person accused of low-value shoplifting was, or was purporting to be, a customer or potential customer of the person offering the goods for sale.

(4) For the purposes of subsection (3)(a)—

    (a) the value of the stolen goods is the price at which they were being offered for sale at the time of the offence, and

    (b) where the accused is charged on the same occasion with two or more offences of low-value shoplifting, the reference to the value involved has effect as if it were a reference to the aggregate of the values involved.

(5) A person guilty of low-value shoplifting is liable on summary conviction to—

    (a) imprisonment for a period not exceeding 51 weeks (or 6 months, if the offence was committed before the commencement of section 281(4) and (5) of the Criminal Justice Act 2003),

    (b) a fine, or

    (c) both.

(6) A person convicted of low-value shoplifting by a magistrates' court may not appeal to the Crown Court against the conviction on the ground that the convicting court was mistaken as to whether the offence was one of low-value shoplifting.

(7) For the purposes of this section, any reference to low-value shoplifting includes aiding, abetting, counselling or procuring the commission of low-value shoplifting.

The amendments made by section 176 have effect in relation to (i) low-value shoplifting committed on or after May 13, 2014, and (ii) low-value shoplifting committed before May 13, 2014, in respect of which proceedings have not yet been instituted on that date (2014 Act, s.176(8)).   ★

### (b) *Procedural rules*

**Criminal Procedure Rules 2013 (S.I. 2013 No. 1554), Pt 9**

*Exercise of magistrates' court's powers*

With effect from April 7, 2014, rule 9.2 of the Criminal Procedure Rules 2013 (S.I. 2013 No. **1-117b** 1554) is amended by rule 6(a) of the Criminal Procedure (Amendment No. 2) Rules 2013 (S.I. 2013 No. 3183), so as (i) to substitute the words "deals with two or more offences alleged against the same defendant, the court must deal with those offences" for the words "deals with more than one offence alleged against the same defendant, it must deal with them" in paragraph (5), and (ii) to insert new paragraphs (6) and (7), as follows—

"(6) Where the court on the same occasion deals with two or more defendants charged jointly with an offence that can be tried in the Crown Court then in the following sequence—

    (a) the court must explain, in terms each defendant can understand (with help, if necessary), that if the court sends one of them to the Crown Court for trial then the court must send for trial in the Crown Court, too, any other of them—

        (i) who is charged with the same offence as the defendant sent for trial, or with an offence which the court decides is related to that offence,

        (ii) who does not wish to plead guilty to each offence with which he or she is charged, and

        (iii) (if that other defendant is under 18, and the court would not otherwise have sent him or her for Crown Court trial) where the court decides that sending is necessary in the interests of justice,

    even if the court by then has decided to allocate that other defendant for magistrates' court trial; and

    (b) the court may ask the defendants questions to help it decide in what order to deal with them.

(7) After following paragraph (5), if it applies, where the court on the same occasion—

    (a) deals with two or more defendants charged jointly with an offence that can be tried in the Crown Court;

    (b) allocates any of them to a magistrates' court for trial; and

    (c) then sends another one of them to the Crown Court for trial,

the court must deal again with each one whom, on that occasion, it has allocated for magistrates' court trial.".

*Sending for Crown Court trial*

With effect from April 7, 2014, rule 9.7(3)(b)(i) of the Criminal Procedure Rules 2013 (S.I. 2013 **1-117g** No. 1554) is amended by rule 6(b) of the Criminal Procedure (Amendment No. 2) Rules 2013 (S.I. 2013 No. 3183), so as to insert the words "or because the court for some other reason is required to send that offence for trial" after the word "there".

(d) *Practice direction*

**1-119**    The 2013 criminal practice directions (see the main work) are now reported at [2013] 1 W.L.R. 3164.

## (5) Penalties on summary conviction

### Magistrates' Courts Act 1980, s.32

★**1-125**    With effect from May 28, 2014, section 85(3) and (17) of the LASPOA 2012 (see the main work) were brought into force: Legal Aid, Sentencing and Punishment of Offenders Act 2012 (Commencement No. 10) Order 2014 (S.I. 2014 No. 1291). Pending the commencement of subsection (1), the commencement of these provisions is relevant only to the rule-making powers under other subsections of section 85, also brought into force on May 28.

## (7) Joinder of certain summary offences in an indictment

### Criminal Justice Act 1988, s.40

*Power to join in indictment count for common assault etc.*

★**1-134**    In *R. v. Lewis* [2014] 1 Cr.App.R. 25, CA, it was held that a properly preferred and signed indictment, containing one count of attempted theft and two counts of common assault (pursuant to the 1988 Act, s.40 (§ 1-133 in the main work)), was not deprived of validity by the fact that the prosecution offered no evidence on the attempted theft count after the defendant had been arraigned. Section 40 contains no indication that, to found jurisdiction in respect of the summary offences listed therein, the defendant must be put in the charge of the jury on charges that include at least one non-summary offence. The section is directed to the stage when the indictment is drawn (*R. v. Plant* (see the main work)).

## IV. AGAINST WHOM AN INDICTMENT LIES

### B. Exemptions

### (3) Sovereign and state immunity

#### State Immunity Act 1978, s.20(1), (2)

**1-155**    There is no interpretational basis for giving the phrase "members of his family forming part of his household", in section 20(1)(b) of the 1978 Act, a wider meaning in relation to heads of state than in relation to diplomats; Parliament chose to limit the extension of immunity to close members of the head of state's family in section 20 by adopting the same formula as had been used in the Vienna Convention on Diplomatic Relations in relation to diplomats; once any extension of the meaning of "household" beyond spouses, civil partners, dependent children and relatives is contemplated, it is impossible to discern as a matter of interpretation of section 20 where the boundary should be set; although section 20 provided for "necessary modifications" in applying the immunities enjoyed by diplomats to heads of state, any attempt to extend the meaning of the household concept in relation to heads of state failed that necessity test; accordingly, the half-brother, and his son, of the King of Saudi Arabia, who both lived separately from the king, with their own households, did not enjoy sovereign immunity: *Apex Global Management Ltd v. Fi Call Ltd* [2014] 1 W.L.R. 492, CA (Civ. Div.) (considering, *inter alia*, *R. v. Bow Street Metropolitan Stipendiary Magistrate, ex p. Pinochet Ugarte (No. 3)* [2000] 1 A.C. 147, HL (as to which, see the main work)).

## (10) Offenders assisting investigations and prosecutions

### Serious Organised Crime and Police Act 2005, s.71

*Assistance by offender: immunity from prosecution*

★**1-162**    With effect from March 27, 2014, the Public Bodies (Merger of the Director of Public Prosecutions and the Director of Revenue and Customs Prosecutions) Order 2014 (S.I. 2014 No. 834), art. 3(3), and Sched. 2, paras 40 and 42, amended section 71 of the 2005 Act, subject to saving and transitional provisions (as to which, see *ante*, § 1-27), so as to repeal subsection (4)(b).

## C. Extraditees and Repatriated Prisoners

### (2) Legislation

#### (a) *Extraditees*

**Extradition Act 2003, ss.145–150, 151A**

*Dealing with person for other offences: Commonwealth countries etc.*

As from a day to be appointed, sections 150 and 151A of the 2003 Act are amended by the Anti-social Behaviour, Crime and Policing Act 2014, s.166(1), so as to insert the words "This is subject to section 151B." at the end of subsection (2) in both sections.  ★**1-170**

*Dealing with person for other offences*

As to the amendment of section 151A of the 2003 Act, see *ante*, § 1-170.  ★**1-171**

It is clear from a reading of the 2003 Act as a whole, and having proper regard to the legislative history relating to extradition, that the reference to an "offence" in section 151A of that Act refers to a criminal offence; a civil contempt is not a criminal offence for this purpose, and thus section 151A does not preclude a fugitive from being dealt with for civil contempt committed before his extradition to the United Kingdom: *Director of the Serious Fraud Office v. O'Brien* [2014] 2 W.L.R. 902, SC. As to this case, see also *post*, §§ 5-846a, 28-118.  ★

*Detention of person for trial in England and Wales for other offences*

As from a day to be appointed, section 166(2) of the Anti-social Behaviour, Crime and Policing Act 2014 inserts a new section 151B in the 2003 Act.  ★**1-171a**

*Detention of person for trial in England and Wales for other offences*

**151B.**—(1) Section 150 or 151A does not prevent a person in whose case that section applies from being detained with a view to trial in England and Wales for an offence if the conditions in subsection (2) are satisfied.

(2) The conditions are that—

    (a) the United Kingdom and the territory from which the person was extradited have each made a declaration under Article 14(3) of the Extradition Convention, and the declarations are still in force;

    (b) the Secretary of State makes a request for the consent referred to in section 150(3)(c) or 151A(3)(c) in respect of the offence ("the consent request");

    (c) the Secretary of State gives notification, which is explicitly acknowledged on behalf of the territory, of the date on which the detention is to begin ("the notified date").

(3) The Extradition Convention is the European Convention on Extradition done at Paris on 13 December 1957.

(4) This section applies only to detention during the period beginning with the notified date and ending with whichever of the following occurs first—

    (a) if a notification of opposition to the detention is given on behalf of the territory, the date on which Secretary of State receives it;

    (b) the date on which the Secretary of State receives notification given on behalf of the territory as to whether the consent request is granted or refused;

    (c) the expiry of the period of 90 days beginning with the date on which the consent request is received.

## V. THE FORM OF AN INDICTMENT

### A. Rules as to Indictments

The 2013 criminal practice directions (see the main work) are now reported at [2013] 1 W.L.R. 3164.  **1-178**

## B. DRAWING THE INDICTMENT

### (1) General

**1-180**  The 2013 criminal practice directions (see the main work) are now reported at [2013] 1 W.L.R. 3164.

### (2) Number of counts

**1-181**  The 2013 criminal practice directions (see the main work) are now reported at [2013] 1 W.L.R. 3164.

## C. CONTENTS

### (2) Statement and particulars of offence(s) and signature

#### Statement of offence

**1-189**  Where it is alleged that a director of a body corporate is guilty of an offence by reason of his consent, connivance or neglect in relation to an offence committed by the body corporate, the statement of offence needs to refer to both the legislative provision creating the index offence and the provision that makes a consenting, etc., director also guilty of that offence: *R. v. Wilson (Michael)* [2014] 1 Cr.App.R. 10, CA (considering the Regulatory Reform (Fire Safety) Order 2005 (S.I. 2005 No. 1541), art. 32(8)).

#### Signature and date

**1-191**  The 2013 criminal practice directions (see the main work) are now reported at [2013] 1 W.L.R. 3164.

#### Prescribed forms of indictment and their use

**1-194**  The 2013 criminal practice directions (see the main work) are now reported at [2013] 1 W.L.R. 3164.

## E. DUPLICITY

### (4) Rule 14.2(2) of the Criminal Procedure Rules 2013 (S.I. 2013 No. 1554)

**1-220**  The 2013 criminal practice directions (see the main work) are now reported at [2013] 1 W.L.R. 3164.

**1-221**  The 2013 criminal practice directions (see the main work) are now reported at [2013] 1 W.L.R. 3164.

## G. JOINDER

### (1) Joinder of counts in one indictment

#### Indictments Act 1915, s.4

#### "founded on the same facts"

**1-238**  *R. v. McGrath* is now reported at [2014] Crim.L.R. 144.

### (2) The effect of misjoinder in contravention of rule 14.2(3)

**1-244**  *R. v. McGrath* is now reported at [2014] Crim.L.R. 144. As to the entry in the main work relating to this case, it should be noted that the cross-reference should be to § 1-238, and not to § 1-138.

## VI. TIME FOR COMMENCEMENT OF PROSECUTION

### C. COMMENCEMENT OF PROSECUTION

**★1-276**  With effect from March 27, 2014, the definition of "public prosecutor" in section 29(5) of the

CJA 2003 was further amended, subject to saving and transitional provisions (as to which, see *ante*, § 1-27), by the Public Bodies (Merger of the Director of Public Prosecutions and the Director of Revenue and Customs Prosecutions) Order 2014 (S.I. 2014 No. 834), art. 3(3), and Sched. 2, paras 37 and 39.

With effect from April 1, 2014, sections 29(1) to (3), (5) and (6) and 30 of the CJA 2003 (§§ 1-272, 1-276 in the main work) came into force, but only for the purposes of criminal proceedings instituted by a public prosecutor within the meaning of section 29(5)(e) (a Secretary of State or a person authorised by a Secretary of State) who is a person authorised to do so on behalf of the Driver and Vehicle Standards Agency, a new executive agency of the Department of Transport (consequent on the merger of the Driving Standards Agency and the Vehicle and Operator Services Agency): Criminal Justice Act 2003 (Commencement No. 32) Order 2014 (S.I. 2014 No. 633). ★

## VII. *PREFERRING THE BILL OF INDICTMENT*

### A. WHEN A BILL OF INDICTMENT MAY BE PREFERRED

#### Administration of Justice (Miscellaneous Provisions) Act 1933, s.2(1), (2)

The provisions of the Crime and Courts Act 2013 referred to in the main work came into force on February 24, 2014: Crime and Courts Act 2013 (Commencement No. 8) Order 2014 (S.I. 2014 No. 258). ★**1-277**

The 2013 criminal practice directions (see the main work) are now reported at [2013] 1 W.L.R. 3164. **1-278**

### Indictment based on sending

The 2013 criminal practice directions (see the main work) are now reported at [2013] 1 W.L.R. 3164. **1-282**

### Indictment based on voluntary bill

The 2013 criminal practice directions (see the main work) are now reported at [2013] 1 W.L.R. 3164. **1-288**

### Joinder of persons or charges separately sent for trial

The 2013 criminal practice directions (see the main work) are now reported at [2013] 1 W.L.R. 3164. **1-293**

### B. RULES AS TO PROCEDURE

The 2013 criminal practice directions (see the main work) are now reported at [2013] 1 W.L.R. 3164. **1-301**

### Voluntary bill procedure

The 2013 criminal practice directions (see the main work) are now reported at [2013] 1 W.L.R. 3164. **1-304**

### C. COPY OF INDICTMENT FOR PARTIES AND JUDGE

The 2013 criminal practice directions (see the main work) are now reported at [2013] 1 W.L.R. 3164. **1-308**

## IX. *PROCEEDINGS AGAINST CORPORATIONS AND OTHER BODIES*

### (2) Deferred prosecutions

### Deferred prosecution agreements

For procedural provision in connection with Schedule 17 to the Crime and Courts Act 2013 (as to which, see the main work), see *post*, § 1-317r. **1-317a**

## Commencement and transitional

**1-317b**   With effect from February 24, 2014, section 45 of, and Schedule 17 to, the Crime and Courts Act 2013 (as to which, see §§ 1-317a *et seq.* in the main work) were brought into force: Crime and Courts Act 2013 (Commencement No. 8) Order 2014 (S.I. 2014 No. 258).

### Crime and Courts Act 2013, Sched. 17, Pt 1

**1-317d**   As to the commencement of Schedule 17 to the 2013 Act, see *ante*, § 1-317b.

*Code of practice*

**1-317i**   On February 14, 2014, the Director of Public Prosecutions and the Director of the Serious Fraud Office together issued a code of practice on deferred prosecution agreements, pursuant to paragraph 6(1) of Schedule 17 to the 2013 Act.

## Procedural provision

**1-317r**   With effect from February 24, 2014, a new Part 12 is inserted into the Criminal Procedure Rules 2013 (S.I. 2013 No. 1554) by rule 7 of the Criminal Procedure (Amendment No. 2) Rules 2013 (S.I. 2013 No. 3183), supplying the procedure for proceedings under Schedule 17 to the Crime and Courts Act 2013 (as to which, see §§ 1-317a *et seq.* in the main work).

### Criminal Procedure Rules 2013 (S.I. 2013 No. 1554), Pt 12 (as inserted by the Criminal Procedure (Amendment No. 2) Rules 2013 (S.I. 2013 No. 3183), r.7)

*When this Part applies*

**1-317s**   **12.1**—(1) This Part applies to proceedings in the Crown Court under Schedule 17 to the Crime and Courts Act 2013.

(2) In this Part—

(a) "agreement" means a deferred prosecution agreement under paragraph 1 of that Schedule;

(b) "prosecutor" means a prosecutor designated by or under paragraph 3 of that Schedule; and

(c) "defendant" means the corporation, partnership or association with whom the prosecutor proposes to enter, or enters, an agreement.

*Exercise of court's powers*

**1-317t**   **12.2**—(1) The court must determine an application to which this Part applies at a hearing, which—

(a) must be in private, under rule 12.3 (application to approve a proposal to enter an agreement);

(b) may be in public or private, under rule 12.4 (application to approve the terms of an agreement), rule 12.6 (application to approve a variation of the terms of an agreement) or rule 12.9 (application to postpone the publication of information by the prosecutor);

(c) must be in public, under rule 12.5 (application on breach of agreement) or rule 12.7 (application to lift suspension of prosecution), unless the court otherwise directs.

(2) If at a hearing in private to which rule 12.4 or rule 12.6 applies the court approves the agreement or the variation proposed, the court must announce its decision and reasons at a hearing in public.

(3) The court must not determine an application under rule 12.3, rule 12.4 or rule 12.6 unless—

(a) both parties are present;

(b) the prosecutor provides the court with a written declaration that, for the purposes of the application—

(i) the investigator enquiring into the alleged offence or offences has certified that no information has been supplied which the investigator knows to be inaccurate, misleading or incomplete, and

(ii) the prosecutor has complied with the prosecution obligation to disclose material to the defendant; and

(c) the defendant provides the court with a written declaration that, for the purposes of the application—

(i) the defendant has not supplied any information which the defendant knows to be inaccurate, misleading or incomplete, and

(ii) the individual through whom the defendant makes the declaration has made reasonable enquiries and believes the defendant's declaration to be true.

(4) The court must not determine an application under rule 12.5 or rule 12.7—
   (a) in the prosecutor's absence; or
   (b) in the absence of the defendant, unless the defendant has had at least 28 days in which to make representations.
(5) If the court approves a proposal to enter an agreement—
   (a) the general rule is that any further application to which this Part applies must be made to the same judge; but
   (b) the court may direct other arrangements.
(6) The court may adjourn a hearing—
   (a) if either party asks, or on its own initiative;
   (b) in particular, if the court requires more information about—
      (i) the facts of an alleged offence,
      (ii) the terms of a proposal to enter an agreement, or of a proposed agreement or variation of an agreement, or
      (iii) the circumstances in which the prosecutor wants the court to decide whether the defendant has failed to comply with the terms of an agreement.
(7) The court may—
   (a) hear an application under rule 12.4 immediately after an application under rule 12.3, if the court approves a proposal to enter an agreement;
   (b) hear an application under rule 12.7 immediately after an application under rule 12.5, if the court terminates an agreement.

*Application to approve a proposal to enter an agreement*
**12.3**—(1) This rule applies where a prosecutor wants the court to approve a proposal to enter an   **1-317u**
agreement.
(2) The prosecutor must—
   (a) apply in writing after the commencement of negotiations between the parties but before the terms of agreement have been settled; and
   (b) serve the application on—
      (i) the court officer, and
      (ii) the defendant.
(3) The application must—
   (a) identify the parties to the proposed agreement;
   (b) attach a proposed indictment setting out such of the offences listed in Part 2 of Schedule 17 to the Crime and Courts Act 2013 as the prosecutor is considering;
   (c) include or attach a statement of facts proposed for inclusion in the agreement, which must give full particulars of each alleged offence, including details of any alleged financial gain or loss;
   (d) include any information about the defendant that would be relevant to sentence in the event of conviction for the offence or offences;
   (e) specify the proposed expiry date of the agreement;
   (f) describe the proposed terms of the agreement, including details of any—
      (i) monetary penalty to be paid by the defendant, and the time within which any such penalty is to be paid,
      (ii) compensation, reparation or donation to be made by the defendant, the identity of the recipient of any such payment and the time within which any such payment is to be made,
      (iii) surrender of profits or other financial benefit by the defendant, and the time within which any such sum is to be surrendered,
      (iv) arrangement to be made in relation to the management or conduct of the defendant's business,
      (v) co-operation required of the defendant in any investigation related to the offence or offences,
      (vi) other action required of the defendant,
      (vii) arrangement to monitor the defendant's compliance with a term,
      (viii) consequence of the defendant's failure to comply with a term, and
      (ix) prosecution costs to be paid by the defendant, and the time within which any such costs are to be paid;
   (g) in relation to those terms, explain how they comply with—

     (i)  the requirements of the code issued under paragraph 6 of Schedule 17 to the Crime and Courts Act 2013, and

     (ii)  any sentencing guidelines or guideline cases which apply;

  (h)  contain or attach the defendant's written consent to the proposal; and

  (i)  explain why—

     (i)  entering into an agreement is likely to be in the interests of justice, and

     (ii)  the proposed terms of the agreement are fair, reasonable and proportionate.

(4) If the proposed statement of facts includes assertions that the defendant does not admit, the application must—

  (a)  specify the facts that are not admitted; and

  (b)  explain why that is immaterial for the purposes of the proposal to enter an agreement.

*Application to approve the terms of an agreement*

**1-317v**    **12.4**—(1) This rule applies where—

  (a)  the court has approved a proposal to enter an agreement on an application under rule 12.3; and

  (b)  the prosecutor wants the court to approve the terms of the agreement.

(2) The prosecutor must—

  (a)  apply in writing as soon as practicable after the parties have settled the terms; and

  (b)  serve the application on—

     (i)  the court officer, and

     (ii)  the defendant.

(3) The application must—

  (a)  attach the agreement;

  (b)  indicate in what respect, if any, the terms of the agreement differ from those proposed in the application under rule 12.3;

  (c)  contain or attach the defendant's written consent to the agreement;

  (d)  explain why—

     (i)  the agreement is in the interests of justice, and

     (ii)  the terms of the agreement are fair, reasonable and proportionate;

  (e)  attach a draft indictment, charging the defendant with the offence or offences the subject of the agreement; and

  (f)  include any application for the hearing to be in private.

(4) If the court approves the agreement and the draft indictment, the court officer must—

  (a)  sign and date the indictment, as if the draft had been served under rule 14.1 (service and signature of indictment); and

  (b)  treat the case as if it had been suspended by order of the court.

*Application on breach of agreement*

**1-317w**    **12.5**—(1) This rule applies where—

  (a)  the prosecutor believes that the defendant has failed to comply with the terms of an agreement; and

  (b)  the prosecutor wants the court to decide—

     (i)  whether the defendant has failed to comply, and

     (ii)  if so, whether to terminate the agreement, or to invite the parties to agree proposals to remedy that failure.

(2) The prosecutor must—

  (a)  apply in writing, as soon as practicable after becoming aware of the grounds for doing so; and

  (b)  serve the application on—

     (i)  the court officer, and

     (ii)  the defendant.

(3) The application must—

  (a)  specify each respect in which the prosecutor believes the defendant has failed to comply with the terms of the agreement, and explain the reasons for the prosecutor's belief; and

  (b)  attach a copy of any document containing evidence on which the prosecutor relies.

(4) A defendant who wants to make representations in response to the application must serve the representations on—

  (a)  the court officer; and

(b)  the prosecutor,

not more than 28 days after service of the application.

*Application to approve a variation of the terms of an agreement*

**12.6**—(1) This rule applies where the parties have agreed to vary the terms of an agreement because—

(a)  on an application under rule 12.5 (application on breach of agreement), the court has invited them to do so; or

(b)  variation of the agreement is necessary to avoid a failure by the defendant to comply with its terms in circumstances that were not, and could not have been, foreseen by either party at the time the agreement was made.

(2) The prosecutor must—

(a)  apply in writing, as soon as practicable after the parties have settled the terms of the variation; and

(b)  serve the application on—

(i)  the court officer, and

(ii)  the defendant.

(3) The application must—

(a)  specify each variation proposed;

(b)  contain or attach the defendant's written consent to the variation;

(c)  explain why—

(i)  the variation is in the interests of justice, and

(ii)  the terms of the agreement as varied are fair, reasonable and proportionate; and

(d)  include any application for the hearing to be in private.

*Application to lift suspension of prosecution*

**12.7**—(1) This rule applies where—

**1-317x**

(a)  the court terminates an agreement before its expiry date; and

(b)  the prosecutor wants the court to lift the suspension of the prosecution that applied when the court approved the terms of the agreement.

(2) The prosecutor must—

(a)  apply in writing, as soon as practicable after the termination of the agreement; and

(b)  serve the application on—

(i)  the court officer, and

(ii)  the defendant.

(3) [*Identical to r.12.5(4), ante, § 1-317w.*]

*Notice to discontinue prosecution*

**12.8**—(1) This rule applies where an agreement expires—

(a)  on its expiry date, or on a date treated as its expiry date; and

(b)  without having been terminated by the court.

(2) The prosecutor must—

(a)  as soon as practicable give notice in writing discontinuing the prosecution on the indictment approved by the court under rule 12.4 (application to approve the terms of an agreement); and

(b)  serve the notice on—

(i)  the court officer, and

(ii)  the defendant.

*Application to postpone the publication of information by the prosecutor*

**12.9**—(1) This rule applies where the prosecutor—

**1-317y**

(a)  makes an application under rule 12.4 (application to approve the terms of an agreement), rule 12.5 (application on breach of agreement) or rule 12.6 (application to approve a variation of the terms of an agreement);

(b)  decides not to make an application under rule 12.5, despite believing that the defendant has failed to comply with the terms of the agreement; or

(c)  gives a notice under rule 12.8 (notice to discontinue prosecution).

(2) A party who wants the court to order that the publication of information by the prosecutor about the court's or the prosecutor's decision should be postponed must—

    (a)   apply in writing, as soon as practicable and in any event before such publication occurs;

    (b)   serve the application on—

        (i)   the court officer, and

        (ii)   the other party; and

    (c)   in the application—

        (i)   specify the proposed terms of the order, and for how long it should last, and

        (ii)   explain why an order in the terms proposed is necessary.

*Duty of court officer, etc.*

**1-317z**      **12.10**—(1) Unless the court otherwise directs, the court officer must—

    (a)   arrange for the recording of proceedings on an application to which this Part applies;

    (b)   arrange for the transcription of such a recording if—

        (i)   a party wants such a transcript, or

        (ii)   anyone else wants such a transcript (but that is subject to the restrictions in paragraph (2)).

(2) Unless the court otherwise directs, a person who transcribes a recording of proceedings under such arrangements—

    (a)   must not supply anyone other than a party with a transcript of a recording of—

        (i)   a hearing in private, or

        (ii)   a hearing in public to which reporting restrictions apply;

    (b)   subject to that, must supply any person with any transcript for which that person asks—

        (i)   in accordance with the transcription arrangements made by the court officer, and

        (ii)   on payment by that person of any fee prescribed.

(3) The court officer must not identify either party to a hearing in private under rule 12.3 (application to approve a proposal to enter an agreement) or rule 12.4 (application to approve the terms of an agreement)—

    (a)   in any notice displayed in the vicinity of the courtroom; or

    (b)   in any other information published by the court officer.

*Court's power to vary requirements under this Part*

     **12.11**—(1) The court may—

    (a)   shorten or extend (even after it has expired) a time limit under this Part;

    (b)   allow there to be made orally—

        (i)   an application under rule 12.4 (application to approve the terms of an agreement), or

        (ii)   an application under rule 12.7 (application to lift suspension of prosecution)

        where the court exercises its power under rule 12.2(7) to hear one application immediately after another.

(2) A party who wants an extension of time must—

    (a)   apply when serving the application or notice for which it is needed; and

    (b)   explain the delay.

## XI. POWERS AND DUTIES OF PARTICULAR PROSECUTION AGENCIES

### A. CROWN PROSECUTION SERVICE

### (2) Functions of Director of Public Prosecutions

#### Prosecution of Offences Act 1985, s.3

**★1-326**      With effect from March 27, 2014, the Public Bodies (Merger of the Director of Public Prosecutions and the Director of Revenue and Customs Prosecutions) Order 2014 (S.I. 2014 No. 834), art. 3(3), and Sched. 1, paras 1 and 2(1) and (2), amended section 3(2) of the 1985 Act, subject to saving and transitional provisions (as to which, see *ante*, § 1-27), so as to insert, after paragraph (aa), new paragraph (ab), as follows—

     "(ab)   to take over the conduct of any criminal proceedings instituted in England and Wales by the Revenue and Customs;".

**★**      With effect from March 27, 2014, S.I. 2014 No. 834 (*ante*), art. 3(3), and Sched. 1, paras 1 and 2(1) and (3), amended section 3(2) of the 1985 Act, subject to saving and transitional provisions (as to which, see *ante*, § 1-27), so as to insert, after paragraph (ba), new paragraph (bb), as follows—

> "(bb) where it appears to him appropriate to do so, to institute and have the conduct of any criminal proceedings in England and Wales relating to a criminal investigation by the Revenue and Customs;".

With effect from March 27, 2014, S.I. 2014 No. 834 (*ante*), art. 3(3), and Sched. 1, paras 1 and ★ 2(1) and (4), amended section 3(2) of the 1985 Act, subject to saving and transitional provisions (as to which, see *ante*, § 1-27), so as to insert, after paragraph (ed), new paragraph (ee), as follows—

> "(ee) to give, to such extent as he considers appropriate, and to such persons as he considers appropriate, advice on matters relating to—
> (i) a criminal investigation by the Revenue and Customs; or
> (ii) criminal proceedings instituted in England and Wales relating to a criminal investigation by the Revenue and Customs;".

With effect from March 27, 2014, S.I. 2014 No. 834 (*ante*), art. 3(3), and Sched. 1, paras 1 and ★ 2(1) and (5), amended section 3(3) of the 1985 Act, subject to saving and transitional provisions (as to which, see *ante*, § 1-27), so as to insert a new definition as follows, after the definition of "the court"—

> "'criminal investigation' means any process—
> (i) for considering whether an offence has been committed;
> (ii) for discovering by whom an offence has been committed; or
> (iii) as a result of which an offence is alleged to have been committed;".

With effect from March 27, 2014, S.I. 2014 No. 834 (*ante*), art. 3(3), and Sched. 1, paras 1 and ★ 2(1) and (6), amended section 3 of the 1985 Act, subject to saving and transitional provisions (as to which, see *ante*, § 1-27), so as to insert, after subsection (3), a new subsection (3A) as follows—

> "(3A) In this section a reference to the Revenue and Customs is a reference to—
> (a) the Commissioners for Her Majesty's Revenue and Customs;
> (b) an officer of Revenue and Customs; or
> (c) a person acting on behalf of the Commissioners or an officer of Revenue and Customs.".

As from a day to be appointed, the Anti-social Behaviour, Crime and Policing Act 2014, ★ s.181(1), and Sched. 11, para. 5, amend section 3(2) of the 1985 Act so as (i) in paragraph (fa), to substitute the words "section 22 of the Anti-social Behaviour, Crime and Policing Act 2014 (criminal behaviour orders made on conviction)" for the words from "section 1C" to "proceedings)", (ii) in paragraph (fb), to substitute the words "section 27 of the Anti-social Behaviour, Crime and Policing Act 2014" for the words "section 1CA(3) of the Crime and Disorder Act 1998", and the words "section 22" for the words "section 1C", (iii) in paragraph (fc), to substitute the words "section 27" for the words "section 1CA" and the words "section 22" for the words "section 1C", and (iv) to repeal paragraphs (fd) and (fe).

As from a day to be appointed, sections 7 and 8 of the VCRA 2006 are repealed by the Anti- ★ social Behaviour, Crime and Policing Act 2014, s.181(1), and Sched. 11, paras 44 and 50.

### Specified proceedings

The Prosecution of Offences Act 1985 (Specified Proceedings) Order 1999 (S.I. 1999 No. 904) ★**1-329** (see the main work) was further amended, with effect from June 9, 2014, by the Prosecution of Offences Act 1985 (Specified Proceedings) (Amendment) Order 2014 (S.I. 2014 No. 1229).

## (4) Conduct of prosecutions on behalf of the service

### Prosecution of Offences Act 1985, s.5

With effect from March 27, 2014, the Public Bodies (Merger of the Director of Public Prosecu- ★**1-331** tions and the Director of Revenue and Customs Prosecutions) Order 2014 (S.I. 2014 No. 834), art. 3(3), and Sched. 1, paras 1 and 3(1) and (2), amended section 5 of the 1985 Act, subject to saving and transitional provisions (as to which, see *ante*, § 1-27), so as to insert, after subsection (1), new subsections (1A) and (1B), as follows—

"(1A) The Director may at any time appoint such a person—

(a) to exercise a function of the Director under section 3(2)(ab) or (bb) in relation to a class or description of criminal proceedings specified in the appointment;

(b) to exercise a function of the Director under section 3(2)(ee) in relation to—

(i) such criminal proceedings as are specified in the appointment, or

(ii) a class or description of criminal proceedings specified in the appointment; or

(c) to appear in—

(i) Revenue and Customs cash recovery proceedings specified in the appointment, or

(ii) a class or description of Revenue and Customs cash recovery proceedings specified in the appointment.

(1B) In subsection (1A)—

'Revenue and Customs cash recovery proceedings' means proceedings in which the Director or a Crown Prosecutor would otherwise appear by virtue of section 302A(2) of the Proceeds of Crime Act 2002 (cash recovery proceedings relating to revenue and customs matters).".

★ With effect from March 27, 2014, S.I. 2014 No. 834 (*ante*), art. 3(3), and Sched. 1, paras 1 and 3(1) and (3), amended section 5(2) of the 1985 Act, subject to saving and transitional provisions (as to which, see *ante*, § 1-27), so as to substitute the words "subsection (1) or exercising functions by virtue of an appointment made under subsection (1A)" for the words "this section".

## (7) Bail applications

### Prosecution of Offences Act 1985, s.7A

★1-335 With effect from March 27, 2014, the Public Bodies (Merger of the Director of Public Prosecutions and the Director of Revenue and Customs Prosecutions) Order 2014 (S.I. 2014 No. 834), art. 3(3), and Sched. 1, paras 1 and 4(1) and (2), amended section 7A(1) of the 1985 Act, subject to saving and transitional provisions (as to which, see *ante*, § 1-27), so as to substitute the words "under this subsection" for the words ", for the purposes of this section,".

★ With effect from March 27, 2014, S.I. 2014 No. 834 (*ante*), art. 3(3), and Sched. 1, paras 1 and 4(1) and (3), amended section 7A(2) of the 1985 Act, subject to saving and transitional provisions (as to which, see *ante*, § 1-27), so as to insert the words "under subsection (1)" for the words "the designation".

★ With effect from March 27, 2014, S.I. 2014 No. 834 (*ante*), art. 3(3), and Sched. 1, paras 1 and 4(1) and (4), amended section 7A of the 1985 Act, subject to saving and transitional provisions (as to which, see *ante*, § 1-27), so as to insert, after subsection (2), new subsections (2A) and (2B) as follows—

"(2A) The Director may designate under this subsection members of the staff of the Crown Prosecution Service who are not Crown Prosecutors.

(2B) A person designated under subsection (2A) has the powers and rights of audience of a Crown Prosecutor in relation to—

(a) Revenue and Customs cash recovery proceedings specified in the designation under subsection (2A), or

(b) a class or description of Revenue and Customs cash recovery proceedings specified in the designation under subsection (2A).".

★ With effect from March 27, 2014, S.I. 2014 No. 834 (*ante*), art. 3(3), and Sched. 1, paras 1 and 4(1) and (5), amended section 7A(3) of the 1985 Act, subject to saving and transitional provisions (as to which, see *ante*, § 1-27), so as to substitute the words "designated under subsection (1) or (2A)" for the words "so designated", and the words "any powers so conferred" for the words "any such powers".

★ With effect from March 27, 2014, S.I. 2014 No. 834 (*ante*), art. 3(3), and Sched. 1, paras 1 and 4(1) and (6), amended section 7A(5) of the 1985 Act, subject to saving and transitional provisions (as to which, see *ante*, § 1-27), so as to insert a new definition as follows, after the definition of "preventative civil orders"—

"'Revenue and Customs cash recovery proceedings' has the meaning given by section 5(1B)".

★ With effect from March 27, 2014, S.I. 2014 No. 834 (ante), art. 3(3), and Sched. 1, paras 1 and 4(1) and (7) to (10), amended subsections (7)(a), (8), (9) and (10) of section 7A of the 1985 Act, subject to saving and transitional provisions (as to which, see *ante*, § 1-27), so as to substitute in each of those subsections the words "under subsection (1) or (2A)" for the words "under this section".

As from a day to be appointed, section 41 of the Crime and Security Act 2010 (see the main ★ work) is repealed by the Anti-social Behaviour, Crime and Policing Act 2014, s.181(1), and Sched. 11, para. 46.

### (10) Interpretation of Part I

#### Prosecution of Offences Act 1985, s.15

The provisions of the Crime and Courts Act 2013 referred to in the main work came into force ★1-341 on February 24, 2014: Crime and Courts Act 2013 (Commencement No. 8) Order 2014 (S.I. 2014 No. 258).

### (11) Power of Secretary of State to set time limits in relation to preliminary stages of criminal proceedings

## Custody time limits: general and procedure

*Laing v. The Queen* is now reported at [2014] 1 Cr.App.R. 2.                  1-353

### (14) Restriction of vexatious prosecutions

The provisions of the Crime and Courts Act 2013 referred to in the main work came into force ★1-364 on April 22, 2014: Crime and Courts Act 2013 (Commencement No. 10 and Transitional Provision) Order 2014 (S.I. 2014 No. 954).

### B. SERIOUS FRAUD OFFICE

### (4) Disclosure of information

#### Criminal Justice Act 1987, s.3

*Disclosure of information*

With effect from March 27, 2014, the Public Bodies (Merger of the Director of Public Prosecu- ★1-378 tions and the Director of Revenue and Customs Prosecutions) Order 2014 (S.I. 2014 No. 834), art. 3(3), and Sched. 2, para. 7, amended section 3(1)(b) of the 1987 Act, subject to saving and transitional provisions (as to which, see *ante*, § 1-27), so as to substitute the words "the Crown Prosecution Service" for the words "the Revenue and Customs Prosecutions Office".

With effect from June 2, 2014 (Anti-social Behaviour, Crime and Policing Act 2014 (Com- ★ mencement No. 3) Order 2014 (S.I. 2014 No. 1226)), the Anti-social Behaviour, Crime and Policing Act 2014, s.149(2)(a) and (b), amended section 3(1) of the 1987 Act so as to omit the word "and" before paragraph (c), to insert the word "and" after that paragraph, and to insert a new paragraph (d) as follows—

> "(d)  in order to comply with a requirement imposed under paragraph 7 of the Schedule to the Crown Prosecution Service Inspectorate Act 2000,".

With effect from June 2, 2014 (S.I. 2014 No. 1226 (*ante*)), the 2014 Act, s.149(2)(c), amended section 3(3) of the 1987 Act so as to substitute, for the words from "by a member of the Serious Fraud Office" to the words "or elsewhere and", the following words—

"by a member of the Serious Fraud Office—
> (a)  for the purposes of any prosecution in England and Wales, Northern Ireland or elsewhere, or
> (b)  in order to comply with a requirement imposed under paragraph 7 of the Schedule to the Crown Prosecution Service Inspectorate Act 2000,

and".

*Tchenguiz v. Director of the Serious Fraud Office (Deutsche Bank A.G., third party)*; *Rawlinson and* ★1-379 *Hunter Trustees S.A. v. Same (Same, third party)* is now reported at [2014] 1 W.L.R. 1476, *sub nom.* *Tchenguiz v. Director of the Serious Fraud Office*; *Rawlinson and Hunter Trustees S.A. v. Same.*

## C. Revenue and Customs Prosecutions Office

### (1) Establishment

**Commissioners for Revenue and Customs Act 2005, s.34**

*The Revenue and Customs Prosecution Office*

★**1-382**    With effect from March 27, 2014, the Public Bodies (Merger of the Director of Public Prosecutions and the Director of Revenue and Customs Prosecutions) Order 2014 (S.I. 2014 No. 834), art. 3(3), and Sched. 1, paras 5 and 9, repealed sections 34 to 39 of the 2005 Act, subject to savings and transitional provisions (as to which, see *ante*, § 1-27).

### (2) Functions

**Commissioners for Revenue and Customs Act 2005, ss.35–39**

*Functions*

★**1-383**    As to the repeal of section 35 of the 2005 Act, see *ante*, § 1-382.

*Functions: supplemental*

★**1-384**    As to the repeal of section 36 of the 2005 Act, see *ante*, § 1-382.

*Prosecutors*

★**1-385**    As to the repeal of section 37 of the 2005 Act, see *ante*, § 1-382.

*Conduct of prosecutions on behalf of the Office*

★**1-386**    As to the repeal of section 38 of the 2005 Act, see *ante*, § 1-382.

*Designation of non-legal staff*

★**1-387**    As to the repeal of section 39 of the 2005 Act, see *ante*, § 1-382.

### (3) Confidentiality of information

**Commissioners for Revenue and Customs Act 2005, ss.40, 41**

*Confidentiality*

★**1-388**    With effect from March 27, 2014, the Public Bodies (Merger of the Director of Public Prosecutions and the Director of Revenue and Customs Prosecutions) Order 2014 (S.I. 2014 No. 834), art. 3(3), and Sched. 1, paras 5 and 10(1) and (2), amended section 40(1) of the 2005 Act, subject to saving and transitional provisions (as to which, see *ante*, § 1-27), so as (i) to substitute the words "The Crown Prosecution Service" for the words "The Revenue and Customs Prosecutions Office", (ii) in paragraph (a), to substitute the words "the Service in connection with any of the Director of Public Prosecution's [*sic*] functions" for the words "the Prosecutions Office in connection with any of its functions", (iii) to omit the word "and" following paragraph (a), (iv) to insert the word ", and" at the end of paragraph (b), and (v) to insert, after paragraph (b), a new paragraph (c) as follows—

> "(c)    was disclosed to the Director of Public Prosecutions by Her Majesty's Revenue and Customs for use in connection with a Revenue and Customs function of the Director of Public Prosecutions".

★    With effect from March 27, 2014, S.I. 2014 No. 834 (*ante*), art. 3(3), and Sched. 1, paras 5 and 10(1) and (3), amended section 40(2) of the 2005 Act, subject to saving and transitional provisions (as to which, see *ante*, § 1-27), so as (i) in paragraph (a)(i), to substitute the words "the Director of Public Prosecutions" for the words "the Prosecutions Office", (ii) in paragraph (a)(ii), after the words "the Director", to insert the words "of Public Prosecutions", (iii) in paragraph (ca)(iii), to omit the words "the Director of Public Prosecutions,", (iv) to repeal paragraph (cb), (v) in paragraph (d), after the words "the Director", to insert the words "of Public Prosecutions", and (vi) to insert, after paragraph (e), a new paragraph (ea) as follows—

"(ea) does not apply to a disclosure made with the consent of the Commissioners (which may be general or specific),".

With effect from March 27, 2014, S.I. 2014 No. 834 (*ante*), art. 3(3), and Sched. 1, paras 5 and 10(1) and (4), amended section 40(4) of the 2005 Act, subject to saving and transitional provisions (as to which, see *ante*, § 1-27), so as (i) to substitute the words "the Crown Prosecution Service" for the words "the Revenue and Customs Prosecutions Office", and (ii) to substitute the words "the Service" for the words "the Office". ★

With effect from March 27, 2014, S.I. 2014 No. 834 (*ante*), art. 3(3), and Sched. 1, paras 5 and 10(1) and (5), amended section 40(6) of the 2005 Act, subject to saving and transitional provisions (as to which, see *ante*, § 1-27), so as (i) to substitute the words "the Crown Prosecution Service" for the words "the Revenue and Customs Prosecutions Office", (ii) to insert, before paragraph (a), new paragraphs (za) and (zb) as follows— ★

"(za) former members of the Crown Prosecution Service,
(zb) persons who hold or have held appointment under section 5 of the Prosecution of Offences Act 1985.".

(iii) in paragraph (a), to substitute the words "the Revenue and Customs Prosecutions Office" for the words "the Office", and (iv) in paragraph (b), to omit the words "hold or".

With effect from March 27, 2014, S.I. 2014 No. 834 (*ante*), art. 3(3), and Sched. 1, paras 5 and 10(1) and (6), amended section 40 of the 2005 Act, subject to saving and transitional provisions (as to which, see *ante*, § 1-27), so as to insert, after subsection (6), new subsection (6A) as follows— ★

"(6A) In this section 'Revenue and Customs function of the Director of Public Prosecutions' means—
(a) a function of the Director of Public Prosecutions under section 3(2)(ab), (bb) or (ee) of the Prosecution of Offences Act 1985, or
(b) a function of the Director of Public Prosecutions under the Proceeds of Crime Act 2002 that relates to a function of the Commissioners for Her Majesty's Revenue and Customs or an officer of Revenue and Customs.".

With effect from March 27, 2014, S.I. 2014 No. 834 (*ante*), art. 3(3), and Sched. 1, paras 5 and 10(1) and (7), amended section 40(8) of the 2005 Act, subject to saving and transitional provisions (as to which, see *ante*, § 1-27), by substituting the words "only by or with the consent of the Director of Public Prosecutions" for the words from "only—" to the end. ★

With effect from March 27, 2014, S.I. 2014 No. 834 (*ante*), art. 3(3), and Sched. 1, paras 5 and 10(1) and (8), repealed section 40(10A) of the 2005 Act, subject to saving and transitional provisions (as to which, see *ante*, § 1-27). ★

*Disclosure of information to Director of Revenue and Customs Prosecutions*

With effect from March 27, 2014, the Public Bodies (Merger of the Director of Public Prosecutions and the Director of Revenue and Customs Prosecutions) Order 2014 (S.I. 2014 No. 834), art. 3(3), and Sched. 1, paras 5 and 11, repealed section 41 of the 2005 Act, subject to saving and transitional provisions (as to which, see *ante*, § 1-27). ★1-389

## CHAPTER 2

# THE CRIMINAL JURISDICTION OF THE CROWN COURT

### I. THE CROWN COURT

### C. CONSTITUTION

### (1) Judges of the Crown Court

**Criminal Procedure Rules 2013 (S.I. 2013 No. 1554), r.63.10**

*Appeals and committals for sentence - constitution of the Crown Court*

Whereas rule 63.10 of the 2013 rules provides that an appeal to the Crown Court may be **2-6** heard with only one justice of the peace if the presiding judge "decides that otherwise the start of the appeal hearing will be delayed unreasonably", no other conclusion would have been appropriate where an appeal against conviction was listed for hearing (before a bench including two justices, one of whom had to recuse herself) nine months after the date of conviction in the magistrates' court, where the matter had twice previously been listed for hearing in the Crown Court but had had to be adjourned on account of the non-availability of witnesses, and where the next available date for a hearing would have been one year after the date of conviction in the lower court: *R. (Chinaka) v. Southwark Crown Court, CPS (interested party)*, 177 J.P. 683, DC (decided by reference to an earlier, but materially identical, version of the rules).

### (2) Additional powers

#### Courts Act 2003, s.66

*Judges having powers of District Judges (Magistrates' Courts)*

★**2-8**    With effect from April 22, 2014, the Crime and Courts Act 2013, s.17(6), and Sched. 10, paras 83 and 90, were brought into force: Crime and Courts Act 2013 (Commencement No. 10 and Transitional Provision) Order 2014 (S.I. 2014 No. 954).

### (3) Mode of address

**2-9**    The 2013 criminal practice directions (see the main work) are now reported at [2013] 1 W.L.R. 3164.

With effect from December 10, 2013, *Criminal Practice Direction (General application) B* (see the main work, and *ante*), is amended to clarify that any senior circuit judge who is an honorary recorder should be addressed, when sitting in court, as "My Lord" or "My Lady" regardless of where he or she is sitting: *Practice Direction (Criminal Proceedings: Various Changes)* [2014] 1 W.L.R. 35.

## E.  RIGHTS OF AUDIENCE AND COURT DRESS

### Court dress of advocates

**2-28**    The 2013 criminal practice directions (see the main work) are now reported at [2013] 1 W.L.R. 3164.

## III. JURISDICTION IN RESPECT OF ACTS PERFORMED ABROAD AND IN RESPECT OF FOREIGN NATIONALS

### D.  PARTICULAR OFFENCES

### (11) Offences in the Admiralty jurisdiction

#### Territorial sea

**2-70**    With effect from March 31, 2014, the Territorial Sea (Limits) Order 1989 (S.I. 1989 No. 482) was amended by the Territorial Sea (Limits) (Amendment) Order 2013 (S.I. 2013 No. 3164) to reflect an agreement between the United Kingdom and France that the coordinates of the points defining the territorial sea boundary between the two countries in the Straits of Dover should be reformulated in World Geodetic Datum System 1984 (WGS84).

★    With effect from June 30, 2014, the Territorial Sea (Baselines) Order 2014 (S.I. 2014 No. 1353) revoked the Territorial Waters Order in Council 1964 and established the baselines from which the breadth of the territorial sea adjacent to the United Kingdom, the Channel Islands and the Isle of Man is measured in accordance with the United Nations Convention on the Law of the Sea.

## IV. JURISDICTION TO OBTAIN EVIDENCE FOR USE OVERSEAS

### Crime (International Co-operation) Act 2003

★**2-154**    As to entry, search and seizure to obtain evidence for use in foreign proceedings, see *Van der Pijl v. Secretary of State for the Home Department*, *post*, §§ 15-72a, 15-112.

The ambit of section 13 of the 2003 Act (as to which, see the main work) was considered in *R.*   ★
*(Secretary of State for the Home Department) v. Southwark Crown Court* [2014] A.C.D. 51, DC ([2013]
EWHC 4366 (Admin.)).

## V. APPELLATE JURISDICTION OF CROWN COURT IN CRIMINAL CASES

### B. RIGHTS OF APPEAL TO CROWN COURT

### (10) Appeal against drinking banning order

#### Violent Crime Reduction Act 2006, s.10

*Appeals*

As from a day to be appointed, Part 2 (ss.22–33) of the Anti-social Behaviour, Crime and Polic-   ★**2-172b**
ing Act 2014 makes provision for criminal behaviour orders. Such orders replace drinking banning orders (and anti-social behaviour orders) made on conviction of a criminal offence. In
consequence, sections 1 to 14 of the VCRA 2006 are repealed as from a day to be appointed:
2014 Act, s.181(1), and Sched. 11, paras 44 and 50. For the replacement provisions, see *post*, §§
5-1210a *et seq.* For saving and transitional provisions, see the 2014 Act, s.33 (*post*, § 5-1210l).

### D. CESSATION AND ABANDONMENT OF RIGHT OF APPEAL

### (3) Abandonment of appeal

The 2013 criminal practice directions (see the main work) are now reported at [2013] 1 W.L.R.   **2-176**
3164.

## VI. CRIMINAL PROCEDURE RULES

#### Criminal Procedure Rules 2013 (S.I. 2013 No. 1554), Pt 2

*Definitions*

The 2013 criminal practice directions (see the main work) are now reported at [2013] 1 W.L.R.   **2-206**
3164.

With effect from April 7, 2014, rule 2.2 of the Criminal Procedure Rules 2013 (S.I. 2013 No.
1554) is amended by rule 4 of the Criminal Procedure (Amendment No. 2) Rules 2013 (S.I. 2013
No. 3183) so as to substitute "Criminal Practice Directions" for "Consolidated Criminal Practice
Direction".

#### Criminal Procedure Rules 2013 (S.I. 2013 No. 1554), Pt 5

*Forms*

The 2013 criminal practice directions (see the main work) are now reported at [2013] 1 W.L.R.   **2-219**
3164.

*Court records*

With effect from October 27, 2013, rule 5.4(1) of the 2013 rules has been amended by the   **2-219c**
Criminal Procedure (Amendment) Rules 2013 (S.I. 2013 No. 2525), r.4, so as: (i) to omit the word
"and" at the end of sub-paragraph (k); (ii) to insert, after sub-paragraph (l)(iii)—

> "(iv)  any interpreter or intermediary,".

(iii) to re-number (l)(iv) and (v) accordingly; and (iv) to insert new sub-paragraphs (m) and (n),
after sub-paragraph (l), as follows—

> "(m) where a defendant is entitled to attend a hearing, any agreement by the defendant to
> waive that right; and
> (n) where interpretation is required for a defendant, any agreement by that defendant to do
> without the written translation of a document."

*Supply to the public, including reporters, of information about a case*

With effect from April 7, 2014, rule 5.8(1) of the Criminal Procedure Rules 2013 (S.I. 2013 No.   **2-219g**

1554) is substituted by rule 5(a) of the Criminal Procedure (Amendment No. 2) Rules 2013 (S.I. 2013 No. 3183), as follows—

"(1) This rule—

    (a) applies where a member of the public, including a reporter, wants information about a case from the court officer;

    (b) requires the court officer to publish information about cases due to be heard."

With effect from April 7, 2014, rule 5.8(2) of the Criminal Procedure Rules 2013 (S.I. 2013 No. 1554) is amended by rule 5(b) of the Criminal Procedure (Amendment No. 2) Rules 2013 (S.I. 2013 No. 3183), so as to substitute the words "A person who wants information about a case from the court officer must" for the words "Such a person".

With effect from April 7, 2014, rule 5(c) of the Criminal Procedure (Amendment No. 2) Rules 2013 (S.I. 2013 No. 3183) amends rule 5.8 of the Criminal Procedure Rules 2013 (S.I. 2013 No. 1554), so as to insert new paragraphs (9) to (11), as follows—

"(9) The court officer must publish the information listed in paragraph (11) if—

    (a) the information is available to the court officer;

    (b) the hearing to which the information relates is due to take place in public; and

    (c) the publication of the information is not prohibited by a reporting restriction.

(10) The court officer must publish that information—

    (a) by notice displayed somewhere prominent in the vicinity of the court room in which the hearing is due to take place;

    (b) by such other arrangements as the Lord Chancellor directs, including arrangements for publication by electronic means; and

    (c) for no longer than 2 business days.

(11) The information that paragraph (9) requires the court officer to publish is—

    (a) the date, time and place of the hearing;

    (b) the identity of the defendant; and

    (c) such other information as it may be practicable to publish concerning—

      (i) the type of hearing,

      (ii) the identity of the court,

      (iii) the offence or offences alleged, and

      (iv) whether any reporting restriction applies.".

*Access to information held by court*

**2-220**    The 2013 criminal practice directions (see the main work) are now reported at [2013] 1 W.L.R. 3164.

*Documents read aloud in their entirety*

**2-221**    With effect from December 10, 2013, Criminal Practice Direction (General matters) 5B, para. 5B.11 (see the main work), is amended to clarify that the legislation being referred to is the *CJA 1967: Practice Direction (Criminal Proceedings: Various Changes)* [2014] 1 W.L.R. 35.

*References to the European Court of Justice*

**2-233**    The 2013 criminal practice directions (see the main work) are now reported at [2013] 1 W.L.R. 3164.

CHAPTER 3

# BAIL, APPEARANCE OF ACCUSED FOR TRIAL, PRESENCE DURING TRIAL

## *I. BAIL*

### A. GENERAL

### (2) The Bail Act 1976

#### (c) *Text of the Act*

**Practice directions**

The 2013 criminal practice directions (see the main work) are now reported at [2013] 1 W.L.R. **3-35** 3164.

*Failure to surrender and trials in absence*

The 2013 criminal practice directions (see the main work) are now reported at [2013] 1 W.L.R. **3-36** 3164.

*Penalties for failure to surrender*

The 2013 criminal practice directions (see the main work) are now reported at [2013] 1 W.L.R. **3-37** 3164.

*Relationship between the Bail Act offence and further remands on bail or in custody*

The 2013 criminal practice directions (see the main work) are now reported at [2013] 1 W.L.R. **3-42** 3164.

*Forfeiture of monies lodged as security or pledged by a surety/estreatment of recognizances*

The 2013 criminal practice directions (see the main work) are now reported at [2013] 1 W.L.R. **3-53a** 3164.

### (6) Place of remand

#### (b) *Persons under 21 years*

**Secure accommodation for children remanded to local authority accommodation**

The provisions of the Crime and Courts Act 2013 referred to in the main work came into force **★3-107** on April 22, 2014: Crime and Courts Act 2013 (Commencement No. 10 and Transitional Provision) Order 2014 (S.I. 2014 No. 954).

### (8) Appeal against grant of bail

**Bail (Amendment) Act 1993, s.1**

*Prosecution right of appeal*

With effect from March 27, 2014, the Public Bodies (Merger of the Director of Public Prosecu- **★3-114** tions and the Director of Revenue and Customs Prosecutions) Order 2014 (S.I. 2014 No. 834), art. 3(3), and Sched. 3, para. 2, amended the Bail (Amendment) Act 1993 (Prescription of Prosecuting Authorities) Order 1994 (S.I. 1994 No. 1438), subject to saving and transitional provisions (as to which, see *ante*, § 1-27), so as to omit from the list of authorities prescribed for the purposes of section 1 of the 1993 Act (§ 3-113 in the main work), the Director of Revenue and Customs Prosecutions and any person designated under section 37(1) of the Commissioners for Revenue and Customs Act 2005.

## B. Specific Provisions

### (2) Magistrates' courts

#### (h) *Recognizances*

**Magistrates' Courts Act 1980, s.120**

*Forfeiture of recognizance*

★3-189    With effect from April 6, 2014, the provisions of the Tribunals, Courts and Enforcement Act 2007 referred to in the main work were brought into force: Tribunals, Courts and Enforcement Act 2007 (Commencement No. 11) Order 2014 (S.I. 2014 No. 768).

### (3) The Crown Court

#### (a) *Preliminaries*

*Bail during trial*

3-204    The 2013 criminal practice directions (see the main work) are now reported at [2013] 1 W.L.R. 3164.

#### (b) *Jurisdiction in respect of cases before magistrates*

*Bail before sending for trial*

3-206    The 2013 criminal practice directions (see the main work) are now reported at [2013] 1 W.L.R. 3164.

### (4) The High Court

#### (a) *Abolition of inherent jurisdiction*

3-212    *R. (M.) v. Isleworth Crown Court and H.M. Customs and Excise* (as to which, see the main work and § 7-11 in the main work), was considered in *R. (Uddin) v Crown Court at Leeds* [2014] 1 Cr.App.R. 13, QBD (H.H. Judge Richardson Q.C., sitting as a deputy High Court judge), in which it was held that section 29(3) of the Senior Courts Act 1981 (§ 7-4 in the main work) does operate so as to prevent judicial review of a decision by a judge during a Crown Court trial to revoke the defendant's bail.

## III. PRESENCE OF THE ACCUSED IN COURT DURING THE TRIAL

### A. General Rule

**Trial**

★3-223    To avoid a trial in his absence, a defendant has a responsibility to maintain contact with his lawyers by means that allow for communication at short notice, and he must ensure that he is aware of the date of his trial or the period of any relevant warned list; if his case is in a warned list, he will need to contact his solicitors or the court on a daily basis to find out whether the case has been listed for the following day; and, as a matter of good practice, defendants should be reminded in terms of these obligations by the judge at the plea and case management hearing: *R. v. Lopez* [2014] Crim.L.R. 384, CA.

**Proceedings relating to sentence and/or confiscation of assets**

*Trials in absence*

3-225a    The 2013 criminal practice directions (see the main work) are now reported at [2013] 1 W.L.R. 3164.

CHAPTER 4

## TRIAL

### I. PRELIMINARIES

### B. HEARING IN OPEN COURT

#### (1) European Convention on Human Rights and common law

**Applications to sit in camera, in chambers, or in private**

Where there is tension between the principle of open justice and the needs of national security,    ★**4-6**
(a) considerations of national security will not by themselves justify a departure from the principle
of open justice, (b) open justice must, however, give way to the yet more fundamental principle
that the paramount object of the court is to do justice; accordingly, where there is a serious possibility that an insistence on open justice in the national security context would frustrate the
administration of justice, *e.g.*, by deterring the Crown from prosecuting a case where it otherwise
would do so, a departure from open justice may be justified, and (c) the question whether to give
effect to a ministerial certificate (asserting a need for privacy) is ultimately for the court, not a
minister; however, in the field of national security, a court will not lightly depart from the assessment made by a minister: *Re Guardian News and Media Ltd*, *The Times*, June 18, 2014, CA (observing that it was difficult to conceive of a situation where the holding of the entirety of a criminal
trial *in camera* and the anonymisation of the defendants would be justified).

### C. PUBLICITY

#### (1) General right to publish reports

When making orders restricting publication, whether as to the identity of the defendant or as    **4-15**
to the details of the evidence, the duty of a court is to ensure (a) compliance with the principles of
open justice, (b) that there be no interference with an individual's rights under Articles 2 (right to
life (§ 16-36 in the main work)) or 3 (prohibition on inhuman or degrading treatment (*ibid.*, § 16-
39)) of the ECHR, and (c) that there be no unnecessary or disproportionate interference with the
rights of the public under Article 10 (freedom of expression (*ibid.*, § 16-119)) or of any relevant
individual under Article 8 (right to privacy and family life (*ibid.*, § 16-101)), see *R. v. Marine A.*; *Re
Guardian News and Media*; *R. (Marine A.) v. Judge Advocate General* [2014] 1 Cr.App.R. 26, DC &
CMAC. The court emphasised that even where a court concludes that there is a relevant risk to a
convention right of the defendant, a witness or a third party, it will still have to ask itself whether
an order restricting publication will be effective to guard against the risk and whether any
alternative measure was available effectively to protect the relevant rights without a derogation
from open justice.

#### (2) Restrictions

(b) *Child or young person as victim, witness or defendant*

**Children and Young Persons Act 1933, s.39**

*Power to prohibit publication*

Whereas, under section 39 of the 1933 Act, a court may prohibit publication of information    **4-24**
"calculated to lead to the identification, of any child or young person concerned in the proceedings, either as being the person by or against or in respect of whom the proceedings are taken, or
as being a witness therein", in relation to criminal proceedings, this can only include a child or
young person who is the victim of an alleged offence, or who is the defendant or a witness; it does
not extend to children or young persons who may be concerned in the more general sense of be-

23

ing affected by the proceedings (as here, where the child in question was the youngest son of a person being tried for tax fraud, by wrongfully claiming military education allowance, in order to send his children to an independent boarding school): *Re Press Association (Robert Jolleys)* [2014] 1 Cr.App.R. 15, CA. It was further held that the particular order also fell to be discharged, first, because the judge had failed to provide the press with an opportunity to make representations prior to making it, contrary to the express provision of rule 16.2(3) of the Criminal Procedure Rules 2012 (S.I. 2012 No. 1726) (see now r.16.2(3) of the 2013 rules (S.I. 2013 No. 1554) (§ 4-47 in the main work)), secondly, because he had asked what the need for identifying the son was, whereas it is for anyone seeking to derogate from open justice to justify derogation by clear and cogent evidence (*R. v. Central Criminal Court, ex p. W., B. and C.* (as to which, see § 4-28 in the main work)), and, thirdly, because the order extended somewhat loosely to a "media report", whereas orders should reflect the language of the legislation, *viz.* newspaper reports and (by virtue of the CYPA 1963, s.57(4)) sound and television reports. The court added that the requirements of open justice demand that judges are fully mindful of these underlying principles; in most cases, the application of the law will be obvious; where, however, there is the slightest doubt, or any novel approach is suggested, it should, the court said, be identified in good time and notice provided so that the press can also consider the matter; even then, judges cannot expect local reporters to be in a position to instruct lawyers or argue the principles in depth, and, in any event, counsel should be required to research and develop the arguments to assist the court in a balanced manner, which is not to limit the right of reporters or their lawyers to advance argument on their own behalf.

★    In *J.C. and R.T. v. Central Criminal Court, CPS and British Broadcasting Corporation (interested parties) and Just for Kids Law (intervener)*, 178 J.P. 188, DC, it was held that a direction under section 39 of the CYPA 1933 (see § 4-24 in the main work) prohibiting the identification of (among others) a defendant under the age of 18 years, will expire automatically when the person attains the age of 18 years; it is not the case of "once a child or young person, always a child or young person".

★**4-25**    *R. (A.) v. Lowestoft Magistrates' Court, CPS and Archant Community Media Ltd (interested parties)* is now reported at [2014] 1 W.L.R. 1489, *sub nom. R. (A.) v. Lowestoft Magistrates' Court.*

### (d) *Photographs*

**4-40**    The Court of Appeal (Recording and Broadcasting) Order 2013 (S.I. 2013 No. 2786) disapplies section 41 of the CJA 1925 (see the main work) and section 9 of the Contempt of Court Act 1981 (§ 28-74 in the main work) in relation to the recording of proceedings in the Court of Appeal that are made in accordance with articles 5 to 7 and the broadcasting of such recordings, if made in accordance with articles 9 to 11. For further details, see *post*, § 7-36a.

### D. IDENTITY AND IMPARTIALITY OF JUDGE

**Impartiality**

**4-56**    *O'Neill v. H.M. Advocate (No. 2)*; *Lauchlan v. Same* is now reported at [2013] 2 Cr.App.R. 34.

### E. PROCEEDINGS ORDINARILY CONDUCTED IN ENGLISH

**4-57**    The 2013 criminal practice directions (see the main work) are now reported at [2013] 1 W.L.R. 3164.

### F. INTERPRETERS

### (7) **Courts in Wales and Monmouthshire**

**4-64**    The 2013 criminal practice directions (see the main work) are now reported at [2013] 1 W.L.R. 3164.

### G. REPRESENTATION OF THE DEFENDANT

### (1) **Legal representation**

★**4-65**    Where a defendant's legal representatives withdraw part-way through criminal proceedings on account of non-payment of fees (in this case, after trial but prior to confiscation proceedings) and then decline to release the case papers to the defendant's new solicitors on the basis that they have a lien over them, an application to the High Court for that court to exercise its equitable jurisdiction to order the production of papers over which a solicitor's lien is being exercised should result in an order for production of the papers; where the interests of an accused person in criminal proceedings are concerned, the solicitor's right to rely on a lien may have to give way: *R. v. Onuigbo (also known as Okoronkwo)* [2014] Lloyd's Rep. F.C. 302, CA.

For a case considering whether it was appropriate to stay a prosecution where no counsel of ★ suitable experience were available to conduct the defence because of the alleged inadequacy of the fees payable under the arrangements for the public funding of criminal defence work, see *R. v. Crawley, post,* § 4-81.

### K. Limited Discretionary Power to Prevent Prosecution Proceeding

### (2) Abuse of process

### (b) *Where it will be impossible to give the defendant a fair trial*

**Evidential matters**

The approach taken in *R. (Ebrahim) v. Feltham Magistrates' Court*; *Mouat v. DPP* (see the main ★**4-78** work) in respect of an application to stay proceedings for abuse of process by reason of non-availability of evidence was followed in *Morris v. DPP* [2014] 2 *Archbold Review* 2, QBD (Wyn Williams J.), in which it was held that, where the appellant, who had been suspected of assault, identified eye-witnesses in interview and thereafter provided the police with their contact information, the police had been under a duty to contact the witnesses and obtain such information as they were able to provide; while this was ultimately an issue of judgment for the police, in relation to which they were entitled to take into account factors such as resources, time and what other evidence may or may not have been available, in a case involving potential eye-witnesses to a single incident where there were sharply conflicting versions of events, they should have attempted to contact the witnesses with a view to taking statements from them. However, the appeal by way of case stated against the magistrates' refusal of the application to stay the proceedings was dismissed, the High Court finding that the opportunity to obtain and retain the relevant evidence was just as much available to the defence as to the prosecution, and that, accordingly, the appellant had not established that the failure of the prosecution to obtain or retain evidence had rendered it impossible for the trial to be fair.

**Delay and the right to trial "within a reasonable time"**

*Application of principles*

Where the respondents had been charged with offences of serious fraud, where, after the court ★**4-81** had made the appropriate representation orders, the case was classified as a "Very High Cost Case", where, meanwhile, the Ministry of Justice announced a cut of 30 per cent in the rate of remuneration paid to counsel in such cases, where the trial was fixed for April 28, 2014 (with a time estimate of three months), at which date no suitably qualified advocate was prepared to sign a VHCC contract, the judge erred in refusing an adjournment and staying the prosecution on the ground that the failure of the state (of which the prosecuting authority (the Financial Conduct Authority) was held to be an arm) to provide the necessary resources for a fair trial to take place within a reasonable time (having found that there was no realistic prospect that sufficient advocates would be available for the case to be tried in January, 2015) constituted an abuse of the court's process: *R. v. Crawley,* unreported, May 21, 2014, CA. The Court of Appeal held, first, that it was quite wrong, for present purposes, to seek to link, effectively as one, the Financial Conduct Authority as prosecuting authority and those responsible for the provision of legal aid; and, secondly, that the judge's finding that there was no realistic prospect of competent Public Defender Service advocates (including Queen's Counsel) with enough time to prepare being available in the foreseeable future could not be sustained.

### (c) *Where a stay is necessary to protect the integrity of the criminal justice system*

**Situations akin to autrefois**

In *R. (Gavigan (Michael) and Gavigan (Connor)) v. Enfield Magistrates' Court, CPS (interested party),* **4-89**

177 J.P. 609, DC, it was held that whereas a penalty notice is a notice offering the person to whom it is addressed the opportunity to pay a fixed penalty "to discharge any liability to be convicted of the offence to which the notice relates" (CJPA 2001, s.2(4)), there is no principle or policy that precludes a person, who has rejected the opportunity to pay a fixed penalty, from being prosecuted for any offence (including, as here, a more serious offence) arising out of the same set of facts as those in respect of which the notice was issued. Referring to *R. v. Gore and Maher* (see the main work), the court said that the law is clear. It added, however, that if the claimants had paid the penalty and not exercised their right to have the issue determined by a court, then, if the evidence of the more serious offence had been available when the notice had been served, it might, by analogy with *R. v. Beedie* (see § 4-88 in the main work), have been unfair subsequently to have prosecuted them for a more serious offence, but that was not this case.

### The decision to institute or continue proceedings

*Private prosecutions*

4-91     Where a private company bringing a prosecution for conspiracy to defraud enlisted the assistance of the police in making arrests and obtaining search warrants, then entered an agreement with the relevant police authority to make a cash donation to the authority of 25 per cent of any sums recovered under a compensation order, and, following conviction, began confiscation proceedings (its quest for compensation was abandoned), given the fact that the only beneficiary of a confiscation order would be the state, the agreement gave rise to no abuse of process; however, in light of *R. v. Hounsham, Mayes and Blake* [2005] Crim.L.R. 991, CA, the agreement provided the police with an incentive to devote resources to assisting the company and gave rise to a perception that their independence was being compromised; it was essential that the Association of Chief Police Officers, the Association of Police and Crime Commissioners and the Home Office gave urgent consideration to the issuing of clear guidance on what the police may or may not do when approached by commercial enterprises to lend assistance in proceedings for confiscation and claims for compensation; where there is cause for concern that the prosecutor's duty to act in the public interest may conflict with his private interest, it will be for the court to ensure that its proceedings are not abused: *R. v. Zinga* [2014] 1 Cr.App.R. 27, CA. As to this case, see also *post*, § 5-806.

### Prosecution/investigators contributing to commission of offence

★4-96    As to the question whether, where it is alleged that the defendant was lured into the commission of an offence (in the sense described in *R. v. Looseley*; *Att.-Gen.'s Reference (No. 3 of 2000)* (see the main work)), the conduct of the police was so seriously improper as to bring the administration of justice into disrepute, the following five considerations (as set out by David Ormerod in "Recent Developments in Entrapment" [2006] Covert Policing Review 65) were of particular relevance, (i) whether the police operation was triggered by a reasonable suspicion of criminal activity, (ii) whether the operation was properly authorised and supervised, (iii) whether the means employed were necessary and proportionate, having regard to the types of offence being investigated, (iv) whether the police caused the offence or merely presented the defendant with an "unexceptional opportunity" to commit it, and (v) whether the evidence of the police was properly authenticated: *R. v. Moore*; *R. v. Burrows* [2014] Crim.L.R. 364, CA.

### (d) *Procedure*

*Abuse of process stay applications*

4-101    The 2013 criminal practice directions (see the main work) are now reported at [2013] 1 W.L.R. 3164.

### L. ACCESS TO THE JUDGE

### (1) General

4-107    The 2013 criminal practice directions (see the main work) are now reported at [2013] 1 W.L.R. 3164.

### M. VIEW OF LOCUS IN QUO

4-111    The 2013 criminal practice directions (see the main work) are now reported at [2013] 1 W.L.R. 3164.

## N. Pre-Trial Hearings

### (1) The court's case management powers and duties

The 2013 criminal practice directions (see the main work) are now reported at [2013] 1 W.L.R. **4-114**
3164.

#### Criminal Procedure Rules 2013 (S.I. 2013 No. 1554), Pt 3

*Case preparation and progression*

With effect from October 27, 2013, rule 3.8 of the 2013 rules has been amended by the **4-117**
Criminal Procedure (Amendment) Rules 2013 (S.I. 2013 No. 2525), r.3, so as to insert new
paragraphs (5) and (6) at the end, as follows—

"(5) Facilitating the participation of the defendant includes finding out whether the defendant
needs interpretation because—
    (a) the defendant does not speak or understand English; or
    (b) the defendant has a hearing or speech impediment.
(6) Where the defendant needs interpretation—
    (a) the court officer must arrange for interpretation to be provided at every hearing which the
       defendant is due to attend;
    (b) interpretation may be by an intermediary where the defendant has a speech impediment,
       without the need for a defendant's evidence direction;
    (c) on application or on its own initiative, the court may require a written translation to be
       provided for the defendant of any document or part of a document, unless—
       (i) translation of that document, or part, is not needed to explain the case against the
         defendant, or
       (ii) the defendant agrees to do without and the court is satisfied that the agreement is
         clear and voluntary and that the defendant has had legal advice or otherwise
         understands the consequences;
    (d) on application by the defendant, the court must give any direction which the court thinks
       appropriate, including a direction for interpretation by a different interpreter, where—
       (i) no interpretation is provided,
       (ii) no translation is ordered or provided in response to a previous application by the
         defendant, or
       (iii) the defendant complains about the quality of interpretation or of any translation.".

### (2) Preliminary hearings and plea and case management hearings

*Case management*

The 2013 criminal practice directions (see the main work) are now reported at [2013] 1 W.L.R. **4-121**
3164.

The 2013 criminal practice directions (see the main work) are now reported at [2013] 1 W.L.R. **4-123b**
3164.

### (3) Preparatory hearings

(b) *Long, complex or serious cases*

#### Criminal Procedure and Investigations Act 1996, s.28

*Introduction*

The provisions of the Crime and Courts Act 2013 referred to in the main work came into force **★4-130**
on February 24, 2014: Crime and Courts Act 2013 (Commencement No. 8) Order 2014 (S.I.
2014 No. 258).

(d) *Authorities (all cases)*

### The purpose and ambit of preparatory hearings

A retrial involving sexual allegations against three defendants (five counts, the most serious of **4-144**
which was rape), relating to a single evening and dependent on the evidence of the complainant,

did not meet the criteria for ordering a preparatory hearing in section 29(1) of the CPIA 1996 (§ 4-131 in the main work) where the trial would be completed in the space of a week or a little more, and where the sentences imposed in the original trial were in the region of eight years' imprisonment: *R. v. Lawrence (Joseph)* [2014] 1 Cr.App.R. 5, CA. As to this case, see also *post*, §§ 10-25, 11-3.

### (4) Statutory pre-trial hearings

#### Criminal Procedure and Investigations Act 1996, ss.39–42

*Meaning of pre-trial hearing*

★**4-152**    The provisions of the Crime and Courts Act 2013 referred to in the main work came into force on February 24, 2014: Crime and Courts Act 2013 (Commencement No. 8) Order 2014 (S.I. 2014 No. 258).

### R. VULNERABLE DEFENDANTS SPECIAL ARRANGEMENTS

**4-162**    The 2013 criminal practice directions (see the main work) are now reported at [2013] 1 W.L.R. 3164.

**4-165**    *R. v. Dixon* is now reported at [2014] 1 W.L.R. 525, *sub nom. R. v. Dixon (Jordan)*.

## II. ARRAIGNMENT AND PLEA

### B. PLEA

### (4) Plea of guilty

#### (b) *To lesser offence*

**4-175**    The 2013 criminal practice directions (see the main work) are now reported at [2013] 1 W.L.R. 3164.

### (9) Autrefois acquit and autrefois convict

#### (d) *Adjudication upon guilt or innocence*

### Summary proceedings

★**4-207**    A plea of *autrefois acquit* will not lie so as to bar the institution of fresh proceedings for the same offence where a magistrates' court dismisses an information for a summary offence under section 15 of the MCA 1980 (failure of prosecutor to appear), and the institution of fresh proceedings in such circumstances could not amount to an abuse of process where there was no prejudice to the accused: *DPP v. Jarman*, 178 J.P. 89, DC (considering *Holmes v. Campbell* (see the main work), *R. (O.) v. Stratford Youth Court* (§ 4-206 in the main work), and *R. v. J. (J.F.)* (§ 4-185 in the main work)). For criticism of this decision, see CLW/14/09/1.

### (13) Defendant unfit to plead or take his trial

#### (a) *Procedure, evidence and burden of proof*

### "did the act or made the omission charged"

**4-237**    Where a defendant was found to be unfit to be tried, pursuant to section 4(5) of the Criminal Procedure (Insanity) Act 1964 (§ 4-231 in the main work), the contents of his police interview should not then have gone before the jury who were to determine whether he did the act charged against him as the offence, pursuant to section 4A(2) of the 1964 Act (*ibid.*, § 4-232), given that his mental impairment in all likelihood resulted in a failure on his part to understand the real significance of the caution given to him before interview; before admitting interview evidence in such circumstances, the court will usually need to be persuaded by expert evidence that, notwithstanding the finding of unfitness, the defendant understood the caution and that, generally, it was safe to interview him; the same considerations would apply to those rare occasions when it is suggested such a defendant should give evidence on the trial of the facts; where an interview under caution is introduced, it is likely that the judge will need to give the jury a specially-crafted direction warning them of the need for particular care, given the risk that what was said in interview may be the result of the defendant's disability rather than because he was lying or otherwise attempting to mislead the police; a direction that is broader than, or different from, a conventional Lucas lies direction (*R. v. Lucas (R.)* (*ibid.*, § 4-461)) will be required, tailored to the circumstances of the case: *R. v. Swinbourne*, 178 J.P. 34, CA (in which it was assumed that where the allegation is one of rape "the act ... charged" against defendant will include not just penetration of the complainant by the defendant with his penis, but also lack of consent on the complainant's part).

## VI. THE JURY

### A. INTRODUCTION

The 2013 criminal practice directions (see the main work) are now reported at [2013] 1 W.L.R.　**4-266**
3164.

### B. QUALIFICATION

#### Juries Act 1974, s.1

The provisions of the Crime and Courts Act 2013 referred to in the main work came into force　**★4-267**
on April 22, 2014: Crime and Courts Act 2013 (Commencement No. 10 and Transitional Provision) Order 2014 (S.I. 2014 No. 954).

### C. SUMMONING AND PANELS

#### Juries Act 1974, s.2

The provisions of the Crime and Courts Act 2013 referred to in the main work came into force　**★4-272**
on April 22, 2014: Crime and Courts Act 2013 (Commencement No. 10 and Transitional Provision) Order 2014 (S.I. 2014 No. 954).

### D. ATTENDANCE, SERVICE, EXCUSALS, DEFERRAL

#### Juries Act 1974, ss.7–9

*Attendance and service*

The provisions of the Crime and Courts Act 2013 referred to in the main work came into force　**★4-280**
on April 22, 2014: Crime and Courts Act 2013 (Commencement No. 10 and Transitional Provision) Order 2014 (S.I. 2014 No. 954).

*Juries: preliminary matters arising before jury service commences*

The 2013 criminal practice directions (see the main work) are now reported at [2013] 1 W.L.R.　**4-288**
3164.

#### Criminal Procedure Rules 2013 (S.I. 2013 No. 1554), r.39.2

*Appeal against refusal to excuse from jury service or to defer attendance*

The provisions of the Crime and Courts Act 2013 referred to in the main work came into force　**★4-289**
on April 22, 2014: Crime and Courts Act 2013 (Commencement No. 10 and Transitional Provision) Order 2014 (S.I. 2014 No. 954).

*Juries: eligibility*

The 2013 criminal practice directions (see the main work) are now reported at [2013] 1 W.L.R.　**4-291a**
3164.

*Juries: precautionary measures before swearing*

The 2013 criminal practice directions (see the main work) are now reported at [2013] 1 W.L.R.　**4-291d**
3164.

### E. THE BALLOT

#### Juries Act 1974, s.11

Where a judge decided to empanel a jury by number rather than name, in accordance with　**4-292** that location of the Crown Court's standard practice in all cases anticipated to last more than two weeks (irrespective of any evidence of risk of jury nobbling), where special arrangements were also made in relation to jury transportation and refreshments and where the jury were directed by the judge that such practices were normal for cases of this length, they could not have had any effect on the perception of the jury in light of the explanation given to them by the judge (considering *R. v. Comerford* (as to which, see the main work)); while the fairness of the trial was not affected and the safety of the conviction was not in any way impaired, such local practices can no longer be justified; practice and procedure in the Crown Court should be the same wherever it may sit, unless there is an objectively justifiable basis for such a variation in practice based on local conditions, in which case details of any such local practice and its justification should be submitted to the office of the Lord Chief Justice before it is implemented: *R. v. Baybasin* [2014] 1 Cr.App.R. 19, CA. As to this case, see also *post*, § 7-97.

## G. Challenge

### (1) Statute

#### Juries Act 1974, s.12

★**4-296**    The provisions of the Crime and Courts Act 2013 referred to in the main work came into force on April 22, 2014: Crime and Courts Act 2013 (Commencement No. 10 and Transitional Provision) Order 2014 (S.I. 2014 No. 954).

## I. Swearing

*Juries: swearing in juries*

**4-306**    The 2013 criminal practice directions (see the main work) are now reported at [2013] 1 W.L.R. 3164.

## J. Discharge of Juror or Jury

### (1) Where a necessity arises

*Juries: discharge of a juror for personal reasons*

**4-307a**    The 2013 criminal practice directions (see the main work) are now reported at [2013] 1 W.L.R. 3164.

### (2) Investigation

*Juries: jury irregularities*

**4-308**    The 2013 criminal practice directions (see the main work) are now reported at [2013] 1 W.L.R. 3164.

**4-309**    In *R. v. Connors* [2013] Crim.L.R. 854, CA, where the jury panel had been asked before trial whether, in the context of the defendants being members of the travelling community, they had any views that would make it difficult to return verdicts based solely on the evidence, before the case of the fourth defendant was about to start, the judge received a letter from a juror alleging prejudice against travellers among some of the other jurors. In the nine weeks of the trial up to that point, nothing had given the judge cause to suspect the possibility of prejudice among the jurors, and he decided that a stern and clear direction was the right remedy in the circumstances. On appeal it was held (having considered, *inter alia*, *R. v. Smith and Mercieca* (see the main work), and *R. v. Thompson; R. v. Crawford; R. v. Gomulu; R. v. Allen; R. v. Blake; R. v. Kasunga* (*ibid.*, § 4-325a)) that he had handled the problem impeccably, and his assessment of the integrity of the particular jury was amply justified; he had not been bound to discharge the jury because of the letter, however troublesome its contents; equally it would have been inappropriate for him to try to conduct an investigation into what was happening in the jury room; and the verdicts, far from being a blanket series of verdicts suggestive of prejudice, were consistent with a conscientious and unimpeachable approach to the jury's responsibilities.

## L. Miscellaneous

### (2) Direction to jury as to how to approach their role

*Juries: preliminary instructions to jurors*

The 2013 criminal practice directions (see the main work) are now reported at [2013] 1 W.L.R.    **4-325**
3164.

## X. DUTIES OF THE PROSECUTION RELATING TO THE PRESENTATION OF THE EVIDENCE AND THE CALLING OF WITNESSES

### A. Preparation of Bundles

*Pagination and indexing of served evidence*

The 2013 criminal practice directions (see the main work) are now reported at [2013] 1 W.L.R.    **4-344**
3164.

### F. "Editing" of Witness's Statement

*Evidence by written statement*

The 2013 criminal practice directions (see the main work) are now reported at [2013] 1 W.L.R.    **4-354**
3164.

## XI. EVIDENCE USUALLY TENDERED IN PRESENCE OF JURY

### B. Exceptions

### (3) Determining the admissibility of tape recordings

Where the prosecution seek to rely on a recorded conversation and allege that one of the    **4-360**
participants was the defendant, while the best way of establishing the authenticity of the recording is through evidence of its provenance and history, this is not the only way. Authenticity can be
proved circumstantially, the test being whether there is sufficient material for the tribunal of fact
to conclude that the recorded sounds reproduce a conversation that occurred and which would
be admissible if proved by oral testimony: *H.K.S.A.R. v Yeung Ka Ho*, unreported, September 26,
2013, Hong Kong Court of Final Appeal ([2013] HKCFA 82). As to this case, see also *post*, § 14-
73a.

## XII. SUBMISSION OF INSUFFICIENT EVIDENCE

### E. Particular Applications

#### Evidence equivocal as to which of two people, jointly indicted, committed the offence

For an example of a case where the evidence, at the close of the Crown's case in respect of a    **4-367**
charge of murder against two defendants, was as consistent with either defendant acting alone,
later assisted by the other with post-mortem activities, as it was with the joint enterprise to kill the
deceased that was alleged (*viz.* that both were present and either acting as principal or as an aider
and abettor), see *R. v. Banfield (Shirley) and Banfield (Lynette)* [2014] Crim.L.R. 147, CA (quashing
the convictions of both appellants on the ground that their submissions of no case should have
been upheld).

## XIII. THE DEFENCE CASE

### B. Warning as to Giving of Evidence by Defendant

*Effect of accused's silence at trial*

    *R. v. Dixon* is now reported at [2014] 1 W.L.R. 525, *sub nom. R. v. Dixon (Jordan)*.    **4-379**

*Defendant's right to give or not to give evidence*

**4-380**    The 2013 criminal practice directions (see the main work) are now reported at [2013] 1 W.L.R. 3164.

## C. Defence Counsel's Duty

**4-382**    In *R. v. Farooqi* [2014] 1 Cr.App.R. 8, CA, the court reiterated (i) that an advocate is not the client's mouthpiece, obliged to conduct the case in accordance with whatever the client, or when the advocate is a barrister, the solicitor, "instructs" him; the advocate is bound to advance the defendant's case on the basis that what his client tells him is the truth, but, save for well-established principles, like the personal responsibility of the defendant to enter his own plea, and to make his own decision whether to give evidence, and perhaps whether a witness who appears to be able to give evidence favourable to the defendant should or should not be called, the advocate, and the advocate alone, remains responsible for the forensic decisions and strategy; (ii) that an advocate must not give evidence or, in the guise of a submission to the jury, make assertions about facts that were not adduced in evidence, the importance of this rule being particularly stark whenever the defendant elects not to give evidence; (iii) that it is unfair to a witness to postpone criticism of his conduct until closing submissions to the jury, not least because, if given the opportunity, the witness whose behaviour is impugned may have a complete or partial answer to the criticism; but fairness to a witness does not require the somewhat dated formulaic use of the word "put" as integral to the process; what should be avoided is the increasing modern habit of assertion (often in tendentious terms or incorporating comment), which is not true cross-examination; this is unfair to the witness and blurs the line from a jury's perspective between evidence from the witness and inadmissible comment from the advocate; the place for comment or assertion, provided a proper foundation has been laid or fairly arises from the evidence, is during closing arguments; and (iv) that the advocate must abide, and ensure that his professional and lay clients understand that he must abide, by procedural requirements and practice directions and court orders. The court noted that where there is incompetence or misconduct on the part of an advocate, the preferable course is for the trial to continue with the judge taking the responsibility to ensure, by appropriate instructions to the jury or otherwise, that the integrity and fairness of the trial are not compromised.

## H. Duty to Stop Irrelevant Evidence

**★4-388**    Counsel are prohibited from asking questions of a witness, the answers to which would permit the jury to consider the appropriate disposal of a case upon conviction; where, therefore, the defence to murder was diminished responsibility, the judge had been correct in stopping defence counsel from questioning a forensic psychiatrist called as a defence witness as to whether there was any prospect that the defendant would ever be released, whatever the verdict and whatever the disposal (the jury knew that she had previously been convicted of manslaughter on the ground of diminished responsibility and had been released not long before the killing for which she was being tried, along with a charge of attempted murder); permitting the jury to consider such matters would violate the principle that judge and jury have separate duties, and the further principle that the jury should address themselves only to matters relevant to the question of whether the offence charged has been proved: *R. v. Edgington (Nicola)* [2014] 1 Cr.App.R. 24, CA.

## XVII. SUMMING UP

## G. Comment

### (6) On a defendant's lies and/or an untrue alibi

**4-461**    As to whether a direction in accordance with *R. v. Lucas (R.)* (as to which, see the main work) should be given in a case where a jury are trying the issue whether a defendant who has been found unfit to be tried did the act charged against him as the offence, and where the contents of his police interview under caution have been introduced in evidence during the trial of that issue, see *R. v. Swinbourne, ante,* § 4-237.

## I. Corroboration

### (2) Statute

## Children

In *R. v. M.H.* [2013] Crim.L.R. 849, CA, a case involving a three-year-old complainant, the    **4-472**
court firmly rejected a suggestion that the judge should have directed the jury that children may
imagine or fantasise or misunderstand a situation, may be easily coached, may say what they think
their mother wants to hear, or may merely repeat by rote that which has been said on a previous
occasion, and should have warned the jury not to be beguiled by the attractiveness of the child
and to bear in mind his extreme youth. It would, the court said, have been quite wrong for the
judge to have engaged in generalisations remote from the facts of the case. As to this case, see also
*post*, §§ 8-59, 11-3d.

## M. Direction as to Unanimity

*Juries: directions to jury before retirement*

The 2013 criminal practice directions (see the main work) are now reported at [2013] 1 W.L.R.    **4-491**
3164.

## N. Direction Concerning Necessary "Give and Take"

Once the jury are in retirement, it is of the first importance that no individual juror should feel    **4-492**
under any pressure to conform with the views of the majority, if to do so would compromise his
conscience and, therefore, his oath; furthermore, the jury as a whole, despite the cost and
inconvenience of a retrial, should not feel under any pressure to return a verdict if, conscien-
tiously, they are not unanimous or cannot reach the required majority; it is undesirable to give a
*R. v. Watson* "give and take" direction (as to which, see the main work) before or at the time of the
majority verdict direction, because its effect may be to undo the benefit of the majority verdict
direction for which Parliament has provided (*i.e.* alleviating pressure on the jury to be unanimous);
exceptional circumstances may arise that will require the judge to deal with the exigencies of the
moment but, in general, there is no occasion to make exhortations to the jury to arrive at a
verdict; this is why a Watson direction is rarely given and, when it is, only as a last resort following a prolonged retirement after the majority verdict direction has been given; as the authorities
subsequent to *Watson* demonstrate (*e.g. R. v. Morgan* and *R. v Atlan* (as to both of which, see the
main work), and *R. v. Farooqi* [2014] 1 Cr.App.R. 8, CA), if complaint is made about the judge's
words of explanation, encouragement or exhortation, the question on appeal is whether the
words used were appropriate in the circumstances or carried with them the risk that jurors would
feel undue pressure to reach a verdict; if the effect of the judge's direction is to create a significant
risk that the jury or individual jurors may have felt under pressure to compromise their oaths,
the verdict is likely to be unsafe; the closer the jury are to unanimity or to an acceptable majority,
the greater is the pressure to which the minority may feel exposed: *R. v. Arthur* [2014] Crim.L.R.
229, CA (ruling that it would have been better if the judge had not referred to "give and take"
and "honest consideration of the evidence" when giving the conventional majority direction,
because such references were unnecessary; but they did not constitute a full *Watson* direction and
did not render the jury's guilty verdict unsafe).

## XVIII. RETIREMENT OF JURY UNTIL VERDICT

### A. No Further Evidence after Enclosure

*Juries: jury access to exhibits and evidence in retirement*

The 2013 criminal practice directions (see the main work) are now reported at [2013] 1 W.L.R.    **4-495a**
3164.

### D. Majority Verdicts

The 2013 criminal practice directions (see the main work) are now reported at [2013] 1 W.L.R.    **4-510**
3164.

## XIX. VERDICT

### C. Verdict Obtained by Threat or Pressure

**4-518**    As to the consequence of a direction that would have created a significant risk that the jury or individual jurors may have felt under pressure to compromise their oaths, see *R. v. Arthur, ante*, § 4-492.

### I. Special Verdict

**4-534**    The taking of special verdicts has fallen into virtual desuetude; on rare occasions, it may be appropriate in the context of a trial for murder where the alternative defences include, for example, diminished responsibility, loss of control and lack of the necessary intent; but even then a special verdict should continue to be a rarity; in particular, it is inappropriate for such a verdict to be sought in the context of section 5 of the Domestic Violence, Crime and Victims Act 2004 (causing or allowing a child or vulnerable adult to die or suffer serious physical harm (§ 19-163 in the main work)), which was deliberately created just because of the inevitable difficulties of proving which of two defendants was responsible for the infliction of fatal injuries on a child (or vulnerable adult) when there are no other candidates and neither defendant appears to be willing to tell the truth about the incident: *R. v. Hopkinson* [2014] 1 Cr.App.R. 3, CA.

CHAPTER 5

# SENTENCES AND ORDERS ON CONVICTION

## I. GENERAL INTERPRETATION

### (2) Legislation

**Powers of Criminal Courts (Sentencing) Act 2000, ss.161, 163, 164**

*General definitions*

★**5-4**    The provisions of the Tribunals, Courts and Enforcement Act 2007 referred to in the main work came into force on April 6, 2014: Tribunals, Courts and Enforcement Act 2007 (Commencement No. 11) Order 2014 (S.I. 2014 No. 768).

**Criminal Justice Act 2003, ss.176, 305**

*Interpretation of Part 12*

★**5-8**    The provisions of the Tribunals, Courts and Enforcement Act 2007 referred to in the main work came into force on April 6, 2014: Tribunals, Courts and Enforcement Act 2007 (Commencement No. 11) Order 2014 (S.I. 2014 No. 768).

★    As from a day to be appointed, the Offender Rehabilitation Act 2014, s.15(5), and Sched. 5, paras 1 and 6, amend section 305(1) of the 2003 Act so as to repeal the definitions of "activity requirement" and "supervision requirement", and to insert a new definition, after "prohibited activity requirement", as follows—

"'rehabilitation activity requirement', in relation to a community order or suspended sentence order, has the meaning given by section 200A;".

★    The amendments made by the 2014 Act do not apply in relation to an order made in respect of an offence committed before they come into force; and where an offence is found to have been committed over a period of two or more days, or at some time during a period of two or more days, it must, for these purposes, be taken to have been committed on the last of those days: 2014 Act, s.21, and Sched. 7, paras 1, 7 and 8.

## II. PRELIMINARIES

### (6) Committal for sentence

**Powers of Criminal Courts (Sentencing) Act 2000, ss.3–7**

*Committal for sentence of dangerous young offenders*

Where, in the case of a child or young person charged with an offence falling within section 91 **5-28** of the PCC(S)A 2000 (offenders under 18 convicted of certain serious offences (§ 5-610 in the main work)), a youth court accepts jurisdiction (on the basis that a sentence of detention in excess of two years is unlikely to be called for (as to which, see § 1-116 in the main work)), it is nevertheless possible that, either in the course of evidence or upon the production of pre-sentence reports, information will emerge that drives the court to conclude that the criteria for the imposition of an extended sentence under section 226B of the CJA 2003 (§ 5-499 in the main work) would be met (including the seriousness of the offence warranting a custodial sentence of at least four years), so as to make committal for sentence under section 3C of the 2000 Act obligatory; but such would be an exceptional situation: *R. (W.) v. Caernarfon Youth Court and CPS (interested party)*, 177 J.P. 534, DC.

**Information to be supplied on committal for sentence, etc.**

The 2013 criminal practice directions (see the main work) are now reported at [2013] 1 W.L.R. **5-39** 3164.

### (8) Deferment of sentence

**Powers of Criminal Courts (Sentencing) Act 2000, ss.1-1D**

*Undertakings to participate in restorative justice activities*

The provisions of the Crime and Courts Act 2013 referred to in the main work came into force **5-45a** on December 11, 2013: Crime and Courts Act 2013 (Commencement No. 6) Order 2013 (S.I. 2013 No. 2981).

## III. GENERAL PRINCIPLES

### B. DETERMINING THE SERIOUSNESS OF AN OFFENCE

#### (1) Statute

**Previous convictions**

The 2013 criminal practice directions (see the main work) are now reported at [2013] 1 W.L.R. **5-72** 3164.

#### (2) Factual basis of sentence

(b) *Following plea of guilty*

*Determining the factual basis of sentence*

The 2013 criminal practice directions (see the main work) are now reported at [2013] 1 W.L.R. **5-91** 3164.

### (3) Information about the effect of the offence on the victim

**Criminal Practice Direction (Sentencing) F [2013] 1 W.L.R. 3164 (as substituted by Practice Direction (Criminal Proceedings: Various Changes) [2014] 1 W.L.R. 35)**

VICTIM PERSONAL STATEMENTS

**F.1** Victims of crime are invited to make a statement, known as a victim personal statement ("VPS"). **5-104** The statement gives victims a formal opportunity to say how a crime has affected them. It may help to identify whether they have a particular need for information, support and protection. The court will

35

take the statement into account when determining sentence. In some circumstances, it may be appropriate for relatives of a victim to make a VPS, for example where the victim has died as a result of the relevant criminal conduct. The revised Code of Practice for Victims of Crime, published on 29 October 2013, gives further information about victims' entitlements within the criminal justice system, and the duties placed on criminal justice agencies when dealing with victims of crime.

**F.2** When a police officer takes a statement from a victim, the victim should be told about the scheme and given the chance to make a VPS. The decision about whether or not to make a VPS is entirely a matter for the victim; no pressure should be brought to bear on their decision, and no conclusion should be drawn if they choose not to make such a statement. A VPS or a further VPS may be made (in proper s.9 form, see below) at any time prior to the disposal of the case. It will not normally be appropriate for a VPS to be made after the disposal of the case; there may be rare occasions between sentence and appeal when a further VPS may be necessary, for example, when the victim was injured and the original prognosis was not available at the date of sentence. However, VPS after disposal should be confined to presenting up-to-date factual material, such as medical information, and should be used sparingly.

**F.3** If the court is presented with a VPS the following approach, subject to the further guidance given by the Court of Appeal in *R. v. Perkins* [see § 5-106 in the main work], should be adopted:

(a) the VPS and any evidence in support should be considered and taken into account by the court, prior to passing sentence;

(b) evidence of the effects of an offence on the victim contained in the VPS or other statement, must be in proper form, that is a witness statement made under section 9 of the CJA 1967 or an expert's report; and served in good time on the defendant's solicitor or the defendant, if he or she is not represented; except where inferences can properly be drawn from the nature of or circumstances surrounding the offence, a sentencing court must not make assumptions unsupported by evidence about the effects of an offence on the victim; the maker of a VPS may be cross-examined on its content;

(c) at the discretion of the court, the VPS may also be read aloud or played in open court, in whole or in part, or it may be summarised; if the VPS is to be read aloud, the court should also determine who should do so; in making these decisions, the court should take account of the victim's preferences, and follow them unless there is good reason not to do so; examples of this include the inadmissibility of the content or the potentially harmful consequences for the victim or others; court hearings should not be adjourned solely to allow the victim to attend court to read the VPS; for the purposes of CPD (General matters) 5B (access to information held by the court) [§§ 5-220 *et seq.* in the main work] a VPS that is read aloud or played in open court in whole or in part should be considered as such, and no longer treated as a confidential document;

(d) in all cases it will be appropriate for a VPS to be referred to in the course of the sentencing hearing and/or in the sentencing remarks;

(e) the court must pass what it judges to be the appropriate sentence having regard to the circumstances of the offence and of the offender, taking into account, so far as the court considers it appropriate, the impact on the victim; the opinions of the victim or the victim's close relatives as to what the sentence should be are therefore not relevant, unlike the consequences of the offence on them; victims should be advised of this; if, despite the advice, opinions as to sentence are included in the statement, the court should pay no attention to them.

**5-104a**   The 2013 criminal practice directions (see the main work) are now reported at [2013] 1 W.L.R. 3164.

**5-106a**   With effect from December 10, 2013, *Criminal Practice Direction (Sentencing) I* takes effect: *Practice Direction (Criminal Proceedings: Various Changes)* [2014] 1 W.L.R. 35. This provides for the making of an impact statement for business by a nominated representative of a business or enterprise, where the business or enterprise is a victim of a crime.

**Criminal Practice Direction (Sentencing) I [2013] 1 W.L.R. 3164 (as inserted in the 2013 criminal practice directions by Practice Direction (Criminal Proceedings: Various Changes) [2014] 1 W.L.R. 35)**

IMPACT STATEMENTS FOR BUSINESSES

**I.1** Individual victims of crime are invited to make a statement, known as a victim personal statement ("VPS") ... If the victim, or one of the victims, is a business or enterprise (including charities but excluding public sector bodies), of any size, a nominated representative may make an impact statement for business ("ISB"). The ISB gives a formal opportunity for the court to be informed how a crime has affected a business. The court will take the statement into account when determining sentence. This does not prevent individual employees from making a VPS about the impact of the same crime on them as individuals. Indeed the ISB should be about the impact on the business exclusively, and the impact on any individual included within a VPS.

**I.2** When a police officer takes statements about the alleged offence, he or she should also inform the business about the scheme. An ISB may be made to the police at that time, or the ISB template may be downloaded from www.police.uk, completed and e-mailed or posted to the relevant police contact. Guidance on how to complete the form is available on www.police.uk and on the CPS website. There is no obligation on any business to make an ISB.

**I.3** An ISB or an updated ISB may be made (in proper s.9 form, see below) at any time prior to the disposal of the case. It will not be appropriate for an ISB to be made after disposal of the case but before an appeal.

**I.4** A business wishing to make an ISB should consider carefully who to nominate as the representative to make the statement on its behalf. A person making an ISB on behalf of a business, the nominated representative, must be authorised to do so on behalf of the business, either by nature of their position within the business, such as a director or owner, or by having been suitably authorised, such as by the owner or board of directors. The nominated representative must also be in a position to give admissible evidence about the impact of the crime on the business. This will usually be through first-hand personal knowledge, or using business documents (as defined in s.117 of the CJA 2003). The most appropriate person will vary depending on the nature of the crime, and the size and structure of the business and may for example include a manager, director, chief executive or shop owner.

**I.5** If the nominated representative leaves the business before the case comes to court, he or she will usually remain the representative, as the ISB made by him or her will still provide the best evidence of the impact of the crime, and he or she could still be asked to attend court. Nominated representatives should be made aware of the on-going nature of the role at the time of making the ISB.

**I.6** If necessary a further ISB may be provided to the police if there is a change in circumstances. This could be made by an alternative nominated representative. However, the new ISB will usually supplement, not replace, the original ISB and again must contain admissible evidence. The prosecutor will decide which ISB to serve on the defence as evidence, and any ISB that is not served in evidence will be included in the unused material and considered for disclosure to the defence.

**I.7** The ISB must be made in proper form, that is as a witness statement made under section 9 of the CJA 1967 or an expert's report; and served in good time on the defendant's solicitor or the defendant, if he or she is not represented. The maker of an ISB can be cross-examined on its content.

**I.8** The ISB and any evidence in support should be considered and taken into account by the court, prior to passing sentence. The statement should be referred to in the course of the sentencing hearing and/or in the sentencing remarks. Subject to the court's discretion, the contents of the statement may be summarised or read out in open court; the views of the business should be taken into account in reaching a decision.

**I.9** The court must pass what it judges to be the appropriate sentence having regard to the circumstances of the offence and of the offender, taking into account, so far as the court considers it appropriate, the impact on the victims, including any business victim. Opinions as to what the sentence should be are therefore not relevant. If, despite the advice, opinions as to sentence are included in the statement, the court should pay no attention to them.

**I.10** Except where inferences can properly be drawn from the nature of or circumstances surrounding the offence, a sentencing court must not make assumptions unsupported by evidence about the e›ects of an offence on a business.

## C. Reduction in Sentence for Guilty Plea

### Facts to be stated

The 2013 criminal practice directions (see the main work) are now reported at [2013] 1 W.L.R.   **5-108**
3164.

### Advance indication of sentence

Discussions about possible sentence in the event of a plea should not take place in the judge's   **★5-110**
chambers, whether or not they are properly recorded; the whole purpose of the *Goodyear* procedure (*R. v. Goodyear* (as to which, see the main work)) is to avoid exactly the sort of problem that arose in this case, where it had been submitted that, as a result of such discussions, the appellant had a legitimate expectation that the judge would take a starting point that was significantly lower than the one actually adopted: *R. v. Ibori* [2014] 1 Cr.App.R.(S.) 15, CA.

It was wrong in principle for a judge to be influenced in any way as to the extent of the credit to which a defendant was entitled by the fact that he had exercised his right to seek a *Goodyear* indication (*R. v. Goodyear* (*ante*)) from the court; this legitimate use of court procedure should not result in any loss of credit for a plea (which should be that appropriate to the stage in the proceedings at which it is entered): *R. v. Hackney* [2014] 1 Cr.App.R.(S.) 41, CA.

**5-111**     The 2013 criminal practice directions (see the main work) are now reported at [2013] 1 W.L.R. 3164.

### General entitlement to discount

**★5-112**     The principle that lies told by an accused, whether in interview or during trial, are not an aggravating factor as regards sentence was emphatically restated in *R. v. Lowndes* [2014] 1 Cr.App.R.(S.) 75, CA (considering *R. v. Scott* and *R. v. Hercules* (as to both of which, see the main work)).

### Extent of discount

**★5-113**     An offender who pleads guilty after having initially failed to answer to police bail cannot expect to receive the same credit as he would have done had he not absconded: *R. v. Ward* [2014] 1 Cr.App.R.(S.) 74, CA.

### First reasonable opportunity

**★5-114**     In *R. v. Kovvali* [2014] 1 Cr.App.R.(S.) 33, CA, a case of gross medical negligence manslaughter where it was submitted that the defendant was entitled to a greater discount for his guilty plea because it was not unreasonable for him to await expert advice as to the level of his breach before entering the plea, the judge's decision that the defendant had not needed such expert advice, and so to limit the discount, was not unreasonable or unfounded; as an experienced practitioner of many years standing, the defendant would have realised that his treatment of the victim fell so far below the accepted standards that it could be properly categorised as grossly negligent.

### Withholding the discount

**★5-115**     In *R. v. Abdul, Hamed and Mustafa* [2014] 1 Cr.App.R.(S.) 30, CA, it was held that the judge erred in reducing the offender's discount for a guilty plea because he later gave evidence, seemingly rejected by the jury, in support of his co-defendants at their trial. When he had pleaded guilty he had not tendered to the court any basis of plea, nor later mitigation, with an intention mendaciously to reduce his culpability and to avoid being sentenced on the factual basis advanced by the prosecution. He was therefore entitled to the discount recommended by the Sentencing Guidelines Council's guideline on reduction in sentence for a guilty plea (*post*, Appendix K-7), and should not have been deprived of that because of later evidence that he gave, designed not, in terms, to reduce his sentence but to assist his co-defendants.

### Plea offered in relation to a lesser included offence

**★5-116**     While a defendant who offers to plead guilty to a lesser offence, conditional upon the prosecution not proceeding with a more serious offence, should expect no credit for the offer where it is rejected by the prosecution and a plea of not guilty is entered or maintained, even if the end result is that the defendant is convicted only of the lesser offence, there was limited force in the submission that the sentence of a defendant who maintains his not guilty plea for purely tactical reasons, but nevertheless accepts his responsibility for the acts alleged (not disputing his guilt of the lesser offence), and who is in due course convicted of the lesser offence on the basis of his admission and acquitted of the more serious offence, should attract a lower starting point than one who accepts no responsibility whatsoever: *R. v. Wilson (Lee)* [2014] 1 Cr.App.R.(S.) 19, CA.

### Minimum sentence cases

**★5-117**     When imposing a minimum sentence with a maximum discount for a guilty plea, both of which are fixed by statute, as under the PCC(S)A 2000, ss.110 and 111 (minimum sentences for third drug trafficking offence or third domestic burglary (§§ 5-443, 5-444 in the main work)), and the

CJA 2003, s.144(2) (maximum discount for plea in case of an offender liable to minimum sentence under s.110 or 111 of the 2000 Act (§ 5-107 in the main work)), the judge should take an arithmetical approach to sentencing: *R. v. Goodale* [2014] 1 Cr.App.R.(S.) 37, CA.

## E. Mitigation

### (3) Selected mitigating factors

#### Assistance to law enforcement agencies

*Assistance given otherwise than in accordance with the 2005 Act*

In *R. v. Lingu* [2014] 1 Cr.App.R.(S.) 21, CA, it was held that the fact that assistance has been given, even where the results of that assistance were minimal, is a proper mitigating factor. ★5-139

#### Entrapment

In *R. v. Dyer* [2014] 1 *Archbold Review* 3, CA, it was said that, in light of the issuing by the Sentencing Council for England and Wales of its definitive guideline on sentencing for drugs offences (as to which, see *post*, Appendix K-271 *et seq.*), it was no longer appropriate to make reference to pre-guideline cases, such as *R. v. Afonso*; *R. v. Sajid*; *R. v. Andrews* (as to which, see the main work (and it should be noted that the cross-reference to § 27-113 is no longer apposite)). The court held that the fact that drugs have been supplied to a test purchase or undercover officer is not a reason to reduce the category within the guideline into which a case would otherwise fall. As to this case, see also *post*, § 5-159 and Appendix K-629. 5-141

## F. Sentencing Guidelines

#### Sentencing Council for England and Wales

The Sentencing Council has now issued nine definitive guidelines. Those issued since the publication of the main work are the guideline on sexual offences (as to which, see *post*, Appendix K-84 *et seq.*), the guideline for the sentencing of offences of fraud, bribery and money laundering committed by corporate offenders (which has now been incorporated into the most recent guideline, *post*), the guideline on environmental offences for which sentence falls to be imposed after June 30, 2014, covering the unauthorised or harmful deposit, treatment or disposal, *etc.*, of waste (Environmental Protection Act 1990, s.33), illegal discharges to air, land and water (Environmental Permitting (England and Wales) Regulations 2010 (S.I. 2010 No. 675), regs 12 and 38(1)–(3)), and certain related offences (not set out in this work), and the guideline for offences of fraud, bribery and money laundering (as to which, see, *post*, Appendix K-297 *et seq.*). ★5-147

#### Effect of guidelines

As to the effect of following the approach set out in an applicable guideline on disparity of sentence as a ground of appeal, see *R. v. Dyer, post*, § 5-159. 5-152

## G. Parity of Sentence

#### Disparity of sentence as a ground of appeal

Save where right-thinking members of the public would think that an offender would have a legitimate sense of grievance, he cannot justifiably complain if a co-offender (*a fortiori* an offender in separate proceedings) fortuitously received an unduly lenient sentence (*R. v. Fawcett* and *R. v. Broadbridge* (as to both of which, see the main work)): *R. v. Dyer* [2014] 1 *Archbold Review* 3, CA (pointing out that arguments surrounding disparity flowing from different outcomes should effectively be precluded where sentencers follow any relevant guideline). As to this case, see also *ante*, § 5-141; and *post*, Appendix K-629, K-1000. 5-159

## IV. DISCHARGE AND BINDING OVER

### (1) Discharge

#### Powers of Criminal Courts (Sentencing) Act 2000, s.12

*Absolute and conditional discharge*

The Prevention of Social Housing Fraud Act 2013 came into force in England (to the extent 5-169 that it was not already in force) on October 15, 2013: Prevention of Social Housing Fraud Act 2013 (Commencement) (England) Order 2013 (S.I. 2013 No. 2622).

The 2013 Act was brought into force in Wales, to the extent that it was not already in force, on November 5, 2013: Prevention of Social Housing Fraud Act 2013 (Commencement) (Wales) Order 2013 (S.I. 2013 No. 2861).

### Combined with other orders

**5-174**    As to the commencement of the Prevention of Social Housing Fraud Act 2013, see *ante*, § 5-169.

### Security for good behaviour

**5-174a**    The 2013 criminal practice directions (see the main work) are now reported at [2013] 1 W.L.R. 3164.

## (2) Binding over

### (b) *To keep the peace*

### Practice direction

**5-184b**    The 2013 criminal practice directions (see the main work) are now reported at [2013] 1 W.L.R. 3164.

## V. COMMUNITY SENTENCES

### B. GENERAL RESTRICTIONS

#### Criminal Justice Act 2003, ss.147–151

*Restrictions on imposing community sentences*

**5-248**    The provisions of the Crime and Courts Act 2013 referred to in the main work came into force on December 11, 2013: Crime and Courts Act 2013 (Commencement No. 6) Order 2013 (S.I. 2013 No. 2981).

*Community sentences not available where sentence fixed by law, etc.*

**5-250**    The provisions of the Crime and Courts Act 2013 referred to in the main work came into force on December 11, 2013: Crime and Courts Act 2013 (Commencement No. 6) Order 2013 (S.I. 2013 No. 2981).

*Community order or youth rehabilitation order for persistent offender previously fined*

**5-252**    As to the commencement of the Prevention of Social Housing Fraud Act 2013, see *ante*, § 5-169.

### C. COMMUNITY ORDERS

### (1) General

#### Criminal Justice Act 2003, s.177

*Community orders*

**5-253**    Paragraphs 1, 2, 4, 31 to 33 and 35 of Schedule 16 to the Crime and Courts Act 2013 came into force on December 11, 2013: Crime and Courts Act 2013 (Commencement No. 6) Order 2013 (S.I. 2013 No. 2981). Paragraphs 11 and 12 of Schedule 16 (all the amendments of s.177 of the 2003 Act noted in the main work, other than the insertion of subss. (2A) and (2B)) remain to be brought into force.

★    As from a day to be appointed, the Offender Rehabilitation Act 2014, s.15(1) and (2), amend section 177(1) of the 2003 Act so as to insert, after paragraph (a), new paragraph (aa), as follows—

"(aa)   a rehabilitation activity requirement (as defined by section 200A),".

As from a day to be appointed, the 2014 Act, s.15(5), and Sched. 5, paras 1 and 2, further ★ amend section 177 of the 2003 Act so as (i) to repeal paragraphs (b) and (k) of subsection (1), (ii) to repeal paragraph (b) of subsection (2), and (iii) in subsection (4), to insert the words "a rehabilitation activity requirement," after "unpaid work requirement," and to omit the words "an activity requirement," and ", a supervision requirement".

The amendments made by the 2014 Act do not apply in relation to an order made in respect of ★ an offence committed before they come into force; and where an offence is found to have been committed over a period of two or more days, or at some time during a period of two or more days, it must, for these purposes, be taken to have been committed on the last of those days: 2014 Act, s.21, and Sched. 7, paras 1, 7 and 8.

### (2)  Definitions

With effect from June 1, 2014 (Offender Rehabilitation Act 2014 (Commencement No. 1) ★**5-262** Order 2014 (S.I. 2014 No. 1287)), section 183 of the AFA 2006 (see the main work) was amended by the Offender Rehabilitation Act 2014, s.19, and Sched. 6, paras 1 and 4 (although note that S.I. 2014 No. 1287, in an apparent oversight, did not bring para. 1 into force).

As from a day to be appointed, the 2014 Act, s.19, and Sched. 6, paras 1 and 8, further amend ★ section 183 of the 2006 Act (see the main work and *ante*). This amendment does not apply in relation to an order made in respect of an offence committed before the amendment comes into force; and where an offence is found to have been committed over a period of two or more days, or at some time during a period of two or more days, it must, for these purposes, be taken to have been committed on the last of those days: 2014 Act, s.21, and Sched. 7, paras 1, 7 and 8.

## Meaning of "responsible officer"

With effect from June 1, 2014, the Offender Rehabilitation Act 2014, s.14(1), substituted, for ★**5-263** section 197 of the CJA 2003, a new section 197 as follows—

*Meaning of "the responsible officer"*
    **197.**—(1) For the purposes of this Part, "the responsible officer", in relation to an offender to whom a relevant order relates, means the person who is for the time being responsible for discharging the functions conferred by this Part on the responsible officer in accordance with arrangements made by the Secretary of State.
    (2) The responsible officer must be—
        (a)  an officer of a provider of probation services, or
        (b)  a person responsible for monitoring the offender in accordance with an electronic monitoring requirement imposed by the relevant order.

## Duties of responsible officer

With effect from June 1, 2014 (Offender Rehabilitation Act 2014 (Commencement No. 1) ★**5-264** Order 2014 (S.I. 2014 No. 1287)), the Offender Rehabilitation Act 2014, s.14(2), and Sched. 4, paras 10 and 11, amended section 198(1) of the CJA 2003 so as to remove the responsible officer's duty to take steps to enforce requirements imposed by a relevant order.

### (3)  Requirements available in the case of all offenders

**Criminal Justice Act 2003, ss.199–213**

*Rehabilitation activity requirement*
    As from a day to be appointed, section 15(1) and (3) of the Offender Rehabilitation Act 2014 ★**5-266a** insert a new section 200A in the 2003 Act.

*Rehabilitation activity requirement*
    **200A.**—(1) In this Part "rehabilitation activity requirement", in relation to a relevant order, means a requirement that, during the relevant period, the offender must comply with any instructions given by the responsible officer to attend appointments or participate in activities or both.

(2) A relevant order imposing a rehabilitation activity requirement must specify the maximum number of days for which the offender may be instructed to participate in activities.

(3) Any instructions given by the responsible officer must be given with a view to promoting the offender's rehabilitation; but this does not prevent the responsible officer giving instructions with a view to other purposes in addition to rehabilitation.

(4) The responsible officer may instruct the offender to attend appointments with the responsible officer or with someone else.

(5) The responsible officer, when instructing the offender to participate in activities, may require the offender to—

    (a) participate in specified activities and, while doing so, comply with instructions given by the person in charge of the activities, or

    (b) go to a specified place and, while there, comply with any instructions given by the person in charge of the place.

(6) The references in subsection (5)(a) and (b) to instructions given by a person include instructions given by anyone acting under the person's authority.

(7) The activities that responsible officers may instruct offenders to participate in include—

    (a) activities forming an accredited programme (see section 202(2));

    (b) activities whose purpose is reparative, such as restorative justice activities.

(8) For the purposes of subsection (7)(b) an activity is a restorative justice activity if—

    (a) the participants consist of, or include, the offender and one or more of the victims,

    (b) the aim of the activity is to maximise the offender's awareness of the impact of the offending concerned on the victims, and

    (c) the activity gives a victim or victims an opportunity to talk about, or by other means express experience of, the offending and its impact.

(9) In subsection (8) "victim" means a victim of, or other person affected by, the offending concerned.

(10) Where compliance with an instruction would require the co-operation of a person other than the offender, the responsible officer may give the instruction only if that person agrees.

(11) In this section "the relevant period" means—

    (a) in relation to a community order, the period for which the community order remains in force, and

    (b) in relation to a suspended sentence order, the supervision period as defined by section 189(1A).

★    This amendment does not apply in relation to an order made in respect of an offence committed before they come into force; and where an offence is found to have been committed over a period of two or more days, or at some time during a period of two or more days, it must, for these purposes, be taken to have been committed on the last of those days: 2014 Act, s.21, and Sched. 7, paras 1, 7 and 8.

*Activity requirement*

★5-267    As from a day to be appointed, the Offender Rehabilitation Act 2014, s.15(1) and (4), repeal sections 201 and 213 (§ 5-279 in the main work) of the 2003 Act. These amendments do not apply in relation to an order made in respect of an offence committed before they come into force; and where an offence is found to have been committed over a period of two or more days, or at some time during a period of two or more days, it must, for these purposes, be taken to have been committed on the last of those days: 2014 Act, s.21, and Sched. 7, paras 1, 7 and 8.

*Programme requirement*

★5-268    As from a day to be appointed, the Offender Rehabilitation Act 2014, s.16(1) and (2), repeal section 202(7) of the 2003 Act.

*Drug rehabilitation requirement: provision for review by court*

★5-276    With effect from June 1, 2014 (Offender Rehabilitation Act 2014 (Commencement No. 1) Order 2014 (S.I. 2014 No. 1287)), the Offender Rehabilitation Act 2014, s.14(2), and Sched. 4, paras 1 and 4, amended section 210(1)(d) of the 2003 Act so as to substitute the words "an officer of a provider of probation services" for the words "the responsible officer".

*Periodic review of drug rehabilitation requirement*

★5-277    With effect from June 1, 2014 (Offender Rehabilitation Act 2014 (Commencement No. 1)

Order 2014 (S.I. 2014 No. 1287)), the Offender Rehabilitation Act 2014, s.14(2), and Sched. 4, paras 1 and 5, amended section 211 of the 2003 Act so as (i) in subsection (1), to omit the word "responsible" and insert, after the word "subsection", the words "('the review officer's report')", and (ii) in each of subsections (6) and (7), to substitute the word "review" for the word "responsible".

*Supervision requirement*

As to the repeal of section 213 of the 2003 Act, see *ante*, § 5-267.  ★5-279

### (4) Requirements available only in case of offenders aged under 25

**Criminal Justice Act 2003, s.214**

*Attendance centre requirement*

As from a day to be appointed, the Offender Rehabilitation Act 2014, s.17(1)–(5), amend sec-  ★5-280
tion 214 of the 2003 Act so as (i) in subsection (1), to omit the words "specified in the relevant order", and to substitute the words "specified in the relevant order" for the words "so specified", (ii) in subsection (3), to substitute the words "an attendance centre which is available for persons of the offender's description" for the words "the attendance centre to be specified in it", and (iii) to insert, after subsection (3), new subsections (3A) and (3B), as follows—

> "(3A) The attendance centre at which the offender is required to attend is to be notified to the offender by the responsible officer from time to time.
> (3B) When choosing an attendance centre, the responsible officer must consider—
>> (a) the accessibility of the attendance centre to the offender, having regard to the means of access available to the offender and any other circumstances, and
>> (b) the description of persons for whom it is available.".

These amendments do not apply in relation to an order made in respect of an offence commit-  ★
ted before they come into force; and where an offence is found to have been committed over a period of two or more days, or at some time during a period of two or more days, it must, for these purposes, be taken to have been committed on the last of those days: 2014 Act, s.21, and Sched. 7, paras 1, 7 and 8.

### (6) Provisions applying to relevant orders generally

**Criminal Justice Act 2003, ss.216–220**

*Availability of arrangements in local area*

As from a day to be appointed, the Offender Rehabilitation Act 2014, s.15(5) and Sched. 5,  ★5-284
paras 1 and 4, repeal section 218(2) of the 2003 Act.

As from a day to be appointed, the 2014 Act, s.17(1) and (6) to (8), further amend section 218  ★
of the 2003 Act, so as (i) in subsection (4)(a), to substitute the words "the relevant area (see subsections (5) to (7))" for the words "the relevant areas mentioned in subsections (5) to (7)", and (ii) in subsection (6), to substitute the words "an area in which there is an attendance centre which is available for persons of the offender's description and which the court is satisfied is reasonably accessible to the offender" for the words "the area in which the attendance centre proposed to be specified in the order is situated".

The amendments made by the 2014 Act to section 218 do not apply in relation to an order  ★
made in respect of an offence committed before they come into force; and where an offence is found to have been committed over a period of two or more days, or at some time during a period of two or more days, it must, for these purposes, be taken to have been committed on the last of those days: 2014 Act, s.21, and Sched. 7, paras 1, 7 and 8.

*Duty to obtain permission before changing residence*

As from a day to be appointed, section 18(1) and (2) of the Offender Rehabilitation Act 2014  ★5-286a
insert a new 220A in the 2003 Act.

> *Duty to obtain permission before changing residence*
> **220A.**—(1) An offender in respect of whom a relevant order is in force must not change residence without permission given in accordance with this section by—

(a) the responsible officer, or

(b) a court.

(2) The appropriate court may, on an application by the offender, give permission in a case in which the responsible officer has refused.

(3) A court may also give permission in any proceedings before it under Schedule 8 or 12 (breach or amendment of orders etc).

(4) The grounds on which the responsible officer or court may refuse an application for permission are that, in the opinion of the officer or court, the change in residence—

(a) is likely to prevent the offender complying with a requirement imposed by the relevant order, or

(b) would hinder the offender's rehabilitation.

(5) The obligation imposed by subsection (1) is enforceable as if it were a requirement imposed by the relevant order.

(6) This section does not apply if the relevant order includes a residence requirement imposed under section 206.

(7) For cases in which a relevant order has to be amended because of permission given under this section, see paragraph 16 of Schedule 8 and paragraph 14 of Schedule 12 (amendment to reflect change in local justice area).

(8) In this section "the appropriate court" has the same meaning as in paragraph 16 of Schedule 8 or paragraph 14 of Schedule 12.

★ The amendments made by section 18 of the 2014 Act do not apply in relation to an order made in respect of an offence committed before they come into force; and where an offence is found to have been committed over a period of two or more days, or at some time during a period of two or more days, it must, for these purposes, be taken to have been committed on the last of those days: 2014 Act, s.21, and Sched. 7, paras 1, 7 and 8.

## D. Youth Community Orders

### Introduction

**5-291**    Attendance centre orders under section 60 of the PCC(S)A 2000 were just one of several "youth community orders" that could be made under that Act. As explained in the main work, however, the sections of the Act that provided for the making of a curfew order (s.37), an exclusion order (s.40A), a supervision order (ss.63, 64 and 67, and Sched. 6) and an action plan order (ss.69–71) were repealed by the CJIA 2008, and these repeals came fully into force on November 30, 2009, except that they continue to apply to offences committed before that date. With the passage of time, it was unlikely that, by the time of publication of the 2013 edition of this work, further reference would need to be made to these provisions. Should it be necessary, however, they can be found in the supplements to the 2012 edition. The position with regard to section 60 is rather different (see the annotations thereto (*post*, § 5-292)).

**Powers of Criminal Courts (Sentencing) Act 2000, s.60**

*Attendance centre orders*

**5-292**    **60.**—(1) Where—

(a) (subject to 148, 150 and 156 of the Criminal Justice Act 2003) a person aged under *21* [16] is convicted by or before a court of an offence punishable with imprisonment, or

(b) a court [has power or] would have power, but for section 89 below (restrictions on imprisonment of young offenders and defaulters), to commit a person aged under *21* [16] to prison in default of payment of any sum of money or for failing to do or abstain from doing anything required to be done or left undone, *or*

(c) *a court has power to commit a person aged at least 21 but under 25 to prison in default of payment of any sum of money,*

the court may, if it has been notified by the Secretary of State that an attendance centre is available for the reception of persons of his description, order him to attend at such a centre, to be specified in the order, for such number of hours as may be so specified.

(2) An order under subsection (1) above is in this Act referred to as an "attendance centre order".

(3) The aggregate number of hours for which an attendance centre order may require a person to attend at an attendance centre shall not be less than 12 except where—

(a) he is aged under 14; and

(b) the court is of the opinion that 12 hours would be excessive, having regard to his age or any other circumstances.

(4) The aggregate number of hours shall not exceed 12 except where the court is of the opinion, having regard to all the circumstances, that 12 hours would be inadequate, and in that case [shall not exceed 24]—

(a) *shall not exceed 24 where the person is aged under 16; and*

(b) *shall not exceed 36 where the person is aged 16 or over but under 21 or (where subsection (1)(c) above applies) under 25.*

(5) A court may make an attendance centre order in respect of a person before a previous attendance centre order made in respect of him has ceased to have effect, and may determine the number of hours to be specified in the order without regard—

(a) to the number specified in the previous order; or

(b) to the fact that order is still in effect.

(6) An attendance centre order shall not be made unless the court is satisfied that the attendance centre to be specified in it is reasonably accessible to the person concerned, having regard to his age, the means of access available to him and any other circumstances.

(7) The times at which a person is required to attend at an attendance centre shall, as for as practicable, be such as to avoid—

(a) any conflict with his religious beliefs or with the requirements of any other [youth] community order to which he may be subject; and

(b) any interference with the times, if any, at which he normally works or attends school or any other educational establishment.

(8) The first time at which the person is required to attend at an attendance centre shall be a time at which the centre is available for his attendance in accordance with the notification of the Secretary of State, and shall be specified in the order.

(9) The subsequent times shall be fixed by the officer in charge of the centre, having regard to the person's circumstances.

(10) A person shall not be required under this section to attend at an attendance centre on more than one occasion on any day, or for more than three hours on any occasion.

(11) Where a court makes an attendance centre order, the clerk of the court shall—

(a) deliver or send a copy of the order to the officer in charge of the attendance centre specified in it; and

(b) deliver a copy of the order to the person in respect of whom it is made or send a copy by registered post or the recorded delivery service addressed to his last or usual place of abode.

(12) Where a person ("the defaulter") has been ordered to attend at an attendance centre in default of the payment of any sum of money—

(a) on payment of the whole sum to any person authorised to receive it, the attendance centre order shall cease to have effect;

(b) on payment of a part of the sum to any such person, the total number of hours for which the defaulter is required to attend at the centre shall be reduced proportionately, that is to say by such number of complete hours as bears to the total number the proportion most nearly approximating to, without exceeding, the proportion which the part bears to the whole sum.

[This section is printed as amended by the CJA 2003, s.304, and Sched. 32, para. 102(1), (2)(a) (substitution of references to sections 148, 150 and 156 of the 2003 Act for references to corresponding provisions of the 2000 Act, and substitution of "16" for "21" in subs. (1)(a)), and (4) (substitution of "youth community order" for "community order" in subs. (7)); and as amended, as from a day to be appointed, by the CJCSA 2000, s.74 and Sched. 7, para. 173 (insertion of words in first set of square brackets in subs. (1)(b)); and the CJA 2003, s.304, and Sched. 32, paras 90 and 102(1), and (2)(b) and (c), and (3) (substitution of "16" for "21" in subs. (1)(b), omission of subs. (1)(c) and the word "or" immediately preceding it, substitution of words in square brackets for italicised words in subs. (4)). The amendments to subss. (1)(a) and (7) came into force on April 4, 2005: Criminal Justice Act 2003 (Commencement No. 8 and Transitional and Saving Provisions) Order 2005 (S.I. 2005 No. 950), save that, in the case of persons aged 16 or 17 upon conviction, the substitution of "16" for "21" in subs. (1)(a) and the insertion of the word "youth" before "community order" in subs. (7) have no application in relation to offences committed before November 30, 2009, or in relation to any failure to comply with an order made in respect of an offence committed before that date: *ibid.*, Sched. 2, paras 12 and 13. The whole of this sec-

45

tion is repealed as from a day to be appointed (as to which, see §§ 5-1, 5-185, 5-186 in the main work) by the CJIA 2008, ss.6(1) and 149, and Sched. 28, Pt 1. To the extent that this repeal relates to subs. (1)(a), it was brought into force on November 30, 2009: Criminal Justice and Immigration Act 2008 (Commencement No. 13 and Transitory Provision) Order 2009 (S.I. 2009 No. 3074).]

**5-293**   As to the requirements to be complied with before imposing an attendance centre order, see (for offences committed before April 4, 2005) sections 35 and 36 of the PCC(S)A 2000 (§§ 5-189, 5-190 in the supplements to the 2012 edition) (it being a "community order" within that Act), and (for offences committed after that date) section 148 of the CJA 2003 (§ 5-248 in the main work) (it being a "community sentence" within that Act).

It is not entirely clear whether a court may make attendance centre orders on the same occasion in respect of a number of offences with an aggregate in excess of the limits in subsection (4). It is submitted that the better view is that it cannot; section 60(1) appears to be concerned with defining an *occasion* when an attendance centre order may be made. On any such occasion *one* order may be made. Subsection (5) appears to confirm the correctness of this approach: if it were incorrect, subsection (5) would not be needed.

Section 61 gives effect to Schedule 5 (*post*, §§ 5-365 *et seq.*).

## E. YOUTH REHABILITATION ORDERS

### Criminal Justice and Immigration Act 2008, Sched. 1

*Electronic monitoring requirement*

★**5-333**   For the most recent order made under paragraph 26(5) of Schedule 1 to the 2008 Act, see the Criminal Justice (Electronic Monitoring) (Responsible Person) (No. 2) Order 2014 (S.I. 2014 No. 669), which revoked, with effect from 7.00 a.m. on March 23, 2014, the Youth Rehabilitation Order (Electronic Monitoring Requirement) Order 2009 (S.I. 2009 No. 2950), and the Criminal Justice (Electronic Monitoring) (Responsible Person) Order 2014 (S.I. 2014 No. 163).

## F. ENFORCEMENT

### (1) Of community orders

### Criminal Justice Act 2003, Sched. 8

*Interpretation*

★**5-339a**   With effect from June 1, 2014 (Offender Rehabilitation Act 2014 (Commencement No. 1) Order 2014 (S.I. 2014 No. 1287)), the Offender Rehabilitation Act 2014, s.14(2), and Sched. 4, paras 1 and 6(1) and (2), amended Schedule 8 to the 2003 Act so as to insert, after paragraph 1, a new paragraph 1A, as follows—

> "1A.—(1) In this Schedule 'enforcement officer' means a person who is for the time being responsible for discharging the functions conferred by this Schedule on an enforcement officer in accordance with arrangements made by the Secretary of State.
> (2) An enforcement officer must be an officer of a provider of probation services that is a public sector provider.
> (3) In sub-paragraph (2) 'public sector provider' means—
> > (a) a probation trust or other public body, or
> > (b) the Secretary of State.".

*Duty to give warning*

★**5-341**   With effect from June 1, 2014 (Offender Rehabilitation Act 2014 (Commencement No. 1) Order 2014 (S.I. 2014 No. 1287)), the Offender Rehabilitation Act 2014, s.14(2), and Sched. 4, paras 1 and 6(1) and (3), substituted, for paragraph 5(1)(b) of Schedule 8 to the 2003 Act, a new paragraph 5(1)(b), as follows—

> "(b) the officer refers the matter to an enforcement officer (see paragraph 6A)".

*Breach of order after warning*

★**5-342**   With effect from June 1, 2014 (Offender Rehabilitation Act 2014 (Commencement No. 1)

Order 2014 (S.I. 2014 No. 1287)), the Offender Rehabilitation Act 2014, s.14(2), and Sched. 4, paras 1 and 6(1) and (4), amended paragraph 6(1) of Schedule 8 to the 2003 Act so as to substitute the words "must refer the matter to an enforcement officer (see paragraph 6A)" for the words "must cause an information" to the end.

*Role of enforcement officer*

With effect from June 1, 2014 (Offender Rehabilitation Act 2014 (Commencement No. 1)  ★**5-342a**
Order 2014 (S.I. 2014 No. 1287)), the Offender Rehabilitation Act 2014, s.14(2), and Sched. 4, paras 1 and 6(1) and (5), inserted, after paragraph 6, a new paragraph 6A into Schedule 8 to the 2003 Act, as follows—

> *"Role of enforcement officer*
>
> 6A.—(1) Where a matter is referred to an enforcement officer under paragraph 5(1)(b) or 6(1), it is the duty of the enforcement officer to consider the case and, where appropriate, to cause an information to be laid before a justice of the peace in respect of the offender's failure to comply with the requirement.
>
> (2) In relation to any community order which was made by the Crown Court and does not include a direction that any failure to comply with the requirements of the order is to be dealt with by a magistrates' court, the reference in sub-paragraph (1) to a justice of the peace is to be read as a reference to the Crown Court.".

*Powers of magistrates' courts*

As to the amendment of paragraph 9(6) of Schedule 8 to the 2003 Act by the Crime and Courts  **5-345**
Act 2013, see *post*, § 5-357.

As from a day to be appointed, the Offender Rehabilitation Act 2014, s.18(1) and (4), repeal  ★
paragraph 9(5A) of Schedule 8 to the 2003 Act. The amendments made by section 18 of the 2014 Act do not apply in relation to an order made in respect of an offence committed before they come into force; and where an offence is found to have been committed over a period of two or more days, or at some time during a period of two or more days, it must, for these purposes, be taken to have been committed on the last of those days: 2014 Act, s.21, and Sched. 7, paras 1, 7 and 8.

*Revocation of order with or without re-sentencing: powers of magistrates' court*

With effect from June 1, 2014 (Offender Rehabilitation Act 2014 (Commencement No. 1)  ★**5-348**
Order 2014 (S.I. 2014 No. 1287)), the Offender Rehabilitation Act 2014, s.14(2), and Sched. 4, paras 1 and 6(1) and (6), amended paragraphs 13(1), 14(1)(b), 17(1), 19, 19A(1), 20(1)(b) and 24(2)(b) of Schedule 8 to the 2003 Act so as to substitute, in each provision, the words "an officer of a provider of probation services" for the words "the responsible officer".

*Revocation of order with or without re-sentencing: powers of Crown Court*

As to the amendment of paragraph 14 of Schedule 8 to the 2003 Act, see *ante*, § 5-348.  ★**5-349**

*Amendment by reason of change of residence*

As from a day to be appointed, the Offender Rehabilitation Act 2014, s.18(1) and (5), amend  ★**5-350**
Schedule 8 to the 2003 Act so as to substitute, for paragraph 16, new paragraphs 16 and 16A, as follows—

> "16.—(1) This paragraph applies where at any time while a community order is in force in respect of an offender—
>
> (a) the offender is given permission under section 220A to change residence, and
> (b) the local justice area in which the new residence is situated ('the new local justice area') is different from the local justice area specified in the order.
>
> (2) If the permission is given by a court, the court must amend the order to specify the new local justice area.
>
> (3) If the permission is given by the responsible officer—
>
> (a) the officer must apply to the appropriate court to amend the order to specify the new local justice area, and
> (b) the court must make that amendment.
>
> (4) In this paragraph 'the appropriate court' means—

(a) in relation to a community order imposing a drug rehabilitation requirement which is subject to review, the court responsible for the order,

(b) in relation to a community order which was made by the Crown Court and does not include a direction that any failure to comply with the requirements of the order is to be dealt with by a magistrates' court, the Crown Court, and

(c) in relation to any other community order, a magistrates' court acting in the local justice area specified in the order.

16A.—(1) This paragraph applies where at any time while a community order is in force in respect of an offender—

(a) a court amends the order,

(b) the order as amended includes a residence requirement requiring the offender to reside at a specified place, and

(c) the local justice area in which that place is situated ('the new local justice area') is different from the local justice area specified in the order.

(2) The court must amend the order to specify the new local justice area.".

★ The amendments made by section 18 of the 2014 Act do not apply in relation to an order made in respect of an offence committed before they come into force; and where an offence is found to have been committed over a period of two or more days, or at some time during a period of two or more days, it must, for these purposes, be taken to have been committed on the last of those days: 2014 Act, s.21, and Sched. 7, paras 1, 7 and 8.

*Amendment of requirements of community order*

★5-351    As to the amendment of paragraph 17 of Schedule 8 to the 2003 Act, see *ante*, § 5-348.

*Amendment of treatment requirements of community order on report of practitioner*

★5-352    With effect from June 1, 2014 (Offender Rehabilitation Act 2014 (Commencement No. 1) Order 2014 (S.I. 2014 No. 1287)), the Offender Rehabilitation Act 2014, s.14(2), and Sched. 4, paras 1 and 6(1) and (7), amended paragraph 18(1) of Schedule 8 to the 2003 Act so as to substitute the words "cause an application to be made" for the word "apply".

*Amendment in relation to review of drug rehabilitation requirement*

★5-353    As to the amendment of paragraph 19 of Schedule 8 to the 2003 Act, see *ante*, § 5-348.

*Extension of order*

★5-353a    As to the amendment of paragraph 19A of Schedule 8 to the 2003 Act, see *ante*, § 5-348.

*Extension of unpaid work requirement*

★5-354    As to the amendment of paragraph 20 of Schedule 8 to the 2003 Act, see *ante*, § 5-348.

*Supplementary*

5-357    Paragraph 22 of Schedule 16 (the amendment of para. 9(6) of Sched. 8 to the 2003 Act (§ 5-345 in the main work)) to the Crime and Courts Act 2013 came into force on December 11, 2013: Crime and Courts Act 2013 (Commencement No. 6) Order 2013 (S.I. 2013 No. 2981). This corrects the oversight referred to in the main work.

★ As to one amendment of paragraph 24 of Schedule 8 to the 2003 Act (effective June 1, 2014), see *ante*, § 5-348.

★ As from a day to be appointed, the Offender Rehabilitation Act 2014, s.18(1) and (6), further amend paragraph 24 of Schedule 8 to the 2003 Act (*ante*) so as to omit the words "No order may be made under paragraph 16, and". The amendments made by section 18 of the 2014 Act do not apply in relation to an order made in respect of an offence committed before they come into force; and where an offence is found to have been committed over a period of two or more days, or at some time during a period of two or more days, it must, for these purposes, be taken to have been committed on the last of those days: 2014 Act, s.21, and Sched. 7, paras 1, 7 and 8.

★ With effect from June 1, 2014 (Offender Rehabilitation Act 2014 (Commencement No. 1) Order 2014 (S.I. 2014 No. 1287)), the 2014 Act, s.14(2), and Sched. 4, paras 10 and 14(1) and (2), amended paragraph 25A(4)(b) of Schedule 8 to the 2003 Act so as to substitute the words "any officer of a provider of probation services who the court thinks has an interest in the proceedings" for the words "the responsible officer".

With effect from June 1, 2014 (S.I. 2014 No. 1287 (*ante*)), the 2014 Act, s.14(2), and Sched. 4,     ★
paras 10 and 14(1) and (3), amended paragraph 27(1)(b) of Schedule 8 to the 2003 Act so as to
substitute, for sub-paragraph (i), a new sub-paragraph (i) as follows—

> "(i)   a provider of probation services that is a public sector provider operating in that area,
> and".

With effect from June 1, 2014 (S.I. 2014 No. 1287 (*ante*)), the 2014 Act, s.14(2), and Sched. 4,     ★
paras 10 and 14(1) and (4), further amended paragraph 27 of Schedule 8 to the 2003 Act so as to
insert, after sub-paragraph (3), a new sub-paragraph (4), as follows—

> "(4) In this paragraph 'public sector provider' means—
>    (a) a probation trust or other public body, or
>    (b) the Secretary of State.".

With effect from June 1, 2014 (Offender Rehabilitation Act 2014 (Commencement No. 1)     ★5-358
Order 2014 (S.I. 2014 No. 1287)), the Offender Rehabilitation Act 2014, s.19, and Sched. 6, paras
1 and 5, amended Schedule 5 to the AFA 2006 (see the main work) so as (i) to include a reference
to paragraph 6A(2) of Schedule 8 to the 2003 Act (*ante*, § 5-342a) in paragraph 1(2), (ii) to repeal
paragraph 2, and (iii) to insert a new paragraph 2A, providing that paragraph 6A(1) of Schedule
8 has effect in relation to a service community order as if the reference to a justice of the peace
were to the Crown Court; but note that S.I. 2014 No. 1287, in an apparent oversight, did not
bring para. 1 of Schedule 6 to the 2014 Act into force.

As from a day to be appointed, the 2014 Act, s.19, and Sched. 6, paras 1 and 10, further     ★
amend paragraph 1(2) of Schedule 5 to the 2006 Act (see the main work and *ante*) so as to
substitute a reference to paragraph 16(4) of Schedule 8 to the 2003 Act (*ante*, § 5-350) for the
reference to paragraph 16(5). This amendment does not apply in relation to an order made in
respect of an offence committed before the amendment comes into force; and where an offence is
found to have been committed over a period of two or more days, or at some time during a
period of two or more days, it must, for these purposes, be taken to have been committed on the
last of those days: 2014 Act, s.21, and Sched. 7, paras 1, 7 and 8.

### Warning (paras 5 and 6)

As to the amendment of paragraphs 5 and 6 of Schedule 8 to the CJA 2003, and as to the     ★5-359
insertion of paragraph 6A in Schedule 8, see *ante*, §§ 5-341, 5-342, 5-342a; and as to the amendment of paragraphs 4 and 5 of Schedule 12 to the CJA 2003, and as to the insertion of paragraph
5A in Schedule 12, see *post*, §§ 5-566, 5-567, 5-567a.

### No power to sentence for subsequent offence

Where a subsequent offence has been committed by a person subject to a community order     ★5-363a
imposed by the Crown Court, and a magistrates' court commits the person to the Crown Court
for that court to deal with the original offence under paragraph 22 of Schedule 8 to the CJA 2003
(§ 5-355 in the main work), paragraph 23 (§ 5-356 in the main work) does not give the Crown
Court power to sentence for the subsequent offence: *R. v. De Brito* [2014] 1 Cr.App.R.(S.) 38, CA.

### (2)  Of youth community orders

### Curfew, exclusion and supervision orders

As to curfew and exclusion orders, see Schedule 3 to the PCC(S)A 2000 (§§ 5-228 *et seq.* in the     **5-364**
supplements to the 2012 edition); and as to supervision orders, see Schedule 7 to that Act (§§
5-371 *et seq.* in the supplements to the 2012 edition).

**Powers of Criminal Courts (Sentencing) Act 2000, Sched. 5**

Section 61                    SCHEDULE 5

Breach, Revocation and Amendment of Attendance Centre Orders

*Breach of order or attendance centre rules*

1.—(1) Where an attendance centre order is in force and it appears on information to a justice     **5-365**
that the offender—

    (a)  has failed to attend in accordance with the order, or

    (b)  while attending has committed a breach of rules made under section 222(1)(d) or (e) of the Criminal Justice Act 2003 which cannot be adequately dealt with under those rules,

the justice may issue a summons requiring the offender to appear at the place and time specified in the summons or, if the information is in writing and on oath, may issue a warrant for the offender's arrest.

(2) Any summons or warrant issued under this paragraph shall direct the offender to appear or be brought—

    (a)  before a magistrates' court acting for the petty sessions area in which the offender resides; or

    (b)  if it is not known where the offender resides, before a magistrates' court acting for the petty sessions area in which is situated the attendance centre which the offender is required to attend by the order or by virtue of an order under paragraph 5(1)(b) below.

2.—(1) If it is proved to the satisfaction of the magistrates' court before which an offender appears or is brought under paragraph 1 above that he has failed without reasonable excuse to attend as mentioned in sub-paragraph (1)(a) of that paragraph or has committed such a breach of rules as is mentioned in sub-paragraph (1)(b) of that paragraph, that court may deal with him in any one of the following ways—

    (a)  it may impose on him a fine not exceeding £1,000;

    (b)  where the attendance centre order was made by a magistrates' court, it may deal with him, for the offence in respect of which the order was made, in any way in which he could have been dealt with for that offence by the court which made the order if the order had not been made; or

    (c)  where the order was made by the Crown Court, it may commit him to custody or release him on bail until he can be brought or appear before the Crown Court.

(2) Any exercise by the court of its power under sub-paragraph (1)(a) above shall be without prejudice to the continuation of the order.

(3) A fine imposed under sub-paragraph (1)(a) above shall be deemed, for the purposes of any enactment, to be a sum adjudged to be paid by a conviction.

(4) Where a magistrates' court deals with an offender under sub-paragraph (1)(b) above, it shall revoke the attendance centre order if it is still in force.

(5) In dealing with an offender under sub-paragraph (1)(b) above, a magistrates' court—

    (a)  shall take into account the extent to which the offender has complied with the requirements of the attendance centre order; and

    (b)  in the case of an offender who has wilfully and persistently failed to comply with those requirements, may impose a custodial sentence notwithstanding anything in section 152(2) of the Criminal Justice Act 2003.

(5A) Where a magistrates' court dealing with an offender under sub-paragraph (1)(a) above would not otherwise have the power to amend the order under paragraph 5(1)(b) below (substitution of different attendance centre), that paragraph has effect as if references to an appropriate magistrates' court were references to the court dealing with an offender.

(6) A person sentenced under sub-paragraph (1)(b) above for an offence may appeal to the Crown Court against the sentence.

(7) A magistrates' court which deals with an offender's case under sub-paragraph (1)(c) above shall send to the Crown Court—

    (a)  a certificate signed by a justice of the peace giving particulars of the offender's failure to attend or, as the case may be, the breach of the rules which he has committed; and

    (b)  such other particulars of the case as may be desirable;

and a certificate purporting to be so signed shall be admissible as evidence of the failure or the breach before the Crown Court.

3.—(1) Where by virtue of paragraph 2(1)(c) above the offender is brought or appears before the Crown Court and it is proved to the satisfaction of the court—

    (a)  that he has failed without reasonable excuse to attend as mentioned in paragraph 1(1)(a) above, or

    (b)  that he has committed such a breach of rules as is mentioned in paragraph 1(1)(b) above,

that court may deal with him, for the offence in respect of which the order was made, in any way in which it could have dealt with him for that offence if it had not made the order.

(2) Where the Crown Court deals with an offender under sub-paragraph (1) above, it shall revoke the attendance centre order if it is still in force.

(3) In in dealing with an offender under sub-paragraph (1) above, the Crown Court—

(a) shall take into account the extent to which the offender has complied with the requirements of the attendance centre order; and

(b) in the case of an offender who has willfully and persistently failed to comply with those requirements, may impose a custodial sentence notwithstanding anything in section 152(2) of the Criminal Justice Act 2003.

(4) In proceedings before the Crown Court under this paragraph any question whether there has been a failure to attend or a breach of the rules shall be determined by the court and not by the verdict of a jury.

*Revocation of order with or without re-sentencing*

4.—(1) Where an attendance centre order is in force in respect of an offender, an appropriate    **5-366** court may, on an application made by the offender or by the officer in charge of the relevant attendance centre, revoke the order.

(2) In sub-paragraph (1) above "an appropriate court" means—

(a) where the court which made the order was the Crown Court and there is included in the order a direction that the power to revoke the order is reserved to that court, the Crown Court;

(b) in any other case, either of the following—

(i) a magistrates' court acting for the petty sessions area in which the relevant attendance centre is situated;

(ii) the court which made the order.

(3) Any power conferred by this paragraph—

(a) on a magistrates' court to revoke an attendance centre order made by such a court, or

(b) on the Crown Court to revoke an attendance centre order made by the Crown Court,

includes power to deal with the offender, for the offence in respect of which the order was made, in any way in which he could have been dealt with for that offence by the court which made the order if the order had not been made.

(4) A person sentenced by a magistrates' court under sub-paragraph (3) above for an offence may appeal to the Crown Court against the sentence.

(5) The proper officer of a court which makes an order under this paragraph revoking an attendance centre order shall—

(a) deliver a copy of the revoking order to the offender or send a copy by registered post or the recorded delivery service addressed to the offender's last or usual place of abode; and

(b) deliver or send a copy to the officer in charge of the relevant attendance centre.

(6) In this paragraph "the relevant attendance centre", in relation to an attendance centre order, means the attendance centre specified in the order or substituted for the attendance centre so specified by an order made by virtue of paragraph 5(1)(b) below.

(7) In this paragraph "proper officer" means—

(a) in relation to a magistrates' court, the justices' chief executive for the court; and

(b) in relation to the Crown Court, the appropriate officer.

*Amendment of order*

5.—(1) Where an attendance centre order is in force in respect of an offender, an appropriate    **5-367** magistrates' court may, on application made by the offender or by the officer in charge of the relevant attendance centre, by order—

(a) vary the day or hour specified in the order for the offender's first attendance at the relevant attendance centre; or

(b) substitute for the relevant attendance centre an attendance centre which the court is satisfied is reasonably accessible to the offender, having regard to his age, the means of access available to him and any other circumstances.

(2) In sub-paragraph (1) above "an appropriate magistrates' court" means—

(a) a magistrates' court acting for the petty sessions area in which the relevant attendance centre is situated; or

(b) (except where the attendance centre order was made by the Crown Court) the magistrates' court which made the order.

(3) The justices' chief executive for a court which makes an order under this paragraph shall—

(a) deliver a copy to the offender or send a copy by registered post or the recorded delivery service addressed to the offender's last or usual place of abode; and

(b) deliver or send a copy—

(i) if the order is made by virtue of sub-paragraph (1)(a) above, to the officer in charge of the relevant attendance centre; and

(ii)   if it is made by virtue of sub-paragraph (1)(b) above, to the officer in charge of the attendance centre which the order as amended will require the offender to attend.

(4) In this paragraph "the relevant attendance centre" has the meaning given by paragraph 4(6) above.

*Orders made on appeal*

**5-368**    6.—(1) Where an attendance centre order has been made on appeal, for the purposes of this Schedule it shall be deemed—

(a)   if it was made on an appeal brought from a magistrates' court, to have been made by that magistrates' court;

(b)   if it was made on an appeal brought from the Crown Court or from the criminal division of the Court of Appeal, to have been made by the Crown Court.

(2) In relation to an attendance centre order made on appeal, paragraphs 2(1)(b) and 4(3) above shall each have effect as if the words "if the order had not been made" were omitted and paragraph 3(1) above shall have effect as if the words "if it had not made the order" were omitted.

*Orders for defaulters*

**5-369**    7.—(1) References in this Schedule to an "offender" include a person who has been ordered to attend at an attendance centre for such a default or failure as is mentioned in section 60(1)(b) or (c) of this Act.

(2) Where a person has been ordered to attend at an attendance centre for such a default or failure—

(a)   paragraphs 2(1)(b), 3(1) and 4(3) above shall each have effect in relation to the order as if the words ", for the offence in respect of which the order was made," and "for that offence" were omitted; and

(b)   paragraphs 2(5)(b) and 3(3)(b) above (which relate to custodial sentences for offences) do not apply.

[This schedule is printed as amended by the CJA 2003, s.304, and Sched. 32, paras 90 and 126; and the Domestic Violence, Crime and Victims Act 2004, s.29, and Sched. 5, para. 6. The whole schedule is repealed as from a day to be appointed (as to which, see §§ 5-1, 5-185, 5-186 in the main work) by the CJIA 2008, ss.6(1) and 149, and Sched. 28, Pt 1.]

**5-370**    When dealing with an offender under paragraph 3(1), the court must observe any limitations related to his age which applied at the time when he was sentenced: he must be sentenced on the basis of his age when he was originally convicted of the offence for which the attendance centre order was made.

In a case coming within paragraph 4, the failure to attend the attendance centre, or breach of the rules, must be proved to the satisfaction of the Crown Court: the certificate of the magistrates' court is merely evidence.

## VI.  CUSTODIAL SENTENCES

### A.  MANDATORY LIFE SENTENCE

### (2) Legislation

## Fixing the minimum term

*The whole life starting point*

**5-406**    *Vinter v. U.K. (No. 2)* is now reported at [2014] Crim.L.R. 81, *sub nom. Vinter v U.K.*

★    For the Court of Appeal's response to *Vinter v. U.K. (No. 2)* (*ante*), see *R. v. Newell*; *Att.-Gen.'s Reference (No. 69 of 2013) (R. v. McLoughlin)* [2014] Crim.L.R. 471, CA, in which it was held that the statutory regime relating to whole life orders was compatible with Article 3 of the ECHR.

### Crime (Sentences) Act 1997, s.28

**5-423**    *R. (Sturnham) v. Parole Board (No. 2)* is now reported at [2013] 2 A.C. 254, *sub nom. R. (Faulkner) v. Secretary of State for Justice*; *R. (Sturnham) v. Parole Board (Nos 1 and 2)*.

**Criminal Justice Act 2003, Sched. 22, paras 1, 2, 9 and 10**

Section 276                    SCHEDULE 22

Mandatory Life Sentences: Transitional Cases

*Interpretation*

1. In this Schedule—                                                                              **5-428**

"the commencement date" means the day on which section 269 comes into force;

"the early release provisions" means the provisions of section 28(5) to (8) of the Crime (Sentences) Act 1997;

"existing prisoner" means a person serving one or more mandatory life sentences passed before the commencement date (whether or not he is also serving any other sentence);

"life sentence" means a sentence of imprisonment for life or custody for life passed in England and Wales or by a court-martial outside England and Wales;

"mandatory life sentence" means a life sentence passed in circumstances where the sentence was fixed by law.

*Existing prisoners notified by Secretary of State*

2. Paragraph 3 applies in relation to any existing prisoner who, in respect of any mandatory life   **5-429**
sentence, has before the commencement date been notified in writing by the Secretary of State
(otherwise than in a notice that is expressed to be provisional) either—

(a) of a minimum period which in the view of the Secretary of State should be served before the prisoner's release on licence, or

(b) that the Secretary of State does not intend that the prisoner should ever be released on licence.

*Sentences passed on or after commencement date in respect of offences committed before that date*

9. Paragraph 10 applies where—                                                                   **5-430**

(a) on or after the commencement date a court passes a life sentence in circumstances where the sentence is fixed by law, and

(b) the offence to which the sentence relates was committed before the commencement date.

10. The court—

(a) may not make an order under subsection (2) of section 269 specifying a part of the sentence which in the opinion of the court is greater than that which, under the practice followed by the Secretary of State before December 2002, the Secretary of State would have been likely to notify as mentioned in paragraph 2(a), and

(b) may not make an order under subsection (4) of section 269 unless the court is of the opinion that, under the practice followed by the Secretary of State before December 2002, the Secretary of State would have been likely to give the prisoner a notification falling within paragraph 2(b).

## (3) Practice

The 2013 criminal practice directions (see the main work) are now reported at [2013] 1 W.L.R.   **5-431**
3164.

**Criminal Practice Direction (Sentencing) N [2013] 1 W.L.R. 3164**

TRANSITIONAL ARRANGEMENTS FOR SENTENCES WHERE THE OFFENCE WAS COMMITTED BEFORE 18 DECEMBER 2003

**N.1** Where the court is passing a sentence of mandatory life imprisonment for an offence committed   **5-432**
before 18 December 2003, the court should take a fourth step in determining the minimum term in accordance with section 276 and Schedule 22 ... .

**N.2** The purpose of those provisions is to ensure that the sentence does not breach the principle of
non-retroactivity by ensuring that a lower minimum term would not have been imposed for the offence
when it was committed. Before setting the minimum term the court must check whether the proposed
term is greater than that which the Secretary of State would probably have notified under the practice
followed by the Secretary of State before December 2002.

**N.3** The decision in *Sullivan* ... gives detailed guidance as to the correct approach to this practice
and judges passing mandatory life sentences where the murder was committed prior to 18 December
2003 are well advised to read that judgment before proceeding.

**N.4** The practical result of that judgment is that in sentences where the murder was committed before 31 May 2002, the best guide to what would have been the practice of the Secretary of State is the letter sent to judges by Lord Bingham C.J. on 10th February 1997, the relevant parts of which are set out below.

**N.5** The practice of Lord Bingham, as set out in his letter ... was to take 14 years as the period actually to be served for the "average", "normal" or "unexceptional" murder. Examples of factors he outlined as capable, in appropriate cases, of mitigating the normal penalty were:

> youth;
> age (where relevant to physical capacity on release or the likelihood of the defendant dying in prison);
> intellectual disability or mental disorder;
> provocation (in a non-technical sense), or an excessive response to a personal threat;
> the absence of an intention to kill;
> spontaneity and lack of premeditation (beyond that necessary to constitute the offence: *e.g.* a sudden response to family pressure or to prolonged and eventually insupportable stress);
> mercy killing;
> a plea of guilty, or hard evidence of remorse or contrition.

**N.6** Lord Bingham then listed the following factors as likely to call for a sentence more severe than the norm:

> evidence of a planned, professional, revenge or contract killing;
> the killing of a child or a very old or otherwise vulnerable victim;
> evidence of sadism, gratuitous violence, or sexual maltreatment, humiliation or degradation before the killing;
> killing for gain (in the course of burglary, robbery, blackmail, insurance fraud, *etc.*);
> multiple killings;
> the killing of a witness or potential witness to defeat the ends of justice;
> the killing of those doing their public duty (policemen, prison officers, postmasters, firemen, judges, *etc*);
> terrorist or politically motivated killings;
> the killing of those doing their public duty (policemen, prison officers, postmasters, firemen, judges, etc);
> terrorist or politically motivated killings;
> the use of firearms or other dangerous weapons, whether carried for defensive or offensive reasons;
> a substantial record of serious violence;
> macabre attempts to dismember or conceal the body.

**N.7** Lord Bingham further stated that the fact that a defendant was under the influence of drink or drugs at the time of the killing is so common he would be inclined to treat it as neutral. But in the not unfamiliar case in which a couple, inflamed by drink, indulge in a violent quarrel in which one dies, often against a background of long-standing drunken violence, then he would tend to recommend a term somewhat below the norm.

**N.8** Lord Bingham went on to say that given the intent necessary for proof of murder, the consequences of taking life and the understandable reaction of relatives to the deceased, a substantial term will almost always be called for, save perhaps in a truly venial case of mercy killing. While a recommendation of a punitive term longer than, say, 30 years will be very rare indeed, there should not be any upper limit. Some crimes will certainly call for terms very well in excess of the norm.

**5-433**   **N.9** For the purposes of sentences where the murder was committed after 31 May 2002 and before 18 December 2003, the judge should apply the practice statement handed down on 31 May 2002 reproduced at paras N.10 to N.20 below.

**N.10** This statement replaces the previous single normal tariff of 14 years by substituting a higher and a normal starting point of respectively 16 (comparable to 32 years) and 12 years (comparable to 24 years). These starting points have then to be increased or reduced because of aggravating or mitigating factors such as those referred to below. It is emphasised that they are no more than starting points.

*The normal starting point of 12 years*

**5-434**   **N.11** Cases falling within this starting point will normally involve the killing of an adult victim, arising from a quarrel or loss of temper between two people known to each other. It will not have the characteristics referred to in paragraph N.13. Exceptionally, the starting point may be reduced because of the sort of circumstances described in the next paragraph.

**N.12** The normal starting point can be reduced because the murder is one where the offender's culpability is significantly reduced, for example, because: (a) the case came close to the borderline between murder and manslaughter; or (b) the offender suffered from mental disorder, or from a mental disability which lowered the degree of his criminal responsibility for the killing, although not affording a defence of diminished responsibility; or (c) the offender was provoked (in a non-technical sense), such as by prolonged and eventually unsupportable stress; or (d) the case involved an over reaction in self-defence; or (e) the offence was a mercy killing. These factors could justify a reduction to 8/9 years (equivalent to 16/18 years).

*The higher starting point of 15/16 years*

**N.13** The higher starting point will apply to cases where the offender's culpability was exceptionally **5-435** high or the victim was in a particularly vulnerable position. Such cases will be characterised by a feature which makes the crime especially serious, such as: (a) the killing was "professional" or a contract killing; (b) the killing was politically motivated; (c) the killing was done for gain (in the course of a burglary, robbery *etc.*); (d) the killing was intended to defeat the ends of justice (as in the killing of a witness or potential witness); (e) the victim was providing a public service; (f) the victim was a child or was otherwise vulnerable; (g) the killing was racially aggravated; (h) the victim was deliberately targeted because of his or her religion or sexual orientation; (i) there was evidence of sadism, gratuitous violence or sexual maltreatment, humiliation or degradation of the victim before the killing; (j) extensive and/or multiple injuries were inflicted on the victim before death; (k) the offender committed multiple murders.

*Variation of the starting point*

**N.14** Whichever starting point is selected in a particular case, it may be appropriate for the trial **5-436** judge to vary the starting point upwards or downwards, to take account of aggravating or mitigating factors, which relate to either the offence or the offender, in the particular case.

**N.15** Aggravating factors relating to the offence can include: (a) the fact that the killing was planned; (b) the use of a firearm; (c) arming with a weapon in advance; (d) concealment of the body, destruction of the crime scene and/or dismemberment of the body; (e) particularly in domestic violence cases, the fact that the murder was the culmination of cruel and violent behaviour by the offender over a period of time.

**N.16** Aggravating factors relating to the offender will include the offender's previous record and failures to respond to previous sentences, to the extent that this is relevant to culpability rather than to risk.

**N.17** Mitigating factors relating to the offence will include: (a) an intention to cause grievous bodily harm, rather than to kill; (b) spontaneity and lack of pre-meditation.

**N.18** Mitigating factors relating to the offender may include: (a) the offender's age; (b) clear evidence of remorse or contrition; (c) a timely plea of guilt.

*Very serious cases*

**N.19** A substantial upward adjustment may be appropriate in the most serious cases, for example, **5-437** those involving a substantial number of murders, or if there are several factors identified as attracting the higher starting point present. In suitable cases, the result might even be a minimum term of 30 years (equivalent to 60 years) which would offer little or no hope of the offender's eventual release. In cases of exceptional gravity, the judge, rather than setting a whole life minimum term, can state that there is no minimum period which could properly be set in that particular case.

**N.20** Among the categories of case referred to in paragraph N.13 some offences may be especially grave. These include cases where the victim was performing his duties as a prison officer at the time of the crime or the offence was a terrorist or sexual or sadistic murder or involved a young child. In such a case, a term of 20 years and upwards could be appropriate.

**N.21** In following this guidance, judges should bear in mind the conclusion of the court in *Sullivan* that the general effect of both these statements is the same. While Lord Bingham does not identify as many starting points, it is open to the judge to come to exactly the same decision irrespective of which was followed. Both pieces of guidance give the judge a considerable degree of discretion.

For *Criminal Practice Direction (Sentencing) P* (procedure for announcing the minimum term in **5-438** open court), see § 5-439 in the main work.

As to the authority referred to in paragraph N.3, see *R. v. Sullivan*; *R. v. Gibbs*; *R. v. Elener (Barry) and Elener (Derek)* [2005] 1 Cr.App.R. 3, CA.

*Announcing the minimum term*

The 2013 criminal practice directions (see the main work) are now reported at [2013] 1 W.L.R. **5-439** 3164.

## B. Automatic Life Sentences

### Powers of Criminal Courts (Sentencing) Act 2000, s.109

*Life sentence for second serious offence*

**5-440**    **109.**—(1) This section applies where—

    (a) a person is convicted of a serious offence committed after 30th September 1997; and

    (b) at the time when that offence was committed, he was 18 or over and had been convicted in any part of the United Kingdom of another serious offence.

(2) The court shall impose a life sentence, that is to say—

    (a) *where the offender is 21 or over when convicted of the offence mentioned in subsection (1)(a) above, a sentence of imprisonment for life,*

    (b) where he is under 21 at that time, a sentence of custody for life under section 94 above,

[a sentence of imprisonment for life] unless the court is of the opinion that there are exceptional circumstances relating to either of the offences or to the offender which justify its not doing so.

(3) Where the court does not impose a life sentence, it shall state in open court that it is of that opinion and what the exceptional circumstances are.

(4) An offence the sentence for which is imposed under *subsection (2)* above shall not be regarded as an offence the sentence for which is fixed by law.

(5) An offence committed in England and Wales is a serious offence for the purposes of this section if it is any of the following, namely—

    (a) an attempt to commit murder, a conspiracy to commit murder or an incitement to murder;

    (b) an offence under section 4 of the Offences Against the Person Act 1861 (soliciting murder);

    (c) manslaughter;

    (d) an offence under section 18 of the Offences Against the Person Act 1861 (wounding, or causing grievous bodily harm, with intent);

    (e) rape or an attempt to commit rape;

    (f) an offence under section 5 of the Sexual Offences Act 1956 (intercourse with a girl under 13);

    (g) an offence under section 16 (possession of a firearm with intent to injure), section 17 (use of a firearm to resist arrest) or section 18 (carrying a firearm with criminal intent) of the Firearms Act 1968; and

    (h) robbery where, at some time during the commission of the offence, the offender had in his possession a firearm or imitation firearm within the meaning of that Act.

(6) An offence committed in Scotland is a serious offence for the purposes of this section if the conviction for it was obtained on indictment in the High Court of Justiciary and it is any of the following, namely—

    (a) culpable homicide;

    (b) attempted murder, incitement to commit murder or conspiracy to commit murder;

    (c) rape or attempted rape;

    (d) clandestine injury to women or an attempt to cause such injury;

    (e) sodomy, or an attempt to commit sodomy, where the complainer, that is to say, the person against whom the offence was committed, did not consent;

    (f) assault where the assault—

        (i) is aggravated because it was carried out to the victim's severe injury or the danger of the victim's life; or

        (ii) was carried out with an intention to rape or to ravish the victim;

    (g) robbery where, at some time during the commission of the offence, the offender had in his possession a firearm or imitation firearm within the meaning of the Firearms Act 1968;

    (h) an offence under section 16 (possession of a firearm with intent to injure), section 17 (use of a firearm to resist arrest) or section 18 (carrying a firearm with criminal intent) of that Act;

    (i) lewd, libidinous or indecent behaviour or practices; and

    (j) an offence under section 5(1) of the Criminal Law (Consolidation) (Scotland) Act 1995 (unlawful intercourse with a girl under 13).

(7) An offence committed in Northern Ireland is a serious offence for the purposes of this section if it is any of the following, namely—

    (a) an offence falling within any of paragraphs (a) to (e) of subsection (5) above;

    (b) an offence under section 4 of the Criminal Law Amendment Act 1885 (intercourse with a girl under 14);

    (c)   an offence under Article 17 (possession of a firearm with intent to injure), Article 18(1) (use of a firearm to resist arrest) or Article 19 (carrying a firearm with criminal intent) of the Firearms (Northern Ireland) Order 1981; and

    (d)   robbery where, at some time during the commission of the offence, the offender had in his possession a firearm or imitation firearm within the meaning of that Order.

[This section is printed as amended, as from a day to be appointed, by the CJCSA 2000, s.74, and Sched. 7, para. 189 (substitution of words in square brackets for paras (a) and (b) in subs. (2)). It is repealed, as from April 4, 2005 (Criminal Justice Act 2003 (Commencement No. 8 and Transitional and Saving Provisions) Order 2005 (S.I. 2005 No. 950), by the CJA 2003, s.332, and Sched. 37 Pt 7. For the saving provisions in relation to an offence committed before April 4, 2005, see § 5-2 in the main work.]

## Serious offences

The only attempts which are serious offences are those specifically mentioned: *R. v. Buckland*;   **5-441**
*R. v. Newman* [2000] 1 Cr.App.R. 471, CA. Offences under the Firearms Act 1968, s.17(2) are serious offences: *ibid.*; as are offences under sections 16, 17 and 18 of that Act where the firearm was an imitation only: *ibid.*

An offence of robbery is a "serious offence" within section 109(2)(h) if the offence was committed as a joint enterprise where a firearm or imitation was used, even though the offender himself had never had possession of it, provided that there was joint possession of it; where, in relation to the alleged index offence, there is an issue as to whether this was established against the offender, the court must be satisfied that at the earlier hearing the offender admitted, or it was admitted on his behalf, that he was in joint possession of the firearm: *R. v. Flamson* [2002] 2 Cr.App.R.(S.) 48, CA. The court considered that *R. v. Eubank* [2002] 1 Cr.App.R.(S.) 4, CA (§ 24-49 in the main work) had no application to the facts of the case. In *R. v. Murphy* [2003] 1 Cr.App.R.(S.) 39, CA, however, it was held, without reference to *Flamson*, that where there was an issue as to whether the defendant had been in possession of a firearm, the proper way to resolve the issue was, in accordance with *Eubank*, for an appropriate count under the Firearms Act 1968 to be included in the indictment. Where this course had not been adopted, it was not open to the judge to conclude in relation to either the index offence or the fresh offence that it fell within section 109(1)(h); absent an unequivocal admission on the part of the defendant (see *R. v. Benfield*; *R. v. Sobers* [2004] 1 Cr.App.R.(S.) 52, CA).

*R. v. Benfield*; *R. v. Sobers* was followed in *R. v. Hylands* [2005] 2 Cr.App.R.(S.) 25, CA, where it was said that for an offence of robbery to fall within section 109(5)(h) of the 2000 Act, the qualifying condition relating to a firearm or imitation firearm had to be established either by means of an appropriate count under the Firearms Act 1968 being included in the indictment, or there had to be an unequivocal admission in relation thereto; and this applies where the only issue in relation to the robbery is identity (there being unchallenged evidence before the jury that the robber was in possession of a firearm at the time of the robbery); if there was any doubt about the matter, it was to be resolved in favour of the defendant.

As to whether a conviction at a court-martial in Germany for an offence of wounding with intent to cause grievous bodily harm committed whilst a serving member of the armed forces in Germany may qualify as a "serious offence" within the meaning of section 109(1)(a) of the PC-C(S)A 2000, see *R. v. Sanders, post*, § 5-447.

## "exceptional circumstances"

The meaning of "exceptional circumstances" (s.109(2)) was reconsidered in *R. v. Offen* [2001] 1   **5-442**
W.L.R. 253, CA. Lord Woolf C.J. said that quite apart from the impact of the Human Rights Act 1998, the rationale of the section should be highly relevant in deciding whether or not exceptional circumstances existed. The question whether circumstances were appropriately regarded as "exceptional" must be influenced by the context in which the question was being asked. The policy and intention of Parliament were to protect the public against a person who had committed two serious offences. It therefore could be assumed that the section was not intended to apply to someone in relation to whom it was established that there would be no need for protection in the future. In other words, if the facts showed the statutory assumption was misplaced, then this,

in the statutory context, was not the normal situation and in consequence, for the purposes of the section, the position was exceptional. The time that elapsed between the two offences could, but would not necessarily, reflect on whether, after the second serious offence was committed, there was any danger against which the public would need protection. The same was true of two differing offences, and the age of the offender. These were all circumstances which could give rise to the conclusion that what could be normal and not exceptional in a different context was exceptional in this context. If this approach was not adopted, then in the case of the serious offences listed in the section, the gravity of which could vary greatly, the approach to "exceptional circumstances" could be unduly restrictive. The aim of section 2 was not to increase the time offenders spent in prison as a punishment for the offence they had committed, but to provide for an assessment to be made to see whether the offender posed a real risk to the public, in which event his release was deferred. Section 109 established a norm. The norm was that those who commit two serious offences were a danger or risk to the public. If in fact, taking into account all the circumstances relating to a particular offender, he did not create an unacceptable risk to the public, he was an exception to this norm.

Construing section 109 in accordance with the duty imposed on the court by section 3 of the 1998 Act, and taking into account the rationale of the section, gave content to "exceptional circumstances". In the court's judgment, section 109 would not contravene Convention rights if courts applied the section so that it did not result in offenders being sentenced to life imprisonment when they did not constitute a significant risk to the public. Whether there was a significant risk would depend on the evidence which was before the court. If the offender was a significant risk, the court could impose a life sentence under section 109 without contravening the Convention. It would be part of the responsibility of judges to assess the risk to the public that offenders constituted. In many cases the degree of risk that an offender constituted would be established by his record, with or without the assistance of assessments made in reports which were available to the court. If courts needed further assistance, they could call for it when deciding whether a discretionary life sentence should be imposed. There should be no undue difficulty in making a similar assessment when considering whether the court was required to impose an automatic life sentence, although the task would not be straightforward, because of the lack of information as to the first serious offence which will sometimes exist because of the passage of time. This did not mean that the court was approaching the passing of an automatic life sentence as if it was no different from the imposition of a discretionary life sentence. Notwithstanding the interpretation resulting from the application of section 3(1) of the 1998 Act suggested, section 109 would give effect to the intention of Parliament. It would do so, however, in a more just, less arbitrary and more proportionate manner. Section 109 would still mean that a judge was obliged to pass a life sentence in accordance with its terms unless, in all the circumstances, the offender posed no significant risk to the public. There was no such obligation in cases where section 109 did not apply. In addition, if the judge decided not to impose a life sentence under section 109, he would have to give reasons as required by section 109(3). Furthermore, the issue of dangerousness would have to be addressed in every case and a decision made as to whether or not to impose a life sentence.

*Offen* has since been applied in *R. v. McDonald* [2001] 2 Cr.App.R.(S.) 127, CA (having regard, in particular, to the length of time since the appellant's conviction for his previous "serious" offences (14 years) and to the fact that it was not the appellant but a co-defendant who had produced an imitation firearm in the course of the robbery, although it belonged to the appellant, it would be wrong to conclude that the appellant presented a serious risk of harm to the public so as to justify the imposition of an automatic life sentence); and in *R. v. Kelly (No. 2)* [2002] 1 Cr.App.R.(S.) 85, CA, it was held that the statutory presumption that arises under section 109(2), and which flows from the existence of two qualifying offences remains in place, and has to be displaced by the defendant in any given case; and such displacement may be achieved in a number of ways, including scrutiny of the offending and behaviour pattern, or by positive psychiatric or similar evidence, such evidence being likely to be required if the court is to be persuaded that the presumption cannot apply since the criterion to be established is that there is "no need to protect the public in the future" or "no significant risk to the public".

In *R. v. Baff* [2003] 2 Cr.App.R.(S.) 37, CA, it was said that the use of imitation firearms for the purpose of robbery caused as much fear and alarm to vulnerable members of the public as robbery with a real firearm; and that, if the court were to rule that section 109 did not as a matter of principle apply where the offender limited his offending to robberies with an imitation firearm, it would be creating an exception to an express provision flatly contradicting an aspect of sentencing policy laid down by Parliament.

In *R. v. Richards* [2002] 2 Cr.App.R.(S.) 26, CA, it was held that in considering whether a defendant who qualifies for an automatic life sentence under section 109 presents a significant risk to the public, the judge may take account of a significant risk of the commission of serious offences other than those listed as "serious" in the section itself, for example, burglaries of dwellings or a conspiracy to import hard drugs. For a criticism of this decision, see the commentary in the *Criminal Law Review*. It is inconsistent with the view of the court in *R. v. Fletcher*; *R. v. Smith* [2002] 1 Cr.App.R.(S.) 82, CA, to the effect that the "danger in point is that of violent or sexual offending."

*Richards* was not cited in *R. v. Stark* [2002] 2 Cr.App.R.(S.) 104, CA, where there was a high risk of further offences being committed by the appellant, but no significant risk of danger to the public by way of either violent or sexual offences; accordingly, it was held that the case was to be regarded as an exception to the norm, which was that those who committed two serious offences were a danger or risk to the public.

The approach in *R. v. Stark* and *R. v. Fletcher*; *R. v. Smith* was followed, and that in *Richards* expressly disapproved in *R. v. Magalhaes* [2005] 2 Cr.App.R.(S.) 13, CA.

In *R. v. Frost* [2001] 2 Cr.App.R.(S.) 26, CA, the appellant had been found guilty by a youth court in 1991 of wounding with intent to resist arrest. He was later convicted of wounding with intent to cause grievous bodily harm. The court held that the finding of guilt by the youth court amounted to a "conviction" for the purposes of PCC(S)A 2000, s.109(1), by virtue of the CYPA 1933, s.59. If the appellant had been older and had been subject to a probation order, the "conviction" would have been deemed not to be a conviction by virtue of the PCCA 1973, s.13(1) (*rep.*), but this provision did not apply to a supervision order. The anomaly which resulted from this amounted to an "exceptional circumstance" for the purposes of section 109, and the sentence of life imprisonment was quashed, even though it could not be said that the offender presented no significant risk to the public.

The fact that the offender is mentally ill and eligible for a hospital order does not in itself amount to an "exceptional circumstance" for this purpose: see *R. v. Newman* [2000] 2 Cr.App.R.(S.) 227, CA; *R. v. Drew* [2003] 2 Cr.App.R. 24, HL (where a submission that an automatic life sentence on conviction of wounding with intent constituted inhuman or degrading treatment was rejected; having been transferred administratively to hospital within a few days of the passing of sentence, the appellant was receiving the same treatment as he would have received had he been made subject to a hospital order, and he could not complain of the stigma attaching to the sentence as he had been convicted by a jury, who must therefore have been satisfied as to his intent).

On appeal, the issue is whether the offender created an unacceptable risk to the public at the time when he was sentenced, not at the time when the Court of Appeal is considering the matter: see *R. v. Watkins* [2003] 1 Cr.App.R.(S.) 16, CA; *R. v. Noorkoiv* [2002] 2 Cr.App.R.(S.) 91, CA.

## C. MINIMUM FIXED TERM SENTENCES

### (1) Legislation

**Powers of Criminal Courts (Sentencing) Act 2000, ss.110, 111**

*Minimum of three years for third domestic burglary*

    *R. v. Coleman* is now reported at [2013] 2 Cr.App.R.(S.) 79.      **5-444**

**Powers of Criminal Courts (Sentencing) Act 2000, ss.112–115**

*Offences under service law*

    In *R. v. Sanders* [2007] 1 Cr.App.R.(S.) 74, CA, it was held that the effect of section 114 of the **5-447** PCC(S)A 2000 was limited to deeming the conviction to have been in England and Wales; it did not deem the offence to have been committed in England and Wales; where, therefore, the appellant had previously been convicted of an offence under section 70 of the Army Act 1955 and the corresponding civil offence had been one of those listed in section 109(5), but the offence had been committed abroad, he was not to be regarded as having previously been convicted of a serious offence, since, under section 109(5), an offence would only be "serious" if committed in England and Wales; section 114 would bite only in relation to convictions under section 70 where the offence occurred in England and Wales. It should be noted that the repeal of the words "a serious offence" in section 114(1)(b) is of no effect where an offender is being dealt with for an offence committed prior to April 4, 2005.

Firearms Act 1968, s.51A

*Minimum sentence for certain offences under s.5*

★5-449    With effect from July 14, 2014 (Anti-social Behaviour, Crime and Policing Act 2014 (Commencement No. 2, Transitional and Transitory Provisions) Order 2014 (S.I. 2014 No. 949)), the Anti-social Behaviour, Crime and Policing Act 2014, s.108(1) and (6), amended section 51A(1A) of the 1968 Act so as to insert, before paragraph (a), a new paragraph (za) as follows—

> "(za) section 5(2A) (manufacture, sale or transfer of firearm, or possession etc. for sale or transfer);".

(2) Practice

### "exceptional circumstances" (1968 Act, s.51A(2))

★5-453    There were exceptional circumstances for the purposes of section 51A(2) of the Firearms Act 1968 (as to which, see § 5-449 in the main work), so as to free the sentencer from the straitjacket of the minimum term of five years' imprisonment for certain firearms offences, where the offender, who had a history of suicide attempts, said that he had been hearing voices that told him to harm himself, had taken guns from his father's collection (his father being a Wild West enthusiast) and threatened staff at a fast food restaurant with a pistol in order to create a situation in which he expected the police to shoot him dead; but an immediate custodial sentence was required, given that, even on his own case, he had set out to frighten others: *R. v. Bate* [2014] 1 Cr.App.R.(S.) 48, CA.

★    Where the offender had, some years previously, ordered from the internet a stun gun disguised as a mobile phone, where the gun could not be used as it was not charged and incapable of being so, where no use had been made of it, and where the offender did not know that possession of such a stun gun was illegal, there were exceptional circumstances for the purposes of section 51A(2) of the 1968 Act (*ante*); as to the appropriate sentence, while stun guns can be a dangerous weapon in the wrong hands, and they can get into the wrong hands easily if left in a house, a deterrent sentence is no deterrent if the offender does not know that what he has done is illegal: *R. v. Stoker* [2014] 1 Cr.App.R.(S.) 47, CA. In *Stoker*, the court substituted a sentence of two years' imprisonment, but in *R. v. Zhekov* [2014] 1 Cr.App.R.(S.) 69, CA, the court substituted a suspended sentence in the case of a Bulgarian lorry driver of "exemplary character" who had a stun gun that also operated as a torch in his cab. He had bought it in Bulgaria where its possession was legal, and he did not know it was illegal to possess it in the United Kingdom. The court said that, given the exceptionality of the case, it was necessary to approach the question of deterrence with a degree of caution; hereafter, those carrying such stun guns to the United Kingdom will know, if this case or similar ones are publicised, that it is illegal to do so and that there is a clear prospect of immediate custody if they are detected.

★    Agreeing to store a prohibited weapon out of fear following pressure and threats by criminals did not, however, amount to exceptional circumstances for the purposes of section 51A(2) (*ante*); the use by criminals of individuals apparently unconnected to them to store firearms or ammunition was a common feature of this type of offending; the courts should assume that citizens, even if subjected to threats, would, if necessary, turn to the authorities for protection; that the offender declined (out of fear) to tell the police who gave him the gun should not be seen as inevitable, acceptable or a factor that had any bearing on exceptional circumstances; to conclude that pressure brought to bear in such a case amounted to exceptional circumstances would largely blunt section 51A: *Att.-Gen.'s Reference (No. 37 of 2013) (R. v. Culpeper)* [2014] 1 Cr.App.R.(S.) 62, CA.

In *Att.-Gen.'s Reference (No. 51 of 2013) (R. v. Wright)* [2014] 1 Cr.App.R.(S.) 83, CA, it was said ★ that certain principles could be distilled from the authorities, especially *R. v. Rehman*; *R. v. Wood* (as to which, see the main work); first, a guilty plea is irrelevant; secondly, cases where exceptional circumstances arise will be rare; thirdly, the necessary assessment involves a consideration of all the circumstances; fourthly, if an offender is unfit to serve a five-year term, or is of very advanced years, this may amount to exceptional circumstances; fifthly, unless the sentencing court was clearly wrong (one way or the other), the Court of Appeal will be slow to interfere; sixthly, circumstances are exceptional where imposition of the minimum term would result in an "arbitrary and disproportionate" sentence. On the facts, the court set aside the judge's finding that there were exceptional circumstances, saying that he had placed far too much weight on the appellant's physical and mental condition, and also erred in ignoring a suspended sentence for fraud; that sentence may have been imposed for an entirely different kind of offence, but the offender was doubtless warned of the consequences of offending in any way.

## D. Discretionary Custodial Sentences

### (1) General restrictions

### (a) *Legislation*

#### Powers of Criminal Courts (Sentencing) Act 2000, s.78

*General limit on magistrates' court's power to impose imprisonment or detention in a young offender institution*
With effect from April 6, 2014, the provisions of the Tribunals, Courts and Enforcement Act ★**5-460** 2007 referred to in the main work were brought into force: Tribunals, Courts and Enforcement Act 2007 (Commencement No. 11) Order 2014 (S.I. 2014 No. 768).

#### Criminal Justice Act 2003, s.154

*General limit on magistrates' court's power to impose imprisonment*
With effect from April 6, 2014, the provisions of the Tribunals, Courts and Enforcement Act ★**5-461** 2007 referred to in the main work were brought into force: Tribunals, Courts and Enforcement Act 2007 (Commencement No. 11) Order 2014 (S.I. 2014 No. 768).

#### Magistrates' Courts Act 1980, ss.132, 133

*Consecutive terms of imprisonment*
With effect from April 6, 2014, the provisions of the Tribunals, Courts and Enforcement Act ★**5-463** 2007 referred to in the main work were brought into force: Tribunals, Courts and Enforcement Act 2007 (Commencement No. 11) Order 2014 (S.I. 2014 No. 768).

### (b) *Authorities*

## Deterrence/prevalence

*Community impact statements*
The 2013 criminal practice directions (see the main work) are now reported at [2013] 1 W.L.R. **5-467a** 3164.

For a case considering the relevance of a community impact statement from a police officer ★ when applying the Sentencing Council's guideline on drugs (as to which, see *post*, Appendix K-271 *et seq.*), see *R. v. Wicks, post*, Appendix K-628b.

### (c) *Legislation (offences committed before April 4, 2005)*

#### Powers of Criminal Courts (Sentencing) Act 2000, ss.79, 80

*General restrictions on imposing discretionary custodial sentences*
**79.**—(1) This section applies where a person is convicted of an offence punishable with a custodial **5-469** sentence other than one—

    (a)  fixed by law; or

    (b)  falling to be imposed under section 109(2), 110(2) or 111(2) below.

  (2) Subject to subsection (3) below, the court shall not pass a custodial sentence on the offender unless it is of the opinion—

    (a)  that the offence, or the combination of the offence and one or more offences associated with it, was so serious that only such a sentence can be justified for the offence; or

    (b)  where the offence is a violent or sexual offence, that only such a sentence would be adequate to protect the public from serious harm from him.

  (3) Nothing in subsection (2) above shall prevent the court from passing a custodial sentence on the offender if he fails to express his willingness to comply with—

    (a)  a requirement which is proposed by the court to be included in a community rehabilitation order or supervision order and which requires an expression of such willingness; or

    (b)  a requirement which is proposed by the court to be included in a drug treatment and testing order or an order under section 52(4) above (order to provide samples). In relation to an offence committed before 1st October 1997:

  (4) Where a court passes a custodial sentence, it shall—

    (a)  in a case not falling within subsection (3) above, state in open court that it is of the opinion that either or both of paragraphs (a) and (b) of subsection (2) above apply and why it is of that opinion; and

    (b)  in any case, explain to the offender in open court and in ordinary language why it is passing a custodial sentence on him.

  (5) A magistrates' court shall cause a reason stated by it under subsection (4) above to be specified in the warrant of commitment and to be entered in the register.

[This section is printed as amended by the CJCSA 2000, s.74 and Sched. 7, para. 1. It is repealed, as from April 4, 2005 (Criminal Justice Act 2003 (Commencement No. 8 and Transitional and Saving Provisions) Order 2005 (S.I. 2005 No. 950)), by the CJA 2003, s.332, and Sched. 37, Pt 7. As to the saving provision in relation to offences committed before April 4, 2005, see § 5-2 in the main work.]

In relation to an offence committed before October 1, 1997, see the transitional provision in Sched. 11, para. 4(d).

*Length of discretionary custodial sentences: general provision.*

**5-470**    **80.**—(1) This section applies where a court passes a custodial sentence other than one fixed by law or falling to be imposed under section 109(2) below.

  (2) Subject to sections 110(2) and 111(2) below, the custodial sentence shall be—

    (a)  for such term (not exceeding the permitted maximum) as in the opinion of the court is commensurate with the seriousness of the offence, or the combination of the offence and one or more offences associated with it; or

    (b)  where the offence is a violent or sexual offence, for such longer term (not exceeding that maximum) as in the opinion of the court is necessary to protect the public from serious harm from the offender.

  (3) Where the court passes a custodial sentence for a term longer than is commensurate with the seriousness of the offence, or the combination of the offence and one or more offences associated with it, the court shall—

    (a)  state in open court that it is of the opinion that subsection (2)(b) above applies and why it is of that opinion; and

    (b)  explain to the offender in open court and in ordinary language why the sentence is for such a term.

  (4) A custodial sentence for an indeterminate period shall be regarded for the purposes of subsections (2) and (3) above as a custodial sentence for a term longer than any actual term.

  (5) Subsection (3) above shall not apply in any case where the court passes a custodial sentence falling to be imposed under subsection (2) of section 110 or 111 below which is for the minimum term specified in that subsection.

[This section is repealed, as from April 4, 2005 (Criminal Justice Act 2003 (Commencement No. 8 and Transitional and Saving Provisions) Order 2005 (S.I. 2005 No. 950)), by the CJA 2003, s.332, and Sched. 37, Pt 7. As to the saving provision in relation to offences committed before April 4, 2005, see § 5-2 in the main work.]

**Powers of Criminal Courts (Sentencing) Act 2000, s.161**

*Meaning of "associated offence", "sexual offence", "violent offence" and "protecting the public from serious harm".*

**161.**—(1) [*See § 5-2 in the main work.*]        **5-471**

(2) In this Act, "sexual offence" means any of the following—

    (f)   an offence under the Protection of Children Act 1978;

    (fa)  an offence under section 3 of the Sexual Offences (Amendment) Act 2000;

    (fa)  an offence under any provision of Part 1 of the Sexual Offences Act 2003; except section 52, 53 or 71

    (g)  an offence under section 1 of the Criminal Law Act 1977; of conspiracy to commit any of the offences in paragraphs (a) to (f) above;

    (h)  an offence under section 1 of the Criminal Attempts Act 1981; of attempting to commit any of those offences;

    (i)  an offence of inciting another to commit any of those offences.

(3) In this Act, "violent offence" means an offence which leads, or is intended or likely to lead, to a person's death or to physical injury to a person, and includes an offence which is required to be charged as arson (whether or not it would otherwise fall within this definition).

(4) In this Act any reference, in relation to an offender convicted of a violent or sexual offence, to protecting the public from serious harm from him shall be construed as a reference to protecting members of the public from death or serious personal injury, whether physical or psychological, occasioned by further such offences committed by him.

[Subss. (2) to (4) are printed as amended and repealed in part, by the Sexual Offences (Amendment) Act 2000, s.6(1); and the SOA 2003, ss.139 and 140, and Sched. 6, para. 4 (insertion of second para. (fa) in subs. (2)), and Sched. 7 (repeal of subs. (2)(a)–(e), the failure to repeal the first para. (fa) being accounted for by the draftsman having overlooked the amendment made by the 2000 Act). The amendments effected by the 2003 Act took effect on May 1, 2004 (Sexual Offences Act 2003 (Commencement) Order 2004 (S.I. 2004 No. 874)). For the former provisions, which will continue to apply in relation to offences committed before that date (Interpretation Act 1978, s.16 (Appendix B-16)), see the 2004 edition of this work. Subss. (2) to (4) are repealed, as from April 4, 2005 (Criminal Justice Act 2003 (Commencement No. 8 and Transitional and Saving Provisions) Order 2005 (S.I. 2005 No. 950)), by the CJA 2003, s.332, and Sched. 7. As to the saving provision in relation to offences committed before April 4, 2005, see § 5-2 in the main work.]

## "Violent" and "sexual" offences

Whether any particular offence is a violent offence depends on the facts of the individual        **5-472**
offence. An offence which leads to or is intended to lead only to psychological injury is not a "violent offence" but it is not necessary that serious harm should have been caused (see *R. v. Robinson* [1994] 1 W.L.R. 168, CA). Nor does it have to be established that physical injury was a probability: *R. v. Szczerba* [2002] 2 Cr.App.R.(S.) 86, CA.

In *R. v. Cochrane*, 15 Cr.App.R.(S.) 708, CA, it was held that a robbery in which the victim was threatened with a knife was a "violent offence" as the incident could have resulted in injury, either accidentally or if the victim had resisted. See also *R. v. Bibby*, 16 Cr.App.R.(S.) 127, CA. For cases of robbery by persons armed with a firearm, see *R. v. Touriq Khan*, 16 Cr.App.R.(S.) 180, CA, *R. v. Palin*, 16 Cr.App.R.(S.) 888, CA, and *R. v. Baker* [2001] 1 Cr.App.R.(S.) 55, CA. An offence of threatening to kill which does not involve the infliction of physical injury will not normally be a "violent offence": see *R. v. Richart*, 16 Cr.App.R.(S.) 977, CA, *R. v. Ragg* [1996] 1 Cr.App.R.(S.) 176, CA and *R. v. Birch* [2002] 1 Cr.App.R.(S.) 129, CA; but see *R. v. Wilson* [1998] 1 Cr.App.R.(S.) 341, CA.

Attempted arson is "an offence which is required to be charged as arson" and is accordingly a "violent offence" within section 161(3): *R. v. Guirke* [1997] 1 Cr.App.R.(S.) 170, CA.

## "Serious harm" (s.161(4) of the Act of 2000)

See § 5-495 in the main work.        **5-473**

## The criterion of seriousness

For discussion of the relevant authorities in relation to section 79(1), see § 5-465 in the main        **5-474**
work.

### Sentences commensurate with the seriousness of the offence

**5-475**    For relevant considerations where a court is deciding what term of custody is commensurate with an offence or group of offences, see § 5-466 in the main work.

### Longer than normal sentences

**5-476**    For the definitions of "sexual offence" and "violent offence", see section 161(2) and (3) of the PCC(S)A 2000 (*ante*, § 5-471); and for the authorities in relation thereto, see *ante*, § 5-472. For the construction of references to "protecting the public from serious harm", see section 161(4) of the 2000 Act (*ante*, § 5-471); and the authorities referred to at §§ 5-495 *et seq.* in the main work.

An isolated offence, however serious, will rarely be sufficient to justify a longer than normal sentence under section 80(2)(b), whether the offence is violent or sexual, or both: *R. v. Walsh*, 16 Cr.App.R.(S.) 204, CA; *R. v. Mumtaz Ali*, 16 Cr.App.R.(S.) 692, CA. A longer than commensurate sentence may be passed on an offender with no previous convictions: *R. v. Thomas*, 16 Cr.App.R.(S.) 616, CA.

A court deciding whether to draw the inference that the offender is likely to commit further violent or sexual offences may need to examine the circumstances of the current offence in some detail, going beyond what would be necessary if only a commensurate sentence were in issue: *R. v. Oudkerk*, 16 Cr.App.R.(S.) 172, CA. Equally, if the inference is to be based on a previous conviction, the court may need to examine the circumstances of that offence in detail: *R. v. Samuels*, 16 Cr.App.R.(S.) 856, CA.

An offender may satisfy the requirements of section 80(2)(b) even though the members of the public who are at risk from him are a small group, or possibly an individual: *R. v. Hashi*, 16 Cr.App.R.(S.) 121, CA. Where the offender's behaviour is directed at a small group of people, who can be protected from him by other means, a longer than commensurate sentence may not be justified: *R. v. Nicholas*, 15 Cr.App.R.(S.) 381, CA; *R. v. Swain*, 15 Cr.App.R.(S.) 765, CA; *R. v. L.*, 15 Cr.App.R.(S.) 501, CA.

In many cases the inference of dangerousness will be based in part on psychiatric evidence: *R. v. Lyons*, 15 Cr.App.R.(S.) 460, CA; *R. v. Fawcett*, 16 Cr.App.R.(S.) 55, CA; *R. v. Etchells* [1996] 1 Cr.App.R.(S.) 163, CA.

The principles which should be applied in deciding the length of a longer than commensurate sentence were considered in *R. v. Mansell*, 15 Cr.App.R.(S.) 771, CA; and *R. v. Crow*; *R. v. Pennington*, 16 Cr.App.R.(S.) 409, CA. Lord Taylor C.J. said that some allowance should usually be made, even in the worst cases, for a plea of guilty. A sentence imposed under section 80(2)(b), whilst long enough to give necessary protection for the public, should still bear a reasonable relationship to the offence for which it was imposed.

This principle was not applied in *R. v. Chapman* [2000] 1 Cr.App.R. 77, CA, where it was said that there was no necessary ratio between the part of the sentence intended to punish and the part intended to protect. There was no objection in principle if the court regarded a sentence of two years as necessary to punish, but an additional term of six or eight years as necessary to protect, making a total term of eight or 10 years. *Chapman* was followed in *R. v. Wilson* [2000] 2 Cr.App.R.(S.) 323, CA, but not apparently in *R. v. De Silva* [2000] 2 Cr.App.R.(S.) 408, CA.

**5-477**    The question whether a longer than commensurate sentence may properly be imposed to run consecutively to a sentence of imprisonment was considered by the Court of Appeal in *R. v. Everleigh* [2002] 1 Cr.App.R.(S.) 32. The court considered *R. v. King*, 16 Cr.App.R.(S.) 987; *R. v. Walters* [1997] 2 Cr.App.R.(S.) 87; *R. v. Johnson* [1998] 1 Cr.App.R.(S.) 126; *R. v. Cuthbertson and Jenks* [2000] 1 Cr.App.R.(S.) 359; *R. v. Parsons* [2000] 1 Cr.App.R.(S.) 428; *R. v. Blades* [2000] 1 Cr.App.R.(S.) 463; *R. v. Sullivan* [2000] 2 Cr.App.R.(S.) 318; *R. v. Sowden* [2000] 2 Cr.App.R.(S.) 360; *R. v. Wilson* [2000] 2 Cr.App.R.(S.) 323; and *R. v. Ellis* [2001] 1 Cr.App.R.(S.) 43. Accepting that not all of these of authorities could be reconciled, the court held that they showed that it was inappropriate to pass a longer than the normal sentence to run consecutively to another sentence imposed on the same occasion, because a longer than normal sentence is intended in itself to protect the public from serious harm, without the need for any additional penalty in relation to other conduct punishable at the same time. Secondly, there was nothing inappropriate, but on the contrary it might be desirable, for a longer than normal sentence to be passed consecutively either to a sentence passed on an earlier occasion (*Wilson*) or to a period of return to custody ordered under the PCC(S)A 2000, s.116 (*post*, § 5-633), which was a consequence of a sentence passed on an earlier occasion (*Blades*). As was pointed out in *Blades*, it was important that both the public and the defendant should know that a sentence once passed would have to be served (subject to any reduction which might be appropriate in accordance with *R. v. Taylor* [1998] 1 Cr.App.R.(S.) 312). It was desirable that the sentencing judge, if imposing a consecutive sentence, should make it plain what were the factors which he had taken into consideration in so passing the sentence under section 80(2)(b).

In *R. v. Christie*, 16 Cr.App.R.(S.) 469, CA, it was said to be wrong to add an additional period to the sentence under section 80(2)(b) if the commensurate sentence already incorporated an element for the protection of the public. In *R. v. Campbell* [1997] 1 Cr.App.R.(S.) 119, CA, it was held that if the sentencing guidelines for a particular offence included an element for the protection of the public, the sentencer should decide what was the appropriate sentence, leaving out of account any element for the protection of the public, and should then add the greater element needed for the protection of the public from serious harm under section 80(2)(b). This would avoid the risk of imposing an element of the sentence twice over. In *R. v. Gabbidon and Bramble* [1997] 2 Cr.App.R.(S.) 19, CA, this approach was described as too difficult an exercise in forensic archaeology; it was better that the sentencer simply applied the principle of balance stated by Lord Taylor C.J. in *R. v. Mansell*, 15 Cr.App.R.(S.) 771.

In a case where a longer than normal sentence is passed on one offender and a commensurate sentence on the other, it does not necessarily follow that there is any disparity of sentence, provided that there is evidence of continuing dangerousness on the part of one offender and not in the case of the other: *R. v. Bestwick and Huddlestone*, 16 Cr.App.R.(S.) 168, CA.

A longer than commensurate sentence may be imposed on an offender under section 80(2)(b) even though he does not qualify for a sentence of life imprisonment under the criteria established for that form of sentence: *R. v. Helm*, 16 Cr.App.R.(S.) 834, CA. The enactment of section 80(2)(b) has not reduced the requirements for a life sentence: *R. v. Roche*, 16 Cr.App.R.(S.) 849, CA.

Where a sentencer has in mind the possibility of passing a longer than commensurate sentence, he should warn counsel for the defendant of his intentions and invite submissions on the question: *R. v. Baverstock*, 96 Cr.App.R. 435, CA. This point has been repeated in many cases; it is particularly important when any question arises as to whether the offence is a "violent offence" for the purposes of the Act. Where a court passes a longer than commensurate sentence it is required by the PCC(S)A 2000, s.80(3) to state in open court that it is of the opinion that subsection (2)(b) applies and why it is of that opinion, and explain to the offender in open court and in ordinary language why the sentence is for such a term. Failure to comply with this obligation does not invalidate the sentence: *Baverstock, ante*; *R. v. Thomas*, 16 Cr.App.R.(S.) 616, CA. Even where the nature of the expected future harm is obvious, the sentencer should ensure that he has properly identified what the harm was before he proceeded to sentence, and should point out clearly and in straightforward terms what it was that he considered to be the serious harm in question: *R. v. Bacon*, 16 Cr.App.R.(S.) 1031, CA.

Where a court fails to pass a longer than commensurate sentence where such a sentence should be passed, the resulting sentence may be "unduly lenient" and may be the subject of a reference by the Attorney-General under the CJA 1988, s.36: *Att-Gen.'s Reference (No. 9 of 1994) (R. v. Groves)*, 16 Cr.App.R.(S.) 366, CA. Where a person sentenced to a longer than commensurate sentence persuades the Court of Appeal that the case is not one in which a longer than commensurate sentence should have been passed, the court is not bound to substitute a shorter sentence; its powers are at large, and it may approve the sentence passed as a commensurate sentence if it considers it appropriate to do so: *R. v. Palmer* [1996] 2 Cr.App.R.(S.) 68, CA; and see also *R. v. Henshaw* [1996] 2 Cr.App.R.(S.) 310, CA; and *R. v. Rai and Robinson* [2000] 2 Cr.App.R.(S.) 120, CA.

### (2) Imprisonment

#### (a) *Age*

Where an offender is convicted at the age of 18 of an offence committed when he was 17, it is ★5-479 not the case that he must be sentenced in accordance with any guidelines applicable to young offenders, but regard should be had to the sentence that would have been appropriate had he been sentenced as a young offender, and this would be a powerful factor, albeit not the sole determining one, in deciding what his sentence should be: *R. v. Y.* [2014] 1 Cr.App.R.(S.) 39, CA (considering *R. v. Ghafoor* and *R. v. Bowker* (see the main work)).

(c) *Life sentences and extended sentences for dangerous offenders*

## Introduction

**5-488**    *R. v. Saunders* is now reported at [2014] 1 Cr.App.R.(S.) 45, *sub nom. R. v. Saunders*; *R. v. G.*; *R. v. Edwards.*

### Criminal Justice Act 2003, ss.224–229

*Life sentence for second listed offence*

**★5-495a**    The question of whether an offender is dangerous must be considered prior to considering whether he is liable to a life sentence under section 224A of the 2003 Act; and any temptation immediately to consider section 224A should be resisted: *Att.-Gen.'s Reference (No. 27 of 2013) (R. v. Burinskas)*; *R. v Phillips* [2014] 3 *Archbold Review* 4, CA. As to this case, see also *post*, §§ 5-496, 5-510.

*Life sentence for serious offence*

**★5-496**    Consideration of whether the seriousness of an offence and any associated offences justifies a life sentence under section 225 of the 2003 Act (as amended by the LASPOA 2012) entails consideration, first, of the seriousness of the offence itself, alone or with any associated offences, in accordance with section 143(1) of the 2003 Act (determining the seriousness of an offence (§ 5-67 in the main work)), secondly, of the defendant's previous convictions in accordance with section 143(2), thirdly, of the level of danger the defendant poses to the public, and whether there is a reliable estimate of the length of time he will remain a danger, and fourthly, of the alternative sentences available: *Att.-Gen.'s Reference (No. 27 of 2013) (R. v. Burinskas)*; *R. v Phillips* [2014] 3 *Archbold Review* 4, CA. As to this case, see also *ante*, § 5-495a; and *post*, § 5-510.

*Extended sentence for certain violent or sexual offences: persons 18 or over*

**★5-498**    As from a day to be appointed, the Offender Rehabilitation Act 2014, s.8(1) and (2), amend section 226A of the 2003 Act, so as (i) in subsection (7), to substitute the words "subsections (7A) to (9)" for the words "subsections (8) and (9)", and (ii) to insert, after subsection (7), a new subsection (7A) as follows—

"(7A) The extension period must be at least 1 year.".

★    The amendments made by the 2014 Act to section 226A do not apply in relation to an offence committed before they come into force; and where an offence is found to have been committed over a period of two or more days, or at some time during a period of two or more days, it must, for these purposes, be taken to have been committed on the last of those days: 2014 Act, s.21, and Sched. 7, paras 1, 4 and 8.

*Extended sentence for certain violent or sexual offences: persons under 18*

**★5-499**    As from a day to be appointed, the Offender Rehabilitation Act 2014, s.8(1) and (3), amend section 226B of the 2003 Act, so as (i) in subsection (5), to substitute the words "subsections (5A) to (7)" for the words "subsections (6) and (7)", and (ii) to insert, after subsection (5), a new subsection (5A) as follows—

"(5A) The extension period must be at least 1 year.".

★    The amendments made by the 2014 Act to section 226B do not apply in relation to an offence committed before they come into force; and where an offence is found to have been committed over a period of two or more days, or at some time during a period of two or more days, it must, for these purposes, be taken to have been committed on the last of those days: 2014 Act, s.21, and Sched. 7, paras 1, 4 and 8.

## Life sentences and extended sentences

(ii) *Imposition of life imprisonment or detention for life*

**5-510**    *R. v. Saunders* is now reported at [2014] 1 Cr.App.R.(S.) 45, *sub nom. R. v. Saunders*; *R. v. G.*; *R. v. Edwards.*

The approach taken in *R. v. Kehoe* (see the main work) was described in *Att.-Gen.'s Reference (No. 27 of 2013) (R. v. Burinskas)*; *R. v Phillips* [2014] 3 *Archbold Review* 4, CA, as being of "limited assistance" after the taking effect of the LASPOA 2012 amendments. The court expressed its general approval of what had been said in *R. v. Saunders* (see the main work, and *ante*). As to this case, see also *ante*, §§ 5-495a, 5-496.

(iv) *Assessment of significant risk*

As to the inter-relationship between the assessment of dangerousness under section 229 of the CJA 2003 (as to which, see § 5-500 in the main work) and automatic deportation under section 32 of the U.K. Borders Act 2007, see *Att.-Gen.'s Reference (No. 41 of 2013) (R. v. M.)*, *post*, § 5-528a. ★5-512

*R. (Sturnham) v. Parole Board (No. 2)* is now reported at [2013] 2 A.C. 254, *sub nom. R. (Faulkner) v. Secretary of State for Justice*; *R. (Sturnham) v. Parole Board (Nos 1 and 2)*. 5-515

**Inter-relationship with automatic deportation**

Where an offender is convicted of a "specified offence" (CJA 2003, s.224 (as to which, see § 5-495 in the main work)), a court must consider the question of dangerousness under section 229 of the CJA 2003 (as to which, see § 5-500 in the main work) regardless of the fact that the offender will be liable to automatic deportation as a "foreign criminal" under section 32 of the U.K. Borders Act 2007 (as to which, see § 5-1267 in the main work); a court is bound to pass sentence without regard to the possibility that the offender would one day be deported: *Att.-Gen.'s Reference (No. 41 of 2013) (R. v. M.)* [2014] 1 Cr.App.R.(S.) 80, CA. ★5-528a

**Fixing the minimum term (life sentences not fixed by law)**

*Imposition of life sentences*

The 2013 criminal practice directions (see the main work) are now reported at [2013] 1 W.L.R. 3164. 5-532

(e) *Suspended sentence ("new style")*

**Criminal Justice Act 2003, ss.189–192**

*Imposition of requirements by suspended sentence order*

As from a day to be appointed, the Offender Rehabilitation Act 2014, s.15(1) and (2) amend section 190(1) of the 2003 Act so as to insert, after paragraph (a), new paragraph (aa) as follows— ★5-550

"(aa) a rehabilitation activity requirement (as defined by section 200A),".

As from a day to be appointed, the 2014 Act, s.15(5), and Sched. 5, paras 1 and 3, further amend section 190 of the 2003 Act so as (i) to repeal paragraphs (b) and (k) of subsection (1), (ii) to repeal paragraph (b) of subsection (2), and (iii) in subsection (4), to insert the words "a rehabilitation activity requirement," after the words "unpaid work requirement," and to omit the words "an activity requirement," and ", a supervision requirement". ★

These amendments do not apply in relation to an order made in respect of an offence committed before they come into force; and where an offence is found to have been committed over a period of two or more days, or at some time during a period of two or more days, it must, for these purposes, be taken to have been committed on the last of those days: 2014 Act, s.21, and Sched. 7, paras 1, 7 and 8. ★

*Power to provide for review of suspended sentence order*

With effect from June 1, 2014 (Offender Rehabilitation Act 2014 (Commencement No. 1) Order 2014 (S.I. 2014 No. 1287)), the Offender Rehabilitation Act 2014, s.14(2), and Sched. 4, paras 1 and 2, amended section 191(1)(d) of the 2003 Act so as to substitute the words "an officer of a provider of probation services" for the words "the responsible officer". ★5-551

*Periodic reviews of suspended sentence order*

With effect from June 1, 2014 (Offender Rehabilitation Act 2014 (Commencement No. 1) Order 2014 (S.I. 2014 No. 1287)), the Offender Rehabilitation Act 2014, s.14(2), and Sched. 4, ★5-552 paras 1 and 3, amended section 192 of the 2003 Act so as (i) in subsection (1), to omit the word "responsible", and insert, after the word "subsection", the words "('the review officer's report')", and (ii) in each of subsections (4) and (5), to substitute the word "review" for the word "responsible".

**Criminal Justice Act 2003, Sched. 12**

*Interpretation*

★5-565a      With effect from June 1, 2014 (Offender Rehabilitation Act 2014 (Commencement No. 1) Order 2014 (S.I. 2014 No. 1287)), the Offender Rehabilitation Act 2014, s.14(2), and Sched. 4, paras 1 and 7(1) and (2), amended Schedule 12 to the 2003 Act so as to insert, after paragraph 1, a new paragraph 1A as follows—

> "1A.—(1) In this Schedule 'enforcement officer' means a person who is for the time being responsible for discharging the functions conferred by this Schedule on an enforcement officer in accordance with arrangements made by the Secretary of State.
> (2) An enforcement officer must be an officer of a provider of probation services that is a public sector provider.
> (3) In sub-paragraph (2) 'public sector provider' means—
>> (a) a probation trust or other public body, or
>> (b) the Secretary of State.".

*Duty to give warning in relation to community requirement*

★5-566      With effect from June 1, 2014 (Offender Rehabilitation Act 2014 (Commencement No. 1) Order 2014 (S.I. 2014 No. 1287)), the Offender Rehabilitation Act 2014, s.14(2), and Sched. 4, paras 1 and 7(1) and (3), amended paragraph 4(1) of Schedule 12 to the 2003 Act so as to substitute, for paragraph (b), a new paragraph (b) as follows—

> "(b) the officer refers the matter to an enforcement officer (see paragraph 5A)".

*Breach of order after warning*

★5-567      With effect from June 1, 2014 (Offender Rehabilitation Act 2014 (Commencement No. 1) Order 2014 (S.I. 2014 No. 1287)), the Offender Rehabilitation Act 2014, s.14(2), and Sched. 4, paras 1 and 7(1) and (4), amended paragraph 5(1) of Schedule 12 to the 2003 Act so as to substitute the words "must refer the matter to an enforcement officer (see paragraph 5A)" for the words "must cause an information" to the end.

*Role of enforcement officer*

★5-567a      With effect from June 1, 2014 (Offender Rehabilitation Act 2014 (Commencement No. 1) Order 2014 (S.I. 2014 No. 1287)), the Offender Rehabilitation Act 2014, s.14(2), and Sched. 4, paras 1 and 7(1) and (5), amended Schedule 12 to the 2003 Act so as to insert, after paragraph 5, a new paragraph 5A as follows—

> *"Role of enforcement officer*
> 5A.—(1) Where a matter is referred to an enforcement officer under paragraph 4(1)(b) or 5(1) , it is the duty of the enforcement officer to consider the case and, where appropriate, to cause an information to be laid before a justice of the peace in respect of the offender's failure to comply with the requirement.
> (2) In relation to any suspended sentence order which was made by the Crown Court and does not include a direction that any failure to comply with the requirements of the order is to be dealt with by a magistrates' court, the reference in sub-paragraph (1) to a justice of the peace is to be read as a reference to the Crown Court.".

*Powers of court on breach of community requirement or conviction of further offence*

★5-570      As from a day to be appointed, the Offender Rehabilitation Act 2014, s.18(1) and (7), repeal paragraph 8(4A) of Schedule 12 to the 2003 Act. The amendments made by section 18 of the 2014 Act do not apply in relation to an order made in respect of an offence committed before they come into force; and where an offence is found to have been committed over a period of two or more days, or at some time during a period of two or more days, it must, for these purposes, be taken to have been committed on the last of those days: 2014 Act, s.21, and Sched. 7, paras 1, 7 and 8.

*Cancellation of community requirements of suspended sentence order*

With effect from June 1, 2014 (Offender Rehabilitation Act 2014 (Commencement No. 1) **★5-575**
Order 2014 (S.I. 2014 No. 1287)), the Offender Rehabilitation Act 2014, s.14(2), and Sched. 4,
paras 1 and 7(1) and (6), amended paragraphs 13(1), 15(1), 17, 18(1)(b) and 19(2)(b) of Schedule
12 to the 2003 Act so as to substitute, in each of those provisions, the words "an officer of a
provider of probation services" for the words "the responsible officer".

*Amendment by reason of change of residence*

As from a day to be appointed, the Offender Rehabilitation Act 2014, s.18(1) and (8), amend **★5-576**
Schedule 12 to the 2003 Act so as to substitute, for paragraph 14, new paragraphs 14 and 14A as
follows—

"14.—(1) This paragraph applies where at any time while a suspended sentence order is in force
in respect of an offender—
  (a) the offender is given permission under section 220A to change residence, and
  (b) the local justice area in which the new residence is situated ('the new local justice area') is
      different from the local justice area specified in the order.
(2) If the permission is given by a court, the court must amend the order to specify the new local
justice area.
(3) If the permission is given by the responsible officer—
  (a) the officer must apply to the appropriate court to amend the order to specify the new local
      justice area, and
  (b) the court must make that amendment.
(4) In this paragraph 'the appropriate court' has the same meaning as in paragraph 13.
14A.—(1) This paragraph applies where at any time while a suspended sentence order is in force
in respect of an offender—
  (a) a court amends the order,
  (b) the order as amended includes a residence requirement requiring the offender to reside at
      a specified place, and
  (c) the local justice area in which that place is situated ('the new local justice area') is different
      from the local justice area specified in the order.
(2) The court must amend the order to specify the new local justice area.".

The amendments made by section 18 of the 2014 Act do not apply in relation to an order ★
made in respect of an offence committed before they come into force; and where an offence is
found to have been committed over a period of two or more days, or at some time during a
period of two or more days, it must, for these purposes, be taken to have been committed on the
last of those days: 2014 Act, s.21, and Sched. 7, paras 1, 7 and 8.

*Amendment of community requirements of suspended sentence order*

As to the amendment of paragraph 15 of Schedule 12 to the 2003 Act, see *ante*, § 5-575. **★5-577**

*Amendment of treatment requirements on report of practitioner*

With effect from June 1, 2014 (Offender Rehabilitation Act 2014 (Commencement No. 1) **★5-578**
Order 2014 (S.I. 2014 No. 1287)), the Offender Rehabilitation Act 2014, s.14(2), and Sched. 4,
paras 1 and 7(1) and (7), amended paragraph 16(1) of Schedule 12 to the 2003 Act so as to
substitute the words "cause an application to be made" for the word "apply".

*Amendment in relation to review of drug rehabilitation requirement*

As to the amendment of paragraph 17 of Schedule 12 to the 2003 Act, see *ante*, § 5-575. **★5-579**

*Extension of unpaid work requirement*

As to the amendment of paragraph 18 of Schedule 12 to the 2003 Act, see *ante*, § 5-575. **★5-580**

*Supplementary*

As to one amendment of paragraph 19 of Schedule 12 to the 2003 Act, see *ante*, § 5-575. **★5-581**

As from a day to be appointed, the Offender Rehabilitation Act 2014, s.18(1) and (9), amend ★
paragraph 19(1) of Schedule 12 to the 2003 Act so as to omit the words ", and no order may be
made under paragraph 14,". The amendments made by section 18 of the 2014 Act do not apply
in relation to an order made in respect of an offence committed before they come into force; and

where an offence is found to have been committed over a period of two or more days, or at some time during a period of two or more days, it must, for these purposes, be taken to have been committed on the last of those days: 2014 Act, s.21, and Sched. 7, paras 1, 7 and 8.

★   With effect from June 1, 2014 (Offender Rehabilitation Act 2014 (Commencement No. 1) Order 2014 (S.I. 2014 No. 1287)), the Offender Rehabilitation Act 2014, s.14(2), and Sched. 4, paras 10 and 15(1) and (2), amended paragraph 22(1) of Schedule 12 to the 2003 Act so as to substitute, for sub-paragraph (b), a new paragraph (b) as follows—

> "(b) in the case of an amending order which substitutes a new local justice area, provide a copy of the amending order to—
>   (i)  a provider of probation services that is a public sector provider operating in that area, and
>   (ii) the magistrates' court acting in that area, and".

★   With effect from June 1, 2014 (Offender Rehabilitation Act 2014 (Commencement No. 1) Order 2014 (S.I. 2014 No. 1287)), the Offender Rehabilitation Act 2014, s.14(2), and Sched. 4, paras 10 and 15(1) and (3), further amended paragraph 22 of Schedule 12 to the 2003 Act so as to insert, after sub-paragraph (3), a new sub-paragraph (4) as follows—

> "(4) In this paragraph 'public sector provider' means—
>   (a) a probation trust or other public body, or
>   (b) the Secretary of State.".

★**5-582**   As from a day to be appointed, the Offender Rehabilitation Act 2014, s.19, and Sched. 6, paras 1 and 9, amend section 205(1)(c) of the AFA 2006 so as to substitute the reference to paragraph 14(5) of Schedule 12 to the CJA 2003 with a reference to paragraph 14(4) of that schedule. This amendment does not apply in relation to an order made in respect of an offence committed before the amendment comes into force; and where an offence is found to have been committed over a period of two or more days, or at some time during a period of two or more days, it must, for these purposes, be taken to have been committed on the last of those days: 2014 Act, s.21, and Sched. 7, paras 1, 7 and 8.

★   With effect from June 1, 2014 (Offender Rehabilitation Act 2014 (Commencement No. 1) Order 2014 (S.I. 2014 No. 1287)), the 2014 Act, s.19, and Sched. 6, paras 1 and 7, further amended Schedule 7 to the 2006 Act (although note that S.I. 2014 No. 1287, in an apparent oversight, did not bring para. 1 into force).

### (f) *Consecutive sentences*

**5-586**   The 2013 criminal practice directions (see the main work) are now reported at [2013] 1 W.L.R. 3164.

## (4) Detention and training orders

### Powers of Criminal Courts (Sentencing) Act 2000, ss.101, 102

*Term of order, consecutive terms and taking account of remands*

★**5-598**   As from a day to be appointed, the Offender Rehabilitation Act 2014, s.6(1) and (2), amend section 101(13) of the 2000 Act so as to insert the words "and 106B" after the word "105".

★   As from a day to be appointed, the 2014 Act, s.19, and Sched. 6, paras 1 and 2, amend section 213(1) of the AFA 2006 (see the main work) so as to substitute the words "106A to 107" for the words "106A and 107".

★   These amendments apply in relation to any person who falls to be released under a detention and training order (including an order under s.211 of the 2006 Act) on or after the day on which they come into force: 2014 Act, s.21, and Sched. 7, paras 1 and 2.

### Powers of Criminal Courts (Sentencing) Act 2000, ss.103, 104

*The period of supervision*

★**5-600**   As from a day to be appointed, the Offender Rehabilitation Act 2014, s.6(1) and (3), amend section 103 of the 2000 Act so as to insert, at the beginning of subsection (2), the words "Subject to subsection (2A),", and, after subsection (2), a new subsection (2A) as follows—

"(2A) An order under subsection (2) may not include provision about cases in which—

    (a) the offender is aged 18 or over at the half-way point of the term of the detention and training order, and

    (b) the order was imposed in respect of an offence committed on or after the day on which section 6(4) of the Offender Rehabilitation Act 2014 came into force.".

As from a day to be appointed, the 2014 Act, s.7(1), and Sched. 3, paras 10 and 11, further ★ amend section 103 of the 2000 Act so as (i) in subsection (3), to repeal paragraph (b) (but not the "or" at the end), and (ii) in subsection (5), to repeal paragraph (a), and, in the words following paragraph (b), to omit the words "social worker or" and "a social worker of, or".

These amendments apply in relation to any person who falls to be released under a detention ★ and training order (including an order under s.211 of the AFA 2006) on or after the day on which they come into force: 2014 Act, s.21, and Sched. 7, paras 1 and 2.

### Powers of Criminal Courts (Sentencing) Act 2000, ss.105–107

*Further supervision after end of term of detention and training order*

As from a day to be appointed, section 6(1) and (4) of the Offender Rehabilitation Act 2014 ★**5-604a** insert a new section 106B in the 2000 Act, after section 106A.

*Further supervision after end of term of detention and training order*

**106B.**—(1) This section applies where a detention and training order is made in respect of an offender if—

    (a) the offender is aged 18 or over at the half-way point of the term of the order,

    (b) the term of the order is less than 24 months, and

    (c) the order was imposed in respect of an offence committed on or after the day on which section 6(4) of the Offender Rehabilitation Act 2014 came into force.

(2) The following provisions of the Criminal Justice Act 2003 (which relate to supervision after end of sentence) apply as they apply in cases described in section 256AA(1) of that Act—

    (a) sections 256AA(2) to (11), 256AB and 256AC,

    (b) sections 256D and 256E, and

    (c) Schedule 19A,

but with the following modifications.

(3) "The supervision period", in relation to the offender, is the period which—

    (a) begins on the expiry of the term of the detention and training order, and

    (b) ends on the expiry of the period of 12 months beginning immediately after the half-way point of the term of the order.

(4) "The supervisor", in relation to the offender, must be—

    (a) an officer of a provider of probation services, or

    (b) a member of the youth offending team established by the local authority in whose area the offender resides for the time being.

(5) The power under section 256AB(4) includes power to make provision about the supervision requirements that may be imposed under section 256AA as applied by this section and to amend this Act.

(6) Subsection (7) applies where the term of the detention and training order is determined by section 101(13) (consecutive and concurrent orders).

(7) The offender is subject to supervision under section 256AA (as applied by this section) if that section (as applied) so requires in respect of one or more of the consecutive or concurrent orders.

The amendments made by section 6 of the 2014 Act apply in relation to any person who falls to ★ be released under a detention and training order (including an order under s.211 of the AFA 2006) on or after the day on which they come into force: 2014 Act, s.21, and Sched. 7, paras 1 and 2.

*Meaning of "youth detention accommodation" and references to terms*

As from a day to be appointed, the Offender Rehabilitation Act 2014, s.7(1), and Sched. 3, ★**5-605** paras 10 and 12, amend section 107 of the 2000 Act so as (i) in subsection (2), to insert the words "and 106B" after the word "105", and (ii) to insert, after subsection (2), a new subsection (3) as follows—

"(3) For the purposes of sections 103(2A) and 106B(1), where an offence is found to have been committed over a period of 2 or more days, or at some time during a period of 2 or more days, it must be taken to have been committed on the last of those days.".

★     The amendments made by Schedule 3 to the 2014 Act apply in relation to any person who falls to be released under a detention and training order (including an order under s.211 of the AFA 2006) on or after the day on which they come into force: 2014 Act, s.21, and Sched. 7, paras 1 and 2.

## E. Release on Licence

### Criminal Justice Act 2003, s.237

*Meaning of "fixed-term prisoner" etc.*

★5-637     As from a day to be appointed, the Offender Rehabilitation Act 2014, s.2(1) and (3), amend section 237(1) of the 2003 Act so as to insert, at the end, "and 'fixed-term sentence' means a sentence falling within paragraph (a) or (b)". This amendment applies in relation to any person who falls to be released under Chapter 6 of Part 12 of the 2003 Act on or after it comes into force: 2014 Act, s.21, and Sched. 7, paras 1 and 2.

## Crediting of periods of remand in custody

5-639     To the accumulated case law on section 240 of the CJA 2003 (as to which, see the 2012 edition of this work) should now be added *R. (Hicks) v. Crown Court at Snaresbrook*, unreported, November 27, 2012, DC & CA ([2012] EWHC 3348 (Admin.) & [2012] EWCA Crim. 2515) (a direction that whole of period spent on remand should count towards sentence cannot be "corrected" administratively where order should have been for only part of that period to count); and *R. v. Leacock*; *R. v. Blacker*; *R. v. Trevis*; *R. v. Nutting*; *R. v. Morin*, unreported, November 12, 2013, CA ([2013] EWCA Crim. 1994) (*Hicks* was decided without the benefit of full argument and should not be followed). As to the relative merits of the two decisions, see CLW/13/43/2.

### Criminal Justice Act 2003, s.240ZA

*Time remanded in custody to count as time served: terms of imprisonment and detention*

★5-644     As from a day to be appointed, the Offender Rehabilitation Act 2014, s.9(1) and (6), amend section 240ZA(6) of the 2003 Act so as to substitute the words "automatic release period served by the offender" for the words "period of 28 days served by the offender before automatic release". This amendment applies only where an offender is recalled on or after the day on which it comes into force: 2014 Act, s.21, and Sched. 7, paras 1 and 5.

### Criminal Justice Act 2003, s.240A

*Time remanded on bail to count as time served: terms of imprisonment and detention*

★5-645     As from a day to be appointed, the Offender Rehabilitation Act 2014, s.9(1) and (7), amend section 240A(3B) so as to substitute the words "automatic release period served by the offender" for the words "period of 28 days served by the offender before automatic release". This amendments applies only where an offender is recalled on or after the day on which it comes into force: 2014 Act, s.21, and Sched. 7, paras 1 and 5.

## Calculation of credit period

★5-649     *R. v. Hoggard* is now reported at [2014] 1 Cr.App.R.(S.) 42.

### Criminal Justice Act 2003, ss.242–243A

*Duty to release prisoners serving less than 12 months*

★5-652a     As from a day to be appointed, the Offender Rehabilitation Act 2014, s.1, amends section 243A of the 2003 Act so as to substitute, for subsection (1), new subsections (1) and (1A) as follows—

> "(1) This section applies to a fixed-term prisoner if—
>> (a) the prisoner is serving a sentence which is for a term of 1 day, or
>> (b) the prisoner—
>>> (i) is serving a sentence which is for a term of less than 12 months, and

(ii) is aged under 18 on the last day of the requisite custodial period.

(1A) This section also applies to a fixed-term prisoner if—

(a) the prisoner is serving a sentence which is for a term of less than 12 months, and

(b) the sentence was imposed in respect of an offence committed before the day on which section 1 of the Offender Rehabilitation Act 2014 came into force.".

As from a day to be appointed, the 2014 Act, s.7(1), and Sched. 3, paras 14, 16 and 17, amend ★ section 243A of the 2003 Act so as (i) to insert the word "certain" after the word "release" in the heading, and (ii) in subsection (3)(a), to substitute the words "in relation to a person serving one sentence" for the words from "in relation to" to "such a term".

The amendments to section 243A made by the 2014 Act apply in relation to any person who ★ falls to be released under Chapter 6 of Part 12 of the 2003 Act on or after the day on which the amendments come into force: 2014 Act, s.21, and Sched. 7, paras 1 and 2.

### Criminal Justice Act 2003, s.244

*Duty to release prisoners*

With effect from December 3, 2012 (Legal Aid, Sentencing and Punishment of Offenders Act ★**5-653** 2012 (Commencement No. 4 and Saving Provisions) Order 2012 (S.I. 2012 No. 2906)), the Legal Aid, Sentencing and Punishment of Offenders Act 2012, s.114(2), amended section 244 of the 2003 Act so as to insert, after subsection (1), new subsection (1A) as follows—

"(1A) Subsection (1) does not apply if the prisoner has been released on licence under section 246 and recalled under section 254 (provision for the release of such persons being made by sections 255B and 255C).".

As from a day to be appointed, the Offender Rehabilitation Act 2014, s.9(1) and (2), amend sec- ★ tion 244(1A) of the 2003 Act (*ante*) so as to insert the words "or 248" after the words "section 246". The amendments made section 9 of the 2014 Act apply only where an offender is recalled on or after the day on which they come into force: 2014 Act, s.21, and Sched. 7, paras 1 and 5.

As from a day to be appointed, the Offender Rehabilitation Act 2014, s.7(1), and Sched. 3, ★ paras 14 and 18, amend section 244(3)(a) of the 2003 Act so as to substitute the words "in relation to a prisoner serving one sentence" for the words from "in relation to" to "such a term". The amendment of section 244(3) applies in relation to any person who falls to be released under Chapter 6 of Part 12 of the 2003 Act on or after it comes into force: 2014 Act, s.21, and Sched. 7, paras 1 and 2.

### Criminal Justice Act 2003, ss.246A, 247, 249

*Duration of licence*

As from a day to be appointed, the Offender Rehabilitation Act 2014, s.5(1) and (4), amend sec- ★**5-658** tion 249(3) of the 2003 Act so as to substitute the word "section" for the word "sections", and the words "and sections 264(3C)(a) and 264B" for the words "and 264(3)". The amendments made by section 5 of the 2014 Act apply in relation to any person who falls to be released under Chapter 6 of Part 12 of the 2003 Act on or after the day on which they come into force: 2014 Act, s.21, and Sched. 7, paras 1 and 2.

*Supervision after end of sentence*

As from a day to be appointed, section 2(1) and (2) of the Offender Rehabilitation Act 2014 ★**5-659** insert a new section 256AA in the 2003 Act, after section 256A.

*Supervision of offenders*

*Supervision after end of sentence of prisoners serving less than 2 years*

**256AA.**—(1) This section applies where a person ("the offender") has served a fixed-term sentence which was for a term of more than 1 day but less than 2 years, except where—

(a) the offender was aged under 18 on the last day of the requisite custodial period (as defined in section 243A(3)),

(b) the sentence was an extended sentence imposed under section 226A or 226B, or

(c) the sentence was imposed in respect of an offence committed before the day on which section 2(2) of the Offender Rehabilitation Act 2014 came into force.

(2) The offender must comply with the supervision requirements during the supervision period, except at any time when the offender is—

(a)  in legal custody,

(b)  subject to a licence under this Chapter or Chapter 2 of Part 2 of the 1997 Act, or

(c)  subject to DTO supervision.

(3) The supervision requirements are the requirements for the time being specified in a notice given to the offender by the Secretary of State (but see the restrictions in section 256AB).

(4) "The supervision period" is the period which—

(a)  begins on the expiry of the sentence, and

(b)  ends on the expiry of the period of 12 months beginning immediately after the offender has served the requisite custodial period (as defined in section 244(3)).

(5) The purpose of the supervision period is the rehabilitation of the offender.

(6) The Secretary of State must have regard to that purpose when specifying requirements under this section.

(7) The supervisor must have regard to that purpose when carrying out functions in relation to the requirements.

(8) In this Chapter, "the supervisor", in relation to a person subject to supervision requirements under this section, means a person who is for the time being responsible for discharging the functions conferred by this Chapter on the supervisor in accordance with arrangements made by the Secretary of State.

(9) In relation to a person subject to supervision requirements under this section following a sentence of detention under section 91 of the Sentencing Act, the supervisor must be—

(a)  an officer of a provider of probation services, or

(b)  a member of the youth offending team established by the local authority in whose area the offender resides for the time being.

(10) In relation to any other person, the supervisor must be an officer of a provider of probation services.

(11) In this section "DTO supervision" means supervision under—

(a)  a detention and training order (including an order under section 211 of the Armed Forces Act 2006 ), or

(b)  an order under section 104(3)(aa) of the Powers of Criminal Courts (Sentencing) Act 2002 (breach of supervision requirements of detention and training order).

(12) This section has effect subject to section 264(3C)(b) and (3D).

★      The amendments made by section 2 of the 2014 Act apply in relation to any person who falls to be released under Chapter 6 of Part 12 of the 2003 Act on or after the day on which they come into force, and any person who falls to be released under a detention and training order (including an order under s.211 of the AFA 2006) on or after the day on which they come into force: 2014 Act, s.21, and Sched. 7, paras 1 and 2.

★**5-660**      As from a day to be appointed, the 2014 Act, s.2(4), and Sched. 1, para. 1, insert a new section 256AB in the 2003 Act, after section 256AA (*ante*).

*Supervision requirements under section 256AA*

**256AB.**—(1) The only requirements that the Secretary of State may specify in a notice under section 256AA are—

(a)  a requirement to be of good behaviour and not to behave in a way which undermines the purpose of the supervision period;

(b)  a requirement not to commit any offence;

(c)  a requirement to keep in touch with the supervisor in accordance with instructions given by the supervisor;

(d)  a requirement to receive visits from the supervisor in accordance with instructions given by the supervisor;

(e)  a requirement to reside permanently at an address approved by the supervisor and to obtain the prior permission of the supervisor for any stay of one or more nights at a different address;

(f)  a requirement not to undertake work, or a particular type of work, unless it is approved by the supervisor and to notify the supervisor in advance of any proposal to undertake work or a particular type of work;

(g)  a requirement not to travel outside the British Islands, except with the prior permission of the supervisor or in order to comply with a legal obligation (whether or not arising under the law of any part of the British Islands);

   (h)  a requirement to participate in activities in accordance with any instructions given by the supervisor;

   (i)  a drug testing requirement (see section 256D);

   (j)  a drug appointment requirement (see section 256E).

(2) Where a requirement is imposed under subsection (1)(h), section 200A(5) to (10) apply in relation to the requirement (reading references to the responsible officer as references to the supervisor).

(3) Paragraphs (i) and (j) of subsection (1) have effect subject to the restrictions in sections 256D(2) and 256E(2).

(4) The Secretary of State may by order—

   (a)  add requirements that may be specified in a notice under section 256AA,

   (b)  remove or amend such requirements,

   (c)  make provision about such requirements, including about the circumstances in which they may be imposed, and

   (d)  make provision about instructions given for the purposes of such requirements.

(5) An order under subsection (4) may amend this Act.

(6) In this section "work" includes paid and unpaid work.

The insertion of section 256AB has effect in relation to any person who falls to be released ★ under Chapter 6 of Part 12 of the 2003 Act on or after it takes effect: 2014 Act, s.21, and Sched. 7, paras 1 and 2.

As from a day to be appointed, section 3(1) of the 2014 Act inserts a new section 256AC in the   ★**5-661** 2003 Act, after section 256AB (*ante*).

*Breach of supervision requirements imposed under section 256AA*

**256AC.**—(1) Where it appears on information to a justice of the peace that a person has failed to comply with a supervision requirement imposed under section 256AA, the justice may—

   (a)  issue a summons requiring the offender to appear at the place and time specified in the summons, or

   (b)  if the information is in writing and on oath, issue a warrant for the offender's arrest.

(2) Any summons or warrant issued under this section must direct the person to appear or be brought—

   (a)  before a magistrates' court acting for the local justice area in which the offender resides, or

   (b)  if it is not known where the person resides, before a magistrates' court acting for the same local justice area as the justice who issued the summons or warrant.

(3) Where the person does not appear in answer to a summons issued under subsection (1)(a), the court may issue a warrant for the person's arrest.

(4) If it is proved to the satisfaction of the court that the person has failed without reasonable excuse to comply with a supervision requirement imposed under section 256AA, the court may—

   (a)  order the person to be committed to prison for a period not exceeding 14 days (subject to subsection (7)),

   (b)  order the person to pay a fine not exceeding level 3 on the standard scale, or

   (c)  make an order (a "supervision default order") imposing on the person—

      (i)  an unpaid work requirement (as defined by section 199), or

     (ii)  a curfew requirement (as defined by section 204).

(5) Section 177(3) (obligation to impose electronic monitoring requirement) applies in relation to a supervision default order that imposes a curfew requirement as it applies in relation to a community order that imposes such a requirement.

(6) If the court deals with the person under subsection (4), it must revoke any supervision default order which is in force at that time in respect of that person.

(7) Where the person is under the age of 21—

   (a)  an order under subsection (4)(a) in respect of the person must be for committal to a young offender institution instead of to prison, but

   (b)  the Secretary of State may from time to time direct that a person committed to a young offender institution by such an order is to be detained in a prison or remand centre instead.

(8) A person committed to prison or a young offender institution by an order under subsection (4)(a) is to be regarded as being in legal custody.

(9) A fine imposed under subsection (4)(b) is to be treated, for the purposes of any enactment, as being a sum adjudged to be paid by a conviction.

(10) In Schedule 19A (supervision default orders)—

   (a)  Part 1 makes provision about requirements of supervision default orders, and

(b) Part 2 makes provision about the breach, revocation and amendment of supervision default orders.

(11) A person dealt with under this section may appeal to the Crown Court against the order made by the court.

★ The amendments made by section 3 of the 2014 Act apply in relation to any person who falls to be released under Chapter 6 of Part 12 of the 2003 Act on or after the day on which they come into force: 2014 Act, s.21, and Sched. 7, paras 1 and 2.

*Revocation of supervision default order on imposition of further sentence*

**★5-662** As from a day to be appointed, the 2014 Act, s.3(2), and Sched. 2, amend the 2003 Act so as to insert, after Schedule 19, a new Schedule 19A (supervision default orders (see s.256AC(10), *ante*)). Schedule 19A applies only in relation to any person who falls to be released under Chapter 6 of Part 12 of the 2003 Act after it comes into force: 2014 Act, s.21, and Sched. 7, paras 1 and 2. For the Crown Court, the two paragraphs of Schedule 19A that matter are paragraphs 12 and 13. Paragraph 12 applies where the Crown Court or a magistrates' court is sentencing a person for an offence, and a supervision default order is in force in respect of the person (sub-para (1)). If the court imposes a sentence of imprisonment or detention (other than a suspended sentence) it must revoke the supervision default order (sub-para. (2)). If it makes a community order or suspended sentence order it may revoke the supervision default order and deal with the person under section 256AC(4) *(ante)* in any way in which the person could be dealt with under that subsection if the supervision default order had never been made (sub-para. (3)). Paragraph 13 provides that where the Crown Court or a magistrates' court orders that a suspended sentence or any part of it is to take effect in relation to a person, and a supervision default order is in force in respect of that person, it must revoke the supervision default order.

**Criminal Justice Act 2003, ss.263, 264**

*Consecutive terms*

**★5-666** As from a day to be appointed, the Offender Rehabilitation Act 2014, s.5(1) and (2), amend section 264 of the 2003 Act so as to substitute, for subsections (3) and (3A), new subsections (3B) to (3E), as follows—

"(3B) The offender's release under this Chapter is to be unconditional if—
(a) the aggregate length of the terms of imprisonment is less than 12 months, and
(b) section 243A so requires in respect of each of the sentences, but in any other case is to be on licence.
(3C) If the offender is released on licence under this Chapter—
(a) the offender is to be on licence, on and after the release, until the offender would, but for the release, have served a term equal in length to the aggregate length of the terms of imprisonment (but see section 264B);
(b) the offender is to be subject to supervision requirements under section 256AA if (and only if)—
(i) section 256AA so requires in respect of one or more of the sentences, and
(ii) the aggregate length of the terms of imprisonment is less than 2 years.
(3D) If the offender is subject to supervision requirements under section 256AA, the supervision period for the purposes of that section begins on the expiry of the period during which the offender is on licence by virtue of subsection (3C)(a).
(3E) When the offender is released under this Chapter (whether unconditionally or on licence), the offender is to be subject to supervision requirements under section 256B if that section so requires in respect of one or more of the sentences.".

★ The amendments made by section 5 of the 2014 Act apply in relation to any person who falls to be released under Chapter 6 of Part 12 of the 2003 Act on or after the day on which the amendments come into force: 2014 Act, s.21, and Sched. 7, paras 1 and 2.

*Consecutive terms: supplementary*

**★5-666a** As from a day to be appointed, section 5(1) and (3) of the Offender Rehabilitation Act 2014 insert a new section 264B in the 2003 Act, after section 264 (s.264A was repealed by the LASPOA 2012, s.89, and Sched. 10, paras 12 and 33).

*Consecutive terms: supplementary*

**264B.**—(1) This section applies in a case in which section 264 applies where—

(a) the offender is released on licence under this Chapter,

(b) the aggregate length of the terms of imprisonment mentioned in section 264(1)(a) is less than 12 months, and

(c) those terms include one or more terms of imprisonment ("short transitional terms") which were imposed in respect of an offence committed before the day on which section 1 of the Offender Rehabilitation Act 2014 came into force, as well as one or more terms imposed in respect of an offence committed on or after that day.

(2) The offender is to be on licence until the offender would, but for the release, have served a term equal in length to the aggregate of—

(a) the custodial period in relation to each of the short transitional terms, and

(b) the full length of each of the other terms.

(3) In this section "custodial period" has the same meaning as in section 264.

The amendments made by section 5 of the 2014 Act apply in relation to any person who falls to ★ be released under Chapter 6 of Part 12 of the 2003 Act after the amendments come into force: 2014 Act, s.21, and Sched. 7, paras 1 and 2.

### Criminal Justice Act 2003, s.268

*Interpretation of Chapter 6*

As from a day to be appointed, the Offender Rehabilitation Act 2014, s.7(1), and Sched. 3, ★**5-670** paras 14 and 23(1) to (3), amend section 268 of the 2003 Act so as to re-number the existing text as subsection (1), and to substitute, in the definition of "fixed term prisoner", the words "'fixed-term prisoner' and 'fixed-term sentence' have" for the words "'fixed-term prisoner' has".

As from a day to be appointed, the 2014 Act, s.7(1), and Sched. 3, paras 14 and 23(1) and (4), ★ further amend section 268(1) of the 2003 Act (*ante*) so as to insert, at the appropriate places, new definitions as follows—

"'offender subject to supervision under this Chapter' means a person who is subject to supervision requirements under section 256AA or 256B;";

"'supervision default order' means an order described in section 256AC(4)(c), whether made under that provision or under paragraph 9 of Schedule 19A;"

"'the supervision period', in relation to an offender subject to supervision under this Chapter, has the meaning given in section 256AA or 256B (as appropriate);"

"'the supervisor'—

(a) in relation to an offender subject to supervision requirements under section 256AA, has the meaning given in that section, and

(b) in relation to an offender subject to supervision requirements under section 256B, means the person who provides supervision under that section;".

As from a day to be appointed, the 2014 Act, s.7(1), and Sched. 3, paras 14 and 23(1) and (5), ★ further amend section 268 of the 2003 Act so as to insert, after subsection (1) (*ante*), a new subsection (2) as follows—

"(2) For the purposes of sections 243A(1A), 256AA(1), 256B(1A) and 264B(1), where an offence is found to have been committed over a period of 2 or more days, or at some time during a period of 2 or more days, it must be taken to have been committed on the last of those days.".

The amendments to section 268 of the 2003 Act made by the 2014 Act apply in relation to any ★ person who falls to be released under Chapter 6 of Part 12 of the 2003 Act on or after the day on which the amendments come into force: 2014 Act, s.21, and Sched. 7, paras 1 and 2.

### Modifications of Chapter 6 in certain transitional cases

As explained in the main work (see § 5-619), the effect of LASPOA 2012 (when the relevant **5-670a** provisions are in force) is to apply Chapter 6 of Part 12 of the CJA 2003 to all prisoners regardless of the date of their offence or the date of sentence. However, two new Schedules (20A and 20B) are inserted into the 2003 Act (by the 2012 Act, s.121(5) and (6), and Scheds 16, paras 1 and 3, and 17, paras 1 and 10) for the purpose of preserving the transitional provisions that existed prior to their commencement. These have the effect of modifying Chapter 6 where they apply. It is submitted that they now only have potential relevance to the release date of an offender sentenced after their commencement in one situation, *viz.* where an offender serving a "1991 Act sentence" who has never been released from that sentence (and theoretically also an offender serving a "1967 Act sentence" who has never been released) is sentenced to a consecutive term for a fresh offence (see paras 22 and 33, *post*).

As to the commencement of these provisions of the 2012 Act, see § 5-2a in the main work.

### Criminal Justice Act 2003, Sched. 20B, paras 1–3, 7, 8, 18–20, 22, 23, 30, 33

PART 1

INTRODUCTORY

*Interpretation*

**5-670b**  1.—(1) The following provisions apply for the purposes of this Schedule.

(2) "The commencement date" means the date on which section 121 of the Legal Aid, Sentencing and Punishment of Offenders Act 2012 comes into force.

(3) "The 1967 Act" means the Criminal Justice Act 1967.

(4) "The 1991 Act" means the Criminal Justice Act 1991.

(5) A "section 85 extended sentence" means an extended sentence under section 85 of the Sentencing Act and includes (in accordance with paragraph 1(3) of Schedule 11 to that Act) a sentence under section 58 of the Crime and Disorder Act 1998.

(6) In relation to a section 85 extended sentence, "the custodial term" and "the extension period" have the meaning given by that section.

(7) References to section 86 of the Sentencing Act include (in accordance with paragraph 1(3) of Schedule 11 to that Act) section 44 of the 1991 Act as originally enacted.

(8) A "1967 Act sentence" is a sentence imposed before 1 October 1992.

(9) A "1991 Act sentence" is a sentence which is—

(a)  imposed on or after 1 October 1992 but before 4 April 2005, or

(b)  imposed on or after 4 April 2005 but before the commencement date and is either—

(i)   imposed in respect of an offence committed before 4 April 2005, or

(ii)  for a term of less than 12 months.

(10) A "2003 Act sentence" is a sentence which is—

(a)  imposed on or after the commencement date, or

(b)  imposed on or after 4 April 2005 but before the commencement date and is both—

(i)   imposed in respect of an offence committed on or after 4 April 2005, and

(ii)  for a term of 12 months or more.

(11) Where an offence is found to have been committed over a period of two or more days, or at some time during a period of two or more days, it is to be taken for the purposes of this Schedule to have been committed on the last of those days.

*Explanation of dates*

**5-670c**  2. The following dates (which are mentioned in this Schedule) are dates on which changes to the law relating to the release and recall of prisoners came into force—

1 October 1992 is the date on which Part 2 of the 1991 Act came into force;

30 September 1998 is the date on which certain provisions of the Crime and Disorder Act 1998 came into force;

4 April 2005 is the date on which this Chapter came into force;

9 June 2008 is the date on which section 26 of the Criminal Justice and Immigration Act 2008 came into force;

14 July 2008 is the date on which certain other provisions of that Act came into force;

2 August 2010 is the date on which section 145 of the Coroners and Justice Act 2009 came into force.

PART 2

PRISONERS SERVING 1991 ACT SENTENCES, ETC.

**5-670d**  3.—(1) This Part applies to certain persons serving a 1991 Act sentence.

(2) This Part also applies to a person serving a 2003 Act sentence which is—

(a)  a section 85 extended sentence, or

(b)  an extended sentence imposed under section 227 or 228 before 14 July 2008.

(3) But this Part does not apply to a person who—

(a)  has been released on licence under Part 2 of the 1991 Act,

(b) has been recalled to prison, and

(c) (whether or not having returned to custody in consequence of that recall) is unlawfully at large on the commencement date.

*Release on licence at one-half of sentence: section 85 extended sentence prisoners*

7. This paragraph applies to a person if— **5-670e**

    (a) the person has been convicted of an offence committed on or after 30 September 1998 but before 4 April 2005,

    (b) the person is serving a section 85 extended sentence in respect of that offence,

    (c) the person has not previously been released from prison on licence in respect of that sentence, and

    (d) paragraph 4 does not apply to the person.

8.—(1) As soon as a person to whom paragraph 7 applies has served one-half of the custodial **5-670f** term, it is the duty of the Secretary of State to release the person on licence under this paragraph.

(2) Sub-paragraph (1) applies in place of section 243A or 244, as the case may be (release of prisoners serving less than 12 months, or serving 12 months or more).

It should be noted that paragraph 4 (see para. 7(d)) has no application to a person sentenced after "the commencement date".

*Period for which licence to remain in force: section 85 extended sentence prisoners*

18. This paragraph applies to a person who— **5-670g**

    (a) has been convicted of an offence committed on or after 30 September 1998 but before 4 April 2005,

    (b) is serving a section 85 extended sentence imposed in respect of that offence, and

    (c) has not previously been released from prison on licence in respect of that sentence.

19.—(1) Where a person to whom paragraph 18 applies is released on licence and the custodial **5-670h** term is less than 12 months, the licence shall remain in force until the end of the period found by adding—

    (a) one-half of the custodial term, and

    (b) the extension period.

(2) Where a person to whom paragraph 18 applies is released on licence and the custodial term is 12 months or more, the licence shall remain in force until the end of the period found by adding—

    (a) three-quarters of the custodial term, and

    (b) the extension period.

(3) Sub-paragraphs (1) and (2) are subject to any revocation under section 254.

(4) Sub-paragraphs (1) to (3) apply in place of section 249 (duration of licence).

*Concurrent or consecutive terms*

20. Paragraphs 21 and 22 apply where a person ("P") is serving two or more sentences of imprison- **5-670i** ment imposed on or after 1 October 1992 and—

    (a) the sentences were passed on the same occasion, or

    (b) where they were passed on different occasions, the person has not been released under Part 2 of the 1991 Act or under this Chapter at any time during the period beginning with the first and ending with the last of those occasions.

22.—(1) This paragraph applies where two or more sentences are to be served consecutively on **5-670j** each other and—

    (a) one or more of those sentences is a 1991 Act sentence, and

    (b) one or more of them is a 2003 Act sentence.

(2) Section 264 does not affect the length of the period which P must serve in prison in respect of the 1991 Act sentence or sentences.

(3) Nothing in this Chapter requires the Secretary of State to release P until P has served a period equal in length to the aggregate of the length of the periods which P must serve in relation to each of the sentences mentioned in sub-paragraph (1).

[(3A) If P is subject to supervision requirements under section 256AA (by virtue of section 264(3C)(b)), section 256AA(4)(b) (end of supervision period) applies in relation to P as if the reference to the requisite custodial period were to the period described in sub-paragraph (3) of this paragraph.]

(4) If P is also serving one or more 1967 Act sentences, paragraphs 32 and 33 apply instead of this paragraph.

[Sub-para. (3A) is inserted, as from a day to be appointed by the Offender Rehabilitation Act ★

2014, s.5(1), (6) and (7). This amendment applies only in relation to any person who falls to be released under Chapter 6 of Part 12 of the 2003 Act on or after the day on which it comes into force: 2014 Act, s.21, and Sched. 7, paras 1 and 2.]

PART 3

PRISONERS SERVING 1967 ACT SENTENCES

**5-670k**      23.—(1) This Part applies to certain persons serving a 1967 Act sentence.

(2) But this Part does not apply to a person who—

(a) has been released on licence,

(b) has been recalled to prison, and

(c) (whether or not having returned to custody in consequence of that recall) is unlawfully at large on the commencement date.

(3) In this Part, references to release under Part 2 of the 1991 Act include release under section 60 of the 1967 Act.

*Concurrent or consecutive terms*

**5-670l**      30. Paragraphs 31 to 33 apply where a person ("P") is serving two or more sentences of imprisonment and—

(a) the sentences were passed on the same occasion, or

(b) where they were passed on different occasions, the person has not been released under Part 2 of the 1991 Act or under this Chapter at any time during the period beginning with the first and ending with the last of those occasions.

**5-670m**      33.—(1) This paragraph applies where two or more sentences are to be served consecutively on each other and—

(a) one or more of those sentences is a 1967 Act sentence, and

(b) one or more of them is a 2003 Act sentence.

(2) Section 264 does not affect the length of the period which P must serve in prison in respect of the 1967 Act sentence or sentences.

(3) Nothing in this Chapter requires the Secretary of State to release P until P has served a period equal in length to the aggregate of the length of the periods which P must serve in relation to each of the sentences mentioned in sub-paragraph (1).

[(4) If P is subject to supervision requirements under section 256AA (by virtue of section 264(3C)(b)), section 256AA(4)(b) (end of supervision period) applies in relation to P as if the reference to the requisite custodial period were to the period described in sub-paragraph (3) of this paragraph.]

★      [Sub-para. (4) is inserted, as from a day to be appointed by the Offender Rehabilitation Act 2014, s.5(1), (6) and (8). This amendment applies only in relation to any person who falls to be released under Chapter 6 of Part 12 of the 2003 Act on or after the day on which it comes into force: 2014 Act, s.21, and Sched. 7, paras 1 and 2.]

## VII. FINES

**Criminal Justice Act 2003, s.162**

*Powers to order statement as to offender's financial circumstances*

**5-672**      The provisions of the Crime and Courts Act 2013 referred to in the main work came into force on December 11, 2013: Crime and Courts Act 2013 (Commencement No. 6) Order 2013 (S.I. 2013 No. 2981).

**Criminal Justice Act 2003, ss.163–165**

*Remission of fines*

**★5-675**      With effect from June 1, 2014 (Anti-social Behaviour, Crime and Policing Act 2014 (Commencement No. 2, Transitional and Transitory Provisions) Order 2014 (S.I. 2014 No. 949)), the Anti-social Behaviour, Crime and Policing Act 2014, s.179(3), amended section 165 of the 2003 Act so as to insert, after subsection (4), a new subsection (5) as follows—

"(5) Where—

(a) under this section the court remits the whole or part of a fine, and

(b) the offender was ordered under section 161A to pay a surcharge the amount of which was set by reference to the amount of the fine, the court must determine how much the surcharge would have been if the fine had not included the amount remitted, and remit the balance of the surcharge.".

Section 165(5) of the 2003 Act applies in any case where the fine, or part of it, is remitted on or after June 1, 2014: 2014 Act, s.179(4).     ★

### Powers of Criminal Courts (Sentencing) Act 2000, ss.139, 140, 142

*Power of Crown Court to order search of persons before it*

As to the commencement of the Prevention of Social Housing Fraud Act 2013, see *ante*, §     **5-678**
5-169.

### Magistrates' Courts Act 1980, ss.36, 75, 82(1)

*Restriction on power to impose imprisonment for default*

With effect from June 1, 2014 (Anti-social Behaviour, Crime and Policing Act 2014 (Commencement No. 2, Transitional and Transitory Provisions) Order 2014 (S.I. 2014 No. 949)), the Anti-social Behaviour, Crime and Policing Act 2014, s.179(1), amended section 82 of the 1980 Act so as to insert, after subsection (1), a new subsection (1A) as follows—     ★**5-682**

"(1A) Subsection (1)(c) above does not apply in relation to a surcharge ordered to be paid under section 161A of the Criminal Justice Act 2003.".

*The standard scale of fines for summary offences*

With effect from May 28, 2014, section 87 of the LASPOA 2012 (see the main work) was brought into force: Legal Aid, Sentencing and Punishment of Offenders Act 2012 (Commencement No. 10) Order 2014 (S.I. 2014 No. 1291).     ★**5-683**

## VIII.  COMPENSATION, RESTITUTION AND REPARATION

### A.  Compensation Orders

#### Powers of Criminal Courts (Sentencing) Act 2000, ss.130–132

*Limit on amount payable under compensation order of magistrates' court in case of young offender*

The provisions of the Crime and Courts Act 2013 referred to in the main work came into force     **5-692**
on December 11, 2013: Crime and Courts Act 2013 (Commencement No. 6) Order 2013 (S.I. 2013 No. 2981).

## IX.  DEPRIVATION AND CONFISCATION

### B.  Confiscation under the Drug Trafficking Act 1994

**Assessment of benefit**

When determining for the purposes of section 2 of the DTA 1994 (confiscation orders) whether     **5-737**
an offender has benefited from an offence of drug trafficking in respect of which he has not been convicted at trial, the statutory assumptions provided for in section 4(3) are not the only way in which the Act permits the court to determine the fact (or extent) of such benefit; where those assumptions are not applicable, the court is entitled to rely on other evidence led at trial to show that one or more offences of drug trafficking (other than those charged) have been committed (and then to estimate the benefit that must have been obtained from those offences): *R. v. Briggs-Price* [2009] 1 A.C. 1026, HL. A majority of their Lordships held, however, that a judge should only rely on evidence of other offences not charged if he was satisfied to the criminal standard that they had been proved (the minority taking the view that the civil standard was the applicable standard).

## Valuation of property

**5-738**     Where a judge assessed the value of the defendant's proceeds of drug trafficking at £3.2 million, he was correct in taking the view that he was required by the DTA 1994 to make a confiscation order in that amount, unless the defendant satisfied him (to the civil standard) that his realisable assets were less than that amount; and where the defendant had failed to do so, there was no obligation on the judge to assume that the defendant would have incurred some expenses to be set against that figure, and to make some discount in respect thereof; such approach was misconceived; his task under the statute was to assess the value of the proceeds in accord with the provisions of the statute (which was not the same as profit), and to make an order in that amount unless the value of the realisable assets was less than that amount, and the burden of proof in that regard was on the defendant: *R. v. Versluis* [2005] 2 Cr.App.R.(S.) 26, CA.

## "drug trafficking offence"

**5-739**     Where the defendant was convicted of a conspiracy to convert the proceeds of drug trafficking "or" the proceeds of criminal conduct (the substantive offences being created by the DTA 1994, s.49, and the CJA 1988, s.93C, respectively), this was to be construed as a finding that the agreement was not restricted to the laundering of the proceeds of drug trafficking or to the proceeds of criminal conduct other than drug trafficking, but was an agreement to launder money, whatever its provenance; it was, in effect, an agreement to launder both the proceeds of drug trafficking and the proceeds of other criminal conduct; accordingly, the defendant was properly to be regarded as having been convicted of a "drug trafficking offence" for the purposes of the confiscation provisions of the 1994 Act as the definition of that expression extended to a conspiracy to commit an offence contrary to section 49; and the judge had, therefore, erred in declining to conduct confiscation proceedings under the 1994 Act: *R. v. Suchedina (Att.-Gen.'s Reference (No. 4 of 2003))* [2005] 1 Cr.App.R. 2, CA.

## Increase in realisable property

**5-740**     In *Re Peacock (Secretary of State for the Home Department intervening)* [2012] 2 Cr.App.R.(S.) 81, SC, it was held that the High Court has power, under section 16(2) of the 1994 Act, to certify that the amount that might be realised is greater than the amount taken into account at the time a confiscation order under that Act was made, and to do so by reference to assets honestly acquired since the date of the making of the order. As to the argument that increasing a confiscation order by reference to after-acquired assets would militate against a defendant's reform and rehabilitation, and be likely to discourage him from engaging in lawful and openly profitable employment, the court pointed out that section 16(4) confers a discretion on the Crown Court, rather than obliging it to order an increase in the amount of the confiscation order in parallel with the assessment of the amount of increase in the defendant's realisable property under section 16(2).

## Certificate of inadequacy

**5-741**     It is unambiguously clear from the wording of sections 6 and 8(1) of the 1994 Act that the value of a gift made by a defendant will be included in the amount of a confiscation order and will constitute "realisable property", even though it may not itself be realisable by the defendant because it is no longer in his power or control; and it is implicit in the statutory scheme that, where the value of a gift has been included in the amount of a confiscation order pursuant to section 6(1), it will not then be open to the defendant to seek a certificate of inadequacy under section 17(1) on the basis that he cannot realise or recover that gift; section 17 cannot be used as a device for upsetting an original finding that an item is "realisable property" within section 6(2), and thus to be included in the "amount that might be realised" under section 6(1), and thus within the amount of the confiscation order: *Re L.*, unreported, June 23, 2010, QBD (Hickinbottom J.) ([2010] EWHC 1531 (Admin.)).

## Variation of realisable amount

**5-742**     Where, following the grant of a certificate of inadequacy by the High Court under section 17 of the 1994 Act, the Crown Court had, pursuant to subsection (4) of that section, substituted a nil amount as the amount to be recovered, it was possible, if the defendant thereafter came into funds, for the amount to be varied upwards again if the High Court issued a certificate under section 16(2) that the amount that might be realised was now more than the amount that had been substituted for the original amount; but the Crown Court had a discretion as to whether to accede to an application for the amount to be increased following such certification, and one factor to be taken into account by it in deciding how to exercise its discretion would be whether the state had sat on its hands after significant and clear evidence about the defendant's change in financial circumstances had come to its attention or had unreasonably delayed in re-opening the issue: *R. v. Griffin* [2009] 2 Cr.App.R.(S.) 89, CA.

### Restraint orders; payment of legal expenses out of restrained assets

See *Revenue and Customs Prosecution Office v. Briggs-Price and O'Reilly, post,* § 5-761.    **5-743**

## C. Confiscation under the Criminal Justice Act 1988

### Postponement of determinations

In *R. v. Haisman* [2004] 1 Cr.App.R.(S.) 63, CA, it was held that where prosecuting counsel had    **5-756** invited the judge to postpone confiscation proceedings and to proceed to sentence, and the judge responded by saying, "If everyone agrees to that, I will do that" and there was no dissent from any counsel to that course, the judge had "manifestly reached a decision" (*R. v. Ross* [2001] 2 Cr.App.R.(S.) 109, CA) to postpone the confiscation proceedings under section 72A of the CJA 1988, with the consequence that the confiscation orders made subsequent to the imposition of sentence were lawful.

In *R. v. Paivarinta-Taylor* [2010] 2 Cr.App.R.(S.) 64, CA, the court said that whereas section 72A(1) of the CJA 1988 enables a court to postpone making a determination as to a defendant's benefit for the purpose of a confiscation order, or as to the amount to be recovered from him under such an order, for such period as it may specify in certain circumstances, and whereas section 72A(9) provides that, in sentencing the defendant at any time during the specified postponement period, the court shall not impose any fine on him, the decision in *R. v. Soneji* [2006] 1 A.C. 340, HL (that where there is a breach of a procedural requirement in a statute, a court should ask itself what Parliament intended should be the consequences and whether it fairly could be taken to have intended total invalidity), remains binding authority, as do *R. v. Ruddick* [2004] 1 Cr.App.R.(S.) 7, CA, *R. v. Simpson* [2003] 2 Cr.App.R. 36, CA, and *R. v. Donohoe* [2007] 1 Cr.App.R.(S.) 88, CA, in so far as they add to the principles identified in *Soneji* as to the correct approach to the consequences of a breach of the procedural provisions relating to confiscation orders under the 1988 Act. Cases such as *R. v. Threapleton* [2002] 2 Cr.App.R.(S.) 46, CA, were decided without reference to *Soneji*, and the Court of Appeal said that they should in future be disregarded when considering the consequences of such a breach. It was held that Parliament could not be taken to have intended that a breach of section 72A(9) would lead to total invalidity, that the imposition of a fine before making a confiscation order would render the fine itself invalid, that, having imposed such a fine, the court could then no longer proceed to consider the making of a confiscation order, or that any confiscation order so made would itself be rendered invalid.

### Assessment of benefit/making of assumptions

The assumption provided for in section 72AA(4)(a) of the 1988 Act (*viz.* that any property    **5-757** transferred to the defendant since the beginning of the relevant period was received by him "in connection with the commission of offences to which this Part of this Act applies") includes within its scope offences committed by persons other than the defendant; thus it is not sufficient to rebut the presumption to show that the property was obtained by the defendant as a result of somebody else's criminal conduct; but the defendant's knowledge or lack of knowledge would be highly material in deciding whether to apply the safety valve in subsection (5) (assumption not to be made if court is satisfied that there would be a serious risk of injustice): *R. v. Ilyas* [2009] 1 Cr.App.R.(S.) 59, CA. See the commentary by David Thomas Q.C. in the *Criminal Law Review* ([2008] Crim.L.R. 908) for the suggestion that this decision will not carry across to the PCA 2002 regime; and see the commentary in CLW/08/39/9 as to the limitations of the actual decision, and, in particular, for the suggestion that it is out of kilter with the decision of the House of Lords in *R. v. May* (§ 5-1044 in the main work).

Whereas section 72AA of the 1988 Act provided that in certain cases it was to be assumed against the defendant that he had committed offences other than those of which he had been convicted or which he had asked to be taken into consideration, and that this assumed criminal conduct should be included within his "relevant criminal conduct" (the assessed benefit from which would form the basis of any confiscation order, subject only to his realisable assets being insufficient), there was nothing objectionable in imposing on the defendant the burden of showing in the particular case that the assumptions should not be made; the assumptions were founded on his holding of property or expenditure of money, and there was nothing unfair in requiring him to show that the source of his property was legitimate: *R. v. Bagnall and Sharma* [2013] 1 W.L.R. 204, CA.

As to the assessment of benefit under the 1988 Act, see also *R. v. Ahmad (Shakeel) and Ahmad (Syed Mubarak)* (§ 5-1051 in the main work and *post*).

### Factual basis for making order

**5-758**    Where an agreement is reached as to the amount of a confiscation order, that agreement will be binding on the defendant unless there are the sort of exceptional circumstances referred to in *R. v. Hirani*, unreported, June 11, 2008, CA ([2008] EWCA Crim. 1463) (save in most exceptional circumstances, a confiscation order based on an agreed amount will not be set aside where the essence of complaint is that, in seeking to secure the best deal available, erroneous advice was given to a party to the agreement; without exhaustively identifying such circumstances, there would need to be a well-founded submission that the whole process was unfair): *R. v. Ayankoya*, unreported, May 24, 2011, CA ([2011] EWCA Crim. 1488). The circumstances had, however, been wholly exceptional where: (i) the defendant had agreed to the amount after being incorrectly informed by his counsel that the judge had ruled that an adjournment to await bank statements supporting his claims would be impossible and that he therefore had a choice of either agreeing the amount or giving evidence without the statements with the inherent risk that a higher amount would result, and (ii) where the bank statements had in fact shown that there was force in the defendant's claims; in these circumstances, the erroneous advice had been of a potentially fundamental nature: *ibid.*

### Amount that might be realised

**5-759**    In *R. v. Blee* [2004] 1 Cr.App.R.(S.) 33, CA, it was held that whereas section 74(3) of the CJA 1988 provides that "the amount that might be realised at the time a confiscation order is made" includes "the total of the values at that time of all gifts caught by this Part of this Act" and whereas section 74(10) provides that a gift is caught by that part of the Act if "(a) it was made by the defendant at any time after the commission of the offence ...; and (b) the court considers it appropriate in all the circumstances to take the gift into account" it follows that the fact that the property held by the donee at the time of the confiscation order is less than the value of the gift does not *per se* preclude the court from taking the full value of the gift into account; the court is given a discretion by section 74(10) and the question for it to decide is whether it is "appropriate" to take the gift into account; if it considers it appropriate to take it into account (in whole or in part), then to the extent that it does so, the value of the gift is to be included in the computation of the amount that might be realised; in exercising the discretion, the court may have regard to the timing of the gift (here, made when the defendant, having been on the run, had decided to surrender), to the fact that it was made to a person from whom the defendant would be likely to be able to receive an equivalent benefit in return, if he wished, and to the fact that whilst the donee currently had assets worth considerably less than the value of the gift, he was in highly paid employment and would be likely again to hold substantial assets; and, where it is said that the gift has been dissipated prior to the confiscation order, this is a matter to be considered under section 74(10), rather than on a subsequent application for a certificate of inadequacy.

As to the approach to be taken where the prosecution allege that the defendant is the beneficial owner of property registered in the name of a third party, see *Revenue and Customs Prosecutions Office v. May* [2010] 3 All E.R. 1173, CA (Civ. Div.) (§ 5-1059 in the main work).

### Valuation of property

**5-760**    In *R. v. Hedges* (2004) 148 S.J. 974, CA, it was held that in making a confiscation order against a defendant whose only realisable asset was the house which he owned jointly with his wife, the correct approach to valuation of his interest in the property had been to determine the market value of the property, then deduct the outstanding mortgage and the reasonable costs of sale before making a confiscation order in respect of half the remaining amount; such an approach properly reflected the intention of section 74(4) of the CJA 1988 and was to be preferred to that of dividing the value of the house and then deducting the remaining mortgage and costs of sale from the defendant's half share, on the basis that he was responsible for payment of the mortgage; whilst it was true that the defendant was in theory liable to repay the whole mortgage, being jointly and severally liable, the reality was that the mortgage and the costs of sale would be discharged out of the proceeds of sale, the net effect of which would be to reduce his share in the value of the house by half the amount of the mortgage and costs of sale.

In *R. v. Ahmed* [2005] 1 All E.R. 128, CA, it was held that where a court concludes that an offender has benefited from relevant criminal conduct (CJA 1988, s.71(1A)), the court has no discretion, in valuing the realisable assets for the purposes of determining the amount of the confiscation order, to exclude from the computation, the value of the defendant's share in the matrimonial home, notwithstanding the probability that the home would have to be sold to meet the confiscation order; the words "the amount appearing to the court" in subsection (6)(b) ("... the sum which an order made by a court under this section requires an offender to pay shall be equal to (a) ...; or (b) the amount appearing to the court to be the amount that might be realised at the time the order is made, whichever is the less") did not give the court a discretion; it merely referred to the valuation process to be carried out under section 74, and section 3 of the Human Rights Act 1998 (§ 16-15 in the main work) did not require it to be read as construing such a discretion on the court on account of the possible interference with innocent third parties' rights under Article 8 of the ECHR (*ibid.*, § 16-101); the court is merely concerned with the arithmetic exercise of computing what is, in effect, a statutory debt; such process does not involve any assessment of the way in which the debt may ultimately be paid; different considerations would apply if the debt is not met and the prosecution determine to take enforcement action; if a court is asked to make an order for the sale of the matrimonial home then the third party's rights under Article 8 would clearly be engaged; and it would be at that stage that the court would have to consider whether or not it would be proportionate to make an order for the sale of the home. In connection with this case, see *Webber v. Webber (CPS intervening)*, § 5-1063 in the main work.

In the earlier case of *R. v. Goodenough* [2005] 1 Cr.App.R.(S.) 88, CA, it was held that where a defendant's only realisable asset was his equity in the matrimonial home, the making of a confiscation order in accordance with the requirements of the 1988 Act for the amount by which he had benefited from his offending (being an amount less than the value of his equity) did not infringe or interfere with his rights under Article 8 or under Article 1 of the First Protocol (right to peaceful enjoyment of possessions); the rights of the defendant's wife might be infringed if the house were to be sold in order to raise the money to pay the amount of the confiscation order, and it would be open to the wife to oppose any application to appoint a receiver to enforce the order.

### Restraint orders; payment of legal expenses out of restrained assets

In *Revenue and Customs Prosecution Office v. Briggs-Price and O'Reilly* [2007] L.S. Gazette, June 28, **5-761** 32, CA (Civ. Div.) ([2007] EWCA Civ. 568) it was held, in relation to the confiscation regimes under the CJA 1988 and the DTA 1994, that the principle in *Customs and Excise Commrs v. Norris* [1991] 2 Q.B. 293, CA (Civ. Div.) (defendant's legal expenses may be met from restrained assets), applies both to legal expenses incurred prior to conviction (and any appeal against conviction) and to legal expenses incurred in connection with the making of a confiscation order and an appeal against such order; there is a discretion in such cases, which will be exercised for a proper and legitimate purpose within the scope of the statutory regime where the released assets are to meet expenses for a prospective appeal which are neither excessive nor improperly incurred (such amount as is released being capable of control by assessment).

### Restraint orders; appointment of receiver

See *Revenue and Customs Prosecutions Office v. Pigott (Lamb, interested party)* [2010] S.T.C. 1190, CA **5-762** (Civ. Div.) (§ 5-874 in the main work).

### Certificate of inadequacy

There is no rule of law that says that, on an application under section 83 of the 1988 Act for a **5-763** certificate of inadequacy, the High Court could not be persuaded that a defendant was unable to pay the outstanding amount by reason of a worsening of his financial circumstances unless he gave full disclosure of what had happened in the meantime to all his assets, including previously unidentified assets (that the Crown Court had found to exist when making the confiscation order); any such rule would trammel the width of section 83 by imposing a restriction which was not in the statute; and it would also be capable of causing not merely hardship, but hardship amounting to injustice; in the case of previously unidentified assets, it is possible that a defendant may genuinely have no idea or only a dim recollection of what originally happened to them; he should be allowed to try to persuade the court, if this be the case, that his identified assets have shrunk in value and that as a result he is not able to pay the amount outstanding: *Glaves v. CPS* [2011] Costs L.R. 556, CA (Civ. Div.) (considering *Telli v. Revenue and Customs Prosecutions Office* (see § 5-1057 in the main work)).

It was held in *Escobar v. DPP* [2009] 1 W.L.R. 64, DC, that when making an order under section 83(4) of the CJA 1988 for the reduction of a sum payable under a confiscation order (following the issue of a certificate of inadequacy), the Crown Court has jurisdiction to fix a time for payment (by way of extension of the original date). The court said that although there is no express power to extend time in section 83, section 75(1) ("(1) Where the Crown Court orders the defendant to pay an amount under this Part ..., sections 139(1) to (4) ... of the Powers of Criminal Courts (Sentencing) Act 2000 (powers of Crown Court in relation to fines and enforcement of Crown Court fines) shall have effect as if that amount were a fine imposed on him by the Crown Court.") operates so as to incorporate section 139(1) of the 2000 Act (§ 5-676 in the main work), which in turn gives the court power to extend the time for payment when it substitutes a lesser sum under section 83. When read as a whole, section 75 is generally concerned to make provision for orders made under section 83 as well as those under other provisions in Part VI, and this is consistent with the natural and grammatical meaning of the relevant provisions, in that the Crown Court is making an order under section 83(4) and the effect of that order is that the defendant has to pay an amount due under Part VI. For the suggestion that the court's conclusion is out of kilter with the legislative structure, see CLW/09/02/5. For the relevant provisions of the PCA 2002, see sections 23 and 39 (§§ 5-824, 5-840 in the main work), neither of which contain any provision for an extension of the time allowed to pay.

### Enforcement

**5-764**    See *Revenue and Customs Prosecutions Office v. May* [2010] 3 All E.R. 1173, CA (Civ. Div.) (§ 5-1059 in the main work).

### Presence of the accused

**5-765**    See *R. v. Spearing* (§ 3-225 in the main work).

### D. CONFISCATION UNDER THE PROCEEDS OF CRIME ACT 2002

### (1) Summary

### Guidance to prosecutors

**★5-803**    For the decision of the European Court of Human Rights in the case of one of the appellants in *CPS v. Nelson*; *CPS v. Pathak*; *R. v. Paulet* (see the main work), see *Paulet v. U.K.*, *post*, § 5-1041.

### (2) Legislation

#### (a) *Statute*

**Proceeds of Crime Act 2002, ss.6–91**

*Making of order*

**5-805**    The Prevention of Social Housing Fraud Act 2013 came into force in England (to the extent that it was not already in force) on October 15, 2013: Prevention of Social Housing Fraud Act 2013 (Commencement) (England) Order 2013 (S.I. 2013 No. 2622).

**5-806**    *R. v. Jawad* is now reported at [2014] 1 Cr.App.R.(S.) 16.

"Prosecutor" in section 6 of the 2002 Act includes a private prosecutor: *R. v. Zinga* [2014] 1 Cr.App.R. 27, CA. The court observed that while the 2002 Act draws a distinction between those who can investigate and those who can prosecute, the fact that a prosecutor cannot investigate does not prevent him from participating fully in confiscation proceedings, provided that an "appropriate officer", as defined in the 2002 Act (see s.378(1) (§ 15-265 in the main work)), assists him by exercising the various investigatory powers. As to this case, see also *ante*, § 4-91.

As to whether a defendant's consent to a confiscation order can confer jurisdiction to make one, see *R. v. Mackle (Patrick), Mackle (Plunkett Jude) and Mackle (Benedict)*; *R. v. McLaughlin (Henry)*, *post*, § 5-1043.

### *Recoverable amount*

As to the commencement of the Prevention of Social Housing Fraud Act 2013, see *ante*, § 5-805. **5-807**

### *Effect of order on court's other powers*

As to the commencement of the Prevention of Social Housing Fraud Act 2013, see *ante*, § 5-805. **5-813**

*R. v. Jawad* is now reported at [2014] 1 Cr.App.R.(S.) 16.

### *Postponement*

As to the commencement of the Prevention of Social Housing Fraud Act 2013, see *ante*, § 5-805. **5-814**

Whereas section 14 of the 2002 Act (§ 5-814 in the main work) provides that the court may **5-815** postpone confiscation proceedings under section 6 (*ibid.*, § 5-805) "for a specified period" (subs. (1)(b)), that a period of postponement may be extended (subs. (2)), that a period of postponement must not end after the permitted period ends (subs. (3)), that subsection (3) does not apply where there are "exceptional circumstances" (subs. (4)), that the permitted period is the period of two years from the date of conviction (subs. (5)), that a postponement or extension may be made on application by either party or by the court of its own motion (subs. (7)), that if confiscation proceedings are postponed for a period and an application is made to extend the period before it ends, the application may be granted even after the period ends (subs. (8)), and that a confiscation order must not be quashed "only on the ground that there was a defect or omission in the procedure connected with the application for or the granting of a postponement" (subs. (11)), it was held in *R. v. Johal* [2014] 1 W.L.R. 146, CA: (i) in accordance with the intention of Parliament, a broad approach should be taken to what may constitute "exceptional circumstances" (considering *R. v. Soneji* (§§ 1-266, 1-267 in the main work)); and listing difficulties may constitute "exceptional circumstances" in light of the history of a particular case; (ii) where the Crown Court, before the expiry of the permitted period, adjourns the case beyond the permitted period without a hearing and without any consideration as to whether there existed "exceptional circumstances", it was permissible for a judge to rule subsequently that there had in fact existed exceptional circumstances at the time of the adjournment and thus to legitimise retrospectively the postponement beyond the permitted period (distinguishing *Revenue and Customs Prosecution Office v. Iqbal* (as to which, see the main work)); and (iii) as to the effect of a failure to specify a period of postponement, if this is not a procedural error within section 14(11), it is still a procedural error to which *R. v. Soneji* should be applied; Parliament could not have intended that the court should be deprived of its duty to make a confiscation order for a breach which typically will not prejudice the defendant in any way; if substantial prejudice were to arise as a result of such a decision, then the abuse of process jurisdiction could be deployed.

### *Effect of postponement*

As to the commencement of the Prevention of Social Housing Fraud Act 2013, see *ante*, § 5-805. **5-816**

### *No order made: reconsideration of case*

As to the commencement of the Prevention of Social Housing Fraud Act 2013, see *ante*, § 5-805. **5-820**

### *No order made: reconsideration of benefit*

As to the commencement of the Prevention of Social Housing Fraud Act 2013, see *ante*, § 5-805. **5-821**

*Order made: reconsideration of benefit*

**5-822**     As to the commencement of the Prevention of Social Housing Fraud Act 2013, see *ante*, §
5-805.

*Order made: reconsideration of available amount*

**5-823**     Whereas section 22 of the 2002 Act enables a court to vary a confiscation order where (a) the
available amount at the time of making the original order was less than the offender's benefit, and
(b) the offender is subsequently found to have a greater available amount, the obligation of the
court under section 22(4)(a) ("(4) If the amount found under the new calculation exceeds the
relevant amount the court may vary the order by substituting for the amount required to be paid
such amount as— (a) it believes is just, ...") is, in the exercise of its discretion, to make a "just"
order, not merely an obligation to avoid infringement of Article 1 of the First Protocol to the
ECHR (peaceful enjoyment of possessions) (as per *R. v. Waya* (as to which, see § 5-1042 in the
main work)); to this end, the court can take all relevant circumstances into account when deciding
this issue (*e.g.* amount outstanding, additional amount that might now be available for a further
payment, length of time since the original order, impact on the offender of any further order for
payment), and must also take into account the legislative policy in favour of maximising the
recovery of the proceeds of crime, even from legitimately acquired assets: *R. v. Padda* [2014] 1
W.L.R. 1920, CA (considering also *Re Peacock (Secretary of State for the Home Department intervening)*
(as to which, see *post*, § 5-939)). The court accordingly held that even though the offender had not
concealed his assets at the time of the original order, the passage of time since that order was six-
and-a-half years and he had gained the subsequent assets by hard work in a legitimate enterprise,
a variation under section 22 to increase the amount payable under the confiscation order in light
of the subsequently acquired assets was neither wrong in principle nor manifestly excessive;
although the passage of time was important, the proper exercise of the discretion must always
turn on the particular facts.

*Defendant neither convicted nor acquitted*

**★5-829**     Sections 6 (making of a confiscation order (§ 5-805 in the main work)) and 28 of the 2002 Act
allow confiscation proceedings to be taken in a defendant's absence where he absconds during
trial and is then convicted in his absence: *R. v. Okedare* (2014) 158(20) S.J. 37, CA.

*Court's powers on appeal*

**5-833**     As to the commencement of the Prevention of Social Housing Fraud Act 2013, see *ante*, §
5-805.

*Appeal to Supreme Court*

**5-834**     As to the commencement of the Prevention of Social Housing Fraud Act 2013, see *ante*, §
5-805.

*Restraint orders*

**★5-844**     It was held in *Barnes v. Eastenders Cash and Carry plc*; *Eastenders Cash and Carry plc v CPS* [2014]
2 W.L.R. 1269, SC, that when the prosecution propose to seek a restraint order under section 41
of the 2002 Act, particularly when coupled with a receivership order under section 48 (§ 5-874 in
the main work), they should give as much notice to the listing office as they reasonably can,
together with a properly considered estimate of the time likely to be required for pre-reading and
for the hearing of the application. It was further held that the fact that such applications are
made *ex parte* places a special burden of candour on the prosecution and responsibility on the
court, and failure to observe the duty of candour may be regarded as serious misconduct within
section 72 of the 2002 Act (compensation: serious default (§ 5-903 in the main work)). As to this
case, see also *post*, §§ 5-874, 5-875, 16-17.

**★5-846a**     The decision of the Court of Appeal in *Director of the Serious Fraud Office v. B.* has been upheld
on appeal: *Director of the Serious Fraud Office v. O'Brien* [2014] 2 W.L.R. 902, SC. As to this case, see
also *ante*, § 1-171; and *post*, § 28-118.

*Appointment*

**★5-874**     *Revenue and Customs Prosecutions Office v. Pigott (Lamb, interested party)* (as to which, see the main work) was considered in *Barnes v. Eastenders Cash and Carry plc*; *Eastenders Cash and Carry plc v. CPS* [2014] 2 W.L.R. 1269, SC, in which the court held that (i) a receivership order should never be a rubber-stamping exercise and the court has a responsibility to consider what conditions it should contain, and (ii) there may be cases where it would be appropriate to include a condition, such as that suggested in *Pigott*, to the effect that if property is shown not to be realisable property, but wholly in the legal and beneficial ownership of a third party, the receiver's costs should fall on the prosecution. As to this case, see also *ante*, § 5-844; and *post*, §§ 5-875, 16-17.

### Powers

While it is an established general common law principle of receivership that a court-appointed ★**5-875** receiver is entitled to look for payment of his proper expenses and remuneration to the assets placed by the court in his control, and that he has a lien over these assets for that purpose, and while it is also established that this principle applies as much to a receiver appointed under a statutory scheme as to any other court-appointed receiver, unless the statute otherwise provides, where the relevant assets were not the property of the defendant (or prospective defendant) and ought never to have been put into the hands of the receiver, allowing the receiver to recover from the receivership assets would involve a disproportionate interference with the rights of the owners of those assets under Article 1 of the First Protocol to the ECHR (peaceful enjoyment of possessions): *Barnes v. Eastenders Cash and Carry plc*; *Eastenders Cash and Carry plc v. CPS* [2014] 2 W.L.R. 1269, SC (on appeal from *CPS v. Eastenders Cash and Carry plc* (see the main work)) (the Supreme Court also holding, however, that to deprive the receiver of his lien would violate his rights under Article 1 of the First Protocol; here there had been an agreement between the receiver and the CPS, and although this did not itself make provision for his remuneration or his lien, it was their mutual expectation that he would have such a lien, and this was the premise upon which he agreed to act; although the CPS had discharged their contractual obligation to the receiver by ensuring that the court order appointing him conformed with the terms of the underlying agreement between them, there had been a total failure of the basis on which the receiver was asked to act and agreed to do so, and thus he should be entitled to recover his proper remuneration and expenses from the CPS under the doctrine of unjust enrichment (enrichment may include the obtaining of services)). As to this case, see also *ante*, §§ 5-844, 5-874; and *post*, § 16-17.

### Sums received by justices' chief executive

As to the commencement of the Prevention of Social Housing Fraud Act 2013, see *ante*, § **5-881** 5-805.

With effect from March 27, 2014, the Public Bodies (Merger of the Director of Public Prosecu- ★ tions and the Director of Revenue and Customs Prosecutions) Order 2014 (S.I. 2014 No. 834), art. 3(3), and Sched. 2, paras 19 and 22, repealed section 55(8)(f) of the 2002 Act, subject to sav- ing and transitional provisions (as to which, see *ante*, § 1-27).

### Restraint orders

With effect from April 6, 2014, the provisions of the Tribunals, Courts and Enforcement Act ★**5-884** 2007 referred to in the main work were brought into force: Tribunals, Courts and Enforcement Act 2007 (Commencement No. 11) Order 2014 (S.I. 2014 No. 768).

### Enforcement receivers

With effect from April 6, 2014, the provisions of the Tribunals, Courts and Enforcement Act ★**5-885** 2007 referred to in the main work were brought into force: Tribunals, Courts and Enforcement Act 2007 (Commencement No. 11) Order 2014 (S.I. 2014 No. 768).

### Serious default

The reference to "SOCA" in section 72(9)(ba) of the 2002 Act should be to the "the National **5-903** Crime Agency" (this is one of the amendments effected by the provisions of the Crime and Courts Act 2013 cited in the main work).

With effect from March 27, 2014, the Public Bodies (Merger of the Director of Public Prosecu- ★ tions and the Director of Revenue and Customs Prosecutions) Order 2014 (S.I. 2014 No. 834), art. 3(3), and Sched. 2, paras 19 and 23, repealed section 72(9)(d) of the 2002 Act, subject to sav- ing and transitional provisions (as to which, see *ante*, § 1-27).

★        In connection with section 72 of the 2002 Act, see *Barnes v. Eastenders Cash and Carry plc*; *Eastenders Cash and Carry plc v. CPS, ante*, § 5-844.

*Criminal lifestyle*

★**5-906**   Where the appellant was convicted of obtaining a money transfer by deception, contrary to section 15A of the Theft Act 1968, where the particulars of offence alleged it to have occurred between January 1, 2006, and December 31, 2006, and where the evidence showed that the fraudulent application for a mortgage loan had been made in June, 2006, and that money, pursuant to that application, had been paid by way of money transfer into the appellant's conveyancer's client account on July 17, 2006, the offence did not come within section 75(2)(c) of the 2002 Act because it was not committed over a period of at least six months; how the debt so acquired was serviced thereafter was an entirely different matter and not encompassed by the specific criminality identified in the count in question: *R. v. Odamo* [2014] 1 Cr.App.R.(S.) 44, CA.

*Conduct and benefit*

**5-907**   As to section 76(2) of the 2002 Act, see *R. v. Oyebola, post*, § 5-1046.

*Value of tainted gifts*

**5-912**   *R. v. Smith* is now reported at [2013] 2 Cr.App.R.(S.) 77.

*Proceedings*

★**5-916**   The provisions of the Crime and Courts Act 2013 referred to in the main work came into force on February 24, 2014: Crime and Courts Act 2013 (Commencement No. 8) Order 2014 (S.I. 2014 No. 258).

(b) *Subordinate legislation*

**Commencement**

**Proceeds of Crime Act 2002 (Commencement No. 5, Transitional Provisions, Savings and Amendment) Order 2003 (S.I. 2003 No. 333)**

*Citation and interpretation*

**5-937**   1.—(1) [*Citation.*]

(2) In this Order, "the Act" means the Proceeds of Crime Act 2002.

(3) Where an offence is found to have been committed over a period of two or more days, or at some time during a period of two or more days, it shall be taken for the purposes of this order to have been committed on the earliest of those days.

*Commencement of provisions*

**5-938**   2.—(1) The provisions of the Act listed in column 1 of the Schedule to this Order shall come into force on 24th March 2003, subject to the transitional provisions and savings contained in this order.

(2) But where a particular purpose is specified in relation to any such provision in column 2 of that Schedule, the provision concerned shall come into force only for that purpose.

*Transitional provisions relating to confiscation orders—England and Wales*

**5-939**   3.—(1) Section 6 of the Act (making of confiscation order) shall not have effect where the offence, or any of the offences, mentioned in section 6(2) was committed before 24th March 2003.

(2) Section 27 of the Act (defendant convicted or committed absconds) shall not have effect where the offence, or any of the offences, mentioned in section 27(2) was committed before 24th March 2003.

(3) Section 28 of the Act (defendant neither convicted nor acquitted absconds) shall not have effect where the offence, or any of the offences, in respect of which proceedings have been started but not concluded was committed before 24th March 2003.

4. [*Transitional provisions relating to confiscation orders—Northern Ireland.*]

It was held in *R. v. Moulden* [2009] 1 Cr.App.R. 27, CA, that where the respondent appeared before the Crown Court to be dealt with in respect of two indictments, one alleging offences committed before March 24, 2003, and the other alleging offences committed after that date, each indictment represented a separate set of "proceedings" for the purposes of section 6(2)(a) of the 2002 Act (see § 5-805 in the main work) and accordingly, by virtue of article 3(1), the 2002 Act had no application to the pre-March 24, 2003, indictment, but did apply to the post-March 24, 2003, indictment. The judge had, therefore, been correct to apply the confiscation provisions of the CJA 1988 to the one indictment and the confiscation provisions of the 2002 Act to the other indictment, and to reject the prosecution submission that the effect of these provisions was to disapply the 2002 Act in relation to both indictments, thereby triggering the assumptions provided for by section 72AA of the 1988 Act.

Where the defendant pleaded guilty to a count of conspiracy to make false instruments, the particulars of offence alleging that the offence took place "between the 1st day of January 2003 and the 16th day of May 2007", and where his written basis of plea was to the effect that his first admitted act in pursuance of the criminal agreement took place only on October 29, 2003, his offence had begun before March 24, 2003, for the purposes of article 3(1) (having regard to article 1(3)), such that the applicable confiscation provisions were those under Part VI of the CJA 1988, not Part 2 of the PCA 2002, see *R. v. Evwierhowa* [2011] 2 Cr.App.R.(S.) 77, CA.

As to whether, in principle, rental income from criminally-obtained properties could properly be regarded as benefit even though it was derived from properties obtained subject to offences, in respect of which there were convictions, that were committed before the commencement of Part 2 of the 2002 Act, see *R. v. Oyebola, post,* § 5-1046.

By virtue of articles 3(1) and 10(1)(e) (*post,* § 5-942), section 16 of the DTA 1994 (increase in realisable property) continues to have effect where an offence mentioned in section 6(2) of the PCA Act 2002 (making of confiscation order (§ 5-805 in the main work)) was committed before March 24, 2003: *Re Peacock (Secretary of State for the Home Department intervening)* [2012] 2 Cr.App.R.(S.) 81, SC. For the suggestion that the court misconstrued the order (albeit reaching the correct result), see CLW/12/08/5.

*Transitional provisions relating to restraint orders and enforcement abroad—England and Wales*

**5.** Sections 41 (restraint orders) and 74 (enforcement abroad) of the Act shall not have effect where—     **5-940**

    (a)  the powers in those sections would otherwise be exercisable by virtue of a condition in section 40(2) or (3) of the Act being satisfied; and

    (b)  the offence mentioned in section 40(2)(a) or 40(3)(a), as the case may be, was committed before 24th March 2003.

**6.** [*Transitional provisions relating to restraint orders and enforcement abroad—Northern Ireland.*]

*Transitional provisions relating to criminal lifestyle—England and Wales*

**7.**—(1) This article applies where the court is determining under section 6(4)(a) of the Act whether the defendant has a criminal lifestyle.     **5-941**

(2) Conduct shall not form part of a course of criminal activity under section 75(3)(a) of the Act where any of the three or more offences mentioned in section 75(3)(a) was committed before 24th March 2003.

(3) Where the court is applying the rule in section 75(5) of the Act on the calculation of relevant benefit for the purposes of determining whether or not the test in section 75(2)(b) of the Act is satisfied by virtue of conduct forming part of a course of criminal activity under section 75(3)(a) of the Act, the court must not take into account benefit from conduct constituting an offence mentioned in section 75(5)(c) of the Act which was committed before 24th March 2003.

(4) Conduct shall form part of a course of criminal activity under section 75(3)(b) of the Act, notwithstanding that any of the offences of which the defendant was convicted on at least two separate occasions in the period mentioned in section 75(3)(b) were committed before 24th March 2003.

(5) Where the court is applying the rule in section 75(5) of the Act on the calculation of relevant benefit for the purposes of determining whether or not the test in section 75(2)(b) of the Act is satisfied by virtue of conduct forming part of a course of criminal activity under section 75(3)(b) of the Act, the court may take into account benefit from conduct constituting an offence committed before 24th March 2003.

(6) Where the court is applying the rule in section 75(6) of the Act on the calculation of relevant benefit for the purposes of determining whether or not the test in section 75(2)(c) of the Act is satisfied, the court must not take into account benefit from conduct constituting an offence mentioned in section 75(6)(b) of the Act which was committed before 24th March 2003.

[This article is printed as substituted by the Proceeds of Crime Act 2002 (Commencement No. 5) (Amendment of Transitional Provisions) Order 2003 (S.I. 2003 No. 531).]

  **8.** [*Transitional provisions relating to criminal lifestyle—Northern Ireland.*]

*Transitional provisions relating to particular criminal conduct*
  **9.** Conduct which constitutes an offence which was committed before 24th March 2003 is not particular criminal conduct under section 76(3) or 224(3) of the Act.

*Savings for England and Wales*
**5-942**    **10.**—(1) Where, under article 3 or 5, a provision of the Act does not have effect, the following provisions shall continue to have effect—
  (a)  sections 71 to 89 (including Schedule 4) and 102 of the Criminal Justice Act 1988;
  (b)  paragraphs 83 and 84 of Schedule 17 to the Housing Act 1988;
  (c)  sections 21(3)(e) to (g), 27, 28 and 34 of the Criminal Justice Act 1993;
  (d)  paragraph 36 of Schedule 9 to the Criminal Justice and Public Order Act 1994;
  (e)  sections 1 to 36 and 41 of the Drug Trafficking Act 1994;
  (f)  sections 1 to 10, 15(1) and (3) (including Schedule 1), 16(2), (5) and (6) of the Proceeds of Crime Act 1995;
  (g)  section 4(3) of the Private International Law (Miscellaneous Provisions) Act 1995;
  (h)  sections 35 to 38 of the Proceeds of Crime (Scotland) Act 1995;
  (i)  the Proceeds of Crime (Enforcement of Confiscation Orders made in England and Wales or Scotland) Order (Northern Ireland) 1997 and the Proceeds of Crime (Northern Ireland) Order 1996, so far as necessary for the continued operation of the Proceeds of Crime (Enforcement of Confiscation Orders made in England and Wales or Scotland) Order (Northern Ireland) 1997;
  (j)  paragraphs 23 and 36 of Schedule 5 to the Justices of the Peace Act 1997;
  (k)  section 83 of, paragraph 114 of Schedule 8 to and paragraph 8 of Schedule 9 to the Crime and Disorder Act 1998;
  (l)  paragraphs 139 and 172 of Schedule 13 to the Access to Justice Act 1999;
  (m)  paragraphs 105 to 113 and 163 to 173 of Schedule 9 to the Powers of Criminal Courts (Sentencing) Act 2000;
  (n)  paragraphs 6(1) to (3) and 10 of Schedule 15 to the Terrorism Act 2000.
  (2) Where under article 3 or 5, a provision of the Act does not have effect, the following provisions shall continue to have effect as if they had not been amended by Schedule 11 to the Act—
  (a)  section 13(6) of the Criminal Justice (International Co-operation) Act 1990;
  (b)  paragraph 17(3) of Schedule 8 to the Terrorism Act 2000.
  **11.** [*Savings for Northern Ireland.*]
  **12.** [*Savings for enforcement of Scottish orders in England, Wales and Northern Ireland.*]
  **13.** [*Savings in relation to external orders.*]
  **14.** [*Amendment of arts 3 and 5 of S.I. 2003 No. 120, §§ 26-4, 26-5 in the main work.*]

Article 2

THE SCHEDULE

**5-943**

| *Column 1* | *Column 2* |
|---|---|
| Part 2 (sections 6 to 91, including Schedule 2) (Confiscation: England and Wales). | So far as not already in force. |
| Part 4 (sections 156 to 239, including Schedule 5) (Confiscation: Northern Ireland). | |
| Part 9 (sections 417 to 434) (Insolvency *etc.*). | |
| Part 10 (sections 435 to 442) (Information). | So far as not already in force. |
| Section 444 (External requests and orders). | |
| Section 445 (External investigations). | |
| Section 447 (Interpretation). | |
| Section 456 (Amendments). | Commenced for the purposes of the provisions of Schedule 11 to the Act commenced by this Order. |

Column 1

Section 457 (Repeals).

In Schedule 11, paragraphs 1, 4, 5, 7, 8, 9, 11, 14(2) and
(3), 15, 16, 17(2), (4) and (6), 19(2) and (3), 20, 21,
25(2)(a) and (h) to (j), 26, 27, 28(1) and (2)(e) and (g),
31(2) and (3)(a) to (c), 32, 37 and 39.

In Schedule 12, the following entries; the entry relating to
the Criminal Appeal (Northern Ireland) Act 1980; the
entry relating to the Police and Criminal Evidence Act
1984; the entry relating to the Criminal Justice Act 1988;
the entry relating to the Housing Act 1988; the entry
relating to the Police and Criminal Evidence (Northern
Ireland) Order 1989; in the entry relating to the Criminal
Justice (International Co-operation) Act 1990, the entry in
the second column concerning section 13 of that Act; the
entry relating to the Criminal Justice (Confiscation)
(Northern Ireland) Order 1990; the entry relating to the
Criminal Justice Act 1993; the entry relating to the Drug
Traficking Act 1994; the entry relating to the Proceeds of
Crime Act 1995; in the entry relating to the Criminal
Procedure (Consequential Provisions) (Scotland) Act 1995,
the entry in the second column concerning Schedule 4 of
that Act; the entry relating to the Private International
Law (Miscellaneous Provisions) Act 1995; in the entry
relating to the Proceeds of Crime (Scotland) Act 1995, the
entry in the second column concerning sections 35 to 39
of that Act, the entry in the second column concerning
section 40 of that Act and the entry in the second column
concerning section 42 of that Act; the entry relating to the
Proceeds of Crime (Northern Ireland) Order 1996; the
entry relating to the Justices of the Peace Act 1997; in the
entry relating to the Crime and Disorder Act 1998, the
entry in the second column concerning section 83 of that
Act, the entry in the second column concerning Schedule
8 of that Act and the entry in the second column
concerning Schedule 9 of that Act; the entry relating to
the Access to Justice Act 1999; the entry relating to the
Powers of Criminal Courts (Sentencing) Act 2000; the
entry relating to the Terrorism Act 2000; and the entry
relating to the Criminal Justice and Police Act 2001.

Column 2

Commenced for the purposes of the
provisions of Schedule 12 to the Act
commenced by this Order.

Paragraphs 7, 11, 15, 16, 20, 21 and
39 are commenced except to the
extent that they relate to Part 3 of the
Act. Paragraph 17(2) is commenced so
far as it repeals sections 71 to 89, 94
and 99 to 102 of the Criminal Justice
Act 1988. Paragraph 25(2)(a) is
commenced so far as it repeals sections
1 to 38 and 41 of the Drug Traficking
Act 1994. Paragraph 27 is commenced
so far as not already in force.
Paragraph 31(2) is commenced so far
as it repeals articles 4 to 41 of the
Proceeds of Crime (Northern Ireland)
Order 1996.

The entry relating to sections 71 to
102 of the Criminal Justice Act 1988 is
commenced so far as it repeals sections
71 to 89, 94 and 99 to 102 of that Act.
The entries relating to the Criminal
Justice Act 1993, the Proceeds of
Crime Act 1995 and the Access to
Justice Act 1999 are commenced so far
as not already in force. The entry
relating to sections 1 to 54 of the Drug
Traficking Act 1994 is commenced so
far as it repeals sections 1 to 38 and 41
of that Act. The entry relating to Parts
II and III of the Proceeds of Crime
(Northern Ireland) Order 1996 is
commenced so far as it repeals articles
4 to 41 of that Order. The entry
relating to the Terrorism Act 2000 is
commenced so far as it repeals
paragraphs 6 and 10 of Schedule 15 to
that Act.

## Rules of court relating to confiscation, restraint and receivership proceedings

### Criminal Procedure Rules 2013 (S.I. 2013 No. 1554), Pt 60

*Remuneration*

As to the Supreme Court's decision on appeal from *CPS v. Eastenders Cash and Carry plc*, see      ★**5-981**
*ante*, § 5-875.

*Forms*

**5-1038**    The 2013 criminal practice directions (see the main work) are now reported at [2013] 1 W.L.R. 3164.

## (3) Authorities

### Effect of postponement

**5-1040**    *R. v. Gordon* (see the main work) is no longer cited at § 5-644 in the main work. Its reference is [2007] 2 Cr.App.R.(S.) 66, CA.

### Lack of discretion/abuse of process/proportionality

**★5-1041**    In *Paulet v U.K., The Times,* May 19, 2014, ECtHR, the court considered the case of one of the appellants in *CPS v. Nelson; CPS v. Pathak; R. v. Paulet* (see the main work), and held that his rights under Article 1 of the First Protocol to the ECHR (peaceful enjoyment of possessions) had been breached where he was an illegal immigrant, where he pleaded guilty to, *inter alia*, obtaining a pecuniary advantage by deception (relating to his obtaining of employment), where a confiscation order under section 6 of the PCA 2002 (§ 5-805 in the main work) deprived him of all the savings he had accumulated while employed illegally in the United Kingdom, and where the order had only been subject to review on the grounds of oppression and abuse of process, rather than proportionality; at the time of the domestic proceedings (which had taken place prior to *R. v. Waya* (§ 5-1042 in the main work)), the scope of the review carried out by the domestic courts was too narrow to satisfy the requirement that a "fair balance" be struck under Article 1 between the protection of the right to property and the general interest.

**★**    As to proportionality considerations in a case of jointly obtained benefit, see *R. v. Ahmad; R. v. Fields, post,* § 5-1046.

**5-1042**    As to *R. v. Waya,* and the approach of the Court of Appeal to applications based thereon for an extension of time in which to appeal against a confiscation order, see *R. v. Bestel; R. v. Raza; R. v. Bashir, post,* § 5-1055.

As to the role of the court where there is cause for concern that a prosecutor's duty in confiscation proceedings to act in the public interest may conflict with his private interest, see *R. v. Zinga, ante,* § 4-91.

### Factual basis for making order

**5-1043**    Under the PCA 2002, the power to make a confiscation order can only arise after the court itself has determined that the defendant has benefited from his particular criminal conduct; a defendant's consent to a confiscation order cannot confer jurisdiction to make one, particularly where the facts that the consent is based upon cannot as a matter of law support the conclusion that he has benefited; however, if the terms on which a defendant consents make it clear that he accepts facts justifying the order, a judge is then entitled to rely on that consent, provided he is satisfied that there has been an unambiguous acceptance of those facts from which the defendant should not be permitted to resile; this is not because the defendant has consented but because his acceptance of the facts constitutes evidence upon which the judge is entitled to rely; the judge need not mount any further investigation, provided the defendant has accepted the facts unequivocally, and particularly where the acceptance was given after legal advice that proves to be sound: *R. v. Mackle (Patrick), Mackle (Plunkett Jude) and Mackle (Benedict); R. v. McLaughlin (Henry)* [2014] 2 W.L.R. 267, SC. As to this case, see also *post,* §§ 5-1046, 7-135.

### Benefit

*Property*

**★5-1046**    In *R. v. Ahmad; R. v. Fields,* unreported, June 18, 2014, SC ([2014] UKSC 36), it was held that: (i) whereas the PCA 2002, s.76(4), provides that a person benefits from conduct "if he obtains property as a result of or in connection with the conduct", the word "obtains" should be given a broad, normal meaning connoting a power of disposition or control rather than ownership; in many cases, it is unclear how many people were involved in a crime, what their roles were, and where the money went; as result, if the court could not proceed on the basis that the participants should be treated as having acquired the proceeds of the crime together, so that each of them "obtained" the "property", it would often be impossible to decide what part of the proceeds had been "obtained" by all or any of the defendants; (ii) where property is obtained as a result of a joint enterprise, it will often be appropriate for a court to hold that each participant "obtained" the whole of that property (see *R. v. May* (§ 5-1044 in the main work), *R. v. Green* (see the main work), and *R. v. Allpress* (§ 5-1045 in the main work)); however, judges in confiscation proceedings should be ready to investigate and make findings as to whether there were separate obtainings; sometimes this is too difficult or impossible, although a court should never make a finding that there has been joint obtaining from convenience, or worse, laziness; (iii) when it comes to enforcement, however, to take the same proceeds twice over would not serve the legitimate aim of the 2002 Act, and even if that were not so, it would be disproportionate; if the state sought to enforce an order for the confiscation of proceeds of crime that have already been paid, this would violate Article 1 of the First Protocol to the ECHR (peaceful enjoyment of possessions). The appeals of the defendants were allowed to the extent that the confiscation orders made against them were amended to provide they could be enforced only to the extent that the same sum had not been recovered through another confiscation order made in relation to the same joint benefit.

A defendant who knowingly comes into physical possession of dutiable goods in relation to which he knows the duty has been evaded, and who plays an active role in handling the goods to assist in their commercial realisation (and who is therefore guilty of an offence of being knowingly concerned in the fraudulent evasion of duty, contrary to the CEMA 1979, s.170(2)(a) (§ 25-474 in the main work)), does not necessarily benefit from his offence for the purposes of section 6 of the 2002 Act (*ibid.*, § 5-805); playing such a role does not alone establish that a person has benefited from his criminal conduct; in order to have benefited therefrom for the purposes of section 6, he must have obtained property as a result of or in connection therewith (s.76 (*ibid.*, § 5-907)), with the approach to the question whether he has "obtained" property being that dictated by *R. v. May* and *Jennings v. CPS* (as to which, see the main work); this must be established by the evidence or reasonable inferences drawn therefrom; it is not to be assumed that because someone has handled contraband that he has had possession of it in the manner necessary to meet the requirements of the legislation: *R. v. Mackle (Patrick), Mackle (Plunkett Jude) and Mackle (Benedict); R. v. McLaughlin (Henry)* [2014] 2 W.L.R. 267, SC (decided in relation to the corresponding provisions of the 2002 Act relating to Northern Ireland, and also considering *R. v. Allpress* (as to which, see the main work), and *R. v. White and other appeals* (as to which, see § 5-1052 in the main work)). As to this case, see also *ante*, § 5-1043; and *post*, § 7-135.

A business which is founded entirely on the infringement of other people's property rights, and which involves the commission of criminal offences, will result in confiscation of the proceeds of the business; where, therefore, the offenders were convicted of offences under section 92 of the Trade Marks Act 1994 (unauthorised use of a trade mark, *etc.*) in respect of their business importing and selling car wheel trims specifically designed for various makes of motor-car and bearing the logo of the relevant manufacturer, even though the trims had been marketed as "non-genuine replacement parts" and it was made clear that they were not produced by the relevant manufacturer, it had not been appropriate to stay confiscation proceedings as an abuse of process; such offences were lifestyle offences within Schedule 2 to the PCA 2002 (§§ 5-924 *et seq.* in the main work); that the offences did not require proof of either bad faith or dishonesty was irrelevant, since the essence of the confiscation regime is to get at the proceeds of crime, not to impose punishment; that the manufacturers of the trims had not been prosecuted was also irrelevant, as was the fact that the offenders were conducting a "proper business", keeping records and paying tax, and that a confiscation order would potentially strip them of all their available assets; furthermore, as decided in *R. v. Waya* (as to which, see §§ 5-1042, 5-1055 in the main work), resort to a stay for abuse is no longer the appropriate response to confiscation proceedings; rather, any potential order should be assessed to ensure that it is proportionate in light of Article 1 of the First Protocol to the ECHR (peaceful enjoyment of possessions); there was nothing remotely disproportionate about removing from an unlawful business the proceeds that it had generated; there may be special cases in which a confiscation order can properly be described as disproportionate, but the fact that it is based on gross proceeds is not one of them: *Hampshire C.C. v. Beazley* [2013] 1 W.L.R. 3331, CA.

In *R. v. Oyebola* [2014] 1 Cr.App.R.(S.) 58, CA, it was held that: (i) rental income from a criminally-obtained property constitutes a "benefit" for the purposes of the confiscation regime under the 2002 Act; there was nothing in *R. v. Waya, ante*, to undermine the common-sense of that conclusion in *R. v. Pattison* (as to which, see § 5-1055 in the main work); and (ii) in principle, rental income here (a criminal lifestyle case) was properly regarded as benefit even though it derived from properties obtained subject to offences (in respect of which there were convictions) committed before the commencement of Part 2 of the 2002 Act (March 24, 2003). As to (i), the court conceded that it would be open to argument that, if an offender obtained a property with the assistance of a fraudulently obtained mortgage, but put up half the purchase price from entirely legitimate sources, there should be some apportionment of the rental income when assessing criminal benefit. As to (ii), because of the effect of the transitional provisions in article 3 of the Proceeds of Crime Act 2002 (Commencement No. 5, Transitional Provisions, Savings and Amendment) Order 2003 (S.I. 2003 No. 333) (*ante*, § 5-939), the prosecution had abandoned reliance on the pre-March 24, 2003, counts in reliance on *R. v. Stapleton* [2009] 1 Cr.App.R.(S.) 38, CA (as to which, see CLW/08/34/18), but then managed to bring the rental income derived from the properties in those counts back into the reckoning by reference to section 76(2) of the 2002 Act ("(2) General criminal conduct of the defendant is all his criminal conduct, and it is immaterial (a) whether conduct occurred before or after the passing of this Act; (b) whether property constituting a benefit from conduct was obtained before or after the passing of this Act." (§ 5-907 in the main work)), when taken in conjunction with section 10 of the Act (assumptions to be made in a criminal lifestyle case (*ibid.*, § 5-810)).

5-1050    *R. v. Seager*; *R. v. Blatch* (see the main work) was considered in *R. v. Sale* [2014] 1 Cr.App.R.(S.) 60, CA. It was said that, having regard to what was said in *Prest v. Petrodel Resources Ltd* [2013] 2 A.C. 415, SC, the three situations identified in *R. v. Seager*; *R. v. Blatch* as situations in which a criminal court would pierce the corporate veil, should now be read as three cases where a benefit obtained by a company is treated in law by the PCA 2002 as a benefit also obtained by the individual criminal. In the instant case, where the offender was the managing director and sole shareholder of a company, where an employee of Network Rail arranged for the award of high value contracts to the company in return for gifts or hospitality paid for by the defendant and the company, and where the offender pleaded guilty to corruption (Prevention of Corruption Act 1906, s.1), the close inter-relationship between his corrupt actions and steps taken by the company in advancing those corrupt acts and intentions meant that in reality the activities of the offender and company were so interlinked as to be indivisible; section 76(4) of the 2002 Act ("(4) A person benefits from conduct if he obtains property as a result of or in connection with the conduct." (§ 5-907 in the main work)) was apt to capture the full amount of the invoices paid to the company by Network Rail (£1.9 million); and a pecuniary advantage, within section 76(5) ("(5) If a person obtains a pecuniary advantage as a result of or in connection with conduct, he is to be taken to obtain as a result of or in connection with the conduct a sum of money equal to the value of the pecuniary advantage."), was also obtained in that the corrupt conduct would have improperly enhanced the company's place in the market; prior to *R. v. Waya* (§§ 5-1042, 5-1055 in the main work), the judge's conclusion as to a benefit figure of £1.9 million would have been upheld; however, applying *R. v. Jawad* (§ 5-813 in the main work), and *Waya*, had this been an offence whose only criminal effect was upon Network Rail, which had been provided with value for money achieved by the performance of a contract in the ordinary course of business, it would have seemed proportionate to limit the confiscation order to the profit made by the company, and to treat the full value given under the contract as analogous to full restoration to the loser; but it was unrealistic to regard Network Rail as the only victim; therefore, an order for profit gained under the contracts, together with the value of the pecuniary advantage obtained (obtaining market share, excluding competitors, and saving on the costs of preparing proper tenders), would represent a proportionate order that would avoid double counting.

In *R. v. Harvey* [2014] 1 Cr.App.R.(S.) 46, CA, it was held: (i) that *R. v. del Basso* (see the main work) is binding authority that, in the context of a criminal lifestyle case, where the appellant owner of a plant hire and contracting business had knowingly made extensive use of stolen plant, VAT received from customers should not be deducted from the turn-over figure of the business (and thus excluded from the calculation of benefit); the total sum received from a customer belonged to the appellant's business when he received it; the VAT element was not held on trust for Revenue and Customs; and it would be wrong in principle to carry out an accounting exercise in respect of VAT collected through the use of stolen property in order to identify such element of it as had been accounted to Revenue and Customs; and (ii) that where a defendant obtains chattels as a result of his criminal conduct, uses those chattels for a substantial period, thereby materially reducing their value, and the chattels are ultimately restored to their true owners, in assessing benefit, a judge should not give credit for their residual value.

The aspect of the Court of Appeal's decision in *R. v. Ahmad (Shakeel) and Ahmad (Syed Mubarak)* that is referred to in the main work was not the subject of challenge when the matter went to the Supreme Court: see *R. v. Ahmad*; *R. v. Fields*, *ante*, § 5-1046. ★**5-1051**

### Pecuniary advantage

As to valuation of the pecuniary advantage accruing to a company awarded contracts by a large company with a nationwide operation and a turnover of £6 billion following the making of corrupt payments to an employee of the latter company, see *R. v. Sale*, *ante*, § 5-1050. **5-1052**

*R. v. White and other appeals* (as to which, see the main work) was considered in *R. v. Mackle (Patrick)*, *Mackle (Plunkett Jude)* and *Mackle (Benedict)*; *R. v. McLaughlin (Henry)*, *ante*, § 5-1046.

The aspect of the Court of Appeal's decision in *R. v. Ahmad (Shakeel) and Ahmad (Syed Mubarak)* that is referred to in the main work was not the subject of challenge when the matter went to the Supreme Court: see *R. v. Ahmad*; *R. v. Fields*, *ante*, § 5-1046. ★

For the decision of the European Court of Human Rights in the case of one of the appellants in *CPS v. Nelson*; *CPS v. Pathak*; *R. v. Paulet* (see the main work), see *Paulet v. U.K.*, *ante*, § 5-1041. ★**5-1053**

### Assumptions to be made in case of a criminal lifestyle

Where money has been expended in furtherance of a conspiracy, section 10(4) of the PCA 2002 (§ 5-810 in the main work) does not have the effect that it is to be assumed against any conspirator that the expenditure was incurred by him; it is necessary first to prove that the expenditure was actually incurred by the particular defendant before the assumption in section 10(4) (that it was met from property obtained by him as a result of his general criminal conduct) can be made: *R. v. Mahmood (Shaukat)* [2013] 1 W.L.R. 3146, CA. **5-1054**

### Valuation of benefit

Where the applicants, each convicted of mortgage fraud, were made subject to confiscation orders, where the Crown Court judge in each case assessed their benefit by reference to sums received by the applicant as a loan from the mortgagee secured by a charge over property purchased with a deposit and the mortgage advance, and where they sought an extension of time within which to apply for leave to appeal against the confiscation orders in reliance on *R. v. Waya* (see the main work), the primacy of the principle of finality had the effect of requiring the most exceptional circumstances before a defendant should be permitted to argue that the new law should apply to his old case and that, if no extension were granted, a substantial injustice would be caused (considering, *inter alia*, *R. v. R.* and *R. v. Cottrell*; *R. v. Fletcher* (as to both of which, see § 7-171 in the main work)); the relevant date for this purpose was the date of the confiscation order and not of any enforcement proceedings, although enforcement proceedings and their consequences are a relevant factor when considering whether a substantial injustice might follow should an extension of time be refused; but so, also, is the availability of an application to the Crown Court under section 23 of the 2002 Act (inadequacy of available amount: variation of order (§ 5-824 in the main work)): *R. v. Bestel*; *R. v. Raza*; *R. v. Bashir* [2013] 2 Cr.App.R. 30, CA (also considering *R. v. Jawad* (§ 5-813 in the main work)). **5-1055**

As to the effect of *R. v. Waya* (*ante*) on the conclusion in *R. v. Pattison* (see the main work) that rental income from a criminally-obtained property constitutes a "benefit" for the purposes of the 2002 Act, see *R. v. Oyebola*, *ante*, § 5-1046.

As to valuation of benefit where property is obtained as a result of a joint enterprise, see *R. v. Ahmad*; *R. v. Fields*, *ante*, § 5-1046. ★

As to whether, where a defendant obtains chattels as a result of his criminal conduct, uses those chattels for a substantial period, thereby materially reducing their value, and the chattels are ultimately restored to their true owners, in assessing benefit, a judge should give credit for their residual value, see *R. v. Harvey*, *ante*, § 5-1050.

### "Free property" (s.82), "realisable property" (s.83) and "property" (s.84)

#### Burden on defendant

The aspect of the Court of Appeal's decision in *R. v. Ahmad (Shakeel) and Ahmad (Syed Mubarak)* ★**5-1057** that is referred to in the main work was not the subject of challenge when the matter went to the Supreme Court: see *R. v. Ahmad*; *R. v. Fields*, *ante*, § 5-1046.

*R. v. McIntosh* (see the main work) and *R. v. Ahmad (Shakeel) and Ahmad (Syed Mubarak)* (see the main work and *ante*) show that when a judge is addressing the question of undisclosed or hidden assets that have to be included in the available amount, he is not bound, simply because he disbelieves a defendant, to decide that they must equal the full amount of the benefit; however, section 7(2) of the PCA 2002 (§ 5-802 in the main work) does lay upon the defendant the obligation to show that the available amount is less than the benefit; whilst those authorities show that one cannot move directly from disbelieving the defendant to finding that his assets that are hidden are necessarily the same sum as his benefit, the court must look at the whole of the evidence and, if there is nothing other than evidence that is disbelieved, it is likely that it will come back to the original conclusion: *R. v. Lee* [2013] Lloyd's Rep. F.C. 453, CA.

### Peaceful enjoyment of possessions

★**5-1065**   For consideration by the European Court of Human Rights of Article 1 of the First Protocol to the ECHR (peaceful enjoyment of possessions) where a confiscation order deprived an illegal immigrant (convicted of obtaining a pecuniary advantage (employment) by deception) of all the savings he had accumulated while employed illegally in the United Kingdom, see *Paulet v. U.K.*, *ante*, § 5-1041.

★   As to the relevance of Article 1 of the First Protocol to the ECHR in a case of jointly-obtained benefit, see *R. v. Ahmad*; *R. v. Fields*, *ante*, § 5-1046.

## X. DISQUALIFICATION, RESTRICTION, EXCLUSION, ETC., ORDERS

### A. BANNING ORDERS UNDER THE FOOTBALL SPECTATORS ACT 1989

#### (2) Legislation

##### Football Spectators Act 1989, s.14

*Main definitions*

**5-1070**   The Football Spectators (2014 World Cup Control Period) Order 2014 (S.I. 2014 No. 144), as amended by the Football Spectators (2014 World Cup Control Period) (Amendment) Order 2014 (S.I. 2014 No. 220), provides that, in relation to the FIFA World Cup in Brazil, section 14(6) of the 1989 Act (definition of "control period" in relation to an external tournament (§ 5-1069 in the main work)) shall have effect as if, for the reference to five days, there were substituted a reference to 10 days, and that the period beginning on June 2, 2014 (which is 10 days before the first match) and ending when the last match included in the tournament is finished or cancelled (which, subject to postponement, is due to be on July 13, 2014) is a control period for the purposes of Part II of the 1989 Act.

##### Football Spectators Act 1989, ss.14A–14H

*Banning orders made on conviction of an offence*

★**5-1071**   Section 14A of the 1989 Act was amended by section 86(5) of the Anti-social Behaviour Act 2003, not by section 86(4) (as stated in the main work).

### C. DRINKING BANNING ORDERS

#### (1) Summary

★**5-1093**   As from a day to be appointed, Part 2 (ss.22–33) of the Anti-social Behaviour, Crime and Policing Act 2014 (*post*, §§ 5-1210a *et seq.*), makes provision for criminal behaviour orders. Criminal behaviour orders replace anti-social behaviour orders on conviction under section 1C of the CDA 1998 (§ 5-1198 in the main work, and *post*) and drinking banning orders made on conviction of a criminal offence.

★   As from a day to be appointed, the 2014 Act, s.181(1), and Sched. 11, paras 44 and 50, repeal sections 1 to 14 of the VCRA 2006 (§§ 5-1094 *et seq.* in the main work). For saving and transitional provisions, see the 2014 Act, s.33 (*post*, § 5-1210l).

## (2) Legislation

### Violent Crime Reduction Act 2006, ss.1, 2

*Drinking banning orders*
 As to the repeal of section 1 of the 2006 Act, see *ante*, § 5-1093.                ★5-1094

*Duration of drinking banning orders*
 As to the repeal of section 2 of the 2006 Act, see *ante*, § 5-1093.                ★5-1095

### Violent Crime Reduction Act 2006, ss.6–9

*Orders on conviction in criminal proceedings*
 As to the repeal of section 6 of the 2006 Act, see *ante*, § 5-1093.                ★5-1096

*Supplementary provision about orders on conviction*
 As to the repeal of section 7 of the 2006 Act, see *ante*, § 5-1093.                ★5-1097

*Variation or discharge of orders under s.6*
 As to the repeal of section 8 of the 2006 Act, see *ante*, § 5-1093.                ★5-1098

*Interim orders*
 As to the repeal of section 9 of the 2006 Act, see *ante*, § 5-1093.                ★5-1099

**Breach of drinking banning orders**

 As to the repeal of section 11 of the 2006 Act, see *ante*, § 5-1093.                ★5-1100

**Approved courses**

 As to the repeal of section 12 of the 2006 Act, see *ante*, § 5-1093.                ★5-1101

### Violent Crime Reduction Act 2006, ss.13, 14

*Certificates of completion of approved courses*
 As to the repeal of section 13 of the 2006 Act, see *ante*, § 5-1093.                ★5-1102

*Interpretation of Chapter 1*
 As to the repeal of section 14 of the 2006 Act, see *ante*, § 5-1093.                ★5-1103

## F. Disqualification or Being Barred from Working with Children or Vulnerable Adults

### (2) Bars on working with children or vulnerable adults

#### Summary

 The Independent Safeguarding Authority was replaced by the "Disclosure and Barring Service"   **5-1123**
not the "Independent Barring Service" (as mistakenly stated in the main work).

## I. Serious Crime Prevention Orders

### (2) Legislation

#### Serious Crime Act 2007, ss.6–10

*Limited class of applicants for making of orders*
 With effect from March 27, 2014, the Public Bodies (Merger of the Director of Public Prosecu-   ★5-1157

tions and the Director of Revenue and Customs Prosecutions) Order 2014 (S.I. 2014 No. 834), art. 3(3), and Sched. 2, paras 45 and 46, repealed section 8(a)(ii) of the 2007 Act, subject to saving and transitional provisions (as to which, see *ante*, § 1-27).

*Notice requirements in relation to orders*

★**5-1159**     With effect from March 27, 2014, the Public Bodies (Merger of the Director of Public Prosecutions and the Director of Revenue and Customs Prosecutions) Order 2014 (S.I. 2014 No. 834), art. 3(3), and Sched. 2, paras 45 and 47, repealed section 10(4)(a)(ii) of the 2007 Act, subject to saving and transitional provisions (as to which, see *ante*, § 1-27).

### Serious Crime Act 2007, ss.42, 43

*Index of defined expressions: Part 1*

★**5-1191**     With effect from March 27, 2014, the Public Bodies (Merger of the Director of Public Prosecutions and the Director of Revenue and Customs Prosecutions) Order 2014 (S.I. 2014 No. 834), art. 3(3), and Sched. 2, paras 45 and 49, amended the table in section 43 of the 2007 Act, subject to saving and transitional provisions (as to which, see *ante*, § 1-27), so as to omit, in the entry relating to the Director of Public Prosecutions and other prosecutors, "Director of Revenue and Customs Prosecutions" and "7(2)".

### Serious Crime Act 2007, Sched. 2

*Functions of applicant authorities under Part 1*

★**5-1193**     With effect from March 27, 2014, the Public Bodies (Merger of the Director of Public Prosecutions and the Director of Revenue and Customs Prosecutions) Order 2014 (S.I. 2014 No. 834), art. 3(3), and Sched. 2, paras 45 and 52(1) and (2), amended Schedule 2 to the 2007 Act, subject to saving and transitional provisions (as to which, see *ante*, § 1-27), so as to insert, after paragraph 5, new paragraph 5A as follows—

> "5A. Section 21 of the Commissioners for Revenue and Customs Act 2005 (disclosure to prosecuting authority) has effect as if the purpose mentioned in subsection (1)(b) included the purpose of enabling the Director to exercise the Director's functions under this Part.".

★**5-1194**     With effect from March 27, 2014, the Public Bodies (Merger of the Director of Public Prosecutions and the Director of Revenue and Customs Prosecutions) Order 2014 (S.I. 2014 No. 834), art. 3(3), and Sched. 2, paras 45 and 52(1) and (4), repealed paragraphs 6 to 11 of Schedule 2 to the 2007 Act, subject to saving and transitional provisions (as to which, see *ante*, § 1-27).

## J. Anti-Social Behaviour Orders

### Crime and Disorder Act 1998, s.1C

*Orders on conviction in criminal proceedings*

★**5-1198**     As from a day to be appointed, the Anti-social Behaviour, Crime and Policing Act 2014, s.181(1), and Sched. 11, para. 24(a), repeal sections 1 to 1K of the 1998 Act (§§ 5-1198 *et seq.* in the main work). For saving and transitional provisions, see the 2014 Act, s.33 (*post*, § 5-1210l).

★     As from a day to be appointed, the 2014 Act, s.181(1), and Sched. 11, para. 50, repeal section 64 of the Police Reform Act 2002, section 86(1) to (4) of the Anti-social Behaviour Act 2003, sections 139(1) and (4), 140(1) and (3), and 141 of the SOCPA 2005, and sections 123 and 124 of the CJIA 2008 (see the main work).

★     As from a day to be appointed, Part 2 (ss.22-33) of the 2014 Act makes provision for criminal behaviour orders. These replace anti-social behaviour orders on conviction under section 1C of the 1998 Act (see the main work) and drinking banning orders on conviction (§§ 5-1093 *et seq.* in the main work, and *ante*). For Part 2 of the 2014 Act, see *post*, §§ 5-1210a *et seq.*

### Crime and Disorder Act 1998, s.1(5A), (7), (10), (10A), (10B), (10C), (10D), (10E), (11), (12)

★**5-1199**     As to the repeal of section 1 of the 1998 Act, see *ante*, § 5-1198.

As from a day to be appointed, the Anti-social Behaviour, Crime and Policing Act 2014, s.181(1), and Sched. 11, para. 50, repeal paragraph 192 of Schedule 9 to the PCC(S)A 2000, section 61 of the Police Reform Act 2002, section 85(4) of the Anti-social Behaviour Act 2003, sections 139(1) and (2) and 141 of the SOCPA 2005, and section 59(1) of the VCRA 2006 (see the main work).

**Crime and Disorder Act 1998, ss.1AA, 1AB**

*Individual support orders*

As to the repeal of section 1AA of the 1998 Act, see *ante*, § 5-1198.

★5-1200

As from a day to be appointed, the Anti-social Behaviour, Crime and Policing Act 2014, s.181(1), and Sched. 11, para. 50, repeal section 322 of the CJA 2003, paragraph 8 of Schedule 2 to the Children Act 2004, and section 124 of the CJIA 2008 (see the main work).

*Individual support orders: explanation, breach, amendment, etc.*

As to the repeal of section 1AB of the 1998 Act, see *ante*, § 5-1198.

★5-1201

As from a day to be appointed, the Anti-social Behaviour, Crime and Policing Act 2014, s.181(1), and Sched. 11, para. 50, repeal section 322 of the CJA 2003 and section 124 of the CJIA 2008 (see the main work).

## Authorities

*Necessity for, and ambit of, order*

For a case following *R. (Cooke) v. DPP* (see the main work), see *Pender v. DPP*, 177 J.P. 662, DC, where the court stressed the importance of the distinction between a likelihood or inevitability of disobeying an anti-social behaviour order under section 1C of the CDA 1998 (§ 5-1198 in the main work) and a lack of capacity to obey it.

5-1203

**Crime and Disorder Act 1998, ss.1CA, 1D, 1I**

*Variation and discharge of orders under section 1C*

As to the repeal of section 1CA of the 1998 Act, see *ante*, § 5-1198.

★5-1206

As from a day to be appointed, the Anti-social Behaviour, Crime and Policing Act 2014, s.181(1), and Sched. 11, para. 50, repeal section 140(1) and (4) of the SOCPA 2005 (see the main work).

*Interim orders*

As to the repeal of section 1D of the 1998 Act, see *ante*, § 5-1198.

★5-1208

As from a day to be appointed, the Anti-social Behaviour, Crime and Policing Act 2014, s.181(1), and Sched. 11, para. 50, repeal section 65 of the Police Reform Act 2002, and section 139(1) and (5) to (9) of the SOCPA 2005 (see the main work).

*Special measures for witnesses*

As to the repeal of section 1I of the 1998 Act, see *ante*, § 5-1198.

★5-1209

As from a day to be appointed, the Anti-social Behaviour, Crime and Policing Act 2014, s.181(1), and Sched. 11, para. 50, repeal section 143 of the SOCPA 2005, and paragraph 72 of Schedule 21 to the Coroners and Justice Act 2009 (see the main work).

## Review of anti-social behaviour orders

As to the repeal of sections 1 to 1K of the 1998 Act, see *ante*, § 5-1198.

★5-1210

As from a day to be appointed, the Anti-social Behaviour, Crime and Policing Act 2014, s.181(1), and Sched. 11, para. 50, repeal section 123 of the CJIA 2008 (see the main work).

JA. Criminal Behaviour Orders

**Anti-Social Behaviour, Crime and Policing Act 2014, ss.22–33**

[*Power to make orders*

**22.**—(1) This section applies where a person ("the offender") is convicted of an offence.

★5-1210a

(2) The court may make a criminal behaviour order against the offender if two conditions are met.

(3) The first condition is that the court is satisfied, beyond reasonable doubt, that the offender has engaged in behaviour that caused or was likely to cause harassment, alarm or distress to any person.

(4) The second condition is that the court considers that making the order will help in preventing the offender from engaging in such behaviour.

(5) A criminal behaviour order is an order which, for the purpose of preventing the offender from engaging in such behaviour—

(a)  prohibits the offender from doing anything described in the order;

(b)  requires the offender to do anything described in the order.

(6) The court may make a criminal behaviour order against the offender only if it is made in addition to—

(a)  a sentence imposed in respect of the offence, or

(b)  an order discharging the offender conditionally.

(7) The court may make a criminal behaviour order against the offender only on the application of the prosecution.

(8) The prosecution must find out the views of the local youth offending team before applying for a criminal behaviour order to be made if the offender will be under the age of 18 when the application is made.

(9) Prohibitions and requirements in a criminal behaviour order must, so far as practicable, be such as to avoid—

(a)  any interference with the times, if any, at which the offender normally works or attends school or any other educational establishment;

(b)  any conflict with the requirements of any other court order or injunction to which the offender may be subject.

(10) In this section "local youth offending team" means—

(a)  the youth offending team in whose area it appears to the prosecution that the offender lives, or

(b)  if it appears to the prosecution that the offender lives in more than one such area, whichever one or more of the relevant youth offending teams the prosecution thinks appropriate.]

Sections 22 to 33 of the 2014 Act come into force on a day to be appointed.

*[Proceedings on an application for an order*

★**5-1210b**   23.—(1) For the purpose of deciding whether to make a criminal behaviour order the court may consider evidence led by the prosecution and evidence led by the offender.

(2) It does not matter whether the evidence would have been admissible in the proceedings in which the offender was convicted.

(3) The court may adjourn any proceedings on an application for a criminal behaviour order even after sentencing the offender.

(4) If the offender does not appear for any adjourned proceedings the court may—

(a)  further adjourn the proceedings,

(b)  issue a warrant for the offender's arrest, or

(c)  hear the proceedings in the offender's absence.

(5) The court may not act under paragraph (b) of subsection (4) unless it is satisfied that the offender has had adequate notice of the time and place of the adjourned proceedings.

(6) The court may not act under paragraph (c) of subsection (4) unless it is satisfied that the offender—

(a)  has had adequate notice of the time and place of the adjourned proceedings, and

(b)  has been informed that if the offender does not appear for those proceedings the court may hear the proceedings in his or her absence.

(7) Subsection (8) applies in relation to proceedings in which a criminal behaviour order is made against an offender who is under the age of 18.

(8) In so far as the proceedings relate to the making of the order—

(a)  section 49 of the Children and Young Persons Act 1933 (restrictions on reports of proceedings in which children and young persons are concerned) does not apply in respect of the offender;

(b)  section 39 of that Act (power to prohibit publication of certain matters) does so apply.]

Sections 22 to 33 of the 2014 Act come into force on a day to be appointed.

*[Requirements included in orders*

**24.**—(1) A criminal behaviour order that includes a requirement must specify the person who is to     **★5-1210c**
be responsible for supervising compliance with the requirement.

The person may be an individual or an organisation.

(2) Before including a requirement, the court must receive evidence about its suitability and
enforceability from—

    (a)  the individual to be specified under subsection (1), if an individual is to be specified;

    (b)  an individual representing the organisation to be specified under subsection (1), if an
        organisation is to be specified.

(3) Before including two or more requirements, the court must consider their compatibility with
each other.

(4) It is the duty of a person specified under subsection (1)—

    (a)  to make any necessary arrangements in connection with the requirements for which the
        person has responsibility (the "relevant requirements");

    (b)  to promote the offender's compliance with the relevant requirements;

    (c)  if the person considers that the offender—

        (i)  has complied with all the relevant requirements, or

        (ii)  has failed to comply with a relevant requirement,

        to inform the prosecution and the appropriate chief officer of police.

(5) In subsection (4)(c) "the appropriate chief officer of police" means—

    (a)  the chief officer of police for the police area in which it appears to the person specified
        under subsection (1) that the offender lives, or

    (b)  if it appears to that person that the offender lives in more than one police area, whichever
        of the relevant chief officers of police that person thinks it most appropriate to inform.

(6) An offender subject to a requirement in a criminal behaviour order must—

    (a)  keep in touch with the person specified under subsection (1) in relation to that require-
        ment, in accordance with any instructions given by that person from time to time;

    (b)  notify the person of any change of address.

These obligations have effect as requirements of the order.]

Sections 22 to 33 of the 2014 Act come into force on a day to be appointed.

*[Duration of order etc*

**25.**—(1) A criminal behaviour order takes effect on the day it is made, subject to subsection (2).     **★5-1210d**

(2) If on the day a criminal behaviour order ("the new order") is made the offender is subject to
another criminal behaviour order ("the previous order"), the new order may be made so as to take
effect on the day on which the previous order ceases to have effect.

(3) A criminal behaviour order must specify the period ("the order period") for which it has effect.

(4) In the case of a criminal behaviour order made before the offender has reached the age of 18,
the order period must be a fixed period of—

    (a)  not less than 1 year, and

    (b)  not more than 3 years.

(5) In the case of a criminal behaviour order made after the offender has reached the age of 18,
the order period must be—

    (a)  a fixed period of not less than 2 years, or

    (b)  an indefinite period (so that the order has effect until further order).

(6) A criminal behaviour order may specify periods for which particular prohibitions or requirements have effect.]

Sections 22 to 33 of the 2014 Act come into force on a day to be appointed.

*[Interim orders*

**26.**—(1) This section applies where a court adjourns the hearing of an application for a criminal     **★5-1210e**
behaviour order.

(2) The court may make a criminal behaviour order that lasts until the final hearing of the application or until further order ("an interim order") if the court thinks it just to do so.

(3) Section 22(6) to (8) and section 25(3) to (5) do not apply in relation to the making of an interim
order.

(4) Subject to that, the court has the same powers whether or not the criminal behaviour order is
an interim order.]

Sections 22 to 33 of the 2014 Act come into force on a day to be appointed.

*[Variation or discharge of orders*

**★5-1210f**   **27.**—(1) A criminal behaviour order may be varied or discharged by the court which made it on the application of—

    (a)  the offender, or

    (b)  the prosecution.

(2) If an application by the offender under this section is dismissed, the offender may make no further application under this section without—

    (a)  the consent of the court which made the order, or

    (b)  the agreement of the prosecution.

(3) If an application by the prosecution under this section is dismissed, the prosecution may make no further application under this section without—

    (a)  the consent of the court which made the order, or

    (b)  the agreement of the offender.

(4) The power to vary an order includes power to include an additional prohibition or requirement in the order or to extend the period for which a prohibition or requirement has effect.

(5) Section 24 applies to additional requirements included under subsection (4) as it applies to requirements included in a new order.

(6) In the case of a criminal behaviour order made by a magistrates' court, the references in this section to the court which made the order include a reference to any magistrates' court acting in the same local justice area as that court.]

Sections 22 to 33 of the 2014 Act come into force on a day to be appointed.

*[Review of orders*

**★5-1210g**   **28.**—(1) If—

    (a)  a person subject to a criminal behaviour order will be under the age of 18 at the end of a review period (see subsection (2)),

    (b)  the term of the order runs until the end of that period or beyond, and

    (c)  the order is not discharged before the end of that period,

a review of the operation of the order must be carried out before the end of that period.

(2) The "review periods" are—

    (a)  the period of 12 months beginning with—

      (i)  the day on which the criminal behaviour order takes effect, or

      (ii)  if during that period the order is varied under section 27, the day on which it is varied (or most recently varied, if the order is varied more than once);

    (b)  a period of 12 months beginning with—

      (i)  the day after the end of the previous review period, or

      (ii)  if during that period of 12 months the order is varied under section 27, the day on which it is varied (or most recently varied, if the order is varied more than once).

(3) A review under this section must include consideration of—

    (a)  the extent to which the offender has complied with the order;

    (b)  the adequacy of any support available to the offender to help him or her comply with it;

    (c)  any matters relevant to the question whether an application should be made for the order to be varied or discharged.

(4) Those carrying out or participating in a review under this section must have regard to any relevant guidance issued by the Secretary of State under section 32 when considering—

    (a)  how the review should be carried out;

    (b)  what particular matters the review should deal with;

    (c)  what action (if any) it would be appropriate to take as a result of the findings of the review.]

Sections 22 to 33 of the 2014 Act come into force on a day to be appointed.

*[Carrying out and participating in reviews*

**★5-1210h**   **29.**—(1) A review under section 28 is to be carried out by the chief officer of police of the police force maintained for the police area in which the offender lives or appears to be living.

(2) The chief officer, in carrying out a review under section 28, must act in co-operation with the council for the local government area in which the offender lives or appears to be living; and the council must co-operate in the carrying out of the review.

(3) The chief officer may invite the participation in the review of any other person or body.

(4) In this section "local government area" means—

    (a)  in relation to England, a district or London borough, the City of London, the Isle of Wight and the Isles of Scilly;

    (b)  in relation to Wales, a county or a county borough.

For the purposes of this section, the council for the Inner and Middle Temples is the Common Council of the City of London.]

Sections 22 to 33 of the 2014 Act come into force on a day to be appointed.

*[Breach of order*

    **30.**—(1) A person who without reasonable excuse—     ★**5-1210i**

    (a)  does anything he or she is prohibited from doing by a criminal behaviour order, or

    (b)  fails to do anything he or she is required to do by a criminal behaviour order,

commits an offence.

(2) A person guilty of an offence under this section is liable—

    (a)  on summary conviction, to imprisonment for a period not exceeding 6 months or to a fine, or to both;

    (b)  on conviction on indictment, to imprisonment for a period not exceeding 5 years or to a fine, or to both.

(3) If a person is convicted of an offence under this section, it is not open to the court by or before which the person is convicted to make an order under subsection (1)(b) of section 12 of the Powers of Criminal Courts (Sentencing) Act 2000 (conditional discharge).

(4) In proceedings for an offence under this section, a copy of the original criminal behaviour order, certified by the proper officer of the court which made it, is admissible as evidence of its having been made and of its contents to the same extent that oral evidence of those things is admissible in those proceedings.

(5) In relation to any proceedings for an offence under this section that are brought against a person under the age of 18—

    (a)  section 49 of the Children and Young Persons Act 1933 (restrictions on reports of proceedings in which children and young persons are concerned) does not apply in respect of the person;

    (b)  section 45 of the Youth Justice and Criminal Evidence Act 1999 (power to restrict reporting of criminal proceedings involving persons under 18) does so apply.

(6) If, in relation to any proceedings mentioned in subsection (5), the court does exercise its power to give a direction under section 45 of the Youth Justice and Criminal Evidence Act 1999, it must give its reasons for doing so.]

Sections 22 to 33 of the 2014 Act come into force on a day to be appointed.

*[Special measures for witnesses*

    **31.**—(1) Chapter 1 of Part 2 of the Youth Justice and Criminal Evidence Act 1999 (special measures   ★**5-1210j** directions in the case of vulnerable and intimidated witnesses) applies to criminal behaviour order proceedings as it applies to criminal proceedings, but with—

    (a)  the omission of the provisions of that Act mentioned in subsection (2) (which make provision appropriate only in the context of criminal proceedings), and

    (b)  any other necessary modifications.

(2) The provisions are—

    (a)  section 17(4) to (7);

    (b)  section 21(4C)(e);

    (c)  section 22A;

    (d)  section 27(10);

    (e)  section 32.

(3) Rules of court made under or for the purposes of Chapter 1 of Part 2 of that Act apply to criminal behaviour order proceedings—

    (a)  to the extent provided by rules of court, and

    (b)  subject to any modifications provided by rules of court.

(4) Section 47 of that Act (restrictions on reporting special measures directions etc) applies with any necessary modifications—

    (a)  to a direction under section 19 of that Act as applied by this section;

    (b)  to a direction discharging or varying such a direction.

Sections 49 and 51 of that Act (offences) apply accordingly.

(5) In this section "criminal behaviour order proceedings" means proceedings in a magistrates' court or the Crown Court so far as relating to the issue whether to make a criminal behaviour order.]

Sections 22 to 33 of the 2014 Act come into force on a day to be appointed.

*[Guidance*

**★5-1210k**      **32.**—(1) The Secretary of State may issue guidance to—

    (a) chief officers of police, and

    (b) the councils mentioned in section 29(2),

about the exercise of their functions under this Part.

(2) The Secretary of State may revise any guidance issued under this section.

(3) The Secretary of State must arrange for any guidance issued or revised under this section to be published.]

Sections 22 to 33 of the 2014 Act come into force on a day to be appointed.

*[Saving and transitional provision*

**★5-1210l**      **33.**—(1) The repeal or amendment by this Act of provisions about any of the orders specified in subsection (2) does not—

    (a) prevent an order specified in that subsection from being made in connection with criminal proceedings begun before the commencement day;

    (b) apply in relation to an order specified in that subsection which is made in connection with criminal proceedings begun before that day;

    (c) apply in relation to anything done in connection with such an order.

(2) The orders are—

    (a) an order under section 1C of the Crime and Disorder Act 1998 (orders on conviction in criminal proceedings);

    (b) an individual support order under section 1AA of that Act made in connection with an order under section 1C of that Act;

    (c) a drinking banning order under section 6 of the Violent Crime Reduction Act 2006 (orders on conviction in criminal proceedings).

(3) As from the commencement day there may be no variation of an order specified in subsection (2) that extends the period of the order or of any provision of the order.

(4) At the end of the period of 5 years beginning with the commencement day—

    (a) this Part has effect in relation to any order specified in subsection (2) that is still in force as if the provisions of the order were provisions of a criminal behaviour order;

    (b) subsections (1) to (3) cease to have effect.

This Part, as it applies by virtue of paragraph (a), has effect with any necessary modifications (and with any modifications specified in an order under section 185(7)).

(5) In deciding whether to make a criminal behaviour order a court may take account of conduct occurring up to 1 year before the commencement day.

(6) In this section "commencement day" means the day on which this Part comes into force.]

Sections 22 to 33 of the 2014 Act come into force on a day to be appointed.

# XI. ORDERS UNDER THE MENTAL HEALTH ACT 1983

## (1) Hospital and guardianship orders

### Inter-relationship with discretionary life sentences

**5-1238**      *R. v. Saunders* is now reported at [2014] 1 Cr.App.R.(S.) 45, *sub nom. R. v. Saunders; R. v. G.; R. v. Edwards.*

# XII. RECOMMENDATION FOR DEPORTATION

**Immigration Act 1971, Sched. 3, paras 2–6**

*Detention or control pending deportation*

**★5-1261**      As from a day to be appointed, the Immigration Act 2014, s.4 and Sched. 1, para. 2(2), amend paragraph 2(4) of Schedule 3 to the 1971 Act so as to substitute the words "to 18A" for ", 18".

Paragraph 2 of Schedule 3 to the 1971 Act was considered in *R. (Francis) v. Secretary of State for the Home Department, post,* § 5-1265.

*Effect of appeals*

As from a day to be appointed, the Immigration Act 2014, s.73(6), and Sched. 9, para. 9, amend paragraph 3 of Schedule 3 to the 1971 Act so as to substitute the number "33A" for the number "33". ★**5-1262**

A failure by the Secretary of State to follow a policy, or the application of an unlawful policy, will not undermine the lawfulness of a person's detention under paragraph 2(1) or (3) (detention pending deportation following recommendation for deportation by court; detention pending removal) of Schedule 3 to the 1971 Act (§ 5-1261 in the main work): *R. (Francis) v. Secretary of State for the Home Department* [2014] 1 All E.R. 68, QBD (H.H. Judge McKenna, sitting as a deputy High Court judge) (considering, *inter alia, R. (Lumba) v. Secretary of State for the Home Department (JUSTICE intervening); Same v. Same (No. 2) (Same intervening); R. (Mighty) v. Same (Same intervening)* (as to which, see the main work)). **5-1265**

## Criteria for exercise of power to make recommendation

*F.V. (Italy) v. Secretary of State for the Home Department* is now reported at [2013] 1 W.L.R. 3339. **5-1268**

## Criterion of "potential detriment"

In *R. v. Ul Haq* [2014] 1 Cr.App.R.(S.) 52, CA, it was found that an offender's continued presence in the United Kingdom would be to its detriment such as to justify a recommendation for deportation under section 6 of the Immigration Act 1971 (§ 5-1257 in the main work), notwithstanding that he was not a "foreign criminal" within the UK Borders Act 2007 (§ 5-1267 in the main work) and that he would also be subject to a sexual offences prevention order; he had committed a series of offences (four offences of sexual assault (indecent touching over clothing) and one of outraging public decency (masturbating under his clothing for a prolonged period on a tube train), arising out of his targeting of lone women on the London public transport system) that were not insignificant in nature, particularly for the victims, and the judge had found him to be a sexual predator; the sexual offences prevention order, which prohibited him from travelling on specified public transport routes for five years, could provide only partial protection, as it was limited in its duration and geographic extent. ★**5-1271**

## XIV. ORDERS AGAINST PARENTS OR GUARDIANS

### (2) Binding over orders

#### Power of Criminal Courts (Sentencing) Act 2000, s.150

## Binding over of parent or guardian

The 2013 criminal practice directions (see the main work) are now reported at [2013] 1 W.L.R. 3164. **5-1281**

### (3) Parenting orders

#### Crime and Disorder Act 1998, ss.8–10

*Parenting orders*

As from a day to be appointed, the Anti-social Behaviour, Crime and Policing Act 2014, s.181(1), and Sched. 11, para 25, amend section 8 of the 1998 Act so as (i) in subsection (1)(b), to substitute the words "an injunction is granted under section 1 of the Anti-social Behaviour, Crime and Policing Act 2014, an order is made under section 22 of that Act or a" for the words "an anti-social behaviour order or", (ii) in subsection (1)(c), to omit the words ", except in a case where section 8A below applies (parenting order on breach of anti-social behaviour order)", and (iii) in subsection (6)(a), to substitute the words "the order being made or the injunction granted" for the words "behaviour which led to". ★**5-1282**

★　As from a day to be appointed, the 2014 Act, s.181(1), and Sched. 11, para 55, further amend section 8 of the 1998 Act so as (i) in each of subsections (1)(b) and (6)(a), to substitute the words "sexual harm prevention order" for the words "sexual offences prevention order", and (ii) to substitute, for subsection (9), new subsection (9) as follows—

"(9) In this section 'sexual harm prevention order' means an order under section 103A of the Sexual Offences Act 2003 (sexual harm prevention orders).".

★　As to the repeal of section 41 of the Crime and Security Act 2010, see *post*, § 5-1284.

*Parenting order on breach of anti-social behaviour order*

★5-1283　As from a day to be appointed, the Anti-social Behaviour, Crime and Policing Act 2014, s.181(1), and Sched. 11, para. 24(c), repeal section 8A of the 1998 Act. For saving and transitional provision, see the 2014 Act, s.33, *ante*, § 5-1210l.

★　As to the repeal of section 41 of the Crime and Security Act 2010, see *post*, § 5-1284.

*Parenting orders: supplemental*

★5-1284　Subsection (1B) of section 9 of the CDA 1998 was inserted by the Anti-social Behaviour Act 2003, s.85(1) and (8), as follows—

"(1B) If an anti-social behaviour order is made in respect of a person under the age of 16 the court which makes the order—
(a)　must make a parenting order if it is satisfied that the relevant condition is fulfilled;
(b)　if it is not so satisfied, must state in open court that it is not and why it is not.".

★　As from a day to be appointed, the Anti-social Behaviour, Crime and Policing Act 2014, s.181(1), and Sched. 11, para. 26, amend section 9 of the 1998 Act so as (i) in subsection (1) (see the main work), to omit the words ", other than an offence under section 1(10) above in respect of an anti-social behaviour order,", (ii) in subsection (1B) (*ante*), to substitute the words "an injunction under section 1 of the Anti-social Behaviour, Crime and Policing Act 2014 is granted or an order is made under section 22 of that Act" for the words "an anti-social behaviour order", and to insert the words "grants the injunction or" after the word "which", (iii) in subsection (2) (see the main work), to omit paragraph (d) and the word "or" before it, and to omit the words "(including any report prepared under section 1(1C))" in the text after paragraph (d), and (iv) to repeal subsection (2AA) (which is not yet in force (see the main work)).

As from a day to be appointed, the 2014 Act, s.181(1), and Sched. 11, para. 46, repeal sections 40 and 41 of the Crime and Security Act 2010 (see the main work).

*Appeals against parenting orders*

★5-1285　As to the repeal of section 41 of the Crime and Security Act 2010, see *ante*, § 5-1284.

★　With effect from April 22, 2014, the provisions of the Crime and Courts Act 2013 referred to in the main work were brought into force: Crime and Courts Act 2013 (Commencement No. 10 and Transitional Provision) Order 2014 (S.I. 2014 No. 954).

## XV. MISCELLANEOUS MATTERS

### B. ALTERATION OF SENTENCE

### Variation after expiration of relevant time limit

5-1293　*R. v. Gordon* (see the main work) is no longer cited at § 5-646 in the main work. Its reference is [2007] 2 Cr.App.R.(S.) 66, CA.

### D. SURCHARGES

### Criminal Justice Act 2003, ss.161A, 161B

*Court's duty to order payment of surcharge*

5-1298　The Prevention of Social Housing Fraud Act 2013 came into force in England (to the extent that it was not already in force) on October 15, 2013: Prevention of Social Housing Fraud Act 2013 (Commencement) (England) Order 2013 (S.I. 2013 No. 2622).

As to the further commencement of the Prevention of Social Housing Fraud Act 2013, see *ante*, § 5-169.

In *R. v. Bailey*; *R. v. Kirk*; *R. v. Tote* [2014] 1 Cr.App.R.(S.) 59, CA, it was held: (i) the Criminal Justice Act 2003 (Surcharge) Order 2012 (S.I. 2012 No. 1696) (§§ 5-1300 *et seq.* in the main work) does not apply where the court deals with a person for any offence committed before October 1, 2012 (art. 7(2)); where it is alleged that an offence was committed between dates that straddle October 1, 2012, although the amount of judicial time to be taken on this issue should reflect its relative importance, by analogy with *R. v. Harries* (as to which, see § 5-529 in the main work), the court should take a view on the evidence so that the appropriate order can be made; in the absence of a clear answer, lengthy analysis is unnecessary and the issue should be resolved in favour of the offender; (ii) if any single offence for which the court is dealing with an offender was committed when the offender was under 18, the relevant table for assessing the surcharge is Table 1 in the schedule (arts 3 and 5); (iii) offences taken into consideration are not "dealt with" in the sense expressed in the 2012 order, and should be ignored when considering a victim surcharge; (iv) on the basis that the amount of the surcharge is driven entirely by the sentence, where a court makes an order in these terms, "The surcharge provisions apply to this case and the order can be drawn up accordingly.", it will be the duty of the advocates to ensure that the sum identified is correct, and this should be done on the day that sentence is passed; this should be confirmed with the clerk of the court but, in the absence of agreement, the matter should be referred to the court; however, if submissions based on section 161A(3) of the CJA 2003 (surcharge to be reduced if it would be appropriate to make a compensation order and offender has insufficient means to pay both) are to be made, a judicial decision will be required; (v) by analogy with *R. v. Gordon* [2007] 2 Cr.App.R.(S.) 66, CA (making allowance for time spent in custody on remand), if an error has been made in the record, it should be possible for the record to be corrected well within "the appropriate time", but if it is not, and an appeal becomes necessary, the prosecution should be notified and an attempt made to agree the position; the application for leave to appeal should then set out both the facts and the agreement; if the position is agreed, the matter will then be remitted by the Registrar of Criminal Appeals directly to the Crown Court for the error to be corrected; there will be no need for a representation order and the offender should be informed that as no purpose would be served by attendance, the court will assume that he does not intend to exercise his right to attend unless informed to the contrary within 28 days; this approach will only apply where the mistake has been to the detriment of the offender, as section 11(3) of the CAA 1968 (*ibid.*, § 7-125) will prevent the court from imposing or increasing a surcharge that is less than the order mandates, unless it reduces some other element of the sentence. As to (v), see CLW/13/42/2.

*Amount of surcharge*

As to the provisions of S.I. 2012 No. 1696 (as to which, see the main work), see *ante*, § 5-1298.   **5-1300**

CHAPTER 6

# COSTS AND CRIMINAL DEFENCE

## I. COSTS

### A. INTRODUCTION

**Practice Direction**

*Practice Direction (Costs in Criminal Proceedings)* (see the main work) is now reported at [2013] 1   **6-2** W.L.R. 3255, *sub nom. Practice Direction (Criminal Proceedings: Costs)*.

## B. Prosecution of Offences Act 1985

### (1) Award of costs out of central funds

#### (a) *Defence costs*

##### Prosecution of Offences Act 1985, ss.16, 16A

**6-4**     With effect from January 27, 2014, section 16A of the 1985 Act was amended by the Costs in Criminal Cases (Legal Costs) (Exceptions) Regulations 2014 (S.I. 2014 No. 130) so as (i) to substitute ", C or D" for "or C" in subsection (2), and (ii) to insert new subsections (5A) and (11) as follows—

"(5A) Condition D is that—
    (a) the accused is an individual,
    (b) the order is made under section 16(2),
    (c) the legal costs were incurred in relevant Crown Court proceedings, and
    (d) the Director of Legal Aid Casework has made a determination of financial ineligibility in relation to the accused and those proceedings
(and condition D continues to be met if the determination is withdrawn).";
    "(11) In subsection (5A)—
      'determination of financial ineligibility', in relation to an individual and proceedings, means a determination under section 21 of the Legal Aid, Sentencing and Punishment of Offenders Act 2012 that the individual's financial resources are such that the individual is not eligible for representation under section 16 of that Act for the purposes of the proceedings;
      'Director of Legal Aid Casework' means the civil servant designated under section 4(1) of the Legal Aid, Sentencing and Punishment of Offenders Act 2012;
      'relevant Crown Court proceedings' means any of the following—
    (a) proceedings in the Crown Court in respect of an offence for which the accused has been sent by a magistrates' court to the Crown Court for trial;
    (b) proceedings in the Crown Court relating to an offence in respect of which a bill of indictment has been preferred by virtue of section 2(2)(b) of the Administration of Justice (Miscellaneous Provisions) Act 1933;
    (c) proceedings in the Crown Court following an order by the Court of Appeal or the Supreme Court for a retrial.".

### Principles governing the exercise of the discretion

**6-11**     *Practice Direction (Costs in Criminal Proceedings)* (see the main work) is now reported at [2013] 1 W.L.R. 3255, *sub nom. Practice Direction (Criminal Proceedings: Costs).*

### Amount of award

**6-15**     *Practice Direction (Costs in Criminal Proceedings)* (see the main work) is now reported at [2013] 1 W.L.R. 3255, *sub nom. Practice Direction (Criminal Proceedings: Costs).*

#### (b) *Prosecution costs*

### Principles governing the exercise of the discretion

**6-24**     *Practice Direction (Costs in Criminal Proceedings)* (see the main work) is now reported at [2013] 1 W.L.R. 3255, *sub nom. Practice Direction (Criminal Proceedings: Costs).*

### (2) Award of costs against accused

### Relevance of means

**6-29**     *Practice Direction (Costs in Criminal Proceedings)* (see the main work) is now reported at [2013] 1 W.L.R. 3255, *sub nom. Practice Direction (Criminal Proceedings: Costs).*
  ★     *R. (Gray) v. Aylesbury Crown Court* is now reported at [2014] 1 W.L.R. 818, *sub nom. R. (Gray) v. Crown Court at Aylesbury.*

## Several defendants

*Practice Direction (Costs in Criminal Proceedings)* (see the main work) is now reported at [2013] 1    **6-31**
W.L.R. 3255, *sub nom. Practice Direction (Criminal Proceedings: Costs)*.

*R. (Gray) v. Aylesbury Crown Court* is now reported at [2014] 1 W.L.R. 818, *sub nom. R. (Gray) v.*    ★
*Crown Court at Aylesbury*.

## The relationship between sentence and costs

*R. (Gray) v. Aylesbury Crown Court* is now reported at [2014] 1 W.L.R. 818, *sub nom. R. (Gray) v.*    **★6-36**
*Crown Court at Aylesbury*.

## Practice and procedure

*Practice Direction (Costs in Criminal Proceedings)* (see the main work) is now reported at [2013] 1    **6-38**
W.L.R. 3255, *sub nom. Practice Direction (Criminal Proceedings: Costs)*.

### (4) Costs against legal representatives, etc.

## Procedure

*Practice Direction (Costs in Criminal Proceedings)* (see the main work) is now reported at [2013] 1    **6-42**
W.L.R. 3255, *sub nom. Practice Direction (Criminal Proceedings: Costs)*.

## "improper", "unreasonable", "negligent"

*Evidential issues*

The 2013 criminal practice directions (see the main work) are now reported at [2013] 1 W.L.R.    **6-48**
3164.

## C. Costs in Criminal Cases (General) Regulations 1986 (S.I. 1986 No. 1335)

### Part II – Costs unnecessarily or improperly incurred (reg. 3)

In *R. (Maninder Singh) v. Ealing Magistrates' Court and CPS*, 178 J.P. 253, DC, it was held that a    **★6-57**
mere mistake without repetition can be grounds for a costs order under section 19 of the Prosecution of Offences Act 1985 (costs unnecessarily or improperly incurred (§ 6-39 in the main work))
and regulation 3 of the 1986 regulations (see the main work), neither of which say anything about
the improper act or omission having to be repeated. There is no doctrine in this area that every
dog is entitled to one bite. While, in the leading case on the interpretation of section 19 to date
(*DPP v. Denning* (see the main work)), there had been repeated failures, that case predated the
introduction of the overriding objective in the Criminal Procedure Rules (see now the Criminal
Procedure Rules 2013 (S.I. 2013 No. 1554), Pt 1 (§ 4-114 in the main work)), of dealing with a
case justly, which includes dealing with it efficiently and expeditiously. In that context, the culture
of adjournment plaguing the criminal justice system will not be defeated unless, in appropriate
cases, courts are prepared to use their powers to make orders for costs under section 19. The
court also held that, where it is clear that someone on the prosecution side was at fault, an order
cannot be resisted on the basis that it is not possible to say whether it was the police or the CPS
who were at fault, as the prosecution are indivisible for this purpose.

### Part III—Costs out of central funds (regs 4–13)

*Application and definitions*

With effect from January 27, 2014, regulation 4 of S.I. 1986 No. 1335 is amended by the Costs    **6-67**
in Criminal Cases (General) (Amendment) (No. 2) Regulations 2013 (S.I. 2013 No. 2830), so as to
insert three new definitions as follows, the first two after the definition of "costs order" and the
third after the definition of "presiding judge"—

> "'determination of financial ineligibility' in relation to an individual and proceedings, means a
> determination under section 21 of the Legal Aid, Sentencing and Punishment of Offenders
> Act 2012 that the individual's financial resources are such that the individual is not eligible
> for representation under section 16 of that Act for the purposes of the proceedings;

'Director of Legal Aid Casework' means the civil servant designated under section 4(1) of the Legal Aid, Sentencing and Punishment of Offenders Act 2012;

'relevant Crown Court proceedings' means any of the following—

(a) proceedings in the Crown Court in respect of an offence for which the accused has been sent by a magistrates' court to the Crown Court for trial;

(b) proceedings in the Crown Court relating to an offence in respect of which a bill of indictment has been preferred by virtue of section 2(2)(b) of the Administration of Justice (Miscellaneous Provisions) Act 1933;

(c) proceedings in the Crown Court following an order by the Court of Appeal or the Supreme Court for a retrial.".

### Determination of costs

**6-71**   With effect from January 27, 2014, regulation 7(6) of S.I. 1986 No. 1335 is amended by S.I. 2013 No. 2830 (*ante*, § 6-67), so as to omit "or" at the end of paragraph (b), to insert "; or" at the end of paragraph (c), and to insert a new paragraph (d) as follows—

"(d) the order was made under section 16(2) of the Act and—

(i) the legal costs were incurred in relevant Crown Court proceedings; and

(ii) the Director of Legal Aid Casework has made a determination of financial ineligibility in relation to the accused and those proceedings".

### Appeals to the High Court

**6-76**   *Practice Direction (Costs in Criminal Proceedings)* (see the main work) is now reported at [2013] 1 W.L.R. 3255, *sub nom. Practice Direction (Criminal Proceedings: Costs)*.

#### Part IV—Miscellaneous applications of the Act (reg. 14)

### Application of sections 16, 17 and 18 of the Act

**6-81**   Regulation 14(2) of the 1986 regulations has been amended by the Costs in Criminal Cases (General) (Amendment) Regulations 2013 (S.I. 2013 No. 2526), so as, in paragraph (a), to substitute "sent" for the second "committed" and to omit the words from "and as if" to the end, and, in paragraph (b), to omit the words from "and as if" to the end.

#### Part V—Allowances to witnesses (regs 15–25)

### Definitions

**6-82**   Regulation 15 of the 1986 regulations has been amended by the Costs in Criminal Cases (General) (Amendment) Regulations 2013 (S.I. 2013 No. 2526), so as to substitute "sent" for "committed" in the definition of "proceedings in a criminal cause or matter".

### General

**6-83**   Regulation 16(1) of the 1986 regulations has been amended by the Costs in Criminal Cases (General) (Amendment) Regulations 2013 (S.I. 2013 No. 2526), so as to insert a new paragraph (bb), as follows—

"(bb) an intermediary is required to assist the defendant; or".

## D. MISCELLANEOUS ENACTMENTS

## (12) Criminal Procedure Rules 2013 (S.I. 2013 No. 1554)

#### Criminal Procedure Rules 2013 (S.I. 2013 No. 1554), Pt 76

### When this Part applies

**6-109**   With effect from April 7, 2014, rule 76.1 of the 2013 rules is amended by rule 9(a) of the Criminal Procedure (Amendment No. 2) Rules 2013 (S.I. 2013 No. 3183), so as to insert "or rule 76.7" after "rule 76.6" in paragraph (1)(c).

### Costs on an application

**6-115**   With effect from April 7, 2014, rule 76.7 of the 2013 rules is amended by rule 9(d) of the Criminal Procedure (Amendment No. 2) Rules 2013 (S.I. 2013 No. 3183), so as to substitute a new paragraph (1), as follows—

"(1) This rule—

    (a) applies where the court can order a party to pay another person's costs in a case in which—

        (i) the court decides an application for the production in evidence of a copy of a bank record,

        (ii) a magistrates' court or the Crown Court decides an application to terminate a football banning order,

        (iii) a magistrates' court or the Crown Court decides an application to terminate a disqualification for having custody of a dog,

        (iv) the Crown Court allows an application to withdraw a witness summons, or

        (v) the Crown Court decides an application relating to a deferred prosecution agreement under rule 12.5 (breach), rule 12.6 (variation) or rule 12.7 (lifting suspension of prosecution);

    (b) authorises the Crown Court, in addition to its other powers, to order a party to pay another party's costs on an application to that court under rule 12.5, 12.6 or 12.7.".

### E. PRACTICE DIRECTION

*Practice Direction (Costs in Criminal Proceedings)* (see the main work) is now reported at [2013] 1    **6-123**
W.L.R. 3255, *sub nom. Practice Direction (Criminal Proceedings: Costs)*.

### F. ENFORCING ORDERS AS TO COSTS (AND COMPENSATION)

### (1) Statute

#### Administration of Justice Act 1970, s.41

The Prevention of Social Housing Fraud Act 2013 came into force in England (to the extent    **6-161**
that it was not already in force) on October 15, 2013: Prevention of Social Housing Fraud Act
2013 (Commencement) (England) Order 2013 (S.I. 2013 No. 2622).

The provisions of the Crime and Courts Act 2013 referred to in the main work came into force    ★
on April 22, 2014: Crime and Courts Act 2013 (Commencement No. 10 and Transitional Provision) Order 2014 (S.I. 2014 No. 954).

#### Administration of Justice Act 1970, Sched. 9

*Miscellaneous orders for costs, compensation, etc.*

As to the commencement of the Prevention of Social Housing Fraud Act 2013, see *ante*, §    **6-165**
6-161.

*Costs awarded by the Court of Appeal (Criminal Division)*

As to the commencement of the Prevention of Social Housing Fraud Act 2013, see *ante*, §    **6-168**
6-161.

#### Magistrates' Courts Act 1980, ss.75A, 76

*Enforcement of sums adjudged to be paid*

The provisions of the Tribunals, Courts and Enforcement Act 2007 referred to in the main    **★6-169**
work came into force on April 6, 2014: Tribunals, Courts and Enforcement Act 2007 (Commencement No. 11) Order 2014 (S.I. 2014 No. 768).

The provisions of the Crime and Courts Act 2013 referred to in the main work came into force    ★
on April 22, 2014: Crime and Courts Act 2013 (Commencement No. 10 and Transitional Provision) Order 2014 (S.I. 2014 No. 954).

### II. LEGAL AID

### A. INTRODUCTION

**Right to legal representation**

For a case considering whether it had been appropriate to stay a prosecution of what was al-    **★6-172** leged to be a substantial and complex fraud where no counsel were available to conduct the defence at the date fixed for trial or, in the trial judge's view, for the foreseeable future, on account of the alleged inadequacy of the fees payable to counsel appearing for legally-aided defendants, see *R. v. Crawley, ante*, § 4-81.

## B. Primary Legislation

### Legal Aid, Sentencing and Punishment of Offenders Act 2012, ss.21–24, 27

*Information about financial resources*

**6-218**    The Legal Aid (Information about Financial Resources) Regulations 2013 (S.I. 2013 No. 628) (as to which, see the main work) have been amended by the Legal Aid (Information about Financial Resources) (Amendment) Regulations 2013 (S.I. 2013 No. 2726), *inter alia*, to prescribe additional information that may be requested for the purposes of facilitating a determination about an individual's financial eligibility for legal aid.

★    The Legal Aid (Information about Financial Resources) Regulations 2013 (*ante*) have been further amended by the Legal Aid (Information about Financial Resources) (Amendment) Regulations 2014 (S.I. 2014 No. 901), so as to add maternity benefit to the list of prescribed benefits.

*Enforcement*

★**6-220**    The provisions of the Crime and Courts Act 2013 referred to in the main work came into force on April 22, 2014: Crime and Courts Act 2013 (Commencement No. 10 and Transitional Provision) Order 2014 (S.I. 2014 No. 954).

## C. Secondary Legislation

### Criminal legal aid

**6-231**    The Criminal Legal Aid (General) (Amendment) Regulations 2013 (S.I. 2013 No. 2790) have amended regulations 2 (interpretation), 12 (advice and assistance for criminal proceedings: prescribed conditions), 24 (determinations for representation: proceedings in the magistrates' court) and 25 (determinations for representation: certain proceedings in the Crown Court) of the Criminal Legal Aid (General) Regulations 2013 (S.I. 2013 No. 9).

### Criminal Legal Aid (General) Regulations 2013 (S.I. 2013 No. 9), Pt 1

*Interpretation*

**6-233**    With effect from January 27, 2014, the Criminal Legal Aid (General) (Amendment) Regulations 2013 (S.I. 2013 No. 2790), reg. 3, amended regulation 2 of S.I. 2013 No. 9, so as to insert a new definition after the definition of "criminal legal aid", as follows—

> "'Financial Resources Regulations' means the Criminal Legal Aid (Financial Resources) Regulations 2013;".

### Criminal Legal Aid (General) Regulations 2013 (S.I. 2013 No. 9), Pt 3

*Criminal proceedings*

★**6-240**    Committal proceedings for contempt other than in the face of the court are eligible for criminal legal aid by virtue of regulation 9(v) of the 2013 regulations (as to which, see the main work): *King's Lynn and West Norfolk Council v. Bunning (Legal Aid Agency, interested party)* [2014] 2 All E.R. 1095, QBD (Blake J.). As to this case, see also *post*, § 6-277.

### Criminal Legal Aid (General) Regulations 2013 (S.I. 2013 No. 9), Pt 4

*Prescribed conditions*

**6-243**    With effect from December 2, 2013, the Criminal Legal Aid (General) (Amendment) Regulations 2013 (S.I. 2013 No. 2790), reg. 4(1) and (2), amended regulation 12 of S.I. 2013 No. 9, so as to substitute a new paragraph (2)(d), as follows—

> "(d)  require advice and assistance regarding—
> > (i)  the application of the provisions in Chapter 6 of Part 12 of the Criminal Justice Act

2003 or in Chapter 2 of Part 2 of the Crime (Sentences) Act 1997, which determine
when a prisoner is either entitled to be released by the Secretary of State or eligible for
consideration by the Parole Board for a direction to be released; or

(ii) the application of the provisions in Chapter 2 of Part 5 of the Powers of Criminal
Courts (Sentencing) Act 2000, which determine when an offender is entitled to be
released by the Secretary of State;".

With effect from December 2, 2013, the Criminal Legal Aid (General) (Amendment) Regulations 2013 (S.I. 2013 No. 2790), reg. 4(1) and (3), amended regulation 12 of S.I. 2013 No. 9, so as
to substitute a new paragraph (2)(f), as follows—

"(f) require advice and assistance regarding a disciplinary hearing in a prison or young offender
institution where—
(i) the proceedings involve the determination of a criminal charge for the purposes of
Article 6(1) of the European Convention on Human Rights; or
(ii) the governor has exercised the governor's discretion to allow advice and assistance in
relation to the hearing;".

With effect from December 2, 2013, the Criminal Legal Aid (General) (Amendment) Regulations 2013 (S.I. 2013 No. 2790), reg. 4(1) and (4), amended regulation 12(2)(g) of S.I. 2013 No. 9,
so as to insert the words "where the Parole Board has power to direct that individual's release"
after the words "Parole Board".

With effect from December 2, 2013, the Criminal Legal Aid (General) (Amendment) Regulations 2013 (S.I. 2013 No. 2790), reg. 4(1) and (5), amended regulation 12 of S.I. 2013 No. 9, so as
to omit paragraph (2)(h).

With effect from December 2, 2013, the Criminal Legal Aid (General) (Amendment) Regulations 2013 (S.I. 2013 No. 2790), reg. 4(1) and (6), amended regulation 12 of S.I. 2013 No. 9, so as
to substitute a new paragraph (3), as follows—

"(3) In this regulation—
(a) 'governor' includes—
(i) a director approved by the Secretary of State for the purposes of section 85(1)(a) of the
Criminal Justice Act 1991 ('the 1991 Act'); and
(ii) a controller appointed by the Secretary of State under section 85(1)(b) of the 1991 Act,
where the Secretary of State has entered into a contract for the running of a prison under
section 84 of the 1991 Act; and
(b) 'volunteer' means an individual who, for the purposes of assisting with an investigation,
without having been arrested—
(i) attends voluntarily at a police station, customs office or any other place where a
constable is present; or
(ii) accompanies a constable to a police station, customs office or any other such place.".

The amendments made by regulation 4 do not apply to an application for advice and assistance
under section 15 of the LASPOA 2012 (§ 6-211 in the main work) which was made before
December 2, 2013: S.I. 2013 No. 2790, reg. 7.

**Criminal Legal Aid (General) Regulations 2013 (S.I. 2013 No. 9), Pt 5**

*Determinations: proceedings in the magistrates' court*

With effect from January 27, 2014, the Criminal Legal Aid (General) (Amendment) Regulations **6-255**
2013 (S.I. 2013 No. 2790), reg. 5, amended regulation 24 of S.I. 2013 No. 9, so as to substitute a
new paragraph (1), as follows—

"(1) Subject to paragraph (2), when the Director makes a determination under section 16 of the
Act in accordance with Part 3 of the Financial Resources Regulations that an individual is eligible for
representation for proceedings in the magistrates' court, the Director must also make a determination that the individual is eligible in accordance with Part 4 of the Financial Resources Regulations
for representation in the Crown Court in relation to those proceedings.".

The amendment made by regulation 5 does not apply to an application by an individual for a
determination under section 16 of the LASPOA 2012 (§ 6-212 in the main work) in relation to
representation in Crown Court proceedings which was made (*i.e.* signed and dated) before January 27, 2014: S.I. 2013 No. 2790, reg. 8.

*Determinations: certain proceedings in the Crown Court*

**6-256**   With effect from January 27, 2014, the Criminal Legal Aid (General) (Amendment) Regulations 2013 (S.I. 2013 No. 2790), reg. 6, amended regulation 25 of S.I. 2013 No. 9, so as to substitute a new paragraph (1), as follows—

"(1) In the circumstances described in paragraph (2), the Director must consider the individual's application for a determination under section 16 of the Act for representation for the purposes of criminal proceedings in the Crown Court in accordance with Part 4 of the Financial Resources Regulations.".

The amendment made by regulation 6 does not apply to an application by an individual for a determination under section 16 of the LASPOA 2012 (§ 6-212 in the main work) in relation to representation in Crown Court proceedings which was made (*i.e.* signed and dated) before January 27, 2014: S.I. 2013 No. 2790, reg. 8.

## Determinations by a court and choice of representative

**6-270**   The Criminal Legal Aid (Determinations by a Court and Choice of Representative) (Amendment) Regulations 2013 (S.I. 2013 No. 2814) have amended the Criminal Legal Aid (Determinations by a Court and Choice of Representative) Regulations 2013 (S.I. 2013 No. 614) (see the main work) in relation to the circumstances in which a defendant may select a Queen's Counsel or two or more advocates to represent him. The affected regulations are regulations 18(7) and 19 (which is substituted in its entirety).

### S.I. 2013 No. 614, regs 4–9

*Determinations by the High Court*

★**6-277**   Where committal proceedings for contempt other than in the face of the court take place in the High Court, that court may make a determination that the person whose committal is sought qualifies for legal aid: *King's Lynn and West Norfolk Council v. Bunning (Legal Aid Agency, interested party)* [2014] 2 All E.R. 1095, QBD (Blake J.) (considering regs 4, 5 and 7 of the 2013 regulations (as to which, see §§ 6-274, 6-275 and 6-277 in the main work)). As to this case, see also *ante,* § 6-240; and for critical consideration of the decision, see CLW/14/22/11.

### Criminal Legal Aid (Determinations by a Court and Choice of Representative) Regulations 2013 (S.I. 2013 No. 614)

*Criminal proceedings other than before a magistrates' court*

**6-291**   With effect from December 2, 2013, the Criminal Legal Aid (Determinations by a Court and Choice of Representative) (Amendment) Regulations 2013 (S.I. 2013 No. 2814), reg. 2(1) and (2), amended regulation 18(7) of S.I. 2013 No. 614, so as to insert the words "and the relevant court is satisfied that the individual will be, or will be likely to be, prejudiced if they too are not represented by two or more advocates" after the word "prosecution" in sub-paragraph (a) of the definition of "the prosecution condition". This amendment applies to an application for a determination under regulation 11 of the principal regulations (§ 6-282 in the main work) that is made on or after December 2, 2013: S.I. 2013 No. 2814, reg. 1(2).

*Judges sitting in the relevant court*

**6-292**   With effect from December 2, 2013, the Criminal Legal Aid (Determinations by a Court and Choice of Representative) (Amendment) Regulations 2013 (S.I. 2013 No. 2814), reg. 2(1) and (3), amended S.I. 2013 No. 614, so as to substitute a new regulation 19, as follows—

*"Selection of a Queen's Counsel or multiple advocates*
  **19.**—(1) A determination that an individual is entitled to select a Queen's Counsel or more than one advocate under regulation 18 may only be made by the following judges—
    (a) subject to paragraph (2), in the course of a trial or a preliminary hearing, pre-trial review or plea and directions hearing, the judge who has been assigned as the trial judge;
    (b) where a trial judge has not been assigned, by—
      (i) a High Court judge; or
      (ii) subject to paragraph (2), a resident judge of the Crown Court or, in the absence of a resident judge, a judge nominated by a resident judge of the Crown Court for the purpose of making such a determination; or

(c) where the proceedings are in the Court of Appeal, by the Registrar of Criminal Appeals, a High Court judge or a judge of the Court of Appeal.

(2) A determination made by a judge referred to in paragraph (1)(a) or (b)(ii) does not take effect unless it is approved by a presiding judge of the circuit or by a judge nominated by a presiding judge of the circuit for the purpose of giving such approval.".

The substitution of the new regulation 19 applies to an application for a determination under regulation 11 of the principal regulations (§ 6-282 in the main work) that is made on or after December 2, 2013: S.I. 2013 No. 2814, reg. 1(2).

## Financial eligibility

The Criminal Legal Aid (Financial Resources) Regulations 2013 (S.I. 2013 No. 471) have been **6-321** amended by the Criminal Legal Aid (Financial Resources) (Amendment) Regulations 2013 (S.I. 2013 No. 2791). Whereas Part 3 of the principal regulations governed an individual's financial eligibility for representation under section 16 of the 2012 Act (§ 6-212 in the main work), and whereas regulation 17 provided that the Director of Legal Aid Casework must determine an application under Part 3 without considering the applicant's financial resources for specified criminal proceedings, including certain proceedings in the Crown Court, regulation 17 is now substituted (regs 7 and 9) so that Part 3 now applies only to magistrates' courts proceedings and that, in all such proceedings, the director must consider the applicant's financial resources in accordance with the provisions of that part. A new Part 4 (regs 30-38) is inserted to introduce a financial eligibility threshold for proceedings in the Crown Court, together with a new Part 5 (reg. 39), which establishes that, in criminal proceedings, other than those to which Parts 3 and 4 apply, the authority determining an individual's application for legal aid must still deem the individual to be financially eligible (reg. 13).

In Part 4, new regulation 30 provides that a determination can be made in relation to "Crown Court proceedings" (as to which, see reg. 2) if a determination has been made under Part 3 (which has not been withdrawn) that an individual is eligible for representation under section 16 of the 2012 Act in relation to criminal proceedings in the magistrates' court, or if the individual has been sent to the Crown Court, a bill of indictment has been preferred, or an order for a retrial has been made by the Court of Appeal or the Supreme Court. Regulation 31 provides that an individual with a gross annual income not exceeding £12,475, or (if gross annual income does exceed that amount) disposable annual income not exceeding £37,500, will be eligible for legal aid, as will an individual who is a child or who is, directly or indirectly, properly in receipt of a "qualifying benefit" (as defined in reg. 2). Regulation 32 provides that the financial resources of an applicant's partner must be treated as the individual's financial resources when assessing the individual's financial eligibility unless the partner has a contrary interest in the proceedings. Financial resources made available to the individual or the individual's partner by a third party should also be so treated. Regulation 33 sets out the financial resources that must be taken into account when calculating an applicant's gross annual income and regulation 34 sets out how annual disposable income must be calculated. Regulation 35 empowers the director at any time to require an individual to provide information and documentary evidence in relation to a determination under section 16. Regulation 36 enables an individual to renew an application following a determination that he is not eligible, but only if there has been a change in financial circumstances that might affect that determination or where the initial determination is withdrawn following a review. Regulation 37 provides that an individual may apply for such a review (within 21 days unless otherwise agreed with the director) on the grounds that there has been a miscalculation of his financial resources or an administrative error, or that the individual does not have sufficient financial resources to pay for legal representation, notwithstanding the determination. Regulation 38 relates to the withdrawal of a determination by the director.

An amendment is made to regulation 7 (advocacy assistance for individuals in prison) to reflect the fact that criminal legal aid is no longer available for cases in which a prisoner wishes to challenge his treatment in prison (reg. 5). Regulation 21 is amended (regs 11, 12) to set out how restrained assets and housing benefit payments are to be treated for the purposes of calculating an individual's disposable income under Part 3. Finally, minor and consequential amendments are made to regulations 2 (interpretation (reg. 4)), 14 (deemed eligibility: qualifying benefits (reg. 6)), and 20 (assessment of resources: gross annual income (reg. 10)), and the Schedule (calculation of an individual's gross annual income and cost of living expenses for purposes of Pts 3 and 4 (reg. 14)), and regulation 16 (interpretation of Pt 3) is revoked (reg. 8).

Regulation 15(1) provides that the amendments made in relation to financial eligibility in the Crown Court do not apply to an application by an individual for a determination under section 16 of the 2012 Act that is "made before" January 27, 2014 (as to which, see further reg. 15(2)).

S.I. 2013 No. 2791 came into force on December 2, 2013, save for regulations 4, 7 to 9, and 13 to 15, which came into force on January 27, 2014.

### Contribution orders (Crown Court)

*Summary*

**6-322**    The Criminal Legal Aid (Contribution Orders) (Amendment) Regulations 2013 (S.I. 2013 No. 2792) amend the Criminal Legal Aid (Contribution Orders) Regulations 2013 (S.I. 2013 No. 483) (see the main work) in consequence of the introduction of a financial eligibility threshold for legal aid in the Crown Court. There are substantive amendments to regulations 6 (which is substituted by a new regulation (*post*, § 6-333)), 7 and 8, and there are consequential amendments to regulations 17, 25(c) (*post*, § 6-334) and 34. The amendment to regulation 7 is to clarify that the Director of Legal Aid Casework will only be entitled to require documentary evidence in relation to an applicant's financial resources where he has made a determination that an individual is financially eligible for legal aid and to ensure that the information is then provided within 14 days of the request. The amendment to regulation 8 is to ensure that the income calculations set out in regulations 10 and 11 will only be made in respect of individuals who have been assessed as financially eligible.

**Criminal Legal Aid (Contribution Orders) Regulations 2013 (S.I. 2013 No. 483), regs 2, 3, 5, 6, 25, 26, 37**

*Application of this part*

**6-333**    With effect from January 27, 2014, the Criminal Legal Aid (Contribution Orders) (Amendment) Regulations 2013 (S.I. 2013 No. 2792), reg. 4, substituted a new regulation 6 in S.I. 2013 No. 483, as follows—

"*Application of this Part*
    **6.**—(1) This Part applies where the Director has made a determination that an individual's financial resources are such that the individual is eligible in accordance with section 21 of the Act (financial resources) for representation under section 16 of the Act (representation for criminal proceedings) in relation to Crown Court proceedings.
    (2) In this Part 'Crown Court proceedings' means criminal proceedings—
        (a) in respect of an offence for which an individual may be, or has been, sent by a magistrates' court to the Crown Court for trial;
        (b) relating to an offence in respect of which a bill of indictment has been preferred by virtue of section 2(2)(b) of the Administration of Justice (Miscellaneous Provisions) Act 1933 ; or
        (c) which are to be heard in the Crown Court following an order by the Court of Appeal or the Supreme Court for a retrial.".

*Assessment of the cost of representation on the conclusion of the proceedings*

**6-334**    With effect from January 27, 2014, the Criminal Legal Aid (Contribution Orders) (Amendment) Regulations 2013 (S.I. 2013 No. 2792), reg. 7, amended regulation 25(c) of S.I. 2013 No. 483, so as to substitute "Crown Court proceedings" for "criminal proceedings to which this Part applies".

Chapter 7

# CRIMINAL APPEAL

## II. HIGH COURT JURISDICTION IN CROWN COURT PROCEEDINGS

### A. Jurisdiction

#### (2) Judicial review

(a) *Statute*

**Senior Courts Act 1981, ss.29, 31**

*Mandatory, prohibiting and quashing orders*

The provisions of the Crime and Courts Act 2013 referred to in the main work came into force ★7-4 on April 22, 2014: Crime and Courts Act 2013 (Commencement No. 10 and Transitional Provision) Order 2014 (S.I. 2014 No. 954).

(c) *Matters relating to trial on indictment*

#### Matters not relating to trial on indictment

As to whether a decision about the defendant's bail made during a trial is a matter relating to 7-11 trial on indictment, see *R. (Uddin) v. Crown Court at Leeds, ante,* § 3-212 (considering *R. (M.) v. Isleworth Crown Court and H.M. Customs and Excise* (as to which, see the main work)).

*Hunter v. Newcastle Crown Court* is now reported at [2014] Q.B. 94, *sub nom. Hunter v. Crown* 7-12 *Court at Newcastle upon Tyne.*

#### Matters relating to trial on indictment

*Hunter v. Newcastle Crown Court* is now reported at [2014] Q.B. 94, *sub nom. Hunter v. Crown* 7-13 *Court at Newcastle upon Tyne.*

## III. THE COURT OF APPEAL

### C. Practice and Procedure

*Form of judgment of court of criminal division*

The 2013 criminal practice directions (see the main work) are now reported at [2013] 1 W.L.R. 7-33 3164.

### E. Recording Proceedings and Broadcasting Such Recordings

The Court of Appeal (Recording and Broadcasting) Order 2013 (S.I. 2013 No. 2786) disapplies 7-36a section 41 of the CJA 1925 (see § 4-40 in the main work) and section 9 of the Contempt of Court Act 1981 (*ibid.*, § 28-74) in relation to the recording (as to which, see art. 2) of proceedings in the Court of Appeal that are made in accordance with articles 5 to 7 and the broadcasting (as to which, see art. 2) of such recordings, if made in accordance with articles 9 to 11. A recording may only be of an appeal, an Attorney-General's reference under the CJA 1988, s.36 (*ibid.*, § 7-442), an application by a prosecutor under the CJA 2003, Pt 10 (retrial for serious offences), or an application for leave to appeal or to make a reference, but appeals and applications under the CAA 1968, ss.12 (against a not guilty verdict by reason of insanity (*ibid.*, § 7-146)), 15 (against a finding of disability (*ibid.*, § 7-151)) and 16A (against a hospital order, *etc.* (*ibid.*, § 7-155)), are excluded (art. 5). Recordings may only include a legal representative's submissions, exchanges between a legal representative and the court, and the court giving judgment, but if any party is not legally represented, the only recording allowed is of the court giving judgment (art. 6). On an appeal, or an application for leave to appeal, against conviction, or an application by a prosecutor under Part 10 of the 2003 Act, a recording must not be broadcast unless the court gives permission, but permission is not required where no retrial is ordered (art. 9). A broadcast must not breach any applicable reporting restriction (art. 10); a report that includes a broadcast of a hearing must be fair and accurate having regard to the overall content and the context of the broadcast (art. 11(1)); and a broadcast must not be used for the purposes of a party political broadcast, advertisement or promotion, light entertainment or satire (art. 11(2)).

## IV. APPEAL TO COURT OF APPEAL BY THE DEFENDANT

### A. APPEAL AGAINST CONVICTION ON INDICTMENT

#### (1) The right of appeal

##### Criminal Appeal Act 1968, s.1

*Right of appeal against conviction on indictment*

★7-37    As to there being a right to only one appeal against conviction, see also *R. v. Boughton-Fox* [2014] Lloyd's Rep. F.C. 343, CA (following *R. v. Pinfold* (as to which, see the main work)).

#### Certificate of trial judge

7-38    The 2013 criminal practice directions (see the main work) are now reported at [2013] 1 W.L.R. 3164.

#### (4) Grounds of appeal

**Inconsistent verdicts**

*Of same court*

★7-70    In *R. v. Formhals* [2014] 1 Cr.App.R. 35, CA, it was held that the principles applicable to inconsistent verdicts are capable of applying by analogy to a verdict of guilty on one count and a disagreement on another, and that, therefore, it would be going too far to prohibit a defendant from arguing that the resulting situation gave rise to an unsafe conviction (not following *R. v. S.* (see the main work)). However, it would be a rare case where a failure to reach a verdict could be said to be logically inexplicable when contrasted with, or set against, a verdict or verdicts that had been reached on one or more other counts. Moreover, the principles applicable to inconsistent verdicts were themselves tightly prescribed, and, accordingly, the bar could be set no lower, and perhaps was to be set higher, where the attempt was to compare and contrast a guilty verdict with a failure by the jury to agree.

**Defects in the indictment**

(ii) *Counts not properly included in the indictment*

7-75    *R. v. McGrath* is now reported at [2014] Crim.L.R. 144.

(iv) *Duplicity and other defects of form*

7-77    There is a clear judicial and legislative steer away from quashing an indictment and allowing appeals on the basis of a purely technical defect; such points should be taken at the time of the trial when they can be properly and fairly addressed; where, therefore, the statement of offence in an indictment alleged rape, contrary to the SOA 1956, s.1(1), when it should have referred to the SOA 2003, s.1(1) (contrary to the requirements of the Indictments Act 1915, s.3, and the 2013 rules, r.14.2(1) (§§ 1-187, 1-188 in the main work)), but where the trial proceeded throughout on the basis that the defendant was charged with an offence under the 2003 Act, without anyone noticing the error, this was a purely technical defect that caused no prejudice; such an error was not so fundamental as to render the proceedings a nullity, and the conviction was therefore safe: *R. v. Stocker* [2014] 1 Cr.App.R. 18, CA (distinguishing, in particular, *R. v. Shields* [2012] 1 Cr.App.R. 9, CA, and *R. v. Abdul* (as to which, see § 7-104 in the main work)).

## Miscellaneous

### (ii) *Conduct of counsel*

Before an application for leave to appeal against conviction is made, where the ground of appeal is the alleged failings of the defendant's legal representatives at trial, proper inquiries must be made of those representatives; it was impermissible to proceed on the word of the defendant alone: *R. v. A. (E.O.)* [2014] 2 Cr.App.R. 7, CA. As to this case, see also *post*, § 7-180. **★7-83**

### (xvi) *Irregularity in relation to jury*

Where an allegation of jury impropriety or irregularity is made by a juror after verdict, the court should start with the presumption that if a juror during the trial falls below the standards expected of jurors, the other jurors will report that to the judge during the trial and before the verdict; inquiries therefore should not be ordered in such cases and the finality of the verdict should be accepted, absent other strong and compelling evidence; the inference that complaints after verdict simply represent a protest by a juror at a verdict with which he disagrees is likely to be overwhelming: *R. v. Baybasin* [2014] 1 Cr.App.R. 19, CA (endorsing *R. v. Lewis* (as to which, see the main work)). As to this case, see also *ante*, § 4-292. **7-97**

## Investigation of irregularities

See *R. v. Baybasin*, *ante*, § 7-97. **7-102**

### (5) Substitution of conviction for alternative offence

#### Criminal Appeal Act 1968, s.3A

*Power to substitute conviction of alternative offence after guilty plea*

Where a conviction based on a plea of guilty is quashed, the Court of Appeal, in deciding whether to substitute a conviction for an alternative offence under section 3A of the 1968 Act, is not confined by subsection (1)(c) ("(c) it appears to the Court of Appeal that the plea of guilty indicates an admission by the appellant of facts which prove him guilty of the other offence") to looking at the indictment: *R. v. White* [2014] 4 *Archbold Review* 2, CA. *R. v. Lawrence* (as to which, see the main work) was referred to in argument, but not in the judgment. For critical comment on the judgment in *White*, see CLW/14/16/1. **★7-105**

### (9) Retrials

#### Criminal Appeal Act 1968, Sched. 2

*Sentence on conviction at retrial*

*R. v. Dobson* (see the main work) is now reported at [2014] 1 Cr.App.R.(S.) 54. **★7-118**

### B. Appeal Against Sentence

### (1) Who can appeal

## Certificate of sentencing judge: bail pending appeal

The 2013 criminal practice directions (see the main work) are now reported at [2013] 1 W.L.R. 3164. **7-128**

#### Criminal Appeal Act 1968, s.11

*Proper construction of section 11(3)*

Where the appropriate sentence for an offence would have been six months' imprisonment rather than the community order with a 24-month supervision requirement and programme requirement imposed by the judge, such a custodial sentence could be imposed on appeal in the particular circumstances, notwithstanding section 11(3) of the 1968 Act; imposition of such a sentence would have meant that the offender would have been released at the date of sentence, **7-130** because he had in fact served half the sentence at that date; he would thereafter have been subject to a three-month licence period, but that would have overlapped with a licence period in respect of an earlier sentence for other offences; in such circumstances, the sentence could not be said to be a more severe sentence than the community order imposed by the judge; the community order would put the offender at risk for an extended period of being returned to prison in the event of breach; and to impose a sentence of imprisonment would therefore be far less onerous; it is necessary to look at the particular circumstances of each case pragmatically (following *R. v. Waters and Young* (as to which, see the main work)): *R. v. Price* [2014] 1 Cr.App.R.(S.) 36, CA.

### (2) Notes on appeal against sentence

### Principles on which the court acts

**7-135**    Where a defendant's consent to a confiscation order resulted from erroneous legal advice, he was not precluded from appealing against the order by reason of that consent (*R. v. Emmett* [1998] A.C. 773, HL): *R. v. Mackle (Patrick), Mackle (Plunkett Jude) and Mackle (Benedict); R. v. McLaughlin (Henry)* [2014] 2 W.L.R. 267, SC. The court further ruled that where a confiscation order was originally made on a basis that is no longer legally viable, a decision to confirm the order on different grounds must be made with great care and only when it is clear that the person against whom it is to be made has had ample opportunity to address the altered grounds. As to this case, see also *ante*, §§ 5-1043, 5-1046.

(iii) *Matters improperly taken into account or fresh matters to be taken into account*

**7-138**    The 2013 criminal practice directions (see the main work) are now reported at [2013] 1 W.L.R. 3164.

(v) *Sentence manifestly excessive or wrong in principle*

★**7-141**    Where the judge in the Crown Court had correctly identified the starting point for sentence by reference to the relevant sentencing guideline, but had not then explained how he reached a sentence well above the starting point, the Court of Appeal would carry out the sentencing exercise afresh; there is no reason why a judge should not sentence outside the range of sentences in a guideline, but it is essential that such a course is explained: *R. v. Datsun and Razak* [2014] 1 Cr.App.R.(S.) 25, CA.

**7-142**    Where the offender, having been dealt with in separate proceedings for two similar offences of robbery committed within three days of each other, appealed against the sentences imposed in each of those two proceedings, the proper approach on appeal was to ask what the appropriate sentence would have been if both matters had been dealt with together: *R. v. May* [2014] 1 Cr.App.R.(S.) 13, CA (emphasising the importance of ensuring that serious cases that are related in time and nature are dealt with, where possible, together).

### G. PROCEDURE FROM NOTICE OF APPEAL TO HEARING

### (2) Right to representation

**7-165**    *Practice Direction (Costs in Criminal Proceedings)* (see the main work) is now reported at [2013] 1 W.L.R. 3255, *sub nom. Practice Direction (Criminal Proceedings: Costs).*

### (4) Drafting of grounds

*Appeal notices containing grounds of appeal*

**7-168a**    The 2013 criminal practice directions (see the main work) are now reported at [2013] 1 W.L.R. 3164.

### (7) Extension of time

**7-171**    *R. v. R.* and *R. v. Cottrell; R. v. Fletcher* (as to both of which, see the main work) were among the authorities considered by the Court of Appeal in *R. v. Bestel; R. v. Raza; R. v. Bashir* (as to which, see *ante*, § 5-1055).

## Variation and amplification of grounds

*R. v. Chapman* is now reported at [2014] 1 W.L.R. 1376.　　**7-172**

### (9) Disposal of groundless appeal or application for leave to appeal

#### Criminal Appeal Act 1968, s.20

Where the ground of appeal is the alleged failings of the defendant's legal representatives at　**★7-180** trial, and proper inquiries have not been made of those representatives, the power of the Court of Appeal to dismiss an application for leave to appeal as being frivolous or vexatious under section 20 of the 1968 Act would be exercised more frequently: *R. v. A. (E.O.)* [2014] 2 Cr.App.R. 7, CA. As to this case, see also *ante*, § 7-83.

### (12) Abandonment of appeal

#### Reinstatement

In *R. v. Smith (Paul James)* [2014] 2 Cr.App.R. 1, CA, the court summarised the effect of the　**7-188** authorities, including, in particular, *R. v. Medway* (as to which, see the main work), as follows: (i) a notice of abandonment of appeal is irrevocable, unless it falls to be treated as a nullity; (ii) it will be a nullity if the defendant's mind does not go with the notice which he signs; (iii) if he abandons his appeal after, and because of, receiving incorrect legal advice, then his mind may not go with the notice; whether this is the case will depend upon the circumstances; and (iv) incorrect legal advice for this purpose means advice that is positively wrong; it does not mean the expression of opinion on a difficult point, with which some may agree and others may disagree. The court said that there is a growing and unwelcome tendency of convicted defendants to dismiss their original counsel and then bring in new counsel to criticise their predecessors; this strategy is an attempt to circumvent the restriction on calling fresh evidence and is to be deplored; members of the bar should not lend their support to this strategy unless there really is a proper basis for impugning the conduct of previous counsel. The court noted that rule 65.13 of the Criminal Procedure Rules 2013 (S.I. 2013 No. 1554) (§ 7-185 in the main work) sets out the procedure for applying to reinstate an application or appeal; but that it does not purport to expand the grounds upon which such an application might succeed.

### (13) Case summaries

The 2013 criminal practice directions (see the main work) are now reported at [2013] 1 W.L.R.　**7-189** 3164.

### (14) Listing practice

The 2013 criminal practice directions (see the main work) are now reported at [2013] 1 W.L.R.　**7-190** 3164.

## H. The Hearing

### (5) Skeleton arguments and citation of authorities

*Skeleton arguments*
The 2013 criminal practice directions (see the main work) are now reported at [2013] 1 W.L.R.　**7-200** 3164.

*Citation of authority and provision of copies of judgments to the court*
The 2013 criminal practice directions (see the main work) are now reported at [2013] 1 W.L.R.　**7-200a** 3164.

### (6) Attendance and role of prosecution

*Respondent's notice*
The 2013 criminal practice directions (see the main work) are now reported at [2013] 1 W.L.R.　**7-202** 3164.

*The provision of notice to the prosecution*

**7-203**   The 2013 criminal practice directions (see the main work) are now reported at [2013] 1 W.L.R. 3164.

## (7)  Leave to call additional evidence

### Criminal Appeal Act 1968, s.23

**7-206**   As to whether an inquiry should be ordered where an allegation of jury impropriety or irregularity is made after verdict by a juror, see *R. v. Baybasin, ante,* § 7-97.

## Practical application

*Expert evidence*

**7-211**   In *R. v Lundy, The Times,* December 10, 2013, the Privy Council held: (i) on an appeal against a conviction founded exclusively or principally on scientific evidence, the court should not be astute to exclude new evidence that presents a significant challenge to the trial evidence solely because it might have been obtained before the trial; (ii) whether to admit the fresh evidence should be decided by the application of a sequential series of tests; if the evidence is not credible, it should not be admitted; if it is credible, the question then arises whether it is fresh in the sense that it is evidence which could not have been obtained for the trial with reasonable diligence; if it is both credible and fresh, it should generally be admitted unless the court is satisfied at that stage that, if admitted, it would have no effect on the safety of the conviction; if the evidence is credible but not fresh, the court should assess its strength and its potential impact on the safety of the conviction; if it considers there is a risk of a miscarriage of justice if the evidence is excluded, it should be admitted, notwithstanding that the evidence is not fresh; the requirement that evidence be fresh can be of less critical importance in cases involving scientific evidence.

## I. Notification of Result of Appeal and Matters Depending Thereon

### (4)  Effect of appeal on sentence

*Loss of time*

**7-226**   The 2013 criminal practice directions (see the main work) are now reported at [2013] 1 W.L.R. 3164.

## VIII.  MISCELLANEOUS RIGHTS OF APPEAL

### A. Appeal in Respect of Orders Restricting Reporting or Public Access

#### Criminal Justice Act 1988, s.159

*Crown Court proceedings - orders restricting or preventing reports or restricting public access*

**7-323**   In *R. v. Marine A.; Re Guardian News and Media; R. (Marine A.) v. Judge Advocate General* [2014] 1 Cr.App.R. 26, DC & CMAC, it was said that provisions of the Armed Forces (Court Martial) Rules 2009 (S.I. 2009 No. 2041) that correspond to paragraphs (b) and (c) of section 159(1) of the 1988 Act should be given a "broad and liberal" construction.

## XIII.  REFERENCES TO THE COURT OF APPEAL BY THE ATTORNEY-GENERAL

### B. Of Sentences

#### Criminal Justice Act 1988, s.36

*Double jeopardy*

**7-449**   In *Att.-Gen.'s Reference (No. 38 of 2013) (R. v. Hall)* [2014] 1 Cr.App.R.(S.) 61, CA, it was said that there was no room for the double jeopardy principle to operate where the offender had received a short, immediate custodial sentence, had been made aware at an early stage that the

Attorney-General proposed to refer his sentence to the Court of Appeal and was still in custody at
the time of the hearing of the reference.

CHAPTER 8

# ORAL TESTIMONY OF WITNESSES

## I. PRELIMINARIES

### A. SECURING ATTENDANCE OF WITNESSES, PRODUCTION OF DOCUMENTS, ETC.

#### (1) Summons to witness to attend Crown Court

**Criminal Procedure (Attendance of Witnesses) Act 1965, s.2**

*Issue of witness summons on application to Crown Court*

The provisions of the Crime and Courts Act 2013 referred to in the main work came into force   ★8-1
on February 24, 2014: Crime and Courts Act 2013 (Commencement No. 8) Order 2014 (S.I.
2014 No. 258).

### B. ISSUES ARISING PRIOR TO ENTRY INTO WITNESS BOX

#### (2) Right to read statement

The 2013 criminal practice directions (see the main work) are now reported at [2013] 1 W.L.R.   **8-40**
3164.

## III. COMPETENCE AND COMPELLABILITY

### (3) Determination of competency

**Youth Justice and Criminal Evidence Act 1999, s.54**

**Manner of**

In *R. v. F.* [2013] 2 Cr.App.R. 13, CA, a ruling that the complainant, who was profoundly deaf   **8-56**
and who had mild to moderate learning difficulties, was incompetent was reversed on appeal.
First, the judge had substituted the issue of the interpreter's difficulties in communicating with
the complainant for the test of whether the witness could understand questions and give intelligible answers. Secondly, the judge had based herself on what had transpired when difficulties
had arisen in the hearing, but which had represented a failure by those involved to engage in a
true and fair test of competency. The interests of justice were plainly broad enough to encompass
the interests of the alleged victim in having the opportunity to have her competency to give
evidence properly considered by the court.

### (6) Children and young persons

In *R. v. M.H.* [2013] Crim.L.R. 849, CA, it was said that in the case of an infant complainant,   **8-59**
significant delay between the alleged offence and the trial may render the child incompetent (or,
more accurately, unable) to give evidence about it; that is not, however, merely because time has
passed but because the passage of time may have affected the ability of the child to give intelligible answers to questions about the incident. As to this case, see also *ante,* § 4-472; and *post,* §
11-3d.

**Criminal Practice Direction (Evidence) 28A, unreported, October 7, 2013**

*Wards of court and children subject to current family proceedings*

The 2013 criminal practice directions (see the main work) are now reported at [2013] 1 W.L.R.   **8-60**
3164.

## IV. RULES OF EVIDENCE AND PRACTICE RELATING TO THE QUESTIONING OF WITNESSES

### A. General

### (1) Special measures directions

**Proceedings for anti-social behaviour orders**

★**8-73**    As to the repeal of section 1I of the CDA 1998 (see the main work), see *ante*, § 5-1198.

*Video Recorded Evidence in Chief*

**8-90**    The 2013 criminal practice directions (see the main work) are now reported at [2013] 1 W.L.R. 3164.

#### Youth Justice and Criminal Evidence Act 1999, ss.23–30

*Video recorded cross-examination or re-examination*

**8-93**    With effect from December 30, 2013, section 28 of the 1999 Act (see the main work) was brought into force in relation to proceedings in the Crown Court sitting at Kingston-upon-Thames, Leeds or Liverpool if the witness is eligible for assistance by virtue of section 16(1) (as to which, see § 8-74 in the main work), but in the case of section 16(1)(a) (age), only if the witness is under 16 at the time of the hearing: Youth Justice and Criminal Evidence Act 1999 (Commencement No. 13) Order 2013 (S.I. 2013 No. 3236).

#### Youth Justice and Criminal Evidence Act 1999, ss.31–33

*Interpretation of Chapter I*

**8-98**    Section 33 of the 1999 Act is amended, with effect from December 18, 2013, by the Special Measures for Child Witnesses (Sexual Offences) Regulations 2013 (S.I. 2013 No. 2971), so as (i) to substitute the words "a relevant offence" for the words "a human trafficking offence" in subsection (5), and (ii) to substitute a new subsection (6), as follows—

> "(6) In subsection (5) 'relevant offence' means—
> (a) a sexual offence;
> (b) an offence under section 1 of the Protection of Children Act 1978 ;
> (c) an offence under section 160 of the Criminal Justice Act 1988 ;
> (d) an offence under section 4 of the Asylum and Immigration (Treatment of Claimants, etc) Act 2004.".

*Vulnerable people in the courts*

**8-131e**    The 2013 criminal practice directions (see the main work) are now reported at [2013] 1 W.L.R. 3164.

*Ground rules hearings to plan the questioning of a vulnerable witness or defendant*

**8-131f**    The 2013 criminal practice directions (see the main work) are now reported at [2013] 1 W.L.R. 3164.

*Intermediaries*

**8-131g**    The 2013 criminal practice directions (see the main work) are now reported at [2013] 1 W.L.R. 3164.

*Measures to assist a witness or defendant to give evidence*

**8-131i**    The 2013 criminal practice directions (see the main work) are now reported at [2013] 1 W.L.R. 3164.

*Witnesses giving evidence by live link*

**8-131j**    The 2013 criminal practice directions (see the main work) are now reported at [2013] 1 W.L.R. 3164.

*Visually recorded interviews: memory refreshing and watching at a different time from the jury*
   The 2013 criminal practice directions (see the main work) are now reported at [2013] 1 W.L.R.  **8-131k**
3164.

## (2) Evidence through television link where witness outside United Kingdom

### Criminal Justice Act 1988, s.32

   *R. v. Diane* (as to which, see the main work) was followed and applied in *R. v. Hampson* [2014] 1  **8-133**
Cr.App.R. 4, CA.

## B. Examination-in-Chief

### (2) Identifying the witness

#### (a) *Name*

*Witness anonymity orders*
   The 2013 criminal practice directions (see the main work) are now reported at [2013] 1 W.L.R.  **8-167**
3164.

## C. Cross-Examination

### (3) Restrictions

#### (b) *In proceedings for sexual offences*

**Reasons**

   Where an issue arises under section 41, the judge should give a formal, reasoned judgment at  **★8-242a**
some point in the proceedings; the defendant is entitled to know why evidence has been excluded
and the Court of Appeal is at a disadvantage if it has to glean the reasoning from a transcript of
the argument: *R. v. Gjoni* [2014] 5 *Archbold Review* 1, CA. As to this case, see also *post*, § 8-249.

**Previous complaints and statements about sexual behaviour**

   In connection with the distinction drawn in *R. v. Winter* (as to which, see the main work)  **★8-246**
between a belief that the complainant would consent and a belief that the complainant was
consenting, see *R. v. Gjoni, post*, § 8-249.

**Miscellaneous**

   Asking a female about whether someone has assisted her in and about the obtaining of a lawful  **8-249**
abortion is not to ask a question about her "sexual behaviour" within section 41(1) of the YJCEA
1999 (as to which, see § 8-238 in the main work): *R. v. P. (R.)* [2014] 1 Cr.App.R. 28, CA. The
court said that the fact that an abortion cannot occur unless sexual behaviour has taken place
does not make a question about the fact of the abortion a question "about" any sexual behaviour;
but the court added that there might be cases where such a question was a way of asking about
sexual history and would be a question "about" sexual behaviour so as to fall within the
prohibition. In the instant case, it was held that the judge should have allowed questions to be
asked of the complainant (the step-daughter of the defendant who was charged with a series of
sexual assaults on her when she was about 12) as to whether the defendant had assisted in arranging an abortion for her when she was aged about 17 (after the defendant and her mother
had separated), that he had paid for it and had travelled with her to the clinic, with a view to
rebutting her evidence that, at that time, she had viewed him with distaste.
   The critical difference between a belief that the complainant would consent to sex and a belief  **★**
that the complainant was consenting was emphasised in *R. v. Gjoni* [2014] 5 *Archbold Review* 1, CA.
The latter belief provides a defence whereas a belief that the complainant would consent will not
avail the defendant, although it may have some relevance by way of explaining the defendant's
preliminary conduct. Here, the judge had drawn the line at the correct place where she had allowed the defendant to say, by way of explanation for his having entered the complainant's

bedroom, that he had been encouraged by a friend (present in the house at the time) to believe that the complainant would agree to have sex with him, but not to say that the friend had told him that he had himself had consensual sex with the complainant a week previously, and that this had encouraged him in his belief. The 1999 Act had been intended to outlaw any such reasoning. While the issue was not one of consent (s.41(3)(a)), and the principal purpose of the evidence was not to impugn the credibility of the complainant (s.41(4)), the judge had been entitled to rule that a refusal of leave would not render the jury's conclusion unsafe (s.41(2)(b)). As to this case, see also *ante*, § 8-242a.

CHAPTER 9

# DOCUMENTARY AND REAL EVIDENCE

*II. PUBLIC DOCUMENTS*

D. CATEGORIES OF PUBLIC DOCUMENTS

## (2) Proceedings in Parliament

*Citation Of Hansard*

**9-38** The 2013 criminal practice directions (see the main work) are now reported at [2013] 1 W.L.R. 3164.

## (4) Public registers

**Births, marriages, deaths, etc.**

**9-52** With effect from January 21, 2014, paragraphs 1, 2, 4, 6 to 10, and 12 to 15 of Schedule 6 to the Marriage (Same Sex Couples) Act 2013 (and s.13(1) of the 2013 Act so far as it relates to those paras) (as to which, see the main work) were brought into force, to the extent that they confer or relate to the power to make subordinate legislation; and with effect from June 3, 2014, section 13 of, and Schedule 6 to, the 2013 Act are brought into force, so far as not already in force: Marriage (Same Sex Couples) Act 2013 (Commencement No. 2 and Transitional Provision) Order 2014 (S.I. 2014 No. 93).

## (6) Certificates given under public authority

**General**

**9-65** With effect from June 3, 2014, section 13(2) of the Marriage (Same Sex Couples) Act 2013 (as to which, see the main work) is brought into force: Marriage (Same Sex Couples) Act 2013 (Commencement No. 2 and Transitional Provision) Order 2014 (S.I. 2014 No. 93).

CHAPTER 10

# MISCELLANEOUS SOURCES OF EVIDENCE

*V. TRANSCRIPT OF EVIDENCE*

A. RETRIAL ORDERED BY COURT OF APPEAL

**Criminal Appeal Act 1968, Sched. 2, para. 1**

**10-25** The mere fact of a refusal by a witness who gave evidence at the first trial to give evidence at the retrial is insufficient to satisfy the requirement in sub-paragraph (1)(c) of paragraph 1 of

Schedule 2 to the 1968 Act that the witness be "unavailable"; a trial judge will have to consider the circumstances of refusal with care; among these will be whether all reasonable efforts have been made to obtain oral evidence from the witness at the retrial and the reasons for the refusal; if the conclusion is that the witness is properly to be regarded as "unavailable", then the judge will have to go on to consider whether it is in the "interests of justice" for the witness's evidence at the first trial to be admitted under section 114 of the CJA 2003 (§ 11-2 in the main work), having regard to the matters listed in subsection (2) of that section: *R. v. Lawrence (Joseph)* [2014] 1 Cr.App.R. 5, CA. As to this case, see also *ante*, § 4-144; and *post*, § 11-3.

## VI. LETTERS OF REQUEST

### Designation of prosecuting authorities

With effect from March 27, 2014, the Public Bodies (Merger of the Director of Public Prosecu- **★10-28** tions and the Director of Revenue and Customs Prosecutions) Order 2014 (S.I. 2014 No. 834), art. 3(3), and Sched. 3, para. 7, amended the Crime (International Co-operation) Act 2003 (Designation of Prosecuting Authorities) Order 2004 (S.I. 2004 No. 1034), subject to saving and transitional provisions (as to which, see *ante*, § 1-27), so as to omit the reference to the Director of Revenue and Customs Prosecutions and any person designated under the Commissioners for Revenue and Customs Act 2005, s.37(1).

### Crime (International Co-operation) Act 2003, ss.9, 10

*Use of evidence obtained*
   *Gohil v. Gohil* is now reported at [2013] Fam. 276. **10-30**

## VII. EXPERT EVIDENCE

### B. OPINION EVIDENCE

### Test of admissibility

Where the defendant was convicted of manslaughter following a collision between two vehicles, **★10-47** one of which he was driving, where the key issue at trial was which of the two vehicles had deliberately been steered into the other, and where the defence sought to adduce fresh evidence on appeal (CAA 1968, s.23 (§ 7-205 in the main work)), which the court received *de bene esse*, of a computer modelling technique that showed that it was not possible to reconstruct the collision in accordance with the prosecution expert's opinion so as to re-create the post-impact results as presented to the trial court, such evidence did not reach "anything like the state of robustness necessary for it significantly to undermine" the prosecution case; while the computer modelling covered around 200 different simulations, several thousand simulations would need to be carried out for a typical full stochastic vehicle dynamics analysis, and there were a large number of variables relating to braking, steering, speed, overlap and separation of vehicles and driver inputs that had not been explored and whose exploration would affect the outcome and balance of the modelling report; while financial constraints had prevented fuller modelling, it was unlikely that further work would have provided an accurate outcome; accordingly, the evidence did not satisfy section 23(2)(b) of the 1968 Act ("the evidence may afford any ground for allowing the appeal") and would not be admitted: *R. v. Kwaik* [2014] Crim.L.R. 454, CA.

CHAPTER 11

## HEARSAY EVIDENCE

*II. STATUTE*

A. CRIMINAL JUSTICE ACT 2003

### (1) The basic rules

**Criminal Justice Act 2003, ss.114, 115, 133, 134**

### Hearsay and the right to a fair trial

**11-3**     As to the difficulty in establishing that reliance on the disputed hearsay evidence of an absent witness is "necessary" where the witness has been given an assurance that he or she would not be compelled to attend court, see *R. v. Lawrence (Joseph)* [2014] 1 Cr.App.R. 5, CA (as to which, see also *ante*, §§ 4-144, 10-25). As to this issue, see, *inter alia, R. v. Horncastle; R. v. Marquis; R. v. Carter* (in the main work), *R. v. D.T.* (§ 11-21 in the main work), and *R. v. Shabir* (§ 11-22 in the main work).

### Section 114(1)(d)—admissibility as being "in the interests of justice"

**11-3d**     Where a three-year-old gave evidence that his father, the defendant, had sexually abused him, the circumstances were overwhelmingly in favour of the admissibility, under section 114(1)(d) of the 2003 Act, of evidence of what he had initially said to his mother, and then to a police officer; evidence of the manner and circumstances in which the child made his disclosures had an important bearing upon the reliability of his account; the evidence could not otherwise be received by the court by reason of the tender age of the child, who could not be expected to remember the occasions when he made the disclosures to others; it was in the interests of justice that the jury should not be deprived of evidence that, but for the age of the witness, they would likely have received through section 120(4) and (7) (§ 11-34 in the main work): *R. v. M.H.* [2013] Crim.L.R. 849, CA. As to this case, see also *ante*, §§ 4–472, 8-59.

### (3) Principal categories of admissibility

(a) *Absent witnesses*

**Criminal Justice Act 2003, s.116**

### Witness cannot be found (s.116(2)(d))

**11-21**     As to the importance of being able to show that all reasonable steps to get a missing witness to court have been taken, see *R. v. Lawrence (Joseph)*, *ante*, § 11-3.

### Witness in fear

**11-22**     As to the importance of not giving a witness an assurance that he or she will not be compelled to come to court, see *R. v. Lawrence (Joseph)*, *ante*, § 11-3.

(d) *Previous statements of witnesses*

**Criminal Justice Act 2003, ss.119, 120**

*Recent complaint (s.120(4), (7) and (8))*

**11-40**     As to the possibility of admitting an infant witness's initial complaints under section 114(1)(d) of the 2003 Act (admissibility "in the interests of justice" (§ 11-2 in the main work)) where it is impossible to rely on section 120(4) because of the inability of the witness to satisfy the condition in subsection (4)(b), see *R. v. M.H., ante*, § 11-3d.

CHAPTER 12

# PRIVILEGE, PUBLIC INTEREST IMMUNITY AND DISCLOSURE

## I. PRIVILEGE

### C. LEGAL PROFESSIONAL PRIVILEGE

#### (1) The nature of legal professional privilege

**Litigation privilege**

In *Rawlinson and Hunter Trustees S.A. v. Akers*, unreported, February 20, 2014, CA (Civ. Div.) ([2014] EWCA Civ. 136), it was held: (i) for a communication to be subject to litigation privilege, the party claiming privilege must establish that it was made with the dominant purpose of being used in aid of, or of obtaining legal advice about, actual or anticipated litigation; (ii) where litigation has not been commenced at the time of the communication, it has to be "reasonably in prospect"; this does not require the prospect of litigation to be greater than 50 per cent, but it must be more than a mere possibility; (iii) a mere claim in evidence before the court that the document was for a particular purpose will not be decisive; the court will look at "purpose" from an objective standpoint, considering all relevant evidence, including evidence as to subjective purpose; and (iv) where a document was prepared for multiple purposes, it is necessary for the party asserting privilege to establish that the pursuit of litigation was the dominant purpose, but it is not necessarily the case that if one purpose for which a document was prepared was to conduct an exercise which the person preparing the document was bound to carry out in any event, that such purpose would necessarily be independent of the possible need to pursue litigation, so that any claim to litigation privilege would be defeated.

★**12-9**

**Legal advice privilege**

*R. (Prudential plc) v. Special Commr of Income Tax (Institute of Chartered Accountants in England and Wales intervening)* is now reported at [2013] 2 A.C. 185.

**12-12**

#### (3) Duration and waiver of privilege

**Waiver**

*R. v. Turner* is now reported at [2013] Crim.L.R. 993.

**12-17**

## II. PUBLIC INTEREST IMMUNITY

### B. CATEGORIES OF PUBLIC INTEREST IMMUNITY

**Categories listed in the code of practice**

As to (i) in the categories of sensitive material listed in the code of practice (see § 12-33 in the main work), it was said in *Secretary of State for Foreign and Commonwealth Affairs v. Assistant Deputy Coroner for Inner North London* [2014] A.C.D. 43, DC, that where public interest immunity is claimed on the ground that disclosure would cause serious harm to national security, it was for the courts, not the government, to decide whether or not public interest immunity should prevent disclosure; when the Secretary of State claimed that disclosure would entail a real risk of damaging national security, there had to be evidence to support his assertion; without such evidence, the claim would fail at the first hurdle; if there were such evidence, and its effect was

★**12-33a**

that disclosure would have a sufficiently grave effect on national security, that would normally be an end to the matter, as there could be no disclosure; if the claimed damage to national security was not plain and substantial enough to render it inappropriate to carry out the balancing exercise, then it had to be carried out; when carrying it out, the Secretary of State's view regarding the nature and extent of the damage to national security that would flow from disclosure should be accepted, unless there were cogent reasons to reject it; if such reasons existed, they had to be set out; a real and significant risk of damage to national security would generally, but not invariably, preclude disclosure.

## III. DISCLOSURE

### A. PRELIMINARY

### Introduction

**12-45**     Revised guidelines on disclosure were published by the Attorney-General on December 3, 2013, replacing the 2005 guidelines (see the main work, and *post*, Appendix A-242 *et seq.*), and also the supplementary guidelines on digital material issued in 2011, which are now annexed to these guidelines (*ibid.*, Appendix A-262 *et seq.*). The guidelines had immediate effect. On the same day, the Lord Chief Justice issued a revised protocol on the disclosure of unused material in criminal cases (see the main work, and *post*, Appendix N-52 *et seq.*). The two documents are similarly structured and should be read together.

### Surviving common law

★**12-49**     In *R. (Nunn) v. Chief Constable of Suffolk Constabulary*, unreported, June 18, 2014, SC ([2014] UKSC 37), it was said that whilst the common law principle of fairness informs the duty of disclosure at all stages of the criminal process, it does not require the same level of disclosure at every stage (before arrival in the Crown Court, the duty is limited to evidence that might be relevant at that stage (*ex p. Lee* (§ 12-46 in the main work)); pending sentence, the duty is only to disclose material relevant to sentence; and, pending appeal, it is to disclose material relevant to the appeal); the common law never recognised a duty of disclosure or to make inquiry after conviction that was identical to that prevailing prior to, and during, trial; whilst there is an important public interest in exposing any flaw in a conviction that renders it unsafe, there is also a powerful public interest in the finality of proceedings, and in ensuring that the police's finite resources are applied to current investigations, unless such good reason is established; thus, the post-appeal common law duty of disclosure extends only to material coming to light that might cast doubt on the safety of a conviction (as set out in para. 72 of the Attorney-General's guidelines on disclosure (*post*, Appendix A-260)); but it is open to police and prosecutors to make further inquiry, following representations on behalf of convicted persons, and they ought to exercise sensible judgment in relation to such representations; if there appears to be a real prospect that further inquiry will uncover something that may affect the safety of a conviction, then there should be co-operation in making it. As to this case, see also *post*, § 12-58b.

### Third party disclosure

**12-51**     As to the replacement of the guidelines on disclosure, the supplementary guidelines relating to digitally-stored material and the protocol for the control and management of unused material in the Crown Court, see *ante*, § 12-45. As to the approach to be taken to third party material, see paras 53 *et seq.* of the guidelines on disclosure (*post*, Appendix A-254 *et seq.*), and paras 44 *et seq.* of the protocol (*post*, Appendix N-59 *et seq.*).

### B. LEGISLATION

### (1) Criminal Procedure and Investigations Act 1996

#### Criminal Procedure and Investigations Act 1996, ss.1, 2

*Application of this part*

★**12-52**     The provisions of the Crime and Courts Act 2013 referred to in the main work were brought into force on February 24, 2014: Crime and Courts Act 2013 (Commencement No. 8) Order 2014 (S.I.2014 No. 258).

### Criminal Procedure and Investigations Act 1996, ss.3, 4

*Initial duty of prosecutor to disclose*

As to the replacement of the guidelines on disclosure and the protocol for the control and **12-54a** management of unused material in the Crown Court, see *ante*, § 12-45.

### Criminal Procedure and Investigations Act 1996, ss.6A–6E

*Contents of defence statement*

As to the replacement of the protocol for the control and management of unused material in **12-57a** the Crown Court, see *ante*, § 12-45.

### Criminal Procedure and Investigations Act 1996, ss.7–9

*Continuing duty of prosecutor to disclose*

The decision of the Divisional Court in *Nunn v. Chief Constable of Suffolk* (as to which, see the **★12-58b** main work) has been upheld by the Supreme Court: see *R. (Nunn) v. Chief Constable of Suffolk Constabulary*, unreported, June 18, 2014, SC ([2014] UKSC 37). For the Supreme Court's consideration of the ambit of the post-trial disclosure duty, see *ante*, § 12-49.

*Application by accused for disclosure*

As to the replacement of the protocol for the control and management of unused material in **12-59** the Crown Court, see *ante*, § 12-45.

### Criminal Procedure and Investigations Act 1996, ss.10, 11

*Faults in disclosure by accused*

As to the replacement of the protocol for the control and management of unused material in **12-62** the Crown Court, see *ante*, § 12-45.

## Attorney-General's guidelines on disclosure of information in criminal proceedings

As to the replacement of the Attorney-General's guidelines on disclosure, and the sup- **12-77** plementary guidelines relating to digitally-stored material, see *ante*, § 12-45.

## (2) Rules and regulations

### Criminal Procedure Rules 2013 (S.I. 2013 No. 1554), rr.22.1, 22.2, 22.3

*Prosecutor's application for public interest ruling*

As to the replacement of the protocol for the control and management of unused material in **12-82** the Crown Court, see *ante*, § 12-45.

*R. (Mohammed) v. Secretary of State for Defence* is now reported at [2014] 1 W.L.R. 1071. **★**

## Preparation of defence statements

As to the question mark as to the current status of the guidance in the main work, see *post*, Ap- **12-98** pendix C-46.

## (4) Sexual offences

### Sexual Offences (Protected Material) Act 1997

*Introductory*

*[Meaning of "protected material"*

**1.**—(1) In this Act "protected material", in relation to proceedings for a sexual offence, means a **12-102** copy (in whatever form) of any of the following material, namely—

 (a) a statement relating to that or any other sexual offence made by any victim of the offence (whether the statement is recorded in writing or in any other form),

 (b) a photograph or pseudo-photograph of any such victim, or

 (c) a report of a medical examination of the physical condition of any such victim,

which is a copy given by the prosecutor to any person under this Act.

(2) For the purposes of subsection (1) a person is, in relation to any proceedings for a sexual offence, a victim of that offence if—

 (a) the charge, summons or indictment by which the proceedings are instituted names that person as a person in relation to whom that offence was committed; or

 (b) that offence can, in the prosecutor's opinion, be reasonably regarded as having been committed in relation to that person;

and a person is, in relation to any such proceedings, a victim of any other sexual offence if that offence can, in the prosecutor's opinion, be reasonably regarded as having been committed in relation to that person.

(3) In this Act, where the context so permits (and subject to subsection (4))—

 (a) references to any protected material include references to any part of any such material; and

 (b) references to a copy of any such material include references to any part of any such copy.

(4) Nothing in this Act—

 (a) so far as it refers to a defendant making any copy of—

  (i) any protected material, or

  (ii) a copy of any such material,

 applies to a manuscript copy which is not a verbatim copy of the whole of that material or copy; or

 (b) so far as it refers to a defendant having in his possession any copy of any protected material, applies to a manuscript copy made by him which is not a verbatim copy of the whole of that material.]

*[Meaning of other expressions*

**12-103**    **2.**—(1) In this Act—

 "contracted out prison" means a contracted out prison within the meaning of Part IV of the Criminal Justice Act 1991;

 "defendant", in relation to any proceedings for a sexual offence, means any person charged with that offence (whether or not he has been convicted);

 "governor", in relation to a contracted out prison, means the director of the prison;

 "inform" means inform in writing;

 "legal representative", in relation to a defendant, means a person who, for the purposes of the Legal Services Act 2007, is an authorised person in relation to an activity which constitutes the exercise of a right of audience or the conduct of litigation (within the meaning of that Act) and who is acting for the defendant in connection with any proceedings for the sexual offence in question;

 "photograph" and "pseudo-photograph" shall be construed in accordance with section 7(4) and (7) of the Protection of Children Act 1978;

 "prison" means any prison, young offender institution or remand centre which is under the general superintendence of, or is provided by, the Secretary of State under the Prison Act 1952, including a contracted out prison;

 "proceedings" means (subject to subsection (2)) criminal proceedings;

 "the prosecutor", in relation to any proceedings for a sexual offence, means any person acting as prosecutor (whether an individual or a body);

 "relevant proceedings", in relation to any material which has been disclosed by the prosecutor under this Act, means any proceedings for the purposes of which it has been so disclosed or any further proceedings for the sexual offence in question;

 "sexual offence" means one of the offences listed in the Schedule to this Act.

(2) For the purposes of this Act references to proceedings for a sexual offence include references to—

 (a) any appeal or application for leave to appeal brought or made by or in relation to a defendant in such proceedings;

 (b) any application made to the Criminal Cases Review Commission for the reference under section 9 or 11 of the Criminal Appeal Act 1995 of any conviction, verdict, finding or sentence recorded or imposed in relation to any such defendant; and

(c)  any petition to the Secretary of State requesting him to recommend the exercise of Her Majesty's prerogative of mercy in relation to any such defendant.

(3) In this Act, in the context of the prosecutor giving a copy of any material to any person—

(a)  references to the prosecutor include references to a person acting on behalf of the prosecutor; and

(b)  where any such copy falls to be given to the defendant's legal representative, references to the defendant's legal representative include references to a person acting on behalf of the defendant's legal representative.]

[The definition of "legal representative" is printed as amended by the Legal Services Act 2007, s.208(1), and Sched 21, para. 123.]

*Regulation of disclosures to defendant*

*[Regulation of disclosures by prosecutor*

**3.**—(1) Where, in connection with any proceedings for a sexual offence, any statement or other   **12-104** material falling within any of paragraphs (a) to (c) of section 1(1) would (apart from this section) fall to be disclosed by the prosecutor to the defendant—

(a)  the prosecutor shall not disclose that material to the defendant; and

(b)  it shall instead be disclosed under this Act in accordance with whichever of subsections (2) and (3) below is applicable.

(2) If—

(a)  the defendant has a legal representative, and

(b)  the defendant's legal representative gives the prosecutor the undertaking required by section 4 (disclosure to defendant's legal representative),

the prosecutor shall disclose the material in question by giving a copy of it to the defendant's legal representative.

(3) If subsection (2) is not applicable, the prosecutor shall disclose the material in question by giving a copy of it to the appropriate person for the purposes of section 5 (disclosure to unrepresented defendant) in order for that person to show that copy to the defendant under that section.

(4) Where under this Act a copy of any material falls to be given to any person by the prosecutor, any such copy—

(a)  may be in such form as the prosecutor thinks fit, and

(b)  where the material consists of information which has been recorded in any form, need not be in the same form as that in which the information has already been recorded.

(5) Once a copy of any material is given to any person under this Act by the prosecutor, the copy shall (in accordance with section 1(1)) be protected material for the purposes of this Act.]

*[Disclosure to defendant's legal representative*

**4.**—(1) For the purposes of this Act the undertaking which a defendant's legal representative is   **12-105** required to give in relation to any protected material given to him under this Act is an undertaking by him to discharge the obligations set out in subsections (2) to (7).

(2) He must take reasonable steps to ensure—

(a)  that the protected material, or any copy of it, is only shown to the defendant in circumstances where it is possible to exercise adequate supervision to prevent the defendant retaining possession of the material or copy or making a copy of it, and

(b)  that the protected material is not shown and no copy of it is given, and its contents are not otherwise revealed, to any person other than the defendant, except so far as it appears to him necessary to show the material or give a copy of it to any such person—

(i)  in connection with any relevant proceedings, or

(ii)  for the purposes of any assessment or treatment of the defendant (whether before or after conviction).

(3) He must inform the defendant—

(a)  that the protected material is such material for the purposes of this Act,

(b)  that the defendant can only inspect that material, or any copy of it, in circumstances such as are described in subsection (2)(a), and

(c)  that it would be an offence for the defendant—

(i)  to have that material, or any copy of it, in his possession otherwise than while inspecting it or the copy in such circumstances, or

(ii)  to give that material or any copy of it, or otherwise reveal its contents, to any other person.

(4) He must, where the protected material or a copy of it has been shown or given in accordance with subsection (2)(b)(i) or (ii) to a person other than the defendant, inform that person—

    (a)   that that person must not give any copy of that material, or otherwise reveal its contents—

        (i)   to any other person other than the defendant, or

        (ii)   to the defendant otherwise than in circumstances such as are described in subsection (2)(a); and

    (b)   that it would be an offence for that person to do so.

(5) He must, where he ceases to act as the defendant's legal representative at a time when any relevant proceedings are current or in contemplation—

    (a)   inform the prosecutor of that fact, and

    (b)   if he is informed by the prosecutor that the defendant has a new legal representative who has given the prosecutor the undertaking required by this section, give the protected material, and any copies of it in his possession, to the defendant's new legal representative.

(6) He must, at the time of giving the protected material to the new legal representative under subsection (5), inform that person—

    (a)   that that material is protected material for the purposes of this Act, and

    (b)   of the extent to which—

        (i)   that material has been shown by him, and

        (ii)   any copies of it have been given by him,

        to any other person (including the defendant).

(7) He must keep a record of every occasion on which the protected material was shown, or a copy of it was given, as mentioned in subsection (6)(b).]

*[Disclosure to unrepresented defendant*

**12-106**    **5.**—(1) This section applies where, in accordance with section 3(3), a copy of any material falls to be given by the prosecutor to the appropriate person for the purposes of this section in order for that person to show that copy to the defendant under this section.

(2) Subject to subsection (3), the appropriate person in such a case is—

    (a)   if the defendant is detained in a prison, the governor of the prison or any person nominated by the governor for the purposes of this section; and

    (b)   otherwise the officer in charge of such police station as appears to the prosecutor to be suitable for enabling the defendant to have access to the material in accordance with this section or any person nominated by that officer for the purposes of this section.

(3) The Secretary of State may by regulations provide that, in such circumstances as are specified in the regulations, the appropriate person for the purposes of this section shall be a person of any description so specified.

(4) The appropriate person shall take reasonable steps to ensure—

    (a)   that the protected material, or any copy of it, is only shown to the defendant in circumstances where it is possible to exercise adequate supervision to prevent the defendant retaining possession of the material or copy or making a copy of it,

    (b)   that, subject to paragraph (a), the defendant is given such access to that material, or a copy of it, as he reasonably requires in connection with any relevant proceedings, and

    (c)   that that material is not shown and no copy of it is given, and its contents are not otherwise revealed, to any person other than the defendant.

(5) The prosecutor shall, at the time of giving the protected material to the appropriate person, inform him—

    (a)   that that material is protected material for the purposes of this Act, and

    (b)   that he is required to discharge the obligations set out in subsection (4) in relation to that material.

(6) The prosecutor shall at that time also inform the defendant—

    (a)   that that material is protected material for the purposes of this Act,

    (b)   that the defendant can only inspect that material, or any copy of it, in circumstances such as are described in subsection (4)(a), and

    (c)   that it would be an offence for the defendant—

        (i)   to have that material, or any copy of it, in his possession otherwise than while inspecting it or the copy in such circumstances, or

        (ii)   to give that material or any copy of it, or otherwise reveal its contents, to any other person,

as well as informing him of the effect of subsection (7).

(7) If—
 (a) the defendant requests the prosecutor in writing to give a further copy of the material mentioned in subsection (1) to some other person, and
 (b) it appears to the prosecutor to be necessary to do so—
   (i) in connection with any relevant proceedings, or
   (ii) for the purposes of any assessment or treatment of the defendant (whether before or after conviction),
the prosecutor shall give such a copy to that other person.

(8) The prosecutor may give such a copy to some other person where no request has been made under subsection (7) but it appears to him that in the interests of the defendant it is necessary to do so as mentioned in paragraph (b) of that subsection.

(9) The prosecutor shall, at the time of giving such a copy to a person under subsection (7) or (8), inform that person—
 (a) that the copy is protected material for the purposes of this Act,
 (b) that he must not give any copy of the protected material or otherwise reveal its contents—
   (i) to any person other than the defendant, or
   (ii) to the defendant otherwise than in circumstances such as are described in subsection (4)(a); and
 (c) that it would be an offence for him to do so.

(10) If the prosecutor—
 (a) receives a request from the defendant under subsection (7) to give a further copy of the material in question to another person, but
 (b) does not consider it to be necessary to do so as mentioned in paragraph (b) of that subsection and accordingly refuses the request,
he shall inform the defendant of his refusal.

(11) [*Making of regulations under subs. (3).*]]

[*Further disclosures by prosecutor*

**6.**—(1) Where— **12-107**
 (a) any material has been disclosed in accordance with section 3(2) to the defendant's legal representative, and
 (b) at a time when any relevant proceedings are current or in contemplation the legal representative either—
   (i) ceases to act as the defendant's legal representative in circumstances where section 4(5)(b) does not apply, or
   (ii) dies or becomes incapacitated,
that material shall be further disclosed under this Act in accordance with whichever of section 3(2) or (3) is for the time being applicable.

(2) Where—
 (a) any material has been disclosed in accordance with section 3(3), and
 (b) at a time when any relevant proceedings are current or in contemplation the defendant acquires a legal representative who gives the prosecutor the undertaking required by section 4,
that material shall be further disclosed under this Act, in accordance with section 3(2), to the defendant's legal representative.]

[**7.** [*Regulation of disclosures by Criminal Cases Review Commission.*]] **12-108**

*Supplementary*

[*Offences*

**8.**—(1) Where any material has been disclosed under this Act in connection with any proceedings **12-109** for a sexual offence, it is an offence for the defendant—
 (a) to have the protected material, or any copy of it, in his possession otherwise than while inspecting it or the copy in circumstances such as are described in section 4(2)(a) or 5(4)(a), or
 (b) to give that material or any copy of it, or otherwise reveal its contents, to any other person.

(2) Where any protected material, or any copy of any such material, has been shown or given to any person in accordance with section 4(2)(b)(i) or (ii) or section 5(7) or (8), it is an offence for that person to give any copy of that material or otherwise reveal its contents—
 (a) to any person other than the defendant, or
 (b) to the defendant otherwise than in circumstances such as are described in section 4(2)(a) or 5(4)(a).

(3) Subsections (1) and (2) apply whether or not any relevant proceedings are current or in contemplation (and references to the defendant shall be construed accordingly).

(4) A person guilty of an offence under this section is liable—

    (a)  on summary conviction, to imprisonment for a term not exceeding *six* [12] months or a fine not exceeding the statutory maximum or both;

    (b)  on conviction on indictment, to imprisonment for a term not exceeding two years or a fine or both.

(5) Where a person is charged with an offence under this section relating to any protected material or copy of any such material, it is a defence to prove that, at the time of the alleged offence, he was not aware, and neither suspected nor had reason to suspect, that the material or copy in question was protected material or (as the case may be) a copy of any such material.

(6) The court before which a person is tried for an offence under this section may (whether or not he is convicted of that offence) make an order requiring him to return any protected material, or any copy of any such material, in his possession to the prosecutor.

(7) Nothing in subsection (1) or (2) shall be taken to apply to—

    (a)  any disclosure made in the course of any proceedings before a court or in any report of any such proceedings, or

    (b)  any disclosure made or copy given by a person when returning any protected material, or a copy of any such material, to the prosecutor or the defendant's legal representative;

and accordingly nothing in section 4, or 5 shall be read as precluding the making of any disclosure or the giving of any copy in circumstances falling within paragraph (a) or (as the case may be) paragraph (b) above.]

[In subs. (4)(a), "12" is substituted for "six", as from a day to be appointed, by the CJA 2003, s.282(2) and (3). The increase has no application to offences committed before the substitution takes effect: s.282(4).]

*[Modification and amendment of other enactments*
**12-110**      **9.**—(1) [*Repealed by CJA 2003, s.332, and Sched. 37, Pt 4.*]

(2) Despite section 20(1) of the Criminal Procedure and Investigations Act 1996 (disclosure provisions of the Act not affected by other statutory duties), section 3(3) to (5) of that Act (manner of disclosure) shall not apply in relation to any disclosure required by section 3, 7 or 9 of that Act if section 3(1) above applies in relation to that disclosure.

(3) [*See ss.17 and 18 of the Criminal Procedure and Investigations Act 1996, §§ 12-68 et seq. in the main work*]

(4) [*Inserts subs. 1(6) into the Criminal Procedure and Investigations Act 1996, § 12-52 in the main work.*]]
**12-111**      [**10.** [*Financial provision.*]]

*[Short title, commencement and extent*
**12-112**      **11.**—(1) [*Short title.*]

(2) This Act shall come into force on such day as the Secretary of State may appoint by order made by statutory instrument.

(3) Nothing in this Act applies to any proceedings for a sexual offence where the defendant was charged with the offence before the commencement of this Act.

(4) This Act extends to England and Wales only.]

[Section 2                    SCHEDULE

Sexual Offences for Purposes of This Act

**12-113**      5. Any offence under section 1 of the Protection of Children Act 1978 or section 160 of the Criminal Justice Act 1988 (indecent photographs of children).

5A. Any offence under any provision of Part 1 of the Sexual Offences Act 2003 except section 64, 65, 69 or 71.

6. Any offence under section 1 of the Criminal Law Act 1977 of conspiracy to commit any of the offences mentioned in paragraphs 5 and 5A.

7. Any offence under section 1 of the Criminal Attempts Act 1981 of attempting to commit any of those offences.

8. Any offence of inciting another to commit any of those offences.]

[This schedule is printed as amended by the SOA 2003, ss.139 and 140, and Scheds 6, para. 36, and 7. The reference in para. 8 to inciting another to commit an offence has effect as a reference to the offences under Part 2 of the SCA 2007: 2007 Act, s.63(1), and Sched. 6, para. 34.]

CHAPTER 13

# EVIDENCE OF BAD CHARACTER

## III. DEFENDANTS

### B. THE SEVEN GATEWAYS

#### (2) Evidence adduced or elicited by defendant (s.101(1)(b))

Where a defendant puts his own bad character in evidence pursuant to section 101(1)(b) of the    **13-28**
CJA 2003 (§ 13-25 in the main work), but where the evidence could also have been admitted via
section 101(1)(g) (attack on another person's character), the judge may give the conventional
direction to the jury as to the approach to bad character evidence appropriate to a case where
such evidence is in fact admitted via gateway (g): *R. v. Speed,* 177 J.P. 649, CA.

#### (4) Important matter in issue between defendant and prosecution (ss.101(1)(d), 103)

(b) *Evidence that would have been admissible at common law*

**The unlikelihood of coincidence**

Where the defendant, charged with production of cannabis, had driven two co-accused from    **★13-42**
London to two adjacent houses in Darlington, where the police discovered 591 cannabis plants
there, where the car contained fertilizer, and where the passengers (and a third co-defendant
who had been present in one of the houses) pleaded guilty, it would have been positively surpris-
ing if the judge had not allowed evidence to be adduced of the defendant's previous conviction of
being concerned in the production of cannabis; it was plainly relevant to an important matter in
issue within section 101(1)(d) of the CJA 2003 (§ 13-25 in the main work)); the defence case was
one of innocent association and the jury were entitled to know that the appellant was saying that
it was a coincidence that he had been asked to drive two men plus fertiliser to a cannabis production operation, when he had a previous conviction for cannabis production: *R. v. Vo,* unreported,
November 19, 2013, CA ([2013] EWCA Crim. 2292).

#### (5) Important matter in issue between defendant and co-defendant (ss.101(1)(e), 104)

**Criminal Justice Act 2003, s.104**

Whereas one defendant (D) in a cut-throat case had given interviews to the police that were    **13-70**
particularly damaging to the case of his co-defendants, whereas the judge had refused an application for severance (based on the prejudicial nature of the interview evidence and the likelihood
that D would not give evidence) by his co-defendants, and whereas the judge had, when the
interview was introduced in evidence, given the jury a direction (emphasised again in his
summing-up) that what one defendant said about another could not be evidence against the other
and that they should be particularly careful to exclude the interview evidence of D when considering the case against his co-defendants, D's previous convictions should not have been admitted
under gateway (e) of section 101(1) of the 2003 Act because (as anticipated) he had not given
evidence, and so his interview formed no part of the evidence against his co-defendants, and
therefore the reliability or honesty of what he said in those interviews was not an issue in the trial
as between him and his co-defendants; although there may be circumstances in which a
defendant's previous convictions will be admissible through gateway (e) where he does not give
evidence (e.g. where they go to propensity), that was not this case: *R. v. Whitnell* [2014] 1
Cr.App.R. 9, CA.

# V. REHABILITATION OF OFFENDERS

## (1) Introduction

★**13-120**    With effect from March 27, 2014, the Rehabilitation of Offenders Act 1974 (Exceptions) Order 1975 (S.I. 1975 No. 1023) (see the main work) was further amended, subject to saving and transitional provisions, by the Public Bodies (Merger of the Director of Public Prosecutions and the Director of Revenue and Customs Prosecutions) Order 2014 (S.I. 2014 No. 834), art. 3(3), and Sched. 3, para. 1.

★    The decision of the civil division of the Court of Appeal in *R. (T.) v. Chief Constable of Greater Manchester (Liberty intervening)*; *R. (B.) v. Secretary of State for the Home Department*; *R. (W.) v. Secretary of State for Justice* (as to which, see the main work), that S.I. 1975 No. 1023 (*ante*) was *ultra vires*, has been reversed by the Supreme Court: see *R. (T.) v. Chief Constable of Greater Manchester Police (Liberty intervening)*; *R. (B.) v. Secretary of State for the Home Department*, unreported, June 18, 2014, SC ([2014] UKSC 35). As to this case, see also *post*, §§ 13-131, 16-107.

## (2) Practice direction

**13-121**    The 2013 criminal practice directions (see the main work) are now reported at [2013] 1 W.L.R. 3164.

## (3) Statute

### Rehabilitation of Offenders Act 1974, s.1

*Rehabilitated persons and spent convictions*

★**13-123**    With effect from March 10, 2014, section 141(10) of, and paragraphs 1 and 2 of Schedule 25 to, the LASPOA 2012 (see the main work) were brought into force, subject to the exception that they have no effect in relation to an order for endorsement made by a court in respect of an offence mentioned in Schedule 2 to the RTOA 1988 (§ 32-312 in the main work): Legal Aid, Sentencing and Punishment of Offenders Act 2012 (Commencement No. 9, Saving Provision and Specification of Commencement Date) Order 2014 (S.I. 2014 No. 423).

★    With effect from April 6, 2014, the provisions of the Tribunals, Courts and Enforcement Act 2007 referred to in the main work were brought into force: Tribunals, Courts and Enforcement Act 2007 (Commencement No. 11) Order 2014 (S.I. 2014 No. 768).

### Rehabilitation of Offenders Act 1974, s.2

*Rehabilitation of persons dealt with in service disciplinary proceedings*

★**13-124**    With effect from March 10, 2014, section 141(10) of, and paragraphs 1 and 3 of Schedule 25 to, the LASPOA 2012 (see the main work) were brought into force, subject to the exception that they have no effect in relation to an order for endorsement made by a court in respect of an offence mentioned in Schedule 2 to the RTOA 1988 (§ 32-312 in the main work): Legal Aid, Sentencing and Punishment of Offenders Act 2012 (Commencement No. 9, Saving Provision and Specification of Commencement Date) Order 2014 (S.I. 2014 No. 423).

### Rehabilitation of Offenders Act 1974, s.4

*Effect of rehabilitation*

★**13-126**    With effect from March 10, 2014, section 141(10) of, and paragraphs 1 and 5 of Schedule 25 to, the LASPOA 2012 (see the main work) were brought into force, subject to the exception that they have no effect in relation to an order for endorsement made by a court in respect of an offence mentioned in Schedule 2 to the RTOA 1988 (§ 32-312 in the main work): Legal Aid, Sentencing and Punishment of Offenders Act 2012 (Commencement No. 9, Saving Provision and Specification of Commencement Date) Order 2014 (S.I. 2014 No. 423).

### Rehabilitation of Offenders Act 1974, s.5

*Rehabilitation periods for particular sentences*

★**13-131**    With effect from March 10, 2014, section 139(1) to (4) of the LASPOA 2012 (see the main work) were brought into force, subject to the exception that they are of no effect in relation to an order for endorsement made by a court in respect of an offence mentioned in Schedule 2 to the RTOA 1988 (§ 32-312 in the main work): Legal Aid, Sentencing and Punishment of Offenders Act 2012 (Commencement No. 9, Saving Provision and Specification of Commencement Date) Order 2014 (S.I. 2014 No. 423).

The aspect of the decision of the civil division of the Court of Appeal in *R. (T.) v. Chief Constable* ★ *of Greater Manchester (Liberty intervening)*; *R. (B.) v. Secretary of State for the Home Department*; *R. (W.) v. Secretary of State for Justice* that is referred to in the main work was not the subject of challenge when the matter went to the Supreme Court: see *R. (T.) v. Chief Constable of Greater Manchester Police (Liberty intervening)*; *R. (B.) v. Secretary of State for the Home Department*, unreported, June 18, 2014, SC ([2014] UKSC 35). As to this case, see also *ante*, § 13-120; and *post*, § 16-107.

### Rehabilitation of Offenders Act 1974, s.6

*The rehabilitation period applicable to a conviction*

With effect from March 10, 2014, sections 139(1) and (5) and 141(10) of, and paragraphs 1 and ★**13-132** 11 of Schedule 25 to, the LASPOA 2012 (see the main work) were brought into force, subject to the exception that, except for section 139(5)(b) (omission of the 1974 Act, s.6(6)), they have no effect in respect of an order for endorsement made by a court in relation to an offence mentioned in Schedule 2 to the RTOA 1988 (§ 32-312 in the main work): Legal Aid, Sentencing and Punishment of Offenders Act 2012 (Commencement No. 9, Saving Provision and Specification of Commencement Date) Order 2014 (S.I. 2014 No. 423).

### Rehabilitation of Offenders Act 1974, s.7(1), (2), (4), (5)

*Limitations on rehabilitation under this Act, etc.*

With effect from March 10, 2014, section 141(10) of, and paragraphs 1 and 6 of Schedule 25 ★**13-133** to, the LASPOA 2012 (see the main work) were brought into force, subject to the exception that they have no effect in relation to an order for endorsement made by a court in respect of an offence mentioned in Schedule 2 to the RTOA 1988 (§ 32-312 in the main work): Legal Aid, Sentencing and Punishment of Offenders Act 2012 (Commencement No. 9, Saving Provision and Specification of Commencement Date) Order 2014 (S.I. 2014 No. 423).

## Cautions, etc.

With effect from March 10, 2014, sections 139(1), (6) and (7), and 141(10) of, and paragraphs 1 ★**13-135** and 8 of Schedule 25 to, the LASPOA 2012 (see the main work) were brought into force, subject to the exception that they have no effect in relation to an order for endorsement made by a court in respect of an offence mentioned in Schedule 2 to the RTOA 1988 (see § 32-312 in the main work): Legal Aid, Sentencing and Punishment of Offenders Act 2012 (Commencement No. 9, Saving Provision and Specification of Commencement Date) Order 2014 (S.I. 2014 No. 423).

### Legal Aid, Sentencing and Punishment of Offenders Act 2012, s.141

*Transitional and consequential provision*

By virtue of the Legal Aid, Sentencing and Punishment of Offenders Act 2012 (Commence- ★**13-136** ment No. 9, Saving Provision and Specification of Commencement Date) Order 2014 (S.I. 2014 No. 423), (i) subsections (1) to (6), (10) and (11) of section 141 of the 2012 Act (see the main work) were brought into force with effect from March 10, 2014, subject to the exceptions that (a) they have no effect in relation to an order for endorsement made by a court in respect of an offence mentioned in Schedule 2 to the RTOA 1988 (§ 32-312 in the main work), and (b) paragraph 4 of Schedule 25 (to which s.141(10) gives effect) has not been brought into force, and (ii) March 10, 2014, was specified as the "commencement date" for the purposes of section 141(1) to (6).

CHAPTER 14

# EVIDENCE OF IDENTIFICATION

*I. VISUAL IDENTIFICATION*

C. POLICE AND CRIMINAL EVIDENCE ACT 1984: CODE D

**(8) Effect of breaches of Code D**

**14-57**    A failure to inform the defendant's solicitor of a note of a telephone call made by a witness attending an identification parade to the police the day after an incident, in which she gave a description of the assailant that differed from the description in her witness statement two days later, was a clear breach of (what is now) paragraph D:3.1 of Code D (*post*, Appendix A-120); but the breach was not such as would on its own have led to the exclusion of the identification parade evidence under section 78 of the PACE Act 1984 (see § 15-401 in the main work): *R. v. Cole*, unreported, July 5, 2013, CA ([2013] EWCA Crim. 1149).

*II. IDENTIFICATION BY OTHER PERSONAL CHARACTERISTICS*

A. VOICE IDENTIFICATION

**Content**

**14-73a**    The identity of the speakers in a recorded conversation may, in certain circumstances, be proved by reference to the content of the recording alone: *H.K.S.A.R. v. Yeung Ka Ho*, unreported, September 26, 2013, Hong Kong Court of Final Appeal ([2013] HKCFA 82). As to this case, see also *ante*, § 4-360.

C. BLOOD, BODY SAMPLES, SECRETIONS, SCENT AND ODONTOLOGY

**DNA**

**14-81**    Where the only evidence against the defendant was a scarf left at the scene of a burglary, from which a DNA profile was derived from a small area of blood, which matched the profile of the defendant, but where the DNA could not be dated, so it was possible that another person had carried the scarf to the scene and where it was not possible to say how the DNA came to be on the scarf and there was no independent evidence that the burglar had cut himself, the judge had been wrong to refuse a submission of no case to answer. While, in an appropriate case, the requisite additional evidence could be very limited, there had to be some independent evidence establishing a nexus between the defendant and the crime: *R. v. Ogden*, unreported, June 28, 2013, CA ([2013] EWCA Crim. 1294).

CHAPTER 15

# INVESTIGATORY POWERS; CONFESSIONS; DISCRETION TO EXCLUDE EVIDENCE, ETC.

*I. INVESTIGATORY POWERS*

A. POLICE AND CRIMINAL EVIDENCE ACT 1984

**(2) Codes of practice**

(b) *Commencement*

**15-6**    The Police and Criminal Evidence Act 1984 (Codes of Practice) (Revisions to Codes A, B, C, E,

F and H) Order 2013 (S.I. 2013 No. 2685) brought revised Codes A, B, C, E, F and H into force
on October 27, 2013.

The Police and Criminal Evidence Act 1984 (Codes of Practice) (Revisions to Codes C and H)  ★
Order 2014 (S.I. 2014 No. 1237) brought revised Codes C and H into force on June 2, 2014. The
revisions implement obligations under European Parliament and Council Directive 2012/13/EU,
in relation to the right to information in criminal proceedings. Every detainee must be given a
revised written notice setting out his rights and entitlements whilst in custody. This has been
updated to reflect the new substantive rights conferred by the 2012 directive. In particular, more
information is to be given to the detainee as to the nature of the accusation, about accessing
records and documents about his arrest and detention and about the offence and the evidence, if
charged, about interpretation and translation facilities, about contact with consular authorities,
and about the maximum period of detention, reviews of detention and release. For the text of all
the codes, see *post*, Appendix A-1 *et seq.*

*R. (H.C. (a child, by his litigation friend C.C.)) v. Secretary of State for the Home Department* is now
reported at [2014] 1 W.L.R. 1234, *sub nom. R. (C.) v. Secretary of State for the Home Department.*

### (3) "Reasonable grounds for suspicion"

For a case considering "reasonable suspicion" under Canadian law in the context of the deploy-  **15-14**
ment of a drug sniffer dog in a search, see *R. v. Chehil, post,* § 27-104.

The aspect of *R. (Hicks) v. Commr of Police of the Metropolis*; *R. (M.) v. Same*; *R. (Pearce) v. Same*;  **★15-15**
*R. (Middleton) v. Bromley Magistrates' Court and Commr of Police of the Metropolis* that is referred to in
the main work was not the subject of challenge when the matter went to the Court of Appeal: see
*R. (Hicks) v. Commr of Police of the Metropolis* [2014] 2 Cr.App.R. 4, CA (Civ. Div.).

### (6) Interpretation

#### Police and Criminal Evidence Act 1984, s.118

*General interpretation*

With effect from May 13, 2014 (Anti-social Behaviour, Crime and Policing Act 2014 (Com-  **★15-21**
mencement No. 2, Transitional and Transitory Provisions) Order 2014 (S.I. 2014 No. 949), any
reference in the 1984 Act to an "indictable offence" has effect as if it included a reference to "low-
value shoplifting", as defined in section 22A(3) of the MCA 1980 (as to which, see *ante,* § 1-108a):
Anti-social Behaviour, Crime and Policing Act 2014, s.176(6). The amendments made by section
176 have effect in relation to (i) low-value shoplifting committed on or after May 13, 2014, and (ii)
low-value shoplifting committed before May 13, 2014, in respect of which proceedings have not
yet been instituted on that date (2014 Act, s.176(8)).

### (7) Application of Act to Armed Forces

#### Police and Criminal Evidence Act 1984, s.113

The Police and Criminal Evidence Act 1984 (Armed Forces) Order 2009 (S.I. 2009 No. 1922)  **15-23**
(see the main work) is further amended by the Police and Criminal Evidence Act 1984 (Armed
Forces) (Amendment) Order 2013 (S.I. 2013 No. 2554) with effect from October 31, 2013. The
effect is to substitute article 15 and insert new articles 15A to 15N in order to make provision
equivalent to the amendments to the 1984 Act effected by the Protection of Freedoms Act 2012 in
respect of the retention and destruction of fingerprints, footwear impressions and DNA samples
taken by the police. Articles 15 to 15N equate to sections 63AA, 63D to 63F, 63H, 63I, 63K and
63N to 63U of the 1984 Act (as to which, see §§ 15-189a, 15-197 in the main work).

### (8) Application of Act to Revenue and Customs

#### S.I. 2007 No. 3175

*Modification of section 64 of the Act (destruction of fingerprints and samples)*

With effect from April 11, 2014, article 14 of the Police and Criminal Evidence Act 1984 (Ap-  **★15-30**
plication to Revenue and Customs) Order 2007 (S.I. 2007 No. 3175) was revoked: Police and

Criminal Evidence Act 1984 (Application to Revenue and Customs) (Amendment) Order 2014 (S.I. 2014 No. 788).

### Provisions of the Act applied to Revenue and Customs

★**15-32**    With effect from April 11, 2014, Schedule 1 to the Police and Criminal Evidence Act 1984 (Application to Revenue and Customs) Order 2007 (S.I. 2007 No. 3175) was amended by the Police and Criminal Evidence Act 1984 (Application to Revenue and Customs) (Amendment) Order 2014 (S.I. 2014 No. 788), so as to substitute, for the reference to section 64 of the 1984 Act, a reference to sections 63D, 63E and 63G to 63U.

## B. STOP AND SEARCH

### (2) Criminal Justice and Public Order Act 1994

#### Criminal Justice and Public Order Act 1994, s.60

*Powers to stop and search in anticipation of, or after, violence*

**15-48**    The Divisional Court's decision in *R. (Roberts) v. Commr of Police of the Metropolis* (see the main work) has been upheld: see *R. (Roberts) v. Commr of Police of the Metropolis (Liberty intervening)* [2014] 2 Cr.App.R. 6, CA (Civ. Div.). For a criticism of the appellate court's reasoning, see the commentary at CLW/14/07/6.

## C. ENTRY, SEARCH AND SEIZURE

### (1) Introduction

★**15-53**    With effect from May 13, 2014, the Armed Forces (Powers of Stop and Search, Search, Seizure and Retention) Order 2009 (S.I. 2009 No. 2056) was further amended by the Armed Forces (Powers of Stop and Search, Search, Seizure and Retention) (Amendment) Order 2014 (S.I. 2014 No. 934).

### (2) Statute

#### Police and Criminal Evidence Act 1984, s.8

*Power of justice of the peace to authorise entry and search of premises*

★**15-54**    In *R. (Cheema) v. Nottingham and Newark Magistrates' Court*, unreported, December 11, 2013, DC ([2013] EWHC 3790 (Admin.)), it was held that, since a justice issuing a warrant under section 8 of the 1984 Act must be satisfied that there are reasonable grounds for believing that the material sought "is likely to be relevant evidence" (s.8(1)(c)), a warrant that used the formula "and any other items which appear relevant to the offences under investigation" was bad on its face as it delegated to the executing officer the responsibility for deciding on relevance. As to this case, see also *post*, § 15-112.

**15-55**    For another case in which it was said that, on a failure by an applicant for a search warrant to present accurately and fairly the evidence upon which the application is founded, the test for deciding whether the warrant should be quashed is whether any errors and omissions would in fact have made a difference to the granting of the warrant, see *R. (Goode) v. Nottingham Crown Court* [2014] A.C.D. 6, DC. As to this case, see also *post*, §§ 15-105, 15-112.

★    Where the police sought a warrant under section 8 of the 1984 Act to search the home of the claimants, family members of a missing man wanted for murder, knowing that they were also criminal solicitors whose work included acting as duty solicitors, where the claimants were not under suspicion for any reason related to their work, and where the issuing justice was not informed of their profession, given that there is every likelihood that a solicitor (especially one who works as a duty solicitor) would take his work-based electronic devices home, that it is common knowledge that criminal solicitors may not maintain separate devices for home and work, and that one question for the justice was whether there were reasonable grounds to believe that the material sought would not consist of or include items subject to legal privilege (s.8(1)(d)), it was obviously material to know that the computers and other devices for which the warrant was sought belonged to solicitors practising in the field of criminal law, and there was plainly a duty to disclose that fact; the failure to do so had the consequence that it was highly likely that the terms of the warrant, as drafted, would cover significant quantities of material that was legally privileged; the warrant was thus unlawful: *R. (A.B. and C.D.) v. Huddersfield Magistrates' Court and Chief Constable of West Yorkshire Police*, 178 J.P. 265, DC. As to this case, see also *post*, § 15-85.

**15-56**

As to the necessity of recording applications for search warrants under section 8 of the 1984 Act, see *R. (S.) v. Chief Constable of British Transport Police (Practice Note)*, *post*, § 15-62.

★

A property owner is entitled, in the absence of public interest immunity, to see the information in support of an application for a search warrant: *Commr of Police for the Metropolis v. Bangs*, 178 J.P. 158, DC. Where public interest immunity is raised by way of objection to an application for access to the information (as to which, see *Taylor v. Anderton*, § 15-85 in the main work), the procedure to be followed should be analogous to that adopted in a criminal trial where public interest immunity is raised as a justification for non-disclosure of material that would otherwise fall to be disclosed; and, in all cases where the issue of public interest immunity is raised, what has to be balanced is the public interest that demands the material be withheld, as against the public interest in the administration of justice that the parties and the court should have the fullest possible access to all relevant material: *ibid.* (holding that the magistrates' court had erred in asking whether disclosure would result in the harm identified by the police, when it should have asked whether there was a real risk of it occurring).

### Police and Criminal Evidence Act 1984, Sched. 1

### Procedure

★**15-62**

The decision of the High Court in *R. (British Sky Broadcasting Ltd) v. Central Criminal Court* (as to which, see the main work) has been upheld on appeal: *R. (British Sky Broadcasting Ltd) v. Central Criminal Court (B. intervening)* [2014] 2 W.L.R. 558, SC, where it was said that, Parliament having decreed that an application under paragraph 7 of Schedule 1 to the 1984 Act for a production order in relation to "special procedure" or "excluded" material must be made *inter partes*, equal treatment of the parties requires that each should know what material the other is asking the court to take into account in making its decision and should have a fair opportunity to respond to it; that is inherent in the concept of an *inter partes* hearing; *ex parte* public interest immunity hearings were distinguishable on the basis that, if a claim to public interest immunity is upheld, the material forms no part of the *inter partes* hearing, whereas, here, the judge had relied on the withheld material in making his decision on the application for a production order.

For a comprehensive review of what an information in support of an application for a warrant under Schedule 1 to the 1984 Act (as to which, see §§ 15-58 *et seq.* in the main work) should contain, and as to the correct procedure, see *R. (S.) v. Chief Constable of British Transport Police (Practice Note)* [2014] 1 W.L.R. 1647, DC. The court said: (i) investigating authorities would be well-advised to seek legal advice before drafting informations and making applications for "special procedure" search warrants, especially if the material sought is more than likely to contain legally privileged material; it is clear from Schedule 1 that the information must (a) set out each of the statutory requirements that has to be satisfied in the particular case before a warrant can be granted; there are a number of different routes to a search warrant and only the route actually selected should be dealt with, or else the judge will not know the precise basis of the application; (b) show how each relevant requirement is satisfied by setting out all the relevant facts relied on, including all facts and matters that are said to show that a particular "reasonable belief" is justified and why it is in the public interest for the material to be produced, having regard to the considerations set out in paragraph 2(c); it is not enough to assert that a particular requirement is satisfied without explaining how it is said to be so; (c) state whether there might be a claim for legal privilege in respect of any communication sought and, if so, how and why that would arise, together with precise details of the arrangements for ensuring that there will be an independent supervising lawyer present at the time of the search (in addition to recognising the right of the owner of the material or his representative also to be present, particularly where a solicitor's premises are being searched for material relating to his work and clients); (d) make full and frank disclosure; a prosecutor seeking an *ex parte* order must put on his defence hat (*Re Stanford International Bank Ltd*; *Janvey v. Wastell*; *Serious Fraud Office v. Wastell* (as to which, see § 5-844 in the main work)); this is a heavy burden but a vital safeguard; full details must be given; it is a useful reminder to the person laying the information to state expressly what information is being given pursuant to the duty of full and frank disclosure; and (e) if further information is supplied to the circuit judge during the hearing of the application, whether as a result of judicial questioning or otherwise, the original information should be supplemented by a witness statement or a further information setting out the fresh material; (ii) the judge should give careful scrutiny to the application, give reasons, and explain, at least briefly, which access conditions he has applied and why he is satisfied that they and the other statutory requirements in Schedule 1 have or have not been fulfilled; (iii) as a matter of practice, all applications for a search warrant, whether for a warrant under section 8 of the 1984 Act (power of justice of the peace to authorise entry and search of premises (§ 15-54 in the main work)), or of the special procedure type, must be recorded so that there can be no dispute about what was or was not said; (iv) there must not be unilateral redaction by the investigating authority of a part of an information that is disclosed to a claimant either before or during judicial review proceedings concerning the grant or execution of a search warrant; the same is true of the transcripts of applications for a search warrant; if public interest immunity is sought, it must be obtained using the correct procedure (as to which, see the Civil Procedure Rules 1998 (S.I. 1998 No. 3132), r.31.19).

### Requests for mutual assistance

★**15-72a**     Where, following a request for mutual assistance from a foreign judicial authority, an application is made for a search warrant under Schedule 1 to the 1984 Act (as to which, see §§ 15-58 *et seq.* in the main work) (as extended by the Crime (International Co-operation) Act 2003, s.16), the question whether the material is likely to be relevant and of substantial value (see para. 2(a)(iii) and (iv)) is to be assessed on a necessarily more circumscribed basis than if the material were being sought in aid of a domestic investigation or prosecution; the international instruments, pursuant to which such requests are made, operate on the basis of a high level of mutual trust between the signatory member states, and do not operate on the basis that the courts of the requested state conduct mini-trials of the case to determine what is pivotally relevant to the trial that has yet to occur in the foreign jurisdiction: *Van der Pijl v. Secretary of State for the Home Department* [2014] Lloyd's Rep. F.C. 362, DC. As to this case, see also *post*, § 15-112.

### Police and Criminal Evidence Act 1984, ss.15, 16

*Search warrants—safeguards*

★**15-84**     For the modified application of section 15 of the 1984 Act to search and seizure warrants sought under section 352 of the PCA 2002 for the purposes of a confiscation or money laundering investigation, and the powers of seizure under them, see *post*, § 15-240.

★     For a case considering the appropriateness of continuing with judicial review proceedings seeking the quashing of a search warrant issued under section 8 of the 1984 Act (as to which, see § 15-54 in the main work) and a declaration that the search and seizure pursuant to the warrant were unlawful because of non-compliance with section 15 of that Act, notwithstanding the fact that there was a pending application to the Crown Court under section 59 of the CJPA 2001, see *R. (Cheema) v. Nottingham and Newark Magistrates' Court*, *post*, § 15-112.

★**15-85**     In *R. (A.B. and C.D.) v. Huddersfield Magistrates' Court and Chief Constable of West Yorkshire Police*, 178 J.P. 265, DC, the court said (referring to *R. (Van der Pijl) v. Crown Court at Kingston* (as to which, see the main work)) that, as has frequently been emphasised, a warrant must be capable of being understood as a free-standing document, and that, whilst the court's first instinct may be to consider whether the warrant can reasonably be construed in a manner that is satisfactory, it is necessary to bear in mind that the pragmatic test is that the occupier who reads it should be able to understand its legitimate ambit. As to this case, see also *ante*, § 15-55.

★     In *Lees v. Solihull Magistrates' Court* [2014] Lloyd's Rep. F.C. 233, DC, however, the point was made that, when considering whether the obligation under section 15(6)(b), for the warrant to identify, so far as practicable, the articles sought, has been satisfied, it may be necessary to look back to the information before the magistrates in order to identify what those articles must have been. On the facts, the vague terms of the warrant were in stark contrast to the precise information supplied to the magistrates.

*Execution of warrants*

For the modified application of section 16 of the 1984 Act to search and seizure warrants sought under section 352 of the PCA 2002 for the purposes of a confiscation or money laundering investigation, and the powers of seizure under them, see *post*, § 15-240.    **★15-86**

The existence of a valid and effective search warrant may be inferred, in the absence of any countervailing evidence, from evidence as to the manner in which a search was carried out: *Sykes v. CPS* [2014] Crim.L.R. 542, QBD (Haddon-Cave J.).    **★**

The decision of the Divisional Court in *R. (Hicks) v. Commr of Police of the Metropolis; R. (M.) v. Same; R. (Pearce) v. Same; R. (Middleton) v. Bromley Magistrates' Court and Commr of Police of the Metropolis* (see the main work), in relation to police motivation and "purpose" under section 16(8) of the 1984 Act, has been upheld: *R. (Pearce) v. Metropolitan Police Commr* [2013] 9 *Archbold Review* 3, CA (Civ. Div.) ([2013] EWCA Civ. 866).    **15-87**

In *Finnigan v. Chief Constable of Northumbria Police* [2014] 1 W.L.R. 445, CA (Civ. Div.), it was held that where it was the defendant's practice to conduct searches in spoken English, the effect of sections 20 and 29(7) of the Equality Act 2010 (where a practice of a person exercising a public function put a disabled person at a substantial disadvantage in relation to a relevant matter in comparison with persons who were not disabled, the former was under a duty to take such steps as it was reasonable to have to take to avoid the disadvantage) was to require the defendant to make reasonable adjustments to that practice so that it did not have a detrimental effect on deaf persons; and that it could not be discharged by deciding on an individual basis how to conduct a search with a particular deaf person. The court observed that the duty might be discharged by adopting a policy of having a sign language interpreter on standby every time there was a search of premises of a person known or believed to be deaf, or by taking other reasonable steps, such as, with some classes of deaf people, having available the assistance of officers skilled in lip reading and sign language.

### Police and Criminal Evidence Act 1984, s.19

*General power of seizure, etc.*

The decision of the Divisional Court in *R. (Hicks) v. Commr of Police of the Metropolis; R. (M.) v. Same; R. (Pearce) v. Same; R. (Middleton) v. Bromley Magistrates' Court and Commr of Police of the Metropolis* (see the main work), has been upheld: *R. (Pearce) v. Metropolitan Police Commr* [2013] 9 *Archbold Review* 3, CA (Civ. Div.) ([2013] EWCA Civ. 866).    **15-93**

### Police and Criminal Evidence Act 1984, ss.20, 21

*Access and copying*

For the modified application of section 21 of the 1984 Act to search and seizure warrants sought under section 352 of the PCA 2002 for the purposes of a confiscation or money laundering investigation, and the powers of seizure under them, see *post*, § 15-240.    **★15-95**

### Police and Criminal Evidence Act 1984, s.22

*Retention*

For the modified application of section 22 of the 1984 Act to search and seizure warrants sought under section 352 of the PCA 2002 for the purposes of a confiscation or money laundering investigation, and the powers of seizure under them, see *post*, § 15-240.    **★15-97**

### Criminal Justice and Police Act 2001, ss.50–52

*Notice of exercise of power under s.50 or 51*

*R. (Dulai) v. Chelmsford Magistrates' Court and Essex County Council; R. (Essex County Council) v. Chelmsford Crown Court and Essex Magistrates' Court, Dulai (interested parties)* (see the main work) was followed in *R. (Goode) v. Nottingham Crown Court* [2014] A.C.D. 6, DC, where a section 52 notice referring only to "documents" did not invalidate a seizure of computer equipment pursuant to section 50 of the 2001 Act. As to this case, see also *ante*, § 15-55; and *post*, § 15-112.    **15-105**

### Criminal Justice and Police Act 2001, ss.59–62

*Application to the appropriate judicial authority*

**15-112**     Section 59(3)(a) of the 2001 Act, which provides that one of the grounds for a judge of the Crown Court granting an application under section 59 is that "there was no power to make the seizure", does not allow for challenges to the validity of the warrant itself; such is the business of the High Court: *R. (Goode) v. Nottingham Crown Court* [2014] A.C.D. 6, DC. As to this case, see also *ante*, §§ 15-55, 15-105.

★     In *R. (Cheema) v. Nottingham and Newark Magistrates' Court*, unreported, December 11, 2013, DC ([2013] EWHC 3790 (Admin.)), the claimants sought to have a search warrant issued under section 8 of the PACE Act 1984 (§ 15-54 in the main work) quashed for non-compliance with the access criteria, and to have the search and seizure pursuant thereto declared unlawful for failure of the warrant to comply with section 15(6)(b) of the 1984 Act (*ibid.*, § 15-84). The prosecution contended that the judicial review proceedings should not be allowed to proceed as it was conceded that the warrant did not comply with section 15(6)(b), and an application under section 59 of the 2001 Act to rectify the situation was pending before the Crown Court. It was held: (i) that there was a continuing need to consider the grounds of challenge because the outcome, and any consequential relief granted, would be matters that any court hearing the section 59 application would need to take into account when considering whether to exercise its discretionary power to order retention of the property unlawfully seized; the court hearing the section 59 application would need to look to the extent and nature of the illegality giving rise to the fact that the property would otherwise fall to be returned; the full circumstances required rigorous examination to determine whether it was a case of mere technicality or one involving more serious default on the part of the applicant; the court would need to consider whether any illegality concerned only the way in which the warrant was drawn up, or whether it went also to the grounds for the grant of the warrant and hence the legality of the warrant itself (which could not be challenged in the Crown Court), and whether the High Court had quashed the warrant; (ii) that the warrant not only failed to comply with section 15(6)(b) of the 1984 Act (as conceded by the prosecution), but was also bad on its face for non-compliance with section 8(1)(c) of that Act (as to which, see *ante*, § 15-54); (iii) as to relief, first, it was appropriate to grant a declaration as to the unlawfulness of the searches and seizures notwithstanding the concession made by the prosecution; secondly, it was appropriate to quash the warrant itself; it had been issued in respect of four specified premises, but the information before the justice did not justify issuing a warrant in respect of two of those premises; this was no mere technicality, albeit evidence existed as to the necessary connections between the four premises and the suspects, which evidence would have justified a warrant in respect of all four premises; but, in light of the pending application under section 59, no order would be made for the return of the property seized or of any copies, even though the claimants were entitled to their return; it would be for the Crown Court to decide, if the conditions in section 59(7) were made out, whether the public interest in the investigation of crime should prevail over the countervailing public interest in upholding the requirement for due legal process in the grant and execution of warrants.

★     There is nothing in section 59 of the 2001 Act that precludes its application to the curing of a defective warrant obtained and executed pursuant to a request for assistance from a foreign judicial authority: *Van der Pijl v. Secretary of State for the Home Department* [2014] Lloyd's Rep. F.C. 362, DC. As to this case, see also *ante*, § 15-72a.

## D. ARREST

### (2) The Police and Criminal Evidence Act 1984

#### Police and Criminal Evidence Act 1984, s.32

*Search upon arrest*

**15-152**     The words "any such case" in section 32(2) of the 1984 Act (as to which, see § 15-151 in the main work) refer to "any case where the person to be searched has been arrested at a place other than a police station" (see subs. (1)) and do not import the additional requirement in that subsection that there be reasonable grounds for believing that the arrested person may present a danger to himself or others: *Lord Hanningfield of Chelmsford v. Chief Constable of Essex Police* [2013] 1 W.L.R. 3632, QBD (Eady J.).

## E. Questioning and Treatment of Persons

### (1) Introduction

As to the commencement of revised Codes C and H, see *ante*, § 15-6. ★**15-154**

### (4) Additional rights of children and young persons

#### Children and Young Persons Act 1933, s.34

*R. (H.C. (a child, by his litigation friend C.C.)) v. Secretary of State for the Home Department* is now **15-165**
reported at [2014] 1 W.L.R. 1234, *sub nom. R. (C.) v. Secretary of State for the Home Department*.

### (5) Access to legal advice

#### Police and Criminal Evidence Act 1984, s.58

## Right of access to solicitor

As to there being no obligation on the police to make specific reference to the duty solicitor ★**15-167**
scheme in referring to the right to free legal advice, see *Beeres v. CPS, post*, § 15-422.

### (8) Fingerprints, photographs, intimate and other samples

#### Police and Criminal Evidence Act 1984, s.61

*Fingerprinting*

With effect from May 13, 2014 (Anti-social Behaviour, Crime and Policing Act 2014 (Com- ★**15-178**
mencement No. 2, Transitional and Transitory Provisions) Order 2014 (S.I. 2014 No. 949), section 61 of the 1984 Act was amended by the Anti-social Behaviour, Crime and Policing Act 2014,
s.144(1), so as: (i) in subsections (5A) and (5B), to substitute, for the words after "investigation" in
paragraph (b), the words—

> "but—
> > (i) subsection (3A)(a) or (b) above applies, or
> > (ii) subsection (5C) below applies";

and (ii) to insert a new subsection (5C), as follows—

> "(5C) This subsection applies where—
> > (a) the investigation was discontinued but subsequently resumed, and
> > (b) before the resumption of the investigation the fingerprints were destroyed pursuant to sec-
> > tion 63D(3) below.".

#### Police and Criminal Evidence Act 1984, s.61A

*Impressions of footwear*

For a first instance decision in which prosecution evidence relating to impressions of a **15-180**
defendant's footwear was held to be inadmissible, see *R. v Howe* 78 J.C.L. 6, Crown Court at
Newcastle upon Tyne (H.H. Judge Milford Q.C.) (police force's deliberate disregard of s.61A(5)
and (6) held to be a "flagrant breach" of the rules).

#### Police and Criminal Evidence Act 1984, s.63

*Other samples*

With effect from May 13, 2014 (Anti-social Behaviour, Crime and Policing Act 2014 (Com- ★**15-183**
mencement No. 2, Transitional and Transitory Provisions) Order 2014 (S.I. 2014 No. 949), section 63 of the 1984 Act was amended by the Anti-social Behaviour, Crime and Policing Act 2014,
s.144(2), so as: (i) to insert, at the end of subsection (3ZA)(b)—

", or
(iii)  subsection (3AA) below applies.";

(ii) in subsection (3A)(b), to substitute, for the words "insufficient; or", the words—

"insufficient, or
(iii)  subsection (3AA) below applies; or";

and (iii) to insert a new subsection (3AA) after subsection (3A), as follows—

"(3AA) This subsection applies where the investigation was discontinued but subsequently resumed, and before the resumption of the investigation—
(a) any DNA profile derived from the sample was destroyed pursuant to section 63D(3) below, and
(b) the sample itself was destroyed pursuant to section 63R(4), (5) or (12) below.".

Whereas, under section 63(3B) of the 1984 Act, a non-intimate sample may be taken from a person without consent where certain conditions relating to previous convictions are met, whereas, under subsection (3BB), this may only be done if authorised by an officer of at least the rank of inspector, and whereas, under paragraph 11 of Schedule 2A (§ 15-188 in the main work), a constable may require a person to attend a police station for the purpose of having a sample taken under section 63(3B), paragraph 15 of that schedule (*ibid.*, § 15–189) makes clear that authorisation for the taking of the sample must be obtained before the requirement to attend a police station is made: *R. (R.) v. A Chief Constable* [2014] 1 Cr.App.R. 19, DC. The court further held that the requirement imposed on the claimant (convicted in 1984 of manslaughter, 1993 of kidnapping, 1997 of driving with excess alcohol, and 1999 of a public order offence), as part of a wider police operation ("Operation Nutmeg") aimed at offenders with certain previous convictions, to attend a police station for the purpose of having a non-intimate sample taken for comparison with crime scene profiles held in the national DNA database, was lawful; the authorising officer's conclusion that the requirement was proportionate in the circumstances was correct, and his conclusion that the public interest in the detection of crime outweighed the limited interference with the claimant's rights under Article 8(1) of the ECHR (privacy and family life (*ibid.*, § 16-101)) was justified; the statistical probability that any one of the samples gathered as part of the police operation would produce a match with the crime scene database was not determinative of the issue of proportionality; acceptance of propensity to commit offences as a measure (albeit an imprecise one) of probability in the detection and proof of further offences was now so widespread that the authorising officer was justified in placing weight upon it; and the absence of specific grounds for suspecting the claimant did not render the requirement disproportionate; the essential question was whether the information before the authorising officer, without more, justified the requirement made, which, given the claimant's history, it did. As to the opportunity to make representations, the court said that a person who is asked in the first instance to consent to the supply of a sample should be afforded an opportunity to respond; if he then offers reasons why it would be, in his particular case, unreasonable or disproportionate to authorise the taking of a sample without consent, the inspector would be under a duty to consider them before making his decision whether or not to give the necessary authorisation. For the Home Office response to this decision, see *post*, § 15-189a.

### Police and Criminal Evidence Act 1984, Sched. 2A

*Persons arrested and released*

★**15-186**     With effect from May 13, 2014 (Anti-social Behaviour, Crime and Policing Act 2014 (Commencement No. 2, Transitional and Transitory Provisions) Order 2014 (S.I. 2014 No. 949), paragraph 1 of Schedule 2A to the 1984 Act was amended by the Anti-social Behaviour, Crime and Policing Act 2014, s.181(1), and Sched. 11, para. 86(1) and (2), so as: (i) in sub-paragraph (2), to substitute, for the words "section 61(5A)(b)", the words "section 61(5A)(b)(i)"; and (ii) to insert a new sub-paragraph (4), as follows—

"(4) The power under sub-paragraph (1) above may not be exercised in a case falling within section 61(5A)(b)(ii) (fingerprints destroyed where investigation interrupted) after the end of the period of six months beginning with the day on which the investigation was resumed.".

*Persons charged etc*

★     With effect from May 13, 2014 (Anti-social Behaviour, Crime and Policing Act 2014 (Commencement No. 2, Transitional and Transitory Provisions) Order 2014 (S.I. 2014 No. 949), paragraph 2 of Schedule 2A to the 1984 Act was amended by the Anti-social Behaviour, Crime and Policing Act 2014, s.181(1), and Sched. 11, para. 86(1) and (3), so as: (i) in sub-paragraph (2)(b), to substitute, for the words "section 61(5B)(b)", the words "section 61(5B)(b)(i) "; and (ii) to insert, at the end of sub-paragraph (2)—

> ", or
>> (c) in a case falling within section 61(5B)(b)(ii) (fingerprints destroyed where investigation interrupted), the day on which the investigation was resumed".

*Persons arrested and released*

With effect from May 13, 2014 (Anti-social Behaviour, Crime and Policing Act 2014 (Com- ★**15-188** mencement No. 2, Transitional and Transitory Provisions) Order 2014 (S.I. 2014 No. 949), paragraph 9 of Schedule 2A to the 1984 Act was amended by the Anti-social Behaviour, Crime and Policing Act 2014, s.181(1), and Sched. 11, para. 86(1) and (4), so as: (i) in sub-paragraph (2), to substitute, for the words "within section 63(3ZA)(b)", the words "within section 63(3ZA)(b)(i) or (ii)"; and (ii) to insert a new sub-paragraph (4), as follows—

> "(4) The power under sub-paragraph (1) above may not be exercised in a case falling within section 63(3ZA)(b)(iii) (sample, and any DNA profile, destroyed where investigation interrupted) after the end of the period of six months beginning with the day on which the investigation was resumed.".

*Persons charged etc*

With effect from May 13, 2014 (Anti-social Behaviour, Crime and Policing Act 2014 (Com- ★ mencement No. 2, Transitional and Transitory Provisions) Order 2014 (S.I. 2014 No. 949), paragraph 10 of Schedule 2A to the 1984 Act was amended by the Anti-social Behaviour, Crime and Policing Act 2014, s.181(1), and Sched. 11, para. 86(1) and (5), so as: (i) in sub-paragraph (3), to substitute, for the words "within section 63(3A)(b)", the words "within section 63(3A)(b)(i) or (ii)"; and (ii) to insert a new sub-paragraph (5), as follows—

> "(5) The power under sub-paragraph (1) above may not be exercised in a case falling within section 63(3A)(b)(iii) (sample, and any DNA profile, destroyed where investigation interrupted) after the end of the period of six months beginning with the day on which the investigation was resumed.".

**National DNA database**

As a response to the possible implications of the decision in *R. (R.) v. A Chief Constable, ante,* § **15-189a** 15-183, the government has amended the Protection of Freedoms Act 2012 (Destruction, Retention and Use of Biometric Data) (Transitional, Transitory and Saving Provisions) Order 2013 (S.I. 2013 No. 1813) (see the main work). New articles 2A and 5A were inserted, with effect from October 31, 2013, by the Protection of Freedoms Act 2012 (Destruction, Retention and Use of Biometric Data) (Transitional, Transitory and Saving Provisions) (Amendment) Order 2013 (S.I. 2013 No. 2580). New article 2A provides that fingerprints and DNA profiles derived from a sample taken before that date may be retained, notwithstanding the PACE Act 1984, s.63D(2)(a) (fingerprints and DNA profiles to which s.63D applies must be destroyed if it appears to the responsible chief officer of police that the taking of the fingerprint or, in the case of a DNA profile, the taking of the sample from which the profile was obtained was unlawful), if taken from a person who was convicted of a recordable offence (other than an excluded offence within the 1984 Act, s.63F(11)), and who, at the time the fingerprints or sample were taken, gave purported consent to them being taken. New article 5A provides that in its application to "PACE material" (as to which, see the main work) taken, or (in the case of a DNA profile) derived from a sample taken, before October 31, 2013, from a person who was liable to have material taken from him under section 63(3B) of the 1984 Act (§ 15-183 in the main work), section 65 of the 1984 Act (*ibid.*, § 15-201) is to have effect as if subsection (2A) were not there. Article 5A was intended to guard against the remote possibility that a sample taken under section 63(3B) before October 31, 2013, might be required to be destroyed by virtue of section 63R (s.63R(2)(a) corresponding to s.63D(2)(a), *ante*). Section 65(2A) provides that a sample is not to be regarded as "insufficient" (which it must be for the power under s.63(3B) to be exercised) if it has been destroyed under section 63R. By disapplying section 65(2A), the police will be able to rely on section 63(3B) to take a further sample.

S.I. 2013 No. 1813 (*ante*) was further amended, with effect from October 31, 2013, by the Protection of Freedoms Act 2012 (Destruction, Retention and Use of Biometric Data) (Transitional, Transitory and Saving Provisions) (Amendment) (No. 2) Order 2013 (S.I. 2013 No. 2770) to add a new article 10, which provides that where fingerprints or a DNA sample are taken pursuant to section 63D of the 1984 Act from a person before September 30, 2014, in connection with the investigation of an offence, and, subsequently, the person is arrested for or charged with a different offence, or is convicted of or given a penalty notice for a different offence, then sections 63E to 63O and 63Q to 63T of the 1984 Act have effect in relation to the fingerprints or profile as if the fingerprints or sample from which the profile was derived were taken in connection with the investigation of the latter offence on the date on which the person was arrested for it (or charged with it or given a penalty notice for it, if not arrested).

### Criminal Justice and Court Services Act 2000, s.70

*Interpretation, etc*

★**15-193**     As from a day to be appointed, section 70 of the 2000 Act is amended by the Offender Rehabilitation Act 2014, s.11(1) and (3), so as: (i) to substitute, for the words "'Class A drug' has", the words "'Class A drug' and 'Class B drug' have"; and (ii) to insert, in the definition of "specified", after "Class A drug", the words "or Class B drug ". These amendments apply to persons released before or after they take effect: s.21(1), and Sched. 7, paras 1 and 6.

### Police and Criminal Evidence Act 1984, s.65

*Part V: supplementary*

**15-196**     As to the disapplication of section 65(2A) in certain transitional cases, see S.I. 2013 No. 1813 (*ante*, § 15-189a), art. 5A (as inserted by S.I. 2013 No. 2580 (*ibid.*)).

### Destruction, retention and use of fingerprints etc.

★**15-197**     Under section 63P of the 1984 Act (as substituted on May 13, 2014 (see the Anti-social Behaviour, Crime and Policing Act 2014 (Commencement No. 2, Transitional and Transitory Provisions) Order 2014 (S.I. 2014 No. 949)), with retrospective effect by the Anti-social Behaviour, Crime and Policing Act 2014, s.145), where section 63D material is taken (or, in the case of a DNA profile, derived from a sample taken) from a person in connection with the investigation of an offence, and the person is subsequently arrested for or charged with a different offence, or convicted of or given a penalty notice for a different offence, sections 63E to 63O, 63Q and 63T have effect in relation to the material as if it were also taken (or, in the case of a DNA profile, derived from a sample taken) in connection with the investigation of the other offence on the date on which the person was arrested for that offence (or charged with it or given a penalty notice for it, if he was not arrested).

★          With effect from May 13, 2014 (Anti-social Behaviour, Crime and Policing Act 2014 (Commencement No. 2, Transitional and Transitory Provisions) Order 2014 (S.I. 2014 No. 949)), section 63U of the 1984 Act was amended by the Anti-social Behaviour, Crime and Policing Act 2014, s.146(1). Section 63U(5) provided that material need not be destroyed in accordance with sections 63D to 63Q, 63S and 63T where it fell to be disclosed under the CPIA 1996 or its associated code of practice. This has been amended to include a reference to section 63R (as to which, see the main work). Section 146(1) also inserts new subsections (5A) and (5B) into section 63U. These provide, first, that any sample within subsection (5) that would otherwise have to be destroyed under section 63R, must not be used other than for the purposes of any proceedings for the offence in connection with which it was taken and, secondly, that once it no longer falls within subsection (5), it must be destroyed.

### Police and Criminal Evidence Act 1984, s.64A

*Photographing of suspects etc.*

★**15-199**     As from a day to be appointed, section 64A(1B) of the 1984 Act is amended by the the Anti-social Behaviour, Crime and Policing Act 2014, s.181(1), and Sched. 11, para. 4, to substitute a new paragraph (ca), as follows—

"(ca) given a direction by a constable under section 35 of the Anti-social Behaviour, Crime and Policing Act 2014;".

## (9) Definitions

### Police and Criminal Evidence Act 1984, s.65A

*"Qualifying offence"*

With effect from November 11, 2013, section 65A(2) of the 1984 Act was amended by the Police    **15-203**
and Criminal Evidence Act 1984 (Amendment: Qualifying Offences) Order 2013 (S.I. 2013 No. 2774) to insert the following paragraphs: (da) an offence of indecent exposure, (db) an offence under the Vagrancy Act 1824, s.4, committed by a person wilfully, openly, lewdly and obscenely exposing his person with intent to insult any female, (dc) an offence under the Town Police Clauses Act 1847, s.28, committed by a person wilfully and indecently exposing his person, (fa) an offence under the Infant Life (Preservation) Act 1929, s.1 (child destruction (§ 19-182 in the main work)), (ga) an offence under the Infanticide Act 1938, s.1 (*ibid.*, § 19-189), (gb) an offence under section 12 (buggery) or 13 (indecency between men) of the SOA 1956, other than an offence committed by a person where the other person involved in the conduct constituting the offence consented to it and was aged 16 or over, (gc) an offence under any other section of the 1956 Act, other than sections 18 (fraudulent abduction of heiress from parent or guardian) and 32 (solicitation by men), (gd) an offence under the MHA 1959, s.128 (sexual intercourse with patients), (ge) an offence under the Indecency with Children Act 1960, s.1 (indecent conduct towards young child), (ha) an offence under the SOA 1967, s.5 (living on earnings of male prostitution), (ja) an offence under the Genocide Act 1969, s.1(1), (ka) an offence under the CLA 1977, s.54 (inciting girl under 16 to commit incest), (na) an offence under the Prohibition of Female Circumcision Act 1985, s.1, (nb) an offence under the Public Order Act 1986, s.1 (riot (*ibid.*, § 29-4)), (oa) an offence under the Sexual Offences (Amendment) Act 2000, s.3 (abuse of position of trust), (ob) an offence under the International Criminal Court Act 2001, s.51 (genocide, crimes against humanity and war crimes), and (oc) an offence under section 1 (offence of female genital mutilation (*ibid.*, § 19-364)), 2 (offence of assisting a girl to mutilate her genitalia (*ibid.*, § 19-365)) or 3 (offence of assisting a non-UK person to mutilate overseas a girl's genitalia (*ibid.*, § 19-366)) of the Female Genital Mutilation Act 2003.

## (10) Code of practice

### Introduction

*R. (H.C. (a child, by his litigation friend C.C.)) v. Secretary of State for the Home Department* is now    **15-204**
reported at [2014] 1 W.L.R. 1234, *sub nom. R. (C.) v. Secretary of State for the Home Department.*

As to the commencement of revised Codes C and H, see *ante*, § 15-6.    ★

### F. POLICE ACT 1997 AND REGULATION OF INVESTIGATORY POWERS ACT 2000

With effect from January 1, 2014, the Regulation of Investigatory Powers (Covert Human    **15-205**
Intelligence Sources: Relevant Sources) Order 2013 (S.I. 2013 No. 2788) introduces a notification and prior approval regime in relation to the use of certain categories of covert human intelligence source plus an enhanced authorisation regime. Article 2 defines a "relevant source" as a source holding an office, rank or position in a specified police force, the National Crime Agency, Her Majesty's Revenue and Customs or the Home Office. Article 3 defines a "long term authorisation" as being an authorisation of a relevant source under section 29 of the 2000 Act (covert human intelligence sources) for a period in excess of 12 months taking account of prior periods for which the source has been authorised in relation to the same investigation, but also disregarding certain periods. The relevant period is reduced to three months in relation to an authorisation to which article 8(1)(b) of S.I. 2010 No. 123 (see § 15-205 the main work) applies (i.e. authorisations given otherwise than by a member of the intelligence services in relation to legally privileged material). Part 2 (arts 4–6) of the order requires section 29 authorisations of a relevant source to be notified to an ordinary Surveillance Commissioner; but a long term authorisation is not to be granted or renewed without the approval of such a commissioner. There is provision for an appeal against a refusal of an approval to the Chief Surveillance Commissioner. Part 3 (prescribed offices, ranks

and positions in relation to relevant sources (arts 7–16)) amends the Regulation of Investigatory Powers (Directed Surveillance and Covert Human Intelligence Sources) Order 2010 (S.I. 2010 No. 521). New article 1A corresponds to article 3 of this order. Whereas article 3 of, and the schedule to, the principal order prescribe offices, ranks and positions within the public authorities listed in Schedule 1 to the 2000 Act for the purposes of section 30(1) of that Act (persons entitled to grant authorisations under ss.28 and 29), this order (i) substitutes a new entry in Part 1 of the schedule for the Home Office following the abolition of the United Kingdom Border Agency, and (ii) inserts a new Part 1A, the effect of which is to introduce a higher internal rank for section 29 authorisations of relevant sources, to increase the rank to chief constable or equivalent for long term authorisations of such sources, and to restrict the possible grounds (under s.29(3)) on which office holders in specified agencies may grant authorisations of such sources.

★   The 2000 Act does not contain a comprehensive definition of "surveillance", although section 48 stipulates that it includes certain specified actions. In light of this, the Investigatory Powers Tribunal held in *Re a Complaint of Surveillance* [2014] 2 All E.R. 576, that the correct approach must be to regard "surveillance" as bearing the meaning that it has in ordinary usage. Applying this approach, the tribunal held that, where an individual holding an office or position with a public authority interviews a member of the public in the course of an investigation or operation, where it has been made clear to the interviewee that the interviewer holds an office or position of that kind and that the interview is voluntary, but where a device is used to record the interview without the interviewee's knowledge or consent, the covert recording is not "surveillance" within the meaning of Part II of the 2000 Act.

★   *R. v. Plunkett (Daniel) and Plunkett (James)* (see the main work) was considered in *R. v. Khan (Imran)* [2014] Crim.L.R. 520, CA. The investigating officers in a murder inquiry, prior to any arrests, obtained authorisation under section 28 of the 2000 Act to conduct post-arrest "directed surveillance" by means of a recording device which was to be installed in a van in which it was anticipated that two of the three suspects would be taken to court for an application for an extension of their pre-charge detention to be authorised, the expectation being that some conversation would take place that would reveal a relationship between all three suspects sufficient to warrant charging them. However, the CPS in fact decided that they should be charged the night before the journey to court, but the recording went ahead. It was held, the trial judge having absolved the investigating officers of any bad faith, despite the basis on which the authorisation had been given having disappeared, that the recordings (which contained incriminating remarks) had been correctly admitted into evidence, notwithstanding a violation of the suspects' right to privacy under Article 8 of the ECHR (§ 16-101 in the main work); Article 8 says nothing about the fairness of the trial overall, which is the touchstone of the law in this area (*Khan v. U.K.* (as to which, see §§ 15-463, 16-67 in the main work)); as in *R. v. Plunkett (Daniel) and Plunkett (James)*, there was no misrepresentation, entrapment or trickery; the police had simply made use of the opportunity afforded to the suspects to talk to each other; there was no oppression or coercion, the recordings themselves demonstrated that the suspects were aware of the possibility that their conversation might be bugged, and nothing limited their right to challenge or explain the evidence.

**15-206**   *R. v. Turner* (see the main work) is now reported at [2013] Crim.L.R. 993.

## G. Drug Trafficking Act 1994

### (3) Prosecution of offences, etc.

**Drug Trafficking Act 1994, s.60**

*Revenue and customs prosecutions*

★**15-218**   With effect from March 27, 2014, section 60(1) of the 1994 Act was amended, subject to saving and transitional provisions (as to which, see *ante*, § 1-27), by the Public Bodies (Merger of the Director of Public Prosecutions and the Director of Revenue and Customs Prosecutions) Order 2014 (S.I. 2014 No. 834), art. 3(3), and Sched. 2, para. 9, to substitute, for the words "the Director of Revenue and Customs Prosecutions", the words "the Director of Public Prosecutions".

# H. Proceeds of Crime Act 2002

## (2) Statute

**Proceeds of Crime Act 2002, ss.346–369**

*Search and seizure warrants*

With effect from March 27, 2014, section 352(5A)(a) of the 2002 Act was amended, subject to   ★**15-239**
saving and transitional provisions (as to which, see *ante*, § 1-27), by the Public Bodies (Merger of
the Director of Public Prosecutions and the Director of Revenue and Customs Prosecutions)
Order 2014 (S.I. 2014 No. 834), art. 3(3), and Sched. 2, paras 19 and 26, to omit the words ", the
Director of Revenue and Customs Prosecutions".

The Proceeds of Crime Act 2002 (Application of Police and Criminal Evidence Act 1984 and   ★
Police and Criminal Evidence (Northern Ireland) Order 1989) Order 2003 (S.I. 2003 No. 174)
makes provision for the modified application of sections 15, 16, 21 and 22 of the 1984 Act (as to
which, see §§ 15-84, 15-86, 15-95, 15-97 in the main work) to search and seizure warrants sought
under section 352 of the 2002 Act for the purposes of a confiscation or money laundering
investigation, and powers of seizure under them. The specified provisions are set out in full in
their modified form in Schedules 1 and 2 to the order.

*Further provisions: confiscation and money laundering*

For an order made under section 355 of the 2002 Act, see the Proceeds of Crime Act 2002 (Ap-   **15-242**
plication of Police and Criminal Evidence Act 1984 and Police and Criminal Evidence (Northern
Ireland) Order 1989) Order 2003 (S.I. 2003 No. 174).

*Disclosure orders*

With effect from March 27, 2014, section 357(8)(d) of the 2002 Act was amended, subject to   ★**15-244**
saving and transitional provisions (as to which, see *ante*, § 1-27), by the Public Bodies (Merger of
the Director of Public Prosecutions and the Director of Revenue and Customs Prosecutions)
Order 2014 (S.I. 2014 No. 834), art. 3(3), and Sched. 2, paras 19 and 27, to substitute, for the
words "the Director of Revenue and Customs Prosecutions", the words "the Director of Public
Prosecutions".

**Proceeds of Crime Act 2002, ss.370–379**

*Code of practice of Attorney General or Advocate General for Northern Ireland*

With effect from March 27, 2014, section 377A(1)(a) of the 2002 Act was amended, subject to   ★**15-264**
saving and transitional provisions (as to which, see *ante*, § 1-27), by the Public Bodies (Merger of
the Director of Public Prosecutions and the Director of Revenue and Customs Prosecutions)
Order 2014 (S.I. 2014 No. 834), art. 3(3), and Sched. 2, paras 19 and 28, to omit the words ", the
Director of Revenue and Customs Prosecutions".

# I. Serious Organised Crime and Police Act 2005

## (1) Disclosure notices

### (b) *Legislation*

**Serious Organised Crime and Police Act 2005, ss.60–70**

With effect from March 27, 2014, section 60 of the 2005 Act was amended, subject to saving   ★**15-297**
and transitional provisions (as to which, see *ante*, § 1-27), by the Public Bodies (Merger of the
Director of Public Prosecutions and the Director of Revenue and Customs Prosecutions) Order
2014 (S.I. 2014 No. 834), art. 3(3), and Sched. 2, paras 40 and 41, to omit subsections (1)(b), (3)
and (5)(b), and the reference to subsection (3), in subsection (6).

## II. CONFESSIONS AND RELATED TOPICS

### A. CONFESSIONS

#### (1) Police and Criminal Evidence Act 1984

##### (b) *Words and phrases*

**Police and Criminal Evidence Act 1984, ss.76, 76A**

### "likely ... to render unreliable any confession which might be made by him in consequence thereof"

★**15-322**   Interviewing a suspect who is not fit to be interviewed (as to which, see Annex G to Code C (*post*, Appendix A-109)) may lead to the exclusion of the interview under section 76 of the 1984 Act: *Beeres v. CPS*, unreported, February 13, 2014, QBD (Green J.) ([2014] EWHC 283 (Admin.)). While paragraphs 2(b) and 3 of Annex G focus primarily on physical or mental unfitness, they can apply equally in relation to incapacity resulting from alcohol or sleep deprivation; if a detainee is materially under the influence of alcohol, then there is an obvious risk that answers given may not be rational or logical; and the same applies to a detainee who is sleep-deprived; if the ability of a detainee to perform properly in interview may be impaired for such reasons, then the evidence that they do give may be unreliable: *ibid*. As to *Beeres*, see also *post*, § 15-422.

##### (c) *Codes of practice*

★**15-324**   As to the commencement of a revised Code C, see *ante*, § 15-6.

## III. DISCRETION TO EXCLUDE EVIDENCE

### A. UNDER STATUTE

#### (5) Access to legal advice

★**15-422**   Giving incomplete or partial information about the availability of legal advice may result in a subsequent confession being excluded under section 78, as in *R. v. Vernon* (see the main work), or under section 76 (§ 15-311 in the main work), as suggested *obiter* in *Beeres v. CPS*, unreported, February 13, 2014, QBD (Green J.) ([2014] EWHC 283 (Admin.)); but there is no obligation to make specific reference to the duty solicitor scheme in referring to the right to free legal advice: *ibid*. As to *Beeres*, see also *ante*, § 15-322.

#### (7) Codes C and H and section 78

##### (a) *Introduction*

★**15-424**   As to the commencement of revised Codes C and H, see *ante*, § 15-6.

##### (d) *Particular topics: authorities*

#### Information as to rights

★**15-427**   The revised Code C that came into force on June 2, 2014 (as to which, see *ante*, § 15-6), implemented obligations under European Parliament and Council Directive 2012/13/EU, in relation to the right to information in criminal proceedings. Every detainee must, under the 2014 code, be given a revised written notice setting out his rights and entitlements whilst in custody. This reflects the new substantive rights conferred by the 2012 directive. In particular, more information is to be given to the detainee as to the nature of the accusation, about accessing records and documents about his arrest and detention and about the offence and the evidence, if charged, about interpretation and translation facilities, about contact with consular authorities, and about the maximum period of detention, reviews of detention and release.

#### (11) Evidence obtained through unlawful act or trickery

#### Eavesdropping

★**15-463**   For a case considering whether a covert recording, obtained by means of a recording device that was installed in a van in which it was anticipated that two suspects would be taken to court, had been obtained by misrepresentation, entrapment or trickery, see *R. v. Khan (Imran)*, *ante*, § 15-205.

## Chapter 16

## HUMAN RIGHTS

### II. THE HUMAN RIGHTS ACT 1998

#### C. Application to Legislation

##### Human Rights Act 1998, s.3

The Supreme Court has allowed the receiver's appeal against the refusal by the Court of Appeal in *CPS v. Eastenders Cash and Carry plc* (see the main work) to order the CPS to pay his remuneration and expenses, but this was not on the basis that the PCA 2002 could be read down pursuant to section 3 of the 1998 Act: see *Barnes v. Eastenders Cash and Carry plc*; *Eastenders Cash and Carry plc v. CPS* [2014] 2 W.L.R. 1269, SC. As to this case, see also *ante*, §§ 5-844, 5-874, 5-875.   ★**16-17**

### III. GENERAL PRINCIPLES OF INTERPRETATION

#### B. The European Convention on Human Rights

**Approach to construction**

*Vinter v. U.K. (No. 2)* is now reported at [2014] Crim.L.R. 81, *sub nom. Vinter v U.K.*   **16-29**

### IV. THE RIGHTS GUARANTEED

#### A. Right to Life

**Positive obligations**

See *Sarjantson v. Chief Constable of Humberside Police*, *post*, § 16-40a.   **16-38a**

#### B. Prohibition of Torture

**Scope**

*Vinter v. U.K. (No. 2)* is now reported at [2014] Crim.L.R. 81, *sub nom. Vinter v U.K.*   **16-40**
*Aswat v. U.K.* is now reported at *Aswat v. U.K* (2014) 58 E.H.R.R. 1.

In *R. v. Newell*; *Att.-Gen.'s Reference (No. 69 of 2013) (R. v. McLoughlin)* [2014] Crim.L.R. 471,   ★
CA, the Court of Appeal held that *Vinter v. U.K. (No. 2)* (see the main work and *ante*) did not "in any way" cast doubt on the fact that there are crimes that are so heinous that just punishment may require imprisonment for life, and, in accordance with the constitution of the United Kingdom, it is was for Parliament to establish the framework under which a judge decided in an individual case whether a whole-life order was the just punishment. Consequently, the statutory regime relating to the imposition of whole-life orders (CJA 2003, s.269, and Sched. 21 (§§ 5-403, 5-425 in the main work)) was compatible with Article 3 of the ECHR (§ 16-39 in the main work). The court further held, disagreeing with *Vinter*, and agreeing with *R. v. Bieber* (see the main work), that section 30 of the C(S)A 1997, under which the Secretary of State may release a prisoner if there are exceptional circumstances that justify release on compassionate grounds, met the requirement (if a violation of Article 3 were to be avoided) that a whole-life sentence be reducible, in the sense that there needed to be provision for a review that would allow the domestic

authorities to consider whether any changes in the prisoner were so significant, and such progress towards rehabilitation had been made, as to mean that continued detention could no longer be justified on legitimate penological grounds.

### Positive obligations

16-40a    The positive obligation of the police to take reasonable steps to protect potential victims from a real and immediate threat to their lives that is attributable to the actual or threatened acts of a third party (*Osman v. U.K.* (see § 16-38a in the main work)), as extended to Article 3 by *E. v. Chief Constable of the Royal Ulster Constabulary(Northern Ireland Human Rights Commission intervening)* (as to which, see the main work), may be engaged regardless of whether the risk arises during an incident that has already commenced and regardless of whether the police know or ought to know the identities of actual or potential victims; and it is irrelevant to liability (though not to quantum) that an earlier response on the part of the police would have made no difference: *Sarjantson v. Chief Constable of Humberside Police* [2014] Q.B. 411, CA (Civ. Div.). The Supreme Court has refused permission to appeal: see *Sarjantson v Chief Constable of Humberside Police* [2014] 1 W.L.R. 1856, SC.

### D. Right to Liberty and Security

### Arrest on reasonable suspicion

★16-49    English courts were not bound to follow the proposition in *Ostendorf v. Germany* (see the main work) that Article 5(1)(c) of the ECHR (§ 16-43 in the main work) requires that there must be an intention from the outset to bring a detainee before a court when arresting or detaining him on reasonable suspicion of having committed an offence; arrest and detention for the purpose of bringing the detainee before the competent legal authority, if that were to become necessary so as to prolong detention on a lawful basis, satisfies Article 5(1)(c): *R. (Hicks) v Commr of Police of the Metropolis* [2014] 2 Cr.App.R. 4, CA (Civ. Div.).

### E. Right to a Fair Trial

### "Equality of arms"

16-64    For a Supreme Court case considering *McLean v. Buchanan* (as to which, see the main work) in the context of the legal aid system in Northern Ireland of fixed fees, with no exceptions, for persons instructed for the purposes of mitigation, see *Re Brownlee*, unreported, January 29, 2014, SC ([2014] UKSC 4).

### Independence of the judiciary

16-73a    The 2013 criminal practice directions (see the main work) are now reported at [2013] 1 W.L.R. 3164.

### The right to legal representation and legal aid

*Pre-trial*

16-86a    *O'Neill v. H.M. Advocate (No. 2); Lauchlan v. Same* is now reported at [2013] 2 Cr.App.R. 34.

### G. Right to Respect for Private and Family Life

### Interference

16-106    *R. (H.C. (a child by his litigation friend C.C.)) v. Secretary of State for the Home Department* is now reported at [2014] 1 W.L.R. 1234, *sub nom. R. (C.) v. Secretary of State for the Home Department*. *Kinloch v. H.M. Advocate* is now reported at [2013] 2 A.C. 93.

### Justification

16-107    *R. (Catt) v. Association of Chief Police Officers; R. (T.) v. Metropolitan Police Commr* is now reported at [2013] 1 W.L.R. 3305, *sub nom. R. (Catt) v. Association of Chief Police Officers of England, Wales and*

*Northern Ireland (Equality and Human Rights Commission intervening); R. (T.) v. Commr of Police of the Metropolis (Secretary of State for the Home Department intervening).*

The Supreme Court has given the defendants permission to appeal in the above case: see *R. (on the application of Catt) v Association of Chief Police Officers of England Wales and Northern Ireland (Equality and Human Rights Commission intervening) R. (on the application of T.) v. Commr of Police of the Metropolis (Secretary of State for the Home Department intervening)* [2013] 1 W.L.R. 3601, SC.

For the Supreme Court's decision upholding the decision of the civil division of the Court of ★ Appeal in *R. (T.) v. Chief Constable of Greater Manchester (Liberty intervening); R. (B.) v. Secretary of State for the Home Department; R. (W.) v. Secretary of State for Justice* (as to which, see the main work) that the provisions of Part V of the Police Act 1997 for the issuing of criminal record certificates (s.113A) and enhanced criminal record certificates (s.113B), as they stood prior to amendment by the Police Act 1997 (Criminal Record Certificates: Relevant Matters) (Amendment) (England and Wales) Order 2013 (S.I. 2013 No. 1200) were incompatible with Article 8 of the ECHR, see *R. (T.) v. Chief Constable of Greater Manchester Police (Liberty intervening); R. (B.) v. Secretary of State for the Home Department*, unreported, June 18, 2014, SC ([2014] UKSC 35). As to this case, see also *ante*, §§ 13-120, 13-131.

The Divisional Court's decision in *R. (Roberts) v. Commr of Police of the Metropolis* has been ★ upheld: see *R. (Roberts) v. Commr of Police of the Metropolis (Liberty intervening)* [2014] 2 Cr.App.R. 6, CA (Civ. Div.) (*ante*, § 15-48).

## Other issues

*R. (Nicklinson) v. Ministry of Justice (C.N.K. Alliance Ltd intervening); R. (A.M.) v. DPP (Same* **16-112** *intervening)* is now reported at [2014] 2 All E.R. 32, *sub nom. R. (Nicklinson) v. Ministry of Justice; R. (A.M.) v. DPP.*

CHAPTER 17

# THE MENTAL ELEMENT IN CRIME

## *V. DRINK AND DRUGS*

### E. RELATIONSHIP TO PARTICULAR DEFENCES

#### (1) Insanity

*R. v. Coley; R. v. McGhee; R. v. Harris* is now reported at [2013] Crim.L.R. 923.      **17-113a**

## *VII. NECESSITY*

### Availability and scope

*R. (Nicklinson) v. Ministry of Justice (C.N.K. Alliance Ltd intervening); R. (A.M.) v. DPP (Same* **17-128** *intervening)* is now reported at [2014] 2 All E.R. 32, *sub nom. R. (Nicklinson) v. Ministry of Justice; R. (A.M.) v. DPP.*

## *VIII. COERCION BY HUSBAND*

### Criminal Justice Act 1925, s.47

Section 11 of, and Schedule 3 to, the Marriage (Same Sex Couples) Act 2013 (which provide ★**17-133** that in the law of England and Wales, marriage has the same effect in relation to same sex couples as it has in relation to opposite sex couples (s.11(1)), that the law of England and Wales (including all legislation whenever passed or made) has effect in accordance with s.11(1) (s.11(2)), and that references to persons who are not married but living together as if they were married are to be read as including a same sex couple who are not married but living together as if they were, *etc.*

(Sched. 3)) are disapplied in relation to section 47 of the 1925 Act (see the main work and *post*): Marriage (Same Sex Couples) Act 2013 (Consequential and Contrary Provisions and Scotland) Order 2014 (S.I. 2014 No. 560).

★  With effect from May 13, 2014, the Anti-social Behaviour, Crime and Policing Act 2014, s.177(1) and (2), abolished the defence of marital coercion and repealed section 47 of the 1925 Act (see the main work and *ante*). Section 177 does not have effect in respect of an offence alleged to have been committed before that date: 2014 Act, s.177(3).

CHAPTER 18

# PRINCIPALS AND SECONDARY PARTIES

*III. SECONDARY PARTIES*

B. AIDERS AND ABETTORS

## (4) Presence

**18-13**    *Bauer v. DPP* (see the main work) is now reported at [2013] 1 W.L.R. 3617.

CHAPTER 19

# OFFENCES AGAINST THE PERSON

*I. HOMICIDE*

A. MURDER

## (3) Lawful homicide

**Medical or surgical treatment**

**19-38**    See *Reeves v. The Queen*, *post*, § 19-235.

### Criminal Justice and Immigration Act 2008, s.76

*Reasonable force for purposes of self-defence, etc.*

**19-40**    It is plain that the second limb of self-defence (*viz.* whether the nature and degree of force used was reasonable in the circumstances: see s.76(1)(b) of the 2008 Act) includes an objective element, even if there may also be a subjective element (*cf. R. v. Keane*; *R. v. McGrath* (§ 19-41 in the main work)); an insane person cannot, therefore, set the standard of reasonableness of the degree of force used by reference to his own insanity: *R. v. Oye* [2014] 1 Cr.App.R. 11, CA (considering *R. v. Martin (Anthony)* (§ 19-47 in the main work)).

## (4) Defences

### (a) *"Loss of control"*

**Loss of control**

★**19-56a**    Evidence of loss of control must be distinguished from evidence of anger; anger might be accompanied by loss of control, and in some circumstances it might be evidence from which loss of control could be inferred; but in others, it might indicate the reverse, namely a considered, controlled, retaliation: *Daniel v. State of Trinidad and Tobago* [2014] 2 W.L.R. 1154, PC (a decision on the law of provocation, as to which, see also *post*, §§ 19-59, 19-67, 19-75).

## Qualifying triggers

*Self-induced loss of control*

For a detailed consideration by the Privy Council of the question of self-induced provocative ★**19-59**
conduct in the context of the defence of provocation, much of which has the potential to carry
across to the new defence of loss of control under section 54 of the Coroners and Justice Act 2009
(§ 19-55 in the main work), see *Daniel v State of Trinidad and Tobago, post,* § 19-75. As to this case,
see also *ante,* § 19-56a; and *post,* § 19-67.

### (b) *Provocation*

## Common law

At common law, provocation reduced murder to manslaughter; and was available as a potential **19-65**
defence both for a principal and an accessory: *R. v. Marks* [1998] Crim.L.R. 676, CA. It was irrelevant on the issue of guilt in all other crimes.

The jury should be directed that before they have to consider the issue of provocation the
Crown must have proved beyond reasonable doubt that all the other elements of murder were
present, including the necessary intent: see *Lee Chun-Chuen v. R.* [1963] A.C. 220, PC; and *R. v.
Martindale,* 50 Cr.App.R. 273, Ct-MAC.

The law as to provocation immediately prior to October 4, 2010 (as to which, see § 19-54 in the
main work) was governed by a blend of common law and statute, *viz.* the Homicide Act 1957, s.3
(*post,* § 19-66).

### Homicide Act 1957, s.3

*Provocation*

**3.** Where on a charge of murder there is evidence on which the jury can find that the person **19-66**
charged was provoked (whether by things done or by things said or by both together) to lose his self-
control, the question whether the provocation was enough to make a reasonable man do as he did
shall be left to be determined by the jury; and in determining that question the jury shall take into
account everything both done and said according to the effect which, in their opinion, it would have
on a reasonable man.

This section altered as well as clarified the common law on this subject.

## Duty of judge

Section 3 involves two questions: (a) is there any evidence of specific provoking conduct of the **19-67**
accused, and (b) is there any evidence that the provocation caused him to lose his self-control? If
both questions are answered in the affirmative, the issue of provocation should be left to the jury
notwithstanding the fact that in the opinion of the judge no reasonable jury could conclude on
the evidence that a reasonable person would have been provoked to lose his self-control: *R. v.
Gilbert,* 66 Cr.App.R. 237, CA; *Franco v. R., The Times,* October 11, 2001, PC; notwithstanding that
there may be circumstances suggesting that the accused acted in revenge, rather than as a result
of a sudden and temporary loss of self-control: *R. v. Baillie* [1995] 2 Cr.App.R. 31, CA; and
notwithstanding that the issue has not been raised by the defence: *Bullard v. R.* [1957] A.C. 635,
PC; *DPP v. Camplin* [1978] A.C. 705, HL; *R. v. Rossiter,* 95 Cr.App.R. 326, CA; and would prefer it
not to be left to the jury: *R. v. Dhillon* [1997] 2 Cr.App.R. 104, CA.

Where, however, there is only a speculative possibility of the accused having acted as a result of
provoking conduct, the issue should not be left to the jury: *R. v. Acott* [1997] 2 Cr.App.R. 94, HL
(there must be some evidence of specific provoking conduct resulting in a loss of control by the
accused; the source of such evidence is immaterial as is reliance thereon by the accused); and *R.
v. Evans (John Derek)* [2010] Crim.L.R. 491, CA (§ 19-62 in the main work). Evidence of a loss of
self-control is insufficient, for a loss of self-control might be brought on by fear, panic or sheer
bad temper, as well as by provoking conduct: *ibid.* Questions put in cross-examination are not
evidence: *ibid.* The observations in *Acott* are equally apt when considering whether there is sufficient evidence that a defendant was provoked, as they are when considering whether there was
evidence of provoking conduct: *R. v. Miao, The Times,* November 26, 2003, CA. For the issue to be
left to the jury, there has to be evidence from which a reasonable jury might conclude that the
defendant was or may have been provoked: *R. v. Cambridge,* 99 Cr.App.R. 142, CA. See also *R. v.*

*Jones (Robert James)* [2000] 3 *Archbold News* 2, CA (where the defence is self-defence, with no reliance by the defence on provocation, the judge should not leave provocation to the jury where the evidence of provoking conduct by the deceased, or the evidence that such conduct caused a loss of self-control by the defendant is minimal or fanciful).

★    In *Daniel v. State of Trinidad and Tobago* [2014] 2 W.L.R. 1154, PC, it was held that while, in the event of dispute, it is for the judge to rule whether the issue of provocation arises on the evidence in relation to the first, subjective, limb of the test (namely, whether there was provocative behaviour and whether the defendant was in fact provoked by it to lose his self-control and kill in consequence), it is of great importance that judges respect the clear principle that the question as to whether the second, objective, limb of the test for provocation (namely, whether the provocation was such as might cause a reasonable man to act as the accused had) has been met, is a matter for the jury. Provocation has to be left to the jury, it was held, even if it is not the accused's primary case if, taking the evidence at its most favourable to the accused and remembering that the onus of proof is on the prosecution to rebut it, manslaughter by reason of provocation is a conclusion to which a jury might reasonably come. The board added that a judge could not withdraw the issue simply because he would decide the issue against the accused, nor even if he regarded the answer as obvious; but in a case where no jury, properly directed, could possibly find the test met, it is in the interests of a fair trial and of coherent law that an issue that does not arise ought not to be inserted into the jury's deliberations. As to this case, see also *ante,* § 19-56a; and *post,* § 19-75.

Where a judge is obliged to leave provocation to the jury, he should indicate to them, unless it is obvious, what evidence might support the conclusion that the defendant had lost his self-control; this is particularly important where the defence have not raised the issue: *R. v. Stewart* [1996] 1 Cr.App.R. 229, CA. See also *R. v. Humphreys* [1995] 4 All E.R. 1008, CA (similar duty where there is a complex history with several distinct strands of potentially provocative conduct, building up over time until the final encounter).

Where provocation is not left to the jury when it should have been, a conviction for manslaughter will be substituted unless the court is sure that the jury would inevitably have convicted: *R. v. Dhillon, ante,* but an appellate court should be cautious in drawing inferences or making findings about how the jury would have resolved issues which were never before them; and that is particularly so in the context of section 3, since Parliament had gone out of its way, unusually, to stipulate that resolution of the objective issue should be exclusively reserved to the jury; to the extent that an appellate court took it upon itself to decide that issue, it was doing what Parliament had said that the jury should do, and section 3 could not be read as applying only to the trial court: *Franco v. R., ante.*

In *R. v. Van Dongen and Van Dongen* [2005] 2 Cr.App.R. 38, CA, it was held that: (i) section 3 is concerned with provocative conduct, as opposed to merely causative conduct; yet a judgment that particular conduct was no more than causative risks straying into an evaluation of the objective element of the defence, which statute has left to the jury; accordingly, the prudent course for judges to take, in borderline cases, especially if the defence ask for a provocation direction to be given, is to leave the issue to the jury; (ii) where, therefore, in a case in which the defence had been self-defence and/or lack of intent and/or accident, but not provocation, there was evidence of conduct that was capable of being provoking conduct and there was evidence of a loss of self-control, the matter should have been left to the jury, more particularly as defence counsel had sought such a direction; but (iii) the failure to leave it did not mean that the conviction could not be upheld, notwithstanding that the Act specifically provides for the jury to determine the objective issue; *Franco v. R., ante,* was not authority for the proposition that a conviction could not be upheld in such circumstances; whilst it was necessary to be cautious in drawing inferences or making findings about how the jury would have resolved issues which were never before them, the court must not overlook the matter of justice for those concerned with the victim, nor the requirements of a proportionate appellate system, which included that those who were surely and fairly shown to be guilty of murder, and were so found by a jury, should not escape the consequences on gossamer grounds; where, therefore, the unavoidable facts of the case and the necessary logic of the jury's verdict ruled out any possibility of a miscarriage of justice, the conviction should be upheld.

### Duty of counsel

**19-68**    See *R. v. Cox (A.M.)* [1995] 2 Cr.App.R. 513, CA (§ 19-61 in the main work).

## Onus of proof

Once there is evidence from any source, sufficient to be left to the jury on the issue of provoca-     **19-69**
tion, the onus remains throughout upon the Crown to prove absence of provocation beyond
reasonable doubt: *R. v. McPherson*, 41 Cr.App.R. 213, CCA. As to the necessity for a careful direction on onus of proof, see *R. v. Wheeler*, 52 Cr.App.R. 28, CA (§ 19-48 in the main work).

## "Provoked … to lose his self control"

(i) *Meaning of "provocation"*

In *R. v. Whitfield*, 63 Cr.App.R. 39 at 42, the Court of Appeal said that the meaning of provoca-     **19-70**
tion was still that given to it by Devlin J. in *R. v. Duffy* [1949] 1 All E.R. 932, as cited by Lord Goddard C.J. when giving the judgment of the Court of Criminal Appeal:

> "Provocation is some act, or series of acts, done [or words spoken] [by the dead man to the ac-
> cused] which would cause in any reasonable person, and actually causes in the accused, a sudden
> and temporary loss of self-control, rendering the accused so subject to passion as to make him or
> her for the moment not master of his mind" (at p.932).

The words in the first pair of square brackets were not actually said by Devlin J. but appear in
the quotation of him by Lord Lane C.J. as if spoken by him (presumably to take account of the
express reference to "things said" in section 3 of the 1957 Act, *ante*, § 19-66); the words in the
second pair of square brackets must be ignored in view of the wording of section 3. See also *post*,
§ 19-73.

(ii) *Loss of self-control must be associated with the act which causes death*

The point was considered in *R. v. Ibrams and Gregory*, 74 Cr.App.R. 154, CA. Provocation is     **19-71**
available only in the case of a sudden and temporary loss of self-control of such a kind as to make
the accused for the moment not master of his mind: see *R. v. Duffy* and *R. v. Whitfield, ante*.
Circumstances which induce a desire for revenge are inconsistent with provocation, since the
conscious formulation of a desire for revenge means that a person has had time to think, to
reflect and that would negative a sudden temporary loss of self-control, which is the essence of
provocation. But the mere existence of such circumstances does not mean that the judge should
not leave the issue to the jury if there is evidence that the accused was in fact provoked; it is for
the jury to decide: see *R. v. Baillie* [1995] 2 Cr.App.R. 31, CA.

(iii) *Cumulative provocation*

Although it is established that a temporary and sudden loss of self-control arising from an act     **19-72**
of provocation is essential, it is less clear to what extent previous acts of provocation are admissible.
Each case must be considered against the background of its own particular facts: *R. v. Thornton*,
96 Cr.App.R. 112, CA. In *R. v. Brown* [1972] 2 Q.B. 229, 56 Cr.App.R. 564, CA, a direction that
the jury had to find provocation in something done on the morning of the killing was approved.
In *R. v. Davies (P.)* [1975] Q.B. 691, 60 Cr.App.R. 253, the Court of Appeal described as "too
generous" a direction that the jury could review the whole of the deceased's conduct throughout
the years preceding death: and see *R. v. Ibrams and Gregory, ante*. In *R. v. Pearson* [1992] Crim.L.R.
193, the Court of Appeal substituted manslaughter for a conviction for murder on the grounds,
*inter alia*, that the jury may have been left with the impression that an eight-year history of violent
conduct by the deceased towards his younger son was not to be taken into account when considering the case of the elder son, who had spent much of that time away from home.

A general approach can, however, be discerned from the authorities, namely that evidence of
previous provocative acts or past conduct, particularly in cases of domestic violence, is admissible
in order to place in its appropriate context the reaction of the accused to the alleged provocation
on the occasion of the killing: see *R. v. Thornton, ante*, at p. 118. For the proper approach in relation to a history of provocation leading to a post-traumatic stress syndrome or "battered woman
syndrome", see *R. v. Ahluwalia*, 96 Cr.App.R. 133, CA, and *R. v. Thornton (No. 2)* [1996] 2
Cr.App.R. 108, CA (a jury might more easily find that there was a sudden loss of self-control triggered even by a minor incident if the defendant had endured abuse over a period, on a last-straw
basis).

## "Things done or said"

The things done or said may be done or said by the deceased or anyone else: *R. v. Davies (P.)*,     **19-73**
*ante*; *R. v. Doughty (S.)*, 83 Cr.App.R. 319, CA.

### "Reasonable man"

**19-74**    The "reasonable man" means "an ordinary person of either sex, not exceptionally excitable or pugnacious, but possessed of such powers of self-control as everyone is entitled to expect that his fellow citizens will exercise in society as it is today": *per* Lord Diplock in *DPP v. Camplin* [1978] A.C. 705 at 771, HL; means "a man of ordinary self-control": *ibid., per* Lord Simon at p.726. Both formulations were approved by the majority in *Att.-Gen. for Jersey v. Holley* [2005] 2 A.C. 580, PC, in which an enlarged board of nine was assembled for the purpose of considering the conflict between *Camplin* and *Luc Thiet Thuan v. R.* [1997] A.C. 131, PC, on the one hand, and *R. v. Smith (Morgan)* [2001] 1 A.C. 146, HL, on the other, and to "clarify definitively the present state of English law". That it had done so was accepted by the Court of Appeal in *R. v. James; R. v. Karimi* [2006] 1 Cr.App.R. 29.

   The majority opinion in *Holley* was that the jury, in deciding whether the defendant lost his self-control and, if he did, whether he did so as a result of provocation, should take the defendant exactly as they find him ("warts and all" (including that he had a violent temperament: see *R. v. Mohammed (Faqir)* [2005] 9 *Archbold News* 3, CA)); but, having assessed the gravity of the provocation to the defendant (for which purpose they must, for example, take account of the fact that he is a homosexual if taunted for his homosexuality, that he is disabled if taunted for being a "cripple", *etc.*), the standard of self-control by which his conduct is to be evaluated is the external standard of a person having and exercising the ordinary powers of self-control to be expected of a person of the defendant's age and sex. The majority ruling in *Smith* was held to be wrong in that section 3 of the 1957 Act adopted a uniform, objective standard; whether the provocative act or words and the defendant's response met the "ordinary person" standard prescribed by the statute is the question the jury must consider, not the altogether looser question (suggested by *Smith*) of whether, having regard to all the circumstances, the jury consider the loss of self-control was sufficiently excusable; the statute, it was said, does not leave each jury free to set whatever standard they consider appropriate. Accordingly, it was held to follow that if the defendant had been taunted by reference to his being an alcoholic or a drug addict, his alcoholism or addiction might be relevant to the jury's consideration of the gravity of the taunt to the defendant, but it would not be relevant to the question whether he exercised ordinary self-control.

### Self-induced provocation

**19-75**    The mere fact that the defendant caused a reaction in others which in turn led him to lose his self-control does not preclude a successful defence of provocation: *R. v. Johnson (C.)*, 89 Cr.App.R. 148, CA.

   In *Edwards v. R.* [1973] A.C. 648, PC, the appellant's case was that the man whom he was blackmailing attacked him with a knife and he thereupon lost his temper and killed him. The relevant ordinance in Hong Kong was in the same terms as section 3 of the Homicide Act 1957, *ante*. The Board said (at p. 658):

> "No authority has been cited with regard to what may be called 'self-induced provocation'. On principle it seems reasonable to say that: (1) a blackmailer cannot rely on the predictable results of his own blackmailing conduct as constituting provocation sufficient to reduce his killing of the victim from murder to manslaughter, and the predictable results may include a considerable degree of hostile reaction by the person sought to be blackmailed, for instance vituperous words and even some hostile action such as blows with a fist; (2) but, if the hostile reaction by the person sought to be blackmailed goes to extreme lengths, it might constitute sufficient provocation even for a blackmailer; (3) there would in many cases be a question of degree to be decided by the jury."

★    In *Daniel v. State of Trinidad and Tobago* [2014] 2 W.L.R. 1154, PC, it was held that there is no room for any general rule of law that provocation cannot arise because the accused himself generated the provocative conduct in issue. Subject to the proper role of the judge, the issue is for the jury, and the jury should ordinarily be directed that, if they find conduct by the accused which generates the provocative behaviour in question, that conduct will be directly relevant to both the subjective and the objective limbs of provocation. As to the subjective limb, it will go to both (a) the question whether the accused killed as a result of the provocative behaviour relied upon and (b) whether he lost self-control as a result of that behaviour. Generally, the more he generates the reaction of the deceased, the less likely it will be that he lost control and killed as a result of it; he might have been out of control from the outset, but that is not loss of control as a result of the provocative behaviour of the deceased. As to the objective limb, it will go to whether the provocative behaviour was enough to make a reasonable man in the defendant's position do as he did. Generally, the more he has himself generated the provocative behaviour, the less likely it will be that a reasonable man would have killed in consequence of it, but there may be cases where the jury may judge that the provocative behaviour may have induced a similar reaction in a reasonable man, notwithstanding the origins of the dispute between the accused and the deceased. On both limbs of the test of provocation, the extent to which the provocative behaviour relied upon was or was not a predictable result of what the accused did, *i.e.* how far it was to be expected, is itself a jury question and clearly a relevant factor, which the jury should take into account along with all the other circumstances of the killing. As to this case, see also *ante*, §§ 19-56a, 19-67.

### Provocation and lies

Lies and attempts to cover up a killing are not necessarily inconsistent with provocation. In **19-76** directions about lies, when the issue was murder or manslaughter, the jury should be alerted to the fact that, before they could treat lies as proof of guilt of the offence charged, they had to be sure that there was not some possible explanation which destroyed their potentially probative effect. A failure to give such a direction, coupled with an indication that the jury might regard lies as probative of murder rather than manslaughter, amounted to a material misdirection: *R. v. Richens*, 98 Cr.App.R. 43, CA; *R. v. Taylor* [1998] 7 *Archbold News* 3, CA.

### Provocation and good character

Where there is evidence of the defendant's good character, the judge should direct the jury as **19-77** to the relevance of that both to credibility and propensity; and, in particular, should remind them that, as a man of good character, the defendant might have been unlikely to indulge in serious violence without first being provoked: *Paria v. R.* [2004] Crim.L.R. 228, PC.

### Sentence

See the guideline issued by the Sentencing Guidelines Council (*post*, K-71 *et seq.*). Of the pre- **19-78** guideline authorities, see, in particular, *Att.-Gen.'s References (Nos 74, 95 and 118 of 2002) (R. v. Suratan; R. v. Humes; R. v. Wilkinson)* [2003] 2 Cr.App.R.(S.) 42, CA, which is summarised at paragraph 2.1 of the guideline (Appendix K-74).

See also *R. v. Brook (Neil)*, § 5-520 in the main work.

### (c) *Diminished responsibility*

### Abnormality of "mind"/ "mental functioning"—substantial impairment

#### (i) *Abnormality of mental functioning*

The Court of Appeal has expressly approved the final three sentences of this paragraph in the ★**19-83** main work as to the jury's role in determining whether the accused's case fits within section 2(1) and (1A) of the Homicide Act 1957 (as amended by s.52(1) of the Coroners and Justice Act 2009 (§ 19-79 in the main work)), as to the relevance of medical evidence to this determination, and as to whether the jury will be bound to accept such medical evidence: see *R. v. Bunch*, unreported, December 6, 2013, CA ([2013] EWCA Crim. 2498). As to this case, see also *post*, § 19-94.

#### (iv) *"Substantially"*

*R. v. Ramchurn, R. v. Lloyd, R. v. Mitchell* and *R. v. Brown (Robert)* (as to all of which, see the ★**19-86** main work) were considered in *R. v. Golds* [2014] 5 *Archbold Review* 2, CA. It was held that judges should either direct juries simply by reference to the words of the legislation or, if they do elaborate, they should say that an abnormality of mental functioning would only have "substantially" impaired the defendant's ability to do one of the things mentioned in subsection (2) of section 2 of the Homicide Act 1957 (§ 19-79 in the main work) where it significantly or appreciably impaired that ability, beyond something that was merely more than trivial or minimal, whilst not wholly impairing his ability to do those things. The court expressed the view that the specimen direction in the *Crown Court Bench Book*, as approved in *Ramchurn*, was somewhat ambiguous.

*(v) Drink and mental abnormality*

★**19-88**    In *R. v. Williams (Dean)* [2014] 1 Cr.App.R. 23, CA, a case under section 2(1) of the Homicide Act 1957 (prior to its substitution by the Coroners and Justice Act 2009, s.52(1) (§ 19-79 in the main work)), it was held that the effect of drink will not necessarily bring a case within the defence under section 2(1), for, of itself, the use of drink, even excessive use, is not an "abnormality of mind", but where fresh evidence, which had not been available at trial, showed that, at the time of the killing, the appellant had an abnormality of mind, based on alcohol dependency syndrome, together with associated cognitive impairment, the safety of his conviction for murder was brought into doubt. It was a question for the jury at a retrial whether the abnormality caused a substantial impairment of his "mental responsibility" or, in other words, his ability to bring a free and rational mind to bear on what he did.

## Medical evidence

★**19-94**    The amendment of section 2(1) of the Homicide Act 1957 by section 52(1) of the Coroners and Justice Act 2009 (§ 19-79 in the main work) did not diminish the authority of cases such as *R. v. Byrne* or *R. v. Dix* (as to both of which, see the main work), in which it was held that medical evidence, although not expressly required by section 2 of the 1957 Act, is "a practical necessity" if a defence of diminished responsibility is to succeed, because the onus is on the defendant: *R. v. Bunch*, unreported, December 6, 2013, CA ([2013] EWCA Crim. 2498). As to this case, see also *ante*, § 19-83.

### B. Manslaughter

### (2) Involuntary manslaughter

### (b) *"Unlawful act" manslaughter*

## Unlawful acts

**19-113**    In *R. v. Bristow* [2014] Crim.L.R. 457, CA, the court approved a direction to the jury to the following effect: if, prior to embarking on a burglary, the burglar foresaw the possibility that someone might try to intervene in order to stop the burglary or prevent his escape, and, prior to the burglary taking place, all sober and reasonable people would inevitably have recognised that any such intervention must subject the person intervening to the risk of some physical harm resulting from the burglary and/ or escape, and someone did intervene in the manner contemplated and in doing so suffered injuries from which he died, then the burglar would be guilty of unlawful act manslaughter. For critical comment on this decision, see CLW/13/41/1.

## Recognising the risk of the unlawful act

**19-120**    In connection with *R. v. Watson (C.)* (as to which, see the main work), see *R. v. Bristow, ante*, § 19-113.

### (8) Sentence

## Involuntary manslaughter

★**19-136**    In *R. v. Mahil, Shoker and Peters* [2014] 1 Cr.App.R.(S.) 18, CA, a case of gross negligence manslaughter where the unconscious or semi-conscious victim was put in the boot of a car, where petrol was poured in the back of the car and over the victim, and where the victim died from the effect of the fire, the court held that little assistance could be derived from sentencing cases concerning unlawful act manslaughter by arson, and that it was not possible to infer any hierarchy of sentences between unlawful act manslaughter cases and gross negligence manslaughter cases; they involved different aspects of involuntary manslaughter, and each covered a wide spectrum of cases in respect of which there was no guideline as to what sentence should be imposed.

## C. CORPORATE MANSLAUGHTER

### (1) The offence

With effect from March 27, 2014, the Public Bodies (Merger of the Director of Public Prosecutions and the Director of Revenue and Customs Prosecutions) Order 2014 (S.I. 2014 No. 834), art. 3(3), and Sched. 2, amended Schedule 1 to the Corporate Manslaughter and Corporate Homicide Act 2007 (see the main work), subject to saving and transitional provisions (as to which, see *ante*, § 1-27), so as to omit the Revenue and Customs Prosecutions Office. ★**19-139**

### (2) Relevant duty of care

#### Corporate Manslaughter and Corporate Homicide Act 2007, ss.2–7

*Meaning of "relevant duty of care"*

As from a day to be appointed, the Immigration Act 2014, s.73(6), and Sched. 9, para. 15, amend section 2 of the 2007 Act so as (i) in subsection (2)(b), to substitute the words ", a short-term holding facility or in pre-departure accommodation" for the words "or short-term holding facility", and (ii) in subsection (7), to substitute the words ", 'short-term holding facility' and 'pre-departure accommodation'" for the words "and 'short-term holding facility'". ★**19-141**

### (7) General and supplemental

#### Corporate Manslaughter and Corporate Homicide Act 2007, ss.25, 27, 28

*Interpretation*

As from April 1, 2014 (Energy Act 2013 (Commencement No. 1) Order 2014 (S.I. 2014 No. 251)), section 25 of the 2007 Act is amended by the Energy Act 2013, s.116(1), and Sched. 12, para. 93, so as to insert the words "and provision dealing with health and safety matters contained in Part 3 of the Energy Act 2013 (nuclear regulation)" at the end of the definition of "health and safety legislation". **19-160**

## D. CAUSING OR ALLOWING A CHILD OR VULNERABLE ADULT TO DIE OR SUFFER SERIOUS PHYSICAL HARM

### (6) Evidence and procedure

#### Domestic Violence, Crime and Victims Act 2004, ss.6, 6A

*Evidence and procedure in cases of death: England and Wales*

As to whether it would ever be appropriate, where the father and mother of a child who has died are jointly charged with an offence under section 5 of the 2004 Act (§ 19-163 in the main work), to seek special verdicts from the jury with a view to identifying which defendant was actually responsible for inflicting the injuries from which the child died, see *R. v. Hopkinson*, *ante*, § 4-534. **19-168**

## III. ABORTION

### (5) Sentence

In *R. v. Catt* [2014] 1 Cr.App.R.(S.) 35, CA, a sentence of eight years' imprisonment for an offence under section 58 of the Offences against the Person Act 1861 (§ 19-203 in the main work) was reduced on appeal to 42 months' imprisonment, where the offender, who had a history of concealing pregnancies, ordered the drug misoprostol (an abortifacient) from the internet and took it when she was about 40 weeks' pregnant (early plea). ★**19-209**

## IV. COMMON ASSAULT AND BATTERY

### C. DEFENCES

**Consent**

There is no requirement to explain the "possible major consequences" together with the "op- **19-235** tions" and "alternative treatments" in order to negative a battery arising out of a medical procedure; it is sufficient that the patient consents to the procedure having been advised in broad terms of its nature; a failure to advise as to the consequences or alternatives might expose the practitioner to a suit in negligence but it would not vitiate consent: *Reeves v The Queen*, unreported, December 18, 2013, High Court of Australia ([2013] HCA 57).

## VI. WOUNDING, CAUSING GRIEVOUS BODILY HARM

### (6) Ingredients of the offences

#### (e) *With intent, etc.*

★**19-265**     A person who, intending to kill X, attempted to shoot him but instead hit Y, causing him grievous bodily harm, may be charged with (and convicted of) both attempted murder of X and causing grievous bodily harm to Y with intent to cause grievous bodily harm to X, contrary to section 18 of the Offences against the Person Act 1861 (§ 19-251 in the main work); an intention to kill X (a necessary ingredient of attempted murder) necessarily includes an intention to cause him grievous bodily harm: *R. v. Grant, Kolawole and McCalla* [2014] 2 *Archbold Review* 2, CA.

## X. HARASSMENT

### B. STATUTE

#### Protection from Harassment Act 1997, ss.3–5

*Civil remedy*

★**19-345**     The provisions of the Crime and Courts Act 2013 referred to in the main work came into force on April 22, 2014: Crime and Courts Act 2013 (Commencement No. 10 and Transitional Provision) Order 2014 (S.I. 2014 No. 954).

*Restraining orders on conviction*

**19-350**     It had not been appropriate to make a restraining order under section 5 of the 1997 Act in favour of the complainant, who had a history of making exaggerated or false complaints, where all the important conflicts of evidence had been resolved in favour of the defendant and where there was a real risk that such an order, far from mending affairs for the future, would provide an opportunity for further complaints to be made: *R. v. James (Andrew)* [2013] 2 Cr.App.R.(S.) 85, CA.

## XI. ILL-TREATMENT OR NEGLECT OF PERSONS OF UNSOUND MIND

### B. PERSONS LACKING CAPACITY

### (4) Sentence

★**19-363d**     In *R. v. Kenyon* [2014] 1 Cr.App.R.(S.) 71, CA, a sentence of eight months' imprisonment on conviction of eight counts under section 44 of the Mental Capacity Act 2005 (§ 19-363a in the main work) was upheld where an experienced care assistant had left eight elderly care-home residents sitting in their own urine or urine and faeces in a fit of petulance after learning she had not been promoted.

### (5) Ingredients of the offence

**19-363e**     *R. v. Patel* (see the main work) and *R. v. Sheppard* (§ 17-47 in the main work) were considered in *R. v. Turbill and Broadway* [2014] 1 Cr.App.R. 7, CA, where there was an issue as to the sufficiency of the judge's directions to the jury in relation to the requirement that the neglect must be "wilful". It was held that "wilful" in this context should be interpreted in accordance with the decision of the House of Lords in *R. v. Sheppard* (§ 17-47 in the main work). Where, therefore, the judge's directions, in some places, appeared to equate carelessness or negligence with wilful neglect, and where he used a variety of expressions ("reckless" without defining it, and without directing the jury it is not simply an objective test; and "careless", "carelessness" and "grossly careless" as if they necessarily equated to a "couldn't care less" attitude" (which they do not: even "gross carelessness" would not, of itself, be sufficient to amount to wilful neglect)), however much he may have focussed the jury's attention on the state of mind of each accused, the cumulative effect of these failings might have been to water down the directions, causing real doubts as to whether the jury would have understood the essential elements of the offence. The convictions were accordingly held to be unsafe.

## XIII. OFFENCES RELATING TO CHILDREN AND YOUNG PERSONS

### B. Abduction of Children

**Child Abduction Act 1984, s.1**

*Offence of abduction by parent, etc.*

With effect from April 22, 2014 (Children and Families Act 2014 (Commencement No. 2)   ★**19-395**
Order 2014 (S.I. 2014 No. 889)), the Children and Families Act 2014, s.12(4), and Sched. 2, para. 47(1), (2) and (3), amended section 1 of the 1984 Act so as (i) in subsection (2)(d), to substitute the words "named in a child arrangements order as a person with whom the child is to live; or" for the words after "person", and (ii) in subsection (3)(a), to substitute, for paragraph (iv), a new paragraph (iv) as follows—

> "(iv)  any person named in a child arrangements order as a person with whom the child is
> to live;".

With effect from April 22, 2014 (S.I. 2014 No. 889 (*ante*)), the 2014 Act, s.12(4), and Sched. 2,   ★
para. 47(1), (4) and (5), further amended section 1 of the 1984 Act so as (i) in subsection (4)(a), to substitute the words "named in a child arrangements order as a person with whom the child is to live" for the words "in whose favour there is a residence order in force with respect to the child,", and (ii) in subsection (5A)(a), to substitute, for sub-paragraph (i), a new sub-paragraph (i) as follows—

> "(i)  named in a child arrangements order as a person with whom the child is to live;".

With effect from April 22, 2014 (S.I. 2014 No. 889 (*ante*)), the 2014 Act, s.12(4), and Sched. 2,   ★
para. 47(1) and (6), further amended section 1 of the 1984 Act so as to substitute, in subsection (7)(a), the words "'child arrangements'" for the word "'residence'".

## XIV. FALSE IMPRISONMENT AND KIDNAPPING

### (5) Defences

#### Arrest under criminal process

(i) *By warrant*

For a further order made under section 125A(3) of the MCA 1980 (see the main work), see the   ★**19-427**
Family Court Warrants (Specification of Orders) Order 2014 (S.I. 2014 No. 832).

With effect from April 22, 2014, the Magistrates' Courts Warrants (Specification of Provisions)   ★
Order 2000 (S.I. 2000 No. 3278) (see the main work) was further amended: Crime and Courts Act 2013 (Family Court: Consequential Provision) (No. 2) Order 2014 (S.I. 2014 No. 879).

The provisions of the Crime and Courts Act 2013 referred to in the main work came into force   ★
on April 22, 2014: Crime and Courts Act 2013 (Commencement No. 10 and Transitional Provision) Order 2014 (S.I. 2014 No. 954).

(ii) *Without warrant*

The aspect of *R. (Hicks) v. Commr of Police of the Metropolis*; *R. (M.) v. Same*; *R. (Pearce) v. Same*;   ★**19-430**
*R. (Middleton) v. Bromley Magistrates' Court and Commr of Police of the Metropolis* that is referred to in

the main work was not the subject of challenge when the matter went to the Court of Appeal: see *R. (Hicks) v. Commr of Police of the Metropolis* [2014] 2 Cr.App.R. 4, CA (Civ. Div.).

CHAPTER 20

# SEXUAL OFFENCES

## I. INTRODUCTION

### Sentencing guidelines

**20-9c**      The Sentencing Council for England and Wales has issued a definitive guideline on sexual offences, applying to all offenders aged 18 or over, who are sentenced on or after April 1, 2014, and covering the following offences: rape (SOA 2003, s.1 (§ 20-19 in the main work)); assault by penetration (2003 Act, s.2 (§ 20-28 in the main work)); sexual assault (2003 Act, s.3 (§ 20-29 in the main work)); causing a person to engage in sexual activity without consent (2003 Act, s.4 (§ 20-40 in the main work)); rape of a child under 13 (2003 Act, s.5 (§ 20-49 in the main work)); assault of a child under 13 by penetration (2003 Act, s.6 (§ 20-50 in the main work)); sexual assault of a child under 13 (2003 Act, s.7 (§ 20-51 in the main work)); causing or inciting a child under 13 to engage in sexual activity (2003 Act, s.8 (§ 20-52 in the main work)); sexual activity with a child (2003 Act, s.9 (§ 20-58 in the main work)); causing or inciting a child to engage in sexual activity (2003 Act, s.10 (§ 20-64 in the main work)); sexual activity with a child family member (2003 Act, s.25 (§ 20-110 in the main work)); inciting a child family member to engage in sexual activity (2003 Act, s.26 (§ 20-111 in the main work)); engaging in sexual activity in the presence of a child (2003 Act, s.11 (§ 20-69 in the main work)); causing a child to watch a sexual act (2003 Act, s.12 (§ 20-74 in the main work)); arranging or facilitating the commission of a child sex offence (2003 Act, s.14 (§ 20-85 in the main work)); meeting a child following sexual grooming (2003 Act, s.15 (§ 20-91 in the main work)); abuse of position of trust: sexual activity with a child (2003 Act, s.16 (§ 20-96 in the main work)); abuse of position of trust: causing or inciting a child to engage in sexual activity (2003 Act, s.17 (§ 20-97 in the main work)); abuse of position of trust: sexual activity in the presence of a child (2003 Act, s.18 (§ 20-98 in the main work)); abuse of position of trust: causing a child to watch a sexual act (2003 Act, s.19 (§ 20-99 in the main work)); possession of indecent photograph of child (CJA 1988, s.160 (§ 31-115 in the main work)); indecent photographs of children (Protection of Children Act 1978, s.1 (§ 31-107 in the main work)); causing or inciting prostitution for gain (2003 Act, s.52 (§ 20-172 in the main work)); controlling prostitution for gain (2003 Act, s.63 (§ 20-173 in the main work)); keeping a brothel used for prostitution (SOA 1956, s.33A (§ 20-229 in the main work)); causing or inciting child prostitution or pornography (2003 Act, s.48 (§ 20-160 in the main work)); controlling a child prostitute or child involved in pornography (2003 Act, s.49 (§ 20-167 in the main work)); arranging or facilitating child prostitution or pornography (2003 Act, s.50 (§ 20-161 in the main work)); paying for the sexual services of a child (2003 Act, s.47 (§ 20-155 in the main work)); trafficking people for sexual exploitation (2003 Act, s.59A (§ 20-179 in the main work)) (and also the 2003 Act, ss.57–59, before their replacement by s.59A); sexual activity with a person with a mental disorder impeding choice (2003 Act, s.30 (§ 20-125 in the main work)); causing or inciting such a person to engage in a sexual activity (2003 Act, s.30 (§ 20-126 in the main work)); engaging in sexual activity in the presence of such a person (2003 Act, s.32 (§ 20-127 in the main work)); causing such a person to watch a sexual act (2003 Act, s.33 (§ 20-128 in the main work)); inducement, threat or deception to procure sexual activity with a person with a mental disorder (2003 Act, s.34 (§ 20-134 in the main work)); causing such a person to engage in or agree to engage in sexual activity by inducement, threat or deception (2003 Act, s.35 (§ 20-135 in the main work)); engaging in sexual activity in the presence, procured by inducement, threat or deception, of a person with a mental disorder (2003 Act, s.36 (§ 20-136 in the main work)); causing such a person to watch a sexual act by inducement, threat or deception (2003 Act, s.37 (§ 20-137 in the main work)); care workers: sexual activity with a person with a mental disorder (2003 Act, s.38 (§ 20-143 in the main work));

care workers: causing or inciting sexual activity (2003 Act, s.39 (§ 20-144 in the main work)); care workers: sexual activity in the presence of a person with a mental disorder (2003 Act, s.40 (§ 20-145 in the main work)); care workers: causing such a person to watch a sexual act (2003 Act, s.41 (§ 20-146 in the main work)); exposure (2003 Act, s.66 (§ 20-208 in the main work)); voyeurism (2003 Act, s.67 (§ 20-212 in the main work)); sex with an adult relative: penetration (2003 Act, s.64 (§ 20-202 in the main work)); sex with an adult relative: consenting to penetration (2003 Act, s.65 (§ 20-203 in the main work)); administering a substance with intent (2003 Act, s.61 (§ 20-187 in the main work)); committing an offence with intent to commit a sexual offence (2003 Act, s.62 (§ 20-192 in the main work)); and trespass with intent to commit a sexual offence (2003 Act, s.63 (§ 20-197 in the main work)).

For the detail of the replacement guideline, see *post*, Appendix K-84 *et seq.*

## II. OFFENCES

### A. GENERAL INTERPRETATION

#### (1) Consent

**Sexual Offences Act 2003, s.74**

*"Consent"*

Where, on a prosecution for rape or sexual assault, the prosecution allege that the complainant ★**20-10** lacked capacity to consent, (i) the jury should be directed that a person lacks capacity if he lacks the capacity to choose, whether because he lacks sufficient understanding of the nature or reasonably foreseeable consequences of what is being done, or for any other reason; such an approach aligns the test of incapacity in the civil and criminal jurisdictions (see the Mental Capacity Act 2005, ss.2 and 3, and the SOA 2003, ss.30(2)(a), 31(2)(a), 32(2)(a), 33(2)(a) (§§ 20-125 *et seq.* in the main work), and 74 (see the main work)); the requirement that the complainant should understand the nature of the act will be a relatively simple issue to address; the question relating to the understanding of reasonably foreseeable consequences should not be divorced from the actual decision-making process carried out in that regard on a daily basis by persons of full capacity; the process is largely visceral rather than cerebral, and owes more to instinct and emotion than to analysis; (ii) the burden of proving incapacity rests with the prosecution and the standard is the criminal standard; section 4 of the 2005 Act ("(4) In proceedings under this Act or any other enactment, any question whether a person lacks capacity within the meaning of this Act must be decided on the balance of probabilities.") has no application to criminal proceedings for an offence other than under that Act; and (iii) where expert evidence is called by the prosecution, it is essential that such evidence is "expert", relevant and is strictly confined to the issue of capacity: see *R. v. A. (G.)* [2014] 2 Cr.App.R. 5, CA.

### B. RAPE

#### (2) Indictment

As to a case considering the effect on the safety of a conviction of a statement of offence in an **20-20** indictment alleging rape, contrary to the SOA 1956, s.1(1), when it should have referred to the SOA 2003, s.1(1) (§ 20-19 in the main work), see *R. v. Stocker, ante*, § 7-77.

#### (4) Sentence

**Guidelines**

As to the replacement of the Sentencing Guidelines Council's guideline, see *ante*, § 20-9c. **20-23**

### C. ASSAULTS

#### (4) Sentence

As to the replacement of the Sentencing Guidelines Council's guideline, see *ante*, § 20-9c. **20-33**

### D. CAUSING SEXUAL ACTIVITY WITHOUT CONSENT

#### (4) Sentence

As to the replacement of the Sentencing Guidelines Council's guideline, see *ante*, § 20-9c. **20-43**

## E. Rape and Other Offences against Children Under 13

### (4) Sentence

**20-55**     As to the replacement of the Sentencing Guidelines Council's guideline, see *ante*, § 20-9c.

## F. Child Sex Offences

### (1) Sexual activity with a child

#### (d) *Sentence*

**20-61**     As to the replacement of the Sentencing Guidelines Council's guideline, see *ante*, § 20-9c.

### (2) Causing or inciting a child to engage in sexual activity

#### (d) *Sentence*

**20-67**     As to the replacement of the Sentencing Guidelines Council's guideline, see *ante*, § 20-9c.

### (3) Engaging in sexual activity in the presence of a child

#### (d) *Sentence*

**20-72**     As to the replacement of the Sentencing Guidelines Council's guideline, see *ante*, § 20-9c.

### (4) Causing a child to watch a sexual act

#### (d) *Sentence*

**20-77**     As to the replacement of the Sentencing Guidelines Council's guideline, see *ante*, § 20-9c.

### (5) Child sex offences committed by persons aged under 18

#### (d) *Sentence*

**20-82**     As to the replacement of the Sentencing Guidelines Council's guideline, see *ante*, § 20-9c. The guideline issued by the Sentencing Council is specific about the fact that it has no application to the sentencing of offenders under the age of 18, and that they should be sentenced in accordance with the principles applicable to the sentencing of young offenders generally.

### (6) Arranging or facilitating commission of a child sex offence

#### (d) *Sentence*

**20-88**     As to the replacement of the Sentencing Guidelines Council's guideline, see *ante*, § 20-9c.

### (7) Meeting a child following sexual grooming

#### (d) *Sentence*

**20-94**     As to the replacement of the Sentencing Guidelines Council's guideline, see *ante*, § 20-9c.

## G. Abuse of Position of Trust

### (4) Sentence

**20-107**     As to the replacement of the Sentencing Guidelines Council's guideline, see *ante*, § 20-9c.

## H. Familial Child Sex Offences

### (4) Sentence

### Guidelines

**20-118**     As to the replacement of the Sentencing Guidelines Council's guideline, see *ante*, § 20-9c.

## I. Offences Against Persons with a Mental Disorder Impeding Choice

### (4) Sentence

**20-131**     As to the replacement of the Sentencing Guidelines Council's guideline, see *ante*, § 20-9c.

### (5) Elements of the offences

As to the approach to the question whether the complainant understood the nature of the act ★**20-132** (SOA 2003, ss.30(2)(a), 31(2)(a), 32(2)(a), 33(2)(a)) (as to which, see §§ 20-125 *et seq.* in the main work), or its reasonably foreseeable consequences (ss.30(2)(a), 31(2)(a)), see *R. v. A. (G.), ante,* § 20-10.

## J. Inducements etc. to Persons with a Mental Disorder

### (4) Sentence

As to the replacement of the Sentencing Guidelines Council's guideline, see *ante,* § 20-9c.    **20-140**

## K. Offences by Care Workers for Persons with a Mental Disorder

### (4) Sentence

As to the replacement of the Sentencing Guidelines Council's guideline, see *ante,* § 20-9c.    **20-152**

## L. Abuse of Children through Prostitution and Pornography

### (1) Paying for sexual services of a child

#### (d) *Sentence*

As to the replacement of the Sentencing Guidelines Council's guideline, see *ante,* § 20-9c.    **20-158**

### (2) Causing, inciting, facilitating, etc., child prostitution or pornography

#### (d) *Sentence*

As to the replacement of the Sentencing Guidelines Council's guideline, see *ante,* § 20-9c.    **20-165**

### (3) Controlling a child prostitute or a child involved in pornography

#### (d) *Sentence*

As to the replacement of the Sentencing Guidelines Council's guideline, see *ante,* § 20-9c.    **20-170**

## M. Exploitation of Prostitution

### (4) Sentence

As to the replacement of the Sentencing Guidelines Council's guideline, see *ante,* § 20-9c.    **20-177**

## N. Trafficking

### (4) Sentence

As to the replacement of the Sentencing Guidelines Council's guideline, see *ante,* § 20-9c.    **20-185**

## O. Preparatory Offences

### (1) Administering a substance with intent

#### (d) *Sentence*

As to the replacement of the Sentencing Guidelines Council's guideline, see *ante,* § 20-9c.    **20-190**

### (2) Committing an offence with intent to commit a sexual offence

#### (d) *Sentence*

As to the replacement of the Sentencing Guidelines Council's guideline, see *ante,* § 20-9c.    **20-195**

### (3) Trespass with intent

#### (d) *Sentence*

As to the replacement of the Sentencing Guidelines Council's guideline, see *ante,* § 20-9c.    **20-200**

## P. Sex with an Adult Relative

### (4) Sentence

**20-206**    As to the replacement of the Sentencing Guidelines Council's guideline, see *ante*, § 20-9c.

## Q. Other Statutory Offences

### (1) Exposure

#### (d) *Sentence*

**20-211**    As to the replacement of the Sentencing Guidelines Council's guideline, see *ante*, § 20-9c.

### (2) Voyeurism

#### (d) *Sentence*

**20-216**    As to the replacement of the Sentencing Guidelines Council's guideline, see *ante*, § 20-9c.

### (3) Intercourse with an animal

#### (d) *Sentence*

**20-221**    The Sentencing Council's guideline on sexual offences (*ante*, § 20-9c) does not cover this offence. As the guideline of the Sentencing Guidelines Council is not said to be "revoked", guidance should presumably still be obtained from that guideline (see *post*, Appendix K-83a).

### (4) Sexual penetration of a corpse

#### (d) *Sentence*

**20-226**    The Sentencing Council's guideline on sexual offences (*ante*, § 20-9c) does not cover this offence. As the guideline of the Sentencing Guidelines Council is not said to be "revoked", guidance should presumably still be obtained from that guideline (see *post*, Appendix K-83b).

### (5) Sexual activity in a public lavatory

**20-228**    The Sentencing Council's guideline on sexual offences (*ante*, § 20-9c) does not cover this offence. As the guideline of the Sentencing Guidelines Council is not said to be "revoked", guidance should presumably still be obtained from that guideline (see *post*, Appendix K-83c).

### (6) Suppression of brothels

#### (d) *Sentence*

**20-232**    As to the replacement of the Sentencing Guidelines Council's guideline, see *ante*, § 20-9c.

## R. Common Law Offences

### (1) Acts outraging public decency

**Sentence**

★**20-240**    In *R. v. Hardy* [2014] 1 Cr.App.R.(S.) 70, CA, the court applied the Sentencing Guidelines Council's guideline on the offence of exposure under the SOA 2003, s.66 (§ 20-208 in the main work), to an offence of outraging public decency consisting of exposure in a public place with a suggestion that the defendant was also masturbating. For the guideline of the Sentencing Council, see *post*, Appendix K-100 (under that guideline, the fact that the offender was masturbating is given as an indicator of greater harm).

## IV. NOTIFICATION AND ORDERS

### A. Notification Requirements

#### (3) Legislation

**Sexual Offences Act 2003, ss.81, 82**

**20-267**    *R. (Minter) v. Chief Constable of Hampshire Constabulary (Secretary of State for the Home Department,* *interested party)* is now reported at [2014] 1 W.L.R. 179, *sub nom. R. (Minter) v. Chief Constable of Hampshire Constabulary.*

**Sexual Offences Act 2003, ss.83–86**

*Notification requirements: initial notification*

Regulation 12 of the Sexual Offences Act 2003 (Notification Requirements) (England and Wales) Regulations 2012 (S.I. 2012 No. 1876) is compatible with Article 8 of the ECHR (right to privacy and family life (§ 16-101 in the main work)): *R. (Prothero) v. Secretary of State for the Home Department* [2014] 1 W.L.R. 1195, DC.     **20-268**

**Sexual Offences Act 2003, ss.87–91**

*Section 87: interpretation*

As from a day to be appointed, the Anti-social Behaviour, Crime and Policing Act 2014, s.181(1), and Sched. 11, para. 56, amend section 88(4)(c) of the 2003 Act so as to insert, after the words "interim notification order," the words "sexual harm prevention order, interim sexual harm prevention order,".     **★20-273**

*Young offenders: parental directions*

As from a day to be appointed, the Anti-social Behaviour, Crime and Policing Act 2014, s.181(1), and Sched. 11, para. 57, amend the table in section 89(1) of the 2003 Act so as to insert, after the words "interim notification order," the words "sexual harm prevention order, interim sexual harm prevention order,".     **★20-274**

## Review of notification requirements

As from a day to be appointed, the Anti-social Behaviour, Crime and Policing Act 2014, s.181(1), and Sched. 11, para. 58, amend section 91A of the 2003 Act (see the main work).     **★20-276a**

## CA. SEXUAL HARM PREVENTION ORDERS

As from a day to be appointed, the SOA 2003 is amended, so as to insert, after section 103, sections 103A to 103K, which provide for sexual harm prevention orders: Anti-social Behaviour, Crime and Policing Act 2014, s.113(1), and Sched. 5, para. 2. Sexual harm prevention orders and sexual risk orders (as to which, see *post*, § 20-337a) replace, in England and Wales, sexual offences prevention orders (§§ 20-323 *et seq.* in the main work and *post*), foreign travel orders (as to which, see *post*, § 20-337) and risk of sexual harm orders (as to which, see *post*, § 20-338).     **★20-322a**

**Sexual Offences Act 2003, ss.103A–103K**

*Sexual harm prevention orders (England and Wales)*

*[Sexual harm prevention orders: applications and grounds*

**103A.**—(1) A court may make an order under this section (a "sexual harm prevention order") in respect of a person ("the defendant") where subsection (2) or (3) applies to the defendant.     **★20-322b**

(2) This subsection applies to the defendant where—

  (a)  the court deals with the defendant in respect of—

   (i)  an offence listed in Schedule 3 or 5, or

   (ii)  a finding that the defendant is not guilty of an offence listed in Schedule 3 or 5 by reason of insanity, or

   (iii)  a finding that the defendant is under a disability and has done the act charged against the defendant in respect of an offence listed in Schedule 3 or 5, and

  (b)  the court is satisfied that it is necessary to make a sexual harm prevention order, for the purpose of—

   (i)  protecting the public or any particular members of the public from sexual harm from the defendant, or

   (ii)  protecting children or vulnerable adults generally, or any particular children or vulnerable adults, from sexual harm from the defendant outside the United Kingdom.

(3) This subsection applies to the defendant where—

  (a)  an application under subsection (4) has been made in respect of the defendant and it is proved on the application that the defendant is a qualifying offender, and

175

(b)  the court is satisfied that the defendant's behaviour since the appropriate date makes it necessary to make a sexual harm prevention order, for the purpose of—

    (i)  protecting the public or any particular members of the public from sexual harm from the defendant, or

    (ii)  protecting children or vulnerable adults generally, or any particular children or vulnerable adults, from sexual harm from the defendant outside the United Kingdom.

(4) A chief officer of police or the Director General of the National Crime Agency ("the Director General") may by complaint to a magistrates' court apply for a sexual harm prevention order in respect of a person if it appears to the chief officer or the Director General that—

    (a)  the person is a qualifying offender, and

    (b)  the person has since the appropriate date acted in such a way as to give reasonable cause to believe that it is necessary for such an order to be made.

(5) A chief officer of police may make an application under subsection (4) only in respect of a person—

    (a)  who resides in the chief officer's police area, or

    (b)  who the chief officer believes is in that area or is intending to come to it.

(6) An application under subsection (4) may be made to any magistrates' court acting for a local justice area that includes—

    (a)  any part of a relevant police area, or

    (b)  any place where it is alleged that the person acted in a way mentioned in subsection (4)(b).

(7) The Director General must as soon as practicable notify the chief officer of police for a relevant police area of any application that the Director has made under subsection (4).

(8) Where the defendant is a child, a reference in this section to a magistrates' court is to be taken as referring to a youth court (subject to any rules of court made under section 103K(1)).

(9) In this section "relevant police area" means—

    (a)  where the applicant is a chief officer of police, the officer's police area;

    (b)  where the applicant is the Director General—

        (i)  the police area where the person in question resides, or

        (ii)  a police area which the Director General believes the person is in or is intending to come to.]

As to the insertion, as from a day to be appointed, of sections 103A to 103K of the 2003 Act, see *ante*, § 20-322a.

*[Section 103A: supplemental*

★**20-322c**    **103B.**—(1) In section 103A—

"appropriate date", in relation to a qualifying offender, means the date or (as the case may be) the first date on which the offender was convicted, found or cautioned as mentioned in subsection (2) or (3) below;

"child" means a person under 18;

"the public" means the public in the United Kingdom;

"sexual harm" from a person means physical or psychological harm caused—

    (a)  by the person committing one or more offences listed in Schedule 3, or

    (b)  (in the context of harm outside the United Kingdom) by the person doing, outside the United Kingdom, anything which would constitute an offence listed in Schedule 3 if done in any part of the United Kingdom;

"qualifying offender" means a person within subsection (2) or (3) below;

"vulnerable adult" means a person aged 18 or over whose ability to protect himself or herself from physical or psychological harm is significantly impaired through physical or mental disability or illness, through old age or otherwise.

(2) A person is within this subsection if, whether before or after the commencement of this Part, the person—

    (a)  has been convicted of an offence listed in Schedule 3 (other than at paragraph 60) or in Schedule 5,

    (b)  has been found not guilty of such an offence by reason of insanity,

    (c)  has been found to be under a disability and to have done the act charged against him in respect of such an offence, or

    (d)  has been cautioned in respect of such an offence.

(3) A person is within this subsection if, under the law in force in a country outside the United Kingdom and whether before or after the commencement of this Part—

    (a)   the person has been convicted of a relevant offence (whether or not the person has been punished for it),

    (b)   a court exercising jurisdiction under that law has made in respect of a relevant offence a finding equivalent to a finding that the person is not guilty by reason of insanity,

    (c)   such a court has made in respect of a relevant offence a finding equivalent to a finding that the person is under a disability and did the act charged against the person in respect of the offence, or

    (d)   the person has been cautioned in respect of a relevant offence.

  (4) In subsection (3), "relevant offence" means an act which—

    (a)   constituted an offence under the law in force in the country concerned, and

    (b)   would have constituted an offence listed in Schedule 3 (other than at paragraph 60) or in Schedule 5 if it had been done in any part of the United Kingdom.

For this purpose an act punishable under the law in force in a country outside the United Kingdom constitutes an offence under that law, however it is described in that law.

  (5) For the purposes of section 103A, acts, behaviour, convictions and findings include those occurring before the commencement of this Part.

  (6) Subject to subsection (7), on an application under section 103A(4) the condition in subsection (4)(b) above (where relevant) is to be taken as met unless, not later than rules of court may provide, the defendant serves on the applicant a notice—

    (a)   stating that, on the facts as alleged with respect to the act concerned, the condition is not in the defendant's opinion met,

    (b)   showing the grounds for that opinion, and

    (c)   requiring the applicant to prove that the condition is met.

  (7) The court, if it thinks fit, may permit the defendant to require the applicant to prove that the condition is met without service of a notice under subsection (6).

  (8) Subsection (9) applies for the purposes of section 103A and this section.

  (9) In construing any reference to an offence listed in Schedule 3, any condition subject to which an offence is so listed that relates—

    (a)   to the way in which the defendant is dealt with in respect of an offence so listed or a relevant finding (as defined by section 132(9)), or

    (b)   to the age of any person,

  is to be disregarded.]

As to the insertion, as from a day to be appointed, of sections 103A to 103K of the 2003 Act, see *ante*, § 20-322a.

*[SHPOs: effect*

  **103C.**—(1) A sexual harm prevention order prohibits the defendant from doing anything described   ★**20-322d**
in the order.

  (2) Subject to section 103D(1), a prohibition contained in a sexual harm prevention order has effect—

    (a)   for a fixed period, specified in the order, of at least 5 years, or

    (b)   until further order.

  (3) A sexual harm prevention order—

    (a)   may specify that some of its prohibitions have effect until further order and some for a fixed period;

    (b)   may specify different periods for different prohibitions.

  (4) The only prohibitions that may be included in a sexual harm prevention order are those necessary for the purpose of—

    (a)   protecting the public or any particular members of the public from sexual harm from the defendant, or

    (b)   protecting children or vulnerable adults generally, or any particular children or vulnerable adults, from sexual harm from the defendant outside the United Kingdom.

  (5) In subsection (4) "the public", "sexual harm", "child" and "vulnerable adult" each has the meaning given in section 103B(1).

  (6) Where a court makes a sexual harm prevention order in relation to a person who is already subject to such an order (whether made by that court or another), the earlier order ceases to have effect.]

As to the insertion, as from a day to be appointed, of sections 103A to 103K of the 2003 Act, see *ante*, § 20-322a.

*[SHPOs: prohibitions on foreign travel*

★**20-322e**    **103D.**—(1) A prohibition on foreign travel contained in a sexual harm prevention order must be for a fixed period of not more than 5 years.

(2) A "prohibition on foreign travel" means—

    (a)  a prohibition on travelling to any country outside the United Kingdom named or described in the order,

    (b)  a prohibition on travelling to any country outside the United Kingdom other than a country named or described in the order, or

    (c)  a prohibition on travelling to any country outside the United Kingdom.

(3) Subsection (1) does not prevent a prohibition on foreign travel from being extended for a further period (of no more than 5 years each time) under section 103E.

(4) A sexual harm prevention order that contains a prohibition within subsection (2)(c) must require the defendant to surrender all of the defendant's passports at a police station specified in the order—

    (a)  on or before the date when the prohibition takes effect, or

    (b)  within a period specified in the order.

(5) Any passports surrendered must be returned as soon as reasonably practicable after the person ceases to be subject to a sexual harm prevention order containing a prohibition within subsection (2)(c) (unless the person is subject to an equivalent prohibition under another order).

(6) Subsection (5) does not apply in relation to—

    (a)  a passport issued by or on behalf of the authorities of a country outside the United Kingdom if the passport has been returned to those authorities;

    (b)  a passport issued by or on behalf of an international organisation if the passport has been returned to that organisation.

(7) In this section "passport" means—

    (a)  a United Kingdom passport within the meaning of the Immigration Act 1971;

    (b)  a passport issued by or on behalf of the authorities of a country outside the United Kingdom, or by or on behalf of an international organisation;

    (c)  a document that can be used (in some or all circumstances) instead of a passport.]

As to the insertion, as from a day to be appointed, of sections 103A to 103K of the 2003 Act, see *ante*, § 20-322a.

*[SHPOs: variations, renewals and discharges*

★**20-322f**    **103E.**—(1) A person within subsection (2) may apply to the appropriate court for an order varying, renewing or discharging a sexual harm prevention order.

(2) The persons are—

    (a)  the defendant;

    (b)  the chief officer of police for the area in which the defendant resides;

    (c)  a chief officer of police who believes that the defendant is in, or is intending to come to, that officer's police area;

    (d)  where the order was made on an application by a chief officer of police under section 103A(4), that officer.

(3) An application under subsection (1) may be made—

    (a)  where the appropriate court is the Crown Court, in accordance with rules of court;

    (b)  in any other case, by complaint.

(4) Subject to subsections (5) and (7), on the application the court, after hearing the person making the application and (if they wish to be heard) the other persons mentioned in subsection (2), may make any order, varying, renewing or discharging the sexual harm prevention order, that the court considers appropriate.

(5) An order may be renewed, or varied so as to impose additional prohibitions on the defendant, only if it is necessary to do so for the purpose of—

    (a)  protecting the public or any particular members of the public from sexual harm from the defendant, or

    (b)  protecting children or vulnerable adults generally, or any particular children or vulnerable adults, from sexual harm from the defendant outside the United Kingdom.

Any renewed or varied order may contain only such prohibitions as are necessary for this purpose.

(6) In subsection (5) "the public", "sexual harm", "child" and "vulnerable adult" each has the meaning given in section 103B(1).

(7) The court must not discharge an order before the end of 5 years beginning with the day on which the order was made, without the consent of the defendant and—

(a)   where the application is made by a chief officer of police, that chief officer, or

(b)   in any other case, the chief officer of police for the area in which the defendant resides.

(8) Subsection (7) does not apply to an order containing a prohibition on foreign travel and no other prohibitions.

(9) In this section "the appropriate court" means—

(a)   where the Crown Court or the Court of Appeal made the sexual harm prevention order, the Crown Court;

(b)   where an adult magistrates' court made the order, that court, an adult magistrates' court for the area in which the defendant resides or, where the application is made by a chief officer of police, any adult magistrates' court acting for a local justice area that includes any part of the chief officer's police area;

(c)   where a youth court made the order and the defendant is under the age of 18, that court, a youth court for the area in which the defendant resides or, where the application is made by a chief officer of police, any youth court acting for a local justice area that includes any part of the chief officer's police area;

(d)   where a youth court made the order and the defendant is aged 18 or over, an adult magistrates' court for the area in which the defendant resides or, where the application is made by a chief officer of police, any adult magistrates' court acting for a local justice area that includes any part of the chief officer's police area.

In this subsection "adult magistrates' court" means a magistrates' court that is not a youth court.]

As to the insertion, as from a day to be appointed, of sections 103A to 103K of the 2003 Act, see *ante*, § 20-322a.

*[Interim SHPOs*

**103F.**—(1) This section applies where an application under section 103A(4) ("the main application") has not been determined.   ★**20-322g**

(2) An application for an order under this section ("an interim sexual harm prevention order")—

(a)   may be made by the complaint by which the main application is made, or

(b)   if the main application has been made, may be made by the person who has made that application, by complaint to the court to which that application has been made.

(3) The court may, if it considers it just to do so, make an interim sexual harm prevention order, prohibiting the defendant from doing anything described in the order.

(4) Such an order—

(a)   has effect only for a fixed period, specified in the order;

(b)   ceases to have effect, if it has not already done so, on the determination of the main application.

(5) The applicant or the defendant may by complaint apply to the court that made the interim sexual harm prevention order for the order to be varied, renewed or discharged.]

As to the insertion, as from a day to be appointed, of sections 103A to 103K of the 2003 Act, see *ante*, § 20-322a.

*[SHPOs and interim SHPOs: notification requirements*

**103G.**—(1) Where—   ★**20-322h**

(a)   a sexual harm prevention order is made in respect of a defendant who was a relevant offender immediately before the making of the order, and

(b)   the defendant would (apart from this subsection) cease to be subject to the notification requirements of this Part while the order (as renewed from time to time) has effect,
the defendant remains subject to the notification requirements.

(2) Where a sexual harm prevention order is made in respect of a defendant who was not a relevant offender immediately before the making of the order—

(a)   the order causes the defendant to become subject to the notification requirements of this Part from the making of the order until the order (as renewed from time to time) ceases to have effect, and

(b)   this Part applies to the defendant, subject to the modification set out in subsection (3).

(3) The "relevant date" is the date of service of the order.

(4) Subsections (1) to (3) apply to an interim sexual harm prevention order as if references to a sexual harm prevention order were references to an interim sexual harm prevention order, and with the omission of "(as renewed from time to time)" in both places.

(5) Where—

    (a)  a sexual harm prevention order is in effect in relation to a relevant sex offender (within the meaning of section 88A), and

    (b)  by virtue of section 88F or 88G the relevant sex offender ceases to be subject to the notification requirements of this Part,

the sexual harm prevention order ceases to have effect.

(6) On an application for a sexual harm prevention order made by a chief officer of police, the court must make a notification order in respect of the defendant (either in addition to or instead of a sexual harm prevention order) if—

    (a)  the applicant invites the court to do so, and

    (b)  it is proved that the conditions in section 97(2) to (4) are met.

(7) On an application for an interim sexual harm prevention order made by a chief officer of police, the court may, if it considers it just to do so, make an interim notification order (either in addition to or instead of an interim sexual harm prevention order).]

As to the insertion, as from a day to be appointed, of sections 103A to 103K of the 2003 Act, see *ante*, § 20-322a.

*[SHPOs and interim SHPOs: appeals*

★**20-322i**     **103H.**—(1) A defendant may appeal against the making of a sexual harm prevention order—

    (a)  where the order was made by virtue of section 103A(2)(a)(i), as if the order were a sentence passed on the defendant for the offence;

    (b)  where the order was made by virtue of section 103A(2)(a)(ii) or (iii), as if the defendant had been convicted of the offence and the order were a sentence passed on the defendant for that offence;

    (c)  where the order was made on an application under section 103A(4), to the Crown Court.

(2) A defendant may appeal to the Crown Court against the making of an interim sexual harm prevention order.

(3) A defendant may appeal against the making of an order under section 103E, or the refusal to make such an order—

    (a)  where the application for such an order was made to the Crown Court, to the Court of Appeal;

    (b)  in any other case, to the Crown Court.

(4) On an appeal under subsection (1)(c), (2) or (3)(b), the Crown Court may make such orders as may be necessary to give effect to its determination of the appeal, and may also make such incidental or consequential orders as appear to it to be just.

(5) Any order made by the Crown Court on an appeal under subsection (1)(c) or (2) (other than an order directing that an application be re-heard by a magistrates' court) is for the purposes of section 103E(9) or 103F(5) (respectively) to be treated as if it were an order of the court from which the appeal was brought (and not an order of the Crown Court).]

As to the insertion, as from a day to be appointed, of sections 103A to 103K of the 2003 Act, see *ante*, § 20-322a.

*[Offence: breach of SHPO or interim SHPO etc*

★**20-322j**     **103I.**—(1) A person who, without reasonable excuse, does anything that the person is prohibited from doing by—

    (a)  a sexual harm prevention order,

    (b)  an interim sexual harm prevention order,

    (c)  a sexual offences prevention order,

    (d)  an interim sexual offences prevention order, or

    (e)  a foreign travel order,

commits an offence.

(2) A person commits an offence if, without reasonable excuse, the person fails to comply with a requirement imposed under section 103D(4).

(3) A person guilty of an offence under this section is liable—

    (a)  on summary conviction, to imprisonment for a term not exceeding 6 months or a fine or both;

    (b)  on conviction on indictment, to imprisonment for a term not exceeding 5 years.

(4) Where a person is convicted of an offence under this section, it is not open to the court by or before which the person is convicted to make, in respect of the offence, an order for conditional discharge.]

As to the insertion, as from a day to be appointed, of sections 103A to 103K of the 2003 Act, see *ante*, § 20-322a.

*[SHPOs and interim SHPOs: guidance*

**103J.**—(1) The Secretary of State must issue guidance to chief officers of police and to the Director     ★**20-322k**
General of the National Crime Agency in relation to the exercise by them of their powers with regard
to sexual harm prevention orders and interim sexual harm prevention orders.

(2) The Secretary of State may, from time to time, revise the guidance issued under subsection (1).

(3) The Secretary of State must arrange for any guidance issued or revised under this section to be
published in such manner as the Secretary of State considers appropriate.]

As to the insertion, as from a day to be appointed, of sections 103A to 103K of the 2003 Act, see *ante*, § 20-322a.

*[SHPOs and interim SHPOs: supplementary*

**103K.**—(1) Rules of court—     ★**20-322l**

    (a)  may provide for a youth court to give permission for an application under section 103A(4)
against a person aged 18 or over to be made to the youth court if—

        (i)  an application to the youth court has been made, or is to be made, under that section
against a person aged under 18, and

       (ii)  the youth court thinks that it would be in the interests of justice for the applications to
be heard together;

    (b)  may, in relation to a person attaining the age of 18 after proceedings against that person
by virtue of section 103A, 103E, 103F or 103G(6) or (7) have begun—

        (i)  prescribe circumstances in which the proceedings may or must remain in the youth
court;

       (ii)  make provision for the transfer of the proceedings from the youth court to a
magistrates' court that is not a youth court (including provision applying section 103F
with modifications).

(2) A person's age is treated for the purposes of sections 103A to 103J and this section as being
that which it appears to the court to be after considering any available evidence.]

As to the insertion, as from a day to be appointed, of sections 103A to 103K of the 2003 Act, see *ante*, § 20-322a.

## D. Sexual Offences Prevention Orders

### (1) Introduction

*Replacement of sexual offences prevention orders*

As from a day to be appointed, the Anti-social Behaviour, Crime and Policing Act 2014,     ★**20-323**
s.113(1), and Sched. 5, para. 3, repeal sections 104 to 122 of the SOA 2003 (§§ 20-323 *et seq.* in
the main work) in relation to England and Wales. Sexual offences prevention orders, foreign
travel orders (§ 20-337 in the main work) and risk of sexual harm orders (§ 20-338 in the main
work) are being replaced by sexual harm prevention orders (as to which, see *ante*, §§ 20-322a *et
seq.*) and sexual risk orders (as to which, see *post*, § 20-337a).

*Saving and transitional*

The repeal or amendment by the 2014 Act of sections 104 to 122 and sections 123 to 129 of the     **20-323a**
SOA 2003 (*post*) does not apply in relation to an application made before the day section 114 of
the 2014 Act comes into force for "an existing order" (a sexual offences prevention order under
the 2003 Act, s.104, a foreign travel order under the 2003 Act, s.114, or a risk of sexual harm
order under the 2003 Act, s.123), an existing order (whether made before or after that day) applied for before that day, or anything done in connection with such an application or order: 2014
Act, s.114(2). Sections 103E (*ante*, § 20-322f), 103I (*ante*, § 20-322j), 122D and 122H (*post*, 20-
337a) of the 2003 Act apply (as appropriate) to an "old order" (a restraining order under the Sex
Offenders Act 1997, s.5A, or a sex offender order under the CDA 1998, s.2) as they apply to a
"new order" (a sexual harm prevention order under the 2003 Act, s.103A (*ante*, § 20-322b), and a
sexual risk order under the 2003 Act, s.122A (*post*, § 20-337a)): 2014 Act, s.114(3). As from the
day section 114 of the 2014 Act comes into force, there may be no variation of an existing order
or an old order that extends the period of the order or of any of its provisions: 2014 Act, s.114(4).

At the end of the period of five years beginning with that day, in relation to any existing order or old order that is still in force, sections 103E and 103I of the 2003 Act or sections 122D and 122H of that Act (as appropriate) will have effect, with any necessary modifications (and with any modifications specified in an order under s.185(7) of the 2014 Act), as if the provisions of the order were provisions of a new order; and section 114(2) and (3) will cease to have effect: 2014 Act, s.114(5). See also the 2003 Act, s.136ZB (*post*, § 20-344a).

## (2) Legislation

### Sexual Offences Act 2003, ss.104, 106–110, 113

*Sexual offences prevention orders: applications and grounds*

★**20-324**     As to the repeal of section 104 of the 2003 Act, see *ante*, § 20-323.

*Section 104: supplemental*

★**20-326**     As to the repeal of section 106 of the 2003 Act, see *ante*, § 20-323.

*SOPOs: effect*

★**20-327**     As to the repeal of section 107 of the 2003 Act, see *ante*, § 20-323.

**20-328**     *R. (Richards) v. Teesside Magistrates' Court and Chief Constable of Cleveland* is now reported at 177 J.P. 545.

A sexual offences prevention order made against a predatory offender convicted of serious sexual offences against a 13-year-old boy that (i) restricted unsupervised contact with male children under the age of 17, (ii) prohibited him from undertaking any work likely to bring him into contact with male children aged under 17 save with written permission from the local chief constable, and (iii) required him to make any computer available on request "for removal and inspection by a police officer", was disproportionate: *R. v. Kimpriktzis* [2014] 1 Cr.App.R.(S.) 6, CA. Having considered *R. v. Smith* (as to which, see the main work), the court said that familial offences and abuse of trust cases apart, contact restrictions should be confined to those under 16 (the cut-off date for most child sex offences in the 2003 Act). As to the restriction on work, this would prevent the offender finding work in almost any occupation for which he was qualified, as almost all such occupations would involve a risk of contact with children; in this regard, it was relevant that the offender was subject to the notification requirements of the 2003 Act and also subject to a disqualification order for 10 years under the CJCSA 2000, which would prevent him from working in any sensitive occupation; this prohibition would accordingly be deleted. Finally, the requirement that the offender make a computer available for removal was excessive; it was sufficient that he should be required to make it available for inspection.

*SOPOs: variations, renewals and discharges*

★**20-329**     As to the repeal of section 108 of the 2003 Act, see *ante*, § 20-323.

*Interim SOPOs*

★**20-330**     As to the repeal of section 109 of the 2003 Act, see *ante*, § 20-323.

*SOPOs and interim SOPOs: appeals*

★**20-331**     As to the repeal of section 110 of the 2003 Act, see *ante*, § 20-323.

*Offences: breach of SOPO or interim SOPO*

★**20-333**     As to the repeal of section 113 of the 2003 Act, see *ante*, § 20-323.

## E. FOREIGN TRAVEL ORDERS

★**20-337**     As from a day to be appointed, the Anti-social Behaviour, Crime and Policing Act 2014, s.113(1), and Sched. 5, para. 3, repeal sections 114 to 122 of the SOA 2003 (see the main work) in relation to England and Wales. New sexual harm prevention orders (*ante*, §§ 20-322a *et seq.*) and sexual risk orders (*post*, § 20-337a) make provision for prohibitions on foreign travel. For saving and transitional provisions, see the 2014 Act, s.114 (*ante*, § 20-323a), and the 2003 Act, s.136ZB (*post*, § 20-344a).

## EA. Sexual Risk Orders

As from a day to be appointed, the Anti-social Behaviour, Crime and Policing Act 2014,   ★**20-337a**
s.113(1), and Sched. 5, para. 4, amend the SOA 2003 so as to insert, before section 123, sections
122A to 122K, which provide for sexual risk orders. Sexual harm prevention orders (*ante*, §§ 20-
322a *et seq.*) and sexual risk orders replace, in England and Wales, sexual offences prevention
orders (*ante*, § 20-323), foreign travel orders (*ante*, § 20-337) and risk of sexual harm orders (*post*,
§ 20-338).

A sexual risk order prohibits a person from doing anything specified in the order for a fixed
period of not less than two years or until further order. Section 122A enables the police or the
National Crime Agency to apply to a magistrates' court (or youth court) for an order if at any
time the defendant has done an act of a sexual nature as a result of which there is reasonable
cause to believe that such an order is necessary. The court may make an order if satisfied that that
condition is satisfied and that an order is necessary for the purpose of protecting the public or
any particular members of the public from harm from the defendant, or protecting children or
vulnerable adults generally, or any particular children or vulnerable adults, from harm from the
defendant outside the United Kingdom. The only prohibitions that may be imposed are those
that are for the purpose of protecting members of the public from such harm. Section 122B is an
interpretative provision; "harm" is defined as "physical or psychological harm caused by the
defendant doing an act of a sexual nature". Sections 122C to 122E correspond to sections 103D
to 103F (*ante*, §§ 20-322e *et seq.*). Section 122F imposes notification requirements on persons
subject to sexual risk orders or interim orders. Sections 122G and 122H correspond to section
103H and 103I (*ante*, §§ 20-322i, 20-322j). Section 122I deals with the relationship between these
orders and other notification requirements under Part 2, and section 122J corresponds to section
103J (*ante*, § 20-322k).

## F. Risk of Sexual Harm Orders

As from a day to be appointed, the Anti-social Behaviour, Crime and Policing Act 2014,   ★**20-338**
s.113(1), and Sched. 5, para. 5, repeal sections 123 to 129 of the SOA 2003 (see the main work) in
relation to England and Wales. For saving and transitional provisions, see the 2014 Act, s.114
(*ante*, § 20-323), and the 2003 Act, s.136ZB (*post*, § 20-344a). Sexual harm prevention orders (*ante*,
§§ 20-322a *et seq.*) and sexual risk orders (*ante*, § 20-337a) replace, in England and Wales, sexual
offences prevention orders (*ante*, § 20-323), foreign travel orders (*ante*, § 20-337) and risk of
sexual harm orders.

## G. Interpretation, etc. of Part 2

### Sexual Offences Act 2003, ss.131–136

*Part 2: general interpretation*

As from a day to be appointed, the Anti-social Behaviour, Crime and Policing Act 2014,   ★**20-341**
s.181(1), and Sched. 11, para. 76, amend section 133(1) of the 2003 Act so as to insert, in the appropriate place, the following definitions—

> "'interim sexual harm prevention order' has the meaning given by section 103F(2);";
> "'interim sexual risk order' has the meaning given by section 122E(2);";
> "'prohibition on foreign travel' has the meaning given by section 103D(2) or 122C(2);";
> "'sexual harm prevention order' has the meaning given by section 103A(1);";
> "'sexual risk order' has the meaning given by section 122A(1);".

## Application of orders

As from a day to be appointed, the Anti-social Behaviour, Crime and Policing Act 2014,   ★**20-344a**
s.113(1), and Sched. 5, para. 6, amend the 2003 Act so as to insert, after section 136, new section
136ZA, which provides that, for the purposes of sections 103I, 113, 122, 122H and 128 of the
2003 Act (as to which, see §§ 20-322j (*ante*), 20-333 (in the main work), 20-337 (in the main work
and *ante*), 20-337a (*ante*), and 20-338 (in the main work and *ante*)) existing orders and new orders
apply throughout the United Kingdom unless expressly confined, and new section 136ZB, which
provides that where a court in England and Wales makes a sexual harm prevention order or a

sexual risk order in relation to a person who is already subject to a sexual offences prevention order or a foreign travel order (where the new order is under s.103A), or a risk of sexual harm order or a foreign travel order (where the new order is under s.122A) the earlier order ceases to have effect (whichever part of the United Kingdom it was made in) unless the court orders otherwise.

## V. *CLOSURE OF PREMISES*

★**20-345**     As from a day to be appointed, the Anti-social Behaviour, Crime and Policing Act 2014, s.115(1), and Sched. 6, amend sections 136A to 136D, 136H to 136J, 136O and 136R of the SOA 2003 (see the main work), and insert new section 136BA in that Act. The general effect of the amendments is (i) to remove the power to issue closure notices and make closure orders in respect of prostitution offences under sections 47 to 50 of the 2003 Act (§§ 20-155 *et seq.* in the main work) in England and Wales, but (ii) (new s.136BA) to enable the issue of such notices and the making of such orders in respect of a child sex offence, now defined in section 136A as being offences under sections 5 to 13, 16 to 19, 25, 26 and 47 to 50 of the 2003 Act (§§ 20-49 *et seq.* in the main work), section 1 of the Protection of Children Act 1978 (indecent photographs (§ 31-107 in the main work)), and offences against a person under 18 under sections 1 to 4, 30 to 41, 59A, 61, 66 and 67 of the 2003 Act (§§ 20-19 *et seq.* in the main work). Section 115(2) of the 2014 Act provides that, for the purposes of new sections 136BA and 136D(7A) (power to make a closure order), it does not matter whether the offence or offences in question were committed before, or on or after, the date on which section 115 comes into force.

CHAPTER 21

## OFFENCES UNDER THE THEFT AND FRAUD ACTS

### II. *THEFT*

#### (3) **Class of offence and mode of trial**

★**21-12**     As to the insertion of section 22A into the MCA 1980 ("low-value shoplifting" to be a summary offence), see *ante*, § 1-108a.

### VI. *TAKING CONVEYANCES WITHOUT AUTHORITY*

#### B. THE AGGRAVATED OFFENCE

##### (5) **Sentence**

**21-161**     What was said in *R. v. Bradshaw* (as to which see the main work, and since reported at [2001] R.T.R. 4, *sub nom. R. v. Bradshaw and Waters (Note – 1994)*) was qualified in *R. v. Roberts (Stephen)* [2013] R.T.R. 32, CA, where it was said that each case will depend on its own facts. An order requiring the appellant to take an extended driving test was upheld where he had been a passenger in a car taken for a joy-ride when it was involved in a fatal accident, but had been behind the wheel earlier the same evening.

##### (6) **Elements of the offence**

**"Owing to the driving of the vehicle"**

**21-163**     *R. v. Hughes* is now reported at [2014] 1 Cr.App.R. 6.

### IX. *FALSE ACCOUNTING*

#### (4) **Sentence**

★**21-231**     As to the definitive guideline of the Sentencing Council for England and Wales for the sentencing of offences of false accounting, replacing the Sentencing Guidelines Council's guideline on statutory offences of fraud, and incorporating the Sentencing Council's guideline on fraud, bribery and money laundering offences committed by corporate offenders, see *post*, Appendix K-297 *et seq.*

## XVIII. FRAUD ACT 2006

### A. FRAUD

#### (4) Sentence

**Guideline and authorities**

As to the definitive guideline of the Sentencing Council for England and Wales for the sentenc-　★**21-368**
ing of offences of fraud, replacing the Sentencing Guidelines Council's guideline on statutory offences of fraud, and incorporating the Sentencing Council's guideline on fraud, bribery and money laundering offences committed by corporate offenders, see *post*, Appendix K-297 *et seq.*

#### (5) The elements of the offence

##### (b) *Fraud by false representation*

**Knowledge that the representation is or might be untrue or misleading**

In *R. v. Augunas* [2014] 1 Cr.App.R. 17, CA, it was held that, on a charge of fraud by false　★**21-373**
representation under sections 1 and 2 of the 2006 Act (§§ 21-356, 21-357 in the main work), it is not enough that a reasonable person might have known that the representation was, or might be untrue or misleading, and nor is it enough for the prosecutor to prove that the accused ought to have appreciated this, or that the circumstances must have given rise to a reasonable suspicion that the representation was, or might be, untrue or misleading. What matters is the accused's actual knowledge. However, if a person wilfully shuts his eyes to the obvious doubts as to the genuineness of the representation that he is making, then he knows that it might be untrue or misleading. As to instructing the jury in such cases, the court said that the safest course for a judge to adopt is to pose to the jury the question for them in words as close as possible to those of the statute; elaboration will rarely assist. In conclusion, the court added that it may be that some direction as to the consequences of an accused wilfully shutting his eyes to the obvious may be required, but rarely will more be needed.

### B. ARTICLES FOR USE IN FRAUDS

#### (4) Sentence

As to the definitive guideline of the Sentencing Council for England and Wales for the sentenc-　★**21-396**
ing of offences under sections 6 and 7 of the Fraud Act 2006, replacing the Sentencing Guidelines Council's guideline on statutory offences of fraud, and incorporating the Sentencing Council's guideline on fraud, bribery and money laundering offences committed by corporate offenders, see *post*, Appendix K-297 *et seq.*

#### (5) The elements of the offences

##### (a) *Possession of an article for use in fraud*

**For use in fraud**

The offence under section 6 of the Fraud Act 2006 (as to which, see § 21-390 in the main work)　**21-399**
requires proof that a person found in possession of an article on a particular date intended to use it for the purposes of fraud in the future: *R. v. Sakalauskas* [2014] 1 W.L.R. 1204, CA (following *R. v. Ellames* (as to which, see the main work)).

CHAPTER 22

## FORGERY, PERSONATION AND CHEATING

*I. FORGERY*

B. MISCELLANEOUS OFFENCES AKIN TO FORGERY

### (2) Identity documents

(a) *Offences*

**Identity Documents Act 2010, ss.4–6**

*Possession of false identity documents etc. with improper intention*

★**22-45a**   With effect from March 14, 2014 (Anti-social Behaviour, Crime and Policing Act 2014 (Commencement No. 1) Order 2014 (S.I. 2014 No. 630)), Schedule 8 (given effect by s.147) to the Anti-social Behaviour, Crime and Policing Act 2014 provided for new powers of seizure of travel documents. These powers are conferred on constables, persons appointed as immigration officers under the Immigration Act 1971, Sched. 2, para. 1, and general customs officials designated under the Borders, Citizenship and Immigration Act 2009, s.3(1) (together referred to in Sched. 8 as "examining officers"), and they include, for examining officers other than constables, the same powers of arrest without a warrant as a constable has in relation to an offence under section 4 or 6 of the 2006 Act.

### (4) Judicial documents

**County Courts Act 1984, s.133**

*False certificate of service*

★**22-48**   The provisions of the Crime and Courts Act 2013 referred to in the main work came into force on April 22, 2014: Crime and Courts Act 2013 (Commencement No. 10 and Transitional Provision) Order 2014 (S.I. 2014 No. 954).

**County Courts Act 1984, s.135**

*Penalty for falsely pretending to act under authority of court*

★**22-49**   The provisions of the Crime and Courts Act 2013 referred to in the main work came into force on April 22, 2014: Crime and Courts Act 2013 (Commencement No. 10 and Transitional Provision) Order 2014 (S.I. 2014 No. 954).

CHAPTER 23

## CRIMINAL DAMAGE AND KINDRED OFFENCES

*IV. COMPUTER MISUSE ACT 1990*

A. COMPUTER MISUSE OFFENCES

**Computer Misuse Act 1990, s.1**

*Unauthorised access to computer material*

★**23-87**   In *R. v. Martin* [2014] 1 Cr.App.R.(S.) 63, CA, it was said that sentences of imprisonment for computer misuse offences should be measured in years, not months, where there was evidence of

186

careful planning and intention to cause harm to individuals and organisations, offences against individuals being akin to burglary or identity theft. The court added that *R. v. Mangham* (as to which, see the main work) should not be considered a benchmark for such cases.

CHAPTER 24

## FIREARMS AND OFFENSIVE WEAPONS

*I. FIREARMS*

A. FIREARMS ACT 1968

### (1) Introduction

## Subordinate legislation

The Firearms Rules 1998 (S.I. 1998 No. 1941) have been further amended, with effect from **24-2** December 1, 2013, by the Firearms (Amendment) (No. 2) Rules 2013 (S.I. 2013 No. 2970); and, with effect from May 20, 2014, by the Firearms (Amendment) Rules 2014 (S.I. 2014 No. 1239).

### (4) Prohibited weapons and ammunition

Firearms Act 1968, s.5

Section 5 of the 1968 Act was amended, with effect from July 14, 2014 (Anti-social Behaviour, **★24-24** Crime and Policing Act 2014 (Commencement No. 2, Transitional and Transitory Provisions) Order 2014 (S.I. 2014 No. 949)), by the Anti-social Behaviour, Crime and Policing Act 2014, ss.108(1)-(4), and 109(1), so as: (i) to omit the words " or manufactures, sells or transfers" in subsection (1); (ii) to omit the words "or sells or transfers" in subsection (1A); (iii) to substitute, for the words between "commits an offence if," and ", he has in his possession" in subsections (1) and (1A), the words "without authority"; (iv) to insert a new subsection (2A), as follows—

"(2A) A person commits an offence if without authority—
  (a) he manufactures any weapon or ammunition specified in subsection (1) of this section,
  (b) he sells or transfers any prohibited weapon or prohibited ammunition,
  (c) he has in his possession for sale or transfer any prohibited weapon or prohibited ammunition, or
  (d) he purchases or acquires for sale or transfer any prohibited weapon or prohibited ammunition.";

(v) to substitute a new subsection (3) ("authority" means an authority given in writing, as regards England and Wales, by the Secretary of State); and (vi) to make amendments to subsections (4) and (6) (further provisions about authorities).

## Class of offence and mode of trial

As to the amendment of Schedule 6 to the 2014 Act, see *post*, § 24-29. **★24-28**

## Sentence

With effect from July 14, 2014 (Anti-social Behaviour, Crime and Policing Act 2014 (Com- **★24-29** mencement No. 2, Transitional and Transitory Provisions) Order 2014 (S.I. 2014 No. 949)), the entries in Schedule 6 to the 1968 Act relating to section 5 of that Act are amended by the Anti-social Behaviour, Crime and Policing Act 2014, s.108(1), (7) and (8); the new offence created by subsection (2A), *ante*, § 24-24, carries a maximum sentence of life imprisonment, and attracts the minimum sentence provisions in section 51A (as amended by the 2014 Act, s.108(1) and (6) (see § 5-449 in the main work and *ante*)).

187

### Special exemptions from prohibition of small firearms

★**24-32**    With effect from July 14, 2014 (Anti-social Behaviour, Crime and Policing Act 2014 (Commencement No. 2, Transitional and Transitory Provisions) Order 2014 (S.I. 2014 No. 949)), subsections (7A) and (7B) are inserted into section 1 of the Firearms (Amendment) Act 1997 by the Anti-social Behaviour, Crime and Policing Act 2014, s.108(9). By subsection (7A), in sections 2 to 7 of the 1997 Act, any reference to section 5(1)(aba) of the 1968 Act shall include a reference to section 5(2A) of that Act as it applies in relation to a firearm specified in section 5(1)(aba). By subsection (7B), in section 8 of the 1997 Act, the reference to section 5(1)(aba), (b) or (c) of the 1968 Act shall include a reference to section 5(2A) of that Act as it applies in relation to a firearm specified in section 5(1)(aba), (b) or (c).

**Firearms (Amendment) Act 1997, ss.2-8**

*Slaughtering instruments*

★**24-33**    With effect from July 14, 2014 (Anti-social Behaviour, Crime and Policing Act 2014 (Commencement No. 2, Transitional and Transitory Provisions) Order 2014 (S.I. 2014 No. 949)), sections 2 to 8 of the 1997 Act are amended by the Anti-social Behaviour, Crime and Policing Act 2014, s.109(3). These amendments affect modifications previously made by the Scotland Act 1998 (Transfer of Functions to the Scottish Ministers etc.) Order 1999 (S.I. 1999 No. 1750), which have not been taken in to the main work. The net effect is that sections 2, 3, 4, 5, 6, 7(1) and (3) and 8 all now begin with the words "The authority of the Secretary of State or the Scottish Ministers" and section 7(3) has inserted at the end, the words "or the Scottish Ministers (by virtue of provision made under section 63 of the Scotland Act 1998)". As to the reference to section 5(1)(aba) of the 1968 Act in section 2 of the 1997 Act, see *ante*, § 24-32.

*Firearms used for humane killing of animals*

★**24-34**    As to the amendment of section 3 of the 1997 Act, see *ante*, § 24-33; and as to the reference to section 5(1)(aba) of the 1968 Act in section 3, see *ante*, § 24-32.

*Shot pistols used for killing vermin*

★**24-35**    As to the amendment of section 4 of the 1997 Act, see *ante*, § 24-33; and as to the reference to section 5(1)(aba) of the 1968 Act in section 4, see *ante*, § 24-32.

*Races at athletic meetings*

★**24-36**    As to the amendment of section 5 of the 1997 Act, see *ante*, § 24-33; and as to the reference to section 5(1)(aba) of the 1968 Act in section 5, see *ante*, § 24-32.

*Trophies of war*

★**24-37**    As to the amendment of section 6 of the 1997 Act, see *ante*, § 24-33; and as to the reference to section 5(1)(aba) of the 1968 Act in section 6, see *ante*, § 24-32.

*Firearms of historic interest*

★**24-38**    As to the amendment of section 7 of the 1997 Act, see *ante*, § 24-33; and as to the reference to section 5(1)(aba) of the 1968 Act in section 7, see *ante*, § 24-32.

*Weapons and ammunition used for treating animals*

★**24-39**    As to the amendment of section 8 of the 1997 Act, see *ante*, § 24-33; and as to references to section 5(1)(aba), (b) or (c) of the 1968 Act in section 8, see *ante*, § 24-32.

**Firearms Act 1968, s.5A**

*Exemptions from requirement of authority under s.5*

★**24-40**    Section 5A of the 1968 Act is amended, with effect from July 14, 2014 (Anti-social Behaviour, Crime and Policing Act 2014 (Commencement No. 2, Transitional and Transitory Provisions) Order 2014 (S.I. 2014 No. 949)), by the Anti-social Behaviour, Crime and Policing Act 2014, ss.108(1) and (5), and 109(2), so as: (i) to omit the words "subsection (1A) of" in subsections (1) and (3) to (7); (ii) to substitute, for the words "any prohibited weapon or ammunition" in subsections (1) and (3), the words "any weapon, ammunition or missile specified in subsection (1A) of that section"; and (iii) to amend modifications previously made by the Scotland Act 1998 (Transfer of Functions to the Scottish Ministers etc.) Order 1999 (S.I. 1999 No. 1750), which were not taken in to the main work (the net effect is that the words "or the Scottish Ministers" now appear after the words "the Secretary of State" in subsections (1), (2)(a) and (b), (3) to (5), (6) (in both places) and (7)).

### (6) Prevention of crime and preservation of public safety

(g) *Possession of firearms by persons previously convicted of crime*

#### Firearms Act 1968, s.21

Section 21 of the 1968 Act was amended, with effect from July 14, 2014 (Anti-social Behaviour, Crime and Policing Act 2014 (Commencement No. 2, Transitional and Transitory Provisions) Order 2014 (S.I. 2014 No. 949)), by the Anti-social Behaviour, Crime and Policing Act 2014, s.110(1), so as to insert, before subsection (3), a new subsection (2C), as follows— ★24-80

"(2C) Where—
    (a) a person has been sentenced to imprisonment for a term of three months or more, and
    (b) the sentence is suspended under section 189 of the Criminal Justice Act 2003,
the person shall not have a firearm or ammunition in his possession at any time during the period of five years beginning with the second day after the date on which the sentence is passed.".

### (16) Particular savings

#### Firearms Act 1968, s.58

Section 58(2) of the 1968 Act was amended, with effect from July 14, 2014 (Anti-social Behaviour, Crime and Policing Act 2014 (Commencement No. 2, Transitional and Transitory Provisions) Order 2014 (S.I. 2014 No. 949)), by the Anti-social Behaviour, Crime and Policing Act 2014, s.110(2), so as to substitute, for the words "Nothing in this Act", the following words— ★24-131

"Apart from—
    (a) section 21 and Schedule 3, and
    (b) any other provision of this Act so far as it applies in relation to an offence under section 21,
nothing in this Act".

### II. OFFENSIVE WEAPONS, BLADED ARTICLES, KNIVES

### A. HAVING AN OFFENSIVE WEAPON IN PUBLIC PLACE

### (4) Sentence

As to the importance of youth courts paying close attention to the guidance given in *R. v. Povey* (as to which, see the main work) when sentencing for offences relating to knife crime, see *R. v. Gomes-Monteiro*, 178 J.P. 200, CA. ★24-168

### CHAPTER 25

# OFFENCES AGAINST THE CROWN AND GOVERNMENT

### III. TERRORISM

### A. TERRORISM ACT 2000

#### Terrorism Act 2000, s.1

The decision of the Court of Appeal in *R. v. Gul* has been upheld by the Supreme Court: see *R. v. Gul (Mohamed)* [2013] 3 W.L.R. 1207, SC. **25-13**

**Terrorism Act 2000, ss.15–23B**

**25-26**    With effect from January 1, 2014, Schedule 3A to the 2000 Act (as to which, see the main work) was further amended by the Capital Requirements Regulations 2013 (S.I. 2013 No. 3115).

★    With effect from April 1, 2014, Schedule 3A was further amended by the Enterprise and Regulatory Reform Act 2013 (Competition) (Consequential, Transitional and Saving Provisions) Order 2014 (S.I. 2014 No. 892).

★    With effect from August 1, 2014 (immediately after the Co-operative and Community Benefit Societies and Credit Unions Act 2010, s.1, comes into force), Schedule 3A is further amended by the Co-operative and Community Benefit Societies Act 2014, s.151(1), and Sched. 4, para. 73.

**Terrorism Act 2000, Sched. 2**

*Proscribed organisations*

**25-91**    With effect from October 29, 2013, the Proscribed Organisations (Name Changes) (No. 2) Order 2013 (S.I. 2013 No. 2742) provides that the name "Ahle Sunnat wal Jamaat", not being a name specified in Schedule 2 to the 2000 Act is to be treated as an additional name for the organisation listed in Schedule 2 as both "Lashkar-e Jhangvi" and "Sipah-e Sahaba Pakistan".

With effect from December 13, 2013, the Terrorism Act 2000 (Proscribed Organisations) (Amendment) (No. 2) Order 2013 (S.I. 2013 No. 3172) adds "Imarat Kavkaz (Caucasus Emirate)" to the list of proscribed organisations in Schedule 2.

★    With effect from April 4, 2014, the Terrorism Act 2000 (Proscribed Organisations) (Amendment) Order 2014 (S.I. 2014 No. 927) added "Ansar Bayt al-Maqdis (Ansar Jerusalem)", "Al Murabitun" and "Ansar al Sharia - Tunisia" to the list of proscribed organisations in Schedule 2.

**Terrorism Act 2000, Sched. 5**

★**25-107**    The decision of the High Court in *R. (British Sky Broadcasting Ltd) v. Central Criminal Court* (as to which, see the main work) has been upheld on appeal: see *R. (British Sky Broadcasting Ltd) v. Central Criminal Court (B. intervening)* [2014] 2 W.L.R. 558, SC.

**Terrorism Act 2000, Sched. 7**

*Interpretation*

★**25-123**    As from a day to be appointed, the Anti-social Behaviour, Crime and Policing Act 2014, s.148, and Sched. 9, para. 1(1) and (2), amend paragraph 1(1)(b) of Schedule 7 to the 2000 Act so as to insert, after the word "officer", the words "who is designated for the purpose of this Schedule by the Secretary of State".

*Examining officers, etc.*

★**25-123a**    With effect from May 13, 2014 (Anti-social Behaviour, Crime and Policing Act 2014 (Commencement No. 2, Transitional and Transitory Provisions) Order 2014 (S.I. 2014 No. 949)), the Anti-social Behaviour, Crime and Policing Act 2014, s.148, and Sched. 9, para. 1(1) and (3), inserted a new paragraph 1A in Schedule 7 to the 2000 Act as follows—

*"Examining officers etc*

1A.—(1) The Secretary of State must under paragraph 6 of Schedule 14 issue a code of practice about—

(a) training to be undertaken by constables, immigration officers and customs officers who are to act as examining officers or exercise other functions under this Schedule, and

(b) the procedure for making designations under paragraph 1(1)(b) and (c).

(2) In particular, the code must make provision for consultation with the relevant chief officer of police before designations are made under paragraph 1(1)(b) or (c).

(3) 'Relevant chief officer of police' means—

(a) in England and Wales, the chief officer of police for the police area in which the persons designated would act as examining officers,

(b) in Scotland, the Chief Constable of the Police Service of Scotland, and

(c) in Northern Ireland, the Chief Constable of the Police Service of Northern Ireland.".

*Port and border controls: power to stop, question and detain*

★**25-124**    In connection with *Beghal v. DPP* (as to which, see the main work (and now reported at [2014]

2 W.L.R. 150)), see *R. (Elosta) v. Commr of Police of the Metropolis (Law Society intervening)*, *post*, § 25-139. The Supreme Court has given the defendant leave to appeal from the decision of the Divisional Court in *Beghal v. DPP*: see *Beghal v. DPP* [2014] 1 W.L.R. 1230, SC.

In *R. (Miranda) v. Home Secretary* [2014] 3 *Archbold Review* 2, DC, considering *Beghal v. DPP* (see ★ the main work and *ante*), it was held: (i) whereas paragraph 2(1) of Schedule 7 to the 2000 Act permits an examining officer to question a person at a port "for the purpose of determining whether he appears to be a person falling within section 40(1)(b)" (*i.e.* a terrorist), the purpose in question is not necessarily the purpose in the mind of the examining officers, since there may be a very good reason why examining officers should not be made privy to the intelligence behind a request to stop a person under Schedule 7; the primary evidence for the determination of the stop's purpose is likely to be the terms of the instructions given to the examining officers, which in most cases ought to provide the essential, even if not the whole, rationale for the decision to carry out the stop; but since they may not tell the whole story, it is important that the court should have some evidence of the hierarchy of decision-making behind and above these instructions; (ii) the purpose in this case (*viz.* to ascertain the nature of the material which the claimant, the partner of a journalist, was carrying, and if, on examination, it proved to be, as feared, "stolen encrypted material, the release or compromise of which would be likely to cause very great damage to security interests and possible loss of life", to neutralise the effects of its release (or further release) or dissemination) fell properly within paragraph 2(1); the purpose should not be to determine whether a person is, but only whether he appears to be, a terrorist; the power is given in order to provide a reasonable but limited opportunity for inquiring into the possibility that a traveller may be, in the words of section 40(1)(b), "concerned in the commission, preparation or instigation of acts of terrorism" (see § 25-51 in the main work); on a proper construction of paragraph 2(1), the authorities are not required, as a condition of the power's lawful use, to have concluded before they execute a stop that the person "appears" to fall within section 40(1)(b).

As from a day to be appointed, the Anti-social Behaviour, Crime and Policing Act 2014, s.148, ★ and Sched. 9, paras 2(1) and (2), repeal paragraph 6(4) of Schedule 7 to the 2000 Act.

As from a day to be appointed, the 2014 Act, s.148, and Sched. 9, paras 7(1) and (2), amend ★ paragraph 6(3) of Schedule 7 to the 2000 Act so as to substitute the words "Parts 1 and 1A" for the words "Part I", and so as to insert, after the word "treatment", the words "and review of detention".

*Time limits on examination without detention*

As from a day to be appointed, the Anti-social Behaviour, Crime and Policing Act 2014, s.148, ★**25-124a** and Sched. 9, para. 2(1) and (3), insert a new paragraph 6A in Schedule 7 to the 2000 Act as follows—

"6A.—(1) This paragraph applies where a person is questioned under paragraph 2 or 3.
(2) After the end of the 1 hour period, the person may not be questioned under either of those paragraphs unless the person is detained under paragraph 6.
(3) If the person is detained under paragraph 6 the person must be released not later than the end of the 6 hour period (unless detained under another power).
(4) In this paragraph—
'the 1 hour period' is the period of 1 hour beginning with the time the person is first questioned under paragraph 2 or 3;
'the 6 hour period' is the period of 6 hours beginning with that time.".

*Searches*

As from a day to be appointed, the Anti-social Behaviour, Crime and Policing Act 2014, s.148, ★**25-125** and Sched. 9, para. 3, amend paragraph 8 of Schedule 7 to the 2000 Act so as to insert, after sub-paragraph (3), new sub-paragraphs (4) to (7) as follows—

"(4) An intimate search of a person may not be carried out under this paragraph.
(5) A strip search of a person may not be carried out under this paragraph unless—
(a) the person is detained under paragraph 6,
(b) the examining officer has reasonable grounds to suspect that the person is concealing something which may be evidence that the person falls within section 40(1)(b), and
(c) the search is authorised by a senior officer who has not been directly involved in questioning the person.

(6) 'Senior officer' means—
    (a) where the examining officer is a constable, a constable of a higher rank than the examining officer,
    (b) where the examining officer is an immigration officer, an immigration officer of a higher grade than the examining officer, and
    (c) where the examining officer is a customs officer, a customs officer of a higher grade than the examining officer.
(7) In this paragraph—
    'intimate search' means a search which consists of a physical examination of a person's body orifices other than the mouth;
    'strip search' means a search which is not an intimate search but involves the removal of an article of clothing which—
    (a) is being worn wholly or partly on the trunk, and
    (b) is being so worn either next to the skin or next to an article of underwear.".

*Power to make and retain copies*

★25-126a    As from a day to be appointed, the Anti-social Behaviour, Crime and Policing Act 2014, s.148, and Sched. 9, para. 4, insert a new paragraph 11A in Schedule 7 to the 2000 Act as follows—

*"Power to make and retain copies*

11A.—(1) This paragraph applies where the examining officer is a constable.
(2) The examining officer may copy anything which—
    (a) is given to the examining officer in accordance with paragraph 5,
    (b) is searched or found on a search under paragraph 8, or
    (c) is examined under paragraph 9.
(3) The copy may be retained—
    (a) for so long as is necessary for the purpose of determining whether a person falls within section 40(1)(b),
    (b) while the examining officer believes that it may be needed for use as evidence in criminal proceedings, or
    (c) while the examining officer believes that it may be needed in connection with a decision by the Secretary of State whether to make a deportation order under the Immigration Act 1971.".

## Modifications applicable to Channel Tunnel

25-133    Article 7 of the Channel Tunnel (International Arrangements) Order 1993 (S.I. 1993 No. 1813) (Appendix F-13a, *post*) provides that the enactments mentioned in Schedule 4 to that order shall (a) in their application to France by virtue of article 4(1) or (1B), and (b) in their application to the United Kingdom within the tunnel system and elsewhere for the authorised purposes (as to which, see article 2(2)), have effect with the modifications set out in Schedule 4. As a result of the amendment of that schedule by the Channel Tunnel (International Arrangements) (Amendment) Order 2001 (S.I. 2001 No. 178), Schedule 7 to the 2000 Act, being one of the enactments mentioned therein, has effect with the following modifications—

    (i) in paragraph 1(2) omit the references to "the border area", "captain", "ship" and "vehicle" and for the words "an airport or hoverport" are substituted the words—

    "a railway station or other place where
    (a) persons embark or disembark or
    (b) goods are loaded or unloaded,
    on or from a through train or shuttle train, as the case may be";

    (ii) in paragraph 1(3) for the words "ship or aircraft" wherever occurring, there are substituted the words "through train or shuttle train";

    (iii) in paragraph 2(2), the words "or in the border area", "or in the area" and "or Northern Ireland" are omitted;

    (iv) in paragraph 2(3) for the words "ship or aircraft" there are substituted "through train or shuttle train" and there are omitted the words "or Northern Ireland";

    (v) after paragraph 2(3) there is inserted—

    "**3A.** An examination under sub-paragraph (1) may be commenced in a train during the period when it is a control area.";

(vi) paragraphs 3 and 4 are omitted;

(vii) in paragraph 5 the words "or 3" are omitted;

(viii) in paragraph 6, in sub-paragraph (1), for the word "vehicle" there are substituted the words "through train or shuttle train" and, in sub-paragraph (2), for the words "ship, aircraft or vehicle" there are substituted the words "through train or shuttle train";

(ix) in paragraph 7 for the words "ship or aircraft", wherever occurring, there are substituted the words "through train or shuttle train";

(x) in paragraph 8 for the words "ship or aircraft", wherever occurring, there are substituted the words "through train or shuttle train", and sub-paragraph (2) is omitted;

(xi) in paragraph 9, in sub-paragraph (2), the words "or in Northern Ireland" are omitted and for the words "ship, aircraft or vehicle" there are substituted the words "through train or shuttle train" and, in sub-paragraph (4), for the words "ship or aircraft or enter a vehicle" there are substituted the words "through train or shuttle train";

(xii) paragraph 12 is omitted;

(xiii) in paragraph 13 for the words "ships or aircraft" and the words "ship or aircraft", wherever occurring, there are substituted the words "a through train or shuttle train" and for the words "United Kingdom" there are substituted the words "Tunnel System";

(xiv) for paragraph 14 there is substituted—

> "**14.**—(1) The Secretary of State may from time to time give written notice to persons operating international services designating all or any through trains as control areas while they are within any area in the UK specified in the notice or while they constitute a control zone.
>
> (2) The Secretary of State may from time to time give written notice designating a control area—
>
> > (i) to the Concessionaires as respects any part of the tunnel system in the UK or of a control zone within the tunnel system in France or Belgium, or
> >
> > (ii) to any occupier or person concerned with the management of a terminal control point in the UK.
>
> (3) A notice under sub-paragraph (1) or (2) above may specify facilities to be provided and conditions and restrictions to be observed in a control area, and any persons to whom such a notice is given shall take all reasonable steps to secure that any such facilities, conditions or restrictions are provided or observed.";

(xv) paragraphs 15, 16 and 17 are omitted, and

(xvi) the Table of Designated Ports is omitted.

### Terrorism Act 2000, Sched. 8

*Place of detention*

As from a day to be appointed, the Anti-social Behaviour, Crime and Policing Act 2014, s.148, and Sched. 9, para. 5(1) and (2), amend paragraph 1(5) of Schedule 8 to the 2000 Act so as to substitute the word "Schedule" for the word "paragraph".     ★**25-134**

*Identification*

As from a day to be appointed, the Anti-social Behaviour, Crime and Policing Act 2014, s.148, and Sched. 9, para. 5(1) and (3), amend paragraph 2(2)(d) of Schedule 8 to the 2000 Act so as to omit the words "(within the meaning of that Schedule)".     ★**25-135**

*Rights: England, Wales and Northern Ireland*

As from a day to be appointed, the Anti-social Behaviour, Crime and Policing Act 2014, s.148, and Sched. 9, para. 5(1) and (4), amend paragraph 6 of Schedule 8 to the 2000 Act so as to substitute the word "place" for the words "police station" in each place where they appear.     ★**25-138**

As from a day to be appointed, the 2014 Act, s.148, and Sched. 9, para. 5(1) and (5), amend paragraph 7(1) of Schedule 8 to the 2000 Act so as to omit the words "at a police station".     ★

As from a day to be appointed, the 2014 Act, s.148, and Sched. 9, para. 5(1) and (6), amend Schedule 8 to the 2000 Act so as to insert, after paragraph 7, a new paragraph 7A as follows—     ★

> "**7A.**—(1) This paragraph applies where a person detained under Schedule 7 requests to consult a solicitor.

(2) The examining officer may not question the detained person under paragraph 2 or 3 of Schedule 7 until the person has consulted a solicitor (or no longer wishes to do so).

(3) Sub-paragraph (2) does not apply if the examining officer reasonably believes that postponing the questioning until then would be likely to prejudice determination of the relevant matters.

(4) The powers given by paragraph 8 of Schedule 7 (search powers where a person is questioned under paragraph 2 of Schedule 7) may be used when questioning is postponed because of sub-paragraph (2).

(5) The detained person is entitled to consult a solicitor in person.

(6) Sub-paragraph (5) does not apply if the examining officer reasonably believes that the time it would take to consult a solicitor in person would be likely to prejudice determination of the relevant matters.

(7) In that case the examining officer may require any consultation to take place in another way.

(8) In this paragraph 'the relevant matters' means the matters the examining officer seeks to determine under paragraph 2 or 3 of Schedule 7.".

★ As from a day to be appointed, the 2014 Act, s.148, and Sched. 9, para. 5(1) and (7), amend paragraph 8(1) to the 2000 Act so as to substitute the words "a police officer" for the words "an officer".

*Rights: England, Wales and Northern Ireland*

**25-139** In *R. (Elosta) v. Commr of Police of the Metropolis (Law Society intervening)* [2014] 1 W.L.R. 239, QBD (Bean J.), it was held: (i) even though paragraph 8 of Schedule 8 (§ 25-138 in the main work) to the 2000 Act, which provides that a person detained under Schedule 7 (*ibid.*, §§ 25-123 *et seq.*) shall be entitled, if he so requests, to consult a solicitor as soon as is reasonably practicable, privately and at any time, only applies where a person is detained at a police station, or a place that has been deemed to be a police station by virtue of being designated as a place where a person may be detained under section 41 (Sched. 8, para. 1(2) (*ibid.*, § 25-134)), a person nevertheless has a right to consult a solicitor at any time, wherever detained; the code of practice issued under Schedule 14 (*ibid.*, § 25-167) to the 2000 Act requires a "TACT 2" form to be served when a person is detained, and that form provides that the right to legal advice as soon as is reasonably practicable, privately, and at any time, applies to all detainees under Schedule 7, irrespective of location; the right may be exercised repeatedly, although not in a manner that frustrates the proper purpose of the examination; (ii) whereas TACT 2 also provides that the consultation with a solicitor may be in person, in writing or on the telephone, the choice as to which is the detainee's; (iii) if a solicitor attends in person, he may be present during the interview; a reasonable delay to await the arrival of a solicitor may be required, but again the detainee is not entitled to exercise that right in such a way as to frustrate the proper purpose of the examination; (iv) having detained the claimant, the refusal of examining officers at Heathrow airport to await the arrival of his solicitor, before questioning him further, was therefore unlawful; but this did not render his detention unlawful. As to whether the decision in this case may be squared with that of the Divisional Court in *Beghal v. DPP* (as to which, see § 25-124 the main work, and *ante*), see CLW/ 13/42/3.

★**25-140** As from a day to be appointed, the Anti-social Behaviour, Crime and Policing Act 2014, s.148, and Sched. 9, para. 5(1) and (8), amend paragraph 9(2)(a) and (b) of Schedule 8 to the 2000 Act so as (i) in each, to omit the words "at a police station", and (ii) in each, to substitute the words "a police officer" for the words "an officer".

★ As from a day to be appointed, the 2014 Act, s.148, and Sched. 9, para. 6, amend paragraph 10 of Schedule 8 to the 2000 Act so as (i) in sub-paragraph (5), to substitute the words "a person detained under section 41, but only" for the words "the detained person only", and (ii) in sub-paragraph (6)(b), to insert the words "in which an authorisation under that sub-paragraph may be given" after the words "in any case".

*Destruction and retention of fingerprints and samples etc: United Kingdom*

★**25-145i** With effect from May 13, 2014 (Anti-social Behaviour, Crime and Policing Act 2014 (Commencement No. 2, Transitional and Transitory Provisions) Order 2014 (S.I. 2014 No. 949)), the Anti-social Behaviour, Crime and Policing Act 2014, s.146(2), amended paragraph 20I of Schedule 8 to the 2000 Act so as (i) to substitute the words "Paragraphs 20A to 20H do not apply to material" for the words "Paragraphs 20A to 20F and 20H do not apply to paragraph 20A material", and (ii) at the end of that paragraph (which became sub-paragraph (1)), to insert new sub-paragraphs (2) and (3) as follows—

"(2) A sample that—
  (a) falls within sub-paragraph (1), and
  (b) but for that sub-paragraph would be required to be destroyed under paragraph 20G,
must not be used other than for the purposes of any proceedings for the offence in connection with which the sample was taken.
  (3) A sample that once fell within sub-paragraph (1) but no longer does, and so becomes a sample to which paragraph 20G applies, must be destroyed immediately if the time specified for its destruction under that paragraph has already passed.".

With effect from May 13, 2014 (S.I. 2014 No. 949 (*ante*)), the 2014 Act, s.181(1), and Sched. 11, ★
para. 125(1) and (3)(a), amended paragraph 20J of Schedule 8 to the 2000 Act so as to substitute, for paragraphs (d) and (e) of the definition of "police force", new paragraphs (d) and (e) as follows—

  "(d) the Police Service of Scotland;
  (e) the Scottish Police Authority;".

With effect from May 13, 2014 (S.I. 2014 No. 949 (*ante*)), the 2014 Act, s.181(1), and Sched. 11, ★
para. 125(1) and (3)(b), further amended paragraph 20J of Schedule 8 to the 2000 Act so as, in the second of the three definitions of "responsible chief officer of police", to substitute the words "the Police Service of Scotland" for the words after "the chief constable of".

*Review of detention under Schedule 7*

As from a day to be appointed (but see *post* in relation to para. 20K(8) and (9)), the Anti-social ★**25-145ja**
Behaviour, Crime and Policing Act 2014, s.148, and Sched. 9, para. 7(1) and (3), amend Schedule 8 to the 2000 Act so as to insert, after Part I, a new Part 1A (paras 20K–20N).

[PART 1A

*Review of detention under Schedule 7*

*General requirements*

20K.—(1) A person's detention under Schedule 7 must be periodically reviewed by a review officer.
  (2) The first review must be carried out before the end of the period of one hour beginning with the person's detention under that Schedule.
  (3) Subsequent reviews must be carried out at intervals of not more than two hours.
  (4) The review officer may authorise a person's continued detention under Schedule 7 only if satisfied that it is necessary for the purposes of exercising a power under paragraph 2 or 3 of that Schedule.
  (5) If on a review under this paragraph the review officer does not authorise a person's continued detention, the person must be released (unless detained under another power).
  (6) In this Part of this Schedule "review officer" means a senior officer who has not been directly involved in questioning the detained person under paragraph 2 or 3 of Schedule 7 .
  (7) "Senior officer" means—
    (a) where the examining officer is a constable, a constable of a higher rank than the examining officer,
    (b) where the examining officer is an immigration officer, an immigration officer of a higher grade than the examining officer, and
    (c) where the examining officer is a customs officer, a customs officer of a higher grade than the examining officer.]
  (8) The Secretary of State must under paragraph 6 of Schedule 14 issue a code of practice about reviews under this Part of this Schedule.
  (9) The code of practice must include provision about training to be undertaken by persons who are to act as review officers.

As to the commencement of sub-paragraphs (8) and (9), see *post*, § 25-145jd.

[*Representations*

20L.—(1) Before determining whether to authorise a person's continued detention, a review of- ★**25-145jb**
ficer must give either of the following persons an opportunity to make representations about the detention—

(a)  the detained person, or

(b)  a solicitor representing the detained person who is available at the time of the review.

(2) Representations may be oral or written.

(3) A review officer may refuse to hear oral representations from the detained person if the officer considers that the detained person is unfit to make representations because of the detained person's condition or behaviour.]

*[Rights*

**★25-145jc**    20M.—(1) Where a review officer authorises continued detention the officer must inform the detained person—

(a)  of any of the detained person's rights under paragraphs 6 and 7 which have not yet been exercised, and

(b)  if the exercise of any of those rights is being delayed in accordance with the provisions of paragraph 8, of the fact that it is being delayed.

(2) Where a review of a person's detention is being carried out at a time when the person's exercise of a right under paragraph 6 or 7 is being delayed—

(a)  the review officer must consider whether the reason or reasons for which the delay was authorised continue to subsist, and

(b)  if in the review officer's opinion the reason or reasons have ceased to subsist, the review officer must inform the officer who authorised the delay of that opinion (unless the review officer was that officer).

(3) In the application of this paragraph to Scotland, for the references to paragraphs 6, 7 and 8 substitute references to paragraph 16.]

*[Record*

**★25-145jd**    20N.—(1) A review officer carrying out a review must make a written record of the outcome of the review and of any of the following which apply—

(a)  the fact that the officer is satisfied that continued detention is necessary for the purposes of exercising a power under paragraph 2 or 3 of Schedule 7,

(b)  the fact that the detained person has been informed as required under paragraph 20M(1),

(c)  the officer's conclusion on the matter considered under paragraph 20M(2)(a), and

(d)  the fact that the officer has taken action under paragraph 20M(2)(b).

(2) The review officer must inform the detained person whether the officer is authorising continued detention, and if so that the officer is satisfied that continued detention is necessary for the purposes of exercising a power under paragraph 2 or 3 of Schedule 7.

(3) Sub-paragraph (2) does not apply where the detained person is—

(a)  incapable of understanding what is said,

(b)  violent or likely to become violent, or

(c)  in urgent need of medical attention.]

★    With effect from May 13, 2014, section 148 of, and paragraph 7(1) and (3) of Schedule 9 to, the 2014 Act (see *ante*) were brought into force, to the extent that they insert new paragraph 20K(8) and (9) in Schedule 8 to the 2000 Act: Anti-social Behaviour, Crime and Policing Act 2014 (Commencement No. 2, Transitional and Transitory Provisions) Order 2014 (S.I. 2014 No. 949).

**Terrorism Act 2000, Sched. 14**

*General*

**★25-165**    With effect from May 13, 2014 (Anti-social Behaviour, Crime and Policing Act 2014 (Commencement No. 2, Transitional and Transitory Provisions) Order 2014 (S.I. 2014 No. 949)), the Anti-social Behaviour, Crime and Policing Act 2014, s.148, and Sched. 9, para. 8(1) and (2), amended paragraph 1 of Schedule 14 to the 2000 Act so as to insert, after the words "'officer' means", the words "(subject to paragraph 6A)".

*Code of practice*

**25-167**    Article 7 of the Channel Tunnel (International Arrangements) Order 1993 (S.I. 1993 No. 1813) (Appendix F-13a, *post*) provides that the enactments mentioned in Schedule 4 to that order shall (a) in their application to France by virtue of article 4(1) or (1B), and (b) in their application to the United Kingdom within the tunnel system and elsewhere for the authorised purposes (as to which, see article 2(2)), have effect with the modifications set out in Schedule 4. As a result of the amendment of that schedule by the Channel Tunnel (International Arrangements) (Amendment) Order 2001 (S.I. 2001 No. 178), Schedule 14 to the 2000 Act, being one of the enactments mentioned therein, has effect with the following modifications: in paragraphs 5 and 6, after the words "this Act", in each place where they occur, there are inserted the words "or the Channel Tunnel (International Arrangements) Order 1993".

With effect from May 13, 2014 (Anti-social Behaviour, Crime and Policing Act 2014 (Commencement No. 2, Transitional and Transitory Provisions) Order 2014 (S.I. 2014 No. 949)), the Anti-social Behaviour, Crime and Policing Act 2014, s.148, and Sched. 9, para. 8(1) and (3), amended Schedule 14 to the 2000 Act so as to insert, after paragraph 6, a new paragraph 6A as follows— ★

"6A. In paragraphs 5 and 6, 'officer' includes a constable, immigration officer or customs officer who—
(a) has functions under Schedule 7, or
(b) has functions under Schedule 8 in relation to a person detained under Schedule 7, otherwise than as an examining officer.".

## B. Anti-terrorism, Crime and Security Act 2001

### Anti-terrorism, Crime and Security Act 2001, ss.47–56

*Revenue and customs prosecutions*

With effect from March 27, 2014, the Public Bodies (Merger of the Director of Public Prosecutions and the Director of Revenue and Customs Prosecutions) Order 2014 (S.I. 2014 No. 834), art. 3(3), and Sched. 2, para. 18, amended section 53(1) of the 2001 Act, subject to saving and transitional provisions (as to which, see *ante*, § 1-27), so as to substitute the words "the Director of Public Prosecutions" for the words "the Director of Revenue and Customs Prosecutions".  ★**25-174**

## D. Counter-Terrorism Act 2008

### (4) Notification requirements

*R. (Irfan) v. Secretary of State for the Home Department* is now reported at [2013] Q.B. 885. The Supreme Court has refused the claimant permission to appeal: see [2013] 1 W.L.R. 3601, SC.  **25-215**

## IV. IMMIGRATION

As from a day to be appointed, section 27 of the Immigration Act 1971 (see the main work) is amended by the Immigration Act 2014, s.67, and Sched. 8, para. 7.  ★**25-280**

### Immigration and Asylum Act 1999, s.31

*Defences based on Article 31(1) of the Refugee Convention*

*R. v. Mateta* is now reported at [2013] 2 Cr.App.R. 35, *sub nom. R. v. Mateta*; *R. v. Ghavami and Afshar*; *R. v. Bashir*; *R. v. Andukwa*.  **25-285**

### Immigration Act 1971, ss.25–25C

There is nothing in section 25 of the 1971 Act to exclude its application to asylum seekers (distinguishing *R. v. Kapoor* (§ 25-290 in the main work)); and section 25(3) (proof of foreign law) is permissive; foreign law may be proved by other methods, such as expert evidence or admission: *R. v. Bina* (2014) 158(24) S.J. 53, CA.  ★**25-286**

## XI. OFFENCES RELATING TO POSTS AND TELECOMMUNICATIONS

### C. Regulation of Investigatory Powers Act 2000

#### Regulation of Investigatory Powers Act 2000, ss.1–5

*Meaning and location of "interception" etc.*

*R. v. Edmondson, Weatherup, Brooks, Coulson and Kuttner* is now reported at [2013] 2 Cr.App.R. 32, *sub nom. R. v. Coulson (Andrew)*.  **25-387**

*Power to provide for lawful interception*

★25-389    Whereas section 4(4) of the 2000 Act authorises interception of communications "if it is conduct in exercise of any power conferred by or under any rules made under section 47 of the Prison Act 1952", and whereas rule 35A(1) of the Prison Rules 1999 (S.I. 1999 No. 728) provides that the Secretary of State "may give directions to any governor concerning the interception in a prison of any communication by any prisoner or class of prisoners if the Secretary of State considers that the directions are (a) necessary on grounds specified in paragraph (4) below, and (b) proportionate to what is sought to be achieved", a direction that all calls by prisoners other than those to legal advisers or the Samaritans be intercepted was not *ultra vires* rule 35A: *R. v. Mahmood (Asad)* [2014] 1 Cr.App.R. 31, CA.

### Regulation of Investigatory Powers Act 2000, s.25

★25-402    With effect from April 1, 2014, the Regulation of Investigatory Powers (Communications Data) Order 2010 (S.I. 2010 No. 480) (see the main work) was further amended by the Enterprise and Regulatory Reform Act 2013 (Competition) (Consequential, Transitional and Saving Provisions) (No. 2) Order 2014 (S.I. 2014 No. 549).

## XII. MISCONDUCT IN JUDICIAL OR PUBLIC OFFICE

### Misfeasance

★25-403    In *R. v. Mitchell (William)* [2014] 2 Cr.App.R. 2, CA, it was held (considering *R. v. Belton* and *R. v. Cosford, Falloon and Flynn* (as to both of which, see the main work)): (i) that the proper approach to the question whether an individual holds public office is to consider, first, the position held, secondly, the nature of the duties undertaken, and, thirdly, whether the fulfilment of those duties represents (as it must) the fulfilment of one of the responsibilities of government such that the public have a significant interest in the discharge of that duty that is additional to or beyond an interest in anyone who might be directly affected by a serious failure in the performance of that duty; and (ii) that the defendant, a paramedic employed by an NHS trust, was not a public officer; the duty of ambulance paramedics is to treat and provide emergency health care to the individual patients whose care they become responsible for due to the circumstances in which they come into contact with them; it is a duty to the individual; in a general sense, the public would be concerned by any example of a breach of the individual duty, but there is not a duty to the public that is different from, or additional to, the general duty owed to the individual.

## XIII. REVENUE AND CUSTOMS OFFENCES

### A. CHEATING THE PUBLIC REVENUE

### Indictment

25-410    In *R. v. Dosanjh (Sandeep)* [2014] 1 W.L.R. 1780, CA, it was said that the common law offence of conspiracy to cheat the public revenue supplements the statutory framework and is the appropriate charge for a small number of the most serious revenue frauds, where statutory offences will not adequately reflect the criminality involved and where a sentence at large is appropriate; and, accordingly, it is not wrong in principle to pass a sentence on a common law conspiracy to cheat the public revenue that is longer than the maximum available for statutory fraud (Fraud Act 2006, s.1 (§ 21-356 in the main work)) or fraudulent evasion of value added tax (Value Added Tax Act 1994, s.72 (*ibid.*, § 25-352)).

★    As to the definitive guideline of the Sentencing Council for England and Wales for the sentencing of offences of fraud, including cheating the public revenue, incorporating the council's earlier guideline on such offences committed by corporate offenders, see *post*, Appendix K-297 *et seq.*

### B. CUSTOMS AND EXCISE MANAGEMENT ACT 1979

#### (1) Introduction

### Principal powers

25-413    The Crime (International Co-operation) Act 2003 (Exercise of Functions) Order 2005 (S.I.

2005 No. 425) has been revoked and replaced by the Crime (International Co-operation) Act 2003 (Exercise of Functions) Order 2013 (S.I. 2013 No. 2733).

## (4) Illegal importation

### Customs and Excise Management Act 1979, s.50

*Penalty for improper importation of goods*

With effect from July 14, 2014 (Anti-social Behaviour, Crime and Policing Act 2014 (Commencement No. 2, Transitional and Transitory Provisions) Order 2014 (S.I. 2014 No. 949)), the Anti-social Behaviour, Crime and Policing Act 2014, s.111(1) and (3)(a), amended section 50(4) of the 1979 Act so as to insert, after "(5A),", "(5AA),". ★**25-430**

With effect from July 14, 2014 (S.I. 2014 No. 949 (ante)), the 2014 Act, s.111(1), (2) and (3)(b) and (c), amended section 50(5A) of the 1979 Act so as (i) to insert the word "or" at the end of paragraph (a), (ii) to repeal paragraph (c) and the word "or" before it, and (iii) to substitute the words "as if for the words 'imprisonment for a term not exceeding 7 years' there were substituted the words 'imprisonment for life'" for the words after "shall have effect". ★

With effect from July 14, 2014 (S.I. 2014 No. 949 (*ante*)), the 2014 Act, s.111(1) and (3)(d), amended section 50 of the 1979 Act so as to insert, after subsection (5A), a new subsection (5AA) as follows— ★

"(5AA) In the case of an offence under subsection (2) or (3) above committed in connection with the prohibition contained in section 20 of the Forgery and Counterfeiting Act 1981, subsection (4)(b) above shall have effect as if for the words '7 years' there were substituted the words '10 years'.".

With effect from January 7, 2014, the Export Control (North Korea and Ivory Coast Sanctions and Syria Amendment) Order 2013 (S.I. 2013 No. 3182), *inter alia*, provides that in the case of an offence committed in connection with the prohibitions on importation in articles 2(3) or 4a(1)(b) of Council Regulation (EU) No. 329/2007, sections 50(4)(b) and 170(3)(b) of the 1979 Act (§§ 25-430, 25-474 in the main work) have effect as if the maximum penalty on conviction on indictment were 10 years' imprisonment, instead of seven years.

As to the definitive guideline of the Sentencing Council for England and Wales for the sentencing of offences under the CEMA 1979, s.50, replacing the Sentencing Guidelines Council's guideline on statutory offences of fraud, and incorporating the Sentencing Council's guideline on fraud, bribery and money laundering offences committed by corporate offenders, see *post*, Appendix K-297 *et seq.* ★

## (5) Illegal exportation

### Customs and Excise Management Act 1979, s.68

*Offences in relation to exportation of prohibited or restricted goods*

With effect from July 14, 2014 (Anti-social Behaviour, Crime and Policing Act 2014 (Commencement No. 2, Transitional and Transitory Provisions) Order 2014 (S.I. 2014 No. 949)), the Anti-social Behaviour, Crime and Policing Act 2014, s.111(1) and (7)(a), amended section 68(3) of the 1979 Act so as to insert, after "(4A)", ", (4AA)". ★**25-435**

With effect from July 14, 2014 (S.I. 2014 No. 949 (*ante*)), the 2014 Act, s.111(1), (6) and (7)(b) and (c), amended section 68(4A) of the 1979 Act so as (i) in paragraph (a), to omit the words "or (3)", (ii) to insert the word "or" at the end of paragraph (a), (iii) to repeal paragraph (c) and the word "or" before it, and (iv) to substitute the words "as if for the words 'imprisonment for a term not exceeding 7 years' there were substituted the words 'imprisonment for life'" for the words after "shall have effect". ★

With effect from July 14, 2014 (S.I. 2014 No. 949 (*ante*)), the 2014 Act, s.111(1) and (3)(d), amended section 68 of the 1979 Act so as to insert, after subsection (4A), a new subsection (4AA) as follows— ★

"(4AA) In the case of an offence under subsection (2) above committed in connection with the prohibition contained in section 21 of the Forgery and Counterfeiting Act 1981, subsection (3)(b) above shall have effect as if for the words '7 years' there were substituted the words '10 years'.".

With effect from January 7, 2014, the Export Control (North Korea and Ivory Coast Sanctions **25-436** and Syria Amendment) Order 2013 (S.I. 2013 No. 3182), *inter alia*, (i) amends the Export Control (Syria Sanctions) Order 2013 (S.I. 2013 No. 2012), and (ii) provides that in the case of an offence committed in connection with the prohibitions on exportation in specified articles of Council Regulation (EU) No. 329/2007 or Council Regulation (EC) No. 174/2005, sections 68(3)(b) and 170(3)(b) of the 1979 Act (§§ 25-435, 25-474 in the main work) have effect as if the maximum penalty on conviction on indictment were 10 years' imprisonment, instead of seven years.

### (9) Powers to seize and detain goods, etc.

**Customs and Excise Management Act 1979, s.139**

★**25-444**     In *R. (Eastenders Cash and Carry plc) v. Revenue and Customs Commrs; R. (First Stop Wholesale Ltd) v. Same* [2014] 2 W.L.R. 1580, SC, it was held that the right to seize or detain property under section 139(1) of the 1979 Act is dependent on the property actually being liable to forfeiture under one of the forfeiture provisions of the customs and excise Acts. On this point, therefore, the Supreme Court upheld the decisions of the Court of Appeal in *Eastenders* and *First Stop* (see the main work). However, the Supreme Court also held (allowing the commissioners' appeal in *Eastenders* on another ground) that the various powers of examination of goods given to officers of revenue and customs under the 1979 Act carried with them a power to detain the goods being examined for as long as was reasonably necessary for the purposes of the examination, and this power was not dependent on the goods being examined actually being liable to forfeiture. The claimants' appeal in *First Stop* was dismissed on the basis that the commissioners had power to detain their goods for examination, and that the reasons given ("pending further inquiries into their duty status"), "although certainly not expansive, were sufficient for them to exercise their rights" (at [52]).

### (10) General provisions as to legal proceedings

**Customs and Excise Management Act 1979, s.145**

*Institution of proceedings*

★**25-445**     With effect from March 27, 2014, the Public Bodies (Merger of the Director of Public Prosecutions and the Director of Revenue and Customs Prosecutions) Order 2014 (S.I. 2014 No. 834), art. 3(3), and Sched. 2, para 2(a), amended section 145(1)(a) of the 1979 Act, subject to saving and transitional provisions (as to which, see *ante*, § 1-27), so as to substitute the words "the Director of Public Prosecutions" for the words "the Director of Revenue and Customs Prosecutions".

**Customs and Excise Management Act 1979, s.146A**

*Time limits for proceedings*

★**25-448**     With effect from March 27, 2014, the Public Bodies (Merger of the Director of Public Prosecutions and the Director of Revenue and Customs Prosecutions) Order 2014 (S.I. 2014 No. 834), art. 3(3), and Sched. 2, para 2(b), amended section 146A(7)(a) of the 1979 Act, subject to saving and transitional provisions (as to which, see *ante*, § 1-27), so as to substitute the words "the Director of Public Prosecutions" for the words "the Director of Revenue and Customs Prosecutions".

**Customs and Excise Management Act 1979, ss.147-149**

*Non-payment of penalties, etc.: maximum terms of imprisonment*

★**25-451**     With effect from April 6, 2014, the provisions of the Tribunals, Courts and Enforcement Act 2007 referred to in the main work were brought into force: Tribunals, Courts and Enforcement Act 2007 (Commencement No. 11) Order 2014 (S.I. 2014 No. 768).

**Customs and Excise Management Act 1979, ss.150, 152**

*Incidental provisions as to legal proceedings*

★**25-452**     With effect from March 27, 2014, the Public Bodies (Merger of the Director of Public Prosecutions and the Director of Revenue and Customs Prosecutions) Order 2014 (S.I. 2014 No. 834),

art. 3(3), and Sched. 2, para 2(c), amended section 150(1) of the 1979 Act, subject to saving and
transitional provisions (as to which, see *ante*, § 1-27), so as to substitute the words "the Director of
Public Prosecutions" for the words "the Director of Revenue and Customs Prosecutions".

### (13) Fraudulent evasion offences

#### Customs and Excise Management Act 1979, s.170

*Penalty for fraudulent evasion of duty, etc.*

With effect from July 14, 2014 (Anti-social Behaviour, Crime and Policing Act 2014 (Com-    ★**25-474**
mencement No. 2, Transitional and Transitory Provisions) Order 2014 (S.I. 2014 No. 949)), the
Anti-social Behaviour, Crime and Policing Act 2014, s.111(1) and (5)(a), amended section 170(3)
of the 1979 Act so as to insert, after "(4A)", ", (4AA)".

With effect from July 14, 2014 (S.I. 2014 No. 949 (*ante*)), the 2014 Act, s.111(1), (4) and (5)(b)    ★
and (c), amended section 170(4A) of the 1979 Act so as (i) in paragraph (a), to substitute the
words "subsection (1) or (2)" for the words "subsection (2) or (3)", (ii) to insert the word "or" at
the end of paragraph (a), (iii) to repeal paragraph (c) and the word "or" before it, and (iv) to
substitute the words "as if for the words 'imprisonment for a term not exceeding 7 years' there
were substituted the words 'imprisonment for life'" for the words after "shall have effect".

With effect from July 14, 2014 (S.I. 2014 No. 949 (*ante*)), the 2014 Act, s.111(1) and (3)(d),    ★
amended section 170 of the 1979 Act so as to insert, after subsection (4A), a new subsection (4AA)
as follows—

"(4AA) In the case of an offence under subsection (1) or (2) above committed in connection with
the prohibitions contained in sections 20 and 21 of the Forgery and Counterfeiting Act 1981, subsection (3)(b) above shall have effect as if for the words '7 years' there were substituted the words '10
years'.".

Where an offence under section 170 (§ 25-474 in the main work) is committed in connection    **25-475**
with specified prohibitions (as to which, see *ante*, § 25-431) on importation in Council Regulation
(EU) No. 329/2007, or on exportation in that regulation or Council Regulation (EC) No. 174/
2005, section 170(3)(b) has effect with the substitution of "10 years" for "7 years": see art. 12(4)
and (5) of the Export Control (North Korea and Ivory Coast Sanctions and Syria Amendment)
Order 2013 (S.I. 2013 No. 3182). Article 15(1) of that order effects a drafting amendment to
article 4 of the Export Control (Syria Sanctions) Order 2013 (S.I. 2013 No. 2012).

As to the definitive guideline of the Sentencing Council for England and Wales for the sentenc-    ★
ing of offences under the CEMA 1979, s.170, replacing the Sentencing Guidelines Council's
guideline on statutory offences of fraud, and incorporating the Sentencing Council's guideline on
fraud, bribery and money laundering offences committed by corporate offenders, see *post*,
Appendix K-297 *et seq.*

### Taking steps to evade excise duty

As to the definitive guideline of the Sentencing Council for England and Wales for the sentenc-    ★**25-505**
ing of offences under the CEMA 1979, s.170B, replacing the Sentencing Guidelines Council's
guideline on statutory offences of fraud, and incorporating the Sentencing Council's guideline on
fraud, bribery and money laundering offences committed by corporate offenders, see *post*,
Appendix K-297 *et seq.*

### (14) Penalties and sentencing

### Authorities

The guidelines in *R. v. Czyzewski* (see the main work) have been superseded "to some extent" by    ★**25-507**
the Sentencing Guidelines Council's definitive guideline on statutory offences of fraud (as to
which, see *post*, Appendix K-228 *et seq.*): *R. v. Hareem and Salih* [2014] 1 Cr.App.R.(S.) 50, CA. As
to this case, see also *post*, Appendix K-530.

As to the definitive guideline of the Sentencing Council for England and Wales for the sentenc-    ★
ing of offences under sections 50, 170 and 170B of the CEMA 1979 (evasion of duty or improper
importation of goods (§§ 25-430, 25-474, 25-505 in the main work)), replacing the Sentencing

201

Guidelines Council's guideline on statutory offences of fraud, and incorporating the Sentencing Council's guideline on fraud, bribery and money laundering offences committed by corporate offenders, see *post*, Appendix K-297 *et seq.*

## C. Criminal Justice (International Co-operation) Act 1990

### (3) Offences at sea

### (c) *Jurisdiction and interpretation*

**Criminal Justice (International Co-operation) Act 1990, ss.21, 24**

*Jurisdiction and prosecutions*

★**25-528**    With effect from March 27, 2014, the Public Bodies (Merger of the Director of Public Prosecutions and the Director of Revenue and Customs Prosecutions) Order 2014 (S.I. 2014 No. 834), art. 3(3), and Sched. 2, amended section 21(2)(a) of the 1990 Act, subject to saving and transitional provisions (as to which, see *ante*, § 1-27), so as to omit the words "or the Director of Revenue and Customs Prosecutions".

## D. Value Added Tax Offences

### (2) Offences and penalties

**Sentence**

★**25-538**    As to the guideline of the Sentencing Council for England and Wales for the sentencing of offences of fraudulent evasion of value added tax, contrary to section 72 of the Value Added Tax Act 1994 (§ 25-532 in the main work), incorporating the Sentencing Council's guideline on fraud, bribery and money laundering offences committed by corporate offenders, see *post*, Appendix K-297 *et seq.*

CHAPTER 26

# MONEY LAUNDERING OFFENCES

## I. PROCEEDS OF CRIME ACT 2002

### B. Offences

### (4) Legislation

**Proceeds of Crime Act 2002, s.327**

**26-11**    For a case considering the *mens rea* requirement where the offence charged is one of attempting to commit an offence under section 327(1) of the 2002 Act, see *R. v Pace*, *post*, § 33-136.

**Proceeds of Crime Act 2002, s.328**

*Arrangements*

★**26-12**    In *Holt v. Att.-Gen.* [2014] 2 All E.R. 397, PC, the Privy Council considered the level of knowledge or suspicion required for an offence under the Proceeds of Crime Act (Isle of Man) 2008 corresponding to the offence under section 328(1) of the 2002 Act. It was alleged that the defendant, who was an advocate for prominent clients in a criminal case, had committed such an offence in that she had become concerned in an arrangement under which the clients' fees, due to both counsel and the firm for which she worked, had been paid out of money from a trust that had constituted the proceeds of crime in the hands of her clients who were trustees of the trust.

The Privy Council held that actual knowledge or suspicion that there was criminal conduct of some kind involved was an essential element of the offence; it was not enough to show that the defendant ought to have realised that some crime, such as theft or obtaining by deception, might well have been involved. The prosecution had to prove that the defendant had applied her mind to the circumstances in which the money had been produced. Knowledge or suspicion that it would be irregular to receive trust money (one of the clients had told the defendant that he would need to borrow money from the trust, and had asked her to prepare the loan documentation, but before that was done, the clients put her in funds), in the sense of a breach of trust, was not automatically the same as knowledge or suspicion that a crime was involved.

### Proceeds of Crime Act 2002, s.330

## The regulated sector and supervisory authorities

With effect from January 1, 2014, Schedule 9 to the 2002 Act (as to which, see the main work) is further amended by the Capital Requirements Regulations 2013 (S.I. 2013 No. 3115). **26-16**

With effect from April 1, 2014, Schedule 9 to the 2002 Act was further amended by the Enterprise and Regulatory Reform Act 2013 (Competition) (Consequential, Transitional and Saving Provisions) Order 2014 (S.I. 2014 No. 892). ★

With effect from August 1, 2014 (immediately after the Co-operative and Community Benefit Societies and Credit Unions Act 2010, s.1, comes into force), Schedule 9 to the 2002 Act is further amended by the Co-operative and Community Benefit Societies Act 2014, s.151(1), and Sched. 4, para. 81. ★

## E. SENTENCE

### Proceeds of Crime Act 2002, s.334

Where there was no clear evidence in a money laundering case to identify the crimes that generated the proceeds being laundered, the offender should not have been sentenced on the basis that the laundered money was the product of the worst type of serious crime: *R. v. Allen* [2014] 1 Cr.App.R.(S.) 28, CA. ★**26-42**

As to the guideline of the Sentencing Council for England and Wales for the sentencing of offences of money laundering, incorporating the Sentencing Council's guideline on such offences committed by corporate offenders, see *post*, Appendix K-297 *et seq*. ★

## F. MISCELLANEOUS

### Proceeds of Crime Act 2002, ss.451, 452

*Revenue and Customs prosecutions*

With effect from March 27, 2014, the Public Bodies (Merger of the Director of Public Prosecutions and the Director of Revenue and Customs Prosecutions) Order 2014 (S.I. 2014 No. 834), art. 3(3), and Sched. 2, paras 19 and 34, amended section 451(1) of the 2002 Act, subject to saving and transitional provisions (as to which, see *ante*, § 1-27), so as to substitute the words "the Director of Public Prosecutions" for the words "the Director of Revenue and Customs Prosecutions". ★**26-43**

## II. MONEY LAUNDERING REGULATIONS 2007

With effect from January 1, 2014, the 2007 regulations (S.I. 2007 No. 2157) are further amended by the Capital Requirements Regulations 2013 (S.I. 2013 No. 3115). **26-45**

With effect from March 27, 2014, the 2007 regulations (*ante*) were further amended, subject to saving and transitional provisions (as to which, see *ante*, § 1-27), by the Public Bodies (Merger of the Director of Public Prosecutions and the Director of Revenue and Customs Prosecutions) Order 2014 (S.I. 2014 No. 834), art. 3(3), and Sched. 3. ★

With effect from March 31, 2014, the 2007 regulations (*ante*) were further amended by the Public Bodies (Abolition of the National Consumer Council and Transfer of the Office of Fair Trading's Functions in relation to Estate Agents etc.) Order 2014 (S.I. 2014 No. 631). ★

★     With effect from April 1, 2014, the 2007 regulations (*ante*) were further amended by the Financial Services and Markets Act 2000 (Consumer Credit) (Miscellaneous Provisions) (No. 2) Order 2014 (S.I. 2014 No. 506).

★**26-49**     With effect from April 1, 2014, section 26(2) of the Enterprise and Regulatory Reform Act 2013 (see the main work) was brought into force, subject to transitional provisions and savings: Enterprise and Regulatory Reform Act 2013 (Commencement No. 6, Transitional Provisions and Savings) Order 2014 (S.I. 2014 No. 416).

CHAPTER 27

# HARMFUL OR DANGEROUS DRUGS

A. INTRODUCTION

### (3) Definition of a "controlled drug"

**Misuse of Drugs Act 1971, s.2**

### Temporary class drug orders

★**27-5a**     Whereas the Misuse of Drugs Act 1971 (Temporary Class Drug) Order 2013 (S.I. 2013 No. 1294) (as to which, see the main work) ceased to have effect at the end of June 9, 2014, the groups of "NBOMe" compounds and groups of benzofuran compounds specified in that order are included within the substances that are prescribed as controlled drugs within the Misuse of Drugs Act 1971 by the Misuse of Drugs Act 1971 (Ketamine etc.) (Amendment) Order 2014 (S.I. 2014 No. 1106) (see *post*, §§ 27-7, 27-9), which has effect from June 10, 2014.

### (4) Classification of controlled drugs

**Misuse of Drugs Act 1971, Sched. 2**

*Class A drugs*

★**27-7**     With effect from June 10, 2014, the Misuse of Drugs Act 1971 (Ketamine etc.) (Amendment) Order 2014 (S.I. 2014 No. 1106) amends Part I of Schedule 2 to the 1971 Act so as to insert new paragraph 1(f), as follows—

> "(f) any compound (not being benzyl(α-methyl-3,4-methylenedioxyphenethyl)amine) structurally derived from mescaline, 4-bromo-2,5-dimethoxy-α-methylphenethylamine, 2,5-dimethoxy-α,4-dimethylphenethylamine, *N*hydroxytenamphetamine, or a compound specified in sub-paragraph (ba) or (c) above, by substitution at the nitrogen atom of the amino group with a benzyl substituent, whether or not substituted in the phenyl ring of the benzyl group to any extent.".

*Class B drugs*

★**27-9**     As from June 10, 2014, the Misuse of Drugs Act 1971 (Ketamine etc.) (Amendment) Order 2014 (S.I. 2014 No. 1106) amends Part II of Schedule 2 to the 1971 Act so as (i) to insert "Ketamine" after "Glutethimide" and "Lisdexamphetamine" after "Lefetamine" in paragraph 1(a), and (ii) to insert new paragraph 1(e), as follows—

> "(e) any compound (not being a compound for the time being specified in paragraph 1(ba) of Part 1 of this Schedule) structurally derived from 1-benzofuran, 2,3-dihydro-1-benzofuran, 1H-indole, indoline, 1H-indene, or indane by substitution in the 6-membered ring with a 2-ethylamino substituent whether or not further substituted in the ring system to any extent with alkyl, alkoxy, halide or haloalkyl substituents and whether or not substituted in the ethylamino side-chain with one or more alkyl substituents".

*Class C drugs*

★**27-10**     As from June 10, 2014, the Misuse of Drugs Act 1971 (Ketamine etc.) (Amendment) Order

2014 (S.I. 2014 No. 1106) amends paragraph 1(a) of Part III of Schedule 2 to the 1971 Act so as (i) to omit "Ketamine", and (ii) to insert "Tramadol" after "Tetrazepam", "Zaleplon" after "N-Ethylamphetamine", and "Zopiclone" after "Zolpidem".

As from June 24, 2014, the Misuse of Drugs Act 1971 (Amendment) Order 2014 (S.I. 2014 No.  ★
1352) amends Part III of Schedule 2 to the 1971 Act by the insertion of "Khat" after "Ketazolam" in paragraph 1(a).

*Meaning of certain expressions used in this Schedule*

As from June 24, 2014, the Misuse of Drugs Act 1971 (Amendment) Order 2014 (S.I. 2014 No.  ★**27-11**
1352) amends Part IV of Schedule 2 to the 1971 Act by the insertion, after the entry for "concentrate of poppy-straw", of—

> "'khat' means the leaves, stems or shoots of the plant of the species *Catha edulis*".

## C. Restriction of Production and Supply of Controlled Drugs

### (2) Production

### (c) *Ingredients of the offences*

**Participation**

A person who is concerned in the production by another of a controlled drug, contrary to sec-  ★**27-35**
tion 4(2)(b) of the Misuse of Drugs Act 1971 (§ 27-28 in the main work), is a principal offender and not merely an aider and abettor of the producer of the drug, who is also a principal offender, contrary to section 4(2)(a). It is therefore possible for two or more persons to be guilty of an offence of conspiracy to be concerned in the production of a controlled drug by another, contrary to section 1 of the CLA 1977 (see § 33-2 in the main work), by agreeing to a course of conduct that will necessarily involve at least one of them being concerned in the production of a controlled drug by a person outside the conspiracy: *R. v. Dang (Manh Toan)* [2014] 2 Cr.App.R. 3, CA. A mere agreement to sell equipment that could be used in the production of a controlled drug would be insufficient; it would have to be proved that the shared objective of the conspirators was to supply equipment to be used in the production of a controlled drug by another. However, the concept of "being concerned in" an activity was a wide one, with it being possible for the relevant act to take place before or after production of the drug: *ibid*. As to this case, see also *post*, § 33-13.

## F. Authorisation of Activities Otherwise Unlawful Under Sections 3 to 6

### Misuse of Drugs Act 1971, ss.7, 7A

The Misuse of Drugs Regulations 2001 (S.I. 2001 No. 3998) were further amended by the  ★**27-83**
Misuse of Drugs and Misuse of Drugs (Safe Custody) (Amendment) (England, Wales and Scotland) Regulations 2014 (S.I. 2014 No. 1275), with effect from June 10, 2014, and by the Misuse of Drugs (Amendment) (England, Wales and Scotland) Regulations 2014 (S.I. 2014 No. 1377), with effect from June 24, 2014.

The Misuse of Drugs (Designation) Order 2001 (S.I. 2001 No. 3997) was further amended by  ★
the Misuse of Drugs (Designation) (Amendment) (England, Wales and Scotland) Order 2014 (S.I. 2014 No. 1274), with effect from June 10, 2014, and by the Misuse of Drugs (Designation) (Amendment) (No. 2) (England, Wales and Scotland) Order 2014 (S.I. 2014 No. 1376), with effect from June 24, 2014.

## J. Powers of Secretary of State for Preventing Misuse of Controlled Drugs

### Misuse of Drugs Act 1971, s.10

The Misuse of Drugs (Safe Custody) Regulations 1973 (S.I. 1973 No. 798) were further  ★**27-91**
amended by the Misuse of Drugs and Misuse of Drugs (Safe Custody) (Amendment) (England, Wales and Scotland) Regulations 2014 (S.I. No. 1275), with effect from June 10, 2014.

## R. Law Enforcement and Punishment of Offenders

### (1) Search and seizure

#### Misuse of Drugs Act 1971, s.23

**27-104**    For a case considering the nature of "reasonable suspicion" (such as to justify the deployment of a sniffer dog in a drug search), the role of "profiles" as grounds for such suspicion, the nature of the judicial scrutiny required where it is asserted that there was no basis for the police to have a "reasonable suspicion", and the requirement that such a search should be conducted reasonably, see *R. v. Chehil*, 301 C.C.C. (3d) 157, Supreme Court of Canada (2013 SCC 49).

### (2) Procedure and penalties

#### Sentencing guidelines

*Sentencing Council for England and Wales*

**27-107**    The inappropriateness of citing pre-guideline authorities was emphasised in *R. v. Dyer* [2014] 1 *Archbold Review* 3, CA. As to this case, see also *ante*, §§ 5-141, 5-159; and *post*, Appendix K-629, K-1000.

*Conspiracy*

**27-109**    *R. v. Khan* is now reported at [2014] 1 Cr.App.R.(S.) 10, *sub nom. R. v. Khan (Kazim Ali), Khan (Umar), Khan (Mohammed Arfan) and Khan (Mohammed Ahsan)*.

## Chapter 28

# OFFENCES AGAINST PUBLIC JUSTICE

## I. PERVERTING THE COURSE OF PUBLIC JUSTICE

### B. Conduct Capable of Amounting to the Offence

#### (9) Interfering with witnesses, evidence and jurors

**Witnesses**

**28-10**    An attempt to persuade a witness that giving evidence in accordance with her witness statement would be a breach of legal professional privilege was not a contempt of court; if the court had upheld the assertion of privilege, it would have been deprived of the witness's evidence by virtue of the law of privilege, not because the course of justice had been perverted: *H.K.S.A.R. v. Wong Chi Wai*, unreported, September 23, 2013, Hong Kong Court of Final Appeal ([2013] HKCFA 80).

### G. Sentence

**★28-25**    In *R. v. Evans-Keady* [2014] 1 Cr.App.R.(S.) 66, CA, where a young police officer had failed to act in accordance with his duty out of sympathy for the predicament of a person whom he had arrested for possession of a controlled drug, the court emphasised the need to reflect the offender's motive when passing sentence for an offence of perverting the course of justice.

## III. CONTEMPT OF COURT

### B. Common Law

#### (2) Civil and criminal contempts

**★28-33**    The distinction between civil contempt, *i.e.* conduct which is not in itself a crime but which is punishable by a court, and criminal contempt was described as "long recognised" in *Director of the*

*Serious Fraud Office v. O'Brien* [2014] 2 W.L.R. 902, SC. Breach of an order made (or undertaking obtained) in the course of legal proceedings may result in punishment as a form of contempt; however, a contempt of that kind does not constitute a criminal offence; although the penalty contains a punitive element, its primary purpose is to make the order of the court effective; a criminal contempt is conduct that goes beyond mere non-compliance with a court order or undertaking and involves a serious interference with the administration of justice; contempt of court constituted by a breach of a restraint order made under the PCA 2002, s.41 (*ante*, § 5-842), is therefore not itself a crime; it is fallacious to argue that, because the order was made by a criminal court, rather than a civil court, disobedience to the order amounts to a crime, whereas it would not have been a crime to disobey a similar order imposed by a civil court; the question whether a contempt is a criminal contempt does not depend on the nature of the court to which the contempt was displayed, but on the nature of the conduct: *ibid*. As to this case, see also *post*, § 28-118.

### (7) Contempt by jurors

*Att.-Gen. v. Davey; Att.-Gen. v. Beard* is now reported at [2014] 1 Cr.App.R. 1. **28-40**

## C. Contempt of Court Act 1981

### (2) The strict liability rule

#### Contempt of Court Act 1981, Sched. 1

*Time when proceedings are active for purposes of section 2*
The provisions of the Crime and Courts Act 2013 referred to in the main work came into force **★28-57** on February 24, 2014: Crime and Courts Act 2013 (Commencement No. 8) Order 2014 (S.I. 2014 No. 258).

#### Contempt of Court Act 1981, ss.3, 4

### Defences and power to order postponement of reporting

The 2013 criminal practice directions (see the main work) are now reported at [2013] 1 W.L.R. **28-67** 3164.

### (3) Miscellaneous offences

#### Contempt of Court Act 1981, s.9

*Use of tape recorders*
As to the disapplication of section 9 of the 1981 Act in relation to the recording of certain **28-74** proceedings in the Court of Appeal and the broadcasting of such recordings, see the Court of Appeal (Recording and Broadcasting) Order 2013 (S.I. 2013 No. 2786), *ante*, § 7-36a.
The 2013 criminal practice directions (see the main work) are now reported at [2013] 1 W.L.R. 3164.

*Unofficial sound recordings of proceedings*
The 2013 criminal practice directions (see the main work) are now reported at [2013] 1 W.L.R. **28-75** 3164.

### (5) Restriction of publication of matters exempted from disclosure

#### Contempt of Court Act 1981, s.11

*Publication of matters exempted from disclosure in court*
The 2013 criminal practice directions (see the main work) are now reported at [2013] 1 W.L.R. **28-79** 3164.
An application made to a court to allow a name or matter to be withheld is not an application ★

for relief made against any person, no remedy or order being sought against any respondent; ancillary directions made under section 11 of the 1981 Act are similarly not made against any person; there is therefore no obligation under section 12(2) of the Human Rights Act 1998 (court orders that might affect exercise of right to freedom of expression) to allow the media an opportunity to be heard before such an order can be granted; but fairness to those who may be affected by an order can be achieved by enabling any such person to seek the recall of the order or directions promptly at an *inter partes* hearing: *A. v. British Broadcasting Corporation (Secretary of State for the Home Department intervening)* [2014] 2 W.L.R. 1243, SC.

## (6) Magistrates' courts

**28-81**     The 2013 criminal practice directions (see the main work) are now reported at [2013] 1 W.L.R. 3164.

## (7) Sentencing

### Contempt of Court Act 1981, s.14

*Proceedings in England and Wales*

★**28-82**     The provisions of the Crime and Courts Act 2013 mentioned in the main work came into force on April 22, 2014: Crime and Courts Act 2013 (Commencement No. 10 and Transitional Provision) Order 2014 (S.I. 2014 No. 954).

## E. Procedural Rules

## (1) Applications to magistrates' courts, the Crown Court and the Court of Appeal

### Criminal Procedure Rules 2013 (S.I. 2013 No. 1554), Pt 62

*Initial procedure on obstruction, disruption, etc.*

**28-105**     The 2013 criminal practice directions (see the main work) are now reported at [2013] 1 W.L.R. 3164.

*Postponement of enquiry*

**28-107**     *R. v. McGrath* is now reported at [2014] Crim.L.R. 144.

★**28-118**     As to the distinction between civil contempt and criminal contempt, see *Director of the Serious Fraud Office v. O'Brien, ante,* § 28-33, in which the Supreme Court upheld the decision of the Court of Appeal in *Director of the Serious Fraud Office v. B.* (as to which, see the main work).

## (2) Applications to Divisional Court

### Civil Procedure Rules 1998 (S.I. 1998 No. 3132), Pt 81, rr.81.1–81.3, 81.12–81.14, 81.16, 81.28, 81.29

*Scope*

★**28-123**     The provisions of the Crime and Courts Act 2013 mentioned in the main work came into force on April 22, 2014: Crime and Courts Act 2013 (Commencement No. 10 and Transitional Provision) Order 2014 (S.I. 2014 No. 954).

## F. Appeals

### Administration of Justice Act 1960, s.13

★**28-130**     The provisions of the Crime and Courts Act 2013 mentioned in the main work came into force on April 22, 2014: Crime and Courts Act 2013 (Commencement No. 10 and Transitional Provision) Order 2014 (S.I. 2014 No. 954).

## IV. INTIMIDATION OF WITNESSES, JURORS AND OTHERS

### Criminal Justice and Public Order Act 1994, s.51

★**28-132**     The provisions of the Crime and Courts Act 2013 referred to in the main work came into force on February 24, 2014: Crime and Courts Act 2013 (Commencement No. 8) Order 2014 (S.I. 2014 No. 258).

## VII. PRISON SECURITY

### A. Escape

### (4) Sentence

Relevant factors in sentencing for escape include whether the escape was planned, what level of violence was used and what injury was suffered by officers or others, whether the escape attempt was successful, and, if so, for how long the defendant was at large, the seriousness of the underlying charge, and whether the escape was from a court or a place of detention, such as a prison: *R. v. Baverstock* [2014] 1 Cr.App.R.(S.) 64, CA.    ★28-181

## Chapter 29

# PUBLIC ORDER OFFENCES

## I. PUBLIC ORDER ACT 1986

### B. Offences (Pt I (ss.1–10))

### (5) Harassment, alarm or distress

With effect from February 1, 2014 (Crime and Courts Act 2013 (Commencement No. 6) Order 2013 (S.I. 2013 No. 2981)), section 57 of the 2013 Act was brought into force.    **29-34a**

Where the appellant had walked naked through a town centre, and where the magistrates' court found that that behaviour had caused alarm or distress to members of the public and that the defendant was at least aware that his behaviour could have been threatening, abusive, insulting or disorderly, a conviction under section 5 of the 1986 Act was proportionate. Although the defendant's right to freedom of expression under Article 10 of the ECHR (see § 16-119 in the main work) was engaged, the court had been entitled to find that there was a pressing social need for the restriction of his right to be naked, and the restriction imposed by section 5(1), under which the maximum penalty was a fine, corresponded to this need and was a proportionate response: *Gough v. DPP*, 177 J.P. 669, DC.

### (6) Mental element: miscellaneous

#### Public Order Act 1986, s.6

With effect from February 1, 2014 (Crime and Courts Act 2013 (Commencement No. 6) Order 2013 (S.I. 2013 No. 2981)), section 57 of the 2013 Act was brought into force.    **29-35**

### E. Religious Hatred and Hatred on the Grounds of Sexual Orientation (Pt 3A (ss.29A–29N))

#### Criminal Justice and Immigration Act 2008

The provisions of the Marriage (Same Sex Couples) Act 2013 referred to in the main work came into force on March 13, 2014: Marriage (Same Sex Couples) Act 2013 (Commencement No. 2 and Transitional Provision) Order 2014 (S.I. 2014 No. 93).    **29-57**

CHAPTER 30

## COMMERCE, FINANCIAL MARKETS AND INSOLVENCY

### *I. INVESTIGATIVE POWERS*

### B. INSOLVENCY ACT 1986

#### (8) Application to bank insolvency

**Banking Act 2009**

★**30-75a**     With effect from June 5, 2014, the Financial Services Act 2012 (Commencement No. 4) Order 2014 (S.I. 2014 No. 1447) brought into force certain provisions of the Financial Services Act 2012 (as to which, see the main work), as follows: (i) sections 100(1), (6) and (7), 101(1) and (7) to (9), and 102(1), (ii) section 100(5), so far as it inserts sections 81C(2) and 81D of the Banking Act 2009 (but s.81C(2) only for the purpose of enabling the power conferred by s.47 of the 2009 Act to be exercised in relation to banking group companies within the meaning of s.81D), (iii) section 101(5), so far as it inserts section 89A(1) of the 2009 Act (but only for the purpose of enabling the powers conferred by ss.47, 60 and 81D(1) to be exercised in relation to investment firms and companies in the same group as an investment firm which are group companies), and (iv) section 102(6), so far as it inserts sections 89B(1) and 89G of the 2009 Act (but s.89B(1) only for the purpose of enabling the powers conferred by ss.47, 48 and 81D(1) to be exercised in relation to recognised central counterparties and companies in the same group as a recognised central counterparty which are group companies).

★     As from March 1, 2014 (Financial Services (Banking Reform) Act 2013 (Commencement No. 1) Order 2014 (S.I. 2014 No. 377)), for limited purposes only, otherwise as from a day or days to be appointed, the 2009 Act is extensively amended by the Financial Services (Banking Reform) Act 2013 (see, in particular, Sched. 2). Among the affected provisions are several of those listed in the main work. A new option has been added to the three stabilisation options under the permanent special resolution regime provided for by Part 1 of the 2009 Act, namely "bail-in"; this is now the third stabilisation option, with the original third option (temporary public ownership) becoming the fourth.

### C. FINANCIAL SERVICES AND MARKETS ACT 2000

#### (2) General inquiries by the regulatory authorities

**Financial Services and Markets Act 2000, ss.165–177**

*Appointment of persons to carry out investigations in particular cases*

**30-80**     With effect from January 1, 2014, the Financial Services and Markets Act 2000 (Qualifying EU Provisions) (No. 2) Order 2013 (S.I. 2013 No. 3116), *inter alia*, specifies further EU measures as "qualifying EU provisions" for the purposes of section 168(4)(k) of the 2000 Act. These are in addition to those specified in the Financial Services and Markets Act 2000 (Qualifying EU Provisions) Order 2013 (S.I. 2013 No. 419) (as to which, see the main work).

### D. ENTERPRISE ACT 2002

#### (1) Introduction

★**30-89**     With effect from April 1, 2014, section 26(1) and (2) of the Enterprise and Regulatory Reform Act 2013 were brought into force, subject to transitional provisions and savings: Enterprise and Regulatory Reform Act 2013 (Commencement No. 6, Transitional Provisions and Savings) Order 2014 (S.I. 2014 No. 416).

## (2) Investigation of cartel offences

### Enterprise Act 2002, ss.192–202

*Investigation of offences under section 188*

With effect from April 1, 2014, section 26(3) of, and paragraph 211 of Schedule 5 to, the ★**30-90**
Enterprise and Regulatory Reform Act 2013 were brought into force, subject to transitional provisions and savings: Enterprise and Regulatory Reform Act 2013 (Commencement No. 6, Transitional Provisions and Savings) Order 2014 (S.I. 2014 No. 416).

*Powers when conducting an investigation*

With effect from April 1, 2014, section 26(3) of, and paragraph 212 of Schedule 5 to, the ★**30-91**
Enterprise and Regulatory Reform Act 2013 were brought into force, subject to transitional provisions and savings: Enterprise and Regulatory Reform Act 2013 (Commencement No. 6, Transitional Provisions and Savings) Order 2014 (S.I. 2014 No. 416).

*Power to enter premises under a warrant*

With effect from April 1, 2014, section 26(3) of, and paragraph 213 of Schedule 5 to, the ★**30-92**
Enterprise and Regulatory Reform Act 2013 were brought into force, subject to transitional provisions and savings: Enterprise and Regulatory Reform Act 2013 (Commencement No. 6, Transitional Provisions and Savings) Order 2014 (S.I. 2014 No. 416).

*Exercise of powers by authorised person*

With effect from April 1, 2014, section 26(3) of, and paragraph 214 of Schedule 5 to, the ★**30-93**
Enterprise and Regulatory Reform Act 2013 were brought into force, subject to transitional provisions and savings: Enterprise and Regulatory Reform Act 2013 (Commencement No. 6, Transitional Provisions and Savings) Order 2014 (S.I. 2014 No. 416).

*Privileged information etc.*

With effect from April 1, 2014, section 26(3) of, and paragraph 215 of Schedule 5 to, the ★**30-94**
Enterprise and Regulatory Reform Act 2013 were brought into force, subject to transitional provisions and savings: Enterprise and Regulatory Reform Act 2013 (Commencement No. 6, Transitional Provisions and Savings) Order 2014 (S.I. 2014 No. 416).

*Offences*

With effect from April 1, 2014, section 26(3) of, and paragraph 216 of Schedule 5 to, the ★**30-96**
Enterprise and Regulatory Reform Act 2013 were brought into force, subject to transitional provisions and savings: Enterprise and Regulatory Reform Act 2013 (Commencement No. 6, Transitional Provisions and Savings) Order 2014 (S.I. 2014 No. 416).

## II. OFFENCES IN RELATION TO COMMERCE, FINANCIAL MARKETS AND INSOLVENCY

### A. COMPANIES ACTS 1985 AND 2006

#### (5) Fraudulent trading

##### Companies Act 2006, s.993

**The nature of the offence**

*Jetivia S.A. v. Bilta (U.K.) Ltd* is now reported at [2014] Ch. 52, *sub nom. Bilta (U.K.) Ltd (in* **30-118**
*liquidation) v. Nazir (No. 2)*. The Supreme Court has given the sixth and seventh defendants
permission to appeal from the the Court of Appeal's decision: see *Bilta (U.K.) Ltd (in liquidation) v.
Nazir (No. 2)* [2014] 1 W.L.R. 1230, SC.

## D. Company Directors Disqualification Act 1986

**30-201**  With effect from April 6, 2014 (Co-operative and Community Benefit Societies and Credit Unions Act 2010 (Commencement No. 2) Order 2014 (S.I. 2014 No. 183)), section 3 of the Co-operative and Community Benefit Societies and Credit Unions Act 2010 is brought into force.

★  With effect from August 1, 2014 (immediately after the Co-operative and Community Benefit Societies and Credit Unions Act 2010, s.1, comes into force), section 22E of the 1986 Act (as to which, see the main work) is amended, and the Industrial and Provident Societies Act 1965 (see the main work) is repealed in its entirety: Co-operative and Community Benefit Societies Act 2014, s.151(1) and (4), Sched. 4, para. 38, and Sched. 7.

## E. Financial Services and Markets Act 2000

### (3) Carrying on unauthorised investment business

**Financial Services and Markets Act 2000, ss.19, 21–25**

*Designation of activities requiring prudential regulation by PRA*

**30-208a**  With effect from January 1, 2014, the Capital Requirements Regulations 2013 (S.I. 2013 No. 3115) amend the Financial Services and Markets Act 2000 (PRA-regulated Activities) Order 2013 (S.I. 2013 No. 556).

*Contravention of the general prohibition or section 20(1) or (1A)*

**30-209**  The Financial Services and Markets Act 2000 (Consumer Credit) (Designated Activities) Order 2014 (S.I. 2014 No. 334) has been made under section 23(1B) of the 2000 Act. It takes effect on April 1, 2014, and designates specified activities as credit-related regulated activities for the purposes of the 2000 Act.

★  For a case in which a wife was held to have aided and abetted her husband's offence under section 23 of the 2000 Act (§ 30-209 in the main work), notwithstanding her lack of knowledge about the requirements of the 2000 Act, and in particular knowledge that her husband needed to be an authorised person under section 19 (§ 30-207 in the main work), and notwithstanding her lack of dishonesty, see *O'Neil v. Gale* [2014] Lloyd's Rep. F.C. 202, CA (Civ. Div.).

★**30-212**  The Financial Services and Markets Act 2000 (Exemption) Order 2001 (S.I. 2001 No. 1201) is further amended by the Financial Services and Markets Act 2000 (Regulated Activities) (Amendment) Order 2014 (S.I. 2014 No. 366) with effect from April 1, 2014, and by the Financial Services and Markets Act 2000 (Consumer Credit) (Miscellaneous Provisions) (No. 2) Order 2014 (S.I. 2014 No. 506), with effect immediately after article 14(4) of the Financial Services and Markets Act 2000 (Regulated Activities) (Amendment No. 2) Order 2013 (S.I. 2013 No. 1881) (as to which, see the main work) comes into force.

★  The Financial Services and Markets Act 2000 (Regulated Activities) Order 2001 (S.I. 2001 No. 544) is further amended by the Capital Requirements Regulations 2013 (S.I. 2013 No. 3115) with effect from January 1, 2014; by S.I. 2014 No. 366 (*ante*) with effect from April 1, 2014; and by the Financial Services and Markets Act 2000 (Regulated Activities) (Amendment) (No. 2) Order 2014 (S.I. 2014 No. 1448), with effect from June 27, 2014.

★  With effect from February 26, 2014 (for the purpose of the Financial Conduct Authority making rules, giving guidance and imposing requirements or giving directions), and April 1, 2014 (otherwise, and immediately after the Financial Services and Markets Act 2000 (Regulated Activities) (Amendment) (No. 2) Order 2013 (S.I. 2013 No. 1881) and the Financial Services Act 2012 (Consumer Credit) Order 2013 (S.I. 2013 No. 1882) are brought into force on that date), the Financial Services and Markets Act 2000 (Financial Promotion) Order 2005 (S.I. 2005 No. 1529) is further amended by the Financial Services and Markets Act 2000 (Consumer Credit) (Miscellaneous Provisions) Order 2014 (S.I. 2014 No. 208). It is further amended, also from April 1, 2014, by S.I. 2014 No. 366 (*ante*), and by S.I. 2014 No. 506 (*ante*).

### Sentence

**30-212a**  The approach to sentencing adopted in *R. v. Powell and Hinkson* (see the main work) was

adopted in *R. v. Dallimore, Weeks and Miah* [2014] 1 Cr.App.R.(S.) 31, CA (court is entitled to take
account of dishonesty or grossly reckless behaviour relating to an offence of carrying on an
unauthorised investment business, notwithstanding the fact that it is a strict liability offence, since
such considerations are plainly relevant to culpability).

## F. Enterprise Act 2002

### (2) Cartel offence

**Enterprise Act 2002, ss.188–190**

*Cartel offence*

With effect from April 1, 2014, section 47(1) to (4), (7) and (8) of the Enterprise and Regulatory    ★**30-217**
Reform Act 2013 were brought into force: Enterprise and Regulatory Reform Act 2013 (Commencement No. 6, Transitional Provisions and Savings) Order 2014 (S.I. 2014 No. 416).

**Enterprise Act 2002, ss.188A, 188B**

*Circumstances in which cartel offence not committed*

For an order made under section 188A(1)(c) of the 2002 Act, see the Enterprise Act 2002    ★**30-217a**
(Publishing of Relevant Information under section 188A) Order 2014 (S.I. 2014 No. 535), which
provides that relevant information about arrangements coming within section 188 of that Act
(cartel offence (as to which, see § 30-217 in the main work)) will be considered published for the
purposes of section 188A(1)(c) if it is advertised once in either the London Gazette, the Edinburgh
Gazette or the Belfast Gazette.

*Defences to commission of cartel offence*

With effect from April 1, 2014, section 47(5) and (6) of the Enterprise and Regulatory Reform    ★**30-217b**
Act 2013 were brought into force: Enterprise and Regulatory Reform Act 2013 (Commencement
No. 6, Transitional Provisions and Savings) Order 2014 (S.I. 2014 No. 416).

*Cartel offence: penalty and prosecution*

With effect from April 1, 2014, section 26(3) of, and paragraph 210 of Schedule 5 to, the    ★**30-219**
Enterprise and Regulatory Reform Act 2013 were brought into force: Enterprise and Regulatory
Reform Act 2013 (Commencement No. 6, Transitional Provisions and Savings) Order 2014 (S.I.
2014 No. 416).

## G. Insider Dealing

**Spread betting**

For an analysis of how spread betting on share prices can amount to insider dealing, see *Patel*    **30-258a**
*v. Mirza* [2013] Lloyd's Rep. F.C. 525, Ch D (David Donaldson Q.C., sitting as a deputy High
Court judge): a spread bet is a contract for differences as defined in Schedule 2 to the 1993 Act (§
30-249 in the main work) and therefore constitutes a "security" for the purposes of section 52 of
the Act (*ibid.*, § 30-231); and the spread betting company is a "professional intermediary" upon
which the person placing the bets would be "relying" so as to satisfy sections 52(3) (person having
inside information is guilty of an offence if, in dealing in price-affected securities, he relies on a
professional intermediary), 55(1) (person deals in securities if he acquires securities whether as
principal or agent (*ibid.*, § 30-234)) and 59(1) (definition of "professional intermediary" (*ibid.*, §
30-238)) of the Act.

CHAPTER 31

## OFFENCES AGAINST PUBLIC MORALS AND POLICY

*I. BIGAMY*

### (6) Evidence

### Marriages abroad

**31-17**  With effect from June 3, 2014 (Marriage (Same Sex Couples) Act 2013 (Commencement No. 2 and Transitional Provision) Order 2014 (S.I. 2014 No. 93)), section 13(2) of the 2013 Act is brought into force.

★  As to the solemnization of marriages abroad, see *post*, § 31-19.

### Marriages in England and abroad

**31-19**  With effect from January 21, 2014, paragraphs 1, 2, 4, 6 to 10, and 12 to 15 of Schedule 6 to the Marriage (Same Sex Couples) Act 2013, and section 13(1) of the 2013 Act insofar as it relates to those paragraphs, were brought into force, to the extent that they confer or relate to the power to make subordinate legislation; and with effect from June 3, 2014, section 13 of, and Schedule 6 to, the 2013 Act are brought into force, so far as not already in force: Marriage (Same Sex Couples) Act 2013 (Commencement No. 2 and Transitional Provision) Order 2014 (S.I. 2014 No. 93).

★  With effect from June 3, 2014, the Consular Marriages and Marriages under Foreign Law Order 2014 (S.I. 2014 No. 1110) makes provision for the solemnization according to the law of England and Wales or of Scotland of consular marriages in countries or territories outside the United Kingdom, and for providing conclusive proof of the same.

★  With effect from June 3, 2014, the Overseas Marriage (Armed Forces) Order 2014 (S.I. 2014 No. 1108) makes provision for the solemnization of marriages in countries or territories outside the United Kingdom, where one of the proposed parties to the marriage is a member of Her Majesty's armed forces serving in that country or territory or is a person subject to service discipline, or is a child of such a person and whose home is with that person in that country or territory.

### Void and voidable marriages

**31-25**  With effect from March 13, 2014 (Marriage (Same Sex Couples) Act 2013 (Commencement No. 2 and Transitional Provision) Order 2014 (S.I. 2014 No. 93)), paragraphs 26 and 27 of Schedule 7 to the 2013 Act, and section 17(4) insofar as it relates to those paragraphs, are brought into force.

*II. PUBLIC NUISANCE*

### A. STATUTE

### (2) Dangerous Dogs Act 1991

#### Dangerous Dogs Act 1991, s.3(1)–(4)

*Keeping dogs under proper control*

★**31-35**  With effect from May 13, 2014 (Anti-social Behaviour, Crime and Policing Act 2014 (Commencement No. 2, Transitional and Transitory Provisions) Order 2014 (S.I. 2014 No. 949)), section 3 of the 1991 Act is amended by the Anti-social Behaviour, Crime and Policing Act 2014, s.106(1) and (2), so as: (i) in subsection (1), to substitute the words "any place in England or Wales (whether or not a public place)" for the words "a public place", and to insert the words "or assistance dog" after the words "injures any person"; (ii) to insert new subsections (1A) and (1B) after subsection (1), as follows—

"(1A) A person ('D') is not guilty of an offence under subsection (1) in a case which is a householder case.
(1B) For the purposes of subsection (1A) 'a householder case' is a case where—
(a) the dog is dangerously out of control while in or partly in a building, or part of a building, that is a dwelling or is forces accommodation (or is both), and
(b) at that time—
(i) the person in relation to whom the dog is dangerously out of control ('V') is in, or is entering, the building or part as a trespasser, or
(ii) D (if present at that time) believed V to be in, or entering, the building or part as a trespasser.
Section 76(8B) to (8F) of the Criminal Justice and Immigration Act 2008 (use of force at place of residence) apply for the purposes of this subsection as they apply for the purposes of subsection (8A) of that section (and for those purposes the reference in section 76(8D) to subsection (8A)(d) is to be read as if it were a reference to paragraph (b)(ii) of this subsection).";

(iii) to repeal subsection (3); (iv) in subsection (4), to omit the words "or (3)", to substitute the words "that subsection" for "either of those subsections", and, in paragraph (b), to substitute the words "the relevant maximum specified in subsection (4A)" for the words "two years"; and (v) to insert new subsection (4A), after subsection 4, as follows—

"(4A) For the purposes of subsection (4)(b), the relevant maximum is—
(a) 14 years if a person dies as a result of being injured;
(b) 5 years in any other case where a person is injured;
(c) 3 years in any case where an assistance dog is injured (whether or not it dies).".

Article 9 of the commencement order (*ante*), provides that the revised penalty provisions do not apply to offences committed before May 13, 2014.

## Interpretation

With effect from May 13, 2014 (Anti-social Behaviour, Crime and Policing Act 2014 (Commencement No. 2, Transitional and Transitory Provisions) Order 2014 (S.I. 2014 No. 949)), section 10(2) of the 1991 Act is amended by the insertion of a definition of "assistance dog" (it has the meaning given by the Equality Act 2010, s.173(1)) and section 10(3) is amended by the insertion of the words "or assistance dog" after "injure any person" and "injuring a person": Anti-social Behaviour, Crime and Policing Act 2014, s.106(1) and (6).   ★**31-36**

While section 3(1) of the 1991 Act creates a strict liability offence, the prosecution are nonetheless required to prove that an act or omission of the defendant, with or without fault, to more than a minimal degree, caused or permitted the dog to be dangerously out of control. Parliament did not intend to render the dog owner absolutely liable in all circumstances for the dog being dangerously out of control, or to create an offence without regard to the ability of the owner, or someone to whom he had entrusted responsibility, to take and keep control of the animal. There must be some causal connection between having control of the dog and the prohibited state of affairs that has arisen: *R. v. Robinson-Pierre* [2014] 1 Cr.App.R. 22, CA (considering, *inter alia*, *Greener v. DPP*, *Rafiq v. DPP*, *R. v. Gedminintaite and Collier* (as to which, see the main work), and *R. v. Bezzina* (as to which, see § 31-37 in the main work)).

In *Criminal Injuries Compensation Authority v. First-tier Tribunal (Social Entitlement Chamber)* (2014) 158(6) S.J. 37, CA (Civ. Div.), it was said, with reference to the provision in section 10(3) of the 1991 Act that, for the purposes of the Act, a dog is "dangerously out of control" if there are grounds for reasonable apprehension that it will injure any person, if a dog is behaving aggressively towards a person, there will almost always be such grounds.

### Dangerous Dogs Act 1991, s.4(1)–(7)

*Destruction and disqualification orders*

With effect from May 13, 2014 (Anti-social Behaviour, Crime and Policing Act 2014 (Com-   ★**31-38** mencement No. 2, Transitional and Transitory Provisions) Order 2014 (S.I. 2014 No. 949)), section 4 of the 1991 Act is amended by the Anti-social Behaviour, Crime and Policing Act 2014, ss.106(1) and (3) and 107(1) and (3) so as: (i) to omit "or (3)" from both places in subsection (1); and (ii) to insert a new subsection (1B), as follows—

> "(1B) For the purposes of subsection (1A)(a), when deciding whether a dog would constitute a danger to public safety, the court—
>> (a) must consider—
>>> (i) the temperament of the dog and its past behaviour, and
>>> (ii) whether the owner of the dog, or the person for the time being in charge of it, is a fit and proper person to be in charge of the dog, and
>> (b) may consider any other relevant circumstances.".

### Dangerous Dogs Act 1991, s.4A

*Contingent destruction orders*

★**31-38a**    With effect from May 13, 2014 (Anti-social Behaviour, Crime and Policing Act 2014 (Commencement No. 2, Transitional and Transitory Provisions) Order 2014 (S.I. 2014 No. 949)), section 4A of the 1991 Act is amended by the Anti-Social Behaviour, Crime and Policing Act 2014, s.106(1) and (4), so as to omit "or (3)" from subsections (1)(a) and (4).

★**31-38b**    With effect from May 13, 2014 (Anti-social Behaviour, Crime and Policing Act 2014 (Commencement No. 2, Transitional and Transitory Provisions) Order 2014 (S.I. 2014 No. 949)), section 1 of the 1991 Act is amended by the Anti-social Behaviour, Crime and Policing Act 2014, s.107(1) and (2), so as to provide (in new subs. (6)) that a scheme under subsection (3) or (5) may in particular include provision requiring a court to consider whether a person is a fit and proper person to be in charge of a dog.

### Search and seizure

★**31-39**    With effect from May 13, 2014 (Anti-social Behaviour, Crime and Policing Act 2014 (Commencement No. 2, Transitional and Transitory Provisions) Order 2014 (S.I. 2014 No. 949)), section 5 of the 1991 Act is amended by the Anti-Social Behaviour, Crime and Policing Act 2014, s.106(1) and (5), so as to extend the power of seizure to any dog which appears to be dangerously out of control in a place which is not a public place.

## III. OBSCENE OR INDECENT PUBLICATIONS AND DISPLAYS, ETC.

### B. STATUTE

### (4) Protection of Children Act 1978

### Protection of Children Act 1978, ss.6, 7

*Punishments*

**31-113**    As to the replacement of the Sentencing Guidelines Council's guideline, see *ante*, § 20-9c; and for the detail of the new guideline, see *post*, Appendix K-84 *et seq.*

### (5) Criminal Justice Act 1988

### Criminal Justice Act 1988, ss.160, 160A

*Possession of indecent photograph of a child*

**31-115**    The Sentencing Council for England and Wales has issued a definitive guideline on sexual offences, applying to all offenders aged 18 or over, who are sentenced on or after April 1, 2014, and covering, *inter alia*, the offence of possession of an indecent photograph of a child, contrary to section 160 of the 1988 Act. For the detail of the guideline, see *post*, Appendix K-84 *et seq.*

### IV. BRIBERY AND CORRUPTION

## B. STATUTE

### (2) Public Bodies Corrupt Practices Act 1889 and Prevention of Corruption Acts 1906 and 1916

The prosecution do not have to prove as an ingredient of the offences under section 1 of the ★**31-140** Prevention of Corruption Act 1906 that the principal did not know of the payment and did not give his informed consent; they need do no more than prove that the payment made for the prohibited purpose was made corruptly, though whether the principal knew of the payment and had given any informed consent might be highly material to the issue whether the payment was corrupt: *R. v. J. (P.) (D. intervening)* [2014] 1 Cr.App.R. 21, CA.

### (3) Bribery Act 2010

#### (c) *Statute*

#### Bribery Act 2010, s.10

With effect from March 27, 2014, section 10 of the 2010 Act is amended by the removal of ★**31-180** references to the Director of Revenue and Customs Prosecutions: Public Bodies (Merger of the Director of Public Prosecutions and the Director of Revenue and Customs Prosecutions) Order 2014 (S.I. 2014 No. 834). The amendments are subject to saving and transitional provisions, as to which, see *ante*, § 1-27.

#### (f) *Sentence*

The Sentencing Council for England and Wales has issued a definitive guideline on offences of ★**31-198** bribery, applying to all offenders aged 18 or older and to organisations falling to be sentenced on or after October 1, 2014, and covering offences contrary to sections 1, 2 and 6 of the 2010 Act (see §§ 31-171, 31-172 and 31-176 in the main work), and failure of commercial organizations to prevent bribery, contrary to section 7 (see § 31-177 in the main work). For the detail of the guideline, see *post*, Appendix K-297 *et seq.* The guideline incorporates the guideline on offences of bribery committed by corporate offenders.

### CHAPTER 32

# MOTOR VEHICLE OFFENCES

## II. DRIVING OFFENCES

### G. CAUSING DEATH BY DRIVING: UNLICENSED, DISQUALIFIED OR UNINSURED DRIVERS

#### (6) Ingredients of the offence

*R. v. Hughes* is now reported at [2014] 1 Cr.App.R. 6.   **32-76**

### I. DRIVING, BEING IN CHARGE, WHILST ABOVE THE PRESCRIBED LIMIT

#### (7) Evidence

**Specimen of breath, blood or urine**

For a case in which it was said, *obiter*, that a specimen taken otherwise than in accordance with  **32-100** the procedure laid down in section 7 of the RTA 1988 (see § 32-126 in the main work) would be admissible in evidence on a charge under section 5 of that Act (§ 32-89 in the main work), subject only to the discretion given to the court to exclude it under section 78 of the PACE Act 1984 (§ 15-401 in the main work), see *Bodhaniya v. CPS*, 178 J.P. 1, DC. For a criticism of this reasoning, and in particular a submission that it overlooks *Howard v. Hallett* and *Fox v. Chief Constable of Gwent* (as to both of which, see the main work), see the commentary at CLW/14/02/5. As to this case, see also *post*, § 32-135.

## L. Failing to Provide Evidential Specimen

### (5) Procedure

### Samples other than breath

*When such a specimen may be required*

**32-135**  For an example of a case being brought within section 7(3)(a) of the RTA 1988 (see § 32-126 in the main work) (constable requiring specimen of blood or urine had reasonable cause to believe that for medical reasons a specimen of breath could not be provided or should not be required) where the constable making the requirement for a specimen of blood or urine did not himself formulate in his own mind the case as being a "medical reasons" case, see *Bodhaniya v. CPS*, 178 J.P. 1, DC. For a criticism of the court's factual reasoning, see the commentary at CLW/14/02/5. As to this case, see also *ante*, § 32-100.

## O. Driving Without a Licence

### (5) Grant and form of licences

#### Road Traffic Act 1988, s.97

*Grant of licences*

**★32-159**  As from a day to be appointed, section 97 of the 1988 Act is amended by the Immigration Act 2014, s.46(1), so as to insert, in the opening words of subsection (1), the words "meets the relevant residence requirement (see section 97A) and" after the word "who".

**★32-160**  The Motor Vehicles (Driving Licences) Regulations 1999 (S.I. 1999 No. 2864) (as to which, see the main work) are further amended by the Driving Standards Agency and the Vehicle and Operator Services Agency (Merger) (Consequential Amendments) Regulations 2014 (S.I. 2014 No. 480), with effect from April 1, 2014, and by the Motor Vehicles (Driving Licences) (Amendment) Regulations 2014 (S.I. 2014 No. 613), with effect from April 10, 2014.

*Residence requirement*

**★32-161**  As from a day to be appointed, a new section 97A is inserted in the RTA 1988 by section 46(2) of the Immigration Act 2014. This sets out when a person is to be regarded as meeting the residence requirement for the purposes of section 97 (as to which, see *ante*, § 32-159).

It should be noted that the section set out as section 97A of the RTA 1988 in the main work is in fact section 97A of the RTOA 1988, and should appear at § 32-307a in the main work.

## S. Failing to Give Information as to Identity of Driver

### (1) Statute

#### Road Traffic Act 1988, s.172

*Duty to give information as to identity of driver, etc., in certain circumstances*

**32-187**  In *Foster v. DPP*, 178 J.P. 15, DC, it was held that Part 4 of the Criminal Procedure Rules 2013 (S.I. 2013 No. 1554) (service of documents) (as to which, see §§ 2-207 *et seq.* in the main work) applies to the calculation of time in section 172(7) of the 1988 Act (requirement to supply information as to identity of driver of vehicle within 28 days of notice being served (*ibid.*, § 32-185)). For a criticism of this decision, and, in particular, a submission that on its correct construction Part 4 of the 2013 rules does not apply in this situation, and that the relevant statutory provision is the Interpretation Act 1978, s.7, *post*, Appendix B-7, see the commentary at CLW/14/02/4.

## V. Disqualification and Endorsement

### (19) Interpretation

#### Road Traffic Offenders Act 1988, ss.96, 97

*Meaning of "driving record"*

The provision currently set out at § 32-161 in the main work as section 97A of the RTA 1988 is in fact section 97A of the RTOA 1988, which was inserted by the RSA 2006, s.8, and came into force on April 1, 2009 (Road Safety Act 2006 (Commencement No. 5) Order 2008 (S.I. 2008 No. 3164)). ★**32-307a**

## Chapter 33

# CONSPIRACY, ENCOURAGEMENT AND ATTEMPT TO COMMIT CRIME

## I. CONSPIRACY

### B. Statutory Offence of Conspiracy

#### (2) The ingredients of conspiracy

##### (a) *Agreement*

**Agreement to aid and abet/aiding and abetting an agreement**

*R. v. Kenning* (as to which, see the main work) was distinguished in *R. v. Dang (Manh Toan)* [2014] 2 Cr.App.R. 3, CA, where it was held that conspiracy to be concerned in the production of a controlled drug by another is an offence known to law. As to this case, see also *ante*, § 27-35. ★**33-13**

### C. Saving of Certain Conspiracies at Common Law, etc.

#### (2) Conspiracy to defraud

**Sentence**

*Att.-Gen.'s References (Nos 7 and 8 of 2013) (R. v. Kallakis and Williams)*; *R. v. Levene* is now reported at [2014] 1 Cr.App.R.(S.) 26. **33-40**

As to the guideline of the Sentencing Council for England and Wales for the sentencing of offences of conspiracy to defraud, incorporating the Sentencing Council's guideline on offences of fraud, bribery and money laundering committed by corporate offenders, see *post*, Appendix K-297 *et seq.*

### D. Pleading, Evidence and Practice

#### (2) The indictment

**Election by prosecution**

The 2013 criminal practice directions (see the main work) are now reported at [2013] 1 W.L.R. 3164. **33-59**

## II. SOLICITING OR INCITING A CRIME

### (1) Common law

#### (a) *Introduction*

**Definition**

To solicit or incite another to commit a crime was indictable at common law. A person was **33-75** guilty of incitement to commit an offence or offences if (a) he incited another to do or cause to be done an act or acts which, if done, would involve the commission of an offence or offences by the other; and (b) he intended or believed that the other, if he acted as incited, should or would do so with the fault required for the offence or offences: *DPP v. Armstrong (Andrew)* [2000] Crim.L.R. 379, DC; *R. v. Claydon* [2006] 1 Cr.App.R. 20, CA (approving, in both cases, the Law Commission's definition (*Criminal Law: A Criminal Code*, Law Com. No. 177, 1989)). In *Invicta Plastics Ltd v. Clare* [1976] R.T.R. 251, the Divisional Court adopted *dicta* of Lord Denning M.R. in *Race Relations Board v. Applin* [1973] 1 Q.B. 815 at 825, CA (Civ. Div.), to the effect that "to incite" was not limited to urging or spurring on by advice, encouragement or persuasion but included inciting another to do an act by threats or by pressure. Incitement also included an offer of a bribe to a person to commit an offence: *Wade v. Broughton* (1814) 3 V. & B. 172.

It was irrelevant whether the solicitation or incitement was effective: *Armstrong, ante*; or whether the principal offence existed under the common law or was created by statute: see 1 Russ.Cr. 12th ed., 176. However, the offence had to be one which was capable of being committed by the person incited: *R. v. Claydon, ante*.

### Agents provocateurs

**33-76**   See §§ 15-452 *et seq.* in the main work, and see *R. v. Anderson* [1986] 1 A.C. 27 at 38, HL, and *R. v. Jones (James)* (§ 27-37a in the main work).

### Mens rea

**33-77**   A person accused of incitement must be shown to have intended or believed that the person incited would, if he acted as incited to do, do so with the *mens rea* appropriate to the offence (*ante*, § 33-75). As with conspiracy (§ 33-15 in the main work), it is submitted that laudable ulterior motives are irrelevant. To the extent that *R. v. Shaw* [1994] Crim.L.R. 365, CA (93 05976 W2) is authority to the contrary, it is submitted that it is wrong (see the commentary in the *Criminal Law Review*); and it was disapproved in *Claydon, ante*, § 33-75. The explanation for the decision (that a person charged with inciting an offence of dishonesty had to be proved to have been dishonest himself) may lie in the fact that the prosecution had so put their case (transcript p.7F).

In *R. v. Curr*, 51 Cr.App.R. 113, CA, it was held that a person could only be convicted of incitement if the person incited knew that the conduct incited amounted to an offence. This was also disapproved of in *R. v. Claydon, ante*, where it was said that the actual knowledge or state of mind of the person incited was irrelevant. Albeit that this was *obiter*, it is submitted that this view is to be preferred, the offence being concerned with the state of mind of the incitor, not of the incitee.

### (b) *Jurisdiction*

**33-78**   The common law jurisdiction in respect of incitement appears to be the same as that for conspiracy, as to which see §§ 33-21 *et seq.* in the main work. In *R. v. Tompkins* [2007] Crim.L.R. 235, CA, it was assumed that the courts of England and Wales have jurisdiction to try an allegation of incitement where the incitor was at all material times within the jurisdiction and the incitee was at all material times without the jurisdiction, provided that the *actus reus* of the offence was to occur, at least in part, within the jurisdiction.

As to the extended jurisdiction of the courts in relation to allegations of incitement to commit certain sexual acts outside the United Kingdom, see the Sexual Offences (Conspiracy and Incitement) Act 1996, s.2 (§ 2-36b in the main work); and as to their extended jurisdiction in relation to incitement to commit fraud and related offences, see Part I of the CJA 1993 (§§ 2-37 *et seq.* in the main work).

### (c) *Indictment*

**Statement of Offence**

*Incitement to steal.*

**Particulars of Offence**

*A B, on the* _____ *day of* _____, *20____, unlawfully incited J N to steal property belonging to Y Z.*

Penalty—fine and/or imprisonment: *R. v. Higgins*, 2 East 5.

### (d) *Particular offences*

## To conspire or to incite

Section 5(7) of the CLA 1977 (§ 33-35 in the main work) abolished the offence of incitement to conspire.

In the course of giving the Court of Appeal's judgment in *R. v. Sirat*, 83 Cr.App.R. 41, Parker L.J. said:

> "There is no doubt that at comm on law incitement to commit a crime is an offence. This being so, it follows logically that if A incites B to incite C to commit a crime, *e.g.* to wound D, A is guilty of incitement to commit a crime, namely, incitement" (at p. 43).

Later in the judgment, however, his Lordship said, having read out the terms of section 5(7) of the 1977 Act:

> "If, therefore, A incites B to agree with C that C will wound D, A's incitement of B is by statute not an offence ... . Where however the facts are that the accused's incitement of B is actually to enter into an agreement with C for the commission of a crime, it would in our judgment be impossible to hold that the accused can be guilty of incitement, on the ground that B must of necessity propose the crime to C on the way to making the agreement. Whether other forms of incitement to incite survive will fall for decision when the question arises. It may appear to be absurd that, where a person is inciting actual agreement to be made for the commission of a crime, he should be guilty of no offence, but that where he does not seek actual agreement but mere encouragement he should be guilty. This however is not necessarily absurd, for there may well be circumstances where there is no question of an agreement being sought but where the particular form of incitement is more effective than any attempt to secure agreement" (at pp. 44–45).

## To attempt, and attempt to incite

On an indictment charging the defendants with inciting, counselling and procuring a pregnant woman to administer to herself a noxious thing, namely an abortifacient, with intent to procure a miscarriage (see the Offences against the Person Act 1861, s.58 (§ 19-203 in the main work)), and with conspiracy to incite her to do the same, it was held (a) that if the woman, believing that she was taking a noxious thing within the meaning of the statute, did, with intent to procure her own abortion, take a thing in fact harmless, she was guilty of an attempt to commit an offence against section 58; but (b) that if the defendants in supplying the drug to the woman, though they well knew that she would take it in the belief that it was an abortifacient did not themselves believe that it was capable of procuring her own abortion, they could not be convicted of inciting her to commit the said offence, although if they had so believed it would have been otherwise: *R. v. Brown*, 63 J.P. 790.

In logic, it would seem that an incitement to attempt to commit an offence must necessarily be an incitement to commit that offence.

Where a letter was sent soliciting and inciting the addressee to commit a crime, but was not proved to have reached the intended recipient, the sender could properly be convicted of an attempt to incite the commission of the crime: *R. v. Banks* (1873) 12 Cox 393; *R. v. Ransford* (1874) 13 Cox 9; *R. v. Krause*, 66 J.P. 121; *R. v. Cope*, 16 Cr.App.R. 77, which may be distinguished from *R. v. Woods*, 22 Cr.App.R. 41, because in the former case the intended recipient of the letter would, if he had received it, have understood that he was being instigated to the commission of a crime, whereas in the latter case he would not; and *R. v. Goldman* [2001] Crim.L.R. 822, CA (defendant guilty of attempt to incite addressee to distribute indecent photographs of children, even where he was responding to an offer made by the addressee).

### To do the impossible

**33-82**    A person cannot be convicted of incitement to commit a particular offence if the person incited was incapable as a matter of law of committing the offence: *R. v. Claydon* [2006] 1 Cr.App.R. 20, CA. Nor can a person be convicted of incitement to commit a particular offence if its commission is factually impossible: see *R. v. Fitzmaurice* [1983] Q.B. 1083, 76 Cr.App.R. 17, CA (giving as an example incitement to murder a person who turned out to have been dead at the time of the incitement). Where it is contended that the offence incited was factually impossible, it is necessary to analyse the evidence with care to decide the precise offence which the defendant is alleged to have incited: *ibid.* At common law, the position was the same for conspiracy and attempts, but see now the CLA 1977, s.1(1)(b) (§ 33-2 in the main work), and the Criminal Attempts Act 1981, s.1(2) (§ 33-128 in the main work).

### To commit a summary offence

**33-83**    Incitement to commit a summary offence was a summary offence, punishable as for the offence incited: MCA 1980, s.45(1), (3).

### To commit an offence triable either way

**33-84**    See the MCA 1980, s.17(1), and Sched. 1, paras 33 and 35. The effect is that incitement to commit an offence triable either way is generally itself triable either way. Note that whilst paragraph 35 of Schedule 1 to the 1980 Act was repealed by the SCA 2007, ss.63(2) and 92, Sched. 6, para. 55(1) and (4), and Sched. 14, its effect has been preserved in relation to pre-commencement offences by the 2007 Act, s.91(1), and Sched. 13, para. 5(1)(b) (§ 33-116 in the main work).

### (e) *Evidence*

**33-85**    Prove the soliciting or inciting as alleged in the indictment. Prove it in the same manner as the offence of being a counsellor and procurer would be proved, except that this offence is committed even though the offence solicited was not in fact committed. It is no defence to the above indictment that the person incited purposely submitted himself to the incitement with intent to betray the inciter: *R. v. Quail* (1866) 4 F. & F. 1076.

On a charge of inciting a person to receive stolen goods it is no defence that at the time of the incitement there did not exist stolen goods of the type mentioned: *R. v. McDonough*, 47 Cr.App.R. 37, CCA.

A charge of incitement to distribute indecent photographs of children could be founded on the defendant's entering the website of a commercial child pornography business and paying the required entrance fee with his credit card; it mattered not that the process was entirely automated by the computer; the computer merely facilitated the business, and it was irrelevant to say that only the computer was incited; someone lay behind the computer: *R. (O.) v. Coventry Magistrates' Court* [2004] Crim.L.R. 948, DC.

## III. ENCOURAGING OR ASSISTING CRIME

### (2) Legislation

#### (a) *Inchoate offences*

**Serious Crime Act 2007, ss.44–46**

*Encouraging or assisting offences believing one or more will be committed*

**33-96**    *R. v. Sadique* (see the main work) is now reported [2013] 2 Cr.App.R. 31, *sub nom. R. v. Sadique (Omar) (No. 2)*.

#### (d) *Jurisdiction and procedure*

**Serious Crime Act 2007, ss.52–58**

*Penalties*

**★33-110**    Where a person is convicted of an offence of encouraging or assisting crime, contrary to section 44 or 45 of the 2007 Act (§§ 33-93, 33-94 in the main work), he is liable to the same maximum penalty as for the full offence (s.58(3) (see the main work)); accordingly, any relevant guideline applicable to the full offence must be taken into account when sentencing for an offence under the 2007 Act: *R. v. Woodford* [2014] 1 Cr.App.R.(S.) 32, CA.

## IV. ENCOURAGING OR ASSISTING SUICIDE

### (2) Statute

#### (a) *The offence*

#### Suicide Act 1961, s.2

*Criminal liability for complicity in another's suicide*

In *R. v. Howe* (2014) 158(8) S.J. 37, CA, the following guidance was given, in relation to the assessment of seriousness for the purposes of sentencing, in cases of face to face encouragement or assistance, as opposed to cases involving remote encouragement over the internet: as to harm, the most serious cases will be those where death resulted; next will be attempted suicides where serious harm resulted; if serious harm has occurred, the court should assess whether the harm has been resolved, or whether it will continue into the foreseeable future; the court will need in addition to take account of adverse consequences for people other than the primary victim; harm in this context will include psychological as well as physical harm; risk of harm to others will be a less serious, but relevant factor; cases where, despite encouragement with the necessary intent, the victim does not go on to attempt suicide, will be at the bottom of the harm range, whereas cases where a substance is provided with intent, but which in fact turns out to be harmless, will be a little higher up the scale (and there will be cases which fall between the levels of harm just described and the upper end of the range); as to culpability, the court should consider the presence of premeditation, persistence, the extent of the encouragement or assistance, and the means by which the suicide is to take place; the offender's motivation may be important, with compassion at one end of the range, and malice or the prospect of gain at the other; the existence of a duty of care or trust may play a part in determining the extent of culpability; consideration should also be given to whether the victim had a settled, voluntary and informed intention to commit suicide, and whether the victim solicited assistance or encouragement; the victim's capacity to make a decision as to suicide will be relevant (the offender's knowledge of any vulnerability of the victim will be important); evidence of threats, pressure or persuasion applied to the victim will also have a bearing on culpability. Once an assessment of the seriousness of the offence has been made, the court will need to consider aggravating and mitigating features of a more generic nature. In conclusion, the Court of Appeal expressed the opinion that, where the custody threshold has been crossed, the range would extend from three to 12 years' custody or more where an attempt at suicide or actual suicide has taken place; where the victim has not attempted suicide, the custody threshold may not have been crossed; each case must, however, be considered on its own facts, and the above factors are non-inclusive.

★**33-118**

### (4) Compatibility with the European Convention on Human Rights

*R. (Nicklinson) v. Ministry of Justice (C.N.K. Alliance Ltd intervening); R. (A.M.) v. DPP (Same intervening)* is now reported at [2014] 2 All E.R. 32, *sub nom. R. (Nicklinson) v. Ministry of Justice; R. (A.M.) v. DPP.*

**33-125**

### (5) The discretion to prosecute

*R. (Nicklinson) v. Ministry of Justice (C.N.K. Alliance Ltd intervening); R. (A.M.) v. DPP (Same intervening)* is now reported at [2014] 2 All E.R. 32, *sub nom. R. (Nicklinson) v. Ministry of Justice; R. (A.M.) v. DPP.*

**33-126**

## V. ATTEMPT TO COMMIT CRIME

### B. STATUTORY OFFENCE OF ATTEMPT

#### Criminal Attempts Act 1981, ss.1, 1A

*Attempting to commit an offence*

With effect from May 13, 2014 (Anti-social Behaviour, Crime and Policing Act 2014 (Com-

★**33-128**

mencement No. 2, Transitional and Transitory Provisions) Order 2014 (S.I. 2014 No. 949), section 1 of the 1981 Act is amended by the Anti-social Behaviour, Crime and Policing Act 2014, s.176(5)(a), so as to insert a new subsection (5), as follows—

> "(5) This section also applies to low-value shoplifting (which is defined in, and is triable only summarily by virtue of, section 22A of the Magistrates' Courts Act 1980).".

★     The amendments made by section 176 of the 2014 Act have effect in relation to (i) low-value shoplifting committed on or after May 13, 2014, and (ii) low-value shoplifting committed before May 13, 2014, in respect of which proceedings have not yet been instituted on that date (2014 Act, s.176(8)).

**Criminal Attempts Act 1981, s.4**

*Trial and penalties*

★**33-132**     With effect from May 13, 2014 (Anti-social Behaviour, Crime and Policing Act 2014 (Commencement No. 2, Transitional and Transitory Provisions) Order 2014 (S.I. 2014 No. 949), section 4(1)(c) of the 1981 Act is amended by the Anti-social Behaviour, Crime and Policing Act 2014, s.176(5)(b), so as to insert, after the words "either way", the words "or is low-value shoplifting (which is defined in, and is triable only summarily by virtue of, section 22A of the Magistrates' Courts Act 1980),". For transitional provision in relation to this amendment, see section 176(8) of the 2014 Act (*ante*, § 33-128).

## "With intent to commit an offence"

**33-136**     In *R. v. Pace* [2014] 1 Cr.App.R. 34, CA, it was held that section 1(1) of the 1981 Act requires proof of an intent to commit all elements of the index offence; and that, accordingly, the necessary mental element to prove the offence of attempting to convert criminal property is not mere suspicion, even though that would be sufficient to prove the substantive offence of conversion under the PCA 2002, s.327(1) (§ 26-11 in the main work). It is not clear from the judgment whether the requisite mental element for attempted conversion should be just intention, or whether belief would suffice. Section 1(3) of the 1981 Act would appear to support the latter where, as in the instant case, the property in question was not in fact a person's benefit from criminal conduct (the prosecution followed a police sting operation to identify rogue scrap metal traders).

# APPENDIX A
## Codes of Practice and Attorney-General's Guidelines

# I. CODES OF PRACTICE

## A. Under the Police and Criminal Evidence Act 1984

### (1) Introduction

The Police and Criminal Evidence Act 1984 makes provision for the issuing by the Secretary of **A-1** State of codes of practice in connection with the tape-recording of interviews (s.60,§ 15-173 in the main work), the visual recording of interviews (s.60A, § 15-177 in the main work), the exercise by police officers of statutory powers of "stop and search" (s.66(1)(a)(i) and (ii), § 15-2 in the main work), the exercise by police officers of statutory powers to arrest a person (s.66(1)(a)(iii), § 15-2 in the main work) the detention, treatment, questioning and identification of persons by police officers (s.66(1)(b), § 15-2 in the main work), and searches of premises and seizure of property (s.66(1)(c) and (d), § 15-2 in the main work).

There are eight extant codes: Code A (stop and search); Code B (search and seizure); Code C (detention, treatment and questioning of persons), Code D (identification), Code E (tape-recording of interviews), Code F (visual recording of interviews), Code G (arrest) and Code H (detention, treatment and questioning of persons under section 41 of, and Schedule 8 to, the Terrorism Act 2000).

Code D came into force on March 7, 2011: Police and Criminal Evidence Act 1984 (Codes of Practice) (Revision of Codes A, B and D) Order 2011 (S.I. 2011 No. 412). Code G came into force on November 12, 2012: Police and Criminal Evidence Act 1984 (Codes of Practice) (Revision of Codes C, G and H) Order 2012 (S.I. 2012 No. 1798).

The Police and Criminal Evidence Act 1984 (Codes of Practice) (Revisions to Codes A, B, C, E, F and H) Order 2013 (S.I. 2013 No. 2685) brought revised Codes A, B, C, E, F and H into force on October 27, 2013. The revisions were required in order to give effect to (i) the United Kingdom's obligations under European Parliament and Council Directive 2010/64/EU on the right to interpretation and translation in criminal proceedings, and (ii) the decision of the Divisional Court in *R. (H.C. (a child, by his litigation friend C.C.)) v. Secretary of State for the Home Department* (as to which, see §§ 15-6, 15-165, 15-204, 16-106 in the main work (and now reported at [2014] 1 W.L.R. 1234, *sub nom. R. (C.) v. Secretary of State for the Home Department*)).

The Police and Criminal Evidence Act 1984 (Codes of Practice) (Revisions to Codes C and H) ★ Order 2014 (S.I. 2014 No. 1237) brought revised Codes C and H into force on June 2, 2014. The revisions implemented obligations under European Parliament and Council Directive 2012/13/EU, in relation to the right to information in criminal proceedings. In particular, every detainee must be given a revised written notice setting out his rights and entitlements whilst in custody, which has been updated to reflect the new substantive rights conferred by the 2012 directive.

For further details of the various versions of the codes and their revisions, see §§ 15-5, 15-6 in the main work. For further details in relation to the codes generally, see the main work at §§ 15-2 *et seq.* (primary legislation), § 15-5 (commencement), § 15-7 (status of codes), § 15-8 (who is bound by the codes), § 15-10 (admissibility), and § 15-11 (breaches).

It should be noted that the original text of the codes has a series of errors. Only in the most obvious cases has any change been made to the wording, but the punctuation, use of case, use of number and paragraphing have been amended with a view to injecting consistency and intelligibility.

## (2) Stop and search

### A. CODE OF PRACTICE FOR THE EXERCISE BY: POLICE OFFICERS OF STATUTORY POWERS OF STOP AND SEARCH; POLICE OFFICERS AND POLICE STAFF OF REQUIREMENTS TO RECORD PUBLIC ENCOUNTERS

#### Commencement—transitional arrangements

This code applies to any search by a police officer and the recording of public encounters taking place after 00.00 on 27 October 2013.

#### A:1.0 General

A-2    A:1.01 This code of practice must be readily available at all police stations for consultation by police officers, police staff, detained persons and members of the public.

A:1.02 The notes for guidance included are not provisions of this code, but are guidance to police officers and others about its application and interpretation. Provisions in the annexes to the code are provisions of this code.

A:1.03 This code governs the exercise by police officers of statutory powers to search a person or a vehicle without first making an arrest. The main stop and search powers to which this code applies are set out in Annex A, but that list should not be regarded as definitive [see *Note 1*]. In addition, it covers requirements on police officers and police staff to record encounters not governed by statutory powers. This code does not apply to:

(a) the powers of stop and search under:
    (i) the Aviation Security Act 1982, s.27(2), and
    (ii) the Police and Criminal Evidence Act 1984, s.6(1) (which relates specifically to powers of constables employed by statutory undertakers on the premises of the statutory undertakers);

(b) searches carried out for the purposes of examination under Schedule 7 to the Terrorism Act 2000 and to which the code of practice issued under paragraph 6 of Schedule 14 to the Terrorism Act 2000 applies;

(c) the powers to search persons and vehicles and to stop and search in specified locations to which the code of practice issued under section 47AB of the Terrorism Act 2000 applies.

#### A:1 Principles governing stop and search

A-3    A:1.1 Powers to stop and search must be used fairly, responsibly, with respect for people being searched and without unlawful discrimination. Under the Equality Act 2010, s.149, when police officers are carrying out their functions, they also have a duty to have due regard to the need to eliminate unlawful discrimination, harassment and victimisation, to advance equality of opportunity between people who share a relevant protected characteristic and people who do not share it, and to take steps to foster good relations between those persons. [See *Notes 1* and *1A*.]

A:1.2 The intrusion on the liberty of the person stopped or searched must be brief and detention for the purposes of a search must take place at or near the location of the stop.

A:1.3 If these fundamental principles are not observed the use of powers to stop and search may be drawn into question. Failure to use the powers in the proper manner reduces their effectiveness. Stop and search can play an important role in the detection and prevention of crime, and using the powers fairly makes them more effective.

A:1.4 The primary purpose of stop and search powers is to enable officers to allay or confirm suspicions about individuals without exercising their power of arrest. Officers may be required to justify the use or authorisation of such powers, in relation both to individual searches and the overall pattern of their activity in this regard, to their supervisory officers or in court. Any misuse of the powers is likely to be harmful to policing and lead to mistrust of the police. Officers must also be able to explain their actions to the member of the public searched. The misuse of these powers can lead to disciplinary action.

A:1.5 An officer must not search a person, even with his or her consent, where no power to search is applicable. Even where a person is prepared to submit to a search voluntarily, the person must not be searched unless the necessary legal power exists, and the search must be in accordance with the relevant power and the provisions of this code. The only exception, where an officer does not require a specific power, applies to searches of persons entering sports grounds or other premises carried out with their consent given as a condition of entry.

### A:2 **Explanation of powers to stop and search**

A:2.1 This code applies, subject to paragraph 1.03, to powers of stop and search as follows:  **A-4**

(a) powers which require reasonable grounds for suspicion, before they may be exercised; that articles unlawfully obtained or possessed are being carried [*sic*];

(b) authorised under section 60 of the Criminal Justice and Public Order Act 1994, based upon a reasonable belief that incidents involving serious violence may take place or that people are carrying dangerous instruments or offensive weapons within any locality in the police area, or that it is expedient to use the powers to find such instruments or weapons that have been used in incidents of serious violence;

(c) [*not used*];

(d) powers to search a person who has not been arrested in the exercise of a power to search premises (see Code B, para. 2.4); and

(e) the powers in Schedule 5 to the Terrorism Prevention and Investigation Measures (TPIM) Act 2011 to search an individual who has not been arrested, conferred by:

(i) paragraph 6(2)(a) at the time of serving a TPIM notice;

(ii) paragraph 8(2)(a) under a search warrant for compliance purposes; and

(iii) paragraph 10 for public safety purposes.

See paragraph 2.18A.

*Searches requiring reasonable grounds for suspicion*

A:2.2 Reasonable grounds for suspicion depend on the circumstances in each case. There must be  **A-5** an objective basis for that suspicion based on facts, information, and/or intelligence which are relevant to the likelihood of finding an article of a certain kind. Reasonable suspicion can never be supported on the basis of personal factors. It must rely on intelligence or information about, or some specific behaviour by the person concerned. For example, unless the police have a description of a suspect, a person's physical appearance (including any of the relevant "protected characteristics" set out in the Equality Act 2010 (see para. 1.1 and *Note 1A*)), or the fact that the person is known to have a previous conviction, cannot be used alone or in combination with each other, or in combination with any other factor, as the reason for searching that person. Reasonable suspicion cannot be based on generalisations or stereotypical images of certain groups or categories of people as more likely to be involved in criminal activity.

A:2.3 Reasonable suspicion can sometimes exist without specific information or intelligence and on the basis of the behaviour of a person. For example, if an officer encounters someone on the street at night who is obviously trying to hide something, the officer may (depending on the other surrounding circumstances) base such suspicion on the fact that this kind of behaviour is often linked to stolen or prohibited articles being carried.

A:2.4 However, reasonable suspicion should normally be linked to accurate and current intelligence or information, such as information describing an article being carried, a suspected offender, or a person who has been seen carrying a type of article known to have been stolen recently from premises in the area. Searches based on accurate and current intelligence or information are more likely to be effective. Targeting searches in a particular area at specified crime problems increases their effectiveness and minimises inconvenience to law-abiding members of the public. It also helps in justifying the use of searches both to those who are searched and to the public. This does not however prevent stop and search powers being exercised in other locations where such powers may be exercised and reasonable suspicion exists.

A:2.5 Searches are more likely to be effective, legitimate, and secure public confidence when reasonable suspicion is based on a range of factors. The overall use of these powers is more likely to be effective when up to date and accurate intelligence or information is communicated to officers and they are well-informed about local crime patterns.

A:2.6 Where there is reliable information or intelligence that members of a group or gang habitually carry knives unlawfully or weapons or controlled drugs, and wear a distinctive item of clothing or other means of identification to indicate their membership of the group or gang, that distinctive item of clothing or other means of identification may provide reasonable grounds to stop and search a person. [See *Note 9*.]

A:2.7 A police officer may have reasonable grounds to suspect that a person is in innocent possession of a stolen or prohibited article or other item for which the officer is empowered to search. In that case the officer may stop and search the person even though there would be no power of arrest.

A:2.8 [*Not used.*]

A:2.9 An officer who has reasonable grounds for suspicion may detain the person concerned in order to carry out a search. Before carrying out a search the officer may ask questions about the person's behaviour or presence in circumstances which gave rise to the suspicion. As a result of questioning the detained person, the reasonable grounds for suspicion necessary to detain that person may be confirmed or, because of a satisfactory explanation, be eliminated. [See *Notes 2* and *3.*] Questioning may also reveal reasonable grounds to suspect the possession of a different kind of unlawful article from that originally suspected. Reasonable grounds for suspicion however cannot be provided retrospectively by such questioning during a person's detention or by refusal to answer any questions put.

A:2.10 If, as a result of questioning before a search, or other circumstances which come to the attention of the officer, there cease to be reasonable grounds for suspecting that an article is being carried of a kind for which there is a power to stop and search, no search may take place. [See *Note 3.*] In the absence of any other lawful power to detain, the person is free to leave at will and must be so informed.

A:2.11 There is no power to stop or detain a person in order to find grounds for a search. Police officers have many encounters with members of the public which do not involve detaining people against their will. If reasonable grounds for suspicion emerge during such an encounter, the officer may search the person, even though no grounds existed when the encounter began. If an officer is detaining someone for the purpose of a search, he or she should inform the person as soon as detention begins.

*Searches authorised under section 60 of the Criminal Justice and Public Order Act 1994*

A:2.12 Authority for a constable in uniform to stop and search under section 60 of the Criminal Justice and Public Order Act 1994 may be given if the authorising officer reasonably believes:

(a) that incidents involving serious violence may take place in any locality in the officer's police area, and it is expedient to use these powers to prevent their occurrence;

(b) that persons are carrying dangerous instruments or offensive weapons without good reason in any locality in the officer's police area; or

(c) that an incident involving serious violence has taken place in the officer's police area, a dangerous incident or offensive weapon used in the incident is being carried by a person in any locality in that police area, and it is expedient to use these powers to find that instrument or weapon.

A:2.13 An authorisation under section 60 may only be given by an officer of the rank of inspector or above, in writing, or orally if paragraph 2.12(c) applies and it is not practicable to give the authorisation in writing. The authorisation (whether written or oral) must specify the grounds on which it was given, the locality in which the powers may be exercised and the period of time for which they are in force. The period authorised shall be no longer than appears reasonably necessary to prevent, or seek to prevent incidents of serious violence, or to deal with the problem of carrying dangerous instruments or offensive weapons. It may not exceed 24 hours. An oral authorisation given where paragraph 2.12(c) applies must be recorded in writing as soon as practicable. [See *Notes 10–13.*]

A:2.14 If an inspector gives an authorisation, he or she must, as soon as practicable, inform an officer of or above the rank of superintendent. This officer may direct that the authorisation shall be extended for a further 24 hours, if violence or the carrying of dangerous instruments or offensive weapons has occurred, or is suspected to have occurred, and the continued use of the powers is considered necessary to prevent or deal with further such activity. That direction must also be given in writing at the time or as soon as practicable afterwards. [See *Note 12.*]

A:2.14A The selection of persons and vehicles under section 60 to be stopped and, if appropriate, searched should reflect an objective assessment of the nature of the incident or weapon in question and the individuals and vehicles thought likely to be associated with that incident or those weapons [see *Notes 10* and *11*]. The powers must not be used to stop and search persons and vehicles for reasons unconnected with the purpose of the authorisation. When selecting persons and vehicles to be stopped in response to a specific threat or incident, officers must take care not to discriminate unlawfully against anyone on the grounds of any of the protected characteristics set out in the Equality Act 2010 (see paragraph 1.1).

A:2.14B The driver of a vehicle which is stopped under section 60 and any person who is searched under section 60 are entitled to a written statement to that effect if they apply within twelve months from the day the vehicle was stopped or the person was searched. This statement is a record which states that the vehicle was stopped or (as the case may be) that the person was searched under section 60 and it may form part of the search record or be supplied as a separate record.

*Powers to require removal of face coverings*

A:2.15 Section 60AA of the Criminal Justice and Public Order Act 1994 also provides a power to **A-6**
demand the removal of disguises. The officer exercising the power must reasonably believe that
someone is wearing an item wholly or mainly for the purpose of concealing identity. There is also a
power to seize such items where the officer believes that a person intends to wear them for this
purpose. There is no power to stop and search for disguises. An officer may seize any such item
which is discovered when exercising a power of search for something else, or which is being carried,
and which the officer reasonably believes is intended to be used for concealing anyone's identity. This
power can only be used if an authorisation given under section 60, or under section 60AA, is in
force. [See *Note 4.*]

A:2.16 Authority under section 60AA for a constable in uniform to require the removal of disguises
and to seize them may be given if the authorising officer reasonably believes that activities may take
place in any locality in the officer's police area that are likely to involve the commission of offences
and it is expedient to use these powers to prevent or control these activities.

A:2.17 An authorisation under section 60AA may only be given by an officer of the rank of inspector or above, in writing, specifying the grounds on which it was given, the locality in which the powers may be exercised and the period of time for which they are in force. The period authorised shall
be no longer than appears reasonably necessary to prevent, or seek to prevent the commission of
offences. It may not exceed 24 hours. [See *Notes 10–13.*]

A:2.18 An inspector who gives an authorisation must, as soon as practicable, inform an officer of or
above the rank of superintendent. This officer may direct that the authorisation shall be extended for
a further 24 hours, if crimes have been committed, or are suspected to have been committed, and
the continued use of the powers is considered necessary to prevent or deal with further such activity.
This direction must also be given in writing at the time or as soon as practicable afterwards. [See *Note
12.*]

As to this paragraph, see, *ante*, A-1 in relation to the effect of S.I. 2011 No. 631.

*Searches under Schedule 5 to the Terrorism Prevention and Investigation Measures Act 2011*

A:2.18A Paragraph 3 of Schedule 5 to the TPIM Act 2011 allows a constable to detain an individual **A-7**
to be searched under the following powers:
  (i) paragraph 6(2)(a) when a TPIM notice is being, or has just been, served on the individual
      for the purpose of ascertaining whether there is anything on the individual that
      contravenes measures specified in the notice;
  (ii) paragraph 8(2)(a) in accordance with a warrant to search the individual issued by a justice
       of the peace in England and Wales, a sheriff in Scotland or a lay magistrate in Northern
       Ireland who is satisfied that a search is necessary for the purpose of determining whether
       an individual in respect of whom a TPIM notice is in force is complying with measures
       specified in the notice (see para. 2.20); and
  (iii) paragraph 10 to ascertain whether an individual in respect of whom a TPIM notice is in
        force is in possession of anything that could be used to threaten or harm any person.
See paragraph 2.1(e).

A:2.19 The exercise of the powers mentioned in paragraph 2.18A does not require the constable
to have reasonable grounds to suspect that the individual:
  (a) has been, or is, contravening any of the measures specified in the TPIM notice; or
  (b) has on them anything which:
    • in the case of the power in sub-paragraph (i), contravenes measures specified in the
      TPIM notice;
    • in the case of the power in sub-paragraph (ii) is not complying with measures specified
      in the TPIM notice; or
    • in the case of the power in sub-paragraph (iii), could be used to threaten or harm any
      person.

A:2.20 A search of an individual on warrant under the power mentioned in paragraph 2.18A(ii)
must carried [*sic*] out within 28 days of the issue of the warrant and:
    • the individual may be searched on one occasion only within that period;
    • the search must take place at a reasonable hour unless it appears that this would frustrate
      the purposes of the search.

A:2.21–2.25 [*Not used.*]

A:2.26 The powers under Schedule 5 only allow a constable to conduct a search of an individual
only for specified purposes relating to a TPIM notice as set out above. However, anything found may

be seized and retained if there are reasonable grounds for believing that it is or it contains evidence of any offence for use at a trial for that offence or to prevent it being concealed, lost, damaged, altered, or destroyed. However, this would not prevent a search being carried out under other search powers if, in the course of exercising these powers, the officer formed reasonable grounds for suspicion.

*Powers to search in the exercise of a power to search premises*

A:2.27 The following powers to search premises also authorise the search of a person, not under arrest, who is found on the premises during the course of the search:

    (a) section 139B of the Criminal Justice Act 1988 under which a constable may enter school premises and search the premises and any person on those premises for any bladed or pointed article or offensive weapon;

    (b) under a warrant issued under section 23(3) of the Misuse of Drugs Act 1971 to search premises for drugs or documents but only if the warrant specifically authorises the search of persons found on the premises; and

    (c) under a search warrant or order issued under paragraph 1, 3 or 11 of Schedule 5 to the Terrorism Act 2000 to search premises and any person found there for material likely to be of substantial value to a terrorist investigation.

A:2.28 Before the power under section 139B of the Criminal Justice Act 1988 may be exercised, the constable must have reasonable grounds to suspect that an offence under section 139A or 139AA of the Criminal Justice Act 1988 (having a bladed or pointed article or offensive weapon on school premises) has been or is being committed. A warrant to search premises and persons found therein may be issued under section 23(3) of the Misuse of Drugs Act 1971 if there are reasonable grounds to suspect that controlled drugs or certain documents are in the possession of a person on the premises.

A:2.29 The powers in paragraph 2.27 do not require prior specific grounds to suspect that the person to be searched is in possession of an item for which there is an existing power to search. However, it is still necessary to ensure that the selection and treatment of those searched under these powers is based upon objective factors connected with the search of the premises, and not upon personal prejudice.

### A:3 Conduct of searches

A:3.1 All stops and searches must be carried out with courtesy, consideration and respect for the person concerned. This has a significant impact on public confidence in the police. Every reasonable effort must be made to minimise the embarrassment that a person being searched may experience. [See *Note 4*.]

A:3.2 The co-operation of the person to be searched must be sought in every case, even if the person initially objects to the search. A forcible search may be made only if it has been established that the person is unwilling to co-operate or resists. Reasonable force may be used as a last resort if necessary to conduct a search or to detain a person or vehicle for the purposes of a search.

As to this paragraph, see *James v. DPP* (§ 15-41 in the main work).

A:3.3 The length of time for which a person or vehicle may be detained must be reasonable and kept to a minimum. Where the exercise of the power requires reasonable suspicion, the thoroughness and extent of a search must depend on what is suspected of being carried, and by whom. If the suspicion relates to a particular article which is seen to be slipped into a person's pocket, then, in the absence of other grounds for suspicion or an opportunity for the article to be moved elsewhere, the search must be confined to that pocket. In the case of a small article which can readily be concealed, such as a drug, and which might be concealed anywhere on the person, a more extensive search may be necessary. In the case of searches mentioned in paragraph 2.1(b) and (d), which do not require reasonable grounds for suspicion, officers may make any reasonable search to look for items for which they are empowered to search. [See *Note 5*.]

A:3.4 The search must be carried out at or near the place where the person or vehicle was first detained. [See *Note 6*.]

A:3.5 There is no power to require a person to remove any clothing in public other than an outer coat, jacket or gloves, except under section 60AA of the Criminal Justice and Public Order Act 1994 (which empowers a constable to require a person to remove any item worn to conceal identity). [See *Notes 4* and *6*.] A search in public of a person's clothing which has not been removed must be restricted to superficial examination of outer garments. This does not, however, prevent an officer from placing his or her hand inside the pockets of the outer clothing, or feeling round the inside of collars, socks and shoes if this is reasonably necessary in the circumstances to look for the object of the search or to remove and examine any item reasonably suspected to be the object of the search.

For the same reasons, subject to the restrictions on the removal of headgear, a person's hair may also be searched in public (see paragraphs 3.1 and 3.3).

A:3.6 Where on reasonable grounds it is considered necessary to conduct a more thorough search (*e.g.* by requiring a person to take off a T-shirt), this must be done out of public view, for example, in a police van unless paragraph 3.7 applies, or police station if there is one nearby. [See *Note 6*.] Any search involving the removal of more than an outer coat, jacket, gloves, headgear or footwear, or any other item concealing identity, may only be made by an officer of the same sex as the person searched and may not be made in the presence of anyone of the opposite sex unless the person being searched specifically requests it. [See Code C, Annex L and *Notes 4* and 7.]

A:3.7 Searches involving exposure of intimate parts of the body must not be conducted as a routine extension of a less thorough search, simply because nothing is found in the course of the initial search. Searches involving exposure of intimate parts of the body may be carried out only at a nearby police station or other nearby location which is out of public view (but not a police vehicle). These searches must be conducted in accordance with paragraph 11 of Annex A to Code C except that an intimate search mentioned in paragraph 11(f) of Annex A to Code C may not be authorised or carried out under any stop and search powers. The other provisions of Code C do not apply to the conduct and recording of searches of persons detained at police stations in the exercise of stop and search powers. [See *Note 7*.]

*Steps to be taken prior to a search*

A:3.8 Before any search of a detained person or attended vehicle takes place the officer must take reasonable steps, if not in uniform (see paragraph 3.9), to show their warrant card to the person to be searched or in charge of the vehicle to be searched and whether or not in uniform, to give that person the following information:　　**A-10**

(a) that they are being detained for the purposes of a search;
(b) the officer's name (except in the case of enquiries linked to the investigation of terrorism, or otherwise where the officer reasonably believes that giving their name might put them in danger, in which case a warrant or other identification number shall be given) and the name of the police station to which the officer is attached;
(c) the legal search power which is being exercised; and
(d) a clear explanation of:
   (i) the object of the search in terms of the article or articles for which there is a power to search; and
   (ii) in the case of:
     • the power under section 60 of the Criminal Justice and Public Order Act 1994 (see para. 2.1(b)), the nature of the power, the authorisation and the fact that it has been given;
     • the powers under Schedule 5 to the Terrorism Prevention and Investigation Measures Act 2011 (see paras 2.1(e) and 2.18A):
      – the fact that a TPIM notice is in force or (in the case of para. 6(2)(a)) that a TPIM notice is being served;
      – the nature of the power being exercised (for a search under para. 8 of Schedule 5, the warrant must be produced and the person provided with a copy of it);
     • all other powers requiring reasonable suspicion (see para. 2.1(a)), the grounds for that suspicion;
(e) that they are entitled to a copy of the record of the search if one is made (see section 4 below) if they ask within 3 months from the date of the search and:
   (i) if they are not arrested and taken to a police station as a result of the search and it is practicable to make the record on the spot, that immediately after the search is completed they will be given, if they request, either:
     • a copy of the record, or
     • receipt which explains how they can obtain a copy of the full record or access to an electronic copy of the record; or
   (ii) if they are arrested and taken to a police station as a result of the search, that the record will be made at the station as part of their custody record and they will be given, if they request, a copy of their custody record which includes a record of the search as soon as practicable whilst they are at the station. [See *Note 16*.]

A:3.9 Stops and searches under the power mentioned in paragraph 2.1(b) may be undertaken only by a constable in uniform.

A:3.10 The person should also be given information about police powers to stop and search and the individual's rights in these circumstances.

A:3.11 If the person to be searched, or in charge of a vehicle to be searched, does not appear to understand what is being said, or there is any doubt about the person's ability to understand English, the officer must take reasonable steps to bring information regarding the person's rights and any relevant provisions of this code to his or her attention. If the person is deaf or cannot understand English and is accompanied by someone, then the officer must try to establish whether that person can interpret or otherwise help the officer to give the required information.

### A:4 Recording requirements

*(a) Searches which do not result in an arrest*

A:4.1 When an officer carries out a search in the exercise of any power to which this code applies and the search does not result in the person searched or person in charge of the vehicle searched being arrested and taken to a police station, a record must be made of it, electronically or on paper, unless there are exceptional circumstances which make this wholly impracticable (*e.g.* in situations involving public disorder or when the recording officer's presence is urgently required elsewhere). If a record is to be made, the officer carrying out the search must make the record on the spot unless this is not practicable, in which case the officer must make the record as soon as practicable after the search is completed. [See *Note 16.*]

A:4.2 If the record is made at the time, the person who has been searched or who is in charge of the vehicle that has been searched must be asked if they want a copy and if they do, they must be given immediately, either:

- a copy of the record, or
- a receipt which explains how they can obtain a copy of the full record or access to an electronic copy of the record.

A:4.2A An officer is not required to provide a copy of the full record or a receipt at the time if they are called to an incident of higher priority. [See *Note 21.*]

*(b) Searches which result in an arrest*

A:4.2B If a search in the exercise of any power to which this code applies results in a person being arrested and taken to a police station, the officer carrying out the search is responsible for ensuring that a record of the search is made as part of their custody record. The custody officer must then ensure that the person is asked if they want a copy of the record and if they do, that they are given a copy as soon as practicable. [See *Note 16.*]

*(c) Record of search*

A:4.3 The record of a search must always include the following information:

(a) a note of the self-defined ethnicity, and if different, the ethnicity as perceived by the officer making the search, of the person searched or of the person in charge of the vehicle searched (as the case may be) [see *Note 18*];

(b) the date, time and place the person or vehicle was searched [see *Note 6*];

(c) the object of the search in terms of the article or articles for which there is a power to search;

(d) in the case of:

- the power under section 60 of the Criminal Justice and Public Order Act 1994 (see paragraph 2.1(b)), the nature of the power, the authorisation and the fact that it has been given [see *Note 17*];

- the powers under Schedule 5 to the Terrorism Prevention and Investigation Measures Act 2011 (see paras 2.1(e) and 2.18A):

  – the fact that a TPIM notice is in force or (in the case of para. 6(2)(a)) that a TPIM notice is being served;

  – the nature of the power, and

  – for a search under paragraph 8, the date the search warrant was issued, the fact that the warrant was produced and a copy of it provided and the warrant must also be endorsed by the constable executing it to state whether anything was found and whether anything was seized, and

- all other powers requiring reasonable suspicion (see para. 2.1(a)), the grounds for that suspicion;

(e) subject to paragraph 3.8(b), the identity of the officer carrying out the search. [See *Note 15.*]

A:4.3A For the purposes of completing the search record, there is no requirement to record the name, address and date of birth of the person searched or the person in charge of a vehicle which is searched and the person is under no obligation to provide this information.

A:4.4 Nothing in paragraph 4.3 requires the names of police officers to be shown on the search record or any other record required to be made under this code in the case of enquiries linked to the investigation of terrorism or otherwise where an officer reasonably believes that recording names might endanger the officers. In such cases the record must show the officers' warrant or other identification number and duty station.

A:4.5 A record is required for each person and each vehicle searched. However, if a person is in a vehicle and both are searched, and the object and grounds of the search are the same, only one record need be completed. If more than one person in a vehicle is searched, separate records for each search of a person must be made. If only a vehicle is searched, the self-defined ethnic background of the person in charge of the vehicle must be recorded, unless the vehicle is unattended.

A:4.6 The record of the grounds for making a search must, briefly but informatively, explain the reason for suspecting the person concerned, by reference to the person's behaviour and/or other circumstances.

A:4.7 Where officers detain an individual with a view to performing a search, but the need to search is eliminated as a result of questioning the person detained, a search should not be carried out and a record is not required. [See paragraph 2.10, *Notes 3* and *22A.*]

A:4.8 After searching an unattended vehicle, or anything in or on it, an officer must leave a notice in it (or on it, if things on it have been searched without opening it) recording the fact that it has been searched.

A:4.9 The notice must include the name of the police station to which the officer concerned is attached and state where a copy of the record of the search may be obtained and how (if applicable) an electronic copy may be accessed and where any application for compensation should be directed.

A:4.10 The vehicle must if practicable be left secure.

*Recording of encounters not governed by statutory powers*

A:4.11 [*Not used.*]

A:4.12 There is no national requirement for an officer who requests a person in a public place to account for themselves, *i.e.* their actions, behaviour, presence in an area or possession of anything, to make any record of the encounter or to give the person a receipt. [See *Notes 22A* and *22B.*]

**A:5  Monitoring and supervising the use of stop and search powers**

A:5.1 Supervising officers must monitor the use of stop and search powers and should consider in particular whether there is any evidence that they are being exercised on the basis of stereotyped images or inappropriate generalisations. Supervising officers should satisfy themselves that the practice of officers under their supervision in stopping, searching and recording is fully in accordance with this code. Supervisors must also examine whether the records reveal any trends or patterns which give cause for concern, and if so take appropriate action to address this.     **A-12**

A:5.2 Senior officers with area or force-wide responsibilities must also monitor the broader use of stop and search powers and, where necessary, take action at the relevant level.

A:5.3 Supervision and monitoring must be supported by the compilation of comprehensive statistical records of stops and searches at force, area and local level. Any apparently disproportionate use of the powers by particular officers or groups of officers or in relation to specific sections of the community should be identified and investigated.

A:5.4 In order to promote public confidence in the use of the powers, forces in consultation with police and crime commissioners must make arrangements for the records to be scrutinised by representatives of the community, and to explain the use of the powers at a local level. [See *Note 19.*]

*Notes for Guidance*

*Officers exercising stop and search powers*

A:1 *This code does not affect the ability of an officer to speak to or question a person in the ordinary course of*     **A-13**
*the officer's duties without detaining the person or exercising any element of compulsion. It is not the purpose of the code to prohibit such encounters between the police and the community with the co-operation of the person concerned and neither does it affect the principle that all citizens have a duty to help police officers to prevent crime and discover offenders. This is a civic rather than a legal duty; but when a police officer is trying to discover*

*whether, or by whom, an offence has been committed he or she may question any person from whom useful information might be obtained, subject to the restrictions imposed by Code C. A person's unwillingness to reply does not alter this entitlement, but in the absence of a power to arrest, or to detain in order to search, the person is free to leave at will and cannot be compelled to remain with the officer.*

A:1A *In paragraphs 1.1 and 2.2, "relevant protected characteristic" includes: age, disability, gender reassignment, pregnancy and maternity, race, religion/belief, sex and sexual orientation.*

A:2 *In some circumstances preparatory questioning may be unnecessary, but in general a brief conversation or exchange will be desirable not only as a means of avoiding unsuccessful searches, but to explain the grounds for the stop/search, to gain cooperation and reduce any tension there might be surrounding the stop/ search.*

A:3 *Where a person is lawfully detained for the purpose of a search, but no search in the event takes place, the detention will not thereby have been rendered unlawful.*

A:4 *Many people customarily cover their heads or faces for religious reasons—for example, Muslim women, Sikh men, Sikh or Hindu women, or Rastafarian men or women. A police officer cannot order the removal of a head or face covering except where there is reason to believe that the item is being worn by the individual wholly or mainly for the purpose of disguising identity, not simply because it disguises identity. Where there may be religious sensitivities about ordering the removal of such an item, the officer should permit the item to be removed out of public view. Where practicable, the item should be removed in the presence of an officer of the same sex as the person and out of sight of anyone of the opposite sex (see Code C, Annex L).*

A:5 *A search of a person in public should be completed as soon as possible.*

A:6 *A person may be detained under a stop and search power at a place other than where the person was first detained, only if that place, be it a police station or elsewhere, is nearby. Such a place should be located within a reasonable travelling distance using whatever mode of travel (on foot or by car) is appropriate. This applies to all searches under stop and search powers, whether or not they involve the removal of clothing or exposure of intimate parts of the body (see paragraphs 3.6 and 3.7) or take place in or out of public view. It means, for example, that a search under the stop and search power in section 23 of the Misuse of Drugs Act 1971 which involves the compulsory removal of more than a person's outer coat, jacket or gloves cannot be carried out unless a place which is both nearby the place they were first detained and out of public view, is available. If a search involves exposure of intimate parts of the body and a police station is not nearby, particular care must be taken to ensure that the location is suitable in that it enables the search to be conducted in accordance with the requirements of paragraph 11 of Annex A to Code C.*

A:7 *A search in the street itself should be regarded as being in public for the purposes of paragraphs 3.6 and 3.7 above, even though it may be empty at the time a search begins. Although there is no power to require a person to do so, there is nothing to prevent an officer from asking a person voluntarily to remove more than an outer coat, jacket or gloves in public.*

A:8 [Not used.]

A:9 *Other means of identification might include jewellery, insignias, tattoos or other features which are known to identify members of the particular gang or group.*

*Authorising officers*

A:10 *The powers under section 60 are separate from and additional to the normal stop and search powers which require reasonable grounds to suspect an individual of carrying an offensive weapon (or other article). Their overall purpose is to prevent serious violence and the widespread carrying of weapons which might lead to persons being seriously injured by disarming potential offenders or finding weapons that have been used in circumstances where other powers would not be sufficient. They should not therefore be used to replace or circumvent the normal powers for dealing with routine crime problems. A particular example might be an authorisation to prevent serious violence or the carrying of offensive weapons at a sports event by rival team supporters when the expected general appearance and age range of those likely to be responsible, alone, would not be sufficiently distinctive to support reasonable suspicion (see paragraph 2.6). The purpose of the powers under section 60AA is to prevent those involved in intimidatory or violent protests using face coverings to disguise identity.*

A:11 *Authorisations under section 60 require a reasonable belief on the part of the authorising officer. This must have an objective basis, for example: intelligence or relevant information such as a history of antagonism and violence between particular groups; previous incidents of violence at, or connected with, particular events or locations; a significant increase in knife-point robberies in a limited area; reports that individuals are regularly carrying weapons in a particular locality; information following an incident in which weapons were used about where the weapons might be found or in the case of section 60AA previous incidents of crimes being committed while wearing face coverings to conceal identity.*

A:12 *It is for the authorising officer to determine the period of time during which the powers mentioned in paragraph 2.1(b) may be exercised. The officer should set the minimum period he or she considers necessary to deal with the risk of violence, the carrying of knives or offensive weapons, or to find dangerous instruments or weapons that have been used. A direction to extend the period authorised under the powers mentioned in paragraph 2.1(b) may be given only once. Thereafter further use of the powers requires a new authorisation.*

A:13 *It is for the authorising officer to determine the geographical area in which the use of the powers is to be authorised. In doing so the officer may wish to take into account factors such as the nature and venue of the anticipated incident or the incident which has taken place, the number of people who may be in the immediate area of that incident, their access to surrounding areas and the anticipated or actual level of violence. The officer should not set a geographical area which is wider than that he or she believes necessary for the purpose of preventing anticipated violence, the carrying of knives or offensive weapons, or for finding a dangerous instrument or weapon that has been used or, in the case of section 60AA, the prevention of commission of offences. It is particularly important to ensure that constables exercising such powers are fully aware of where they may be used. If the area specified is smaller than the whole force area, the officer giving the authorisation should specify either the streets which form the boundary of the area or a divisional boundary within the force area. If the power is to be used in response to a threat or incident that straddles police force areas, an officer from each of the forces concerned will need to give an authorisation.*

A:14 [Not used.]

*Recording*

A:15 *Where a stop and search is conducted by more than one officer the identity of all the officers engaged in the search must be recorded on the record. Nothing prevents an officer who is present but not directly involved in searching from completing the record during the course of the encounter.* **A-15**

A:16 *When the search results in the person searched or in charge of a vehicle which is searched being arrested, the requirement to make the record of the search as part of the person's custody record does not apply if the person is granted "street bail" after arrest (see section 30A of PACE) to attend a police station and is not taken in custody to the police station. An arrested person's entitlement to a copy of the search record which is made as part of their custody record does not affect their entitlement to a copy of their custody record or any other provisions of PACE Code C section 2 (custody records).*

A:17 *It is important for monitoring purposes to specify when authority is given for exercising the stop and search power under section 60 of the Criminal Justice and Public Order Act 1994.*

A:18 *Officers should record the self-defined ethnicity of every person stopped according to the categories used in the 2001 census question listed in Annex B. The person should be asked to select one of the five main categories representing broad ethnic groups and then a more specific cultural background from within this group. The ethnic classification should be coded for recording purposes using the coding system in Annex B. An additional "Not stated" box is available but should not be offered to respondents explicitly. Officers should be aware and explain to members of the public, especially where concerns are raised, that this information is required to obtain a true picture of stop and search activity and to help improve ethnic monitoring, tackle discriminatory practice, and promote effective use of the powers. If the person gives what appears to the officer to be an "incorrect" answer (e.g. a person who appears to be white states that they are black), the officer should record the response that has been given and then record their own perception of the person's ethnic background by using the PNC classification system. If the "Not stated" category is used the reason for this must be recorded on the form.*

A:19 *Arrangements for public scrutiny of records should take account of the right to confidentiality of those stopped and searched. Anonymised forms and/or statistics generated from records should be the focus of the examinations by members of the public.*

A:20 [Not used.]

A:21 *In situations where it is not practicable to provide a written copy of the record or immediate access to an electronic copy of the record or a receipt of the search at the time (see paragraph 4.2A above), the officer should consider giving the person details of the station which they may attend for a copy of the record. A receipt may take the form of a simple business card which includes sufficient information to locate the record should the person ask for copy [sic], for example, the date and place of the search, and a reference number or the name of the officer who carried out the search (unless paragraph 4.4 applies).*

A:22 [Not used.]

A:22A *Where there are concerns which make it necessary to monitor any local disproportionality, forces have discretion to direct officers to record the self-defined ethnicity of persons they request to account for themselves in a public place or who they detain with a view to searching but do not search. Guidance should be provided locally and efforts made to minimise the bureaucracy involved. Records should be closely monitored and supervised in line with paragraphs 5.1 to 5.4, and forces can suspend or re-instate recording of these encounters as appropriate.*

A:22B *A person who is asked to account for themselves should, if they request, be given information about how they can report their dissatisfaction about how they have been treated.*

*Definition of offensive weapon*

A:23 *"Offensive weapon" is defined as any article made or adapted for use for causing injury to the person, or intended by the person having it with him for such use or by someone else. There are three categories of offensive weapons: those made for causing injury to the person; those adapted for such a purpose; and those not so made or adapted, but carried with the intention of causing injury to the person. A firearm, as defined by section 57 of the Firearms Act 1968, would fall within the definition of offensive weapon if any of the criteria above apply.*

## ANNEX A

### Summary of main stop and search powers to which Code A applies

This table relates to stop and search powers only. Individual statutes below may contain other police powers of entry, search and seizure.

| Power | Object of search | Extent of Search | Where Exercisable |
|---|---|---|---|
| **Unlawful articles general** | | | |
| 1. Public Stores Act 1875, s.6 | HM Stores stolen or unlawfully obtained | Persons, vehicles and vessels | Anywhere where the constabulary powers are exercisable |
| 2. Firearms Act 1968, s.47 | Firearms | Persons and vehicles | A public place, or anywhere in the case of reasonable suspicion of offences of carrying rearms with criminal intent or trespassing with rearms |
| 3. Misuse of Drugs Act 1971, s.23 | Controlled drugs | Persons and vehicles | Anywhere |
| 4. Customs and Excise Management Act 1979, s.163 | Goods: (a) on which duty has not been paid; (b) being unlawfully removed, imported or exported; (c) otherwise liable to forfeiture to HM Revenue and Customs | Vehicles and vessels only | Anywhere |
| 5. Aviation Security Act 1982, s.27(1) | Stolen or unlawfully obtained goods | Airport employees and vehicles carrying airport employees or aircraft or any vehicle in a cargo area whether or not carrying an employee | Any designated airport |
| 6. Police and Criminal Evidence Act 1984, s.1 | Stolen goods; articles for use in certain Theft Act offences; offensive weapons, including bladed or sharply-pointed articles (except folding pocket knives with a bladed cutting edge not exceeding 3 inches); prohibited possession of a category 4 (display grade) rework, any person under 18 in possession of an adult rework in a public place. | Persons and vehicles | Where there is public access |
| | Criminal damage: articles made, adapted or intended for use in destroying or damaging property | Persons and vehicles | Where there is public access |

239

| Power | Object of search | Extent of Search | Where Exercisable |
|---|---|---|---|
| 7. Sporting Events (Control of Alcohol etc.) Act 1985, s.7 | Intoxicating liquor | Persons, coaches and trains | Designated sports grounds or coaches and trains travelling to or from a designated sporting event. |
| 8. Crossbows Act 1987, s.4 | Crossbows or parts of crossbows (except crossbows with a draw weight of less than 1.4 kilograms) | Persons and vehicles | Anywhere except dwellings |
| 9. Criminal Justice Act 1988 s.139B | Offensive weapons, bladed or sharply pointed article | Persons | School premises |
| **Evidence of game and wildlife offences** | | | |
| 10. Poaching Prevention Act 1862, s.2 | Game or poaching equipment | Persons and vehicles | A public place |
| 11. Deer Act 1991, s.12 | Evidence of offences under the Act | Persons and vehicles | Anywhere except dwellings |
| 12. Conservation of Seals Act 1970, s.4 | Seals or hunting equipment | Vehicles only | Anywhere |
| 13. Protection of Badgers Act 1992, s.11 | Evidence offences under the Act | Persons and vehicles | Anywhere |
| 14. Wildlife and Countryside Act 1981, s.19 | Evidence of wildlife offences | Persons and vehicles | Anywhere except dwellings |
| **Other** | | | |
| 15. Paragraphs 6 & 8 of Schedule 5 to the Terrorism Prevention and Investigation Measures Act 2011 | Anything that contravenes measures specied in a TPIM notice. | Persons in respect of whom a TPIM notice is being served or is in force | Anywhere |
| 16. Paragraph 10 of Schedule 5 to the Terrorism Prevention and Investigation Measures Act 2011 | Anything that could be used to threaten or harm any person. | Persons in respect of whom a TPIM notice is in force. | Anywhere |
| 17. [*Not used.*] | | | |
| 18. Paragraphs 7 and 8 of Schedule 7 to the Terrorism Act 2000 | Anything relevant to determining if a person being examined falls within section 40(1)(b) | Persons, vehicles, vessels *etc. (Note: these searches are subject to the code of practice and issued under paragraph 6 of Schedule 14 to the Terrorism Act 2000)* | Ports and airports |
| 19. Section 60 Criminal Justice and Public Order Act 1994 | Offensive weapons or dangerous instruments to prevent incidents of serious violence or to deal with the carrying of such items or nd such items which have been used in incidents of serious violence | Persons and vehicles | Anywhere within a locality authorised under subsection (1) |

**ANNEX B**

**Self-defined ethnic classification categories**

| | | |
|---|---|---|
| **White** | **W** | **A-17** |
| A. White—British | W1 | |
| B. White—Irish | W2 | |
| C. Any other White background | W9 | |
| **Mixed** | **M** | |
| D. White and Black Caribbean | M1 | |
| E. White and Black African | M2 | |
| F. White and Asian | M3 | |
| G. Any other Mixed background | M9 | |
| **Asian/ Asian—British** | **A** | |
| H. Asian—Indian | A1 | |
| I. Asian—Pakistani | A2 | |
| J. Asian—Bangladeshi | A3 | |
| K. Any other Asian background | A9 | |
| **Black / Black—British** | **B** | |
| L. Black—Caribbean | B1 | |
| M. Black African | B2 | |
| N. Any other Black background | B9 | |
| **Other** | **O** | |
| O. Chinese | O1 | |
| P. Any other | O9 | |
| **Not stated** | **NS** | |

Archbold
paragraph
numbers

A-17a

*Archbold's Criminal Pleading—2014 ed.*

A-17a

# ANNEX C

## Summary of powers of community support officers to search and seize

The following is a summary of the search and seizure powers that may be exercised by a community support officer (CSO) who has been designated with the relevant powers in accordance with Part 4 of the Police Reform Act 2002.

When exercising any of these powers, a CSO must have regard to any relevant provisions of this code, including section 3 governing the conduct of searches and the steps to be taken prior to a search.

**1.** [*Not used.*]

**2. Powers to search requiring the consent of the person and seizure**

A CSO may detain a person using reasonable force where necessary as set out in Part 1 of Schedule 4 to the Police Reform Act 2002. If the person has been lawfully detained, the CSO may search the person provided that person gives consent to such a search in relation to the following:

| Designation | Powers conferred | Object of Search | Extent of Search | Where Exercisable |
|---|---|---|---|---|
| Police Reform Act 2002, Schedule 4, paragraph 7A | (a) Criminal Justice and Police Act 2001, s.12(2) | (a) Alcohol or a container for alcohol | (a) Persons | (a) Designated public place |
| | (b) Confiscation of Alcohol (Young Persons) Act 1997, s.1 | (b) Alcohol | (b) Persons under 18 years old | (b) Public place |
| | (c) Children and Young Persons Act 1933, s.7(3) | (c) Tobacco or cigarette papers | (c) Persons under 16 years old and found smoking | (c) Public place |

**3. Powers to search not requiring the consent of the person and seizure**

A CSO may detain a person using reasonable force where necessary as set out in Part 1 of Schedule 4 to the Police Reform Act 2002. If the person has been lawfully detained, the CSO may search the person without the need for that person's consent in relation to the following:

| Designation | Power conferred | Object of Search | Extent of Search | Where Exercisable |
|---|---|---|---|---|
| Police Reform Act 2002, Schedule 4, paragraph 2A | Police and Criminal Evidence Act 1984, s.32 | (a) Objects that might be used to cause physical injury to the person or the CSO. (b) Items that might be used to assist escape. | Persons made subject to a requirement to wait. | Any place where the requirement to wait has been made. |

**4. Powers to seize without consent**

This power applies when drugs are found in the course of any search mentioned above.

| Designation | Power conferred | Object of Seizure | | Where Exercisable |
|---|---|---|---|---|
| Police Reform Act 2002, Schedule 4, paragraph 7B | Police Reform Act 2002, Schedule 4, paragraph 7B | Controlled drugs in a person's possession. | | Any place where the person is in possession of the drug. |

Annex D—Deleted
Annex E—Deleted

**ANNEX F**

**Establishing gender of persons for the purpose of searching**

See Code C, Annex L.                                                    **A-17b**

## (3) Search and seizure

The text that follows is of the version of the code that came into force on October 27, 2013: see    **A-18**
*ante*, Appendix A-1.

For authorities in relation to Code B, see, in particular, §§ 15-104 and 15-151 in the main
work.

**B. CODE OF PRACTICE FOR SEARCHES OF PREMISES BY POLICE OFFICERS AND THE
SEIZURE OF PROPERTY FOUND BY POLICE OFFICERS ON PERSONS OR PREMISES**

### Commencement—transitional arrangements

This code applies to applications for warrants made after 00.00 on 27 October 2013 and to    **A-19**
searches and seizures taking place after 00.00 on 27 October 2013.

### B:1 Introduction

B:1.1 This code of practice deals with police powers to:                        **A-20**
- search premises
- seize and retain property found on premises and persons.

B:1.1A These powers may be used to find:
- property and material relating to a crime
- wanted persons
- children who abscond from local authority accommodation where they have been
  remanded or committed by a court.

B:1.2 A justice of the peace may issue a search warrant granting powers of entry, search and
seizure, *e.g.* warrants to search for stolen property, drugs, firearms and evidence of serious offences.
Police also have powers without a search warrant. The main ones provided by the Police and
Criminal Evidence Act 1984 (PACE) include powers to search premises:
- to make an arrest
- after an arrest.

B:1.3 The right to privacy and respect for personal property are key principles of the Human
Rights Act 1998. Powers of entry, search and seizure should be fully and clearly justified before use
because they may significantly interfere with the occupier's privacy. Officers should consider if the
necessary objectives can be met by less intrusive means.

B:1.3A Powers to search and seize must be used fairly, responsibly, with respect for people who
occupy premises being searched or are in charge of property being seized and without unlawful
discrimination. Under the Equality Act 2010, s.149, when police officers are carrying out their functions, they also have a duty to have due regard to the need to eliminate unlawful discrimination,
harassment and victimisation, to advance equality of opportunity between people who share a
relevant protected characteristic and people who do not share it, and to take steps to foster good
relations between those persons. [See *Note 1A.*]

B:1.4 In all cases, police should therefore:
- exercise their powers courteously and with respect for persons and property
- only use reasonable force when this is considered necessary and proportionate to the
  circumstances.

B:1.5 If the provisions of PACE and this code are not observed, evidence obtained from a search
may be open to question.

*Notes for guidance*

B:1A *In paragraph 1.3A, "relevant protected characteristic" includes: age, disability, gender reassignment,
pregnancy and maternity, race, religion/belief, sex and sexual orientation.*

**B:2  General**

A-21 B:2.1 This code must be readily available at all police stations for consultation by:

- police officers
- police staff
- detained persons
- members of the public.

B:2.2 The *Notes for Guidance* included are not provisions of this code.

B:2.3 This code applies to searches of premises:

(a) by police for the purposes of an investigation into an alleged offence, with the occupier's consent, other than:
- routine scene of crime searches;
- calls to a fire or burglary made by or on behalf of an occupier or searches following the activation of fire or burglar alarms or discovery of insecure premises;
- searches when paragraph 5.4 applies;
- bomb threat calls;

(b) under powers conferred on police officers by PACE, ss.17, 18 and 32;

(c) undertaken in pursuance of search warrants issued to and executed by constables in accordance with PACE, ss.15 and 16 [see *Note 2A*];

(d) subject to paragraph 2.6, under any other power given to police to enter premises with or without a search warrant for any purpose connected with the investigation into an alleged or suspected offence. [See *Note 2B*.]

For the purposes of this code, "premises" as defined in PACE, s.23, includes any place, vehicle, vessel, aircraft, hovercraft, tent or movable structure and any offshore installation as defined in the Mineral Workings (Offshore Installations) Act 1971, s.1. [See *Note 2D*.]

B:2.4 A person who has not been arrested but is searched during a search of premises should be searched in accordance with Code A. [See *Note 2C*.]

B:2.5 This code does not apply to the exercise of a statutory power to enter premises or to inspect goods, equipment or procedures if the exercise of that power is not dependent on the existence of grounds for suspecting that an offence may have been committed and the person exercising the power has no reasonable grounds for such suspicion.

B:2.6 This code does not affect any directions or requirements of a search warrant, order or other power to search and seize lawfully exercised in England or Wales that any item or evidence seized under that warrant, order or power be handed over to a police force, court, tribunal, or other authority outside England or Wales. For example, warrants and orders issued in Scotland or Northern Ireland [see *Note 2B(f)*] and search warrants and powers provided for in sections 14 to 17 of the Crime (International Co-operation) Act 2003.

B:2.7 When this code requires the prior authority or agreement of an officer of at least inspector or superintendent rank, that authority may be given by a sergeant or chief inspector authorised to perform the functions of the higher rank under PACE, s.107.

B:2.8 Written records required under this code not made in the search record shall, unless otherwise specified, be made:

- in the recording officer's pocket book ("pocket book" includes any official report book issued to police officers), or
- on forms provided for the purpose.

B:2.9 Nothing in this code requires the identity of officers, or anyone accompanying them during a search of premises, to be recorded or disclosed:

(a) in the case of enquiries linked to the investigation of terrorism; or

(b) if officers reasonably believe recording or disclosing their names might put them in danger.

In these cases officers should use warrant or other identification numbers and the name of their police station. Police staff should use any identification number provided to them by the police force. [See *Note 2E*.]

B:2.10 The "officer in charge of the search" means the officer assigned specific duties and responsibilities under this code. Whenever there is a search of premises to which this code applies one officer must act as the officer in charge of the search. [See *Note 2F*.]

B:2.11 In this code:

(a) "designated person" means a person other than a police officer, designated under the Police Reform Act 2002, Pt 4 who has specified powers and duties of police officers conferred or imposed on them [see Note 2G];

(b) any reference to a police officer includes a designated person acting in the exercise or performance of the powers and duties conferred or imposed on them by their designation;

(c) a person authorised to accompany police officers or designated persons in the execution of a warrant has the same powers as a constable in the execution of the warrant and the search and seizure of anything related to the warrant. These powers must be exercised in the company and under the supervision of a police officer. [See *Note 3C.*]

B:2.12 If a power conferred on a designated person:

(a) allows reasonable force to be used when exercised by a police officer, a designated person exercising that power has the same entitlement to use force;

(b) includes power to use force to enter any premises, that power is not exercisable by that designated person except:

(i) in the company and under the supervision of a police officer; or

(ii) for the purpose of:

- saving life or limb; or
- preventing serious damage to property.

B:2.13 Designated persons must have regard to any relevant provisions of the codes of practice.

*Notes for guidance*

B:2A *PACE ss.15 and 16 apply to all search warrants issued to and executed by constables under any enact-* **A-22** *ment, e.g. search warrants issued by a:*

(a) *justice of the peace under the:*

- *Theft Act 1968, s.26—stolen property;*
- *Misuse of Drugs Act 1971, s.23—controlled drugs;*
- *PACE, s.8—evidence of an indictable offence;*
- *Terrorism Act 2000, Sched. 5, para. 1;*
- *Terrorism Prevention and Investigation Measures Act 2011, Sched. 5, para. 8(2)(b)— search of premises for compliance purposes (see para. 10.1);*

(b) *circuit judge under:*

- *PACE, Sched. 1;*
- *Terrorism Act 2000, Sched. 5, para. 11.*

B:2B *Examples of the other powers in paragraph 2.3(d) include:*

(a) *Road Traffic Act 1988, s.6E(1) giving police power to enter premises under section 6E(1) to:*

- *require a person to provide a specimen of breath; or*
- *arrest a person following:*
  - *a positive breath test;*
  - *failure to provide a specimen of breath;*

(b) *Transport and Works Act 1992, s.30(4) giving police powers to enter premises mirroring the powers in (a) in relation to specified persons working on transport systems to which the Act applies;*

(c) *Criminal Justice Act 1988, s.139B giving police power to enter and search school premises for offensive weapons, bladed or pointed articles;*

(d) *Terrorism Act 2000, Sched. 5, paras 3 and 15 empowering a superintendent in urgent cases to give written authority for police to enter and search premises for the purposes of a terrorist investigation;*

(e) *Explosives Act 1875, s.73(b) empowering a superintendent to give written authority for police to enter premises, examine and search them for explosives;*

(f) *search warrants and production orders or the equivalent issued in Scotland or Northern Ireland endorsed under the Summary Jurisdiction (Process) Act 1881 or the Petty Sessions (Ireland) Act 1851 respectively for execution in England and Wales;*

(g) *Terrorism Prevention and Investigation Measures Act 2011, Sched. 5, paras 5(1), 6(2)(b) and 7(2), searches relating to TPIM notices (see para. 10.1).*

B:2C *The Criminal Justice Act 1988, s.139B provides that a constable who has reasonable grounds to suspect an offence under the Criminal Justice Act 1988, s.139A or 139AA has or is being committed may enter school premises and search the premises and any persons on the premises for any bladed or pointed article or offensive weapon. Persons may be searched under a warrant issued under the Misuse of Drugs Act 1971, s.23(3) to search premises for drugs or documents only if the warrant specifically authorises the search of persons on the premises. Powers to search premises under certain terrorism provisions also authorise the search of persons on the premises, for example, under paragraphs 1, 2, 11 and 15 of Schedule 5 to the Terrorism Act 2000 and section 52 of the Anti-terrorism, Crime and Security Act 2001.*

B:2D *The Immigration Act 1971, Pt III and Sched. 2 gives immigration officers powers to enter and search premises, seize and retain property, with and without a search warrant. These are similar to the powers available to police under search warrants issued by a justice of the peace and without a warrant under PACE, ss.17, 18, 19 and 32 except they only apply to specified offences under the Immigration Act 1971 and immigration control powers. For certain types of investigations and enquiries these powers avoid the need for the Immigration Service to rely on police officers becoming directly involved. When exercising these powers, immigration officers are required by the Immigration and Asylum Act 1999, s.145 to have regard to this code's corresponding provisions. When immigration officers are dealing with persons or property at police stations, police officers should give appropriate assistance to help them discharge their specific duties and responsibilities.*

B:2E *The purpose of paragraph 2.9(b) is to protect those involved in serious organised crime investigations or arrests of particularly violent suspects when there is reliable information that those arrested or their associates may threaten or cause harm to the officers or anyone accompanying them during a search of premises. In cases of doubt, an officer of inspector rank or above should be consulted.*

B:2F *For the purposes of paragraph 2.10, the officer in charge of the search should normally be the most senior officer present. Some exceptions are:*

(a) *a supervising officer who attends or assists at the scene of a premises search may appoint an officer of lower rank as officer in charge of the search if that officer is:*
- *more conversant with the facts;*
- *a more appropriate officer to be in charge of the search;*

(b) *when all officers in a premises search are the same rank. The supervising officer if available, must make sure one of them is appointed officer in charge of the search, otherwise the officers themselves must nominate one of their number as the officer in charge;*

(c) *a senior officer assisting in a specialist role. This officer need not be regarded as having a general supervisory role over the conduct of the search or be appointed or expected to act as the officer in charge of the search.*

*Except in (c), nothing in this note diminishes the role and responsibilities of a supervisory officer who is present at the search or knows of a search taking place.*

B:2G *An officer of the rank of inspector or above may direct a designated investigating officer not to wear a uniform for the purposes of a specific operation.*

### B:3 Search warrants and production orders

#### (a) *Before making an application*

B:3.1 When information appears to justify an application, the officer must take reasonable steps to check the information is accurate, recent and not provided maliciously or irresponsibly. An application may not be made on the basis of information from an anonymous source if corroboration has not been sought. See *Note 3A*.

B:3.2 The officer shall ascertain as specifically as possible the nature of the articles concerned and their location.

B:3.3 The officer shall make reasonable enquiries to:
- (i) establish if:
  - anything is known about the likely occupier of the premises and the nature of the premises themselves;
  - the premises have been searched previously and how recently;
- (ii) obtain any other relevant information.

B:3.4 An application:

(a) to a justice of the peace for a search warrant or to a circuit judge for a search warrant or production order under PACE, Sched. 1 must be supported by a signed written authority from an officer of inspector rank or above; [Note: if the case is an urgent application to a justice of the peace and an inspector or above is not readily available, the next most senior officer on duty can give the written authority];

(b) to a circuit judge under the Terrorism Act 2000, Sched. 5 for:
- a production order;
- search warrant; or
- an order requiring an explanation of material seized or produced under such a warrant or production order,

must be supported by a signed written authority from an officer of superintendent rank or above.

B:3.5 Except in a case of urgency, if there is reason to believe a search might have an adverse effect on relations between the police and the community, the officer in charge shall consult the local police/community liaison officer:

- before the search; or
- in urgent cases, as soon as practicable after the search.

(b) *Making an application*

B:3.6 A search warrant application must be supported in writing, specifying:

(a) the enactment under which the application is made [see *Note 2A*];

(b) (i) whether the warrant is to authorise entry and search of:
- one set of premises; or
- if the application is under PACE, s.8, or Sched. 1, para. 12, more than one set of specified premises or all premises occupied or controlled by a specified person, and

(ii) the premises to be searched;

(c) the object of the search [see *Note 3B*];

(d) the grounds for the application, including, when the purpose of the proposed search is to find evidence of an alleged offence, an indication of how the evidence relates to the investigation;

(da) where the application is under PACE, s.8, or Sched. 1, para. 12 for a single warrant to enter and search:

(i) more than one set of specified premises, the officer must specify each set of premises which it is desired to enter and search;

(ii) all premises occupied or controlled by a specified person, the officer must specify:
- as many sets of premises which it is desired to enter and search as it is reasonably practicable to specify;
- the person who is in occupation or control of those premises and any others which it is desired to search;
- why it is necessary to search more premises than those which can be specified;
- why it is not reasonably practicable to specify all the premises which it is desired to enter and search;

(db) whether an application under PACE, s.8 is for a warrant authorising entry and search on more than one occasion, and if so, the officer must state the grounds for this and whether the desired number of entries authorised is unlimited or a specified maximum;

(e) that there are no reasonable grounds to believe the material to be sought, when making application to a:

(i) justice of the peace or a circuit judge consists of or includes items subject to legal privilege;

(ii) justice of the peace, consists of or includes excluded material or special procedure material;

[Note: this does not affect the additional powers of seizure in the Criminal Justice and Police Act 2001, Pt 2 covered in paragraph 7.7 [see *Note 3B*]];

(f) if applicable, a request for the warrant to authorise a person or persons to accompany the officer who executes the warrant [see *Note 3C*].

B:3.7 A search warrant application under PACE, Sched. 1, para. 12(a), shall if appropriate indicate why it is believed service of notice of an application for a production order may seriously prejudice the investigation. Applications for search warrants under the Terrorism Act 2000, Schedule 5, paragraph 11 must indicate why a production order would not be appropriate.

B:3.8 If a search warrant application is refused, a further application may not be made for those premises unless supported by additional grounds.

*Notes for guidance*

B:3A *The identity of an informant need not be disclosed when making an application, but the officer should be prepared to answer any questions the magistrate or judge may have about:*     **A-24'**
- *the accuracy of previous information from that source, and*
- *any other related matters.*

B:3B *The information supporting a search warrant application should be as specific as possible, particularly in relation to the articles or persons being sought and where in the premises it is suspected they may be found. The meaning of "items subject to legal privilege", "excluded material" and "special procedure material" are defined by PACE, ss.10, 11 and 14 respectively.*

B:3C *Under PACE, s.16(2), a search warrant may authorise persons other than police officers to accompany the constable who executes the warrant. This includes, e.g. any suitably qualified or skilled person or an expert in a particular field whose presence is needed to help accurately identify the material sought or to advise where certain evidence is most likely to be found and how it should be dealt with. It does not give them any right to force entry, but it gives them the right to be on the premises during the search and to search for or seize property without the occupier's permission.*

### B:4 Entry without warrant—particular powers

(a) *Making an arrest etc*

**A-25**    B:4.1 The conditions under which an officer may enter and search premises without a warrant are set out in PACE, s.17. It should be noted that this section does not create or confer any powers of arrest. See other powers in *Note 2B(a)*.

(b) *Search of premises where arrest takes place or the arrested person was immediately before arrest*

B:4.2 When a person has been arrested for an indictable offence, a police officer has power under PACE, s.32 to search the premises where the person was arrested or where the person was immediately before being arrested.

(c) *Search of premises occupied or controlled by the arrested person*

B:4.3 The specific powers to search premises which are occupied or controlled by a person arrested for an indictable offence are set out in PACE, s.18. They may not be exercised, except if section 18 (5) applies, unless an officer of inspector rank or above has given written authority. That authority should only be given when the authorising officer is satisfied that the premises are occupied or controlled by the arrested person and that the necessary grounds exist. If possible the authorising officer should record the authority on the Notice of Powers and Rights and, subject to paragraph 2.9, sign the notice. The record of the grounds for the search and the nature of the evidence sought as required by section 18(7) of the Act should be made in:

- the custody record if there is one, otherwise
- the officer's pocket book, or
- the search record.

### B:5 Search with consent

**A-26**    B:5.1 Subject to paragraph 5.4, if it is proposed to search premises with the consent of a person entitled to grant entry the consent must, if practicable, be given in writing on the Notice of Powers and Rights before the search. The officer must make any necessary enquiries to be satisfied the person is in a position to give such consent. [See *Notes 5A* and *5B*.]

B:5.2 Before seeking consent the officer in charge of the search shall state the purpose of the proposed search and its extent. This information must be as specific as possible, particularly regarding the articles or persons being sought and the parts of the premises to be searched. The person concerned must be clearly informed they are not obliged to consent, that any consent given can be withdrawn at any time, including before the search starts or while it is under way and anything seized may be produced in evidence. If at the time the person is not suspected of an offence, the officer shall say this when stating the purpose of the search.

B:5.3 An officer cannot enter and search or continue to search premises under paragraph 5.1 if consent is given under duress or withdrawn before the search is completed.

B:5.4 It is unnecessary to seek consent under paragraphs 5.1 and 5.2 if this would cause disproportionate inconvenience to the person concerned. [See *Note 5C*.]

*Notes for guidance*

**A-27**    B:5A *In a lodging house, hostel or similar accommodation, every reasonable effort should be made to obtain the consent of the tenant, lodger or occupier. A search should not be made solely on the basis of the landlord's consent.*

B:5B *If the intention is to search premises under the authority of a warrant or a power of entry and search without warrant, and the occupier of the premises co-operates in accordance with paragraph 6.4, there is no need to obtain written consent.*

B:5C *Paragraph 5.4 is intended to apply when it is reasonable to assume innocent occupiers would agree to, and expect, police to take the proposed action, e.g. if:*

- *a suspect has fled the scene of a crime or to evade arrest and it is necessary quickly to check surrounding gardens and readily accessible places to see if the suspect is hiding, or*
- *police have arrested someone in the night after a pursuit and it is necessary to make a brief check of gardens along the pursuit route to see if stolen or incriminating articles have been discarded.*

### B:6 Searching premises—general considerations

#### (a) *Time of searches*

B:6.1 Searches made under warrant must be made within three calendar months of the date the **A-28** warrant is issued or within the period specified in the enactment under which the warrant is issued if this is shorter.

B:6.2 Searches must be made at a reasonable hour unless this might frustrate the purpose of the search.

B:6.3 When the extent or complexity of a search mean it is likely to take a long time, the officer in charge of the search may consider using the seize and sift powers referred to in section 7.

B:6.3A A warrant under PACE, s.8 may authorise entry to and search of premises on more than one occasion if, on the application, the justice of the peace is satisfied that it is necessary to authorise multiple entries in order to achieve the purpose for which the warrant is issued. No premises may be entered or searched on any subsequent occasions without the prior written authority of an officer of the rank of inspector who is not involved in the investigation. All other warrants authorise entry on one occasion only.

B:6.3B Where a warrant under PACE, s.8, or Sched. 1, para. 12 authorises entry to and search of all premises occupied or controlled by a specified person, no premises which are not specified in the warrant may be entered and searched without the prior written authority of an officer of the rank of inspector who is not involved in the investigation.

#### (b) *Entry other than with consent*

B:6.4 The officer in charge of the search shall first try to communicate with the occupier, or any other person entitled to grant access to the premises, explain the authority under which entry is sought and ask the occupier to allow entry, unless:

    (i) the search premises are unoccupied;

    (ii) the occupier and any other person entitled to grant access are absent;

    (iii) there are reasonable grounds for believing that alerting the occupier or any other person entitled to grant access would frustrate the object of the search or endanger officers or other people.

B:6.5 Unless sub-paragraph 6.4(iii) applies, if the premises are occupied the officer, subject to paragraph 2.9, shall, before the search begins:

    (i) identify him or herself, show their warrant card (if not in uniform) and state the purpose of, and grounds for, the search; and

    (ii) identify and introduce any person accompanying the officer on the search (such persons should carry identification for production on request) and briefly describe that person's role in the process.

B:6.6 Reasonable and proportionate force may be used if necessary to enter premises if the officer in charge of the search is satisfied the premises are those specified in any warrant, or in exercise of the powers described in paragraph 4.1 to 4.3, and if:

    (i) the occupier or any other person entitled to grant access has refused entry;

    (ii) it is impossible to communicate with the occupier or any other person entitled to grant access; or

    (iii) any of the provisions of paragraph 6.4 apply.

#### (c) *Notice of powers and rights*

B:6.7 If an officer conducts a search to which this code applies the officer shall, unless it is **A-29** impracticable to do so, provide the occupier with a copy of a notice in a standard format:

    (i) specifying if the search is made under warrant, with consent, or in the exercise of the powers described in paragraphs 4.1 to 4.3. Note: the notice format shall provide for authority or consent to be indicated (see paragraphs 4.3 and 5.1);

    (ii) summarising the extent of the powers of search and seizure conferred by PACE and other relevant legislation as appropriate;

    (iii) explaining the rights of the occupier and the owner of the property seized;

    (iv) explaining compensation may be payable in appropriate cases for damages [*sic*] caused entering and searching premises, and giving the address to send a compensation application [see *Note 6A*]; and

    (v) stating this code is available at any police station.

B:6.8 If the occupier is:

    • present, copies of the notice and warrant shall, if practicable, be given to them before the

search begins, unless the officer in charge of the search reasonably believes this would frustrate the object of the search or endanger officers or other people;
- not present, copies of the notice and warrant shall be left in a prominent place on the premises or appropriate part of the premises and endorsed, subject to paragraph 2.9 with the name of the officer in charge of the search, the date and time of the search.

The warrant shall be endorsed to show this has been done.

### (d) *Conduct of searches*

B:6.9 Premises may be searched only to the extent necessary to achieve the purpose of the search, having regard to the size and nature of whatever is sought.

B:6.9A A search may not continue under:
- a warrant's authority once all the things specified in that warrant have been found;
- any other power once the object of that search has been achieved.

B:6.9B No search may continue once the officer in charge of the search is satisfied whatever is being sought is not on the premises [see *Note 6B*]. This does not prevent a further search of the same premises if additional grounds come to light supporting a further application for a search warrant or exercise or further exercise of another power. For example, when, as a result of new information, it is believed articles previously not found or additional articles are on the premises.

B:6.10 Searches must be conducted with due consideration for the property and privacy of the occupier and with no more disturbance than necessary. Reasonable force may be used only when necessary and proportionate because the co-operation of the occupier cannot be obtained or is insufficient for the purpose. [See *Note 6C*.]

B:6.11 A friend, neighbour or other person must be allowed to witness the search if the occupier wishes unless the officer in charge of the search has reasonable grounds for believing the presence of the person asked for would seriously hinder the investigation or endanger officers or other people. A search need not be unreasonably delayed for this purpose. A record of the action taken should be made on the premises search record including the grounds for refusing the occupier's request.

B:6.12 A person is not required to be cautioned prior to being asked questions that are solely necessary for the purpose of furthering the proper and effective conduct of a search, see Code C, paragraph 10.1(c). For example, questions to discover the occupier of specified premises, to find a key to open a locked drawer or cupboard or to otherwise seek co-operation during the search or to determine if a particular item is liable to be seized.

B:6.12A If questioning goes beyond what is necessary for the purpose of the exemption in Code C, the exchange is likely to constitute an interview as defined by Code C, paragraph 11.1A and would require the associated safeguards included in Code C, section 10.

### (e) *Leaving premises*

B:6.13 If premises have been entered by force, before leaving the officer in charge of the search must make sure they are secure by:
- arranging for the occupier or their agent to be present;
- any other appropriate means.

### (f) *Searches under PACE, Schedule 1 or the Terrorism Act 2000, Schedule 5*

B:6.14 An officer shall be appointed as the officer in charge of the search (see paragraph 2.10), in respect of any search made under a warrant issued under PACE Act 1984, Sched. 1 or the Terrorism Act 2000, Sched. 5. They are responsible for making sure the search is conducted with discretion and in a manner that causes the least possible disruption to any business or other activities carried out on the premises.

B:6.15 Once the officer in charge of the search is satisfied material may not be taken from the premises without their knowledge, they shall ask for the documents or other records concerned. The officer in charge of the search may also ask to see the index to files held on the premises, and the officers conducting the search may inspect any files which, according to the index, appear to contain the material sought. A more extensive search of the premises may be made only if:
- the person responsible for them refuses to:
  - produce the material sought, or
  - allow access to the index;
- it appears the index is:
  - inaccurate, or
  - incomplete;

- for any other reason the officer in charge of the search has reasonable grounds for believing such a search is necessary in order to find the material sought.

### Notes for guidance

B:6A *Whether compensation is appropriate depends on the circumstances in each case. Compensation for damage caused when effecting entry is unlikely to be appropriate if the search was lawful, and the force used can be shown to be reasonable, proportionate and necessary to effect entry. If the wrong premises are searched by mistake everything possible should be done at the earliest opportunity to allay any sense of grievance and there should normally be a strong presumption in favour of paying compensation.*    **A-31**

B:6B *It is important that, when possible, all those involved in a search are fully briefed about any powers to be exercised and the extent and limits within which it should be conducted.*

B:6C *In all cases the number of officers and other persons involved in executing the warrant should be determined by what is reasonable and necessary according to the particular circumstances.*

### B:7 Seizure and retention of property

#### (a) *Seizure*

B:7.1 Subject to paragraph 7.2, an officer who is searching any person or premises under any statutory power or with the consent of the occupier may seize anything:    **A-32**

   (a) covered by a warrant;

   (b) the officer has reasonable grounds for believing is evidence of an offence or has been obtained in consequence of the commission of an offence but only if seizure is necessary to prevent the items being concealed, lost, disposed of, altered, damaged, destroyed or tampered with;

   (c) covered by the powers in the Criminal Justice and Police Act 2001, Pt 2 allowing an officer to seize property from persons or premises and retain it for sifting or examination elsewhere.

See *Note 7B*.

B:7.2 No item may be seized which an officer has reasonable grounds for believing to be subject to legal privilege, as defined in PACE, s.10, other than under the Criminal Justice and Police Act 2001, Pt 2.

B:7.3 Officers must be aware of the provisions in the Criminal Justice and Police Act 2001, s.59, allowing for applications to a judicial authority for the return of property seized and the subsequent duty to secure in section 60 (see paragraph 7.12(iii)).

B:7.4 An officer may decide it is not appropriate to seize property because of an explanation from the person holding it but may nevertheless have reasonable grounds for believing it was obtained in consequence of an offence by some person. In these circumstances, the officer should identify the property to the holder, inform the holder of their suspicions and explain the holder may be liable to civil or criminal proceedings if they dispose of, alter or destroy the property.

B:7.5 An officer may arrange to photograph, image or copy, any document or other article they have the power to seize in accordance with paragraph 7.1. This is subject to specific restrictions on the examination, imaging or copying of certain property seized under the Criminal Justice and Police Act 2001, Pt 2. An officer must have regard to their statutory obligation to retain an original document or other article only when a photograph or copy is not sufficient.

B:7.6 If an officer considers information stored in any electronic form and accessible from the premises could be used in evidence, they may require the information to be produced in a form:

- which can be taken away and in which it is visible and legible; or
- from which it can readily be produced in a visible and legible form.

#### (b) *Criminal Justice and Police Act 2001: specific procedures for seize and sift powers*

B:7.7 The Criminal Justice and Police Act 2001, Pt 2 gives officers limited powers to seize property from premises or persons so they can sift or examine it elsewhere. Officers must be careful they only exercise these powers when it is essential and they do not remove any more material than necessary. The removal of large volumes of material, much of which may not ultimately be retainable, may have serious implications for the owners, particularly when they are involved in business or activities such as journalism or the provision of medical services. Officers must carefully consider if removing copies or images of relevant material or data would be a satisfactory alternative to removing originals. When originals are taken, officers must be prepared to facilitate the provision of copies or images for the owners when reasonably practicable. [See *Note 7C*.]    **A-33**

B:7.8 Property seized under the Criminal Justice and Police Act 2001, s.50 or 51 must be kept securely and separately from any material seized under other powers. An examination under section

53 to determine which elements may be retained must be carried out at the earliest practicable time, having due regard to the desirability of allowing the person from whom the property was seized, or a person with an interest in the property, an opportunity of being present or represented at the examination.

B:7.8A All reasonable steps should be taken to accommodate an interested person's request to be present, provided the request is reasonable and subject to the need to prevent harm to, interference with, or unreasonable delay to the investigatory process. If an examination proceeds in the absence of an interested person who asked to attend or their representative, the officer who exercised the relevant seizure power must give that person a written notice of why the examination was carried out in those circumstances. If it is necessary for security reasons or to maintain confidentiality officers may exclude interested persons from decryption or other processes which facilitate the examination but do not form part of it. [See *Note 7D*.]

B:7.9 It is the responsibility of the officer in charge of the investigation to make sure property is returned in accordance with sections 53 to 55. Material which there is no power to retain must be:

- separated from the rest of the seized property; and
- returned as soon as reasonably practicable after examination of all the seized property.

B:7.9A Delay is only warranted if very clear and compelling reasons exist, for example:

- the unavailability of the person to whom the material is to be returned; or
- the need to agree a convenient time to return a large volume of material.

B:7.9B Legally privileged, excluded or special procedure material which cannot be retained must be returned:

- as soon as reasonably practicable; and
- without waiting for the whole examination.

B:7.9C As set out in section 58, material must be returned to the person from whom it was seized, except when it is clear some other person has a better right to it. [See *Note 7E*.]

B:7.10 When an officer involved in the investigation has reasonable grounds to believe a person with a relevant interest in property seized under section 50 or 51 intends to make an application under section 59 for the return of any legally privileged, special procedure or excluded material, the officer in charge of the investigation should be informed as soon as practicable and the material seized should be kept secure in accordance with section 61. [See *Note 7C*.]

B:7.11 The officer in charge of the investigation is responsible for making sure property is properly secured. Securing involves making sure the property is not examined, copied, imaged or put to any other use except at the request, or with the consent, of the applicant or in accordance with the directions of the appropriate judicial authority. Any request, consent or directions must be recorded in writing and signed by both the initiator and the officer in charge of the investigation. [See *Notes 7F* and *7G*.]

B:7.12 When an officer exercises a power of seizure conferred by sections 50 or 51 they shall provide the occupier of the premises or the person from whom the property is being seized with a written notice:

  (i) specifying what has been seized under the powers conferred by that section;
  (ii) specifying the grounds for those powers;
  (iii) setting out the effect of sections 59 to 61 covering the grounds for a person with a relevant interest in seized property to apply to a judicial authority for its return and the duty of officers to secure property in certain circumstances when an application is made; and
  (iv) specifying the name and address of the person to whom:
    - notice of an application to the appropriate judicial authority in respect of any of the seized property must be given;
    - an application may be made to allow attendance at the initial examination of the property.

B:7.13 If the occupier is not present but there is someone in charge of the premises, the notice shall be given to them. If no suitable person is available, so the notice will easily be found it should either be:

- left in a prominent place on the premises; or
- attached to the exterior of the premises.

## (c) *Retention*

B:7.14 Subject to paragraph 7.15, anything seized in accordance with the above provisions may be **A-34** retained only for as long as is necessary. It may be retained, among other purposes:

(i) for use as evidence at a trial for an offence;

(ii) to facilitate the use in any investigation or proceedings of anything to which it is inextricably linked [see *Note 7H*];

(iii) for forensic examination or other investigation in connection with an offence;

(iv) in order to establish its lawful owner when there are reasonable grounds for believing it has been stolen or obtained by the commission of an offence.

B:7.15 Property shall not be retained under paragraph 7.14(i), (ii) or (iii) if a copy or image would be sufficient.

## (d) *Rights of owners etc*

B:7.16 If property is retained, the person who had custody or control of it immediately before seizure must, on request, be provided with a list or description of the property within a reasonable time.

B:7.17 That person or their representative must be allowed supervised access to the property to examine it or have it photographed or copied, or must be provided with a photograph or copy, in either case within a reasonable time of any request and at their own expense, unless the officer in charge of an investigation has reasonable grounds for believing this would:

(i) prejudice the investigation of any offence or criminal proceedings; or

(ii) lead to the commission of an offence by providing access to unlawful material such as pornography.

A record of the grounds shall be made when access is denied.

## *Notes for guidance*

B:7A *Any person claiming property seized by the police may apply to a magistrates' court under the Police* **A-35** *(Property) Act 1897 for its possession and should, if appropriate, be advised of this procedure.*

B:7B *The powers of seizure conferred by PACE, ss.18(2) and 19(3) extend to the seizure of the whole premises when it is physically possible to seize and retain the premises in their totality and practical considerations make seizure desirable. For example, police may remove premises such as tents, vehicles or caravans to a police station for the purpose of preserving evidence.*

B:7C *Officers should consider reaching agreement with owners and/or other interested parties on the procedures for examining a specific set of property, rather than awaiting the judicial authority's determination. Agreement can sometimes give a quicker and more satisfactory route for all concerned and minimise costs and legal complexities.*

B:7D *What constitutes a relevant interest in specific material may depend on the nature of that material and the circumstances in which it is seized. Anyone with a reasonable claim to ownership of the material and anyone entrusted with its safe keeping by the owner should be considered.*

B:7E *Requirements to secure and return property apply equally to all copies, images or other material created because of seizure of the original property.*

B:7F *The mechanics of securing property vary according to the circumstances; "bagging up", i.e. placing material in sealed bags or containers and strict subsequent control of access is the appropriate procedure in many cases.*

B:7G *When material is seized under the powers of seizure conferred by PACE, the duty to retain it under the code of practice issued under the Criminal Procedure and Investigations Act 1996 is subject to the provisions on retention of seized material in PACE, s.22.*

B:7H *Paragraph 7.14(ii) applies if inextricably linked material is seized under the Criminal Justice and Police Act 2001, s.50 or 51. Inextricably linked material is material it is not reasonably practicable to separate from other linked material without prejudicing the use of that other material in any investigation or proceedings. For example, it may not be possible to separate items of data held on computer disk without damaging their evidential integrity. Inextricably linked material must not be examined, imaged, copied or used for any purpose other than for proving the source and/or integrity of the linked material.*

## B:8 Action after searches

B:8.1 If premises are searched in circumstances where this code applies, unless the exceptions in **A-36** paragraph 2.3(a) apply, on arrival at a police station the officer in charge of the search shall make or have made a record of the search, to include:

(i) the address of the searched premises;

(ii) the date, time and duration of the search;

(iii) the authority used for the search:
- if the search was made in exercise of a statutory power to search premises without warrant, the power which was used for the search:
- if the search was made under a warrant or with written consent;
  – a copy of the warrant and the written authority to apply for it, see paragraph 3.4; or
  – the written consent;

shall be appended to the record or the record shall show the location of the copy warrant or consent;

(iv) subject to paragraph 2.9, the names of:
- the officer(s) in charge of the search;
- all other officers and any authorised persons who conducted the search;

(v) the names of any people on the premises if they are known;

(vi) any grounds for refusing the occupier's request to have someone present during the search, see paragraph 6.11;

(vii) a list of any articles seized or the location of a list and, if not covered by a warrant, the grounds for their seizure;

(viii) whether force was used, and the reason;

(ix) details of any damage caused during the search, and the circumstances;

(x) if applicable, the reason it was not practicable:
  (a) to give the occupier a copy of the notice of powers and rights, see paragraph 6.7;
  (b) before the search to give the occupier a copy of the notice, see paragraph 6.8;

(xi) when the occupier was not present, the place where copies of the notice of powers and rights and search warrant were left on the premises, see paragraph 6.8.

B:8.2 On each occasion when premises are searched under warrant, the warrant authorising the search on that occasion shall be endorsed to show:

(i) if any articles specified in the warrant were found and the address where found;

(ii) if any other articles were seized;

(iii) the date and time it was executed and if present, the name of the occupier or if the occupier is not present the name of the person in charge of the premises;

(iv) subject to paragraph 2.9, the names of the officers who executed it and any authorised persons who accompanied them; and

(v) if a copy, together with a copy of the notice of powers and rights was:
- handed to the occupier; or
- endorsed as required by paragraph 6.8; and left on the premises and where.

B:8.3 Any warrant shall be returned within three calendar months of its issue or sooner on completion of the search(es) authorised by that warrant, if it was issued by a:
- justice of the peace, to the designated officer for the local justice area in which the justice was acting when issuing the warrant; or
- judge, to the appropriate officer of the court concerned.

### B:9 Search registers

**A-37**    B:9.1 A search register will be maintained at each sub-divisional or equivalent police station. All search records required under paragraph 8.1 shall be made, copied, or referred to in the register. [See *Note 9A.*]

*Note for guidance*

B:9A *Paragraph 9.1 also applies to search records made by immigration officers. In these cases, a search register must also be maintained at an immigration office. [See also Note 2D.]*

### B:10 Searches under Schedule 5 to the Terrorism Prevention and Investigation Measures Act 2011

**A-37a**    B:10.1 This code applies to the powers of constables under Schedule 5 to the Terrorism Prevention and Investigation Measures Act 2011 relating to TPIM notices to enter and search premises subject to the modifications in the following paragraphs.

B:10.2 In paragraph 2.3(d), the reference to the investigation into an alleged or suspected offence include [*sic*] the enforcement of terrorism prevention and investigation measures which may be imposed on an individual by a TPIM notice in accordance with the Terrorism Prevention and Investigation Measures Act 2011.

B:10.3 References to the purpose and object of the entry and search of premises, the nature of articles sought and what may be seized and retained include (as appropriate):

(a) in relation to the power to search without a search warrant in paragraph 5 (for purposes of serving TPIM notice), finding the individual on whom the notice is to be served;

(b) in relation to the power to search without a search warrant in paragraph 6 (at time of serving TPIM notice), ascertaining whether there is anything in the premises, that contravenes measures specified in the notice [see *Note 10A*];

(c) in relation to the power to search without a search warrant under paragraph 7 (suspected absconding), ascertaining whether a person has absconded or if there is anything on the premises which will assist in the pursuit or arrest of an individual in respect of whom a TPIM notice is force who is reasonably suspected of having absconded;

(d) in relation to the power to search under a search warrant issued under paragraph 8 (for compliance purposes), determining whether an individual in respect of whom a notice is in force is complying with measures specified in the notice [see *Note 10A*].

*Note for guidance*

B:10A *Searches of individuals under Schedule 5, paras 6(2)(a) (at time of serving TPIM notice) and 8(2)(a) (for compliance purposes) must be conducted and recorded in accordance with Code A. See Code A, para. 2.18A for details.*

## (4) Detention, treatment and questioning of persons

The text that follows is of the version of the code that came into force on June 2, 2014: see ★**A-38** *ante*, A-1.

For authorities in relation to Code C, see, in particular, §§ 15-167 *et seq.* (right of access to solicitor), § 15-204 (general), § 15-311 (confessions), § 15-372 (sufficient evidence for prosecution to succeed), §§ 15-401 *et seq.* (discretionary exclusion of evidence) in the main work.

## C. CODE OF PRACTICE FOR THE DETENTION, TREATMENT AND QUESTIONING OF PERSONS BY POLICE OFFICERS

### Commencement—transitional arrangements

This code applies to people in police detention after 00.00 on 27 October 2013, notwithstanding **A-39** that their period of detention may have commenced before that time.

### C:1 General

C:1.0 The powers and procedures in this code must be used fairly, responsibly, with respect for **A-40** the people to whom they apply and without unlawful discrimination. Under the Equality Act 2010, s.149, when police officers are carrying out their functions, they also have a duty to have due regard to the need to eliminate unlawful discrimination, harassment and victimisation, to advance equality of opportunity between people who share a relevant protected characteristic and people who do not share it, and to take steps to foster good relations between those persons. See *Notes 1A* and *1AA*.

C:1.1 All persons in custody must be dealt with expeditiously, and released as soon as the need for detention no longer applies.

C:1.1A A custody officer must perform the functions in this code as soon as practicable. A custody officer will not be in breach of this code if delay is justifiable and reasonable steps are taken to prevent unnecessary delay. The custody record shall show when a delay has occurred and the reason. See *Note 1H*.

C:1.2 This code of practice must be readily available at all police stations for consultation by:

• police officers;
• police staff;
• detained persons;
• members of the public.

C:1.3 The provisions of this code:

• include the *Annexes*;
• do not include the *Notes for Guidance*.

C:1.4 If an officer has any suspicion, or is told in good faith, that a person of any age may be mentally disordered or otherwise mentally vulnerable, in the absence of clear evidence to dispel that suspicion, the person shall be treated as such for the purposes of this code. See *Note 1G*.

C:1.5 If anyone appears to be under 17, they shall in the absence of clear evidence that they are older, be treated as a juvenile for the purposes of this code and any other code.

C:1.5A If anyone appears to have attained the age of 17 and to be under the age of 18, they shall in the absence of clear evidence that they are older, be treated as a 17-year-old for the purposes of this and any other code. The provisions and *Notes for Guidance* which in accordance with paragraph 1.5 apply to a juvenile and the way they are to be treated shall also apply to them, except as described in sub-paragraphs (a) and (b) below:

(a) the statutory provisions in section 38 of PACE (detention after charge) which apply only to an arrested juvenile as defined in section 37(15) of PACE and to which paragraphs 16.7 and 16.10 and *Note 16D* of this code relate, shall not apply to a person who appears to have attained the age of 17 for the purposes of:

(i) the grounds to keep them in police detention after charge; and

(ii) the requirement to transfer a person who has been kept in police detention after charge to local authority accommodation and the power of the local authority to detain them pending appearance at court;

(b) the statutory provisions in section 65(1) of PACE (appropriate consent) which require appropriate consent for a person who has not attained the age of 17 to be given by them and their parent or guardian shall not apply to a person who appears to have attained the age of 17 and whose consent alone shall be sufficient. In this code, section 65(1) applies to Annex A, paras 2(b) and 2B (intimate searches), and Annex K, paras 1(b) and 3 (X-Ray and ultrasound scan), and in Code D (identification), to para. 2.12 and *Note 2A* with regards to taking fingerprints, samples, footwear impressions, photographs and evidential searches and examinations.

See *Notes 1L* and *1M*.

C:1.6 If a person appears to be blind, seriously visually impaired, deaf, unable to read or speak or has difficulty orally because of a speech impediment, they shall be treated as such for the purposes of this code in the absence of clear evidence to the contrary.

**A-41**

C:1.7 The "appropriate adult" means, in the case of a:

(a) juvenile:

(i) the parent, guardian or, if the juvenile is in the care of a local authority or voluntary organisation, a person representing that authority or organisation (see *Note 1B*);

(ii) a social worker of a local authority (see *Note 1C*);

(iii) failing these, some other responsible adult aged 18 or over who is not a police officer or employed by the police;

note: paragraph 1.5A extends sub-paragraph (a) to the person called to fulfil the role of the appropriate adult for a 17-year-old detainee [*sic*];

(b) person who is mentally disordered or mentally vulnerable (see *Note 1D*);

(i) a relative, guardian or other person responsible for their care or custody;

(ii) someone experienced in dealing with mentally disordered or mentally vulnerable people but who is not a police officer or employed by the police;

(iii) failing these, some other responsible adult aged 18 or over who is not a police officer or employed by the police.

C:1.8 If this code requires a person be given certain information, they do not have to be given it if at the time they are incapable of understanding what is said, are violent or may become violent or in urgent need of medical attention, but they must be given it as soon as practicable.

C:1.9 References to a custody officer include any police officer who for the time being, is performing the functions of a custody officer.

C:1.9A When this code requires the prior authority or agreement of an officer of at least inspector or superintendent rank, that authority may be given by a sergeant or chief inspector authorised to perform the functions of the higher rank under the Police and Criminal Evidence Act 1984 (PACE), s.107.

C:1.10 Subject to paragraph 1.12, this code applies to people in custody at police stations in England and Wales, whether or not they have been arrested, and to those removed to a police station as a place of safety under the Mental Health Act 1983, ss.135 and 136, as a last resort (see paragraph 3.16). Section 15 applies solely to people in police detention, *e.g.* those brought to a police station under arrest or arrested at a police station for an offence after going there voluntarily.

C:1.11 No part of this code applies to a detained person:

(a) to whom PACE Code H applies because:

• they are detained following arrest under section 41 of the Terrorism Act 2000 (TACT) and not charged; or

• an authorisation has been given under section 22 of the Counter-Terrorism Act 2008 (CTACT) (post-charge questioning of terrorist suspects) to interview them;

(b) to whom the code of practice issued under paragraph 6 of Schedule 14 to TACT applies because they are detained for examination under Schedule 7 to TACT.

C:1.12 This code does not apply to people in custody:

(i) arrested by officers under the Criminal Justice and Public Order Act 1994, s.136(2), on warrants issued in Scotland, or arrested or detained without warrant under section 137(2) by officers from a police force in Scotland; in these cases, police powers and duties and the person's rights and entitlements whilst at a police station in England or Wales are the same as those in Scotland;

(ii) arrested under the Immigration and Asylum Act 1999, s.142(3), in order to have their fingerprints taken;

(iii) whose detention is authorised under Schedules 2 or 3 to the Immigration Act 1971 or section 62 of the Nationality, Immigration and Asylum Act 2002;

(iv) who are convicted or remanded prisoners held in police cells on behalf of the Prison Service under the Imprisonment (Temporary Provisions) Act 1980;

(v) [*not used*];

(vi) detained for searches under stop and search powers except as required by Code A.

The provisions on conditions of detention and treatment in sections 8 and 9 must be considered as the minimum standards of treatment for such detainees.

C:1.13 In this code:

(a) "designated person" means a person other than a police officer, designated under the Police Reform Act 2002, Pt 4, who has specified powers and duties of police officers conferred or imposed on them;

(b) reference to a police officer includes a designated person acting in the exercise or performance of the powers and duties conferred or imposed on them by their designation;

(c) where a search or other procedure to which this code applies may only be carried out or observed by a person of the same sex as the detainee, the gender of the detainee and other parties present should be established and recorded in line with Annex L of this code.

C:1.14 Designated persons are entitled to use reasonable force as follows:— **A-42**

(a) when exercising a power conferred on them which allows a police officer exercising that power to use reasonable force, a designated person has the same entitlement to use force; and

(b) at other times when carrying out duties conferred or imposed on them that also entitle them to use reasonable force, for example:

- when at a police station carrying out the duty to keep detainees for whom they are responsible under control and to assist any police officer or designated person to keep any detainee under control and to prevent their escape;
- when securing, or assisting any police officer or designated person in securing, the detention of a person at a police station;
- when escorting, or assisting any police officer or designated person in escorting, a detainee within a police station;
- for the purpose of saving life or limb; or
- preventing serious damage to property.

C:1.15 Nothing in this code prevents the custody officer, or other officer given custody of the detainee, from allowing police staff who are not designated persons to carry out individual procedures or tasks at the police station if the law allows. However, the officer remains responsible for making sure the procedures and tasks are carried out correctly in accordance with the codes of practice (see *Note 3F*). Any such person must be:

(a) a person employed by a police force and under the direction and control of the chief officer of that force; or

(b) employed by a person with whom a police force has a contract for the provision of services relating to persons arrested or otherwise in custody.

C:1.16 Designated persons and other police staff must have regard to any relevant provisions of the codes of practice.

C:1.17 References to pocket books include any official report book issued to police officers or other police staff.

*Notes for guidance*

C:1A *Although certain sections of this code apply specifically to people in custody at police stations, those there voluntarily to assist with an investigation should be treated with no less consideration, e.g. offered refreshments at appropriate times, and enjoy an absolute right to obtain legal advice or communicate with anyone outside the police station.*

C:1AA *In paragraph 1.0, "relevant protected characteristic" includes: age, disability, gender reassignment, pregnancy and maternity, race, religion/belief, sex and sexual orientation.*

C:1B *A person, including a parent or guardian, should not be an appropriate adult if they:*
- *are*
  - *suspected of involvement in the offence;*
  - *the victim;*
  - *a witness;*
  - *involved in the investigation;*
- *received admissions prior to attending to act as the appropriate adult.*

*Note: if a juvenile's parent is estranged from the juvenile, they should not be asked to act as the appropriate adult if the juvenile expressly and specifically objects to their presence.*

*Note: Paragraph 1.5A applies this note to 17-year-old detainees.*

C:1C *If a juvenile admits an offence to, or in the presence of, a social worker or member of a youth offending team other than during the time that person is acting as the juvenile's appropriate adult, another appropriate adult should be appointed in the interest of fairness.*

*Note: Paragraph 1.5A applies this note to 17-year-old detainees.*

C:1D *In the case of people who are mentally disordered or otherwise mentally vulnerable, it may be more satisfactory if the appropriate adult is someone experienced or trained in their care rather than a relative lacking such qualifications. But if the detainee prefers a relative to a better qualified stranger or objects to a particular person their wishes should, if practicable, be respected.*

C:1E *A detainee should always be given an opportunity, when an appropriate adult is called to the police station, to consult privately with a solicitor in the appropriate adult's absence if they want. An appropriate adult is not subject to legal privilege.*

C:1F *A solicitor or independent custody visitor present at the police station in that capacity may not be the appropriate adult.*

C:1G *"Mentally vulnerable" applies to any detainee who, because of their mental state or capacity, may not understand the significance of what is said, of questions or of their replies. "Mental disorder" is defined in the Mental Health Act 1983, s.1(2), as "any disorder or disability of mind". When the custody officer has any doubt about the mental state or capacity of a detainee, that detainee should be treated as mentally vulnerable and an appropriate adult called.*

C:1H *Paragraph 1.1A is intended to cover delays which may occur in processing detainees, e.g. if:*
- *a large number of suspects are brought into the station simultaneously to be placed in custody;*
- *interview rooms are all being used;*
- *there are difficulties contacting an appropriate adult, solicitor or interpreter.*

C:1I *The custody officer must remind the appropriate adult and detainee about the right to legal advice and record any reasons for waiving it in accordance with section 6.*

C:1J *[Not used.]*

C:1K *This code does not affect the principle that all citizens have a duty to help police officers to prevent crime and discover offenders. This is a civic rather than a legal duty; but when police officers are trying to discover whether, or by whom, offences have been committed they are entitled to question any person from whom they think useful information can be obtained, subject to the restrictions imposed by this code. A person's declaration that they are unwilling to reply does not alter this entitlement.*

C:1L *Paragraph 1.5A does not amend section 37(15) of PACE which defines the term "arrested juvenile" for the purposes of sections 34 to 51 of PACE, or provisions in any other enactment which expressly refer and apply to persons under the age of 17. Until amended by Parliament, these statutory provisions alone do not extend to persons who have attained the age of 17.*

C:1M *The purpose of paragraph 1.5A is to extend the safeguards for juveniles to 17-year-olds unless this is precluded by any statutory provisions. Sub-paragraphs 1.5A(a) and (b) identify the provisions of sections 38 and 65 of PACE concerning detention after charge and appropriate consent which for this reason do not extend to 17-year-olds. All other safeguards in this and other codes are extended and the requirements which are indicated in the relevant provisions and Notes for Guidance are as follows:*
- (a) *under paragraph 3.13 of this code, to identify and inform someone responsible for the welfare of a 17-year-old which is in addition to their right in section 5 of this code not to be held incommunicado;*
- (b) *under paragraph 3.14 of this code to notify a person who has statutory responsibility under a court order to supervise or monitor a 17-year-old;*

(c) *under paragraph 8.8 with regard to cell accommodation and keeping 17-year-old detainees separate from adults;*

(d) *to call a person described by paragraph 1.7(a) or Note 17G in relation to testing for the presence of Class A drugs, to fulfil the role of the appropriate adult for the purposes of this or any other code to support and assist a 17-year-old:*

(i) *by being present when:*

- *they are informed of their rights and entitlements and the grounds for their detention (see paras 3.17 and 3.18);*
- *they are cautioned or given a special warning (see paras 10.12 and 10.11A);*
- *they are being interviewed in accordance with this code (see sections 11 and 12) or Codes E or F unless paragraph 11.15 of this code allows the interview to go ahead without the adult being present;*
- *their detention is being reviewed or an extension is being considered (see paras 15.3(c) and 15.3C(a)):*
- *they are charged and related action is taken (see paras 16.1, 16.3, 16.4A and 16.6);*
- *samples to test for Class A drugs are requested from a person who has not attained the age of 18 (see para. 17.7);*
- *an intimate search is carried out (see Annex A, paras 2A, 2B and 5);*
- *a strip search is carried out (see Annex A, para. 11(c));*
- *an x-ray or ultrasound scan is carried out (see Annex K, paras 2 and 3);*
- *procedures in Code D involving witness identification, taking fingerprints, samples, footwear impressions and photographs and when evidential searches and examinations are carried out (see paras 2.14 and 2.15).*

(ii) *by allowing:*

- *the adult to inspect their custody record and to have a copy of their record (see paras 2.4, 2.4A and 2.5);*
- *a 17-year-old to consult the adult in private (see para. 3.18);*
- *the adult to request legal advice on their behalf to advise and assist them (see paras 3.19, 6.5A and 11.17).*

### C:2 Custody records

C:2.1A When a person:

- is brought to a police station under arrest
- is arrested at the police station having attended there voluntarily or
- attends a police station to answer bail

they must be brought before the custody officer as soon as practicable after their arrival at the station or if applicable, following their arrest after attending the police station voluntarily. This applies to both designated and non-designated police stations. A person is deemed to be "at a police station" for these purposes if they are within the boundary of any building or enclosed yard which forms part of that police station.

C:2.1 A separate custody record must be opened as soon as practicable for each person brought to a police station under arrest or arrested at the station having gone there voluntarily or attending a police station in answer to street bail. All information recorded under this code must be recorded as soon as practicable in the custody record unless otherwise specified. Any audio or video recording made in the custody area is not part of the custody record.

C:2.2 If any action requires the authority of an officer of a specified rank, subject to paragraph 2.6A, their name and rank must be noted in the custody record.

C:2.3 The custody officer is responsible for the custody record's accuracy and completeness and for making sure the record or copy of the record accompanies a detainee if they are transferred to another police station. The record shall show the:

- time and reason for transfer;
- time a person is released from detention.

C:2.3A If a person is arrested and taken to a police station as a result of a search in the exercise of any stop and search power to which PACE Code A (stop and search) or the "search powers code" issued under TACT applies, the officer carrying out the search is responsible for ensuring that the record of that stop and search, is made as part of the person's custody record. The custody officer must then ensure that the person is asked if they want a copy of the search record and if they do, that they are given a copy as soon as practicable. The person's entitlement to a copy of the search record which is made as part of their custody record is in addition to, and does not affect, their entitlement to a copy of their custody record or any other provisions of section 2 (custody records) of this code. (See Code A, para. 4.2B, and the TACT search powers code, para. 5.3.5.)

**A-44**

C:2.4 The detainee's solicitor and appropriate adult must be permitted to inspect the whole of the detainee's custody record as soon as practicable after their arrival at the station and at any other time on request, whilst the person is detained. This includes the following specific records relating to the reasons for the detainee's arrest and detention and the offence concerned, to which paragraph 3.1(b) refers:

> (a) the information about the circumstances and reasons for the detainee's arrest as recorded in the custody record in accordance with paragraph 4.3 of Code G; this applies to any further offences for which the detainee is arrested whilst in custody;
>
> (b) the record of the grounds for each authorisation to keep the person in custody; the authorisations to which this applies are the same as those described at items (i)(a) to (d) in the table in paragraph 2 of Annex M [*sic*] of this code.

Access to the records in sub-paragraphs (a) and (b) is in addition to the requirements in paragraphs 3.4(b), 11.1A, 15.0, 15.7A(c) and 16.7A to make certain documents and materials available and to provide information about the offence and the reasons for arrest and detention.

Access to the custody record for the purposes of this paragraph must be arranged and agreed with the custody officer and may not unreasonably interfere with the custody officer's duties. A record shall be made when access is allowed and whether it includes the records described in sub-paragraphs (a) and (b) above.

Note: paragraph 1.5A extends this paragraph to the person called to fulfil the role of the appropriate adult for a 17-year-old detainee.

C:2.4A When a detainee leaves police detention or is taken before a court they, their legal representative or appropriate adult shall be given, on request, a copy of the custody record as soon as practicable. This entitlement lasts for 12 months after release.

Note: paragraph 1.5A extends this paragraph to the person called to fulfil the role of the appropriate adult for a 17-year-old detainee.

C:2.5 The detainee, appropriate adult or legal representative shall be permitted to inspect the original custody record after the detainee has left police detention provided they give reasonable notice of their request. Any such inspection shall be noted in the custody record.

Note: paragraph 1.5A extends this paragraph to the person called to fulfil the role of the appropriate adult for a 17-year-old detainee.

C:2.6 Subject to paragraph 2.6A, all entries in custody records must be timed and signed by the maker. Records entered on computer shall be timed and contain the operator's identification.

C:2.6A Nothing in this code requires the identity of officers or other police staff to be recorded or disclosed:

> (a) [*not used*];
>
> (b) if the officer or police staff reasonably believe recording or disclosing their name might put them in danger.

In these cases, they shall use their warrant or other identification numbers and the name of their police station. See *Note 2A*.

C:2.7 The fact and time of any detainee's refusal to sign a custody record, when asked in accordance with this code, must be recorded.

*Note for guidance*

A-45        C:2A *The purpose of paragraph 2.6A(b) is to protect those involved in serious organised crime investigations or arrests of particularly violent suspects when there is reliable information that those arrested or their associates may threaten or cause harm to those involved. In cases of doubt, an officer of inspector rank or above should be consulted.*

### C:3  Initial action

(a) *Detained persons—normal procedure*

A-46        C:3.1 When a person is brought to a police station under arrest or arrested at the station having gone there voluntarily, the custody officer must make sure the person is told clearly about:

> (a) the following continuing rights, which may be exercised at any stage during the period in custody:
>
> > (i) their right to consult privately with a solicitor and that free independent legal advice is available as in section 6;
> >
> > (ii) their right to have someone informed of their arrest as in section 5;
> >
> > (iii) their right to consult the codes of practice (see *Note 3D*); and
> >
> > (iv) if applicable, their right to interpretation and translation (see para. 3.12) and their

right to communicate with their high commission, embassy or consulate (see para. 3.12A).

(b) their right to be informed about the offence and (as the case may be) any further of-fences for which they are arrested whilst in custody and why they have been arrested and detained in accordance with paragraphs 2.4, 3.4(a) and 11.1A of this code and paragraph 3.3 of Code G.

C:3.2 The detainee must also be given a written notice, which contains information:

(a) setting out:

(i) their rights under paragraph 3.1, paragraph 3.12 and 3.12A;

(ii) the arrangements for obtaining legal advice, see section 6;

(iii) their right to a copy of the custody record as in paragraph 2.4A;

(iv) their right to remain silent as set out in the caution in the terms prescribed in section 10;

(v) their right to have access to materials and documents which are essential to effectively challenging the lawfulness of their arrest and detention for any offence and (as the case may be) any further offences for which they are arrested whilst in custody, in ac-cordance with paragraphs 3.4(b), 15.0, 15.7A(c) and 16.7A of this code;

(vi) the maximum period for which they may be kept in police detention without being charged, when detention must be reviewed and when release is required;

(vii) their right to medical assistance in accordance with section 9 of this code;

(viii) their right, if they are prosecuted, to have access to the evidence in the case before their trial in accordance with the Criminal Procedure and Investigations Act 1996, the Attorney General's Guidelines on Disclosure, the common law and the Criminal Procedure Rules;

(b) briefly setting out their other entitlements while in custody, by:

(i) mentioning:

– the provisions relating to the conduct of interviews;

– the circumstances in which an appropriate adult should be available to assist the detainee and their statutory rights to make representations whenever the need for their detention is reviewed;

(ii) listing the entitlements in this code, concerning:

– reasonable standards of physical comfort;

– adequate food and drink;

– access to toilets and washing facilities, clothing, medical attention, and exercise when practicable.

See *Note 3A*.

C:3.2A The detainee must be given an opportunity to read the notice and shall be asked to sign the custody record to acknowledge receipt of the notice. Any refusal to sign must be recorded on the custody record.

C:3.3 [*Not used.*]

C:3.3A An "easy read" illustrated version should also be provided if available (see *Note 3A*).

C:3.4 (a) The custody officer shall:

• record the offence(s) that the detainee has been arrested for and the reason(s) for the arrest on the custody record (see para. 10.3 and Code G, paras 2.2 and 4.3);

• note on the custody record any comment the detainee makes in relation to the arrest-ing officer's account but shall not invite comment; if the arresting officer is not physi-cally present when the detainee is brought to a police station, the arresting officer's ac-count must be made available to the custody officer remotely or by a third party on the arresting officer's behalf; if the custody officer authorises a person's detention, subject to paragraph 1.8, that officer must record the grounds for detention in the detainee's presence and at the same time, inform them of the grounds; the detainee must be informed of the grounds for their detention before they are questioned about any offence;

• note any comment the detainee makes in respect of the decision to detain them but shall not invite comment;

• not put specific questions to the detainee regarding their involvement in any offence, nor in respect of any comments they may make in response to the arresting officer's account or the decision to place them in detention; such an exchange is likely to constitute an interview as in paragraph 11.1A and require the associated safeguards in section 11.

Note: this sub-paragraph also applies to any further offences and grounds for detention which come to light whilst the person is detained.

See paragraph 11.13 in respect of unsolicited comments.

(b) Documents and materials which are essential to effectively challenging the lawfulness of the detainee's arrest and detention must be made available to the detainee or their solicitor. Documents and materials will be "essential" for this purpose if they are capable of undermining the reasons and grounds which make the detainee's arrest and detention necessary. The decision about whether particular documents or materials must be made available for the purpose of this requirement therefore rests with the custody officer who determines whether detention is necessary, in consultation with the investigating officer who has the knowledge of the documents and materials in a particular case necessary to inform that decision. A note should be made in the detainee's custody record of the fact that documents or materials have been made available under this sub-paragraph and when. The investigating officer should make a separate note of what is made available and how it is made available in a particular case. This sub-paragraph also applies (with modifications) for the purposes of sections 15 (reviews and extensions of detention) and 16 (charging detained persons). See *Note 3ZA* and paragraphs 15.0 and 16.7A.

C:3.5 The custody officer or other custody staff as directed by the custody officer shall:

(a) ask the detainee, whether at this time, they:
  (i) would like legal advice, see paragraph 6.5;
  (ii) want someone informed of their detention, see section 5;

(b) ask the detainee to sign the custody record to confirm their decisions in respect of (a);

(c) determine whether the detainee:
  (i) is, or might be, in need of medical treatment or attention, see section 9;
  (ii) requires:
    • an appropriate adult (see paras 1.4, 1.5, 1.5A and 3.15);
    • help to check documentation (see para. 3.20);
    • an interpreter (see para. 3.12 and *Note 13B*);

(d) record the decision in respect of (c).

Where any duties under this paragraph have been carried out by custody staff at the direction of the custody officer, the outcomes shall, as soon as practicable, be reported to the custody officer who retains overall responsibility for the detainee's care and treatment and ensuring that it complies with this code. See *Note 3F*.

C:3.6 When these needs are determined, the custody officer is responsible for initiating an assessment to consider whether the detainee is likely to present specific risks to custody staff or themselves. Such assessments should always include a check on the Police National Computer, to be carried out as soon as practicable, to identify any risks highlighted in relation to the detainee. Although such assessments are primarily the custody officer's responsibility, it may be necessary for them to consult and involve others, *e.g.* the arresting officer or an appropriate healthcare professional, see paragraph 9.13. Reasons for delaying the initiation or completion of the assessment must be recorded.

C:3.7 Chief officers should ensure that arrangements for proper and effective risk assessments required by paragraph 3.6 are implemented in respect of all detainees at police stations in their area.

C:3.8 Risk assessments must follow a structured process which clearly defines the categories of risk to be considered and the results must be incorporated in the detainee's custody record. The custody officer is responsible for making sure those responsible for the detainee's custody are appropriately briefed about the risks. If no specific risks are identified by the assessment, that should be noted in the custody record. See *Note 3E* and paragraph 9.14.

C:3.8A The content of any risk assessment and any analysis of the level of risk relating to the person's detention is not required to be shown or provided to the detainee or any person acting on behalf of the detainee. But information should not be withheld from any person acting on the detainee's behalf, for example, an appropriate adult, solicitor or interpreter, if to do so might put that person at risk.

C:3.9 The custody officer is responsible for implementing the response to any specific risk assessment, *e.g.*:
    • reducing opportunities for self harm;
    • calling an appropriate healthcare professional;
    • increasing levels of monitoring or observation;
    • reducing the risk to those who come into contact with the detainee.

See *Note 3E*.

C:3.10 Risk assessment is an ongoing process and assessments must always be subject to review if circumstances change.

C:3.11 If video cameras are installed in the custody area, notices shall be prominently displayed showing cameras are in use. Any request to have video cameras switched off shall be refused.

(b) *Detained persons—special groups*

C:3.12 If the detainee appears to be someone who does not speak or understand English or who    **A-47** has a hearing or speech impediment, the custody officer must ensure:

    (a) that without delay, an interpreter is called for assistance in the action under paragraphs 3.1 to 3.5; if the person appears to have a hearing or speech impediment, the reference to "interpreter" includes appropriate assistance necessary to comply with paragraphs 3.1 to 3.5 (see para. 13.1C if the detainee is in Wales) (see section 13 and *Note 13B*);

    (b) that in addition to the continuing rights set out in paragraph 3.1(a)(i) to (iv), the detainee is told clearly about their right to interpretation and translation;

    (c) that the written notice given to the detainee in accordance with paragraph 3.2 is in a language the detainee understands and includes the right to interpretation and translation together with information about the provisions in section 13 and Annex M, which explain how the right applies (see *Note 3A*); and

    (d) that if the translation of the notice is not available, the information in the notice is given through an interpreter and a written translation provided without undue delay.

C:3.12A If the detainee is a citizen of an independent Commonwealth country or a national of a foreign country, including the Republic of Ireland, the custody officer must ensure that in addition to the continuing rights set out in paragraph 3.1(a)(i) to (iv), they are informed as soon as practicable about their rights of communication with their high commission, embassy or consulate set out in section 7. This right must be included in the written notice given to the detainee in accordance with paragraph 3.2.

C:3.13 If the detainee is a juvenile, the custody officer must, if it is practicable, ascertain the identity of a person responsible for their welfare. That person:

- may be:
  - the parent or guardian;
  - if the juvenile is in local authority or voluntary organisation care, or is otherwise being looked after under the Children Act 1989, a person appointed by that authority or organisation to have responsibility for the juvenile's welfare;
  - any other person who has, for the time being, assumed responsibility for the juvenile's welfare;
- must be informed as soon as practicable that the juvenile has been arrested, why they have been arrested and where they are detained. This right is in addition to the juvenile's right in section 5 not to be held incommunicado. See *Note 3C*.

Note: paragraph 1.5A extends the obligations in this paragraph to 17-year-old detainees.

C:3.14 If a juvenile is known to be subject to a court order under which a person or organisation is given any degree of statutory responsibility to supervise or otherwise monitor them, reasonable steps must also be taken to notify that person or organisation (the "responsible officer"). The responsible officer will normally be a member of a youth offending team, except for a curfew order which involves electronic monitoring when the contractor providing the monitoring will normally be the responsible officer.

Note: paragraph 1.5A extends the obligations in this paragraph to 17-year-old detainees.

C:3.15 If the detainee is a juvenile, mentally disordered or otherwise mentally vulnerable, the custody officer must, as soon as practicable:

- inform the appropriate adult, who in the case of a juvenile may or may not be a person responsible for their welfare, as in paragraph 3.13, of:
  - the grounds for their detention;
  - their whereabouts;
- ask the adult to come to the police station to see the detainee.

Note: paragraph 1.5A extends the obligation to call someone to fulfil the role of the appropriate adult to 17-year-old detainees.

C:3.16 It is imperative that a mentally disordered or otherwise mentally vulnerable person, detained under the Mental Health Act 1983, s.136, be assessed as soon as possible. A police station should only be used as a place of safety as a last resort but if that assessment is to take place at the police station, an approved mental health professional and a registered medical practitioner shall be called to the station as soon as possible to carry it out. See *Note 9D*. The appropriate adult has no role in the assessment process and their presence is not required. Once the detainee has been assessed and suitable arrangements made for their treatment or care, they can no longer be detained under section 136. A detainee must be immediately discharged from detention under section 136 if a registered medical practitioner, having examined them, concludes they are not mentally disordered within the meaning of the Act.

C:3.17 If the appropriate adult is:

- already at the police station, the provisions of paragraphs 3.1 to 3.5 must be complied with in the appropriate adult's presence;
- not at the station when these provisions are complied with, they must be complied with again in the presence of the appropriate adult when they arrive,

and a copy of the notice given to the detainee in accordance with paragraph 3.2, shall also be given to the appropriate adult.

Note: paragraph 1.5A extends the obligations in this paragraph to 17-year-old detainees.

C:3.18 The detainee shall be advised that:

- the duties of the appropriate adult include giving advice and assistance;
- they can consult privately with the appropriate adult at any time.

Note: paragraph 1.5A extends the obligations in this paragraph to 17-year-old detainees.

C:3.19 If the detainee, or appropriate adult on the detainee's behalf, asks for a solicitor to be called to give legal advice, the provisions of section 6 apply.

Note: paragraph 1.5A extends the obligations in this paragraph to 17-year-old detainees.

C:3.20 If the detainee is blind, seriously visually impaired or unable to read, the custody officer shall make sure their solicitor, relative, appropriate adult or some other person likely to take an interest in them and not involved in the investigation is available to help check any documentation. When this code requires written consent or signing the person assisting may be asked to sign instead, if the detainee prefers. This paragraph does not require an appropriate adult to be called solely to assist in checking and signing documentation for a person who is not a juvenile, or mentally disordered or otherwise mentally vulnerable (see para. 3.15 and *Note 13C*).

### (c) *Persons attending a police station or elsewhere voluntarily*

A-48

C:3.21 Anybody attending a police station or other location (see para. 3.22) voluntarily to assist police with the investigation of an offence may leave at will unless arrested. See *Note 1K*. The person may only be prevented from leaving at will if their arrest on suspicion of committing the offence is necessary in accordance with Code G. See Code G, *Note 2G*.

(a) If during an interview it is decided that their arrest is necessary, they must:

- be informed at once that they are under arrest and of the grounds and reasons as required by Code G, and
- be brought before the custody officer at the police station where they are arrested or, as the case may be, at the police station to which they are taken after being arrested elsewhere. The custody officer is then responsible for making sure that a custody record is opened and that they are notified of their rights in the same way as other detainees as required by this code.

(b) If they are not arrested but are cautioned as in section 10, the person who gives the caution must, at the same time, inform them they are not under arrest, they are not obliged to remain at the station or other location but if they agree to remain, they may obtain free and independent legal advice if they want. They shall also be given a copy of the notice explaining the arrangements for obtaining legal advice and told that the right to legal advice includes the right to speak with a solicitor on the telephone and be asked if they want advice. If advice is requested, the interviewer is responsible for securing its provision without delay by contacting the defence solicitor call centre. The interviewer must ensure that other provisions of this code and Codes E and F concerning the conduct and recording of interviews of suspects and the rights and entitlements and safeguards for suspects who have been arrested and detained are followed insofar as they can be applied to suspects who are not under arrest. This includes:

- informing them of the offence and, as the case may be, any further offences, they are suspected of and the grounds and reasons for that suspicion and their right to be so informed (see para. 3.1(b));
- the caution as required in section 10;
- determining whether they require an appropriate adult and help to check documentation (see para. 3.5(c)(ii)); and
- determining whether they require an interpreter and the provision of interpretation and translation services and informing them of that right (see paras 3.1(a)(iv), 3.5(c)(ii) and 3.12, *Note 6B* and section 13),

but does not include any requirement to provide a written notice in addition to that above which concerns the arrangements for obtaining legal advice.

C:3.22 If the other location mentioned in paragraph 3.21 is any place or premises for which the interviewer requires the person's informed consent to remain, for example, the person's home, then the references that the person is "not obliged to remain" and that they "may leave at will" mean that the person may also withdraw their consent and require the officer to leave.

### (d) *Documentation*

C:3.23 The grounds for a person's detention shall be recorded, in the person's presence if practicable. See paragraph 1.8.

C:3.24 Action taken under paragraphs 3.12 to 3.20 shall be recorded.

### (e) *Persons answering street bail*

C:3.25 When a person is answering street bail, the custody officer should link any documentation held in relation to arrest with the custody record. Any further action shall be recorded on the custody record in accordance with paragraphs 3.23 and 3.24 above.

### (f) *Requirements for suspects to be informed of certain rights*

C:3.26 The provisions of this section identify the information which must be given to suspects who have been cautioned in accordance with section 10 of this code according to whether or not they have been arrested and detained. It includes information required by EU Directive 2012/13 on the right to information in criminal proceedings. If a complaint is made by or on behalf of such a suspect that the information and (as the case may be) access to records and documents has not been provided as required, the matter shall be reported to an inspector to deal with as a complaint for the purposes of paragraph 9.2, or paragraph 12.9 if the challenge is made during an interview. This would include, for example:

(a) in the case of a detained suspect:
  • not informing them of their rights (see para. 3.1);
  • not giving them a copy of the notice (see para. 3.2(a));
  • not providing an opportunity to read the notice (see para. 3.2A);
  • not providing the required information (see paras 3.2(a), 3.12(b) and, 3.12A);
  • not allowing access to the custody record (see para. 2.4);
  • not providing a translation of the notice (see para. 3.12(c) and (d)); and
(b) in the case of a suspect who is not detained:
  • not informing them of their rights or providing the required information (see para. 3.21(b)).

### *Notes for guidance*

C:3ZA *For the purposes of paragraphs 3.4(b) and 15.0:*                                      **A-49**

(a) *investigating officers are responsible for bringing to the attention of the officer who is responsible for authorising the suspect's detention or (as the case may be) continued detention (before or after charge), any documents and materials in their possession or control which appear to undermine the need to keep the suspect in custody; in accordance with Part IV of PACE, this officer will be either the custody officer, the officer reviewing the need for detention before or after charge (PACE, s.40), or the officer considering the need to extend detention without charge from 24 to 36 hours (PACE, s.42) who is then responsible for determining, which, if any, of those documents and materials are capable of undermining the need to detain the suspect and must therefore be made available to the suspect or their solicitor;*

(b) *the way in which documents and materials are "made available", is a matter for the investigating officer to determine on a case by case basis and having regard to the nature and volume of the documents and materials involved: for example, they may be made available by supplying a copy or allowing supervised access to view; however, for view only access, it will be necessary to demonstrate that sufficient time is allowed for the suspect and solicitor to view and consider the documents and materials in question.*

C:3A *For access to currently available notices, including "easy-read" versions, see https://www.gov.uk/notice-of-rights-and-entitlements-a-persons-rights-in-police-detention.*

C:3B *[Not used.]*

C:3C *If the juvenile is in local authority or voluntary organisation care but living with their parents or other adults responsible for their welfare, although there is no legal obligation to inform them, they should normally be contacted, as well as the authority or organisation unless they are suspected of involvement in the offence concerned. Even if the juvenile is not living with their parents, consideration should be given to informing them.*

C:3D *The right to consult the codes of practice does not entitle the person concerned to delay unreasonably any necessary investigative or administrative action whilst they do so. Examples of action which need not be delayed unreasonably include:*

- *procedures requiring the provision of breath, blood or urine specimens under the Road Traffic Act 1988 or the Transport and Works Act 1992;*
- *searching detainees at the police station;*
- *taking fingerprints, footwear impressions or non-intimate samples without consent for evidential purposes.*

C:3E *The Detention and Custody Authorised Professional Practice (APP) produced by the College of Policing (see http://www.app.college.police.uk) provides more detailed guidance on risk assessments and identifies key risk areas which should always be considered.*

C:3F *A custody officer or other officer who, in accordance with this code, allows or directs the carrying out of any task or action relating to a detainee's care, treatment, rights and entitlements to another officer or any police staff must be satisfied that the officer or police staff concerned are suitable, trained and competent to carry out the task or action in question.*

### C:4 Detainee's property

(a) *Action*

A-50      C:4.1 The custody officer is responsible for:

(a) ascertaining what property a detainee:

(i) has with them when they come to the police station, whether on:
- arrest or re-detention on answering to bail;
- commitment to prison custody on the order or sentence of a court;
- lodgement at the police station with a view to their production in court from prison custody;
- transfer from detention at another station or hospital;
- detention under the Mental Health Act 1983, s.135 or 136;
- remand into police custody on the authority of a court;

(ii) might have acquired for an unlawful or harmful purpose while in custody;

(b) the safekeeping of any property taken from a detainee which remains at the police station.

The custody officer may search the detainee or authorise their being searched to the extent they consider necessary, provided a search of intimate parts of the body or involving the removal of more than outer clothing is only made as in Annex A. A search may only be carried out by an officer of the same sex as the detainee. See *Note 4A* and Annex L.

C:4.2 Detainees may retain clothing and personal effects at their own risk unless the custody officer considers they may use them to cause harm to themselves or others, interfere with evidence, damage property, effect an escape or they are needed as evidence. In this event the custody officer may withhold such articles as they consider necessary and must tell the detainee why.

C:4.3 Personal effects are those items a detainee may lawfully need, use or refer to while in detention but do not include cash and other items of value.

(b) *Documentation*

C:4.4 It is a matter for the custody officer to determine whether a record should be made of the property a detained person has with him or had taken from him on arrest. Any record made is not required to be kept as part of the custody record but the custody record should be noted as to where such a record exists. Whenever a record is made the detainee shall be allowed to check and sign the record of property as correct. Any refusal to sign shall be recorded.

C:4.5 If a detainee is not allowed to keep any article of clothing or personal effects, the reason must be recorded.

*Notes for guidance*

A-51      C:4A *PACE, s.54(1), and paragraph 4.1 require a detainee to be searched when it is clear the custody officer will have continuing duties in relation to that detainee or when that detainee's behaviour or offence makes an inventory appropriate. They do not require every detainee to be searched, e.g. if it is clear a person will only be detained for a short period and is not to be placed in a cell, the custody officer may decide not to search them. In such a case the custody record will be endorsed "not searched", paragraph 4.4 will not apply, and the detainee will be invited to sign the entry. If the detainee refuses, the custody officer will be obliged to ascertain what property they have in accordance with paragraph 4.1.*

C:4B *Paragraph 4.4 does not require the custody officer to record on the custody record property in the* detainee's possession on arrest if, by virtue of its nature, quantity or size, it is not practicable to remove it to the police station.

C:4C *Paragraph 4.4 does not require items of clothing worn by the person to be recorded unless withheld by the custody officer as in paragraph 4.2.*

### C:5 Right not to be held incommunicado

(a) *Action*

C:5.1 Subject to paragraph 5.7B, any person arrested and held in custody at a police station or **A-52** other premises may, on request, have one person known to them or likely to take an interest in their welfare informed at public expense of their whereabouts as soon as practicable. If the person cannot be contacted the detainee may choose up to two alternatives. If they cannot be contacted, the person in charge of detention or the investigation has discretion to allow further attempts until the information has been conveyed. See *Notes 5C* and *5D.*

C:5.2 The exercise of the above right in respect of each person nominated may be delayed only in accordance with Annex B.

C:5.3 The above right may be exercised each time a detainee is taken to another police station.

C:5.4 If the detainee agrees, they may at the custody officer's discretion, receive visits from friends, family or others likely to take an interest in their welfare, or in whose welfare the detainee has an interest. See *Note 5B.*

C:5.5 If a friend, relative or person with an interest in the detainee's welfare enquires about their whereabouts, this information shall be given if the suspect agrees and Annex B does not apply. See *Note 5D.*

C:5.6 The detainee shall be given writing materials, on request, and allowed to telephone one person for a reasonable time, see *Notes 5A* and *5E.* Either or both of these privileges may be denied or delayed if an officer of inspector rank or above considers sending a letter or making a telephone call may result in any of the consequences in:

> (a) Annex B, paragraphs 1 and 2 and the person is detained in connection with an indictable offence;
>
> (b) [*Not used.*]

Nothing in this paragraph permits the restriction or denial of the rights in paragraphs 5.1 and 6.1.

C:5.7 Before any letter or message is sent, or telephone call made, the detainee shall be informed that what they say in any letter, call or message (other than in a communication to a solicitor) may be read or listened to and may be given in evidence. A telephone call may be terminated if it is being abused. The costs can be at public expense at the custody officer's discretion.

C:5.7A Any delay or denial of the rights in this section should be proportionate and should last no longer than necessary.

C:5.7B In the case of a person in police custody for specific purposes and periods in accordance with a direction under the Crime (Sentences) Act 1997, Sched. 1 (productions from prison *etc.*), the exercise of the rights in this section shall be subject to any additional conditions specified in the direction for the purpose of regulating the detainee's contact and communication with others whilst in police custody. See *Note 5F.*

(b) *Documentation*

C:5.8 A record must be kept of any:

> (a) request made under this section and the action taken;
>
> (b) letters, messages or telephone calls made or received or visit received;
>
> (c) refusal by the detainee to have information about them given to an outside enquirer. The detainee must be asked to countersign the record accordingly and any refusal recorded.

*Notes for guidance*

C:5A *A person may request an interpreter to interpret a telephone call or translate a letter.* **A-53**

C:5B *At the custody officer's discretion and subject to the detainee's consent, visits should be allowed when possible, subject to having sufficient personnel to supervise a visit and any possible hindrance to the investigation.*

C:5C *If the detainee does not know anyone to contact for advice or support or cannot contact a friend or relative, the custody officer should bear in mind any local voluntary bodies or other organisations who might be able to help. Paragraph 6.1 applies if legal advice is required.*

C:5D *In some circumstances it may not be appropriate to use the telephone to disclose information under paragraphs 5.1 and 5.5.*

C:5E *The telephone call at paragraph 5.6 is in addition to any communication under paragraphs 5.1 and 6.1.*

C:5F *Prison Service Instruction 26/2012 (Production of Prisoners at the Request of Warranted Law Enforcement Agencies) provides detailed guidance and instructions for police officers and governors and directors of prisons regarding applications for prisoners to be transferred to police custody and their safe custody and treatments while in police custody.*

### C:6 Right to legal advice

#### (a) *Action*

**A-54**    C:6.1 Unless Annex B applies, all detainees must be informed that they may at any time consult and communicate privately with a solicitor, whether in person, in writing or by telephone, and that free independent legal advice is available. See paragraph 3.1, *Notes 1I, 6B* and *6J*.

C:6.2 [*Not used.*]

C:6.3 A poster advertising the right to legal advice must be prominently displayed in the charging area of every police station. See *Note 6H*.

C:6.4 No police officer should, at any time, do or say anything with the intention of dissuading any person who is entitled to legal advice in accordance with this code, whether or not they have been arrested and are detained, from obtaining legal advice. See *Note 6ZA*.

C:6.5 The exercise of the right of access to legal advice may be delayed only as in Annex B. Whenever legal advice is requested, and unless Annex B applies, the custody officer must act without delay to secure the provision of such advice. If the detainee has the right to speak to a solicitor in person but declines to exercise the right the officer should point out that the right includes the right to speak with a solicitor on the telephone. If the detainee continues to waive this right, or a detainee whose right to free legal advice is limited to telephone advice from the Criminal Defence Service (CDS) Direct (see *Note 6B*) declines to exercise that right, the officer should ask them why and any reasons should be recorded on the custody record or the interview record as appropriate. Reminders of the right to legal advice must be given as in paragraphs 3.5, 11.2, 15.4, 16.4, 16.5, 2B of Annex A, 3 of Annex K and 5 of Annex M of this code and Code D, paragraphs 3.17(ii) and 6.3. Once it is clear a detainee does not want to speak to a solicitor in person or by telephone they should cease to be asked their reasons. See *Note 6K*.

C:6.5A In the case of a person who is a juvenile or is mentally disordered or otherwise mentally vulnerable, an appropriate adult should consider whether legal advice from a solicitor is required. If the person indicates that they do not want legal advice, the appropriate adult has the right to ask for a solicitor to attend if this would be in the best interests of the person. However, the person cannot be forced to see the solicitor if they are adamant that they do not wish to do so.

Note: paragraph 1.5A applies this paragraph to 17-year-old detainees.

C:6.6 A detainee who wants legal advice may not be interviewed or continue to be interviewed until they have received such advice unless:

> (a) Annex B applies, when the restriction on drawing adverse inferences from silence in Annex C will apply because the detainee is not allowed an opportunity to consult a solicitor; or
>
> (b) an officer of superintendent rank or above has reasonable grounds for believing that:
>> (i) the consequent delay might:
>>> • lead to interference with, or harm to, evidence connected with an offence;
>>> • lead to interference with, or physical harm to, other people;
>>> • lead to serious loss of, or damage to, property;
>>> • lead to alerting other people suspected of having committed an offence but not yet arrested for it;
>>> • hinder the recovery of property obtained in consequence of the commission of an offence; see *Note 6A*;
>>
>> (ii) when a solicitor, including a duty solicitor, has been contacted and has agreed to attend, awaiting their arrival would cause unreasonable delay to the process of investigation;
>>
>> note: in these cases the restriction on drawing adverse inferences from silence in Annex C will apply because the detainee is not allowed an opportunity to consult a solicitor;
>
> (c) the solicitor the detainee has nominated or selected from a list:
>> (i) cannot be contacted;
>> (ii) has previously indicated they do not wish to be contacted; or
>> (iii) having been contacted, has declined to attend; and
>>> • the detainee has been advised of the duty solicitor scheme but has declined to ask for the duty solicitor;

- in these circumstances the interview may be started or continued without further delay provided an officer of inspector rank or above has agreed to the interview proceeding;

note: the restriction on drawing adverse inferences from silence in Annex C will not apply because the detainee is allowed an opportunity to consult the duty solicitor;

(d) the detainee changes their mind about wanting legal advice or (as the case may be) about wanting a solicitor present at the interview and states that they no longer wish to speak to a solicitor; in these circumstances, the interview may be started or continued without delay provided that:

(i) an officer of inspector rank or above:
- speaks to the detainee to enquire about the reasons for their change of mind (see *Note 6K*), and
- makes, or directs the making of, reasonable efforts to ascertain the solicitor's expected time of arrival and to inform the solicitor that the suspect has stated that they wish to change their mind and the reason (if given);

(ii) the detainee's reason for their change of mind (if given) and the outcome of the action in (i) are recorded in the custody record;

(iii) the detainee, after being informed of the outcome of the action in (i) above, confirms in writing that they want the interview to proceed without speaking or further speaking to a solicitor or (as the case may be) without a solicitor being present and do not wish to wait for a solicitor by signing an entry to this effect in the custody record;

(iv) an officer of inspector rank or above is satisfied that it is proper for the interview to proceed in these circumstances and:
- gives authority in writing for the interview to proceed and, if the authority is not recorded in the custody record, the officer must ensure that the custody record shows the date and time of authority and where it is recorded, and
- takes, or directs the taking of, reasonable steps to inform the solicitor that the authority has been given and the time when the interview is expected to commence and records or causes to be recorded, the outcome of this action in the custody record;

(v) when the interview starts and the interviewer reminds the suspect of their right to legal advice (see paragraph 11.2, Code E, paragraph 4.5, and Code F, paragraph 4.5), the interviewer shall then ensure that the following is recorded in the written interview record or the interview record made in accordance with Code E or F:
- confirmation that the detainee has changed their mind about wanting legal advice or (as the case may be) about wanting a solicitor present and the reasons for it if given;
- the fact that authority for the interview to proceed has been given and, subject to paragraph 2.6A, the name of the authorising officer;
- that if the solicitor arrives at the station before the interview is completed, the detainee will be so informed without delay and a break will be taken to allow them to speak to the solicitor if they wish, unless paragraph 6.6(a) applies; and
- that at any time during the interview, the detainee may again ask for legal advice and that if they do, a break will be taken to allow them to speak to the solicitor, unless paragraph 6.6(a), (b), or (c) applies;

note: in these circumstances, the restriction on drawing adverse inferences from silence in Annex C will not apply because the detainee is allowed an opportunity to consult a solicitor if they wish.

C:6.7 If paragraph 6.6(a) applies, where the reason for authorising the delay ceases to apply, there **A-55** may be no further delay in permitting the exercise of the right in the absence of a further authorisation unless paragraph 6.6(b), (c) or (d) applies. If paragraph 6.6(b)(i) applies, once sufficient information has been obtained to avert the risk, questioning must cease until the detainee has received legal advice unless paragraph 6.6(a), (b)(ii), (c) or (d) applies.

C:6.8 A detainee who has been permitted to consult a solicitor shall be entitled on request to have the solicitor present when they are interviewed unless one of the exceptions in paragraph 6.6 applies.

C:6.9 The solicitor may only be required to leave the interview if their conduct is such that the interviewer is unable properly to put questions to the suspect. See *Notes 6D* and *6E*.

C:6.10 If the interviewer considers a solicitor is acting in such a way, they will stop the interview and consult an officer not below superintendent rank, if one is readily available, and otherwise an officer not below inspector rank not connected with the investigation. After speaking to the solicitor, the officer consulted will decide if the interview should continue in the presence of that solicitor. If they decide it should not, the suspect will be given the opportunity to consult another solicitor before the interview continues and that solicitor given an opportunity to be present at the interview. See *Note 6E.*

C:6.11 The removal of a solicitor from an interview is a serious step and, if it occurs, the officer of superintendent rank or above who took the decision will consider if the incident should be reported to the Solicitors Regulation Authority. If the decision to remove the solicitor has been taken by an officer below superintendent rank, the facts must be reported to an officer of superintendent rank or above who will similarly consider whether a report to the Solicitors Regulation Authority would be appropriate. When the solicitor concerned is a duty solicitor, the report should be both to the Solicitors Regulation Authority and to the Legal Aid Agency.

C:6.12 "Solicitor" in this code means:

- a solicitor who holds a current practising certificate;
- an accredited or probationary representative included on the register of representatives maintained by the Legal Aid Agency.

C:6.12A An accredited or probationary representative sent to provide advice by, and on behalf of, a solicitor shall be admitted to the police station for this purpose unless an officer of inspector rank or above considers such a visit will hinder the investigation and directs otherwise. Hindering the investigation does not include giving proper legal advice to a detainee as in *Note 6D.* Once admitted to the police station, paragraphs 6.6 to 6.10 apply.

C:6.13 In exercising their discretion under paragraph 6.12A, the officer should take into account in particular:

- whether:
  - the identity and status of an accredited or probationary representative have been satisfactorily established;
  - they are of suitable character to provide legal advice, *e.g.* a person with a criminal record is unlikely to be suitable unless the conviction was for a minor offence and not recent;
- any other matters in any written letter of authorisation provided by the solicitor on whose behalf the person is attending the police station. See *Note 6F.*

C:6.14 If the inspector refuses access to an accredited or probationary representative or a decision is taken that such a person should not be permitted to remain at an interview, the inspector must notify the solicitor on whose behalf the representative was acting and give them an opportunity to make alternative arrangements. The detainee must be informed and the custody record noted.

C:6.15 If a solicitor arrives at the station to see a particular person, that person must, unless Annex B applies, be so informed whether or not they are being interviewed and asked if they would like to see the solicitor. This applies even if the detainee has declined legal advice or, having requested it, subsequently agreed to be interviewed without receiving advice. The solicitor's attendance and the detainee's decision must be noted in the custody record.

(b) *Documentation*

C:6.16 Any request for legal advice and the action taken shall be recorded.

C:6.17 A record shall be made in the interview record if a detainee asks for legal advice and an interview is begun either in the absence of a solicitor or their representative, or they have been required to leave an interview.

*Notes for guidance*

**A-56**

C:6ZA *No police officer or police staff shall indicate to any suspect, except to answer a direct question, that period for which they are liable to be detained, or if not detained, the time taken to complete the interview, might be reduced:*

- *if they do not ask for legal advice or do not want a solicitor present when they are interviewed; or*
- *if they have asked for legal advice or (as the case may be) asked for a solicitor to be present when they are interviewed but change their mind and agree to be interviewed without waiting for a solicitor.*

C:6A *In considering if paragraph 6.6(b) applies, the officer should, if practicable, ask the solicitor for an estimate of how long it will take to come to the station and relate this to the time detention is permitted, the time of day (i.e. whether the rest period under paragraph 12.2 is imminent) and the requirements of other investigations. If the solicitor is on their way or is to set off immediately, it will not normally be appropriate to begin an interview before they arrive. If it appears necessary to begin an interview before the solicitor's arrival, they should be given an indication of how long the police would be able to wait before 6.6(b) applies so there is an opportunity to make arrangements for someone else to provide legal advice.*

**C:6B** *A detainee has a right to free legal advice and to be represented by a solicitor. This note for guidance explains the arrangements which enable detainees to obtain legal advice. An outline of these arrangements is also included in the Notice of Rights and Entitlements given to detainees in accordance with paragraph 3.2. The arrangements also apply, with appropriate modifications, to persons attending a police station or other location voluntarily who are cautioned prior to being interviewed. See paragraph 3.21.*

*When a detainee asks for free legal advice, the Defence Solicitor Call Centre (DSCC) must be informed of the request.*

*Free legal advice will be limited to telephone advice provided by CDS Direct if a detainee is:*

- *detained for a non-imprisonable offence;*
- *arrested on a bench warrant for failing to appear and being held for production at court (except where the solicitor has clear documentary evidence available that would result in the client being released from custody);*
- *arrested for drink driving (driving/in charge with excess alcohol, failing to provide a specimen, driving/in charge whilst unfit through drink); or*
- *detained in relation to breach of police or court bail conditions;*

*unless one or more exceptions apply, in which case the DSCC should arrange for advice to be given by a solicitor at the police station, for example:*

- *the police want to interview the detainee or carry out an eye-witness identification procedure;*
- *the detainee needs an appropriate adult;*
- *the detainee is unable to communicate over the telephone;*
- *the detainee alleges serious misconduct by the police;*
- *the investigation includes another offence not included in the list;*
- *the solicitor to be assigned is already at the police station.*

*When free advice is not limited to telephone advice, a detainee can ask for free advice from a solicitor they know or if they do not know a solicitor or the solicitor they know cannot be contacted, from the duty solicitor.*

*To arrange free legal advice, the police should telephone the DSCC. The call centre will decide whether legal advice should be limited to telephone advice from CDS Direct, or whether a solicitor known to the detainee or the duty solicitor should speak to the detainee.*

*When a detainee wants to pay for legal advice themselves:*

- *the DSCC will contact a solicitor of their choice on their behalf;*
- *they may, when free advice is only available by telephone from CDS Direct, still speak to a solicitor of their choice on the telephone for advice, but the solicitor would not be paid by legal aid and may ask the person to pay for the advice;*
- *they should be given an opportunity to consult a specific solicitor or another solicitor from that solicitor's firm; if this solicitor is not available, they may choose up to two alternatives; if these alternatives are not available, the custody officer has discretion to allow further attempts until a solicitor has been contacted and agreed to provide advice;*
- *they are entitled to a private consultation with their chosen solicitor on the telephone or the solicitor may decide to come to the police station;*
- *if their chosen solicitor cannot be contacted, the DSCC may still be called to arrange free legal advice.*

*Apart from carrying out duties necessary to implement these arrangements, an officer must not advise the suspect about any particular firm of solicitors.*

**C:6C** [*Not used.*]

**C:6D** *The solicitor's only role in the police station is to protect and advance the legal rights of their client. On occasions this may require the solicitor to give advice which has the effect of the client avoiding giving evidence which strengthens a prosecution case. The solicitor may intervene in order to seek clarification, challenge an improper question to their client or the manner in which it is put, advise their client not to reply to particular questions, or if they wish to give their client further legal advice. Paragraph 6.9 only applies if the solicitor's approach or conduct prevents or unreasonably obstructs proper questions being put to the suspect or the suspect's response being recorded. Examples of unacceptable conduct include answering questions on a suspect's behalf or providing written replies for the suspect to quote.*

**C:6E** *An officer who takes the decision to exclude a solicitor must be in a position to satisfy the court the decision was properly made. In order to do this they may need to witness what is happening.*

**C:6F** *If an officer of at least inspector rank considers a particular solicitor or firm of solicitors is persistently sending probationary representatives who are unsuited to provide legal advice, they should inform an officer of at least superintendent rank, who may wish to take the matter up with the Solicitors Regulation Authority.*

**C:6G** *Subject to the constraints of Annex B, a solicitor may advise more than one client in an investigation if they wish. Any question of a conflict of interest is for the solicitor under their professional code of conduct. If, however, waiting for a solicitor to give advice to one client may lead to unreasonable delay to the interview with another, the provisions of paragraph 6.6(b) may apply.* **A-57**

C:6H *In addition to a poster in English, a poster or posters containing translations into Welsh, the main minority ethnic languages and the principal European languages should be displayed wherever they are likely to be helpful and it is practicable to do so.*

C:6I [*Not used.*]

C:6J *Whenever a detainee exercises their right to legal advice by consulting or communicating with a solicitor, they must be allowed to do so in private. This right to consult or communicate in private is fundamental. If the requirement for privacy is compromised because what is said or written by the detainee or solicitor for the purpose of giving and receiving legal advice is overheard, listened to, or read by others without the informed consent of the detainee, the right will effectively have been denied. When a detainee speaks to a solicitor on the telephone, they should be allowed to do so in private unless this is impractical because of the design and layout of the custody area or the location of telephones. However, the normal expectation should be that facilities will be available, unless they are being used, at all police stations to enable detainees to speak in private to a solicitor either face to face or over the telephone.*

C:6K *A detainee is not obliged to give reasons for declining legal advice and should not be pressed to do so.*

### C:7 Citizens of independent Commonwealth countries or foreign nationals

#### (a) *Action*

**A-58**

C:7.1 A detainee who is a citizen of an independent Commonwealth country or a national of a foreign country, including the Republic of Ireland, has the right, upon request, to communicate at any time with the appropriate high commission, embassy or consulate. That detainee must be informed as soon as practicable of this right and asked if they want to have their high commission, embassy or consulate told of their whereabouts and the grounds for their detention. Such a request should be acted upon as soon as practicable. See *Note 7A.*

C:7.2 A detainee who is a citizen of a country with which a bilateral consular convention or agreement is in force requiring notification of arrest, must also be informed that subject to paragraph 7.4, notification of their arrest will be sent to the appropriate high commission, embassy or consulate as soon as practicable, whether or not they request it. A list of the countries to which this requirement currently applies and contact details for the relevant high commissions, embassies and consulates can be obtained from the Consular Directorate of the Foreign and Commonwealth Office (FCO) as follows:

- from the FCO web pages:
  - https://gov.uk/government/publications/table-of-consular-conventions-and-mandatory-notification-obligations, and
  - https://www.gov.uk/government/publications/foreign-embassies-in-the-uk
- by telephone to 020 7008 3100,
- by email to fcocorrespondence@fco.gov.uk.
- or by letter to the Foreign and Commonwealth Office, King Charles Street, London, SW1A 2AH.

C:7.3 Consular officers may, if the detainee agrees, visit one of their nationals in police detention to talk to them and, if required, to arrange for legal advice. Such visits shall take place out of the hearing of a police officer.

C:7.4 Notwithstanding the provisions of consular conventions, if the detainee claims that they are a refugee or have applied or intend to apply for asylum, the custody officer must ensure that the UK Visas and Immigration (UKVI) (formerly the UK Border Agency) is informed as soon as practicable of the claim. UKVI will then determine whether compliance with relevant international obligations requires notification of the arrest to be sent and will inform the custody officer as to what action police need to take.

#### (b) *Documentation*

**A-59**

C:7.5 A record shall be made:

- when a detainee is informed of their rights under this section and of any requirement in paragraph 7.2;
- of any communications with a high commission, embassy or consulate; and
- of any communications with UKVI about a detainee's claim to be a refugee or to be seeking asylum and the resulting action taken by police.

Archbold paragraph numbers

*Note for guidance*

C:7A *The exercise of the rights in this section may not be interfered with even though Annex B applies.*  **A-60**

### C:8 Conditions of detention

(a) *Action*

C:8.1 So far as it is practicable, not more than one detainee should be detained in each cell. See  **A-61**
*Note 8C.*

C:8.2 Cells in use must be adequately heated, cleaned and ventilated. They must be adequately lit, subject to such dimming as is compatible with safety and security to allow people detained overnight to sleep. No additional restraints shall be used within a locked cell unless absolutely necessary and then only restraint equipment, approved for use in that force by the chief officer, which is reasonable and necessary in the circumstances having regard to the detainee's demeanour and with a view to ensuring their safety and the safety of others. If a detainee is deaf, mentally disordered or otherwise mentally vulnerable, particular care must be taken when deciding whether to use any form of approved restraints.

C:8.3 Blankets, mattresses, pillows and other bedding supplied shall be of a reasonable standard and in a clean and sanitary condition. See *Note 8A.*

C:8.4 Access to toilet and washing facilities must be provided.

C:8.5 If it is necessary to remove a detainee's clothes for the purposes of investigation, for hygiene, health reasons or cleaning, replacement clothing of a reasonable standard of comfort and cleanliness shall be provided. A detainee may not be interviewed unless adequate clothing has been offered.

C:8.6 At least two light meals and one main meal should be offered in any 24-hour period. See *Note 8B.* Drinks should be provided at meal times and upon reasonable request between meals. Whenever necessary, advice shall be sought from the appropriate healthcare professional, see *Note 9A,* on medical and dietary matters. As far as practicable, meals provided shall offer a varied diet and meet any specific dietary needs or religious beliefs the detainee may have. The detainee may, at the custody officer's discretion, have meals supplied by their family or friends at their expense. See *Note 8A.*

C:8.7 Brief outdoor exercise shall be offered daily if practicable.

C:8.8 A juvenile shall not be placed in a police cell unless no other secure accommodation is available and the custody officer considers it is not practicable to supervise them if they are not placed in a cell or that a cell provides more comfortable accommodation than other secure accommodation in the station. A juvenile may not be placed in a cell with a detained adult.

Note: paragraph 1.5A extends these requirements to 17-year-old detainees.

(b) *Documentation*

C:8.9 A record must be kept of replacement clothing and meals offered.  **A-62**

C:8.10 If a juvenile is placed in a cell, the reason must be recorded.

Note: paragraph 1.5A extends this requirement to 17-year-old detainees.

C:8.11 The use of any restraints on a detainee whilst in a cell, the reasons for it and, if appropriate, the arrangements for enhanced supervision of the detainee whilst so restrained, shall be recorded. See paragraph 3.9.

*Notes for guidance*

C:8A *The provisions in paragraph 8.3 and 8.6 respectively are of particular importance in the case of a*  **A-63**
*person likely to be detained for an extended period. In deciding whether to allow meals to be supplied by family or friends, the custody officer is entitled to take account of the risk of items being concealed in any food or package and the officer's duties and responsibilities under food handling legislation.*

C:8B *Meals should, so far as practicable, be offered at recognised meal times, or at other times that take account of when the detainee last had a meal.*

C:8C *The Detention and Custody Authorised Professional Practice (APP) produced by the College of Policing (see* http://www.app.college.police.uk*) provides more detailed guidance on matters concerning detainee healthcare and treatment and associated f orensic issues which should be read in conjunction with sections 8 and 9 of this code.*

## C:9 Care and treatment of detained persons

### (a) *General*

**A-64**     C:9.1 Nothing in this section prevents the police from calling an appropriate healthcare professional to examine a detainee for the purposes of obtaining evidence relating to any offence in which the detainee is suspected of being involved. See *Notes 9A* and *8C*.

C:9.2 If a complaint is made by, or on behalf of, a detainee about their treatment since their arrest, or it comes to notice that a detainee may have been treated improperly, a report must be made as soon as practicable to an officer of inspector rank or above not connected with the investigation. If the matter concerns a possible assault or the possibility of the unnecessary or unreasonable use of force, an appropriate healthcare professional must also be called as soon as practicable.

C:9.3 Detainees should be visited at least every hour. If no reasonably foreseeable risk was identified in a risk assessment, see paragraphs 3.6-3.10, there is no need to wake a sleeping detainee. Those suspected of being under the influence of drink or drugs or both or of having swallowed drugs, see *Note 9CA*, or whose level of consciousness causes concern must, subject to any clinical directions given by the appropriate healthcare professional, see paragraph 9.13:

- be visited and roused at least every half hour;
- have their condition assessed as in Annex H;
- and clinical treatment arranged if appropriate.

See *Notes 9B, 9C* and *9H*.

C:9.4 When arrangements are made to secure clinical attention for a detainee, the custody officer must make sure all relevant information which might assist in the treatment of the detainee's condition is made available to the responsible healthcare professional. This applies whether or not the healthcare professional asks for such information. Any officer or police staff with relevant information must inform the custody officer as soon as practicable.

### (b) *Clinical treatment and attention*

**A-65**     C:9.5 The custody officer must make sure a detainee receives appropriate clinical attention as soon as reasonably practicable if the person:

(a) appears to be suffering from physical illness; or

(b) is injured; or

(c) appears to be suffering from a mental disorder; or

(d) appears to need clinical attention.

C:9.5A This applies even if the detainee makes no request for clinical attention and whether or not they have already received clinical attention elsewhere. If the need for attention appears urgent, *e.g.* when indicated as in Annex H, the nearest available healthcare professional or an ambulance must be called immediately.

C:9.5B The custody officer must also consider the need for clinical attention as set out in *Note for Guidance 9C* in relation to those suffering the effects of alcohol or drugs.

C:9.6 Paragraph 9.5 is not meant to prevent or delay the transfer to a hospital if necessary of a person detained under the Mental Health Act 1983, s.136. See *Note 9D*. When an assessment under that Act is to take place at a police station, see paragraph 3.16, the custody officer must consider whether an appropriate healthcare professional should be called to conduct an initial clinical check on the detainee. This applies particularly when there is likely to be any significant delay in the arrival of a suitably qualified medical practitioner.

C:9.7 If it appears to the custody officer, or they are told, that a person brought to a station under arrest may be suffering from an infectious disease or condition, the custody officer must take reasonable steps to safeguard the health of the detainee and others at the station. In deciding what action to take, advice must be sought from an appropriate healthcare professional. See *Note 9E*. The custody officer has discretion to isolate the person and their property until clinical directions have been obtained.

**A-66**     C:9.8 If a detainee requests a clinical examination, an appropriate healthcare professional must be called as soon as practicable to assess the detainee's clinical needs. If a safe and appropriate care plan cannot be provided, the appropriate healthcare professional's advice must be sought. The detainee may also be examined by a medical practitioner of their choice at their expense.

C:9.9 If a detainee is required to take or apply any medication in compliance with clinical directions prescribed before their detention, the custody officer must consult the appropriate healthcare professional before the use of the medication. Subject to the restrictions in paragraph 9.10, the custody officer is responsible for the safekeeping of any medication and for making sure the detainee is given the opportunity to take or apply prescribed or approved medication. Any such consultation and its outcome shall be noted in the custody record.

C:9.10 No police officer may administer or supervise the self-administration of medically prescribed controlled drugs of the types and forms listed in the Misuse of Drugs Regulations 2001, Sched. 2 or 3. A detainee may only self-administer such drugs under the personal supervision of the registered medical practitioner authorising their use or other appropriate healthcare professional. The custody officer may supervise the self-administration of, or authorise other custody staff to supervise the self-administration of, drugs listed in Schedule 4 or 5 for self-administration if the officer has consulted the appropriate healthcare professional authorising their use and both are satisfied self-administration will not expose the detainee, police officers or anyone else to the risk of harm or injury.

C:9.11 When appropriate healthcare professionals administer drugs or authorise the use of other medications, supervise their self-administration or consult with the custody officer about allowing self-administration of drugs listed in Schedule 4 or 5, it must be within current medicines legislation and the scope of practice as determined by their relevant statutory regulatory body.

C:9.12 If a detainee has in their possession, or claims to need, medication relating to a heart condition, diabetes, epilepsy or a condition of comparable potential seriousness then, even though paragraph 9.5 may not apply, the advice of the appropriate healthcare professional must be obtained.

C:9.13 Whenever the appropriate healthcare professional is called in accordance with this section to examine or treat a detainee, the custody officer shall ask for their opinion about:

- any risks or problems which police need to take into account when making decisions about the detainee's continued detention;
- when to carry out an interview if applicable; and
- the need for safeguards.

C:9.14 When clinical directions are given by the appropriate healthcare professional, whether orally or in writing, and the custody officer has any doubts or is in any way uncertain about any aspect of the directions, the custody officer shall ask for clarification. It is particularly important that directions concerning the frequency of visits are clear, precise and capable of being implemented. See *Note 9F*.

### (c) *Documentation*

C:9.15 A record must be made in the custody record of: **A-67**

- (a) the arrangements made for an examination by an appropriate healthcare professional under paragraph 9.2 and of any complaint reported under that paragraph together with any relevant remarks by the custody officer;
- (b) any arrangements made in accordance with paragraph 9.5;
- (c) any request for a clinical examination under paragraph 9.8 and any arrangements made in response;
- (d) the injury, ailment, condition or other reason which made it necessary to make the arrangements in (a) to (c); see *Note 9G*;
- (e) any clinical directions and advice, including any further clarifications, given to police by a healthcare professional concerning the care and treatment of the detainee in connection with any of the arrangements made in (a) to (c); see *Notes E* and *9F*;
- (f) if applicable, the responses received when attempting to rouse a person using the procedure in Annex H. See *Note 9H*.

C:9.16 If a healthcare professional does not record their clinical findings in the custody record, the record must show where they are recorded. See *Note 9G*. However, information which is necessary to custody staff to ensure the effective ongoing care and well-being of the detainee must be recorded openly in the custody record, see paragraph 3.8 and Annex G, paragraph 7.

C:9.17 Subject to the requirements of section 4, the custody record shall include:

- a record of all medication a detainee has in their possession on arrival at the police station;
- a note of any such medication they claim to need but do not have with them.

### Notes for guidance

C:9A *A "healthcare professional" means a clinically qualified person working within the scope of practice as* **A-68** *determined by their relevant statutory regulatory body. Whether a healthcare professional is "appropriate" depends on the circumstances of the duties they carry out at the time.*

C:9B *Whenever possible juveniles and mentally vulnerable detainees should be visited more frequently. Note: paragraph 1.5A extends this note to 17-year-old detainees.*

C:9C *A detainee who appears drunk or behaves abnormally may be suffering from illness, the effects of drugs or may have sustained injury, particularly a head injury which is not apparent. A detainee needing or dependent on certain drugs, including alcohol, may experience harmful effects within a short time of being deprived of their* supply. *In these circumstances, when there is any doubt, police should always act urgently to call an appropriate healthcare professional or an ambulance. Paragraph 9.5 does not apply to minor ailments or injuries which do not need attention. However, all such ailments or injuries must be recorded in the custody record and any doubt must be resolved in favour of calling the appropriate healthcare professional.*

C:9CA *Paragraph 9.3 would apply to a person in police custody by order of a magistrates' court under the Criminal Justice Act 1988, s.152 (as amended by the Drugs Act 2005, s.8) to facilitate the recovery of evidence after being charged with drug possession or drug trafficking and suspected of having swallowed drugs. In the case of the healthcare needs of a person who has swallowed drugs, the custody officer subject to any clinical directions, should consider the necessity for rousing every half hour. This does not negate the need for regular visiting of the suspect in the cell.*

C:9D *Whenever practicable, arrangements should be made for persons detained for assessment under the Mental Health Act 1983, s.136 to be taken to a hospital. Chapter 10 of the Mental Health Act 1983 Code of Practice (as revised) provides more detailed guidance about arranging assessments under section 136 and transferring detainees from police stations to other places of safety.*

C:9E *It is important to respect a person's right to privacy and information about their health must be kept confidential and only disclosed with their consent or in accordance with clinical advice when it is necessary to protect the detainee's health or that of others who come into contact with them.*

C:9F *The custody officer should always seek to clarify directions that the detainee requires constant observation or supervision and should ask the appropriate healthcare professional to explain precisely what action needs to be taken to implement such directions.*

C:9G *Paragraphs 9.15 and 9.16 do not require any information about the cause of any injury, ailment or condition to be recorded on the custody record if it appears capable of providing evidence of an offence.*

C:9H *The purpose of recording a person's responses when attempting to rouse them using the procedure in Annex H is to enable any change in the individual's consciousness level to be noted and clinical treatment arranged if appropriate.*

### C:10 Cautions

#### (a) *When a caution must be given*

**A-69**

C:10.1 A person whom there are grounds to suspect of an offence, see *Note 10A*, must be cautioned before any questions about an offence, or further questions if the answers provide the grounds for suspicion, are put to them if either the suspect's answers or silence (*i.e.* failure or refusal to answer or answer satisfactorily) may be given in evidence to a court in a prosecution. A person need not be cautioned if questions are for other necessary purposes, *e.g.*:

(a) solely to establish their identity or ownership of any vehicle;

(b) to obtain information in accordance with any relevant statutory requirement, see paragraph 10.9;

(c) in furtherance of the proper and effective conduct of a search, *e.g.* to determine the need to search in the exercise of powers of stop and search or to seek co-operation while carrying out a search; or

(d) to seek verification of a written record as in paragraph 11.13.

C:10.2 Whenever a person not under arrest is initially cautioned, or reminded they are under caution, that person must at the same time be told they are not under arrest and informed of the provisions of paragraph 3.21 which explain how they may obtain legal advice according to whether they are at a police station or elsewhere. See *Note 10C.*

C:10.3 A person who is arrested, or further arrested, must be informed at the time if practicable or, if not, as soon as it becomes practicable thereafter, that they are under arrest and of the grounds and reasons for their arrest, see paragraph 3.4, *Note 10B* and Code G, paragraphs 2.2 and 4.3.

C:10.4 As required by Code G, section 3, a person who is arrested, or further arrested, must also be cautioned unless:

(a) it is impracticable to do so by reason of their condition or behaviour at the time;

(b) they have already been cautioned immediately prior to arrest as in paragraph 10.1.

#### (b) *Terms of the cautions*

C:10.5 The caution which must be given on:

(a) arrest; or

(b) all other occasions before a person is charged or informed they may be prosecuted; see section 16,

should, unless the restriction on drawing adverse inferences from silence applies, see Annex C, be in the following terms:

*"You do not have to say anything. But it may harm your defence if you do not mention when questioned something which you later rely on in court. Anything you do say may be given in evidence.".*

Where the use of the Welsh language is appropriate, a constable may provide the caution directly in Welsh in the following terms:

*"Does dim rhaid i chi ddweud dim byd. Ond gall niweidio eich amddiffyniad os na fyddwch chi'n sôn, wrth gael eich holi, am rywbeth y byddwch chi'n dibynnu arno nes ymlaen yn y Llys. Gall unrhyw beth yr ydych yn ei ddweud gael ei roi fel tystiolaeth.".*

See *Note 10G*.

C:10.6 Annex C, paragraph 2, sets out the alternative terms of the caution to be used when the **A-70** restriction on drawing adverse inferences from silence applies.

C:10.7 Minor deviations from the words of any caution given in accordance with this code do not constitute a breach of this code, provided the sense of the relevant caution is preserved. See *Note 10D*.

C:10.8 After any break in questioning under caution, the person being questioned must be made aware they remain under caution. If there is any doubt the relevant caution should be given again in full when the interview resumes. See *Note 10E*.

C:10.9 When, despite being cautioned, a person fails to co-operate or to answer particular questions which may affect their immediate treatment, the person should be informed of any relevant consequences and that those consequences are not affected by the caution. Examples are when a person's refusal to provide:

- their name and address when charged may make them liable to detention;
- particulars and information in accordance with a statutory requirement, *e.g.* under the Road Traffic Act 1988, may amount to an offence or may make the person liable to a further arrest.

(c) *Special warnings under the Criminal Justice and Public Order Act 1994, ss.36 and 37*

C:10.10 When a suspect interviewed at a police station or authorised place of detention after ar- **A-71** rest fails or refuses to answer certain questions, or to answer satisfactorily, after due warning, see *Note 10F*, a court or jury may draw such inferences as appear proper under the Criminal Justice and Public Order Act 1994, ss.36 and 37. Such inferences may only be drawn when:

(a) the restriction on drawing adverse inferences from silence, see Annex C, does not apply; and
(b) the suspect is arrested by a constable and fails or refuses to account for any objects, marks or substances, or marks on such objects found:
  - on their person;
  - in or on their clothing or footwear;
  - otherwise in their possession; or
  - in the place they were arrested;
(c) the arrested suspect was found by a constable at a place at or about the time the offence for which that officer has arrested them is alleged to have been committed, and the suspect fails or refuses to account for their presence there.

When the restriction on drawing adverse inferences from silence applies, the suspect may still be asked to account for any of the matters in (b) or (c) but the special warning described in paragraph 10.11 will not apply and must not be given.

C: 10.11 For an inference to be drawn when a suspect fails or refuses to answer a question about one of these matters or to answer it satisfactorily, the suspect must first be told in ordinary language:

(a) what offence is being investigated;
(b) what fact they are being asked to account for;
(c) this fact may be due to them taking part in the commission of the offence;
(d) a court may draw a proper inference if they fail or refuse to account for this fact; and
(e) a record is being made of the interview and it may be given in evidence if they are brought to trial.

(d) *Juveniles and persons who are mentally disordered or otherwise mentally vulnerable*

C:10.11A The information required in paragraph 10.11 must not be given to a suspect who is a juvenile or who is mentally disordered or otherwise mentally vulnerable unless the appropriate adult is present.

C:10.12 If a juvenile or a person who is mentally disordered or otherwise mentally vulnerable is cautioned in the absence of the appropriate adult, the caution must be repeated in the adult's presence.

C:10.12A Paragraph 1.5A extends the requirements in paragraphs 10.11A and 10.12 to 17-year-old detainees.

### (e) *Documentation*

C:10.13 A record shall be made when a caution is given under this section, either in the interviewer's pocket book or in the interview record.

### Notes for guidance

**A-72**

C:10A *There must be some reasonable, objective grounds for the suspicion, based on known facts or information which are relevant to the likelihood the offence has been committed and the person to be questioned committed it.*

C:10B *An arrested person must be given sufficient information to enable them to understand that they have been deprived of their liberty and the reason they have been arrested, e.g. when a person is arrested on suspicion of committing an offence they must be informed of the suspected offence's nature, when and where it was committed. The suspect must also be informed of the reason or reasons why the arrest is considered necessary. Vague or technical language should be avoided.*

C:10C *The restriction on drawing inferences from silence, see Annex C, paragraph 1, does not apply to a person who has not been detained and who therefore cannot be prevented from seeking legal advice if they want, see paragraph 3.21.*

C:10D *If it appears a person does not understand the caution, the person giving it should explain it in their own words.*

C:10E *It may be necessary to show to the court that nothing occurred during an interview break or between interviews which influenced the suspect's recorded evidence. After a break in an interview or at the beginning of a subsequent interview, the interviewing officer should summarise the reason for the break and confirm this with the suspect.*

C:10F *The Criminal Justice and Public Order Act 1994, ss.36 and 37, apply only to suspects who have been arrested by a constable or an officer of Revenue and Customs and are given the relevant warning by the police or Revenue and Customs officer who made the arrest or who is investigating the offence. They do not apply to any interviews with suspects who have not been arrested.*

C:10G *Nothing in this code requires a caution to be given or repeated when informing a person not under arrest they may be prosecuted for an offence. However, a court will not be able to draw any inferences under the Criminal Justice and Public Order Act 1994, s.34, if the person was not cautioned.*

### C:11 Interviews—general

#### (a) *Action*

★**A-73**

C:11.1A An interview is the questioning of a person regarding their involvement or suspected involvement in a criminal offence or offences which, under paragraph 10.1, must be carried out under caution. Before a person is interviewed, they and, if they are represented, their solicitor must be given sufficient information to enable them to understand the nature of any such offence, and why they are suspected of committing it (see paras 3.4(a) and 10.3), in order to allow for the effective exercise of the rights of the defence. However, whilst the information must always be sufficient for the person to understand the nature of any offence (see *Note 11ZA*), this does not require the disclosure of details at a time which might prejudice the criminal investigation. The decision about what needs to be disclosed for the purpose of this requirement therefore rests with the investigating officer who has sufficient knowledge of the case to make that decision. The officer who discloses the information shall make a record of the information disclosed and when it was disclosed. This record may be made in the interview record, in the officer's pocket book or other form provided for this purpose. Procedures under the Road Traffic Act 1988, s.7, or the Transport and Works Act 1992, s.31, do not constitute interviewing for the purpose of this code.

C:11.1 Following a decision to arrest a suspect, they must not be interviewed about the relevant offence except at a police station or other authorised place of detention, unless the consequent delay would be likely to:

  (a) lead to:
- interference with, or harm to, evidence connected with an offence;
- interference with, or physical harm to, other people; or
- serious loss of, or damage to, property;

  (b) lead to alerting other people suspected of committing an offence but not yet arrested for it; or

(c) hinder the recovery of property obtained in consequence of the commission of an offence. Interviewing in any of these circumstances shall cease once the relevant risk has been averted or the necessary questions have been put in order to attempt to avert that risk.

C:11.2 Immediately prior to the commencement or re-commencement of any interview at a police station or other authorised place of detention, the interviewer should remind the suspect of their entitlement to free legal advice and that the interview can be delayed for legal advice to be obtained, unless one of the exceptions in paragraph 6.6 applies. It is the interviewer's responsibility to make sure all reminders are recorded in the interview record.

C:11.3 [*Not used.*]

C:11.4 At the beginning of an interview the interviewer, after cautioning the suspect, see section 10, shall put to them any significant statement or silence which occurred in the presence and hearing of a police officer or other police staff before the start of the interview and which have not been put to the suspect in the course of a previous interview. See *Note 11A*. The interviewer shall ask the suspect whether they confirm or deny that earlier statement or silence and if they want to add anything.

C:11.4A A significant statement is one which appears capable of being used in evidence against the suspect, in particular a direct admission of guilt. A significant silence is a failure or refusal to answer a question or answer satisfactorily when under caution, which might, allowing for the restriction on drawing adverse inferences from silence, see Annex C, give rise to an inference under the Criminal Justice and Public Order Act 1994, Pt III.

C:11.5 No interviewer may try to obtain answers or elicit a statement by the use of oppression. Except as in paragraph 10.9, no interviewer shall indicate, except to answer a direct question, what action will be taken by the police if the person being questioned answers questions, makes a statement or refuses to do either. If the person asks directly what action will be taken if they answer questions, make a statement or refuse to do either, the interviewer may inform them what action the police propose to take provided that action is itself proper and warranted.

C:11.6 The interview or further interview of a person about an offence with which that person has not been charged or for which they have not been informed they may be prosecuted, must cease when:

  (a) the officer in charge of the investigation is satisfied all the questions they consider relevant to obtaining accurate and reliable information about the offence have been put to the suspect, this includes allowing the suspect an opportunity to give an innocent explanation and asking questions to test if the explanation is accurate and reliable, *e.g.* to clear up ambiguities or clarify what the suspect said;

  (b) the officer in charge of the investigation has taken account of any other available evidence; and

  (c) the officer in charge of the investigation, or in the case of a detained suspect, the custody officer, see paragraph 16.1, reasonably believes there is sufficient evidence to provide a realistic prospect of conviction for that offence. See *Note 11B*.

This paragraph does not prevent officers in revenue cases or acting under the confiscation provisions of the Criminal Justice Act 1988 or the Drug Trafficking Act 1994 from inviting suspects to complete a formal question and answer record after the interview is concluded.

(b) *Interview records*

C:11.7 (a) An accurate record must be made of each interview, whether or not the interview takes **A-74** place at a police station.

  (b) The record must state the place of interview, the time it begins and ends, any interview breaks and, subject to paragraph 2.6A, the names of all those present; and must be made on the forms provided for this purpose or in the interviewer's pocket book or in accordance with Codes of Practice E or F.

  (c) Any written record must be made and completed during the interview, unless this would not be practicable or would interfere with the conduct of the interview, and must constitute either a verbatim record of what has been said or, failing this, an account of the interview which adequately and accurately summarises it.

C:11.8 If a written record is not made during the interview it must be made as soon as practicable after its completion.

C:11.9 Written interview records must be timed and signed by the maker.

C:11.10 If a written record is not completed during the interview the reason must be recorded in the interview record.

C:11.11 Unless it is impracticable, the person interviewed shall be given the opportunity to read the interview record and to sign it as correct or to indicate how they consider it inaccurate. If the person interviewed cannot read or refuses to read the record or sign it, the senior interviewer present shall read it to them and ask whether they would like to sign it as correct or make their mark or to indicate how they consider it inaccurate. The interviewer shall certify on the interview record itself what has occurred. See *Note 11E.*

C:11.12 If the appropriate adult or the person's solicitor is present during the interview, they should also be given an opportunity to read and sign the interview record or any written statement taken down during the interview.

Note: paragraph 1.5A extends the requirement in this paragraph to interviews of 17-year-old suspects.

C:11.13 A written record shall be made of any comments made by a suspect, including unsolicited comments, which are outside the context of an interview but which might be relevant to the offence. Any such record must be timed and signed by the maker. When practicable the suspect shall be given the opportunity to read that record and to sign it as correct or to indicate how they consider it inaccurate. See *Note 11E.*

C:11.14 Any refusal by a person to sign an interview record when asked in accordance with this code must itself be recorded.

### (c) *Juveniles and mentally disordered or otherwise mentally vulnerable people*

A-75 C:11.15 A juvenile or person who is mentally disordered or otherwise mentally vulnerable must not be interviewed regarding their involvement or suspected involvement in a criminal offence or offences, or asked to provide or sign a written statement under caution or record of interview, in the absence of the appropriate adult unless paragraphs 11.1, 11.18 to 11.20 apply. See *Note 11C.*

Note: paragraph 1.5A extends the requirement in this paragraph to 17-year-old suspects.

C:11.16 Juveniles may only be interviewed at their place of education in exceptional circumstances and only when the principal or their nominee agrees. Every effort should be made to notify the parent(s) or other person responsible for the juvenile's welfare and the appropriate adult, if this is a different person, that the police want to interview the juvenile and reasonable time should be allowed to enable the appropriate adult to be present at the interview. If awaiting the appropriate adult would cause unreasonable delay, and unless the juvenile is suspected of an offence against the educational establishment, the principal or their nominee can act as the appropriate adult for the purposes of the interview.

Note: paragraph 1.5A extends the requirement in this paragraph to 17-year-old suspects.

C:11.17 If an appropriate adult is present at an interview, they shall be informed:
- that they are not expected to act simply as an observer; and
- that the purpose of their presence is to:
  - advise the person being interviewed;
  - observe whether the interview is being conducted properly and fairly; and
  - facilitate communication with the person being interviewed.

### (d) *Vulnerable suspects—urgent interviews at police stations*

C:11.18 The following interviews may take place only if an officer of superintendent rank or above considers delaying the interview will lead to the consequences in paragraph 11.1(a) to (c), and is satisfied the interview would not significantly harm the person's physical or mental state (see Annex G):
- (a) an interview of a juvenile or person who is mentally disordered or otherwise mentally vulnerable without the appropriate adult being present (note: paragraph 1.5A extends this requirement to 17-year-old detainees);
- (b) an interview of anyone other than in (a) who appears unable to:
  - appreciate the significance of questions and their answers; or
  - understand what is happening because of the effects of drink, drugs or any illness, ailment or condition;
- (c) an interview, without an interpreter being present, of a person whom the custody officer has determined requires an interpreter (see paras 3.5(c)(ii) and 3.12) which is carried out by an interviewer speaking the suspect's own language or (as the case may be) otherwise establishing effective communication which is sufficient to enable the necessary questions to be asked and answered in order to avert the consequences. See paragraphs 13.2 and 13.5.

C:11.19 These interviews may not continue once sufficient information has been obtained to avert the consequences in paragraph 11.1(a) to (c).

C:11.20 A record shall be made of the grounds for any decision to interview a person under paragraph 11.18.

*Notes for guidance*

C:11ZA *The requirement in paragraph 11.1A for a suspect to be given sufficient information about the offence* ★**A-76** *applies prior to the interview and whether or not they are legally represented. What is sufficient will depend on the circumstances of the case, but it should normally include, as a minimum, a description of the facts relating to the suspected offence that are known to the officer, including the time and place in question. This aims to avoid suspects being confused or unclear about what they are supposed to have done and to help an innocent suspect to clear the matter up more quickly.*

C:11A *Paragraph 11.4 does not prevent the interviewer from putting significant statements and silences to a suspect again at a later stage or a further interview.*

C:11B *The Criminal Procedure and Investigations Act 1996 code of practice, paragraph 3.5 states "In conducting an investigation, the investigator should pursue all reasonable lines of enquiry, whether these point towards or away from the suspect. What is reasonable will depend on the particular circumstances." Interviewers should keep this in mind when deciding what questions to ask in an interview.*

C:11C *Although juveniles or people who are mentally disordered or otherwise mentally vulnerable are often capable of providing reliable evidence, they may, without knowing or wishing to do so, be particularly prone in certain circumstances to provide information that may be unreliable, misleading or self-incriminating. Special care should always be taken when questioning such a person, and the appropriate adult should be involved if there is any doubt about a person's age, mental state or capacity. Because of the risk of unreliable evidence it is also important to obtain corroboration of any facts admitted whenever possible. Paragraph 1.5A extends this note to 17-year-old suspects.*

C:11D *Juveniles should not be arrested at their place of education unless this is unavoidable. When a juvenile is arrested at their place of education, the principal or their nominee must be informed. Paragraph 1.5A extends this note to 17-year-old suspects.*

C:11E *Significant statements described in paragraph 11.4 will always be relevant to the offence and must be recorded. When a suspect agrees to read records of interviews and other comments and sign them as correct, they should be asked to endorse the record with, e.g. "I agree that this is a correct record of what was said" and add their signature. If the suspect does not agree with the record, the interviewer should record the details of any disagreement and ask the suspect to read these details and sign them to the effect that they accurately reflect their disagreement. Any refusal to sign should be recorded.*

### C:12 Interviews in police stations

(a) *Action*

C:12.1 If a police officer wants to interview or conduct enquiries which require the presence of a **A-77** detainee, the custody officer is responsible for deciding whether to deliver the detainee into the officer's custody. An investigating officer who is given custody of a detainee takes over responsibility for the detainee's care and safe custody for the purposes of this code until they return the detainee to the custody officer when they must report the manner in which they complied with the code whilst having custody of the detainee.

C:12.2 Except as below, in any period of 24 hours a detainee must be allowed a continuous period of at least 8 hours for rest, free from questioning, travel or any interruption in connection with the investigation concerned. This period should normally be at night or other appropriate time which takes account of when the detainee last slept or rested. If a detainee is arrested at a police station after going there voluntarily, the period of 24 hours runs from the time of their arrest and not the time of arrival at the police station. The period may not be interrupted or delayed, except:

    (a) when there are reasonable grounds for believing not delaying or interrupting the period would:

        (i) involve a risk of harm to people or serious loss of, or damage to, property;

        (ii) delay unnecessarily the person's release from custody; or

        (iii) otherwise prejudice the outcome of the investigation;

    (b) at the request of the detainee, their appropriate adult or legal representative;

    (c) when a delay or interruption is necessary in order to:

        (i) comply with the legal obligations and duties arising under section 15; or

        (ii) to take action required under section 9 or in accordance with medical advice.

If the period is interrupted in accordance with (a), a fresh period must be allowed. Interruptions under (b) and (c) do not require a fresh period to be allowed.

C:12.3 Before a detainee is interviewed the custody officer, in consultation with the officer in charge of the investigation and appropriate healthcare professionals as necessary, shall assess whether the detainee is fit enough to be interviewed. This means determining and considering the risks to the detainee's physical and mental state if the interview took place and determining what safeguards are needed to allow the interview to take place. See Annex G. The custody officer shall not allow a detainee to be interviewed if the custody officer considers it would cause significant harm to the detainee's physical or mental state. Vulnerable suspects listed at paragraph 11.18 shall be treated as always being at some risk during an interview and these persons may not be interviewed except in accordance with paragraphs 11.18 to 11.20.

C:12.4 As far as practicable interviews shall take place in interview rooms which are adequately heated, lit and ventilated.

C:12.5 A suspect whose detention without charge has been authorised under PACE because the detention is necessary for an interview to obtain evidence of the offence for which they have been arrested may choose not to answer questions but police do not require the suspect's consent or agreement to interview them for this purpose. If a suspect takes steps to prevent themselves being questioned or further questioned, *e.g.* by refusing to leave their cell to go to a suitable interview room or by trying to leave the interview room, they shall be advised their consent or agreement to interview is not required. The suspect shall be cautioned as in section 10, and informed if they fail or refuse to co-operate, the interview may take place in the cell and that their failure or refusal to co-operate may be given in evidence. The suspect shall then be invited to co-operate and go into the interview room.

C:12.6 People being questioned or making statements shall not be required to stand.

A-78 C:12.7 Before the interview commences each interviewer shall, subject to paragraph 2.6A, identify themselves and any other persons present to the interviewee.

C:12.8 Breaks from interviewing should be made at recognised meal times or at other times that take account of when an interviewee last had a meal. Short refreshment breaks shall be provided at approximately two hour intervals, subject to the interviewer's discretion to delay a break if there are reasonable grounds for believing it would:

    (i) involve a:

        • risk of harm to people;

        • serious loss of, or damage to, property;

    (ii) unnecessarily delay the detainee's release; or

    (iii) otherwise prejudice the outcome of the investigation.

See *Note 12B*.

C:12.9 If during the interview a complaint is made by or on behalf of the interviewee concerning the provisions of any of the codes, or it comes to the interviewer's notice that the interviewee may have been treated improperly, the interviewer should:

    (i) record the matter in the interview record; and

    (ii) inform the custody officer, who is then responsible for dealing with it as in section 9.

(b) *Documentation*

A-79 C:12.10 A record must be made of the:

    • time a detainee is not in the custody of the custody officer, and why;

    • reason for any refusal to deliver the detainee out of that custody.

C:12.11 A record shall be made of:

    (a) the reasons it was not practicable to use an interview room; and

    (b) any action taken as in paragraph 12.5.

The record shall be made on the custody record or in the interview record for action taken whilst an interview record is being kept, with a brief reference to this effect in the custody record.

C:12.12 Any decision to delay a break in an interview must be recorded, with reasons, in the interview record.

C:12.13 All written statements made at police stations under caution shall be written on forms provided for the purpose.

C:12.14 All written statements made under caution shall be taken in accordance with Annex D. Before a person makes a written statement under caution at a police station, they shall be reminded about the right to legal advice. See *Note 12A*.

*Notes for guidance*

A-80 C:12A *It is not normally necessary to ask for a written statement if the interview was recorded in writing and the record signed in accordance with paragraph 11.11 or audibly or visually recorded in accordance with Code E or F. Statements under caution should normally be taken in these circumstances only at the person's express wish. A person may however be asked if they want to make such a statement.*

C:12B *Meal breaks should normally last at least 45 minutes and shorter breaks after two hours should last at least 15 minutes. If the interviewer delays a break in accordance with paragraph 12.8 and prolongs the interview, a longer break should be provided. If there is a short interview and another short interview is contemplated, the length of the break may be reduced if there are reasonable grounds to believe this is necessary to avoid any of the consequences in paragraph 12.8(i) to (iii).*

### C:13 Interpreters

(a) *General*

C:13.1 Chief officers are responsible for making arrangements to provide appropriately qualified **A-81** independent persons to act as interpreters and to provide translations of essential documents for:

- detained suspects who, in accordance with paragraph 3.5(c)(ii), the custody officer has determined require an interpreter, and
- suspects who are not under arrest but are cautioned as in section 10 who, in accordance with paragraph 3.21, the interviewer has determined require an interpreter. In these cases, the responsibilities of the custody officer are, if appropriate, assigned to the interviewer. An interviewer who has any doubts about whether an interpreter is required or about how the provisions of this section should be applied to a suspect who is not under arrest should seek advice from an officer of the rank of sergeant or above.

If the suspect has a hearing or speech impediment, references to "interpreter" and "interpretation" in this code include appropriate assistance necessary to establish effective communication with that person. See paragraph 13.1C below if the person is in Wales.

C:13.1A The arrangements must comply with the minimum requirements set out in Directive 2010/64/EU of the European Parliament and of the Council of 20 October 2010 on the right to interpretation and translation in criminal proceedings (see *Note 13A*). The provisions of this code implement the requirements for those to whom this code applies. These requirements include the following:

- that the arrangements made and the quality of interpretation and translation provided shall be sufficient to "*safeguard the fairness of the proceedings, in particular by ensuring that suspected or accused persons have knowledge of the cases against them and are able to exercise their right of defence*"; this term which is used by the directive means that the suspect must be able to understand their position and be able to communicate effectively with police officers, interviewers, solicitors and appropriate adults as provided for by this and any other code in the same way as a suspect who can speak and understand English and who does not have a hearing or speech impediment and who would therefore not require an interpreter;
- the provision of a written translation of all documents considered essential for the person to exercise their right of defence and to "*safeguard the fairness of the proceedings*" as described above; for the purposes of this code, this includes any decision to authorise a person to be detained and details of any offence(s) with which the person has been charged or for which they have been told they may be prosecuted, see Annex M;
- procedures to help determine:
  - whether a suspect can speak and understand English and needs the assistance of an interpreter, see paragraph 13.1 and *Notes 13B* and *13C*; and
  - whether another interpreter should be called or another translation should be provided when a suspect complains about the quality of either or both, see paragraphs 13.10A and 13.10C.

C:13.1B All reasonable attempts should be made to make the suspect understand that interpretation and translation will be provided at public expense.

C:13.1C With regard to persons in Wales, nothing in this or any other code affects the application of the Welsh language schemes produced by police and crime commissioners in Wales in accordance with the Welsh Language Act 1993: see paragraphs 3.12 and 13.1.

(b) *Interviewing suspects—foreign languages*

C:13.2 Unless paragraphs 11.1 or 11.18(c) apply, a suspect who for the purposes of this code requires an interpreter because they do not appear to speak or understand English (see paras 3.5(c)(ii) and 3.12) must not be interviewed in the absence of a person capable of interpreting.

C:13.2A An interpreter should also be called if a juvenile is interviewed and their parent or guardian, present as the appropriate adult, does not appear to speak or understand English, unless the interview is urgent and paragraphs 11.1 or 11.18(c) apply.

Note: paragraph 1.5A extends the requirement in this paragraph to interviews of 17-year-old suspects.

C:13.3 When a written record of the interview is made (see para. 11.7), the interviewer shall make sure the interpreter makes a note of the interview at the time in the person's language for use in the event of the interpreter being called to give evidence, and certifies its accuracy. The interviewer should allow sufficient time for the interpreter to note each question and answer after each is put, given and interpreted. The person should be allowed to read the record or have it read to them and sign it as correct or indicate the respects in which they consider it inaccurate. If an audio or visual record of the interview is made, the arrangements in Code E or F shall apply.

C:13.4 In the case of a person making a statement under caution to a police officer or other police staff other than in English:

    (a) the interpreter shall record the statement in the language it is made;

    (b) the person shall be invited to sign it;

    (c) an official English translation shall be made in due course.

### (c) *Interviewing suspects who have a hearing or speech impediment*

**A-82**    C:13.5 Unless paragraphs 11.1 or 11.18(c) (urgent interviews) apply, a suspect who for the purposes of this code requires an interpreter or other appropriate assistance to enable effective communication with them because they appear to have a hearing or speech impediment (see paras 3.5(c)(ii) and 3.12) must not be interviewed in the absence of an independent person capable of interpreting or without that assistance.

C:13.6 An interpreter should also be called if a juvenile is interviewed and their parent or guardian, present as the appropriate adult, appears to have a hearing or speech impediment, unless the interview is urgent and paragraphs 11.1 or 11.18(c) apply.

Note: paragraph 1.5A extends the requirement in this paragraph to interviews of 17-year-old suspects.

C:13.7 The interviewer shall make sure the interpreter is allowed to read the interview record and certify its accuracy in the event of the interpreter being called to give evidence. If the interview is audibly recorded or visually recorded, the arrangements in Code E or F apply.

### (d) *Additional rules for detained persons*

C:13.8 [*Not used.*]

C:13.9 If paragraph 6.1 applies and the detainee cannot communicate with the solicitor because of language, hearing or speech difficulties, an interpreter must be called. A police officer or any other police staff may not be used for this purpose.

C:13.10 After the custody officer has determined that a detainee requires an interpreter (see para. 3.5(c)(ii)) and following the initial action in paragraphs 3.1 to 3.5, arrangements must also be made for an interpreter to:

    • explain the grounds and reasons for any authorisation for their continued detention, before or after charge and any information about the authorisation given to them by the authorising officer and which is recorded in the custody record (see paras 15.3, 15.4 and 15.16(a) and (b));

    • be present at the magistrates' court for the hearing of an application for a warrant of further detention or any extension or further extension of such warrant to explain any grounds and reasons for the application and any information about the authorisation of their further detention given to them by the court (see PACE, ss.43 and 44 and paras 15.2 and 15.16(c)), and

    • explain any offence with which the detainee is charged or for which they are informed they may be prosecuted and any other information about the offence given to them by or on behalf of the custody officer (see paras 16.1 and 16.3).

C:13.10A If a detainee complains that they are not satisfied with the quality of interpretation, the custody officer or (as the case may be) the interviewer, is responsible for deciding whether a different interpreter should be called in accordance with the procedures set out in the arrangements made by the chief officer (see para. 13.1A).

### (e) *Translations of essential documents*

C:13.10B Written translations, oral translations and oral summaries of essential documents in a language the detainee understands shall be provided in accordance with Annex M (translations of documents and records).

C:13.10C If a detainee complains that they are not satisfied with the quality of the translation, the custody officer or (as the case may be) the interviewer, is responsible for deciding whether a further translation should be provided in accordance with the procedures set out in the arrangements made by the chief officer (see para. 13.1A).

(f) *Decisions not to provide interpretation and translation.*

C:13.10D If a suspect challenges a decision:

- made by the custody officer or (as the case may be) by the interviewer, in accordance with this code (see paras 3.5(c)(ii) and 3.21) that they do not require an interpreter; or
- made in accordance with paragraphs 13.10A, 13.10B or 13.10C not to provide a different interpreter or another translation or not to translate a requested document,

the matter shall be reported to an inspector to deal with as a complaint for the purposes of paragraph 9.2 or paragraph 12.9 if the challenge is made during an interview.

(g) *Documentation*

C:13.11 The following must be recorded in the custody record or, as applicable, the interview record:

- (a) action taken to call an interpreter;
- (b) action taken when a detainee is not satisfied about the standard of interpretation or translation provided (see paras 13.10A and 13.10C);
- (c) when an urgent interview is carried out in accordance with paragraph 13.2 or 13.5 in the absence of an interpreter;
- (d) when a detainee has been assisted by an interpreter for the purpose of providing or being given information or being interviewed;
- (e) action taken in accordance with Annex M when:
  - a written translation of an essential document is provided;
  - an oral translation or oral summary of an essential document is provided instead of a written translation and the authorising officer's reason(s) why this would not prejudice the fairness of the proceedings (see Annex M, para. 3);
  - a suspect waives their right to a translation of an essential document (see Annex M, para. 4);
  - when representations that a document which is not included in the table is essential and that a translation should be provided are refused and the reason for the refusal (see Annex M, para. 8).

*Notes for guidance*

C:13A *Chief officers have discretion when determining the individuals or organisations they use to provide interpretation and translation services for their forces provided that these services are compatible with the requirements of the directive. One example which chief officers may wish to consider is the Ministry of Justice framework agreement for interpretation and translation services.*

C:13B *A procedure for determining whether a person needs an interpreter might involve a telephone interpreter service or using cue cards or similar visual aids which enable the detainee to indicate their ability to speak and understand English and their preferred language. This could be confirmed through an interpreter who could also assess the extent to which the person can speak and understand English.*

C:13C *There should also be a procedure for determining whether a suspect who requires an interpreter requires assistance in accordance with paragraph 3.20 to help them check and, if applicable, sign any documentation.*

### C:14 Questioning—special restrictions

C:14.1 If a person is arrested by one police force on behalf of another and the lawful period of detention in respect of that offence has not yet commenced in accordance with PACE, s.41, no questions may be put to them about the offence while they are in transit between the forces except to clarify any voluntary statement they make.  **A-83**

C:14.2 If a person is in police detention at a hospital, they may not be questioned without the agreement of a responsible doctor. See *Note 14A*.

*Note for guidance*

C:14A *If questioning takes place at a hospital under paragraph 14.2, or on the way to or from a hospital, the period of questioning concerned counts towards the total period of detention permitted.*  **A-84**

## C:15 Reviews and extensions of detention

### (a) *Persons detained under PACE*

★A-85     C:15.0 The requirement in paragraph 3.4(b) that documents and materials essential to challenging the lawfulness of the detainee's arrest and detention must be made available to the detainee or their solicitor, applies for the purposes of this section as follows:

    (a) the officer reviewing the need for detention without charge (PACE, s.40), or (as the case may be) the officer considering the need to extend detention without charge from 24 to 36 hours (PACE, s.42), is responsible, in consultation with the investigating officer, for deciding which documents and materials are essential and must be made available;

    (b) when paragraph 15.7A applies (application for a warrant of further detention or extension of such a warrant), the officer making the application is responsible for deciding which documents and materials are essential and must be made available before the hearing. See *Note 3ZA*.

    C:15.1 The review officer is responsible under PACE, s.40, for periodically determining if a person's detention, before or after charge, continues to be necessary. This requirement continues throughout the detention period and, except as in paragraph 15.10, the review officer must be present at the police station holding the detainee. See *Notes 15A* and *15B*.

    C:15.2 Under PACE, s.42, an officer of superintendent rank or above who is responsible for the station holding the detainee may give authority any time after the second review to extend the maximum period the person may be detained without charge by up to 12 hours. Further detention without charge may be authorised only by a magistrates' court in accordance with PACE, ss.43 and 44. See *Notes 15C, 15D* and *15E*.

    C:15.2A An authorisation under section 42(1) of PACE extends the maximum period of detention permitted before charge for indictable offences from 24 hours to 36 hours. Detaining a juvenile or mentally vulnerable person for longer than 24 hours will be dependent on the circumstances of the case and with regard to the person's:

    (a) special vulnerability;

    (b) the legal obligation to provide an opportunity for representations to be made prior to a decision about extending detention;

    (c) the need to consult and consider the views of any appropriate adult; and

    (d) any alternatives to police custody.

Note: paragraph 1.5A extends sub-paragraph (c) to 17-year-old detainees.

    C:15.3 Before deciding whether to authorise continued detention the officer responsible under paragraph 15.1 or 15.2 shall give an opportunity to make representations about the detention to:

    (a) the detainee, unless in the case of a review as in paragraph 15.1, the detainee is asleep;

    (b) the detainee's solicitor if available at the time; and

    (c) the appropriate adult if available at the time.

Note: paragraph 1.5A extends the requirement in sub-paragraph (c) to 17-year-old detainees.
See *Note 15CA*.

    C:15.3A Other people having an interest in the detainee's welfare may also make representations at the authorising officer's discretion.

    C:15.3B Subject to paragraph 15.10, the representations may be made orally in person or by telephone or in writing. The authorising officer may, however, refuse to hear oral representations from the detainee if the officer considers them unfit to make representations because of their condition or behaviour. See *Note 15C*.

    C:15.3C The decision on whether the review takes place in person or by telephone or by video conferencing (see *Note 15G*) is a matter for the review officer. In determining the form the review may take, the review officer must always take full account of the needs of the person in custody. The benefits of carrying out a review in person should always be considered, based on the individual circumstances of each case with specific additional consideration if the person is:

    (a) a juvenile (and the age of the juvenile); or (note: para. 1.5A extends this sub-paragraph to 17-year-old detainees)

    (b) suspected of being mentally vulnerable; or

    (c) in need of medical attention for other than routine minor ailments; or

    (d) subject to presentational or community issues around their detention.

A-86     C:15.4 Before conducting a review or determining whether to extend the maximum period of detention without charge, the officer responsible must make sure the detainee is reminded of their entitlement to free legal advice, see paragraph 6.5, unless in the case of a review the person is asleep.

    C:15.5 If, after considering any representations, the review officer under paragraph 15.1 decides to keep the detainee in detention or the superintendent under paragraph 15.2 extends the maximum period for which they may be detained without charge, then any comment made by the detainee shall be recorded. If applicable, the officer shall be informed of the comment as soon as practicable. See also paragraphs 11.4 and 11.13.

C:15.6 No officer shall put specific questions to the detainee:
- regarding their involvement in any offence; or
- in respect of any comments they may make:
  - when given the opportunity to make representations; or
  - in response to a decision to keep them in detention or extend the maximum period of detention.

Such an exchange could constitute an interview as in paragraph 11.1A and would be subject to the associated safeguards in section 11 and, in respect of a person who has been charged, paragraph 16.5. See also paragraph 11.13.

C:15.7 A detainee who is asleep at a review, see paragraph 15.1, and whose continued detention is authorised must be informed about the decision and reason as soon as practicable after waking.

C:15.7A When an application is made to a magistrates' court under PACE, s.43, for a warrant of further detention to extend detention without charge of a person arrested for an indictable offence, or under section 44, to extend or further extend that warrant, the detainee:
- (a) must be brought to court for the hearing of the application;
- (b) is entitled to be legally represented if they wish, in which case, Annex B cannot apply;
- (c) must be given a copy of the information which supports the application and states:
  - (i) the nature of the offence for which the person to whom the application relates has been arrested;
  - (ii) the general nature of the evidence on which the person was arrested;
  - (iii) what inquiries about the offence have been made and what further inquiries are proposed;
  - (iv) the reasons for believing continued detention is necessary for the purposes of the further inquiries.

Note: a warrant of further detention can only be issued or extended if the court has reasonable grounds for believing that the person's further detention is necessary for the purpose of obtaining evidence of an indictable offence for which the person has been arrested and that the investigation is being conducted diligently and expeditiously.

See paragraph 15.0(b).

C:15.8 [*Not used.*]

(b) *Review of detention by telephone and video conferencing facilities*

C:15.9 PACE, s.40A, provides that the officer responsible under section 40 for reviewing the deten- **A-87** tion of a person who has not been charged, need not attend the police station holding the detainee and may carry out the review by telephone.

C:15.9A PACE, s.45A(2), provides that the officer responsible under section 40 for reviewing the detention of a person who has not been charged, need not attend the police station holding the detainee and may carry out the review by video conferencing facilities. (See *Note 15G.*)

C:15.9B A telephone review is not permitted where facilities for review by video conferencing exist and it is practicable to use them.

C:15.9C The review officer can decide at any stage that a telephone review or review by video conferencing should be terminated and that the review will be conducted in person. The reasons for doing so should be noted in the custody record. See *Note 15F.*

C:15.10 When a review is carried out by telephone or by video conferencing facilities, an officer at the station holding the detainee shall be required by the review officer to fulfil that officer's obligations under PACE, s.40, and this code by:
- (a) making any record connected with the review in the detainee's custody record;
- (b) if applicable, making the record in (a) in the presence of the detainee; and
- (c) for a review by telephone, giving the detainee information about the review.

C:15.11 When a review is carried out by telephone or by video conferencing facilities, the requirement in paragraph 15.3 will be satisfied:
- (a) if facilities exist for the immediate transmission of written representations to the review officer, *e.g.* fax or email message, by allowing those who are given the opportunity to make representations, to make their representations:
  - (i) orally by telephone or (as the case may be) by means of the video conferencing facilities; or

      (ii) in writing using the facilities for the immediate transmission of written representations; and

  (b) in all other cases, by allowing those who are given the opportunity to make representations, to make their representations orally by telephone or by means of the video conferencing facilities.

(c) Documentation

C:15.12 It is the officer's responsibility to make sure all reminders given under paragraph 15.4 are noted in the custody record.

C:15.13 The grounds for, and extent of, any delay in conducting a review shall be recorded.

C:15.14 When a review is carried out by telephone or video conferencing facilities, a record shall be made of:

  (a) the reason the review officer did not attend the station holding the detainee;

  (b) the place the review officer was;

  (c) the method representations, oral or written, were made to the review officer, see paragraph 15.11.

C:15.15 Any written representations shall be retained.

C:15.16 A record shall be made as soon as practicable of:

  (a) the outcome of each review of detention before or after charge, and if paragraph 15.7 applies, of when the person was informed and by whom;

  (b) the outcome of any determination under PACE, s.42, by a superintendent whether to extend the maximum period of detention without charge beyond 24 hours from the relevant time; if an authorisation is given, the record shall state the number of hours and minutes by which the detention period is extended or further extended;

  (c) the outcome of each application under PACE, s.43, for a warrant of further detention or under section 44, for an extension or further extension of that warrant; if a warrant for further detention is granted under section 43 or extended or further extended under 44, the record shall state the detention period authorised by the warrant and the date and time it was granted or (as the case may be) the period by which the warrant is extended or further extended.

Note: any period during which a person is released on bail does not count towards the maximum period of detention without charge allowed under PACE, ss.41 to 44.

Notes for guidance

**A-88**

C:15A *Review officer for the purposes of:*

  • *PACE, ss.40, 40A and 45A means, in the case of a person arrested but not charged, an officer of at least inspector rank not directly involved in the investigation and, if a person has been arrested and charged, the custody officer.*

C:15B *The detention of persons in police custody not subject to the statutory review requirement in paragraph 15.1 should still be reviewed periodically as a matter of good practice. Such reviews can be carried out by an officer of the rank of sergeant or above. The purpose of such reviews is to check the particular power under which a detainee is held continues to apply, any associated conditions are complied with and to make sure appropriate action is taken to deal with any changes. This includes the detainee's prompt release when the power no longer applies, or their transfer if the power requires the detainee be taken elsewhere as soon as the necessary arrangements are made. Examples include persons:*

  (a) *arrested on warrant because they failed to answer bail to appear at court;*

  (b) *arrested under the Bail Act 1976, s.7(3), for breaching a condition of bail granted after charge;*

  (c) *in police custody for specific purposes and periods under the Crime (Sentences) Act 1997, Sched. 1;*

  (d) *convicted, or remand prisoners, held in police stations on behalf of the Prison Service under the Imprisonment (Temporary Provisions) Act 1980, s.6;*

  (e) *being detained to prevent them causing a breach of the peace;*

  (f) *detained at police stations on behalf of Immigration Enforcement (formerly the UK Immigration Service);*

  (g) *detained by order of a magistrates' court under the Criminal Justice Act 1988, s.152 (as amended by the Drugs Act 2005, s.8) to facilitate the recovery of evidence after being charged with drug possession or drug trafficking and suspected of having swallowed drugs.*

    *The detention of persons remanded into police detention by order of a court under the Magistrates' Courts Act 1980, s.128, is subject to a statutory requirement to review that detention. This is to make sure the detainee is taken back to court no later than the end of the period authorised by the court or when the need for their detention by police ceases, whichever is the sooner.*

C:15C *In the case of a review of detention, but not an extension, the detainee need not be woken for the review. However, if the detainee is likely to be asleep, e.g. during a period of rest allowed as in paragraph 12.2, at the latest time a review or authorisation to extend detention may take place, the officer should, if the legal obligations and time constraints permit, bring forward the procedure to allow the detainee to make representations. A detainee not asleep during the review must be present when the grounds for their continued detention are recorded and must at the same time be informed of those grounds unless the review officer considers the person is incapable of understanding what is said, violent or likely to become violent or in urgent need of medical attention.*

C:15CA *In paragraph 15.3(b) and (c), "available" includes being contactable in time to enable them to make representations remotely by telephone or other electronic means or in person by attending the station. Reasonable efforts should therefore be made to give the solicitor and appropriate adult sufficient notice of the time the decision is expected to be made so that they can make themselves available.*

C:15D *An application to a magistrates' court under PACE, s.43 or 44, for a warrant of further detention or its extension should be made between 10am and 9pm, and if possible during normal court hours. It will not usually be practicable to arrange for a court to sit specially outside the hours of 10am to 9pm. If it appears a special sitting may be needed outside normal court hours but between 10am and 9pm, the clerk to the justices should be given notice and informed of this possibility, while the court is sitting if possible.*

C:15E *In paragraph 15.2, the officer responsible for the station holding the detainee includes a superintendent or above who, in accordance with their force operational policy or police regulations, is given that responsibility on a temporary basis whilst the appointed long-term holder is off duty or otherwise unavailable.*

C:15F *The provisions of PACE, s.40A, allowing telephone reviews do not apply to reviews of detention after charge by the custody officer. When video conferencing is not required, they allow the use of a telephone to carry out a review of detention before charge. The procedure under PACE, s.42, must be done in person.*

C:15G *Video conferencing facilities means any facilities (whether a live television link or other facilities) by means of which the review can be carried out with the review officer, the detainee concerned and the detainee's solicitor all being able to both see and to hear each other. The use of video conferencing facilities for decisions about detention under section 45A of PACE is subject to regulations made by the Secretary of State being in force.*

### C:16 Charging detained persons

*(a) Action*

C:16.1 When the officer in charge of the investigation reasonably believes there is sufficient **A-89** evidence to provide a realistic prospect of conviction for the offence (see paragraph 11.6), they shall without delay, and subject to the following qualification, inform the custody officer who will be responsible for considering whether the detainee should be charged. See *Notes 11B* and *16A*. When a person is detained in respect of more than one offence it is permissible to delay informing the custody officer until the above conditions are satisfied in respect of all the offences, but see paragraph 11.6. If the detainee is a juvenile, mentally disordered or otherwise mentally vulnerable, any resulting action shall be taken in the presence of the appropriate adult if they are present at the time.

Note: paragraph 1.5A requires someone to fulfil the role of the appropriate adult to be present when the action applies to a 17-year-old detainee.

See *Notes 16B* and *16C*.

C:16.1A Where guidance issued by the Director of Public Prosecutions under PACE, s.37A, is in force the custody officer must comply with that guidance in deciding how to act in dealing with the detainee. See *Notes 16AA* and *16AB*.

C:16.1B Where in compliance with the DPP's guidance the custody officer decides that the case should be immediately referred to the CPS to make the charging decision, consultation should take place with a crown prosecutor as soon as is reasonably practicable. Where the crown prosecutor is unable to make the charging decision on the information available at that time, the detainee may be released without charge and on bail (with conditions if necessary) under section 37(7)(a). In such circumstances, the detainee should be informed that they are being released to enable the Director of Public Prosecutions to make a decision under section 37B.

C:16.2 When a detainee is charged with or informed they may be prosecuted for an offence, see *Note 16B*, they shall, unless the restriction on drawing adverse inferences from silence applies, see Annex C, be cautioned as follows:

*"You do not have to say anything. But it may harm your defence if you do not mention now something which you later rely on in court. Anything you do say may be given in evidence.".*

Where the use of the Welsh language is appropriate, a constable may provide the caution directly in Welsh in the following terms:

*"Does dim rhaid i chi ddweud dim byd. Ond gall niweidio eich amddiffyniad os na fyddwch chi'n sôn, yn awr, am rywbeth y byddwch chi'n dibynnu arno nes ymlaen yn y llys. Gall unrhyw beth yr ydych yn ei ddweud gael ei*

*roi fel tystiolaeth.".*

Annex C, paragraph 2, sets out the alternative terms of the caution to be used when the restriction on drawing adverse inferences from silence applies.

C:16.3 When a detainee is charged they shall be given a written notice showing particulars of the offence and, subject to paragraph 2.6A, the officer's name and the case reference number. As far as possible the particulars of the charge shall be stated in simple terms, but they shall also show the precise offence in law with which the detainee is charged. The notice shall begin:

*"You are charged with the offence(s) shown below."* Followed by the caution.

If the detainee is a juvenile, mentally disordered or otherwise mentally vulnerable, a copy of the notice should also be given to the appropriate adult.

Note: paragraph 1.5A provides that a copy of the notice should be given to the person called to fulfil the role of the appropriate adult when a 17-year-old detainee is charged.

C:16.4 If, after a detainee has been charged with or informed they may be prosecuted for an offence, an officer wants to tell them about any written statement or interview with another person relating to such an offence, the detainee shall either be handed a true copy of the written statement or the content of the interview record brought to their attention. Nothing shall be done to invite any reply or comment except to:

(a) caution the detainee, *"You do not have to say anything, but anything you do say may be given in evidence.";*

where the use of the Welsh Language is appropriate, caution the detainee in the following terms:

*"Does dim rhaid i chi ddweud dim byd, ond gall unrhyw beth yr ydych yn ei ddweud gael ei roi fel tystiolaeth.";* and

(b) remind the detainee about their right to legal advice.

C:16.4A If the detainee:

• cannot read, the document may be read to them;

• is a juvenile, mentally disordered or otherwise mentally vulnerable, the appropriate adult shall also be given a copy, or the interview record shall be brought to their attention.

Note: paragraph 1.5A requires a copy of the record to be given to, or brought to the attention of, the person called to fulfil the role of the appropriate adult for a 17-year-old detainee.

C:16.5 A detainee may not be interviewed about an offence after they have been charged with, or informed they may be prosecuted for it, unless the interview is necessary:

• to prevent or minimise harm or loss to some other person, or the public;

• to clear up an ambiguity in a previous answer or statement;

• in the interests of justice for the detainee to have put to them, and have an opportunity to comment on, information concerning the offence which has come to light since they were charged or informed they might be prosecuted.

Before any such interview, the interviewer shall:

(a) caution the detainee, *"You do not have to say anything, but anything you do say may be given in evidence.";*

where the use of the Welsh language is appropriate, the interviewer shall caution the detainee: *"Does dim rhaid i chi ddweud dim byd, ond gall unrhyw beth yr ydych yn ei ddweud gael ei roi fel tystiolaeth.";*

(b) remind the detainee about their right to legal advice.

See *Note 16B.*

C:16.6 The provisions of paragraphs 16.2 to 16.5 must be complied with in the appropriate adult's presence if they are already at the police station. If they are not at the police station then these provisions must be complied with again in their presence when they arrive unless the detainee has been released. See *Note 16C.*

Note: Paragraph 1.5A extends the requirement in this paragraph to 17-year-old detainees.

C:16.7 When a juvenile is charged with an offence and the custody officer authorises their continued detention after charge, the custody officer must make arrangements for the juvenile to be taken into the care of a local authority to be detained pending appearance in court unless the custody officer certifies in accordance with PACE, s.38(6), that:

(a) for any juvenile, it is impracticable to do so; or

(b) in the case of a juvenile of at least 12 years old, no secure accommodation is available and other accommodation would not be adequate to protect the public from serious harm from that juvenile. See *Note 16D.*

Note: the 16-year-old maximum age limit for transfer to local authority accommodation, the power of the local authority to detain the person transferred and take over responsibility for that person from the police are determined by section 38 of PACE. For this reason, this paragraph and *Note 16D* do <u>not</u> apply to detainees who appear to have attained the age of 17 (see para. 1.5A(a)).

C:16.7A The requirement in paragraph 3.4(b) that documents and materials essential to effectively    ★
challenging the lawfulness of the detainee's arrest and detention must be made available to the detainee and, if they are represented, their solicitor, applies for the purposes of this section and a person's detention after charge. This means that the custody officer making the bail decision (PACE, s.38) or reviewing the need for detention after charge (PACE, s.40), is responsible for determining what, if any, documents or materials are essential and must be made available to the detainee or their solicitor. See *Note 3ZA*.

### (b) *Documentation*

C:16.8 A record shall be made of anything a detainee says when charged.

C:16.9 Any questions put in an interview after charge and answers given relating to the offence shall be recorded in full during the interview on forms for that purpose and the record signed by the detainee or, if they refuse, by the interviewer and any third parties present. If the questions are audibly recorded or visually recorded the arrangements in Code E or F apply.

C:16.10 If arrangements for a juvenile's transfer into local authority care as in paragraph 16.7 are not made, the custody officer must record the reasons in a certificate which must be produced before the court with the juvenile. See *Note 16D*.

### *Notes for guidance*

C:16A *The custody officer must take into account alternatives to prosecution under the Crime and Disorder Act*    **A-91**
*1998 applicable to persons under 18, and in national guidance on the cautioning of offenders applicable to persons aged 18 and over.*

C:16AA *When a person is arrested under the provisions of the Criminal Justice Act 2003 which allow a person to be re-tried after being acquitted of a serious offence which is a qualifying offence specified in Schedule 5 to that Act and not precluded from further prosecution by virtue of section 75(3) of that Act the detention provisions of PACE are modified and make an officer of the rank of superintendent or above who has not been directly involved in the investigation responsible for determining whether the evidence is sufficient to charge.*

C:16AB *Where guidance issued by the Director of Public Prosecutions under section 37B is in force, a custody officer who determines in accordance with that guidance that there is sufficient evidence to charge the detainee, may detain that person for no longer than is reasonably necessary to decide how that person is to be dealt with under PACE, s.37(7)(a) to (d), including, where appropriate, consultation with the duty prosecutor. The period is subject to the maximum period of detention before charge determined by PACE, ss.41 to 44. Where in accordance with the guidance the case is referred to the CPS for decision, the custody officer should ensure that an officer involved in the investigation sends to the CPS such information as is specified in the guidance.*

C:16B *The giving of a warning or the service of the notice of intended prosecution required by the Road Traffic Offenders Act 1988, s.1 does not amount to informing a detainee they may be prosecuted for an offence and so does not preclude further questioning in relation to that offence.*

C:16C *There is no power under PACE to detain a person and delay action under paragraphs 16.2 to 16.5 solely to await the arrival of the appropriate adult. Reasonable efforts should therefore be made to give the appropriate adult sufficient notice of the time the decision (charge etc.) is to be implemented so that they can be present. If the appropriate adult is not, or cannot be, present at that time, the detainee should be released on bail to return for the decision to be implemented when the adult is present, unless the custody officer determines that the absence of the appropriate adult makes the detainee unsuitable for bail for this purpose. After charge, bail cannot be refused, or release on bail delayed, simply because an appropriate adult is not available, unless the absence of that adult provides the custody officer with the necessary grounds to authorise detention after charge under PACE, s.38.*

C:16D *Except as in paragraph 16.7, neither a juvenile's behaviour nor the nature of the offence provides grounds for the custody officer to decide it is impracticable to arrange the juvenile's transfer to local authority care. Impracticability concerns the transport and travel requirements and the lack of secure accommodation which is provided for the purposes of restricting liberty does not make it impracticable to transfer the juvenile. The availability of secure accommodation is only a factor in relation to a juvenile aged 12 or over when other local authority accommodation would not be adequate to protect the public from serious harm from them. The obligation to transfer a juvenile to local authority accommodation applies as much to a juvenile charged during the daytime as to a juvenile to be held overnight, subject to a requirement to bring the juvenile before a court under PACE, s.46.*

*This note does not apply to 17-year-old detainees (see para. 16.7).*

### C:17 Testing persons for the presence of specified Class A drugs

#### (a) *Action*

A-91a    C:17.1 This section of Code C applies only in selected police stations in police areas where the provisions for drug testing under section 63B of PACE (as amended by section 5 of the Criminal Justice Act 2003 and section 7 of the Drugs Act 2005) are in force and in respect of which the Secretary of State has given a notification to the relevant chief officer of police that arrangements for the taking of samples have been made. Such a notification will cover either a police area as a whole or particular stations within a police area. The notification indicates whether the testing applies to those arrested or charged or under the age of 18 as the case may be and testing can only take place in respect of the persons so indicated in the notification. Testing cannot be carried out unless the relevant notification has been given and has not been withdrawn. See *Note 17F*.

C:17.2 A sample of urine or a non-intimate sample may be taken from a person in police detention for the purpose of ascertaining whether they have any specified Class A drug in their body only where they have been brought before the custody officer and:

(a) either the arrest condition, see paragraph 17.3, or the charge condition, see paragraph 17.4, is met;

(b) the age condition, see paragraph 17.5, is met;

(c) the notification condition is met in relation to the arrest condition, the charge condition, or the age condition, as the case may be (testing on charge and/or arrest must be specifically provided for in the notification for the power to apply; in addition, the fact that testing of under 18s is authorised must be expressly provided for in the notification before the power to test such persons applies); see paragraph 17.1; and

(d) a police officer has requested the person concerned to give the sample (the request condition).

C:17.3 The arrest condition is met where the detainee:

(a) has been arrested for a trigger offence, see *Note 17E*, but not charged with that offence; or

(b) has been arrested for any other offence but not charged with that offence and a police officer of inspector rank or above, who has reasonable grounds for suspecting that their misuse of any specified Class A drug caused or contributed to the offence, has authorised the sample to be taken.

C:17.4 The charge condition is met where the detainee:

(a) has been charged with a trigger offence; or

(b) has been charged with any other offence and a police officer of inspector rank or above, who has reasonable grounds for suspecting that the detainee's misuse of any specified Class A drug caused or contributed to the offence, has authorised the sample to be taken.

C:17.5 The age condition is met where:

(a) in the case of a detainee who has been arrested but not charged as in paragraph 17.3, they are aged 18 or over;

(b) in the case of a detainee who has been charged as in paragraph 17.4, they are aged 14 or over.

C:17.6 Before requesting a sample from the person concerned, an officer must:

(a) inform them that the purpose of taking the sample is for drug testing under PACE; this is to ascertain whether they have a specified Class A drug present in their body;

(b) warn them that if, when so requested, they fail without good cause to provide a sample they may be liable to prosecution;

(c) where the taking of the sample has been authorised by an inspector or above in accordance with paragraph 17.3(b) or 17.4(b) above, inform them that the authorisation has been given and the grounds for giving it;

(d) remind them of the following rights, which may be exercised at any stage during the period in custody:

(i) the right to have someone informed of their arrest [see section 5];

(ii) the right to consult privately with a solicitor and that free independent legal advice is available [see section 6]; and

(iii) the right to consult these codes of practice [see section 3].

C:17.7 In the case of a person who has not attained the age of 17—

(a) the making of the request for a sample under paragraph 17.2(d) above;

(b) the giving of the warning and the information under paragraph 17.6 above; and

(c) the taking of the sample,

may not take place except in the presence of an appropriate adult. See *Note 17G*.

Note: paragraph 1.5A requires someone to fulfil the role of the appropriate adult to be present if the person to be tested appears to be under the age of 18.

C:17.8 Authorisation by an officer of the rank of inspector or above within paragraph 17.3(b) or 17.4(b) may be given orally or in writing but, if it is given orally, it must be confirmed in writing as soon as practicable.

C:17.9 If a sample is taken from a detainee who has been arrested for an offence but not charged with that offence as in paragraph 17.3, no further sample may be taken during the same continuous period of detention. If during that same period the charge condition is also met in respect of that detainee, the sample which has been taken shall be treated as being taken by virtue of the charge condition, see paragraph 17.4, being met.

C:17.10 A detainee from whom a sample may be taken may be detained for up to six hours from the time of charge if the custody officer reasonably believes the detention is necessary to enable a sample to be taken. Where the arrest condition is met, a detainee whom the custody officer has decided to release on bail without charge may continue to be detained, but not beyond 24 hours from the relevant time (as defined in section 41(2) of PACE), to enable a sample to be taken.

C:17.11 A detainee in respect of whom the arrest condition is met, but not the charge condition, see paragraphs 17.3 and 17.4, and whose release would be required before a sample can be taken had they not continued to be detained as a result of being arrested for a further offence which does not satisfy the arrest condition, may have a sample taken at any time within 24 hours after the arrest for the offence that satisfies the arrest condition.

#### (b) *Documentation*

C:17.12 The following must be recorded in the custody record:
(a) if a sample is taken following authorisation by an officer of the rank of inspector or above, the authorisation and the grounds for suspicion;
(b) the giving of a warning of the consequences of failure to provide a sample;
(c) the time at which the sample was given; and
(d) the time of charge or, where the arrest condition is being relied upon, the time of arrest and, where applicable, the fact that a sample taken after arrest but before charge is to be treated as being taken by virtue of the charge condition, where that is met in the same period of continuous detention. See paragraph 17.9.

#### (c) *General*

C:17.13 A sample may only be taken by a prescribed person. See *Note 17C*.

C:17.14 Force may not be used to take any sample for the purpose of drug testing.

C:17.15 The terms "Class A drug" and "misuse" have the same meanings as in the Misuse of Drugs Act 1971. "Specified" (in relation to a Class A drug) and "trigger offence" have the same meanings as in Part III of the Criminal Justice and Court Services Act 2000.

C:17.16 Any sample taken:
(a) may not be used for any purpose other than to ascertain whether the person concerned has a specified Class A drug present in his body; and
(b) can be disposed of as clinical waste unless it is to be sent for further analysis in cases where the test result is disputed at the point when the result is known, including on the basis that medication has been taken, or for quality assurance purposes.

#### (d) *Assessment of misuse of drugs*

C:17.17 Under the provisions of Part 3 of the Drugs Act 2005, where a detainee has tested positive for a specified Class A drug under section 63B of PACE a police officer may, at any time before the person's release from the police station, impose a requirement on the detainee to attend an initial assessment of their drug misuse by a suitably qualified person and to remain for its duration. Where such a requirement is imposed, the officer must, at the same time, impose a second requirement on the detainee to attend and remain for a follow-up assessment. The officer must inform the detainee that the second requirement will cease to have effect if, at the initial assessment they are informed that a follow-up assessment is not necessary. These requirements may only be imposed on a person if:
(a) they have reached the age of 18;
(b) notification has been given by the Secretary of State to the relevant chief officer of police that arrangements for conducting initial and follow-up assessments have been made for those from whom samples for testing have been taken at the police station where the detainee is in custody.

C:17.18 When imposing a requirement to attend an initial assessment and a follow-up assessment the police officer must:

    (a) inform the person of the time and place at which the initial assessment is to take place;

    (b) explain that this information will be confirmed in writing; and

    (c) warn the person that they may be liable to prosecution if they fail without good cause to attend the initial assessment and remain for its duration and if they fail to attend the follow-up assessment and remain for its duration (if so required).

C:17.19 Where a police officer has imposed a requirement to attend an initial assessment and a follow-up assessment in accordance with paragraph 17.17, he must, before the person is released from detention, give the person notice in writing which:

    (a) confirms their requirement to attend and remain for the duration of the assessments; and

    (b) the information and repeats the warning referred to in paragraph 17.18.

C:17.20 The following must be recorded in the custody record:

    (a) that the requirement to attend an initial assessment and a follow-up assessment has been imposed; and

    (b) the information, explanation, warning and notice given in accordance with paragraphs 17.17 and 17.19.

C:17.21 Where a notice is given in accordance with paragraph 17.19, a police officer can give the person a further notice in writing which informs the person of any change to the time or place at which the initial assessment is to take place and which repeats the warning referred to in paragraph 17.18(c).

C:17.22 Part 3 of the Drugs Act 2005 also requires police officers to have regard to any guidance issued by the Secretary of State in respect of the assessment provisions.

*Notes for guidance*

C:17A *When warning a person who is asked to provide a urine or non-intimate sample in accordance with paragraph 17.6(b), the following form of words may be used:*

"*You do not have to provide a sample, but I must warn you that if you fail or refuse without good cause to do so, you will commit an offence for which you may be imprisoned, or fined, or both*".

*Where the Welsh language is appropriate, the following form of words may be used:*

"*Does dim rhaid i chi roi sampl, ond mae'n rhaid i mi eich rhybuddio y byddwch chin cyflawni trosedd os byddwch chi'n methu neu yn gwrthod gwneud hynny heb reswm da, ac y gellir, oherwydd hynny, eich carcharu, eich dirwyo, neu'r ddau.*"

C:17B *A sample has to be sufficient and suitable. A sufficient sample is sufficient in quantity and quality to enable drug-testing analysis to take place. A suitable sample is one which by its nature, is suitable for a particular form of drug analysis.*

C:17C *A prescribed person in paragraph 17.13 is one who is prescribed in regulations made by the Secretary of State under section 63B(6) of the Police and Criminal Evidence Act 1984. [The regulations are currently contained in regulation S.I. 2001 No. 2645, the Police and Criminal Evidence Act 1984 (Drug Testing Persons in Police Detention) (Prescribed Persons) Regulations 2001.]*

C:17D *Samples, and the information derived from them, may not be subsequently used in the investigation of any offence or in evidence against the persons from whom they were taken.*

C:17E *Trigger offences are:*

    1.  *Offences under the following provisions of the Theft Act 1968:*

| | |
|---|---|
| *section 1* | *(theft)* |
| *section 8* | *(robbery)* |
| *section 9* | *(burglary)* |
| *section 10* | *(aggravated burglary)* |
| *section 12* | *(taking a motor vehicle or other conveyance without authority)* |
| *section 12A* | *(aggravated vehicle-taking)* |
| *section 22* | *(handling stolen goods)* |
| *section 25* | *(going equipped for stealing, etc.).* |

    2.  *Offences under the following provisions of the Misuse of Drugs Act 1971, if committed in respect of a specified Class A drug:*

| | |
|---|---|
| *section 4* | *(restriction on production and supply of controlled drugs)* |

| section 5(2) | *(possession of a controlled drug)* |
| section 5(3) | *(possession of a controlled drug with intent to supply).* |

3. *Offences under the following provisions of the Fraud Act 2006:*

| section 1 | *(fraud)* |
| section 6 | *(possession etc. of articles for use in frauds)* |
| section 7 | *(making or supplying articles for use in frauds).* |

3A. *An offence under section 1(1) of the Criminal Attempts Act 1981 if committed in respect of an offence under:*

(a) *any of the following provisions of the Theft Act 1968:*

| section 1 | *(theft)* |
| section 8 | *(robbery)* |
| section 9 | *(burglary)* |
| section 22 | *(handling stolen goods)* |

(b) *section 1 of the Fraud Act 2006 (fraud).*

4. *Offences under the following provisions of the Vagrancy Act 1824:*

| section 3 | *(begging)* |
| section 4 | *(persistent begging).* |

C:17F *The power to take samples is subject to notification by the Secretary of State that appropriate arrangements for the taking of samples have been made for the police area as a whole or for the particular police station concerned for whichever of the following is specified in the notification:*

    (a) *persons in respect of whom the arrest condition is met;*
    (b) *persons in respect of whom the charge condition is met;*
    (c) *persons who have not attained the age of 18.*

*Note: notification is treated as having been given for the purposes of the charge condition in relation to a police area, if testing (on charge) under section 63B(2) of PACE was in force immediately before section 7 of the Drugs Act 2005 was brought into force; and for the purposes of the age condition, in relation to a police area or police station, if immediately before that day, notification that arrangements had been made for the taking of samples from persons under the age of 18 (those aged 14-17) had been given and had not been withdrawn.*

C:17G *Appropriate adult in paragraph 17.7 means the person's—*

    (a) *parent or guardian or, if they are in the care of a local authority or voluntary organisation, a person representing that authority or organisation; or*

    (b) *a social worker of a local authority; or*

    (c) *if no person falling within (a) or (b) above is available, any responsible person aged 18 or over who is not a police officer or a person employed by the police.*

*Note: paragraph 1.5A extends this note to the person called to fulfil the role of the appropriate adult for a 17-year-old detainee for the purposes of paragraph 17.7.*

## ANNEX A

**Intimate and strip searches**

A *Intimate search*

    C:1. An intimate search consists of the physical examination of a person's body orifices other than **A-92** the mouth. The intrusive nature of such searches means the actual and potential risks associated with intimate searches must never be underestimated.

*(a) Action*
    C:2. Body orifices other than the mouth may be searched only: **A-93**

    (a) if authorised by an officer of inspector rank or above who has reasonable grounds for believing that the person may have concealed on themselves:

        (i) anything which they could and might use to cause physical injury to themselves or others at the station; or

        (ii) a Class A drug which they intended to supply to another or to export;

        and the officer has reasonable grounds for believing that an intimate search is the only means of removing those items; and

    (b) if the search is under paragraph 2(a)(ii) (a drug offence search), the detainee's appropriate consent has been given in writing.

C:2A. Before the search begins, a police officer or designated detention officer, must tell the detainee:

    (a) that the authority to carry out the search has been given;

    (b) the grounds for giving the authorisation and for believing that the article cannot be removed without an intimate search.

Note: paragraph 1.5A of this code requires someone to fulfil the role of the appropriate adult to be present when a 17-year-old is told about the authority and grounds for an intimate search.

C:2B. Before a detainee is asked to give appropriate consent to a search under paragraph 2(a)(ii) (a drug offence search) they must be warned that if they refuse without good cause their refusal may harm their case if it comes to trial, see *Note A6*. This warning may be given by a police officer or member of police staff. In the case of juveniles, mentally vulnerable or mentally disordered suspects the seeking and giving of consent must take place in the presence of the appropriate adult. A juvenile's consent is only valid if their parent's or guardian's consent is also obtained unless the juvenile is under 14, when their parent's or guardian's consent is sufficient in its own right. A detainee who is not legally represented must be reminded of their entitlement to have free legal advice, see Code C, paragraph 6.5, and the reminder noted in the custody record.

Note: paragraph 1.5A of this code requires someone to fulfil the role of the appropriate adult to be present when the warning is given to a 17-year-old and their consent to a drug offence search is sought and given but the consent of their parent or guardian is not required.

C:3. An intimate search may only be carried out by a registered medical practitioner or registered nurse, unless an officer of at least inspector rank considers this is not practicable and the search is to take place under paragraph 2(a)(i), in which case a police officer may carry out the search. See *Notes A1 to A5*.

C:3A. Any proposal for a search under paragraph 2(a)(i) to be carried out by someone other than a registered medical practitioner or registered nurse must only be considered as a last resort and when the authorising officer is satisfied the risks associated with allowing the item to remain with the detainee outweigh the risks associated with removing it. See *Notes A1 to A5*.

C:4. An intimate search under:

    • paragraph 2(a)(i) may take place only at a hospital, surgery, other medical premises or police station;

    • paragraph 2(a)(ii) may take place only at a hospital, surgery or other medical premises and must be carried out by a registered medical practitioner or a registered nurse.

C:5. An intimate search at a police station of a juvenile or mentally disordered or otherwise mentally vulnerable person may take place only in the presence of an appropriate adult of the same sex (see Annex L), unless the detainee specifically requests a particular adult of the opposite sex who is readily available. In the case of a juvenile, the search may take place in the absence of the appropriate adult only if the juvenile signifies in the presence of the appropriate adult they do not want the adult present during the search and the adult agrees. A record shall be made of the juvenile's decision and signed by the appropriate adult.

Note: paragraph 1.5A of this code extends the requirement in this paragraph to an intimate search of a 17-year-old.

C:6. When an intimate search under paragraph 2(a)(i) is carried out by a police officer, the officer must be of the same sex as the detainee (see Annex L). A minimum of two people, other than the detainee, must be present during the search. Subject to paragraph 5, no person of the opposite sex who is not a medical practitioner or nurse shall be present, nor shall anyone whose presence is unnecessary. The search shall be conducted with proper regard to the sensitivity and vulnerability of the detainee.

*(b) Documentation*

**A-94**    C:7. In the case of an intimate search, the following shall be recorded as soon as practicable in the detainee's custody record:

    (a) for searches under paragraphs 2(a)(i) and (ii);

      • the authorisation to carry out the search;

      • the grounds for giving the authorisation;

      • the grounds for believing the article could not be removed without an intimate search;

      • which parts of the detainee's body were searched;

      • who carried out the search;

      • who was present;

- the result;
(b) for searches under paragraph 2(a)(ii):
   - the giving of the warning required by paragraph 2B;
   - the fact that the appropriate consent was given or (as the case may be) refused, and if refused, the reason given for the refusal (if any).

C:8. If an intimate search is carried out by a police officer, the reason why it was impracticable for a registered medical practitioner or registered nurse to conduct it must be recorded.

## B *Strip search*

C:9. A strip search is a search involving the removal of more than outer clothing. In this code, **A-95** outer clothing includes shoes and socks.

### (a) Action

C:10. A strip search may take place only if it is considered necessary to remove an article which a **A-96** detainee would not be allowed to keep and the officer reasonably considers the detainee might have concealed such an article. Strip searches shall not be routinely carried out if there is no reason to consider that articles are concealed.

### *The conduct of strip searches*

C:11. When strip searches are conducted:
(a) a police officer carrying out a strip search must be the same sex as the detainee (see Annex L);
(b) the search shall take place in an area where the detainee cannot be seen by anyone who does not need to be present, nor by a member of the opposite sex (see Annex L) except an appropriate adult who has been specifically requested by the detainee;
(c) except in cases of urgency, where there is risk of serious harm to the detainee or to others, whenever a strip search involves exposure of intimate body parts, there must be at least two people present other than the detainee, and if the search is of a juvenile or mentally disordered or otherwise mentally vulnerable person, one of the people must be the appropriate adult; except in urgent cases as above, a search of a juvenile may take place in the absence of the appropriate adult only if the juvenile signifies in the presence of the appropriate adult that they do not want the adult to be present during the search and the adult agrees; a record shall be made of the juvenile's decision and signed by the appropriate adult; the presence of more than two people, other than an appropriate adult, shall be permitted only in the most exceptional circumstances (note: para. 1.5A of this code extends the requirement in this sub-paragraph to a strip search of a 17-year-old);
(d) the search shall be conducted with proper regard to the sensitivity and vulnerability of the detainee in these circumstances and every reasonable effort shall be made to secure the detainee's co-operation and minimise embarrassment; detainees who are searched shall not normally be required to remove all their clothes at the same time, *e.g.* a person should be allowed to remove clothing above the waist and redress before removing further clothing;
(e) if necessary to assist the search, the detainee may be required to hold their arms in the air or to stand with their legs apart and bend forward so a visual examination may be made of the genital and anal areas provided no physical contact is made with any body orifice;
(f) if articles are found, the detainee shall be asked to hand them over; if articles are found within any body orifice other than the mouth, and the detainee refuses to hand them over, their removal would constitute an intimate search, which must be carried out as in Part A;
(g) a strip search shall be conducted as quickly as possible, and the detainee allowed to dress as soon as the procedure is complete.

### (b) Documentation

C:12. A record shall be made on the custody record of a strip search including the reason it was **A-97** considered necessary, those present and any result.

*Notes for guidance*

A-98        C:A1 *Before authorising any intimate search, the authorising officer must make every reasonable effort to persuade the detainee to hand the article over without a search. If the detainee agrees, a registered medical practitioner or registered nurse should whenever possible be asked to assess the risks involved and, if necessary, attend to assist the detainee.*

C:A2 *If the detainee does not agree to hand the article over without a search, the authorising officer must carefully review all the relevant factors before authorising an intimate search. In particular, the officer must consider whether the grounds for believing an article may be concealed are reasonable.*

C:A3 *If authority is given for a search under paragraph 2(a)(i), a registered medical practitioner or registered nurse shall be consulted whenever possible. The presumption should be that the search will be conducted by the registered medical practitioner or registered nurse and the authorising officer must make every reasonable effort to persuade the detainee to allow the medical practitioner or nurse to conduct the search.*

C:A4 *A constable should only be authorised to carry out a search as a last resort and when all other approaches have failed. In these circumstances, the authorising officer must be satisfied the detainee might use the article for one or more of the purposes in paragraph 2(a)(i) and the physical injury likely to be caused is sufficiently severe to justify authorising a constable to carry out the search.*

C:A5 *If an officer has any doubts whether to authorise an intimate search by a constable, the officer should seek advice from an officer of superintendent rank or above.*

C:A6 *In warning a detainee who is asked to consent to an intimate drug offence search, as in paragraph 2B, the following form of words may be used:*

"You do not have to allow yourself to be searched, but I must warn you that if you refuse without good cause, your refusal may harm your case if it comes to trial.".

*Where the use of the Welsh language is appropriate, the following form of words may be used:*

"Nid oes rhaid i chi roi caniatâd i gael eich archwilio, ond mae'n rhaid i mi eich rhybuddio os gwrthodwch heb reswm da, y gallai eich penderfyniad i wrthod wneud niwed i'ch achos pe bai'n dod gerbron llys.".

## ANNEX B

### Delay in notifying arrest or allowing access to legal advice

*A Persons detained under PACE*

A-99        C:1. The exercise of the rights in section 5 or section 6, or both, may be delayed if the person is in police detention, as in PACE, section 118(2), in connection with an indictable offence, has not yet been charged with an offence and an officer of superintendent rank or above, or inspector rank or above only for the rights in section 5, has reasonable grounds for believing their exercise will:
  (i) lead to:
    • interference with, or harm to, evidence connected with an indictable offence; or
    • interference with, or physical harm to, other people; or
  (ii) lead to alerting other people suspected of having committed an indictable offence but not yet arrested for it; or
  (iii) hinder the recovery of property obtained in consequence of the commission of such an offence.
C:2. These rights may also be delayed if the officer has reasonable grounds to believe that:
  (i) the person detained for an indictable offence has benefited from their criminal conduct (decided in accordance with Part 2 of the Proceeds of Crime Act 2002); and
  (ii) the recovery of the value of the property constituting that benefit will be hindered by the exercise of either right.
C:3. Authority to delay a detainee's right to consult privately with a solicitor may be given only if the authorising officer has reasonable grounds to believe the solicitor the detainee wants to consult will, inadvertently or otherwise, pass on a message from the detainee or act in some other way which will have any of the consequences specified under paragraphs 1 or 2. In these circumstances, the detainee must be allowed to choose another solicitor. See *Note B3.*
C:4. If the detainee wishes to see a solicitor, access to that solicitor may not be delayed on the grounds they might advise the detainee not to answer questions or the solicitor was initially asked to attend the police station by someone else. In the latter case, the detainee must be told the solicitor has come to the police station at another person's request, and must be asked to sign the custody record to signify whether they want to see the solicitor.
C:5. The fact the grounds for delaying notification of arrest may be satisfied does not automatically mean the grounds for delaying access to legal advice will also be satisfied.

C:6. These rights may be delayed only for as long as grounds exist and in no case beyond 36 hours after the relevant time as in PACE, s.41. If the grounds cease to apply within this time, the detainee must, as soon as practicable, be asked if they want to exercise either right, the custody record must be noted accordingly, and action taken in accordance with the relevant section of the code.

C:7. A detained person must be permitted to consult a solicitor for a reasonable time before any court hearing.

B [*Not used.*]

C *Documentation*

C:13. The grounds for action under this annex shall be recorded and the detainee informed of them as soon as practicable.     **A-100**

C:14. Any reply given by a detainee under paragraphs 6 or 11 must be recorded and the detainee asked to endorse the record in relation to whether they want to receive legal advice at this point.

D *Cautions and special warnings*

C:15. When a suspect detained at a police station is interviewed during any period for which access to legal advice has been delayed under this annex, the court or jury may not draw adverse inferences from their silence.

*Notes for guidance*

C:B1 *Even if Annex B applies in the case of a juvenile, or a person who is mentally disordered or otherwise mentally vulnerable, action to inform the appropriate adult and the person responsible for a juvenile's welfare if that is a different person, must nevertheless be taken as in paragraph 3.13 and 3.15.*     **A-101**

*Note: paragraph 1.5A of this code extends this note to 17-year-old detainees.*

C:B2 *In the case of Commonwealth citizens and foreign nationals, see Note 7A.*

C:B3 *A decision to delay access to a specific solicitor is likely to be a rare occurrence and only when it can be shown the suspect is capable of misleading that particular solicitor and there is more than a substantial risk that the suspect will succeed in causing information to be conveyed which will lead to one or more of the specified consequences.*

## ANNEX C

### Restriction on drawing adverse inferences from silence and terms of the caution when the restriction applies

(a) *The restriction on drawing adverse inferences from silence*

C:1. The Criminal Justice and Public Order Act 1994, ss.34, 36 and 37 as amended by the Youth Justice and Criminal Evidence Act 1999, s.58 describe the conditions under which adverse inferences may be drawn from a person's failure or refusal to say anything about their involvement in the offence when interviewed, after being charged or informed they may be prosecuted. These provisions are subject to an overriding restriction on the ability of a court or jury to draw adverse inferences from a person's silence. This restriction applies:     **A-102**

    (a) to any detainee at a police station, see *Note 10C*, who, before being interviewed, see section 11, or being charged or informed they may be prosecuted, see section 16, has:

        (i) asked for legal advice, see section 6, paragraph 6.1;

        (ii) not been allowed an opportunity to consult a solicitor, including the duty solicitor, as in this code; and

        (iii) not changed their mind about wanting legal advice, see section 6, paragraph 6.6(d);

            – [note the condition in (ii) will

                – apply when a detainee who has asked for legal advice is interviewed before speaking to a solicitor as in section 6, paragraph 6.6(a) or (b);

                – not apply if the detained person declines to ask for the duty solicitor, see section 6, paragraphs 6.6(c) and (d)];

    (b) to any person charged with, or informed they may be prosecuted for, an offence who:

        (i) has had brought to their notice a written statement made by another person or the content of an interview with another person which relates to that offence, see section 16, paragraph 16.4;

        (ii) is interviewed about that offence, see section 16, paragraph 16.5; or

(iii) makes a written statement about that offence, see Annex D paragraphs 4 and 9.

(b) *Terms of the caution when the restriction applies*

C:2. When a requirement to caution arises at a time when the restriction on drawing adverse inferences from silence applies, the caution shall be:

*"You do not have to say anything, but anything you do say may be given in evidence.".*

Where the use of the Welsh language is appropriate, the caution may be used directly in Welsh in the following terms:

*"Does dim rhaid i chi ddweud dim byd, ond gall unrhyw beth yr ydych chi'n ei ddweud gael ei roi fel tystiolaeth.".*

C:3. Whenever the restriction either begins to apply or ceases to apply after a caution has already been given, the person shall be re-cautioned in the appropriate terms. The changed position on drawing inferences and that the previous caution no longer applies shall also be explained to the detainee in ordinary language. See *Note C2.*

*Notes for guidance*

C:C1 *The restriction on drawing inferences from silence does not apply to a person who has not been detained and who therefore cannot be prevented from seeking legal advice if they want to, see paragraphs 10.2 and 3.15.*

C:C2 *The following is suggested as a framework to help explain changes in the position on drawing adverse inferences if the restriction on drawing adverse inferences from silence:*

    (a) *begins to apply:*

        *"The caution you were previously given no longer applies. This is because after that caution:*
          (i) *you asked to speak to a solicitor but have not yet been allowed an opportunity to speak to a solicitor;" see paragraph 1(a); or*
        *"(ii) you have been charged with/informed you may be prosecuted." See paragraph 1(b).*
        *"This means that from now on, adverse inferences cannot be drawn at court and your defence will not be harmed just because you choose to say nothing. Please listen carefully to the caution I am about to give you because it will apply from now on. You will see that it does not say anything about your defence being harmed.";*

    (b) *ceases to apply before or at the time the person is charged or informed they may be prosecuted, see paragraph 1(a);*

        *"The caution you were previously given no longer applies. This is because after that caution you have been allowed an opportunity to speak to a solicitor. Please listen carefully to the caution I am about to give you because it will apply from now on. It explains how your defence at court may be affected if you choose to say nothing.".*

## ANNEX D

### Written statements under caution

(a) *Written by a person under caution*

C:1. A person shall always be invited to write down what they want to say.

C:2. A person who has not been charged with, or informed they may be prosecuted for, any offence to which the statement they want to write relates, shall:

    (a) unless the statement is made at a time when the restriction on drawing adverse inferences from silence applies, see Annex C, be asked to write out and sign the following before writing what they want to say:

        *"I make this statement of my own free will. I understand that I do not have to say anything but that it may harm my defence if I do not mention when questioned something which I later rely on in court. This statement may be given in evidence.";*

    (b) if the statement is made at a time when the restriction on drawing adverse inferences from silence applies, be asked to write out and sign the following before writing what they want to say;

        *"I make this statement of my own free will. I understand that I do not have to say anything. This statement may be given in evidence.".*

C:3. When a person, on the occasion of being charged with or informed they may be prosecuted for any offence, asks to make a statement which relates to any such offence and wants to write it they shall:

    (a) unless the restriction on drawing adverse inferences from silence, see Annex C, applied when they were so charged or informed they may be prosecuted, be asked to write out and sign the following before writing what they want to say:

        *"I make this statement of my own free will. I understand that I do not have to say anything but that it may harm my defence if I do not mention when questioned something which I later rely on in court. This statement may be given in evidence.";*

    (b) if the restriction on drawing adverse inferences from silence applied when they were so charged or informed they may be prosecuted, be asked to write out and sign the following before writing what they want to say:

        *"I make this statement of my own free will. I understand that I do not have to say anything. This statement may be given in evidence.".*

C:4. When a person who has already been charged with or informed they may be prosecuted for any offence asks to make a statement which relates to any such offence and wants to write it, they shall be asked to write out and sign the following before writing what they want to say:

*"I make this statement of my own free will. I understand that I do not have to say anything. This statement may be given in evidence.".*

C:5. Any person writing their own statement shall be allowed to do so without any prompting except a police officer or police staff may indicate to them which matters are material or question any ambiguity in the statement.

(b) *Written by a police officer or other police staff*

C:6. If a person says they would like someone to write the statement for them, a police officer, or **A-104** other police staff shall write the statement.

C:7. If the person has not been charged with, or informed they may be prosecuted for, any offence to which the statement they want to make relates they shall, before starting, be asked to sign, or make their mark, to the following:

    (a) unless the statement is made at a time when the restriction on drawing adverse inferences from silence applies, see Annex C:

        *"I, ................., wish to make a statement. I want someone to write down what I say. I understand that I do not have to say anything but that it may harm my defence if I do not mention when questioned something which I later rely on in court. This statement may be given in evidence.";*

    (b) if the statement is made at a time when the restriction on drawing adverse inferences from silence applies:

        *"I, ................., wish to make a statement. I want someone to write down what I say. I understand that I do not have to say anything. This statement may be given in evidence.".*

C:8. If, on the occasion of being charged with or informed they may be prosecuted for any offence, the person asks to make a statement which relates to any such offence they shall before starting be asked to sign, or make their mark to, the following:

    (a) unless the restriction on drawing adverse inferences from silence applied, see Annex C, when they were so charged or informed they may be prosecuted:

        *"I, ................., wish to make a statement. I want someone to write down what I say. I understand that I do not have to say anything but that it may harm my defence if I do not mention when questioned something which I later rely on in court. This statement may be given in evidence.";*

    (b) if the restriction on drawing adverse inferences from silence applied when they were so charged or informed they may be prosecuted:

        *"I, ................., wish to make a statement. I want someone to write down what I say. I understand that I do not have to say anything. This statement may be given in evidence.".*

C:9. If, having already been charged with or informed they may be prosecuted for any offence, a person asks to make a statement which relates to any such offence they shall before starting, be asked to sign, or make their mark to:

*"I, ................., wish to make a statement. I want someone to write down what I say. I understand that I do*

*not have to say anything. This statement may be given in evidence.".*

C:10. The person writing the statement must take down the exact words spoken by the person making it and must not edit or paraphrase it. Any questions that are necessary, *e.g.* to make it more intelligible, and the answers given must be recorded at the same time on the statement form.

C:11. When the writing of a statement is finished the person making it shall be asked to read it and to make any corrections, alterations or additions they want. When they have finished reading they shall be asked to write and sign or make their mark on the following certificate at the end of the statement:

*"I have read the above statement, and I have been able to correct, alter or add anything I wish. This statement is true. I have made it of my own free will.".*

C:12. If the person making the statement cannot read, or refuses to read it, or to write the above mentioned certificate at the end of it or to sign it, the person taking the statement shall read it to them and ask them if they would like to correct, alter or add anything and to put their signature or make their mark at the end. The person taking the statement shall certify on the statement itself what has occurred.

### ANNEX E

**Summary of provisions relating to mentally disordered and otherwise mentally vulnerable people**

**A-105**

C:1. If an officer has any suspicion, or is told in good faith, that a person of any age may be mentally disordered or otherwise mentally vulnerable, or mentally incapable of understanding the significance of questions or their replies that person shall be treated as mentally disordered or otherwise mentally vulnerable for the purposes of this code. See paragraph 1.4 and *Note E4*.

C:2. In the case of a person who is mentally disordered or otherwise mentally vulnerable, "the appropriate adult" means:

   (a) a relative, guardian or other person responsible for their care or custody;
   (b) someone experienced in dealing with mentally disordered or mentally vulnerable people but who is not a police officer or employed by the police;
   (c) failing these, some other responsible adult aged 18 or over who is not a police officer or employed by the police.

See paragraph 1.7(b) and *Note 1D*.

C:3. If the custody officer authorises the detention of a person who is mentally vulnerable or appears to be suffering from a mental disorder, the custody officer must as soon as practicable inform the appropriate adult of the grounds for detention and the person's whereabouts, and ask the adult to come to the police station to see them. If the appropriate adult:

   • is already at the station when information is given as in paragraphs 3.1 to 3.5 the information must be given in their presence;
   • is not at the station when the provisions of paragraph 3.1 to 3.5 are complied with these provisions must be complied with again in their presence once they arrive.

See paragraphs 3.15 to 3.17.

C:4. If the appropriate adult, having been informed of the right to legal advice, considers legal advice should be taken, the provisions of section 6 apply as if the mentally disordered or otherwise mentally vulnerable person had requested access to legal advice. See paragraph 3.19 and *Note E1*.

C:5. The custody officer must make sure a person receives appropriate clinical attention as soon as reasonably practicable if the person appears to be suffering from a mental disorder or in urgent cases immediately call the nearest appropriate healthcare professional or an ambulance. It is not intended these provisions delay the transfer of a detainee to a place of safety under the Mental Health Act 1983, s.136, if that is applicable. If an assessment under that Act is to take place at a police station, the custody officer must consider whether an appropriate healthcare professional should be called to conduct an initial clinical check on the detainee. See paragraph 9.5 and 9.6.

C:6. It is imperative a mentally disordered or otherwise mentally vulnerable person detained under the Mental Health Act 1983, s.136, be assessed as soon as possible. A police station should only be used as a place of safety as a last resort but if that assessment is to take place at the police station, an approved social worker and registered medical practitioner shall be called to the station as soon as possible to carry it out. Once the detainee has been assessed and suitable arrangements been made for their treatment or care, they can no longer be detained under section 136. A detainee should be immediately discharged from detention if a registered medical practitioner having examined them, concludes they are not mentally disordered within the meaning of the Act. See paragraph 3.16.

C:7. If a mentally disordered or otherwise mentally vulnerable person is cautioned in the absence of the appropriate adult, the caution must be repeated in the appropriate adult's presence. See paragraph 10.12.

C:8. A mentally disordered or otherwise mentally vulnerable person must not be interviewed or asked to provide or sign a written statement in the absence of the appropriate adult unless the provisions of paragraphs 11.1 or 11.18 to 11.20 apply. Questioning in these circumstances may not continue in the absence of the appropriate adult once sufficient information to avert the risk has been obtained. A record shall be made of the grounds for any decision to begin an interview in these circumstances. See paragraphs 11.1, 11.15 and 11.18 to 11.20.

C:9. If the appropriate adult is present at an interview, they shall be informed they are not expected to act simply as an observer and the purposes of their presence are to:

- advise the interviewee;
- observe whether or not the interview is being conducted properly and fairly;
- facilitate communication with the interviewee.

See paragraph 11.17.

C:10. If the detention of a mentally disordered or otherwise mentally vulnerable person is **A-106** reviewed by a review officer or a superintendent, the appropriate adult must, if available at the time, be given an opportunity to make representations to the officer about the need for continuing detention. See paragraph 15.3.

C:11. If the custody officer charges a mentally disordered or otherwise mentally vulnerable person with an offence or takes such other action as is appropriate when there is sufficient evidence for a prosecution this must be carried out in the presence of the appropriate adult if they are at the police station. A copy of the written notice embodying any charge must also be given to the appropriate adult. See paragraphs 16.1 to 16.4A.

C:12. An intimate or strip search of a mentally disordered or otherwise mentally vulnerable person may take place only in the presence of the appropriate adult of the same sex, unless the detainee specifically requests the presence of a particular adult of the opposite sex. A strip search may take place in the absence of an appropriate adult only in cases of urgency when there is a risk of serious harm to the detainee or others. See Annex A, paragraphs 5 and 11(c).

C:13. Particular care must be taken when deciding whether to use any form of approved restraints on a mentally disordered or otherwise mentally vulnerable person in a locked cell. See paragraph 8.2.

*Notes for guidance*

C:E1 *The purpose of the provision at paragraph 3.19 is to protect the rights of a mentally disordered or* **A-107** *otherwise mentally vulnerable detained person who does not understand the significance of what is said to them. If the detained person wants to exercise the right to legal advice, the appropriate action should be taken and not delayed until the appropriate adult arrives. A mentally disordered or otherwise mentally vulnerable detained person should always be given an opportunity, when an appropriate adult is called to the police station, to consult privately with a solicitor in the absence of the appropriate adult if they want.*

C:E2 *Although people who are mentally disordered or otherwise mentally vulnerable are often capable of providing reliable evidence, they may, without knowing or wanting to do so, be particularly prone in certain circumstances to provide information that may be unreliable, misleading or self-incriminating. Special care should always be taken when questioning such a person, and the appropriate adult should be involved if there is any doubt about a person's mental state or capacity. Because of the risk of unreliable evidence, it is important to obtain corroboration of any facts admitted whenever possible.*

C:E3 *Because of the risks referred to in Note E2, which the presence of the appropriate adult is intended to minimise, officers of superintendent rank or above should exercise their discretion to authorise the commencement of an interview in the appropriate adult's absence only in exceptional cases, if it is necessary to avert an immediate risk of serious harm. See paragraphs 11.1, 11.18 to 11.20.*

C:E4 *There is no requirement for an appropriate adult to be present if a person is detained under section 136 of the Mental Health Act 1983 for assessment.*

**ANNEX F**

[*Not used.*] **A-108**

**ANNEX G**

**Fitness to be interviewed**

C:1. This annex contains general guidance to help police officers and health care professionals as- **A-109** sess whether a detainee might be at risk in an interview.

C:2. A detainee may be at risk in an interview if it is considered that:

(a) conducting the interview could significantly harm the detainee's physical or mental state;

(b) anything the detainee says in the interview about their involvement or suspected involvement in the offence about which they are being interviewed **might** be considered unreliable in subsequent court proceedings because of their physical or mental state.

C:3. In assessing whether the detainee should be interviewed, the following must be considered:

(a) how the detainee's physical or mental state might affect their ability to understand the nature and purpose of the interview, to comprehend what is being asked and to appreciate the significance of any answers given and make rational decisions about whether they want to say anything;

(b) the extent to which the detainee's replies may be affected by their physical or mental condition rather than representing a rational and accurate explanation of their involvement in the offence;

(c) how the nature of the interview, which could include particularly probing questions, might affect the detainee.

**A-110**
C:4. It is essential health care professionals who are consulted consider the functional ability of the detainee rather than simply relying on a medical diagnosis, *e.g.* it is possible for a person with severe mental illness to be fit for interview.

C:5. Health care professionals should advise on the need for an appropriate adult to be present, whether reassessment of the person's fitness for interview may be necessary if the interview lasts beyond a specified time, and whether a further specialist opinion may be required.

C:6. When health care professionals identify risks they should be asked to quantify the risks. They should inform the custody officer:

- whether the person's condition:
  - is likely to improve;
  - will require or be amenable to treatment; and
- indicate how long it may take for such improvement to take effect.

C:7. The role of the health care professional is to consider the risks and advise the custody officer of the outcome of that consideration. The health care professional's determination and any advice or recommendations should be made in writing and form part of the custody record.

C:8. Once the health care professional has provided that information, it is a matter for the custody officer to decide whether or not to allow the interview to go ahead and if the interview is to proceed, to determine what safeguards are needed. Nothing prevents safeguards being provided in addition to those required under the code. An example might be to have an appropriate health care professional present during the interview, in addition to an appropriate adult, in order constantly to monitor the person's condition and how it is being affected by the interview.

## ANNEX H

### Detained person: observation list

**A-111**
C:1. If any detainee fails to meet any of the following criteria, an appropriate health care professional or an ambulance must be called.

C:2. When assessing the level of rousability, consider:

*Rousability*—can they be woken?
- go into the cell
- call their name
- shake gently

*Response to questions*—can they give appropriate answers to questions such as:
- What's your name?
- Where do you live?
- Where do you think you are?

*Response to commands*—can they respond appropriately to commands such as:
- Open your eyes!
- Lift one arm, now the other arm!

C:3. Remember to take into account the possibility or presence of other illnesses, injury, or mental condition; a person who is drowsy and smells of alcohol may also have the following:

- Diabetes
- Epilepsy
- Head injury
- Drug intoxication or overdose
- Stroke

**ANNEX I**

[*Not used.*]

**ANNEX J**

[*Not used.*]

**ANNEX K**

**X-rays and ultrasound scans**

(a) *Action*

C:1. PACE, s.55A allows a person who has been arrested and is in police detention to have an **A-111a**
x-ray taken of them or an ultrasound scan to be carried out on them (or both) if:
>    (a) authorised by an officer of inspector rank or above who has reasonably grounds for
>    believing that the detainee:
>    >    (i) may have swallowed a Class A drug; and
>    >    (ii) was in possession of that Class A drug with the intention of supplying it to another or
>    >    to export; and
>    (b) the detainee's appropriate consent has been given in writing.

C:2. Before an x-ray is taken or an ultrasound scan carried out, a police officer or designated
detention officer must tell the detainee:
>    (a) that the authority has been given; and
>    (b) the grounds for giving the authorisation.

Note: paragraph 1.5A in this code requires someone to fulfil the role of the appropriate adult to
be present when a 17-year-old is told about the authority and grounds for an x-ray and ultrasound
scan.

C:3. Before a detainee is asked to give appropriate consent to an x-ray or an ultrasound scan, they
must be warned that if they refuse without good cause their refusal may harm their case if it comes
to trial, see *Notes K1* and *K2*. This warning may be given by a police officer or member of police staff.
In the case of juveniles, mentally vulnerable or mentally disordered suspects the seeking and giving
of consent must take place in the presence of the appropriate adult. A juvenile's consent is only valid
if their parent's or guardian's consent is also obtained unless the juvenile is under 14, when their
parent's or guardian's consent is sufficient in its own right. A detainee who is not legally represented
must be reminded of their entitlement to have free legal advice, see Code C, paragraph 6.5, and the
reminder noted in the custody record.

Note: paragraph 1.5A in this code requires someone to fulfil the role of the appropriate adult to
be present when the warning is given to a 17-year-old and their consent to an x-ray or ultrasound
scan is sought and given but the consent of their parent or guardian is not required.

C:4. An x-ray may be taken, or an ultrasound scan may be carried out, only by a registered medical practitioner or registered nurse, and only at a hospital, surgery or other medical premises.

(b) *Documentation*

C:5. The following shall be recorded as soon as practicable in the detainee's custody record:
>    (a) the authorisation to take the x-ray or carry out the ultrasound scan (or both);
>    (b) the grounds for giving the authorisation;
>    (c) the giving of the warning required by paragraph 3; and
>    (d) the fact that the appropriate consent was given or (as the case may be) refused, and if
>    refused, the reason given for the refusal (if any); and
>    (e) if an x-ray is taken or an ultrasound scan carried out:
>    >    • where it was taken or carried out;
>    >    • who took it or carried it out;
>    >    • who was present;
>    >    • the result.

*Notes for guidance*

C:K1 *If authority is given for an x-ray to be taken or an ultrasound scan to be carried out (or both),* **A-111b**
*consideration should be given to asking a registered medical practitioner or registered nurse to explain to the
detainee what is involved and to allay any concerns the detainee might have about the effect which taking an x-ray
or carrying out an ultrasound scan might have on them. If appropriate consent is not given, evidence of the*

*explanation may, if the case comes to trial, be relevant to determining whether the detainee had a good cause for refusing.*

C:K2 *In warning a detainee who is asked to consent to an x-ray being taken or an ultrasound scan being carried out (or both), as in paragraph 3, the following form of words may be used:*

"*You do not have to allow an x-ray of you to be taken or an ultrasound scan to be carried out on you, but I must warn you that if you refuse without good cause, your refusal may harm your case if it comes to trial.*".

*Where the use of the Welsh language is appropriate, the following form of words may be provided in Welsh:*

"*Does dim rhaid i chi ganiatáu cymryd sgan uwchsain neu belydr-x (neu'r ddau) arnoch, ond mae'n rhaid i mi eich rhybuddio os byddwch chin gwrthod gwneud hynny heb reswm da, fe allai hynny niweidio eich achos pe bai'n dod gerbron llys.*".

## ANNEX L

### Establishing gender of persons for the purpose of searching

A-111c        C:1. 1. Certain provisions of this and other PACE codes explicitly state that searches and other procedures may only be carried out by, or in the presence of, persons of the same sex as the person subject to the search or other procedure. See *Note L1*.

C:2. All searches and procedures must be carried out with courtesy, consideration and respect for the person concerned. Police officers should show particular sensitivity when dealing with transgender individuals (including transsexual persons) and transvestite persons (see *Notes L2, L3* and *L4*).

(a) *Consideration*

A-111d        C:3. In law, the gender (and accordingly the sex) of an individual is their gender as registered at birth unless they have been issued with a gender recognition certificate (GRC) under the Gender Recognition Act 2004 (GRA), in which case the person's gender is their acquired gender. This means that if the acquired gender is the male gender, the person's sex becomes that of a man and, if it is the female gender, the person's sex becomes that of a woman and they must be treated as their acquired gender.

C:4. When establishing whether the person concerned should be treated as being male or female for the purposes of these searches and procedures, the following approach which is designed to minimise embarrassment and secure the person's co-operation should be followed:

(a) the person must not be asked whether they have a GRC (see paragraph 8);

(b) if there is no doubt as to as to whether the person concerned should be treated as being male or female, they should be dealt with as being of that sex;

(c) if at any time (including during the search or carrying out the procedure) there is doubt as to whether the person should be treated, or continue to be treated, as being male or female:

  (i) the person should be asked what gender they consider themselves to be; if they express a preference to be dealt with as a particular gender, they should be asked to indicate and confirm their preference by signing the custody record or, if a custody record has not been opened, the search record or the officer's notebook; subject to (ii) below, the person should be treated according to their preference;

  (ii) if there are grounds to doubt that the preference in (i) accurately reflects the person's predominant lifestyle, for example, if they ask to be treated as a woman but documents and other information make it clear that they live predominantly as a man, or vice versa, they should be treated according to what appears to be their predominant lifestyle and not their stated preference;

  (iii) if the person is unwilling to express a preference as in (i) above, efforts should be made to determine their predominant lifestyle and they should be treated as such; for example, if they appear to live predominantly as a woman, they should be treated as being female; or

  (iv) if none of the above apply, the person should be dealt with according to what reasonably appears to have been their sex as registered at birth.

C:5. Once a decision has been made about which gender an individual is to be treated as, each officer responsible for the search or procedure should where possible be advised before the search or procedure starts of any doubts as to the person's gender and the person informed that the doubts have been disclosed. This is important so as to maintain the dignity of the person and any officers concerned.

(b) *Documentation*

C:6. The person's gender as established under paragraph 4(c)(i) to (iv) above must be recorded in **A-111e** the person's custody record or, if a custody record has not been opened, on the search record or in the officer's notebook.

C:7. Where the person elects which gender they consider themselves to be under paragraph 4(b)(i) but, following 4(b)(ii) is not treated in accordance with their preference, the reason must be recorded in the search record, in the officer's notebook or, if applicable, in the person's custody record.

(c) *Disclosure of information*

C:8. Section 22 of the GRA defines any information relating to a person's application for a GRC or **A-111f** to a successful applicant's gender before it became their acquired gender as "protected information". Nothing in this annex is to be read as authorising or permitting any police officer or any police staff who has acquired such information when acting in their official capacity to disclose that information to any other person in contravention of the GRA. Disclosure includes making a record of "protected information" which is read by others.

*Notes for guidance*

C:L1 *Provisions to which paragraph 1 applies include:* **A-111g**

- *in Code C; paragraph 4.1 and Annex A, paragraphs 5, 6 and 11 (searches, strip and intimate searches of detainees under sections 54 and 55 of PACE);*
- *in Code A; paragraphs 2.8 and 3.6 and Note 4;*
- *in Code D; paragraph 5.5 and Note 5F (searches, examinations and photographing of detainees under section 54A of PACE) and paragraph 6.9 (taking samples);*
- *in Code H; paragraph 4.1 and Annex A, paragraphs 6, 7 and 12 (searches, strip and intimate searches under sections 54 and 55 of PACE of persons arrested under section 41 of the Terrorism Act 2000).*

C:L2 *While there is no agreed definition of transgender (or trans), it is generally used as an umbrella term to describe people whose gender identity (self-identification as being a woman, man, neither or both) differs from the sex they were registered as at birth. The term includes, but is not limited to, transsexual people.*

C:L3 *Transsexual means a person who is proposing to undergo, is undergoing or has undergone a process (or part of a process) for the purpose of gender reassignment, which is a protected characteristic under the Equality Act 2010 (see paragraph 1.0) by changing physiological or other attributes of their sex. This includes aspects of gender such as dress and title. It would apply to a woman making the transition to being a man and a man making the transition to being a woman, as well as to a person who has only just started out on the process of gender reassignment and to a person who has completed the process. Both would share the characteristic of gender reassignment with each having the characteristics of one sex, but with certain characteristics of the other sex.*

C:L4 *Transvestite means a person of one gender who dresses in the clothes of a person of the opposite gender. However, a transvestite does not live permanently in the gender opposite to their birth sex.*

C:L5 *Chief officers are responsible for providing corresponding operational guidance and instructions for the deployment of transgender officers and staff under their direction and control to duties which involve carrying out, or being present at, any of the searches and procedures described in paragraph 1. The guidance and instructions must comply with the Equality Act 2010 and should therefore complement the approach in this annex.*

## ANNEX M

### Documents and records to be translated

C:1. For the purposes of Directive 2010/64/EU of the European Parliament and of the Council of **A-111h** 20 October 2010 and this code, essential documents comprise records required to be made in accordance with this code which are relevant to decisions to deprive a person of their liberty, to any charge and to any record considered necessary to enable a detainee to defend themselves in criminal proceedings and to safeguard the fairness of the proceedings. Passages of essential documents which are not relevant need not be translated. See *Note M1*.

C:2. The table below lists the documents considered essential for the purposes of this code and when (subject to paras 3 to 7) written translations must be created and provided.

*Table of essential documents:*

| | Essential documents for the purposes of this code | When translation to be created | When translation to be provided. |
|---|---|---|---|
| (i) | The grounds for each of the following authorisations to keep the person in custody as they are described and referred to in the custody record:<br><br>(a) authorisation for detention before and after charge given by the custody o cer and by the review officer, see Code C, paras 3.4 and 15.16(a);<br><br>(b) authorisation to extend deten-tion without charge beyond 24 hours given by a superin-tendent, see Code C, para. 15.16(b);<br><br>(c) a warrant of further detention issued by a magistrates' court and any extension(s) of the warrant, see Code C, para. 15.16(c);<br><br>(d) an authority to detain in ac-cordance with the directions in a warrant of arrest issued in connection with criminal proceedings including the court issuing the warrant. | As soon as practicable after each authorisation has been recorded in the custody record. | As soon as practicable after the translation has been created, whilst the person is detained or after they have been released (see *Note M3*). |
| (ii) | Written notice showing particulars of the offence charged required by Code C, para. 16.3, or the offence for which the suspect has been told they may be prosecuted. | As soon as practicable after the person has been charged or reported. | |
| (iii) | Written interview records: Code C:11.11, 13.3, 13.4 & Code E4.7 Written statement under caution: Code C, Annex D. | To be created contemporaneously by the interpreter for the person to check and sign. | As soon as practicable after the person has been charged or told they may be prosecuted. |

C:3. The custody officer may authorise an oral translation or oral summary of documents (i) to (ii) in the table (but not (iii)) to be provided (through an interpreter) instead of a written translation. Such an oral translation or summary may only be provided if it would not prejudice the fairness of the proceedings by in any way adversely affecting or otherwise undermining or limiting the ability of the suspect in question to understand their position and to communicate effectively with police offic-ers, interviewers, solicitors and appropriate adults with regard to their detention and the investiga-tion of the offence in question and to defend themselves in the event of criminal proceedings. The quantity and complexity of the information in the document should always be considered and specific additional consideration given if the suspect is mentally disordered or otherwise mentally vulnerable or is a juvenile or a 17-year-old (see Code C, para. 1.5A). The reason for the decision must be recorded (see para. 13.11(e))

C:4. Subject to paragraphs 5 to 7 below, a suspect may waive their right to a written translation of the essential documents described in the table but only if they do so voluntarily after receiving legal advice or having full knowledge of the consequences and give their unconditional and fully informed consent in writing (see para. 9).

C:5. The suspect may be asked if they wish to waive their right to a written translation and before giving their consent, they must be reminded of their right to legal advice and asked whether they wish to speak to a solicitor.

C:6. No police officer or police staff should do or say anything with the intention of persuading a suspect who is entitled to a written translation of an essential document to waive that right. See *Notes M2* and *M3*.

C:7. For the purpose of the waiver:

(a) the consent of a person who is mentally disordered or otherwise mentally vulnerable person is only valid if the information about the circumstances under which they can waive the right and the reminder about their right to legal advice mentioned in paragraphs 3 to 5 and their consent is given in the presence of the appropriate adult (note: para. 1.5A in Code C requires someone to fulfil the role of the appropriate adult to be present when a 17-year-old is given the information and reminder mentioned in sub-para. (a) above and gives their consent to waive their right; the consent of their parent or guardian is not required);

(b) the consent of a juvenile is only valid if their parent's or guardian's consent is also obtained unless the juvenile is under 14, when their parent's or guardian's consent is sufficient in its own right and the information and reminder mentioned in sub-paragraph (a) above and their consent is also given in the presence of the appropriate adult (who may or may not be a parent or guardian).

C:8. The detainee, their solicitor or appropriate adult may make representations to the custody officer that a document which is not included in the table is essential and that a translation should be provided. The request may be refused if the officer is satisfied that the translation requested is not essential for the purposes described in paragraph 1 above.

C:9. If the custody officer has any doubts about—

• providing an oral translation or summary of an essential document instead of a written translation (see para. 3),

• whether the suspect fully understands the consequences of waiving their right to a written translation of an essential document (see para. 4), or

• about refusing to provide a translation of a requested document (see para. 7),

the officer should seek advice from an inspector or above.

*Documentation*

C:10. Action taken in accordance with this annex shall be recorded in the detainee's custody **A-111j** record or interview record as appropriate (see Code C, para. 13.11(e)).

*Notes for guidance*

C:M1 *It is not necessary to disclose information in any translation which is capable of undermining or* **A-111k** *otherwise adversely affecting any investigative processes, for example, by enabling the suspect to fabricate an innocent explanation or to conceal lies from the interviewer.*

C:M2 *No police officer or police staff shall indicate to any suspect, except to answer a direct question, whether the period for which they are liable to be detained or if not detained, the time taken to complete the interview, might be reduced:*

• *if they do not ask for legal advice before deciding whether they wish to waive their right to a written translation of an essential document; or*

• *if they decide to waive their right to a written translation of an essential document.*

C:M3 *There is no power under PACE to detain a person or to delay their release solely to create and provide a written translation of any essential document.*

## (5) Identification

The text that follows is of the version of the code that came into force on March 7, 2011 see **A-112** *ante*, Appendix A-1.

In connection with Code D, see also §§ 14-39 *et seq.* (application of code), §§ 14-45 *et seq.* (identification parades), § 14-55 (group identification, confrontation and video identification), §§ 14-57 *et seq.* (effect of breaches), §§ 14-60 *et seq.* (photographs), §§ 14-64 *et seq.* (video recordings), and § 15-179 (photographs) in the main work.

## D. CODE OF PRACTICE FOR THE IDENTIFICATION OF PERSONS BY POLICE OFFICERS

### Commencement—Transitional arrangements

**A-113**     This code has effect in relation to any identification procedure carried out after midnight, twenty-one days after the day on which the Police and Criminal Evidence Act 1984 (Codes of Practice) (Revision of Codes A, B and D) Order 2010 [*sic*] is made.

### D:1 Introduction

**A-114**     D:1.1 This code of practice concerns the principal methods used by police to identify people in connection with the investigation of offences and the keeping of accurate and reliable criminal records. The powers and procedures in this code must be used fairly, responsibly, with respect for the people to whom they apply and without unlawful discrimination. The Equality Act 2010 makes it unlawful for police officers to discriminate against, harass or victimise any person on the grounds of the "protected characteristics" of age, disability, gender reassignment, race, religion or belief, sex and sexual orientation, marriage and civil partnership, pregnancy and maternity when using their powers. When police forces are carrying out their functions they also have a duty to have regard to the need to eliminate unlawful discrimination, harassment and victimisation and to take steps to foster good relations.

D:1.2 In this code, identification by an eye-witness arises when a witness who has seen the offender committing the crime and is given an opportunity to identify a person suspected of involvement in the offence in a video identification, identification parade or similar procedure. These eyewitness identification procedures (see Part A of section 3 below) are designed to:

- test the witness's ability to identify the suspect as the person they saw on a previous occasion;
- provide safeguards against mistaken identification.

While this code concentrates on visual identification procedures, it does not preclude the police making use of aural identification procedures such as a "voice identification parade", where they judge that appropriate.

D:1.2A In this code, separate provisions in Part B of section 3 below apply when any person, including a police officer, is asked if they recognise anyone they see in an image as being someone they know and to test their claim that they recognise that person as someone who is known to them. Except where stated, these separate provisions are not subject to the eye-witnesses identification procedures described in paragraph 1.2.

D:1.3 Identification by fingerprints applies when a person's fingerprints are taken to:

- compare with fingerprints found at the scene of a crime;
- check and prove convictions;
- help to ascertain a person's identity.

D:1.3A Identification using footwear impressions applies when a person's footwear impressions are taken to compare with impressions found at the scene of a crime.

D:1.4 Identification by body samples and impressions includes taking samples such as blood or hair to generate a DNA profile for comparison with material obtained from the scene of a crime, or a victim.

D:1.5 Taking photographs of arrested people applies to recording and checking identity and locating and tracing persons who:

- are wanted for offences;
- fail to answer their bail.

D:1.6 Another method of identification involves searching and examining detained suspects to find, *e.g.*, marks such as tattoos or scars which may help establish their identity or whether they have been involved in committing an offence.

D:1.7 The provisions of the Police and Criminal Evidence Act 1984 (PACE) and this code are designed to make sure fingerprints, samples, impressions and photographs are taken, used and retained, and identification procedures carried out, only when justified and necessary for preventing, detecting or investigating crime. If these provisions are not observed, the application of the relevant procedures in particular cases may be open to question.

### D:2 General

**A-115**     D:2.1 This code must be readily available at all police stations for consultation by:

- police officers and police staff;
- detained persons;
- members of the public.

D:2.2 The provisions of this code:

- include the Annexes;

- do not include the *Notes for guidance*.

D:2.3 Code C, paragraph 1.4, regarding a person who may be mentally disordered or otherwise mentally vulnerable and the *Notes for guidance* applicable to those provisions apply to this code.

D:2.4 Code C, paragraph 1.5, regarding a person who appears to be under the age of 17 applies to this code.

D:2.5 Code C, paragraph 1.6, regarding a person who appears to be blind, seriously visually impaired, deaf, unable to read or speak or has difficulty communicating orally because of a speech impediment applies to this code.

D:2.6 In this code:　　　　　　　　　　　　　　　　　　　　　　　　　　　　　　　　 **A-116**
- "appropriate adult" means the same as in Code C, paragraph 1.7;
- "solicitor" means the same as in Code C, paragraph 6.12;

and the *Notes for guidance* applicable to those provisions apply to this code;
- where a search or other procedure under this code may only be carried out or observed by a person of the same sex as the person to whom the search or procedure applies, the gender of the detainee and other persons present should be established and recorded in line with Annex F of Code A.

D:2.7 References to custody officers include those performing the functions of custody officer, see paragraph 1.9 of Code C.

D:2.8 When a record of any action requiring the authority of an officer of a specified rank is made under this code, subject to paragraph 2.18, the officer's name and rank must be recorded.

D:2.9 When this code requires the prior authority or agreement of an officer of at least inspector or superintendent rank, that authority may be given by a sergeant or chief inspector who has been authorised to perform the functions of the higher rank under PACE, s.107.

D:2.10 Subject to paragraph 2.18, all records must be timed and signed by the maker.

D:2.11 Records must be made in the custody record, unless otherwise specified. References to  **A-117** "pocket book" include any official report book issued to police officers or police staff.

D:2.12 If any procedure in this code requires a person's consent, the consent of a:
- mentally disordered or otherwise mentally vulnerable person is only valid if given in the presence of the appropriate adult;
- juvenile is only valid if their parent's or guardian's consent is also obtained unless the juvenile is under 14, when their parent's or guardian's consent is sufficient in its own right. If the only obstacle to an identification procedure in section 3 is that a juvenile's parent or guardian refuses consent or reasonable efforts to obtain it have failed, the identification officer may apply the provisions of paragraph 3.21. See *Note 2A*.

D:2.13 If a person is blind, seriously visually impaired or unable to read, the custody officer or identification officer shall make sure their solicitor, relative, appropriate adult or some other person likely to take an interest in them and not involved in the investigation is available to help check any documentation. When this code requires written consent or signing, the person assisting may be asked to sign instead, if the detainee prefers. This paragraph does not require an appropriate adult to be called solely to assist in checking and signing documentation for a person who is not a juvenile, or mentally disordered or otherwise mentally vulnerable (see *Note 2B* and Code C, paragraph 3.15).

D:2.14 If any procedure in this code requires information to be given to or sought from a suspect, it must be given or sought in the appropriate adult's presence if the suspect is mentally disordered, otherwise mentally vulnerable or a juvenile. If the appropriate adult is not present when the information is first given or sought, the procedure must be repeated in the presence of the appropriate adult when they arrive. If the suspect appears deaf or there is doubt about their hearing or speaking ability or ability to understand English, and effective communication cannot be established, the information must be given or sought through an interpreter.

D:2.15 Any procedure in this code involving the participation of a suspect who is mentally disordered, otherwise mentally vulnerable or a juvenile must take place in the presence of the appropriate adult. See Code C, paragraph 1.4.

D:2.15A Any procedure in this code involving the participation of a witness who is or appears to be mentally disordered, otherwise mentally vulnerable or a juvenile should take place in the presence of a pre-trial support person unless the witness states that they do not want a support person to be present. A support person must not be allowed to prompt any identification of a suspect by a witness. See *Note 2AB*.

D:2.16 References to:
- "taking a photograph", include the use of any process to produce a single, still or moving, visual image;
- "photographing a person", should be construed accordingly;

- "photographs", "films", "negatives" and "copies" include relevant visual images recorded, stored, or reproduced through any medium;
- "destruction" includes the deletion of computer data relating to such images or making access to that data impossible.

D:2.17 Except as described, nothing in this code affects the powers and procedures:

(i) for requiring and taking samples of breath, blood and urine in relation to driving offences, etc, when under the influence of drink, drugs or excess alcohol under the:
- Road Traffic Act 1988, ss.4 to 11;
- Road Traffic Offenders Act 1988, ss.15 and 16;
- Transport and Works Act 1992, ss.26 to 38;

(ii) under the Immigration Act 1971, Sched. 2, para. 18, for taking photographs and fingerprints from persons detained under that Act, Schedule 2, paragraph 16 (administrative controls as to control on entry *etc.*); for taking fingerprints in accordance with the Immigration and Asylum Act 1999, ss.141 and 142(3), or other methods for collecting information about a person's external physical characteristics provided for by regulations made under that Act, section 144;

(iii) under the Terrorism Act 2000, Sched. 8, for taking photographs, fingerprints, skin impressions, body samples or impressions from people:
- arrested under that Act, section 41,
- detained for the purposes of examination under that Act, Schedule 7, and to whom the code of practice issued under that Act, Schedule 14, paragraph 6, applies ("the terrorism provisions"); see *Note 2C*;

(iv) for taking photographs, fingerprints, skin impressions, body samples or impressions from people who have been:
- arrested on warrants issued in Scotland, by officers exercising powers under the Criminal Justice and Public Order Act 1994, s.136(2);
- arrested or detained without warrant by officers from a police force in Scotland exercising their powers of arrest or detention under the Criminal Justice and Public Order Act 1994, s.137(2) (cross border powers of arrest *etc.*).

Note: in these cases, police powers and duties and the person's rights and entitlements whilst at a police station in England and Wales are the same as if the person had been arrested in Scotland by a Scottish police officer.

D:2.18 Nothing in this code requires the identity of officers or police staff to be recorded or disclosed:

(a) in the case of enquiries linked to the investigation of terrorism;
(b) if the officers or police staff reasonably believe recording or disclosing their names might put them in danger.

In these cases, they shall use warrant or other identification numbers and the name of their police station. See *Note 2D*.

A-118    D:2.19 In this code:

(a) "designated person" means a person other than a police officer, designated under the Police Reform Act 2002, Pt 4, who has specified powers and duties of police officers conferred or imposed on them;
(b) any reference to a police officer includes a designated person acting in the exercise or performance of the powers and duties conferred or imposed on them by their designation.

D:2.20 If a power conferred on a designated person:

(a) allows reasonable force to be used when exercised by a police officer, a designated person exercising that power has the same entitlement to use force;
(b) includes power to use force to enter any premises, that power is not exercisable by that designated person except:
(i) in the company, and under the supervision, of a police officer; or
(ii) for the purpose of:
- saving life or limb; or
- preventing serious damage to property.

D:2.21 Nothing in this code prevents the custody officer, or other officer given custody of the detainee, from allowing police staff who are not designated persons to carry out individual procedures or tasks at the police station if the law allows. However, the officer remains responsible for making sure the procedures and tasks are carried out correctly in accordance with the codes of practice. Any such person must be:

(a) a person employed by a police authority maintaining a police force and under the control and direction of the chief officer of that force;

(b) employed by a person with whom a police authority has a contract for the provision of services relating to persons arrested or otherwise in custody.

D:2.22 Designated persons and other police staff must have regard to any relevant provisions of the codes of practice.

*Notes for guidance*

D:2A *For the purposes of paragraph 2.12, the consent required from a parent or guardian may, for a juvenile* **A-119** *in the care of a local authority or voluntary organisation, be given by that authority or organisation. In the case of a juvenile, nothing in paragraph 2.12 requires the parent, guardian or representative of a local authority or voluntary organisation to be present to give their consent, unless they are acting as the appropriate adult under paragraphs 2.14 or 2.15. However, it is important that a parent or guardian not present is fully informed before being asked to consent. They must be given the same information about the procedure and the juvenile's suspected involvement in the offence as the juvenile and appropriate adult. The parent or guardian must also be allowed to speak to the juvenile and the appropriate adult if they wish. Provided the consent is fully informed and is not withdrawn, it may be obtained at any time before the procedure takes place.*

D:2AB *The Youth Justice and Criminal Evidence Act 1999 guidance "Achieving Best Evidence in Criminal Proceedings" indicates that a pre-trial support person should accompany a vulnerable witness during any identification procedure unless the witness states that they do not want a support person to be present. It states that this support person should not be (or not be likely to be) a witness in the investigation.*

D:2B *People who are seriously visually impaired or unable to read may be unwilling to sign police documents. The alternative, i.e. their representative signing on their behalf, seeks to protect the interests of both police and suspects.*

D:2C *Photographs, fingerprints, samples and impressions may be taken from a person detained under the terrorism provisions to help determine whether they are, or have been, involved in terrorism, as well as when there are reasonable grounds for suspecting their involvement in a particular offence.*

D:2D *The purpose of paragraph 2.18(b) is to protect those involved in serious organised crime investigations or arrests of particularly violent suspects when there is reliable information that those arrested or their associates may threaten or cause harm to the officers. In cases of doubt, an officer of inspector rank or above should be consulted.*

### D:3 Identification and recognition of suspects

#### (a) *Identification of a suspect by an eye-witness*

D:3.0 This part applies when an eye-witness has seen the offender committing the crime or in any **A-120** other circumstances which tend to prove or disprove the involvement of the person they saw in the crime, for example, close to the scene of the crime, immediately before or immediately after it was committed. It sets out the procedures to be used to test the ability of that eye-witness to identify a person suspected of involvement in the offence as the person they saw on the previous occasion. Except where stated, this part does not apply to the procedures described in Part B and *Note 3AA*.

D:3.1 A record shall be made of the suspect's description as first given by a potential witness. This record must:

(a) be made and kept in a form which enables details of that description to be accurately produced from it, in a visible and legible form, which can be given to the suspect or the suspect's solicitor in accordance with this code; and

(b) unless otherwise specified, be made before the witness takes part in any identification procedures under paragraphs 3.5 to 3.10, 3.21 or 3.23.

A copy of the record shall where practicable, be given to the suspect or their solicitor before any procedures under paragraphs 3.5 to 3.10, 3.21 or 3.23 are carried out. See *Note 3E*.

#### (a) Cases when the suspect's identity is not known

D:3.2 In cases when the suspect's identity is not known, a witness may be taken to a particular neighbourhood or place to see whether they can identify the person they saw on a previous occasion. Although the number, age, sex, race, general description and style of clothing of other people present at the location and the way in which any identification is made cannot be controlled, the principles applicable to the formal procedures under paragraphs 3.5 to 3.10 shall be followed as far as practicable. For example:

(a) where it is practicable to do so, a record should be made of the witness's description of the suspect, as in paragraph 3.1(a), before asking the witness to make an identification;

(b) care must be taken not to direct the witness's attention to any individual unless, taking into account all the circumstances, this cannot be avoided; however, this does not prevent a witness being asked to look carefully at the people around at the time or to look towards a group or in a particular direction, if this appears necessary to make sure that the witness does not overlook a possible suspect simply because the witness is looking in the opposite direction and also to enable the witness to make comparisons between any suspect and others who are in the area; see *Note 3F*;

(c) where there is more than one witness, every effort should be made to keep them separate and witnesses should be taken to see whether they can identify a person independently;

(d) once there is sufficient information to justify the arrest of a particular individual for suspected involvement in the offence, *e.g.*, after a witness makes a positive identification, the provisions set out from paragraph 3.4 onwards shall apply for any other witnesses in relation to that individual;

(e) the officer or police staff accompanying the witness must record, in their pocket book, the action taken as soon as, and in as much detail, as possible. The record should include: the date, time and place of the relevant occasion the witness claims to have previously seen the suspect; where any identification was made; how it was made and the conditions at the time (*e.g.* the distance the witness was from the suspect, the weather and light); if the witness's attention was drawn to the suspect; the reason for this; and anything said by the witness or the suspect about the identification or the conduct of the procedure.

D:3.3 A witness must not be shown photographs, computerised or artist's composite likenesses or similar likenesses or pictures (including "E-fit" images) if the identity of the suspect is known to the police and the suspect is available to take part in a video identification, an identification parade or a group identification. If the suspect's identity is not known, the showing of such images to a witness to obtain identification evidence must be done in accordance with Annex E.

### (b) Cases when the suspect is known and available

**A-121**

D:3.4 If the suspect's identity is known to the police and they are available, the identification procedures set out in paragraphs 3.5 to 3.10 may be used. References in this section to a suspect being "known" mean there is sufficient information known to the police to justify the arrest of a particular person for suspected involvement in the offence. A suspect being "available" means they are immediately available or will be within a reasonably short time and willing to take an effective part in at least one of the following which it is practicable to arrange:

- video identification;
- identification parade; or
- group identification.

*Video identification*

D:3.5 A "video identification" is when the witness is shown moving images of a known suspect, together with similar images of others who resemble the suspect. Moving images must be used unless:

- the suspect is known but not available (see paragraph 3.21 of this code); or
- in accordance with paragraph 2A of Annex A of this code, the identification officer does not consider that replication of a physical feature can be achieved or that it is not possible to conceal the location of the feature on the image of the suspect.

The identification officer may then decide to make use of video identification but using **still** images.

D:3.6 Video identifications must be carried out in accordance with Annex A.

*Identification parade*

D:3.7 An "identification parade" is when the witness sees the suspect in a line of others who resemble the suspect.

D:3.8 Identification parades must be carried out in accordance with Annex B.

*Group identification*

D:3.9 A "group identification" is when the witness sees the suspect in an informal group of people.

D:3.10 Group identifications must be carried out in accordance with Annex C.

*Arranging identification procedures*

D:3.11 Except for the provisions in paragraph 3.19, the arrangements for, and conduct of, the identification procedures in paragraphs 3.5 to 3.10 and circumstances in which an identification procedure must be held shall be the responsibility of an officer not below inspector rank who is not involved with the investigation, "the identification officer". Unless otherwise specified, the identification officer may allow another officer or police staff, see paragraph 2.21, to make arrangements for, and conduct, any of these identification procedures. In delegating these procedures, the identification officer must be able to supervise effectively and either intervene or be contacted for advice. No officer or any other person involved with the investigation of the case against the suspect, beyond the extent required by these procedures, may take any part in these procedures or act as the identification officer. This does not prevent the identification officer from consulting the officer in charge of the investigation to determine which procedure to use. When an identification procedure is required, in the interest of fairness to suspects and witnesses, it must be held as soon as practicable.

*Circumstances in which an eye-witness identification procedure must be held*

D:3.12 Whenever:     **A-122**
> (i) an eye witness has identified a suspect or purported to have identified them prior to any identification procedure set out in paragraphs 3.5 to 3.10 having been held; or
> (ii) there is a witness available who expresses an ability to identify the suspect, or where there is a reasonable chance of the witness being able to do so, and they have not been given an opportunity to identify the suspect in any of the procedures set out in paragraphs 3.5 to 3.10,

and the suspect disputes being the person the witness claims to have seen, an identification procedure shall be held unless it is not practicable or it would serve no useful purpose in proving or disproving whether the suspect was involved in committing the offence, for example:
> • where the suspect admits being at the scene of the crime and gives an account of what took place and the eye-witness does not see anything which contradicts that;
> • when it is not disputed that the suspect is already known to the witness who claims to have recognised them when seeing them commit the crime.

D:3.13 An eye-witness identification procedure may also be held if the officer in charge of the investigation considers it would be useful.

*Selecting an identification procedure*

D:3.14 If, because of paragraph 3.12, an identification procedure is to be held, the suspect shall initially be offered a video identification unless:
> (a) a video identification is not practicable; or
> (b) an identification parade is both practicable and more suitable than a video identification; or
> (c) paragraph 3.16 applies.

The identification officer and the officer in charge of the investigation shall consult each other to determine which option is to be offered. An identification parade may not be practicable because of factors relating to the witnesses, such as their number, state of health, availability and travelling requirements. A video identification would normally be more suitable if it could be arranged and completed sooner than an identification parade. Before an option is offered the suspect must also be reminded of their entitlement to have free legal advice, see Code C, paragraph 6.5.

D:3.15 A suspect who refuses the identification procedure first offered shall be asked to state their reason for refusing and may get advice from their solicitor and/or if present, their appropriate adult. The suspect, solicitor and/or appropriate adult shall be allowed to make representations about why another procedure should be used. A record should be made of the reasons for refusal and any representations made. After considering any reasons given, and representations made, the identification officer shall, if appropriate, arrange for the suspect to be offered an alternative which the officer considers suitable and practicable. If the officer decides it is not suitable and practicable to offer an alternative identification procedure, the reasons for that decision shall be recorded.

D:3.16 A group identification may initially be offered if the officer in charge of the investigation considers it is more suitable than a video identification or an identification parade and the identification officer considers it practicable to arrange.

*Notice to suspect*

D:3.17 Unless paragraph 3.20 applies, before a video identification, an identification parade or     **A-123**
group identification is arranged, the following shall be explained to the suspect:
> (i) the purposes of the video identification, identification parade or group identification;
> (ii) their entitlement to free legal advice; see Code C, paragraph 6.5;
> (iii) the procedures for holding it, including their right to have a solicitor or friend present;
> (iv) that they do not have to consent to or co-operate in a video identification, identification parade or group identification;

(v) that if they do not consent to, and co-operate in, a video identification, identification parade or group identification, their refusal may be given in evidence in any subsequent trial and police may proceed covertly without their consent or make other arrangements to test whether a witness can identify them, see paragraph 3.21;

(vi) whether, for the purposes of the video identification procedure, images of them have previously been obtained, see paragraph 3.20, and if so, that they may co-operate in providing further, suitable images to be used instead;

(vii) if appropriate, the special arrangements for juveniles;

(viii) if appropriate, the special arrangements for mentally disordered or otherwise mentally vulnerable people;

(ix) that if they significantly alter their appearance between being offered an identification procedure and any attempt to hold an identification procedure, this may be given in evidence if the case comes to trial, and the identification officer may then consider other forms of identification, see paragraph 3.21 and *Note 3C*;

(x) that a moving image or photograph may be taken of them when they attend for any identification procedure;

(xi) whether, before their identity became known, the witness was shown photographs, a computerised or artist's composite likeness or similar likeness or image by the police, see *Note 3B*;

(xii) that if they change their appearance before an identification parade, it may not be practicable to arrange one on the day or subsequently and, because of the appearance change, the identification officer may consider alternative methods of identification, see *Note 3C*;

(xiii) that they or their solicitor will be provided with details of the description of the suspect as first given by any witnesses who are to attend the video identification, identification parade, group identification or confrontation, see paragraph 3.1.

D:3.18 This information must also be recorded in a written notice handed to the suspect. The suspect must be given a reasonable opportunity to read the notice, after which, they should be asked to sign a second copy to indicate if they are willing to co-operate with the making of a video or take part in the identification parade or group identification. The signed copy shall be retained by the identification officer.

D:3.19 The duties of the identification officer under paragraphs 3.17 and 3.18 may be performed by the custody officer or other officer not involved in the investigation if:

(a) it is proposed to release the suspect in order that an identification procedure can be arranged and carried out and an inspector is not available to act as the identification officer, see paragraph 3.11, before the suspect leaves the station; or

(b) it is proposed to keep the suspect in police detention whilst the procedure is arranged and carried out and waiting for an inspector to act as the identification officer, see paragraph 3.11, would cause unreasonable delay to the investigation.

The officer concerned shall inform the identification officer of the action taken and give them the signed copy of the notice. See *Note 3C*.

D:3.20 If the identification officer and officer in charge of the investigation suspect, on reasonable grounds that if the suspect was given the information and notice as in paragraphs 3.17 and 3.18, they would then take steps to avoid being seen by a witness in any identification procedure, the identification officer may arrange for images of the suspect suitable for use in a video identification procedure to be obtained before giving the information and notice. If suspect's [*sic*] images are obtained in these circumstances, the suspect may, for the purposes of a video identification procedure, co-operate in providing new images which if suitable, would be used instead, see paragraph 3.17(vi).

### (c) Cases when the suspect is known but not available

A-124

D:3.21 When a known suspect is not available or has ceased to be available, see paragraph 3.4, the identification officer may make arrangements for a video identification (see Annex A). If necessary, the identification officer may follow the video identification procedures but using still images. Any suitable moving or still images may be used and these may be obtained covertly if necessary. Alternatively, the identification officer may make arrangements for a group identification. See *Note 3D*. These provisions may also be applied to juveniles where the consent of their parent or guardian is either refused or reasonable efforts to obtain that consent have failed (see paragraph 2.12).

D:3.22 Any covert activity should be strictly limited to that necessary to test the ability of the witness to identify the suspect.

D:3.23 The identification officer may arrange for the suspect to be confronted by the witness if none of the options referred to in paragraphs 3.5 to 3.10 or 3.21 are practicable. A "confrontation" is when the suspect is directly confronted by the witness. A confrontation does not require the suspect's consent. Confrontations must be carried out in accordance with Annex D.

D:3.24 Requirements for information to be given to, or sought from, a suspect or for the suspect to be given an opportunity to view images before they are shown to a witness, do not apply if the suspect's lack of co-operation prevents the necessary action.

### (d) Documentation

D:3.25 A record shall be made of the video identification, identification parade, group identifica-  **A-125** tion or confrontation on forms provided for the purpose.

D:3.26 If the identification officer considers it is not practicable to hold a video identification or identification parade requested by the suspect, the reasons shall be recorded and explained to the suspect.

D:3.27 A record shall be made of a person's failure or refusal to co-operate in a video identification, identification parade or group identification and, if applicable, of the grounds for obtaining images in accordance with paragraph 3.20.

### (e) Showing films and photographs of incidents and information released to the media

D:3.28 Nothing in this code inhibits showing films, photographs or other images to the public  **A-126** through the national or local media, or to police officers for the purposes of recognition and tracing suspects. However, when such material is shown to obtain evidence of recognition, the procedures in Part B will apply. See *Note 3AA*.

D:3.29 When a broadcast or publication is made, see paragraph 3.28, a copy of the relevant material released to the media for the purposes of recognising or tracing the suspect, shall be kept. The suspect or their solicitor shall be allowed to view such material before any eye-witness identification procedures under paragraphs 3.5 to 3.10, 3.21 or 3.23 of Part A are carried out, provided it is practicable and would not unreasonably delay the investigation. Each eye-witness involved in the procedure shall be asked, after they have taken part, whether they have seen any film, photograph or image relating to the offence or any description of the suspect which has been broadcast or published in any national or local media or on any social networking site and if they have, they should be asked to give details of the circumstances, such as the date and place as relevant. Their replies shall be recorded. This paragraph does not affect any separate requirement under the Criminal Procedure and Investigations Act 1996 to retain material in connection with criminal investigations.

### (f) Destruction and retention of photographs taken or used in eye-witness identification procedures

D:3.30 PACE, s.64A, see paragraph 5.12, provides powers to take photographs of suspects and allows these photographs to be used or disclosed only for purposes related to the prevention or detection of crime, the investigation of offences or the conduct of prosecutions by, or on behalf of, police or other law enforcement and prosecuting authorities inside and outside the United Kingdom or the enforcement of a sentence. After being so used or disclosed, they may be retained but can only be used or disclosed for the same purposes.

D:3.31 Subject to paragraph 3.33, the photographs (and all negatives and copies), of suspects not taken in accordance with the provisions in paragraph 5.12 which are taken for the purposes of, or in connection with, the identification procedures in paragraphs 3.5 to 3.10, 3.21 or 3.23 must be destroyed unless the suspect:

(a) is charged with, or informed they may be prosecuted for, a recordable offence;

(b) is prosecuted for a recordable offence;

(c) is cautioned for a recordable offence or given a warning or reprimand in accordance with the Crime and Disorder Act 1998 for a recordable offence; or

(d) gives informed consent, in writing, for the photograph or images to be retained for purposes described in paragraph 3.30.

D:3.32 When paragraph 3.31 requires the destruction of any photograph, the person must be given an opportunity to witness the destruction or to have a certificate confirming the destruction if they request one within five days of being informed that the destruction is required.

D:3.33 Nothing in paragraph 3.31 affects any separate requirement under the Criminal Procedure and Investigations Act 1996 to retain material in connection with criminal investigations.

(b) *Evidence of recognition by showing films, photographs and other images*

D:3.34 This part of this section applies when, for the purposes of obtaining evidence of recognition, any person, including a police officer:

(a) views the image of an individual in a film, photograph or any other visual medium; and

(b) is asked whether they recognise that individual as someone who is known to them.

See *Notes 3AA* and *3G*.

D:3.35 The films, photographs and other images shall be shown on an individual basis to avoid any possibility of collusion and to provide safeguards against mistaken recognition (see *Note 3G*), the showing shall as far as possible follow the principles for video identification if the suspect is known, see Annex A, or identification by photographs if the suspect is not known, see Annex E.

D:3.36 A record of the circumstances and conditions under which the person is given an opportunity to recognise the individual must be made and the record must include:

(a) whether the person knew or was given information concerning the name or identity of any suspect;

(b) what the person has been told *before* the viewing about the offence, the person(s) depicted in the images or the offender and by whom;

(c) how and by whom the witness was asked to view the image or look at the individual;

(d) whether the viewing was alone or with others and if with others, the reason for it;

(e) the arrangements under which the person viewed the film or saw the individual and by whom those arrangements were made;

(f) whether the viewing of any images was arranged as part of a mass circulation to police and the public or for selected persons;

(g) the date time and place images were viewed or further viewed or the individual was seen;

(h) the times between which the images were viewed or the individual was seen;

(i) how the viewing of images or sighting of the individual was controlled and by whom;

(j) whether the person was familiar with the location shown in any images or the place where they saw the individual and if so, why;

(k) whether or not on this occasion, the person claims to recognise any image shown, or any individual seen, as being someone known to them, and if they do:

(i) the reason;

(ii) the words of recognition;

(iii) any expressions of doubt;

(iv) what features of the image or the individual triggered the recognition.

D:3.37 The record under paragraph 3.36 may be made by:

• the person who views the image or sees the individual and makes the recognition;

• the officer or police staff in charge of showing the images to the person or in charge of the conditions under which the person sees the individual.

*Notes for guidance*

D:3AA *The eye-witness identification procedures in Part A should not be used to test whether a witness can recognise a person as someone they know and would be able to give evidence of recognition along the lines that "On (describe date, time location) I saw an image of an individual who I recognised as AB." In these cases, the procedures in Part B shall apply.*

D:3A *Except for the provisions of Annex E, paragraph 1, a police officer who is a witness for the purposes of this part of the code is subject to the same principles and procedures as a civilian witness.*

D:3B *When a witness attending an identification procedure has previously been shown photographs, or been shown or provided with computerised or artist's composite likenesses, or similar likenesses or pictures, it is the officer in charge of the investigation's responsibility to make the identification officer aware of this.*

D:3C *The purpose of paragraph 3.19 is to avoid or reduce delay in arranging identification procedures by enabling the required information and warnings, see sub-paragraphs 3.17(ix) and 3.17(xii), to be given at the earliest opportunity.*

D:3D *Paragraph 3.21 would apply when a known suspect deliberately makes themselves "unavailable" in order to delay or frustrate arrangements for obtaining identification evidence. It also applies when a suspect refuses or fails to take part in a video identification, an identification parade or a group identification, or refuses or fails to take part in the only practicable options from that list. It enables any suitable images of the suspect, moving or still, which are available or can be obtained, to be used in an identification procedure. Examples include images from custody and other CCTV systems and from visually recorded interview records, see Code F, Note for Guidance 2D.*

D:3E *When it is proposed to show photographs to a witness in accordance with Annex E, it is the responsibility of the officer in charge of the investigation to confirm to the officer responsible for supervising and directing the showing, that the first description of the suspect given by that witness has been recorded. If this description has not been recorded, the procedure under Annex E must be postponed. See Annex E, paragraph 2.*

D:3F *The admissibility and value of identification evidence obtained when carrying out the procedure under paragraph 3.2 may be compromised if:*

(a) *before a person is identified, the witness's attention is specifically drawn to that person; or*

(b) *the suspect's identity becomes known before the procedure.*

D:3G *The admissibility and value of evidence of recognition obtained when carrying out the procedures in Part B may be compromised if before the person is recognised, the witness who has claimed to know them is given or is made, or becomes aware of, information about the person which was not previously known to them personally but which they have purported to rely on to support their claim that the person is in fact known to them.*

## D:4 Identification by fingerprints and footwear impressions

(a) *Taking fingerprints in connection with a criminal investigation*

### (a) General

D:4.1 References to "fingerprints" means any record, produced by any method, of the skin pattern and other physical characteristics or features of a person's:          **A-128**

(i) fingers; or

(ii) palms.

### (b) Action

D:4.2 A person's fingerprints may be taken in connection with the investigation of an offence only with their consent or if paragraph 4.3 applies. If the person is at a police station consent must be in writing.

D:4.3 PACE, s.61, provides powers to take fingerprints without consent from any person over the age of ten years:

(a) under section 61(3), from a person detained at a police station in consequence of being arrested for a recordable offence, see *Note 4A*, if they have not had their fingerprints taken in the course of the investigation of the offence unless those previously taken fingerprints are not a complete set or some or all of those fingerprints are not of sufficient quality to allow satisfactory analysis, comparison or matching;

(b) under section 61(4), from a person detained at a police station who has been charged with a recordable offence, see *Note 4A*, or informed they will be reported for such an offence if they have not had their fingerprints taken in the course of the investigation of the offence unless those previously taken fingerprints are not a complete set or some or all of those fingerprints are not of sufficient quality to allow satisfactory analysis, comparison or matching;

(c) under section 61(4A), from a person who has been bailed to appear at a court or police station if the person:

(i) has answered to bail for a person whose fingerprints were taken previously and there are reasonable grounds for believing they are not the same person; or

(ii) who has answered to bail claims to be a different person from a person whose fingerprints were previously taken;

and in either case, the court or an officer of inspector rank or above, authorises the fingerprints to be taken at the court or police station (an inspector's authority may be given in writing or orally and confirmed in writing, as soon as practicable);

(ca) under section 61(5A) from a person who has been arrested for a recordable offence and released if the person:

(i) is on bail and has not had their fingerprints taken in the course of the investigation of the offence; or

(ii) has had their fingerprints taken in the course of the investigation of the offence, but they do not constitute a complete set or some, or all, of the fingerprints are not of sufficient quality to allow satisfactory analysis, comparison or matching;

(cb) under section 61(5B) from a person not detained at a police station who has been charged with a recordable offence or informed they will be reported for such an offence if they have not had their fingerprints taken in the course of the investigation or their fingerprints have been taken in the course of the investigation of the offence, but they do not constitute a complete set or some, or all, of the fingerprints are not of sufficient quality to allow satisfactory analysis, comparison or matching;

(d) under section 61(6), from a person who has been:
  (i) convicted of a recordable offence;
  (ii) given a caution in respect of a recordable offence which, at the time of the caution, the person admitted; or
  (iii) warned or reprimanded under the Crime and Disorder Act 1998, s.65, for a recordable offence, if, since their conviction, caution, warning or reprimand their fingerprints have not been taken or their fingerprints which have been taken since then do not constitute a complete set or some, or all, of the fingerprints are not of sufficient quality to allow satisfactory analysis, comparison or matching, and in either case, an officer of inspector rank or above, is satisfied that taking the fingerprints is necessary to assist in the prevention or detection of crime and authorises the taking;
(e) under section 61(6A) from a person a constable reasonably suspects is committing or attempting to commit, or has committed or attempted to commit, any offence if either:
  • the person's name is unknown and cannot be readily ascertained by the constable; or
  • the constable has reasonable grounds for doubting whether a name given by the person is their real name; note: fingerprints taken under this power are not regarded as having been taken in the course of the investigation of an offence; [see *Note 4C*];
(f) under section 61(6D) from a person who has been convicted outside England and Wales of an offence which if committed in England and Wales would be a qualifying offence as defined by PACE, s.65A [see *Note 4AB*] if:
  (i) the person's fingerprints have not been taken previously under this power or their fingerprints have been so taken on a previous occasion but they do not constitute a complete set or some, or all, of the fingerprints are not of sufficient quality to allow satisfactory analysis, comparison or matching; and
  (ii) a police officer of inspector rank or above is satisfied that taking fingerprints is necessary to assist in the prevention or detection of crime and authorises them to be taken.

D:4.4 PACE, s.63A(4), and Sched. 2A, provide powers to:
(a) make a requirement (in accordance with Annex G) for a person to attend a police station to have their fingerprints taken in the exercise of certain powers in paragraph 4.3 above when that power applies at the time the fingerprints would be taken in accordance with the requirement; those powers are:
  (i) section 61(5A)—persons arrested for a recordable offence and released, see paragraph 4.3(ca): the requirement may not be made more than six months from the day the investigating officer was informed that the fingerprints previously taken were incomplete or below standard;
  (ii) section 61(5B)—persons charged *etc.* with a recordable offence, see paragraph 4.3(cb): the requirement may not be made more than six months from:
    • the day the person was charged or reported if fingerprints have not been taken since then; or
    • the day the investigating officer was informed that the fingerprints previously taken were incomplete or below standard;
  (iii) section 61(6)—person convicted, cautioned, warned or reprimanded for a recordable offence in England and Wales, see paragraph 4.3(d): where the offence for which the person was convicted etc is also a qualifying offence (see *Note 4AB*), there is no time limit for the exercise of this power; where the conviction *etc.* is for a recordable offence which is not a qualifying offence, the requirement may not be made more than two years from:
    • the day the person was convicted, cautioned, warned or reprimanded, or the day Schedule 2A comes into force (if later), if fingerprints have not been taken since then; or
    • the day an officer from the force investigating the offence was informed that the fingerprints previously taken were incomplete or below standard or the day Schedule 2A comes into force (if later);
  (v) [*sic*] section 61(6D)—a person who has been convicted of a qualifying offence (see *Note 4AB*) outside England and Wales, see paragraph 4.3(g): there is no time limit for making the requirement;
  note: a person who has had their fingerprints taken under any of the powers in section 61 mentioned in paragraph 4.3 on two occasions in relation to any offence may not be required under Schedule 2A to attend a police station for their fingerprints to be taken again under section 61 in relation to that offence, unless authorised by an officer of

inspector rank or above; the fact of the authorisation and the reasons for giving it must
be recorded as soon as practicable;

(b) arrest, without warrant, a person who fails to comply with the requirement.

D:4.5 A person's fingerprints may be taken, as above, electronically.

D:4.6 Reasonable force may be used, if necessary, to take a person's fingerprints without their
consent under the powers as in paragraphs 4.3 and 4.4.

D:4.7 Before any fingerprints are taken:

(a) without consent under any power mentioned in paragraphs 4.3 and 4.4 above, the
person must be informed of:

(i) the reason their fingerprints are to be taken;

(ii) the power under which they are to be taken; and

(iii) the fact that the relevant authority has been given if any power mentioned in
paragraph 4.3(c), (d) or (f) applies;

(b) with or without consent at a police station or elsewhere, the person must be informed:

(i) that their fingerprints may be subject of a speculative search against other fingerprints,
see *Note 4B*; and

(ii) that their fingerprints may be retained in accordance with Annex F, Part (a) unless
they were taken under the power mentioned in paragraph 4.3(e) when they must be
destroyed after they have being [*sic*] checked (see *Note 4C*).

#### (c) Documentation

D:4.8A A record must be made as soon as practicable after the fingerprints are taken, of:

- the matters in paragraph 4.7(a)(i) to (iii) and the fact that the person has been informed
of those matters; and

- the fact that the person has been informed of the matters in paragraph 4.7(b)(i) and (ii).

The record must be made in the person's custody record if they are detained at a police station when
the fingerprints are taken.

D:4.8 If force is used, a record shall be made of the circumstances and those present.

D:4.9 [*Not used.*]

#### (b) *Taking fingerprints in connection with immigration enquiries*

#### Action

D:4.10 A person's fingerprints may be taken and retained for the purposes of immigration law   **A-129**
enforcement and control in accordance with powers and procedures other than under PACE and for
which the UK Border Agency (not the police) are responsible. Details of these powers and procedures
which are under the Immigration Act 1971, Sched. 2 and Immigration and Asylum Act 1999, s.141,
including modifications to the *PACE Codes of Practice* are contained in Chapter 24 of the operational
instructions and guidance manual which is published by the UK Border Agency (see *Note 4D*).

D:4.11–15 [*Not used.*]

#### (c) *Taking footwear impressions in connection with a criminal investigation*

#### (a) Action

D:4.16 Impressions of a person's footwear may be taken in connection with the investigation of an
offence only with their consent or if paragraph 4.17 applies. If the person is at a police station
consent must be in writing.

D:4.17 PACE, s.61A, provides power for a police officer to take footwear impressions without
consent from any person over the age of ten years who is detained at a police station:

(a) in consequence of being arrested for a recordable offence, see *Note 4A*; or if the detainee
has been charged with a recordable offence, or informed they will be reported for such
an offence; and

(b) the detainee has not had an impression of their footwear taken in the course of the
investigation of the offence unless the previously taken impression is not complete or is
not of sufficient quality to allow satisfactory analysis, comparison or matching (whether in
the case in question or generally).

D:4.18 Reasonable force may be used, if necessary, to take a footwear impression from a detainee
without consent under the power in paragraph 4.17.

D:4.19 Before any footwear impression is taken with, or without, consent as above, the person
must be informed:

(a) of the reason the impression is to be taken;

(b) that the impression may be retained and may be subject of a speculative search against other impressions, see *Note 4B*, unless destruction of the impression is required in accordance with Annex F, Part (a); and

(c) that if their footwear impressions are required to be destroyed, they may witness their destruction as provided for in Annex F, Part (a).

**(b) Documentation**

D:4.20 A record must be made as soon as possible, of the reason for taking a person's footwear impressions without consent. If force is used, a record shall be made of the circumstances and those present.

D:4.21 A record shall be made when a person has been informed under the terms of paragraph 4.19(b), of the possibility that their footwear impressions may be subject of a speculative search.

*Notes for guidance*

D:4A *References to "recordable offences" in this code relate to those offences for which convictions, cautions, reprimands and warnings may be recorded in national police records: see PACE, s.27(4). The recordable offences current at the time when this code was prepared, are any offences which carry a sentence of imprisonment on conviction (irrespective of the period, or the age of the offender or actual sentence passed) as well as the non-imprisonable offences under the Vagrancy Act 1824, ss.3 and 4 (begging and persistent begging), the Street Offences Act 1959, s.1 (loitering or soliciting for purposes of prostitution), the Road Traffic Act 1988, s.25 (tampering with motor vehicles), the Criminal Justice and Public Order Act 1994, s.167 (touting for car hire services) and others listed in the National Police Records (Recordable Offences) Regulations 2000 as amended.*

D:4AB *A qualifying offence is one of the offences specified in PACE, s.65A. These indictable offences which concern the use or threat of violence or unlawful force against persons, sexual offences and offences against children include, for example, murder, manslaughter, false imprisonment, kidnapping and other offences such as:*

- *sections 4, 16, 18, 20 to 24 or 47 of the Offences Against the Person Act 1861;*
- *sections 16 to 18 of the Firearms Act 1968;*
- *sections 9 or 10 of the Theft Act 1968 or under section 12A of that Act involving an accident which caused a person's death;*
- *section 1 of the Criminal Damage Act 1971 required to be charged as arson;*
- *section 1 of the Protection of Children Act 1978 and;*
- *sections 1 to 19, 25, 26, 30 to 41, 47 to 50, 52, 53, 57 to 59, 61 to 67, 69 and 70 of the Sexual Offences Act 2003.*

D:4B *Fingerprints, footwear impressions or a DNA sample (and the information derived from it) taken from a person arrested on suspicion of being involved in a recordable offence, or charged with such an offence, or informed they will be reported for such an offence, may be subject of a speculative search. This means the fingerprints, footwear impressions or DNA sample may be checked against other fingerprints, footwear impressions and DNA records held by, or on behalf of, the police and other law enforcement authorities in, or outside, the UK, or held in connection with, or as a result of, an investigation of an offence inside or outside the UK. Fingerprints, footwear impressions and samples taken from a person suspected of committing a recordable offence but not arrested, charged or informed they will be reported for it, may be subject to a speculative search only if the person consents in writing. The following is an example of a basic form of words:*

*"I consent to my fingerprints, footwear impressions and DNA sample and information derived from it being retained and used only for purposes related to the prevention and detection of a crime, the investigation of an offence or the conduct of a prosecution either nationally or internationally.*

*I understand that my fingerprints, footwear impressions or DNA sample may be checked against other fingerprint, footwear impressions and DNA records held by or on behalf of relevant law enforcement authorities, either nationally or internationally.*

*I understand that once I have given my consent for my fingerprints, footwear impressions or DNA sample to be retained and used I cannot withdraw this consent."*

*See Annex F regarding the retention and use of fingerprints and footwear impressions taken with consent for elimination purposes.*

D:4C *The power under section 61(6A) of PACE described in paragraph 4.3(e) allows fingerprints of a suspect who has not been arrested to be taken in connection with any offence (whether recordable or not) using a mobile device and then checked on the street against the database containing the national fingerprint collection. Fingerprints taken under this power cannot be retained after they have been checked. The results may make an arrest for the suspected offence based on the name condition unnecessary (see code G, paragraph 2.9(a)) and enable the offence to be disposed of without arrest, for example, by summons/charging by post, penalty notice or words of advice. If arrest for a non-recordable offence is necessary for any other reasons, this power may also be exercised at the station. Before the power is exercised, the officer should:*

- *inform the person of the nature of the suspected offence and why they are suspected of committing it;*
- *give them a reasonable opportunity to establish their real name before deciding that their name is unknown and cannot be readily ascertained or that there are reasonable grounds to doubt that a name they have given is their real name;*
- *as applicable, inform the person of the reason why their name is not known and cannot be readily ascertained or of the grounds for doubting that a name they have given is their real name, including, for example, the reason why a particular document the person has produced to verify their real name, is not sufficient.*

D:4D *Powers to take fingerprints without consent for immigration purposes are given to police and immigration officers under the:*

(a) *Immigration Act 1971, Sched. 2, para. 18(2), when it is reasonably necessary for the purposes of identifying a person detained under the Immigration Act 1971, Sched. 2, para. 16 (detention of person liable to examination or removal), and*

(b) *Immigration and Asylum Act 1999, s.141(7) when a person:*

- *fails without reasonable excuse to produce, on arrival, a valid passport with a photograph or some other document satisfactorily establishing their identity and nationality;*
- *is refused entry to the UK but is temporarily admitted if an immigration officer reasonably suspects the person might break a residence or reporting condition;*
- *is subject to directions for removal from the UK;*
- *has been arrested under the Immigration Act 1971, Sched. 2, para. 17;*
- *has made a claim for asylum;*
- *is a dependant of any of the above.*

*The Immigration and Asylum Act 1999, s.142(3), also gives police and immigration officers power to arrest without warrant a person who fails to comply with a requirement imposed by the Secretary of State to attend a specified place for fingerprinting.*

### D:5 Examinations to establish identity and the taking of photographs

(a) *Detainees at police stations*

#### (a) Searching or examination of detainees at police stations

D:5.1 PACE, s.54A(1), allows a detainee at a police station to be searched or examined or both, to **A-130** establish:

(a) whether they have any marks, features or injuries that would tend to identify them as a person involved in the commission of an offence and to photograph any identifying marks, see paragraph 5.5; or

(b) their identity, see *Note 5A.*

A person detained at a police station to be searched under a stop and search power, see Code A, is not a detainee for the purposes of these powers.

D:5.2 A search and/or examination to find marks under section 54A(1)(a) may be carried out without the detainee's consent, see paragraph 2.12, only if authorised by an officer of at least inspector rank when consent has been withheld or it is not practicable to obtain consent, see *Note 5D.*

D:5.3 A search or examination to establish a suspect's identity under section 54A(1)(b) may be carried out without the detainee's consent, see paragraph 2.12, only if authorised by an officer of at least inspector rank when the detainee has refused to identify themselves or the authorising officer has reasonable grounds for suspecting the person is not who they claim to be.

D:5.4 Any marks that assist in establishing the detainee's identity, or their identification as a person involved in the commission of an offence, are identifying marks. Such marks may be photographed with the detainee's consent, see paragraph 2.12; or without their consent if it is withheld or it is not practicable to obtain it, see *Note 5D.*

D:5.5 A detainee may only be searched, examined and photographed under section 54A, by a police officer of the same sex.

D:5.6 Any photographs of identifying marks, taken under section 54A, may be used or disclosed only for purposes related to the prevention or detection of crime, the investigation of offences or the conduct of prosecutions by, or on behalf of, police or other law enforcement and prosecuting authorities inside, and outside, the UK. After being so used or disclosed, the photograph may be retained but must not be used or disclosed except for these purposes, see *Note 5B.*

D:5.7 The powers, as in paragraph 5.1, do not affect any separate requirement under the Criminal Procedure and Investigations Act 1996 to retain material in connection with criminal investigations.

D:5.8 Authority for the search and/or examination for the purposes of paragraphs 5.2 and 5.3

may be given orally or in writing. If given orally, the authorising officer must confirm it in writing as soon as practicable. A separate authority is required for each purpose which applies.

D:5.9 If it is established a person is unwilling to co-operate sufficiently to enable a search and/or examination to take place or a suitable photograph to be taken, an officer may use reasonable force to:

    (a) search and/or examine a detainee without their consent; and

    (b) photograph any identifying marks without their consent.

D:5.10 The thoroughness and extent of any search or examination carried out in accordance with the powers in section 54A must be no more than the officer considers necessary to achieve the required purpose. Any search or examination which involves the removal of more than the person's outer clothing shall be conducted in accordance with Code C, Annex A, paragraph 11.

D:5.11 An intimate search may not be carried out under the powers in section 54A.

**(b) Photographing detainees at police stations and other persons elsewhere than at a police station**

**A-131**

D:5.12 Under PACE, s.64A, an officer may photograph:

    (a) any person whilst they are detained at a police station; and

    (b) any person who is elsewhere than at a police station and who has been:

       (i) arrested by a constable for an offence;

      (ii) taken into custody by a constable after being arrested for an offence by a person other than a constable;

      (iii) made subject to a requirement to wait with a community support officer under paragraph 2(3) or (3B) of Schedule 4 to the Police Reform Act 2002;

     (iiia) given a direction by a constable under section 27 of the Violent Crime Reduction Act 2006;

      (iv) given a penalty notice by a constable in uniform under Chapter 1 of Part 1 of the Criminal Justice and Police Act 2001, a penalty notice by a constable under section 444A of the Education Act 1996, or a fixed penalty notice by a constable in uniform under section 54 of the Road Traffic Offenders Act 1988;

      (v) given a notice in relation to a relevant fixed penalty offence (within the meaning of paragraph 1 of Schedule 4 to the Police Reform Act 2002) by a community support officer by virtue of a designation applying that paragraph to him;

      (vi) given a notice in relation to a relevant fixed penalty offence (within the meaning of paragraph 1 of Schedule 5 to the Police Reform Act 2002) by an accredited person by virtue of accreditation specifying that that paragraph applies to him; or

     (vii) given a direction to leave and not return to a specified location for up to 48 hours by a police constable (under section 27 of the Violent Crime Reduction Act 2006).

D:5.12A Photographs taken under PACE, s.64A:

    (a) may be taken with the person's consent, or without their consent if consent is withheld or it is not practicable to obtain their consent, see *Note 5E*; and

    (b) may be used or disclosed only for purposes related to the prevention or detection of crime, the investigation of offences or the conduct of prosecutions by, or on behalf of, police or other law enforcement and prosecuting authorities inside and outside the United Kingdom or the enforcement of any sentence or order made by a court when dealing with an offence. After being so used or disclosed, they may be retained but can only be used or disclosed for the same purposes. See *Note 5B*.

D:5.13 The officer proposing to take a detainee's photograph may, for this purpose, require the person to remove any item or substance worn on, or over, all, or any part of, their head or face. If they do not comply with such a requirement, the officer may remove the item or substance.

D:5.14 If it is established the detainee is unwilling to co-operate sufficiently to enable a suitable photograph to be taken and it is not reasonably practicable to take the photograph covertly, an officer may use reasonable force, see *Note 5F*:

    (a) to take their photograph without their consent; and

    (b) for the purpose of taking the photograph, remove any item or substance worn on, or over, all, or any part of, the person's head or face which they have failed to remove when asked.

D:5.15 For the purposes of this code, a photograph may be obtained without the person's consent by making a copy of an image of them taken at any time on a camera system installed anywhere in the police station.

**(c) Information to be given**

**A-132**

D:5.16 When a person is searched, examined or photographed under the provisions as in paragraph 5.1 and 5.12, or their photograph obtained as in paragraph 5.15, they must be informed of the:

    (a) purpose of the search, examination or photograph;

    (b) grounds on which the relevant authority, if applicable, has been given; and

    (c) purposes for which the photograph may be used, disclosed or retained.

This information must be given before the search or examination commences or the photograph is taken, except if the photograph is:

    (i) to be taken covertly;

    (ii) obtained as in paragraph 5.15, in which case the person must be informed as soon as practicable after the photograph is taken or obtained.

**(d) Documentation**

D:5.17 A record must be made when a detainee is searched, examined, or a photograph of the person, or any identifying marks found on them, are [*sic*] taken. The record must include the:

    (a) identity, subject to paragraph 2.18, of the officer carrying out the search, examination or taking the photograph;

    (b) purpose of the search, examination or photograph and the outcome;

    (c) detainee's consent to the search, examination or photograph, or the reason the person was searched, examined or photographed without consent;

    (d) giving of any authority as in paragraphs 5.2 and 5.3, the grounds for giving it and the authorising officer.

D:5.18 If force is used when searching, examining or taking a photograph in accordance with this section, a record shall be made of the circumstances and those present.

(b) *Persons at police stations not detained*

D:5.19 When there are reasonable grounds for suspecting the involvement of a person in a criminal offence, but that person is at a police station *voluntarily* and not detained, the provisions of paragraphs 5.1 to 5.18 should apply, subject to the modifications in the following paragraphs.    **A-133**

D:5.20 References to the "person being detained" and to the powers mentioned in paragraph 5.1 which apply only to detainees at police stations shall be omitted.

D:5.21 Force may not be used to:

    (a) search and/or examine the person to:

        (i) discover whether they have any marks that would tend to identify them as a person involved in the commission of an offence; or

        (ii) establish their identity, see *Note 5A*;

    (b) take photographs of any identifying marks, see paragraph 5.4; or

    (c) take a photograph of the person.

D:5.22 Subject to paragraph 5.24, the photographs of persons or of their identifying marks which are not taken in accordance with the provisions mentioned in paragraphs 5.1 or 5.12, must be destroyed (together with any negatives and copies) unless the person:

    (a) is charged with, or informed they may be prosecuted for, a recordable offence;

    (b) is prosecuted for a recordable offence;

    (c) is cautioned for a recordable offence or given a warning or reprimand in accordance with the Crime and Disorder Act 1998 for a recordable offence; or

    (d) gives informed consent, in writing, for the photograph or image to be retained as in paragraph 5.6.

D:5.23 When paragraph 5.22 requires the destruction of any photograph, the person must be given an opportunity to witness the destruction or to have a certificate confirming the destruction provided they so request the certificate within five days of being informed the destruction is required.

D:5.24 Nothing in paragraph 5.22 affects any separate requirement under the Criminal Procedure and Investigations Act 1996 to retain material in connection with criminal investigations.

*Notes for guidance*

D:5A *The conditions under which fingerprints may be taken to assist in establishing a person's identity, are*    **A-134**
*described in section 4.*

D:5B *Examples of purposes related to the prevention or detection of crime, the investigation of offences or the conduct of prosecutions include:*

    (a) *checking the photograph against other photographs held in records or in connection with, or as a result of, an investigation of an offence to establish whether the person is liable to arrest for other offences;*

(b) *when the person is arrested at the same time as other people, or at a time when it is likely that other people will be arrested, using the photograph to help establish who was arrested, at what time and where;*

(c) *when the real identity of the person is not known and cannot be readily ascertained or there are reasonable grounds for doubting a name and other personal details given by the person are their real name and personal details; in these circumstances, using or disclosing the photograph to help to establish or verify their real identity or determine whether they are liable to arrest for some other offence, e.g. by checking it against other photographs held in records or in connection with, or as a result of, an investigation of an offence;*

(d) *when it appears any identification procedure in section 3 may need to be arranged for which the person's photograph would assist;*

(e) *when the person's release without charge may be required, and if the release is:*

(i) *on bail to appear at a police station, using the photograph to help verify the person's identity when they answer their bail and if the person does not answer their bail, to assist in arresting them; or*

(ii) *without bail, using the photograph to help verify their identity or assist in locating them for the purposes of serving them with a summons to appear at court in criminal proceedings;*

(f) *when the person has answered to bail at a police station and there are reasonable grounds for doubting they are the person who was previously granted bail, using the photograph to help establish or verify their identity;*

(g) *when the person arrested on a warrant claims to be a different person from the person named on the warrant and a photograph would help to confirm or disprove their claim;*

(h) *when the person has been charged with, reported for, or convicted of, a recordable offence and their photograph is not already on record as a result of (a) to (f) or their photograph is on record but their appearance has changed since it was taken and the person has not yet been released or brought before a court.*

**D:5C** *There is no power to arrest a person convicted of a recordable offence solely to take their photograph. The power to take photographs in this section applies only where the person is in custody as a result of the exercise of another power, e.g. arrest for fingerprinting under PACE, s.27.*

**D:5D** *Examples of when it would not be practicable to obtain a detainee's consent, see paragraph 2.12, to a search, examination or the taking of a photograph of an identifying mark include:*

(a) *when the person is drunk or otherwise unfit to give consent;*

(b) *when there are reasonable grounds to suspect that if the person became aware a search or examination was to take place or an identifying mark was to be photographed, they would take steps to prevent this happening, e.g. by violently resisting, covering or concealing the mark etc and it would not otherwise be possible to carry out the search or examination or to photograph any identifying mark;*

(c) *in the case of a juvenile, if the parent or guardian cannot be contacted in sufficient time to allow the search or examination to be carried out or the photograph to be taken.*

**D:5E** *Examples of when it would not be practicable to obtain the person's consent, see paragraph 2.12, to a photograph being taken include:*

(a) *when the person is drunk or otherwise unfit to give consent;*

(b) *when there are reasonable grounds to suspect that if the person became aware a photograph, suitable to be used or disclosed for the use and disclosure described in paragraph 5.6, was to be taken, they would take steps to prevent it being taken, e.g. by violently resisting, covering or distorting their face etc, and it would not otherwise be possible to take a suitable photograph;*

(c) *when, in order to obtain a suitable photograph, it is necessary to take it covertly; and*

(d) *in the case of a juvenile, if the parent or guardian cannot be contacted in sufficient time to allow the photograph to be taken.*

**D:5F** *The use of reasonable force to take the photograph of a suspect elsewhere than at a police station must be carefully considered. In order to obtain a suspect's consent and co-operation to remove an item of religious headwear to take their photograph, a constable should consider whether in the circumstances of the situation the removal of the headwear and the taking of the photograph should be by an officer of the same sex as the person. It would be appropriate for these actions to be conducted out of public view.*

## D:6 Identification by body samples and impressions

### (a) *General*

D:6.1 References to:  **A-135**

(a) an "intimate sample" mean a dental impression or sample of blood, semen or any other tissue fluid, urine, or pubic hair, or a swab taken from any part of a person's genitals or from a person's body orifice other than the mouth;

(b) a "non-intimate sample" means:

(i) a sample of hair, other than pubic hair, which includes hair plucked with the root, see Note 6A;

(ii) a sample taken from a nail or from under a nail;

(iii) a swab taken from any part of a person's body other than a part from which a swab taken would be an intimate sample;

(iv) saliva;

(v) a skin impression which means any record, other than a fingerprint, which is a record, in any form and produced by any method, of the skin pattern and other physical characteristics or features of the whole, or any part of, a person's foot or of any other part of their body.

### (b) *Action*

### (a) Intimate samples

D:6.2 PACE, s.62, provides that intimate samples may be taken under:  **A-136**

(a) section 62(1), from a person in police detention only:

(i) if a police officer of inspector rank or above has reasonable grounds to believe such an impression or sample will tend to confirm or disprove the suspect's involvement in a recordable offence, see *Note 4A*, and gives authorisation for a sample to be taken; and

(ii) with the suspect's written consent;

(b) section 62(1A), from a person not in police detention but from whom two or more non-intimate samples have been taken in the course of an investigation of an offence and the samples, though suitable, have proved insufficient if:

(i) a police officer of inspector rank or above authorises it to be taken; and

(ii) the person concerned gives their written consent; see *Notes 6B* and *6C*;

(c) section 62(2A), from a person convicted outside England and Wales of an offence which if committed in England and Wales would be qualifying offence [*sic*] as defined by PACE, s.65A (see *Note 4AB*) from whom two or more non-intimate samples taken under section 63(3E) (see paragraph 6.6(h)) have proved insufficient if:

(i) a police officer of inspector rank or above is satisfied that taking the sample is necessary to assist in the prevention or detection of crime and authorises it to be taken; and

(ii) the person concerned gives their written consent.

D:6.2A PACE, s.63A(4), and Sched. 2A, provide powers [*sic*] to:

(a) [*sic*] make a requirement (in accordance with Annex G) for a person to attend a police station to have an intimate sample taken in the exercise of one of the following powers in paragraph 6.2 when that power applies at the time the sample is to be taken in accordance with the requirement or after the person's arrest if they fail to comply with the requirement:

(i) section 62(1A)—persons from whom two or more non-intimate samples have been taken and proved to be insufficient, see paragraph 6.2(b); there is no time limit for making the requirement;

(ii) section 62(2A)—persons convicted outside England and Wales from whom two or more non-intimate samples taken under section 63(3E) (see paragraph 6.6(h)) have proved insufficient, see paragraph 6.2(c); there is no time limit for making the requirement.

D:6.3 Before a suspect is asked to provide an intimate sample, they must be:

(a) informed:

(i) of the reason, including the nature of the suspected offence (except if taken under paragraph 6.2(c) from a person convicted outside England and Wales;

(ii) that authorisation has been given and the provisions under which given;

(iii) that a sample taken at a police station may be subject of a speculative search;

(b) warned that if they refuse without good cause their refusal may harm their case if it comes to trial, see *Note 6D*. If the suspect is in police detention and not legally represented, they must also be reminded of their entitlement to have free legal advice, see Code C, paragraph 6.5, and the reminder noted in the custody record. If paragraph 6.2(b) applies and the person is attending a station voluntarily, their entitlement to free legal advice as in Code C, paragraph 3.21 shall be explained to them.

D:6.4 Dental impressions may only be taken by a registered dentist. Other intimate samples, except for samples of urine, may only be taken by a registered medical practitioner or registered nurse or registered paramedic.

### (b) Non-intimate samples

**A-137**

D:6.5 A non-intimate sample may be taken from a detainee only with their written consent or if paragraph 6.6 applies.

D:6.6 A non-intimate sample may be taken from a person without the appropriate consent in the following circumstances:

(a) under section 63(2A) from a person who is in police detention as a consequence of being arrested for a recordable offence and who has not had a non-intimate sample of the same type and from the same part of the body taken in the course of the investigation of the offence by the police or they have had such a sample taken but it proved insufficient;

(b) under section 63(3) from a person who is being held in custody by the police on the authority of a court if an officer of at least the rank of inspector authorises it to be taken; an authorisation may be given:

  (i) if the authorising officer has reasonable grounds for suspecting the person of involvement in a recordable offence and for believing that the sample will tend to confirm or disprove that involvement; and

  (ii) in writing or orally and confirmed in writing, as soon as practicable; but an authorisation may not be given to take from the same part of the body a further non-intimate sample consisting of a skin impression unless the previously taken impression proved insufficient;

(c) under section 63(3ZA) from a person who has been arrested for a recordable offence and released if the person:

  (i) is on bail and has not had a sample of the same type and from the same part of the body taken in the course of the investigation of the offence; or

  (ii) has had such a sample taken in the course of the investigation of the offence, but it proved unsuitable or insufficient;

(d) under section 63(3A), from a person (whether or not in police detention or held in custody by the police on the authority of a court) who has been charged with a recordable offence or informed they will be reported for such an offence if the person:

  (i) has not had a non-intimate sample taken from them in the course of the investigation of the offence;

  (ii) has had a sample so taken, but it proved unsuitable or insufficient, see *Note 6B*; or

  (iii) has had a sample taken in the course of the investigation of the offence and the sample has been destroyed and in proceedings relating to that offence there is a dispute as to whether a DNA profile relevant to the proceedings was derived from the destroyed sample;

(e) under section 63(3B), from a person who has been:

  (i) convicted of a recordable offence;

  (ii) given a caution in respect of a recordable offence which, at the time of the caution, the person admitted; or

  (iii) warned or reprimanded under the Crime and Disorder Act 1998, s.65, for a recordable offence,

  if, since their conviction, caution, warning or reprimand a non-intimate sample has not been taken from them or a sample which has been taken since then has proved to be unsuitable or insufficient and in either case, an officer of inspector rank or above, is satisfied that taking the fingerprints [*sic*] is necessary to assist in the prevention or detection of crime and authorises the taking;

(f) under section 63(3C) from a person to whom section 2 of the Criminal Evidence (Amendment) Act 1997 applies (persons detained following acquittal on grounds of insanity or finding of unfitness to plead);

(g) under section 63(3E) from a person who has been convicted outside England and Wales of an offence which if committed in England and Wales would be a qualifying offence as defined by PACE, s.65A (see *Note 4AB*) if:

(i) a non-intimate sample has not been taken previously under this power or unless a sample was so taken but was unsuitable or insufficient; and

(ii) a police officer of inspector rank or above is satisfied that taking a sample is necessary to assist in the prevention or detection of crime and authorises it to be taken.

D:6.6A PACE, s.63A(4), and Sched. 2A, provide powers to:

(a) make a requirement (in accordance with Annex G) for a person to attend a police station to have a non-intimate sample taken in the exercise of one of the following powers in paragraph 6.6 when that power applies at the time the sample would be taken in accordance with the requirement:

(i) section 63(3ZA)—persons arrested for a recordable offence and released, see paragraph 6.6(c); the requirement may not be made more than six months from the day the investigating officer was informed that the sample previously taken was unsuitable or insufficient;

(ii) section 63(3A)—persons charged *etc.* with a recordable offence, see paragraph 6.6(d); the requirement may not be made more than six months from:

• the day the person was charged or reported if a sample has not been taken since then; or

• the day the investigating officer was informed that the sample previously taken was unsuitable or insufficient;

(iii) section 63(3B)—person convicted, cautioned, warned or reprimanded for a recordable offence in England and Wales, see paragraph 6.6(e); where the offence for which the person was convicted etc is also a qualifying offence (see *Note 4AB*), there is no time limit for the exercise of this power; where the conviction etc was for a recordable offence that is not a qualifying offence, the requirement may not be made more than two years from:

• the day the person was convicted, cautioned, warned or reprimanded, or the day Schedule 2A comes into force (if later), if a samples [*sic*] has not been taken since then; or

• the day an officer from the force investigating the offence was informed that the sample previously taken was unsuitable or insufficient or the day Schedule 2A comes into force (if later);

(iv) section 63(3E)—a person who has been convicted of qualifying offence (see *Note 4AB*) outside England and Wales, see paragraph 6.6(h); there is no time limit for making the requirement;

note: a person who has had a non-intimate sample taken under any of the powers in section 63 mentioned in paragraph 6.6 on two occasions in relation to any offence may not be required under Schedule 2A to attend a police station for a sample to be taken again under section 63 in relation to that offence, unless authorised by an officer of inspector rank or above; the fact of the authorisation and the reasons for giving it must be recorded as soon as practicable;

(b) arrest, without warrant, a person who fails to comply with the requirement.

D:6.7 Reasonable force may be used, if necessary, to take a non-intimate sample from a person without their consent under the powers mentioned in paragraph 6.6.

D:6.8 Before any non-intimate sample is taken:

(a) without consent under any power mentioned in paragraphs 6.6 and 6.6A, the person must be informed of:

(i) the reason for taking the sample;

(ii) the power under which the sample is to be taken;

(iii) the fact that the relevant authority has been given if any power mentioned in paragraph 6.6(b), (e) or (h) applies;

(b) with or without consent at a police station or elsewhere, the person must be informed:

(i) that their sample or information derived from it may be subject of a speculative search against other samples and information derived from them, see *Note 6E*; and

(ii) that their sample and the information derived from it may be retained in accordance with Annex F, Part (a).

D:6.9 When clothing needs to be removed in circumstances likely to cause embarrassment to the person, no person of the opposite sex who is not a registered medical practitioner or registered health care professional shall be present (unless in the case of a juvenile, mentally disordered or mentally vulnerable person, that person specifically requests the presence of an appropriate adult of the opposite sex who is readily available), nor shall anyone whose presence is unnecessary. However, in the case of a juvenile, this is subject to the overriding proviso that such a removal of clothing may take place in the absence of the appropriate adult only if the juvenile signifies in their presence, that they prefer the adult's absence and they agree.

**(c) Documentation**

D:6.10  A record must be made as soon as practicable after the sample is taken of:
- the matters in paragraph 6.8(a)(i) to (iii) and the fact that the person has been informed of those matters; and
- the fact that the person has been informed of the matters in paragraph 6.8(b)(i) and (ii).

D:6.10A  If force is used, a record shall be made of the circumstances and those present.

D:6.11  A record must be made of a warning given as required by paragraph 6.3.

*Notes for guidance*

**A-138**    D:6A *When hair samples are taken for the purpose of DNA analysis (rather than for other purposes such as making a visual match), the suspect should be permitted a reasonable choice as to what part of the body the hairs are taken from. When hairs are plucked, they should be plucked individually, unless the suspect prefers otherwise and no more should be plucked than the person taking them reasonably considers necessary for a sufficient sample.*

   (a) *An insufficient sample is one which is not sufficient either in quantity or quality to provide informa-tion for a particular form of analysis, such as DNA analysis. A sample may also be insufficient if enough information cannot be obtained from it by analysis because of loss, destruction, damage or contamination of the sample or as a result of an earlier, unsuccessful attempt at analysis.*

   (b) *An unsuitable sample is one which, by its nature, is not suitable for a particular form of analysis.*

D:6C *Nothing in paragraph 6.2 prevents intimate samples being taken for elimination purposes with the consent of the person concerned but the provisions of paragraph 2.12 relating to the role of the appropriate adult, should be applied. Paragraph 6.2(b) does not, however, apply where the non-intimate samples were previously taken under the Terrorism Act 2000, Sched. 8, para. 10.*

D:6D *In warning a person who is asked to provide an intimate sample as in paragraph 6.3, the following form of words may be used:*

*"You do not have to provide this sample/allow this swab or impression to be taken, but I must warn you that if you refuse without good cause, your refusal may harm your case if it comes to trial."*

D:6E *Fingerprints or a DNA sample and the information derived from it taken from a person arrested on suspicion of being involved in a recordable offence, or charged with such an offence, or informed they will be reported for such an offence, may be subject of a speculative search. This means they may be checked against other fingerprints and DNA records held by, or on behalf of, the police and other law enforcement authorities in or outside the UK or held in connection with, or as a result of, an investigation of an offence inside or outside the UK. Fingerprints and samples taken from any other person, e.g. a person suspected of committing a recordable offence but who has not been arrested, charged or informed they will be reported for it, may be subject to a specula-tive search only if the person consents in writing to their fingerprints being subject of such a search. The following is an example of a basic form of words:*

*"I consent to my fingerprints/DNA sample and information derived from it being retained and used only for purposes related to the prevention and detection of a crime, the investigation of an offence or the conduct of a prosecution either nationally or internationally.*

   *I understand that this sample may be checked against other fingerprint/DNA records held by or on behalf of relevant law enforcement authorities, either nationally or internationally.*

   *I understand that once I have given my consent for the sample to be retained and used I cannot withdraw this consent."*

*See Annex F regarding the retention and use of fingerprints and samples taken with consent for elimination purposes.*

D:6F *Samples of urine and non-intimate samples taken in accordance with sections 63B and 63C of PACE may not be used for identification purposes in accordance with this code. See Code C note for guidance 17D.*

**ANNEX A**

**Video identification**

(a) *General*

D:1 The arrangements for obtaining and ensuring the availability of a suitable set of images to be   **A-139**
used in a video identification must be the responsibility of an identification officer, who has no direct
involvement with the case.

D:2 The set of images must include the suspect and at least eight other people who, so far as possible, resemble the suspect in age, general appearance and position in life. Only one suspect shall appear in any set unless there are two suspects of roughly similar appearance, in which case they may
be shown together with at least twelve other people.

D:2A If the suspect has an unusual physical feature, *e.g.* a facial scar, tattoo or distinctive hairstyle
or hair colour which does not appear on the images of the other people that are available to be used,
steps may be taken to:

    (a) conceal the location of the feature on the images of the suspect and the other people; or

    (b) replicate that feature on the images of the other people.

For these purposes, the feature may be concealed or replicated electronically or by any other method
which it is practicable to use to ensure that the images of the suspect and other people resemble each
other. The identification officer has discretion to choose whether to conceal or replicate the feature
and the method to be used. If an unusual physical feature has been described by the witness, the
identification officer should, if practicable, have that feature replicated. If it has not been described,
concealment may be more appropriate.

D:2B If the identification officer decides that a feature should be concealed or replicated, the
reason for the decision and whether the feature was concealed or replicated in the images shown to
any witness shall be recorded.

D:2C If the witness requests to view an image where an unusual physical feature has been
concealed or replicated without the feature being concealed or replicated, the witness may be allowed
to do so.

D:3 The images used to conduct a video identification shall, as far as possible, show the suspect
and other people in the same positions or carrying out the same sequence of movements. They shall
also show the suspect and other people under identical conditions unless the identification officer
reasonably believes:

    (a) because of the suspect's failure or refusal to co-operate or other reasons, it is not
        practicable for the conditions to be identical; and

    (b) any difference in the conditions would not direct a witness's attention to any individual
        image.

D:4 The reasons identical conditions are not practicable shall be recorded on forms provided for
the purpose.

D:5 Provision must be made for each person shown to be identified by number.

D:6 If police officers are shown, any numerals or other identifying badges must be concealed. If a
prison inmate is shown, either as a suspect or not, then either all, or none of, the people shown
should be in prison clothing.

D:7 The suspect or their solicitor, friend, or appropriate adult must be given a reasonable op-   **A-140**
portunity to see the complete set of images before it is shown to any witness. If the suspect has a
reasonable objection to the set of images or any of the participants, the suspect shall be asked to state
the reasons for the objection. Steps shall, if practicable, be taken to remove the grounds for objection.
If this is not practicable, the suspect and/or their representative shall be told why their objections
cannot be met and the objection, the reason given for it and why it cannot be met shall be recorded
on forms provided for the purpose.

D:8 Before the images are shown in accordance with paragraph 7, the suspect or their solicitor
shall be provided with details of the first description of the suspect by any witnesses who are to attend
the video identification. When a broadcast or publication is made, as in paragraph 3.28, the suspect
or their solicitor must also be allowed to view any material released to the media by the police for the
purpose of recognising or tracing the suspect, provided it is practicable and would not unreasonably
delay the investigation.

D:9 The suspect's solicitor, if practicable, shall be given reasonable notification of the time and
place the video identification is to be conducted so a representative may attend on behalf of the
suspect. The suspect may not be present when the images are shown to the witness(es). In the
absence of the suspect's solicitor, the viewing itself shall be recorded on video. No unauthorised
people may be present.

(b) *Conducting the video identification*

**A-141**   D:10 The identification officer is responsible for making the appropriate arrangements to make sure, before they see the set of images, witnesses are not able to communicate with each other about the case, see any of the images which are to be shown, see, or be reminded of, any photograph or description of the suspect or be given any other indication as to the suspect's identity, or overhear a witness who has already seen the material. There must be no discussion with the witness about the composition of the set of images and they must not be told whether a previous witness has made any identification.

D:11 Only one witness may see the set of images at a time. Immediately before the images are shown, the witness shall be told that the person they saw on a specified earlier occasion may, or may not, appear in the images they are shown and that if they cannot make a positive identification, they should say so. The witness shall be advised that at any point, they may ask to see a particular part of the set of images or to have a particular image frozen for them to study. Furthermore, it should be pointed out to the witness that there is no limit on how many times they can view the whole set of images or any part of them. However, they should be asked not to make any decision as to whether the person they saw is on the set of images until they have seen the whole set at least twice.

D:12 Once the witness has seen the whole set of images at least twice and has indicated that they do not want to view the images, or any part of them, again, the witness shall be asked to say whether the individual they saw in person on a specified earlier occasion has been shown and, if so, to identify them by number of the image. The witness will then be shown that image to confirm the identification, see paragraph 17.

D:13 Care must be taken not to direct the witness's attention to any one individual image or give any indication of the suspect's identity. Where a witness has previously made an identification by photographs, or a computerised or artist's composite or similar likeness, the witness must not be reminded of such a photograph or composite likeness once a suspect is available for identification by other means in accordance with this code. Nor must the witness be reminded of any description of the suspect.

D:14 After the procedure, each witness shall be asked whether they have seen any broadcast or published films or photographs, or any descriptions of suspects relating to the offence and their reply shall be recorded.

(c) *Image security and destruction*

D:15 Arrangements shall be made for all relevant material containing sets of images used for specific identification procedures to be kept securely and their movements accounted for. In particular, no-one involved in the investigation shall be permitted to view the material prior to it being shown to any witness.

D:16 As appropriate, paragraph 3.30 or 3.31 applies to the destruction or retention of relevant sets of images.

(d) *Documentation*

D:17 A record must be made of all those participating in, or seeing, the set of images whose names are known to the police.

D:18 A record of the conduct of the video identification must be made on forms provided for the purpose. This shall include anything said by the witness about any identifications or the conduct of the procedure and any reasons it was not practicable to comply with any of the provisions of this code governing the conduct of video identifications.

**ANNEX B**

**Identification parades**

(a) *General*

**A-142**   D:1 A suspect must be given a reasonable opportunity to have a solicitor or friend present, and the suspect shall be asked to indicate on a second copy of the notice whether or not they wish to do so.

D:2 An identification parade may take place either in a normal room or one equipped with a screen permitting witnesses to see members of the identification parade without being seen. The procedures for the composition and conduct of the identification parade are the same in both cases, subject to paragraph 8 (except that an identification parade involving a screen may take place only when the suspect's solicitor, friend or appropriate adult is present or the identification parade is recorded on video).

D:3 Before the identification parade takes place, the suspect or their solicitor shall be provided with details of the first description of the suspect by any witnesses who are attending the identification parade. When a broadcast or publication is made as in paragraph 3.28, the suspect or their solicitor should also be allowed to view any material released to the media by the police for the purpose of recognising or tracing the suspect, provided it is practicable to do so and would not unreasonably delay the investigation.

(b) *Identification parades involving prison inmates*

D:4 If a prison inmate is required for identification, and there are no security problems about the person leaving the establishment, they may be asked to participate in an identification parade or video identification.

D:5 An identification parade may be held in a Prison Department establishment but shall be conducted, as far as practicable under normal identification parade rules. Members of the public shall make up the identification parade unless there are serious security, or control, objections to their admission to the establishment. In such cases, or if a group or video identification is arranged within the establishment, other inmates may participate. If an inmate is the suspect, they are not required to wear prison clothing for the identification parade unless the other people taking part are other inmates in similar clothing, or are members of the public who are prepared to wear prison clothing for the occasion.

(c) *Conduct of the identification parade*

D:6 Immediately before the identification parade, the suspect must be reminded of the procedures     **A-143**
governing its conduct and cautioned in the terms of Code C, paragraphs 10.5 or 10.6, as appropriate.

D:7 All unauthorised people must be excluded from the place where the identification parade is held.

D:8 Once the identification parade has been formed, everything afterwards, in respect of it, shall take place in the presence and hearing of the suspect and any interpreter, solicitor, friend or appropriate adult who is present (unless the identification parade involves a screen, in which case everything said to, or by, any witness at the place where the identification parade is held, must be said in the hearing and presence of the suspect's solicitor, friend or appropriate adult or be recorded on video).

D:9 The identification parade shall consist of at least eight people (in addition to the suspect) who, so far as possible, resemble the suspect in age, height, general appearance and position in life. Only one suspect shall be included in an identification parade unless there are two suspects of roughly similar appearance, in which case they may be paraded together with at least twelve other people. In no circumstances shall more than two suspects be included in one identification parade and where there are separate identification parades, they shall be made up of different people.

D:10 If the suspect has an unusual physical feature, *e.g.*, a facial scar, tattoo or distinctive hairstyle or hair colour which cannot be replicated on other members of the identification parade, steps may be taken to conceal the location of that feature on the suspect and the other members of the identification parade if the suspect and their solicitor, or appropriate adult, agree. For example, by use of a plaster or a hat, so that all members of the identification parade resemble each other in general appearance.

D:11 When all members of a similar group are possible suspects, separate identification parades shall be held for each unless there are two suspects of similar appearance when they may appear on the same identification parade with at least twelve other members of the group who are not suspects. When police officers in uniform form an identification parade any numerals or other identifying badges shall be concealed.

D:12 When the suspect is brought to the place where the identification parade is to be held, they shall be asked if they have any objection to the arrangements for the identification parade or to any of the other participants in it and to state the reasons for the objection. The suspect may obtain advice from their solicitor or friend, if present, before the identification parade proceeds. If the suspect has a reasonable objection to the arrangements or any of the participants, steps shall, if practicable, be taken to remove the grounds for objection. When it is not practicable to do so, the suspect shall be told why their objections cannot be met and the objection, the reason given for it and why it cannot be met, shall be recorded on forms provided for the purpose.

D:13 The suspect may select their own position in the line, but may not otherwise interfere with the order of the people forming the line. When there is more than one witness, the suspect must be told, after each witness has left the room, that they can, if they wish, change position in the line. Each position in the line must be clearly numbered, whether by means of a number laid on the floor in front of each identification parade member or by other means.

D:14 Appropriate arrangements must be made to make sure, before witnesses attend the identifica-     **A-144**
tion parade, they are not able to:

    (i) communicate with each other about the case or overhear a witness who has already seen the identification parade;

    (ii) see any member of the identification parade;

    (iii) see, or be reminded of, any photograph or description of the suspect or be given any other indication as to the suspect's identity; or

    (iv) see the suspect before or after the identification parade.

D:15 The person conducting a witness to an identification parade must not discuss with them the composition of the identification parade and, in particular, must not disclose whether a previous witness has made any identification.

D:16 Witnesses shall be brought in one at a time. Immediately before the witness inspects the identification parade, they shall be told the person they saw on a specified earlier occasion may, or may not, be present and if they cannot make a positive identification, they should say so. The witness must also be told they should not make any decision about whether the person they saw is on the identification parade until they have looked at each member at least twice.

D:17 When the officer or police staff (see paragraph 3.11) conducting the identification procedure is satisfied the witness has properly looked at each member of the identification parade, they shall ask the witness whether the person they saw on a specified earlier occasion is on the identification parade and, if so, to indicate the number of the person concerned, see paragraph 28.

D:18 If the witness wishes to hear any identification parade member speak, adopt any specified posture or move, they shall first be asked whether they can identify any person(s) on the identification parade on the basis of appearance only. When the request is to hear members of the identification parade speak, the witness shall be reminded that the participants in the identification parade have been chosen on the basis of physical appearance only. Members of the identification parade may then be asked to comply with the witness's request to hear them speak, see them move or adopt any specified posture.

D:19 If the witness requests that the person they have indicated remove anything used for the purposes of paragraph 10 to conceal the location of an unusual physical feature, that person may be asked to remove it.

D:20 If the witness makes an identification after the identification parade has ended, the suspect and, if present, their solicitor, interpreter or friend shall be informed. When this occurs, consideration should be given to allowing the witness a second opportunity to identify the suspect.

D:21 After the procedure, each witness shall be asked whether they have seen any broadcast or published films or photographs or any descriptions of suspects relating to the offence and their reply shall be recorded.

D:22 When the last witness has left, the suspect shall be asked whether they wish to make any comments on the conduct of the identification parade.

(d) *Documentation*

D:23 A video recording must normally be taken of the identification parade. If that is impracticable, a colour photograph must be taken. A copy of the video recording or photograph shall be supplied, on request, to the suspect or their solicitor within a reasonable time.

D:24 As appropriate, paragraph 3.30 or 3.31, should apply to any photograph or video taken as in paragraph 23.

D:25 If any person is asked to leave an identification parade because they are interfering with its conduct, the circumstances shall be recorded.

D:26 A record must be made of all those present at an identification parade whose names are known to the police.

D:27 If prison inmates make up an identification parade, the circumstances must be recorded.

D:28 A record of the conduct of any identification parade must be made on forms provided for the purpose. This shall include anything said by the witness or the suspect about any identifications or the conduct of the procedure, and any reasons it was not practicable to comply with any of this code's provisions.

## ANNEX C

### Group identification

(a) *General*

D:1 The purpose of this annex is to make sure, as far as possible, group identifications follow the **A-146** principles and procedures for identification parades so the conditions are fair to the suspect in the way they test the witness's ability to make an identification.

D:2 Group identifications may take place either with the suspect's consent and co-operation or covertly without their consent.

D:3 The location of the group identification is a matter for the identification officer, although the officer may take into account any representations made by the suspect, appropriate adult, their solicitor or friend.

D:4 The place where the group identification is held should be one where other people are either passing by or waiting around informally, in groups such that the suspect is able to join them and be capable of being seen by the witness at the same time as others in the group. For example people leaving an escalator, pedestrians walking through a shopping centre, passengers on railway and bus stations, waiting in queues or groups or where people are standing or sitting in groups in other public places.

D:5 If the group identification is to be held covertly, the choice of locations will be limited by the places where the suspect can be found and the number of other people present at that time. In these cases, suitable locations might be along regular routes travelled by the suspect, including buses or trains or public places frequented by the suspect.

D:6 Although the number, age, sex, race and general description and style of clothing of other **A-147** people present at the location cannot be controlled by the identification officer, in selecting the location the officer must consider the general appearance and numbers of people likely to be present. In particular, the officer must reasonably expect that over the period the witness observes the group, they will be able to see, from time to time, a number of others whose appearance is broadly similar to that of the suspect.

D:7 A group identification need not be held if the identification officer believes, because of the unusual appearance of the suspect, none of the locations it would be practicable to use, satisfy the requirements of paragraph 6 necessary to make the identification fair.

D:8 Immediately after a group identification procedure has taken place (with or without the suspect's consent), a colour photograph or video should be taken of the general scene, if practicable, to give a general impression of the scene and the number of people present. Alternatively, if it is practicable, the group identification may be video recorded.

D:9 If it is not practicable to take the photograph or video in accordance with paragraph 8, a photograph or film of the scene should be taken later at a time determined by the identification officer if the officer considers it practicable to do so.

D:10 An identification carried out in accordance with this code remains a group identification even though, at the time of being seen by the witness, the suspect was on their own rather than in a group.

D:11 Before the group identification takes place, the suspect or their solicitor shall be provided with details of the first description of the suspect by any witnesses who are to attend the identification. When a broadcast or publication is made, as in paragraph 3.28, the suspect or their solicitor should also be allowed to view any material released by the police to the media for the purposes of recognising or tracing the suspect, provided that it is practicable and would not unreasonably delay the investigation.

D:12 After the procedure, each witness shall be asked whether they have seen any broadcast or published films or photographs or any descriptions of suspects relating to the offence and their reply recorded.

(b) *Identification with the consent of the suspect*

D:13 A suspect must be given a reasonable opportunity to have a solicitor or friend present. They **A-148** shall be asked to indicate on a second copy of the notice whether or not they wish to do so.

D:14 The witness, the person carrying out the procedure and the suspect's solicitor, appropriate adult, friend or any interpreter for the witness, may be concealed from the sight of the individuals in the group they are observing, if the person carrying out the procedure considers this assists the conduct of the identification.

D:15 The person conducting a witness to a group identification must not discuss with them the forthcoming group identification and, in particular, must not disclose whether a previous witness has made any identification.

D:16 Anything said to, or by, the witness during the procedure about the identification should be said in the presence and hearing of those present at the procedure.

D:17 Appropriate arrangements must be made to make sure, before witnesses attend the group identification, they are not able to:

    (i) communicate with each other about the case or overhear a witness who has already been given an opportunity to see the suspect in the group;

    (ii) see the suspect; or

    (iii) see, or be reminded of, any photographs or description of the suspect or be given any other indication of the suspect's identity.

D:18 Witnesses shall be brought one at a time to the place where they are to observe the group. Immediately before the witness is asked to look at the group, the person conducting the procedure shall tell them that the person they saw may, or may not, be in the group and that if they cannot make a positive identification, they should say so. The witness shall be asked to observe the group in which the suspect is to appear. The way in which the witness should do this will depend on whether the group is moving or stationary.

### Moving group

**A-149**  D:19 When the group in which the suspect is to appear is moving, *e.g.* leaving an escalator, the provisions of paragraphs 20 to 24 should be followed.

D:20 If two or more suspects consent to a group identification, each should be the subject of separate identification procedures. These may be conducted consecutively on the same occasion.

D:21 The person conducting the procedure shall tell the witness to observe the group and ask them to point out any person they think they saw on the specified earlier occasion.

D:22 Once the witness has been informed as in paragraph 21 the suspect should be allowed to take whatever position in the group they wish.

D:23 When the witness points out a person as in paragraph 21 they shall, if practicable, be asked to take a closer look at the person to confirm the identification. If this is not practicable, or they cannot confirm the identification, they shall be asked how sure they are that the person they have indicated is the relevant person.

D:24 The witness should continue to observe the group for the period which the person conducting the procedure reasonably believes is necessary in the circumstances for them to be able to make comparisons between the suspect and other individuals of broadly similar appearance to the suspect as in paragraph 6.

### Stationary groups

**A-150**  D:25 When the group in which the suspect is to appear is stationary, *e.g.* people waiting in a queue, the provisions of paragraphs 26 to 29 should be followed.

D:26 If two or more suspects consent to a group identification, each should be subject to separate identification procedures unless they are of broadly similar appearance when they may appear in the same group. When separate group identifications are held, the groups must be made up of different people.

D:27 The suspect may take whatever position in the group they wish. If there is more than one witness, the suspect must be told, out of the sight and hearing of any witness, that they can, if they wish, change their position in the group.

D:28 The witness shall be asked to pass along, or amongst, the group and to look at each person in the group at least twice, taking as much care and time as possible according to the circumstances, before making an identification. Once the witness has done this, they shall be asked whether the person they saw on the specified earlier occasion is in the group and to indicate any such person by whatever means the person conducting the procedure considers appropriate in the circumstances. If this is not practicable, the witness shall be asked to point out any person they think they saw on the earlier occasion.

D:29 When the witness makes an indication as in paragraph 28, arrangements shall be made, if practicable, for the witness to take a closer look at the person to confirm the identification. If this is not practicable, or the witness is unable to confirm the identification, they shall be asked how sure they are that the person they have indicated is the relevant person.

### All cases

**A-151**  D:30 If the suspect unreasonably delays joining the group, or having joined the group, deliberately conceals themselves [*sic*] from the sight of the witness, this may be treated as a refusal to co-operate in a group identification.

D:31 If the witness identifies a person other than the suspect, that person should be informed what has happened and asked if they are prepared to give their name and address. There is no obligation upon any member of the public to give these details. There shall be no duty to record any details of any other member of the public present in the group or at the place where the procedure is conducted.

D:32 When the group identification has been completed, the suspect shall be asked whether they wish to make any comments on the conduct of the procedure.

D:33 If the suspect has not been previously informed, they shall be told of any identifications made by the witnesses.

(c) *Identification without the suspect's consent*

D:34 Group identifications held covertly without the suspect's consent should, as far as practicable, **A-152** follow the rules for conduct of group identification by consent.

D:35 A suspect has no right to have a solicitor, appropriate adult or friend present as the identification will take place without the knowledge of the suspect.

D:36 Any number of suspects may be identified at the same time.

(d) *Identifications in police stations*

D:37 Group identifications should only take place in police stations for reasons of safety, security or because it is not practicable to hold them elsewhere.

D:38 The group identification may take place either in a room equipped with a screen permitting witnesses to see members of the group without being seen, or anywhere else in the police station that the identification officer considers appropriate.

D:39 Any of the additional safeguards applicable to identification parades should be followed if the identification officer considers it is practicable to do so in the circumstances.

(e) *Identifications involving prison inmates*

D:40 A group identification involving a prison inmate may only be arranged in the prison or at a **A-153** police station.

D:41 When a group identification takes place involving a prison inmate, whether in a prison or in a police station, the arrangements should follow those in paragraphs 37 to 39. If a group identification takes place within a prison, other inmates may participate. If an inmate is the suspect, they do not have to wear prison clothing for the group identification unless the other participants are wearing the same clothing.

(f) *Documentation*

D:42 When a photograph or video is taken as in paragraph 8 or 9, a copy of the photograph or video shall be supplied on request to the suspect or their solicitor within a reasonable time.

D:43 Paragraph 3.30 or 3.31, as appropriate, shall apply when the photograph or film taken in accordance with paragraph 8 or 9 includes the suspect.

D:44 A record of the conduct of any group identification must be made on forms provided for the purpose. This shall include anything said by the witness or suspect about any identifications or the conduct of the procedure and any reasons why it was not practicable to comply with any of the provisions of this code governing the conduct of group identifications.

## ANNEX D

### Confrontation by a witness

D:1 Before the confrontation takes place, the witness must be told that the person they saw may, **A-154** or may not, be the person they are to confront and that if they are not that person, then the witness should say so.

D:2 Before the confrontation takes place the suspect or their solicitor shall be provided with details of the first description of the suspect given by any witness who is to attend. When a broadcast or publication is made, as in paragraph 3.28, the suspect or their solicitor should also be allowed to view any material released to the media for the purposes of recognising or tracing the suspect, provided it is practicable to do so and would not unreasonably delay the investigation.

D:3 Force may not be used to make the suspect's face visible to the witness.

D:4 Confrontation must take place in the presence of the suspect's solicitor, interpreter or friend unless this would cause unreasonable delay.

D:5 The suspect shall be confronted independently by each witness, who shall be asked "Is this the person?". If the witness identifies the person but is unable to confirm the identification, they shall be asked how sure they are that the person is the one they saw on the earlier occasion.

D:6 The confrontation should normally take place in the police station, either in a normal room or one equipped with a screen permitting a witness to see the suspect without being seen. In both cases, the procedures are the same except that a room equipped with a screen may be used only when the suspect's solicitor, friend or appropriate adult is present or the confrontation is recorded on video.

D:7 After the procedure, each witness shall be asked whether they have seen any broadcast or published films or photographs or any descriptions of suspects relating to the offence and their reply shall be recorded.

## ANNEX E

### Showing photographs

(a) *Action*

**A-155**     D:1 An officer of sergeant rank or above shall be responsible for supervising and directing the showing of photographs. The actual showing may be done by another officer or police staff, see paragraph 3.11.

D:2 The supervising officer must confirm the first description of the suspect given by the witness has been recorded before they are shown the photographs. If the supervising officer is unable to confirm the description has been recorded they shall postpone showing the photographs.

D:3 Only one witness shall be shown photographs at any one time. Each witness shall be given as much privacy as practicable and shall not be allowed to communicate with any other witness in the case.

D:4 The witness shall be shown not less than twelve photographs at a time, which shall, as far as possible, all be of a similar type.

D:5 When the witness is shown the photographs, they shall be told the photograph of the person they saw may, or may not, be amongst them and if they cannot make a positive identification, they should say so. The witness shall also be told they should not make a decision until they have viewed at least twelve photographs. The witness shall not be prompted or guided in any way but shall be left to make any selection without help.

D:6 If a witness makes a positive identification from photographs, unless the person identified is otherwise eliminated from enquiries or is not available, other witnesses shall not be shown photographs. But both they, and the witness who has made the identification, shall be asked to attend a video identification, an identification parade or group identification unless there is no dispute about the suspect's identification.

**A-156**     D:7 If the witness makes a selection but is unable to confirm the identification, the person showing the photographs shall ask them how sure they are that the photograph they have indicated is the person they saw on the specified earlier occasion.

D:8 When the use of a computerised or artist's composite or similar likeness has led to there being a known suspect who can be asked to participate in a video identification, appear on an identification parade or participate in a group identification, that likeness shall not be shown to other potential witnesses.

D:9 When a witness attending a video identification, an identification parade or group identification has previously been shown photographs or computerised or artist's composite or similar likeness (and it is the responsibility of the officer in charge of the investigation to make the identification officer aware that this is the case), the suspect and their solicitor must be informed of this fact before the identification procedure takes place.

D:10 None of the photographs shown shall be destroyed, whether or not an identification is made, since they may be required for production in court. The photographs shall be numbered and a separate photograph taken of the frame or part of the album from which the witness made an identification as an aid to reconstituting it.

(b) *Documentation*

**A-157**     D:11 Whether or not an identification is made, a record shall be kept of the showing of photographs on forms provided for the purpose. This shall include anything said by the witness about any identification or the conduct of the procedure, any reasons it was not practicable to comply with any of the provisions of this code governing the showing of photographs and the name and rank of the supervising officer.

D:12 The supervising officer shall inspect and sign the record as soon as practicable.

## ANNEX F

### Fingerprints, footwear impressions and samples—destruction and speculative searches

(a) *Fingerprints, footwear impressions and samples taken in connection with a criminal investigation from a person suspected of committing the offence under investigation*

D:1 The retention and destruction of fingerprints, footwear impressions and samples taken in connection with a criminal investigation from a person suspected of committing the offence under investigation is subject to PACE, s.64.

(b) *Fingerprints, footwear impressions and samples taken in connection with a criminal investigation from a person not suspected of committing the offence under investigation*

D:2 When fingerprints, footwear impressions or DNA samples are taken from a person in connection with an investigation and the person is not suspected of having committed the offence, see *Note F1*, they must be destroyed as soon as they have fulfilled the purpose for which they were taken unless:

(a) they were taken for the purposes of an investigation of an offence for which a person has been convicted; and

(b) fingerprints, footwear impressions or samples were also taken from the convicted person for the purposes of that investigation.

However, subject to paragraph 2, the fingerprints, footwear impressions and samples, and the information derived from samples, may not be used in the investigation of any offence or in evidence against the person who is, or would be, entitled to the destruction of the fingerprints, footwear impressions and samples, see *Note F2*.

D:3 The requirement to destroy fingerprints, footwear impressions and DNA samples, and information derived from samples, and restrictions on their retention and use in paragraph 1 do not apply if the person gives their written consent for their fingerprints, footwear impressions or sample to be retained and used after they have fulfilled the purpose for which they were taken, see *Note F1*.

D:4 When a person's fingerprints, footwear impressions or sample are to be destroyed:

(a) any copies of the fingerprints and footwear impressions must also be destroyed;

(b) the person may witness the destruction of their fingerprints, footwear impressions or copies if they ask to do so within five days of being informed destruction is required;

(c) access to relevant computer fingerprint data shall be made impossible as soon as it is practicable to do so and the person shall be given a certificate to this effect within three months of asking; and

(d) neither the fingerprints, footwear impressions, the sample, or any information derived from the sample, may be used in the investigation of any offence or in evidence against the person who is, or would be, entitled to its destruction.

D:5 Fingerprints, footwear impressions or samples, and the information derived from samples, taken in connection with the investigation of an offence which are not required to be destroyed, may be retained after they have fulfilled the purposes for which they were taken but may be used only for purposes related to the prevention or detection of crime, the investigation of an offence or the conduct of a prosecution in, as well as outside, the UK and may also be subject to a speculative search. This includes checking them against other fingerprints, footwear impressions and DNA records held by, or on behalf of, the police and other law enforcement authorities in, as well as outside, the UK.

(b) [*sic*] *Fingerprints taken in connection with Immigration Service enquiries*

D:6 See paragraph 4.10.

*Notes for guidance*

D:F1 *Fingerprints, footwear impressions and samples given voluntarily for the purposes of elimination play an important part in many police investigations. It is, therefore, important to make sure innocent volunteers are not deterred from participating and their consent to their fingerprints, footwear impressions and DNA being used for the purposes of a specific investigation is fully informed and voluntary. If the police or volunteer seek to have the fingerprints, footwear impressions or samples retained for use after the specific investigation ends, it is important the volunteer's consent to this is also fully informed and voluntary.*

*Examples of consent for:*

- *DNA/fingerprints/footwear impressions—to be used only for the purposes of a specific investigation;*
- *DNA/fingerprints/footwear impressions—to be used in the specific investigation and retained by the police for future use.*

*To minimise the risk of confusion, each consent should be physically separate and the volunteer should be asked to sign* **each consent**.

     (a) *DNA:*

        (i) *DNA sample taken for the purposes of elimination or as part of an intelligence-led screening and to be used only for the purposes of that investigation and destroyed afterwards:*

        "*I consent to my DNA/mouth swab being taken for forensic analysis. I understand that the sample will be destroyed at the end of the case and that my profile will only be compared to the crime stain profile from this enquiry. I have been advised that the person taking the sample may be required to give evidence and/or provide a written statement to the police in relation to the taking of it.*".

       (ii) *DNA sample to be retained on the National DNA database and used in the future:*

        "*I consent to my DNA sample and information derived from it being retained and used only for purposes related to the prevention and detection of a crime, the investigation of an offence or the conduct of a prosecution either nationally or internationally.*

        *I understand that this sample may be checked against other DNA records held by, or on behalf of, relevant law enforcement authorities, either nationally or internationally.*

        *I understand that once I have given my consent for the sample to be retained and used I cannot withdraw this consent.*".

     (b) *Fingerprints:*

        (i) *Fingerprints taken for the purposes of elimination or as part of an intelligence-led screening and to be used only for the purposes of that investigation and destroyed afterwards:*

        "*I consent to my fingerprints being taken for elimination purposes. I understand that the fingerprints will be destroyed at the end of the case and that my fingerprints will only be compared to the fingerprints from this enquiry. I have been advised that the person taking the fingerprints may be required to give evidence and/or provide a written statement to the police in relation to the taking of it.*".

       (ii) *Fingerprints to be retained for future use:*

        "*I consent to my fingerprints being retained and used only for purposes related to the prevention and detection of a crime, the investigation of an offence or the conduct of a prosecution either nationally or internationally.*

        *I understand that my fingerprints may be checked against other records held by, or on behalf of, relevant law enforcement authorities, either nationally or internationally.*

        *I understand that once I have given my consent for my fingerprints to be retained and used I cannot withdraw this consent.*".

     (c) *Footwear impressions:*

        (i) *Footwear impressions taken for the purposes of elimination or as part of an intelligence-led screening and to be used only for the purposes of that investigation and destroyed afterwards:*

        "*I consent to my footwear impressions being taken for elimination purposes. I understand that the footwear impressions will be destroyed at the end of the case and that my footwear impressions will only be compared to the footwear impressions from this enquiry. I have been advised that the person taking the footwear impressions may be required to give evidence and/or provide a writtens statement to the police in relation to the taking of it.*".

       (ii) *Footwear impressions to be retained for future use:*

        "*I consent to my footwear impressions being retained and used only for purposes related to the prevention and detection of a crime, the investigation of an offence or the conduct of a prosecution, either nationally or internationally.*

        *I understand that my footwear impressions may be checked against other records held by, or on behalf of, relevant law enforcement authorities, either nationally or internationally.*

        *I understand that once I have given my consent for my footwear impressions to be retained and used I cannot withdraw this consent.*".

**A-161**      D:F2 *The provisions for the retention of fingerprints, footwear impressions and samples in paragraph 1 allow for all fingerprints, footwear impressions and samples in a case to be available for any subsequent miscarriage of justice investigation.*

**ANNEX G**

**Requirement for a person to attend a police station for fingerprints and samples**

D:1 A requirement under Schedule 2A for a person to attend a police station to have fingerprints **A-161a**
or samples taken:

    (a) must give the person a period of at least seven days within which to attend the police station; and

    (b) may direct them to attend at a specified time of day or between specified times of day.

D:2 When specifying the period and times of attendance, the officer making the requirements must consider whether the fingerprints or samples could reasonably be taken at a time when the person is required to attend the police station for any other reason. See *Note G1*.

D:3 An officer of the rank of inspector or above may authorise a period shorter than 7 days if there is an urgent need for person's fingerprints or sample for the purposes of the investigation of an offence. The fact of the authorisation and the reasons for giving it must be recorded as soon as practicable.

D:4 The constable making a requirement and the person to whom it applies may agree to vary it so as to specify any period within which, or date or time at which, the person is to attend. However, variation shall not have effect for the purposes of enforcement, unless it is confirmed by the constable in writing.

*Notes for guidance*

D:G1 *The specified period within which the person is to attend need not fall within the period allowed (if applicable) for making the requirement.* **A-161b**

D:G2 *To justify the arrest without warrant of a person who fails to comply with a requirement, (see paragraph 4.4(b) above), the officer making the requirement, or confirming a variation, should be prepared to explain how, when and where the requirement was made or the variation was confirmed and what steps were taken to ensure the person understood what to do and the consequences of not complying with the requirement.*

## (6) Tape-recording of interviews

The text that follows is of the version of the code that came into force on October 27, 2013: see **A-162**
*ante*, Appendix A-1.

For further details of the application of the code, and as to commencement of the governing legislation, see § 15-174, *ante*.

### E. CODE OF PRACTICE ON AUDIO RECORDING INTERVIEWS WITH SUSPECTS

#### Commencement—transitional arrangements

This code applies to interviews carried out after 00.00 on 27 October 2013 notwithstanding that **A-162a**
the interview may have commenced before that time.

#### E:1 General

E:1.0 The procedures in this code must be used fairly, responsibly, with respect for the people to **A-163**
whom they apply and without unlawful discrimination. Under the Equality Act 2010, s.149, when police officers are carrying out their functions, they also have a duty to have due regard to the need to eliminate unlawful discrimination, harassment and victimisation, to advance equality of opportunity between people who share a relevant protected characteristic and people who do not share it, and to take steps to foster good relations between those persons. See *Note 1B*.

E:1.1 This code of practice must be readily available for consultation by:
- police officers;
- police staff;
- detained persons;
- members of the public.

E:1.2 The *Notes for Guidance* included are not provisions of this code.

E:1.3 Nothing in this code shall detract from the requirements of Code C, the code of practice for the detention, treatment and questioning of persons by police officers.

E:1.4 The interviews to which this code applies are described in section 3.

E:1.5 The term:
- "appropriate adult" has the same meaning as in Code C, para. 1.7, and in the case of a 17-year-old suspect, includes the person called to fulfil that role in accordance with paragraph 1.5A of Code C;

- "solicitor" has the same meaning as in Code C, para. 6.12;
- "interview" has the same meaning as in Code C, para. 11.1A.

E:1.5A Recording of interviews shall be carried out openly to instil confidence in its reliability as an impartial and accurate record of the interview.

**A-164**

E:1.6 In this code:

   (aa) "recording media" means any removable, physical audio recording medium (such as magnetic tape, optical disc or solid state memory) which can be played and copied;

   (a) "designated person" means a person other than a police officer, designated under the Police Reform Act 2002, Pt 4, who has specified powers and duties of police officers conferred or imposed on them;

   (b) any reference to a police officer includes a designated person acting in the exercise or performance of the powers and duties conferred or imposed on them by their designation; and

   (c) "secure digital network" is a computer network system which enables an original interview recording to be stored as a digital multi media file or a series of such files, on a secure file server which is accredited by the National Accreditor for Police Information Systems in accordance with the UK Government Protective Marking Scheme. (See section 7 of this code.).

E:1.7 Sections 2 to 6 of this code set out the procedures and requirements which apply to all interviews together with the provisions which apply only to interviews recorded using removable media. Section 7 sets out the provisions which apply to interviews recorded using a secure digital network and specifies the provisions in sections 2 to 6 which do not apply to secure digital network recording.

**A-165**

E:1.8 Nothing in this code prevents the custody officer, or other officer given custody of the detainee, from allowing police staff who are not designated persons to carry out individual procedures or tasks at the police station if the law allows. However, the officer remains responsible for making sure the procedures and tasks are carried out correctly in accordance with this code. Any such police staff must be:

   (a) a person employed by a police force and under the control and direction of the chief officer of that force; or

   (b) employed by a person with whom a police force has a contract for the provision of services relating to persons arrested or otherwise in custody.

E:1.9 Designated persons and other police staff must have regard to any relevant provisions of the codes of practice.

E:1.10 References to pocket book [*sic*] include any official report book issued to police officers or police staff.

E:1.11 References to a custody officer include those performing the functions of a custody officer as in paragraph 1.9 of Code C.

E:1.12 In the application of this code to the conduct and recording of an interview of a suspect who has not been arrested:

   (a) references to the "custody officer" include references to an officer of the rank of sergeant or above who is not directly involved in the investigation of the offence(s);

   (b) if the interview takes place elsewhere than at a police station, references to "interview room" include any place or location which the interviewer is satisfied will enable the interview to be conducted and recorded in accordance with this code and where the suspect is present voluntarily (see Note 1A); and

   (c) provisions in addition to those which expressly apply to these interviews shall be followed insofar as they are relevant and can be applied in practice.

*Notes for guidance*

E:1A *An interviewer who is not sure, or has any doubt, about the suitability of a place or location of an interview to be carried out elsewhere than at a police station, should consult an officer of the rank of sergeant or above for advice.*

E:1B *In paragraph 1.0, "relevant protected characteristic" includes: age, disability, gender reassignment, pregnancy and maternity, race, religion/belief, sex and sexual orientation.*

## E:2 Recording and sealing master recordings

E:2.1 [*Not used.*]

**A-166**

E:2.2 One recording, the master recording, will be sealed in the suspect's presence. A second recording will be used as a working copy. The master recording is any of the recordings made by a multi-deck/drive machine or the only recording made by a single deck/drive machine. The working copy is one of the other recordings made by a multi-deck/drive machine or a copy of the master recording made by a single deck/drive machine. (See *Note 2A*.)

[This paragraph does not apply to interviews recorded using a secure digital network, see paras 7.4 to 7.6.]

E:2.3 Nothing in this code requires the identity of officers or police staff conducting interviews to be recorded or disclosed:

  (a) [*not used*];
  (b) if the interviewer reasonably believes recording or disclosing their name might put them in danger.

In these cases interviewers should use warrant or other identification numbers and the name of their police station. Such instances and the reasons for them shall be recorded in the custody record or the interviewer's pocket book. See *Note 2C*.

### Notes for guidance

E:2A *The purpose of sealing the master recording before it leaves the suspect's presence is to establish their confidence that the integrity of the recording is preserved. If a single deck/drive machine is used the working copy of the master recording must be made in the suspect's presence and without the master recording leaving their sight. The working copy shall be used for making further copies if needed.*

**A-167**

E:2B [*Not used.*]

E:2C *The purpose of paragraph 2.3(b) is to protect those involved in serious organised crime investigations or arrests of particularly violent suspects when there is reliable information that those arrested or their associates may threaten or cause harm to those involved. In cases of doubt, an officer of inspector rank or above should be consulted.*

## E:3 Interviews to be audio recorded

E:3.1 Subject to paragraphs 3.3 and 3.4, audio recording shall be used for any interview:

**A-168**

  (a) with a person cautioned under Code C, section 10 in respect of any indictable offence, which includes any offence triable either way, except where that person has been arrested and the interview takes place elsewhere than at a police station in accordance with Code C, para. 11.1, for which a written record would be required (see *Note 3A*);
  (b) which takes place as a result of an interviewer exceptionally putting further questions to a suspect about an offence described in paragraph 3.1(a) after they have been charged with, or told they may be prosecuted for, that offence, see Code C, para. 16.5;
  (c) when an interviewer wants to tell a person, after they have been charged with, or informed they may be prosecuted for, an offence described in paragraph 3.1(a), about any written statement or interview with another person, see Code C, para. 16.4.

E:3.2 The Terrorism Act 2000 and the Counter-Terrorism Act 2008 make separate provisions for a code of practice for the video recording with sound of:

  • interviews of persons detained under section 41 of, or Schedule 7 to, the 2000 Act; and
  • post-charge questioning of persons authorised under section 22 or 23 of the 2008 Act.

The provisions of this code do not apply to such interviews. (See *Note 3C*.)

E:3.3 If the conditions in paragraph 3.3A are satisfied, authority not to audio record an interview to which paragraph 3.1 applies may be given by:

  (a) the custody officer in the case of a detained suspect, or
  (b) an officer of the rank of sergeant or above in the case of a suspect who has not been arrested and to whom paragraphs 3.21 and 3.22 of Code C (persons attending a police station or elsewhere voluntarily) apply.

E:3.3A The conditions referred to in paragraph 3.3 are:

  (a) it is not reasonably practicable to audio record, or as the case may be, continue to audio record, the interview because of equipment failure or the unavailability of a suitable interview room or recording equipment; and
  (b) the authorising officer considers, on reasonable grounds, that the interview or continuation of the interview should not be delayed until the failure has been rectified or until a suitable room or recording equipment becomes available.

In these cases:

- the interview must be recorded or continue to be recorded in writing in accordance with Code C, section 11; and
- the authorising officer shall record the specific reasons for not audio recording and the interviewer is responsible for ensuring that the written interview record shows the date and time of the authority, the authorising officer and where the authority is recorded. (See *Note 3B*.)

E:3.4 If a detainee refuses to go into or remain in a suitable interview room, see Code C, paragraph 12.5, and the custody officer considers, on reasonable grounds, that the interview should not be delayed the interview may, at the custody officer's discretion, be conducted in a cell using portable recording equipment or, if none is available, recorded in writing as in Code C, section 11. The reasons for this shall be recorded.

E:3.5 The whole of each interview shall be audio recorded, including the taking and reading back of any statement.

E:3.6 A sign or indicator which is visible to the suspect must show when the recording equipment is recording.

### Notes for guidance

E:3A *Nothing in this code is intended to preclude audio recording at police discretion of interviews at police stations or elsewhere with people cautioned in respect of offences not covered by paragraph 3.1, or responses made by persons after they have been charged with, or told they may be prosecuted for, an offence, provided this code is complied with.*

E:3B *A decision not to audio record an interview for any reason may be the subject of comment in court. The authorising officer should be prepared to justify that decision.*

E:3C *If, during the course of an interview under this code, it becomes apparent that the interview should be conducted under the terrorism code for the video recording with sound of interviews, the interview should only continue in accordance with that code.*

E:3D *Attention is drawn to the provisions set out in Code C about the matters to be considered when deciding whether a detained person is fit to be interviewed.*

E:3E *Code C sets out the circumstances in which a suspect may be questioned about an offence after being charged with it.*

E:3F *Code C sets out the procedures to be followed when a person's attention is drawn after charge, to a statement made by another person. One method of bringing the content of an interview with another person to the notice of a suspect may be to play them a recording of that interview.*

### E:4 The interview

#### (a) *General*

E:4.1 The provisions of Code C:
- sections 10 and 11, and the applicable *Notes for Guidance* apply to the conduct of interviews to which this code applies;
- paragraphs 11.7 to 11.14 apply only when a written record is needed.

E:4.2 Code C, paragraphs 10.10, 10.11 and Annex C describe the restriction on drawing adverse inferences from an arrested suspect's failure or refusal to say anything about their involvement in the offence when interviewed or after being charged or informed they may be prosecuted, and how it affects the terms of the caution and determines if and by whom a special warning under sections 36 and 37 of the Criminal Justice and Public Order Act 1994 can be given.

#### (b) *Commencement of interviews*

E:4.3 When the suspect is brought into the interview room the interviewer shall, without delay but in the suspect's sight, load the recorder with new recording media and set it to record. The recording media must be unwrapped or opened in the suspect's presence.

[This paragraph does not apply to interviews recorded using a secure digital network, see paras 7.4 and 7.5.]

E:4.4 The interviewer should tell the suspect about the recording process and point out the sign or indicator which shows that the recording equipment is activated and recording. See paragraph 3.6. The interviewer shall:
- (a) explain that the interview is being audibly recorded;
- (b) subject to paragraph 2.3, give their name and rank and that of any other interviewer present;
- (c) ask the suspect and any other party present, *e.g.* the appropriate adult, a solicitor or interpreter, to identify themselves;

(d) state the date, time of commencement and place of the interview; and

(e) state the suspect will be given a notice about what will happen to the recording. [This sub-paragraph does not apply to interviews recorded using a secure digital network, see paras 7.4 and 7.6 to 7.7.]

See *Note 4A*.

E:4.4A Any person entering the interview room after the interview has commenced shall be invited by the interviewer to identify themselves for the purpose of the audio recording and state the reason why they have entered the interview room.

E:4.5 The interviewer shall:

- caution the suspect, see Code C, section 10; and
- if they are detained, remind them of their entitlement to free legal advice, see Code C, para. 11.2; or
- if they are not detained under arrest, explain this and their entitlement to free legal advice, see Code C, para. 3.21.

E:4.6 The interviewer shall put to the suspect any significant statement or silence, see Code C, paragraph 11.4.

### (c) *Interviews with suspects who appear to have a hearing impediment*

E:4.7 If the suspect appears to have a hearing impediment, the interviewer shall make a written note of the interview in accordance with Code C, at the same time as audio recording it in accordance with this code. (See *Notes 4B* and *4C*.) **A-171**

### (d) *Objections and complaints by the suspect*

E:4.8 If the suspect or an appropriate adult on their behalf objects to the interview being audibly recorded either at the outset, during the interview or during a break, the interviewer shall explain that the interview is being audibly recorded and that this code requires the objections to be recorded on the audio recording. When any objections have been audibly recorded or the suspect or appropriate adult have refused to have their objections recorded, the interviewer shall say they are turning off the recorder, give their reasons and turn it off. The interviewer shall then make a written record of the interview as in Code C, section 11. If, however, the interviewer reasonably considers they may proceed to question the suspect with the audio recording still on, the interviewer may do so. This procedure also applies in cases where the suspect has previously objected to the interview being visually recorded, see Code F, para. 4.8, and the investigating officer has decided to audibly record the interview. (See *Note 4D*.)

E:4.9 If in the course of an interview a complaint is made by or on behalf of the person being questioned concerning the provisions of this or any other codes, or it comes to the interviewer's notice that the person may have been treated improperly, the interviewer shall act as in Code C, para. 12.9. (See *Notes 4E* and *4F*.)

E:4.10 If the suspect indicates they want to tell the interviewer about matters not directly connected with the offence of which they are suspected and they are unwilling for these matters to be audio recorded, the suspect should be given the opportunity to tell the interviewer about these matter [*sic*] after the conclusion of the formal interview.

### (e) *Changing recording media*

E:4.11 When the recorder shows the recording media only has a short time left to run, the interviewer shall so inform the person being interviewed and round off that part of the interview. If the interviewer leaves the room for a second set of recording media, the suspect shall not be left unattended. The interviewer will remove the recording media from the recorder and insert the new recording media which shall be unwrapped or opened in the suspect's presence. The recorder should be set to record on the new media. To avoid confusion between the recording media, the interviewer shall mark the media with an identification number immediately after it is removed from the recorder.

[This paragraph does not apply to interviews recorded using a secure digital network as this does not use removable media, see paras 1.6(c), 7.4 and 7.14 to 7.15.]

### (f) *Taking a break during interview*

E:4.12 When a break is taken, the fact that a break is to be taken, the reason for it and the time shall be recorded on the audio recording. **A-172**

E:4.12A When the break is taken and the interview room vacated by the suspect, the recording media shall be removed from the recorder and the procedures for the conclusion of an interview followed, see paragraph 4.18.

E:4.13 When a break is a short one and both the suspect and an interviewer remain in the interview room, the recording may be stopped. There is no need to remove the recording media and when the interview recommences the recording should continue on the same recording media. The time the interview recommences shall be recorded on the audio recording.

E:4.14 After any break in the interview the interviewer must, before resuming the interview, remind the person being questioned of their right to legal advice if they have not exercised it and that they remain under caution or, if there is any doubt, give the caution in full again. (See *Note 4G*.)

[Paragraphs 4.12 to 4.14 do not apply to interviews recorded using a secure digital network, see paras 7.4 and 7.8 to 7.10.]

### (g) *Failure of recording equipment*

E:4.15 If there is an equipment failure which can be rectified quickly, *e.g.* by inserting new recording media, the interviewer shall follow the appropriate procedures as in paragraph 4.11. When the recording is resumed the interviewer shall explain what happened and record the time the interview recommences. If, however, it will not be possible to continue recording on that recorder and no replacement recorder is readily available, the interview may continue without being audibly recorded. If this happens, the interviewer shall seek the authority as in paragraph 3.3 of the custody officer, or as applicable, a sergeant or above. (See *Note 4H*.)

[This paragraph does not apply to interviews recorded using a secure digital network, see paras 7.4 and 7.11.]

### (h) *Removing recording media from the recorder*

E:4.16 Recording media which is removed from the recorder during the interview shall be retained and the procedures in paragraph 4.18 followed.

[This paragraph does not apply to interviews recorded using a secure digital network as this does not use removable media, see 1.6(c), 7.4 and 7.14 to 7.15.]

### (i) *Conclusion of interview*

E:4.17 At the conclusion of the interview, the suspect shall be offered the opportunity to clarify anything they have said and asked if there is anything they want to add.

E:4.18 At the conclusion of the interview, including the taking and reading back of any written statement, the time shall be recorded and the recording shall be stopped. The interviewer shall seal the master recording with a master recording label and treat it as an exhibit in accordance with force standing orders. The interviewer shall sign the label and ask the suspect and any third party present during the interview to sign it. If the suspect or third party refuse to sign the label an officer of at least the rank of inspector, or if not available the custody officer, or if the suspect has not been arrested, a sergeant, shall be called into the interview room and asked, subject to paragraph 2.3, to sign it.

E:4.19 The suspect shall be handed a notice which explains:
* how the audio recording will be used;
* the arrangements for access to it;
* that if they are charged or informed they will be prosecuted, a copy of the audio recording will be supplied as soon as practicable or as otherwise agreed between the suspect and the police or on the order of the court.

[Paragraphs 4.17 to 4.19 do not apply to interviews recorded using a secure digital network, see paras 7.4 and 7.12 to 7.13.]

### *Notes for guidance*

**A-173**  E:4A *For the purpose of voice identification the interviewer should ask the suspect and any other people present to identify themselves.*

E:4B *This provision is to give a person who is deaf or has impaired hearing equivalent rights of access to the full interview record as far as this is possible using audio recording.*

E:4C *The provisions of Code C on interpreters for suspects who do not appear to speak or understand English, or who appear to have a hearing or speech impediment, continue to apply.*

E:4D *The interviewer should remember that a decision to continue recording against the wishes of the suspect may be the subject of comment in court.*

E:4E *If the custody officer, or in the case of a person who has not been arrested, a sergeant, is called to deal with the complaint, the recorder should, if possible, be left on until the officer has entered the room and spoken to the person being interviewed. Continuation or termination of the interview should be at the interviewer's discretion pending action by an inspector under Code C, paragraph 9.2.*

**E:4F** *If the complaint is about a matter not connected with this code or Code C, the decision to continue is at* **A-174**
*the interviewer's discretion. When the interviewer decides to continue the interview, they shall tell the suspect that*
*at the conclusion of the interview, the complaint will be brought to the attention of the custody officer, or in the*
*case of a person who has not been arrested, a sergeant. When the interview is concluded the interviewer must, as*
*soon as practicable, inform the custody officer or, as the case may be, the sergeant, about the existence and nature*
*of the complaint made.*

**E:4G** *In considering whether to caution again after a break, the interviewer should bear in mind that they may*
*have to satisfy a court that the person understood that they were still under caution when the interview resumed.*
*The interviewer should also remember that it may be necessary to show to the court that nothing occurred during a*
*break or between interviews which influenced the suspect's recorded evidence. After a break or at the beginning of*
*a subsequent interview, the interviewer should consider summarising on the record the reason for the break and*
*confirming this with the suspect.*

**E:4H** *Where the interview is being recorded and the media or the recording equipment fails, the interviewer*
*should stop the interview immediately. Where part of the interview is unaffected by the error and is still accessible*
*on the media, that part shall be copied and sealed in the suspect's presence as a master copy and the interview*
*recommenced using new equipment/media as required. Where the content of the interview has been lost in its*
*entirety, the media should be sealed in the suspect's presence and the interview begun again. If the recording*
*equipment cannot be fixed or no replacement is immediately available, the interview should be recorded in accord-*
*ance with Code C, section 11.*

### E:5 After the interview

**E:5.1** The interviewer shall make a note in their pocket book that the interview has taken place **A-175**
and that it was audibly recorded, the time it commenced, its duration and date and identification
number of the master recording.

**E:5.2** If no proceedings follow in respect of the person whose interview was recorded, the recording media must be kept securely as in paragraph 6.1 and *Note 6A.*

[This section (paras 5.1, 5.2 and Note 5A) does not apply to interviews recorded using a secure
digital network, see paras 7.4 and 7.14 to 7.15.]

*Note for guidance*

**E:5A** *Any written record of an audio recorded interview should be made in accordance with current national* **A-176**
*guidelines for police officers, police staff and CPS prosecutors concerned with the preparation, processing and*
*submission of prosecution files.*

### E:6 Master recording security

(a) *General*

**E:6.1** The officer in charge of each police station at which interviews with suspects are recorded or **A-177**
as the case may be, where recordings of interviews carried out elsewhere than at a police station are
held, shall make arrangements for master recordings to be kept securely and their movements accounted for on the same basis as material which may be used for evidential purposes, in accordance
with force standing orders. (See *Note 6A.*)

(b) *Breaking master recording seal for criminal proceedings*

**E:6.2** A police officer has no authority to break the seal on a master recording which is required
for criminal trial or appeal proceedings. If it is necessary to gain access to the master recording, the
police officer shall arrange for its seal to be broken in the presence of a representative of the Crown
Prosecution Service. The defendant or their legal adviser should be informed and given a reasonable
opportunity to be present. If the defendant or their legal representative is present they shall be
invited to re-seal and sign the master recording. If either refuses or neither is present this should be
done by the representative of the Crown Prosecution Service. (See *Notes 6B* and *6C.*)

(c) *Breaking master recording seal: other cases*

**E:6.3** The chief officer of police is responsible for establishing arrangements for breaking the seal
of the master copy where no criminal proceedings result, or the criminal proceedings to which the
interview relates have been concluded and it becomes necessary to break the seal. These arrangements should be those which the chief officer considers are reasonably necessary to demonstrate to
the person interviewed and any other party who may wish to use or refer to the interview record
that the master copy has not been tampered with and that the interview record remains accurate.
(See *Note 6D.*)

**E:6.3A** Subject to paragraph 6.3C, a representative of each party must be given a reasonable opportunity to be present when the seal is broken and the master recording copied and resealed.

E:6.3B If one or more of the parties is not present when the master copy seal is broken because they cannot be contacted or refuse to attend or paragraph 6.6 applies, arrangements should be made for an independent person such as a custody visitor, to be present. Alternatively, or as an additional safeguard, arrangement should be made for a film or photographs to be taken of the procedure.

E:6.3C Paragraph 6.3A does not require a person to be given an opportunity to be present when:

(a) it is necessary to break the master copy seal for the proper and effective further investigation of the original offence or the investigation of some other offence; and

(b) the officer in charge of the investigation has reasonable grounds to suspect that allowing an opportunity might prejudice any such an investigation or criminal proceedings which may be brought as a result or endanger any person. (See *Note 6E*.)

(d) *Documentation*

E:6.4 When the master recording seal is broken, a record must be made of the procedure followed, including the date, time, place and persons present.

[This section (paras 6.1 to 6.4 and *Notes 6A* to *6E*) does not apply to interviews recorded using a secure digital network, see paras 7.4 and 7.14 to 7.15.]

*Notes for guidance*

A-178
E:6A *This section is concerned with the security of the master recording sealed at the conclusion of the interview. Care must be taken of working recordings because their loss or destruction may lead unnecessarily to the need to access master recordings.*

E:6B *If the master recording has been delivered to the Crown Court for their keeping after committal for trial the crown prosecutor will apply to the chief clerk of the Crown Court centre for the release of the recording for unsealing by the crown prosecutor.*

A-179
E:6C *Reference to the Crown Prosecution Service or to the crown prosecutor in this part of the code should be taken to include any other body or person with a statutory responsibility for the proceedings for which the police recorded interview is required.*

E:6D *The most common reasons for needing access to master copies that are not required for criminal proceedings arise from civil actions and complaints against police and civil actions between individuals arising out of allegations of crime investigated by police.*

E:6E *Paragraph 6.3C could apply, for example, when one or more of the outcomes or likely outcomes of the investigation might be: (i) the prosecution of one or more of the original suspects; (ii) the prosecution of someone previously not suspected, including someone who was originally a witness; and (iii) any original suspect being treated as a prosecution witness and when premature disclosure of any police action, particularly through contact with any parties involved, could lead to a real risk of compromising the investigation and endangering witnesses.*

### E:7 Recording of interviews by secure digital network

A-179a
E:7.1 A secure digital network does not use removable media and this section specifies the provisions which will apply when a secure digital network is used.

E:7.2 [*Not used.*]

E:7.3 The following requirements are solely applicable to the use of a secure digital network for the recording of interviews.

(a) *Application of sections 1 to 6 of Code E*

A-179b
E:7.4 Sections 1 to 6 of CodeE above apply except for the following paragraphs:

• paragraph 2.2 under "Recording and sealing of master recordings";
• paragraph 4.3 under "(b) Commencement of interviews";
• paragraph 4.4 (e) under "(b) Commencement of interviews";
• paragraphs 4.11 to 4.19 under "(e) Changing recording media", "(f) Taking a break during interview", "(g) Failure of recording equipment", "(h) Removing recording media from the recorder" and (i) "Conclusion of the interview"; and
• paragraphs 6.1 to 6.4 and *Notes 6A* to *6C* under "Media security".

(b) *Commencement of interviews*

A-179c
E:7.5 When the suspect is brought into the interview room, the interviewer shall without delay and in the sight of the suspect, switch on the recording equipment and enter the information necessary to log on to the secure network and start recording.

E:7.6 The interviewer must then provide inform the suspect that the interview is being recorded using a secure digital network and that recording has commenced.

E:7.7 In addition to the requirements of paragraph 4.4(a) to (d) above, the interviewer must inform the person that:

- they will be given access to the recording of the interview in the event that they are charged or informed that they will be prosecuted but if they are not charged or informed that they will be prosecuted they will only be given access as agreed with the police or on the order of a court; and
- they will be given a written notice at the end of the interview setting out their rights to access the recording and what will happen to the recording.

### (c) *Taking a break during interview*

E:7.8 When a break is taken, the fact that a break is to be taken, the reason for it and the time shall be recorded on the audio recording. The recording shall be stopped and the procedures in paragraphs 7.12 and 7.13 for the conclusion of an interview followed. **A-179d**

E:7.9 When the interview recommences the procedures in paragraphs 7.5 to 7.7 for commencing an interview shall be followed to create a new file to record the continuation of the interview. The time the interview recommences shall be recorded on the audio recording.

E:7.10 After any break in the interview the interviewer must, before resuming the interview, remind the person being questioned that they remain under caution or, if there is any doubt, give the caution in full again. (See *Note 4G*.)

### (d) *Failure of recording equipment*

E:7.11 If there is an equipment failure which can be rectified quickly, *e.g.* by commencing a new secure digital network recording, the interviewer shall follow the appropriate procedures as in paragraphs 7.8 to 7.10. When the recording is resumed the interviewer shall explain what happened and record the time the interview recommences. If, however, it is not possible to continue recording on the secure digital network the interview should be recorded on removable media as in paragraph 4.3 unless the necessary equipment is not available. If this happens the interview may continue without being audibly recorded and the interviewer shall seek the authority of the custody officer or a sergeant as in paragraph 3.3(a) or (b). (See *Note 4H*.) **A-179e**

### (e) *Conclusion of interview*

E:7.12 At the conclusion of the interview, the suspect shall be offered the opportunity to clarify anything he or she has said and asked if there is anything they want to add. **A-179f**

E:7.13 At the conclusion of the interview, including the taking and reading back of any written statement:

(a) the time shall be orally recorded;

(b) the suspect shall be handed a notice (see *Note 7A*) which explains:

- how the audio recording will be used,
- the arrangements for access to it,
- that if they are charged or informed that they will be prosecuted, they will be given access to the recording of the interview either electronically or by being given a copy on removable recording media, but if they are not charged or informed that they will prosecuted, they will only be given access as agreed with the police or on the order of a court;

(c) the suspect must be asked to confirm that he or she has received a copy of the notice at sub-paragraph (b) above; if the suspect fails to accept or to acknowledge receipt of the notice, the interviewer will state for the recording that a copy of the notice has been provided to the suspect and that he or she has refused to take a copy of the notice or has refused to acknowledge receipt;

(d) the time shall be recorded and the interviewer shall notify the suspect that the recording is being saved to the secure network. The interviewer must save the recording in the presence of the suspect. The suspect should then be informed that the interview is terminated.

### (f) *After the interview*

E:7.14 The interviewer shall make a note in their pocket book that the interview has taken place and that it was audibly recorded, the time it commenced, its duration and date and the identification number of the original recording.

E:7.15 If no proceedings follow in respect of the person whose interview was recorded, the recordings must be kept securely as in paragraphs 7.16 and 7.17. (See *Note 5A*.)

(g) *Security of secure digital network interview records*

E:7.16 Interview record files are stored in read only format on non-removable storage devices, for example, hard disk drives, to ensure their integrity. The recordings are first saved locally to a secure non-removable device before being transferred to the remote network device. If for any reason the network connection fails, the recording remains on the local device and will be transferred when the network connections are restored.

E:7.17 Access to interview recordings, including copying to removable media, must be strictly controlled and monitored to ensure that access is restricted to those who have been given specific permission to access for specified purposes when this is necessary. For example, police officers and CPS lawyers involved in the preparation of any prosecution case, persons interviewed if they have been charged or informed they may be prosecuted and their legal representatives.

*Note for guidance*

**A-179g**    E:7A *The notice at paragraph 7.13 above should provide a brief explanation of the secure digital network and how access is strictly limited to the recording. The notice should also explain the access rights of the suspect, his or her legal representative, the police and the prosecutor to the recording of the interview. Space should be provided on the form to insert the date and the file reference number for the interview.*

## (7) Visual recording of interviews

**A-180**    The text that follows is of the version of the code that came into force on October 27, 2013: see *ante*, Appendix A-1.

As at July 7, 2014, there was no requirement on any police force to make visual recordings of interviews, but police officers who choose to make such recordings will still be required to have regard to the provisions of this code.

### F. CODE OF PRACTICE ON VISUAL RECORDINGS WITH SOUND OF INTERVIEWS WITH SUSPECTS

#### Commencement—transitional arrangements

**A-180a**    The contents of this code should be considered if an interviewer decides to make a visual recording with sound of an interview with a suspect after 00.00 on 27 October 2013. There is no statutory requirement under *PACE* to visually record interviews.

#### F:1 General

**A-181**    F:1.0 The procedures in this code must be used fairly, responsibly, with respect for the people to whom they apply and without unlawful discrimination. Under the Equality Act 2010, section 149, when police officers are carrying out their functions, they also have a duty to have due regard to the need to eliminate unlawful discrimination, harassment and victimisation, to advance equality of opportunity between people who share a relevant protected characteristic and people who do not share it, and to take steps to foster good relations between those persons. [See *Note 1C*.]

F:1.1 This code of practice must be readily available for consultation by police officers and other police staff, detained persons and members of the public.

F:1.2 The notes for guidance included are not provisions of this code. They form guidance to police officers and others about its application and interpretation.

F:1.3 Nothing in this code shall be taken as detracting in any way from the requirements of the Code of Practice for the Detention, Treatment and Questioning of Persons by Police Officers (Code C). [See *Note 1A*.]

F:1.4 The interviews to which this code applies are described in section 3.

F:1.5 In this code, the term "appropriate adult", "solicitor" and "interview" have the same meaning as those set out in Code C and in the case of a 17-year-old suspect, "appropriate adult" includes the person called to fulfil that role in accordance with paragraph 1.5A of Code C. The corresponding provisions and *Notes for Guidance* in Code C applicable to those terms shall also apply where appropriate.

F:1.5A The visual recording of interviews shall be carried out openly to instil confidence in its reliability as an impartial and accurate record of the interview.

F:1.6 Any reference in this code to visual recording shall be taken to mean visual recording with sound and in this code:

    (aa) "recording media" means any removable, physical audio recording medium (such as magnetic tape, optical disc or solid state memory) which can be played and copied;

(a) "designated person" means a person other than a police officer, designated under the Police Reform Act 2002, Pt 4, who has specified powers and duties of police officers conferred or imposed on them;

(b) any reference to a police officer includes a designated person acting in the exercise or performance of the powers and duties conferred or imposed on them by their designation;

(c) "secure digital network" is a computer network system which enables an original interview recording to be stored as a digital multi media file or a series of such files, on a secure file server which is accredited by the National Accreditor for Police Information Systems in accordance with the UK Government Protective Marking Scheme. See paragraph 1.6A and section 7 of this code.

F:1.6A Section 7 below sets out the provisions which apply to interviews visually recorded using a secure digital network by reference to Code E and by excluding provisions of sections 1 to 6 of this code which relate or apply only to removable media.

F:1.7 References to "pocket book" in this code include any official report book issued to police officers.

F:1.8 In the application of this code to the conduct and visual recording of an interview of a suspect who has not been arrested:

(a) references to the "custody officer" include references to an officer of the rank of sergeant or above who is not directly involved in the investigation of the offence(s);

(b) if the interview takes place elsewhere than at a police station, references to "interview room" include any place or location which the interviewer is satisfied will enable the interview to be conducted and recorded in accordance with this code and where the suspect is present voluntarily [see *Note 1B*]; and

(c) provisions in addition to those which expressly apply to these interviews shall be followed insofar as they are relevant and can be applied in practice.

*Notes for guidance*

F:1A *As in paragraph 1.9 of Code C, references to custody officers include those carrying out the functions of a custody officer.*

F:1B *An interviewer who is not sure, or has any doubt, about the suitability of a place or location of an interview to be carried out elsewhere than at a police station, should consult an officer of the rank of sergeant or above for advice.*

F:1C *In paragraph 1.0, "relevant protected characteristic" includes: age, disability, gender reassignment, pregnancy and maternity, race, religion/belief, sex and sexual orientation.*

### F:2 Recording and sealing of master recordings

F:2.1 [*Not used.*]                                                                                    **A-182**

F:2.2 The camera(s) shall be placed in the interview room so as to ensure coverage of as much of the room as is practicably possible whilst the interviews are taking place. [See *Note 2A*.]

F:2.3 When the recording medium is placed in the recorder and it is switched on to record, the correct date and time, in hours, minutes and seconds will be superimposed automatically, second by second, during the whole recording, see *Note 2B*. See section 7 regarding the use of a secure digital network to record the interview.

F:2.4 One recording, referred to in this code as the master recording copy, will be sealed before it leaves the presence of the suspect. A second recording will be used as a working copy. [See *Notes 2C* and *2D*.]

F:2.5 Nothing in this code requires the identity of an officer or police staff to be recorded or disclosed:

(a) [*not used*];

(b) if the interviewer reasonably believes that recording or disclosing their name might put them in danger.

In these cases, the interviewer will have their back to the camera and shall use their warrant or other identification number and the name of the police station to which they are attached. Such instances and the reasons for them shall be recorded in the custody record or the interviewer's pocket book. [See *Note 2E*.]

**A-183**       F:2A *Interviewers will wish to arrange that, as far as possible, visual recording arrangements are unobtrusive. It must be clear to the suspect, however, that there is no opportunity to interfere with the recording equipment or the recording media.*

F:2B *In this context, the recording medium should be capable of having an image of the date and time superimposed as the interview is recorded.*

F:2C *The purpose of sealing the master recording before it leaves the presence of the suspect is to establish their confidence that the integrity of the recording is preserved.*

F:2D *The visual recording of the interview may be used for identification procedures in accordance with paragraph 3.21 or Annex E of Code D.*

F:2E *The purpose of the [sic] paragraph 2.5(b) is to protect police officers and others involved in the investigation of serious organised crime or the arrest of particularly violent suspects when there is reliable information that those arrested or their associates may threaten or cause harm to the officers, their families or their personal property. In cases of doubt, an officer of inspector rank should be consulted.*

### F:3 Interviews to be visually recorded

**A-184**       F:3.1 Subject to paragraph 3.2 below, when an interviewer is deciding whether to make a visual recording, these are the areas where it might be appropriate:

(a) with a suspect in respect of an indictable offence (including an offence triable either way) [see *Notes 3A* and *3B*];

(b) which takes place as a result of an interviewer exceptionally putting further questions to a suspect about an offence described in sub-paragraph (a) above after they have been charged with, or informed they may be prosecuted for, that offence [see *Note 3C*];

(c) in which an interviewer wishes to bring to the notice of a person, after that person has been charged with, or informed they may be prosecuted for an offence described in subparagraph (a) above, any written statement made by another person, or the content of an interview with another person [see *Note 3D*];

(d) with, or in the presence of, a deaf or deaf/blind or speech impaired person who uses sign language to communicate;

(e) with, or in the presence of anyone who requires an "appropriate adult"; or

(f) in any case where the suspect or their representative requests that the interview be recorded visually.

**A-185**       F:3.2 The Terrorism Act 2000 and the Counter-Terrorism Act 2008 make separate provisions for a code of practice for the video recording with sound of:

• interviews of persons detained under section 41 of, or Schedule 7 to, the 2000 Act; and

• post-charge questioning of persons authorised under section 22 or 23 of the 2008 Act.

The provisions of this code do not therefore apply to such interviews. [See *Note 3E*.]

F:3.3 Following a decision by an interviewer to visually record any interview mentioned in paragraph 3.1 above, the custody officer in the case of a detained person, or a sergeant in the case of a suspect who has not been arrested, may authorise the interviewer not to make a visual record and for the purpose of this code (F), the provisions of Code E, paras 3.1, 3.2, 3.3, 3.3A and 3.4 shall apply as appropriate. However, authority not to make a visual recording does not detract in any way from the requirement for audio recording. This would require a further authorisation not to make in accordance with Code E. [See *Note 3F*.]

F:3.4 [*Not used.*]

F:3.5 The whole of each interview shall be recorded visually, including the taking and reading back of any statement.

F:3.6 A sign or indicator which is visible to the suspect must show when the visual recording equipment is recording.

**A-186**       F:3A *Nothing in the code is intended to preclude visual recording at police discretion of interviews at police stations or elsewhere with people cautioned in respect of offences not covered by paragraph 3.1, or responses made by persons after they have been charged with or informed they may be prosecuted for, an offence, provided that this code is complied with.*

F:3B *Attention is drawn to the provisions set out in Code C about the matters to be considered when deciding whether a detained person is fit to be interviewed.*

F:3C *Code C sets out the circumstances in which a suspect may be questioned about an offence after being charged with it.*

F:3D *Code C sets out the procedures to be followed when a person's attention is drawn after charge, to a state-*

*ment made by another person. One method of bringing the content of an interview with another person to the notice of a suspect may be to play them a recording of that interview.*

F:3E *If during the course of an interview under this code, it becomes apparent that the interview should be conducted under the terrorism code for the video recording with sound of interviews, the interview should only continue in accordance with that code.*

F:3F *A decision not to record an interview visually for any reason may be the subject of comment in court. The authorising officer should therefore be prepared to justify their decision in each case.*

### F:4  The interview

#### (a) *General*

F:4.1 The provisions of Code C in relation to cautions and interviews and the Notes for Guidance   **A-187**
applicable to those provisions shall apply to the conduct of interviews to which this code applies.

F:4.2 Particular attention is drawn to those parts of Code C that describe the restrictions on drawing adverse inferences from an arrested suspect's failure or refusal to say anything about their involvement in the offence when interviewed, or after being charged or informed they may be prosecuted and how those restrictions affect the terms of the caution and determine whether a special warning under sections 36 and 37 of the Criminal Justice and Public Order Act 1994 can be given.

#### (b) *Commencement of interviews*

F:4.3 When the suspect is brought into the interview room the interviewer shall without delay, but   **A-188**
in sight of the suspect, load the recording equipment and set it to record. The recording media must be unwrapped or otherwise opened in the presence of the suspect. [See *Note 4A*.]

F:4.4 The interviewer shall then tell the suspect formally about the visual recording and point out the sign or indicator which shows that the recording equipment is activated and recording. See paragraph 3.6. The interviewer shall:

    (a) explain that the interview is being visually recorded;

    (b) subject to paragraph 2.5, give their name and rank, and that of any other interviewer present;

    (c) ask the suspect and any other party present (*e.g.* the appropriate adult, a solicitor or interpreter) to identify themselves;

    (d) state the date, time of commencement and place of the interview; and

    (e) state that the suspect will be given a notice about what will happen to the recording.

[See *Note 4AA*.]

F:4.4A Any person entering the interview room after the interview has commenced shall be invited by the interviewer to identify themselves for the purpose of the recording and state the reason why they have entered the interview room.

F:4.5 The interviewer shall then caution the suspect, see Code C, section 10, and:

    • if they are detained, remind them of their entitlement to free legal advice, see Code C, para. 11.2, or

    • if they are not detained under arrest, explain this and their entitlement to free legal advice, see Code C, para. 3.21.

F:4.6 The interviewer shall then put to the suspect any significant statement or silence, see Code C, para. 11.4.

#### (c) *Interviews with suspects who appear to require an interpreter*

F:4.7 The provisions of Code C on interpreters for suspects who do not appear to speak or   **A-189**
understand English, or who appear to have a hearing or speech impediment, continue to apply.

#### (d) *Objections and complaints by the suspect*

F:4.8 If the suspect or an appropriate adult on their behalf, objects to the interview being visually   **A-190**
recorded either at the outset or during the interview or during a break in the interview, the interviewer shall explain that the interview is being visually recorded and that this code requires the objections to be recorded on the visual recording. When any objections have been recorded or the suspect or the appropriate adult have refused to have their objections recorded, the interviewer shall say that they are turning off the visual recording, give their reasons and turn it off. If a separate audio recording is being maintained, the interviewer shall ask the person to record the reasons for refusing to agree to the interview being visually recorded. Paragraph 4.8 of Code E will apply if the person also objects to the interview being audio recorded. If the interviewer reasonably considers

they may proceed to question the suspect with the visual recording still on, the interviewer may do so. [See *Note 4G.*]

F:4.9 If in the course of an interview a complaint is made by the person being questioned, or on their behalf, concerning the provisions of this or any other code, or it comes to the interviewer's notice that the person may have been treated improperly, then the interviewer shall act as in Code C, para. 12.9. [See *Notes 4B* and *4C.*]

F:4.10 If the suspect indicates that they wish to tell the interviewer about matters not directly connected with the offence of which they are suspected and that they are unwilling for these matters to be visually recorded, the suspect should be given the opportunity to tell the interviewer about these matters after the conclusion of the formal interview.

### (e) *Changing the recording media*

A-191

F:4.11 In instances where the recording medium is not of sufficient length to record all of the interview with the suspect, further certified recording medium will be used. When the recording equipment indicates that the recording medium has only a short time left to run, the interviewer shall advise the suspect and round off that part of the interview. If the interviewer wishes to continue the interview but does not already have further certified recording media with him, they shall obtain a set. The suspect should not be left unattended in the interview room. The interviewer will remove the recording media from the recording equipment and insert the new ones which have been unwrapped or otherwise opened in the suspect's presence. The recording equipment shall then be set to record. Care must be taken, particularly when a number of sets of recording media have been used, to ensure that there is no confusion between them. This could be achieved by marking the sets of recording media with consecutive identification numbers.

### (f) *Taking a break during the interview*

A-192

F:4.12 When a break is taken, the fact that a break is to be taken, the reason for it and the time shall be recorded on the visual record.

F:4.12A When the break is taken and the interview room vacated by the suspect, the recording media shall be removed from the recorder and the procedures for the conclusion of an interview followed. (See para. 4.18.)

F:4.13 When a break is a short one and both the suspect and an interviewer remain in the interview room, the recording may be stopped. There is no need to remove the recording media and when the interview recommences the recording should continue on the same recording media. The time at which the interview recommences shall be recorded.

F:4.14 After any break in the interview the interviewer must, before resuming the interview, remind the person being questioned of their right to legal advice if they have not exercised it and that they remain under caution or, if there is any doubt, give the caution in full again. [See *Notes 4D* and *4E.*]

### (g) *Failure of recording equipment*

A-193

F:4.15 If there is a failure of equipment which can be rectified quickly, the appropriate procedures set out in paragraph 4.12 shall be followed. When the recording is resumed the interviewer shall explain what has happened and record the time the interview recommences. If, however, it is not possible to continue recording on that particular recorder and no alternative equipment is readily available, the interview may continue without being recorded visually. In such circumstances, the procedures set out in paragraph 3.3 of this code for seeking the authority of the custody officer or a sergeant will be followed. [See *Note 4F.*]

### (h) *Removing used recording media from recording equipment*

A-194

F:4.16 Where used recording media are removed from the recording equipment during the course of an interview, they shall be retained and the procedures set out in paragraph 4.18 below followed.

### (i) *Conclusion of interview*

A-195

F:4.17 Before the conclusion of the interview, the suspect shall be offered the opportunity to clarify anything he or she has said and asked if there is anything that they wish to add.

F:4.18 At the conclusion of the interview, including the taking and reading back of any written statement, the time shall be recorded and the recording equipment switched off. The master recording shall be removed from the recording equipment, sealed with a master recording label and treated as an exhibit in accordance with the force standing orders. The interviewer shall sign the label and also ask the suspect and any third party present during the interview to sign it. If the suspect or third party refuses to sign the label, an officer of at least the rank of inspector, or if one is not available, the custody officer or, if the suspect has not been arrested, a sergeant, shall be called into the interview room and asked, subject to paragraph 2.5, to sign it.

F:4.19 The suspect shall be handed a notice which explains the use which will be made of the recording and the arrangements for access to it. The notice will also advise the suspect that a copy of the tape shall be supplied as soon as practicable if the person is charged or informed that he will be prosecuted.

*Notes for guidance*

F:4AA *For the purpose of voice identification the interviewer should ask the suspect and any other people*     **A-196**
*present to identify themselves.*

F:4A *The interviewer should attempt to estimate the likely length of the interview and ensure that an appropriate quantity of certified recording media and labels with which to seal the master copies are available in the interview room.*

F:4B *Where the custody offcer, or in the case of a person who has not been arrested, a sergeant, is called to deal with the complaint, wherever possible the recorder should be left to run until the offcer has entered the interview room and spoken to the person being interviewed. Continuation or termination of the interview should be at the discretion of the interviewer pending action by an inspector under Code C, para.9.2.*

F:4C *Where the complaint is about a matter not connected with this code or Code C, the decision to continue with the interview is at the interviewer's discretion. Where the interviewer decides to continue with the interview, the person being interviewed shall be told that at the conclusion of the interview, the complaint will be brought to the attention of the custody officer, or in the case of a person who has not been arrested, a sergeant. When the interview is concluded, the interviewer must, as soon as practicable, inform the custody officer or the sergeant of the existence and nature of the complaint made.*

F:4D *In considering whether to caution again after a break, the interviewer should bear in mind that they may have to satisfy a court that the person understood that they were still under caution when the interview resumed.*

F:4E *The officer should bear in mind that it may be necessary to satisfy the court that nothing occurred during a break in an interview or between interviews which influenced the suspect's recorded evidence. On the recommencement of an interview, the interviewer should consider summarising on the record the reason for the break and confirming this with the suspect.*

F:4F *Where the interview is being recorded and the media or the recording equipment fails, the interviewer should stop the interview immediately. Where part of the interview is unaffected by the error and is still accessible on the media, that part shall be copied and sealed in the suspect's presence as a master copy and the interview recommenced using new equipment/media as required. Where the content of the interview has been lost in its entirety, the media should be sealed in the suspect's presence and the interview begun again. If the recording equipment cannot be fixed or no replacement is immediately available, the interview should be audio recorded in accordance with Code E.*

F:4G *The interviewer should be aware that a decision to continue recording against the wishes of the suspect may be the subject of comment in court.*

### F:5  After the interview

F:5.1 The interviewer shall make a note in his or her pocket book of the fact that the interview     **A-197**
has taken place and has been recorded, its time, duration and date and the identification number of the master copy of the recording media.

F:5.2 Where no proceedings follow in respect of the person whose interview was recorded, the recording media must nevertheless be kept securely in accordance with paragraph 6.1 and *Note 6A.*

*Note for guidance*

F:5A *Any written record of a recorded interview shall be made in accordance with current national guidelines for police offcers, police staff and CPS prosecutors concerned with the preparation, processing and submission of files.*

### F:6  Master recording security

(a) *General*

F:6.1 The officer in charge of the police station at which interviews with suspects are recorded or     **A-198**
as the case may be, where recordings of interviews carried out elsewhere than at a police station are held, shall make arrangements for the master copies to be kept securely and their movements accounted for on the same basis as other material which may be used for evidential purposes, in accordance with force standing orders. [See *Note 6A.*]

(b) *Breaking master recording seal for criminal proceedings*

**A-199**     F:6.2 A police officer has no authority to break the seal on a master copy which is required for criminal trial or appeal proceedings. If it is necessary to gain access to the master copy, the police officer shall arrange for its seal to be broken in the presence of a representative of the Crown Prosecution Service. The defendant or their legal adviser shall be informed and given a reasonable opportunity to be present. If the defendant or their legal representative is present they shall be invited to reseal and sign the master copy. If either refuses or neither is present, this shall be done by the representative of the Crown Prosecution Service. [See *Notes 6B* and *6C.*]

(c) *Breaking master recording seal: other cases*

**A-200**     F:6.3 The chief officer of police is responsible for establishing arrangements for breaking the seal of the master copy where no criminal proceedings result, or the criminal proceedings, to which the interview relates, have been concluded and it becomes necessary to break the seal. These arrangements should be those which the chief officer considers are reasonably necessary to demonstrate to the person interviewed and any other party who may wish to use or refer to the interview record that the master copy has not been tampered with and that the interview record remains accurate. [See *Note 6D.*]

F:6.4 Subject to paragraph 6.6, a representative of each party must be given a reasonable opportunity to be present when the seal is broken and the master recording copied and re-sealed.

F:6.5 If one or more of the parties is not present when the master copy seal is broken because they cannot be contacted or refuse to attend or paragraph 6.6 applies, arrangements should be made for an independent person such as a custody visitor, to be present. Alternatively, or as an additional safeguard, arrangement should be made for a film or photographs to be taken of the procedure.

F:6.6 Paragraph 6.4 does not require a person to be given an opportunity to be present when:

(a) it is necessary to break the master copy seal for the proper and effective further investigation of the original offence or the investigation of some other offence; and

(b) the officer in charge of the investigation has reasonable grounds to suspect that allowing an opportunity might prejudice any such an investigation or criminal proceedings which may be brought as a result or endanger any person. [See *Note 6E.*]

(d) *Documentation*

**A-201**     F:6.7 When the master copy seal is broken, copied and re-sealed, a record must be made of the procedure followed, including the date time and place and persons present.

*Notes for guidance*

**A-202**     F:6A *This section is concerned with the security of the master recordings which will have been sealed at the conclusion of the interview. Care should, however, be taken of working recordings since their loss or destruction may lead unnecessarily to the need to have access to master copies.*

F:6B *If the master recording has been delivered to the Crown Court for their keeping after committal for trial the crown prosecutor will apply to the chief clerk of the Crown Court centre for its release for unsealing by the crown prosecutor.*

F:6C *Reference to the Crown Prosecution Service or to the crown prosecutor in this part of the code shall be taken to include any other body or person with a statutory responsibility for prosecution for whom the police conduct any recorded interviews.*

F:6D *The most common reasons for needing access to master recordings that are not required for criminal proceedings arise from civil actions and complaints against police and civil actions between individuals arising out of allegations of crime investigated by police.*

F:6E *Paragraph 6.6 could apply, for example, when one or more of the outcomes or likely outcomes of the investigation might be: (i) the prosecution of one or more of the original suspects; (ii) the prosecution of someone previously not suspected, including someone who was originally a witness; and (iii) any original suspect being treated as a prosecution witness and when premature disclosure of any police action, particularly through contact with any parties involved, could lead to a real risk of compromising the investigation and endangering witnesses.*

### F:7 Visual recording of interviews by secure digital network

**A-202a**     F:7.1 This section applies if an officer wishes to make a visual recording with sound of an interview mentioned in section 3 of this code using a secure digital network which does not use removable media (see paragraph 1.6(c) above).

F:7.3 [*sic*] The provisions of sections 1 to 6 of this code which relate or apply only to removable media will not apply to a secure digital network recording.

F:7.4 The statutory requirement and provisions for the audio recording of interviews using a secure digital network set out in section 7 of Code E should be applied to the visual recording with sound of interviews mentioned in section 3 of this code as if references to audio recordings of interviews include visual recordings with sound.

## (8) Statutory power of arrest

The first version of Code G came into force on January 1, 2006, to coincide with the com- **A-203** mencement of the substantial changes to the provisions of the PACE Act 1984 relating to the powers of arrest of police constables. As from that date, all offences became arrestable offences, but the lawfulness of an arrest by a constable for an offence became dependent on the constable having "reasonable grounds for believing that for any of the reasons mentioned in subsection (5) [of section 24] it is necessary to arrest the person in question". For the substituted section 24, see § 15-131 in the main work.

A revised code G came into force on November 12, 2012 (see *ante*, A-1).

### G. CODE OF PRACTICE FOR THE STATUTORY POWER OF ARREST BY POLICE OFFICERS

#### Commencement

This code applies to any arrest made by a police officer after 00.00 on 12 November 2012. **A-203a**

#### G:1 Introduction

G:1.1 This code of practice deals with statutory power of police to arrest a person who is involved, **A-204** or suspected of being involved, in a criminal offence. The power of arrest must be used fairly, responsibly, with respect for people suspected of committing offences and without unlawful discrimination. The Equality Act 2010 makes it unlawful for police officers to discriminate against, harass or victimise any person on the grounds of the "protected characteristics" of age, disability, gender reassignment, race, religion or belief, sex and sexual orientation, marriage and civil partnership, pregnancy and maternity when using their powers. When police forces are carrying out their functions they also have a duty to have regard to the need to eliminate unlawful discrimination, harassment and victimisation and to take steps to foster good relations.

G:1.2 The exercise of the power of arrest represents an obvious and significant interference with the right to liberty and security under Article 5 of the European Convention on Human Rights set out in Part I of Schedule 1 to the Human Rights Act 1998.

G:1.3 The use of the power must be fully justified and officers exercising the power should consider if the necessary objectives can be met by other, less intrusive means. Absence of justification for exercising the power of arrest may lead to challenges should the case proceed to court. It could also lead to civil claims against police for unlawful arrest and false imprisonment. When the power of arrest is exercised it is essential that it is exercised in a non-discriminatory and proportionate manner which is compatible with the right to liberty under Article 5. See *Note 1B*.

G:1.4 Section 24 of the Police and Criminal Evidence Act 1984 (as substituted by section 110 of the Serious Organised Crime and Police Act 2005) provides the statutory power for a constable to arrest without warrant for all offences. If the provisions of the Act and this code are not observed, both the arrest and the conduct of any subsequent investigation may be open to question.

G:1.5 This code of practice must be readily available at all police stations for consultation by police officers and police staff, detained persons and members of the public.

G:1.6 The notes for guidance are not provisions of this code.

#### G:2 Elements of arrest under section 24 PACE

G:2.1 A lawful arrest requires two elements: **A-205**

a person's involvement or suspected involvement or attempted involvement in the commission of a criminal offence; and

reasonable grounds for believing that the person's arrest is necessary.

Both elements must be satisfied, and it can never be necessary to arrest a person unless there are reasonable grounds to suspect them of committing an offence.

G:2.2 The arrested person must be informed that they have been arrested, even if this fact is obvious, and of the relevant circumstances of the arrest in relation to both the above elements. The custody officer must be informed of these matters on arrival at the police station. See paragraphs 2.9, 3.3 and *Note 3* and Code C, para. 3.4.

(a) "Involvement in the commission of an offence"

**A-206**    G:2.3 A constable may arrest without warrant in relation to any offence (see *Notes 1* and *1A*) anyone:

- who is about to commit an offence or is in the act of committing an offence;
- whom the officer has reasonable grounds for suspecting is about to commit an offence or to be committing an offence;
- whom the officer has reasonable grounds to suspect of being guilty of an offence which he or she has reasonable grounds for suspecting has been committed;
- anyone [*sic*] who is guilty of an offence which has been committed or anyone whom the officer has reasonable grounds for suspecting to be guilty of that offence.

G:2.3A There must be some reasonable, objective grounds for the suspicion, based on known facts and information which are relevant to the likelihood the offence has been committed and the person liable to arrest committed it. See *Notes 2* and *2A*.

(b) Necessity criteria

**A-207**    G:2.4 The power of arrest is only exercisable if the constable has reasonable grounds for believing that it is necessary to arrest the person. The statutory criteria for what may constitute necessity are set out in paragraph 2.9 and it remains an operational decision at the discretion of the constable to decide:

- which one or more of the necessity criteria (if any) applies to the individual; and
- if any of the criteria do apply, whether to arrest, grant street bail after arrest, report for summons or for charging by post, issue a penalty notice or take any other action that is open to the officer.

G:2.5 In applying the criteria, the arresting officer has to be satisfied that at least one of the reasons supporting the need for arrest is satisfied.

G:2.6 Extending the power of arrest to all offences provides a constable with the ability to use that power to deal with any situation. However, applying the necessity criteria requires the constable to examine and justify the reason or reasons why a person needs to be arrested or (as the case may be) further arrested, for an offence for the custody officer to decide whether to authorise their detention for that offence. See *Note 2C*.

G:2.7 The criteria in paragraph 2.9 below which are set out in section 24 of PACE, as substituted by section 110 of the Serious Organised Crime and Police Act 2005, are exhaustive. However, the circumstances that may satisfy those criteria remain a matter for the operational discretion of individual officers. Some examples are given to illustrate what those circumstances might be and what officers might consider when deciding whether arrest is necessary.

G:2.8 In considering the individual circumstances, the constable must take into account the situation of the victim, the nature of the offence, the circumstances of the suspect and the needs of the investigative process.

**A-208**    G:2.9 When it is practicable to tell a person why their arrest is necessary (as required by paragraphs 2.2, 3.3 and *Note 3*), the constable should outline the facts, information and other circumstances which provide the grounds for believing that their arrest is necessary and which the officer considers satisfy one or more of the statutory criteria in sub-paragraphs (a) to (f), namely:

(a) to enable the name of the person in question to be ascertained (in the case where the constable does not know, and cannot readily ascertain, the person's name, or has reasonable grounds for doubting whether a name given by the person as his name is his real name):

an officer might decide that a person's name cannot be readily ascertained if they fail or refuse to give it when asked, particularly after being warned that failure or refusal is likely to make their arrest necessary (see *Note 2D*); grounds to doubt a name given may arise if the person appears reluctant or hesitant when asked to give their name or to verify the name they have given;

where mobile fingerprinting is available and the suspect's name cannot be ascertained or is doubted, the officer should consider using the power under section 61(6A) of PACE (see Code D, para. 4.3(e)) to take and check the fingerprints of a suspect as this may avoid the need to arrest solely to enable their name to be ascertained;

(b) correspondingly as regards the person's address:

an officer might decide that a person's address cannot be readily ascertained if they fail or refuse to give it when asked, particularly after being warned that such a failure or refusal is likely to make their arrest necessary (see *Note 2D*); grounds to doubt an address given may arise if the person appears reluctant or hesitant when asked to give their address or is unable to provide verifiable details of the locality they claim to live in;

when considering reporting to consider summons or charging by post as alternatives to arrest, an address would be satisfactory if the person will be at it for a sufficiently long period for it to be possible to serve them with the summons or requisition and charge; or, that some other person at that address specified by the person will accept service on their behalf; when considering issuing a penalty notice, the address should be one where the person will be in the event of enforcement action if the person does not pay the penalty or is convicted and fined after a court hearing;

(c) to prevent the person in question:

(i) causing physical injury to himself or any other person; this might apply where the suspect has already used or threatened violence against others and it is thought likely that they may assault others if they are not arrested (see *Note 2D*);

(ii) suffering physical injury; this might apply where the suspect's behaviour and actions are believed likely to provoke, or have provoked, others to want to assault the suspect unless the suspect is arrested for their own protection (see *Note 2D*);

(iii) causing loss or damage to property; this might apply where the suspect is a known persistent offender with a history of serial offending against property (theft and criminal damage) and it is thought likely that they may continue offending if they are not arrested;

(iv) committing an offence against public decency (only applies where members of the public going about their normal business cannot reasonably be expected to avoid the person in question); this might apply when an offence against public decency is being committed in a place to which the public have access and is likely to be repeated in that or some other public place at a time when the public are likely to encounter the suspect (see *Note 2D*);

(v) causing an unlawful obstruction of the highway; this might apply to any offence where its commission causes an unlawful obstruction which it is believed may continue or be repeated if the person is not arrested, particularly if the person has been warned that they are causing an obstruction (see *Note 2D*);

(d) to protect a child or other vulnerable person from the person in question; this might apply when the health (physical or mental) or welfare of a child or vulnerable person is likely to be harmed or is at risk of being harmed, if the person is not arrested in cases where it is not practicable and appropriate to make alternative arrangements to prevent the suspect from having any harmful or potentially harmful contact with the child or vulnerable person;

(e) to allow the prompt and effective investigation of the offence or of the conduct of the person in question (see *Note 2E*); this may arise when it is thought likely that unless the person is arrested and then either taken in custody to the police station or granted "street bail" to attend the station later (see *Note 2J*), further action considered necessary to properly investigate their involvement in the offence would be frustrated, unreasonably delayed or otherwise hindered and therefore be impracticable; examples of such actions include:

(i) interviewing the suspect on occasions when the person's voluntary attendance is not considered to be a practicable alternative to arrest, because for example:

- it is thought unlikely that the person would attend the police station voluntarily to be interviewed;
- it is necessary to interview the suspect about the outcome of other investigative action for which their arrest is necessary, see (ii) to (v) below;
- arrest would enable the special warning to be given in accordance with Code C, paras 10.10 and 10.11 when the suspect is found:
  - in possession of incriminating objects, or at a place where such objects are found;
  - at or near the scene of the crime at or about the time it was committed;
- the person has made false statements and/or presented false evidence;
- it is thought likely that the person:
  - may steal or destroy evidence;
  - may collude or make contact with, co-suspects or conspirators;
  - may intimidate or threaten or make contact with, witnesses;

(see *Notes 2F* and *2G*);

    (ii) when considering arrest in connection with the investigation of an indictable offence (see *Note 6*), there is a need:

- to enter and search without a search warrant any premises occupied or controlled by the arrested person or where the person was when arrested or immediately before arrest;
- to prevent the arrested person from having contact with others;
- to detain the arrested person for more than 24 hours before charge;

    (iii) when considering arrest in connection with any recordable offence and it is necessary to secure or preserve evidence of that offence by taking fingerprints, footwear impressions or samples from the suspect for evidential comparison or matching with other material relating to that offence, for example, from the crime scene (see *Note 2H*);

    (iv) when considering arrest in connection with any offence and it is necessary to search, examine or photograph the person to obtain evidence (see *Note 2H*);

    (v) when considering arrest in connection with an offence to which the statutory Class A drug testing requirements in Code C, section 17, apply, to enable testing when it is thought that drug misuse might have caused or contributed to the offence (see *Note 2I*);

  (f) to prevent any prosecution for the offence from being hindered by the disappearance of the person in question; this may arise when it is thought that:

- if the person is not arrested they are unlikely to attend court if they are prosecuted;
- the address given is not a satisfactory address for service of a summons or a written charge and requisition to appear at court because the person will not be at it for a sufficiently long period for the summons or charge and requisition to be served and no other person at that specified address will accept service on their behalf.

### G:3 Information to be given on arrest

#### (a) *Cautions—when a caution must be given*

**A-209**
G:3.1 Code C, paras 10.1 and 10.2, set out the requirement for a person whom there are grounds to suspect of an offence (see *Note 2*) to be cautioned before being questioned or further questioned about an offence.

G:3.2 [*Not used.*]

G:3.3 A person who is arrested, or further arrested, must be informed at the time if practicable, or if not, as soon as it becomes practicable thereafter, that they are under arrest and of the grounds and reasons for their arrest (see paragraphs [*sic*] 2.2 and *Note 3*).

G:3.4 A person who is arrested, or further arrested, must be cautioned unless:

  (a) it is impracticable to do so by reason of their condition or behaviour at the time;

  (b) they have already been cautioned immediately prior to arrest as in paragraph 3.1.

#### (b) *Terms of the caution (taken from Code C, section 10)*

**A-210**
G:3.5 The caution, which must be given on arrest, should be in the following terms:

*"You do not have to say anything. But it may harm your defence if you do not mention when questioned something which you later rely on in court. Anything you do say may be given in evidence.".*

Where the use of the Welsh language is appropriate, a constable may provide the caution directly in Welsh in the following terms:

*"Does dim rhaid i chi ddweud dim byd. Ond gall niweidio eich amddiffyniad os na fyddwch chi'n sôn, wrth gael eich holi, am rywbeth y byddwch chi'n dibynnu arno nes ymlaen yn y Llys. Gall unrhyw beth yr ydych yn ei ddweud gael ei roi fel tystiolaeth.".*

See *Note 4*.

G:3.6 Minor deviations from the words of any caution given in accordance with this code do not constitute a breach of this code, provided the sense of the relevant caution is preserved. See *Note 5*.

G:3.7 *Not used.*

## G:4 Records of arrest

### (a) *General*

G:4.1 The arresting officer is required to record in his pocket book or by other methods used for          **A-211**
recording information:

- the nature and circumstances of the offence leading to the arrest;
- the reason or reasons why arrest was necessary;
- the giving of the caution; and
- anything said by the person at the time of the arrest.

G:4.2 Such a record should be made at the time of the arrest unless impracticable to do. If not
made at that time, the record should then be completed as soon as possible thereafter.

G:4.3 On arrival at the police station or after being first arrested at the police station, the arrested
person must be brought before the custody officer as soon as practicable and a custody record must
be opened in accordance with section 2 of Code C. The information given by the arresting officer on
the circumstances and reason or reasons for arrest shall be recorded as part of the custody record.
Alternatively, a copy of the record made by the officer in accordance with paragraph 4.1 above shall
be attached as part of the custody record. See paragraph 2.2 and Code C, paras 3.4 and 10.3.

G:4.4 The custody record will serve as a record of the arrest. Copies of the custody record will be
provided in accordance with paragraphs 2.4 and 2.4A of Code C and access for inspection of the
original record in accordance with paragraph 2.5 of Code C.

### (b) *Interviews and arrests*

G:4.5 Records of interviews, significant statements or silences will be treated in the same way as set
out in sections 10 and 11 of Code C and in Codes E and F (audio and visual recording of interviews).

### *Notes for guidance*

G:1 *For the purposes of this code, "offence" means any statutory or common law offence for which a person may*          **A-212**
*be tried by a magistrates' court or the Crown Court and punished if convicted.* [The note then gives examples
of statutory and common law offences.]

G:1A *This code does not apply to powers of arrest conferred on constables under any arrest warrant, for
example, a warrant issued under the Magistrates' Courts Act 1980, ss.1 or 13, or the Bail Act 1976, s.7(1), or to
the powers of constables to arrest without warrant other than under section 24 of PACE for an offence. These
other powers to arrest without warrant do not depend on the arrested person committing any specific offence and
include:*

- *PACE, s.46A, arrest of person who fails to answer police bail to attend police station or is suspected
  of breaching any condition of that bail for the custody officer to decide whether they should be kept in
  police detention which applies whether or not the person commits an offence under section 6 of the
  Bail Act 1976 (e.g. failing without reasonable cause to surrender to custody);*
- *Bail Act 1976, s.7(3), arrest of person bailed to attend court who is suspected of breaching, or is
  believed likely to breach, any condition of bail to take them to court for bail to be re-considered;*
- *Children and Young Persons Act 1969, s.32(1A) (absconding) – arrest to return the person to the
  place where they are required to reside;*
- *Immigration Act 1971, Sched. 2, to arrest a person liable to examination to determine their right to
  remain in the U.K.;*
- *Mental Health Act 1983, s.136 to remove person suffering from mental disorder to place of safety
  for assessment;*
- *Prison Act 1952, s.49, arrest to return person unlawfully at large to the prison, etc., where they are
  liable to be detained;*
- *Road Traffic Act 1988, s.6D, arrest of driver following the outcome of a preliminary roadside test
  requirement to enable the driver to be required to provide an evidential sample;*
- *common law power to stop or prevent a breach of the peace—after arrest a person aged 18 or over
  may be brought before a justice of the peace court to show cause why they should not be bound over to
  keep the peace – not criminal proceedings.*

G:1B *Juveniles should not be arrested at their place of education unless this is unavoidable. When a juvenile
is arrested at their place of education, the principal or their nominee must be informed (from Code C, Note 11D).*

G:2 *Facts and information relevant to a person's suspected involvement in an offence should not be confined to
those which tend to indicate the person has committed or attempted to commit the offence. Before making a decision
to arrest, a constable should take account of any facts and information that are available, including claims of innocence made by the person, that might dispel the suspicion.*

G:2A *Particular examples of facts and information which might point to a person's innocence and may tend to dispel suspicion include those which relate to the statutory defence provided by the Criminal Law Act 1967, s.3(1) which allows the use of reasonable force in the prevention of crime or making an arrest and the common law of self-defence. This may be relevant when a person appears, or claims, to have been acting reasonably in defence of themselves or others or to prevent their property or the property of others from being stolen, destroyed or damaged, particularly if the offence alleged is based on the use of unlawful force, e.g. a criminal assault. When investigating allegations involving the use of force by school staff, the power given to all school staff under the Education and Inspections Act 2006, s.93, to use reasonable force to prevent their pupils from committing any offence, injuring persons, damaging property or prejudicing the maintenance of good order and discipline may be similarly relevant. The Association of Chief Police Officers and the Crown Prosecution Service have published joint guidance to help the public understand the meaning of reasonable force and what to expect from the police and CPS in cases which involve claims of self-defence. Separate advice for school staff on their powers to use reasonable force is available from the Department for Education.*

**G:2B** *If a constable who is dealing with an allegation of crime and considering the need to arrest becomes an investigator for the purposes of the Code of Practice under the Criminal Procedure and Investigations Act 1996, the officer should, in accordance with paragraph 3.5 of that code, "pursue all reasonable lines of inquiry, whether these point towards or away from the suspect. What is reasonable in each case will depend on the particular circumstances."*

**G:2C** *For a constable to have reasonable grounds for believing it necessary to arrest, he or she is not required to be satisfied that there is no viable alternative to arrest. However, it does mean that in all cases, the officer should consider that arrest is the practical, sensible and proportionate option in all the circumstances at the time the decision is made. This applies equally to a person in police detention after being arrested for an offence who is suspected of involvement in a further offence and the necessity to arrest them for that further offence is being considered.*

**G:2D** *Although a warning is not expressly required, officers should if practicable, consider whether a warning which points out their offending behaviour, and explains why, if they do not stop, the resulting consequences may make their arrest necessary. Such a warning might:*

- *if heeded, avoid the need to arrest, or*
- *if it is ignored, support the need to arrest and also help prove the mental element of certain offences, for example, the person's intent or awareness, or help to rebut a defence that they were acting reasonably.*

*A person who is warned that they may be liable to arrest if their real name and address cannot be ascertained, should be given a reasonable opportunity to establish their real name and address before deciding that either or both are unknown and cannot be readily ascertained or that there are reasonable grounds to doubt that a name and address they have given is their real name and address. They should be told why their name is not known and cannot be readily ascertained and (as the case may be) of the grounds for doubting that a name and address they have given is their real name and address, including, for example, the reason why a particular document the person has produced to verify their real name and/or address, is not sufficient.*

**G:2E** *The meaning of "prompt" should be considered on a case by case basis taking account of all the circumstances. It indicates that the progress of the investigation should not be delayed to the extent that it would adversely affect the effectiveness of the investigation. The arresting officer also has discretion to release the arrested person on "street bail" as an alternative to taking the person directly to the station (see Note 2J).*

**G:2F** *An officer who believes that it is necessary to interview the person suspected of committing the offence must then consider whether their arrest is necessary in order to carry out the interview. The officer is not required to interrogate the suspect to determine whether they will attend a police station voluntarily to be interviewed but they must consider whether the suspect's voluntary attendance is a practicable alternative for carrying out the interview. If it is, then arrest would not be necessary. Conversely, an officer who considers this option but is not satisfied that it is a practicable alternative, may have reasonable grounds for deciding that the arrest is necessary at the outset "on the street". Without such considerations, the officer would not be able to establish that arrest was necessary in order to interview.*

*Circumstances which suggest that a person's arrest "on the street" would not be necessary to interview them might be where the officer:*

- *is satisfied as to their identity and address and that they will attend the police station voluntarily to be interviewed, either immediately or by arrangement at a future date and time; and*
- *is not aware of any other circumstances which indicate that voluntary attendance would not be a practicable alternative (see paragraph 2.9(e)(i) to (v)).*

*When making arrangements for the person's voluntary attendance, the officer should tell the person:*

- *that to properly investigate their suspected involvement in the offence they must be interviewed under caution at the police station, but in the circumstances their arrest for this purpose will not be necessary if they attend the police station voluntarily to be interviewed;*
- *that if they attend voluntarily, they will be entitled to free legal advice before, and to have a solicitor present at, the interview;*

- *that the date and time of the interview will take account of their circumstances and the needs of the investigation; and*
- *that if they do not agree to attend voluntarily at a time which meets the needs of the investigation, or having so agreed, fail to attend, or having attended, fail to remain for the interview to be completed, their arrest will be necessary to enable them to be interviewed.*

G:2G *When the person attends the police station voluntarily for interview by arrangement as in Note 2F above, their arrest on arrival at the station prior to interview would only be justified if:*

- *new information coming to light after the arrangements were made indicates that from that time, voluntary attendance ceased to be a practicable alternative and the person's arrest became necessary; and*
- *it was not reasonably practicable for the person to be arrested before they attended the station.*

*If a person who attends the police station voluntarily to be interviewed decides to leave before the interview is complete, the police would at that point be entitled to consider whether their arrest was necessary to carry out the interview. The possibility that the person might decide to leave during the interview is therefore not a valid reason for arresting them before the interview has commenced (see Code C, para. 3.21).*

G:2H *The necessity criteria do not permit arrest solely to enable the routine taking, checking (speculative searching) and retention of fingerprints, samples, footwear impressions and photographs when there are no prior grounds to believe that checking and comparing the fingerprints, etc., or taking a photograph would provide relevant evidence of the person's involvement in the offence concerned or would help to ascertain or verify their real identity.*

G:2I *The necessity criteria do not permit arrest for an offence solely because it happens to be one of the statutory drug testing "trigger offences" (see Code C, Note 17E) when there is no suspicion that Class A drug misuse might have caused or contributed to the offence.*

G:2J *Having determined that the necessity criteria have been met and having made the arrest, the officer can then consider the use of street bail on the basis of the effective and efficient progress of the investigation of the offence in question. It gives the officer discretion to compel the person to attend a police station at a date/ time that best suits the overall needs of the particular investigation. Its use is not confined to dealing with child care issues or allowing officers to attend to more urgent operational duties and granting street bail does not retrospectively negate the need to arrest.*

G:3 *An arrested person must be given sufficient information to enable them to understand they have been deprived of their liberty and the reason they have been arrested, as soon as practicable after the arrest, e.g. when a person is arrested on suspicion of committing an offence they must be informed of the nature of the suspected offence and when and where it was committed. The suspect must also be informed of the reason or reasons why arrest is considered necessary. Vague or technical language should be avoided. When explaining why one or more of the arrest criteria apply, it is not necessary to disclose any specific details that might undermine or otherwise adversely affect any investigative processes. An example might be the conduct of a formal interview when prior disclosure of such details might give the suspect an opportunity to fabricate an innocent explanation or to otherwise conceal lies from the interviewer.*

G:4 *Nothing in this code requires a caution to be given or repeated when informing a person not under arrest they may be prosecuted for an offence. However, a court will not be able to draw any inferences under the Criminal Justice and Public Order Act 1994, s.34, if the person was not cautioned.*

G:5 *If it appears a person does not understand the caution, the people giving it should explain it in their own words.*

G:6 *Certain powers available as the result of an arrest - for example, entry and search of premises, detention without charge beyond 24 hours, holding a person incommunicado and delaying access to legal advice - only apply in respect of indictable offences and are subject to the specific requirements on authorisation as set out in PACE and the relevant code of practice.*

## (9) Detention treatment and questioning of terrorist suspects

The Police and Criminal Evidence Act 1984 (Code of Practice C and Code of Practice H) Order **A-213** 2006 (S.I. 2006 No. 1938) provided for a revised Code C, and for a new Code H (on detention, treatment and questioning by police officers of persons under section 41 of, and Schedule 8 to, the Terrorism Act 2000), to come into operation on July 25, 2006. The new codes were consequential upon the commencement of the provisions of the Terrorism Act 2006, which were concerned with the 28-day detention of those arrested under section 41 of the 2000 Act. Whereas Code C had previously regulated the detention, treatment and questioning of those detained following arrest under section 41, from that date onwards these matters were regulated by Code H. Code C was revised so as to remove references to detention under the 2000 Act. The new Code H largely mirrored the provisions of Code C, but with various differences.

A revised Code H came into force on July 10, 2012, and a further revision came into force on

October 27, 2013. The text that follows is that of a yet further revision that came into force on June 2, 2014 (see *ante*, A-1).

## H. CODE OF PRACTICE IN CONNECTION WITH THE DETENTION, TREATMENT AND QUESTIONING BY POLICE OFFICERS OF PERSONS UNDER SECTION 41 OF, AND SCHEDULE 8 TO, THE TERRORISM ACT 2000

### Commencement—transitional arrangements

**A-214**   This code applies to people in police detention after 00.00 on 27 October 2013, notwithstanding that their period of detention may have commenced before that time.

### H:1 General

**A-214a**   H:1.0 [*Identical to C1:0.*]

H:1.1 This code of practice applies to, and only to:

(a) persons in police detention after being arrested under section 41 of the Terrorism Act 2000 (TACT) and detained under section 41 of, or Schedule 8 to that Act and not charged; and

(b) detained persons in respect of whom an authorisation has been given under section 22 of the Counter-Terrorism Act 2008 (post-charge questioning of terrorist suspects) to interview them in which case, section 15 of this code will apply.

H:1.2 The provisions in *PACE* Code C apply when a person:

(a) is in custody otherwise than as a result of being arrested under section 41 of TACT or detained for examination under Schedule 7 to TACT (see paragraph 1.4);

(b) is charged with an offence; or

(c) is being questioned about any offence after being charged with that offence without an authorisation being given under section 22 of the Counter-Terrorism Act 2008.
See *Note 1N*.

H:1.3 In this code references to an offence and to a person's involvement or suspected involvement in an offence where the person has not been charged with an offence, include being concerned, or suspected of being concerned, in the commission, preparation or instigation of acts of terrorism.

H:1.4 The code of practice issued under paragraph 6 of Schedule 14 to TACT applies to persons detained for examination under Schedule 7 to TACT. See *Note 1N*.

H:1.5 All persons in custody must be dealt with expeditiously, and released as soon as the need for detention no longer applies.

H:1.6 There is no provision for bail under TACT before or after charge. See *Note 1N*.

H:1.7 An officer must perform the assigned duties in this code as soon as practicable. An officer will not be in breach of this code if delay is justifiable and reasonable steps are taken to prevent unnecessary delay. The custody record shall show when a delay has occurred and the reason. See *Note 1H*.

H:1.8–1.10 [*Identical to C:1.2 to C:1.4, respectively.*]

H:1.11 For the purposes of this code, a juvenile is any person under the age of 17. If anyone appears to be under 17, and there is no clear evidence that they are 17 or over, they shall be treated as a juvenile for the purposes of this code.

H:1.11A If anyone appears to have attained the age of 17 and to be under the age of 18, they shall in the absence of clear evidence that they are older, be treated as a 17-year-old for the purposes of this code and the provisions and *Notes for Guidance* which in accordance with paragraph 1.11 apply to a juvenile and the way they are to be treated shall also apply to them, except for the purposes of the statutory provisions in section 65(1) of PACE (appropriate consent) which by virtue of paragraph 15 of Schedule 8 to the Terrorism Act 2000, applies to the powers in paragraphs 10 to 14 of that schedule to take fingerprints, intimate and non-intimate samples. For these powers, the statutory requirement for appropriate consent for a person who has not attained the age of 17 to be given by them and their parent or guardian shall not apply to a person who appears to have attained the age of 17 and whose consent alone is sufficient. (See *Notes 1O* and *1P*.)

H:1.12 [*Identical to C:1.6.*]

H:1.13 [*Identical to C:1.7, save for reference to "paragraph 1.11A" in lieu of reference to "paragraph 1.5A".*]

H:1.14 [*Identical to C:1.8.*]

H:1.15 [*Identical to C:1.9.*]

H:1.16 When this code requires the prior authority or agreement of an officer of at least inspector or superintendent rank, that authority may be given by a sergeant or chief inspector authorised by section 107 of PACE to perform the functions of the higher rank under TACT.

H:1.17 In this code:

    (a) "designated person" means a person other than a police officer, designated under the Police Reform Act 2002, Pt 4, who has specified powers and duties of police officers conferred or imposed on them;

    (b) reference to a police officer includes a designated person acting in the exercise or performance of the powers and duties conferred or imposed on them by their designation;

    (c) where a search or other procedure to which this code applies may only be carried out or observed by a person of the same sex as the detainee, the gender of the detainee and other parties present should be established and recorded in line with Annex I of this code.

H:1.18 [*Identical to C:1.14.*]

H:1.19 [*Identical to C:1.15.*]

H:1.20 Designated persons and other police staff must have regard to any relevant provisions of this code.

H:1.21 [*Identical to C:1.17.*]

*Notes for guidance*

H:1A *Although certain sections of this code apply specifically to people in custody at police stations, those there* **A-214b** *voluntarily to assist with an investigation should be treated with no less consideration, e.g. offered refreshments at appropriate times, and enjoy an absolute right to obtain legal advice or communicate with anyone outside the police station.*

H:1AA [*Identical to C:1AA.*]

H:1B *A person, including a parent or guardian, should not be an appropriate adult if they:*

    • *are:*

        – *suspected of involvement in the offence or involvement in the commission, preparation or instigation of acts of terrorism;*

        – *the victim;*

        – *a witness;*

        – *involved in the investigation;*

    • *received admissions prior to attending to act as the appropriate adult.*

*Note: if a juvenile's parent is estranged from the juvenile, they should not be asked to act as the appropriate adult if the juvenile expressly and specifically objects to their presence.*

*Note: Paragraph 1.11A applies this note to 17-year-old detainees.*

H:1C *If a juvenile admits an offence to, or in the presence of, a social worker or member of a youth offending team other than during the time that person is acting as the juvenile's appropriate adult, another appropriate adult should be appointed in the interest of fairness.*

*Note: Paragraph 1.11A applies this note to 17-year-old detainees.*

H:1D–1G [*Identical to C:1D–G.*]

H:1H *Paragraph 1.7 is intended to cover delays which may occur in processing detainees e.g if:*

    • *a large number of suspects are brought into the station simultaneously to be placed in custody;*

    • *interview rooms are all being used;*

    • *there are difficulties contacting an appropriate adult, solicitor or interpreter.*

H:1I–1K [*Identical to C:1I to C:1K, respectively.*]

H:1L *If a person is moved from a police station to receive medical treatment, or for any other reason, the period of detention is still calculated from the time of arrest under section 41 of TACT (or, if a person was being detained under TACT, Sched. 7, when arrested, from the time at which the examination under Schedule 7 began).*

H:1M *Under paragraph 1 of Schedule 8 to TACT, all police stations are designated for detention of persons arrested under section 41 of TACT. Paragraph 4 of Schedule 8 requires that the constable who arrests a person under section 41 takes him as soon as practicable to the police station which the officer considers is "most appropriate".*

H:1N *The powers under Part IV of PACE to detain and release on bail (before or after charge) a person arrested under section 24 of PACE for any offence (see PACE Code G (Arrest)) do not apply to persons whilst they are detained under the terrorism powers following their arrest/detention under section 41 of, or Schedule 7 to, TACT. If when the grounds for detention under these powers cease the person is arrested under section 24 of PACE for a specific offence, the detention and bail provisions of PACE will apply and must be considered from the time of that arrest.*

H:1O *Paragraph 1.11A does not amend the provisions in any enactment or statutory instrument which expressly refer and apply to persons under the age of 17. Until amended by Parliament, these statutory provisions alone do not extend to persons who have attained the age of 17.*

H:1P *The purpose of paragraph 1.11A is to extend the safeguards for juveniles to 17-year-olds unless this is precluded by any statutory provisions. The exception identifies section 65 of PACE (appropriate consent) which by virtue of paragraph 15 of Schedule 8 to the Terrorism Act 2000, is applied to the powers under that schedule to take fingerprints and samples. All other safeguards in this code are extended and the requirements which are indicated in the relevant provisions and Notes for Guidance are as follows:*

(a) *under paragraph 3.15 of this code, to identify and inform someone responsible for the welfare of a 17-year-old which is in addition to their right in section 5 of this code not to be held incommunicado;*

(b) *under paragraph 3.16 of this code to notify a person who has statutory responsibility under a court order to supervise or monitor a 17-year-old;*

(c) *under paragraph 8.9 with regard to cell accommodation and keeping 17-year-old detainees separate from adults;*

(d) *to call a person described by paragraph 1.13(a) to fulfil the role of the appropriate adult for the purposes of this or any other code to support and assist a 17-year-old:*

(i) *by being present when:*

• *they are informed of their rights and entitlements and the grounds for their detention (see paras 3.17 and 3.18);*

• *they are cautioned or given a special warning (see paras 10.10 and 10.11A);*

• *they are being interviewed unless paragraph 11.11 of this code allows the interview to go ahead without the adult being present;*

• *an intimate search is carried out (see Annex A, paras 3 and 6);*

• *a strip search is carried out (see Annex A, para. 12);*

(ii) *by allowing:*

• *the adult to inspect their custody record and to have a copy of their record (see paras 2.5, 2.6 and 2.7);*

• *a 17-year-old to consult the adult in private (see para. 3.19);*

• *the adult to request legal advice on their behalf to advise and assist them (see paras 3.20, 6.6 and 11.10).*

### H:2  Custody records

H:2.1  When a person is:

• brought to a police station following arrest under TACT, s.41;

• arrested under TACT, s.41 at a police station having attended there voluntarily;

• brought to a police station and there detained to be questioned in accordance with an authorisation under section 22 of the Counter-Terrorism Act 2008 (post-charge questioning) (see *Notes 15A* and *15B*); or

• at a police station and there detained when authority for post-charge questioning is given under section 22 of the Counter-Terrorism Act 2008 (see *Notes 15A* and *15B*),

they should be brought before the custody officer as soon as practicable after their arrival at the station or, if appropriate, following the authorisation of post-charge questioning or following arrest after attending the police station voluntarily: see *Note 3H*. A person is deemed to be "at a police station" for these purposes if they are within the boundary of any building or enclosed yard which forms part of that police station.

H:2.2  A separate custody record must be opened as soon as practicable for each person described in paragraph 2.1. All information recorded under this code must be recorded as soon as practicable in the custody record unless otherwise specified. Any audio or video recording made in the custody area is not part of the custody record.

H:2.3  If any action requires the authority of an officer of a specified rank, this must be noted in the custody record, subject to paragraph 2.8.

H:2.3A  If a person is arrested under TACT, s.41, and taken to a police station as a result of a search in the exercise of any stop and search power to which PACE Code A (stop and search) or the "search powers code" issued under TACT applies, the officer carrying out the search is responsible for ensuring that the record of that stop and search is made as part of the person's custody record. The custody officer must then ensure that the person is asked if they want a copy of the search record and if they do, that they are given a copy as soon as practicable. The person's entitlement to a copy of the search record which is made as part of their custody record is in addition to, and does not affect, their entitlement to a copy of their custody record or any other provisions of section 2 (custody records) of this code. See Code A, para. 4.2B, and the TACT search powers code para. 5.3.5.

H:2.4  *[Identical to C:2.3.]*

H:2.5  The detainee's solicitor and appropriate adult must be permitted to inspect the whole of the detainee's custody record as soon as practicable after their arrival at the station and at any other time on request whilst the person is detained. This includes the following specific records relating to the reasons for the detainee's arrest and detention and the offence concerned to which paragraph 3.1(b) refers:

    (a) the information about the circumstances and reasons for the detainee's arrest as recorded in the custody record in accordance with paragraph 3.4; this applies to any further reasons which come to light and are recorded whilst the detainee is detained;

    (b) the record of the grounds for each authorisation to keep the person in custody; the authorisations to which this applies are the same as those described in paragraph 2 of Annex M [*sic*] of this code.

Access to the records in sub-paragraphs (a) and (b) is in addition to the requirements in paragraphs 3.4(b), 11.1 and 14.0 (to make certain documents and materials available and to provide information about the reasons for arrest and detention) and in paragraph 14.4A to provide written information about the grounds for continued detention when an application for a warrant of further detention (or for an extension of such a warrant) is made.

Access to the custody record for the purposes of this paragraph must be arranged and agreed with the custody officer and may not unreasonably interfere with the custody officer's duties or the justifiable needs of the investigation. A record shall be made when access is allowed and whether it includes the records described in sub-paragraphs (a) and (b) above.

Note: paragraph 1.11A extends this paragraph to the person called to fulfil the role of the appropriate adult for a 17-year-old detainee.

H:2.6 [*Identical to C:2.4A, save for reference to "paragraph 1.11A" in lieu of reference to "paragraph 1.5A".*]

H:2.7 The detainee, appropriate adult or legal representative shall be permitted to inspect the original custody record once the detained person is no longer being held under the provisions of TACT, s.41, and Sched. 8, or being questioned after charge as authorised under section 22 of the Counter-Terrorism Act 2008 (see section 15), provided they give reasonable notice of their request. Any such inspection shall be noted in the custody record.

Note: paragraph 1.11A extends this paragraph to the person called to fulfil the role of the appropriate adult for a 17-year-old detainee.

H:2.8 All entries in custody records must be timed and identified by the maker. Nothing in this code requires the identity of officers or other police staff to be recorded or disclosed in the case of enquiries linked to the investigation of terrorism. In these cases, they shall use their warrant or other identification numbers and the name of their police station: see *Note 2A*. Records entered on computer shall be timed and contain the operator's identification.

H:2.9 [*Identical to C:2.7.*]

### *Note for guidance*

H:2A *The purpose of paragraph 2.8 is to protect those involved in terrorist investigations or arrests of terrorist suspects from the possibility that those arrested, their associates or other individuals or groups may threaten or cause harm to those involved.*     **A-215a**

### H:3  Initial action

#### (a) *Detained persons—normal procedure*

H:3.1 When a person to whom paragraph 2.1 applies is at a police station, the custody officer must make sure the person is told clearly about:     **★A-215b**

    (a) the following continuing rights which may be exercised at any stage during the period in custody:

        (i) their right to consult privately with a solicitor and that free independent legal advice is available as in section 6;

        (ii) their right to have someone informed of their arrest as in section 5;

        (iii) the right to consult this code of practice (see *Note 3D*); and

        (iv) if applicable, their right to interpretation and translation (see para. 3.14) and their right to communicate with their high commission, embassy or consulate (see para. 3.14A);

    (b) their right to be informed about why they have been arrested and detained on suspicion of being involved in the commission, preparation or instigation of acts of terrorism in accordance with paragraphs 2.5, 3.4(a) and 11.1A of this code.

H:3.2 The detainee must also be given a written notice, which contains information:

(a) setting out:
    (i) their rights under paragraphs 3.1, 3.14 and 3.14A;
    (ii) the arrangements for obtaining legal advice, see section 6;
    (iii) their right to a copy of the custody record as in paragraph 2.6;
    (iv) their right to remain silent as set out in the caution in the terms prescribed in section 10;
    (v) their right to have access to records and documents which are essential to effectively challenging the lawfulness of their arrest and detention as required in accordance with paragraphs 3.4(b) and 14.0 of this code;
    (vi) the maximum period for which they may be kept in police detention without being charged, when detention must be reviewed and when release is required;
    (vii) their right to medical assistance in accordance with section 9 of this code;
    (viii) their right, if they are prosecuted, to have access to the evidence in the case before their trial in accordance with the Criminal Procedure and Investigations Act 1996, the Attorney General's Guidelines on Disclosure, the common law and the Criminal Procedure Rules;

(b) briefly setting out their other entitlements while in custody, by:
    (i) mentioning:
      – the provisions relating to the conduct of interviews;
      – the circumstances in which an appropriate adult should be available to assist the detainee and their statutory rights to make representations whenever the need for their detention is reviewed;
    (ii) listing the entitlements in this code, concerning:
      – reasonable standards of physical comfort;
      – adequate food and drink;
      – access to toilets and washing facilities, clothing, medical attention, and exercise when practicable.

See *Note 3A*.

H:3.2A The detainee must be given an opportunity to read the notice and shall be asked to sign the custody record to acknowledge receipt of these notices. Any refusal must be recorded on the custody record.

H:3.3 [*Not used.*]

H:3.3A [*Identical to C:3.3A.*]

H:3.4 (a) The custody officer shall:
- record that the person was arrested under section 41 of TACT and the reason(s) for the arrest on the custody record (see para. 10.2 and *Note 3G*);
- note on the custody record any comment the detainee makes in relation to the arresting officer's account but shall not invite comment; if the arresting officer is not physically present when the detainee is brought to a police station, the arresting officer's account must be made available to the custody officer remotely or by a third party on the arresting officer's behalf;
- note any comment the detainee makes in respect of the decision to detain them but shall not invite comment;
- not put specific questions to the detainee regarding their involvement in any offence (see para. 1.3), nor in respect of any comments they may make in response to the arresting officer's account or the decision to place them in detention (see paras 14.1 and 14.2 and *Notes 3H, 14A* and *14B*); such an exchange is likely to constitute an interview as in paragraph 11.1 and require the associated safeguards in section 11.

Note: this sub-paragraph also applies to any further reasons and grounds for detention which come to light whilst the person is detained.

See paragraph 11.8A in respect of unsolicited comments.

If the first review of detention is carried out at this time, see paragraphs 14.1 and 14.2, and Part II of Schedule 8 to the Terrorism Act 2000 in respect of action by the review officer.

(b) Any available documents and materials which are essential to effectively challenging the lawfulness the detainee's arrest and detention must be made available to the detainee or their solicitor. Documents and material will be "essential" for this purpose if they are capable of undermining the reasons and grounds which make the detainee's arrest and detention necessary. The decision about whether particular documents or materials must made [*sic*] available for the purpose of this requirement rests with the officer responsible under Schedule 8 to the Terrorism Act 2000 for determining whether detention is necessary, in consultation with the investigating officer who has the knowledge of the documents and materials in a particular case necessary to inform that decision (see *Note 3G*). A note should be made in the detainee's custody record of the fact that documents or materials have been made available under this sub-paragraph and when. The investigating officer should make a separate note of what is made available in a particular case. This sub-paragraph also applies for the purposes of section 14 (reviews and extensions of detention under the Terrorism Act 2000). See *Note 3ZA* and paragraph 14.0.

H:3.5 The custody officer or other custody staff as directed by the custody officer shall:

    (a) ask the detainee, whether at this time, they:

        (i) would like legal advice, see paragraph 6.4;

        (ii) want someone informed of their detention, see section 5;

    (b) ask the detainee to sign the custody record to confirm their decisions in respect of (a);

    (c) determine whether the detainee:

        (i) is, or might be, in need of medical treatment or attention, see section 9;

        (ii) requires:

            • an appropriate adult (see paras 1.10, 1.11A, and 3.15);

            • help to check documentation (see para. 3.21);

            • an interpreter (see para. 3.14 and *Note 13B*).

    (d) record the decision in respect of (c).

Where any duties under this paragraph have been carried out by custody staff at the direction of the custody officer, the outcomes shall, as soon as practicable, be reported to the custody officer who retains overall responsibility for the detainee's care and safe custody and ensuring it complies with this code. See *Note 3I*.

H:3.6 When these needs are determined, the custody officer is responsible for initiating an assessment to consider whether the detainee is likely to present specific risks to custody staff, any individual who may have contact with the detainee (*e.g.* legal advisers, medical staff), or themselves. Such assessments should always include a check on the Police National Computer, to be carried out as soon as practicable, to identify any risks highlighted in relation to the detainee. Although such assessments are primarily the custody officer's responsibility, it will be necessary to obtain information from other sources, especially the investigation team (see *Note 3E*), the arresting officer or an appropriate healthcare professional (see paragraph 9.15). Reasons for delaying the initiation or completion of the assessment must be recorded.

H:3.7 [*Identical to C:3.7.*]

H:3.8 Risk assessments must follow a structured process which clearly defines the categories of risk to be considered and the results must be incorporated in the detainee's custody record. The custody officer is responsible for making sure those responsible for the detainee's custody are appropriately briefed about the risks. The content of any risk assessment and any analysis of the level of risk relating to the person's detention is not required to be shown or provided to the detainee or any person acting on behalf of the detainee. If no specific risks are identified by the assessment, that should be noted in the custody record. See *Note 3F* and paragraph 9.15.

H:3.8A The content of any risk assessment and any analysis of the level of risk relating to the person's detention is not required to be shown or provided to the detainee or any person acting on behalf of the detainee. But information should not be withheld from any person acting on the detainee's behalf, for example, an appropriate adult, solicitor or interpreter, if to do so might put that person at risk.

H:3.9 Custody officers are responsible for implementing the response to any specific risk assessment, which should include for example:

    • reducing opportunities for self harm;

    • calling a health care professional;

    • increasing levels of monitoring or observation;

    • reducing the risk to those who come into contact with the detainee.

See *Note 3F*.

H:3.10, 3.11 [*Identical to C:3.10 and C:3.11, respectively.*]

H:3.12 A constable, prison officer or other person authorised by the Secretary of State may take any steps which are reasonably necessary for—

    (a) photographing the detained person,

    (b) measuring the person, or

    (c) identifying the person.

H:3.13 Paragraph 3.12 concerns the power in TACT, Sched. 8, para. 2. The power in TACT,

Sched. 8, para. 2, does not cover the taking of fingerprints, intimate samples or non-intimate samples, which is covered in TACT, Sched. 8, paras 10-15.

### (b) *Detained persons—special groups*

H:3.14 [*Identical to C:3.12, save for reference to "Annex K" in lieu of reference to "Annex M".*]

H:3.14A [*Identical to C:3.12A.*]

H:3.15, 3.16 [*Identical to C:3.13 and C:3.14 respectively, save for references to "paragraph 1.11A" in lieu of references to "paragraph 1.5A".*]

H:3.17 [*Identical to C:3.15, save for references to "paragraph 3.15" and "paragraph 1.11A" in lieu of references to "paragraph 3.13" and "paragraph 1.5A" respectively.*]

H:3.18–3.20 [*Identical to C:3.17 to C:3.19 respectively, save for references to "paragraph 1.11A" in lieu of references to "paragraph 1.5A".*]

H:3.21 [*Identical to C:3.20, save for reference to "paragraph 3.17" in lieu of reference to "paragraph 3.15".*]

### (d) [*sic*] *Documentation*

H:3.22 The grounds for a person's detention shall be recorded, in the person's presence if practicable.

H:3.23 Action taken under paragraphs 3.14 to 3.22 shall be recorded.

### (e) *Requirements for suspects to be informed of certain rights*

H:3.24 The provisions of this section identify the information which must be given to suspects who have been arrested under section 41of the Terrorism Act and cautioned in accordance with section 10 of this code. It includes information required by EU Directive 2012/13 on the right to information in criminal proceedings. If a complaint is made by or on behalf of such a suspect that the information and (as the case may be) access to records and documents has not been provided as required, the matter shall be reported to an inspector to deal with as a complaint for the purposes of paragraph 9.3, or paragraph 12.10 if the challenge is made during an interview. This would include, for example:

- not informing them of their rights (see para. 3.1);
- not giving them a copy of the notice (see para. 3.2(a));
- not providing an opportunity to read the notice (see para. 3.2A);
- not providing the required information (see paras 3.2(a), 3.14(b) and, 3.14A);
- not allowing access to the custody record (see para. 2.5);
- not providing a translation of the notice (see para. 3.14(c) and (d)).

### *Notes for guidance*

**A-216**

H:3ZA *For the purposes of paragraphs 3.4(b) and 14.0:*

(a) *investigating officers are responsible for bringing to the attention of the officer who is responsible for authorising the suspect's detention or (as the case may be) continued detention, any documents and materials in their possession or control which appear to undermine the need to keep the suspect in custody; in accordance with Part II of Schedule 8 to the Terrorism Act 2000, this officer will be either the inspector or superintendent reviewing the need for detention; this officer is then responsible for determining which, if any, of those documents and materials are capable of undermining the need to detain the suspect and must therefore be made available to the suspect or their solicitor;*

(b) *the way in which documents and materials are "made available", is a matter for the investigating officer to determine on a case by case basis and having regard to the nature and volume of the documents and materials involved; for example, they may be made available by supplying a copy or allowing supervised access to view; however, for view only access, it will be necessary to demonstrate that sufficient time is allowed for the suspect and solicitor to view and consider the documents and materials in question.*

H:3A [*Identical to C:3A.*]

H:3B [*Not used.*]

H:3C [*Identical to C:3C.*]

H:3D *The right to consult this or other relevant codes of practice does not entitle the person concerned to delay unreasonably any necessary investigative or administrative action whilst they do so. Examples of action which need not be delayed unreasonably include:*

- *searching detainees at the police station;*
- *taking fingerprints or non-intimate samples without consent for evidential purposes.*

H:3E *The investigation team will include any officer involved in questioning a suspect, gathering or analysing evidence in relation to the offences of which the detainee is suspected of having committed. Should a custody officer require information from the investigation team, the first point of contact should be the officer in charge of the investigation.*

H:3F *Home Office Circular 32/2000 provides more detailed guidance on risk assessments and identifies key risk areas which should always be considered.*

H:3G *Arrests under TACT, s.41, can only be made where an officer has reasonable grounds to suspect that the individual concerned is a "terrorist". This differs from the PACE power of arrest in that it need not be linked to a specific offence. There may also be circumstances where an arrest under TACT is made on the grounds of sensitive information which cannot be disclosed. In such circumstances, the grounds for arrest may be given in terms of the interpretation of a "terrorist" set out in TACT, s.40(1)(a) or (b).*

H:3H *For the purpose of arrests under TACT, s.41, the review officer is responsible for authorising detention (see paragraphs 14.1 and 14.2, and Notes for Guidance 14A and 14B). The review officer's role is explained in TACT, Sched. 8, Pt II. A person may be detained after arrest pending the first review, which must take place as soon as practicable after the person's arrest.*

H:3I *A custody officer or other officer who, in accordance with this code, allows or directs the carrying out of any task or action relating to a detainee's care, treatment, rights and entitlements by another officer or any police staff must be satisfied that the officer or police staff concerned are suitable, trained and competent to carry out the task or action in question.*

### H:4 Detainee's property

#### (a) *Action*

H:4.1 The custody officer is responsible for: **A-216a**
    (a) ascertaining what property a detainee:
        (i) has with them when they come to the police station, either on first arrival at the police station or any subsequent arrivals at a police station in connection with that detention;
        (ii) might have acquired for an unlawful or harmful purpose while in custody;
    (b) the safekeeping of any property taken from a detainee which remains at the police station.
The custody officer may search the detainee or authorise their being searched to the extent they consider necessary, provided a search of intimate parts of the body or involving the removal of more than outer clothing is only made as in Annex A. A search may only be carried out by an officer of the same sex as the detainee. See *Note 4A* and Annex I.

H:4.2, 4.3 *[Identical to C:4.2 and C:4.3, respectively.]*

#### (b) *Documentation*

H:4.4 It is a matter for the custody officer to determine whether a record should be made of the property a detained person has with him or had taken from him on arrest [see *Note 4D*]. Any record made is not required to be kept as part of the custody record but the custody record should be noted as to where such a record exists. Whenever a record is made the detainee shall be allowed to check and sign the record of property as correct. Any refusal to sign shall be recorded.

H:4.5 *[Identical to C:4.5.]*

#### *Notes for guidance*

H:4A–4C *[Identical to C:4A to C:4C, respectively.]* **A-216b**

H:4D *Section 43(2) of TACT allows a constable to search a person who has been arrested under section 41 to discover whether they have anything in their possession that may constitute evidence that they are a terrorist.*

### H:5 Right not to be held incommunicado

#### (a) *Action*

H:5.1 Any person to whom this code applies who is held in custody at a police station or other **A-217** premises may, on request, have one named person who is a friend, relative or a person known to them who is likely to take an interest in their welfare informed at public expense of their whereabouts as soon as practicable. If the person cannot be contacted the detainee may choose up to two alternatives. If they cannot be contacted, the person in charge of detention or the investigation has discretion to allow further attempts until the information has been conveyed. See *Notes 5D* and *5E*.

H:5.2 *[Identical to C:5.2.]*

H:5.3 The above right may be exercised each time a detainee is taken to another police station or returned to a police station having been previously transferred to prison. This code does not afford such a right to a person on transfer to a prison, where a detainee's rights will be governed by prison rules [see paragraph 14.8].

H:5.4 If the detainee agrees, they may at the custody officer's discretion receive visits from friends, family or others likely to take an interest in their welfare, or in whose welfare the detainee has an interest. Custody officers should liaise closely with the investigation team [see *Note 3E*] to allow risk assessments to be made where particular visitors have been requested by the detainee or identified themselves to police. In circumstances where the nature of the investigation means that such requests cannot be met, consideration should be given, in conjunction with a representative of the relevant scheme, to increasing the frequency of visits from independent visitor schemes. See *Notes 5B* and *5C*.

H:5.5 [*Identical to C:5.5, save for reference to "Note 5E" in lieu of reference to "Note 5D".*]

H:5.6 The detainee shall be given writing materials, on request, and allowed to telephone one person for a reasonable time, see *Notes 5A* and *5F*. Either or both these privileges may be denied or delayed if an officer of inspector rank or above considers sending a letter or making a telephone call may result in any of the consequences in Annex B, paras 1 and 2, particularly in relation to the making of a telephone call in a language which an officer listening to the call [see paragraph 5.7] does not understand. See *Note 5G*.

Nothing in this paragraph permits the restriction or denial of the rights in paragraphs 5.1 and 6.1.

H:5.7 Before any letter or message is sent, or telephone call made, the detainee shall be informed that what they say in any letter, call or message (other than in a communication to a solicitor) may be read or listened to and may be given in evidence. A telephone call may be terminated if it is being abused [see *Note 5G*]. The costs can be at public expense at the custody officer's discretion.

H:5.8 [*Identical to C:5.7A.*]

### (b) Documentation

H:5.9 A record must be kept of any:

(a) request made under this section and the action taken;

(b) letters, messages or telephone calls made or received or visit received;

(c) refusal by the detainee to have information about them given to an outside enquirer, or any refusal to see a visitor. The detainee must be asked to countersign the record accordingly and any refusal recorded.

### Notes for guidance

H:5A *A person may request an interpreter to interpret a telephone call or translate a letter.*

H:5B *At the custody officer's discretion (and subject to the detainee's consent), visits should be allowed when possible, subject to sufficient personnel being available to supervise a visit and any possible hindrance to the investigation. Custody officers should bear in mind the exceptional nature of prolonged TACT detention and consider the potential benefits that visits may bring to the health and welfare of detainees who are held for extended periods.*

H:5C *Official visitors should be given access following consultation with the officer who has overall responsibility for the investigation provided the detainee consents, and they do not compromise safety or security or unduly delay or interfere with the progress of an investigation. Official visitors should still be required to provide appropriate identification and subject to any screening process in place at the place of detention. Official visitors may include:*

- *an accredited faith representative;*
- *Members of either House of Parliament;*
- *public officials needing to interview the prisoner in the course of their duties;*
- *other persons visiting with the approval of the officer who has overall responsibility for the investigation;*
- *consular officials visiting a detainee who is a national of the country they represent subject to section 7 of this code.*

*Visits from appropriate members of the Independent Custody Visitors Scheme should be dealt with in accordance with the separate Code of Practice on Independent Custody Visiting.*

H:5D *If the detainee does not know anyone to contact for advice or support or cannot contact a friend or relative, the custody officer should bear in mind any local voluntary bodies or other organisations that might be able to help. Paragraph 6.1 applies if legal advice is required.*

H:5E *In some circumstances it may not be appropriate to use the telephone to disclose information under paragraphs 5.1 and 5.5.*

H:5F *The telephone call at paragraph 5.6 is in addition to any communication under paragraphs 5.1 and 6.1. Further calls may be made at the custody officer's discretion.*

H:5G *The nature of terrorism investigations means that officers should have particular regard to the possibility of suspects attempting to pass information which may be detrimental to public safety, or to an investigation.*

## H:6 Right to legal advice

### (a) *Action*

H:6.1 Unless Annex B applies, all detainees must be informed that they may at any time consult   **A-217b** and communicate privately with a solicitor, whether in person, in writing or by telephone, and that free independent legal advice is available from the duty solicitor. Where an appropriate adult is in attendance, they must also be informed of this right. See paragraph 3.1, *Note 1I, Notes 6B* and *6J*.

H:6.2 A poster advertising the right to legal advice must be prominently displayed in the charging area of every police station. See *Note 6G*.

H:6.3 [*Identical to C:6.4.*]

H:6.4 The exercise of the right of access to legal advice may be delayed exceptionally only as in Annex B. Whenever legal advice is requested, and unless Annex B applies, the custody officer must act without delay to secure the provision of such advice. If, on being informed or reminded of this right, the detainee declines to speak to a solicitor in person, the officer should point out that the right includes the right to speak with a solicitor on the telephone (see paragraph 5.6). If the detainee continues to waive this right the officer should ask them why and any reasons should be recorded on the custody record or the interview record as appropriate. Reminders of the right to legal advice must be given as in paragraphs 3.5, 11.3 and 5 of Annex K [*sic*] of this code and *PACE* Code D on the Identification of Persons by Police Officers, paragraphs 3.17(ii) and 6.3. Once it is clear a detainee does not want to speak to a solicitor in person or by telephone they should cease to be asked their reasons. See *Note 6J*.

H:6.5 An officer of the rank of commander or assistant chief constable or above may give a direction under TACT, Sched. 8, para. 9, that a detainee may only consult a solicitor within the sight and hearing of a qualified officer. Such a direction may only be given if the officer has reasonable grounds to believe that if it were not, it may result in one of the consequences set out in TACT, Sched. 8, para. 8(4) or (5)(c). See Annex B, para. 3, and *Note 6I*. A "qualified officer" means a police officer who:

(a) is at least the rank of inspector;

(b) is of the uniformed branch of the force of which the officer giving the direction is a member; and

(c) in the opinion of the officer giving the direction, has no connection with the detained person's case.

Officers considering the use of this power should first refer to Home Office *Circular 40/2003*.

H:6.6 [*Identical to C:6.5A, save for reference to "paragraph 1.11A" in lieu of reference to "paragraph 1.5A".*]

H:6.7 A detainee who wants legal advice may not be interviewed or continue to be interviewed until they have received such advice unless:

(a) [*identical to C:6.6(a)*];

(b) [*identical to C:6.6(b)*];

(c) [*identical to C:6.6(c)*];

(d) the detainee changes their mind, about wanting legal advice or (as the case may be) about wanting a solicitor present at the interview, and states that they no longer wish to speak to a solicitor; in these circumstances the interview may be started or continued without delay provided that:

   (i) an officer of inspector rank or above:

     • speaks to the detainee to enquire about the reasons for their change of mind (see *Note 6J*); and

     • makes, or directs the making of, reasonable efforts to ascertain the solicitor's expected time of arrival and to inform the solicitor that the suspect has stated that they wish to change their mind and the reason (if given);

   (ii) the detainee's reason for their change of mind (if given) and the outcome of the action in (i) are recorded in the custody record;

   (iii) the detainee, after being informed of the outcome of the action in (i) above, confirms in writing that they want the interview to proceed without speaking or further speaking to a solicitor or (as the case may be) without a solicitor being present and do not wish to wait for a solicitor by signing an entry to this effect in the custody record;

   (iv) an officer of inspector rank or above is satisfied that it is proper for the interview to proceed in these circumstances and:

- gives authority in writing for the interview to proceed and if the authority is not recorded in the custody record, the officer must ensure that the custody record shows the date and time of authority and where it is recorded; and
- takes or directs the taking of, reasonable steps to inform the solicitor that the authority has been given and the time when the interview is expected to commence and records or causes to be recorded, the outcome of this action in the custody record;

(v) when the interview starts and the interviewer reminds the suspect of their right to legal advice (see paragraph 11.3) and the code of practice issued under paragraph 3 of Schedule 8 to the Terrorism Act 2000 for the video recording with sound of interviews, the interviewer shall then ensure that the following is recorded in the interview record made in accordance with that code:

- confirmation that the detainee has changed their mind about wanting legal advice or (as the case may be) about wanting a solicitor present and the reasons for it if given;
- the fact that authority for the interview to proceed has been given and, subject to paragraph 2.8, the name of the authorising officer;
- that if the solicitor arrives at the station before the interview is completed, the detainee will be so informed without delay and a break will be taken to allow them to speak to the solicitor if they wish, unless paragraph 6.7(a) applies; and
- that at any time during the interview, the detainee may again ask for legal advice and that if they do, a break will be taken to allow them to speak to the solicitor, unless paragraph 6.7(a), (b) or (c) applies.

Note: in these circumstances the restriction on drawing adverse inferences from silence in Annex C will not apply because the detainee is allowed an opportunity to consult a solicitor if they wish.

H:6.8 If paragraph 6.7(a) applies, where the reason for authorising the delay ceases to apply, there may be no further delay in permitting the exercise of the right in the absence of a further authorisation unless paragraph 6.7(b), (c) or (d) applies. If paragraph 6.7(b)(i) applies, once sufficient information has been obtained to avert the risk, questioning must cease until the detainee has received legal advice unless paragraph 6.7(a), (b)(ii), (c) or (d) applies.

H:6.9 [*Identical to C:6.8, save for reference to "paragraph 6.7" in lieu of reference to "paragraph 6.6".*]

H:6.10 The solicitor may only be required to leave the interview if their conduct is such that the interviewer is unable properly to put questions to the suspect. See *Notes 6C* and *6D*.

H:6.11 [*Identical to C:6.10, save for reference to "Note 6D" in lieu of reference to "Note 6E".*]

H:6.12 [*Identical to C:6.11.*]

H: 6.13 [*Identical to C:6.12.*]

H:6.14 [*Identical to C:6.12A, save for references to "Note 6C" and to "paragraphs 6.7 to 6.11" in lieu of references to "Note 6D" and "paragraphs 6.6. to 6.10".*]

H:6.15 In exercising their discretion under paragraph 6.14, the officer should take into account in particular:

- whether:
  - the identity and status of an accredited or probationary representative have been satisfactorily established;
  - they are of suitable character to provide legal advice,
- any other matters in any written letter of authorisation provided by the solicitor on whose behalf the person is attending the police station. See *Note 6E*.

H:6.16 If the inspector refuses access to an accredited or probationary representative or a decision is taken that such a person should not be permitted to remain at an interview, the inspector must notify the solicitor on whose behalf the representative was acting and give them an opportunity to make alternative arrangements. The detainee must be informed and the custody record noted.

H:6.17 If a solicitor arrives at the station to see a particular person, that person must, unless Annex B applies, be so informed whether or not they are being interviewed and asked if they would like to see the solicitor. This applies even if the detainee has declined legal advice or, having requested it, subsequently agreed to be interviewed without receiving advice. The solicitor's attendance and the detainee's decision must be noted in the custody record.

(b) *Documentation*

H:6.18, 6.19 [*Identical to C:6.16 and C:6.17, respectively.*]

*Notes for guidance*

H:6ZA *No police officer or police staff shall indicate to any suspect, except to answer a direct question, that* **A-218**
*period for which they are liable to be detained, or the time taken to complete the interview, might be reduced:*

- *if they do not ask for legal advice or do not want a solicitor present when they are interviewed; or*
- *if after asking for legal advice, they change their mind about wanting it or (as the case may be) wanting a solicitor present when they are interviewed and agree to be interviewed without waiting for a solicitor.*

H:6A *In considering if paragraph 6.7(b) applies, the officer should, if practicable, ask the solicitor for an estimate of how long it will take to come to the station and relate this to the time detention is permitted, the time of day (i.e. whether the rest period under paragraph 12.2 is imminent) and the requirements of other investigations. If the solicitor is on their way or is to set off immediately, it will not normally be appropriate to begin an interview before they arrive. If it appears necessary to begin an interview before the solicitor's arrival, they should be given an indication of how long the police would be able to wait so there is an opportunity to make arrangements for someone else to provide legal advice. Nothing within this section is intended to prevent police from ascertaining immediately after the arrest of an individual whether a threat to public safety exists (see paragraph 11.2).*

H:6B *A detainee has a right to free legal advice and to be represented by a solicitor. This note for guidance explains the arrangements which enable detainees to whom this code applies to obtain legal advice. An outline of these arrangements is also included in the Notice of Rights and Entitlements given to detainees in accordance with paragraph 3.2.*

*The detainee can ask for free advice from a solicitor they know or if they do not know a solicitor or the solicitor they know cannot be contacted, from the duty solicitor.*

*To arrange free legal advice, the police should telephone the Defence Solicitor Call Centre (DSCC). The call centre will contact either the duty solicitor or the solicitor requested by the detainee as appropriate.*

*When a detainee wants to pay for legal advice themselves:*

- *the DSCC will contact a solicitor of their choice on their behalf;*
- *they should be given an opportunity to consult a specific solicitor or another solicitor from that solicitor's firm; if this solicitor is not available, they may choose up to two alternatives; if these alternatives are not available, the custody officer has discretion to allow further attempts until a solicitor has been contacted and agreed to provide advice;*
- *they are entitled to a private consultation with their chosen solicitor on the telephone or the solicitor may decide to come to the police station;*
- *if their chosen solicitor cannot be contacted, the DSCC may still be called to arrange free legal advice.*

*Apart from carrying out duties necessary to implement these arrangements, an officer must not advise the suspect about any particular firm of solicitors.*

H:6C [*Identical to C:6D.*]

H:6D [*Identical to C:6E.*]

H:6E [*Identical to C:6F.*]

H:6F [*Identical to C:6G, save for reference to "paragraph 6.7(b)" in lieu of reference to "paragraph 6.6(b)".*]

H:6G [*Identical to C:6H.*]

H:6H [*Not used.*]

H:6I *Whenever a detainee exercises their right to legal advice by consulting or communicating with a solicitor, they must be allowed to do so in private. This right to consult or communicate in private is fundamental. Except as allowed by the Terrorism Act 2000, Sched. 8, para. 9, if the requirement for privacy is compromised because what is said or written by the detainee or solicitor for the purpose of giving and receiving legal advice is overheard, listened to, or read by others without the informed consent of the detainee, the right will effectively have been denied. When a detainee speaks to a solicitor on the telephone, they should be allowed to do so in private unless a direction under Schedule 8, paragraph 9 of the Terrorism Act 2000 has been given or this is impractical because of the design and layout of the custody area, or the location of telephones. However, the normal expectation should be that facilities will be available, unless they are being used, at all police stations to enable detainees to speak in private to a solicitor either face to face or over the telephone.*

H:6J [*Identical to C:6K.*]

### H:7 Citizens of independent Commonwealth countries or foreign nationals

**A-218a**      [*Identical to C:7 (apart from use of "are" instead of "is" in paragraph 7.4).*]

### H:8 Conditions of detention

#### (a) *Action*

**A-218b**      H:8.1, 8.2 [*Identical to C:8.1, save for omission of reference to Note 8C, and C:8.2, respectively.*]

H:8.3 [*Identical to C:8.3, save for omission of reference to Note 8A.*]

H:8.4, 8.5 [*Identical to C:8.4 and C:8.5, respectively.*]

H:8.6 At least two light meals and one main meal should be offered in any 24-hour period. See *Note 8B*. Drinks should be provided at meal times and upon reasonable request between meals. Whenever necessary, advice shall be sought from the appropriate health care professional, see *Note 9A*, on medical and dietary matters. As far as practicable, meals provided shall offer a varied diet and meet any specific dietary needs or religious beliefs the detainee may have. Detainees should also be made aware that the meals offered meet such needs. The detainee may, at the custody officer's discretion, have meals supplied by their family or friends at their expense. See *Note 8A*.

H:8.7 Brief outdoor exercise shall be offered daily if practicable. Where facilities exist, indoor exercise shall be offered as an alternative if outside conditions are such that a detainee cannot be reasonably expected to take outdoor exercise (*e.g.*, in cold or wet weather) or if requested by the detainee or for reasons of security. See *Note 8C*.

H:8.8 Where practicable, provision should be made for detainees to practice [*sic*] religious observance. Consideration should be given to providing a separate room which can be used as a prayer room. The supply of appropriate food and clothing, and suitable provision for prayer facilities, such as uncontaminated copies of religious books, should also be considered. See *Note 8D*.

H:8.9 A juvenile shall not be placed in a cell unless no other secure accommodation is available and the custody officer considers it is not practicable to supervise them if they are not placed in a cell or that a cell provides more comfortable accommodation than other secure accommodation in the station. A juvenile may not be placed in a cell with a detained adult.

Note: paragraph 1.11A extends these requirements to 17-year-old detainees.

H:8.10 Police stations should keep a reasonable supply of reading material available for detainees, including but not limited to, the main religious texts. See *Note 8D*. Detainees should be made aware that such material is available and reasonable requests for such material should be met as soon as practicable unless to do so would:

    (i) interfere with the investigation; or

    (ii) prevent or delay an officer from discharging his statutory duties, or those in this code.

If such a request is refused on the grounds of (i) or (ii) above, this should be noted in the custody record and met as soon as possible after those grounds cease to apply.

#### (b) *Documentation*

H:8.11, 8.12 [*Identical to C:8.9 and C:8.11, respectively.*]

#### *Notes for guidance*

**A-219**      H:8A *In deciding whether to allow meals to be supplied by family or friends, the custody officer is entitled to take account of the risk of items being concealed in any food or package and the officer's duties and responsibilities under food handling legislation. If an officer needs to examine food or other items supplied by family and friends before deciding whether they can be given to the detainee, he should inform the person who has brought the item to the police station of this and the reasons for doing so.*

H:8B [*Identical to C:8B.*]

H:8C *In light of the potential for detaining individuals for extended periods of time, the overriding principle should be to accommodate a period of exercise, except where to do so would hinder the investigation, delay the detainee"s release or charge, or it is declined by the detainee.*

H:8D *Police forces should consult with representatives of the main religious communities to ensure the provision for religious observance is adequate, and to seek advice on the appropriate storage and handling of religious texts or other religious items.*

### H:9 Care and treatment of detained persons

#### (a) *General*

H:9.1 Notwithstanding other requirements for medical attention as set out in this section, detainees **A-219a** who are held for more than 96 hours must be visited by an appropriate healthcare professional at least once every 24 hours.

H:9.2, 9.3 [*Identical to C:9.1, save for omission of reference to Note 8C, and C:9.2, respectively.*]

H:9.4 [*Identical to C:9.3, save for references to "Note 9C", "paragraph 9.15" and "Note 9G" in lieu of references to "Note 9CA", "paragraph 9.13" and "Note 9H", respectively.*]

H:9.5 [*Identical to C:9.4.*]

#### (b) *Clinical treatment and attention*

H:9.6, 9.7, 9.8 [*Identical to C:9.5, C:9.5A and C: 9.5B, respectively.*]

H:9.9 [*Identical to C:9.7, save for reference to "Note 9D" in lieu of reference to "Note 9E".*]

H:9.10 [*Identical to C:9.8.*]

H:9.11 [*Identical to C:9.9, save for reference to "paragraph 9.12" in lieu of reference to "paragraph 9.10".*]

H:9.12 No police officer may administer or supervise the self-administration of medically prescribed controlled drugs of the types and forms listed in the Misuse of Drugs Regulations 2001, Sched. 2 or 3. A detainee may only self-administer such drugs under the personal supervision of the registered medical practitioner authorising their use or other appropriate healthcare professional. The custody officer may supervise the self-administration of, or authorise other custody staff to supervise the self-administration of, drugs listed in Schedule 4 or 5 if the officer has consulted the appropriate healthcare professional authorising their use and both are satisfied self-administration will not expose the detainee, police officers or anyone else to the risk of harm or injury.

H:9.13 When appropriate healthcare professionals administer drugs or authorise the use of other medications, or consult with the custody officer about allowing self-administration of drugs listed in Schedule 4 or 5, it must be within current medicines legislation and the scope of practice as determined by their relevant regulatory body.

H:9.14 [*Identical to C:9.12, save for reference to "paragraph 9.6" in lieu of reference to "paragraph 9.5".*]

H:9.15 [*Identical to C:9.13.*]

H:9.16 [*Identical to C:9.14, save for reference to "Note 9E" in lieu of reference to "Note 9F".*]

#### (c) *Documentation*

H:9.17 [*Identical to C:9.15, save for references to "paragraph 9.3", "paragraph 9.6", "paragraph 9.10", "Note 9F", "Notes 9D and 9E" and "Note 9G" in lieu of references to "paragraph 9.2", "paragraph 9.5", "paragraph 9.8", "Note 9G", "Notes 9E and 9F" and "Note 9H", respectively.*]

H:9.18 [*Identical to C:9.16, save for reference to "Note 9F" in lieu of reference to "Note 9G".*]

H:9.19 [*Identical to C:9.17.*]

#### Notes for guidance

H:9A, 9B [*Identical to C:9A and C:9B (save for reference to "paragraph 1.11A" in lieu of reference to* **A-219b** *"paragraph 1:5A"), respectively.*]

H:9C [*Identical to C:9C, save for reference to "Paragraph 9.6" in lieu of reference to "Paragraph 9.5".*]

H:9D, 9E [*Identical to C:9E and C:9F, respectively.*]

H:9F [*Identical to C:9G, save for reference to "Paragraphs 9.17 and 9.18" in lieu of reference to "Paragraphs 9.15 and 9.16".*]

H:9G [*Identical to C:9H.*]

### H:10 Cautions

#### (a) *When a caution must be given*

H:10.1 A person whom there are grounds to suspect of an offence, see *Note 10A*, must be cautioned **A-220** before any questions about an offence, or further questions if the answers provide the grounds for suspicion, are put to them if either the suspect's answers or silence (*i.e.* failure or refusal to answer or answer satisfactorily) may be given in evidence to a court in a prosecution.

H:10.2 A person who is arrested, or further arrested, must be informed at the time if practicable or, if not, as soon as it becomes practicable thereafter, that they are under arrest and of the grounds and reasons for their arrest, see paragraph 3.4, *Note 3G* and *Note 10B*.

H:10.3 [*Effectively identical to C:10.4.*]

A-220a

(b) *Terms of the cautions*

H:10.4 The caution which must be given:
- (a) on arrest;
- (b) on all other occasions before a person is charged or informed they may be prosecuted; see PACE, Code C, section 16; and
- (c) before post-charge questioning under section 22 of the Counter-Terrorism Act 2008 (see section 15.9);

should, unless the restriction on drawing adverse inferences from silence applies, see Annex C, be in the following terms:

"*You do not have to say anything. But it may harm your defence if you do not mention when questioned something which you later rely on in court. Anything you do say may be given in evidence.*".

Where the use of the Welsh language is appropriate, a constable may provide the caution directly in Welsh in the following terms:

"*Does dim rhaid i chi ddweud dim byd. Ond gall niweidio eich amddiffyniad os na fyddwch chi'n sôn, wrth gael eich holi, am rywbeth y byddwch chi'n dibynnu arno nes ymlaen yn y Llys. Gall unrhyw beth yr ydych yn ei ddweud gael ei roi fel tystiolaeth.*".

See *Note 10F*.

H:10.5 [*Identical to C:10.6.*]
H:10.6 [*Identical to C:10.7, save for reference to "Note 10C" in lieu of reference to "Note 10D".*]
H:10.7 [*Identical to C:10.8, save for reference to "Note 10D" in lieu of reference to "Note 10E".*]
H: 10.8 [*Identical to C:10.9, but the words following "statutory requirement" have been omitted.*]

(c) *Special warnings under the Criminal Justice and Public Order Act 1994, sections 36 and 37*

H:10.9 [*Identical to C:10.10, save for references to "Note 10E" and "paragraph 10.10" in lieu of references to "Note 10F" and "paragraph 10.11", respectively.*]
H:10.10 [*Identical to C:10.11.*]

(d) *Juveniles and persons who are mentally disordered or otherwise mentally vulnerable*

H:10.10A [*Identical to C:10.11A, save for reference to "paragraph 10.10" in lieu of reference to "paragraph 10.11".*]
H:10.11 [*Identical to C:10.12.*]
H:10.11A Paragraph 1.11A extends the requirements in paragraphs 10.10A and 10.11 to 17-year-old detainees.

(e) *Documentation*

H:10.12 [*Identical to C:10.13.*]

*Notes for guidance*

H:10A [*Identical to C:10A.*]
H:10B [*Identical to C:10B, save for inclusion of reference to "Note 3G" after the word "committed".*]
H:10C–10F [*Identical to C:10D to C:10G.*]

**H:11 Interviews—general**

(a) *Action*

H:11.1 An interview in this code is the questioning of a person arrested on suspicion of being a terrorist which, under paragraph 10.1, must be carried out under caution. Before a person is interviewed they and, if they are represented, their solicitor must be informed of the grounds for arrest, and given sufficient information to enable them to understand the nature of their suspected involvement in the commission, preparation or instigation of acts of terrorism (see para. 3.4(a)) in order to allow for the effective exercise of the rights of the defence. However, whilst the information must always be sufficient information for the person to understand the nature of their suspected involvement in the commission, preparation or instigation of acts of terrorism, this does not require the disclosure of details at a time which might prejudice the investigation (see *Notes 3G* and *11ZA*). The decision about what needs to be disclosed for the purpose of this requirement therefore rests with the investigating officer who has sufficient knowledge of the case to make that decision. The officer who discloses the information shall make a record of the information disclosed and when it was disclosed. This record may be made in the interview record, in the officer's pocket book or other form provided for this purpose.

H:11.2 Following the arrest of a person under section 41 TACT, that person must not be interviewed about the relevant offence except at a place designated for detention under Schedule 8, paragraph 1, of the Terrorism Act 2000, unless the consequent delay would be likely to:

    (a) lead to:

- interference with, or harm to, evidence connected with an offence;
- interference with, or physical harm to, other people; or
- serious loss of, or damage to, property;

    (b) lead to alerting other people suspected of committing an offence but not yet arrested for it; or

    (c) hinder the recovery of property obtained in consequence of the commission of an offence. Interviewing in any of these circumstances shall cease once the relevant risk has been averted or the necessary questions have been put in order to attempt to avert that risk.

H:11.3 Immediately prior to the commencement or re-commencement of any interview at a designated place of detention, the interviewer should remind the suspect of their entitlement to free legal advice and that the interview can be delayed for legal advice to be obtained, unless one of the exceptions in paragraph 6.7 applies. It is the interviewer's responsibility to make sure all reminders are recorded in the interview record.

H:11.4, 11.5 [*Identical to C:11.4 and C:11.4A.*]

H:11.6 [*Identical to C:11.5, save for reference "paragraph 10.8" in lieu of reference to "paragraph 10.9".*]

H:11.7 [*Identical to C:11.6, but with the omission of the final sub-paragraph of that paragraph.*]

### (b) *Interview records*

H:11.8 Interviews of a person detained under section 41 of, or Schedule 8 to, TACT must be video recorded with sound in accordance with the code of practice issued under paragraph 3 of Schedule 8 to the Terrorism Act 2000, or in the case of post-charge questioning authorised under section 22 of the Counter-Terrorism Act 2008, the code of practice issued under section 25 of that Act.

H:11.8A [*Identical to C:11.13.*]

### (c) *Juveniles and mentally disordered or otherwise mentally vulnerable people*

H:11.9 [*Identical to C:11.15, save for reference to "paragraphs 11.2, 11.11 to 11.13" in lieu of reference to "paragraphs 11.1, 11.18 to 11.20", and to "paragraph 1.11A" in lieu of reference to "paragraph 1.5A".*]

H:11.10 If an appropriate adult is present at an interview, they shall be informed:

- that they are not expected to act simply as an observer; and
- that the purpose of their presence is to:
  - advise the person being interviewed;
  - observe whether the interview is being conducted properly and fairly;
  - facilitate communication with the person being interviewed.

The appropriate adult may be required to leave the interview if their conduct is such that the interviewer is unable properly to put questions to the suspect. This will include situations where the appropriate adult's approach or conduct prevents or unreasonably obstructs proper questions being put to the suspect or the suspect's responses being recorded. If the interviewer considers an appropriate adult is acting in such a way, they will stop the interview and consult an officer not below superintendent rank, if one is readily available, and otherwise an officer not below inspector rank not connected with the investigation. After speaking to the appropriate adult, the officer consulted will decide if the interview should continue without the attendance of that appropriate adult. If they decide it should not, another appropriate adult should be obtained before the interview continues, unless the provisions of paragraph 11.11 below apply.

### (d) *Vulnerable suspects—urgent interviews at police stations*

H:11.11–11.13 [*Identical to C:11.18 to C:11.20, save for references to "paragraph 11.2(a) to (c)", "paragraph 1.11A", "paragraph 3.14" and "paragraph 11.11", in lieu of references to "paragraph 11.1(a) to (c)", "paragraph 1.5A", paragraph "3.12" and "paragraph 11.18", respectively.*]

*Notes for guidance*

**★A-221**   H:11ZA *The requirement in paragraph 11.1A for a suspect to be given sufficient information about the nature of their suspected involvement in the commission, preparation or instigation of acts of terrorism applies prior to the interview and whether or not they are legally represented. What is sufficient will depend on the circumstances of the case, but it should normally include, as a minimum, enough to avoid suspects being confused or unclear about what they are supposed to have done and to help an innocent suspect to clear the matter up more quickly.*

H:11A–11C *[Identical to C:11A (save for an erroneous reference to para. 3.4 of code of practice under 1996 Act) to C:11C (save for reference to "paragraph 1.11A" in lieu of reference to "paragraph 1.5A"), respectively.]*

H:11B *The Criminal Procedure and Investigations Act 1996 Code of Practice, paragraph 3.4 states 'In conducting an investigation, the investigator should pursue all reasonable lines of enquiry, whether these point towards or away from the suspect. What is reasonable will depend on the particular circumstances.' Interviewers should keep this in mind when deciding what questions to ask in an interview.*

H:11C *Although juveniles or people who are mentally disordered or otherwise mentally vulnerable are often capable of providing reliable evidence, they may, without knowing or wishing to do so, be particularly prone in certain circumstances to provide information that may be unreliable, misleading or self-incriminating. Special care should always be taken when questioning such a person, and the appropriate adult should be involved if there is any doubt about a person's age, mental state or capacity. Because of the risk of unreliable evidence it is also important to obtain corroboration of any facts admitted whenever possible. Paragraph 1.11A extends this note to 17-year-old suspects.*

H:11D *Consideration should be given to the effect of extended detention on a detainee and any subsequent information they provide, especially if it relates to information on matters that they have failed to provide previously in response to similar questioning: see Annex G.*

H:11E *[Identical to C:11E.]*

### H:12 Interviews in police stations

(a) *Action*

**A-221a**   H:12.1 If a police officer wants to interview or conduct enquiries which require the presence of a detainee, the custody officer is responsible for deciding whether to deliver the detainee into the officer's custody. An investigating officer who is given custody of a detainee takes over responsibility for the detainee's care and treatment for the purposes of this code until they return the detainee to the custody officer when they must report the manner in which they complied with the code whilst having custody of the detainee.

H:12.2 Except as below, in any period of 24 hours a detainee must be allowed a continuous period of at least 8 hours for rest, free from questioning, travel or any interruption in connection with the investigation concerned. This period should normally be at night or other appropriate time which takes account of when the detainee last slept or rested. If a detainee is arrested at a police station after going there voluntarily, the period of 24 hours runs from the time of their arrest (or, if a person was being detained under TACT, Sched. 7, when arrested, from the time at which the examination under Schedule 7 began) and not the time of arrival at the police station. The period may not be interrupted or delayed, except:

    (a) when there are reasonable grounds for believing not delaying or interrupting the period would:

        (i) involve a risk of harm to people or serious loss of, or damage to, property;

        (ii) delay unnecessarily the person's release from custody; or

        (iii) otherwise prejudice the outcome of the investigation;

    (b) at the request of the detainee, their appropriate adult or legal representative;

    (c) when a delay or interruption is necessary in order to:

        (i) comply with the legal obligations and duties arising under section 14; or

        (ii) to take action required under section 9 or in accordance with medical advice.

If the period is interrupted in accordance with (a), a fresh period must be allowed. Interruptions under (b) and (c), do not require a fresh period to be allowed.

H:12.3 *[Identical to C:12.3, save that there is no reference to "Annex G" and the references to "paragraph 11.18" and "paragraphs 11.18 to 11.20" are replaced by references to "paragraph 11.11" and "paragraphs 11.11 to 11.13".]*

H:12.4 *[Identical to C:12.4.]*

H:12.5 A suspect whose detention without charge has been authorised under TACT, Sched. 8, because the detention is necessary for an interview to obtain evidence of the offence for which they have been arrested, may choose not to answer questions but police do not require the suspect's consent or agreement to interview them for this purpose. If a suspect takes steps to prevent themselves being questioned or further questioned, *e.g.* by refusing to leave their cell to go to a suitable interview room or by trying to leave the interview room, they shall be advised their consent or agreement to interview is not required. The suspect shall be cautioned as in section 10, and informed if they fail or refuse to co-operate, the interview may take place in the cell and that their failure or refusal to co-operate may be given in evidence. The suspect shall then be invited to co-operate and go into the interview room.

H:12.6 People being questioned or making statements shall not be required to stand.

H:12.7 Before the interview commences each interviewer shall, subject to the qualification at paragraph 2.8, identify themselves and any other persons present to the interviewee.

H:12.8 [*Effectively identical to C:12.8.*]

H:12.9 During extended periods where no interviews take place, because of the need to gather further evidence or analyse existing evidence, detainees and their legal representative shall be informed that the investigation into the relevant offence remains ongoing. If practicable, the detainee and legal representative should also be made aware in general terms of any reasons for long gaps between interviews. Consideration should be given to allowing visits, more frequent exercise, or for reading or writing materials to be offered: see paragraph 5.4, section 8 and *Note 12C*.

H:12.10 [*Identical to C:12.9.*]

### (b) *Documentation*

H:12.11-12.15 [*Identical to C:12.10 to C:12.14, respectively.*]

### Notes for guidance

H:12A *It is not normally necessary to ask for a written statement if the interview was recorded in accordance* **A-221b** *with the code of practice issued under TACT, Sched. 8, para. 3. Statements under caution should normally be taken in these circumstances only at the person's express wish. A person may however be asked if they want to make such a statement.*

H:12B [*Identical to C:12B.*]

H:12C *Consideration should be given to the matters referred to in paragraph 12.9 after a period of over 24 hours without questioning. This is to ensure that extended periods of detention without an indication that the investigation remains ongoing do not contribute to a deterioration of the detainee's well-being.*

### H:13 Interpreters

### (a) *General*

H:13.1 Chief officers are responsible for making arrangements to provide appropriately qualified independent persons to act as interpreters and to provide translations of essential documents for detained suspects who, in accordance with paragraph 3.5(c)(ii), the custody officer has determined require an interpreter.

If the suspect has a hearing or speech impediment, references to "interpreter" and "interpretation" in this code include appropriate assistance necessary to establish effective communication with that person. See paragraph 13.1C if the detainee is in Wales.

H:13.1A [*Identical to C:13.1A, save for reference to "Annex K" in lieu of reference to "Annex M".*]

H:13.1B [*Identical to C:13.1B.*]

H:13.1C [*Identical to C:13.1C, save for reference to paragraph "3.14" in lieu of reference to paragraph "3.12".*]

### (b) *Interviewing suspects—foreign languages*

H:13.2 Unless paragraphs 11.2 or 11.11(c) apply, a suspect who for the purposes of this code requires an interpreter because they do not appear to speak or understand English (see paras 3.5(c)(ii) and 3.14) must not be interviewed in the absence of a person capable of interpreting.

H:13.3 An interpreter should also be called if a juvenile is interviewed and their parent or guardian, present as the appropriate adult, does not appear to speak or understand English, unless the interview is urgent and paragraphs 11.2 or 11.11(c) apply.

Note: paragraph 1.11A extends the requirement in this paragraph to interviews of 17-year-old suspects.

H:13.4 [*Identical to C:13.4.*]

(c) *Interviewing suspects who have a hearing or speech impediment*

H:13.5 [*Identical to C:13.5, save for reference to paragraph "3.14" in lieu of reference to paragraph "3.12".*]

H:13.6 An interpreter should also be called if a juvenile is interviewed and their parent or guardian present as the appropriate adult appears to have a hearing or speech impediment, unless the interview is urgent and paragraphs 11.2 or 11.11(c) apply.

Note: paragraph 1.11A extends the requirement in this paragraph to interviews of 17-year-old suspects.

H:13.7 [*Not used.*]

(d) *Additional rules for detained persons*

H:13.8 [*Not used.*]

H:13.9 [*Identical to C:13.9.*]

H:13.10 After the custody officer has determined that a detainee requires an interpreter (see para. 3.5(c)(ii)) and following the initial action in paragraphs 3.1 to 3.5, arrangements must also be made for an interpreter to explain:

- the grounds and reasons for any authorisation of their detention under the provisions of the Terrorism Act 2000 or the Counter Terrorism Act 2008 (post-charge questioning) to which this code applies, and
- any information about the authorisation given to them by the authorising officer or (as the case may be) the court and which is recorded in the custody record.

See sections 14 and 15 of this code.

H:13.10A [*Identical to C:13.10A.*]

(e) *Translations of essential documents*

H:13.10B [*Identical to C:13.10B, save for reference to "Annex K" in lieu of reference to "Annex M".*]

H:13.10C [*Identical to C:13.10C.*]

(f) *Decisions not to provide interpretation and translation.*

H:13.10D If a suspect challenges a decision:

- made by the custody officer in accordance with this code (see para. 3.5(c)(ii)) that they do not require an interpreter, or
- made in accordance with paragraphs 13.10A, 13.10B or 13.10C not to provide a different interpreter or another translation or not to translate a requested document,

the matter shall be reported to an inspector to deal with as a complaint for the purposes of paragraph 9.3 or 12.10 if the challenge is made during an interview.

(g) *Documentation*

H:13.11 [*Identical to C:13.11, save for references to "Annex K" in lieu of references to "Annex M".*]

*Notes for guidance*

H:13A–13C [*Identical to C:13A to C:13C, respectively.*]

**H:14 Reviews and extensions of detention under the Terrorism Act 2000**

(a) *General*

★A-222    H:14.0 The requirement in paragraph 3.4(b) that documents and materials essential to challenging the lawfulness of the detainee's arrest and detention must be made available to the detainee or their solicitor, applies for the purposes of this section as follows:

- (a) the officer reviewing the need for detention (TACT, Sched. 8) is responsible, in consultation with the investigating officer, for deciding which documents and materials are essential and must be made available;
- (b) when an application is to be made for a warrant as described in paragraph 14.3, the person making the application is responsible for deciding which documents and materials are essential and must be made available before the hearing. See *Note 3ZA.*

H:14.1 The powers and duties of the review officer are in the Terrorism Act 2000, Sched. 8, Pt II. See *Notes 14A* and *14B.* A review officer should carry out their duties at the police station where the detainee is held, and be allowed such access to the detainee as is necessary to exercise those duties.

H:14.2 For the purposes of reviewing a person's detention, no officer shall put specific questions to the detainee:

- regarding their involvement in any offence; or
- in respect of any comments they may make:
  – when given the opportunity to make representations; or
  – in response to a decision to keep them in detention or extend the maximum period of detention.

Such an exchange could constitute an interview as in paragraph 11.1 and would be subject to the associated safeguards in section 11.

H:14.3 If detention is necessary for longer than 48 hours from the time of arrest or, if a person was being detained under TACT, Sched. 7, from the time at which the examination under Schedule 7 began), a police officer of at least superintendent rank, or a crown prosecutor may apply for a warrant of further detention or for an extension or further extension of such a warrant under paragraph 29 or (as the case may be) 36 of Part III of Schedule 8 to the Terrorism Act 2000. See paragraph 14.0(b) and *Note 14C.*

H:14.4 When an application is made for a warrant as described in paragraph 14.3, the detained person and their representative must be informed of their rights in respect of the application. These include:

(i) the right to a written notice of the application (see para. 14.4 [*sic*]);
(ii) the right to make oral or written representations to the judicial authority/High Court judge about the application;
(iii) the right to be present and legally represented at the hearing of the application, unless specifically excluded by the judicial authority/High Court judge;
(iv) their right to free legal advice (see section 6 of this code).

H:14.4A TACT, Sched. 8, para. 31, requires the notice of the application for a warrant of further detention to be provided before the judicial hearing of the application for that warrant and that the notice must include:

(a) notification that the application for a warrant has been made;
(b) the time at which the application was made;
(c) the time at which the application is to be heard;
(d) the grounds on which further detention is sought.

A notice must also be provided each time an application is made to extend or further extend an existing warrant.

(b) *Transfer of persons detained for more than 14 days to prison*

H:14.5 If the *Detention of Terrorists Suspects (Temporary Extension) Bill* is enacted and in force, a High Court judge may extend or further extend a warrant of further detention to authorise a person to be detained beyond a period of 14 days from the time of their arrest (or if they were being detained under TACT, Sched. 7, from the time at which their examination under Schedule 7 began). The provisions of Annex J will apply when a warrant of further detention is so extended or further extended.

H:14.6–14.10 [*Not used.*]

(c) *Documentation*

H:14.11 It is the responsibility of the officer who gives any reminders as at paragraph 14.4, to ensure that these are noted in the custody record, as well any comments made by the detained person upon being told of those rights.

H:14.12 The grounds for, and extent of, any delay in conducting a review shall be recorded.

H:14.13 Any written representations shall be retained.

H:14.14 A record shall be made as soon as practicable about the outcome of each review and, if applicable, the grounds on which the review officer authorises continued detention. A record shall also be made as soon as practicable about the outcome of an application for a warrant of further detention or its extension.

H:14.15 [*Not used.*]

*Notes for guidance*

H:14A *TACT, Sched. 8, Pt II, sets out the procedures for review of detention up to 48 hours from the time of arrest under TACT, s.41 (or if a person was being detained under TACT, Sched. 7, from the time at which the examination under Schedule 7 began). These include provisions for the requirement to review detention, postponing a review, grounds for continued detention, designating a review officer, representations, rights of the detained person and keeping a record. The review officer's role ends after a warrant has been issued for extension of detention under Part III of Schedule 8.* **A-222a**

H:14B *A review officer may authorise a person's continued detention if satisfied that detention is necessary—*

   (a) *to obtain relevant evidence whether by questioning the person or otherwise;*

   (b) *to preserve relevant evidence;*

   (c) *while awaiting the result of an examination or analysis of relevant evidence;*

   (d) *for the examination or analysis of anything with a view to obtaining relevant evidence;*

   (e) *pending a decision to apply to the Secretary of State for a deportation notice to be served on the detainee, the making of any such application, or the consideration of any such application by the Secretary of State;*

   (f) *pending a decision to charge the detainee with an offence.*

H:14C *Applications for warrants to extend detention beyond 48 hours, may be made for periods of 7 days at a time (initially under TACT, Sched. 8, para. 29, and extensions thereafter under TACT, Sched. 8, para. 36), up to a maximum period of 14 days (or 28 days if the Detention of Terrorists Suspects (Temporary Extension) Bill is enacted and in force) from the time of their arrest (or if they were being detained under TACT, Sched. 7, from the time at which their examination under Schedule 7 began). Applications may be made for shorter periods than 7 days, which must be specified. The judicial authority or High Court judge may also substitute a shorter period if they feel a period of 7 days is inappropriate.*

H:14D *Unless Note 14F applies, applications for warrants that would take the total period of detention up to 14 days or less should be made to a judicial authority, meaning a District Judge (Magistrates' Court) designated by the Lord Chief Justice to hear such applications.*

H:14E *If by virtue of the relevant provisions described in Note 14C being enacted the maximum period of detention is extended to 28 days, any application for a warrant which would take the period of detention beyond 14 days from the time of arrest (or if a person was being detained under TACT, Sched. 7, from the time at which the examination under Schedule 7 began), must be made to a High Court Judge.*

H:14F *If, when the Detention of Terrorists Suspects (Temporary Extension) Bill is enacted and in force, an application is made to a High Court judge for a warrant which would take detention beyond 14 days and the High Court judge instead issues a warrant for a period of time which would not take detention beyond 14 days, further applications for extension of detention must also be made to a High Court judge, regardless of the period of time to which they refer.*

H:14G *[Not used.]*

H:14H *An officer applying for an order under TACT, Sched. 8, para. 34, to withhold specified information on which he intends to rely when applying for a warrant of further detention or the extension or further extension of such a warrant, may make the application for the order orally or in writing. The most appropriate method of application will depend on the circumstances of the case and the need to ensure fairness to the detainee.*

H:14I *After hearing any representations by or on behalf of the detainee and the applicant, the judicial authority or High Court judge may direct that the hearing relating to the extension of detention under Part III of Schedule 8 is to take place using video conferencing facilities. However, if the judicial authority requires the detained person to be physically present at any hearing, this should be complied with as soon as practicable. Paragraph 33(4) to (9) of TACT, Sched. 8, govern the hearing of applications via video-link or other means.*

H:14J *[Not used.]*

H:14K *[Not used.]*

## H:15 Charging and post-charge questioning in terrorism cases

### (a) *Charging*

H:15.1 Charging of detained persons is covered by PACE and guidance issued under PACE by the Director of Public Prosecutions. Decisions to charge persons to whom this code (H) applies, the charging process and related matters are subject to section 16 of PACE Code C.

### (b) *Post-charge questioning*

H:15.2 Under section 22 of the Counter-Terrorism Act 2008, a judge of the Crown Court may authorise the questioning of a person about an offence for which they have been charged, informed that they may be prosecuted or sent for trial, if the offence:

   • is a terrorism offence as set out in section 27 of the Counter-Terrorism Act 2008; or

   • is an offence which appears to the judge to have a terrorist connection (see *Note 15C*).

The decision on whether to apply for such questioning will be based on the needs of the investigation. There is no power to detain a person solely for the purposes of post-charge questioning. A person can only be detained whilst being so questioned (whether at a police station or in prison) if they are already there in lawful custody under some existing power. If at a police station the contents of sections 8 and 9 of this code must be considered the minimum standards of treatment for such detainees.

H:15.3 The Crown Court judge may authorise the questioning if they are satisfied that:

- further questioning is necessary in the interests of justice;
- the investigation for the purposes of which the further questioning is being proposed is being conducted diligently and expeditiously; and
- the questioning would not interfere unduly with the preparation of the person's defence to the charge or any other criminal charge that they may be facing.

See *Note 15E*.

H:15.4 The judge authorising questioning may specify the location of the questioning.

H:15.5 The judge may only authorise a period up to a maximum of 48 hours before further authorisation must be sought. The 48 hour period would run continuously from the commencement of questioning. This period must include breaks in questioning in accordance with paragraphs 8.6 and 12.2 of this code (see *Note 15B*).

H:15.6 Nothing in this code shall be taken to prevent a suspect seeking a voluntary interview with the police at any time.

H:15.7 For the purposes of this section, any reference in sections 6, 10, 11, 12 and 13 of this code to:

- "suspect" means the person in respect of whom an authorisation has been given under section 22 of the Counter-Terrorism Act 2008 (post-charge questioning of terrorist suspects) to interview them;
- "interview" means post-charge questioning authorised under section 22 of the CounterTerrorism Act 2008;
- "offence" means an offence for which the person has been charged, informed that they may be prosecuted or sent for trial and about which the person is being questioned; and
- "place of detention" means the location of the questioning specified by the judge (see paragraph 15.4),

and the provisions of those sections apply (as appropriate), to such questioning (whether at a police station or in prison) subject to the further modifications in the following paragraphs:

**Right to legal advice**

H:15.8 In section 6 of this code, for the purposes of post-charge questioning:

- access to a solicitor may not be delayed under Annex B; and
- paragraph 6.5 (direction that a detainee may only consult a solicitor within the sight and hearing of a qualified officer) does not apply.

**Cautions**

H:15.9 In section 10 of this code, unless the restriction on drawing adverse inferences from silence applies (see paragraph 15.10), for the purposes of post-charge questioning, the caution must be given in the following terms before any such questions are asked:

"*You do not have to say anything. But it may harm your defence if you do not mention when questioned something which you later rely on in court. Anything you do say may be given in evidence.*".

Where the use of the Welsh language is appropriate, a constable may provide the caution directly in Welsh in the following terms:

"*Does dim rhaid i chi ddweud dim byd. Ond gall niweidio eich amddiffyniad os na fyddwch chi'n sôn, yn awr, am rywbeth y byddwch chi'n dibynnu arno nes ymlaen yn y llys. Gall unrhyw beth yr ydych yn ei ddweud gael ei roi fel tystiolaeth.*".

H:15.10 The only restriction on drawing adverse inferences from silence, see Annex C, applies in those situations where a person has asked for legal advice and is questioned before receiving such advice in accordance with paragraph 6.7(b).

**Interviews**

H:15.11 In section 11, for the purposes of post-charge questioning, whenever a person is questioned, they must be informed of the offence for which they have been charged or informed that they may be prosecuted, or that they have been sent for trial and about which they are being questioned.

H:15.12 Paragraph 11.2 (place where questioning may take place) does not apply to postcharge questioning.

**Recording post-charge questioning**

H:15.13 All interviews must be video recorded with sound in accordance with the separate code of practice issued under section 25 of the Counter-Terrorism Act 2008 for the video recording with sound of post-charge questioning authorised under section 22 of the Counter-Terrorism Act 2008 (see paragraph 11.8).

*Notes for guidance*

**A-222d**

H:15A *If a person is detained at a police station for the purposes of post-charge questioning, a custody record must be opened in accordance with section 2 of this code. The custody record must note the power under which the person is being detained, the time at which the person was transferred into police custody, their time of arrival at the police station and their time of being presented to the custody officer.*

H:15B *The custody record must note the time at which the interview process commences. This shall be regarded as the relevant time for any period of questioning in accordance with paragraph 15.5 of this code.*

H:15C *Where reference is made to "terrorist connection" in paragraph 15.2, this is determined in accordance with section 30 of the Counter-Terrorism Act 2008. Under section 30 of that Act a court must in certain circumstances determine whether an offence has a terrorist connection. These are offences under general criminal law which may be prosecuted in terrorism cases (for example explosives-related offences and conspiracy to murder). An offence has a terrorist connection if the offence is, or takes place in the course of, an act of terrorism or is committed for the purposes of terrorism (section 98 of the Act). Normally the court will make the determination during the sentencing process, however for the purposes of post-charge questioning, a Crown Court judge must determine whether the offence could have a terrorist connection.*

H:15D *The powers under section 22 of the Counter-Terrorism Act 2008 are separate from and additional to the normal questioning procedures within this code. Their overall purpose is to enable the further questioning of a terrorist suspect after charge. They should not therefore be used to replace or circumvent the normal powers for dealing with routine questioning.*

H:15E *Post-charge questioning has been created because it is acknowledged that terrorist investigations can be large and complex and that a great deal of evidence can come to light following the charge of a terrorism suspect. This can occur, for instance, from the translation of material or as the result of additional investigation. When considering an application for post-charge questioning, the police must "satisfy" the judge on all three points under paragraph 15.3. This means that the judge will either authorise or refuse an application on the balance of whether the conditions in paragraph 15.3 are all met. It is important therefore, when making the application, to consider the following questions:*

- *What further evidence is the questioning expected to provide?*
- *Why was it not possible to obtain this evidence before charge?*
- *How and why was the need to question after charge first recognised ?*
- *How is the questioning expected to contribute further to the case ?*
- *To what extent could the time and place for further questioning interfere with the preparation of the person's defence (for example if authorisation is sought close to the time of a trial)?*
- *What steps will be taken to minimise any risk that questioning might interfere with the preparation of the person's defence ?*

*This list is not exhaustive but outlines the type of questions that could be relevant to any asked by a judge in considering an application.*

### H:16 Testing persons for the presence of specified Class A drugs

**A-223**

H:16.1 The provisions for drug testing under section 63B of PACE (as amended by section 5 of the Criminal Justice Act 2003 and section 7 of the Drugs Act 2005), do not apply to persons to whom this code applies. Guidance on these provisions can be found in section 17 of PACE Code C.

### ANNEX A

### Intimate and strip searches

A *Intimate search*

**A-223a**

H:1. [*Identical to Code C, Annex A, para. 1.*]

### (a) Action

H:2. Body orifices other than the mouth may be searched if authorised by an officer of inspector rank or above who has reasonable grounds for believing that the person may have concealed on themselves anything which they could and might use to cause physical injury to themselves or others at the station and the officer has reasonable grounds for believing that an intimate search is the only means of removing those items.

H:3. [*Identical to Code C, Annex A, para. 2A, save for reference to "paragraph 1.11A" in lieu of reference to "paragraph 1.5A".*]

H:4. An intimate search may only be carried out by a registered medical practitioner or registered nurse, unless an officer of at least inspector rank considers this is not practicable, in which case a police officer may carry out the search. See *Notes A1 to A5.*

H:5. Any proposal for a search under paragraph 2 to be carried out by someone other than a registered medical practitioner or registered nurse must only be considered as a last resort and when the authorising officer is satisfied the risks associated with allowing the item to remain with the detainee outweigh the risks associated with removing it. See *Notes A1 to A5.*

H:6. An intimate search at a police station of a juvenile or mentally disordered or otherwise mentally vulnerable person may take place only in the presence of an appropriate adult of the same sex (see Annex I), unless the detainee specifically requests a particular adult of the opposite sex who is readily available. In the case of a juvenile the search may take place in the absence of the appropriate adult only if the juvenile signifies in the presence of the appropriate adult they do not want the adult present during the search and the adult agrees. A record shall be made of the juvenile's decision and signed by the appropriate adult.

Note: paragraph 1.11A of this code extends the requirement in this paragraph to an intimate search of a 17-year-old.

H:7. When an intimate search under paragraph 2 is carried out by a police officer, the officer must be of the same sex as the detainee (see Annex I). A minimum of two people, other than the detainee, must be present during the search. Subject to paragraph 6, no person of the opposite sex who is not a medical practitioner or nurse shall be present, nor shall anyone whose presence is unnecessary. The search shall be conducted with proper regard to the sensitivity and vulnerability of the detainee.

**(b) Documentation**

H:8. In the case of an intimate search under paragraph 2, the following shall be recorded as soon as practicable, in the detainee's custody record:

- the authorisation to carry out the search;
- the grounds for giving the authorisation;
- the grounds for believing the article could not be removed without an intimate search;
- which parts of the detainee's body were searched;
- who carried out the search;
- who was present;
- the result.

H:9. [*Identical to Code C, Annex A, para. 8.*]

B *Strip search*

H:10. [*Identical to Code C, Annex A, para. 9.*]

**(a) Action**

H:11. [*Identical to Code C, Annex A, para. 10.*]

*The conduct of strip searches*

H:12. [*Identical to Code C, Annex A, para. 11, save for references to "Annex I" in lieu of references to "Annex L", and reference to "paragraph 1.11A" in lieu of reference to "paragraph 1.5A".*]

**(b) Documentation**

H:13. [*Identical to Code C, Annex A, para. 12.*]

*Notes for guidance*

H:A1 [*Identical to Code C, Annex A, A1.*]　　　　　　　　　　　　　　　　　　　　　　　　**A-223b**

H:A2 [*Identical to Code C, Annex A, A2.*]

H:A3 [*Identical to Code C, Annex A, A3, save for reference to "paragraph 2" in lieu of reference to "paragraph 2(a)(i)".*]

H:A4 [*Identical to Code C, Annex A, A4, save for reference to "paragraph 2" in lieu of reference to "paragraph 2(a)(i)".*]

H:A5 [*Identical to Code C, Annex A, A5.*]

**ANNEX B**

**Delay in notifying arrest or allowing access to legal advice for persons detained under the Terrorism Act 2000**

A-224     H:1. The rights as in sections 5 or 6, may be delayed if the person is detained under the Terrorism Act 2000, s.41, has not yet been charged with an offence and an officer of superintendent rank or above has reasonable grounds for believing the exercise of either right will have one of the following consequences:

(a) interference with or harm to evidence of a serious offence;

(b) interference with or physical injury to any person;

(c) the alerting of persons who are suspected of having committed a serious offence but who have not been arrested for it;

(d) the hindering of the recovery of property obtained as a result of a serious offence or in respect of which a forfeiture order could be made under section 23;

(e) interference with the gathering of information about the commission, preparation or instigation of acts of terrorism;

(f) the alerting of a person and thereby making it more difficult to prevent an act of terrorism; or

(g) the alerting of a person and thereby making it more difficult to secure a person's apprehension, prosecution or conviction in connection with the commission, preparation or instigation of an act of terrorism.

H:2. These rights may also be delayed if the officer has reasonable grounds for believing that:

(a) the detained person has benefited from his criminal conduct (to be decided in accordance with Part 2 of the Proceeds of Crime Act 2002); and

(b) the recovery of the value of the property constituting the benefit will be hindered by—

(i) informing the named person of the detained person's detention (in the case of an authorisation under paragraph 8(1)(a) of Schedule 8 to TACT); or

(ii) the exercise of the right under paragraph 7 (in the case of an authorisation under paragraph 8(1)(b) of Schedule 8 to TACT).

H:3. Authority to delay a detainee's right to consult privately with a solicitor may be given only if the authorising officer has reasonable grounds to believe the solicitor the detainee wants to consult will, inadvertently or otherwise, pass on a message from the detainee or act in some other way which will have any of the consequences specified under paragraph 8 of Schedule 8 to the Terrorism Act 2000. In these circumstances, the detainee must be allowed to choose another solicitor. See *Note B3.*

H:4. [*Identical to Code C, Annex B, para. 4.*]

H:5. [*Identical to Code C, Annex B, para. 5.*]

H:6. These rights may be delayed only for as long as is necessary but not beyond 48 hours from the time of arrest (or if a person was being detained under TACT, Sched. 7, from the time at which the examination under Schedule 7 began). If the above grounds cease to apply within this time the detainee must as soon as practicable be asked if they wish to exercise either right, the custody record noted accordingly, and action taken in accordance with the relevant section of this code.

H:7. A person must be allowed to consult a solicitor for a reasonable time before any court hearing.

*Documentation*

H:8. [*Identical to Code C, Annex B, para. 13.*]

H:9. [*Identical to Code C, Annex B, para. 14, save for reference to "paragraph 6" in lieu of reference to "paragraphs 6 or 11".*]

*Cautions and special warnings*

H:10. [*Identical to Code C, Annex B, para. 15.*]

*Notes for guidance*

A-224a     H:B1 [*Identical to Code C, Annex B, B1, save for reference to "paragraph 3.15 and 3.17" in lieu of reference to "paragraph 3.13 and 3.15" and reference to "paragraph 1.11A" in lieu of reference to "paragraph 1.5A".*]

H:B2 [*Identical to Code C, Annex B, B2.*]

H:B3 [*Identical to Code C, Annex B, B3.*]

## ANNEX C

**Restriction on drawing adverse inferences from silence and terms of the caution when the restriction applies**

(a) *The restriction on drawing adverse inferences from silence*

H:1. The Criminal Justice and Public Order Act 1994, ss.34, 36 and 37 as amended by the Youth **A-224b** Justice and Criminal Evidence Act 1999, s.58 describe the conditions under which adverse inferences may be drawn from a person's failure or refusal to say anything about their involvement in the offence when interviewed, after being charged or informed they may be prosecuted. These provisions are subject to an overriding restriction on the ability of a court or jury to draw adverse inferences from a person's silence. This restriction applies:

(a) to any detainee at a police station who, before being interviewed, see section 11 or being charged or informed they may be prosecuted, see section 15, has:

(i) asked for legal advice, see section 6, paragraph 6.1;

(ii) not been allowed an opportunity to consult a solicitor, including the duty solicitor, as in this code; and

(iii) not changed their mind about wanting legal advice, see section 6, paragraph 6.7(d);

Note the condition in (ii) will:

− apply when a detainee who has asked for legal advice is interviewed before speaking to a solicitor as in section 6, paragraph 6.6(a) or (b);

− not apply if the detained person declines to ask for the duty solicitor, see section 6, paragraphs 6.7(b) and (c);

(b) to any person who has been charged with, or informed they may be prosecuted for, an offence who:

(i) has had brought to their notice a written statement made by another person or the content of an interview with another person which relates to that offence, see PACE Code C, section 16, paragraph 16.4;

(ii) is interviewed about that offence, see *PACE* Code C, section 16, paragraph 16.5; or

(iii) makes a written statement about that offence, see Annex D, paragraphs 4 and 9, unless post-charge questioning has been authorised in accordance with section 22 of the Counter-Terrorism Act 2008, in which case the restriction will apply only if the person has asked for legal advice, see section 6, paragraph 6.1, and is questioned before receiving such advice in accordance with paragraph 6.7(b). See paragraph 15.11.

(b) *Terms of the caution when the restriction applies*

H:2. [*Identical to Code C, Annex C, para. 2.*]

H:3. [*Identical to Code C, Annex C, para. 3, save for reference to "Note C1" in lieu of reference to "Note C2".*]

*Notes for guidance*

H:C1 [*Identical to Code C, Annex C, C2.*] **A-225**

## ANNEX D

**Written statements under caution**

[*Identical to Annex D to Code C.*] **A-225a**

## ANNEX E

**Summary of provisions relating to mentally disordered and otherwise mentally vulnerable people**

H:1. [*Identical to Code C, Annex E, para. 1, save for reference to "paragraph 1.10" in lieu of reference to* **A-225b** *"paragraph 1.4" and absence of any reference to Note E4.*]

H:2. [*Identical to Code C, Annex E, para. 2, save for reference to "paragraph 1.13(b)" in lieu of reference to "paragraph 1.7(b)".*]

H:3. If the detention of a person who is mentally vulnerable or appears to be suffering from a mental disorder is authorised by the review officer (see paragraphs 14.1 and 14.2 and *Notes for Guidance 14A and 14B*), the custody officer must as soon as practicable inform the appropriate adult of the grounds for detention and the person's whereabouts, and ask the adult to come to the police station to see them. If the appropriate adult:

- is already at the station when information is given as in paragraphs 3.1 to 3.5 the information must be given in their presence
    - is not at the station when the provisions of paragraph 3.1 to 3.5 are complied with these provisions must be complied with again in their presence once they arrive.

See paragraphs 3.15 to 3.16.

H:4. [*Identical to Code C, Annex E, para. 4, save for reference to "paragraph 3.20" in lieu of reference to "paragraph 3.19".*]

H:5. [*Identical to Code C, Annex E, para. 5, save for reference to "paragraph 9.6 and 9.8" in lieu of reference to "paragraph 9.5 and 9.6".*]

H:6. If a mentally disordered or otherwise mentally vulnerable person is cautioned in the absence of the appropriate adult, the caution must be repeated in the appropriate adult's presence. See paragraph 10.11.

H:7. A mentally disordered or otherwise mentally vulnerable person must not be interviewed or asked to provide or sign a written statement in the absence of the appropriate adult unless the provisions of paragraphs 11.2 or 11.11 to 11.13 apply. Questioning in these circumstances may not continue in the absence of the appropriate adult once sufficient information to avert the risk has been obtained. A record shall be made of the grounds for any decision to begin an interview in these circumstances. See paragraphs 11.2, 11.9 and 11.11 to 11.13.

H:8. If the appropriate adult is present at an interview, they shall be informed they are not expected to act simply as an observer and the purposes of their presence are to:
- advise the interviewee;
- observe whether or not the interview is being conducted properly and fairly;
- facilitate communication with the interviewee.

See paragraph 11.10.

H:9. If the custody officer charges a mentally disordered or otherwise mentally vulnerable person with an offence or takes such other action as is appropriate when there is sufficient evidence for a prosecution this must be carried out in the presence of the appropriate adult if they are at the police station. A copy of the written notice embodying any charge must be given to the appropriate adult. See *PACE* Code C, section 16.

H:10. [*Identical to Code C, Annex E, para. 12, save for reference to "paragraphs 6 and 12(c)" in lieu of reference to "paragraphs 5 and 11(c)".*]

H:11. [*Identical to Code C, Annex E, para. 13.*]

*Notes for guidance*

**A-226**      H:E1 [*Identical to Code C, Annex E, E1, save for reference to "paragraph 3.20" in lieu of reference to "paragraph 3.19".*]

H:E2 [*Identical to Code C, Annex E, E2.*]

H:E3 [*Identical to Code C, Annex E, E3, save for reference to "paragraphs 11.2, 11.11 to 11.13" in lieu of reference to "paragraphs 11.1, 11.18 to 11.20".*]

**ANNEX F**

**A-226a**      [*Not used.*]

**ANNEX G**

**Fitness to be interviewed**

**A-226b**      [*Identical to Annex G to Code C.*]

**ANNEX H**

**Detained person: observation list**

**A-227**      [*Identical to Annex H to Code C.*]

**ANNEX I**

**Establishing gender of persons for the purpose of searching**

**A-228**      [*Identical to Annex L to Code C, save that the references to notes are to Note I1, I2 and so on, rather than to Note L1, L2 and so on.*]

**ANNEX J**

**Transfer of persons detained for more than 14 days to prison**

H:1. When a warrant of further detention is extended or further extended by a High Court judge **A-229** to authorise a person's detention beyond a period of 14 days from the time of their arrest (or if they were being detained under TACT, Sched. 7, from the time at which their examination under Schedule 7 began), the person must be transferred from detention in a police station to detention in a designated prison as soon as is practicable after the warrant is issued, unless:

    (a) the detainee specifically requests to remain in detention at a police station and that request can be accommodated; or

    (b) there are reasonable grounds to believe that transferring the detainee to a prison would:

        (i) significantly hinder a terrorism investigation;

        (ii) delay charging of the detainee or their release from custody; or

        (iii) otherwise prevent the investigation from being conducted diligently and expeditiously.

Any grounds in (b)(i) to (iii) above which are relied upon for not transferring the detainee to prison must be presented to the senior judge as part of the application for the extension or further extension of the warrant. See *Note J1*.

H:2 If at any time during which a person remains in detention at a police station under the warrant, the grounds at (b)(i) to (iii) cease to apply, the person must be transferred to a prison as soon as practicable.

H:3 Police should maintain an agreement with the National Offender Management Service (NOMS) that stipulates named prisons to which individuals may be transferred under this paragraph. This should be made with regard to ensuring detainees are moved to the most suitable prison for the purposes of the investigation and their welfare, and should include provision for the transfer of male, female and juvenile detainees. Police should ensure that the governor of a prison to which they intend to transfer a detainee is given reasonable notice of this. Where practicable, this should be no later than the point at which a warrant is applied for that would take the period of detention beyond 14 days.

H:4 Following a detainee's transfer to a designated prison, their detention will be governed by the terms of Schedule 8 to TACT 2000 and the *Prison Rules* and this code of practice will not apply during any period that the person remains in prison detention. The code will once more apply if the person is transferred back from prison detention to police detention. In order to enable the governor to arrange for the production of the detainee back into police custody, police should give notice to the governor of the relevant prison as soon as possible of any decision to transfer a detainee from prison back to a police station. Any transfer between a prison and a police station should be conducted by police and this code will be applicable during the period of transit. See *Note 2J*. A detainee should only remain in police custody having been transferred back from a prison, for as long as is necessary for the purpose of the investigation.

H:5 The investigating team and custody officer should provide as much information as necessary to enable the relevant prison authorities to provide appropriate facilities to detain an individual. This should include, but not be limited to:

    (i) medical assessments;

    (ii) security and risk assessments;

    (iii) details of the detained person's legal representatives;

    (iv) details of any individuals from whom the detained person has requested visits, or who have requested to visit the detained person.

H:6 Where a detainee is to be transferred to prison, the custody officer should inform the detainee's legal adviser beforehand that the transfer is to take place (including the name of the prison). The custody officer should also make all reasonable attempts to inform:

    • family or friends who have been informed previously of the detainee's detention; and

    • the person who was initially informed of the detainee's detention in accordance with paragraph 5.1.

H:7 Any decision not to transfer a detained person to a designated prison under paragraph 1, must be recorded, along with the reasons for this decision. If a request under paragraph 1(a) is not accommodated, the reasons for this should also be recorded.

*Notes for guidance*

A-230       H:J1 *Transfer to prison is intended to ensure that individuals who are detained for extended periods of time are held in a place designed for longer periods of detention than police stations. Prison will provide detainees with a greater range of facilities more appropriate to longer detention periods.*

H:J2 *This code will only apply as is appropriate to the conditions of detention during the period of transit. There is obviously no requirement to provide such things as bed linen or reading materials for the journey between prison and police station.*

## ANNEX K

### Documents and records to be translated

A-230a       H:1. [*Identical to Code C, Annex M, para. 1.*]

H:2. The documents considered essential for the purposes of this code and for which (subject to paragraphs 3 to 7) written translations must be created are the records made in accordance with this code of the grounds and reasons for any authorisation of a suspect's detention under the provisions of the Terrorism Act 2000 or the Counter Terrorism Act 2008 (post-charge questioning) to which this code applies as they are described and referred to in the suspect's custody record. Translations should be created as soon as practicable after the authorisation has been recorded and provided as soon as practicable thereafter, whilst the person is detained or after they have been released (see *Note K3*).

H:3. [*Identical to Code C, Annex M, para. 3, save for reference to "Code H, paragraph 1.11A" in lieu of reference to "Code C, paragraph 1.5A".*]

H:4. [*Identical to Code C, Annex M, para. 4 (but note that there is no table in Annex K (unlike Annex M to Code C)).*]

H:5. [*Identical to Code C, Annex M, para. 5.*]

H:6. [*Identical to Code C, Annex M, para. 6, save for reference to "Notes K2 and K3" in lieu of reference to "Notes M2 and M3".*]

H:7. For the purpose of the waiver:

(a) the consent of a person who is mentally disordered or otherwise mentally vulnerable person is only valid if the information about the circumstances under which they can waive the right and the reminder about their right to legal advice mentioned in paragraphs 3 to 5 and their consent is given in the presence of the appropriate adult, and the appropriate adult also agrees;

(b) the consent of a juvenile is only valid if their parent's or guardian's consent is also obtained unless the juvenile is under 14, when their parent's or guardian's consent is sufficient in its own right and the information and reminder mentioned in sub-paragraph (a) above and their consent is also given in the presence of the appropriate adult (who may or may not be a parent or guardian).

Note: paragraph 1.11A in Code C [*sic*] requires someone to fulfil the role of the appropriate adult to be present when a 17-year-old is given the information and reminder mentioned in sub paragraph (a) above and gives their consent to waive their right. The consent of their parent or guardian is not required.

H:8. [*Identical to Code C, Annex M, para. 8 (but note that there is no table in Annex K (unlike Annex M to Code C)).*]

H:9. [*Identical to Code C, Annex M, para. 9.*]

*Documentation*

H:10. [*Identical to Code C, Annex M, para. 10, save for reference to "Code H" in lieu of reference to "Code C".*]

*Note for guidance*

H:K1–K3 [*Identical to Code C, Annex M, M1–M3, save for reference to 2000 Act in lieu of reference to 1984 Act.*]

## B. Under the Criminal Procedure and Investigations Act 1996

### (1) As to the recording and retention by the police of material obtained during an investigation and its supply to the prosecutor

### Introduction

A-231       Pursuant to sections 23 and 25 of the 1996 Act (§§ 12-73, 12-74 in the main work), the Secretary of State has prepared and published two codes of practice governing the action the police must take in recording and retaining material obtained in the course of a criminal investigation and regulating its supply to the prosecutor for a decision on disclosure.

The first code came into force on the day appointed for the purpose of Part I of the 1996 Act, namely April 1, 1997 (S.I. 1997 No. 1033). The revised code (set out post) came into force on April 4, 2005: Criminal Procedure and Investigations Act 1996 (Code of Practice) Order 2005 (S.I. 2005 No. 985).

In connection with this code, see also § 12-72 in the main work (meaning of "investigation").

As to the significance of the code of practice in relation to material held overseas, outside the European Union, by entities not subject to the jurisdiction of the United Kingdom, see *R. v. Flook* [2010] 1 Cr.App.R. 30, CA (*ante*, § 12-77).

## CRIMINAL PROCEDURE AND INVESTIGATIONS ACT 1996 CODE OF PRACTICE UNDER PART II

### Preamble

This code of practice is issued under Part II of the Criminal Procedure and Investigations Act 1996 ("the Act"). It sets out the manner in which police officers are to record, retain and reveal to the prosecutor material obtained in a criminal investigation and which may be relevant to the investigation, and related matters.   **A-232**

### Introduction

1.1 This code of practice applies in respect of criminal investigations conducted by police officers **A-232a** which begin on or after the day on which this code comes into effect. Persons other than police officers who are charged with the duty of conducting an investigation as defined in the Act are to have regard to the relevant provisions of the code, and should take these into account in applying their own operating procedures.

1.2 This code does not apply to persons who are not charged with the duty of conducting an investigation as defined in the Act.

1.3 Nothing in this code applies to material intercepted in obedience to a warrant issued under section 2 of the Interception of Communications Act 1985 or section 5 of the Regulation of Investigatory Powers Act 2000, or to any copy of that material as defined in section 10 of the 1985 Act or section 15 of the 2000 Act.

1.4 This code extends only to England and Wales.

### Definitions

2.1 In this code:   **A-233**
   — a *criminal investigation* is an investigation conducted by police officers with a view to it being ascertained whether a person should be charged with an offence, or whether a person charged with an offence is guilty of it. This will include:
      — investigations into crimes that have been committed;
      — investigations whose purpose is to ascertain whether a crime has been committed, with a view to the possible institution of criminal proceedings; and
      — investigations which begin in the belief that a crime may be committed, for example when the police keep premises or individuals under observation for a period of time, with a view to the possible institution of criminal proceedings;
   — charging a person with an offence includes prosecution by way of summons;
   — an *investigator* is any police officer involved in the conduct of a criminal investigation. All investigators have a responsibility for carrying out the duties imposed on them under this code, including in particular recording information, and retaining records of information and other material;
   — the *officer in charge of an investigation* is the police officer responsible for directing a criminal investigation. He is also responsible for ensuring that proper procedures are in place for recording information, and retaining records of information and other material, in the investigation;
   — the *disclosure officer* is the person responsible for examining material retained by the police during the investigation; revealing material to the prosecutor during the investigation and any criminal proceedings resulting from it, and certifying that he has done this; and disclosing material to the accused at the request of the prosecutor;

— the *prosecutor* is the authority responsible for the conduct, on behalf of the Crown, of criminal proceedings resulting from a specific criminal investigation;

— *material* is material of any kind, including information and objects, which is obtained in the course of a criminal investigation and which may be relevant to the investigation. This includes not only material coming into the possession of the investigator (such as documents seized in the course of searching premises) but also material generated by him (such as interview records);

— material may be *relevant to the investigation* if it appears to an investigator, or to the officer in charge of an investigation, or to the disclosure officer, that it has some bearing on any offence under investigation or any person being investigated, or on the surrounding circumstances of the case, unless it is incapable of having any impact on the case;

— *sensitive material* is material, the disclosure of which, the disclosure officer believes, would give rise to a real risk of serious prejudice to an important public interest;

— references to *prosecution disclosure* are to the duty of the prosecutor under sections 3 and 7A of the Act to disclose material which is in his possession or which he has inspected in pursuance of this code, and which might reasonably be considered capable of undermining the case against the accused, or of assisting the case for the accused;

— references to the disclosure of material to a person accused of an offence include references to the disclosure of material to his legal representative;

— references to police officers and to the chief officer of police include those employed in a police force as defined in section 3(3) of the Prosecution of Offences Act 1985.

As to the meaning of "criminal investigation", see *DPP v. Metten*, unreported, January 22, 1999, DC (§ 12-72 in the main work).

### General responsibilities

A-234    3.1 The functions of the investigator, the officer in charge of an investigation and the disclosure officer are separate. Whether they are undertaken by one, two or more persons will depend on the complexity of the case and the administrative arrangements within each police force. Where they are undertaken by more than one person, close consultation between them is essential to the effective performance of the duties imposed by this code.

3.2 In any criminal investigation, one or more deputy disclosure officers may be appointed to assist the disclosure officer, and a deputy disclosure officer may perform any function of a disclosure officer as defined in paragraph 2.1.

3.3 The chief officer of police for each police force is responsible for putting in place arrangements to ensure that in every investigation the identity of the officer in charge of an investigation and the disclosure officer is recorded. The chief officer of police for each police force shall ensure that disclosure officers and deputy disclosure officers have sufficient skills and authority, commensurate with the complexity of the investigation, to discharge their functions effectively. An individual must not be appointed as disclosure officer, or continue in that role, if that is likely to result in a conflict of interest, for instance, if the disclosure officer is the victim of the alleged crime which is the subject of the investigation. The advice of a more senior officer must always be sought if there is doubt as to whether a conflict of interest precludes an individual acting as disclosure officer. If thereafter the doubt remains, the advice of a prosecutor should be sought.

3.4 The officer in charge of an investigation may delegate tasks to another investigator, to civilians employed by the police force, or to other persons participating in the investigation under arrangements for joint investigations, but he remains responsible for ensuring that these have been carried out and for accounting for any general policies followed in the investigation. In particular, it is an essential part of his duties to ensure that all material which may be relevant to an investigation is retained, and either made available to the disclosure officer or (in exceptional circumstances) revealed directly to the prosecutor.

3.5 In conducting an investigation, the investigator should pursue all reasonable lines of inquiry, whether these point towards or away from the suspect. What is reasonable in each case will depend on the particular circumstances. For example, where material is held on computer, it is a matter for the investigator to decide which material on the computer it is reasonable to inquire into, and in what manner.

3.6 If the officer in charge of an investigation believes that other persons may be in possession of material that may be relevant to the investigation, and if this has not been obtained under paragraph 3.5 above, he should ask the disclosure officer to inform them of the existence of the investigation and to invite them to retain the material in case they receive a request for its disclosure. The disclosure officer should inform the prosecutor that they may have such material. However, the officer in charge of an investigation is not required to make speculative enquiries of other persons; there must be some reason to believe that they may have relevant material. That reason may come from information provided to the police by the accused or from other inquiries made or from some other source.

3.7 If, during a criminal investigation, the officer in charge of an investigation or disclosure officer for any reason no longer has responsibility for the functions falling to him, either his supervisor or the police officer in charge of criminal investigations for the police force concerned must assign someone else to assume that responsibility. That person's identity must be recorded, as with those initially responsible for these functions in each investigation.

As to the meaning of "criminal investigation", see *DPP v. Metten*, unreported, January 22, 1999, DC (§ 12-72 in the main work).

Where, in the run-up to an election, there was an arrangement that a local electoral office would notify the police of any suspected fraudulent applications for postal votes, where that office submitted 1,600 suspected fraudulent applications to the police (out of a total of 10,000 applications), where the criminal investigation that ensued resulted in the prosecution of the appellants for conspiracy to defraud the electoral officer, and where complaint was made about the non-disclosure of the 8,400 postal vote applications that had been examined by the electoral office, but had not been submitted to the police, there was no duty of disclosure on the electoral office as either a delegate of the investigator or as a joint investigator within paragraph 3.4; the role of the electoral office was in the nature of an examination by a complainant of suspicious documents subsequently handed to the police, comparable to that of a bank handing over suspicious cheques to the police: *R. v. Khan* [2011] L.S. Gazette, October 20, 23, CA ([2011] EWCA Crim. 2240).

### Recording of information

4.1 If material which may be relevant to the investigation consists of information which is not **A-235** recorded in any form, the officer in charge of an investigation must ensure that it is recorded in a durable or retrievable form (whether in writing, on video or audio tape, or on computer disk).

4.2 Where it is not practicable to retain the initial record of information because it forms part of a larger record which is to be destroyed, its contents should be transferred as a true record to a durable and more easily-stored form before that happens.

4.3 Negative information is often relevant to an investigation. If it may be relevant it must be recorded. An example might be a number of people present in a particular place at a particular time who state that they saw nothing unusual.

4.4 Where information which may be relevant is obtained, it must be recorded at the time it is obtained or as soon as practicable after that time. This includes, for example, information obtained in house-to-house enquiries, although the requirement to record information promptly does not require an investigator to take a statement from a potential witness where it would not otherwise be taken.

### Retention of material

#### (a) Duty to retain material

5.1 The investigator must retain material obtained in a criminal investigation which may be **A-236** relevant to the investigation. Material may be photographed, video-recorded, captured digitally or otherwise retained in the form of a copy rather than the original at any time, if the original is perishable; the original was supplied to the investigator rather than generated by him and is to be returned to its owner; or the retention of a copy rather than the original is reasonable in all the circumstances.

5.2 Where material has been seized in the exercise of the powers of seizure conferred by the Police and Criminal Evidence Act 1984, the duty to retain it under this code is subject to the provisions on the retention of seized material in section 22 of that Act.

5.3 If the officer in charge of an investigation becomes aware as a result of developments in the case that material previously examined but not retained (because it was not thought to be relevant) may now be relevant to the investigation, he should, wherever practicable, take steps to obtain it or ensure that it is retained for further inspection or for production in court if required.

5.4 The duty to retain material includes in particular the duty to retain material falling into the following categories, where it may be relevant to the investigation:

— crime reports (including crime report forms, relevant parts of incident report books or police officer's notebooks);
— custody records;

— records which are derived from tapes of telephone messages (for example, 999 calls) containing descriptions of an alleged offence or offender;
— final versions of witness statements (and draft versions where their content differs from the final version), including any exhibits mentioned (unless these have been returned to their owner on the understanding that they will be produced in court if required);
— interview records (written records, or audio or video tapes, of interviews with actual or potential witnesses or suspects);
— communications between the police and experts such as forensic scientists, reports of work carried out by experts, and schedules of scientific material prepared by the expert for the investigator, for the purposes of criminal proceedings;
— records of the first description of a suspect by each potential witness who purports to identify or describe the suspect, whether or not the description differs from that of subsequent descriptions by that or other witnesses;
— any material casting doubt on the reliability of a witness.

5.5 The duty to retain material, where it may be relevant to the investigation, also includes in particular the duty to retain material which may satisfy the test for prosecution disclosure in the Act, such as:

— information provided by an accused person which indicates an explanation for the offence with which he has been charged;
— any material casting doubt on the reliability of a confession;
— any material casting doubt on the reliability of a prosecution witness.

5.6 The duty to retain material falling into these categories does not extend to items which are purely ancillary to such material and possess no independent significance (for example, duplicate copies of records or reports).

*(b) Length of time for which material is to be retained*

5.7 All material which may be relevant to the investigation must be retained until a decision is taken whether to institute proceedings against a person for an offence.

5.8 If a criminal investigation results in proceedings being instituted, all material which may be relevant must be retained at least until the accused is acquitted or convicted or the prosecutor decides not to proceed with the case.

5.9 Where the accused is convicted, all material which may be relevant must be retained at least until:

— the convicted person is released from custody, or discharged from hospital, in cases where the court imposes a custodial sentence or a hospital order;
— six months from the date of conviction, in all other cases.

If the court imposes a custodial sentence or hospital order and the convicted person is released from custody or discharged from hospital earlier than six months from the date of conviction, all material which may be relevant must be retained at least until six months from the date of conviction.

5.10 If an appeal against conviction is in progress when the release or discharge occurs, or at the end of the period of six months specified in paragraph 5.9, all material which may be relevant must be retained until the appeal is determined. Similarly, if the Criminal Cases Review Commission is considering an application at that point in time, all material which may be relevant must be retained at least until the Commission decides not to refer the case to the Court.

**Preparation of material for prosecutor**

*(a) Introduction*

A-237    6.1 The officer in charge of the investigation, the disclosure officer or an investigator may seek advice from the prosecutor about whether any particular item of material may be relevant to the investigation.

6.2 Material which may be relevant to an investigation, which has been retained in accordance with this code, and which the disclosure officer believes will not form part of the prosecution case, must be listed on a schedule.

6.3 Material which the disclosure officer does not believe is sensitive must be listed on a schedule of non-sensitive material. The schedule must include a statement that the disclosure officer does not believe the material is sensitive.

6.4 Any material which is believed to be sensitive must be either listed on a schedule of sensitive material or, in exceptional circumstances, revealed to the prosecutor separately. If there is no sensitive material, the disclosure officer must record this fact on a schedule of sensitive material.

6.5 Paragraphs 6.6 to 6.11 below apply to both sensitive and non-sensitive material. Paragraphs 6.12 to 6.14 apply to sensitive material only.

*(b) Circumstances in which a schedule is to be prepared*

6.6 The disclosure officer must ensure that a schedule is prepared in the following circumstances:
— the accused is charged with an offence which is triable only on indictment;
— the accused is charged with an offence which is triable either way, and it is considered either that the case is likely to be tried on indictment or that the accused is likely to plead not guilty at a summary trial;
— the accused is charged with a summary offence, and it is considered that he is likely to plead not guilty.

6.7 In respect of either way and summary offences, a schedule may not be needed if a person has admitted the offence, or if a police officer witnessed the offence and that person has not denied it.

6.8 If it is believed that the accused is likely to plead guilty at a summary trial, it is not necessary to prepare a schedule in advance. If, contrary to this belief, the accused pleads not guilty at a summary trial, or the offence is to be tried on indictment, the disclosure officer must ensure that a schedule is prepared as soon as is reasonably practicable after that happens.

*(c) Way in which material is to be listed on schedule*

6.9 The disclosure officer should ensure that each item of material is listed separately on the schedule, and is numbered consecutively. The description of each item should make clear the nature of the item and should contain sufficient detail to enable the prosecutor to decide whether he needs to inspect the material before deciding whether or not it should be disclosed.

6.10 In some enquiries it may not be practicable to list each item of material separately. For example, there may be many items of a similar or repetitive nature. These may be listed in a block and described by quantity and generic title.

6.11 Even if some material is listed in a block, the disclosure officer must ensure that any items among that material which might satisfy the test for prosecution disclosure are listed and described individually.

*(d) Treatment of sensitive material*

6.12 Subject to paragraph 6.13 below, the disclosure officer must list on a sensitive schedule any material, the disclosure of which he believes would give rise to a real risk of serious prejudice to an important public interest, and the reason for that belief. The schedule must include a statement that the disclosure officer believes the material is sensitive. Depending on the circumstances, examples of such material may include the following among others:
— material relating to national security;
— material received from the intelligence and security agencies;
— material relating to intelligence from foreign sources which reveals sensitive intelligence gathering methods;
— material given in confidence;
— material relating to the identity or activities of informants, or undercover police officers, or witnesses, or other persons supplying information to the police who may be in danger if their identities are revealed;
— material revealing the location of any premises or other place used for police surveillance, or the identity of any person allowing a police officer to use them for surveillance;
— material revealing, either directly or indirectly, techniques and methods relied upon by a police officer in the course of a criminal investigation, for example covert surveillance techniques, or other methods of detecting crime;
— material whose disclosure might facilitate the commission of other offences or hinder the prevention and detection of crime;
— material upon the strength of which search warrants were obtained;
— material containing details of persons taking part in identification parades;
— material supplied to an investigator during a criminal investigation which has been generated by an official of a body concerned with the regulation or supervision of bodies corporate or of persons engaged in financial activities, or which has been generated by a person retained by such a body;
— material supplied to an investigator during a criminal investigation which relates to a

child or young person and which has been generated by a local authority social services department, an Area Child Protection Committee or other party contacted by an investigator during the investigation;

— material relating to the private life of a witness.

6.13 In exceptional circumstances, where an investigator considers that material is so sensitive that its revelation to the prosecutor by means of an entry on the sensitive schedule is inappropriate, the existence of the material must be revealed to the prosecutor separately. This will apply only where compromising the material would be likely to lead directly to the loss of life, or directly threaten national security.

6.14 In such circumstances, the responsibility for informing the prosecutor lies with the investigator who knows the detail of the sensitive material. The investigator should act as soon as is reasonably practicable after the file containing the prosecution case is sent to the prosecutor. The investigator must also ensure that the prosecutor is able to inspect the material so that he can assess whether it is disclosable and, if so, whether it needs to be brought before a court for a ruling on disclosure.

### Revelation of material to prosecutor

A-238

7.1 The disclosure officer must give the schedules to the prosecutor. Wherever practicable this should be at the same time as he gives him the file containing the material for the prosecution case (or as soon as is reasonably practicable after the decision on mode of trial or the plea, in cases to which paragraph 6.8 applies).

7.2 The disclosure officer should draw the attention of the prosecutor to any material an investigator has retained (including material to which paragraph 6.13 applies) which may satisfy the test for prosecution disclosure in the Act, and should explain why he has come to that view.

7.3 At the same time as complying with the duties in paragraphs 7.1 and 7.2, the disclosure officer must give the prosecutor a copy of any material which falls into the following categories (unless such material has already been given to the prosecutor as part of the file containing the material for the prosecution case):

— information provided by an accused person which indicates an explanation for the offence with which he has been charged;

— any material casting doubt on the reliability of a confession;

— any material casting doubt on the reliability of a prosecution witness;

— any other material which the investigator believes may satisfy the test for prosecution disclosure in the Act;

— any other material which the investigator believes may fall within the test for primary prosecution disclosure in the Act.

7.4 If the prosecutor asks to inspect material which has not already been copied to him, the disclosure officer must allow him to inspect it. If the prosecutor asks for a copy of material which has not already been copied to him, the disclosure officer must give him a copy. However, this does not apply where the disclosure officer believes, having consulted the officer in charge of the investigation, that the material is too sensitive to be copied and can only be inspected.

7.5 If material consists of information which is recorded other than in writing, whether it should be given to the prosecutor in its original form as a whole, or by way of relevant extracts recorded in the same form, or in the form of a transcript, is a matter for agreement between the disclosure officer and the prosecutor.

### Subsequent action by disclosure officer

A-239

8.1 At the time a schedule of non-sensitive material is prepared, the disclosure officer may not know exactly what material will form the case against the accused, and the prosecutor may not have given advice about the likely relevance of particular items of material. Once these matters have been determined, the disclosure officer must give the prosecutor, where necessary, an amended schedule listing any additional material:

— which may be relevant to the investigation;

— which does not form part of the case against the accused;

— which is not already listed on the schedule; and

— which he believes is not sensitive,

unless he is informed in writing by the prosecutor that the prosecutor intends to disclose the material to the defence.

8.2 Section 7A of the Act imposes a continuing duty on the prosecutor, for the duration of criminal proceedings against the accused, to disclose material which satisfies the test for disclosure (subject to public interest considerations). To enable him to do this, any new material coming to light should be treated in the same way as the earlier material.

8.3 In particular, after a defence statement has been given, the disclosure officer must look again at the material which has been retained and must draw the attention of the prosecutor to any material which might reasonably be considered capable of undermining the case for the prosecution against the accused or of assisting the case for the accused; and he must reveal it to him in accordance with paragraphs 7.4 and 7.5 above.

### Certification by disclosure officer

9.1 The disclosure officer must certify to the prosecutor that to the best of his knowledge andbelief, all relevant material which has been retained and made available to him has been revealed to the prosecutor in accordance with this code. He must sign and date the certificate. It will be necessary to certify not only at the time when the schedule and accompanying material is submitted to the prosecutor, and when relevant material which has been retained is reconsidered after the accused has given a defence statement, but also whenever a schedule is otherwise given or material is otherwise revealed to the prosecutor. **A-240**

### Disclosure of material to accused

10.1 If material has not already been copied to the prosecutor, and he requests its disclosure to the accused on the ground that: **A-241**
    — it satisfies the test for prosecution disclosure; or
    — it satisfies the test for prosecution disclosure; or
the disclosure officer must disclose it to the accused.

10.2 If material has been copied to the prosecutor, and it is to be disclosed, whether it is disclosed by the prosecutor or the disclosure officer is a matter of agreement between the two of them.

10.3 The disclosure officer must disclose material to the accused either by giving him a copy or by allowing him to inspect it. If the accused person asks for a copy of any material which he has been allowed to inspect, the disclosure officer must give it to him, unless in the opinion of the disclosure officer that is either not practicable (for example because the material consists of an object which cannot be copied, or because the volume of material is so great), or not desirable (for example because the material is a statement by a child witness in relation to a sexual offence).

10.4 If material which the accused has been allowed to inspect consists of information which is recorded other than in writing, whether it should be given to the accused in its original form or in the form of a transcript is matter for the discretion of the disclosure officer. If the material is transcribed, the disclosure officer must ensure that the transcript is certified to the accused as a true record of the material which has been transcribed.

10.5 If a court concludes that an item of sensitive material satisfies the prosecution disclosure test and that the interests of the defence outweigh the public interest in withholding disclosure, it will be necessary to disclose the material if the case is to proceed. This does not mean that sensitive documents must always be disclosed in their original form: for example, the court may agree that sensitive details still requiring protection should be blocked out, or that documents may be summarised, or that the prosecutor may make an admission about the substance of the material under section 10 of the Criminal Justice Act 1967.

## (2) As to the practice for arranging and conducting interviews of witnesses notified by the accused

### Introduction

As from May 1, 2010, a new code of practice entitled "Code of Practice for Arranging and Conducting Interviews of Witnesses Notified by the Accused", which was prepared under section 21A of the CPIA 1996, was brought into force by the Criminal Procedure and Investigations Act 1996 (Code of Practice for Interviews of Witnesses Notified by Accused) Order 2010 (S.I. 2010 No. 1223). **A-241a**

## CODE OF PRACTICE FOR ARRANGING AND CONDUCTING INTERVIEWS OF WITNESSES NOTIFIED BY THE ACCUSED

### Preamble

**A-241b**    This code of practice is issued under section 21A of the Criminal Procedure and Investigations Act 1996 ("the Act"). It sets out guidance that police officers and other persons charged with investigating offences must follow if they arrange or conduct interviews of proposed witnesses whose details are disclosed to the prosecution by an accused person pursuant to the disclosure provisions in Part I of the Act.

### Introduction

**A-241c**    1.1 Part I of the Act sets out rules governing disclosure of information in the course of criminal proceedings by both the prosecution and persons accused of offences to which that Part of the Act applies.

1.2. Sections 5 and 6 of the Act provide for accused persons to give defence statements to the prosecution and to the court and section 6A sets out what those defence statements must contain. Section 6A(2) requires that any defence statement that discloses an alibi must give particulars of it, including prescribed details of any witness who the accused believes is able to give evidence in support of the alibi and any information the accused has which may assist in identifying or finding such a witness.

1.3. Section 6C of the Act requires the accused to give to the prosecutor and the court a notice indicating whether he intends to call any witnesses at trial and giving details of those witnesses.

1.4. This code of practice sets out guidance that police officers and other persons charged with investigating offences must have regard to when they are arranging and conducting interviews of proposed witnesses identified in a defence statement given under section 6A(2) of the Act or a notice given under section 6C of the Act.

### Definitions

**A-241d**    2. In this code:—

– *the accused* means a person mentioned in section 1(1) or (2) of the Act;

– "an appropriate person" means:

(a) in the case of a witness under the age of 18:

(i) the parent, guardian or, if the witness is in local authority or voluntary organisation care, or is otherwise being looked after under the Children Act 1989, a person representing that authority or organisation; or

(ii) a social worker of a local authority; or

(iii) failing these, some other responsible person aged 18 or over who is not a police officer or employed by the police; and

(b) in the case of a witness who is mentally disordered or mentally vulnerable:

(i) a relative, guardian or other person responsible for the witness's care or custody; or

(ii) someone experienced in dealing with mentally disordered or mentally vulnerable people but who is not a police officer or employed by the police; or

(iii) failing these, some other responsible person aged 18 or over who is not a police officer or employed by the police.

– *an investigator* is a police officer or any other person charged with the duty of investigating offences.

– *a witness* is a potential witness identified by an accused person either:

– in a defence statement under section 6A(2) of the Act as being a witness that he believes is able to give evidence in support of an alibi disclosed in the statement; or

– in a notice given to the court and the prosecutor under section 6C of the Act as being a person that he intends to call as a witness at his trial.

### Arrangement of the interview

*Information to be provided to the witness before any interview may take place*

**A-241e**    3.1. If an investigator wishes to interview a witness, the witness must be asked whether he consents to being interviewed and informed that:

• an interview is being requested following his identification by the accused as a proposed witness under section 6A(2) or section 6C of the Act;

- he is not obliged to attend the proposed interview;
- he is entitled to be accompanied by a solicitor at the interview (but nothing in this code of practice creates any duty on the part of the Legal Services Commission to provide funding for any such attendance); and
- a record will be made of the interview and he will subsequently be sent a copy of the record.

3.2. If the witness consents to being interviewed, the witness must be asked:

- whether he wishes to have a solicitor present at the interview;
- whether he consents to a solicitor attending the interview on behalf of the accused, as an observer; and
- whether he consents to a copy of the record being sent to the accused. If he does not consent, the witness must be informed that the effect of disclosure requirements in criminal proceedings may nevertheless require the prosecution to disclose the record to the accused (and any co-accused) in the course of the proceedings.

### *Information to be provided to the accused before any interview may take place*

4.1. The investigator must notify the accused or, if the accused is legally represented in the **A-241f** proceedings, the accused's representatives:

- that the investigator requested an interview with the witness;
- whether the witness consented to the interview; and
- if the witness consented to the interview, whether the witness also consented to a solicitor attending the interview on behalf of the accused, as an observer.

4.2. If the accused is not legally represented in the proceedings, and if the witness consents to a solicitor attending the interview on behalf of the accused, the accused must be offered the opportunity, a reasonable time before the interview is held, to appoint a solicitor to attend it.

### *Identification of the date, time and venue for the interview*

5. The investigator must nominate a reasonable date, time and venue for the interview and notify **A-241g** the witness of them and any subsequent changes to them.

### *Notification to the accused's solicitor of the date, time and venue of the interview*

6. If the witness has consented to the presence of the accused's solicitor, the accused's solicitor **A-241h** must be notified that the interview is taking place, invited to observe, and provided with reasonable notice of the date, time and venue of the interview and any subsequent changes.

### Conduct of the interview

#### *The investigator conducting the interview*

7. The identity of the investigator conducting the interview must be recorded. That person must **A-241i** have sufficient skills and authority, commensurate with the complexity of the investigation, to discharge his functions effectively. That person must not conduct the interview if that is likely to result in a conflict of interest, for instance, if that person is the victim of the alleged crime which is the subject of the proceedings. The advice of a more senior officer must always be sought if there is doubt as to whether a conflict of interest precludes an individual conducting the interview. If thereafter the doubt remains, the advice of a prosecutor must be sought.

#### *Attendance of the accused's solicitor*

8.1. The accused's solicitor may only attend the interview if the witness has consented to his presence as an observer. Provided that the accused's solicitor was given reasonable notice of the date, **A-241j** time and place of the interview, the fact that the accused's solicitor is not present will not prevent the interview from being conducted. If the witness at any time withdraws consent to the accused's solicitor being present at the interview, the interview may continue without the presence of the accused's solicitor.

8.2. The accused's solicitor may attend only as an observer.

#### *Attendance of the witness's solicitor*

9. Where a witness has indicated that he wishes to appoint a solicitor to be present, that solicitor **A-241k** must be permitted to attend the interview.

*Attendance of any other appropriate person*

10. A witness under the age of 18 or a witness who is mentally disordered or otherwise mentally vulnerable must be interviewed in the presence of an appropriate person.

*Recording of the interview*

11.1. An accurate record must be made of the interview, whether it takes place at a police station or elsewhere. The record must be made, where practicable, by audio recording or by visual recording with sound, or otherwise in writing. Any written record must be made and completed during the interview, unless this would not be practicable or would interfere with the conduct of the interview, and must constitute either a verbatim record of what has been said or, failing this, an account of the interview which adequately and accurately summarises it. If a written record is not made during the interview it must be made as soon as practicable after its completion. Written interview records must be timed and signed by the maker.

11.2 A copy of the record must be given, within a reasonable time of the interview, to:

(a) the witness; and

(b) if the witness consents, to the accused or the accused's solicitor.

## II. ATTORNEY-GENERAL'S GUIDELINES

### A. DISCLOSURE

**Introduction**

On December 3, 2013, the Attorney-General published revised guidelines on disclosure, replacing the 2005 guidelines, and also the supplementary guidelines on digital material issued in 2011, which are now annexed to the new guidelines. The new guidelines should be read together with the revised protocol on the disclosure of unused material in criminal cases (*post*, Appendix N-52 *et seq.*), and are not designed to be a substitute for a thorough understanding of the relevant legislation, codes of practice, case law and procedure. They have immediate effect (para. 73).

Paragraphs 1 to 3 emphasise the importance of disclosure and a "timely dialogue between the prosecution, defence and the court", and are a shortened version of the introductory section to the 2005 guidelines. Paragraphs 4 to 14 relate to general principles and incorporate most of the corresponding section in the 2005 guidelines, but also stress the role the defence have to play in ensuring that the prosecution are directed towards appropriate material, the importance of communication within the prosecution team and the role of the reviewing lawyer. Paragraphs 15 to 27 relate to the duties on investigators and disclosure officers, incorporating a shortened version of the corresponding section in the 2005 guidelines. They underline that thought must be given to defining and limiting the scope of investigations under the guidance of the reviewing lawyer and prosecutor where appropriate, the need to keep full records of meetings and decisions taken and that, whilst there will be some cases where detailed examination of all material seized will be necessary, there will be others where this is impossible. Paragraphs 28 to 34 set out the disclosure duties on prosecutors, again incorporating a shortened version of the corresponding section in the 2005 guidelines, and also highlighting that prosecutors should challenge the lack of, or inadequate, defence statements in writing, copying the document to the court. Paragraphs 35 to 37 set out the disclosure duties on prosecution advocates, incorporating a shortened version of the corresponding section in the 2005 guidelines, and make clear the duty to keep disclosure under review, whenever possible in consultation with the reviewing prosecutor. Paragraphs 39 to 43 deal with the defence, and emphasise the importance of early and meaningful defence engagement and defence statements, including in the magistrates' courts.

Paragraphs 44 to 47 relate to disclosure obligations in magistrates' courts where a not guilty plea is entered. Paragraphs 48 and 49 relate to the Crown Court, particularly cases which involve digital material. Paragraphs 50 to 52 deal with large and complex cases in the Crown Court. Paragraphs 53 to 55 relate to material held by government departments and third parties and paragraphs 56 and 57 to material held by other domestic bodies. Both largely replicate the corresponding sections in the 2005 guidelines. Paragraphs 59 to 64 concern material held overseas (and correspond to paras 58-63 of the 2011 supplementary guidelines on digital material). Paragraphs 65 to 69 deal with applications for non-disclosure in the public interest and largely reproduce the corresponding section in the 2005 guidelines. Finally, paragraphs 70 to 72 ("other disclosure", "material relevant to sentence" and "post-conviction") correspond to the sections relating to material relevant to sentence and the post-conviction period in the 2005 guidelines.

As to the significance of the guidelines in relation to material held overseas, outside the European Union, by entities not subject to the jurisdiction of the United Kingdom, see *R. v. Flook* [2010] 1 Cr.App.R. 30, CA (§§ 12-51, 12-77 in the main work).

### Foreword

We are pleased to publish a revised judicial protocol and revised guidance on the disclosure of **A-242a** unused material in criminal cases. Proper disclosure of unused material, made through a rigorous and carefully considered application of the law, remains a crucial part of a fair trial, and essential to avoiding miscarriages of justice. These new documents are intended to clarify the procedures to be followed and to encourage the active participation of all parties.

They have been prepared following the recommendations of Lord Justice Gross in his September 2011 "Review of Disclosure in Criminal Proceedings" and take account of Lord Justice Gross and Lord Justice Treacy's "Further review of disclosure in criminal proceedings: sanctions for disclosure failure", published in November 2012.

There are important roles for the prosecution, the defence and the court in ensuring that disclosure is conducted properly, including on the part of the investigating, case progression and disclosure officers, as well as the lawyers and advocates. Lord Justice Gross particularly recommended that the guidance on disclosure of unused material in criminal cases should be consolidated and abbreviated. Given all of those involved in this process have separate constitutional roles, the judiciary and the Attorney-General have worked together to produce complementary guidance that is shorter than the previous iterations, but remains comprehensive. The two documents are similarly structured for ease of reference and should be read together.

The Rt. Hon. Dominic Grieve Q.C. M.P., Attorney General

The Rt. Hon. The Lord Thomas, Lord Chief Justice of England and Wales

### Introduction

These guidelines are issued by the Attorney General for investigators, prosecutors and defence **A-243** practitioners on the application of the disclosure regime contained in the Criminal Procedure and Investigations Act 1996 ("CPIA"). The guidelines emphasise the importance of prosecution-led disclosure and the importance of applying the CPIA regime in a "thinking manner", tailored, where appropriate, to the type of investigation or prosecution in question.

The guidelines do not contain the detail of the disclosure regime; they outline the high level principles which should be followed when the disclosure regime is applied.

These guidelines replace the existing Attorney General's Guidelines on Disclosure issued in 2005 and the Supplementary Guidelines on Digital Material issued in 2011, which is an annex to the general guidelines.

The guidelines are intended to operate alongside the Judicial Protocol on the Disclosure of Unused Material in Criminal Cases. They are not designed to be an unequivocal statement of the law at any one time, nor are they a substitute for a thorough understanding of the relevant legislation, codes of practice, case law and procedure.

Readers should note that a review of disclosure in the magistrates' courts is currently being undertaken by H.H.J. Kinch Q.C. and the Chief Magistrate, on behalf of Lord Justice Gross, the Senior Presiding Judge. Amendments may therefore be made to these documents following the recommendations of that review, and in accordance with other forthcoming changes to the criminal justice system.

### The importance of disclosure

1. The statutory framework for criminal investigations and disclosure is contained in the Criminal **A-244** Procedure and Investigations Act 1996 (the CPIA) and the *CPIA Code of Practice*. The CPIA aims to ensure that criminal investigations are conducted in a fair, objective and thorough manner, and requires prosecutors to disclose to the defence material which has not previously been disclosed to the accused and which might reasonably be considered capable of undermining the case for the prosecution against the accused or of assisting the case for the accused. The CPIA requires a timely dialogue between the prosecution, defence and the court to enable the prosecution properly to identify such material.

2. Every accused person has a right to a fair trial, a right long embodied in our law and guaranteed by Article 6 of the European Convention on Human Rights (ECHR). A fair trial is the proper object and expectation of all participants in the trial process. Fair disclosure to the accused is an inseparable

part of a fair trial. A fair trial should not require consideration of irrelevant material and should not involve spurious applications or arguments which serve to divert the trial process from examining the real issues before the court.

3. Properly applied, the CPIA should ensure that material is not disclosed which overburdens the participants in the trial process, diverts attention from the relevant issues, leads to unjustifiable delay, and is wasteful of resources. Consideration of disclosure issues should be an integral part of a good investigation and not something that exists separately.

### Disclosure: general principles

**A-245**     4. Disclosure refers to providing the defence with copies of, or access to, any prosecution material which might reasonably be considered capable of undermining the case for the prosecution against the accused, or of assisting the case for the accused, and which has not previously been disclosed (s.3 CPIA).

5. Prosecutors will only be expected to anticipate what material might undermine their case or strengthen the defence in the light of information available at the time of the disclosure decision, and they may take into account information revealed during questioning.

6. In deciding whether material satisfies the disclosure test, consideration should be given amongst other things to:

    a. the use that might be made of it in cross-examination;

    b. its capacity to support submissions that could lead to:

      (i) the exclusion of evidence;

      (ii) a stay of proceedings, where the material is required to allow a proper application to be made;

      (iii) a court or tribunal finding that any public authority had acted incompatibly with the accused's rights under the ECHR;

    c. its capacity to suggest an explanation or partial explanation of the accused's actions;

    d. the capacity of the material to have a bearing on scientific or medical evidence in the case.

7. It should also be borne in mind that while items of material viewed in isolation may not be reasonably considered to be capable of undermining the prosecution case or assisting the accused, several items together can have that effect.

8. Material relating to the accused's mental or physical health, intellectual capacity, or to any ill treatment which the accused may have suffered when in the investigator's custody is likely to fall within the test for disclosure set out in paragraph 4 above.

9. Disclosure must not be an open-ended trawl of unused material. A critical element to fair and proper disclosure is that the defence play their role to ensure that the prosecution are directed to material which might reasonably be considered capable of undermining the prosecution case or assisting the case for the accused. This process is key to ensuring prosecutors make informed determinations about disclosure of unused material. The defence statement is important in identifying the issues in the case and why it is suggested that the material meets the test for disclosure.

10. Disclosure should be conducted in a thinking manner and never be reduced to a box-ticking exercise[1]; at all stages of the process, there should be consideration of **why** the CPIA disclosure regime requires a particular course of action and what should be done to achieve that aim.

11. There will always be a number of participants in prosecutions and investigations: senior investigation officers, disclosure officers, investigation officers, reviewing prosecutors, leading counsel, junior counsel, and sometimes disclosure counsel. Communication within the "prosecution team" is vital to ensure that all matters which could have a bearing on disclosure issues are given sufficient attention by the right person. This is especially so given many reviewing lawyers will be unable to sit behind the trial advocate throughout the trial. In practice, this is likely to mean that a full log of disclosure decisions (with reasons) must be kept on the file and made available as appropriate to the prosecution team.

12. The role of the reviewing lawyer will be central to ensuring all members of the prosecution team are aware of, and carry out, their duties and role(s). Where this involves counsel or more than one reviewing lawyer, this should be done by giving clear written instructions and record keeping.

13. The centrality of the reviewing lawyer does not mean that he or she has to do all the work personally; on the contrary, it will often mean effective delegation. Where the conduct of a prosecution is assigned to more than one prosecutor, steps must be taken to ensure that all involved in the case properly record their decisions. Subsequent prosecutors must be able to see and understand previous disclosure decisions before carrying out their continuous review function.

14. Investigators must always be alive to the potential need to reveal and prosecutors to the

---

[1] *R. v. Olu, Wilson and Brooks* [2010] EWCA Crim. 2975, [2011] 1 Cr.App.R. 33, CA (at [42]).

potential need to disclose material, in the interests of justice and fairness in the particular circumstances of any case, after the commencement of proceedings but before their duty arises under the Act. For instance, disclosure ought to be made of significant information that might affect a bail decision. This is likely to depend on what the defence chooses to reveal at that stage.

### Investigators and disclosure officers

15. Investigators and disclosure officers must be fair and objective and must work together with **A-246** prosecutors to ensure that disclosure obligations are met. Investigators and disclosure officers should be familiar with the CPIA Code of Practice, in particular their obligations to **retain** and **record** relevant material, to **review** it and to **reveal** it to the prosecutor.

16. Whether a case is a summary only matter or a long and complex trial on indictment, it is important that investigators and disclosure officers should approach their duties in a "thinking manner" and not as a box ticking exercise. Where necessary, the reviewing lawyer should be consulted. It is important that investigators and disclosure officers are deployed on cases which are commensurate with their training, skills and experience. The conduct of an investigation provides the foundation for the entire case, and may even impact the conduct of linked cases. It is vital that there is always consideration of disclosure matters at the outset of an investigation, regardless of its size.

17. A fair investigation involves the pursuit of material following all reasonable lines of enquiry, whether they point towards or away from the suspect. What is "reasonable" will depend on the context of the case. A fair investigation does not mean an endless investigation: investigators and disclosure officers must give thought to defining, and thereby limiting, the scope of their investigations, seeking the guidance of the prosecutor where appropriate.

18. Where there are a number of disclosure officers assigned to a case, there should be a lead disclosure officer who is the focus for enquiries and whose responsibility it is to ensure that the investigator's disclosure obligations are complied with. Where appropriate, regular case conferences and other meetings should be held to ensure prosecutors are apprised of all relevant developments in investigations. Full records should be kept of such meetings.

19. The *CPIA Code of Practice* encourages investigators and disclosure officers to seek advice from prosecutors about whether any particular item of material may be relevant to the investigation, and if so, how. Investigators and disclosure officers should record key decisions taken on these matters and be prepared to account for their actions later. An identical approach is not called for in each and every case.

20. Investigators are to approach their task seeking to establish what actually happened. They are to be fair and objective.

21. Disclosure officers (or their deputies) must inspect, view, listen to or search all relevant material that has been retained by the investigator and the disclosure officer must provide a personal declaration to the effect that this task has been undertaken. In some cases, a detailed examination of all material seized may be required. In others, however, a detailed examination of every item of material seized would be virtually impossible: see the **Annex**.

22. Prosecutors only have knowledge of matters which are revealed to them by investigators and disclosure officers, and the schedules are the written means by which that revelation takes place. Whatever the approach taken by investigators or disclosure officers to examining the material gathered or generated in the course of an investigation, it is crucial that disclosure officers record their reasons for a particular approach in writing.

23. In meeting the obligations in paragraph 6.9 and 8.1 of the code, schedules must be completed in a form which not only reveals sufficient information to the prosecutor, but which demonstrates a transparent and thinking approach to the disclosure exercise, to command the confidence of the defence and the court. Descriptions on non-sensitive schedules must be clear and accurate, and must contain sufficient detail to enable the prosecutor to make an informed decision on disclosure. The use of abbreviations and acronyms can be problematic and lead to difficulties in appreciating the significance of the material.

24. Sensitive schedules must contain sufficiently clear descriptions to enable the prosecutor to make an informed decision as to whether or not the material itself should be viewed, to the extent possible without compromising the confidentiality of the information.

25. It may become apparent to an investigator that some material obtained in the course of an investigation, either because it was considered to be potentially relevant, or because it was inextricably linked to material that was relevant, is, in fact, incapable of impact. It is not necessary to retain such material, although the investigator should err on the side of caution in reaching that conclusion and should be particularly mindful of the fact that some investigations continue over some time and that what is incapable of impact may change over time. The advice of the prosecutor should be sought where appropriate.

26. Disclosure officers must specifically draw material to the attention of the prosecutor for consideration where they have any doubt as to whether it might reasonably be considered capable of undermining the prosecution case or of assisting the case for the accused.

27. Disclosure officers must seek the advice and assistance of prosecutors when in doubt as to their responsibility as early as possible. They must deal expeditiously with requests by the prosecutor for further information on material, which may lead to disclosure.

### Prosecutors

A-247     28. Prosecutors are responsible for making proper disclosure in consultation with the disclosure officer. The duty of disclosure is a continuing one and disclosure should be kept under review. In addition, prosecutors should ensure that advocates in court are properly instructed as to disclosure issues. Prosecutors must also be alert to the need to provide advice to, and where necessary probe actions taken by, disclosure officers to ensure that disclosure obligations are met. There should be no aspects of an investigation about which prosecutors are unable to ask probing questions.

29. Prosecutors must review schedules prepared by disclosure officers thoroughly and must be alert to the possibility that relevant material may exist which has not been revealed to them or material included which should not have been. If no schedules have been provided, or there are apparent omissions from the schedules, or documents or other items are inadequately described or are unclear, the prosecutor must at once take action to obtain properly completed schedules. Likewise schedules should be returned for amendment if irrelevant items are included. If prosecutors remain dissatisfied with the quality or content of the schedules they must raise the matter with a senior investigator to resolve the matter satisfactorily.

30. Where prosecutors have reason to believe that the disclosure officer has not discharged the obligation in paragraph 21 to inspect, view, listen to or search relevant material, they must at once raise the matter with the disclosure officer and request that it be done. Where appropriate the matter should be raised with the officer in the case or a senior officer.

31. Prosecutors should copy the defence statement to the disclosure officer and investigator as soon as reasonably practicable and prosecutors should advise the investigator if, in their view, reasonable and relevant lines of further enquiry should be pursued. If the defence statement does point to other reasonable lines of enquiry, further investigation is required and evidence obtained as a result of these enquiries may be used as part of the prosecution case or to rebut the defence.

32. It is vital that prosecutors consider defence statements thoroughly. Prosecutors cannot comment upon, or invite inferences to be drawn from, failures in defence disclosure otherwise than in accordance with section 11 of the CPIA. Prosecutors may cross-examine the accused on differences between the defence case put at trial and that set out in his or her defence statement. In doing so, it may be appropriate to apply to the judge under section 6E of the CPIA for copies of the statement to be given to a jury, edited if necessary to remove inadmissible material. Prosecutors should examine the defence statement to see whether it points to other lines of enquiry.

33. Prosecutors should challenge the lack of, or inadequate, defence statements in writing, copying the document to the court and the defence and seeking directions from the court to require the provision of an adequate statement from the defence.

34. If the material does not fulfil the disclosure test there is no requirement to disclose it. For this purpose, the parties' respective cases should not be restrictively analysed but must be carefully analysed to ascertain the specific facts the prosecution seek to establish and the specific grounds on which the charges are resisted.

### Prosecution advocates

A-248     35. Prosecution advocates should ensure that all material which ought to be disclosed under the Act is disclosed to the defence. However, prosecution advocates cannot be expected to disclose material if they are not aware of its existence. As far as is possible, prosecution advocates must place themselves in a fully informed position to enable them to make decisions on disclosure.

36. Upon receipt of instructions, prosecution advocates should consider as a priority all the information provided regarding disclosure of material. Prosecution advocates should consider, in every case, whether they can be satisfied that they are in possession of all relevant documentation and that they have been fully instructed regarding disclosure matters. If as a result the advocate considers that further information or action is required, written advice should promptly be provided setting out the aspects that need clarification or action.

37. The prosecution advocate must keep decisions regarding disclosure under review until the conclusion of the trial, whenever possible in consultation with the reviewing prosecutor. The prosecution advocate must in every case specifically consider whether he or she can satisfactorily discharge the duty of continuing review on the basis of the material supplied already, or whether it is necessary

to inspect further material or to reconsider material already inspected. Prosecution advocates must not abrogate their responsibility under the CPIA by disclosing material which does not pass the test for disclosure, set out in paragraph 4, above.

38. There remains no basis in practice or law for counsel to counsel disclosure.

### Defence

39. Defence engagement must be early and meaningful for the CPIA regime to function as **A-249** intended. Defence statements are an integral part of this and are intended to help focus the attention of the prosecutor, court and co-defendants on the relevant issues in order to identify exculpatory unused material. Defence statements should be drafted in accordance with the relevant provisions of the CPIA.

40. Defence requests for further disclosure should ordinarily only be answered by the prosecution if the request is relevant to and directed to an issue identified in the defence statement. If it is not, then a further or amended defence statement should be sought by the prosecutor and obtained before considering the request for further disclosure.

41. In some cases that involve extensive unused material that is within the knowledge of a defendant, the defence will be expected to provide the prosecution and the court with assistance in identifying material which is suggested to pass the test for disclosure.

42. The prosecution's continuing duty to keep disclosure under review is crucial, and particular attention must be paid to understanding the significance of developments in the case on the unused material and earlier disclosure decisions. Meaningful defence engagement will help the prosecution to keep disclosure under review. The continuing duty of review for prosecutors is less likely to require the disclosure of further material to the defence if the defence have clarified and articulated their case, as required by the CPIA.

43. In the magistrates' courts, where the provision of a defence statement is not mandatory, early identification of the material issues by the defence, whether through a defence statement, case management form or otherwise, will help the prosecution to focus its preparation of the case and allow any defence disclosure queries to be dealt with promptly and accurately.

### Magistrates' courts (including the youth court)

44. The majority of criminal cases are heard in the magistrates' court. The requirement for the **A-250** prosecution to provide initial disclosure only arises after a not guilty plea has been entered but prosecutors should be alert to the possibility that material may exist which should be disclosed to the defendant prior to the CPIA requirements applying to the case.[2]

45. Where a not guilty plea is entered in the magistrates' court, prosecutors should ensure that any issues of dispute which are raised are noted on the file. They should also seek to obtain a copy of any Magistrates' Court Trial Preparation Form. Consideration of the issues raised in court and on the trial preparation form will assist in deciding what material undermines the prosecution case or assists the defendant.

46. Where a matter is set down for trial in the magistrates' court, prosecutors should ensure that the investigator is requested to supply any outstanding disclosure schedules as a matter of urgency. Prosecutors should serve initial disclosure in sufficient time to ensure that the trial date is effective.

47. There is no requirement for a defence statement to be served in the magistrates' court but it should be noted that if none is given the court has no power to hear an application for further prosecution disclosure under section 8 of the CPIA and the Criminal Procedure Rules.

### Cases in the Crown Court

48. The exponential increase in the use of technology in society means that many routine Crown **A-251** Court cases are increasingly likely to have to engage with digital material of some form. It is not only in large and complex cases that there may be large quantities of such material. Where such investigations involve digital material, it will be virtually impossible for investigators (or prosecutors) to examine every item of such material individually and there should be no expectation that such material will be so examined. Having consulted with the prosecution as appropriate, disclosure officers should determine what their approach should be to the examination of the material. Investigators or disclosure officers should decide how best to pursue a reasonable line of enquiry in relation to the relevant digital material, and ensure that the extent and manner of the examination are commensurate with the issues in the case.

49. Consideration should be given to any local or national agreements in relation to disclosure in "Early Guilty Plea Scheme" cases.

---

[2] See for example *R. v. DPP, ex p. Lee* [1999] 2 Cr.App.R. 304, DC.

## Large and complex cases in the Crown Court

**A-252**      50. The particular challenges presented by large and complex criminal prosecutions require an approach to disclosure which is specifically tailored to the needs of such cases. In these cases more than any other is the need for careful thought to be given to prosecution-led disclosure matters from the very earliest stage. It is essential that the prosecution takes a grip on the case and its disclosure requirements from the very outset of the investigation, which must continue throughout all aspects of the case preparation.

*Disclosure management documents*

**A-253**      51. Accordingly, investigations and prosecutions of large and complex cases should be carefully defined and accompanied by a clear investigation and prosecution strategy. The approach to disclosure in such cases should be outlined in a document which should be served on the defence and the court at an early stage. Such documents, sometimes known as disclosure management documents, will require careful preparation and presentation, tailored to the individual case. They may include:

     a. where prosecutors and investigators operate in an integrated office, an explanation as to how the disclosure responsibilities have been managed;

     b. a brief summary of the prosecution case and a statement outlining how the prosecutor's general approach will comply with the CPIA regime, these guidelines and the Judicial Protocol on the Disclosure of Unused Material in Criminal Cases;

     c. the prosecutor's understanding of the defence case, including information revealed during interview;

     d. an outline of the prosecution's general approach to disclosure, which may include detail relating to:

        (i) digital material: explaining the method and extent of examination, in accordance with the **Annex** to these guidelines;

        (ii) video footage;

        (iii) linked investigations: explaining the nexus between investigations, any memoranda of understanding or disclosure agreements between investigators;

        (iv) third party and foreign material, including steps taken to obtain the material;

        (v) reasonable lines of enquiry: a summary of the lines pursued, particularly those that point away from the suspect, or which may assist the defence;

        (vi) credibility of a witness: confirmation that witness checks, including those of professional witnesses have, or will be, carried out.

     52. Thereafter the prosecution should follow the disclosure management document. They are living documents and should be amended in light of developments in the case; they should be kept up to date as the case progresses. Their use will assist the court in its own case management and will enable the defence to engage from an early stage with the prosecution's proposed approach to disclosure.

## Material not held by the prosecution

*Involvement of other agencies: material held by other government departments and third parties*

**A-254**      53. Where it appears to an investigator, disclosure officer or prosecutor that a government department or other Crown body has material that may be relevant to an issue in the case, reasonable steps should be taken to identify and consider such material. Although what is reasonable will vary from case to case, the prosecution should inform the department or other body of the nature of its case and of relevant issues in the case in respect of which the department or body might possess material, and ask whether it has any such material.

     54. It should be remembered that investigators, disclosure officers and prosecutors cannot be regarded to be in constructive possession of material held by government departments or Crown bodies simply by virtue of their status as government departments or Crown bodies.

     55. Where, after reasonable steps have been taken to secure access to such material, access is denied, the investigator, disclosure officer or prosecutor should consider what if any further steps might be taken to obtain the material or inform the defence. The final decision on any further steps will be for the prosecutor.

*Third party material: other domestic bodies*

**A-255**      56. There may be cases where the investigator, disclosure officer or prosecutor believes that a third party (for example, a local authority, a social services department, a hospital, a doctor, a school, a provider of forensic services) has material or information which might be relevant to the prosecution case. In such cases, investigators, disclosure officers and prosecutors should take reasonable steps to identify, secure and consider material held by any third party where it appears to the investigator, disclosure officer or prosecutor that (a) such material exists and (b) that it may be relevant to an issue in the case.

57. If the investigator, disclosure officer or prosecutor seeks access to the material or information but the third party declines or refuses to allow access to it, the matter should not be left. If despite any reasons offered by the third party it is still believed that it is reasonable to seek production of the material or information, and the requirements of section 2 of the Criminal Procedure (Attendance of Witnesses) Act 1965 or as appropriate section 97 of the Magistrates' Courts Act 1980 are satisfied (or any other relevant power), then the prosecutor or investigator should apply for a witness summons causing a representative of the third party to produce the material to the court.

58. Sometimes, for example through multi-agency working arrangements, investigators, disclosure officers or prosecutors may become aware of the content or nature of material held by a third party. Consultation with the relevant third party must always take place before disclosure is made; there may be public interest reasons to apply to the court for an order for non-disclosure in the public interest, in accordance with the procedure outlined in paragraph 65 and following.

### International matters

59. The obligations under the CPIA Code to pursue all reasonable lines of enquiry apply to material held overseas.                                                                                      **A-256**

60. Where it appears that there is relevant material, the prosecutor must take reasonable steps to obtain it, either informally or making use of the powers contained in the Crime (International Co-operation) Act 2003 and any EU and international conventions. See CPS Guidance "Obtaining Evidence and Information from Abroad".

61. There may be cases where a foreign state or a foreign court refuses to make the material available to the investigator or prosecutor. There may be other cases where the foreign state, though willing to show the material to investigators, will not allow the material to be copied or otherwise made available and the courts of the foreign state will not order its provision.

62. It is for these reasons that there is no absolute duty on the prosecutor to disclose relevant material held overseas by entities not subject to the jurisdiction of the courts in England and Wales. However consideration should be given to whether the type of material believed to be held can be provided to the defence.

63. The obligation on the investigator and prosecutor under the CPIA is to take reasonable steps. Where investigators are allowed to examine files of a foreign state but are not allowed to take copies or notes or list the documents held, there is no breach by the prosecution in its duty of disclosure by reason of its failure to obtain such material, provided reasonable steps have been taken to try and obtain the material. Prosecutors have a margin of consideration as to what steps are appropriate in the particular case but prosecutors must be alive to their duties and there may be some circumstances where these duties cannot be met. Whether the prosecutor has taken reasonable steps is for the court to determine in each case if the matter is raised.

64. In these circumstances it is important that the position is clearly set out in writing so that the court and the defence know what the position is. Investigators and prosecutors must record and explain the situation and set out, insofar as they are permitted by the foreign state, such information as they can and the steps they have taken.

### Applications for non-disclosure in the public interest

65. The CPIA allows prosecutors to apply to the court for an order to withhold material which would otherwise fall to be disclosed if disclosure would give rise to a real risk of serious prejudice to an important public interest. Before making such an application, prosecutors should aim to disclose as much of the material as they properly can (for example, by giving the defence redacted or edited copies or summaries). Neutral material or material damaging to the defendant need not be disclosed and there is no need to bring it to the attention of the court. Only in truly borderline cases should the prosecution seek a judicial ruling on whether material in its possession should be disclosed.    **A-257**

66. Prior to the hearing, the prosecutor and the prosecution advocate must examine all material which is the subject matter of the application and make any necessary enquiries of the investigator. The investigator must be frank with the prosecutor about the full extent of the sensitive material. Prior to or at the hearing, the court must be provided with full and accurate information about the material.

67. The prosecutor (or representative) and/or investigator should attend such applications. Section 16 of the CPIA allows a person claiming to have an interest in the sensitive material to apply to the court for the opportunity to be heard at the application.

68. The principles set out at paragraph 36 of *R. v. H.* [2004] 2 A.C. 134, [2004] UKHL 3, should be applied rigorously, firstly by the prosecutor and then by the court considering the material. It is essential that these principles are scrupulously adhered to, to ensure that the procedure for examination of material in the absence of the accused is compliant with Article 6.

69. If prosecutors conclude that a fair trial cannot take place because material which satisfies the test for disclosure cannot be disclosed, and that this cannot be remedied by the above procedure; how the case is presented; or by any other means, they should not continue with the case.

### Other disclosure

**A-258**

70. Disclosure of any material that is made outside the ambit of CPIA will attract confidentiality by virtue of *Taylor v. Serious Fraud Office* [1999] 2 A.C. 177, HL.

### *Material relevant to sentence*

**A-259**

71. In all cases the prosecutor must consider disclosing in the interests of justice any material which is relevant to sentence (*e.g.* information which might mitigate the seriousness of the offence or assist the accused to lay blame in part upon a co-accused or another person).

### *Post-conviction*

**A-260**

72. Where, after the conclusion of the proceedings, material comes to light, that might cast doubt upon the safety of the conviction, the prosecutor must consider disclosure of such material.

### *Applicability of these guidelines*

**A-261**

73. These guidelines shall have immediate effect.

### Annex: Attorney General's Guidelines on Disclosure: Supplementary Guidelines on Digitally Stored Material (2011)

**A-262**

A1. The guidelines are intended to supplement the Attorney General's Guidelines on Disclosure.

A2. As a result of the number of cases now involving digitally stored material and the scale of the digital material that may be involved, more detailed guidance is considered to be needed. The objective of these guidelines is to set out how material satisfying the tests for disclosure can best be identified and disclosed to the defence without imposing unrealistic or disproportionate demands on the investigator and prosecutor.

A3. The approach set out in these guidelines is in line with existing best practice, in that:

   a. investigating and prosecuting agencies, especially in large and complex cases, will apply their respective case management and disclosure strategies and policies and be transparent with the defence and the courts about how the prosecution has approached complying with its disclosure obligations in the context of the individual case; and,

   b. the defence will be expected to play their part in defining the real issues in the case. In this context, the defence will be invited to participate in defining the scope of the reasonable searches that may be made of digitally stored material by the investigator to identify material that might reasonably be expected to undermine the prosecution case or assist the defence.

A4. Only if this approach is followed can the courts be in a position to use their case management powers effectively and to determine applications for disclosure fairly.

A5. The Attorney General's Guidelines are not detailed operational guidelines. They are intended to set out a common approach to be adopted in the context of digitally stored material.

### Types of digital material

**A-263**

A6. Digital material falls into two categories: the first category is material which is created natively within an electronic environment (*e.g.* email, office files, system files, digital photographs, audio, etc.); the second category is material which has been digitised from an analogue form (*e.g.* scanned copy of a document, scanned photograph, a faxed document). Irrespective of the way in which technology changes, the categorisation of digital material will remain the same.

A7. Digital material is usually held on one of the three types of media. Optical media (e.g. CD, DVD, Blu-ray) and solid-state media (*e.g.* removable memory cards, solid-state music players or mobile devices, etc.) cater for usually lower volume storage. Magnetic media (*e.g.* disk drives and back up tapes) usually cater for high volume storage.

## General principles for investigators

A8. The general principles[3] to be followed by investigators in handling and examining digital material are:   **A-264**

    a. no action taken by investigators or their agents should change data held on a computer or storage media which may subsequently be relied upon in court;

    b. in circumstances where a person finds it necessary to access original data held on computer or storage media, that person must be competent to do so and be able to give evidence explaining the relevance and implications of their actions;

    c. an audit trail or other record of all processes applied to computer-based electronic evidence should be created and preserved; an independent third party should be able to examine those processes (see further the sections headed "Record keeping" and "Scheduling" below); and

    d. the person in charge of the investigation has overall responsibility for ensuring that the law and these principles are followed.

A9. Where an investigator has reasonable grounds for believing that digital material may contain material subject to legal professional privilege, very strong legal constraints apply. No digital material may be seized which an investigator has reasonable grounds for believing to be subject to legal privilege, other than where the provisions of the Criminal Justice and Police Act 2001 apply. Strict controls need to be applied where privileged material is seized. See the more detailed section on legal professional privilege starting at paragraph A28, below.

## Seizure, relevance and retention

A10. The legal obligations are to be found in a combination of the Police and Criminal Evidence Act 1984 (PACE), the Criminal Justice and Police Act 2001 (CJPA 2001) and the Criminal Procedure and Investigations Act 1996 (the CPIA 1996).   **A-265**

A11. These guidelines also apply to digital material seized or imaged under other statutory provisions. For example, the Serious Fraud Office has distinct powers of seizure under warrant obtained under section 2(4) of the Criminal Justice Act 1987. In cases concerning indecent images of children and obscene material, special provisions apply to the handling, storage and copying of such material. Practitioners should refer to specific guidance on the application of those provisions.

## Seizure

A12. Before searching a suspect's premises where digital evidence is likely to be found, consideration must be given to what sort of evidence is likely to be found and in what volume, whether it is likely to be possible to view and copy, if relevant, the material at the location (it is not uncommon with the advent of cloud computing for digital material to be hosted by a third party) and to what should be seized. Business and commercial premises will often have very substantial amounts of digital material stored on computers and other media. Investigators will need to consider the practicalities of seizing computer hard drives and other media, the effect this may have on the business and, where it is not feasible to obtain an image of digital material, the likely timescale for returning seized items.   **A-266**

A13. In deciding whether to seize and retain digital material it is important that the investigator either complies with the procedure under the relevant statutory authority, relying either on statutory powers or a search warrant, or obtains the owner's consent. In particular, investigators need to be aware of the constraints applying to legally privileged material.

A14. A computer hard drive or single item of media, such as a back up tape, is a single storage entity. This means that if any digital material found on the hard drive or other media can lawfully be seized the computer hard drive or single item of media may, if appropriate, be seized or imaged. In some circumstances investigators may wish to image specific folders, files or categories of data where it is feasible to do so without seizing the hard drive or other media, or instead of taking an image of all data on the hard drive or other media. In practice, the configuration of most systems means that data may be contained across a number of hard drives and more than one hard drive or item of media may be required in order to access the information sought.

A15. Digital material must not be seized if an investigator has reasonable grounds for believing it is subject to legal professional privilege, other than where sections 50 or 51 of the CJPA 2001 apply. If such material is seized it must be isolated from other seized material and any other investigation material in the possession of the investigating authority.

---

[3] Based on: Association of Chief Police Officers: Good Practice Guide for Computer Based Electronic Evidence Version 0.1.4.

## The Police and Criminal Evidence Act 1984

A16. PACE 1984 provides powers to seize and retain anything for which the search has been authorised or after arrest, other than items attracting legal professional privilege.[4] In addition, there is a general power to seize anything which is on the premises if there are reasonable grounds to believe that it has been obtained in the commission of an offence, or that it is evidence and that it is necessary to seize it to prevent it being concealed, lost, altered or destroyed.[5] There is another related power to require information which is stored in any electronic form and is accessible from the premises to be produced in a form in which it can be taken away and in which it is visible and legible or from which it can readily be produced in a visible and legible form.[6]

A17. An image (a forensically sound copy) of the digital material may be taken at the location of the search. Where the investigator makes an image of the digital material at the location, the original need not be seized. Alternatively, when originals are taken, investigators must be prepared to copy or image the material for the owners when reasonably practicable in accordance with PACE 1984, Code B 7.17.

A18. Where it is not possible or reasonably practicable to image the computer or hard drive, it will need to be removed from the location or premises for examination elsewhere. This allows the investigator to seize and sift material for the purpose of identifying that which meets the tests for retention in accordance with the 1984 PACE.[7]

## The Criminal Justice and Police Act 2001

A19. The additional powers of seizure in sections 50 and 51 of the CJPA 2001 Act [*sic*] only extend the scope of existing powers of search and seizure under the PACE and other specified statutory authorities[8] where the relevant conditions and circumstances apply.

A20. Investigators must be careful only to exercise powers under the CJPA 2001 when it is necessary and not to remove any more material than is justified. The removal of large volumes of material, much of which may not ultimately be retainable, may have serious consequences for the owner of the material, particularly when they are involved in business or other commercial activities.

A21. A written notice must be given to the occupier of the premises where items are seized under sections 50 and 51.[9]

A22. Until material seized under the CJPA 2001 has been examined, it must be kept securely and separately from any material seized under other powers. Any such material must be examined as soon as reasonably practicable to determine which elements may be retained and which should be returned. Regard must be had to the desirability of allowing the person from whom the property was seized — or a person with an interest in the property — an opportunity of being present or represented at the examination.

## Retention

A23. Where material is seized under the powers conferred by PACE the duty to retain it under the code of practice issued under the CPIA is subject to the provisions on retention under section 22 of PACE. Material seized under sections 50 and 51 of the CJPA 2001 may be retained or returned in accordance with sections 53–58 of that Act.

A24. Retention is limited to evidence and relevant material (as defined in the code of practice issued under the CPIA). Where either evidence or relevant material is inextricably linked to nonrelevant material which is not reasonably practicable to separate, that material can also be retained. Inextricably linked material is material that is not reasonably practicable to separate from other linked material without prejudicing the use of that other material in any investigation or proceedings.

A25. However, inextricably linked material must not be examined, imaged, copied or used for any purpose other than for providing the source of or the integrity of the linked material.

A26. There are four categories of material that may be retained:

    a. material that is evidence or potential evidence in the case; where material is retained for evidential purposes there will be a strong argument that the whole thing (or an authenticated image or copy) should be retained for the purpose of proving provenance and continuity;

---

[4] By warrant under s.8, and Sched. 1 and s.18.
[5] S.19.
[6] S.20.
[7] Special provision exists for investigations conducted by Her Majesty's Revenue and Customs in the application of their powers under PACE — see s.114(2)(b) — and the CJPA 2001.
[8] Sched. 1 to the CJPA 2001.
[9] S.52.

b. where evidential material has been retained, inextricably linked non-relevant material which is not reasonably practicable to separate can also be retained (PACE, Code B, para. 7);

c. an investigator should retain material that is relevant to the investigation and required to be scheduled as unused material; this is broader than but includes the duty to retain material which may satisfy the test for prosecution disclosure; the general duty to retain relevant material is set out in the CPIA code at paragraph 5; or

d. material which is inextricably linked to relevant unused material which of itself may not be relevant material; such material should be retained (PACE, Code B, para. 7).

A27. The balance of any digital material should be returned in accordance with sections 53–55 of the CJPA 2001 if seized under that Act.

### Legal professional privilege (LPP)

A28. No digital material may be seized which an investigator has reasonable grounds for believing to be subject to LPP, other than under the additional powers of seizure in the CJPA 2001.    **A-270**

A29. The CJPA 2001 enables an investigator to seize relevant items which contain LPP material where it is not reasonably practicable on the search premises to separate LPP material from non-LPP material.

A30. Where LPP material or material suspected of containing LPP is seized, it must be isolated from the other material which has been seized in the investigation. The mechanics of securing property vary according to the circumstances; "bagging up", *i.e.* placing materials in sealed bags or containers, and strict subsequent control of access, is the appropriate procedure in many cases.

A31. Where material has been identified as potentially containing LPP it must be reviewed by a lawyer independent of the prosecuting authority. No member of the investigative or prosecution team involved in either the current investigation or, if the LPP material relates to other criminal proceedings, in those proceedings should have sight of or access to the LPP material.

A32. If the material is voluminous, search terms or other filters may have to be used to identify the LPP material. If so this will also have to be done by someone independent and not connected with the investigation.

A33. It is essential that anyone dealing with LPP material maintains proper records showing the way in which the material has been handled and those who have had access to it as well as decisions taken in relation to that material.

A34. LPP material can only be retained in specific circumstances in accordance with section 54 of the CJPA 2001, *i.e.* where the property which comprises the LPP material has been lawfully seized and it is not reasonably practicable for the item to be separated from the rest of the property without prejudicing the use of the rest of the property. LPP material which cannot be retained must be returned as soon as practicable after the seizure without waiting for the whole examination of the seized material.

### Excluded and special procedure material

A35. Similar principles to those that apply to LPP material apply to excluded or special procedure material, as set out in section 55 of the CJPA 2001.[10]    **A-271**

### Encryption

A36. Part III of the Regulation of Investigatory Powers Act 2000 (RIPA) and the *Investigation of Protected Electronic Information Code of Practice* govern encryption. See the CPS's Guidance RIPA, Part III.    **A-272**

A37. RIPA enables specified law enforcement agencies to compel individuals or companies to provide passwords or encryption keys for the purpose of rendering protected material readable. Failure to comply with RIPA, Part III orders is a criminal offence. The code of practice provides guidance when exercising powers under RIPA, to require disclosure of protected electronic data in an intelligible form or to acquire the means by which protected electronic data may be accessed or put in an intelligible form.

### Sifting/examination

A38. In complying with its duty of disclosure, the prosecution should follow the procedure as outlined below.    **A-273**

A39. Where digital material is examined, the extent and manner of inspecting, viewing or listening will depend on the nature of the material and its form.

---

[10] Special provision exists for investigations conducted by Her Majesty's Revenue and Customs in the application of their powers under PACE — see s.114(2)(b) — and the CJPA.

A40. It is important for investigators and prosecutors to remember that the duty under the CPIA code of practice is to "pursue all reasonable lines of enquiry including those that point away from the suspect". Lines of enquiry, of whatever kind, should be pursued only if they are reasonable in the context of the individual case. It is not the duty of the prosecution to comb through all the material in its possession – *e.g.* every word or byte of computer material – on the look out for anything which might conceivably or speculatively assist the defence. The duty of the prosecution is to disclose material which might reasonably be considered capable of undermining its case or assisting the case for the accused which they become aware of, or to which their attention is drawn.

A41. In some cases the sift may be conducted by an investigator/disclosure officer manually assessing the content of the computer or other digital material from its directory and determining which files are relevant and should be retained for evidence or unused material.

A42. In other cases such an approach may not be feasible. Where there is an enormous volume of material it is perfectly proper for the investigator/disclosure officer to search it by sample, key words, or other appropriate search tools or analytical techniques to locate relevant passages, phrases and identifiers.

A43. In cases involving very large quantities of data, the person in charge of the investigation will develop a strategy setting out how the material should be analysed or searched to identify categories of data. Where search tools are used to examine digital material it will usually be appropriate to provide the accused and his or her legal representative with a copy of reasonable search terms used, or to be used, and invite them to suggest any further reasonable search terms. If search terms are suggested which the investigator or prosecutor believes will not be productive – for example because of the use of common words that are likely to identify a mass of irrelevant material, the investigator or prosecutor is entitled to open a dialogue with the defence representative with a view to agreeing sensible refinements. The purpose of this dialogue is to ensure that reasonable and proportionate searches can be carried out.

A44. It may be necessary to carry out sampling and searches on more than one occasion, especially as there is a duty on the prosecutor to keep duties of disclosure under review. To comply with this duty it may be appropriate (and should be considered) where further evidence or unused material is obtained in the course of the investigation; the defence statement is served on the prosecutor; the defendant makes an application under section 8 of the CPIA for disclosure; or the defendant requests that further sampling or searches be carried out (provided it is a reasonable line of enquiry).

### Record keeping

**A-274**

A45. A record or log must be made of all digital material seized or imaged and subsequently retained as relevant to the investigation.

A46. In cases involving very large quantities of data where the person in charge of the investigation has developed a strategy setting out how the material should be analysed or searched to identify categories of data, a record should be made of the strategy and the analytical techniques used to search the data. The record should include details of the person who has carried out the process and the date and time it was carried out. In such cases the strategy should record the reasons why certain categories have been searched for (such as names, companies, dates, etc).

A47. In any case it is important that any searching or analytical processing of digital material, as well as the data identified by that process, is properly recorded. So far as practicable, what is required is a record of the terms of the searches or processing that has been carried out. This means that in principle the following details may be recorded:

    a. a record of all searches carried out, including the date of each search and the person(s) who conducted it;

    b. a record of all search words or terms used on each search; however where it is impracticable to record each word or terms (such as where Boolean searches or search strings or conceptual searches are used) it will usually be sufficient to record each broad category of search;

    c. a log of the key judgements made while refining the search strategy in the light of what is found, or deciding not to carry out further searches; and

    d. where material relating to a "hit" is not examined, the decision not to examine should be explained in the record of examination or in a statement; for instance, a large number of "hits" may be obtained in relation to a particular search word or term, but material relating to the "hits" is not examined because they do not appear to be relevant to the investigation; any subsequent refinement of the search terms and further hits should also be noted and explained as above.

A48. Just as it is not necessary for the investigator or prosecutor to produce records of every search made of hard copy material, it is not necessary to produce records of what may be many hundreds of searches or analyses that have been carried out on digitally stored material, simply to demonstrate that these have been done. It should be sufficient for the prosecution to explain how the disclosure exercise has been approached and to give the accused or suspect's legal representative an opportunity to participate in defining the reasonable searches to be made, as described in the section on sifting/examination.

### Scheduling

A49. The disclosure officer should ensure that scheduling of relevant material is carried out in ac- **A-275** cordance with the CPIA code of practice. This requires each item of unused material to be listed separately on the unused material schedule and numbered consecutively. The description of each item should make clear the nature of the item and should contain sufficient detail to enable the prosecutor to decide whether he needs to inspect the material before deciding whether or not it should be disclosed (see para. A24).

A50. In some enquiries it may not be practicable to list each item of material separately. If so, these may be listed in a block and described by quantity and generic title. Even if the material is listed in a block, the search terms used and any items of material which might satisfy the disclosure test are listed and described separately. In practical terms this will mean, where appropriate, cross referencing the schedules to your disclosure management document.

A51. The remainder of any computer hard drive/media containing material which is not responsive to search terms or other analytical technique or not identified by any "hits", and material identified by "hits" but not examined, is unused material and should be recorded (if appropriate by a generic description) and retained.

A52. Where continuation sheets of the unused material schedule are used, or additional schedules are sent subsequently, the item numbering must be, where possible, sequential to all other items on earlier schedules.

### Third party material

A53. Third party material is material held by a person, organisation, or government department **A-275a** other than the investigator and prosecutor within the UK or outside the UK.

### Within the UK

A54. The CPIA code and the AG's Guidelines make clear the obligation on the prosecution to **A-275b** pursue all reasonable lines of enquiry in relation to material held by third parties within the UK.

A55. If as a result of the duty to pursue all reasonable lines of enquiry, the investigator or prosecutor obtains or receives the material from the third party, then it must be dealt with in accordance with the CPIA, *i.e.* the prosecutor must disclose material if it meets the disclosure tests, subject to any public interest immunity claim. The person who has an interest in the material (the third party) may make representations to the court concerning public interest immunity (see s.16 of the CPIA 1996).

A56. Material not in the possession of an investigator or prosecutor falls outside the CPIA. In such cases the Attorney General's Guidelines on Disclosure prescribe the approach to be taken to disclosure of material held by third parties as does the judicial disclosure protocol.

## B. Acceptance of Pleas

### Introduction

The Attorney-General issued revised guidelines on the acceptance of pleas, which came into **A-276** force on December 1, 2009. The principal changes were to Part C (basis of plea). Paragraph C.1 now makes it clear that in multi-handed cases, any bases of plea must be factually consistent with each other. Paragraph C.2 now states that a defence advocate must reduce an acceptable basis of plea to writing in all cases save for those in which the defendant has indicated that the guilty plea has been or will be tendered on the basis of the prosecution case (previously this was not necessary in cases where the issue was "simple"). Paragraph C.4 now additionally provides that, where the basis of plea differs in its implications for sentencing or the making of ancillary orders from the case originally outlined by the prosecution, the prosecution advocate must ensure that such differences are accurately reflected in the written record prior to showing it to the prosecuting authority. New paragraph C.6 provides that in all cases where it is likely to assist the court where the sentencing issues are complex or unfamiliar, the prosecution must add to the written outline of the case served upon the court a summary of the key considerations, taking the form of brief notes on (a) any statutory limitations, (b) any relevant sentencing authorities or guidelines, (c) the scope for any ancillary orders, and (d) the age of the defendant and information regarding any outstanding offences. Paragraph C.7 was new and clarifies that the prosecution are able to provide further written information where they think that it is likely to assist the judge or where the judge requests it. Old paragraph C.7 became new paragraph C.8, and was amended to ensure that the procedure to be followed where the prosecution advocate takes issue with all or part of the written basis of plea is in line with the then consolidated criminal practice direction. Old paragraph C.8 is now paragraph C.11. For the relevant provisions of *Criminal Practice Direction (Sentence) B* [2013] 1 W.L.R. 3164, see §§ 4-109, 4-175 and 5-91 *et seq.* in the main work; and *post*, A-299 *et seq.*

### ATTORNEY-GENERAL'S GUIDELINES ON THE ACCEPTANCE OF PLEAS AND THE PROSECUTOR'S ROLE IN THE SENTENCING EXERCISE

#### A. Foreword

**A-277**    A:1. Prosecutors have an important role in protecting the victim's interests in the criminal justice process, not least in the acceptance of pleas and the sentencing exercise. The basis of plea, particularly in a case that is not contested, is the vehicle through which the victim's voice is heard. Factual inaccuracies in pleas in mitigation cause distress and offence to victims, the families of victims and witnesses. This can take many forms but may be most acutely felt when the victim is dead and the family hears inaccurate assertions about the victim's character or lifestyle. Prosecution advocates are reminded that they are required to adhere to the standards set out in the Victim's Charter, which places the needs of the victim at the heart of the criminal justice process, and that they are subject to a similar obligation in respect of the Code of Practice for Victims of Crime.

A:2. The principle of fairness is central to the administration of justice. The implementation of Human Rights Act 1998 [*sic*] in October 2000 incorporated into domestic law the principle of fairness to the accused articulated in the European Convention on Human Rights. Accuracy and reasonableness of plea plays an important part in ensuring fairness both to the accused and to the victim.

A:3. The Attorney General's Guidelines on the Acceptance of Pleas issued on December 7, 2000 highlighted the importance of transparency in the conduct of justice. The basis of plea agreed by the parties in a criminal trial is central to the sentencing process. An illogical or unsupported basis of plea can lead to an unduly lenient sentence being passed and has a consequential effect where consideration arises as to whether to refer the sentence to the Court of Appeal under section 36 of the Criminal Justice Act 1988.

A:4. These Guidelines, which replace the Guidelines issued in October 2005, give guidance on how prosecutors should meet these objectives of protection of victims' interests and of securing fairness and transparency in the process. They take into account paragraphs IV.45.4 and following of the consolidated criminal practice direction, amended May 2009, and the guidance issued by the Court of Appeal (Criminal) Division [*sic*] in *R. v. Beswick* [1996] 1 Cr.App.R. 343, *R. v. Tolera* [1999] 1 Cr.App.R. 25 and *R. v. Underwood* [2005] 1 Cr.App.R 13. They complement the Bar Council Guidance on Written Standards for the Conduct of Professional Work issued with the 7th edition of the Code of Conduct for the Bar of England and Wales and the Law Society's Professional Conduct Rules. When considering the acceptance of a guilty plea prosecution advocates are also reminded of the need to apply "The Farquharson Guidelines on The Role and Responsibilities of the Prosecution Advocate".

A:5. The Guidelines should be followed by all prosecutors and those persons designated under section 7 of the Prosecution of Offences Act 1985 (designated caseworkers) and apply to prosecutions conducted in England and Wales.

#### B. General Principles

**A-278**    B:1. Justice in this jurisdiction, save in the most exceptional circumstances, is conducted in public. This includes the acceptance of pleas by the prosecution and sentencing.

B:2. The Code for Crown Prosecutors governs the prosecutor's decision-making prior to the commencement of the trial hearing and sets out the circumstances in which pleas to a reduced number of charges, or less serious charges, can be accepted.

B:3. When a case is listed for trial and the prosecution form the view that the appropriate course is to accept a plea before the proceedings commence or continue, or to offer no evidence on the indictment or any part of it, the prosecution should whenever practicable speak to the victim or the victim's family, so that the position can be explained. The views of the victim or the family may assist in informing the prosecutor's decision as to whether it is the [*sic*] public interest, as defined by the

Code for Crown Prosecutors, to accept or reject the plea. The victim or victim's family should then be kept informed and decisions explained once they are made at court.

B:4. The appropriate disposal of a criminal case after conviction is as much a part of the criminal justice process as the trial of guilt or innocence. The prosecution advocate represents the public interest, and should be ready to assist the court to reach its decision as to the appropriate sentence. This will include drawing the court's attention to:

— any victim personal statement or other information available to the prosecution advocate as to the impact of the offence on the victim;

— where appropriate, to any evidence of the impact of the offending on a community;

— any statutory provisions relevant to the offender and the offences under consideration;

— any relevant sentencing guidelines and guideline cases; and

— the aggravating and mitigating factors of the offence under consideration.

The prosecution advocate may also offer assistance to the court by making submissions, in the light of all these factors, as to the appropriate sentencing range.

In all cases, it is the prosecution advocate's duty to apply for appropriate ancillary orders, such as anti-social behaviour orders and confiscation orders. When considering which ancillary orders to apply for, prosecution advocates must always have regard to the victim's needs, including the question of his or her future protection.

### C. The Basis of Plea

C:1. The basis of a guilty plea must not be agreed on a misleading or untrue set of facts and must    **A-279** take proper account of the victim's interests. An illogical or insupportable basis of plea will inevitably result in the imposition of an inappropriate sentence and is capable of damaging public confidence in the criminal justice system. In cases involving multiple defendants the bases of plea for each defendant must be factually consistent with each other.

C:2. When the defendant indicates an acceptable plea, the defence advocate should reduce the basis of the plea to writing. This must be done in all cases save for those in which the defendant has indicated that the guilty plea has been or will be tendered on the basis of the prosecution case.

C:3. The written basis of plea must be considered with great care, taking account of the position of any other relevant defendant where appropriate. The prosecution should not lend itself to any agreement whereby a case is presented to the sentencing judge on a misleading or untrue set of facts or on a basis that is detrimental to the victim's interests. There will be cases where a defendant seeks to mitigate on the basis of assertions of fact which are outside the scope of the prosecution's knowledge. A typical example concerns the defendant's state of mind. If a defendant wishes to be sentenced on this basis, the prosecution advocate should invite the judge not to accept the defendant's version unless he or she gives evidence on oath to be tested in cross- examination. Paragraph IV.45.14 of the consolidated criminal practice direction states that in such circumstances the defence advocate should be prepared to call the defendant and, if the defendant is not willing to testify, subject to any explanation that may be given, the judge may draw such inferences as appear appropriate.

C:4. The prosecution advocate should show the prosecuting authority any written record relating to the plea and agree with them the basis on which the case will be opened to the court. If, as may well be the case, the basis of plea differs in its implications for sentencing or the making of ancillary orders from the case originally outlined by the prosecution, the prosecution advocate must ensure that such differences are accurately reflected in the written record prior to showing it to the prosecuting authority.

C:5. It is the responsibility of the prosecution advocate thereafter to ensure that the defence advocate is aware of the basis on which the plea is accepted by the prosecution and the way in which the prosecution case will be opened to the court.

C:6. In all cases where it is likely to assist the court where the sentencing issues are complex or unfamiliar the prosecution must add to the written outline of the case which is served upon the court a summary of the key considerations. This should take the form of very brief notes on:

— any relevant statutory limitations;

— the names of any relevant sentencing authorities or guidelines;

— the scope for any ancillary orders (*e.g.* concerning anti-social behaviour, confiscation or deportation will need to be considered).

The outline should also include the age of the defendant and information regarding any outstanding offences.

C:7. It remains open to the prosecutor to provide further written information (for example to supplement and update the analysis at later stages of the case) where he or she thought that likely to assist the court, or if the judge requests it.

C:8. When the prosecution advocate has agreed the written basis of plea submitted by the defence advocate, he or she should endorse the document accordingly. If the prosecution advocate takes issue with all or part of the written basis of plea, the procedure set out in the consolidated criminal practice direction (and in Part 37.10(5) of the Criminal Procedure Rules) should be followed. The defendant's basis of plea must be set out in writing identifying what is in dispute; the court may invite the parties to make representations about whether the dispute is material to sentence; and if the court decides that it is a material dispute, the court will invite further representations or evidence as it may require and decide the dispute in accordance with the principles set out in *R. v. Newton*, 77 Cr.App.R.13, CA. The signed original document setting out the disputed factual matters should be made available to the trial judge and thereafter lodged with the court papers, as it will form part of the record of the hearing.

C:9. Where the basis of plea cannot be agreed and the discrepancy between the two accounts is such as to have a potentially significant effect on the level of sentence, it is the duty of the defence advocate so to inform the court before the sentencing process begins. There remains an overriding duty on the prosecution advocate to ensure that the sentencing judge is made aware of the discrepancy and of the consideration which must be given to holding a *Newton* hearing to resolve the issue. The court should be told where a derogatory reference to a victim, witness or third party is not accepted, even though there may be no effect on sentence.

C:10. As emphasised in paragraph IV.45.10 of the consolidated criminal practice direction, whenever an agreement as to the basis of plea is made between the prosecution and defence, any such agreement will be subject to the approval of the trial judge, who may of his or her own motion disregard the agreement and direct that a *Newton* hearing should be held to determine the proper basis on which sentence should be passed.

C:11. Where a defendant declines to admit an offence that he or she previously indicated should be taken into consideration, the prosecution advocate should indicate to the defence advocate and the court that, subject to further review, the offence may now form the basis of a new prosecution.

### D. Sentence Indications

A-280    D:1. Only in the Crown Court may sentence indications be sought. Advocates there are reminded that indications as to sentence should not be sought from the trial judge unless issues between the prosecution and defence have been addressed and resolved. Therefore, in difficult or complicated cases, no less than seven days notice in writing of an intention to seek an indication should normally be given to the prosecution and the court. When deciding whether the circumstances of a case require such notice to be given, defence advocates are reminded that prosecutors should not agree a basis of plea unless and until the necessary consultation has taken place first with the victim and/or the victim's family and second, in the case of an independent prosecution advocate, with the prosecuting authority.

D:2. If there is no final agreement about the plea to the indictment, or the basis of plea, and the defence nevertheless proceeds to seek an indication of sentence, which the judge appears minded to give, the prosecution advocate should remind him or her of the guidance given in *R. v. Goodyear (Karl)* [2005] EWCA 888 [*sic*] that normally speaking an indication of sentence should not be given until the basis of the plea has been agreed or the judge has concluded that he or she can properly deal with the case without the need for a trial of the issue.

D:3. If an indication is sought, the prosecution advocate should normally enquire whether the judge is in possession of or has access to all the evidence relied on by the prosecution, including any victim personal statement, as well as any information about relevant previous convictions recorded against the defendant.

D:4. Before the judge gives the indication, the prosecution advocate should draw the judge's attention to any minimum or mandatory statutory sentencing requirements. Where the prosecution advocate would be expected to offer the judge assistance with relevant guideline cases or the views of the Sentencing Guidelines Council, he or she should invite the judge to allow them to do so. Where it applies, the prosecution advocate should remind the judge that the position [*sic*] of the Attorney General to refer any sentencing decision as unduly lenient is unaffected. In any event, the prosecution advocate should not say anything which may create the impression that the sentence indication has the support or approval of the Crown.

### E. Pleas in Mitigation

A-281    E:1. The prosecution advocate must challenge any assertion by the defence in mitigation which is derogatory to a person's character (for instance, because it suggests that his or her conduct is or has been criminal, immoral or improper) and which is either false or irrelevant to proper sentencing considerations. If the defence advocate persists in that assertion, the prosecution advocate should invite the court to consider holding a *Newton* hearing to determine the issue.

E:2. The defence advocate must not submit in mitigation anything that is derogatory to a person's character without giving advance notice in writing so as to afford the prosecution advocate the opportunity to consider their position under paragraph E:1. When the prosecution advocate is so notified they must take all reasonable steps to establish whether the assertions are true. Reasonable steps will include seeking the views of the victim. This will involve seeking the views of the victim's family if the victim is deceased, and the victim's parents or legal guardian where the victim is a child. Reasonable steps may also include seeking the views of the police or other law enforcement authority, as appropriate. An assertion which is derogatory to a person's character will rarely amount to mitigation unless it has a causal connection to the circumstances of the offence or is otherwise relevant to proper sentencing considerations.

E:3. Where notice has not been given in accordance with paragraph E:2, the prosecution advocate must not acquiesce in permitting mitigation which is derogatory to a person's character. In such circumstances, the prosecution advocate should draw the attention of the court to the failure to give advance notice and seek time, and if necessary, an adjournment to investigate the assertion in the same way as if proper notice had been given. Where, in the opinion of the prosecution advocate, there are substantial grounds for believing that such an assertion is false or irrelevant to sentence, he or she should inform the court of their opinion and invite the court to consider making an order under section 58(8) of the Criminal Procedure and Investigations Act 1996, preventing publication of the assertion.

E:4. Where the prosecution advocate considers that the assertion is, if true, relevant to sentence, or the court has so indicated, he or she should seek time, and if necessary an adjournment, to establish whether the assertion is true. If the matter cannot be resolved to the satisfaction of the parties, the prosecution advocate should invite the court to consider holding a *Newton* hearing to determine the issue.

## C. Jury Checks

### Introduction

For the background to these guidelines, see § 4-275 in the main work. They were updated in November 2012. **A-282**

#### Attorney-General's Guidelines: Jury checks, unreported, November 27, 2012

1. The principles which are generally to be observed are: **A-283**
   (a) that members of a jury should be selected at random from the panel,
   (b) the Juries Act 1974 identifies those classes of persons who alone are either disqualified from or ineligible for service on a jury; no other class of person may be treated as disqualified or ineligible,
   (c) the correct way for the Crown to seek to exclude a member of the panel from sitting as a juror is by the exercise in open court of the right to request a stand by or, if necessary, to challenge for cause.

2. Parliament has provided safeguards against jurors who may be corrupt or biased. In addition to the provision for majority verdicts, there is the sanction of a criminal offence for a disqualified person to serve on a jury. The omission of a disqualified person from the panel is a matter for court officials—they will check criminal records for the purpose of ascertaining whether or not a potential juror is a disqualified person.

3. There are, however, certain exceptional types of case of public importance for which the provisions as to majority verdicts and the disqualification of jurors may not be sufficient to ensure the proper administration of justice. In such cases it is in the interests of both justice and the public that there should be further safeguards against the possibility of bias and in such cases checks which go beyond the investigation of criminal records may be necessary. **A-284**

4. These classes of case may be defined broadly as (a) cases in which national security is involved and part of the evidence is likely to be heard in camera, and (b) security and terrorist cases in which a juror's extreme beliefs could prevent a fair trial.

5. The particular aspects of these cases which may make it desirable to seek extra precautions are:
   (a) in security cases a danger that a juror, either voluntarily or under pressure, may make an improper use of evidence which, because of its sensitivity, has been given in camera,
   (b) in both security and terrorist cases the danger that a juror's personal beliefs are so biased as to go beyond normally reflecting the broad spectrum of views and interests in the community to reflect the extreme views of sectarian interest or pressure group to a degree which might interfere with his fair assessment of the facts of the case or lead him to exert improper pressure on his fellow jurors.

**6.** In order to ascertain whether in exceptional circumstances of the above nature either of these factors might seriously influence a potential juror's impartial performance of his duties or his respecting the secrecy of evidence given in camera, it may be necessary to conduct a limited investigation of the panel. In general, such further investigation beyond one of criminal records made for disqualifications may only be made with the records of the police. However, a check may, additionally, be made against the records of the Security Service. No checks other than on these sources and no general inquiries are to be made save to the limited extent that they may be needed to confirm the identity of a juror about whom the initial check has raised serious doubts.

**7.** No further investigation, as described in paragraph 6 above, should be made save with the personal authority of the Attorney-General on the application of the Director of Public Prosecutions and such checks are hereafter referred to as "authorised checks". When a chief officer of police or the prosecutor has reason to believe that it is likely that an authorised check may be desirable and proper in accordance with these guidelines, he should refer the matter to the Director of Public Prosecutions. In those cases in which the Director of Public Prosecutions believes authorised checks are both proportionate and necessary, the Director will make an application to the Attorney-General.

**8.** The Director of Public Prosecutions will provide the Attorney-General with all relevant information in support of the requested authorised checks. The Attorney-General will consider personally the request and, if appropriate, authorise the check.

**9.** The result of any authorised check will be sent to the Director of Public Prosecutions. The Director will then decide, having regard to the matters set out in paragraph 5 above, what information ought to be brought to the attention of prosecuting counsel. The Director will also provide the Attorney-General with the result of the authorised check.

**10.** Although the right of stand by and the decision to authorise checks are wholly within the discretion of the Attorney-General, when the Attorney-General has agreed to an authorised check being conducted, the Director of Public Prosecutions will write to the presiding judge for the area to advise him that this is being done.

**11.** No right of stand by should be exercised by counsel for the Crown on the basis of information obtained as a result of an authorised check save with the personal authority of the Attorney-General and unless the information is such as, having regard to the facts of the case and the offences charged, to afford strong reason for believing that a particular juror might be a security risk, be susceptible to improper approaches or be influenced in arriving at a verdict for the reasons given above.

**12.** Information revealed in the course of an authorised check must be considered in line with the normal rules on disclosure.

**13.** A record is to be kept by the Director of Public Prosecutions of the use made by counsel of the information passed to him and of the jurors stood by or challenged by the parties to the proceedings. A copy of this record is to be forwarded to the Attorney-General for the sole purpose of enabling him to monitor the operation of these guidelines.

**14.** No use of the information obtained as a result of an authorised check is to be made except as may be necessary in direct relation to or arising out of the trial for which the check was authorised. The information may, however, be used for the prevention of crime or as evidence in a future criminal prosecution, save that material obtained from the Security Service may only be used in those circumstances with the authority of the Security Service.

## D. Prosecution's Right of Stand By

For the background to these guidelines, see §§ 4-304, 4-305 in the main work. They were updated in November, 2012.

### Attorney-General's Guidelines on the Exercise by the Crown of its Right of Stand By, unreported, November 27, 2012

**1.** Although the law has long recognised the right of the Crown to exclude a member of a jury panel from sitting as a juror by the exercise in open court of the right to request a stand by or, if necessary, by challenge for cause, it has been customary for those instructed to prosecute on behalf of the Crown to assert that right only sparingly and in exceptional circumstances. It is generally accepted that the prosecution should not use its right in order to influence the overall composition of a jury or with a view to tactical advantage.

**2.** The approach outlined above is founded on the principles that:

> (a) the members of a jury should be selected at random from the panel subject to any rule of law as to right of challenge by the defence, and

> (b) the Juries Act 1974 identifies those classes of persons who alone are disqualified from or ineligible for service on a jury. No other class of person may be treated as disqualified or ineligible.

**3.** The enactment by Parliament of section 118 of the Criminal Justice Act 1988 abolishing the right of defendants to remove jurors by means of peremptory challenge makes it appropriate that the Crown should assert its right to stand by only on the basis of clearly defined and restrictive criteria. Derogation from the principle that members of a jury should be selected at random should be permitted only where it is essential.

**4.** Primary responsibility for ensuring that an individual does not serve on a jury if he is not competent to discharge properly the duties of a juror rests with the appropriate court officer and, ultimately the trial judge. Current legislation provides, in sections 9 to 10 of the Juries Act 1974, fairly wide discretion to excuse, defer or discharge jurors.

**5.** The circumstances in which it would be proper for the Crown to exercise its right to stand by a member of a jury panel are:

    (a) where a jury check authorised in accordance with the Attorney-General's guidelines on jury checks reveals information justifying exercise of the right to stand by in accordance with paragraph 11 of the guidelines ... and the Attorney-General personally authorises the exercise of the right to stand by; or

    (b) where a person is about to be sworn as a juror who is manifestly unsuitable and the defence agree that, accordingly, the exercise by the prosecution of the right to stand by would be appropriate. An example of the sort of exceptional circumstances which might justify stand by is where it becomes apparent that, despite the provisions mentioned in paragraph 4 above, a juror selected for service to try a complex case is in fact illiterate.

### E. Conspiracy to Defraud

The Attorney-General has issued guidance to prosecuting authorities in relation to charging a **A-290** common law conspiracy to defraud instead of a substantive offence, contrary to the Fraud Act 2006, or a statutory conspiracy to commit a substantive offence, contrary to section 1 of the CLA 1977 (§ 33-2 in the main work); the prosecutor should consider (i) whether the conduct alleged falls within the ambit of a statutory offence, and (ii) whether such a charge or charges would adequately reflect the gravity of the alleged offending; as to (i), non-exhaustive examples of circumstances falling outside of the range of statutory offences, but within the ambit of the common law offence, are: (a) the dishonest obtaining of land or other property which cannot be stolen; (b) the dishonest infringement of another's right (*e.g.* the dishonest exploitation of another's patent); (c) an agreement involving an intention that the final offence be committed by someone outside the conspiracy; and (d) an agreement where the conspirators cannot be proved to have had the necessary degree of knowledge for the substantive offence to be perpetrated; as to (ii), prosecution for the common law offence may be more effective where the interests of justice can only be served by presenting an overall picture which could not be achieved by charging a series of substantive offences or statutory conspiracies (because of a large number of counts and/or the possibility of severed trials and evidence on one count being deemed inadmissible on another); where a case lawyer proposes to charge the common law offence, he must consider, and set out in the review note, how much such a charge would add to the amount of evidence likely to be called by the parties, the justification for using the charge, and why specific statutory offences are inadequate or otherwise inappropriate; a supervising lawyer experienced in fraud cases must also specifically approve the charge: *Attorney-General's guidance on the use of the common law offence of conspiracy to defraud*, unreported, January 9, 2007.

### F. Prosecutor's Role in Applications for Witness Anonymity Orders

On July 21, 2008, the Attorney-General issued guidelines on the overarching principles which **A-291** a prosecutor must consider when deciding whether to apply for witness anonymity orders under the Criminal Evidence (Witness Anonymity) Act 2008 (now the Coroners and Justice Act 2009, ss.86-97 (§§ 8-151 *et seq.* in the main work)).

The guidance is in four parts (Part A (foreword), Part B (prosecutor's duties), Part C (applications by defendants) and Part D (appointment and role of special counsel)), and, to a large extent, highlights various provisions of the Act and restates elementary aspects of fairness at trial. Paragraph A2 makes clear that, given that the defendant's right to confront and challenge those who accuse him is an important aspect of a fair trial, making a witness anonymity order is a serious step which must only be taken where there are genuine grounds to believe that the conditions set out in the Act have been satisfied, which must be evaluated with care on the facts of each case. Paragraph B3 sets out the prosecutor's role, which prosecutors must approach in light of their overriding duties to be fair, independent and objective, and which includes a duty: (a) to examine with care and probe where appropriate, the material provided in support of the application and the evidential basis for it, and (b) to put before the court and to disclose to the defendant all material relevant to the application and the defence, including material which may undermine or qualify the prosecution case. Any such material is particularly relevant if credibility is in issue, for example, if there is a known link between the witness and defendant or a co-accused. Paragraph B4 explains that applications should only be authorised by prosecutors of an appropriately senior level. Paragraph D5 explains that a prosecutor making an application for an order must always be prepared to assist the court to consider whether the circumstances are such that exceptionally the appointment of special counsel may be called for, and, where appropriate, should draw to the attention of the court any aspect of the application which may be relevant to such appointment. Where the court decides to invite the Attorney-General to appoint special counsel, the prosecutor should (regardless of any steps taken by the court or any defendant) ensure that the Attorney-General's office is promptly notified and receives all information needed to take a decision as to whether to make such appointment. If special counsel is appointed, the prosecutor should then provide special counsel with open material made available to the accused regarding the application, and any other open material requested by special counsel. Closed or unredacted material which has been provided to the court should only be given to special counsel after open material has been provided and after special counsel has subsequently sought instructions from the defendant and his legal representative.

## G. Plea Discussions in Cases of Serious or Complex Fraud

### (1) Guidelines

A-292    On March 18, 2009, the Attorney-General issued guidelines setting out the process by which a prosecutor may discuss allegations of serious or complex fraud with a person whom he is prosecuting or expecting to prosecute.

### ATTORNEY GENERAL'S GUIDELINES ON PLEA DISCUSSIONS IN CASES OF SERIOUS OR COMPLEX FRAUD

#### A. Foreword

A-293    A:1  These guidelines set out a process by which a prosecutor may discuss an allegation of serious or complex fraud with a person who he or she is prosecuting or expects to prosecute, or with that person's legal representative. They come into force on the 5th day of May 2009 and apply to plea discussions initiated on or after that date.

A:2  The guidelines will be followed by all prosecutors in England and Wales when conducting plea discussions in cases of serious or complex fraud. For the purposes of the guidelines, fraud means any financial, fiscal or commercial misconduct or corruption which is contrary to the criminal law. Fraud may be serious or complex if at least two of the following factors are present:

- the amount obtained or intended to be obtained is alleged to exceed £500,000;
- there is a significant international dimension;
- the case requires specialised knowledge of financial, commercial, fiscal or regulatory matters such as the operation of markets, banking systems, trusts or tax regimes;
- the case involves allegations of fraudulent activity against numerous victims;
- the case involves an allegation of substantial and significant fraud on a public body;
- the case is likely to be of widespread public concern;
- the alleged misconduct endangered the economic well-being of the United Kingdom, for example by undermining confidence in financial markets.

Taking account of these matters, it is for the prosecutor to decide whether or not a case is one of fraud, and whether or not it is serious or complex.

A:3  The decision whether a person should be charged with a criminal offence rests with the prosecutor. In selecting the appropriate charge or charges, the prosecutor applies principles set out in the Code for Crown Prosecutors ("the code"). Charges should reflect the seriousness and extent of the offending, give the court adequate sentencing powers and enable the case to be presented in a clear and simple way. The code also states that prosecutors should not go ahead with more charges to encourage a defendant to plead guilty to a few; equally, prosecutors should not charge a more serious offence to encourage a defendant to plead to a less serious one.

A:4  Once proceedings are instituted, the accused may plead guilty to all of the charges selected. If the defendant will plead guilty to some, but not all, of the charges or to a different, possibly less serious charge, the code states that a prosecutor is entitled to accept such pleas if he or she assesses that the court could still pass an adequate sentence. In taking these decisions the prosecutor also applies the Attorney General's Guidelines on the Acceptance of Pleas and the Prosecutor's Role in the Sentencing Exercise ("the acceptance of pleas guidelines") [*ante*, A-259 *et seq.*].

A:5 The purpose of plea discussions is to narrow the issues in the case with a view to reaching a just outcome at the earliest possible time, including the possibility of reaching an agreement about acceptable pleas of guilty and preparing a joint submission as to sentence.

A:6 The potential benefits of plea discussions are that:

- early resolution of the case may reduce the anxiety and uncertainty for victims and witnesses, and provide earlier clarity for accused persons who admit their guilt (subject to the court's power to reject the agreement);
- the issues in dispute may be narrowed so that even if the case proceeds to trial, it can be managed more efficiently in accordance with rule 3.2 of the Criminal Procedure Rules 2005. If pleas are agreed, litigation can be kept to a minimum.

A:7 Where plea discussions take place prior to the commencement of proceedings, the charges brought by the prosecutor will reflect those agreed, rather than those that the prosecutor would necessarily have preferred if no agreement had been reached. Also, any criminal investigation may not be complete when these discussions take place. For these reasons it is important that the procedures followed should command public and judicial confidence; that any agreement reached is reasonable, fair and just; that there are safeguards to ensure that defendants are not under improper pressure to make admissions; and that there are proper records of discussions that have taken place.

A:8 The guidelines are not intended to prevent or discourage existing practices by which prosecutors and prosecuting advocates discuss cases with defence legal representatives after charge, in order to narrow the issues or to agree a basis of plea. Neither do they affect the existing practice of judicial sentence indications at the plea and case management hearing or later in accordance with the guidance in *R. v. Goodyear* [2005] 2 Cr.App.R. 20 (§ 5-110 in the main work) (see also the acceptance of pleas guidelines). They complement, and do not detract from or replace, the code and the acceptance of pleas guidelines, or any other relevant guidance such as the Prosecutor's Pledge, the Victim's Charter and the Code of Practice for Victims of Crime.

A:9 Where a plea agreement is reached, it remains entirely a matter for the court to decide how to deal with the case.

### B. General Principles

B:1 In conducting plea discussions and presenting a plea agreement to the court, the prosecutor **A-294** must act openly, fairly and in the interests of justice.

B:2 Acting in the interests of justice means ensuring that the plea agreement reflects the seriousness and extent of the offending, gives the court adequate sentencing powers, and enables the court, the public and the victims to have confidence in the outcome. The prosecutor must consider carefully the impact of a proposed plea or basis of plea on the community and the victim, and on the prospects of successfully prosecuting any other person implicated in the offending. The prosecutor must not agree to a reduced basis of plea which is misleading, untrue or illogical.

B:3 Acting fairly means respecting the rights of the defendant and of any other person who is being or may be prosecuted in relation to the offending. The prosecutor must not put improper pressure on a defendant in the course of plea discussions, for example by exaggerating the strength of the case in order to persuade the defendant to plead guilty, or to plead guilty on a particular basis.

B:4 Acting openly means being transparent with the defendant, the victim and the court. The prosecutor must:

- ensure that a full and accurate record of the plea discussions is prepared and retained;
- ensure that the defendant has sufficient information to enable him or her to play an informed part in the plea discussions;
- communicate with the victim before accepting a reduced basis of plea, wherever it is practicable to do so, so that the position can be explained; and
- ensure that the plea agreement placed before the court fully and fairly reflects the matters agreed. The prosecutor must not agree additional matters with the defendant which are not recorded in the plea agreement and made known to the court.

## C. Initiating Plea Discussions

*When and with whom discussions should be initiated and conducted*

C:1 Where he or she believes it advantageous to do so, the prosecutor may initiate plea discussions with any person who is being prosecuted or investigated with a view to prosecution in connection with a serious or complex fraud, and who is legally represented. The prosecutor will not initiate plea discussions with a defendant who is not legally represented. If the prosecutor receives an approach from such a defendant, he or she may enter into discussions if satisfied that it is appropriate to do so.

C:2 Where proceedings have not yet been instituted, the prosecutor should not initiate plea discussions until he or she and the investigating officer are satisfied that the suspect's criminality is known. This will not usually be the case until after the suspect has been interviewed under caution.

C:3 The prosecutor should be alert to any attempt by the defendant to use plea discussions as a means of delaying the investigation or prosecution, and should not initiate or continue discussions where the defendant's commitment to the process is in doubt. The prosecutor should ensure that the position is preserved during plea discussions by, for example, restraining assets in anticipation of the making of a confiscation order. Where a defendant declines to take part in plea discussions, the prosecutor should not make a second approach unless there is a material change in circumstances.

*Invitation letter*

C:4 In order to initiate the plea discussions, the prosecutor will send the defendant's representatives a letter which:

* asks whether the defence wish to enter into discussions in accordance with these guidelines; and
* sets a deadline for a response from the defence.

*Terms and conditions letter*

C:5 Where the defence agree to engage in plea discussions, the prosecutor should send them a letter setting out the way in which the discussions will be conducted. This letter should deal with:

* the confidentiality of information provided by the prosecutor and defendant in the course of the plea discussions;
* the use which may be made by the prosecutor of information provided by the defendant; and
* the practical means by which the discussions will be conducted.

*Confidentiality and use of information*

C:6 In relation to confidentiality, the prosecutor will indicate that he or she intends to provide an undertaking to the effect that the fact that the defendant has taken part in the plea discussions, and any information provided by the defence in the course of the plea discussions will be treated as confidential and will not be disclosed to any other party other than for the purposes of the plea discussions and plea agreement (applying these guidelines), or as required by law. The undertaking will make it clear that the law in relation to the disclosure of unused material may require the prosecutor to provide information about the plea discussions to another defendant in criminal proceedings.

C:7 The prosecutor will require the defendant's legal representative to provide an undertaking to the effect that information provided by the prosecutor in the course of the plea discussions will be treated as confidential and will not be disclosed to any other party, other than for the purposes of the plea discussion and plea agreement or as required by law.

C:8 In relation to the use of information, the prosecutor will indicate that he or she intends to undertake not to rely upon the fact that the defendant has taken part in the plea discussions, or any information provided by the defendant in the course of the discussions, as evidence in any prosecution of that defendant for the offences under investigation, should the discussions fail. However, this undertaking will make it clear that the prosecutor is not prevented from:

* relying upon a concluded and signed plea agreement as confession evidence or as admissions;
* relying upon any evidence obtained from enquiries made as a result of the provision of information by the defendant;
* relying upon information provided by the defendant as evidence against him or her in any prosecution for an offence other than the fraud which is the subject of the plea discussion and any offence which is consequent upon it, such as money laundering; and
* relying upon information provided by the defendant in a prosecution of any other person for any offence (so far as the rules of evidence allow).

C:9 In exceptional circumstances the prosecutor may agree to different terms regarding the confidentiality and use of information. However, the prosecutor must not surrender the ability to rely upon a concluded and signed plea agreement as evidence against the defendant. The prosecutor may reserve the right to bring other charges (additional to those to which the defendant has indicated a willingness to plead guilty) in specific circumstances, for example if substantial new information comes to light at a later stage, the plea agreement is rejected by the court, or the defendant fails to honour the agreement.

C:10 Until the issues of confidentiality and use of information have been agreed to the satisfaction of both parties, and the agreement reflected in signed undertakings, the prosecutor must not continue with the substantive plea discussions.

## D. Conducting Plea Discussions

### *Statement of case*

D:1 Where plea discussions take place prior to proceedings being instituted, the prosecutor will **A-296** provide a statement of case to the defence. This is a written summary of the nature of the allegation against the suspect and the evidence which has been obtained, or is expected to be obtained, to support it. The statement of case should include a list of the proposed charges. Material in support of the statement of case may also be provided, whether or not in the form of admissible evidence. However, the prosecutor is not obliged to reveal to the suspect all of the information or evidence supporting his case, provided that this does not mislead the suspect to his or her prejudice.

D:2 Where plea discussions are initiated after proceedings have been commenced, but before the prosecutor has provided the defence with a case summary or opening note, the prosecutor may provide a statement of case to assist the defendant in understanding the evidence and identifying the issues.

### *Unused material*

D:3 These guidelines do not affect the prosecutor's existing duties in relation to the disclosure of unused material. Where plea discussions take place prior to the institution of proceedings, the prosecutor should ensure that the suspect is not misled as to the strength of the prosecution case. It will not usually be necessary to provide copies of unused material in order to do this.

### *Conducting and recording the discussions*

D:4 Having provided the defence with the statement of case and supporting material, the parties will then be in a position to conduct the plea discussion proper. Whether this is done by correspondence, by face-to-face meetings or by a combination of the two is a matter for the parties to decide in the individual case.

D:5 It is essential that a full written record is kept of every key action and event in the discussion process, including details of every offer or concession made by each party, and the reasons for every decision taken by the prosecutor. Meetings between the parties should be minuted and the minutes agreed and signed. Particular care should be taken where the defendant is not legally represented. The prosecutor should only meet with a defendant who is not legally represented if the defendant agrees to the meeting being recorded, or to the presence of an independent third party.

### *Queen's evidence*

D:6 If the defendant offers at any stage to provide information, or to give evidence about the criminal activities of others, any such offer will be dealt with in accordance with sections 71 to 75 of the Serious Organised Crime and Police Act 2005 ("SOCPA"), the judgment of the Court of Appeal in *R. v P.; R v Blackburn* [2008] 2 Cr.App.R.(S.) 5 (§ 5-136 in the main work) and the guidance agreed and issued by the Director of Public Prosecutions, the Director of the Serious Fraud Office and the Director of Revenue and Customs Prosecutions.

### *Discussion of pleas*

D:7 In deciding whether or not to accept an offer by the defendant to plead guilty, the prosecutor will follow sections 7 and 10 of the code relating to the selection of charges and the acceptance of guilty pleas. The prosecutor should ensure that:
- the charges reflect the seriousness and extent of the offending;
- they give the court adequate powers to sentence and impose appropriate post-conviction orders;
- they enable the case to be presented in a clear and simple way (bearing in mind that many cases of fraud are necessarily complex);

- the basis of plea enables the court to pass a sentence that matches the seriousness of the offending, particularly if there are aggravating features;
- the interests of the victim, and where possible any views expressed by the victim, are taken into account when deciding whether it is in the public interest to accept the plea; and
- the investigating officer is fully appraised of developments in the plea discussions and his or her views are taken into account.

D:8 In reaching an agreement on pleas, the parties should resolve any factual issues necessary to allow the court to sentence the defendant on a clear, fair and accurate basis. Before agreeing to proposed pleas, the prosecutor should satisfy him or herself that the full code test as set out in the code will be made out in respect of each charge. In considering whether the evidential stage of the test will be met, the prosecutor should assume that the offender will sign a plea agreement amounting to an admission to the charge.

*Discussion of sentence*

D:9 Where agreement is reached as to pleas, the parties should discuss the appropriate sentence with a view to presenting a joint written submission to the court. This document should list the aggravating and mitigating features arising from the agreed facts, set out any personal mitigation available to the defendant, and refer to any relevant sentencing guidelines or authorities. In the light of all of these factors, it should make submissions as to the applicable sentencing range in the relevant guideline. The prosecutor must ensure that the submissions are realistic, taking full account of all relevant material and considerations.

D:10 The prosecutor should bear in mind all of the powers of the court, and seek to include in the joint submission any relevant ancillary orders. It is particularly desirable that measures should be included that achieve redress for victims (such as compensation orders) and protection for the public (such as directors' disqualification orders, serious crime prevention orders or financial reporting orders).

D:11 Due regard should be had to the court's asset recovery powers and the desirability of using these powers both as a deterrent to others and as a means of preventing the defendant from benefiting from the proceeds of crime or funding future offending. The Proceeds of Crime Act 2002 requires the Crown Court to proceed to the making of a confiscation order against a convicted defendant who has benefited from his criminal conduct where the prosecutor asks the court to do so, or the court believes that it is appropriate to do so. Fraud is an acquisitive crime, and the expectation in a fraud case should be that a confiscation order will be sought by the prosecutor reflecting the full benefit to the defendant. However, in doing so it is open to the prosecutor to take a realistic view of the likely approach of the court to the determination of any points in dispute (such as the interest of a third party in any property).

D:12 In the course of the plea discussions the prosecutor must make it clear to the defence that the joint submission as to sentence (including confiscation) is not binding on the court.

*Liaison with another prosecutor or regulator*

D:13 The prosecutor may become aware that another prosecuting authority or regulatory body (either in England and Wales or elsewhere) has an interest in the defendant. The prosecutor should liaise with the other agency, in accordance with the Prosecutors' Convention and any other relevant agreement or guidance. The other agency may wish to take part in the plea discussions, or they may authorise the prosecutor to discuss with the defendant the matters which they are interested in, with a view to resolving all matters in one plea agreement. The prosecutor should warn the defendant that a plea agreement will not bind any other agency which is not a party to it.

### E. The Written Plea Agreement

E:1 All matters agreed between the prosecutor and the defence must be reduced to writing as a plea agreement and signed by both parties. The plea agreement will include:
- a list of the charges;
- a statement of the facts; and
- a declaration, signed by the defendant personally, to the effect that he or she accepts the stated facts and admits he or she is guilty of the agreed charges.

E:2 Any agreement under the SOCPA regarding the giving of assistance to the prosecutor by the defendant should be in a separate document accompanying the plea agreement.

E:3 Once a plea agreement is signed in a case where proceedings have not yet been commenced, the prosecutor will review the case in accordance with the code and, assuming the evidential stage of the full code test is satisfied on the basis of the signed plea agreement and the other available evidence, will arrange for proceedings to be instituted by summons or charge.

**E:4** In advance of the defendant's first appearance in the Crown Court, the prosecutor should send the court sufficient material to allow the judge to understand the facts of the case and the history of the plea discussions, to assess whether the plea agreement is fair and in the interests of justice, and to decide the appropriate sentence. This will include:

- the signed plea agreement;
- a joint submission as to sentence and sentencing considerations;
- any relevant sentencing guidelines or authorities;
- all of the material provided by the prosecution to the defendant in the course of the plea discussions;
- any material provided by the defendant to the prosecution, such as documents relating to personal mitigation; and
- the minutes of any meetings between the parties and any correspondence generated in the plea discussions.

**E:5** It will then be for the court to decide how to deal with the plea agreement. In particular, the court retains an absolute discretion as to whether or not it sentences in accordance with the joint submission from the parties.

### F. Failure of Plea Discussions

**F:1** There are several circumstances in which plea discussions may result in an outcome other than the defendant pleading guilty in accordance with a plea agreement. The prosecutor or the defendant may break off the discussions. They may be unable to reach an agreement. They may reach an agreement, but intervening events may lead the prosecutor to decide that proceedings should not be instituted. Proceedings may be instituted but the court may reject the plea agreement. The defendant may decline to plead guilty in accordance with the plea agreement, either as a result of a sentence indication given under the procedure set out in *R. v. Goodyear*, or for some other reason.    **A-298**

**F:2** If any of these situations arises, the prosecutor may wish for further enquiries to be made with a view to bringing or completing proceedings against the defendant. If proceedings have already been instituted, the prosecutor will use the appropriate means to delay them - either discontinuing under section 23 or 23A of the Prosecution of Offences Act 1985 or (if the indictment has already been preferred) applying for an adjournment or stay of the proceedings. The prosecutor and the defendant's representatives will continue to be bound by the preliminary undertakings made in relation to the confidentiality and use of information provided in the course of the plea discussions.

**F:3** Where plea discussions have broken down for any reason, it will be rare that the prosecutor will wish to re-open them, but he or she may do so if there is a material change in circumstances which warrants it.

## (2) Practice

Paragraphs IV.45.18 to IV.45.28 of the consolidated criminal practice direction, as inserted by *Practice Direction (Criminal proceedings: substituted and additional provisions)* [2009] 1 W.L.R. 1396, with effect from May 14, 2009, made provision as to the practice to be followed where a plea agreement has been reached and a joint sentencing submission is to be placed before the court. Paragraph IV.45 of the consolidated criminal practice direction has now been revoked (*Criminal Practice Direction (General matters) A2* [2013] 1 W.L.R. 3164), with paragraphs IV.45.18 to IV.45.28 being superseded by paragraphs B.17 to B.27 of *Criminal Practice Direction (Sentencing) B* [2013] 1 W.L.R. 3164.    **A-299**

### Criminal Practice Direction (Sentencing) B, paras B.17-27 [2013] 1 W.L.R. 3164

**B.17** In this part—    **A-300**

- (a) "a plea agreement" means a written basis of plea agreed between the prosecution and defendant(s) in accordance with the principles set out in *R v Underwood* [see § 5-90 in the main work, and *ante*, A-277], supported by admissible documentary evidence or admissions under section 10 of the Criminal Justice Act 1967;
- (b) "a sentencing submission" means sentencing submissions made jointly by the prosecution and defence as to the appropriate sentencing authorities and applicable sentencing range in the relevant sentencing guideline relating to the plea agreement;
- (c) "serious or complex fraud" includes, but is not limited to, allegations of fraud where two or more of the following are present [list as per the guidelines, *ante*, A-293]:

*Procedure*
**B.18** The procedure regarding agreed bases of plea outlined above [§§ 5-91 *et seq.* in the main    **A-301**

work], applies with equal rigour to the acceptance of pleas under this procedure. However, because under this procedure the parties will have been discussing the plea agreement and the charges from a much earlier stage, it is vital that the judge is fully informed of all relevant background to the discussions, charges and the eventual basis of plea.

**B.19** Where the defendant has not yet appeared before the Crown Court, the prosecutor must send full details of the plea agreement and sentencing submission(s) to the court, at least 7 days in advance of the defendant's first appearance. Where the defendant has already appeared before the Crown Court, the prosecutor must notify the court as soon as is reasonably practicable that a plea agreement and sentencing submissions under the Attorney-General's Plea Discussion Guidelines are to be submitted. The court should set a date for the matter to be heard, and the prosecutor must send full details of the plea agreement and sentencing submission(s) to the court as soon as practicable, or in accordance with the directions of the court.

**B.20** The provision to the judge of full details of the plea agreement requires sufficient information to be provided to allow the judge to understand the facts of the case and the history of the plea discussions, to assess whether the plea agreement is fair and in the interests of justice, and to decide the appropriate sentence. This will include, but is not limited to: (i) the plea agreement; (ii) the sentencing submission(s); (iii) all of the material provided by the prosecution to the defendant in the course of the plea discussions; (iv) relevant material provided by the defendant, for example documents relating to personal mitigation; and (v) the minutes of any meetings between the parties and any correspondence generated in the plea discussions. The parties should be prepared to provide additional material at the request of the court.

**B.21** The court should at all times have regard to the length of time that has elapsed since the date of the occurrence of the events giving rise to the plea discussions, the time taken to interview the defendant, the date of charge and the prospective trial date (if the matter were to proceed to trial) so as to ensure that its consideration of the plea agreement and sentencing submissions does not cause any unnecessary further delay.

*Status of plea agreement and joint sentencing submissions*

**A-302**     **B.22** Where a plea agreement and joint sentencing submissions are submitted, it remains entirely a matter for the court to decide how to deal with the case. The judge retains the absolute discretion to refuse to accept the plea agreement and to sentence otherwise than in accordance with the sentencing submissions made under the Attorney-General's Plea Discussion Guidelines.

**B.23** Sentencing submissions should draw the court's attention to any applicable range in any relevant guideline, and to any ancillary orders that may be applicable. Sentencing submissions should not include a specific sentence or agreed range other than the ranges set out in sentencing guidelines or authorities.

**B.24** Prior to pleading guilty in accordance with the plea agreement, the defendant(s) may apply to the court for an indication of the likely maximum sentence [in accordance with *R. v. Goodyear*, as to which, see § 5-110 in the main work].

**B.25** In the event that the judge indicates a sentence or passes a sentence which is not within the submissions made on sentencing, the plea agreement remains binding.

**B.26** If the defendant does not plead guilty in accordance with the plea agreement or if a defendant who has pleaded guilty in accordance with a plea agreement successfully applies to withdraw his plea under rule 39.3 of the Criminal Procedure Rules, the signed plea agreement may be treated as confession evidence, and may be used against the defendant at a later stage in these or any other proceedings. Any credit for a timely guilty plea may be lost. The court may exercise its discretion under section 78 of the Police and Criminal Evidence Act 1984 to exclude any such evidence … .

**B.27** Where a defendant has failed to plead guilty in accordance with a plea agreement, the case is unlikely to be ready for trial immediately. The prosecution may have been commenced earlier than it otherwise would have been, in reliance upon the defendant's agreement to plead guilty. This is likely to be a relevant consideration for the court in deciding whether or not to grant an application to adjourn or stay the proceedings to allow the matter to be prepared for trial in accordance with the protocol on the Control and Management of Heavy Fraud and other Complex Criminal Cases, or as required.

### (3) Authorities

**A-303**     As to the limitations on prosecuting authorities' power to enter into agreements (with overseas authorities or a potential accused) as to how a case should be disposed of, see *R. v. Innospec Ltd*, § 1-369 in the main work. As to this case, see also § 5-804 in the main work.

In *R. v. Dougall* [2011] 1 Cr.App.R.(S.) 37, CA, it was said that a joint submission as to sentence pursuant to the Attorney-General's Guidelines on Plea Discussions in Cases of Serious or Complex Fraud, *ante*, should recognise that it is the court alone that decides on sentence, should avoid advocacy of a particular outcome, and should confine itself to the appropriate range within which it is said the sentence should fall. As to this case, see also § 5-138 in the main work.

## H. Asset Recovery Powers of Prosecuting Authorities

The Attorney-General and the Home Secretary have issued joint guidance under section 2A of **A-304** the PCA 2002 to the National Crime Agency, the DPP, the Director of Revenue and Customs Prosecutions, the Director of the Serious Fraud Office and the DPP for Northern Ireland directing them to consider using their civil asset recovery powers under the 2002 Act wherever proceeds of crime have been identified but it is not feasible to secure a conviction, or a conviction has been secured but no confiscation order made (para. 2). They must also consider whether the public interest might be better served by using these powers, rather than by instituting a criminal investigation or prosecution, whilst applying the principle that a criminal disposal will generally make the best contribution to the reduction of crime (para. 3). Paragraph 4 states that the factors listed in the Code for Crown Prosecutors (*post*, Appendix E-6) as being relevant to the question whether a prosecution would be in the public interest might also be relevant when considering at any stage whether or not the civil recovery powers should be used; but it is emphasised that a potential defendant should not be able to escape an appropriate prosecution by the simple device of agreeing to a civil recovery order. Paragraph 5 contains a non-exhaustive list of circumstances in which use of the powers might be appropriate because it is not feasible to secure a conviction and paragraph 6 contains an equivalent list for where a conviction is feasible but where the public interest might be better served by use of these powers. Paragraph 8 sets out the ways in which the relevant authorities should seek to minimise any potential prejudice to a related or potential criminal investigation or proceedings, including through the disclosure of relevant information. Paragraph 9 confirms that the guidance does not prohibit (i) a criminal investigation being carried out by a law enforcement authority at the same time as a civil recovery and/or a tax investigation; (ii) civil recovery and/or tax proceedings being instituted where a criminal investigation by a law enforcement authority is being carried out at the same time into unrelated criminality (subjectto the duty set out in para. 8, *ante*); or (iii) criminal proceedings being instituted or carried on by a prosecuting authority at the same time as a civil recovery and/or tax investigation is being carried out. However, paragraph 10 prohibits in all circumstances criminal and civil/tax proceedings being carried on at the same time in relation to the same criminality. Where criminal proceedings have been stayed by a court, or cannot progress (*e.g.* because the defendant has absconded), they are not being "carried on" for the purposes of this prohibition. Paragraph 11 sets out the circumstances in which a relevant authority may agree to accept a reduced sum in satisfaction of a civil recovery claim. For the full text of the guidance, see http://www.attorneygen eral.gov.uk/Publications/Pages/AttorneyGeneralsGuidelines.aspx.

# APPENDIX B
## Interpretation Act 1978

*General provisions as to enactment and operation*

*Words of enactment*

1. Every section of an Act takes effect as a substantive enactment without introductory words. **B-1**

*Amendment or repeal in same Session*

2. Any Act may be amended or repealed in the Session of Parliament in which it is passed. **B-2**

*Judicial notice*

3. Every Act is a public Act to be judicially noticed as such, unless the contrary is expressly **B-3**
provided by the Act.

*Time of commencement*

4. An Act or provision of an Act comes into force— **B-4**
   (a) where provision is made for it to come into force on a particular day, at the beginning of
       that day;
   (b) where no provision is made for its coming into force, at the beginning of the day on which
       the Act receives the Royal Assent.

*Interpretation and construction*

*Definitions*

5. In any Act, unless the contrary intention appears, words and expressions listed in Schedule 1 to **B-5**
this Act are to be construed according to that Schedule.

*Gender and number*

6. In any Act, unless the contrary intention appears,— **B-6**
   (a) words importing the masculine gender include the feminine;
   (b) words importing the feminine gender include the masculine;
   (c) words in the singular include the plural and words in the plural include the singular.

*References to service by post*

7. Where an Act authorises or requires any document to be served by post (whether the expres- **B-7**
sion "serve" or the expression "give" or "send" or any other expression is used) then, unless the
contrary intention appears, the service is deemed to be effected by properly addressing, prepaying
and posting a letter containing the document and, unless the contrary is proved, to have been effected at the time at which the letter would be delivered in the ordinary course of post.

*References to distance*

8. In the measurement of any distance for the purposes of an Act, that distance shall, unless the **B-8**
contrary intention appears, be measured in a straight line on a horizontal plane.

*References to time of day*

9. Subject to section 3 of the Summer Time Act 1972 (construction of references to points of time **B-9**
during the period of summer time), whenever an expression of time occurs in an Act, the time
referred to shall, unless it is otherwise specifically stated, be held to be Greenwich mean time.

*References to Sovereign*

10. In any Act a reference to the Sovereign reigning at the time of the passing of the Act is to be **B-10**
construed, unless the contrary intention appears, as a reference to the Sovereign for the time being.

*Construction of subordinate legislation*

11. Where an Act confers power to make subordinate legislation, expressions used in that legisla- **B-11**
tion have, unless the contrary intention appears, the meaning which they bear in the Act.

*Statutory powers and duties*

*Continuity of powers and duties*

12.—(1) Where an Act confers a power or imposes a duty it is implied, unless the contrary inten- **B-12**
tion appears, that the power may be exercised, or the duty is to be performed, from time to time as
occasion requires.

(2) Where an Act confers a power or imposes a duty on the holder of an office as such, it is
implied, unless the contrary intention appears, that the power may be exercised, or the duty is to be
performed, by the holder for the time being of the office.

*Anticipatory exercise of powers*

**B-13**    **13.** Where an Act which (or any provision of which) does not come into force immediately on its passing confers power to make subordinate legislation, or to make appointments, give notices, prescribe forms or do any other thing for the purposes of the Act, then, unless the contrary intention appears, the power may be exercised, and any instrument made thereunder may be made so as to come into force, at any time after the passing of the Act so far as may be necessary or expedient for the purpose—

    (a)  of bringing the Act or any provision of the Act into force; or

    (b)  of giving full effect to that Act or any such provision at or after the time when it comes into force.

*Implied power to amend*

**B-14**    **14.** Where an Act confers power to make—

    (a)  rules, regulations or byelaws; or

    (b)  Orders in Council, orders or other subordinate legislation to be made by statutory instrument,

it implies, unless the contrary intention appears, a power exercisable in the same manner and subject to the same conditions or limitations, to revoke, amend or re-enact any instrument made under the power.

*Power to include sunset and review provisions in subordinate legislation*

**B-14a**    **14A.**—(1) This section applies where an Act confers a power or a duty on a person to make subordinate legislation except to the extent that—

    (a)  the power or duty is exercisable by the Scottish Ministers, or

    (b)  the power or duty is exercisable by any other person within devolved competence (within the meaning of the Scotland Act 1998).

(2) The subordinate legislation may include—

    (a)  provision requiring the person to review the effectiveness of the legislation within a specified period or at the end of a specified period;

    (b)  provision for the legislation to cease to have effect at the end of a specified day or a specified period;

    (c)  if the power or duty is being exercised to amend other subordinate legislation, provision of the kind mentioned in paragraph (a) or (b) in relation to that other legislation.

(3) The provision that may be made by virtue of subsection (2)(a) includes provision requiring the person to consider whether the objectives which it was the purpose of the legislation to achieve remain appropriate and, if so, whether they could be achieved in another way.

(4) Subordinate legislation including provision of a kind mentioned in subsection (2) may make such provision generally or only in relation to specified provisions of the legislation or specified cases or circumstances.

(5) Subordinate legislation including provision of a kind mentioned in subsection (2) may make transitional, consequential, incidental or supplementary provision or savings in connection with such provision.

(6) In this section "specified" means specified in the subordinate legislation.

[This section was inserted by the Enterprise and Regulatory Reform Act 2013, s.59(1) and (2).]

*Repealing enactments*

*Repeal of repeal*

**B-15**    **15.** Where an Act repeals a repealing enactment, the repeal does not revive any enactment previously repealed unless words are added reviving it.

*General savings*

**B-16**    **16.**—(1) Without prejudice to section 15, where an Act repeals an enactment, the repeal does not, unless the contrary intention appears,—

    (a)  revive anything not in force or existing at the time at which the repeal takes effect;

    (b)  affect the previous operation of the enactment repealed or anything duly done or suffered under that enactment;

    (c)  affect any right, privilege, obligation or liability acquired, accrued or incurred under that enactment;

    (d)  affect any penalty, forfeiture or punishment incurred in respect of any offence committed against that enactment;

(e)   affect any investigation, legal proceeding or remedy in respect of any such right, privilege, obligation, liability, penalty, forfeiture or punishment;

and any such investigation, legal proceeding or remedy may be instituted, continued or enforced, and any such penalty, forfeiture or punishment may be imposed, as if the repealing Act had not been passed.

(2) This section applies to the expiry of a temporary enactment as if it were repealed by an Act.

[Considered in *R. v. West London Stipendiary Magistrate, ex p. Simeon* [1983] A.C. 234, HL. See also *Hough v. Windus* (1884) 12 Q.B.D. 224, and *R. v. Fisher (Charles)* [1969] 1 W.L.R. 8, CA.]

*Repeal and re-enactment*

**17.**—(1) Where an Act repeals a previous enactment and substitutes provisions for the enactment **B-17** repealed, the repealed enactment remains in force until the substitute provisions come into force.

(2) Where an Act repeals and re-enacts, with or without modification, a previous enactment then, unless the contrary intention appears,—

(a)   any reference in any other enactment to the enactment so repealed shall be construed as a reference to the provision re-enacted;

(b)   in so far as any subordinate legislation made or other thing done under the enactment so repealed, or having effect as if so made or done, could have been made or done under the provision re-enacted, it shall have effect as if made or done under that provision.

*Miscellaneous*

*Duplicated offences*

**18.** Where an act or omission constitutes an offence under two or more Acts, or both under an Act **B-18** and at common law, the offender shall, unless the contrary intention appears, be liable to be prosecuted and punished under either or any of those Acts or at common law, but shall not be liable to be punished more than once for the same offence.

See in the main work, § 4-189.

*Citation of other Acts*

**19.** Where an Act cites another Act by year, statute, session or chapter, or a section or other por- **B-19** tion of another Act by number or letter, the reference shall, unless the contrary intention appears, be read as referring—

(a)   in the case of Acts included in any revised edition of the statutes printed by authority, to that edition;

(b)   in the case of Acts not so included but included in the edition prepared under the direction of the Record Commission, to that edition;

(c)   in any other case, to the Acts printed by the Queen's Printer, or under the superintendence or authority of Her Majesty's Stationery Office.

(2) An Act may continue to be cited by the short title authorised by any enactment notwithstanding the repeal of that enactment.

*References to other enactments*

**20.**—(1) Where an Act describes or cites a portion of an enactment by referring to words, sections **B-20** or other parts from or to which or from and to which the portion extends, the portion described or cited includes the words, sections or other parts referred to unless the contrary intention appears.

(2) Where an Act refers to an enactment, the reference unless the contrary intention appears, is a reference to that enactment as amended, and includes a reference thereto as extended or applied, by or under any other enactment, including any other provision of that Act.

*References to EU instruments*

**20A.** Where an Act passed after the commencement of this section refers to a EU instrument that **B-20a** has been amended, extended or applied by another such instrument, the reference, unless the contrary intention appears, is a reference to that instrument as so amended, extended or applied.

[This section was inserted by the Legislative and Regulatory Reform Act 2006, s.25(1). It is printed as amended by the European Union (Amendment) Act 2008, s.3, and Sched., Pt 2.]

*Supplementary*

*Interpretation, etc.*

**21.**—(1) In this Act "Act" includes a local and personal or private Act; and "subordinate legisla- **B-21**

tion" means Orders in Council, orders, rules, regulations, schemes, warrants, byelaws and other instruments made or to be made under any Act.

(2) This Act binds the Crown.

*Application to Acts and Measures*

**B-22**     **22.**—(1) This Act applies to itself, to any Act passed after the commencement of this Act (subject, in the case of section 20A, to the provision made in that section) and, to the extent specified in Part I of Schedule 2, to Acts passed before the commencement of this Act.

(2) In any of the foregoing provisions of this Act a reference to an Act is a reference to an Act to which that provision applies; but this does not affect the generality of references to enactments or of the references in section 19(1) to other Acts.

(3) This Act applies to Measures of the General Synod of the Church of England (and, so far as it relates to Acts passed before the commencement of this Act, to Measures of the Church Assembly passed after May 28, 1925) as it applies to Acts.

[This section is printed as amended by the Legislative and Regulatory Reform Act 2006, s.25(2).]

*Application to other instruments*

**B-23**     **23.**—(1) The provisions of this Act, except sections 1 to 3 and 4(b), apply, so far as applicable and unless the contrary intention appears, to subordinate legislation made after the commencement of this Act and, to the extent specified in Part II of Schedule 2, to subordinate legislation made before the commencement of this Act, as they apply to Acts.

(2) In the application of this Act to Acts passed or subordinate legislation made after the commencement of this Act, all references to an enactment include an enactment comprised in subordinate legislation whenever made, and references to the passing or repeal of an enactment are to be construed accordingly.

(3) Sections 9 and 19(1) also apply to deeds and other instruments and documents as they apply to Acts and subordinate legislation; and in the application of section 17(2)(a) to Acts passed or subordinate legislation made after the commencement of this Act, the reference to any other enactment includes any deed or other instrument or document.

(4) Subsections (1) and (2) of this section do not apply to Orders in Council made under section 5 of the Statutory Instruments Act 1946, section 1(3) of the Northern Ireland (Temporary Provisions) Act 1972 or Schedule 1 to the Northern Ireland Act 1974.

**B-23a**     **23A.** [*Acts of the Scottish Parliament, etc.*]
**B-23b**     **23B.** [*Measures and Acts of the National Assembly for Wales, etc.*]
**B-24**      **24.** [*Application to Northern Ireland.*]

*Repeals and savings*

**B-25**     **25.**—(1) The enactments described in Schedule 3 are repealed to the extent specified in the third column of that Schedule.

(2) Without prejudice to section 17(2)(a), a reference to the Interpretation Act 1889, to any provision of that Act or to any other enactment repealed by this Act whether occurring in another Act, in subordinate legislation, in Northern Ireland legislation or in any deed or other instrument or document, shall be construed as referring to this Act, or to the corresponding provision of this Act, as it applies to Acts passed at the time of the reference.

(3) The provisions of this Act relating to Acts passed after any particular time do not affect the construction of Acts passed before that time, though continued or amended by Acts passed thereafter.

**B-26**     **26.** [*Commencement.*]
**B-27**     **27.** [*Short title.*]

SCHEDULES

SCHEDULE 1

WORDS AND EXPRESSIONS DEFINED

**B-28**     *Note*: The years or dates which follow certain entries in this Schedule are relevant for the purposes of paragraph 4 of Schedule 2 (application to existing enactments).

*Definitions*

.... .

"Bank of England" means, as the context requires, the Governor and Company of the Bank of England or the bank of the Governor and Company of the Bank of England.

.... .

"British Islands" means the United Kingdom, the Channel Islands and the Isle of Man. [1889]

"British possession" means any part of Her Majesty's dominions outside the United Kingdom; and where parts of such dominions are under both a central and local legislature, all parts under the central legislature are deemed, for the purposes of this definition, to be one British possession. [1889]

.... .

"Central funds", in an enactment providing in relation to England and Wales for the payment of costs out of central funds, means money provided by Parliament.

.... .

"Civil partnership" means a civil partnership which exists under or by virtue of the Civil Partnership Act 2004 (and any reference to a civil partner is to be read accordingly).

[This definition is inserted by the Civil Partnership Act 2004, s.261(1), and Sched. 27, para. 59.]

"Colonial legislature", and "legislature" in relation to a British possession, mean the authority, other than the Parliament of the United Kingdom or Her Majesty in Council, competent to make laws for the possession. [1889]

"Colony" means any part of Her Majesty's dominions outside the British Islands except—

(a) countries having fully responsible status within the Commonwealth;

(b) territories for whose external relations a country other than the United Kingdom is responsible;

(c) associated states; and where parts of such dominions are under both a central and a local legislature, all parts under the central legislature are deemed for the purposes of this definition to be one colony. [1889]

"Commencement", in relation to an Act or enactment, means the time when the Act or enactment comes into force.

"The EU", or "the EU Treaties" and other expressions defined by section 1 of and Schedule 1 to the European Communities Act 1972 have the meanings prescribed by that Act.

[This definition is printed as amended by the European Union (Amendment) Act 2008, s.3, and Sched., Pt 2.]

.... .

"Consular officer" has the meaning assigned by Article 1 of the Vienna Convention set out in Schedule 1 to the Consular Relations Act 1968.

.... .

"County Court" means—

(a) in relation to England and Wales, the County Court established under section A1 of the County Courts Act 1984;

(b) [*Northern Ireland*].

[This definition is printed as amended by the County Courts Act 1984, Sched. 2; and the Crime and Courts Act 2013, s.17(5), and Sched. 9. para. 94.]

"Court of Appeal" means—

(a) in relation to England and Wales, Her Majesty's Court of Appeal in England;

(b) in relation to Northern Ireland, Her Majesty's Court of Appeal in Northern Ireland.

"Court of summary jurisdiction", "summary conviction" and "Summary Jurisdiction Acts", in relation to Northern Ireland, have the same meanings as in Measures of the Northern Ireland Assembly and Acts of the Parliament of Northern Ireland.

"Crown Court" means—

(a) in relation to England and Wales, the Crown Court constituted by section 4 of the Courts Act 1971;

(b) [*Northern Ireland*].

.... .

"EEA agreement" means the agreement on the European Economic Area signed at Oporto on 2nd May 1992, together with the Protocol adjusting that Agreement signed at Brussels on 17th March 1993, as modified or supplemented from time to time. [The date of the coming into force of this paragraph.]

"EEA state", in relation to any time, means—
>     (a) a state which at that time is a member State; or
>     (b) any other state which at that time is a party to the EEA agreement. [The date of the coming into force of this paragraph.]

[These two definitions were inserted, as from January 8, 2007, by the Legislative and Regulatory Reform Act 2006, s.26(1).]

"England" means, subject to any alteration of boundaries under Part IV of the Local Government Act 1972, the area consisting of the counties established by section 1 of that Act, Greater London and the Isles of Scilly. [1st April 1974]
... .

"Governor-General" includes any person who for the time being has the powers of the Governor-General, and "Governor", in relation to any British possession, includes the officer for the time being administering the government of that possession. [1889]

"Her Majesty's Revenue and Customs" has the meaning given by section 4 of the Commissioners for Revenue and Customs Act 2005.

[This definition was inserted by the Commissioners for Revenue and Customs Act 2005, s.4(3).]

"High Court" means—
>     (a) in relation to England and Wales, Her Majesty's High Court of Justice in England;
>     (b) in relation to Northern Ireland, Her Majesty's High Court of Justice in Northern Ireland.
... .

"Land" includes buildings and other structures, land covered with water, and any estate, interest, easement, servitude or right in or over land. [1st January 1979]
... .

"Local policing body" has the meaning given by section 101(1) of the Police Act 1996.

[This definition was inserted by the Police Reform and Social Responsibility Act 2011, s.97(1) and (2).]

"London borough" means a borough described in Schedule 1 to the London Government Act 1963, "inner London borough" means one of the boroughs so described and numbered from 1 to 12 and "outer London borough" means one of the boroughs so described and numbered 13 to 32, subject (in each case) to any alterations made under Part IV of the Local Government Act 1972 or Part II of the Local Government Act 1992.

[This definition is printed as amended by the Local Government Act 1992, s.27(1), and Sched. 3, para. 21.]

"Lord Chancellor" means the Lord High Chancellor of Great Britain.

"Magistrates' court" has the meaning assigned to it—
>     (a) in relation to England and Wales, by section 148 of the Magistrates' Courts Act 1980;
>     (b) [*Northern Ireland*].

[This definition is printed as amended by the MCA 1980, s.154, and Sched. 7, para. 169.]

"Month" means calendar month. [1850]
... .

"Oath" and "affidavit" include affirmation and declaration, and "swear" includes affirm and declare.

"Officer of Revenue and Customs" has the meaning given by section 2(1) of the Commissioners for Revenue and Customs Act 2005.

[This definition was inserted by the Commissioners for Revenue and Customs Act 2005, s.2(7).]

"Ordnance Map" means a map made under powers conferred by the Ordnance Survey Act 1841 or the Boundary Survey (Ireland) Act 1854.

"Parliamentary Election" means the election of a Member to serve in Parliament for a constituency. [1889]

"Person" includes a body of persons corporate or unincorporate. [1889]

"Police and crime commissioner" means a police and crime commissioner established under section 1 of the Police Reform and Social Responsibility Act 2011.

[This definition was inserted by the Police Reform and Social Responsibility Act 2011, s.97(1) and (3).]

"Police area" ... and other expressions relating to the police have the meaning or effect described—

(a) in relation to England and Wales, by section 101(1) of the Police Act 1996; ...

[This definition is printed as amended by the Police Act 1996, Sched. 7, para. 32; the Police Reform and Social Responsibility Act 2011, s.97(1) and (4); and the Police and Fire Reform (Scotland) Act 2012 (Consequential Provisions and Modifications) Order 2013 (S.I. 2013 No. 602).]

"The Privy Council" means the Lords and others of Her Majesty's Most Honourable Privy Council.

"Registered" in relation to nurses, midwives and health visitors, means registered in the register maintained by the United Kingdom Central Council for Nursing, Midwifery and Health Visiting by virtue of qualifications in nursing, midwifery or health visiting, as the case may be.

[This definition was inserted by the Nurses, Midwives and Health Visitors Act 1979, s.23(4), and Sched. 7, para. 30.]

"Registered medical practitioner" means a fully registered person within the meaning of the Medical Act 1983 who holds a licence to practise under that Act. [1st January 1979]

[This definition is printed as amended by the Medical Act 1983, s.56(1), and Sched. 5, para. 18; and the Medical Act 1983 (Amendment) Order 2002 (S.I 2002 No. 3135), Sched.1, para. 10.]

"Rules of Court" in relation to any court means rules made by the authority having power to make rules or orders regulating the practice and procedure of that court, and in Scotland includes Acts of Adjournal and Acts of Sederunt; and the power of the authority to make rules of court (as above defined) includes power to make such rules for the purpose of any Act which directs or authorises anything to be done by rules of court. [1889]

"Secretary of State" means one of Her Majesty's Principal Secretaries of State.

"Senior Courts" means the Senior Courts of England and Wales.

[This definition was inserted by the Constitutional Reform Act 2005, s.59(5), and Sched. 11, para. 24.]

"Sent for trial" means, in relation to England and Wales, sent by a magistrates' court to the Crown Court for trial pursuant to section 51 or 51A of the Crime and Disorder Act 1998.

[This definition was inserted by the CJA 2003, s.41, and Sched. 3, para. 49(b).]

... .

"Sheriff", in relation to Scotland, includes sheriff principal. [1889]

"The standard scale", with reference to a fine or penalty for an offence triable only summarily,—

(a) in relation to England and Wales, has the meaning given by section 37 of the Criminal Justice Act 1982;

(b) [*Scotland*];

(c) [*Northern Ireland*].

[This definition was inserted by the CJA 1988, s.170(1), and Sched. 15, para. 58(a). (For s.37 of the 1982 Act, see the main work, § 5-683.)]

"Statutory declaration" means a declaration made by virtue of the Statutory Declarations Act 1835.

"Statutory maximum", with reference to a fine or penalty on summary conviction for an offence—

(a) in relation to England and Wales, means the prescribed sum within the meaning of section 32 of the Magistrates' Courts Act 1980;

(b) [*Scotland*]; and

(c) [*Northern Ireland*].

[This definition was inserted by the CJA 1988, s.170(1), and Sched. 15, para. 58(b). (For s.32 of the 1980 Act, see the main work, § 1-123.)]

"Supreme Court" means the Supreme Court of the United Kingdom.

[This definition is printed as amended by the Constitutional Reform Act 2005, s.59(5), and Sched. 11, para. 24.]

"The Treasury" means the Commissioners of Her Majesty's Treasury.

"United Kingdom" means Great Britain and Northern Ireland. [12th April 1927]

"Wales" means the combined area of the counties which were created by section 20 of the Local Government Act 1972, as originally enacted, but subject to any alteration made under section

73 of that Act (consequential alteration of boundary following alteration of watercourse) [1st
April 1974]

[This definition was substituted by the Local Government (Wales) Act 1994, Sched. 2, para. 9.]

... .

"Writing" includes typing, printing, lithography, photography and other modes of representing or
reproducing words in avisible form, and expressions referring to writing are construed
accordingly.

*Construction of certain expressions relating to offences*

In relation to England and Wales—
  (a)  "indictable offence" means an offence which, if committed by an adult, is triable on indict-
       ment, whether it is exclusively so triable or triable either way;
  (b)  "summary offence" means an offence which, if committed by an adult, is triable only
       summarily;
  (c)  "offence triable either way" means an offence, other than an offence triable on indictment
       only by virtue of Part V of the Criminal Justice Act 1988 which, if committed by an adult, is
       triable either on indictment or summarily;
and the terms "indictable", "summary" and "triable either way", in their application to offences are to
be construed accordingly.

In the above definitions references to the way or ways in which an offence is triable are to be
construed without regard to the effect, if any, of section 22 of the Magistrates' Courts Act 1980 on the
mode of trial in a particular case.

[This para. is printed as amended by the MCA 1980, Sched. 7; and the CJA 1988, Sched. 15,
para. 59.]

*Construction of certain references to relationships*

In relation to England and Wales—
  (a)  references (however expressed) to any relationship between two persons;
  (b)  references to a person whose father and mother were or were not married to each other at
       the time of his birth; and
  (c)  references cognate with references falling within paragraph (b) above,
shall be construed in accordance with section 1 of the Family Law Reform Act 1987. [The date of the
coming into force of that section.]

[This para. was added by Schedule 2 to the Family Law Reform Act 1987.]

*Construction of certain expressions relating to the police: Scotland*

In relation to Scotland—
  (a)  references to a police force include references to the Police Service of Scotland;
  (b)  references to a chief officer of police include references to the chief constable of the Police
       Service of Scotland;
  (c)  "police authority" means the Scottish Police Authority;
  (d)  the "police area" of the Police Service of Scotland is Scotland and references to a police
       force or police authority for any area include references to the Police Service of Scotland
       or, as the case may be, the Scottish Police Authority;
  (e)  references to a constable or chief constable of, or appointed for, any area are to be
       construed as references to a constable or, as the case may be, the chief constable of, or ap-
       pointed for, the Police Service of Scotland.

[This para. was added by the Police and Fire Reform (Scotland) Act 2012 (Consequential Provisions and Modifications) Order 2013 (S.I. 2013 No. 602).]

*NOTE*: the definitions of the following expressions have been omitted: "Associated state",
"Bank of Ireland", "Building regulations", "Charity Commissioners", "Comptroller and Auditor
General", "Consular officer", "The Corporation Tax Acts", "Crown Estate Commissioners",
"Financial year", "The Income Tax Acts", "Lands Clauses Act", "National Debt Commissioners",
"Northern Ireland legislation", "Sewerage undertaker", "The Tax Acts" and "Water undertaker".

SCHEDULE 2

APPLICATION OF ACT TO EXISTING ENACTMENTS

PART I

ACTS

1. The following provisions of this Act apply to Acts whenever passed:—  **B-29**

    Section 6(a) and (c) so far as applicable to enactments relating to offences punishable on indictment or on summary conviction

    Section 9

    Section 10

    Section 11 so far as it relates to subordinate legislation made after the year 1889

    Section 14A

    Section 18

    Section 19(2).

[Para. 1 is printed as amended by the Enterprise and Regulatory Reform Act 2013, s.59(1) and (3).]

2. The following apply to Acts passed after the year 1850:—

    Section 1

    Section 2

    Section 3

    Section 6(a) and (c) so far as not applicable to such Acts by virtue of paragraph 1

    Section 15

    Section 17(1).

3. The following apply to Acts passed after the year 1889:—

    Section 4

    Section 7

    Section 8

    Section 12

    Section 13

    Section 14 so far as it relates to rules, regulations or byelaws

    Section 16(1)

    Section 17(2)(a)

    Section 19(1)

    Section 20(1).

4.—(1) Subject to the following provisions of this paragraph—

    (a) paragraphs of Schedule 1 at the end of which a year or date is specified or described apply, so far as applicable, to Acts passed on or after the date, or after the year, so specified or described; and

    (b) paragraphs of that Schedule at the end of which no year or date is specified or described apply, so far as applicable, to Acts passed at any time.

(2) The definition of "British Islands", in its application to Acts passed after the establishment of the Irish Free State but before the commencement of this Act, includes the Republic of Ireland.

(3) The definition of "colony", in its application to an Act passed at any time before the commencement of this Act, includes—

    (a) any colony within the meaning of section 18(3) of the Interpretation Act 1889 which was excluded, but in relation only to Acts passed at a later time, by any enactment repealed by this Act;

    (b) any country or territory which ceased after that time to be part of Her Majesty's dominions but subject to a provision for the continuation of existing law as if it had not so ceased;

and paragraph (b) of the definition does not apply.

(4) The definition of "Lord Chancellor" does not apply to Acts passed before 1st October 1921 in which that expression was used in relation to Ireland only.

(5) The definition of "person", so far as it includes bodies corporate, applies to any provision of an Act whenever passed relating to an offence punishable on indictment or on summary conviction.

(6) This paragraph applies to the National Health Service Reorganisation Act 1973 and the Water Act 1973 as if they were passed after 1st April 1974.

[Para. 4 is printed as amended by the Family Law Reform Act 1987, Scheds 2 and 4.]

5. The following definitions shall be treated as included in Schedule 1 for the purposes specified in this paragraph—

    (a) in any Act passed before 1st April 1974, a reference to England includes Berwick upon Tweed and Monmouthshire and, in the case of an Act passed before the Welsh Language Act 1967, Wales;

    (b) in any Act passed before the commencement of this Act and after the year 1850, "land" includes messuages, tenements and hereditaments, houses and buildings of any tenure;

    (c) [*Scotland*].

## PART II

### SUBORDINATE LEGISLATION

**B-30**     6. Sections 4(a), 9 and 19(1), and so much of Schedule 1 as defines the following expressions, namely—

    England;

    Local land charges register and appropriate local land charges register;

    in relation to Scotland, expressions relating to the police;

    United Kingdom;

    Wales;

apply to subordinate legislation made at any time before the commencement of this Act as they apply to Acts passed at that time.

[Para. 6 is printed as amended by the British Nationality Act 1981, Sched. 9; and the Police and Fire Reform (Scotland) Act 2012 (Consequential Provisions and Modifications) Order 2013 (S.I. 2013 No. 602).]

7. The definition in Schedule 1 of "county court", in relation to England and Wales, applies to Orders in Council made after the year 1846.

# APPENDIX C
# The Duties of Advocates

## I. CODE OF CONDUCT

The first edition of the Bar Standards Board Handbook came into force on January 6, 2014. It **C-1** contains (in Part 2) the ninth edition of the Code of Conduct for the Bar of England and Wales. Part 1 of the handbook is an introduction. Parts 3 and 4 contain the scope of practice rules and the qualification rules. Part 5 comprises the enforcement regulations and Part 6 provides for the interpretation of terms used throughout the handbook.

Within the code, there are "core duties", "outcomes", "rules" and "guidance". The significance of each is explained in the introductory section of the handbook. Thus the core duties (italicised words and expressions are defined in Part 6)—

> "underpin the entire regulatory framework and set the mandatory standards that all *BSB regulated persons* are required to meet. They also define the core elements of professional conduct. Disciplinary proceedings may be taken against a *BSB regulated person* if the *Bar Standards Board* believes there has been a breach by that person of the Core Duties set out in this *Handbook* and that such action would be in accordance with the *Enforcement Policy*."

The outcomes—

> "explain the reasons for the regulatory scheme and what it is designed to achieve. They are derived from the *regulatory objectives* as defined in the *LSA* and the risks which must be managed if those objectives are to be achieved. They are not themselves mandatory rules, but they are factors which *BSB regulated persons* should have in mind when considering how the Core Duties, Conduct Rules or Qualification Rules (as appropriate) should be applied in particular circumstances. The *Bar Standards Board* will take into account whether or not an Outcome has, or might have been, adversely affected when considering how to respond to alleged breaches of the Core Duties, Conduct Rules or Qualification Rules."

The conduct rules (*i.e.* those in the code of conduct)—

> "supplement the Core Duties and are mandatory. Disciplinary proceedings may be taken against a *BSB regulated person* if the *Bar Standards Board* believes there has been a breach by that person of the Conduct Rules set out in Part 2 of this *Handbook* and that it would be in accordance with the *Enforcement policy* to take such action. However, the Conduct Rules are not intended to be exhaustive. In any situation where no specific Rule applies, reference should be made to the Core Duties. In situations where specific Rules do apply, it is still necessary to consider the Core Duties, since compliance with the Rules alone will not necessarily be sufficient to comply with the Core Duties."

The guidance is self-explanatory, its principal purpose being to assist in the interpretation of the core duties and rules.

The code of conduct itself is divided into four sections: A - Application, B - The Core Duties, C **C-2** - The Conduct Rules, and D - Rules Applying to Particular Groups of Regulated Persons. The conduct rules are themselves divided into five sections, *viz.* C1 "You and the court", C2 "Behaving ethically", C3 "You and your client", C4 "You and your regulator" and C5 "You and your practice". So far as practice in court is concerned, the most important rules are contained in section C1. These, together with the core duties, are set in full, *post*. The handbook runs to a total of 277 pages and space precludes the inclusion of more detail. However it should be noted that C2 (behaving ethically) contains provisions relating to honesty, integrity and independence, referral fees, undertakings, discrimination and foreign work, and that C3 (you and your client) has rules relating to "best interests of each client, provision of a competent standard of work, and confidentiality", "not misleading clients and potential clients", "personal responsibility", "accepting instructions", "defining terms or basis on which instructions are accepted", "returning instructions", "requirement not to discriminate", "the 'cab-rank rule'" and the "quality assurance scheme for advocates rules".

## Core duties

| | |
|---|---|
| **CD1** | You must observe your duty to the court in the administration of justice. |
| **CD2** | You must act in the best interests of each client. |
| **CD3** | You must act with honesty and integrity. |
| **CD4** | You must maintain your independence. |
| **CD5** | You must not behave in a way which is likely to diminish the trust and confidence which the public places in you or in the profession. |
| **CD6** | You must keep the affairs of each client confidential. |
| **CD7** | You must provide a competent standard of work and service to each client. |
| **CD8** | You must not discriminate unlawfully against any person. |
| **CD9** | You must be open and co-operative with your regulators. |
| **CD10** | You must take reasonable steps to manage your practice, or carry out your role within your practice, competently and in such a way as to achieve compliance with your legal and regulatory obligations. |

*Guidance to the core duties*

gC1 The Core Duties are not presented in order of precedence, subject to the following:

.1 CD1 overrides any other core duty, if and to the extent the two are inconsistent. Rules C3.5 and C4 deal specifically with the relationship between CD1, CD2 and CD6 and you should refer to those rules and to the related Guidance;

.2 in certain other circumstances set out in this Code of Conduct one Core Duty overrides another. Specifically, Rule C16 provides that CD2 (as well as being subject to CD1) is subject to your obligations under CD3, CD4 and CD8.

gC2 Your obligation to take reasonable steps to manage your *practice*, or carry out your role within your *practice*, competently and in such a way as to achieve compliance with your legal and regulatory obligations (CD10) includes an obligation to take all reasonable steps to mitigate the effects of any breach of those legal and regulatory obligations once you become aware of the same.

## The Conduct Rules

*C.1 You and the court*

### Outcomes

oC1 The *court* is able to rely on information provided to it by those conducting litigation and by advocates who appear before it.

oC2 The proper administration of justice is served.

oC3 The interests of *clients* are protected to the extent compatible with outcomes oC1 and oC2 and the Core Duties.

oC4 Both those who appear before the *court* and *clients* understand clearly the extent of the duties owed to the *court* by advocates and those conducting litigation and the circumstances in which duties owed to *clients* will be overridden by the duty owed to the *court*.

oC5 *The public* has confidence in the administration of justice and in those who serve it.

### Rules

rC3 You owe a duty to the *court* to act with independence in the interests of justice. This duty overrides any inconsistent obligations which you may have (other than obligations under the criminal law). It includes the following specific obligations which apply whether you are acting as an advocate or are otherwise involved in the conduct of litigation in whatever role (with the exception of Rule C3.1 below, which applies when acting as an advocate):

.1 you must not knowingly or recklessly mislead or attempt to mislead the *court*;

.2 you must not abuse your role as an advocate;

.3 you must take reasonable steps to avoid wasting the *court's* time;

.4 you must take reasonable steps to ensure that the *court* has before it all relevant decisions and legislative provisions;

.5 you must ensure that your ability to act independently is not compromised.

rC4 Your duty to act in the best interests of each *client* is subject to your duty to the *court*.

rC5 Your duty to the *court* does not require you to act in breach of your duty to keep the affairs of each *client* confidential.

## Not misleading the court

rC6 Your duty not to mislead the *court* or to permit the *court* to be misled will include the following obligations: **C-7**

    .1 you must not:

        .a make submissions, representations or any other statement; or

        .b ask questions which suggest facts to witnesses

    which you know, or are instructed, are untrue or misleading.

    .2 you must not call witnesses to give evidence or put affidavits or witness statements to the *court* which you know, or are *instructed*, are untrue or misleading, unless you make clear to the *court* the true position as known by or instructed to you.

## Not abusing your role as an advocate

rC7 Where you are acting as an advocate, your duty not to abuse your role includes the following obligations: **C-8**

    .1 you must not make statements or ask questions merely to insult, humiliate or annoy a witness or any other person;

    .2 you must not make a serious allegation against a witness whom you have had an opportunity to cross-examine unless you have given that witness a chance to answer the allegation in cross-examination;

    .3 you must not make a serious allegation against any person, or suggest that a person is guilty of a crime with which your *client* is charged unless:

        .a you have reasonable grounds for the allegation; and

        .b the allegation is relevant to your *client's* case or the credibility of a witness; and

        .c where the allegation relates to a third party, you avoid naming them in open *court* unless this is reasonably necessary.

    .4 you must not put forward to the *court* a personal opinion of the facts or the law unless you are invited or required to do so by the *court* or by law.

## Guidance

### Guidance on Rules C3 - C6 and relationship to CD1 and CD2

gC3 Rules C3 - C6 set out some specific aspects of your duty to the *court* (CD1). See CD1 and associated Guidance at gC1. **C-9**

gC4 Knowingly misleading the *court* includes inadvertently misleading the *court* if you later realise that you have misled the *court*, and you fail to correct the position. Recklessness means being indifferent to the truth, or not caring whether something is true or false. The duty continues to apply for the duration of the case.

gC5 Your duty under Rule C3.3 includes drawing to the attention of the *court* any decision or provision which may be adverse to the interests of your *client*. It is particularly important where you are appearing against a litigant who is not legally represented.

gC6 You are obliged by CD2 to promote and to protect your *client's* interests so far as that is consistent with the law and with your overriding duty to the *court* under CD1. Your duty to the *court* does not prevent you from putting forward your *client's* case simply because you do not believe that the facts are as your *client* states them to be (or as you, on your *client's* behalf, state them to be), as long as any positive case you put forward accords with your *instructions* and you do not mislead the *court*. Your role when acting as an advocate or conducting litigation is to present your *client's* case, and it is not for you to decide whether your *client's* case is to be believed.

gC7 For example, you are entitled and it may often be appropriate to draw to the witness's attention other evidence which appears to conflict with what the witness is saying and you are entitled to indicate that a *court* may find a particular piece of evidence difficult to accept. But if the witness maintains that the evidence is true, it should be recorded in the witness statement and you will not be misleading the *court* if you call the witness to confirm their witness statement. Equally, there may be circumstances where you call a hostile witness whose evidence you are instructed is untrue. You will not be in breach of Rule C6 if you make the position clear to the *court*. See further the guidance at gC14.

gC8 As set out in Rule C4, your duty to the *court* does not permit or require you to disclose confidential information which you have obtained in the course of your *instructions* and which your *client* has not authorised you to disclose to the *court*. However, Rule C6 requires you not knowingly to mislead the *court* or to permit the *court* to be misled. There may be situations where you have obligations under both these rules.

gC9 Rule C3.5 makes it clear that your duty to act in the best interests of your *client* is subject to your duty to the *court*. For example, if your *client* were to tell you that he had committed the crime with which he was charged, in order to be able to ensure compliance with Rule C4 on the one hand and Rule C3 and Rule C6 on the other:

    .1 you would not be entitled to disclose that information to the *court* without your *client's* consent; and

    .2 you would not be misleading the *court* if, after your *client* had entered a plea of "not guilty", you were to test in cross-examination the reliability of the evidence of the prosecution witnesses and then address the jury to the effect that the prosecution had not succeeded in making them sure of your *client's* guilt.

gC10 However, you would be misleading the *court* and would therefore be in breach of Rules C3 and C6 if you were to set up a positive case inconsistent with the confession, as for example by:

    .1 suggesting to prosecution witnesses, calling your *client* or your witnesses to show; or submitting to the *jury*, that your *client* did not commit the crime; or

    .2 suggesting that someone else had done so; or

    .3 putting forward an alibi.

gC11 If there is a risk that the *court* will be misled unless you disclose confidential information which you have learned in the course of your *instructions*, you should ask the client for permission to disclose it to the *court*. If your *client* refuses to allow you to make the disclosure you must cease to act, and return your *instructions*: see Rules C25 to C27 below. In these circumstances you must not reveal the information to the *court*.

gC12 For example, if your *client* tells you that he has previous *convictions* of which the prosecution is not aware, you may not disclose this without his consent. However, in a case where mandatory sentences apply, the non-disclosure of the previous *convictions* will result in the *court* failing to pass the sentence that is required by law. In that situation, you must advise your *client* that if consent is refused to your revealing the information you will have to cease to act. In situations where mandatory sentences do not apply, and your *client* does not agree to disclose the previous *convictions*, you can continue to represent your *client* but in doing so must not say anything that misleads the *court*. This will constrain what you can say in mitigation. For example, you could not advance a positive case of previous good character knowing that there are undisclosed prior *convictions*. Moreover, if the *court* asks you a direct question you must not give an untruthful answer and therefore you would have to withdraw if, on your being asked such a question, your *client* still refuses to allow you to answer the question truthfully. You should explain this to your *client*.

gC13 Similarly, if you become aware that your *client* has a document which should be disclosed but has not been disclosed, you cannot continue to act unless your *client* agrees to the disclosure of the document. In these circumstances you must not reveal the existence or contents of the document to the *court*.

**[The next paragraph is C-20.]**

## II. BAR COUNCIL GUIDANCE

### Written standards of work

**C-20**    The Bar Council issued written standards for the conduct of professional work together with the eighth edition of the code of conduct. They did not form part of the code, but paragraph 701(d) obliged a barrister "to have regard to any relevant written standards." They can still be found on the website of the Bar Standards Board, but it does not appear that they are intended to have any continuing effect as there is a statement at the top of the page to the effect that, as from January 6, 2014, barristers should refer to the board's handbook (as to which, see *ante*, C-1) for rules and guidance on their conduct as such.

**[The next paragraph is C-45.]**

### Criticism of previous counsel

**C-45**    In consequence of observations made by the Court of Appeal in *R. v. Clarke and Jones, The*

*Times,* August 19, 1994, and *R. v. Bowler, The Times,* May 9, 1995, the following guidance was approved by Lord Taylor C.J. and the Bar Council. It is still to be found on the website of the Bar Council, but it is emphasised there that it is not "guidance" for the purposes of the Bar Standards Board's handbook (as to which, see *ante,* C-1)), and it is accompanied by a disclaimer to the effect that it does not constitute legal advice and a statement to the effect that it was prepared by the Bar Council to assist barristers on matters of professional conduct and ethics.

1. Allegations against former counsel may receive substantial publicity whether accepted or rejected by the court. Counsel should not settle or sign grounds of appeal unless he is satisfied that they are reasonable, have some real prospect of success and are such that he is prepared to argue before the court (Guide to Proceedings in the Court of Appeal Criminal Division, para. A2-6 [*post,* Appendix J-5]). When such allegations are properly made however, in accordance with the Code of Conduct counsel newly instructed must promote and protect fearlessly by all proper and lawful means his lay client's best interests without regard to others, including fellow members of the legal profession (Code, para. 303(a)).

2. When counsel newly instructed is satisfied that such allegations are made, and a waiver of privilege is necessary, he should advise the lay client fully about the consequences of waiver and should obtain a waiver of privilege in writing signed by the lay client relating to communications with, instructions given to and advice given by former counsel. The allegations should be set out in the Grounds of Application for Leave of Appeal. Both waiver and grounds should be lodged without delay; the grounds may be perfected if necessary in due course.

3. On receipt of the waiver and grounds, the Registrar of Criminal Appeals will send both to former counsel with an invitation on behalf of the court to respond to the allegations made.

4. If former counsel wishes to respond and considers the time for doing so insufficient, he should ask the Registrar for further time. The court will be anxious to have full information and to give counsel adequate time to respond.

5. The response should be sent to the Registrar. On receipt, he will send it to counsel newly instructed who may reply to it. The grounds and the responses will go before the single judge.

6. The Registrar may have received grounds of appeal direct from the applicant, and obtained a waiver of privilege before fresh counsel is assigned. In those circumstances, when assigning counsel, the Registrar will provide copies of the waiver, the grounds of appeal and any response from former counsel.

7. This guidance covers the formal procedures to be followed. It is perfectly proper for counsel newly instructed to speak to former counsel as a matter of courtesy before grounds are lodged to inform him of the position.

As to the need to follow the Bar Council's guidance, see *R. v. Nasser, The Times,* February 19, 1998, CA.

## Preparation of defence statements

On September 24, 1997, the Professional Conduct and Complaints Committee of the Bar Council approved guidance as to the duties of counsel in relation to the preparation of defence statements pursuant to the CPIA 1996. The guidance (as revised by the Bar Standards Board in January, 2011) is set out in full in the main work at § 12-98. As at July 7, 2014, the guidance was still available on the website of the Bar Standards Board, in a section headed "Old Code Guidance". There is, however, a statement at the head of the page to the effect that, as from January 6, 2014, barristers should refer to the board's handbook (as to which, see *ante,* C-1)) for rules and guidance on their conduct as such. Its precise status is, therefore, unclear. On the website of the Bar Council, there is now an item in the "Professional Practice and Ethics" section that is headed "Failure to draft defence statements and skeleton arguments", the first paragraph of which reads as follows— **C-46**

> "1. You cannot, and should not, draft a defence statement without adequate instructions, which amounts to either a signed proof of evidence or having advised the client in conference. These

statements are of increasing importance and defendants are frequently cross-examined, to their detriment, on such documents. You should be formally instructed to draft them. If you fail to comply, there are already sanctions within the BSB handbook."

As to the last sentence, it should be noted that there is no specific reference to defence statements in the handbook. The item is accompanied by a statement that the document was prepared by the Bar Council to assist barristers on matters of professional conduct and ethics and that it does not constitute guidance for the purposes of the board's handbook.

## III. MISCELLANEOUS AUTHORITIES ON DUTIES OF ADVOCATES

### (1) Return of brief or instructions

C-47      Members of the criminal bar have a personal responsibility for compliance with provisions of the Code of Conduct relating to the return of instructions, of which their clerks should be aware. It is open to a court concerned with a problem caused by a late return of a brief to send a complaint to the Professional Conduct Committee of the Bar Council: *R. v. Sutton JJ., ex p. DPP*, 95 Cr.App.R. 180, DC, *per* Brooke J., at p. 186 (decided in relation to paragraphs 507 and 508 of the fifth edition of the Code of Conduct).

The absence of what counsel would regard as sufficient time for preparation does not constitute an exception to the cab-rank rule requiring him to act for his client: see *R. v. Ulcay* (§ 4-67 in the main work).

### (2) Duty not to accept certain instructions

C-48      Counsel should not appear for the prosecution in a case where the defendant is a person he has previously represented; para. 501(f) of the Code of Conduct for the Bar (6th ed.) referred to the risk that the barrister might have considential information or special knowledge disadvantageous to the defendant, his former client; it is contrary to the spirit of the code that a barrister should put himself in a position where such a risk might be perceived: *R. v. Dann* [1997] Crim.L.R. 46, CA. As to *Dann*, see further *Re T. and A. (Children) (Risk of Disclosure)* [2002] 1 F.L.R. 859, CA (Civ.Div.).

### (3) Duty in relation to the giving of advice and taking of instructions

C-48a     Although not laid down in prescriptive form in the codes of conduct governing barristers and solicitors, solicitors and counsel should make a brief note of the advice given and the instructions received in conference on important issues as to the conduct of the defence (such as discussions relating to strategy, including as to whether the defendant should give evidence); such a note would be to the benefit of the client, in that it will serve to ensure that he has been given the appropriate advice; it would also serve to protect the advocate and his instructing solicitors from criticism based on assertions made after the event by a dissatisfied client: *R. v. Anderson*, *The Times*, December 23, 2010, CA.

### (4) Duty of counsel to acquaint themselves with the terms of the indictment

C-49      See *R. v. Peckham*, 25 Cr.App.R. 125, CCA (prosecution), and *R. v. Olivo*, 28 Cr.App.R. 173, CCA (defence).

### (5) Duty concerning recent legislation

C-50      In *R. v. Isaacs*, *The Times*, February 9, 1990, the Court of Appeal said that when presenting cases at first instance or in appellate courts, counsel have a positive duty to inform the court of all relevant commencement dates of recent legislation.

### (6) Duty of counsel to inform themselves of the sentencing powers of the court

C-51      The Court of Appeal has repeatedly emphasised the duty of both counsel to inform themselves before the commencement of proceedings in the Crown Court of the sentencing powers of the court, including powers in relation to ancillary orders, such as costs, compensation, *etc.* The starting point is *R. v. Clarke (R.W.W.)*, 59 Cr.App.R. 298, CA. Lawton L.J. concluded the judgment of the court with the following general observations and guidance. His Lordship's remarks are even more apposite today than when they were made: legislation in relation to sentence has become ever more complex. Sections 28 and 29 of the MCA 1952 were replaced by sections 37 and 38 respectively of the MCA 1980, which have themselves since been subject to extensive amendment. Section 37 was eventually repealed by the CDA 1998, and section 38 was repealed and replaced by section 3 of the PCC(S)A 2000.

> "We adjudge that counsel as a matter of professional duty to the Court, and in the case of defending counsel to their client, should always before starting a criminal case satisfy themselves as to what the maximum sentence is. There can be no excuse for counsel not doing this and they should remember that the performance of this duty is particularly important in a case where a man has been committed to the Crown Court for sentencing pursuant to the provisions of sections 28 and 29 of the Magistrates' Courts Act 1952, and section 56 of the Criminal Justice Act 1967. Those statutory provisions are pregnant with dangers for court and for counsel and above all for accused persons...
>
> Secondly, those who administer the Crown Court should act as follows. Before the Crown Court came into existence..., it was the practice of many clerks of assize and many clerks of the peace to make a note on the documents put before the trial judge of the maximum sentence which could be passed and of the paragraphs in *Archbold's Criminal Pleading, Evidence and Practice* which dealt with the offence. In some Crown Courts this former practice has been followed. On the other hand it is clear from this case and from inquiries which we have made that it is not always followed. It should be; and it is particularly important that it should be when judges are asked to deal with cases committed for sentence under the statutory provisions to which I have already referred" (at pp. 301–302).

A reminder of the duty of counsel for both sides to ensure that sentences imposed, and orders made, are within the powers of the court, and to invite the court to vary a sentence if on subsequent consideration it appears to be unlawful, was given in *R. v. Komsta and Murphy*, 12 Cr.App.R.(S.) 63. Turner J. commented that it could not be too clearly understood that there was positive obligation on counsel, both for the prosecution and the defence, to ensure that no order was made that the court had no power to make. The PCC(S)A 2000, s. 155(1) (see § 5-1289 in the main work) allowed the Crown Court to alter or vary any sentence or order, within the period of 28 [now 56] days of the making of the order. If it appeared to either counsel that the order was one which the court had no power to make, counsel should not hesitate to invite the court to exercise such powers.

See also *R. v. Richards, The Times*, April 1, 1993, CA, *R. v. Hartrey* [1993] Crim.L.R. 230, CA, *R. v. Johnstone (D.), The Times*, June 18, 1996, CA, *R. v. Bruley* [1996] Crim.L.R. 913, CA, *R. v. McDonnell* [1996] Crim.L.R. 914, CA, *R. v. Street*, 161 J.P. 28, CA, *R. v. Blight* [1999] Crim.L.R. 426, CA and, most recently, *R. v. Cain* [2007] 2 Cr.App.R.(S.) 25, CA. In *Blight*, it was said that counsel do not discharge their duty simply by having a copy of *Archbold* "to hand"; it is the duty of both counsel to be aware in advance of the powers of the court so that any error may be recited immediately; as to the defence counsel, it was said to be very difficult to see how mitigation can be done properly without having in the very front of the mind the powers within which the judge must exercise his duty. In *R. v. Cain*, it was said that defence advocates should ascertain and be prepared to assist the judge with any relevant legal restrictions on sentence, and the prosecution advocate should ensure that the sentencer does not, through inadvertence, impose an unlawful sentence; in particular, prosecution advocates should always be ready to assist the court by drawing attention to any statutory provisions that govern the court's sentencing powers and to any sentencing guidelines or guideline decisions of the Court of Appeal.

In *R. v. Reynolds* [2007] 2 Cr.App.R.(S.) 87, CA, it was said that prosecuting and defence **C-52** advocates must ensure that they are fully aware of the potential impact of the provisions of the dangerous offender provisions in Chapter 5 of Part 12 of the CJA 2003 (§§ 5-494 *et seq.* in the main work), that they are able to assist the sentencer in that respect and are alert to any mistakes made in passing sentence so that any problem can be resolved before it is too late.

### (7) Defendant absconding

See generally, §§ 3-222 *et seq.* in the main work, and *R. v. Shaw*, 70 Cr.App.R. 313, CA (§ 7-87 **C-53** in the main work).

### (8) Defendant not giving evidence

In *R. v. Bevan*, 98 Cr.App.R. 354, CA, it was held that where a defendant decides not to give **C-54** evidence, it should be the invariable practice of counsel to record that decision and to cause the defendant to sign that record, indicating clearly first, that he has, of his own free will, decided not to give evidence and, secondly, that he has so decided bearing in mind the advice given to him by counsel. In the light of section 35 of the CJPOA 1994 (§ 4-377 in the main work), the advice of the Court of Appeal in *Bevan* is likely to become of greater importance than at the time of the decision. As to this, see also *Ebanks (Kurt) v. The Queen* [2006] 1 W.L.R. 1827, PC (§ 4-382 in the main work).

### (9) Duties in relation to cross-examination

**C-55**  See §§ 8-216, 8-219 *et seq.* in the main work and, in relation to defence counsel's duty when cross-examining a co-defendant, see *R. v. Fenlon*, 71 Cr.App.R. 307, CA, see § 8-297 in the main work.

### (10) Duties in relation to the summing up

**C-56**  See §§ 4-433 *et seq.* in the main work.

### (11) Duties in relation to appeal

**C-57**  As to the duty to advise in relation to the possibility of an appeal against conviction or sentence, see §§ 7-166 *et seq.* in the main work, and *ante*, C-39, C-45.

As to counsel's general duty in relation to the drafting of grounds of appeal, see § 7-168 in the main work. As to criticism of former counsel, see § 7-83 in the main work and *ante*, and § C-45, *ante*.

As to the duty of counsel for the prosecution, see § 7-201 in the main work.

The duty of a barrister to present his client's case before the Court of Appeal could not extend to advancing the client's assertion, unsubstantiated by any evidence, that the trial judge was corrupt or biased. A barrister's duty in such circumstances is either to decline to comply with the instructions or to withdraw from the case: *Thatcher v. Douglas, The Times,* January 8, 1996, CA (Civ. Div.).

### (12) Duties of prosecuting counsel

**C-58**  Apart from the matters mentioned above, see also (a) *The Role and Responsibilities of the Prosecution Advocate, post*, E-15 *et seq.*; (b) *R. v. Herbert*, 94 Cr.App.R. 230, CA (§ 4-173 in the main work) and *R. v. Richards and Stober*, 96 Cr.App.R. 258, CA (§ 19-103 in the main work), in relation to "plea-bargaining" and the acceptance of pleas, with particular reference to cases where there are two or more defendants; (c) §§ 4-342 *et seq.* in the main work, in relation to the opening of a case generally, and *R. v. Hobstaff*, 14 Cr.App.R.(S.) 605, CA, in relation to opening the facts on a plea of guilty; and (d) the Attorney-General's guidelines on the acceptance of pleas and the prosecutor's role in the sentencing exercise (*ante*, Appendix A-276 *et seq.*).

### (13) Advocate as witness

**C-59**  In *R. v. Jacquith (or Jaquith) and Emode* [1989] Crim.L.R. 508 and 563, CA, junior counsel for one defendant has been called on his behalf to rebut a suggestion of recent invention made against him. The Court of Appeal said that the evidence on this point was admissible but it was very undesirable for counsel to give evidence on this point in court. In addition to the effect on the jury it caused embarrassment and difficulty to other members of the Bar who had to set about cross-examining a colleague.

May L.J. said that the suggestion had been made that the court givesome indication of its views concerning evidence given by counsel and also where a client alleged an attempt to pervert the court of justice by a co-defendant. their Lordships considered, however, that the right course would be to list points for consideration by the Bar Council and the Law Society. It was not sought to lay these maters down as ones of principle; their Lordships merely thought they deserved consideration.

1. No advocate should ever give evidence if that could possibly be avoided. 2. Where it was not possible for an advocate to avoid giving evidence, he should take no further part in the case. It necessarily followed that, if he was not being led, the trial must stop and a retrial be ordered. 3.

There was a duty on counsel to anticipate circumstances in which he might be called upon to give evidence. Experienced counsel ought to be able to anticipate whether such a situation might arise. Where such a situation was anticipated, or envisaged even as a possibility, he should withdraw from the case. 4. Where it came to the notice of a legal adviser, through an accused person, that one of his co-defendants had attempted to pervert the court of justice, there was a duty on the legal adviser, usually the instructing solicitor, to take a detailed proof at once to provide a record and for further investigation. 5. Where the giving of evidence by an advocate caused real embarrassment or inhibition or difficulty regarding cross-examination by other advocates, the judge should exercise his discretion to discharge the jury and order a retrial.

### (14) Co-habiting counsel

It is generally undesirable for husband and wife, or other partners living together, to appear as **C-60** counsel on opposite sides in the same criminal matter since it might give rise to an apprehension that the proper conduct of the case had been in some way affected by that personal relationship: *R. v. Batt, The Times*, May 30, 1996, CA. See also *Re L. (Minors) (Care Proceedings: Solicitors)* [2001] 1 W.L.R. 100, Fam D. (Wilson J.).

# APPENDIX D
## Forms for use at Preliminary Hearings and Plea and Case Management Hearings

**CROWN COURT**

**CASE PROGRESSION**

**PRELIMINARY HEARING**

Date of hearing:  /  /                    Judge:

| Prosecution advocate: | | |
|---|---|---|
| D1 | [bail][custody] represented by: | |
| D2 | [bail][custody] represented by: | |
| D3 | [bail][custody] represented by: | |
| D4 | [bail][custody] represented by: | |
| D5 | [bail][custody] represented by: | |

No. of case in Crown Court: [        ]  URN: [        ]

Has the defendant been advised about credit for pleading guilty?

| D1 | D2 | D3 | D4 | D5 |
|---|---|---|---|---|
| | | | | |

Has the defendant been warned that if he is on bail and fails to attend, the proceedings may continue in his absence?

1) TRIAL JUDGE

Should the future management of the case be under the supervision of the trial judge or a nominated judge?                                                    YES/NO

2) PLEA

a.   Is it likely that the case can be concluded by the defendant pleading guilty?

| D1 | D2 | D3 | D4 | D5 |
|---|---|---|---|---|
| | | | | |

b.   If yes and if the defendant cannot be sentenced at the preliminary hearing, go to 3) and/or 4) as appropriate

3) LIKELY GUILTY PLEA

a.   *The defendant will be sentenced on:  /  /  or at the plea and case management hearing*

b.   *The directions made by the magistrates' court when the case was sent shall apply subject to the following amendments:*

c.   *The pre-sentence report (if required) to be received by the Crown Court and made available to the defence and the prosecution by:*

d.   *The defence to serve any material which it wishes the court to consider when sentencing by:*

e.   Does the defence intend to make "derogatory assertions" against a person's character in the course of mitigation?

| D1 | D2 | D3 | D4 | D5 |
|---|---|---|---|---|
| | | | | |

f.   *If yes, the court orders:*

g. Are there any other matters against a defendant which should be dealt with at the same time as the proceedings in this case (other offences/TIC's)?

| D1 | D2 | D3 | D4 | D5 |
|----|----|----|----|----|
|    |    |    |    |    |

h. If yes, give brief details:

i. *If there are other matters, the court orders:*

j. *Further orders (e.g. orders re medical, psychiatric reports, confiscation proceedings or Newton hearings):*

4) DIRECTIONS FOR PLEA AND CASE MANAGEMENT HEARING

a. *The directions made by the Magistrates' Court when the case was sent shall apply subject to the following amendments:*

b. *Further orders:*

5) EXPERT EVIDENCE

a. **Is this a case in which the parties will rely on expert evidence?**

| P | D1 | D2 | D3 | D4 | D5 |
|---|----|----|----|----|----|
|   |    |    |    |    |    |

b. *If yes, the court orders:*

6) TRIAL

a. **Can the date of the trial or the period during which the trial will take place be fixed now?** YES/NO

b. *If yes, the trial will take place on:*
*or within the period of :*
*and it is estimated that it will last:*

## CROWN COURT
## CASE PROGRESSION
## PRELIMINARY HEARING
## GUIDANCE NOTES

### General notes

These notes accompany the preliminary hearing form.

The parties must ensure that the Court has a copy of the "CASE SENT TO THE CROWN COURT UNDER SECTION 51 OF THE CRIME AND DISORDER ACT 1998" form completed in the Magistrates' Court.

The answers to the questions in bold must be filled in before the hearing. The proposed italicised orders should be filled in before the hearing, if possible (if there are more than five defendants, a further form should be filled in only so far as necessary).

Except where otherwise required, a direction in the form to "serve" material means serve on the other party(ies) and file with the Crown Court.

### Notes relevant to specific sections

1) TRIAL JUDGE OR NOMINATED JUDGE

If the case is due to last for more than 4 weeks or if it seems likely that a preparatory hearing will be ordered, the future case management should normally be under the supervision of the trial judge or a nominated judge. It may also be desirable for the future case management to be under the supervision of the trial judge or a nominated judge in other cases where, for example there are difficult issues of law to be considered or where the prosecution intends to make a public interest immunity application.

If the case fits into this category, the court should normally make the necessary directions for the plea and case management hearing and then direct that the case be considered by the Resident Judge.

2) PLEA

If it is likely that the case can be concluded by all the defendants pleading guilty then 3) should be completed and there should be no need to make any orders under 4). Otherwise any appropriate orders under 3) should be made in respect of those defendants likely to plead guilty and 4) should be completed.

3) LIKELY GUILTY PLEA

3b.The Crown Court has a greater power to vary the time limits than the magistrates' court.

3c. A pre-sentence report will not be required in every case.

3e. Advance notice of the fact that such an assertion is going to be made should be given to the prosecution to enable it to decide whether to challenge the assertion and to enable the sentencing court to consider whether to make an order restricting the publication of the assertion under sections 58-61 of the Criminal Procedure and Investigations Act 1996 ("CPIA").

3i. If the defendant is facing charges in other courts give brief details of offence, court and court number.

4) DIRECTIONS FOR PLEA AND CASE MANAGEMENT HEARING

4a. The Crown Court has a greater power to vary the time limits than the Magistrates' Court.

5) EXPERT EVIDENCE

The court should identify any issues in relation to which it is appropriate to call expert evidence and set a timetable for obtaining, serving, and (if possible) agreeing such evidence or identifying the issues in dispute. See also paragraph 15 of the guidance notes to the PCMH form.

The parties should consider whether orders being considered by the court will involve costs being incurred which may not be met by the Legal Services Commission.

7) TRIAL

The court should consider whether it is possible and desirable to set the trial date or period because, for example, of the health, vulnerability or availability of a witness or the defendant or because the defendant falls within the definition of a persistent young offender, or because experts and/or leading counsel may have to be instructed and, before any such instructions can be expected, it is necessary to know the date.

| The Crown Court | Plea and Case Management Hearing |
|---|---|

**Advocates' Questionnaire**

| CC Case Number    D1 | |
|---|---|

Date of trial

| Fixed | ☐ |
| Warned | ☐ |

■ Parties must complete this form.
■ This form is to be used at all Crown Court Centres, without local variation.
There is an electronic version of the form on the Ministry of Justice website, at:
www.justice.gov.uk/courts/procedure-rules/criminal/formspage

---

**PART ONE**
**(Questions 1 to 15 are to be completed in all cases, together with question 37 'Witness List')**

**1    Date of trial and custody time limits**

1.1    Date of PCMH                                        PTI URN

Judge                                                Estimated length of trial

1.2    What are the custody time limit expiry dates as agreed between the parties? *(If different custody time limits attach to different offences or defendants, please give details.)*

1.3    Can an application to extend any custody time limit be made today?          ☐ No   ☐ Yes

**2    Parties**

Prosecuting authority                              Advocate

P

| Defendant's name | Age | Remand status | Trial Advocate | PCMH Advocate (if different) |
|---|---|---|---|---|
| D1 | | C ☐   B ☐ | | |

## 3  Contact details

3.1    Parties

| P | Office | Name | Phone |
|---|---|---|---|
|   |   | Email |   |

|   | Advocate | Name | Phone |
|---|---|---|---|
|   |   | Email |   |

| D1 | Solicitor | Name | Phone |
|---|---|---|---|
|   |   | Email |   |

|   | Advocate | Name | Phone |
|---|---|---|---|
|   |   | Email |   |

3.2    Case progression officers

| P | Name | Phone |
|---|---|---|
|   | Email |   |

| D1 | Name | Phone |
|---|---|---|
|   | Email |   |

| Court | Name | Phone |
|---|---|---|
|   | Email |   |

## 4  Readiness for PCMH

4.1    Which, if any, of the orders made at the magistrates' court have not been complied with?

P

D1

4.2    Are the parties ready for the PCMH?  If not, why not?

P

D1

## 5    Has the defendant been advised that he or she will receive credit for a guilty plea?

D1                                                                                          ☐ No   ☐ Yes

## 6    Has the defendant been warned that the case may proceed in his or her absence?

D1                                                                                          ☐ No   ☐ Yes

## 7    What guilty plea(s) (if any) is the defendant offering?

D1

8      Should the case be referred to the Resident Judge for a trial judge to be allocated?    ☐ No   ☐ Yes

9      Give details of any issues relating to the defendant's fitness to plead or to stand trial.

*D1*

## 10    Prosecution evidence

10.1    Has the prosecution served the principal evidence on which the prosecution case relies, and if so when (give the date)? If not, why not?

*P*

10.2    What further evidence (if any) does the prosecution expect to serve? By when is it reasonably practicable to serve it (give the date)?

*P*

10.3    Defence comments (if any) on the prosecution replies to 10.1 and 10.2:

*D1*

## 11    Disclosure, defence statement and defence witness notice

11.1    Has the prosecution made statutory disclosure and if so when (give the date)? If not, why not?

*P*

11.2    When does / did the time expire for service of a defence statement and witness notice (give the date)?

*P*

11.3    Defence comments (if any) on the prosecution replies to 11.1 and 11.2:

*D1*

11.4    Has the defence served (a) a defence statement and (b) a witness notice, and if so when (give the date(s))? If not, why not?

*D1*

11.5    Do the defence statement and witness notice comply with the statutory requirements?

*P*    *Prosecution comments (if any):*

11.6    Has the defendant been warned of the consequences of any failure to serve a defence statement and   ☐ No    ☐ Yes
witness notice (a) within the time prescribed and (b) complying with the statutory requirements?

11.7    If the defendant has served a defence statement, does the defendant expect to apply for further    ☐ No    ☐ Yes
prosecution disclosure?

11.8    If not clear from the defence statement, what are the real issues?

*D1*

*P*    *Prosecution comments (if any):*

**12      Expert evidence**

12.1    Give details of any expert evidence likely to be relied upon, including why it is required and by when it is reasonably
        practicable to serve this.

P

D1

12.2    Is a note of agreement / disagreement required?

**13      Witnesses**

13.1    Have the parties completed the Witness List (see **37**)?                                    ☐ No  ☐ Yes

13.2    Are the parties satisfied that all the listed witnesses are needed (see **37**)?             ☐ No  ☐ Yes
        If 'no', give details.

13.3    Are the parties satisfied that the time estimates for questioning witnesses are realistic (see **37**)?  ☐ No  ☐ Yes
        If 'no', give details.

13.4    Is any witness summons necessary?                                                            ☐ No  ☐ Yes
        If 'yes', give particulars:

13.5    Can a timetable be fixed now for the calling of witnesses?                                   ☐ No  ☐ Yes
        If 'no', why not?

**14      Timetabling of the trial**

14.1    Are there matters which need to be determined at the start of the trial, which may affect the timetable?  ☐ No ☐ Yes
        If so, when will (1) the jury and (2) the witnesses be required?

        What timetable can now be set for the conduct of the trial (see rule 3.10)?

### The indictment

14.2

### 15

15.1  Has the indictment been signed and dated as required by Part 14 of the CrimPR?          ☐ No  ☐ Yes

15.2  Is any amendment of the indictment required?          ☐ No  ☐ Yes

> **PART TWO**
> *Question 37 (Witness list) is to be completed in every case*
> *Answer the remaining questions only where relevant*

### 16  Admissions and agreed facts

What matters can usefully be admitted or put into schedules, diagrams, visual aids etc.?

### 17  Case summary

P    Is it proposed to serve a case summary or note of opening?          ☐ No  ☐ Yes

### 18  Measures to assist witnesses and defendants in giving evidence

18A  **Measures to assist a witness in giving evidence.**

*Each of these issues must be addressed separately in respect of each young vulnerable or intimidated witness who is or may be required to give evidence in person. (If completed electronically, the form will expand to deal with each separate witness separately. If completed manually, attach separate sheets if necessary.)*

Name and age of witness:

Name:                                                        Age:

What arrangements have been made for a pre-trial visit?

What arrangements have been made to ensure that the witness sees the video of their evidence BEFORE the trial (i.e. not immediately before giving their evidence over the live link)?

| | | |
|---|---|---|
| Has the witness been offered a 'supporter'?<br>If 'yes', give particulars: | ☐ No | ☐ Yes |

| | | |
|---|---|---|
| Does the witness need an intermediary?<br>If 'yes', give particulars: | ☐ No | ☐ Yes |

What arrangements have been made for the witness to access the court building other than by the main public entrance?

What are the arrangements to ensure that this witness can give evidence without waiting or at least by reducing waiting to a minimum (*e.g. by ensuring that the opening and any preliminary points will be finished before the time appointed for the witness to attend or by agreeing and fixing a timed witness order in advance*)?

| | | |
|---|---|---|
| Have the views of the witness been sought and, if so, has s/he expressed any particular view or concerns? | ☐ No | ☐ Yes |

If 'yes', give particulars:

If views not sought, why not?

What material (if any) needs to be available to the witness in the video suite?

**18B**      **Defendant's evidence direction**

| | | |
|---|---|---|
| Is any defendant's evidence direction to be sought? | ☐ No | ☐ Yes |
| If so, has the necessary application been made, complying with Section 4 of CrimPR Part 29? | ☐ No | ☐ Yes |

---

If so, give details

---

18C    **Witness anonymity order**

| Is any witness anonymity order sought / to be made? | ☐ No ☐ Yes |
|---|---|
| If so, has an application been made, complying with Section 5 of CrimPR Part 29? | ☐ No ☐ Yes |

If so give details (subject to the restrictions in Section 5 of CrimPR Part 29).

---

## 19    Young or vulnerable defendants

Are any other arrangements needed for any young or vulnerable defendants?

*D1*

---

## 20    Reporting restrictions

State type and grounds of any reporting restriction sought.

*P*

*D1*

---

## 21    Third party material

Is any application to be made for the production of third party material?    ☐ No    ☐ Yes

---

## 22    Defendant's interview(s)

22.1    Specify any issue relating to the admissibility of all or any part of the defendant's interview(s). Can the issue be resolved now ? If not, when ? Are skeleton arguments needed and, if so, when ?

22.2    By how much can the interview(s) be shortened by editing / summary for trial ? Give a timetable for the service of any proposed summary by the prosecution and agreement / counter-proposal by the defence.

---

22.3     Specify any other issues concerning the defendant's interview(s).

## 23    Witnesses giving evidence by video or DVD interview

23.1     Is there video or DVD evidence of any young / vulnerable / intimidated witness yet to be served?

23.2     Has each video been transcribed?

23.3     Is there an issue in relation to the accuracy / admissibility / quality / length of any video or transcript?

## 24    Witness interview(s)

24.1     Are there any videos / audio tapes of witness interviews which, if they meet the disclosure test, are yet to be disclosed as unused material?

24.2     If so, is any application made for that video / audio tape to be transcribed and, if so, why?

## 25    CCTV evidence

25.1     Are there any outstanding issues in relation to service or disclosure of CCTV footage? *If the material is in the possession of a third party, complete 21 instead.*

25.2    Is an edited version to be served / used?

## 26    Electronic equipment

26.1    Give details of any special equipment (e.g. CCTV, live link, audio recordings, DVD) required in the trial courtroom.

*P*

*D1*

26.2    Is the evidence in its present form compatible with the equipment in court?

## 27    Cross-examination on sexual history

If an application has not already been made, does the defence intend to make an application under section 41 of the Youth Justice and Criminal Evidence Act 1999 to cross-examine a witness about his or her sexual history?

*D1*

## 28    Bad character

Are any directions necessary in relation to bad character applications? Are there to be any further applications?

*P*

*D1*

**29   Hearsay**

Are any directions necessary in relation to hearsay applications? Are there to be any further applications?

P

D1

**30   Admissibility and legal issues**

What points on admissibility / other legal issues are to be taken? Is it necessary for any to be resolved before trial?

P

D1

**31   Public interest immunity**

Is any 'on notice' public interest immunity application to be made?

P

**32   Jury bundle**

What proposals do the prosecution make for a jury bundle?

P

**33   Concurrent family proceedings**

Give details of any concurrent family proceedings.

**34     Other special arrangements**

Give details of any special arrangements (e.g., interpreter, intermediary, wheelchair access, hearing loop system, breaks) needed for anyone attending the trial.

**35     Linked criminal proceedings**

Are there other criminal proceedings against the defendant or otherwise linked?

**36     Additional orders**

Are any additional orders required?

**37     Witness List**   (see table for completion, over page)

**37    Witness List**

*The parties should indicate here which prosecution witnesses are required to give evidence at trial. The attendance of any witness is subject to the judge's direction.*

| Name of witness | Page No. | Required by | What is the relevant, disputed issue? | Estimated time for questioning | |
|---|---|---|---|---|---|
| | | | | Chief | X - exam |
| | | | | | |
| | | | | | |
| | | | | | |
| | | | | | |
| | | | | | |
| | | | | | |
| | | | | | |
| | | | | | |
| | | | | | |
| | | | | | |
| | | | | | |
| | | | | | |
| | | | | | |
| | | | | | |
| | | | | | |
| | | | | | |
| | | | | | |
| | | | | | |
| | | | | | |
| | | | | | |
| | | | | | |
| | | | | | |

## Plea and Case Management Hearing Form: Guidance Notes

### The need for an effective PCMH

i.    The public, and all those concerned in or affected by a criminal case, have a right to expect that the business of the courts will be conducted fairly but also efficiently and effectively. Delays cost money and adversely impact on the quality of justice. The Plea and Case Management Hearing offers the best, and often the only, opportunity for the judge properly and effectively to manage the case before it is listed for trial. Other hearings – formerly called 'mentions' – are expensive and should actively be discouraged; nearly everything formerly done at a 'mention' can – and should – be done in some other way (usually by telephone or on paper or by an exchange of email, as permitted by CrimPR 3.5(2)(d)). An effective PCMH is therefore vital.

ii.    Advocates should attend the hearing fully prepared to deal with the issues that are likely to arise, and the listing officer should consider reasonable requests to list the PCMH to enable trial counsel to attend.

iii.    Since an effective PCMH can only take place after the defence have had a proper opportunity to consider the papers, it is suggested that at least four weeks should elapse between the service of the prosecution case papers and listing of the PCMH.

iv.    The short guidance given here is intended to be followed in every case but, of course, it is not possible to cover exhaustively all the situations which may be relevant to achieving an effective PCMH. See also Consolidated Criminal Practice Direction (CCPD), paragraph IV.41, Management of Cases to be Heard in the Crown Court; and paragraph V.56, Case Management in Magistrates' Courts.

### How to use the form

v.    The parties should complete only one form for each case. **The form should be used in every Crown Court centre, without any local exception or variation.**

vi.    The form may be completed in manuscript or electronically.

vii.    Questions 1 to 15 (in Part I) must be answered in every case.

viii.    Questions 16-36 (in Part II) need only be answered if they are relevant.

ix.    Question 37, at the end of the form, (the witness list) must be completed in every case.

x.    The advocate may be asked by the court to expand upon or explain an entry, or to account for the absence of an entry, where one is required. The judge will record on the judicial orders template, or on the PCMH form, any orders made and, if practicable, issue a copy to the parties before the hearing ends. The parties must obtain a copy of that record and comply with the orders made by the date given.

### Accessing the form

xi. The current version of the form is available on the Ministry of Justice website at www.justice.gov.uk/guidance/courts-and-tribunals/courts/procedure-rules/criminal/formspage.htm

### Transmitting the form

xii. If you complete the form on the screen, it can still be printed off and used in hard copy. Alternatively, it can be emailed as an attachment.

## Contents of the form

*(The following commentary is to assist with the completion of the questions so numbered on the PCMH form.)*

### 1 Date of trial and custody time limits

The date of trial should normally be fixed at the PCMH (or before). Any application to extend the Custody Time Limit is best dealt with at the PCMH, when the reasons for fixing a case beyond the time limits will be clear; otherwise there will be the avoidable expense of another hearing.

### 2 and 3 Details of case and parties

This section must be fully completed. The parties must be able to contact one another as must case progression officers and the court. Any change in the details must immediately be notified to the other parties and to the court. See CrimPR 3.4.

### 4 Compliance with the directions given by magistrates' courts

The standard / specific directions given by magistrates' courts should be complied with (CrimPR 3.5(3)). The court will need to know which orders have not been complied with, and why.

### 5 Credit for guilty plea

Defendants are entitled to be given the advice that credit is given for guilty pleas and the earlier the plea is entered, the greater is the credit given. The judge needs to know that this advice has been given.

### 6 Trial in absence

Defendants need to be warned that if they waive their right to attend, the trial may proceed in their absence. No one can engineer an adjournment simply by absconding. Those who claim to be ill must support that claim by medical evidence to the effect that they are unfit to attend their trial; it is unlikely that a medical certificate merely suggesting that they are unfit to work will be sufficient. See CCPD, I.13; CrimPR 3.8(2)(a).

### 7 The pleas which the defendant is offering

Recording in writing pleas offered to alternative offences which the prosecution are initially unwilling to accept will be advantageous to the defendant if the prosecution subsequently

Revised 2011

2

changes its position. In such circumstances, it will be easier for a defendant to claim maximum credit if that offer has been recorded. Pleas offered to counts on the indictment must similarly be recorded before credit is claimed.

## 8 Allocation of the case

Most courts have a system to identify before the PCMH those cases which require allocation to a particular judge; this question is intended to seek out those cases which have been missed.

## 9 Fitness to plead

This is self explanatory, but the judge will need assistance to fix a timetable for the service of experts' reports and for the issue to be tried.

## 10 Disclosure, the defence statement and notification of defence witnesses

The parties must identify any outstanding disclosure points. See Part 22 of The Criminal Procedure Rules 2010. The defence must serve a detailed defence statement setting out the issues in the trial; any failure to do so may be the subject of adverse comment at the trial and the judge may issue a warning to this effect, under section 11(3) of the Criminal Procedure and Investigations Act 1996. Pending service of a defence statement, question 10.4 allows the defence to give some notification of the defence. The practice of appending long 'shopping lists' to vague and unspecific defence statements has no legal foundation; any application for further disclosure should be made by way of formal application under section 8 of the Criminal Procedure and Investigations Act 1996 (as amended). The judge will expect compliance with the relevant Practice Directions, Guidelines and Protocols.

Pursuant to section 6C of the Criminal Procedure and Investigations Act 1996, the defence must notify the prosecution and the court whether he intends to call any witnesses at trial, and if so, give their names, addresses and dates of birth. The Practice Direction sets out a form for use by the defence when giving this notice (see rule 22.4). It may be that the time limit for notification has not expired when the PCMH is held but even so the defence might usefully be reminded of their responsibilities under that provision; if even as early as the PCMH the defence can comply, then they should be encouraged to do so.

## 11 and 12 Timetable of further evidence and expert evidence

Advocates should have available proper information as to what remains to be served, together with a realistic timetable for compliance. Parties should be prepared to provide realistic time estimates and not rely on a standard time period of, for example, 28 days if this has little bearing on the true amount of time likely to be required. The court needs detailed and accurate information as to when the evidence will be available. These enquiries should be made before the hearing. Failure to do so is likely to cause unnecessary adjournments. Consideration should be given to CrimPR 33.6 and whether (now or later) the experts should be asked to confer, to identify the real areas of dispute.

## 13 (and 37) Witness list

The mere fact of warning a witness to attend may cause him or her anxiety. Furthermore, the warning of witnesses is time consuming and expensive. When completing the witness list at paragraph 37, it is important to identify the relevant disputed issues to which the evidence of any particular witness is necessary, so that the judge can decide whether their attendance is necessary. The court may decline to order the attendance of witnesses unless their presence is really necessary. Consideration should therefore also be given to those witnesses in respect of whom a summons is required. See CrimPR Part 28 for rules on witness summonses. Thought should always be given to the staggering of witnesses to eliminate or reduce waiting times. The witnesses' availability must be known at the PCMH to ensure that the trial date is convenient.

## 14 Timetabling of the trial

Part 3.10 CrimPR requires the judge to consider timetabling in every case, with a view to improving efficiency; these matters require consideration throughout the trial; it may be possible to make some orders even at the PCMH.

If there are to be preliminary points taken, then consideration must be given to when a jury will be required and arrangements made to stagger the attendance of witnesses. No one should be asked to attend for a 10.30 am start only to find that there is a lengthy legal argument before the case can even be opened.

## 15 The Indictment

CrimPR 14.1(3)(a) requires the indictment to be signed by the court officer. Any amendment to the indictment must be ordered by the court.

## 16 Admissions and agreed facts

Admissions, sometimes more accurately called agreed facts, take time to draft but they can save a great deal of court time and thereby reduce costs. This applies not only to formal evidence (for example of continuity or of the captions to photographs) but also to many other types of evidence, of which these are but examples: lengthy police interviews are often better summarised and agreed; witness statements which are agreed to be read can often be summarised; expert evidence, including medical evidence, is often easier to understand if it is summarised by way of agreement rather than being read; this applies with particular force to evidence of telephone traffic and to cell site analysis; bad character evidence, if admissible, is also often better agreed.

## 17 Case Summary

Case Summaries should have been provided before the PCMH in all Class 1 cases and in any other case of complexity, but they may be needed in other cases as well.

## 18 Measures to assist witnesses and defendants in giving evidence

In accordance with CrimPR Part 29, special measures applications should have been made by the parties and considered by the court before the PCMH. This question addresses other points:

**Question 18A** serves to remind advocates and judges of the needs of vulnerable and intimidated witnesses and of the measures which now exist to assist them in giving evidence;

**Question 18B** serves a similar purpose in relation to defendants, who may require assistance in giving evidence;

**Question 18C** alerts the judge to applications to be made in relation to anonymous witnesses, which are likely to require a separate hearing, ideally before the trial judge.

## 19 Young or vulnerable defendants

Question 18B addresses the assistance which a defendant may need to facilitate giving evidence. This question seeks to identify any other needs of defendants who are children or young people or adults who are 'vulnerable' in that they suffer from a mental disorder or from some other significant impairment of intelligence or social function and for whom special arrangements must be made so that they can effectively understand and participate in the proceedings (as to which see generally paragraph III.30 of the CCPD).

## 20 Reporting restrictions

Reporting restrictions need to be carefully considered and balanced against the rights of the press and other interested parties. The judge is likely to require assistance before making any order. See CCPD I.3. and the JSB and Society of Editors publication, *Reporting Restrictions in the Criminal Courts*, url
hhtp://www.judiciary.gov.uk/Resources/JCO/Documents/crown court reporting restrictions 021009.pdf.)

## 21 Third party material

Such applications must comply with CrimPR Part 28. Careful thought needs to go into identifying the witness to be served, the material sought and the reason that it is said to be relevant to an issue in the case. Any person whose right of confidentiality might be adversely affected must also be identified and information provided as to how and by whom they are to be notified, how they are to be permitted to make representations and when and by whom any rulings are to be made. It is important that such applications are made no later than the PCMH to avoid adjournments at a later stage arising out of delayed applications. Any such application is better made using the appropriate form set out in the Practice Direction for use in connection with an application under Part 28, which directs the applicant and the judge to the relevant criteria.

## 22 Defendant's interviews

Inaccuracies within transcriptions and likely submissions as to admissibility must be identified. Furthermore, the police may interview suspects at length, producing bundles of transcripts, the volume of which may make them unsuitable to put before a jury. The parties must consider producing summaries. The production of the first draft is primarily the responsibility of the advocate for the prosecution. If practicable, interviews should be available in electronic form, so that editing, pagination and copying can be done without delay. Further guidance is given in CCPD IV.43.

## 23 Witnesses giving evidence by video or DVD interview

These questions, each of which raises a separate point, are self-explanatory but failure to address them is a frequent source of adjournments. The quality of the recording, the accuracy of the transcript and the admissibility of the interview (or any particular part or parts of it) are separate points, each of which needs to be addressed at the PCMH.

Any editing of the tape (or disc) takes time. Particular care must be taken to ensure that any editing of the tapes has not diminished its sound quality and that any editing of the tape is precisely reflected in editing to the transcript; again this takes time. It should not be done on the morning of the trial or the day beforehand.

Only if these issues are addressed in advance can young and vulnerable witnesses be called as soon as they arrive at court. It is unacceptable to prolong the anxiety of young and vulnerable witnesses simply because these issues have not been resolved at PCMH. See also CrimPR Part 29 for rules on special measures directions; and CCPD IV.40.

Furthermore, the extreme and unnecessary length of many of these interviews is becoming a matter of great concern. Judges have a responsibility to eliminate undue repetition and may require interviews to be reduced in length, so as to reduce the burden on the jury, and on the witness, whilst not disadvantaging the defendant.

## 24 Witness interviews

The issues raised in this question differ from those raised in question 23. There is a growing practice of recording interviews with witnesses before setting out their evidence in a written witness statement. If this is done, then, subject to the disclosure test, the video or audio recording should be disclosed as unused material. The prosecution advocate therefore needs to know if any witness was interviewed in this way (which may not be clear from the papers served). It will normally suffice for the video or audio recording itself to be disclosed. Transcripts are expensive and any claim for a transcript needs to be justified.

## 25 and 26 CCTV evidence and electronic equipment

Subject to the duties of the prosecution properly to investigate the case under the relevant Guidelines, the prosecution only have duties to consider disclosure of CCTV footage in their possession. If the defence seek footage from third parties, it is for them to do so, rather than the prosecution. Furthermore, much CCTV footage is in a format (e.g. multiplex) which is unsuitable for showing in court without adaptation or editing. This must be sorted out before the trial. Many courts have simple VHS video and DVD playback facilities and the parties must ensure that the material which they want to play is compatible with the court equipment (if not, they must provide their own).

## 27 Cross-examination on sexual history

Section 41 of the Youth Justice and Criminal Evidence Act 1999 enacts an important principle and compliance with its requirements is vital to ensure that those who complain that they are victims of rape (and other sexual offences) receive the protection which the law affords to them. In accordance with CrimPR Part 36, applications should be made and considered – by the trial judge if possible – at or before the PCMH. Applications made on the day of the trial are strongly to be discouraged.

## 28 and 29 Bad character and hearsay

CrimPR at Parts 34 (Hearsay) and 35 (Evidence of bad character) provide for detailed applications to be made in the prescribed forms. Questions 28 and 29 therefore only seek to identify any outstanding issues (or potential future applications).

## 30 Admissibility and legal issues

Issues of admissibility and legal issues should, where possible, be identified before the trial, so that the parties can exchange skeleton arguments and the judge can properly prepare for the hearing. See also section 7 of the Criminal Justice Act 1987; and sections 31 and 40 of the Criminal Procedure and Investigations Act 1996.

## 31 Public Interest Immunity claims

If a claim is to be made on notice, then the necessary arrangements must be made. See CrimPR 22.3.

Revised 2011                                                                 6

## 32 Jury bundle

If a jury bundle will be needed at the trial, then its content will need to be agreed before the trial. Any outstanding issues need to be identified.

## 33 Concurrent family proceedings

It is important to identify those cases where there are concurrent family proceedings, so that the Designated Family Judge can be alerted.

## 34 Special arrangements

Any requirements for an interpreter or for those with a disability must be identified in advance, so that proper arrangements can be made. See CrimPR 10.5(1)(h) and 12.1(1)(e).

## 35 Linked criminal proceedings

These need to be identified, if possible with the court reference numbers.

## 36 Additional orders

It is important to identify additional orders which may be required.

## 37 Witness List

See the note in paragraph 13, above.

**Forms for use in cases with two or more defendants**

**D-3**    An expanded version of the plea and case management hearing form, for use in connection
with cases involving up to 10 defendants is available on the Ministry of Justice website (http://ww
w.justice.gov.uk/courts/procedure-rules/criminal/formspage).

**Criminal practice directions**

**D-4**    The consolidated criminal practice direction has now been revoked: *Criminal Practice Direction
(General matters) A2* [2013] 1 W.L.R. 3164. For paragraph I.3 of that practice direction (referred
to in para. 20 of the guidance notes), see now *Criminal Practice Direction (Preliminary proceedings)
16B* [2013] 1 W.L.R. 3164; for paragraph I.13 of that practice direction (para. 6), see now
*Criminal Practice Direction (Custody and bail) 19B* [2013] 1 W.L.R. 3164; for paragraph III.30 of that
practice direction (para. 19), see now *Criminal Practice Direction (General matters) 3G* [2013] 1
W.L.R. 3164; for paragraph IV.40 of that practice direction (para. 23), see now *Criminal Practice
Direction (Evidence) 27B* [2013] 1 W.L.R. 3164; for paragraph IV.41 of that practice direction
(para. (iv)), see now *Criminal Practice Direction (General matters) 3A and 3B* [2013] 1 W.L.R. 3164;
for paragraph IV.43 of that practice direction (para. 22), see now *Criminal Practice Direction
(Evidence) 27C* [2013] 1 W.L.R. 3164; and for paragraph V.56 of that practice direction (para.
(iv)), see now *Criminal Practice Direction (General matters) 3A* [2013] 1 W.L.R. 3164.

# APPENDIX E
# Crown Prosecution Service

## I. CODE FOR CROWN PROSECUTORS

### A. INTRODUCTION

The Crown Prosecution Service is the principal public prosecuting authority for England and **E-1** Wales and is headed by the Director of Public Prosecutions, who is to discharge his functions under the superintendence of the Attorney-General (Prosecution of Offences Act 1985, s.3(1)). The Attorney-General is accountable to Parliament for the Service.

The Crown Prosecution Service is a national organisation consisting of 42 areas. Each area is headed by a Chief Crown Prosecutor and corresponds to a single police force area, with one for London. It was set up in 1986 to prosecute cases investigated by the police.

Although the Crown Prosecution Service works closely with the police, it is independent of them. The independence of crown prosecutors is of fundamental constitutional importance. Casework decisions taken with fairness, impartiality and integrity help deliver justice for victims, witnesses, defendants and the public.

The Crown Prosecution Service co-operates with the investigating and prosecuting agencies of other jurisdictions.

The Director of Public Prosecutions is responsible for issuing a Code for Crown Prosecutors under section 10 of the Prosecution of Offences Act 1985, giving guidance on the general principles to be applied when making decisions about prosecutions. This is the seventh edition of the code and replaces all earlier versions. It was issued on January 28, 2013.

### B. THE CODE

#### 1. INTRODUCTION

1.1 The Code for Crown Prosecutors (the code) is issued by the Director of Public Prosecutions **E-2** (DPP) under section 10 of the Prosecution of Offences Act 1985. This is the seventh edition of the code and replaces all earlier versions.

1.2 The DPP is the head of the Crown Prosecution Service (CPS), which is the principal public prosecution service for England and Wales. The DPP operates independently, under the superintendence of the Attorney-General who is accountable to Parliament for the work of the CPS.

1.3 The code gives guidance to prosecutors on the general principles to be applied when making decisions about prosecutions. The code is issued primarily for prosecutors in the CPS, but other prosecutors follow the code either through convention or because they are required to do so by law.

1.4 In this code, the term "suspect" is used to describe a person who is not yet the subject of formal criminal proceedings; the term "defendant" is used to describe a person who has been charged or summonsed; and the term "offender" is used to describe a person who has admitted his or her guilt to a police officer or other investigator or prosecutor, or who has been found guilty in a court of law.

#### 2. GENERAL PRINCIPLES

2.1 The decision to prosecute or to recommend an out-of-court disposal is a serious step that af- **E-3** fects suspects, victims, witnesses and the public at large and must be undertaken with the utmost care.

2.2 It is the duty of prosecutors to make sure that the right person is prosecuted for the right offence and to bring offenders to justice wherever possible. Casework decisions taken fairly, impartially and with integrity help to secure justice for victims, witnesses, defendants and the public. Prosecutors must ensure that the law is properly applied; that relevant evidence is put before the court; and that obligations of disclosure are complied with.

2.3 Although each case must be considered on its own facts and on its own merits, there are general principles that apply in every case.

2.4 Prosecutors must be fair, independent and objective. They must not let any personal views about the ethnic or national origin, gender, disability, age, religion or belief, political views, sexual orientation, or gender identity of the suspect, victim or any witness influence their decisions. Neither must prosecutors be affected by improper or undue pressure from any source. Prosecutors must always act in the interests of justice and not solely for the purpose of obtaining a conviction.

2.5 The CPS is a public authority for the purposes of current, relevant equality legislation. Prosecutors are bound by the duties set out in this legislation.

2.6 Prosecutors must apply the principles of the European Convention on Human Rights, in accordance with the Human Rights Act 1998, at each stage of a case. Prosecutors must also comply with any guidelines issued by the Attorney-General; with the *Criminal Procedure Rules* currently in force; and have regard to the obligations arising from international conventions. They must follow the policies and guidance of the CPS issued on behalf of the DPP and available for the public to view on the CPS website.

### 3. The Decision Whether to Prosecute

**E-4**

3.1 In more serious or complex cases, prosecutors decide whether a person should be charged with a criminal offence and, if so, what that offence should be. They make their decisions in accordance with this code and the DPP's guidance on charging. The police apply the same principles in deciding whether to start criminal proceedings against a person in those cases for which they are responsible.

3.2 The police and other investigators are responsible for conducting enquiries into any alleged crime and for deciding how to deploy their resources. This includes decisions to start or continue an investigation and on the scope of the investigation. Prosecutors often advise the police and other investigators about possible lines of inquiry and evidential requirements, and assist with pre-charge procedures. In large scale investigations the prosecutor may be asked to advise on the overall investigation strategy, including decisions to refine or narrow the scope of the criminal conduct and the number of suspects under investigation. This is to assist the police and other investigators to complete the investigation within a reasonable period of time and to build the most effective prosecution case. However, prosecutors cannot direct the police or other investigators.

3.3 Prosecutors should identify and, where possible, seek to rectify evidential weaknesses, but, subject to the threshold test (see section 5), they should swiftly stop cases which do not meet the evidential stage of the full code test (see section 4) and which cannot be strengthened by further investigation, or where the public interest clearly does not require a prosecution (see section 4). Although prosecutors primarily consider the evidence and information supplied by the police and other investigators, the suspect or those acting on his or her behalf may also submit evidence or information to the prosecutor via the police or other investigators, prior to charge, to help inform the prosecutor's decision.

3.4 Prosecutors must only start or continue a prosecution when the case has passed both stages of the full code test (see section 4). The exception is when the threshold test (see section 5) may be applied where it is proposed to apply to the court to keep the suspect in custody after charge, and the evidence required to apply the full code test is not yet available.

3.5 Prosecutors should not start or continue a prosecution which would be regarded by the courts as oppressive or unfair and an abuse of the court's process.

3.6 Prosecutors review every case they receive from the police or other investigators. Review is a continuing process and prosecutors must take account of any change in circumstances that occurs as the case develops, including what becomes known of the defence case. Wherever possible, they should talk to the investigator when thinking about changing the charges or stopping the case. Prosecutors and investigators work closely together, but the final responsibility for the decision whether or not a case should go ahead rests with the CPS.

3.7 Parliament has decided that a limited number of offences should only be taken to court with the agreement of the DPP. These are called consent cases. In such cases the DPP, or prosecutors acting on his or her behalf, apply the code in deciding whether to give consent to a prosecution. There are also certain offences that should only be taken to court with the consent of the Attorney-General. Prosecutors must follow current guidance when referring any such cases to the Attorney-General. Additionally, the Attorney-General will be kept informed of certain cases as part of his or her superintendence of the CPS and accountability to Parliament for its actions.

### 4. The Full Code Test

**E-5**

4.1 The full code test has two stages: (i) the evidential stage; followed by (ii) the public interest stage.

4.2 In most cases, prosecutors should only decide whether to prosecute after the investigation has been completed and after all the available evidence has been reviewed. However there will be cases where it is clear, prior to the collection and consideration of all the likely evidence, that the public interest does not require a prosecution. In these instances, prosecutors may decide that the case should not proceed further.

4.3 Prosecutors should only take such a decision when they are satisfied that the broad extent of the criminality has been determined and that they are able to make a fully informed assessment of the public interest. If prosecutors do not have sufficient information to take such a decision, the investigation should proceed and a decision taken later in accordance with the full code test set out in this section.

### The evidential stage

4.4 Prosecutors must be satisfied that there is sufficient evidence to provide a realistic prospect of    **E-6** conviction against each suspect on each charge. They must consider what the defence case may be, and how it is likely to affect the prospects of conviction. A case which does not pass the evidential stage must not proceed, no matter how serious or sensitive it may be.

4.5 The finding that there is a realistic prospect of conviction is based on the prosecutor's objective assessment of the evidence, including the impact of any defence and any other information that the suspect has put forward or on which he or she might rely. It means that an objective, impartial and reasonable jury or bench of magistrates or judge hearing a case alone, properly directed and acting in accordance with the law, is more likely than not to convict the defendant of the charge alleged. This is a different test from the one that the criminal courts themselves must apply. A court may only convict if it is sure that the defendant is guilty.

4.6 When deciding whether there is sufficient evidence to prosecute, prosecutors should ask themselves the following:

*Can the evidence be used in court?*

Prosecutors should consider whether there is any question over the admissibility of certain evidence. In doing so, prosecutors should assess:

    (a) the likelihood of that evidence being held as inadmissible by the court; and

    (b) the importance of that evidence in relation to the evidence as a whole.

*Is the evidence reliable?*

Prosecutors should consider whether there are any reasons to question the reliability of the evidence, including its accuracy or integrity.

*Is the evidence credible?*

Prosecutors should consider whether there are any reasons to doubt the credibility of the evidence.

### The public interest stage

4.7 In every case where there is sufficient evidence to justify a prosecution, prosecutors must go    **E-7** on to consider whether a prosecution is required in the public interest.

4.8 It has never been the rule that a prosecution will automatically take place once the evidential stage is met. A prosecution will usually take place unless the prosecutor is satisfied that there are public interest factors tending against prosecution which outweigh those tending in favour. In some cases the prosecutor may be satisfied that the public interest can be properly served by offering the offender the opportunity to have the matter dealt with by an out-of-court disposal rather than bringing a prosecution.

4.9 When deciding the public interest, prosecutors should consider each of the questions set out below in paragraphs 4.12(a) to (g) so as to identify and determine the relevant public interest factors tending for and against prosecution. These factors, together with any public interest factors set out in relevant guidance or policy issued by the DPP, should enable prosecutors to form an overall assessment of the public interest.

4.10 The explanatory text below each question in paragraphs 4.12(a) to (g) provides guidance to prosecutors when addressing each particular question and determining whether it identifies public interest factors for or against prosecution. The questions identified are not exhaustive, and not all the questions may be relevant in every case. The weight to be attached to each of the questions, and the factors identified, will also vary according to the facts and merits of each case.

4.11 It is quite possible that one public interest factor alone may outweigh a number of other factors which tend in the opposite direction. Although there may be public interest factors tending against prosecution in a particular case, prosecutors should consider whether nonetheless a prosecution should go ahead and those factors put to the court for consideration when sentence is passed.

4.12  Prosecutors should consider each of the following questions:

(a)  *How serious is the offence committed?*

The more serious the offence, the more likely it is that a prosecution is required. When deciding the level of seriousness of the offence committed, prosecutors should include amongst the factors for consideration the suspect's culpability and the harm to the victim by asking themselves the questions at (b) and (c).

(b)  *What is the level of culpability of the suspect?*

The greater the suspect's level of culpability, the more likely it is that a prosecution is required. Culpability is likely to be determined by the suspect's level of involvement; the extent to which the offending was premeditated and/or planned; whether they have previous criminal convictions and/or out-of-court disposals and any offending whilst on bail or whilst subject to a court order; whether the offending was or is likely to be continued, repeated or escalated; and the suspect's age or maturity (see paragraph (d) below for suspects under 18). Prosecutors should also have regard when considering culpability as to whether the suspect is, or was at the time of the offence, suffering from any significant mental or physical ill-health as in some circumstances this may mean that it is less likely that a prosecution is required. However, prosecutors will also need to consider how serious the offence was, whether it is likely to be repeated and the need to safeguard the public or those providing care to such persons.

(c)  *What are the circumstances of and the harm caused to the victim?*

The circumstances of the victim are highly relevant. The greater the vulnerability of the victim, the more likely it is that a prosecution is required. This includes where a position of trust or authority exists between the suspect and victim. A prosecution is also more likely if the offence has been committed against a victim who was at the time a person serving the public. Prosecutors must also have regard to whether the offence was motivated by any form of discrimination against the victim's ethnic or national origin, gender, disability, age, religion or belief, sexual orientation or gender identity; or the suspect demonstrated hostility towards the victim based on any of those characteristics. The presence of any such motivation or hostility will mean that it is more likely that prosecution is required. In deciding whether a prosecution is required in the public interest, prosecutors should take into account the views expressed by the victim about the impact that the offence has had. In appropriate cases, this may also include the views of the victim's family. Prosecutors also need to consider if a prosecution is likely to have an adverse effect on the victim's physical or mental health, always bearing in mind the seriousness of the offence. If there is evidence that prosecution is likely to have an adverse impact on the victim's health it may make a prosecution less likely, taking into account the victim's views. However, the CPS does not act for victims or their families in the same way as solicitors act for their clients, and prosecutors must form an overall view of the public interest.

(d)  *Was the suspect under the age of 18 at the time of the offence?*

The criminal justice system treats children and young people differently from adults and significant weight must be attached to the age of the suspect if they are a child or young person under 18. The best interests and welfare of the child or young person must be considered including whether a prosecution is likely to have an adverse impact on his or her future prospects that is disproportionate to the seriousness of the offending. Prosecutors must have regard to the principal aim of the youth justice system which is to prevent offending by children and young people. Prosecutors must also have regard to the obligations arising under the United Nations 1989 Convention on the Rights of the Child. As a starting point, the younger the suspect, the less likely it is that a prosecution is required. However, there may be circumstances which mean that notwithstanding the fact that the suspect is under 18, a prosecution is in the public interest. These include where the offence committed is serious, where the suspect's past record suggests that there are no suitable alternatives to prosecution, or where the absence of an admission means that out-of-court disposals which might have addressed the offending behaviour are not available.

(e)  *What is the impact on the community?*

The greater the impact of the offending on the community, the more likely it is that a prosecution is required. In considering this question, prosecutors should have regard to how community is an inclusive term and is not restricted to communities defined by location.

(f)  *Is prosecution a proportionate response?*

Prosecutors should also consider whether prosecution is proportionate to the likely outcome, and in so doing the following may be relevant to the case under consideration:

- the cost to the CPS and the wider criminal justice system, especially where it could be regarded as excessive when weighed against any likely penalty (prosecutors should not decide the public interest on the basis of this factor alone; it is essential that regard is also given to the public interest factors identified when considering the other questions in paragraphs 4.12(a) to (g), but cost is a relevant factor when making an overall assessment of the public interest);
- cases should be capable of being prosecuted in a way that is consistent with principles of effective case management; for example, in a case involving multiple suspects, prosecution might be reserved for the main participants in order to avoid excessively long and complex proceedings.

(g) *Do sources of information require protecting?*

In cases where public interest immunity does not apply, special care should be taken when proceeding with a prosecution where details may need to be made public that could harm sources of information, international relations or national security. It is essential that such cases are kept under continuing review.

## 5. The Threshold Test

5.1 The threshold test may only be applied where the suspect presents a substantial bail risk and not all the evidence is available at the time when he or she must be released from custody unless charged.    **E-8**

### When the threshold test may be applied

5.2 Prosecutors must determine whether the following conditions are met:    **E-8a**

   (a) there is insufficient evidence currently available to apply the evidential stage of the full code test; and

   (b) there are reasonable grounds for believing that further evidence will become available within a reasonable period; and

   (c) the seriousness or the circumstances of the case justifies the making of an immediate charging decision; and

   (d) there are continuing substantial grounds to object to bail in accordance with the Bail Act 1976 and in all the circumstances of the case it is proper to do so.

5.3 Where any of the above conditions is not met, the threshold test cannot be applied and the suspect cannot be charged. The custody officer must determine whether the person may continue to be detained or be released on bail, with or without conditions.

5.4 There are two parts to the evidential consideration of the threshold test.

*The first part of the threshold test—is there reasonable suspicion?*

5.5 Prosecutors must be satisfied that there is at least a reasonable suspicion that the person to be charged has committed the offence.

5.6 In determining this, prosecutors must consider the evidence then available. This may take the form of witness statements, material or other information, provided the prosecutor is satisfied that:

   (a) it is relevant; and

   (b) it is capable of being put into an admissible format for presentation in court; and

   (c) it would be used in the case.

5.7 If satisfied on this the prosecutor should then consider the second part of the threshold test.

*The second part of the threshold test – can further evidence be gathered to provide a realistic prospect of conviction?*

5.8 Prosecutors must be satisfied that there are reasonable grounds for believing that the continuing investigation will provide further evidence, within a reasonable period of time, so that all the evidence together is capable of establishing a realistic prospect of conviction in accordance with the full code test.

5.9 The further evidence must be identifiable and not merely speculative.

5.10 In reaching this decision prosecutors must consider:

   (a) the nature, extent and admissibility of any likely further evidence and the impact it will have on the case;

   (b) the charges that all the evidence will support;

   (c) the reasons why the evidence is not already available;

(d) the time required to obtain the further evidence and whether any consequential delay is reasonable in all the circumstances.

5.11 If both parts of the threshold test are satisfied, prosecutors must apply the public interest stage of the full code test based on the information available at that time.

### Reviewing the threshold test

**E-9**    5.12 A decision to charge under the threshold test must be kept under review. The evidence must be regularly assessed to ensure that the charge is still appropriate and that continued objection to bail is justified. The full code test must be applied as soon as is reasonably practicable and in any event before the expiry of any applicable custody time limit.

### 6. SELECTION OF CHARGES

**E-10**    6.1 Prosecutors should select charges which:

(a) reflect the seriousness and extent of the offending supported by the evidence;

(b) give the court adequate powers to sentence and impose appropriate post-conviction orders; and

(c) enable the case to be presented in a clear and simple way.

6.2 This means that prosecutors may not always choose or continue with the most serious charge where there is a choice.

6.3 Prosecutors should never go ahead with more charges than are necessary just to encourage a defendant to plead guilty to a few. In the same way, they should never go ahead with a more serious charge just to encourage a defendant to plead guilty to a less serious one.

6.4 Prosecutors should not change the charge simply because of the decision made by the court or the defendant about where the case will be heard.

6.5 Prosecutors must take account of any relevant change in circumstances as the case progresses after charge.

### 7. OUT-OF-COURT DISPOSALS

**E-11**    7.1 An out-of-court disposal may take the place of a prosecution in court if it is an appropriate response to the offender and/or the seriousness and consequences of the offending.

7.2 Prosecutors must follow any relevant guidance when asked to advise on or authorise a simple caution, a conditional caution, any appropriate regulatory proceedings, a punitive or civil penalty, or other disposal. They should ensure that the appropriate evidential standard for the specific out-of-court disposal is met including, where required, a clear admission of guilt, and that the public interest would be properly served by such a disposal.

### 8. MODE OF TRIAL

**E-12**    8.1 Prosecutors must have regard to the current guidelines on sentencing and allocation when making submissions to the magistrates' court about where the defendant should be tried.

8.2 Speed must never be the only reason for asking for a case to stay in the magistrates' court. But prosecutors should consider the effect of any likely delay if a case is sent to the Crown Court, and the possible effect on any victim or witness if the case is delayed.

### Venue for trial in cases involving youths

8.3 Prosecutors must bear in mind that youths should be tried in the youth court wherever possible. It is the court which is best designed to meet their specific needs. A trial of a youth in the Crown Court should be reserved for the most serious cases or where the interests of justice require a youth to be jointly tried with an adult.

### 9. ACCEPTING GUILTY PLEAS

**E-12a**    9.1 Defendants may want to plead guilty to some, but not all, of the charges. Alternatively, they may want to plead guilty to a different, possibly less serious, charge because they are admitting only part of the crime.

9.2 Prosecutors should only accept the defendant's plea if they think the court is able to pass a sentence that matches the seriousness of the offending, particularly where there are aggravating features. Prosecutors must never accept a guilty plea just because it is convenient.

9.3 In considering whether the pleas offered are acceptable, prosecutors should ensure that the interests and, where possible, the views of the victim, or in appropriate cases the views of the victim's family, are taken into account when deciding whether it is in the public interest to accept the plea. However, the decision rests with the prosecutor.

9.4 It must be made clear to the court on what basis any plea is advanced and accepted. In cases where a defendant pleads guilty to the charges but on the basis of facts that are different from the prosecution case, and where this may significantly affect sentence, the court should be invited to hear evidence to determine what happened, and then sentence on that basis.

9.5 Where a defendant has previously indicated that he or she will ask the court to take an offence into consideration when sentencing, but then declines to admit that offence at court, prosecutors will consider whether a prosecution is required for that offence. Prosecutors should explain to the defence advocate and the court that the prosecution of that offence may be subject to further review, in consultation with the police or other investigators wherever possible.

9.6 Particular care must be taken when considering pleas which would enable the defendant to avoid the imposition of a mandatory minimum sentence. When pleas are offered, prosecutors must also bear in mind the fact that ancillary orders can be made with some offences but not with others.

### 10. RECONSIDERING A PROSECUTION DECISION

10.1 People should be able to rely on decisions taken by the CPS. Normally, if the CPS tells a **E-12b** suspect or defendant that there will not be a prosecution, or that the prosecution has been stopped, the case will not start again. But occasionally there are reasons why the CPS will overturn a decision not to prosecute or to deal with the case by way of an out-of-court disposal or when it will restart the prosecution, particularly if the case is serious.

10.2 These reasons include:
   (a) cases where a new look at the original decision shows that it was wrong and, in order to maintain confidence in the criminal justice system, a prosecution should be brought despite the earlier decision;
   (b) cases which are stopped so that more evidence which is likely to become available in the fairly near future can be collected and prepared; in these cases, the prosecutor will tell the defendant that the prosecution may well start again;
   (c) cases which are stopped because of a lack of evidence but where more significant evidence is discovered later; and
   (d) cases involving a death in which a review following the findings of an inquest concludes that a prosecution should be brought, notwithstanding any earlier decision not to prosecute.

© Crown Copyright 2013

## C. AUTHORITIES

### Charging of youths

Whereas the code for crown prosecutors requires consideration to be given to the interests of a **E-12c** child or young person when deciding whether it is in the public interest to prosecute (see now para. 4.12(d), *ante*, E-7), there is no requirement that a crown prosecutor should obtain a risk assessment from the youth offending services or that he should contact the potential defendant's school: *R. (A.) v. South Yorkshire Police and CPS*, 171 J.P. 465, DC.

In *D. and B. v. Commr of Police for the Metropolis, CPS, Croydon JJ.* [2008] A.C.D. 47, DC, it was held that it was permissible for a crown prosecutor to decide that the combination of the seriousness of an offence and the public interest warranted prosecution, despite the fact that the particular circumstances of the offence would normally, in accordance with the guidance issued under section 65 of the CDA 1998, be such as to justify only a final warning.

### Charging victims of human trafficking

Where it is possible that a defendant or potential defendant is a victim of human trafficking, a **E-12d** prosecutor should take cognisance of the CPS guidance on (i) the prosecution of defendants charged with immigration offences who might be victims of trafficking, and (ii) the prosecution of young offenders charged with offences who might be such victims; in particular, under (i), when deciding whether to prosecute, or to continue to prosecute, a "credible trafficked victim" for immigration offences, prosecutors should consider whether this would serve the public interest; and under (ii), a case should be discontinued on evidential grounds where there is clear evidence that a youth has a credible defence of duress, but, if the evidence is less certain, further details should be sought from the police and youth offender teams; the defence, on the other hand, should make inquiries wherever there is credible material showing that the defendant might have been a trafficked victim, especially if the client is young; as a signatory to the Council of Europe Convention on Action against Trafficking in Human Beings, the United Kingdom is required to identify and protect victims of trafficking, and, whereas the CPS guidance supports the purpose of the convention, a trial which had failed to have proper regard to it was not fair, either under the principles of the common law or under the principles enshrined in the ECHR: *R. v. O.*, *The Times*, October 2, 2008, CA ([2008] EWCA Crim. 2835).

*R. v. O.* and the issues arising from it were further considered in *R. v. M. (L.), B. (M.) and G. (D.)*; *R. v. Tabot*; *R. v. Tijani* [2011] 1 Cr.App.R. 12, CA. It was held that one way in which the duty under Article 26 of the Council of Europe Convention (to avoid the imposition of penalties on victims of human trafficking for their involvement in unlawful activities to the extent that they were compelled to become so involved) is met in England and Wales, is by means of the guidance given to prosecutors considering whether charges should be brought against those who are or may be victims of trafficking (the court pointed out that whilst the guidance is now set out in the context of immigration offences only, it should be taken to apply whatever the nature of the allegation). The effect of the CPS's guidance, according to the court, is to require of prosecutors a three-stage exercise, asking, first, whether there is reason to believe that the person has been trafficked, secondly, whether there is clear evidence of a common law defence (in which case, any proceedings will be discontinued on evidential grounds) and, thirdly, where there is no such evidence, but the offence may have been committed as a result of compulsion arising from the trafficking, whether the public interest requires a prosecution. It was said that Article 26 does not require a blanket immunity from prosecution for trafficked victims, and that there will normally be no reason not to prosecute a victim of trafficking if the offence appears to have been committed out-with any reasonable nexus of compulsion occasioned by the trafficking. The court said that material considerations for the prosecutor when deciding whether to pursue a prosecution will be the gravity of the offence, the degree of continuing compulsion and the alternatives reasonably available to the defendant. As to this case, see also § 17-119 in the main work.

*R. v. O.* and *R. v. M. (L.), B. (M.) and G. (D.)*; *R. v. Tabot*; *R. v. Tijani* were further considered in *R. v. N. (A.)*; *R. v. Le* [2012] 1 Cr.App.R. 35, CA. It was held that: (i) implementation of Article 26 is normally achieved by the proper exercise of the prosecutorial discretion which enables the Crown, however strong the evidence, to decide that it would be inappropriate to prosecute, or to continue with the prosecution of, a defendant who is unable to advance duress as a defence, but who falls within the protective ambit of that article; this requires a judgment to be made in the light of all the available evidence; the responsibility is not that of the court but of the prosecution; but the court may intervene if its process is abused by using the "ultimate sanction" of a stay; the burden of establishing an improper exercise of the discretion rests on the defendant; that the context is the United Kingdom's convention obligation does not involve the creation of any new principles; apart from the specific jurisdiction to stay proceedings, the court may also, in the exercise of its sentencing responsibilities, implement Article 26 in the language of the article itself, by discharging the defendant absolutely or conditionally; (ii) the only publication likely to be relevant to an inquiry into an alleged abuse is the CPS's guidance on human trafficking and smuggling as it was in force at the time when the relevant decisions were made; unless it is to be argued that the guidance itself is open to question because it has failed to keep itself regularly updated in light of developing knowledge, for the purposes of the court considering an alleged abuse for which the prosecution are responsible, it is that guidance that should be the starting, and in the overwhelming majority of cases, the finishing point; (iii) expert evidence is unlikely to assist on the issue of the correctness of the decision to prosecute; (iv) a defendant has one opportunity to give his instructions to his legal advisers; it is only most exceptionally that the court would, on appeal, consider it appropriate to allow a defendant to advance fresh instructions about the facts; and there is no special category of exceptionality in the context of Article 26; and (v) an abuse argument founded on the convention that is advanced long after conviction is most unlikely to succeed on the basis that subsequent events show that, if the decision whether to prosecute were to be taken now, the result might have been different from the decision actually taken in the light of the standards and guidance existing at the time it was taken.

These issues were further considered in *R. v. L. (C.)*; *R. v. N. (H.V.)*; *R. v. N. (T.H.)*; *R. v. T.*

*(H.D.) (Children's Commr for England and Equality and Human Rights Commission Intervening)* [2013] 2 Cr.App.R. 23, CA. It was held that: (i) whereas Article 8 of European Parliament and Council Directive 2011/36/EU obliges member states to "take the necessary measures to ensure that competent national authorities are entitled not to prosecute or impose penalties on victims of trafficking ... for their involvement in criminal activities which they have been compelled to commit as a direct consequence of being subjected" to trafficking, the courts will give effect to this obligation by reviewing decisions to prosecute, staying inappropriate prosecutions and discharging defendants where prosecution was appropriate but punishment inappropriate; as to the review of the decision to prosecute, this is no mere *Wednesbury* review (*Associated Picture Houses Ltd v. Wednesbury Corporation* [1948] 1 K.B. 223, CA); the court must reach its own conclusion on the evidence presented to it; (ii) if it is found that the defendant is a victim of trafficking, the next question is the extent to which the offences with which he is charged were integral to, or consequent on, the exploitation of which he was the victim; in some cases the facts will show that he was under levels of compulsion that mean that, in reality, culpability was extinguished; if so, a stay is likely to be granted; in other cases, more likely in the case of a defendant who is no longer a child (18 plus), culpability may be diminished but nevertheless be significant; for these individuals, prosecution may well be appropriate, with due allowance to be made in any sentencing decision for their diminished culpability; in yet other cases, the fact that the defendant was a victim of trafficking will provide no more than a colourable excuse for criminality that is unconnected to and does not arise from their victimisation; (iii) as to the question whether the defendant was indeed a victim of trafficking, where there has been a referral to one of the two competent authorities (the U.K. Border Agency and the U.K. Human Tracking Centre), if their conclusion is that the defendant is a victim of trafficking, the court is likely to adopt that view although it is not bound by it, as it is the court that has the ultimate responsibility for making the decision with all the relevant evidence bearing on the issues of trafficking, exploitation, age and culpability being addressed; while there is no obligation to seek assistance from experts in the field, the court may adjourn for further information on the subject, and indeed may require the assistance of various authorities; and (iv) where the defendant is under 18, his best interests are not the only consideration, but they are a primary consideration; and where there is any doubt about whether or not the defendant is under that age, "due inquiry" must be made (CYPA 1933, s.99(1) (§ 19-412 in the main work)); this requires much more than superficial observation of the defendant in the dock; the court must be provided with all the relevant evidence that bears on the issue of age; if, at the end of the inquiry, his age remains in doubt and there are reasons to believe that he is under the age of 18, he must be presumed to be under that age.

**The full code test/evidential stage**

When applying the "realistic prospect of conviction" test, a prosecutor should adopt a "merits based" approach, imagining himself to be the fact finder and asking himself, whether, on balance, the evidence is sufficient to merit a conviction, taking into account what he knows about the defence case, rather than a predictive "bookmaker's" approach, based on past experience of similar cases; questions of how a jury are likely to see a case are not relevant at this stage but at a later stage, under the public interest test in paragraphs 5.6 to 5.13 of the code: *R. (F.B.) v. DPP* [2009] 1 Cr.App.R. 38, DC. As to this case, see also §§ 1-337, 16-40a in the main work. **E-12e**

## II. LEGAL GUIDANCE AND CHARGING STANDARDS

Apart from the code for crown prosecutors, the CPS has prepared legal guidance to prosecutors and caseworkers in relation to many criminal offences and procedural issues. It has never been suggested that such guidance has the force of law, or even parity of standing with the code. It is merely, in the words of the CPS website (where it is available to the public), "an aid to guide crown prosecutors and associate prosecutors in the use of their discretion in making decisions in cases", which "does not create any rights enforceable at law, in any legal proceedings", and is subject to the principles as set out in the code for crown prosecutors. **E-13**

Incorporated within the guidance are various "charging standards" for various offences or groups of offences, such as offences against the person, driving offences, drug offences, public order offences and theft. They contain a mixture of propositions of law (as to the ingredients of **E-14** the various offences, maximum penalties, available alternative verdicts, *etc.*) and guidance as to the various factors that should be taken into consideration in deciding which offence to charge. The standards emphasise that they:

    (a) are not to be used in the determination of any pre-charge decision, such as the decision to arrest;

    (b) do not override any guidance issued on the use of appropriate alternative forms of disposal short of charge, such as cautioning;

    (c) do not override the principles set out in the code for crown prosecutors;

    (d) do not override the need for consideration to be given in every case as to whether a charge or prosecution is in the public interest;

    (e) do not override particular policy guidance involving hate crimes; and

    (f) do not remove the need for each case to be considered on its individual merits or fetter the discretion of the police to charge and the CPS to prosecute the most appropriate offence depending on the particular facts of the case in question.

The following recitation of general charging principles is common to all the standards:

    (a) the charge or charges preferred should accurately reflect the extent of the defendant's involvement and responsibility, thereby allowing the courts the discretion to sentence appropriately;

    (b) the choice of charges should ensure the clear and simple presentation of the case, particularly where there is more than one defendant;

    (c) it is wrong to encourage a defendant to plead guilty to a few charges by selecting more charges than are necessary;

    (d) it is wrong to select a more serious charge which is not supported by the evidence in order to encourage a plea of guilty to a lesser allegation.

## III. THE ROLE AND RESPONSIBILITIES OF THE PROSECUTION ADVOCATE

### Foreword

E-15    The prosecution advocate plays an important public role and as such may be considered a cornerstone of an open and fair criminal justice system. The principles so well articulated by Farquharson L.J. and his committee as to the role of the prosecution advocate have served us well since they were published in 1986. However, the time has come for new guidance which, whilst building on the established principles, reflects the changes that have occurred in the criminal courts, at the Bar and within the Crown Prosecution Service over recent years.

    I welcome and commend the new Guidelines which, whilst not legally binding unless expressly approved by the Court of Appeal, nonetheless provide important practical guidance for practitioners involved in the prosecution process.

    Lord Woolf C.J.

### Introduction

E-16    The work undertaken in 1986 by the committee chaired by Farquharson L.J. has, for over 15 years, provided valuable guidance as to role [*sic*] of the prosecution advocate and their relationship with the Crown Prosecution Service (CPS).

    However, the ever-evolving criminal justice system, changes at the Bar and developments in the CPS brought about by the implementation of Sir Iain Glidewell's Review, mean that the environment in which we all operate has radically changed since the original report was published.

    Whilst the principles established by Farquharson L.J.'s committee have been enormously helpful and will continue to apply, the time has come for new guidance that reflects the changes and emphasises the new relationship that is developing between CPS Areas and the local Bar.

    The new Guidelines have therefore been developed to take account of the changes and are the result of the Bar and CPS working in partnership and in consultation with the judiciary, Bar Council and Law Society.

We commend the Guidelines as providing valuable guidance and a framework within which the Bar and the CPS can work effectively together.

Lord Goldsmith Q.C., Attorney General

David Calvert-Smith Q.C., Director of Public Prosecutions

### 1. Pre-trial preparation

**Farquharson**

(a) *It is the duty of prosecution counsel to read the Instructions delivered to him expeditiously and to advise or confer with those instructing him on all aspects of the case well before its commencement.* **E-17**

1.1 The Crown Prosecution Service (CPS) will deliver instructions at a stage in the proceedings **E-18** that allows sufficient time for the prosecution advocate adequately to consider, prepare and advise on the evidence before the court hearing or draft/agree the indictment.

1.2 Where a CPS higher court advocate represents the prosecution at a Plea and Directions Hearing (PDH), the CPS will deliver instructions to the trial advocate no later than 10 working days after the date of the PDH.

1.3 The CPS will deliver instructions which:

    i. address the issues in the case including any strategic decisions that have been or may need to be made;

    ii. identify relevant case law;

    iii. explain the basis and rationale of any decision made in relation to the disclosure of unused material;

    iv. where practical, provide specific guidance or indicate parameters on acceptable plea(s); and

    v. where a case is an appeal either to the Crown Court from the magistrates' court or is before the Court of Appeal, Divisional Court or House of Lords, address the issues raised in the notice of appeal, case stated, application for judicial review or petition.

**Action on receipt of instructions**

1.4 On receipt of instructions the prosecution advocate will consider the papers and advise the **E-19** CPS, ordinarily in writing, or orally in cases of urgency where:

    i. the prosecution advocate forms a different view to that expressed by the CPS (or where applicable a previous prosecution advocate) on acceptability of plea;

    ii. the indictment as preferred requires amendment;

    iii. additional evidence is required;

    iv. there is an evidential deficiency (which cannot be addressed by the obtaining of further evidence) and, applying the Code for Crown Prosecutors, there is no longer a realistic prospect of conviction; or the prosecution advocate believes that it is not in the public interest to continue the prosecution;

    v. in order to expedite and simplify proceedings certain formal admissions should be made;

    vi. the prosecution advocate, having reviewed previous disclosure decisions, disagrees with a decision that has been made; or is not satisfied that he or she is in possession of all relevant documentation; or considers that he or she has not been fully instructed regarding disclosure matters;

    vii. a case conference is required (particularly where there is a sensitive issue, *e.g.* informant/ PII/ disclosure etc);

    viii. the presentation of the case to the court requires special preparation of material for the jury or presentational aids.

1.5 The prosecution advocate will endeavour to respond within five working days of receiving **E-20** instructions, or within such period as may be specified or agreed where the case is substantial or the issues complex.

1.6 Where the prosecution advocate is to advise on a specific aspect of the case other than 1.4 (i-viii), the advocate should contact the CPS and agree a realistic timescale within which advice is to be provided.

1.7 The prosecution advocate will inform the CPS without delay where the advocate is unlikely to be available to undertake the prosecution or advise within the relevant timescale.

1.8 When returning a brief, the advocate originally instructed must ensure that the case is in good order and should discuss outstanding issues or potential difficulties with the advocate receiving the brief. Where the newly instructed advocate disagrees with a decision or opinion reached by the original advocate, the CPS should be informed so that the matter can be discussed.

### Case summaries

**E-21**       1.9 When a draft case summary is prepared by the CPS, the prosecution advocate will consider the summary and either agree the contents or advise the CPS of any proposed amendment.

1.10 In cases where the prosecution advocate is instructed to settle the case summary or schedules, the document(s) will be prepared and submitted to the CPS without delay.

### Case management plan

**E-22**       1.11 On receipt of a case management plan the prosecution advocate, having considered the papers, will contact the Crown Prosecutor within seven days, or such period as may be specified or agreed where the case is substantial or the issues complex, to discuss and agree the plan. The plan will be maintained and regularly reviewed to reflect the progress of the case.

### Keeping the prosecution advocate informed

**E-23**       1.12 The CPS will inform the prosecution advocate of developments in the case without delay and, where a decision is required which may materially affect the conduct and presentation of the case, will consult with the prosecution advocate prior to that decision.

1.3 Where the CPS is advised by the defence of a plea(s) of guilty or there are developments which suggest that offering no evidence on an indictment or count therein is an appropriate course, the matter should always be discussed with the prosecution advocate without delay unless to do so would be wholly impracticable.

### Victims and witnesses

**E-24**       1.14 When a decision whether or not to prosecute is based on the public interest, the CPS will always consider the consequences of that decision for the victim and will take into account any views expressed by the victim or the victim's family.

1.15 The prosecution advocate will follow agreed procedures and guidance on the care and treatment of victims and witnesses, particularly those who may be vulnerable or have special needs.

### Appeals

**E-25**       1.16 Where the prosecution advocate forms a different view to that expressed by the CPS on the conduct/approach to the appeal, the advocate should advise the CPS within FIVE working days of receiving instructions or such period as may be specified or agreed where the case is substantial or the issues complex.

### PDH and other preliminary hearings

**E-26**       1.17 The principles and procedures applying to trials as set out in the following paragraphs will be equally applicable where the prosecution advocate is conducting a PDH or other preliminary hearing.

## 2. Withdrawal of instructions

### Farquharson

**E-27**       (b) *A solicitor who has briefed counsel to prosecute may withdraw his instructions before the commencement of the trial up to the point when it becomes impracticable to do so, if he disagrees with the advice given by Counsel or for any other proper professional reason.*

2.1 The CPS will consult and take all reasonable steps to resolve any issue or disagreement and will only consider withdrawing instructions from a prosecution advocate as a last resort.

2.2 If the prosecution advocate disagrees with any part of his or her instructions the advocate should contact the responsible Crown Prosecutor to discuss the matter. Until the disagreement has been resolved the matter will remain confidential and must not be discussed by the prosecution advocate with any other party to the proceedings.

### "Proper professional reason"

**E-28**       2.3 The prosecution advocate will keep the CPS informed of any personal concerns, reservations or ethical issues that the advocate considers have the potential to lead to possible conflict with his or her instructions.

2.4 Where the CPS identifies the potential for professional embarrassment or has concerns about the prosecution advocate's ability or experience to present the case effectively to the court, the CPS reserves the right to withdraw instructions.

### Timing

2.5 It is often difficult to define when, in the course of a prosecution it becomes impracticable to   **E-29** withdraw instructions as circumstances will vary according to the case. The nature of the case, its complexity, witness availability and the view of the court will often be factors that will influence the decision.

2.6 In the majority of prosecutions it will not be practicable to withdraw instructions once the judge has called the case before the court as a preliminary step to the swearing of the jury.

2.7 If instructions are withdrawn, the prosecution advocate will be informed in writing and reasons will be given.

2.8 Instructions may only be withdrawn by or with the consent of the Chief Crown Prosecutor, Assistant Chief Crown Prosecutor, Head of a CPS Trials Unit or, in appropriate cases, Head of a CPS Criminal Justice Unit.

2.9 In relation to cases prosecuted by the CPS Casework Directorate, the decision may only be taken by the Director Casework or Head of Division.

### 3. Presentation and conduct

#### Farquharson

(c) *While he remains instructed it is for counsel to take all necessary decisions in the presentation and general*   **E-30** *conduct of the prosecution.*

3.1 The statement at 3(c) applies when the prosecution advocate is conducting the trial, PDH or any other preliminary hearing, but is subject to the principles and procedures relating to matters of policy set out in section 4 below.

#### Disclosure of material

3.2 Until the conclusion of the trial the prosecution advocate and CPS have a continuing duty to   **E-31** keep under review decisions regarding disclosure. The prosecution advocate should in every case specifically consider whether he or she can satisfactorily discharge the duty of continuing review on the basis of the material supplied already, or whether it is necessary to inspect further material or to reconsider material already inspected.

3.3 Disclosure of material must always follow the established law and procedure. Unless consultation is impracticable or cannot be achieved without a delay to the hearing, it is desirable that the CPS, and where appropriate the disclosure officer are consulted over disclosure decisions.

### 4. Policy decisions

#### Farquharson

(d) *Where matters of policy[1] fall to be decided after the point indicated in (b) above (including offering no*   **E-32** *evidence on the indictment or on a particular count, or on the acceptance of pleas to lesser counts), it is the duty of Counsel to consult his Instructing Solicitor/Crown Prosecutor whose views at this stage are of crucial importance.*

(e) *In the rare case where counsel and his instructing solicitor are unable to agree on a matter of policy, it is, subject to (g) below, for prosecution counsel to make the necessary decisions.*

#### Policy issues arising at trial

4.1 The prosecution advocate should alert the CPS at the first opportunity if a matter of policy is   **E-33** likely to arise.

4.2 The prosecution advocate must not give an indication or undertaking which binds the prosecution without first discussing the issue with the CPS.

#### CPS representation at Crown Court

4.3 Whenever possible, an experienced Crown Prosecutor will be available at the Crown Court to   **E-34** discuss and agree any issue involving the conduct or progress of the case.

---

[1] "Policy" decisions should be understood as referring to non-evidential decisions on: the acceptance of pleas of guilty to lesser counts or groups of counts or available alternatives; offering no evidence on particular counts; consideration of a retrial; whether to lodge an appeal; certification of a point of law; and the withdrawal of the prosecution as a whole.

4.4 When it is not possible to provide a Crown Prosecutor at court, an experienced caseworker will attend and facilitate communication between the prosecution advocate and the Crown Prosecutor having responsibility for the case.

4.5 In exceptional circumstances where it is not possible to contact a Crown Prosecutor, the prosecution advocate should ask the court to adjourn the hearing for a realistic period in order to consult with the CPS. Where an adjournment is refused, the prosecution advocate may make the decision but should record his or her reasons in writing.

### Referral to senior CPS representative

4.6 Where an issue remains unresolved following consultation with a Crown Prosecutor; or where the case/issue under consideration is substantial, sensitive or complex; or the prosecution advocate disagrees with the advice of the Crown Prosecutor, the matter may be referred to the Chief Crown Prosecutor, the Director Casework or to a senior Crown Prosecutor with delegated authority to act on their behalf.

4.7 In order to ensure consultation takes place at the highest level appropriate to the circumstances and nature of the case, the court should be asked to adjourn if necessary. When an adjournment is sought, the facts leading to the application should be placed before the court only in so far as they are relevant to that application.

4.8 Where a Chief Crown Prosecutor has been directly involved in the decision making process and the issue remains unresolved, the matter may be referred to the Director of Public Prosecutions.

### Farquharson

(f) *Where counsel has taken a decision on a matter of policy with which his Instructing Solicitor has not agreed, then it would be appropriate for the Attorney General to require Counsel to submit to him a written report of all the circumstances, including his reasons for disagreeing with those who instruct him.*

4.9 It will only be in exceptional circumstances that the Attorney General will require a written report. The prosecution advocate will first discuss the decision with the Chief Crown Prosecutor or the Director, Casework. Where, by agreement, the issue remains one that either party considers should be drawn to the attention of the Director of Public Prosecutions the prosecution advocate will, on request, provide a written report for submission to the Director of Public Prosecutions. If he considers it appropriate to do so, the Director of Public Prosecutions may refer the matter to the Attorney General.

4.10 Where there has been a disagreement on a matter of policy, provided that the CPS is satisfied that the prosecution advocate followed the principles set out in this document, the professional codes of conduct and was not *Wednesbury* unreasonable, the CPS will not apply sanctions in respect of any future work solely as a result of the decision in a particular case.

### 5. Change of advice

### Farquharson

(g) *When counsel has had the opportunity to prepare his brief and to confer with those instructing him, but at the last moment before trial unexpectedly advises that the case should not proceed or that pleas to lesser offences should be accepted, and his Instructing Solicitor does not accept such advice, counsel should apply for an adjournment if instructed so to do.*

5.1 The CPS and the prosecution advocate should agree a period of adjournment that would allow a newly instructed advocate to prepare for trial. The period should be realistic and acknowledge that in such circumstances a case conference will usually be required.

5.2 The facts leading to the application for the adjournment should be placed before the court only in so far as they are relevant to that application.

### 6. Prosecution advocate's role in decision making at trial

### Farquharson

(h) *Subject to the above, it is for prosecution counsel to decide whether to offer no evidence on a particular count or on the indictment as a whole and whether to accept pleas to a lesser count or counts.*

6.1 The prosecution advocate may ask the defence advocate as to whether a plea will be forthcoming but at this initial stage should not suggest or indicate a plea that might be considered acceptable to the prosecution before a plea is offered.

6.2 Where the defence advocate subsequently offers details of a plea, the prosecution advocate may discuss the matter with a view to establishing an acceptable plea that reflects the defendant's criminality and provides the court with sufficient powers to sentence appropriately.

**Responsibility of prosecution advocate to consult**

6.3 Where the prosecution advocate forms the view that the appropriate course is to accept a plea **E-40** before proceedings commence or continue, or to offer no evidence on the indictment or any part of it, the prosecution advocate should:

  i. whenever practicable, speak with the victim or victim's family attending court to explain the position;
  ii. ensure that the interests of the victim or any views expressed by the victim or victim's family are taken into account as part of the decision making process; and
  iii. keep the victim or victim's family attending court informed and explain decisions as they are made.

6.4 Where appropriate the prosecution advocate may seek an adjournment of the court hearing in order to facilitate discussion with the victim or victim's family.

6.5 The prosecution advocate should always comply with paragraph 6.3 and, where practicable, discuss the matter with the CPS before informing the defence advocate or the court that a plea is acceptable.

6.6 Where the defendant indicates an acceptable plea, unless the issue is simple, the defence should reduce the basis of the plea to writing. The prosecution advocate should show the CPS any written record relating to the plea and agree with the CPS the basis on which the case will be opened to the court.

6.7 It is the responsibility of the prosecution advocate to ensure that the defence advocate is aware of the basis on which the plea is accepted by the prosecution and the way in which the prosecution case will be opened to the court.

6.8 It will not be necessary for the prosecution advocate to consult the CPS where the plea or course of action accords with the written instructions received from the CPS, although paragraph 6.3 may still apply.

**Prosecution advocate's role in sentencing**

6.9 The prosecution advocate should always draw the court's attention to any matters, including **E-41** aggravating or mitigating features, that might affect sentence. Additionally, the advocate should be in a position to assist the court, if requested, with any statutory provisions or sentencing guidelines and should always draw attention to potential sentencing errors.

6.10 Where a discussion on plea and sentence takes place, the prosecution advocate must adhere to the Attorney General's Guidelines on the Acceptance of Pleas published on 7 December 2000.

### 7. Seeking judicial approval

**Farquharson**

(i) *If prosecution counsel invites the Judge to approve the course he is proposing to take, then he must abide by* **E-42** *the judge's decision.*

7.1 A discussion with the judge about the acceptability of a plea or conduct of the case should be held in the presence of the defendant unless exceptional circumstances apply.[2]

7.2 In exceptional circumstances, where the prosecution advocate considers it appropriate to communicate with the judge or seek the judge's view in chambers, the CPS should be consulted before such a step is taken.

7.3 Where discussions take place in chambers it is the responsibility of the prosecution advocate to remind the judge, if necessary, that an independent record must always be kept.

7.4 The prosecution advocate should also make a full note of such an event, recording all decisions and comments. This note should be made available to the CPS.

**Farquharson**

(j) *If prosecution counsel does not invite the judge's approval of his decision it is open to the judge to express* **E-43**

---

[2] For the purposes of these guidelines, "exceptional circumstances" would include the following:
  (i) Where there is material or information which should not be made public, *e.g.* a police text, or for some other compelling reason such as a defendant or witness suffering, unkown to them, from a serious or terminal illness; or
  (ii) There are sensitivities surrounding a prosecution decision or proposed action which need to be explained in chambers with a view to obtaining judicial approval. Such approval may be given in open court where it is necessary to explain a prosecution decision or action in order to maintain public confidence in the criminal justice system.

*his dissent with the course proposed and invite counsel to reconsider the matter with those instructing him, but having done so, the final decision remains with counsel.*

7.5 Where a judge expresses a view based on the evidence or public interest, the CPS will carry out a further review of the case.

7.6 The prosecution advocate will inform the CPS in a case where the judge has expressed a dissenting view and will agree the action to be taken. Where there is no CPS representative at court, the prosecution advocate will provide a note of the judge's comments.

7.7 The prosecution advocate will ensure that the judge is aware of all factors that have a bearing on the prosecution decision to adopt a particular course. Where there is a difference of opinion between the prosecution advocate and the CPS the judge will be informed as to the nature of the disagreement.

**Farquharson**

E-44
(k) *In an extreme case where the judge is of the opinion that the course proposed by counsel would lead to serious injustice, he may decline to proceed with the case until counsel has consulted with either the Director or the Attorney General as may be appropriate.*

7.8 As a preliminary step, the prosecution advocate will discuss the judge's observations with the Chief Crown Prosecutor in an attempt to resolve the issue. Where the issue remains unresolved the Director of Public Prosecutions will be consulted. In exceptional circumstances the Director of Public Prosecutions may consult the Attorney General.

E-45
**Note:** These Guidelines are subject to the Code of Conduct of the Bar of England and Wales (barrister advocates) and The Law Society's The Guide to the Professional Conduct of Solicitors (solicitor advocates). Whilst reference is made in the guidelines to the CPS and levels of authority within the Service, the guidelines may be adopted as best practice, with consequential amendments to levels of authority, by other prosecuting authorities.

These Guidelines may be amended at any time and copyright is waived.

These Guidelines are also available on the CPS Website: www.cps.gov.uk.

# APPENDIX F
# The Channel Tunnel

# Introduction

The starting point is the Treaty between the United Kingdom of Great Britain and Northern    **F-1**
Ireland and the French Republic concerning the Construction and Operation by Private Concessionaires of a Channel Fixed Link (the "Treaty of Canterbury") (T.S. No. 15 (1992) (Cm 1827)). It
is only necessary to set out Article 1 thereof, which contains definitions. These are incorporated in
Article 1(1) of Schedule 2 to the Channel Tunnel (International Arrangements) Order 1993 (S.I.
1993 No. 1813) (*post*).

The Channel Tunnel Act 1987 provided, *inter alia*, for the construction and operation of the
tunnel system, for the incorporation of part of the tunnel system into the United Kingdom and
for the application and enforcement of law in relation to, and otherwise for the regulation of, that
system and matters connected with it.

S.I. 1993 No. 1813, *ante*, is made under section 11 of the 1987 Act. It makes detailed provision
in relation, *inter alia*, to the application of the criminal law outside the United Kingdom and in
relation to the powers of constables and other officers. Article 1 provides for it to come into force
on a date to be notified in the London, Edinburgh and Belfast *Gazettes*. The date notified was
August 2, 1993 (*London Gazette*, August 6, 1993).

In relation to rail traffic between the United Kingdom and Belgium, there is a further agree-
ment and a further order. The agreement is the Agreement between the Government of the
Kingdom of Belgium, the Government of the French Republic and the Government of the
United Kingdom of Great Britain and Northern Ireland Concerning Rail Traffic between Belgium
and the United Kingdom Using the Channel Fixed Link. This agreement came into force on
December 1, 1997.

The further order is the Channel Tunnel (Miscellaneous Provisions) Order 1994 (S.I. 1994 No.
1405). Apart from certain amending provisions, which came into force on July 1, 1994, this order
came into force simultaneously with the agreement.

S.I. 1994 No. 1405 is made under section 11 of the Channel Tunnel Act 1987. It gives qualified
effect in United Kingdom law to material provisions (the "tripartite articles" set out in Schedule 2)
of the agreement.

The tripartite articles are by article 3(1) given the force of law within, and for the purposes
specified in article 2(2) outside, the control zones accorded to Belgium ("the Belgian control
zone") and to France by the tripartite articles; article 3(2) affirms that Belgian, and French, officers may to the extent specified in the tripartite articles go about their business in the United
Kingdom, and article 3(3) ensures that Belgian officers can be provided with the required facilities.
Article 4(1) performs the corresponding operation for British officers working in Belgium or
France.

Article 5(1) to (3) extends English criminal jurisdiction to conduct in a United Kingdom control
zone which, if taking place in England, would constitute an offence under a frontier control
enactment as defined in Schedule 1. Article 5(4) creates a presumption as to jurisdiction where it
is uncertain in which of the three states an offence not of that kind was committed.

**Treaty between the United Kingdom of Great Britain and Northern Ireland and the French
Republic Concerning The Construction and Operation by Private Concessionaires of a Channel
Fixed Link (T.S. No. 15 (1992) (Cm. 1827))**

ARTICLE 1

Object and Definitions

(1) The High Contracting Parties undertake to permit the construction and operation by private    **F-2**
concessionaires (hereinafter referred to as "the Concessionaires") of a Channel fixed link in accordance with the provisions of this Treaty, of its supplementary Protocols and arrangements and of a
concession between the two Governments and the Concessionaires (hereinafter referred to as "the
Concession"). The Channel fixed link shall be financed without recourse to government funds or to
government guarantees of a financial or commercial nature.

(2) The Channel fixed link (hereinafter referred to as "the Fixed Link"), which shall be more
particularly described in the Concession, means a twin bored tunnel rail link, with associated service
tunnel under the English Channel between Cheriton in Kent and Fréthun in the Pas-de-Calais,

together with the terminal areas for control of access to, and egress from, the tunnels, and shall include any freight or other facility, and any road link between the United Kingdom and France, which may hereafter be agreed between the High Contracting Parties to form part of the Fixed Link.

**Channel Tunnel Act 1987, s.1(1), (3)–(10)**

*Construction and operation of a tunnel rail link between the United Kingdom and France*

**F-3**      **1.**—(1) The primary purpose of this Act is to provide for the construction and operation of a tunnel rail link (together with associated works, facilities and installations) under the English Channel between the United Kingdom and France, in accordance with—

  (a)  the Treaty between the United Kingdom of Great Britain and Northern Ireland and the French Republic concerning the Construction and Operation by Private Concessionaires of a Channel Fixed Link, signed at Canterbury on 12th February 1986, together with its supplementary protocols and arrangements; and

  (b)  the Concession between Her Majesty's Government in the United Kingdom and the Government of the French Republic on the one hand and private Concessionaires on the other hand which, in accordance with Article 1 of that Treaty, regulates, together with that Treaty, the construction and operation of the Channel fixed link referred to in that Article.

(3) Subject to section 3 of this Act, the expressions defined below in this section have the meanings there given for the purposes of this Act.

(4) "The Treaty" means the Treaty mentioned in paragraph (a) of subsection (1) above, including its supplementary protocols and arrangements, and "the Concession" means the Concession mentioned in paragraph (b) of that subsection.

(5) "Concession agreement" means any agreement or arrangement which for the time being constitutes, or is included among the agreements or arrangements which together for the time being constitute, the Concession.

(6) "Concession lease" means any lease granted by the Secretary of State to the Concessionaires in pursuance of the Concession, and references to a Concession lease include any provisions of a Concession agreement providing for the grant of a lease of any land by the Secretary of State to the Concessionaires.

(7) "The tunnel system" means the tunnel rail link, together with its associated works, facilities and installations, to be constructed in pursuance of the Treaty, and incorporating—

  (a)  tunnels under the English Channel between Cheriton, Folkestone, in Kent and Fréthun in the Pas de Calais, comprising two main tunnels capable of carrying both road traffic on shuttle trains and rail traffic, and an associated service tunnel;

  (b)  two terminal areas, for controlling access to and egress from the tunnels, located at the portals of the tunnels in the vicinity of Cheriton, Folkestone and Fréthun respectively;

  (c)  a service and maintenance area at the Old Dover Colliery site;

  (d)  an inland clearance depot at Ashford, in Kent, for the accommodation, in connection with the application to them of customs and other controls, of freight vehicles which have been or are to be conveyed through the tunnels on shuttle services;

  (e)  necessary links with the road and rail networks of each country; and

  (f)  the fixed and movable equipment needed for the operation of the tunnels and the associated works, facilities and installations mentioned in paragraphs (b) to (e) above or for the operation of shuttle services using the tunnels.

(8) "The Concessionaires" means the person or persons who, under the Concession, have for the time being the function of constructing and operating or (as the case may be) of operating the tunnel system.

(9) "Shuttle train" means a train designed for the purpose of carrying road traffic between Cheriton, Folkestone and Fréthun by way of the tunnels and "shuttle service" means a service operated by means of a shuttle train.

(10) Where the Concessionaires for the time being are two or more persons, any provision of this Act conferring or imposing upon them any right, power, liability or duty shall have effect (except where the context otherwise requires) so as to confer or impose it upon them jointly; but anything done by or in relation to any one of them which purports to be done by or in relation to both or all of them shall have effect for the purposes of this Act as if done by or in relation to them jointly.

**Channel Tunnel Act 1987, s.10(1)**

*Incorporation of part of the tunnel into the United Kingdom and general application of law*

**F-4**      **10.**—(1) The land compromising the tunnel system as far as the frontier, so far as not forming part of the United Kingdom before the passing of this Act, shall, as it becomes occupied by or on behalf of the Concessionaires working from England, together with so much of the surrounding subsoil as is necessary for the security of the part of the system so occupied, be incorporated into England and form part of the district of Dover in the county of Kent, and the law of England shall apply accordingly.

### Channel Tunnel Act 1987, s.11(1), (3), (4)

*Regulation of the tunnel system: application and enforcement of law, etc.*

**11.**—(1) The appropriate Minister may by order make such provision as appears to him to be   **F-5** necessary or expedient—

   (a)   for the purpose of implementing the international arrangements, or enabling those arrangements to be implemented.

   (b)   [*transfer of property*];

   (c)   in relation to the construction, operation or use of the tunnel system or any part of the tunnel system, so far as relates to activities carried on, persons employed or engaged in work, things done or omitted or other matters arising anywhere within the system (whether in England or in France), including in particular (without prejudice to the generality of the preceding provision) provision with respect to controls in relation to persons or goods within the system;

   (d)   for the purpose of applying any provisions of the law of England (with or without modifications), or excluding or modifying any of those provisions, in relation to things done or omitted or other matters arising anywhere within the tunnel system (whether in England or France);

   (e)   with respect to controls in relation to persons or goods—

      (i)   on trains engaged on international services; or

      (ii)   at authorised terminal control points for such services; outside the tunnel system (whether in the United Kingdom or elsewhere);

   (f)   in relation to persons employed or engaged on work outside the tunnel system (whether in the United Kingdom or elsewhere)—

      (i)   on any train engaged on an international service, in or for the purposes of or in connection with the operation of that service; or

      (ii)   in or for the purposes of or in connection with the exercise, on any such train or at any authorised terminal control point for such service, of any controls in relation to persons or goods as are mentioned in paragraph (e) above;

   (g)   for the purpose of dealing with any matters arising out of or connected with any provision within the powers conferred by any of paragraphs (a) to (f) above (whether or not those matters arise within the tunnel system, on any such train or at any such control point); or

   (h)   otherwise in relation to, or for regulating any matters arising out of or connected with, the tunnel system.

(3) Without prejudice to the generality of subsection (1) above, the kind of provision that may be made by an order under this section includes the following—

   (a)   provision creating new criminal offences punishable as may be provided by the order or imposing penalties otherwise than in respect of criminal offences;

   (b)   [*fees and charges*];

   (c)   provision conferring power on any Minister of the Crown or Government department to make orders, rules, regulations or other subordinate instruments of a legislative character;

   (d)   provision for, or authorising any such order, rule, regulation or other subordinate instrument to provide for, the delegation of any functions conferred or imposed by or in pursuance of any order under this section or by any enactment;

   (e)   provision, subject to subsection (4) below, for or in connection with the enforcement or execution outside the United Kingdom of any provision of the law of England or within the United Kingdom of any provision of the law of any other country, including in particular—

      (i)   provision conferring powers on any officer belonging to the United Kingdom to arrest and detain outside the United Kingdom persons suspected of having committed offences under the law of England and bring them to lawful custody in England;

      (ii)   provision conferring powers on any such officer to arrest and detain within the United Kingdom persons suspected of having committed offences under the law of any other country and surrender them to the custody of officers belonging to that country without the authority of any order or a court in any part of the United Kingdom; and

> (iii) provision for or in connection with the exercise in the United Kingdom by officers belonging to any other country of powers corresponding to those mentioned in sub-paragraph (i) above; and

> (f) provision conferring jurisdiction on courts or tribunals in any part of the United Kingdom or limiting the jurisdiction otherwise exercisable by any such courts or tribunals.

(4) An order under this section may not make provision for or in connection with the exercise of powers by officers belonging to one country in any other country except—

> (a) within the tunnel system;
> (b) on trains engaged on international services; or
> (c) at authorised terminal control points for such services.

## Channel Tunnel Act 1987, s.12

*Controls on board trains engaged on international services*

**F-6**  **12.**—(1) It shall be duty of the appropriate Minister to secure that, where this subsection applies, controls exercisable in relation to—

> (a) passengers carried on a train engaged on an international service on a journey beginning or intended to end at a place in Great Britain other than London or Cheriton, Folkestone or any place between those places; or
> (b) things contained in the baggage of such passengers;

shall be exercised on the train.

(2) Subject to subsection (3) below, subsection (1) above applies where—

> (a) the person operating the service has made a request to the appropriate Minister that the controls in question should be exercised on trains engaged on the service in question;
> (b) the appropriate Minister has approved as satisfactory arrangements made by that person for the provision of facilities to enable the controls in question to be exercised on such trains;
> (c) facilities enabling the exercise of the controls in question are provided on the train in question in accordance with such approved arrangements; and
> (d) the controls are exercised by customs officers or immigration officers.

(3) Subsection (1) above does not apply—

> (a) in the case of passengers carried on a particular train or part of a particular train, or things contained in the baggage of such passengers, if in the opinion of a customs officer or immigration officer exercising the controls it is not reasonably practicable effectively to exercise the controls in question on the train or part of a train; and
> (b) in the case of any particular passenger or things contained in the baggage of any particular passenger, if in the opinion of any such officer it is not reasonably practicable effectively to exercise the controls in question in relation to the passenger or his baggage on the train.

(4) [*Fees and charges.*]

(5) In this section—

"customs officer" means an officer or other person acting under the authority of the Commissioners of Customs and Excise; and

"immigration officer" means an immigration officer appointed for the purposes of the Immigration Act 1971.

## Channel Tunnel Act 1987, s.13

*Provisions supplementary to sections 11 and 12*

**F-7**  **13.**—(1) Subject to subsection (2) below, in sections 11 and 12 of this Act "the appropriate Minister" means, in relation to any matter, the Minister in charge of any Government department concerned with that matter or, where more than one such department is concerned with that matter, the Ministers in charge of those departments, acting jointly.

(2) Where the Commissioners of Customs and Excise or the Forestry Commissioners are concerned with any matter (whether alone or together with any other Government department) subsection (1) above shall apply as if the references to the Minister or Ministers in charge of any Government department or departments concerned with that matter were or included references to those Commissioners.

(3) The validity of any order purporting to be made under section 11 of this Act shall not be af-

fected by any question whether or not the order fell by virtue of subsection (1) above to be made by the Minister or department (or any of the Ministers or departments) purporting to make it.

(4) In sections 11 and 12 of this Act "controls" means prohibitions, restrictions or requirements of any descriptions, and any reference to the exercise of controls is a reference to the exercise or performance of any functions conferred or imposed by any enactment, or otherwise under any lawful authority, for or in connection with the enforcement of prohibitions, restrictions or requirements of any description.

(5) For the purposes of those sections a train is engaged on an international service at any time when the whole or any part of the train is being used in the operation of such a service and a place is an authorised terminal control point for international services if it is designated as such in accordance with the international arrangements.

(6) In those sections and this section—

"the international arrangements" includes any agreements or arrangements between Her Majesty's Government in the United Kingdom and the Government of any country on the Continent of Europe other than France which for the time being apply for regulating any matters arising out of or connected with the operation of international services; and

"international service" means any service (including a shuttle service) for the carriage of passengers or goods by way of the tunnel system.

## Policing of tunnel system

This is to be undertaken by constables under the direction of the Chief Constable of Kent **F-8** constabulary: Channel Tunnel Act 1987, s.14(1). The Railways Board may, on the application of the Chief Constable, provide constables or other assistance for the policing of the tunnel system.

### Channel Tunnel Act 1987, s.23

*Control of traffic within the tunnel system*

**23.**—(1) Subject to the following provisions of this section, the enactments relating to road traffic **F-9** shall apply in relation to any tunnel system road to which the public does not have access as they apply in relation to a road which the public does have access.

(2) Those enactments shall apply in relation to any tunnel system road subject to such exceptions and modifications as the Secretary of State may by order specify.

(3) An order under subsection (2) above may, in particular, confer on the Concessionaires functions exercisable under those enactments by a highway authority or a local authority.

(4) The Secretary of State may by order provide that those enactments shall not apply in relation to any tunnel system road specified in the order and may require the Concessionaires to indicate any such road in a manner so specified.

(5) Those enactments shall not, in the case of any tunnel system road, apply in relation to it until such date as the Secretary of State may by order specify.

(6) Before making an order under this section, the Secretary of State shall consult the Concessionaires.

(7) In this section, "tunnel system road" means any length of road comprised in the tunnel system.

### Channel Tunnel Act 1987, s.49(1)

*Interpretation*

**49.**—(1) In this Act, except where the context otherwise requires— **F-10**

"enactment" includes an enactment contained in this Act or in any Act passed on or after the date on which this Act is passed, and any subordinate legislation within meaning of the Interpretation Act 1978;

"footpath" has the same meaning as in the Highways Act 1980;

"frontier" means the frontier between the United Kingdom and France fixed by the Treaty;

"functions" includes powers, duties and obligations;

"goods" includes vehicles (notwithstanding that they may be being used for the carriage of other goods or of persons), animals, plants and any other creature, substance or thing capable of being transported;

"the Intergovernmental Commission" means the Intergovernmental Commission established by the Treaty;

"the international arrangements" means—

(a) the Treaty and the Concession; and

(b) any other agreements or arrangements between Her Majesty's Government in the United Kingdom and the Government of the French Republic which for the time being apply for regulating any matters arising out of or connected with the tunnel system;

"land" includes buildings and other structures, land covered with water, and any estate, interest, easement, servitude or right in or over land;

"modification" includes addition, omission and alteration, and related expressions shall be construed accordingly;

"the Railways Board" has the meaning given by section 5(3);

"the Safety Authority" means the Safety Authority established by the Treaty;

"shuttle service" and "shuttle train" have the meanings given by section 1(9);

"substance" means any natural or artificial substance, whether in solid or liquid form or in the form of a gas or vapour;

"train" includes any locomotive and railway rolling stock of any description;

"the Treaty" has the meaning given by section 1(4);

"the tunnel system" has the meaning given by section 1(7); and

"vehicle" includes a railway vehicle.

**F-11**    The definitions of the following words and expressions have been omitted from this subsection: "A20 improvement works", "the appropriate authority", "the arbitral tribunal", "bridleway", "deposited plans", "deposited sections", "Dover Harbour", "limits of deviation" and "nature conservation". Subsections (2) to (9) contain further interpretative provisions.

### S.I. 1993 No. 1813, art. 1

*Citation and commencement*

**F-12**    **1.** This Order may be cited as the Channel Tunnel (International Arrangements) Order 1993 and shall come into force on the date on which the Protocol between the Government of the United Kingdom of Great Britain and Northern Ireland and the Government of the French Republic Concerning Frontier Controls and Policing, Co-operation in Criminal Justice, Public Safety and Mutual Assistance Relating to the Channel Fixed Link enters into force. That date will be notified in the London, Edinburgh and Belfast *Gazettes*.

[The commencement date was August 2, 1993: see *ante*, Appendix F-1.]

### S.I. 1993 No. 1813, arts 2–7

*Interpretation*

**F-13**    **2.**—(1) In this Order, except for the purpose of construing the international articles or the supplementary articles [or the 2012 Agreement], and in any enactment as applied by it with modifications, any expression for which there is an entry in the first column of Schedule 1 has the meaning given against it in the second column.

(2) In this Order "the authorised purposes" means—

(a) purposes for which provision is authorised by any of paragraphs (a), (d) and (g), and

(b) purposes connected with any matter in relation to or with respect to or for regulating which provision is authorised by any of paragraphs (c), (e), (f) and (h), of section 11(1) of the Channel Tunnel Act 1987.

(3) In this Order "the international articles" means the provisions set out in Schedule 2 (being Articles or parts of Articles of the Protocol mentioned in article 1 above); and in the international articles the expression "the Fixed Link" shall for the purposes of this Order be taken to have the same meaning as is given to "the tunnel system" by section 1(7) of the Channel Tunnel Act 1987.

(4) In this Order "the supplementary articles" means the provisions set out in Schedule 2A (being Articles of the Additional Protocol between the Government of the United Kingdom of Great Britain and Nothern Ireland and the Government of the French Republic and amendments to those Articles made by the amending instrument), and in the supplementary articles "the Protocol signed at Sangatte" and "the Sangatte Protocol" mean the Protocol mentioned in article 1 above.

(5) In paragraph (4) and in the supplementary articles, "Additional Protocol" means the Additional Protocol to the Sangatte Protocol on the Establishment of Bureaux Responsible for Controls on Persons Travelling by Train between France and the United Kingdom, signed at Brussels on 29th May 2000.

(6) In paragraph (4) "the amending instrument" means the Agreement between the Government of the United Kingdom of Great Britain and Northern Ireland and the Government of the French Republic making amendments to the Additional Protocol to the Sangatte Protocol on the Establishment of Bureaux responsible for controls on persons travelling by train between the United Kingdom and France, and to the Agreement concerning the carrying of service weapons by French officers on the territory of the United Kingdom of Great Britain and Northern Ireland, signed in Paris on 18th June 2007.

[(7) In this order, the "2012 Agreement" means the Agreement between the Government of the United Kingdom of Great Britain and Northern Ireland and the Government of the Republic of France on Implementation of the Cyclamen Device in the French Terminal of the Channel Tunnel Situated in Coquelles signed in London on 10th May 2012.]

[This article is printed as amended by the Channel Tunnel (International Arrangements) (Amendment No. 3) Order 2001 (S.I. 2001 No. 1544); and the Channel Tunnel (International Arrangements) (Amendment) Order 2007 (S.I. 2007 No. 2907); and as amended, as from the day after the day on which an agreement between the United Kingdom and France regarding security checks within the Channel Tunnel system comes into force (such date to be notified in the London, Edinburgh and Belfast Gazettes), by the Channel Tunnel (International Arrangements) (Amendment) Order 2012 (S.I. 2012 No. 1264) (insertion of words in square brackets).]

*Application of international articles*

**3.**—(1) The international articles shall have the force of law in the United Kingdom—

    (a)   within the tunnel system,

    (b)   within a control zone, and

    (c)   elsewhere for the authorised purposes only.

(2) Without prejudice to paragraph (1) officers belonging to the French Republic shall to the extent specified in the international articles have rights and obligations and powers to carry out functions in the United Kingdom.

(3) For the purpose of giving full effect to Article 34 of the international articles (accommodation *etc.*, for authorities of adjoining State) the appropriate Minister may by written notice require any occupier or person concerned with the management of a terminal control point to provide free of charge such accommodation, installations and equipment as may be necessary to satisfy requirements determined under Article 33 of the Protocol mentioned in article 1 above (which requires the competent authorities of the two States to determine their respective requirements in consultation with one another).

[This article is printed as amended by the Channel Tunnel (International Arrangements) (Amendment No. 4) Order 2001 (S.I. 2001 No. 3707).]

*Application of supplementary articles*

**3A.**—(1) The supplementary articles shall have the force of law in the United Kingdom within a supplementary control zone.

(2) Subject to paragraph (4), without prejudice to paragraph (1), officers belonging to the French Republic who are responsible for immigration controls shall to the extent specified in the supplementary articles have rights and obligations and powers to carry out functions in the United Kingdom.

(3) Subject to paragraph (4), for the purpose of enabling the authorities of the French Republic to make use in the United Kingdom of the accommodation, installations and equipment necessary for the performance of their functions under the supplementary articles, the Secretary of State for the Home Department may by written notice require any occupier or person concerned with the management of a terminal control point to provide free of charge such accommodation, installations and equipment as may be necessary to satisfy requirements determined by the authorities of the French Republic in consultation with the authorities of the United Kingdom.

(4) Nothing in this article implies the existence of a supplementary control zone in the station of London-Waterloo on British Territory.

[This article was inserted by the Channel Tunnel (International Arrangements) (Amendment No. 3) Order 2001 (S.I. 2001 No. 1544). It is printed as amended by the Channel Tunnel (International Arrangements) (Amendment No. 4) Order 2001 (S.I. 2001 No. 3707); and the Channel Tunnel (International Arrangements) (Amendment) Order 2007 (S.I. 2007 No. 2907).]

*Application of enactments*

**4.**—(1) All frontier control enactments except those relating to transport and road traffic controls shall for the purpose of enabling officers belonging to the United Kingdom to carry out frontier controls extend to France within a control zone.

(1A) All frontier control enactments relating to transport and road traffic controls shall for the purpose of enabling officers belonging to the United Kingdom to carry out such controls extend to France within the control zone in France within the tunnel system.

[(1AA) All security control enactments shall for the purpose of enabling officers belonging to the United Kingdom to carry out security controls extend to France within the tunnel system.]

(1B) All immigration control enactments shall, for the purpose of enabling immigration officers to carry out immigration controls, extend to France within a supplementary control zone.

(1C) The Race Relations Act 1976 shall apply to the carrying out by immigration officers of their functions in a control zone or a supplementary control zone outside the United Kingdom as it applies to the carrying out of their functions within the United Kingdom.

(2), (3) [*Application of Data Protection Act 1984.*]

[This article is printed as amended by the Channel Tunnel (International Arrangements) (Amendment) Order 1996 (S.I. 1996 No. 2283); the Channel Tunnel (International Arrangements) (Amendment No. 3) Order 2001 (S.I. 2001 No. 1544); and the Channel Tunnel (International Arrangements) (Amendment No. 4) Order 2001 (S.I. 2001 No. 3707); and as prospectively amended (insertion of para. (1AA), and of sub-para. (c) in para. (2)) by S.I. 2012 No. 1264 (as to which, see the annotation to article 2, *ante*).]

The Data Protection Act 1984 is repealed and replaced by the Data Protection Act 1998.

*Application of criminal law*

**5.**—(1) Any act or omission which—

    (a)  takes place outside the United Kingdom in a control zone, and

    (b)  would, if taking place in England, constitute an offence under a frontier control enactment,

or any act or omission which—

    (c)  takes place outside the United Kingdom in a supplementary control zone, and

    (d)  would, if taking place in England, constitute an offence under an immigration control enactment

shall be treated for the purposes of that enactment as taking place in England.

(1A) Summary proceedings for anything that is by virtue of paragraph (1) an offence triable summarily or triable either way may be taken, and the offence may for all incidental purposes be treated as having been committed, in the county of Kent or in the inner London area as defined in section 2(1)(a) of the Justices of the Peace Act 1979.

(2) Any jurisdiction conferred by virtue of paragraphs (1) and (1A) on any court is without prejudice to any jurisdiction exercisable apart from this article by that or any other court.

(3) Where it is proposed to institute proceedings in respect of an alleged offence in any court and a question as to the court's jurisdiction arises under Article 38(2)(a) of the international articles, it shall be presumed, unless the contrary is proved, that the court has jurisdiction by virtue of that Article.

[This article is printed as amended by the Channel Tunnel (Miscellaneous Provisions) Order 1994 (S.I. 1994 No. 1405); and the Channel Tunnel (International Arrangements) (Amendment No. 3) Order 2001 (S.I. 2001 No. 1544).]

*Persons boarding a through train*

**5A.** For the purposes of the exercise of any power of an immigration officer in a supplementary control zone in France, any person who seeks to board a through train shall be deemed to be seeking to arrive in the United Kingdom through the tunnel system.

[This article was inserted by the Channel Tunnel (International Arrangements) (Amendment No. 3) Order 2001 (S.I. 2001 No. 1544).]

*Powers of officers and supplementary controls*

**F-13a**    **6.** Schedule 3 (which contains in Part I provision as to powers exercisable by constables and other officers and in Part II provision for meeting obligations under Article 25 of the Protocol mentioned in article 1 above concerning the prevention of animals from straying into the Fixed Link) shall have effect.

*Enactments modified*

**7.**—(1) Without prejudice to the generality of articles 4(1), 4(1B) and 5(1), the frontier control enactments mentioned in Schedule 4 shall—

(a)  in their application to France by virtue of article 4(1) or article 4(1B), and

(b)  in their application to the United Kingdom—

(i)   within the tunnel system, and

(ii)  elsewhere for the authorised purposes,

have effect with the modifications set out in Schedule 4.

(1A) Nothing in paragraph (1)(b)(ii) implies the existence of a supplementary control zone in the station of London-Waterloo on British Territory.

(2) Subject to paragraph (3), within a control zone or a supplementary control zone and on trains within the tunnel system section 54(3) of the Firearms Act 1968 (application to Crown Servants) shall have effect as if the reference to a member of a police force included a reference to an officer belonging to the French Republic exercising functions as mentioned in Article 28(2) of the international articles or functions under Article 3 of the supplementary articles.

(3) As respects officers exercising their functions in a control zone paragraph (2) applies only to the agreed number of specified officers mentioned in Article 28(2)(b) of the international articles.

(4) The frontier control enactments relating to transport and road traffic controls in their application to France within the control zone in the tunnel system by virtue of Article 4(1A) shall have effect as if any reference therein to a "public road" or "road" were a reference to any part of that control zone.

[This paragraph is printed as amended by S.I. 1996 No. 2283, *ante*; S.I. 2001 No. 1544, *ante*; and S.I. 2007 No. 2907, *ante*.]

## Amendment and repeals

Articles 8 and 9 give effect to Schedules 5 and 6, amendments and repeals respectively.          **F-14**

### S.I. 1993 No. 1813, Sched. 1

Article 2(1)                                SCHEDULE 1

EXPRESSIONS DEFINED

| Expression | Meaning | |
|---|---|---|
| ["2012 Agreement"] | [The meaning given by article 2(7).] | **F-15** |
| "The Concessionaires" | The meaning given by section 1(8) (read with section 3(3)) of the Channel Tunnel Act 1987. | |
| "Control zone" | A control zone within the meaning of the international articles. | |
| "Frontier controls" | So far as they constitute frontier controls within the meaning of the international articles and are controls in relation to persons or goods, police, immigration, customs, health, veterinary and phytosanitary, and transport and road traffic controls. | |
| "Frontier control enactment" | An Act, or an instrument made under an Act, for the time being in force, which contains provision relating to frontier controls. | |
| "Immigration control enactment" | An Act, or an instrument made under an Act, for the time being in force, which contains provision relating to immigration controls. | |
| "Immigration officer" | The same meaning as in the Immigration Act 1971. | |
| "The international articles" | The meaning given by article 2(3) above. | |
| "International service" | The meaning given in section 13(6) of the Channel Tunnel Act 1987. | |
| ["Security control enactment"] | [An Act, or an instrument made under an Act, for the time being in force, which contains provision relating to security controls.] | |
| ["Security controls"] | [Controls in relation to customs carried out for the purposes of the 2012 Agreement.] | |
| "Shuttle train" | The meaning given in section 1(9) of the Channel Tunnel Act 1987. | |
| "State of arrival" | The meaning given by the supplementary articles. | |

| *Expression* | *Meaning* |
|---|---|
| "State of departure" | The meaning given by the supplementary articles. |
| "The supplementary articles" | The meaning given by article 2(4) above. |
| "Supplementary control zone" | The part of the territory of the State of departure, determined by mutual agreement between the Governments of the State of departure and the State of arrival but excluding the station of London-Waterloo on British territory, within which the officers of the State of arrival are empowered to effect controls under the supplementary articles. |
| "Terminal control point" | A place which is an authorised terminal control point for international services for the purposes of sections 11 and 12 of the Channel Tunnel Act 1987. |
| "Through train" | A train, other than a shuttle train, which for the purposes of sections 11 and 12 of the Channel Tunnel Act 1987 is engaged on an international service. |
| "Train manager" | In relation to a through train or shuttle train, the person designated as train manager by the person operating the international service on which the train is engaged. |
| "The tunnel system" | The meaning given by section 1(7) of the Channel Tunnel Act 1987. |

[This Schedule is printed as amended by S.I. 1996 No. 2283; S.I. 2001 No. 1544; S.I. 2001 No. 3707; and S.I. 2007 No. 2907 (*ante*, F-13); and as prospectively amended (insertion of definitions in square brackets) by S.I. 2012 No. 1264 (as to which, see the annotation to article 2, *ante*, F-13).]

**S.I. 1993 No. 1813, Sched. 2**

Article 2(3)                                    SCHEDULE 2

INTERNATIONAL ARTICLES

ARTICLE 1

*Definitions*

**F-16**     (1) Any term defined in the Treaty shall have the same meaning in this Protocol.

(2) Otherwise for the purposes of this Protocol the expression:

(a) "frontier controls" means police, immigration, customs, health, veterinary and phytosanitary, consumer protection, and transport and road traffic controls, as well as any other controls provided for in national or European Community laws and regulations;

(b) "host State" means the State in whose territory the controls of the other State are effected;

(c) "adjoining State" means the other State;

(d) "officers" means persons responsible for policing and frontier controls who are under the command of the persons or authorities designated in accordance with Article 2(1);

(e) "rescue services" means the authorities and organisations whose functions are provided for in the emergency arrangements referred to in Part VII of this Protocol who are under the command of the persons or authorities designated in accordance with Article 2(1);

(f) [...]

(g) "control zone" means the part of the territory of the host State determined by the mutual agreement between the two Governments within which the officers of the adjoining State are empowered to effect controls;

(h) "restricted zone" means the part of the Fixed Link situated in each State subject to special protective security measures;

(i) "through trains" means trains travelling the Fixed Link but originating and terminating outside it, as opposed to "shuttle trains" which are trains travelling solely within the Fixed Link.

## Part I

### Authorities and General Principles of Co-operation

### Article 2

(1) Each of the Governments shall designate the authorities or the persons having charge of the **F-16a** services which in its territory have responsibility for the exercise of frontier controls, the maintenance of law and order and fire fighting and rescue within the Fixed Link.

## Part II

### Frontier Controls and Police: General

### Article 5

(1) In order to simplify and speed up the formalities relating to entry into the State of arrival and **F-16b** exit from the State of departure, the two Governments agree to establish juxtaposed national control bureaux in the terminal installations situated at Fréthun in French territory and at Folkestone in British territory. These bureaux shall be so arranged that, for each direction of travel, the frontier controls shall be carried out in the terminal in the State of departure.

(2) Supplementary frontier controls may exceptionally be carried out in the Fixed Link by officers of the State of arrival on its own territory.

### Article 6

The competence of those juxtaposed national control bureaux shall extend to all cross-frontier movements with the exception of customs clearance of commercial traffic.

### Article 7

(1) For through trains, each state may carry out its frontier controls during the journey and may authorise the officers of the other State to carry out their frontier controls in its territory.

(2) The two States may agree to an extension of the control zones for through trains, as far as London and Paris, respectively.

### Article 8

Within the Fixed Link, each Government shall permit officers of the other State to carry out their functions in its own territory in application of their powers relating to frontier controls.

### Article 9

The laws and regulations to frontier controls of the adjoining State shall be applicable in the control zone situated in the host State and shall be put into effect by the officers of the adjoining State in the same way as in their own territory.

### Article 10

(1) The officers of the adjoining State shall, in exercise of their national powers, be permitted in the control zone situated in the host State to detain or arrest persons in accordance with the laws and regulations relating to frontier controls of the adjoining State or persons sought by the authorities of the adjoining State. These officers shall also be permitted to conduct such persons to the territory of the adjoining State.

(2) However, except in exceptional circumstances, no person may be held more than 24 hours in the areas reserved, in the host State, for the frontier controls of the adjoining State. Any such detention shall be subject to the requirements and procedures laid down by the legislation of the adjoining State.

(3) In exceptional circumstances the 24 hour period of detention may be extended for a further period of 24 hours in accordance with the legislation of the adjoining State. The extension of the period of detention shall be notified to the authorities of the host State.

### Article 11

Breaches of the laws and regulations relating to frontier controls of the adjoining State which are detected in the control zone situated in the host State shall be subject to the laws and regulations of the adjoining State, as if the breaches had occurred in the latter's own territory.

### Article 12

(1) The frontier controls of the State of departure shall normally be effected before those of the State of arrival.

511

(2) The officers of the State of arrival are not authorised to carry out such controls before the end of controls of the State of departure. Any form of relinquishment of such controls shall be considered as a control.

(3) The officers of the State of departure may no longer carry out their controls when the officers of the State of arrival have begun their own operations except with the consent of the competent officers of the State of arrival.

(4) If exceptionally, in the course of the frontier controls, the sequence of operations provided for inparagraph (1) of this Article is modified, the officers of the State of arrival may not proceed to detentions, arrests or seizures until the frontier controls of the State of departure are completed. In such a case, these officers shall escort the persons, vehicles, merchandise, animals or other goods, for which the frontier controls of the State of departure are not yet completed, to the officers of that State. If these latter then wish to proceed to detentions, arrests or seizures, they shall have priority.

ARTICLE 14

The detailed plans for the Fixed Link and its means of access, shall, in accordance with the relevant provisions of the Concession, delimit among other things:

(a) the control zones;

(b) the restricted zones and their sub-divisions;

(c) railway lines and their means of access included in the control zones;

(d) the area of the frontier control installations and their means of access.

ARTICLE 16

Where investigations and proceedings concern offences committed in the Fixed Link or having a connection with the Fixed Link, the authorities of the host State shall, at the request of the authorities of the adjoining State, undertake official enquiries, the examination of witnesses and experts and the notification to accused persons of summonses and administrative decisions.

ARTICLE 17

The assistance provided for in Article 16 shall be furnished in accordance with the laws, regulations and procedures in force in the State providing the assistance, and with international agreements to which that State is a party.

ARTICLE 18

If the State of arrival refuses admission to persons, vehicles, animals or goods, or if persons decide not to pass through the frontier controls of the State of arrival, or send or take back any vehicles, animals or goods which are accompanying them, the authorities of the State of departure may not refuse to accept back such persons, vehicles, animals or goods. However, the authorities of the State of departure may take any measures to deal with them in accordance with national law and in a way which does not impose obligations on the other State.

ARTICLE 19

(2) In an emergency, the local representatives of the authorities concerned may by mutual agreement, provisionally bring into effect alterations to the delimitation of the control zones which may prove necessary. Any arrangement so reached shall come into effect immediately.

PART III

HEALTH, VETERINARY AND PHYTOSANITARY CONTROLS

[*Articles 20–24*]

PART IV

OFFICERS

ARTICLE 26

**F-16c**     Officers of both States shall be permitted to circulate freely in the whole of the Fixed Link for official purposes. In carrying out their functions they shall be authorised to pass through the frontier controls simply by producing appropriate evidence of their identity and status.

ARTICLE 28

(1) Officers of the adjoining State may wear their national uniform or visible distinctive insignia in the host State.

(2) In accordance with the laws, regulations and procedures governing the carriage and use of firearms in the host State, the competent authorities of that State will issue permanent licences to carry arms:

    (a)  to officers of the adjoining State exercising their official functions on board trains within the Fixed Link; and

    (b)  to an agreed number of specified officers of the adjoining State exercising their functions within the control zone of the host State.

### ARTICLE 29

(1) The authorities of the host State shall grant the same protection and assistance to officers of the adjoining State, in the exercise of their functions, as they grant to their own officers.

(2) The provisions of the criminal law in force in the host State for the protection of officers in the exercise of their functions shall be equally applicable to the punishment of offences committed against officers of the adjoining State in the exercise of their functions.

### ARTICLE 30

(1) Without prejudice to the application of the provisions of Article 46, claims for compensation for loss, injury or damage caused by or to officers of the adjoining State in the exercise of their functions in the host State shall be subject to the law and jurisdiction of the adjoining State as if the circumstances giving rise to the claim had occurred in that State.

(2) Officers of the adjoining State may not be prosecuted by authorities of the host State for any acts performed in the control zone or within the Fixed Link whilst in the exercise of their functions. In such a case, they shall come under the jurisdiction of the adjoining State, as if the act had been committed in that State.

(3) The judicial authorities or the police of the host State, having taken steps to record the complaint and to assemble the facts relating thereto, shall communicate all the particulars and evidence thereof to the competent authorities of the other State for the purposes of a possible prosecution according to the laws in force in the latter.

### ARTICLE 31

(1) Officers of the adjoining State shall be permitted freely to transfer to that State sums of money levied on behalf of their Government in the control zone situated in the host State, as well as merchandise and other goods seized there.

(2) They may equally sell such merchandise and other goods in the host State in conformity with the provisions in force in the host State, and transfer the proceeds to the adjoining State.

### PART V

### FACILITIES

### ARTICLE 34

The authorities of the adjoining State shall be able to make use in the host State of the accommodation, installations and equipment necessary for the performance of their functions.   **F-16d**

### ARTICLE 35

(1) The officers of the adjoining State are empowered to keep order within the accommodation appointed for their exclusive use in the host State.

(2) The officers of the host State shall not have access to such accommodation, except at the request of the officers of the adjoining State or in accordance with the laws of the host State applicable to entry into and searches of private premises.

### ARTICLE 36

All goods which are necessary to enable the officers of the adjoining State to carry out their functions in the host State shall be exempt from all taxes and dues on entry and exit.

### ARTICLE 37

(1) The officers of the adjoining State whilst exercising their functions in the host State shall be authorised to communicate with their national authorities.

PART VI

CO-OPERATION IN CRIMINAL JUSTICE

ARTICLE 38

**F-16e**     (1) Without prejudice to the provisions of Articles 11 and 30(2), when an offence is committed in the territory of one of the two States, including that lying within the Fixed Link up to its frontier, that State shall have jurisdiction.

(2)

(a)  Within the Fixed Link, each State shall have jurisdiction and shall apply its own law:

(i)   when it cannot be ascertained with certainty where an offence has been committed; or

(ii)  when an offence committed in the territory of one State is related to an offence committed on the territory of the other State; or

(iii) when an offence has begun in or has been continued into its own territory;

(b)  however, the State which first receives the person suspected of having committed such an offence (in this Article referred to as "the receiving State") shall have priority in exercising jurisdiction.

(3) When the receiving State decides not to exercise its priority jurisdiction under paragraph (2) of this Article it shall inform the other State without delay. If the latter decides not to exercise its jurisdiction, the receiving State shall be obliged to exercise its jurisdiction in accordance with its own national law.

ARTICLE 39

Where an arrest has been made for an offence in respect of which a State has jurisdiction under Article 38, that arrest shall not be affected by the fact that it continues in the territory of the other State.

ARTICLE 40

Without prejudice to the application of Article 3 of the Treaty and Part II of this Protocol, the police and customs officers of one State may in accordance with their own national laws make arrests on the territory of the other State in cases where a person is found committing, attempting to commit, or just having committed an offence:

(a)  on board any train which has commenced its journey from one State to the other and is within the Fixed Link; or

(b)  within any tunnel described in Article 1(2) of the Treaty.

ARTICLE 41

In the case of arrests covered by Articles 39 and 40:

(a)  the person arrested shall be presented without delay to the competent authorities of the State of arrival for that State to be responsible for determining the exercise of jurisdiction as required by Article 38; and

(b)  where jurisdiction shall be exercised by the other State in accordance with Article 38, the person arrested may be transferred to the territory of that State. However, any such transfer shall take place within 48 hours of the presentation under paragraph (a) of this Article. Moreover, each State reserves the right not to transfer its nationals.

PART VII

PUBLIC SAFETY AND RESCUE

[*Articles 42–44*]

PART VIII

FINAL CLAUSES

[*Articles 46, 47*]

S.I. 1993 No. 1813, Sched. 2A

Article 2(4)

## SCHEDULE 2A

SUPPLEMENTARY ARTICLES

### ARTICLE 1

Any terms defined in Article 1 of the Protocol signed at Sangatte have the same meaning in this **F-16f** Additional Protocol. For the purposes of this Additional Protocol, the following definitions shall be added:

"State of departure" means the State in which the persons boards the train;

"State of arrival" means the State in which the persons alight from the train.

### ARTICLE 2

The authorities of the two States shall jointly put in place control bureaux, for persons using through trains and wishing to travel to the State of arrival, in the stations of London-Waterloo, London-St Pancras and Ashford on British territory, and the stations of Paris-Gare du Nord, Calais and Lille-Europe on French territory.

The provisions of the Protocol signed at Sangatte concerning the officers of the adjoining State shall be applicable, under the same conditions, to the officers of the State of arrival who are on duty in the stations mentioned in the preceeding paragraph.

#### *Amendments to Article 2*

In addition to the stations referred to in Article 2, control bureaux shall also be established at the station of Ebbsfleet International on British Territory.

The provisions of the Additional Protocol apply to the station of Ebbsfleet International under the same conditions and in accordance with the same procedures as they apply to the stations referred to in the said Article 2.

### ARTICLE 3

The purpose of the controls carried out by the authorities of the State of departure shall be to check whether the person can leave its territory.

The purpose of the controls carried out by the authorities of the State of arrival shall be to check whether the person is in possession of the necessary travel documents and fulfils the other conditions for entry to its territory. If this is not the case, the person shall be immediately handed over to the authorities of the State of departure who shall apply their domestic law procedures.

The authorities of the State of departure and of the State of arrival shall carry out their controls in accordance with this Additional Protocol, with their laws and regulations and with their international obligations.

The controls mentioned in the preceeding paragraphs are without prejudice to customs and security controls.

### ARTICLE 4

Notwithstanding the third paragraph of Article 3 of this Additional Protocol, when a person submits a request for refugee status or any other kind of protection provided for in international law or in the domestic law of the State of departure during a control carried out at the station of the State of departure by the officers of the State of arrival, this request shall be examined by the authorities of the State of departure in accordance with the rules and procedures of its domestic law.

The same provisions shall be applicable when the request is submitted after the person has passed through this control and before the train doors close at the last scheduled stop at a station located in the territory of the State of departure. If such a request is made after the train doors have closed, it shall be processed by the State of arrival in accordance with the rules and procedures of its domestic law.

### ARTICLE 5

The controls referred to in Article 3 of this Additional Protocol shall be carried out in accordance with Article 12 of the Sangatte Protocol.

### ARTICLE 6

The procedures for the implementation of this Additional Protocol may, as far as necessary, be the subject of technical or administrative arrangements between the competent authorities of the two States.

[Sched. 2A was inserted by S.I. 2001 No. 1544 (*ante*, F-13). It is printed as amended by the Channel Tunnel (International Arrangements) (Amendment) Order 2007 (S.I. 2007 No. 2907).]

S.I. 1993 No. 1813, Sched. 3

Article 6                                      SCHEDULE 3

Part I

Powers of Officers

*Power to assist French authorities*

**F-17**  1.—(1) Where—

(a)  an officer belonging to the French Republic has in a control zone in the United Kingdom
or in a supplementary control zone in the United Kingdom arrested or detained a person
as permitted by Article 10(1) of the international articles and Article 2 of the supplementary
articles, and

(b)  such an officer so requests,

a constable or an officer commissioned by the Commissioners of Customs and Excise under section
6(3) of the Customs and Excise Management Act 1979 (in this Schedule referred to as a "customs officer") may make arrangements for the person to be taken into temporary custody.

(2) A person taken into temporary custody under sub-paragraph (1)—

(a)  shall be treated for all purposes as being in lawful custody, and

(b)  may be taken to a police station or such other place as may be appropriate in the
circumstances, and shall in that case be treated as being a person in whose case sections
36(7) and (8), 54 to 56 and 58 of the Police and Criminal Evidence Act 1984 (in this
Schedule referred to as "the 1984 Act"), and in the case of a child or young person section
34(2) to (7), (8) and (9) of the Children and Young Persons Act 1933, apply, and

(c)  must be returned, before the end of the period for which he could in the circumstances be
detained in the United Kingdom under Article 10 of the international articles or Article 2
of the supplementary articles, to a place where detention under that Article could be
resumed.

(3) Where a person falls to be treated as mentioned in sub-paragraph (2)(b) section 56 of the 1984
Act shall be taken to apply as if he were detained for a serious arrestable offence.

[This paragraph is printed as amended by the Channel Tunnel (Miscellaneous Provisions)
Order 1994 (S.I. 1994 No. 1405); and the Channel Tunnel (International Arrangements) (Amendment No. 3) Order 2001 (S.I. 2001 No. 1544).]

*Powers of arrest outside United Kingdom*

**F-17a**  2.—(1) A constable may in a control zone in France—

(a)  exercise any power of arrest conferred by a frontier control enactment or conferred by the
1984 Act in respect of an offence under such an enactment,

(b)  make any arrest authorised by a warrant issued by a court in the United Kingdom, and

(c)  arrest any person whose name or description or both, together with particulars of an
indictable offence of which there are reasonable grounds for suspecting him to be guilty,
have been made available by a chief officer of police to other such officers.

(2) For the purposes of sub-paragraph (1)(a) the reference in sub-paragraph (1) to a constable
shall be construed—

(a)  in relation to the powers of arrest conferred by section 28A(1) and (3) of and paragraph
17(1) of Schedule 2 to the Immigration Act 1971, as including a reference both—

(i)  to an immigration officer appointed for the purposes of that Act under paragraph 1
of that Schedule, and

(ii)  to an officer of customs and excise who is the subject of arrangements for the employment of such officers as immigration officers made under that paragraph by the
Secretary of State,

and where this sub-paragraph applies, the reference in sub-paragraph (1) [*sic*] to a control
zone in France shall be construed as including a reference to a supplementary control zone
in France.

(b)  in relation to the power of arrest conferred by paragraph 6(4) of Schedule 5 to the Prevention of Terrorism (Temporary Provisions) Act 1989, as including a reference to any person
who by virtue of paragraph 1(1) of that Schedule is an examining officer for the purposes
of that Act, and

(c)  in relation to any arrest that may be made by a customs officer by virtue of section 138 of
the Customs and Excise Management Act 1979 and an arrest for a drug trafficking offence
as defined in section 38(1) of the Drug Trafficking Offences Act 1986, as including a reference to a customs officer.

(3) A customs officer may[—

(a)]  in a control zone in France arrest any person whose name or description or both, together with particulars of an arrestable offence (within the meaning of section 24 of the 1984 Act) which is an offence in relation to an assigned matter as defined in section 1(1) of the Customs and Excise Management Act 1979 and of which there are reasonable grounds for suspecting him to be guilty, have been made available to customs officers generally under the authority of the Commissioners for Her Majesty's Revenue and Customs[;

　　(b) within the tunnel system exercise any power of arrest conferred by a security control enactment in connection with the carrying out of security controls].

(4) For the purpose of enabling constables to make arrests in France in the cases described in Article 40 of the international articles sections 24 and 25 of the 1984 Act shall extend to France.

(5) Where—

　　(a) an arrest has been made for an offence of the kind mentioned in Article 39 of the international articles, and

　　(b) it falls to the competent authorities in France to determine the exercise of jurisdiction in accordance with Article 38,

the person arrested shall be treated as continuing to be under arrest while in France until he is presented to those authorities as required by Article 41(a).

(6) Where—

　　(a) an arrest falling within sub-paragraph (4) or (5) above has been made, and

　　(b) the competent authorities in France determine under Article 41 of the international articles that jurisdiction is to be exercised by the United Kingdom,

the person arrested shall be treated as having continued to be under arrest throughout, even if he was for some period in the custody of those authorities, and sections 30 and 41 of the 1984 Act shall apply accordingly.

(7) Any power conferred by an enactment to search an arrested person may be exercised following an arrest authorised by this paragraph as if the person had been arrested in the United Kingdom.

[This paragraph is printed as amended by the Channel Tunnel (International Arrangements) (Amendment No. 3) Order 2001 (S.I. 2001 No. 1544); the Serious Organised Crime and Police Act 2005 (Powers of Arrest) (Consequential Amendments) Order 2005 (S.I. 2005 No. 3389) and the Commissioners for Revenue and Customs Act 2005, s.50(1); and as prospectively amended (insertion of text in square brackets) by S.I. 2012 No. 1264 (as to which, see the annotation to article 2, *ante*, F-13).]

*Arrested persons held in France*

　3.—(1) Where—　　　　　　　　　　　　　　　　　　　　　　　　　　　**F-17b**

　　(a) an arrest of any kind authorised by paragraph 2 above has been made in a control zone in France or in a supplementary control zone in France; or

　　(b) an arrest of any such kind has been made in the United Kingdom and the person arrested enters such a control zone while under arrest,

the person arrested may be held in France for a period of not more than 24 hours and, if there are exceptional circumstances and an officer belonging to the French Republic is notified of the extension, for a further period.

(2) Subject to sub-paragraphs (3) and (4), the person arrested shall be treated as if the place where he is held were for the purposes of the provisions mentioned in paragraph 1(2)(b) above and those of sections 61 to 63 of the 1984 Act a police station, or where the arrest was made by a customs officer, a customs office, in England, not being a police station or customs office designated under section 35 of the 1984 Act.

(3) Where—

　　(a) an arrest falling within paragraph 2(1)(a) or (3)[(a) or (b)] above has been made by a customs officer, and

　　(b) the person arrested is held in France in a place within the tunnel system which would if it were in England be a customs office within the meaning of the 1984 Act,

sections 34(1) to (5), 36, 37, 39 to 42, 50, 54, 55, 56(1) to (9), 58(1) to (11), 62, 63 and 64(1) to (6) of the 1984 Act and in the case of a child or young person section 34(2) to (7), (8) and (9) of the Children and Young Persons Act 1933, shall apply as if the place where he is held were a customs office in England designated under section 35 of the 1984 Act.

(4) Where the power of arrest mentioned in paragraph 2(2)(b) has been exercised any detention in France of the person arrested shall be treated for all purposes as being detention under paragraph 6(1) of Schedule 5 to the Prevention of Terrorism (Temporary Provisions) Act 1989, and section 16(2) of that Act, sections 51(b), 56 and 58 of the 1984 Act and section 34 of the Children and Young Persons Act 1933 as applying accordingly.

[This paragraph is printed as amended by the Channel Tunnel (International Arrangements) (Amendment No. 3) Order 2001 (S.I. 2001 No. 1544); and as prospectively amended (insertion of text in square brackets in para. (3)(a)) by S.I. 2012 No. 1264 (as to which, see the annotation to article 2, *ante*, F-13).]

*Arrested persons arriving in the United Kingdom*

**F-17c**        4.—(1) Where—

    (a)  an arrest falling within Article 39 or 40 of the international articles has been made, and

    (b)  the person arrested enters the United Kingdom while under arrest,

the person arrested shall be taken to a police station.

(2) The custody officer at the police station to which the person is taken shall determine—

    (a)  whether the offence is one over which the United Kingdom has jurisdiction by virtue of Article 38(1), and

    (b)  if he determines that it is not, whether it is one over which the United Kingdom may exercise jurisdiction by virtue of Article 38(2) and if so whether jurisdiction is to be exercised,

and may for the purpose of determining those questions detain the person at the police station for not longer than the permitted period.

(3) The permitted period is the period of 48 hours beginning at the time at which the person arrives at the police station.

(4) Subject to sub-paragraph (6), the person shall be treated—

    (a)  as not being detained at the police station for the purposes of section 37 of the 1984 Act, and

    (b)  as not being in police detention for the purposes of sections 40 to 43 of the 1984 Act.

(5) Where the custody officer determines that the United Kingdom does not have jurisdiction by virtue of Article 38(1) and—

    (a)  that jurisdiction is not exercisable by virtue of Article 38(2), or

    (b)  that jurisdiction is exercisable by virtue of Article 38(2) but is not to be exercised,

he shall immediately inform the competent French authorities of his determination and shall arrange for the person to be transferred to France within the permitted period.

(6) Where the custody officer determines that the United Kingdom has jurisdiction by virtue of Article 38(1) or that jurisdiction is exercisable by virtue of Article 38(2) and is to be exercised—

    (a)  he shall immediately inform the person of his determination,

    (b)  the person shall be treated as being in police detention for all purposes of Part IV of the 1984 Act, and

    (c)  that Part shall have effect in relation to him as if the relevant time mentioned in section 41(1) were the time at which he is informed of the determination.

(7) Where the police station to which the person is taken is not a police station designated under section 35 of the 1984 Act, references in this paragraph to the custody officer are to be construed as references to an officer not below the rank of sergeant.

[The heading of paragraph 4 and sub-paragraph (1) were substituted by the Channel Tunnel (Miscellaneous Provisions) Order 1994: S.I. 1994 No. 1405, art. 8 and Sched. 4, with effect from July 1, 1994: *ibid.*, art. 1(2).]

*Arrests of French officers*

**F-17d**        5.—(1) This paragraph applies where an officer belonging to the French Republic ("the officer") is arrested for an act performed in the United Kingdom in the tunnel system or a control zone or supplementary control zone.

(2) If the officer enters France while under arrest—

    (a)  he shall without delay be handed over for custody to the competent French authorities and shall be treated as continuing to be under arrest until he has been handed over, and

    (b)  if after consultation with those authorities it is then determined that the act was not performed by the officer whilst in the exercise of his functions and he accordingly does not by virtue of Article 30(2) of the international articles come under French jurisdiction, he shall be treated as having continued to be under arrest until sub-paragraph (3) has been complied with.

(3) Where—

    (a)  sub-paragraph (2)(b) applies, or

    (b)  the officer does not enter France while under arrest,

he shall be taken to a police station designated under section 35 of the 1984 Act.

(4) Sub-paragraphs (5) to (9) apply in a case falling within sub-paragraph (3)(b).

(5) The custody officer at the police station to which the officer is taken shall after consultation with the competent French authorities determine whether the act was performed by the officer whilst in the exercise of his functions, and may for the purpose of determining that question detain the officer at the police station for not longer than the permitted period.

(6) The permitted period is the period of 48 hours beginning at the time at which the officer arrives at the police station.

(7) Subject to sub-paragraph (9), the officer shall be treated—

  (a) as not being detained at the police station for the purposes of section 37 of the 1984 Act, and

  (b) as not being in police detention for the purposes of sections 40 to 43 of the 1984 Act.

(8) Where the custody officer determines that the act was performed by the officer whilst in the exercise of his functions and the officer accordingly comes under French jurisdiction by virtue of Article 30(2), he shall immediately inform the competent French authorities and shall arrange for the officer to be transferred to France within the permitted period.

(9) In any other case—

  (a) the custody officer shall immediately inform the officer of his determination,

  (b) the officer shall be treated as being in police detention for all purposes of Part IV of the 1984 Act, and

  (c) that Part shall have effect in relation to him as if the relevant time mentioned in section 41(1) were the time at which he is informed of the determination.

[This paragraph is printed as amended by the Channel Tunnel (International Arrangements) (Amendment No. 3) Order 2001 (S.I. 2001 No. 1544).]

*Arrests of United Kingdom officers*

6.—(1) This paragraph applies where an officer belonging to the United Kingdom ("the officer") is **F-17e** arrested for an act performed in France in the tunnel system or a control zone or supplementary control zone.

(2) If—

  (a) the officer does not enter the United Kingdom while under arrest, and

  (b) the competent French authorities determine that the act was performed by the officer whilst in the exercise of his functions and he accordingly comes under United Kingdom jurisdiction by virtue of Article 30(2) of the international articles,

he shall on being handed over by those authorities to a constable be treated as having been arrested by the constable.

(3) Where—

  (a) sub-paragraph (2)(b) applies, or

  (b) the officer enters the United Kingdom while under the original arrest,

he shall be taken to a police station designated under section 35 of the 1984 Act.

(4) Sub-paragraphs (5) to (9) apply in a case falling within sub-paragraph (3)(b).

(5) The custody officer at the police station to which the officer is taken shall—

  (a) immediately invite the competent French authorities to determine whether the act was performed by the officer whilst in the exercise of his functions, and

  (b) afford those authorities any assistance they may require in determining that question,

and may for the purpose of enabling that question to be determined detain the officer at the police station for not longer than the permitted period.

(6) The permitted period is the period of 48 hours beginning at the time at which the officer arrives at the police station.

(7) Subject to sub-paragraph (9), the officer shall be treated—

  (a) as not being detained at the police station for the purposes of section 37 of the 1984 Act, and

  (b) as not being in police detention for the purposes of sections 40 to 43 of the 1984 Act.

(8) Where the competent French authorities determine that the act was not performed by the officer whilst in the exercise of his functions and the officer accordingly does not by virtue of Article 30(2) come under United Kingdom jurisdiction, the custody officer shall arrange for the officer to be transferred to France within the permitted period.

(9) In any other case—

  (a) the custody officer shall immediately inform the officer of the determination,

  (b) the officer shall be treated as being in police detention for all purposes of Part IV of the 1984 Act, and

(c)   that Part shall have effect in relation to him as if the relevant time mentioned in section 41(1) were the time at which he is informed of the determination.

[This paragraph is printed as amended by the Channel Tunnel (International Arrangements) (Amendment No. 3) Order 2001 (S.I. 2001 No. 1544).]

### Supplementary controls over animals

**F-18**   Part II, consisting of eight paragraphs, imposes controls for the purpose of preventing the spread of the rabies virus through the tunnel to the United Kingdom. Failure by the Concessionaires to carry out the duties imposed is made an offence triable either way (maximum penalty on conviction on indictment is a fine). It is also an offence, punishable in the same way, for any person to interfere with any anti-rabies installation, or to do any act which might impair the effectiveness of any anti-rabies measure, or to obstruct a person authorised to enforce the provisions of this Part.

### Enactments modified

**F-19**   As to Schedule 4, see article 7, *ante*, F-13a. The enactments modified which fall within the compass of this work are the Immigration Act 1971 (as to which, see § 25-233 in the main work) and the Terrorism Act 2000 (as to which, see *ante*, §§ 25-136a, 25-141).

### Amendments, repeals, revocations

**F-20**   Relevant entries in Schedules 5 (amendments) and 6 (repeals and revocations) are noted at the appropriate place elsewhere in this work.

**S.I. 1994 No. 1405, art. 1**

*Citation and commencement*

**F-21**     **1.**—(1) This Order may be cited as the Channel Tunnel (Miscellaneous Provisions) Order 1994 and, except as provided in paragraphs (2) and (3) below, shall come into force on the date on which the Agreement between the Government of the Kingdom of Belgium, the Government of the French Republic and the Government of the United Kingdom and Great Britain and Northern Ireland Concerning Rail Traffic between Belgium and the United Kingdom Using the Channel Fixed Link enters into force. That date will be notified in the London, Edinburgh and Belfast *Gazettes*.

(2) Article 8 shall, to the extent necessary to give effect to those of the amendments specified in Schedule 4 that are mentioned in paragraph (3) below, come into force on 1st July 1994.

(3) The amendments are—

(a)   those specified in paragraphs 6, 8(b), 9, 10 and 12 of Schedule 4, and

(b)   those specified in paragraph 11 of Schedule 4 except the amendments to paragraphs 1(11)(d) and 3(b) of Schedule 4 to the 1993 Order.

**S.I. 1994 No. 1405, arts 2-8**

*Interpretation*

★**F-22**     **2.**—(1) In this Order, except for the purpose of construing the tripartite articles, and in any enactment as applied by it with modifications, any expression for which there is an entry in the first column of Schedule 1 has the meaning given against it in the second column.

(2) In this Order "the authorised purposes" means—

(a)   purposes for which provision is authorised by any of paragraphs (a), (d) and (g), and

(b)   purposes connected with any matter in relation to or with respect to or for regulating which provision is authorised by any of paragraphs (c), (e), (f) and (h),

of section 11(1) of the Channel Tunnel Act 1987.

(3) In this Order "the tripartite articles" means the provisions set out—

(a)   in Part I of Schedule 2 (being Articles or parts of Articles of the Agreement mentioned in article 1 above), and

(b)   in Part II of Schedule 2 (being Articles or parts of Articles of the Protocol attached to and forming part of that Agreement);

(c)   in Part III of Schedule 2 (being Articles or parts of Articles of the Protocol attached to and

520

forming part of the Agreement, as applied by the Administrative Arrangement to immigration controls upon person travelling [between the United Kingdom and Belgium] on international trains making a commercial stop);

[(d) in Part IV of Schedule 2 (being Articles or parts of Articles of the Protocol attached to and forming part of the Agreement as applied by the Bilateral Agreement to immigration controls on passengers travelling on international trains between Belgium and the United Kingdom making a commercial stop);]

and in the tripartite articles the expression "the Fixed Link" shall for the purposes of this Order be taken to have the same meaning as is given to "the tunnel system" by section 1(7) of the Channel Tunnel Act 1987.

[This article is printed as amended by the Channel Tunnel (Miscellaneous Provisions) (Amendment) Order 2004 (S.I. 2004 No. 2589); and as amended, as from the date on which the Agreement signed in December, 2013, between the Government of the United Kingdom of Great Britain and Northern Ireland and the Government of the Kingdom of Belgium, Concerning Immigration Controls on Rail Traffic between Belgium and the United Kingdom Using the Channel Fixed Link enters into force, by the Channel Tunnel (Miscellaneous Provisions) (Amendment) Order 2014 (S.I. 2014 No. 409), arts 2 and 3(1) and (2) (insertion of words in square brackets).]

*Application of tripartite articles*

**3.**—(1) The tripartite articles shall have the force of law in the United Kingdom—
   (a)   within a control zone, and
   (b)   elsewhere for the authorised purposes only.

(2) Subject to paragraph (4), without prejudice to paragraph (1) officers belonging to the Kingdom of Belgium and officers belonging to the French Republic shall to the extent specified in the tripartite articles have rights and obligations and powers to carry out functions in the United Kingdom.

(3) Subject to paragraph (4), for the purpose of giving full effect to Article 17 of the Part II provisions *and to Article 17 of the Part III provisions* [, Article 17 of the Part III provisions and Article 17 of the Part IV provisions] (accommodation, etc., for Belgian authorities) the appropriate Minister may by written notice require any occupier or person concerned with the management of a terminal control point to provide such accommodation, installations and equipment as may be necessary to satisfy requirements determined under Article 16 of the Protocol mentioned in article 2(3)(b) above *and under that Article as applied by Article 3 of the Administrative Arrangement* [, under that Article as applied by Article 3 of the Administrative Arrangement and under that Article as applied by Article 4 of the Bilateral Agreement] (which requires the competent authorities of the Kingdom of Belgium and of the United Kingdom to determine their respective requirements in consultation with one another).

(4) Nothing in this article implies the existence of a control zone in the station of London-Waterloo on British Territory.

[This article is printed as amended by the Channel Tunnel (Miscellaneous Provisions) (Amendment) Order 2004 (S.I. 2004 No. 2589); and the Channel Tunnel (Miscellaneous Provisions) (Amendment) Order 2007 (S.I. 2007 No. 2908); and as amended, as from the date on which the Agreement signed in December, 2013, between the Government of the United Kingdom of Great Britain and Northern Ireland and the Government of the Kingdom of Belgium, Concerning Immigration Controls on Rail Traffic between Belgium and the United Kingdom Using the Channel Fixed Link enters into force, by the Channel Tunnel (Miscellaneous Provisions) (Amendment) Order 2014 (S.I. 2014 No. 409), arts 2 and 3(1) and (3) (insertion of words in square brackets, omission of italicised words that precede them).]

*Application of enactments*

**4.**—(1) All frontier enactments shall for the purpose of enabling officers belonging to the United Kingdom to carry out frontier controls extend—
   (a)   to France within a control zone, and
   (b)   to Belgium within a control zone.

(1A) The Race Relations Act 1976 shall apply to the carrying out by immigration officers of their functions in a control zone outside the United Kingdom as it applies to the carrying out of their functions within the United Kingdom.

(2), (3) [Application of Data Protection Act 1984.]

[This article is printed as amended by S.I. 2007 No. 2908 (*ante*).]

*Application of criminal law*

**5.**—(1) Any act or omission which—

(a) takes place outside the United Kingdom in a control zone, and

(b) would, if taking place in England, constitute an offence under a frontier control enactment,

shall be treated for the purposes of that enactment as taking place in England.

(2) Summary proceedings for anything that is by virtue of paragraph (1) an offence triable summarily or triable either way may be taken, and the offence may for all incidental purposes be treated as having been committed, in the county of Kent or in the inner London area as defined in section 2(1)(a) of the Justices of the Peace Act 1979.

(3) Any jurisdiction conferred by virtue of paragraphs (1) and (2) on any court is without prejudice to any jurisdiction exercisable apart from this article by that or any other court.

(4) Where it is proposed to institute proceedings in respect of an alleged offence in any court and a question as to the court's jurisdiction arises under Article 11(2) of the Part I provisions, it shall be presumed, unless the contrary is proved, that the court has jurisdiction by virtue of that Article.

*Powers of officers*

**6.** Schedule 3 (which contains provision as to powers exercisable by constables and other officers) shall have effect.

*Enactments modified*

**7.**—(1) Without prejudice to the generality of articles 4(1) and 5(1), the enactments specified in paragraph (2) shall—

(a) in their application to France and Belgium by virtue of article 4(1), and

(b) in their application to the United Kingdom for the authorised purposes,

have effect with modifications the same as those set out in Schedule 4 to the 1993 Order.

(2) Nothing in paragraph (1)(b) implies the existence of a control zone in the station of London-Waterloo on British Territory.

(2) The enactments are—

(a) Immigration Act 1971;

(b) Public Health (Control of Disease) Act 1984;

(c) Immigration and Asylum Act 1999;

(d) Terrorism Act 2000; and

(e) Immigration, Asylum and Nationality Act 2006.

[This article is printed as amended by the Channel Tunnel (Miscellaneous Provisions) (Amendment) Order 2006 (S.I. 2006 No. 2627); S.I. 2007 No. 2908 (*ante*); and the Channel Tunnel (International Arrangements and Miscellaneous Provisions) (Amendment) Order 2007 (S.I. 2007 No. 3579) (insertion of second para. (2)).]

*Amendments of instruments*

**8.** The instruments mentioned in Schedule 4 shall have effect with the amendments there specified.

**S.I. 1994 No. 1405, Sched. 1**

Article 2(1)                                    SCHEDULE 1

EXPRESSIONS DEFINED

| *Expression* | *Meaning* |
|---|---|
| ★**F-23** "Administrative arrangement" | The Administrative Arrangement made between the Secretary of State for the Home Department of the United Kingdom of Great Britain and Northern Ireland, the Vice Prime Minister, Minister of Home Affairs of the Kingdom of Belgium, and the Minister of the Interior, of Internal Security and Local Freedoms of the French Republic, concerning the exercise of Immigration Controls by British Officials at the Gare du Midi in Brussels and by Belgian Officials at Waterloo International Staton in London and Ashford International dated 1st October 2004 [as |

| Expression | Meaning |
|---|---|
| | amended by the Amending Administrative Arrangement]. |
| ["Amending Administrative Arrangement" | The Amending Administrative Arrangement signed on 4th and 5th October 2007 between the Secretary of State for the Home Department of the United Kingdom of Great Britain and Northern Ireland, the Vice Prime Minister, Minister for Home Affairs of the Kingdom of Belgium, and the Minister of Immigration, Integration, National Identity and Co-development of the French Republic making Amendments to the Administrative Arrangement signed at the Hague on 1st October 2004. |
| "Bilateral Agreement" | The Agreement between the Government of the United Kingdom of Great Britain and Northern Ireland and the Government of the Kingdom of Belgium, concerning Immigration Controls on Rail Traffic between Belgium and the United Kingdom using the Channel Fixed Link signed at London on 3rd December 2013 and at Brussels on 18th December 2013.] |
| "Control zone" | A control zone defined under Article 1(6) of the Part I provisions but excluding the station of London-Waterloo on British territory. |
| "Frontier controls" | So far as they constitute frontier controls as defined in Article 1(1) of the Part I provisions and are controls in relation to persons or goods, police, immigration, customs, health, veterinary and phytosanitary controls. |
| "Immigration controls" | The controls carried out by the authorities of the State of arrival to check whether passengers making a journey between Belgium and the United Kingdom are in possession of the necessary travel documents and fulfil the other conditions for entry to its territory. |
| "International service" | The meaning given in section 13(6) of the Channel Tunnel Act 1987. |
| "Officers" | Persons responsible for authorising departure from or entry to the State of arrival. |
| "The 1993 Order" | The Channel Tunnel (International Arrangements) Order 1993. |
| "The Part I provisions" | The provisions set out in Part I of Schedule 2. |
| "The Part II provisions" | The provisions set out in Part II of Schedule 2. |
| "The Part III provisions" | The Provisions set out in Part III of Schedule 2. |
| ["The Part IV provisions" | The Provisions set out in Part IV of Schedule 2.] |
| "Through train" | A train, other than a shuttle train as defined in section 1(9) of the Channel Tunnel Act 1987, which for the purposes of sections 11 and 12 of that Act is engaged on an international service. |

[The definitions of "Administrative arrangement", "Immigration controls", "Officers", and "The Part III provisions" were inserted by the Channel Tunnel (Miscellaneous Provisions) (Amendment) Order 2004 (S.I. 2004 No. 2589). The definition of "control zone" is printed as amended by the Channel Tunnel (Miscellaneous Provisions) (Amendment) Order 2007 (S.I. 2007 No. 2908). The words in square brackets in the definition of "Administrative arrangements" and the definitions of "Amending Administrative Arrangement", "Bilateral Agreement", and "The Part IV provisions" are inserted, as from the date on which the Agreement signed in December, 2013, between the Government of the United Kingdom of Great Britain and Northern Ireland and the Government of the Kingdom of Belgium, Concerning Immigration Controls on Rail Traffic between Belgium and the United Kingdom Using the Channel Fixed Link enters into force, by the Channel Tunnel (Miscellaneous Provisions) (Amendment) Order 2014 (S.I. 2014 No. 409), arts 2 and 3(4). In addition to the above definitions, the Schedule also contains definitions of the following expressions, which are identical to those contained in Schedule 1 to the 1993 Order (*ante*, F-15): "Frontier control enactment", "Terminal control point", "Train manager" and "The tunnel system".]

**S.I. 1994 No. 1405, Sched. 2**

Article 2(3)                    SCHEDULE 2

TRIPARTITE ARTICLES

PART I

AGREEMENT

PART I

**General provisions**

ARTICLE 1

*Definitions*

**F-24**        (1) "Frontier controls" means police, immigration, customs, health, veterinary and phytosanitary, consumer protection, and transport controls, as well as any other controls provided for in national or European Community laws and regulations.

(2) "Fixed Link" means the Channel Fixed Link defined in Article 1 of the Treaty done at Canterbury on 12 February 1986.

(3) "Trains" means international trains travelling between Belgium and British territory, using the Fixed Link and passing through French territory.

(4) "Non-stop trains" means international trains travelling between Belgian and British territory, using the Fixed Link and crossing French territory without making a commercial stop, except for technical stops.

(5) "Officers" means persons responsible for policing and frontier controls who are under the command of the persons or authorities designated in accordance with Article 3(2).

(6) "Control Zone" means that part of the territory of the host State and the non-stop trains, within which the officers of the other States are empowered to effect controls. Each control zone shall be defined by mutual agreement between the host State and the State whose officers will be operating in the said zone; however, in the case of non-stop trains, the control zone in French territory shall be determined jointly by the three Governments.

(7) "Host State" means the State in whose territory the controls of the other States are effected.

ARTICLE 2

*Scope*

(1) This Agreement shall apply to rail traffic between the United Kingdom and Belgium travelling via the Fixed Link and passing through French territory.

(3) A Protocol concerning frontier controls and policing on non-stop trains between the United Kingdom and Belgium via the Fixed Link is attached as an annex to this Agreement and shall form an integral part thereof.

PART II

**Authorities and General Principles of Co-operation**

ARTICLE 3

**F-24a**        (2) Each of the Governments shall designate the authorities or persons having charge of the services which in its territory have responsibility for the exercise of frontier controls and the maintenance of law and order.

524

### ARTICLE 4

On non-stop trains, British officers may exercise frontier controls in Belgian and French territory, and Belgian officers in British and French territory.

### ARTICLE 5

It is agreed that the frontier controls relating to non-stop trains shall in principle be effected under the exclusive responsibility of the British and Belgian authorities.

### ARTICLE 9

The officers of the three States shall be authorised to circulate freely over the whole of the route between London and Brussels for official purposes simply by producing appropriate evidence of their identity and status.

### PART III

#### Co-operation in Criminal Justice

##### ARTICLE 11

(1) Without prejudice to the provisions of Articles 4 and 14(2) of the Protocol attached as an annex **F-24b** to this Agreement, when an offence is committed on the territory of one of the three States that State shall have jurisdiction.

(2) When it cannot be ascertained where such an offence has been committed, the State of arrival shall have jurisdiction.

##### ARTICLE 12

Where an arrest is made for an offence in respect of which one State has jurisdiction under Article 11, that arrest shall not be affected by the fact that its effects continue in the territory of the other States.

##### ARTICLE 13

Persons who are found committing, attempting to commit, or just having committed an offence and who are apprehended on the train during the journey shall be handed over as soon as possible to the empowered officers of the State which has jurisdiction under Article 11.

##### ARTICLE 14

(1) In the event that a person is found committing, attempting to commit or just having committed on board a train in the territory of a State one of the following offences: homicide, rape, arson, armed robbery, kidnapping and hostage taking, or use of explosives, the train must be stopped in order to enable the competent authorities of that State to take any measures relevant to their investigations and, where appropriate, detain the person suspected of having committed the offence.

(2) If the train cannot be stopped because it is within the Fixed Link or because it is about to leave the territory of the State in which one of the offences referred to in the preceding paragraph has been committed, authorised officers who are present must take all appropriate interim measures to ensure that, when the train arrives, the officers of the State which has jurisdiction under Article 11 are able to interview witnesses, take evidence or receive information relevant to their investigations and, where appropriate, take charge of the person suspected of having committed the offence.

##### ARTICLE 15

(1) When a person is arrested in a manner covered by Articles 6, 12, 13 and 14(2) of this Agreement, the arrest shall be notified without delay to the authorities of the State of arrival. The person arrested may be transferred to the territory of the State which has jurisdiction under Article 11.

(2) However, any such transfer shall take place within no more than 24 hours of the notification under the preceding paragraph. Moreover, each State reserves the right not to authorise the transfer of its nationals.

### PART V

#### Co-operation Between the Competent Authorities

##### ARTICLE 23

(1) Each State shall waive any claim which it may have against the other States for compensation in **F-24c** respect of damage caused to its officers or its property.

(2) The provisions of this Article shall not affect in any way the rights of third parties under the laws of each State.

PART VI

**Final Clauses**

ARTICLE 24

**F-24d**      In addition to the arrangements provided for under Article 20, the procedures for the implementation of this Agreement and its Protocol may, as far as necessary, be the subject of technical or administrative arrangements between the competent authorities of the three States.

PART II

PROTOCOL

ARTICLE 1

**F-24e**      This Protocol shall apply to non-stop rail traffic between the United Kingdom and Belgium travelling via the Fixed Link and passing through French territory.

ARTICLE 2

(1) The laws and regulations relating to frontier controls of one State shall be applicable in the control zone situated in the other States and shall be put into effect by the officers of that State in the same way as in their own territory.

(2) The officers of each State shall be subject to the legislation of that State on the protection of individuals with regard to automated processing of personal data when using their automated data files and equipment in the control zone situated in either of the other States.

ARTICLE 3

(1) The officers of the other States shall, in exercise of their national powers, be permitted in the control zone situated in the host State to detain or arrest persons in accordance with the laws and regulations relating to frontier controls of their own State or persons sought by the authorities of their own State. These officers shall also be permitted to conduct such persons to the territory of their own State.

(2) However, no person may be held for more than 24 hours in the areas reserved for frontier controls in the host State. Any such detention shall be subject to the requirements and procedures laid down by the legislation of the State of the officers who have made the detention or arrest.

ARTICLE 4

Breaches of the laws and regulations relating to frontier controls of other States which are detected in the control zone situated in the host State shall be subject to the laws and regulations of those other States, as if the breaches had occurred in the territory of the latter.

ARTICLE 5

(1) The frontier controls of the State of departure shall normally be effected before those of the State of arrival.

(2) The officers of the State of arrival are not authorised to begin to carry out such controls before the end of the controls of the State of departure. Any form of relinquishment of such controls shall be considered as a control.

(3) The officers of the State of departure may no longer carry out their controls when the officers of the State of arrival have begun their own operations, except with the consent of the competent officers of the State of arrival.

(4) If exceptionally, in the course of the frontier controls, the sequence of operations provided for in paragraph (1) of this Article is modified, the officers of the State of arrival may not proceed to detentions, arrests or seizures until the frontier controls of the State of departure are completed. In such a case, these officers shall escort the persons, vehicles, merchandise, animals or other goods, for which the frontier controls of the State of departure are not yet completed, to the officers of that State. If these latter then wish to proceed to detentions, arrests or seizure, they shall have priority.

ARTICLE 6

If the State of arrival refuses admission to persons, vehicles, animals or goods, or if persons refuse to submit to the frontier controls of the State of arrival, or send or take back any vehicles, animals or goods which are accompanying them, the authorities of the State of departure may not refuse to accept back such persons, vehicles, animals or goods. However, the authorities of the State of departure may take any measures to deal with them in accordance with the law applicable in that State and in a way which does not impose obligations either on the State of transit or on the State of arrival.

## ARTICLE 7

(2) In an emergency, the local representatives of the authorities concerned may by mutual agreement provisionally bring into effect alterations to the delimitation of the control zones which may prove necessary. Any arrangements so reached shall come into effect immediately.

## ARTICLES 8–11

*[Health, veterinary and phytosanitary controls]*

## ARTICLE 12

Officers of the other States may wear their national uniform or visible distinctive insignia in the host State.

## ARTICLE 13

(1) The authorities of the host State shall grant the same protection and assistance to officers of the other States, in the exercise of their functions, as they grant to their own officers.

(2) The provisions of the criminal law in force in the host State for the protection of officers in the exercise of their functions shall be equally applicable to the punishment of offences committed against officers of the other States in the exercise of their functions.

## ARTICLE 14

(1) Without prejudice to the application of the provisions of Article 23 of the Agreement, claims for compensation for loss, injury or damage caused by or to officers of the other States in the exercise of their functions in the host State shall be subject to the law and jurisdiction of the State to which those officers belong as if the circumstance giving rise to the claim had occurred in that State.

(2) Officers of the other States may not be prosecuted by authorities of the host State for any acts performed in the control zone whilst in the exercise of their functions. In such a case, they shall come under the jurisdiction of their own State as if the act had been committed in that State.

(3) The judicial authorities or police of the host State who take steps to record the complaint and assemble the facts relating thereto shall communicate all the particulars and evidence thereof to the competent authorities of the State to which the accused officer belongs for the purposes of a possible prosecution according to the laws in force in that State.

## ARTICLE 15

(1) Officers of the other States shall be permitted freely to transfer to their own States sums of money levied on behalf of their Governments in the control zone situated in the host State, as well as merchandise and other goods seized there.

(2) They may equally sell such merchandise and other goods in the host State in conformity with the provisions in force in the host State and transfer the proceeds to their own State.

## ARTICLE 17

The authorities of the Kingdom of Belgium and of the United Kingdom shall use their best endeavours to ensure that the authorities of the other Party are able to make use in the host State of the accommodation, installations and equipment necessary for the performance of their functions.

## ARTICLE 18

(1) The officers of the other States are empowered to keep order within the accommodation appointed for their exclusive use in the host State.

(2) The officers of the host State shall not have access to such accommodation, except at the request of the officers of the State concerned or in accordance with the laws of the host State applicable to entry into and searches of private premises.

## ARTICLE 19

All goods which are necessary to enable the officers of the other States to carry out their functions in the host State shall be exempt from all taxes and dues on entry and exit.

## ARTICLE 20

(1) The officers of the other States whilst exercising their functions in the host State shall be authorised to communicate with their national authorities.

PART III

ARTICLES OR PARTS OF ARTICLES OF THE PROTOCOL ATTACHED TO AND FORMING PART OF THE AGREEMENT, AS APPLIED BY THE ADMINISTRATIVE ARRANGEMENT TO IMMIGRATION CONTROLS UPON PASSENGERS TRAVELLING [BETWEEN THE UNITED KINGDOM AND BELGIUM] ON INTERNATIONAL TRAINS MAKING A COMMERCIAL STOP

ARTICLE 1

**F-24f**    *This Protocol shall apply to rail traffic between the United Kingdom and Belgium travelling via the Fixed Link and making a commercial stop in French territory* [This Protocol shall apply to rail traffic between Ashford International, Ebbsfleet International or St Pancras International train stations in the United Kingdom and Belgium, travelling via the Fixed Link and making a commercial stop in French territory].

ARTICLE 2

(1) The laws and regulations relating to immigration controls of one State shall be applicable in the control zone situated in the other States and shall be put into effect by the officers of that State in the same way as in their own territory.

(2) The officers of each State shall be subject to the legislation of that State on the protection of individuals with regard to automated processing of personal data when using their automated data files and equipment in the control zone situated in either of the other States.

ARTICLE 3

(1) The officers of the other States shall, in exercise of their national powers, be permitted in the control zone situated in the host state to detain or arrest persons in accordance with the laws relating to immigration control of their own State. These officers shall also be permitted to conduct such persons to the territory of their own State.

(2) However, no person may be held for more than 24 hours in the areas reserved for immigration controls in the host State. Any such detention shall be subject to the requirements and procedures laid down by the legislation of the State of the officers who have made the detention or arrest.

ARTICLE 4

Breaches of the laws and regulations relating to immigration controls of the other States which are detected in the control zone situated in the host State shall be subject to the laws and regulations of those other States, as if the breaches had occurred in the territory of the latter.

ARTICLE 5

(1) The immigration controls of the State of departure shall normally be effected before those of the *State of arrival* [other States].

(2) The officers of the *State of arrival* [other States] are not authorised to begin to carry out such controls before the end of the controls of the State of departure. Any form of relinquishment of such controls shall be considered as a control.

(3) The officers of the State of departure may no longer carry out their immigration controls when the officers of the *State of arrival* [other States] have begun their own operations, except with the consent of the competent officers of the *State of arrival* [other States].

(4) If exceptionally, in the course of the immigration controls, the sequence of operations provided for in paragraph (1) of this Article is modified, the officers of the *State of arrival* [other States] may not proceed to detentions, arrests or seizures until the immigration controls of the State of departure are completed. In such a case, these officers shall escort any persons and goods for which the immigration controls of the State of departure are not yet completed, to the officers of that State. If these latter then wish to proceed to detentions, arrests or seizures, they shall have priority.

ARTICLE 6

If the *State of arrival refuses* [officers of the other States refuse] admission to persons or goods or if the persons refuse to submit to the immigration controls of the *State of arrival* [other States], or send or take back any goods which are accompanying them, the authorities of the State of departure may not refuse to accept back such persons or goods. However, the authorities of the State of departure may take any measures to deal with them in accordance with the law applicable in that State and in a way which does not impose obligations either on the State of transit or on the State of arrival.

ARTICLE 7

In an emergency, the local representatives of the authorities concerned may by mutual agreement provisionally bring into effect alterations to the delimitation of the control zones which may prove necessary. Any arrangements so reached shall come into effect immediately.

528

ARTICLE 8

Immigration controls on persons for the purpose of safeguarding public health shall be carried out in the control zones situated in the host State by the competent authorities of the *State of arrival* [other States] in conformity with the regulations applicable in *that State* [those States].

ARTICLE 12

Officers of the other States may wear their national uniform or visible distinctive insignia in the host State.

ARTICLE 13

(1) The authorities of the host State shall grant the same protection and assistance to officers of the other States, in the exercise of their functions, as they grant to their own officers.

(2) The provisions of the criminal law in force in the host State for the protection of officers in the exercise of their functions shall be equally applicable to the punishment of offences committed against officers of the other States in the exercise of their functions.

ARTICLE 14

(1) Without prejudice to the application of the provisions of Article 23 of the Agreement, claims for compensation for loss, injury or damage caused by or to officers of the other States in the exercise of their functions in the host State shall be subject to the law and jurisdiction of the State to which those officers belong as if the circumstance giving rise to the claim had occurred there.

(2) Officers of the other States may not be prosecuted by the authorities of the host State for any acts performed in the control zone whilst in the exercise of their functions. In such a case, they shall come under the jurisdiction of their own State as if the act had been committed there.

(3) The judicial authorities or police of the host State who take steps to record the complaint and assemble the facts relating thereto shall communicate all the particulars and evidence thereof to the competent authorities of the State to which the officer belongs for the purposes of a possible prosecution according to the laws in force in that State.

ARTICLE 17

The authorities of the Kingdom of Belgium and of the United Kingdom shall use their best endeavours to ensure that the authorities of the other party are able to make use in the host State of the accommodation, installations and equipment necessary for the performance of their functions.

ARTICLE 18

(1) The officers of the other State are empowered to keep order within the accommodation appointed for their exclusive use in the host State.

(2) The officers of the host State shall not have access to such accommodation except at the request of the officers of the State concerned or in accordance with the laws of the host State applicable to entry into and searches of private premises.

ARTICLE 19

All goods which are necessary to enable the officers of the other State to carry out their functions in the host State shall be exempt from all taxes and duty on entry and exit.

ARTICLE 20

The officers of the other State whilst exercising their functions in the host State shall be authorised to communicate with their national authorities.

[Part III of this schedule was inserted by the Channel Tunnel (Miscellaneous Provisions) Order 2004 (S.I. 2004 No. 2589). It is printed as amended, as from the date on which the Agreement signed in December, 2013, between the Government of the United Kingdom of Great Britain and Northern Ireland and the Government of the Kingdom of Belgium, Concerning Immigration Controls on Rail Traffic between Belgium and the United Kingdom Using the Channel Fixed Link enters into force, by the Channel Tunnel (Miscellaneous Provisions) (Amendment) Order 2014 (S.I. 2014 No. 409), arts 2 and 5 (insertion of words in square brackets, omission of italicised words that precede them).]

[PART IV

ARTICLES OR PARTS OF ARTICLES OF THE PROTOCOL ATTACHED TO AND FORMING PART OF THE AGREEMENT, AS APPLIED BY THE BILATERAL AGREEMENT TO IMMIGRATION CONTROLS UPON PASSENGERS TRAVELLING BETWEEN BELGIUM AND THE UNITED KINGDOM ON INTERNATIONAL TRAINS MAKING A COMMERCIAL STOP

ARTICLE 1

This Protocol shall apply to rail traffic between the Brussels-South train station in Belgium and the United Kingdom, travelling via the Fixed Link and making a commercial stop in French territory.

ARTICLE 2

(1) The laws and regulations relating to immigration controls of one State shall be applicable in the control zones situated in the other State and shall be put into effect by the officers of that State in the same way as in their own territory.

(2) The officers of each State shall be subject to the legislation of that State on the protection of individuals with regard to automated processing of personal data when using their automated data files and equipment in the control zone situated in either of the other State [*sic*].

ARTICLE 3

(1) The officers of the other State shall, in exercise of their national powers, be permitted in the control zone situated in the host state to detain or arrest persons in accordance with the laws relating to immigration control of their own State. These officers shall also be permitted to conduct such persons to the territory of their own State.

(2) However, no person may be held for more than 24 hours in the areas reserved for immigration controls in the host State. Any such detention shall be subject to the requirements and procedures laid down by the legislation of the State of the officers who have made the detention or arrest.

ARTICLE 4

Breaches of the laws and regulations relating to immigration controls of the other State which are detected in the control zone situated in the host State shall be subject to the laws and regulations of the other State, as if the breaches had occurred in the territory of the latter.

ARTICLE 5

(1) The immigration controls of the State of departure shall normally be effected before those of the State of arrival.

(2) The officers of the State of arrival are not authorised to begin to carry out such controls before the end of the controls of the State of departure. Any form of relinquishment of such controls shall be considered as a control.

(3) The officers of the State of departure may no longer carry out their immigration controls when the officers of the State of arrival have begun their own operations, except with the consent of the competent officers of the State of arrival.

(4) If exceptionally, in the course of the immigration controls, the sequence of operations provided for in paragraph (1) of this Article is modified, the officers of the State of arrival may not proceed to detentions, arrests or seizures until the immigration controls of the State of departure are completed. In such a case, these officers shall escort any persons and goods for which the immigration controls of the State of departure are not yet completed, to the officers of that State. If these latter then wish to proceed to detentions, arrests or seizures, they shall have priority.

ARTICLE 6

If the State of arrival refuses admission to persons or goods or if the persons refuse to submit to the immigration controls of the State of arrival, or send or take back any goods which are accompanying them, the authorities of the State of departure may not refuse to accept back such persons or goods. However, the authorities of the State of departure may take any measures to deal with them in accordance with the law applicable in that State and in a way which does not impose obligations either on the State of transit or on the State of arrival.

ARTICLE 7

In an emergency, the local representatives of the authorities concerned may by mutual agreement provisionally bring into effect alterations to the delimitation of the control zones which may prove necessary. Any arrangements so reached shall come into effect immediately.

ARTICLE 8

Immigration controls on persons for the purpose of safeguarding public health shall be carried out in the control zones situated in the host State by the competent authorities of the State of arrival in conformity with the regulations applicable in that State.

ARTICLE 12

Officers of the other State may wear their national uniform or visible distinctive insignia in the host State.

ARTICLE 13

(1) The authorities of the host State shall grant the same protection and assistance to officers of the other State, in the exercise of their functions, as they grant to their own officers.

(2) The provisions of the criminal law in force in the host State for the protection of officers in the exercise of their functions shall be equally applicable to the punishment of offences committed against officers of the other State in the exercise of their functions.

ARTICLE 14

(1) Without prejudice to the application of the provisions of Article 23 of the Agreement, claims for compensation for loss, injury or damage caused by or to officers of the other State in the exercise of their functions in the host State shall be subject to the law and jurisdiction of the State to which those officers belong as if the circumstance giving rise to the claim had occurred there.

(2) Officers of the other State may not be prosecuted by the authorities of the host State for any acts performed in the control zone whilst in the exercise of their functions. In such a case, they shall come under the jurisdiction of their own State as if the act had been committed there.

(3) The judicial authorities or police of the host State who take steps to record the complaint and assemble the facts relating thereto shall communicate all the particulars and evidence thereof to the competent authorities of the State to which the officer belongs for the purposes of a possible prosecution according to the laws in force in that State.

ARTICLE 17

The authorities of the Kingdom of Belgium and of the United Kingdom shall use their best endeavours to ensure that the authorities of the other party are able to make use in the host State of the accommodation, installations and equipment necessary for the performance of their functions.

ARTICLE 18

(1) The officers of the other State are empowered to keep order within the accommodation appointed for their exclusive use in the host State.

(2) The officers of the host State shall not have access to such accommodation except at the request of the officers of the State concerned or in accordance with the laws of the host State applicable to entry into and searches of private premises.

ARTICLE 19

All goods which are necessary to enable the officers of the other State to carry out their functions in the host State shall be exempt from all taxes and duty on entry and exit.

ARTICLE 20

The officers of the other State whilst exercising their functions in the host State shall be authorised to communicate with their national authorities.]

[Part IV of this schedule is inserted, as from the date on which the Agreement signed in December, 2013, between the Government of the United Kingdom of Great Britain and Northern Ireland and the Government of the Kingdom of Belgium, Concerning Immigration Controls on Rail Traffic between Belgium and the United Kingdom Using the Channel Fixed Link enters into force, by the Channel Tunnel (Miscellaneous Provisions) (Amendment) Order 2014 (S.I. 2014 No. 409), arts 2 and 3(6).]

## Powers of officers

Paragraph 1 of Schedule 3 to S.I. 1994 No. 1405 provides that Part I of Schedule 3 to the 1993 **F-25** Order (*ante*, F-17) shall, with the variations set out in paragraphs 2 to 7, be taken to apply as if it were contained in the 1994 Order. Part I of Schedule 3 to the 1993 Order, *as so varied*, is set out below.

**S.I. 1993 No. 1813, Sched. 3, Pt I (as varied by S.I. 1994 No. 1405, Sched. 3)**

SCHEDULE 3

PART I

POWERS OF OFFICERS

*Powers of arrest outside United Kingdom*

**F-26**    2.—(1) A constable may in a control zone in France or Belgium—

    (a) exercise any power of arrest conferred by a frontier control enactment or conferred by the Police and Criminal Evidence Act 1984 (in this Schedule referred to as "the 1984 Act") in respect of an offence under such an enactment,

    (b) make any arrest authorised by a warrant issued by a court in the United Kingdom, and

    (c) arrest any person whose name or description or both, together with particulars of an arrestable offence (within the meaning of section 24 of the 1984 Act) of which there are reasonable grounds for suspecting him to be guilty, have been made available by a chief officer of police to other such officers.

(2) For the purposes of sub-paragraph (1)(a) the reference in sub-paragraph (1) to a constable shall be construed—

    (a) in relation to the powers of arrest conferred by section 25(3) of and paragraph 17(1) of Schedule 2 to the Immigration Act 1971, as including a reference both—

        (i) to an immigration officer appointed for the purposes of that Act under paragraph 1 of that Schedule, and

        (ii) to an officer of customs and excise who is the subject of arrangements for the employment of such officers as immigration officers made under that paragraph by the Secretary of State.

    (b) in relation to the power of arrest conferred by paragraph 6(4) of Schedule 5 to the Prevention of Terrorism (Temporary Provisions) Act 1989, as including a reference to any person who by virtue of paragraph 1(1) of that Schedule is an examining officer for the purposes of that Act, and

    (c) in relation to any arrest that may be made by a customs officer by virtue of section 138 of the Customs and Excise Management Act 1979 and an arrest for a drug trafficking offence as defined in section 38(1) of the Drug Trafficking Offences Act 1986, as including a reference to a customs officer.

(3) A customs officer may in a control zone in France or Belgium arrest any person whose name or description or both, together with particulars of an arrestable offence (within the meaning of section 24 of the 1984 Act) which is an offence in relation to an assigned matter as defined in section 1(1) of the Customs and Excise Management Act 1979 and of which there are reasonable grounds for suspecting him to be guilty, have been made available to customs officers generally under the authority of the Commissioners of Customs and Excise.

(4) Sub-paragraph (5) applies where—

    (a) an arrest has been made for an offence of the kind mentioned in Article 12 of the Part I provisions, and

    (b) the person arrested enters France or Belgium ("the State of arrival") while under arrest.

(5) If jurisdiction is not asserted by the State of arrival, the person arrested shall be treated as having continued to be under arrest throughout, notwithstanding any intervening transfer of Custody to a person other than the person who arrested him, and sections 30 and 41 of the 1984 Act shall apply accordingly.

(6) [*Not printed in this work.*]

(7) Any power conferred by an enactment to search an arrested person may be exercised following an arrest authorised by this paragraph as if the person had been arrested in the United Kingdom.

    3.—(1) Where—

    (a) an arrest of any kind authorised by paragraph 2 above has been made in a control zone in France or Belgium; or

    (b) an arrest of any such kind has been made in the United Kingdom and the person arrested enters such a control zone while under arrest,

the person arrested may be held in France or, as the case may be, Belgium for a period of not more than 24 hours.

(2) Subject to sub-paragraph (4), the person arrested shall be treated as if the place where he is held were for the purposes of sections 36(7) and (8), 54 to 56, 58 and 61 to 63 of the 1984 Act and in

the case of a child or young person section 34(2) to (7), (8) and (9) of the Children and Young Persons Act 1933 a police station, or where the arrest was made by a customs officer, a customs office, in England, not being a police station or customs office designated under section 35 of the 1984 Act.

(4) Where the power of arrest mentioned in paragraph 2(2)(b) has been exercised any detention in France or Belgium of the persons arrested shall be treated for all purposes as being detention under paragraph 6(1) of Schedule 5 to the Prevention of Terrorism (Temporary Provisions) Act 1989, and section 16(2) of that Act, sections 51(b), 56 and 58 of the 1984 Act and section 34 of the Children and Young Persons Act 1933 as applying accordingly.

### *Arrested persons arriving in the United Kingdom*

4.—(1) Where a constable is satisfied that an arrest made outside the United Kingdom on a   **F-26a** through train was one falling within Article 13 or 14 of the Part I provisions (persons found committing, attempting to commit or just having committed an offence) he may arrange for the person arrested to be taken into temporary custody.

(2) A person taken into temporary custody under sub-paragraph (1)—

(a)  shall be treated for all purposes as being in lawful custody, and

(b)  may be taken to a police station or such other place as may be appropriate in the circumstances, and shall in that case be treated as being a person in whose case sections 36(7) and (8), 54 to 56 and 58 of the 1984 Act, and in the case of a child or young person section 34(2) to (7), (8) and (9) of the Children and Young Persons Act 1933, apply;

and arrangements must be made for him to be transferred within 24 hours from the time at which he was taken into custody to the State having jurisdiction by virtue of Article 11(1) of the Part I provisions.

(2A) Where an arrest has been made for an offence in respect of which the United Kingdom may have jurisdiction as the State of arrival by virtue of Article 11(2) of the Part I provisions the person arrested shall be taken to a police station.

(2B) The custody officer at the police station to which the person is taken shall consider whether the offence is one in respect of which the United Kingdom has jurisdiction by virtue of Article 11(2) of the Part I provisions and may for that purpose detain the person at the police station for not longer than the permitted period.

(3) The permitted period is the period of 24 hours beginning at the time at which the person arrives at the police station.

(4) Subject to sub-paragraph (6), the person shall be treated—

(a)  as not being detained at the police station for the purposes of section 37 of the 1984 Act, and

(b)  as not being in police detention for the purposes of sections 40 to 43 of the 1984 Act.

(5) Where the custody officer reaches the conclusion that the United Kingdom does not have jurisdiction by virtue of Article 11(2) he shall immediately inform the competent authorities of the State appearing to him to have jurisdiction by virtue of Article 11(1) that he has reached that conclusion and shall arrange for the person to be transferred to that State within the permitted period.

(6) Where the custody officer reaches the conclusion that the United Kingdom has jurisdiction by virtue of Article 11(2)—

(a)  he shall immediately inform the person of his conclusion,

(b)  the person shall be treated as being in police detention for all purposes of Part IV of the 1984 Act, and

(c)  that Part shall have effect in relation to him as if the relevant time mentioned in section 41(1) were the time at which he is informed of the conclusion.

(7) Where the police station to which the person is taken is not a police station designated under section 34 of the 1984 Act, references in this paragraph to the custody officer are to be construed as references to an officer not below the rank of sergeant.

### *Arrests of French officers*

5.—(1) This paragraph applies where an officer belonging to the French Republic or to the   **F-26b** Kingdom of Belgium ("the officer") is arrested for an act performed in the United Kingdom in a control zone.

(2) If the officer enters the State to which he belongs ("the home State") while under arrest—

(a)  he shall without delay be handed over for custody to the competent authorities of the home State and shall be treated as continuing to be under arrest until he has been handed over, and

(b)  if after consultation with those authorities it is then determined that the act was not performed by the officer whilst in the exercise of his functions and he accordingly does not by virtue of Article 14(2) of the Part II provisions come under the jurisdiction of the home State, he shall be treated as having continued to be under arrest until sub-paragraph (3) has been complied with.

(3) Where—

(a)   sub-paragraph (2)(b) applies, or

(b)   the officer does not leave the United Kingdom whilst under arrest,

he shall be taken to a police station designated under section 35 of the 1984 Act.

(4) Sub-paragraphs (5) to (9) apply in a case falling within sub-paragraph (3)(b).

(5) The custody officer at the police station to which the officer is taken shall after consultation with the competent authorities of the home State determine whether the act was performed by the officer whilst in the exercise of his functions, and may for the purpose of determining that question detain the officer at the police station for not longer than the permitted period.

(6) The permitted period is the period of 24 hours beginning at the time at which the officer arrives at the police station.

(7) Subject to sub-paragraph (9), the officer shall be treated—

(a)   as not being detained at the police station for the purposes of section 37 of the 1984 Act, and

(b)   as not being in police detention for the purposes of sections 40 to 43 of the 1984 Act.

(8) Where the custody officer determines that the act was performed by the officer whilst in the exercise of his functions and the officer accordingly comes under the jurisdiction of the home State by virtue of Article 14(2), he shall immediately inform the competent authorities of the home State and shall arrange for the officer to be transferred to the home State within the permitted period.

(9) In any other case—

(a)   the custody officer shall immediately inform the officer of his determination,

(b)   the officer shall be treated as being in police detention for all purposes of Part IV of the 1984 Act, and

(c)   that Part shall have effect in relation to him as if the relevant time mentioned in section 41(1) were the time at which he is informed of the determination.

*Arrests of United Kingdom officers*

**F-26c**      6.—(1) This paragraph applies where an officer belonging to the United Kingdom ("the officer") is arrested for an act performed in France or Belgium in a control zone.

(2) If—

(a)   the officer does not enter the United Kingdom while under arrest, and

(b)   the competent authorities of the State in which the act was performed ("the State concerned") determine that the act was performed by the officer whilst in the exercise of his functions and he accordingly comes under United Kingdom jurisdiction by virtue of Article 14(2) of the Part II provisions,

he shall on being handed over by those authorities to a constable be treated as having been arrested by the constable.

(3) Where—

(a)   sub-paragraph (2)(b) applies, or

(b)   the officer enters the United Kingdom while under the original arrest,

he shall be taken to a police station designated under section 35 of the 1984 Act.

(4) Sub-paragraphs (5) to (9) apply in a case falling within sub-paragraph (3)(b).

(5) The custody officer at the police station to which the officer is taken shall—

(a)   immediately invite the competent authorities of the State concerned to determine whether the act was performed by the officer whilst in the exercise of his functions, and

(b)   afford those authorities any assistance they may require in determining that question

and may for the purpose of enabling that question to be determined detain the officer at the police station for not longer than the permitted period.

(6) The permitted period is the period of 24 hours beginning at the time at which the officer arrives at the police station.

(7) Subject to sub-paragraph (9), the officer shall be treated—

(a)   as not being detained at the police station for the purposes of section 37 of the 1984 Act, and

(b)   as not being in police detention for the purposes of sections 40 to 43 of the 1984 Act.

(8) Where the competent authorities of the State concerned determine that the act was not performed by the officer whilst in the exercise of his functions and the officer accordingly does not by virtue of Article 14(2) come under United Kingdom jurisdiction, the custody officer shall arrange for the officer to be transferred to the State concerned within the permitted period.

(9) In any other case—

    (a)   the custody officer shall immediately inform the officer of the determination,

    (b)   the officer shall be treated as being in police detention for all purposes of Part IV of the 1984 Act, and

    (c)   that Part shall have effect in relation to him as if the relevant time mentioned in section 41(1) were the time at which he is informed of the determination.

## Amendments

Relevant entries in Schedule 4 are noted at the appropriate place elsewhere in this work. **F-27**

# APPENDIX G
## Guidelines on Claims for Fees under a Crown Court Representation Order and in the Court of Appeal

## A. SUMMARY OF SOURCE MATERIAL

### Legislation

As from April 2, 2001 the relevant provisions of the Legal Aid in Criminal and Care Proceed-   **G-1**
ings (Costs) Regulations 1989 (S.I. 1989 No. 343), as amended, were superseded, virtually
unamended, by the Criminal Defence Service (Funding) Order 2001 (S.I. 2001 No. 855) ("the
Funding Order 2001"). This was significantly amended by a series of amending orders until it was
revoked and replaced, in relation to representation orders granted on or after April 30, 2007, by
the Criminal Defence Service (Funding) Order 2007 (S.I. 2007 No. 1174). The 2007 order was
itself amended on many occasions over the following six years, until it lapsed on April 1, 2013,
with the commencement of the repeal of its enabling legislation by the LASPOA 2012, s.39(1),
and Sched. 5, para. 39. Full details of all the amending instruments for both the 2001 order and
the 2007 order may be found in the second supplement to the 2013 edition of this work, together
with the full text of the 2007 order (as amended).

The Criminal Legal Aid (Remuneration) Regulations 2013 (S.I. 2013 No. 435) (set out in full,
*post*, G-6 *et seq.*) came into force on April 1, 2013. The substance of the 2013 regulations is almost
identical to that of the 2007 order as it read at the time it lapsed, and many, if not all, the
authorities that related to the 2007 order at that time will simply carry across. Where they are
referred to *post* in this appendix, references to provisions of the former legislation have simply
been updated to refer to the corresponding provision of the 2013 regulations.

As to the transitional arrangements in connection with the repeal of the relevant provisions of
the Access to Justice Act 1999 and the commencement of the relevant provisions of the 2012 Act,
see *ante*, § 6-173.

### The current regimes

Apart from a handful of historical cases which will be governed by the former provisions for *ex*   **G-2**
*post facto* taxation (as to which see Appendix G-200 *et seq.* in the supplements to the 2010 edition
of this work), advocates' fees in the Crown Court effectively fall into one of two regimes:

   (i) *Graduated fees.* These were first introduced in 1997 for trials lasting up to 10 days, appeals
      and other minor Crown Court business: Legal Aid in Criminal and Care Proceedings
      (Costs) Regulations 1989 (S.I. 1989 No. 343), Sched. 3. The scheme was then extended to
      cover trials of up to 25 days and, as from 2005, of trials up to 40 days. As from April 30,
      2007, it was intended that the scheme would cover all Crown Court work save for those
      cases contracted under the Very High Costs Case provisions: Criminal Defence Service
      (Funding) Order 2007 (S.I. 2007 No. 1174), art. 3(6A), and Sched. 1, para. 2(1). The 2007
      scheme is sometimes referred to as the Revised Advocacy Graduated Fee Scheme (RAGFS).
      The details were contained in Schedule 1 to the 2007 order, which replaced Schedule 4 to
      the Criminal Defence Service (Funding) Order 2001 (S.I. 2001 No. 855). The 2007 scheme
      (as amended) is now to be found in Schedule 1 to the Criminal Legal Aid (Remuneration)
      Regulations 2013 (S.I. 2013 No. 435).

  (ii) *Very High Cost Cases (VHCC).* This regime came into effect on October 29, 2001. All cases
      estimated to last more than 24 days are capable of being subject to a VHCC contract. As to
      the current VHCC regime, see *post*, G-181 *et seq.*

## Notes for guidance

*(a) Graduated fees*

**G-3**     The Ministry of Justice's *Graduated Fee Scheme Guidance (GFSG)* is updated at regular intervals. In addition, guidance notes have been issued by the Criminal Bar Association, and are available on both the Criminal Bar Association's and the Courts Service's National Taxing Team's websites. The GFSG includes references to costs judges' decisions which are given and commonly referred to and indexed by their "X" references. For convenience these references are used hereafter. The guidance may be cited by advocates when asking for a re-determination: GFSG, Preface. However, while interesting and instructive, it is simply the department's gloss on the wording of the regulations, and does not bind costs judges: *R. v. Phillips*, X1, SCTO 594/97.

The Bar Council has also introduced a *Graduated Fee Payment Protocol*. This is an essential part of the mechanism by which advocates will be remunerated in future, and sets out arrangements to ensure that substitute advocates are paid by instructed advocates. The protocol falls outside the immediate scope of this work. It is available on both the Bar Council's and the Criminal Bar Association's websites.

*(b) Very High Cost Cases*

**G-4**     Very High Cost Cases are governed by the Very High Cost (Crime) Cases Arrangements 2013 (see *post*, G-181 *et seq.*). Additional guidance is contained in the 2013 VHCC Guidance (published by the Legal Aid Agency, an executive agency of the Ministry of Justice).

## Contract Appeals Committee decisions

**G-5**     Summaries of decisions of the Contract Appeals Committee have been collated and appear on the website of the Legal Aid Agency's section of the Ministry of Justice's website.

B. THE REMUNERATION REGULATIONS

**Criminal Legal Aid (Remuneration) Regulations 2013 (S.I. 2013 No. 435)**

*Citation and commencement*

**G-6**     **1.** These Regulations may be cited as the Criminal Legal Aid (Remuneration) Regulations 2013 and shall come into force on 1st April 2013.

*Interpretation*

**G-7**     **2.**—(1) In these Regulations—
     "the Act" means the Legal Aid, Sentencing and Punishment of Offenders Act 2012;
     "advocate" means a barrister, a solicitor advocate or a solicitor who is exercising their automatic rights of audience in the Crown Court;
     "appropriate officer" means—
         (a) in the case of proceedings in the civil division of the Court of Appeal, the head of the civil appeals office;
         (b) in the case of proceedings in the criminal division of the Court of Appeal, the registrar of criminal appeals;
         (c) in the case of proceedings in the Crown Court, the Lord Chancellor;
         (d) in respect of advice or assistance as to an appeal from the Crown Court to the Court of Appeal (except in the case of an appeal under section 9(11) of the Criminal Justice Act 1987 (preparatory hearings)) where, on the advice of any representative instructed, notice of appeal is given, or application for leave to appeal is made, whether or not such appeal is later abandoned, the registrar of criminal appeals;
         (e) in respect of advice or assistance as to an appeal to the Courts-Martial Appeal Court, the registrar of criminal appeals;
         (f) in respect of advice or assistance as to an appeal from the Court of Appeal to the Supreme Court, where the appeal is not lodged with the Supreme Court, the registrar of criminal appeals; and
         (g) in any other case, the Lord Chancellor,
     and, in any case, includes an officer designated by the person who is the appropriate officer by virtue of paragraphs (a) to (g) to act on his behalf for the purposes of these Regulations;

"assisted person" means an individual in whose favour a section 16 determination has been made;

"fee earner" means a litigator, or person employed by a litigator, who undertakes work on a case;

"instructed advocate" means—

    (a) where the section 16 determination provides for representation by a single advocate, the first barrister or solicitor advocate instructed in the case, who has primary responsibility for the case; or

    (b) where the section 16 determination provides for representation by more than one advocate, each of—

        (i) the leading instructed advocate; and

        (ii) the led instructed advocate;

"leading instructed advocate" means the first leading barrister or solicitor advocate instructed in the case who has primary responsibility for those aspects of a case undertaken by a leading advocate;

"led instructed advocate" means the first led barrister or solicitor advocate instructed in the case who has primary responsibility for those aspects of the case undertaken by a led advocate;

"litigator" means the person referred to in the representation order as representing an assisted person, being a solicitor, firm of solicitors or other appropriately qualified person.

"related proceedings" means—

    (a) two or more sets of proceedings involving the same defendant which are prepared, heard or dealt with together; or

    (b) proceedings involving more than one defendant which arise out of the same incident, so that the defendants are charged, tried or disposed of together;

"representation order" means a document which records a section 16 determination;

"representative" means a litigator or an advocate including, where appropriate, an instructed advocate;

"section 16 determination" means a determination made under section 16 of the Act that an individual qualities for representation for the purposes of criminal proceedings;

"senior solicitor" means a solicitor who, in the judgement of the appropriate officer, has the skill, knowledge and experience to deal with the most difficult and complex cases;

"solicitor advocate" means a solicitor who has obtained a higher courts advocacy qualification in accordance with regulations and rules of conduct of the Law Society;

"solicitor, legal executive or fee earner of equivalent experience" means a solicitor, Fellow of the Institute of Legal Executives or equivalent senior fee earner who, in the judgement of the appropriate officer, has good knowledge and experience of the conduct of criminal cases;

"trainee solicitor or fee earner of equivalent experience" means a trainee solicitor or other fee earner who is not a Fellow of the Institute of Legal Executives, who, in the judgement of the appropriate officer, carries out the routine work on a case;

"Very High Cost Case" means a case in which a section 16 determination has been made and which the Director classifies as a Very High Cost Case on the grounds that—

    (a) in relation to fees claimed by litigators—

        (i) if the case were to proceed to trial, the trial would in the opinion of the Director be likely to last for more than 40 days and the Director considers that there are no exceptional circumstances which make it unsuitable to be dealt with under an individual case contract for Very High Cost Cases made by the Lord Chancellor under section 2(1) of the Act; or

        (ii) if the case were to proceed to trial, the trial would in the opinion of the Director be likely to last no fewer than 25 and no more than 40 days and the Director considers that there are circumstances which make it suitable to be dealt with under an individual case contract for Very High Cost Cases made by the Lord Chancellor under section 2(1) of the Act;

    (b) in relation to fees claimed by advocates, if the case were to proceed to trial, the trial would in the opinion of the Director be likely to last for more than 60 days and the Director considers that there are no exceptional circumstances which make it unsuitable to be dealt with under an individual case contract for Very High Cost Cases made by the Lord Chancellor under section 2(1) of the Act;

"Very High Cost Case contract" means the 2013 VHCC contract between the Lord Chancellor and a representative for the provision of representation under section 16 of the Act (criminal legal aid).

(2) The fees and rates set out in the Schedules to these Regulations are exclusive of value added tax.

(3) A function of the Lord Chancellor or Director under these Regulations may be exercised by, or by an employee of, a person authorised for that purpose by the Lord Chancellor or Director respectively.

[This regulation is printed as amended (insertion of definition of "Very High Cost Case contract") by the Criminal Legal Aid (Remuneration) (Amendment) Regulations 2013 (S.I. 2013 No. 2803), reg. 3(1) and (3). The amendment applies in relation to fees for work undertaken on or after December 2, 2013: *ibid.*, reg. 4.]

*Scope*

**G-8**    **3.**—(1) Regulations 5(2), 10 and 14(1) apply to proceedings in magistrates' courts and to proceedings in the Crown Court.

(2) Regulation 8 and Schedule 4 apply to proceedings in magistrates' courts, to proceedings in the Crown Court and to proceedings in the High Court.

(3) Regulations 16 and 31 and Schedule 5 apply to proceedings in magistrates' courts, to proceedings in the Crown Court and to proceedings in the Court of Appeal.

(4) Regulations 4, 5(1) and (3) to (8), 13, 14(2) to (9), 15, 17 to 24 and 28 to 30 and Schedules 1 and 2 apply to proceedings in the Crown Court only.

(5) Regulations 9, 11 and 25 to 27, apply to proceedings in the Crown Court and to proceedings in the Court of Appeal.

(6) Regulation 6 and Schedule 3 apply to proceedings in the Court of Appeal only.

(7) Regulation 7 applies to proceedings in the Supreme Court only.

(8) With the exception of regulations 12 and 12A and paragraphs 13(8) and (9) of Schedule 2 and Schedule 6, these Regulations do not apply to Very High Cost Cases.

(9) For the purpose of these Regulations, any reference to the Court of Appeal includes as appropriate a reference to—

(a)   the criminal division of the Court of Appeal;

(b)   the civil division of the Court of Appeal;

(c)   the Courts-Martial Appeal Court; and

(d)   a Divisional Court of the High Court.

[This regulation is printed as amended (insertion of references to reg. 12A and Sched. 6) by the Criminal Legal Aid (Remuneration) (Amendment) Regulations 2013 (S.I. 2013 No. 2803), reg. 3(1) and (4). The amendment applies in relation to fees for work undertaken on or after December 2, 2013: *ibid.*, reg. 4.]

**[The next paragraph is G-10.]**

*Claims for fees by advocates—Crown Court*

**G-10**    **4.**—(1) Claims for fees by an instructed advocate in proceedings in the Crown Court must be made and determined in accordance with the provisions of Schedule 1 to these Regulations.

(2) A claim for fees under this regulation and Schedule 1 must be made by each instructed advocate.

(3) Subject to regulation 31, a claim by an instructed advocate for fees in respect of work done pursuant to a section 16 determination must not be entertained unless the instructed advocate submits it within three months of the conclusion of the proceedings to which it relates.

(4) An instructed advocate must submit a claim for fees to the appropriate officer in such form and manner as the appropriate officer may direct.

(5) An instructed advocate must supply such further information and documents as the appropriate officer may require.

(6) Where a confiscation hearing under Part 2 of the Proceeds of Crime Act 2002 (confiscation: England and Wales), section 2 of the Drug Trafficking Act 1994 (confiscation orders) or section 71 of the Criminal Justice Act 1988 (confiscation orders) is to be held more than 28 days after—

(a)   the conclusion of the trial to which the section 16 determination relates; or

(b)   the entering of a guilty plea,

an instructed advocate may submit any claim for fees in respect of the trial or guilty plea as soon as the trial has concluded or the guilty plea has been entered.

(7) Where the section 16 determination provides for representation by—

(a) a single advocate other than a QC; or

(b) two or more advocates other than QC,

and a QC agrees to appear as the single advocate or as a leading junior, that QC must be treated for all the purposes of these Regulations as having been instructed in relation to that determination, and the remuneration of that QC must be determined as if the advocate were not a QC.

*Claims for fees and disbursements by litigators—Crown Court*

**5.**—(1) Claims for fees by litigators in proceedings in the Crown Court must be made and **G-11** determined in accordance with the provisions of Schedule 2 to these Regulations.

(2) Claims for disbursements by litigators in proceedings in the Crown Court or in proceedings in a magistrates' court which are subsequently committed or sent for trial to the Crown Court must be made and determined in accordance with the provisions of regulations 14 to 17.

(3) Subject to regulation 31, a claim by a litigator for fees in respect of work done pursuant to a section 16 determination must not be entertained unless the litigator submits it within three months of the conclusion of the proceedings to which it relates.

(4) Subject to paragraph (5), a claim by a litigator for fees in proceedings in the Crown Court must be submitted to the appropriate officer in such form and manner as the appropriate officer may direct and must be accompanied by the representation order and any receipts or other documents in support of any disbursement claimed.

(5) A claim under paragraph 20 or 26 of Schedule 2 to these Regulations must—

(a) summarise the items of work done by a fee earner in respect of which fees are claimed according to the classes specified in paragraph 26(2) of Schedule 2;

(b) state, where appropriate, the dates on which the items of work were done, the time taken, the sums claimed and whether the work was done for more than one assisted person;

(c) specify, where appropriate, the level of fee earner who undertook each of the items of work claimed; and

(d) give particulars of any work done in relation to more than one indictment or a retrial.

(6) Where the litigator claims that paragraph 29 of Schedule 2 applies in relation to an item of work, the litigator must give full particulars in support of the claim.

(7) The litigator must specify any special circumstances which the litigator considers should be drawn to the attention of the appropriate officer.

(8) The litigator must supply such further information and documents as the appropriate officer may require.

### [The next paragraph is G-13.]

*Proceedings in the Court of Appeal*

**6.** Claims for fees by representatives in proceedings in the Court of Appeal must be made and **G-13** determined in accordance with the provisions of Schedule 3 to these Regulations.

*Proceedings in the Supreme Court*

**7.**—(1) In proceedings in the Supreme Court, the fees payable to a representative in respect of **G-14** advice and assistance or representation made available to an individual in accordance with sections 15 or 16 of the Act must be determined by such officer as may be prescribed by order of the Supreme Court.

(2) Subject to paragraph (1), these Regulations do not apply to proceedings in the Supreme Court.

*Claims for fees for certain categories of work to which the Standard Crime Contract applies*

**8.**—(1) This regulation applies to— **G-15**

(a) advice and assistance provided pursuant to a determination made under section 13 or section 15 of the Act;

(b) representation in proceedings in a magistrates' court pursuant to a section 16 determination;

(c) representation pursuant to a section 16 determination in proceedings prescribed as criminal proceedings under section 14(h) of the Act; and

(d) representation in appeals by way of case stated to the High Court.

(2) Claims for fees in cases to which this regulation applies must—

(a) be made and determined in accordance with the 2010 Standard Crime Contract; and

(b) be paid in accordance with the rates set out in Schedule 4.

(3) In this regulation and in Schedule 4, "2010 Standard Crime Contract" means the contract so

named between the Lord Chancellor and a person with whom the Lord Chancellor has made an arrangement under section 2(1) of the Act for the provision of advice, assistance and representation made available under sections 13, 15 and 16 of the Act.

*Payments from other sources*

**G-16**    **9.** Where representation is provided in respect of any proceedings, the representative, whether acting pursuant to a section 16 determination or otherwise, must not receive or be a party to the making of any payment for work done in connection with those proceedings, except such payments as may be made—

(a) by the Lord Chancellor; or

(b) in respect of any expenses or fees incurred in—

(i) preparing, obtaining or considering any report, opinion or further evidence, whether provided by an expert witness or otherwise; or

(ii) obtaining any transcripts or recordings,

where an application under regulation 13 for an authority to incur such fees or expenses has been refused by a committee appointed under arrangements made by the Lord Chancellor to deal with, amongst other things, appeals of, or review of, assessment of costs.

*Cases committed or sent for trial to the Crown Court*

**G-17**    **10.**—(1) Where a case is committed or sent for trial or transferred to the Crown Court, the payment in relation to work carried out in the magistrates' court is included within the applicable fee payable under Schedule 1 or Schedule 2.

(2) Paragraph (1) does not apply where the case is remitted to a magistrates' court.

*Proceedings for contempt*

**G-18**    **11.** Where representation is provided in proceedings referred to in section 14(g) of the Act (proceedings for contempt in the face of a court), the Lord Chancellor may only pay remuneration for services in accordance with Schedules 1, 2 and 3.

*Notification of Very High Cost Cases*

**G-18a**    **12.**—(1) A litigator who has conduct of a case which is, or is likely to be classified as, a Very High Cost Case, must notify the Lord Chancellor in writing as soon as practicable.

(2) Where a litigator fails to comply with this regulation without good reason, and as a result there is a loss to public funds, the Lord Chancellor may refuse payment of the litigator's costs up to the extent of such loss.

(3) The Lord Chancellor must not refuse payment under paragraph (2) unless the litigator has been given a reasonable opportunity to show why the payment should not be refused.

*Fees in Very High Cost Cases*

**12A.** Where services consisting of representation made available under section 16 of the Act (criminal legal aid) are provided in a case which is the subject of a Very High Cost Case contract, fees for that case must be paid—

(a) in accordance with the terms of that contract; and

(b) at the rates set out for the appropriate category and level of representative set out in Schedule 6 to these Regulations.

[This regulation was inserted by the Criminal Legal Aid (Remuneration) (Amendment) Regulations 2013 (S.I. 2013 No. 2803), reg. 3(1) and (5). It applies in relation to fees for work undertaken on or after December 2, 2013: *ibid.*, reg. 4.]

*Authorisation of expenditure*

**G-18b**    **13.**—(1) Where it appears to a litigator necessary for the proper conduct of proceedings in the Crown Court for costs to be incurred in relation to representation by taking any of the following steps—

(a) obtaining a written report or opinion of one or more experts;

(b) employing a person to provide a written report or opinion (otherwise than as an expert);

(c) obtaining any transcripts or recordings; or

(d) performing an act which is either unusual in its nature or involves unusually large expenditure,

the litigator may apply to the Lord Chancellor for prior authority to do so.

(2) Where the Lord Chancellor authorises the taking of any step referred to in paragraph (1), the Lord Chancellor shall also authorise the maximum to be paid in respect of that step.

(3) A representative assigned to an assisted person in any proceedings in the Crown Court may apply to the Lord Chancellor for prior authority for the incurring of travelling and accommodation expenses in order to attend at the trial or other main hearing in those proceedings.

The following authorities were decided under the corresponding provisions in earlier legal aid legislation: see, in particular, regulation 54 of the Legal Aid in Criminal and Care Proceedings (General) Regulations 1989 (S.I. 1989 No. 344).

In *R. v. Silcott, Braithwaite and Raghip, The Times,* December 9, 1991, the Court of Appeal said that all members of the legal profession were under a duty not to involve the legal aid fund in unnecessary expenditure. If an expert consulted by the defence was hostile to the accused's case or his solicitor considered the opinion to be wrong or defective it was most unlikely that legal aid authority would be given on application by the solicitor to consult more than one expert and certainly no more than two. In the instant case, the opinions of two experts had been obtained on behalf of one defendant. They were adverse to the defendant. Neither expert was called, but both changed their views in the light of the opinion of a third expert, who had been consulted after the trial's conclusion. This demonstrated that a third opinion had been necessary in the interests of justice. "Expert shopping" was to be discouraged, but there were exceptional cases where the need for a further expert opinion could be demonstrated. In such cases counsel should be asked to advise on evidence in support of an extension of the legal aid certificate, if he thought it right to do so. The courts and those responsible for the legal aid fund must rely on proper professional standards being observed by all the lawyers concerned.

A judge has no power to authorise the incurring of costs under a legal aid order for an expert witness, although he may express his opinion as to the desirability of legal aid being so extended: *R. v. Donnelly* [1998] Crim.L.R. 131, CA.

**14.**—(1) A litigator may submit a claim to the appropriate officer for payment of a disbursement **G-19** for which the litigator has incurred liability in proceedings in the Crown Court, or in proceedings in a magistrates' court which are subsequently committed or sent for trial or transferred to the Crown Court, in accordance with the provisions of this regulation.

(2) A claim for payment under paragraph (1) may be made where—

    (a)  a litigator has obtained prior authority to incur expenditure of £100 or more under regulation 13; and

    (b)  the litigator has incurred such a liability.

(3) Without prejudice to regulation 17(4) and (5) a claim for payment under paragraph (1) must not exceed the maximum amount authorised under the prior authority.

(4) A claim for payment under paragraph (1) may be made at any time before the litigator submits a claim for fees under regulation 5.

(5) A claim for payment under paragraph (1) must be submitted to the appropriate officer in such form and manner as the appropriate officer may direct and must be accompanied by the authority to incur expenditure and any invoices or other documents in support of the claim.

(6) Subject to regulation 16, the appropriate officer must allow the disbursement subject to the limit in paragraph (3) if it appears to have been reasonably incurred in accordance with the prior authority.

(7) The appropriate officer must notify the litigator and, where the disbursement claimed includes the fees or charges of any person, may notify that person of the appropriate officer's decision.

(8) Where the appropriate officer allows the disbursement, the appropriate officer must notify the litigator and, where the disbursement includes the fees or charges of any person, may notify that person, of the amount payable, and must authorise payment to the litigator accordingly.

(9) Regulations 28 to 30 do not apply to a payment under this regulation.

*Interim disbursements and final determination of fees*

**15.**—(1) On a final determination of fees, regulations 5(2) and 17 apply notwithstanding that a **G-20** payment has been made under regulation 14.

(2) Where the amount found to be due under regulation 17 in respect of a disbursement is less than the amount paid under regulation 14 ("the interim payment"), the appropriate officer must deduct the difference from the sum otherwise payable to the litigator on the determination of fees, and where the amount due under regulation 17 exceeds the interim payment, the appropriate officer must add the difference to the amount otherwise payable to the litigator.

*Expert services*

**16.**—(1) Subject to paragraph (2), the Lord Chancellor may provide for the payment of expert **G-20a** services only at the fixed fees or at rates not exceeding the rates set out in Schedule 5.

(2) The appropriate officer may, in relation to a specific claim, increase the fixed fees or rates set out in Schedule 5 if that officer considers it reasonable to do so in exceptional circumstances.

(3) For the purposes of paragraph (2), exceptional circumstances are where the expert's evidence is key to the client's case and either—

  (a) the complexity of the material is such that an expert with a high level of seniority is required; or

  (b) the material is of such a specialised and unusual nature that only very few experts are available to provide the necessary evidence.

*Determination of litigators' disbursements*

**G-21**   **17.**—(1) Subject to paragraphs (2) to (5), the appropriate officer must allow such disbursements claimed under regulation 5(2) as appear to the appropriate officer to have been reasonably incurred.

(2) If the disbursements claimed are abnormally large by reason of the distance of the court or the assisted person's residence or both from the litigator's place of business, the appropriate officer may limit reimbursement of the disbursements to what otherwise would, having regard to all the circumstances, be a reasonable amount.

(3) No question as to the propriety of any step or act in relation to which prior authority has been obtained under regulation 13 may be raised on any determination of disbursements, unless the litigator knew or ought reasonably to have known that the purpose for which the authority was given had failed or had become irrelevant or unnecessary before the disbursements were incurred.

(4) Where disbursements are reasonably incurred in accordance with and subject to the limit imposed by a prior authority given under regulation 13, no question may be raised on any determination of fees as to the amount of the payment to be allowed for the step or act in relation to which the authority was given.

(5) Where disbursements are incurred in taking any steps or doing any act for which authority may be given under regulation 13, without such authority having been given or in excess of any fee so authorised, payment in respect of those disbursements may nevertheless be allowed on a determination of disbursements payable under regulation 5.

(6) Paragraph (7) applies where the Lord Chancellor receives a request for funding of an expert service of a type not listed in Schedule 5.

(7) In considering the rate at which to fund the expert service the Lord Chancellor—

  (a) must have regard to the rates set out in Schedule 5; and

  (b) may require more than one quotation for provision of the service to be submitted to the Lord Chancellor.

*Interim payments in cases awaiting determination of fees*

**G-22**   **18.**—(1) The appropriate officer must authorise an interim payment in respect of a claim for fees in proceedings in the Crown Court in accordance with this regulation.

(2) Entitlement to a payment arises in respect of a claim for fees by an instructed advocate, where—

  (a) the graduated fee claimed in accordance with Schedule 1 is £4,000 or more (exclusive of value added tax); and

  (b) the claim for fees is for less than the amount mentioned in sub-paragraph (a) but is related to any claim for fees falling under sub-paragraph (a).

(3) For the purposes of this regulation, the following claims for fees are related to each other—

  (a) the claims of instructed advocates acting in the same proceedings for a defendant; and

  (b) the claims of any instructed advocate acting for any assisted person in related proceedings.

(4) Entitlement to a payment under paragraph (1) does not arise until three months have elapsed from the earlier of—

  (a) the date on which the claim for fees is received by the appropriate officer for determination, except that where there are related claims for fees, the date on which the last claim is received by the appropriate officer; or

  (b) three months after the conclusion of the last of any related proceedings.

(5) An instructed advocate may submit a claim for an interim payment under this regulation where—

  (a) no payment has been made under paragraph (1); and

  (b) six months have elapsed from the conclusion of the proceedings against the assisted person.

(6) Subject to regulation 31, payment must not be made under this regulation unless the instructed advocate has submitted a claim for fees in accordance with regulation 4(3).

*Amount of interim payments in cases awaiting determination of fees*

**19.**—(1) Where entitlement to an interim payment arises under regulation 18, the amount payable **G-23** is 40% of the total claim for fees, less any sum already paid.

(2) Regulations 28 to 30 do not apply to an interim payment under this regulation.

*Staged payments in long Crown Court proceedings*

**20.**—(1) An instructed advocate may submit a claim to the appropriate officer for a staged pay- **G-24** ment of the instructed advocate's fees in relation to proceedings in the Crown Court.

(2) Where a claim is submitted in accordance with this regulation, a staged payment must be allowed where the appropriate officer is satisfied—

    (a)  that the claim relates to fees for a period of preparation of 100 hours or more, for which the instructed advocate will, subject to final determination of the fees payable, be entitled to be paid in accordance with Schedule 1; and

    (b)  that the period from committal, or sending for trial or transfer (or from the date of the section 16 determination, if later) to the conclusion of the Crown Court proceedings is likely to exceed 12 months, having regard, amongst other matters, to the number of defendants, the anticipated pleas and the weight and complexity of the case.

(3) In this regulation, "preparation" means—

    (a)  reading the papers in the case;

    (b)  contact with prosecutors;

    (c)  written or oral advice on plea;

    (d)  researching the law, preparation for examination of witnesses and preparation of oral submissions;

    (e)  viewing exhibits or undisclosed material at police stations;

    (f)  written advice on evidence;

    (g)  preparation of written submissions, notices or other documents for use at the trial;

    (h)  attendance at views at the scene of the alleged offence,

and is limited to preparation done before the trial, except in proceedings in which a preparatory hearing has been ordered under section 8 of the Criminal Justice Act 1987 (commencement of trial and arraignment), in which case it is limited to preparation done before the date on which the jury is sworn (or on which it became certain, by reason of pleas of guilty or otherwise, that the matter would not proceed to trial).

(4) The amount allowed for preparation falling within paragraph (3) must be determined by reference to the number of hours of preparation which it appears to the appropriate officer, without prejudice to the final determination of the fees payable, has been reasonably done, multiplied by the hourly rate for special preparation as set out in the table following paragraph 24 of Schedule 1, as appropriate to the category of advocate.

(5) A claim for staged payment of fees under this regulation must be made to the appropriate officer in such form and manner as the appropriate officer may direct, including such case plan as the appropriate officer may require for the purposes of paragraph (2)(a).

(6) An instructed advocate may claim further staged payments in accordance with this regulation in respect of further periods of preparation exceeding 100 hours which were not included in an earlier claim.

(7) Regulations 28 to 30 do not apply to a payment under this regulation.

**[The next paragraph is G-26.]**

*Hardship payments*

**21.**—(1) Subject to paragraphs (5) and (6), the appropriate officer may allow a hardship payment **G-26** to a representative in the circumstances set out in paragraph (2).

(2) Those circumstances are that the representative—

    (a)  represents the assisted person in proceedings in the Crown Court;

    (b)  applies for such payment, in such form and manner as the appropriate officer may direct, not less than six months after the representative was first instructed in those proceedings, or in related proceedings if the representative was instructed in those proceedings earlier than in the proceedings to which the application relates;

    (c)  is unlikely to receive final payment in respect of the proceedings, as determined under Schedule 1 or 2, within the three months following the application for the hardship payment; and

    (d)  satisfies the appropriate officer that, by reason of the circumstance in sub-paragraph (c), the representative is likely to suffer financial hardship.

(3) Every application for a hardship payment by an advocate must be accompanied by such information and documents as the appropriate officer may require as evidence of—

    (a)  the work done by the advocate in relation to the proceedings up to the date of the application; and

    (b)  the likelihood of financial hardship.

(4) Every application for a hardship payment by a litigator must be accompanied by such information and documents as the appropriate officer may require as evidence of—

    (a)  the Class of Offence with which the assisted person is charged, in accordance with Part 7 of Schedule 1;

    (b)  the length of trial, where appropriate;

    (c)  the number of pages of prosecution evidence, determined in accordance with paragraph 1(2) of Schedule 2;

    (d)  the total number of defendants in the proceedings who are represented by the litigator;

    (e)  the likelihood of financial hardship.

(5) The amount of any hardship payment is at the discretion of the appropriate officer, but must not exceed such sum as would be reasonable remuneration for the work done by the representative in the proceedings up to the date of the application.

(6) A hardship payment must not be made if it appears to the appropriate officer that the sum which would be reasonable remuneration for the representative, or the sum required to relieve the representative's financial hardship, is less than £5,000 (excluding value added tax).

(7) Where the appropriate officer allows a hardship payment under paragraph (1), the appropriate officer must authorise payment accordingly.

(8) Where the application for a hardship payment is made by an advocate other than an instructed advocate, and the appropriate officer allows a hardship payment under paragraph (1)—

    (a)  payment must be made to the leading instructed advocate or the led instructed advocate, as appropriate; and

    (b)  the appropriate officer must notify the advocate who made the application that payment has been made to the instructed advocate.

*Computation of final claim where an interim payment has been made*

**G-27**    **22.**—(1) At the conclusion of a case in which one or more payments have been made to an instructed advocate or a litigator under regulations 18 to 21, the instructed advocate or litigator must submit a claim under regulation 4 or 5 for the determination of the overall remuneration, whether or not such a claim will result in any payment additional to those already made.

(2) In the determination of the amount payable to an instructed advocate or litigator under regulation 4 or 5—

    (a)  the appropriate officer must deduct the amount of any payment made under regulations 18 to 21 in respect of the same case from the amount that would otherwise be payable; and

    (b)  if the amount of the interim payment is greater than the amount that would otherwise be payable, the appropriate officer may recover the amount of the difference, either by way of repayment by the instructed advocate or litigator or by way of deduction from any other amount that may be due to the instructed advocate or litigator.

*Payment of fees to advocates—Crown Court*

**G-28**    **23.**—(1) Having determined the fees payable to each instructed advocate, in accordance with Schedule 1, the appropriate officer must notify each instructed advocate of the fees payable and authorise payment accordingly.

(2) Where, as a result of any redetermination or appeal made or brought pursuant to regulations 28 to 30, the fees payable under paragraph (1) are altered—

    (a)  if they are increased, the appropriate officer must authorise payment of the increase; or

    (b)  if they are decreased, the instructed advocate must repay the amount of such decrease.

(3) Where the payment of any fees of an instructed advocate is ordered under regulation 29(12) or regulation 30(8), the appropriate officer must authorise payment.

*Payment of fees to litigators—Crown Court*

**G-29**    **24.**—(1) Having determined the fees payable to a litigator in accordance with Schedule 2, the appropriate officer must authorise payment accordingly.

(2) Where the appropriate officer determines that the fees payable under paragraph (1) are greater than or less than the amount claimed by the litigator under regulation 5(1), the appropriate officer must notify the litigator of the amount the appropriate officer has determined to be payable.

(3) Where, as a result of any redetermination or appeal made or brought pursuant to regulations 28 to 30, the fees payable under paragraph (1) are altered—

(a) if they are increased, the appropriate officer must authorise payment of the increase; or

(b) if they are decreased, the litigator must repay the amount of such decrease.

(4) Where the payment of any fees of the litigator is ordered under regulation 29(12) or regulation 30(8), the appropriate officer must authorise payment.

## [The next paragraph is G-31.]

*Recovery of overpayments*

**25.**—(1) This regulation applies where a representative is entitled to be paid a certain sum ("the **G-31** amount due") by virtue of the provisions of Schedule 1, 2 or 3 and, for whatever reason, the representative is paid an amount greater than that sum.

(2) Where this regulation applies, the appropriate officer may—

(a) require immediate repayment of the amount in excess of the amount due ("the excess amount"); or

(b) deduct the excess amount from any other sum which is or becomes payable to the representative by virtue of the provisions of Schedule 1, 2 or 3,

and where sub-paragraph (a) applies the representative must repay the excess amount to the appropriate officer.

(3) The appropriate officer may proceed under paragraph (2)(b) without first proceeding under paragraph (2)(a).

(4) Paragraph (2) applies notwithstanding that the representative to whom the excess amount was paid is exercising, or may exercise, a right under regulations 28 to 30.

*Adverse observations*

**26.**—(1) Where in any proceedings to which Schedule 1, 2 or 3 applies, the court makes adverse **G-32** observations concerning a representative's conduct of the proceedings, the appropriate officer may reduce any fee which would otherwise be payable in accordance with Schedule 1, 2 or 3 by such proportion as the appropriate officer considers reasonable.

(2) Before reducing the fee payable to a representative in accordance with the provisions of paragraph (1), the appropriate officer must give the representative the opportunity to make representations about whether it is appropriate to reduce the fee and the extent to which the fee should be reduced.

*Wasted costs orders*

**27.**—(1) Subject to paragraph (2), where the court has disallowed the whole or any part of any **G-33** wasted costs under section 19A of the Prosecution of Offences Act 1985 (costs against legal representatives *etc*), the appropriate officer, in determining fees in respect of work done by the representative against whom the wasted costs order was made, may deduct the amount in the wasted costs order from the amount otherwise payable in accordance with these Regulations.

(2) Where the appropriate officer, in accordance with this regulation, is minded to disallow any amount of a claim for work done to which the wasted costs order relates, the appropriate officer must disallow that amount or the amount of the wasted costs order, whichever is the greater.

*Redetermination of fees by appropriate offcer*

**28.**—(1) Where— **G-34**

(a) an advocate in proceedings in the Crown Court is dissatisfied with the decision not to allow any of the following fees, or with the number of hours allowed in the calculation of such a fee, namely—

(i) a special preparation fee under paragraph 17 of Schedule 1; or

(ii) a wasted preparation fee under paragraph 18 of Schedule 1; or

(b) an instructed advocate in proceedings in the Crown Court is dissatisfied with—

(i) the decision not to allow an hourly fee in respect of attendance at conferences or views at the scene of the alleged offence under paragraph 19 of Schedule 1, or with the number of hours allowed in the calculation of such a fee;

(ii) the calculation by the appropriate officer of the fee payable to the instructed advocate in accordance with Schedule 1; or

(iii) the decision of the appropriate officer under paragraph 3(3) of Schedule 1 (reclassification of an offence not specifically listed in the relevant Table of Offences and so deemed to fall within Class H); or

(c) a litigator is dissatisfied with—
  (i) the calculation by the appropriate officer of the fee payable to the litigator in accordance with Schedule 2; or
  (ii) the decision of the appropriate officer under paragraph 3(3) of Schedule 2 (reclassification of an offence not specifically listed in the relevant Table of Offences and so deemed to fall within Class H),

the advocate, instructed advocate or litigator, as the case may be, may apply to the appropriate officer to redetermine those fees, to review that decision or to reclassify the offence, as appropriate.

(2) An application under paragraph (1) may not challenge the quantum of any of the fees set out in Schedule 1 or Schedule 2.

(3) Subject to regulation 31, an application under paragraph (1), or paragraph 11(1) of Schedule 3, must be made—
  (a) within 21 days of the receipt of the fees payable under regulation 23, regulation 24 or paragraph 10 of Schedule 3, as appropriate;
  (b) by giving notice in writing to the appropriate officer, specifying the matters in respect of which the application is made and the grounds of objection; and
  (c) in such form and manner as the appropriate officer may direct.

(4) The notice of application must be accompanied by the information and documents supplied under regulation 4, regulation 5 or Schedule 3, as appropriate.

(5) The notice of application must state whether the applicant wishes to appear or to be represented and, if the applicant so wishes, the appropriate officer must notify the applicant of the hearing date and time.

(6) The applicant must supply such further information and documents as the appropriate officer may require.

(7) The appropriate officer must, in the light of the objections made by the applicant or on behalf of the applicant—
  (a) redetermine the fees, whether by way of confirmation, or increase or decrease in the amount previously determined;
  (b) confirm the classification of the offence within Class H; or
  (c) reclassify the offence,

as the case may be, and must notify the applicant of his decision.

(8) Where the applicant so requests, the appropriate officer must give reasons in writing for the appropriate officer's decision.

(9) Subject to regulation 31, any request under paragraph (8) must be made within 21 days of receiving notification of the appropriate officer's decision under paragraph (7).

*Appeals to a costs judge*

**G-35**

**29.**—(1) Where the appropriate officer has given his reasons for his decision under regulation 28(8), a representative who is dissatisfied with that decision may appeal to a costs judge.

(2) Subject to regulation 31, an appeal under paragraph (1) or paragraph 11(2) of Schedule 3 must be instituted within 21 days of the receipt of the appropriate officer's reasons, by giving notice in writing to the Senior Costs Judge.

(3) The appellant must send a copy of any notice of appeal given under paragraph (2) to the appropriate officer.

(4) The notice of appeal must be accompanied by—
  (a) a copy of any written representations given under regulation 28(3);
  (b) the appropriate officer's reasons for the appropriate officer's decision given under regulation 28(8); and
  (c) the information and documents supplied to the appropriate officer under regulation 28.

(5) The notice of appeal must—
  (a) be in such form as the Senior Costs Judge may direct;
  (b) specify separately each item appealed against, showing (where appropriate) the amount claimed for the item, the amount determined and the grounds of the objection to the determination; and
  (c) state whether the appellant wishes to appear or to be represented or whether the appellant will accept a decision given in the appellant's absence.

(6) The Senior Costs Judge may, and if so directed by the Lord Chancellor either generally or in a particular case must, send to the Lord Chancellor a copy of the notice of appeal together with copies of such other documents as the Lord Chancellor may require.

(7) With a view to ensuring that the public interest is taken into account, the Lord Chancellor may

arrange for written or oral representations to be made on the Lord Chancellor's behalf and, if the Lord Chancellor intends to do so, the Lord Chancellor must inform the Senior Costs Judge and the appellant.

(8) Any written representations made on behalf of the Lord Chancellor under paragraph (7) must be sent to the Senior Costs Judge and the appellant and, in the case of oral representations, the Senior Costs Judge and the appellant must be informed of the grounds on which such representations will be made.

(9) The appellant must be permitted a reasonable opportunity to make representations in reply.

(10) The costs judge must inform the appellant (or the person representing him) and the Lord Chancellor, where representations have been or are to be made on the Lord Chancellor's behalf, of the date of any hearing and, subject to the provisions of this regulation, may give directions as to the conduct of the appeal.

(11) The costs judge may consult the trial judge or the appropriate officer and may require the appellant to provide any further information which the costs judge requires for the purpose of the appeal and, unless the costs judge otherwise directs, no further evidence may be received on the hearing of the appeal and no ground of objection may be raised which was not raised under regulation 28.

(12) The costs judge has the same powers as the appropriate officer under these Regulations and, in the exercise of such powers, may alter the redetermination of the appropriate officer in respect of any sum allowed, whether by increasing or decreasing it, as the costs judge thinks fit.

(13) The costs judge must communicate his decision and the reasons for it in writing to the appellant, the Lord Chancellor and the appropriate officer.

(14) Where the costs judge increases the sums redetermined under regulation 28, the costs judge may allow the appellant a sum in respect of part or all of any reasonable costs incurred by the appellant in connection with the appeal (including any fee payable in respect of an appeal).

*Appeals to the High Court*

**30.**—(1) A representative who is dissatisfied with the decision of a costs judge on an appeal under regulation 29 may apply to a costs judge to certify a point of principle of general importance. **G-36**

(2) Subject to regulation 31, an application under paragraph (1) or paragraph 11(3) of Schedule 3 must be made within 21 days of receiving notification of a costs judge's decision under regulation 29(13).

(3) Where a costs judge certifies a point of principle of general importance the appellant may appeal to the High Court against the decision of a costs judge on an appeal under regulation 29, and the Lord Chancellor must be a respondent to such an appeal.

(4) Subject to regulation 31, an appeal under paragraph (3) must be instituted within 21 days of receiving notification of a costs judge's certificate under paragraph (1).

(5) Where the Lord Chancellor is dissatisfied with the decision of a costs judge on an appeal under regulation 29, the Lord Chancellor may, if no appeal has been made by an appellant under paragraph (3), appeal to the High Court against that decision, and the appellant must be a respondent to the appeal.

(6) Subject to regulation 31, an appeal under paragraph (5) must be instituted within 21 days of receiving notification of the costs judge's decision under regulation 29(13).

(7) An appeal under paragraph (3) or (5) must—

(a) be brought in the Queen's Bench Division;

(b) subject to paragraph (4), follow the procedure set out in Part 52 of the Civil Procedure Rules 1998; and

(c) be heard and determined by a single judge whose decision will be final.

(8) The judge has the same powers as the appropriate officer and a costs judge under these Regulations and may reverse, affirm or amend the decision appealed against or make such other order as the judge thinks fit.

*Time limits*

**31.**—(1) Subject to paragraph (2), the time limit within which any act is required or authorised to be done under these Regulations may, for good reason, be extended— **G-37**

(a) in the case of acts required or authorised to be done under regulations 29 or 30, by a costs judge or the High Court as the case may be; and

(b) in the case of acts required or authorised to be done by a representative under any other regulation, by the appropriate officer.

(2) Where a representative without good reason has failed (or, if an extension were not granted,

would fail) to comply with a time limit, the appropriate officer, a costs judge or the High Court, as the case may be, may, in exceptional circumstances, extend the time limit and must consider whether it is reasonable in the circumstances to reduce the fees payable to the representative under regulations 4, 5 or 6, provided that the fees must not be reduced unless the representative has been allowed a reasonable opportunity to show cause orally or in writing why the fees should not be reduced.

(3) A representative may appeal to a costs judge against a decision made under this regulation by an appropriate officer and such an appeal must be instituted within 21 days of the decision being given by giving notice in writing to the Senior Costs Judge specifying the grounds of appeal.

**[The next paragraph is G-39.]**

Regulation 4

## SCHEDULE 1

ADVOCATES' GRADUATED FEE SCHEME

PART 1

DEFINITIONS AND SCOPE

*Interpretation*

**G-39**    1.—(1) In this Schedule—

"case" means proceedings in the Crown Court against any one assisted person—

    (a) on one or more counts of a single indictment;

    (b) arising out of a single notice of appeal against conviction or sentence, or a single committal for sentence, whether on one or more charges; or

    (c) arising out of a single alleged breach of an order of the Crown Court,

and a case falling within paragraph (c) must be treated as a separate case from the proceedings in which the order was made;

"cracked trial" means a case on indictment in which—

    (a) a plea and case management hearing takes place and—

        (i) the case does not proceed to trial (whether by reason of pleas of guilty or for other reasons) or the prosecution offers no evidence; and

        (ii) either—

            (aa) in respect of one or more counts to which the assisted person pleaded guilty, the assisted person did not so plead at the plea and case management hearing; or

            (bb) in respect of one or more counts which did not proceed, the prosecution did not, before or at the plea and case management hearing, declare an intention of not proceeding with them; or

    (b) the case is listed for trial without a plea and case management hearing taking place;

"guilty plea" means a case on indictment which—

    (a) is disposed of without a trial because the assisted person pleaded guilty to one or more counts; and

    (b) is not a cracked trial;

"main hearing" means—

    (a) in relation to a case which goes to trial, the trial;

    (b) in relation to a guilty plea, the hearing at which pleas are taken or, where there is more than one such hearing, the last such hearing;

    (c) in relation to a cracked trial, the hearing at which—

        (i) the case becomes a cracked trial by meeting the conditions in the definition of a cracked trial, whether or not any pleas were taken at that hearing; or

        (ii) a formal verdict of not guilty was entered as a result of the prosecution offering no evidence, whether or not the parties attended the hearing;

    (d) in relation to an appeal against conviction or sentence in the Crown Court, the hearing of the appeal;

    (e) in relation to proceedings arising out of a committal for sentence in the Crown Court, the sentencing hearing; and

    (f) in relation to proceedings arising out of an alleged breach of an order of the Crown Court, the hearing at which those proceedings are determined;

"*Newton* hearing" means a hearing at which evidence is heard for the purpose of determining the sentence of a convicted person in accordance with the principles of *R. v. Newton* (1982) 77 Cr.App.R. 13;

"standard appearance" means an appearance by the trial advocate or substitute advocate in any of the following hearings which do not form part of the main hearing—

(a) a plea and case management hearing, except the first plea and case management hearing;

(b) a pre-trial review;

(c) the hearing of a case listed for plea which is adjourned for trial;

(d) any hearing (except a trial, a plea and case management hearing, a pre-trial review or a hearing referred to in paragraph 2(1)(b)) which is listed but cannot proceed because of the failure of the assisted person or a witness to attend, the unavailability of a pre-sentence report or other good reason;

(e) custody time limit applications;

(f) bail and other applications (except where any such applications take place in the course of a hearing referred to in paragraph 2(1)(b));

(g) the hearing of the case listed for mention only, including applications relating to the date of the trial (except where an application takes place in the course of a hearing referred to in paragraph 2(1)(b));

(h) a sentencing hearing other than one falling within paragraph 2(1)(b)(ii), paragraph 15(1) or paragraph 34;

(i) a preliminary hearing; or

(j) a hearing, whether contested or not, relating to breach of bail, failure to surrender to bail or execution of a bench warrant,

provided that a fee is not payable elsewhere under this Schedule in respect of the hearing;

"substitute advocate" means an advocate who is not an instructed advocate or the trial advocate but who undertakes work on the case; and

"trial advocate" means an advocate instructed pursuant to a section 16 determination to represent the assisted person at the main hearing in any case, including a QC or a leading junior advocate so instructed after the hearing at which pleas are taken.

(2) For the purposes of this Schedule, the number of pages of prosecution evidence served on the court must be determined in accordance with sub-paragraphs (3) to (5).

(3) The number of pages of prosecution evidence includes all—

(a) witness statements;

(b) documentary and pictorial exhibits;

(c) records of interviews with the assisted person; and

(d) records of interviews with other defendants,

which form part of the committal or served prosecution documents or which are included in any notice of additional evidence.

(4) Subject to sub-paragraph (5), a document served by the prosecution in electronic form is included in the number of pages of prosecution evidence.

(5) A documentary or pictorial exhibit which—

(a) has been served by the prosecution in electronic form; and

(b) has never existed in paper form,

is not included within the number of pages of prosecution evidence unless the appropriate officer decides that it would be appropriate to include it in the pages of prosecution evidence taking into account the nature of the document and any other relevant circumstances.

(6) In proceedings on indictment in the Crown Court initiated otherwise than by committal for trial, the appropriate officer must determine the number of pages of prosecution evidence in accordance with sub-paragraphs (2) to (5) or as nearly in accordance with those sub-paragraphs as possible as the nature of the case permits.

(7) A reference to the Table of Offences in this Schedule is to the Table of Offences in Part 7 and a reference to a Class of Offence in this Schedule is to the Class in which that offence is listed in the Table of Offences.

*Application*

2.—(1) Subject to sub-paragraphs (2) to (11), this Schedule applies to— **G-40**

(a) every case on indictment; and

(b) the following proceedings in the Crown Court—

(i) an appeal against conviction or sentence;

(ii) a sentencing hearing following a committal for sentence to the Crown Court; and

(iii) proceedings arising out of an alleged breach of an order of the Crown Court (whether or not this Schedule applies to the proceedings in which the order was made).

(2) Sub-paragraphs (3) and (4) apply where, following a trial, an order is made for a new trial and the same trial advocate appears at both trials where—

    (a)   the defendant is an assisted person at both trials; or

    (b)   the defendant is an assisted person at the new trial only; or

    (c)   the new trial is a cracked trial or guilty plea.

(3) Subject to sub-paragraph (4), in respect of a new trial, or if the trial advocate so elects, in respect of the first trial, the graduated fee payable to the trial advocate must be calculated in accordance with Part 2 or Part 3, as appropriate, except that the fee must be reduced by—

    (a)   30%, where the new trial started within one month of the conclusion of the first trial;

    (b)   20%, where the new trial did not start within one month of the conclusion of the first trial;

    (c)   40%, where the new trial becomes a cracked trial or guilty plea within one month of the conclusion of the first trial; or

    (d)   25% where the new trial becomes a cracked trial or guilty plea more than one month after the conclusion of the first trial.

(4) Where—

    (a)   in relation to the first trial, the case was committed or sent for trial to the Crown Court on the election of a defendant where the magistrates' court had determined the case to be suitable for summary trial; and

    (b)   the new trial becomes a cracked trial or guilty plea,

the fee payable to the trial advocate must be

        (i)   the graduated fee calculated in accordance with Part 2, in respect of the first trial; and

        (ii)   the fixed fee set out in paragraph 10 in respect of the new trial.

(5) Sub-paragraphs (6) and (7) apply in the circumstances set out in sub-paragraph (2) but where a different trial advocate appears for the assisted person at each trial.

(6) Subject to sub-paragraph (7), in respect of each trial, the graduated fee payable to the trial advocate must be calculated in accordance with Part 2 or Part 3 as appropriate.

(7) Where—

    (a)   in relation to the first trial, the case was committed or sent for trial to the Crown Court on the election of a defendant where the magistrates' court had determined the case to be suitable for summary trial; and

    (b)   the new trial becomes a cracked trial or guilty plea,

the fee payable to the trial advocate at the first trial must be the graduated fee, calculated in accordance with Part 2 and the fee payable to the trial advocate at the new trial must be the fixed fee set out in paragraph 10.

(8) Where following a case on indictment a *Newton* hearing takes place—

    (a)   for the purposes of this Schedule the case is to be treated as having gone to trial;

    (b)   the length of the trial is to be taken to be the combined length of the main hearing and the *Newton* hearing;

    (c)   the provisions of this Schedule relating to cracked trials and guilty pleas do not apply; and

    (d)   no fee is payable under paragraph 15 in respect of the *Newton* hearing.

(9) Sub-paragraph (10) applies where proceedings are—

    (a)   sent for trial to the Crown Court; or

    (b)   transferred to the Crown Court under—

        (i)   section 4 of the Criminal Justice Act 1987 (transfer of serious fraud cases); or

        (ii)   section 53 of the Criminal Justice Act 1991 (transfer of certain cases involving children).

(10) Where, at any time after proceedings are sent or transferred to the Crown Court as referred to in sub-paragraph (9), they are—

    (a)   discontinued by a notice served under section 23A of the Prosecution of Offences Act 1985 (discontinuance of proceedings after accused has been sent for trial); or

    (b)   dismissed pursuant to—

        (i)   paragraph 2 of Schedule 3 to the Crime and Disorder Act 1998 (applications for dismissal);

        (ii)   section 6 of the Criminal Justice Act 1987 (applications for dismissal); or

        (iii)   paragraph 5 of Schedule 6 to the Criminal Justice Act 1991 (applications for dismissal),

the provisions of paragraph 22 apply.

(11) For the purposes of this Schedule, a case on indictment which discontinues at or before the plea and case management hearing otherwise than—

    (a)  by reason of a plea of guilty being entered; or

    (b)  in accordance with sub-paragraph (10),

must be treated as a guilty plea.

*Class of offences*

    3.—(1) For the purposes of this Schedule—          **G-41**

    (a)  every indictable offence falls within the Class under which it is listed in the Table of Offences and, subject to sub-paragraph (2), indictable offences not specifically so listed are deemed to fall within Class H;

    (b)  conspiracy to commit an indictable offence contrary to section 1 of the Criminal Law Act 1977 (the offence of conspiracy), incitement to commit an indictable offence and attempts to commit an indictable offence contrary to section 1 of the Criminal Attempts Act 1981 (attempting to commit an offence) fall within the same Class as the substantive offence to which they relate;

    (c)  where the Table of Offences specifies that the Class within which an offence falls depends on whether the value involved exceeds a stated limit, the value must be presumed not to exceed that limit unless the advocate making the claim under regulation 4 proves otherwise to the satisfaction of the appropriate officer;

    (d)  where more than one count of the indictment is for an offence in relation to which the Class depends on the value involved, that value must be taken to be the total value involved in all those offences, but where two or more counts relate to the same property, the value of that property must be taken into account once only;

    (e)  where an entry in the Table of Offences specifies an offence as being contrary to a statutory provision, then subject to any express limitation in the entry that entry includes every offence contrary to that statutory provision whether or not the words of description in the entry are appropriate to cover all such offences;

    (f)  where in a case on indictment there is a hearing to determine the question of whether an assisted person is unfit to plead or unfit to stand trial, the trial advocate must elect whether that hearing falls within the same Class as the indictable offence to which it relates or within Class D; and

    (g)  where in a case on indictment a restriction order is made under section 41 of the Mental Health Act 1983 (power of higher courts to restrict discharge from hospital), the offence falls within Class A, regardless of the Class under which the offence would be listed in the Table of Offences but for this paragraph.

    (2) Where an advocate in proceedings in the Crown Court is dissatisfied with the classification within Class H of an indictable offence not listed in the Table of Offences, the advocate may apply to the appropriate officer when lodging the claim for fees to reclassify the offence.

    (3) The appropriate officer must, in light of the objections made by the advocate—

    (a)  confirm the classification of the offence within Class H; or

    (b)  reclassify the offence,

and must notify the advocate of the decision.

As to this paragraph, see *post*, G-119.


PART 2

GRADUATED FEES FOR TRIAL

*Calculation of graduated fees*

    4. The amount of the graduated fee for a single trial advocate representing one assisted person be-    **G-42**
ing tried on one indictment in the Crown Court in a trial lasting one to 40 days must be calculated in accordance with the following formula—

$$G = B + (d \times D) + (e \times E) + (w \times W)$$

Where—

- **G** is the amount of the graduated fee;
- **B** is the basic fee specified in the table following paragraph 5 as appropriate to the offence for which the assisted person is tried and the category of trial advocate;
- **d** is the number of days or parts of a day on which the advocate attends at court by which the trial exceeds 2 days but does not exceed 40 days;
- **D** is the fee payable in respect of daily attendance at court for the number of days by which the trial exceeds 2 days but does not exceed 40 days, as appropriate to the offence for which the assisted person is tried and the category of trial advocate;

- **e** is the number of pages of prosecution evidence excluding the first 50, up to a maximum of 10,000;
- **E** is the evidence uplift specified in the table following paragraph 5 as appropriate to the offence for which the assisted person is tried and the category of trial advocate;
- **w** is the number of prosecution witnesses excluding the first 10;
- **W** is the witness uplift specified in the table following paragraph 5 as appropriate to the offence for which the assisted person is tried and the category of trial advocate.

*Table of fees*

**G-43**    5. For the purposes of paragraph 4 the basic fee (B), the daily attendance fee (D), the evidence uplift (E) and the witness uplift (W) appropriate to any offence are those specified in the table following this paragraph in accordance with the Class within which that offence falls.

TABLE OF FEES AND UPLIFTS

| Class of Offence | Basic Fee (B) (£) | Daily attendance fee (D) (£) | Evidence uplift (E) (£) | Witness uplift (W) (£) |
|---|---|---|---|---|
| **QC** | | | | |
| A | 2,856 | 979 | 1.63 | 6.53 |
| B | 2,529 | 857 | 1.63 | 6.53 |
| C | 1,968 | 816 | 1.63 | 6.53 |
| D | 2,284 | 816 | 1.63 | 6.53 |
| E | 1,514 | 612 | 1.63 | 6.53 |
| F | 1,514 | 612 | 1.63 | 6.53 |
| G | 1,514 | 612 | 1.63 | 6.53 |
| H | 1,903 | 816 | 1.63 | 6.53 |
| I | 2,122 | 816 | 1.63 | 6.53 |
| J | 2,856 | 979 | 1.63 | 6.53 |
| K | 2,856 | 979 | 1.63 | 6.53 |
| **Leading Junior** | | | | |
| A | 2,142 | 734 | 1.23 | 4.9 |
| B | 1,897 | 643 | 1.23 | 4.9 |
| C | 1,476 | 612 | 1.23 | 4.9 |
| D | 1,714 | 612 | 1.23 | 4.9 |
| E | 1,136 | 459 | 1.23 | 4.9 |
| F | 1,136 | 459 | 1.23 | 4.9 |
| G | 1,136 | 459 | 1.23 | 4.9 |
| H | 1,427 | 612 | 1.23 | 4.9 |
| I | 1,592 | 612 | 1.23 | 4.9 |
| J | 2,142 | 734 | 1.23 | 4.9 |
| K | 2,142 | 734 | 1.23 | 4.9 |
| **Led Junior** | | | | |
| A | 1,632 | 490 | 0.81 | 3.26 |
| B | 1,265 | 428 | 0.81 | 3.26 |
| C | 898 | 408 | 0.81 | 3.26 |
| D | 1,125 | 408 | 0.81 | 3.26 |
| E | 694 | 306 | 0.81 | 3.26 |
| F | 694 | 306 | 0.81 | 3.26 |
| G | 694 | 306 | 0.81 | 3.26 |
| H | 816 | 408 | 0.81 | 3.26 |
| I | 979 | 408 | 0.81 | 3.26 |

| Class of Offence | Basic Fee (B) (£) | Daily attendance fee (D) (£) | Evidence uplift (E) (£) | Witness uplift (W) (£) |
|---|---|---|---|---|
| J | 1,632 | 490 | 0.81 | 3.26 |
| K | 1,428 | 490 | 0.81 | 3.26 |
| **Junior alone** | | | | |
| A | 1,632 | 530 | 0.98 | 4.9 |
| B | 1,305 | 469 | 0.98 | 4.9 |
| C | 898 | 408 | 0.98 | 4.9 |
| D | 1,125 | 408 | 0.98 | 4.9 |
| E | 653 | 326 | 0.98 | 4.9 |
| F | 694 | 326 | 0.98 | 4.9 |
| G | 694 | 326 | 0.98 | 4.9 |
| H | 816 | 408 | 0.98 | 4.9 |
| I | 979 | 408 | 0.98 | 4.9 |
| J | 1,632 | 530 | 0.98 | 4.9 |
| K | 1,632 | 530 | 0.98 | 4.9 |

PART 3

GRADUATED FEES FOR GUILTY PLEAS AND CRACKED TRIALS

*Scope of Part 3*

6. Subject to paragraph 22, this Part does not apply to a case committed or sent for trial to the   **G-44**
Crown Court on the election of a defendant where the magistrates' court has determined the case to
be suitable for summary trial.

*Calculation of graduated fees in guilty pleas and cracked trials*

7.—(1) The amount of the graduated fee for a single trial advocate representing one assisted   **G-44a**
person in a guilty plea or cracked trial is—

    (a) where the case is a guilty plea or a trial which cracks in the first third—
        (i) the basic fee specified in Table A following paragraph 8 as appropriate to the offence
            with which the assisted person is charged, and the category of trial advocate; and
        (ii) the evidence uplift, as appropriate to the number of pages of prosecution evidence,
            calculated in accordance with that table; and
    (b) where the case is a trial which cracks in the second or last third—
        (i) the basic fee specified in Table B following paragraph 8 as appropriate to the offence
            with which the assisted person is charged and the category of trial advocate; and
        (ii) the evidence uplift, as appropriate to the number of pages of prosecution evidence,
            calculated in accordance with that table.

    (2) Where—
    (a) the trial of a case does not commence on the date first fixed; or
    (b) the case is not taken and disposed of from the first warned list in which it is entered,
the basic fee and evidence uplift for the offence are those specified for the last third in Table B following paragraph 8.

    (3) In this paragraph, and in the tables following paragraph 8, references to the first, second and
last third are references to the first, second and last third—
    (a) where a case is first listed for trial on a fixed date, of the period of time beginning with the
        day after the date on which the case is so listed and ending with the day before the date so
        fixed;
    (b) where the case is first placed in a warned list, of the period of time beginning with the day
        after the date on which the case is so placed and ending with the day before the date of the
        start of that warned list,
and where the number of days in this period of time cannot be divided by three equally, any days
remaining after such division must be added to the last third.

    (4) Where a graduated fee is calculated in accordance with this Part for the purposes of paragraph
2(3), the fee must be calculated as if the trial had cracked in the last third.

*Tables of fees*

8. Subject to paragraph 7, the basic fee and evidence uplift appropriate to any offence are specified   **G-45**

in the tables following this paragraph in accordance with the Class within which that offence falls, the category of trial advocate and whether the case is a guilty plea, a trial which cracks in the first third or a trial which cracks in the second or last third.

TABLE A: FEES AND UPLIFTS IN GUILTY PLEAS AND TRIALS WHICH CRACK IN THE FIRST THIRD

| Class of Offence | Basic fee (£) | Evidence uplift per page of prosecution evidence (pages 1 to 1,000) (£) | Evidence uplift per page of prosecution evidence (1,001 to 10,000) (£) |
|---|---|---|---|
| **QC** | | | |
| A | 1,714 | 2.85 | 1.43 |
| B | 1,305 | 1.8 | 0.9 |
| C | 1,224 | 1.28 | 0.64 |
| D | 1,305 | 2.85 | 1.43 |
| E | 1,081 | 0.92 | 0.46 |
| F | 1,081 | 1.2 | 0.61 |
| G | 1,081 | 1.2 | 0.61 |
| H | 1,224 | 1.65 | 0.82 |
| I | 1,224 | 1.61 | 0.8 |
| J | 1,714 | 2.85 | 1.43 |
| K | 1,714 | 1.59 | 0.8 |
| **Leading Junior** | | | |
| A | 1,285 | 2.15 | 1.07 |
| B | 979 | 1.35 | 0.67 |
| C | 918 | 0.96 | 0.48 |
| D | 979 | 2.15 | 1.07 |
| E | 811 | 0.69 | 0.35 |
| F | 811 | 0.9 | 0.46 |
| G | 811 | 0.9 | 0.46 |
| H | 918 | 1.24 | 0.61 |
| I | 918 | 1.21 | 0.6 |
| J | 1,285 | 2.15 | 1.07 |
| K | 1,285 | 1.19 | 0.6 |
| **Led Junior** | | | |
| A | 857 | 1.43 | 0.72 |
| B | 653 | 0.9 | 0.45 |
| C | 612 | 0.64 | 0.32 |
| D | 653 | 1.43 | 0.72 |
| E | 541 | 0.46 | 0.23 |
| F | 541 | 0.61 | 0.3 |
| G | 541 | 0.61 | 0.3 |
| H | 612 | 0.83 | 0.42 |
| I | 612 | 0.8 | 0.4 |
| J | 857 | 1.43 | 0.72 |
| K | 857 | 0.8 | 0.4 |
| **Junior Alone** | | | |
| A | 979 | 1.19 | 0.59 |
| B | 694 | 0.81 | 0.41 |
| C | 449 | 0.6 | 0.3 |

| Class of Offence | Basic fee (£) | Evidence uplift per page of prosecution evidence (pages 1 to 1,000) (£) | Evidence uplift per page of prosecution evidence (1,001 to 10,000) (£) |
|---|---|---|---|
| D | 694 | 1.19 | 0.59 |
| E | 408 | 0.35 | 0.17 |
| F | 408 | 0.54 | 0.27 |
| G | 408 | 0.54 | 0.27 |
| H | 490 | 0.54 | 0.28 |
| I | 571 | 0.42 | 0.22 |
| J | 979 | 1.19 | 0.59 |
| K | 979 | 1.02 | 0.51 |

TABLE B: FEES AND UPLIFTS IN TRIALS WHICH CRACK IN THE SECOND OR FINAL THIRD

| Class of Offence | Basic Fee (£) | Evidence uplift per page of prosecution evidence (pages 1 to 250) (£) | Evidence up lift per page of prosecutionevidence (pages 251-1000) (£) | Evidence uplift per page of prosecution evidence (pages 1,001 to 10,000) (£) |
|---|---|---|---|---|
| **QC** | | | | |
| A | 2,324 | 5.07 | 1.27 | 1.68 |
| B | 1,743 | 3.2 | 0.8 | 1.06 |
| C | 1,520 | 2.27 | 0.57 | 0.75 |
| D | 1,743 | 5.07 | 1.27 | 1.68 |
| E | 1,232 | 1.63 | 0.41 | 0.54 |
| F | 1,232 | 2.14 | 0.54 | 0.71 |
| G | 1,232 | 2.14 | 0.54 | 0.71 |
| H | 1,540 | 2.93 | 0.73 | 0.96 |
| I | 1,598 | 2.87 | 0.71 | 0.94 |
| J | 2,324 | 5.07 | 1.27 | 1.68 |
| K | 2,324 | 2.83 | 0.71 | 0.94 |
| **Leading Junior** | | | | |
| A | 1,744 | 3.8 | 0.95 | 1.26 |
| B | 1,307 | 2.4 | 0.6 | 0.8 |
| C | 1,140 | 1.7 | 0.43 | 0.56 |
| D | 1,307 | 3.8 | 0.95 | 1.26 |
| E | 924 | 1.22 | 0.31 | 0.41 |
| F | 924 | 1.6 | 0.41 | 0.53 |
| G | 924 | 1.6 | 0.41 | 0.53 |
| H | 1,155 | 2.2 | 0.54 | 0.72 |
| I | 1,198 | 2.14 | 0.53 | 0.71 |
| J | 1,744 | 3.8 | 0.95 | 1.26 |
| K | 1,744 | 2.13 | 0.53 | 0.71 |
| **Led Junior** | | | | |
| A | 1162 | 2.54 | 0.64 | 0.84 |
| B | 871 | 1.6 | 0.4 | 0.53 |
| C | 760 | 1.14 | 0.28 | 0.37 |
| D | 871 | 2.54 | 0.64 | 0.84 |
| E | 616 | 0.82 | 0.2 | 0.27 |

| Class of Offence | Basic Fee (£) | Evidence uplift per page of prosecution evidence (pages 1 to 250) (£) | Evidence up lift per page of prosecutionevidence (pages 251-1000) (£) | Evidence uplift per page of prosecution evidence (pages 1,001 to 10,000) (£) |
|---|---|---|---|---|
| F | 616 | 1.07 | 0.27 | 0.36 |
| G | 616 | 1.07 | 0.27 | 0.36 |
| H | 770 | 1.46 | 0.37 | 0.48 |
| I | 798 | 1.43 | 0.36 | 0.48 |
| J | 1162 | 2.54 | 0.64 | 0.84 |
| K | 1162 | 1.42 | 0.36 | 0.47 |
| **Junior alone** | | | | |
| A | 1307 | 4.52 | 2.1 | 0.69 |
| B | 908 | 3.11 | 1.45 | 0.48 |
| C | 581 | 2.31 | 1.07 | 0.36 |
| D | 808 | 4.52 | 2.1 | 0.69 |
| E | 508 | 1.34 | 0.63 | 0.2 |
| F | 508 | 2.08 | 0.96 | 0.32 |
| G | 508 | 2.08 | 0.96 | 0.32 |
| H | 618 | 2.08 | 0.97 | 0.32 |
| I | 726 | 1.63 | 0.76 | 0.25 |
| J | 1307 | 4.52 | 2.1 | 0.69 |
| K | 1234 | 3.91 | 1.82 | 0.60 |

PART 4

FIXED FEE FOR GUILTY PLEAS AND CRACKED TRIALS

*Scope of Part 4*

**G-46**    9. This Part applies to a case committed or sent for trial to the Crown Court on the election of a defendant where the magistrates' court has determined the case to be suitable for summary trial.

*Fixed fee for guilty pleas or cracked trials*

10. The fee payable to an advocate in relation to a guilty plea or cracked trial to which this Part applies is £194 per proceedings.

PART 5

FIXED FEES

*General provisions*

**G-46a**    11.—(1) All work undertaken by an advocate in a case to which Part 4 applies is included within the fee set out in paragraph 10 except for attendance at a confiscation hearing to which paragraph 14 applies.

(2) Except as provided under this Part, all work undertaken by an advocate in a case to which Part 3 applies is included within the basic fee (B) specified in the table following paragraph 5, or that following paragraph 8, as appropriate to—

    (a)   the offence for which the assisted person is tried;

    (b)   the category of advocate; and

    (c)   whether the case is a cracked trial, guilty plea or trial.

*Fees for plea and case management hearings and standard appearance*

**G-47**    12.—(1) The fee payable in respect of—

    (a)   an appearance by the trial advocate or substitute advocate at the first plea and case management hearing or pre-trial review; and

    (b)   up to four standard appearances by the trial advocate or substitute advocate,

is included within the basic fee (B) specified in the table following paragraph 5, or that following paragraph 8, as appropriate to the offence for which the assisted person is tried and the category of trial advocate.

(2) The fee payable in respect of an appearance by the trial advocate or substitute advocate at a plea and case management hearing or standard appearance not included in sub-paragraph (1) is specified in the table following paragraph 24 as appropriate to the category of trial advocate or substitute advocate.

(3) The fee payable for preparing and filing the plea and case management questionnaire where no oral hearing takes place is specified in the table following paragraph 24 as appropriate to the category of trial advocate or substitute advocate.

(4) This paragraph does not apply to a standard appearance which is or forms part of the main hearing in a case or to a hearing for which a fee is payable elsewhere under this Schedule.

As to whether any appearances can be remunerated under paragraph 12(2) where no basic fee is payable, see *R. v. Metcalf* and *R. v. Muoka, post,* G-129.

*Fees for abuse of process, disclosure, admissibility and withdrawal of plea hearings*

13.—(1) This paragraph applies to— **G-48**
- (a) the hearing of an application to stay the case on indictment or any count on the ground that the proceedings constitute an abuse of the process of the court;
- (b) any hearing relating to the question of whether any material should be disclosed by the prosecution to the defence or the defence to the prosecution (whether or not any claim to public interest immunity is made);
- (c) the hearing of an application under section 2(1) of the Criminal Procedure (Attendance of Witnesses) Act 1965 (issue of witness summons on application to Crown Court) for disclosure of material held by third parties;
- (d) any hearing relating to the question of the admissibility as evidence of any material; and
- (e) the hearing of an application to withdraw a plea of guilty where the application is—
  - (i) made by an advocate other than the advocate who appeared at the hearing at which the plea of guilty was entered; and
  - (ii) unsuccessful.

(2) Where a hearing to which this paragraph applies is held on any day of the main hearing of a case on indictment, no separate fee is payable in respect of attendance at the hearing, but the hearing is included in the length of the main hearing for the purpose of calculating the fees payable.

(3) Where a hearing to which this paragraph applies is held prior to the first or only day of the main hearing, it is not included in the length of the main hearing for the purpose of calculating the fees payable and the trial advocate or substitute advocate must be remunerated for attendance at such a hearing—
- (a) in respect of any day where the hearing begins before and ends after the luncheon adjournment, at the daily rate set out in the table following paragraph 24 as appropriate to the category of trial advocate or substitute advocate; or
- (b) in respect of any day where the hearing begins and ends before the luncheon adjournment, or begins after the luncheon adjournment, at the half-daily rate set out in the table following paragraph 24 as appropriate to the category of trial advocate or substitute advocate.

*Fees for confiscation hearings*

14.—(1) This paragraph applies to— **G-49**
- (a) a hearing under Part 2 of the Proceeds of Crime Act 2002 (confiscation: England and Wales);
- (b) a hearing under section 2 of the Drug Trafficking Act 1994 (confiscation orders); and
- (c) a hearing under section 71 of the Criminal Justice Act 1988 (confiscation orders).

(2) A hearing to which this paragraph applies is not included in the length of the main hearing or of any sentencing hearing for the purpose of calculating the fees payable, and the trial advocate or substitute advocate must be remunerated in respect of such a hearing—
- (a) where the number of pages of evidence is fewer than 51, for attendance—
  - (i) in respect of any day when the hearing begins before and ends after the luncheon adjournment, at the daily rate set out in the first section of the table following this sub-paragraph; or
  - (ii) in respect of any day when the hearing begins and ends before the luncheon adjournment, or begins after the luncheon adjournment, at the half-daily rate set out in the first section of that table,

  as appropriate to the category of trial advocate or substitute advocate;
- (b) where the number of pages of evidence is between 51 and 1000—
  - (i) at the rates for the relevant number of pages set out in the second section of the table following this sub-paragraph; and

    (ii)  where the hearing lasts for more than one day, for attendance on subsequent days or half-days at the daily rate or half-daily rate set out in the first section of that table, as appropriate to the category of trial advocate or substitute advocate; or

  (c)  where the number of pages of evidence exceeds 1000—

    (i)  at the rates for 751 to 1000 pages set out in the second section of the table following this sub-paragraph;

    (ii)  with such fee as the appropriate officer considers reasonable for preparation in respect of the pages in excess of 1000, at the hourly rates for preparation set out in the third section of that table; and

    (iii)  where the hearing lasts for more than one day, for attendance on subsequent days or half-days at the daily rate or half-daily rate set out in the first section of that table, as appropriate to the category of trial advocate or substitute advocate.

FEES FOR CONSFISCATION HEARINGS

| | Fee for QC (£) | Fee for leading junior (£) | Fee for junior alone (£) | Fee for led junior (£) |
|---|---|---|---|---|
| *1. Daily and half-daily rates* | | | | |
| Half-daily rate | 260 | 195 | 130 | 130 |
| Daily rate | 497 | 346 | 238 | 238 |
| *2. Pages of evidence* | | | | |
| 51-250 | 649 | 541 | 433 | 324 |
| 251-500 | 973 | 811 | 649 | 486 |
| 501-750 | 1,298 | 1,081 | 865 | 649 |
| 751-1000 | 1,946 | 1,622 | 1,298 | 973 |
| *3. Preparation* | | | | |
| Hourly rates | 74 | 56 | 39 | 39 |

    (3) In sub-paragraph (2) "evidence" means—

  (a)  the statement of information served under section 16 of the Proceeds of Crime Act 2002 and relied on by the prosecution for the purposes of a hearing under Part 2 of that Act, or a similar statement served and so relied on for the purposes of a hearing under section 2 of the Drug Trafficking Act 1994 or under section 71 of the Criminal Justice Act 1988 and, in each case, any attached annexes and exhibits;

  (b)  any other document which—

    (i)  is served as a statement or an exhibit for the purposes of the trial;

    (ii)  is specifically referred to in, but not served with, a statement mentioned in paragraph (a); and

    (iii)  the prosecution state that they intend to rely on in the hearing; and

  (c)  any written report of an expert obtained with the prior authority of the Lord Chancellor under regulation 13 or allowed by the appropriate officer under these Regulations, and any attached annexes and exhibits, other than documents contained in such annexes or exhibits which have also been served under paragraph (a) or (b) or which consist of financial records or similar data.

*Fees for sentencing hearings*

**G-50**    15.—(1) This paragraph applies to a sentencing hearing following a case on indictment to which this Schedule applies, where sentence has been deferred under section 1 of the Powers of Criminal Courts (Sentencing) Act 2000 (deferment of sentence).

    (2) The fee payable to an advocate for appearing at a hearing to which this paragraph applies is that set out in the table following paragraph 24 as appropriate to the category of trial advocate or substitute advocate and the circumstances of the hearing.

*Fees for ineffective trials*

**G-51**    16. The fee set out in the table following paragraph 24 as appropriate to the category of trial advocate is payable in respect of each day on which the case was listed for trial but did not proceed on the day for which it was listed, for whatever reason.

*Fees for special preparation*

**G-52**    17.—(1) This paragraph applies where, in any case on indictment in the Crown Court in respect of which a graduated fee is payable under Part 2 or Part 3—

(a) it has been necessary for an advocate to do work by way of preparation substantially in excess of the amount normally done for cases of the same type because the case involves a very unusual or novel point of law or factual issue;

(b) the number of pages of prosecution evidence, as defined in paragraph 1(2), exceeds 10,000 and the appropriate officer considers it reasonable to make a payment in excess of the graduated fee payable under this Schedule; or

(c) a documentary or pictorial exhibit is served by the prosecution in electronic form where—
  (i) the exhibit has never existed in paper form; and
  (ii) the appropriate officer—
    (aa) does not consider it appropriate to include the exhibit in the pages of prosecution evidence; and
    (bb) considers it reasonable to make a payment in respect of the exhibit in excess of the graduated fee.

(2) Where this paragraph applies, a special preparation fee may be paid, in addition to the graduated fee payable under Part 2 or Part 3.

(3) The amount of the special preparation fee must be calculated—

(a) where sub-paragraph (1)(a) applies, from the number of hours preparation in excess of the amount the appropriate officer considers reasonable for cases of the same type;

(b) where sub-paragraph (1)(b) applies, from the number of hours which the appropriate officer considers reasonable to read the excess pages; and

(c) where sub-paragraph (1)(c) applies, from the number of hours which the appropriate officer considers reasonable to view the prosecution evidence,

and in each case using the hourly fee rates set out in the table following paragraph 24 as appropriate to the category of trial advocate.

(4) Any claim for a special preparation fee under this paragraph must be made by an instructed advocate, whether or not the instructed advocate did the work claimed for.

(5) An instructed advocate claiming a special preparation fee must supply such information and documents as may be required by the appropriate officer in support of the claim.

(6) In determining a claim under this paragraph, the appropriate officer must take into account all the relevant circumstances of the case, including, where special preparation work has been undertaken by more than one advocate, the benefit of such work to the trial advocate.

*Fees for wasted preparation*

18.—(1) A wasted preparation fee may be claimed where a trial advocate in any case to which this **G-53** paragraph applies is prevented from representing the assisted person in the main hearing by any of the following circumstances—

(a) the trial advocate is instructed to appear in other proceedings at the same time as the main hearing in the case and has been unable to secure a change of date for either the main hearing or the other proceedings;

(b) the date fixed for the main hearing is changed by the court despite the trial advocate's objection;

(c) the trial advocate has withdrawn from the case with the leave of the court because of the trial advocate's professional code of conduct or to avoid embarrassment in the exercise of the trial advocate's profession;

(d) the trial advocate has been dismissed by the assisted person or the litigator; or

(e) the trial advocate is obliged to attend at any place by reason of a judicial office held by the trial advocate or other public duty.

(2) This paragraph applies to every case on indictment to which this Schedule applies provided that—

(a) the case goes to trial, and the trial lasts for five days or more; or

(b) the case is a cracked trial, and the number of pages of prosecution evidence exceeds 150.

(3) The amount of the wasted preparation fee must be calculated from the number of hours of preparation reasonably carried out by the trial advocate, using the hourly fee rates set out in the table following paragraph 24 as appropriate to the category of trial advocate, but no such fee is payable unless the number of hours of preparation is eight or more.

(4) Any claim for a wasted preparation fee under this paragraph must be made by an instructed advocate, whether or not the instructed advocate did the work claimed for.

(5) An instructed advocate claiming a wasted preparation fee must supply such information and documents as may be required by the appropriate officer as proof of the circumstances in which the instructed advocate was prevented from representing the assisted person and of the number of hours of preparation.

*Fees for conferences and views*

**G-54**   19.—(1) This paragraph applies to the following types of work—

    (a)  attendance by the trial advocate at pre-trial conferences with prospective or actual expert witnesses not held at court;

    (b)  attendance by the trial advocate at views at the scene of the alleged offence;

    (c)  attendance by the trial advocate at pre-trial conferences with the assisted person not held at court;

    (d)  reasonable travelling time by the trial advocate for the purpose of attending a view at the scene of the alleged offence; or

    (e)  reasonable travelling time by the trial advocate for the purpose of attending a pre-trial conference with the assisted person or prospective or actual expert witness, where the appropriate officer is satisfied that the assisted person or prospective or actual expert witness was unable or could not reasonably have been expected to attend a conference at the trial advocate's chambers or office.

(2) The fees payable in respect of attendance at the first three pre-trial conferences or views, as set out in sub-paragraph (1)(a) to (c), are included in the basic fee (B) specified in the table following paragraph 5, or that following paragraph 8, as appropriate to the offence for which the assisted person is tried, the category of trial advocate and whether the case is a guilty plea, cracked trial or trial, provided that the trial advocate satisfies the appropriate officer that the work was reasonably necessary.

(3) The fee specified in the table following paragraph 24 as appropriate to the category of trial advocate is payable in the following circumstances, provided that the trial advocate satisfies the appropriate officer that the work was reasonably necessary—

    (a)  for trials lasting not less than 21 and not more than 25 days, and cracked trials where it was accepted by the court at the plea and case management hearing that the trial would last not less than 21 days and not more than 25 days, one further pre-trial conference or view not exceeding two hours;

    (b)  for trials lasting not less than 26 and not more than 35 days, and cracked trials where it was accepted by the court at the plea and case management hearing that the trial would last not less than 26 days and not more than 35 days, two further pre-trial conferences or views each not exceeding two hours; and

    (c)  for trials lasting not less than 36 days, and cracked trials where it was accepted by the court at the plea and case management hearing that the trial would last not less than 36 days and not more than 40 days, three further pre-trial conferences or views each not exceeding two hours.

(4) Travel expenses must be paid for all conferences and views set out in sub-paragraph (1)(a) to (c), provided that the trial advocate satisfies the appropriate officer that they were reasonably incurred.

(5) Travelling time must be paid for all conferences and views set out in sub-paragraph (1)(a) to (c), provided that the trial advocate satisfies the appropriate officer that it was reasonable.

*Fees for appeals, committals for sentence and breach hearings*

**G-55**   20.—(1) Subject to sub-paragraphs (4) and (5) and paragraph 26 the fee payable to a trial advocate in any of the hearings referred to in paragraph 2(1)(b) is the fixed fee specified in the table following paragraph 24.

(2) Where a hearing referred to in paragraph 2(1)(b) is listed but cannot proceed because of the failure of the assisted person or a witness to attend, the unavailability of a pre-sentence report, or other good reason, the fee payable to the advocate is the fixed fee specified in the table following paragraph 24.

(3) Where—

    (a)  a bail application;

    (b)  a mention hearing; or

    (c)  any other application,

takes place in the course of a hearing referred to in paragraph 2(1)(b), the fee payable to the advocate is the fixed fee specified in the table following paragraph 24.

(4) Where it appears to the appropriate officer that the fixed fee allowed under sub-paragraph (1) would be inappropriate taking into account all of the relevant circumstances of the case the appropriate officer may instead allow fees of such amounts as appear to the appropriate officer to be reasonable remuneration for the relevant work in accordance with sub-paragraph (5).

(5) The appropriate officer may allow any of the following classes of fees to an advocate in respect of work allowed by the appropriate officer under this paragraph—

(a)  a fee for preparation including, where appropriate, the first day of the hearing including, where they took place on that day—
  (i)    short conferences;
  (ii)   consultations;
  (iii)  applications and appearances (including bail applications);
  (iv)   views at the scene of the alleged offence; and
  (v)    any other preparation;
(b)  a refresher fee for any day or part of a day for which a hearing continued, including, where they took place on that day—
  (i)    short conferences;
  (ii)   consultations;
  (iii)  applications and appearances (including bail applications);
  (iv)   views at the scene of the alleged offence; and
  (v)    any other preparation; and
(c)  subsidiary fees for—
  (i)    attendance at conferences, consultations and views at the scene of the alleged offence not covered by paragraph (a) or (b);
  (ii)   written advice on evidence, plea, appeal, case stated or other written work; and
  (iii)  attendance at applications and appearances (including bail applications and adjournments for sentence) not covered by paragraph (a) or (b).

*Fees for contempt proceedings*

**G-55a**

21.—(1) Subject to sub-paragraph (2), remuneration for advocates in proceedings referred to in section 14(g) of the Act in the Crown Court must be at the rates specified in the table following this sub-paragraph.

| Category of advocate | Payment rates (£ per day) |
| --- | --- |
| QC | 300 |
| Leading junior | 225 |
| Led junior or junior acting alone | 150 |

(2) Where an advocate and a litigator are instructed in proceedings referred to in section 14(g) of the Act, remuneration must be at the rates specified in the table following this sub-paragraph, as appropriate to the category of advocate.

| Category of advocate | Payment rates (£ per day) |
| --- | --- |
| QC | 175 |
| Leading junior | 125 |
| Led junior or junior acting alone | 100 |

*Discontinuance or dismissal of sent or transferred proceedings*

**G-56**

22.—(1) This paragraph applies to proceedings which are—
(a)  sent for trial to the Crown Court; or
(b)  transferred to the Crown Court under—
  (i)   section 4 of the Criminal Justice Act 1987 (transfer of serious fraud cases); or
  (ii)  section 53 of the Criminal Justice Act 1991 (transfer of certain cases involving children).

(2) Where proceedings referred to in sub-paragraph (1) are discontinued by a notice served under section 23A of the Prosecution of Offences Act 1985 (discontinuance of proceedings after accused has been sent for trial) at any time before the prosecution serves its evidence in accordance with the Crime and Disorder Act 1998 (Service of Prosecution Evidence) Regulations 2005 the advocate must be paid 50% of the basic fee (B) for a guilty plea, as specified in the table following paragraph 8 as appropriate to the offence for which the assisted person is charged and the category of advocate.

(3) Where proceedings referred to in sub-paragraph (1) are discontinued by a notice served under section 23A of the Prosecution of Offences Act 1985 (discontinuance of proceedings after accused has been sent for trial) at any time after the prosecution serves its evidence in accordance with the Crime and Disorder Act 1998 (Service of Prosecution Evidence) Regulations 2005, the advocate must be paid a graduated fee calculated in accordance with paragraph 7, as appropriate for representing an assisted person in a guilty plea.

(4) Sub-paragraph (5) applies to—
    (a)  a plea and case management hearing that takes place after the prosecution serves its evidence; and
    (b)  any other hearing that takes place before a plea and case management hearing has taken place but after the prosecution has served its evidence.
(5) Where, at a hearing to which this sub-paragraph applies—
    (a)  the prosecution offers no evidence and the assisted person is discharged; or
    (b)  the case is remitted to the magistrates' court in accordance with paragraph 10(3)(a), 13(2) or 15(3)(a) of Schedule 3 to the Crime and Disorder Act 1998,
the advocate instructed in the proceedings must be paid a graduated fee calculated in accordance with paragraph 7, as appropriate for representing an assisted person in a guilty plea.

(6) Where an application for dismissal is made under paragraph 2 of Schedule 3 to the Crime and Disorder Act 1998, section 6 of the Criminal Justice Act 1987 or paragraph 5 of Schedule 6 to the Criminal Justice Act 1991 (applications for dismissal), the advocate must be remunerated for attendance at the hearing of the application for dismissal—
    (a)  in respect of any day where the hearing begins before and ends after the luncheon adjournment, at the daily rate set out in the table following paragraph 24 as appropriate to the category of advocate; or
    (b)  in respect of any day where the hearing begins and ends before the luncheon adjournment, or begins after the luncheon adjournment, at the half-daily rate set out in that table as appropriate to the category of advocate,
provided that a fee is not payable elsewhere under this Schedule in respect of any day of the hearing.

(7) Where an application for dismissal is made under paragraph 2 of Schedule 3 to the Crime and Disorder Act 1998, section 6 of the Criminal Justice Act 1987 or paragraph 5 of Schedule 6 to the Criminal Justice Act 1991, and—
    (a)  the charge, or charges, are dismissed and the assisted person is discharged; or
    (b)  the case is remitted to the magistrates' court in accordance with paragraph 10(3)(a), 13(2) or 15(3)(a) of Schedule 3 to the Crime and Disorder Act 1998,
in respect of the first day of the hearing of the application to dismiss, the advocate instructed in the proceedings must be paid a graduated fee calculated in accordance with paragraph 7, as appropriate for representing an assisted person in a guilty plea.

(8) Where an advocate represents more than one assisted person in proceedings referred to in sub-paragraph (1), the advocate must be paid a fixed fee of 20% of—
    (a)  the fee specified in sub-paragraph (2) where that sub-paragraph applies; or
    (b)  the basic fee (B) specified in the table following paragraph 8 where sub-paragraph (3), (4) or (5) applies, as appropriate for the circumstances set out in the relevant sub-paragraph,
in respect of each additional assisted person the advocate represents.

*Noting brief fees*

**G-57**    23. The fee payable to an advocate retained solely for the purpose of making a note of any hearing must be the daily fee set out in the table following paragraph 24.

*Fixed fees*

**G-57a**    24. The table following this paragraph sets out the fixed fees payable in relation to the category of work specified in the first column of the table.

FIXED FEES

| Category of work | Paragraph providing for fee | Fee for QC £ | Fee for leading junior £ | Fee for led junior or junior alone £ |
|---|---|---|---|---|
| Standard appearance | 9(2) | 173 per day | 130 per day | 87 per day |
| Paper plea and case management hearing | 9(3) | 26 per case | 26 per case | 26 per case |
| Abuse of process hearing | 10(1)(a) | 260 Half day | 195 Half day | 130 Half day |
|  |  | 497 Full day | 346 Full day | 238 Full day |

| Category of work | Paragraph providing for fee | Fee for QC £ | Fee for leading junior £ | Fee for led junior or junior alone £ |
|---|---|---|---|---|
| Hearings relating to disclosure | 10(1)(b) and (c) | 260 Half day | 195 Half day | 130 Half day |
| | | 497 Full day | 346 Full day | 238 Full day |
| Hearings relating to the admissibility of evidence | 10(1)(d) | 260 Half day | 195 Half day | 130 Half day |
| | | 497 Full day | 346 Full day | 238 Full day |
| Hearings on withdrawal of guilty plea | 10(1)(e) | 260 Half day | 195 Half day | 130 Half day |
| | | 497 Full day | 346 Full day | 238 Full day |
| Deferred sentencing hearing | 12(1)(a) | 324 per day | 238 per day | 173 per day |
| Ineffective trial payment | 13 | 281 per day | 195 per day | 130 per day |
| Special preparation | 14 | 74 per hour | 56 per hour | 39 per hour |
| Wasted preparation | 15 | 74 per hour | 56 per hour | 39 per hour |
| Conferences and views | 16 | 74 per hour | 56 per hour | 39 per hour |
| Appeals to the Crown Court against conviction | 17(1) | 260 per day | 195 per day | 130 per day |
| Appeals to the Crown Court against sentence | 17(1) | 216 per day | 151 per day | 108 per day |
| Proceedings relating to breach of an order of the Crown Court | 17(1) | 216 per day | 151 per day | 108 per day |
| Committal for sentence | 17(1) | 260 per day | 195 per day | 130 per day |
| Adjourned appeals, committals for sentence and breach hearings | 17(2) | 173 per day | 130 per day | 87 per day |
| Bail applications, mentions and other applications in appeals, committals for sentence and breach hearings | 17(3) | 173 per day | 130 per day | 87 per day |
| Second and subsequent days of an application to dismiss | 18(6) | 260 Half day | 195 Half day | 130 Half day |
| | | 497 Full day | 346 Full day | 238 Full day |
| Noting brief | 19 | — | — | 108 per day |
| Hearing for mitigation of sentence | 29 | 260 per day | 173 per day | 108 per day |

PART 6

MISCELLANEOUS

*Identity of instructed advocate*

25.—(1) Where an instructed advocate is appointed before the plea and case management hear-    **G-58**
ing, the instructed advocate must notify the Court in writing as soon as the appointment is made
and, where appropriate, must confirm whether the instructed advocate is the leading instructed
advocate or the led instructed advocate.

(2) Where the section 16 determination provides for representation by a single advocate and no instructed advocate has been notified to the Court in accordance with sub-paragraph (1)—

    (a)  the barrister or solicitor advocate who attends the plea and case management hearing is deemed to be the instructed advocate; and

    (b)  the Court must make a written record of this fact.

(3) Where the section 16 determination provides for representation by a single advocate and no barrister or solicitor advocate attends the plea and case management hearing—

    (a)  the barrister or solicitor advocate who attends the next hearing in the case is deemed to be the instructed advocate; and

    (b)  the Court must make a written record of this fact.

(4) Where the section 16 determination provides for representation by more than one advocate, and no leading instructed advocate has been notified to the Court in accordance with sub-paragraph (1), the leading advocate who attends—

    (a)  the plea and case management hearing; or

    (b)  where no leading advocate attends the plea and case management hearing, the next hearing in the case attended by a leading advocate,

is deemed to be the leading instructed advocate, and the Court must make a written record of this fact.

(5) Where the section 16 determination provides for representation by more than one advocate, and no led instructed advocate has been notified to the Court in accordance with sub-paragraph (1), the led advocate who attends—

    (a)  the plea and case management hearing; or

    (b)  where no led advocate attends the plea and case management hearing, the next hearing in the case attended by a led advocate,

is deemed to be the led instructed advocate, and the Court must make a written record of this fact.

(6) Where a section 16 determination is amended after the plea and case management hearing to provide for representation by more than one advocate—

    (a)  the additional instructed advocate must notify the Court in writing of the additional instructed advocate's appointment within 7 days of the date on which the section 16 determination is amended; and

    (b)  each instructed advocate must notify the Court whether that instructed advocate is the leading instructed advocate or the led instructed advocate.

(7) Where no additional instructed advocate has been notified to the Court in accordance with sub-paragraph (6)(a), the advocate who attends the next hearing in the case is deemed to be an instructed advocate and the Court must record in writing whether that instructed advocate is the leading instructed advocate or the led instructed advocate, as appropriate to the circumstances of the case.

(8) Where—

    (a)  a case ceases to be a Very High Cost Case (in relation to fees claimed by advocates); and

    (b)  none of sub-paragraphs (1) to (7) applies,

the instructed advocate must notify the Court in writing of the instructed advocate's appointment within 7 days of the case ceasing to be a Very High Cost Case.

(9) The Court must attach—

    (a)  any notice received under sub-paragraph (1), (6) or (8); and

    (b)  any record made by it under sub-paragraph (2), (3), (4), (5) or (7),

to the representation order.

(10) An instructed advocate must remain as instructed advocate at all times, except where—

    (a)  a date for trial is fixed at or before the plea and case management hearing and the instructed advocate is unable to conduct the trial due to the instructed advocate's other pre-existing commitments;

    (b)  the instructed advocate is dismissed by the assisted person or the litigator; or

    (c)  the instructed advocate is required to withdraw because of his professional code of conduct.

(11) Where, in accordance with sub-paragraph (10), an instructed advocate withdraws, the instructed advocate must—

    (a)  immediately notify the court of the withdrawal—

        (i)  in writing; or

        (ii)  where the withdrawal takes place at a plea and case management hearing, orally; and

    (b)  within 7 days of the date of the withdrawal, notify the court in writing of the identity of a replacement instructed advocate, who must fulfil all the functions of an instructed advocate in accordance with these Regulations.

(12) This paragraph does not apply to a claim for fees under paragraph 32, 33 or 34.

*Payment of fees to instructed advocate*

26.—(1) In accordance with regulation 23 the appropriate officer must notify each instructed    **G-59**
advocate of the total fees payable and authorise payment to the instructed advocate accordingly.

(2) Payment of the fees in accordance with sub-paragraph (1) must be made to each instructed
advocate.

(3) Where the section 16 determination provides for representation by a single advocate, the
instructed advocate is responsible for arranging payment of fees to the trial advocate and any
substitute advocate who has undertaken work on the case.

(4) Where there are two instructed advocates for an assisted person, payment must be made to
each instructed advocate individually, and—

     (a)   the leading instructed advocate is responsible for arranging payment of fees to the trial
advocate and any substitute advocate who have undertaken work on the case of a type for
which a leading advocate is responsible; and

     (b)   the led instructed advocate is responsible for arranging payment of fees to the trial advocate
and any substitute advocate who have undertaken work on the case of a type for which a
led advocate is responsible.

(5) This paragraph does not apply to a claim for fees under paragraph 32, 33 or 34.

*Additional charges and additional cases*

27.—(1) Where an assisted person is charged with more than one offence on one indictment, the    **G-60**
fee payable to the trial advocate under this Schedule must be based on whichever of those offences
the trial advocate selects.

(2) Where two or more cases to which this Schedule applies involving the same trial advocate are
heard concurrently (whether involving the same or different assisted persons)—

     (a)   the trial advocate must select one case ("the principal case"), which must be treated for the
purposes of remuneration in accordance with this Schedule;

     (b)   in respect of the main hearing in each of the other cases the trial advocate must be paid a
fixed fee of 20% of—

         (i)   the basic fee (B) specified in the table following paragraph 5 or that following
paragraph 8, as appropriate, for the principal case, where that is a case falling within
paragraph 2(1)(a); or

         (ii)   the fixed fee for the principal case, where that is a case falling within paragraph
2(1)(b) or paragraph 10.

(3) Nothing in sub-paragraphs (4) to (6) permits a fixed fee under Part 5, other than one to which
paragraph 14 applies, to be paid in a case to which Part 4 applies.

(4) Where a trial advocate or substitute advocate appears at a hearing specified in paragraph 12,
13, 14, 15 or 16, forming part of two or more cases involving different assisted persons, the trial
advocate or substitute advocate must be paid—

     (a)   in respect of the first such case, the fixed fee for that hearing specified in the table follow-
ing paragraph 24; and

     (b)   in respect of each of the other cases, 20% of that fee.

(5) Subject to sub-paragraphs (1) to (4), where a trial advocate or substitute advocate appears at a
hearing forming part of two or more cases, the trial advocate or substitute advocate must be paid the
fixed fee for that hearing specified in the table following paragraph 24 in respect of one such case,
without any increase in respect of the other cases.

(6) Where a trial advocate selects—

     (a)   one offence, in preference to another offence, under sub-paragraph (1); or

     (b)   one case as the principal case, in preference to another case, under sub-paragraph (2),

that selection does not affect the trial advocate's right to claim any of the fees set out in the table following paragraph 24 to which the trial advocate would otherwise have been entitled.

*Multiple advocates*

28. Where a section 16 determination provides for representation by three advocates in a case the    **G-61**
provisions of this Schedule apply, and the fees payable to the led juniors in accordance with Part 2 or
Part 3 are payable to each led junior who is instructed in the case.

*Non-local appearances*

29. Where an advocate is instructed to appear in a court which is not within 40 kilometres of the    **G-62**
advocate's office or chambers, the appropriate officer may allow an amount for travelling and other
expenses incidental to that appearance, provided that the amount must not be greater than the

amount, if any, which would be payable to a trial advocate from the nearest local Bar or the nearest advocate's office (whichever is the nearer) unless the advocate instructed to appear has obtained prior approval under regulation 13 for the incurring of such expenses or can justify the attendance having regard to all the relevant circumstances of the case.

*Trials lasting over 40 days*

**G-63**     30. Where a trial exceeds 40 days, the trial advocate must be paid a fee as set out in the table following this paragraph, as appropriate to the category of trial advocate and the Class of Offence, for each day by which the trial exceeds 40 days on which the trial advocate attends at court.

DAILY RATES PAYABLE WHERE A TRIAL LASTS OVER 40 DAYS

| Class of Offence | Daily rate payable for days 41 to 50 (£) | Daily rate payable for days 51 and over (£) |
|---|---|---|
| **QC** | | |
| A–K | 387 | 414 |
| **Leading Junior** | | |
| A–K | 331 | 356 |
| **Led Junior** | | |
| A–K | 221 | 237 |
| **Junior Acting Alone** | | |
| A | 266 | 285 |
| B | 247 | 265 |
| C | 247 | 265 |
| D | 266 | 285 |
| E | 225 | 241 |
| F | 225 | 241 |
| G | 225 | 241 |
| H | 247 | 265 |
| I | 247 | 265 |
| J | 266 | 285 |
| K | 266 | 285 |

*Assisted person unfit to plead or stand trial*

**G-64**     31. Where in any case a hearing is held to determine the question of whether the assisted person is unfit to plead or to stand trial (a "fitness hearing")—

    (a)  if a trial on indictment is held, or continues, at any time thereafter, the length of the fitness hearing is included in determining the length of the trial for the calculation of the graduated fee in accordance with Part 2 or Part 3;

    (b)  if a trial on indictment is not held, or does not continue, thereafter by reason of the assisted person being found unfit to plead or to stand trial, the trial advocate must be paid—

        (i)  a graduated fee calculated in accordance with paragraph 4 as appropriate to the combined length of—

          (aa)  the fitness hearing; and

          (bb)  any hearing under section 4A of the Criminal Procedure (Insanity) Act 1964 (finding that the accused did the act or made the omission charged against him); or

        (ii)  a graduated fee calculated in accordance with paragraph 7 as appropriate for representing an assisted person in a cracked trial,

        whichever the trial advocate elects; and

    (c)  if at any time the assisted person pleads guilty to the indictable offence, the trial advocate must be paid either—

        (i)  a graduated fee calculated in accordance with paragraph 4 as appropriate to the length of the fitness hearing; or

        (ii)  a graduated fee calculated in accordance with paragraph 7 as appropriate for representing an assisted person in a guilty plea,

        whichever the trial advocate elects.

*Cross examination of witness*

**G-65**     32.—(1) Where in any case on indictment an advocate is retained solely for the purpose of cross-examining a witness under section 38 of the Youth Justice and Criminal Evidence Act 1999 (defence representation for purposes of cross-examination), the advocate must be paid a graduated fee calculated in accordance with paragraph 4.

(2) For the purposes of this paragraph the daily attendance fee (D) is as set out in the table following paragraph 5 as appropriate to the number of days of attendance at court by the advocate.

*Provision of written or oral advice*

33.—(1) Where in any case on indictment an advocate is assigned pursuant to a section 16   **G-66** determination solely for the purpose of providing written or oral advice, the advocate must be paid for the reasonable number of hours of preparation for that advice using the hourly fee rates for special preparation set out in the table following paragraph 24 as appropriate to the category of trial advocate.

(2) An advocate claiming a fee for advice under this paragraph may apply to the appropriate officer to redetermine the fee under regulation 28 and the advocate must supply such information and documents as may be required by the appropriate officer as proof of the number of hours of preparation.

*Mitigation of sentence*

34.—(1) Where in any case on indictment an advocate is assigned pursuant to a section 16   **G-67** determination to appear at a sentencing hearing solely for the purpose of applying to the court to mitigate the assisted person's sentence, the advocate must be paid in respect of that appearance the fee specified in the table following paragraph 24 together with a fee calculated from the reasonable number of hours of preparation for that appearance using the hourly fee rates for special preparation set out in the table following paragraph 24 as appropriate to the category of trial advocate.

(2) An advocate claiming an hourly preparation fee under this paragraph may apply to the appropriate officer to redetermine such hourly fee under regulation 28 and the advocate must supply such information and documents as may be required by the appropriate officer as proof of the number of hours of preparation.

## Table of offences

At the end of Schedule 1 to the regulations (in Pt 7), there is a table of offences. For the effect   **G-68** thereof, see *post*, G-119, G-168 *et seq.*

Regulation 5                              SCHEDULE 2

LITIGATORS' GRADUATED FEE SCHEME

PART 1

DEFINITION AND SCOPE

*Interpretation*

1.—(1) In this Schedule—                                                             **G-69**
    "case" means proceedings in the Crown Court against any one assisted person—
        (a) on one or more counts of a single indictment;
        (b) arising out of a single notice of appeal against conviction or sentence, or a single
            committal for sentence, whether on one or more charges; or
        (c) arising out of a single alleged breach of an order of the Crown Court,
    and a case falling within paragraph (c) must be treated as a separate case from the proceedings in which the order was made;
    "cracked trial" means a case on indictment in which—
        (a) a plea and case management hearing takes place and
            (i) the case does not proceed to trial (whether by reason of pleas of guilty or for other
                reasons) or the prosecution offers no evidence; and
            (ii) either—
                (aa) in respect of one or more counts to which the assisted person pleaded guilty,
                    the assisted person did not so plead at the plea and case management hearing; or
                (bb) in respect of one or more counts which did not proceed, the prosecution did
                    not, before or at the plea and case management hearing, declare an intention of not proceeding with them; or
        (b) the case is listed for trial without a plea and case management hearing taking place;
    "guilty plea" means a case on indictment which—

571

(a) is disposed of without a trial because the assisted person pleaded guilty to one or more counts; and

(b) is not a cracked trial;

"main hearing" means—

(a) in relation to a case which goes to trial, the trial;

(b) in relation to a guilty plea, the hearing at which pleas are taken or, where there is more than one such hearing, the last such hearing;

(c) in relation to a cracked trial, the hearing at which—

(i) the case becomes a cracked trial by meeting the conditions in the definition of a cracked trial, whether or not any pleas were taken at that hearing; or

(ii) a formal verdict of not guilty was entered as a result of the prosecution offering no evidence, whether or not the parties attended the hearing;

(d) in relation to an appeal against conviction or sentence in the Crown Court, the hearing of the appeal;

(e) in relation to proceedings arising out of a committal for sentence in the Crown Court, the sentencing hearing; and

(f) in relation to proceedings arising out of an alleged breach of an order of the Crown Court, the hearing at which those proceedings are determined;

"*Newton* hearing" means a hearing at which evidence is heard for the purpose of determining the sentence of a convicted person in accordance with the principles of *R. v. Newton* (1982) 77 Cr.App.R. 13;

"PPE Cut-off" means the minimum number of pages of prosecution evidence for use in calculating the fee payable to a litigator under this Schedule, as set out in the tables following paragraph 5(1) and (2).

(2) For the purposes of this Schedule, the number of pages of prosecution evidence served on the court must be determined in accordance with sub-paragraphs (3) to (5).

(3) The number of pages of prosecution evidence includes all—

(a) witness statements;

(b) documentary and pictorial exhibits;

(c) records of interviews with the assisted person; and

(d) records of interviews with other defendants,

which form part of the committal or served prosecution documents or which are included in any notice of additional evidence.

(4) Subject to sub-paragraph (5), a document served by the prosecution in electronic form is included in the number of pages of prosecution evidence.

(5) A documentary or pictorial exhibit which—

(a) has been served by the prosecution in electronic form; and

(b) has never existed in paper form,

is not included within the number of pages of prosecution evidence unless the appropriate officer decides that it would be appropriate to include it in the pages of prosecution evidence taking into account the nature of the document and any other relevant circumstances.

(6) In proceedings on indictment in the Crown Court initiated otherwise than by committal for trial, the appropriate officer must determine the number of pages of prosecution evidence in accordance with sub-paragraphs (2) to (5) or as nearly in accordance with those sub-paragraphs as possible as the nature of the case permits.

(7) A reference to the Table of Offences in this Schedule is to the Table of Offences in Part 7 of Schedule 1 and a reference to a Class of Offence in this Schedule is to the Class in which that offence is listed in the Table of Offences.

*Application*

**G-69a**

2.—(1) Subject to sub-paragraphs (2) to (7), this Schedule applies to—

(a) every case on indictment;

(b) the following proceedings in the Crown Court—

(i) an appeal against conviction or sentence from the magistrates' court;

(ii) a sentencing hearing following a committal for sentence to the Crown Court;

(iii) proceedings arising out of an alleged breach of an order of the Crown Court (whether or not this Schedule applies to the proceedings in which the order was made);

(c) a sentencing hearing following a case on indictment to which this Schedule applies, where sentence has been deferred under section 1 of the Powers of Criminal Courts (Sentencing) Act 2000 (deferment of sentence);

    (d)  any other post-sentence hearing.

(2) Sub-paragraph (3) applies where proceedings are—

    (a)  sent for trial to the Crown Court; or

    (b)  transferred to the Crown Court under—

        (i)  section 4 of the Criminal Justice Act 1987 (transfer of serious fraud cases); or

        (ii)  section 53 of the Criminal Justice Act 1991 (transfer of certain cases involving children).

(3) Where, at any time after proceedings are sent or transferred to the Crown Court as referred to in sub-paragraph (2), they are—

    (a)  discontinued by a notice served under section 23A of the Prosecution of Offences Act 1985 (discontinuance of proceedings after accused has been sent for trial); or

    (b)  dismissed pursuant to—

        (i)  paragraph 2 of Schedule 3 to the Crime and Disorder Act 1998 (applications for dismissal);

        (ii)  section 6 of the Criminal Justice Act 1987 (applications for dismissal); or

        (iii)  paragraph 5 of Schedule 6 to the Criminal Justice Act 1991 (applications for dismissal),

the provisions of paragraphs 21 and 22 apply.

(4) Where, following a case on indictment, a *Newton* hearing takes place—

    (a)  for the purposes of this Schedule the case is to be treated as having gone to trial;

    (b)  the length of the trial is to be taken to be the combined length of the main hearing and the *Newton* hearing; and

    (c)  the provisions of this Schedule relating to cracked trials and guilty pleas will not apply.

(5) For the purposes of this Schedule, a case on indictment which discontinues at or before the plea and case management hearing otherwise than—

    (a)  by reason of a plea of guilty being entered; or

    (b)  in accordance with sub-paragraph (3),

must be treated as a guilty plea.

(6) For the purposes of this Schedule, where a trial that is not a Very High Cost Case (in relation to fees claimed by litigators) lasts over 200 days, it must be treated as if it had lasted 200 days.

(7) For the purposes of this Schedule, where the number of pages of prosecution evidence in a case which is not a Very High Cost Case (in relation to fees claimed by litigators) exceeds—

    (a)  the PPE Cut-off figure specified in the table following paragraph 5(2) as appropriate to the offence for which the assisted person is to be tried and the length of trial; and

    (b)  10,000,

the case must be treated as though it had 10,000 pages of prosecution evidence.

*Class of offences*

3.—(1) For the purposes of this Schedule— **G-70**

    (a)  every indictable offence falls within the Class under which it is listed in the Table of Offences and, subject to sub-paragraph (2), indictable offences not specifically so listed are deemed to fall within Class H;

    (b)  conspiracy to commit an indictable offence contrary to section 1 of the Criminal Law Act 1977 (the offence of conspiracy), incitement to commit an indictable offence and attempts to commit an indictable offence contrary to section 1 of the Criminal Attempts Act 1981 (attempting to commit an offence) fall within the same Class as the substantive offence to which they relate;

    (c)  where the Table of Offences specifies that the Class within which an offence falls depends on whether the value involved exceeds a stated limit, the value must be presumed not to exceed that limit unless the litigator making the claim under regulation 5 proves otherwise to the satisfaction of the appropriate officer;

    (d)  where more than one count of the indictment is for an offence in relation to which the Class depends on the value involved, that value must be taken to be the total value involved in all those offences, but where two or more counts relate to the same property, the value of that property must be taken into account once only;

    (e)  where an entry in the Table of Offences specifies an offence as being contrary to a statutory provision, then subject to any express limitation in the entry that entry includes every offence contrary to that statutory provision whether or not the words of description in the entry are appropriate to cover all such offences;

    (f)  where in a case on indictment there is a hearing to determine the question of whether an assisted person is unfit to plead or unfit to stand trial, the litigator must elect whether that hearing falls within the same Class as the indictable offence to which it relates or within Class D;

(g) where in a case on indictment a restriction order is made under section 41 of the Mental Health Act 1983 (power of higher courts to restrict discharge from hospital), the offence falls within Class A, regardless of the Class under which the offence would be listed in the Table of Offences, but for this paragraph.

(2) Where a litigator in proceedings in the Crown Court is dissatisfied with the classification within Class H of an indictable offence not listed in the Table of Offences, the litigator may apply to the appropriate officer, when lodging the claim for fees, to reclassify the offence.

(3) The appropriate officer must, in light of the objections made by the litigator—

(a) confirm the classification of the offence within Class H; or

(b) reclassify the offence,

and must notify the litigator of the decision.

As to this paragraph, see *post*, G-119.

PART 2

GRADUATED FEES FOR GUILTY PLEAS, CRACKED TRIALS AND TRIALS

*Scope*

**G-70a**  4. Subject to paragraph 21, this Part does not apply to a guilty plea or cracked trial in a case committed or sent for trial to the Crown Court on the election of a defendant where the magistrates' court has determined the case to be suitable for summary trial.

*Pages of prosecution evidence*

**G-70b**  5.—(1) For the purposes of this Part, the PPE Cut-off figures in a cracked trial or guilty plea are specified in the table following this sub-paragraph, as appropriate to the offence with which the assisted person is charged.

PPE CUT-OFF FIGURES IN CRACKED TRIALS AND GUILTY PLEAS

| *Type of case* | *Class of offence* | | | | | | | | | | |
|---|---|---|---|---|---|---|---|---|---|---|---|
| | *A* | *B* | *C* | *D* | *E* | *F* | *G* | *H* | *I* | *J* | *K* |
| Cracked trial or guilty plea | 80 | 70 | 40 | 80 | 40 | 50 | 50 | 40 | 40 | 80 | 120 |

(2) For the purposes of this Part, the PPE Cut-off figures in a trial are specified in the table following this sub-paragraph, as appropriate to the offence for which the assisted person is tried and the length of trial.

PPE CUT-OFF FIGURES IN TRIALS

| Trial length in days | PPE Cut off A | PPE Cut off B | PPE Cut off C | PPE Cut off D | PPE Cut off E | PPE Cut off F | PPE Cut off G | PPE Cut off H | PPE Cut off I | PPE Cut off J | PPE Cut off K |
|---|---|---|---|---|---|---|---|---|---|---|---|
| 1 | 80 | 70 | 40 | 80 | 40 | 50 | 50 | 40 | 40 | 80 | 120 |
| 2 | 80 | 70 | 40 | 80 | 40 | 50 | 50 | 40 | 40 | 80 | 120 |
| 3 | 95 | 105 | 81 | 95 | 120 | 138 | 138 | 122 | 134 | 95 | 186 |
| 4 | 126 | 139 | 120 | 126 | 158 | 173 | 173 | 157 | 185 | 126 | 252 |
| 5 | 156 | 170 | 157 | 156 | 195 | 206 | 206 | 191 | 232 | 156 | 314 |
| 6 | 186 | 203 | 193 | 186 | 229 | 240 | 240 | 225 | 281 | 186 | 372 |
| 7 | 218 | 238 | 230 | 218 | 265 | 276 | 276 | 260 | 329 | 218 | 433 |
| 8 | 257 | 274 | 267 | 257 | 301 | 310 | 310 | 301 | 376 | 257 | 495 |
| 9 | 293 | 306 | 301 | 293 | 333 | 342 | 342 | 338 | 420 | 293 | 550 |
| 10 | 330 | 338 | 339 | 330 | 365 | 373 | 373 | 374 | 464 | 330 | 606 |
| 11 | 367 | 370 | 378 | 367 | 399 | 405 | 405 | 412 | 509 | 367 | 663 |
| 12 | 404 | 402 | 417 | 404 | 433 | 437 | 437 | 449 | 554 | 404 | 721 |
| 13 | 440 | 434 | 455 | 440 | 467 | 470 | 470 | 486 | 598 | 440 | 779 |
| 14 | 477 | 465 | 493 | 477 | 500 | 501 | 501 | 523 | 642 | 477 | 836 |
| 15 | 514 | 497 | 531 | 514 | 532 | 533 | 533 | 559 | 686 | 514 | 894 |
| 16 | 551 | 535 | 569 | 551 | 565 | 564 | 564 | 596 | 730 | 551 | 951 |
| 17 | 587 | 573 | 607 | 587 | 598 | 596 | 596 | 637 | 774 | 587 | 1,007 |
| 18 | 624 | 611 | 646 | 624 | 646 | 627 | 627 | 687 | 818 | 624 | 1,063 |
| 19 | 661 | 649 | 684 | 661 | 696 | 659 | 659 | 736 | 862 | 661 | 1,119 |
| 20 | 697 | 687 | 722 | 697 | 746 | 690 | 690 | 786 | 907 | 697 | 1,174 |
| 21 | 742 | 722 | 753 | 742 | 787 | 720 | 720 | 826 | 943 | 742 | 1,230 |
| 22 | 786 | 757 | 785 | 786 | 828 | 752 | 752 | 867 | 980 | 786 | 1,286 |
| 23 | 830 | 792 | 819 | 830 | 868 | 784 | 784 | 908 | 1,017 | 830 | 1,341 |
| 24 | 874 | 826 | 857 | 874 | 908 | 816 | 816 | 948 | 1,053 | 874 | 1,396 |
| 25 | 917 | 860 | 894 | 917 | 948 | 848 | 848 | 988 | 1,088 | 917 | 1,451 |
| 26 | 961 | 895 | 931 | 961 | 988 | 880 | 880 | 1,028 | 1,124 | 961 | 1,505 |

| Trial length in days | PPE Cut off A | PPE Cut off B | PPE Cut off C | PPE Cut off D | PPE Cut off E | PPE Cut off F | PPE Cut off G | PPE Cut off H | PPE Cut off I | PPE Cut off J | PPE Cut off K |
|---|---|---|---|---|---|---|---|---|---|---|---|
| 27 | 1,005 | 935 | 967 | 1,005 | 1,028 | 912 | 912 | 1,068 | 1,160 | 1,005 | 1,560 |
| 28 | 1,049 | 975 | 1,004 | 1,049 | 1,068 | 944 | 944 | 1,107 | 1,196 | 1,049 | 1,615 |
| 29 | 1,099 | 1,016 | 1,041 | 1,099 | 1,108 | 976 | 976 | 1,147 | 1,231 | 1,099 | 1,670 |
| 30 | 1,150 | 1,057 | 1,077 | 1,150 | 1,148 | 1,007 | 1,007 | 1,187 | 1,267 | 1,150 | 1,725 |
| 31 | 1,200 | 1,098 | 1,114 | 1,200 | 1,188 | 1,039 | 1,039 | 1,226 | 1,303 | 1,200 | 1,780 |
| 32 | 1,251 | 1,138 | 1,151 | 1,251 | 1,228 | 1,070 | 1,070 | 1,266 | 1,349 | 1,251 | 1,835 |
| 33 | 1,301 | 1,179 | 1,187 | 1,301 | 1,268 | 1,102 | 1,102 | 1,307 | 1,394 | 1,301 | 1,889 |
| 34 | 1,352 | 1,220 | 1,224 | 1,352 | 1,308 | 1,133 | 1,133 | 1,357 | 1,439 | 1,352 | 1,944 |
| 35 | 1,402 | 1,261 | 1,262 | 1,402 | 1,347 | 1,165 | 1,165 | 1,407 | 1,485 | 1,402 | 1,999 |
| 36 | 1,453 | 1,302 | 1,303 | 1,453 | 1,435 | 1,196 | 1,196 | 1,457 | 1,530 | 1,453 | 2,054 |
| 37 | 1,503 | 1,348 | 1,345 | 1,503 | 1,526 | 1,228 | 1,228 | 1,507 | 1,575 | 1,503 | 2,109 |
| 38 | 1,554 | 1,395 | 1,386 | 1,554 | 1,617 | 1,259 | 1,259 | 1,557 | 1,621 | 1,554 | 2,164 |
| 39 | 1,604 | 1,441 | 1,428 | 1,604 | 1,708 | 1,291 | 1,291 | 1,607 | 1,666 | 1,604 | 2,219 |
| 40 | 1,652 | 1,484 | 1,444 | 1,652 | 1,745 | 1,314 | 1,314 | 1,629 | 1,704 | 1,652 | 2,271 |
| 41 | 1,700 | 1,527 | 1,461 | 1,700 | 1,782 | 1,338 | 1,338 | 1,651 | 1,742 | 1,700 | 2,324 |
| 42 | 1,748 | 1,570 | 1,477 | 1,748 | 1,820 | 1,361 | 1,361 | 1,673 | 1,780 | 1,748 | 2,377 |
| 43 | 1,796 | 1,613 | 1,494 | 1,796 | 1,857 | 1,384 | 1,384 | 1,695 | 1,818 | 1,796 | 2,430 |
| 44 | 1,844 | 1,656 | 1,511 | 1,844 | 1,895 | 1,410 | 1,410 | 1,716 | 1,856 | 1,844 | 2,483 |
| 45 | 1,892 | 1,699 | 1,527 | 1,892 | 1,932 | 1,440 | 1,440 | 1,738 | 1,894 | 1,892 | 2,536 |
| 46 | 1,939 | 1,742 | 1,544 | 1,939 | 1,970 | 1,470 | 1,470 | 1,760 | 1,932 | 1,939 | 2,589 |
| 47 | 1,987 | 1,785 | 1,560 | 1,987 | 2,007 | 1,501 | 1,501 | 1,782 | 1,970 | 1,987 | 2,642 |
| 48 | 2,039 | 1,828 | 1,577 | 2,039 | 2,045 | 1,531 | 1,531 | 1,804 | 2,008 | 2,039 | 2,695 |
| 49 | 2,091 | 1,871 | 1,594 | 2,091 | 2,082 | 1,561 | 1,561 | 1,826 | 2,046 | 2,091 | 2,749 |
| 50 | 2,144 | 1,914 | 1,610 | 2,144 | 2,120 | 1,591 | 1,591 | 1,848 | 2,084 | 2,144 | 2,802 |
| 51 | 2,196 | 1,957 | 1,627 | 2,196 | 2,158 | 1,622 | 1,622 | 1,870 | 2,122 | 2,196 | 2,855 |
| 52 | 2,249 | 2,000 | 1,644 | 2,249 | 2,195 | 1,652 | 1,652 | 1,892 | 2,160 | 2,249 | 2,908 |
| 53 | 2,301 | 2,043 | 1,660 | 2,301 | 2,233 | 1,682 | 1,682 | 1,914 | 2,198 | 2,301 | 2,962 |
| 54 | 2,354 | 2,086 | 1,677 | 2,354 | 2,271 | 1,712 | 1,712 | 1,936 | 2,236 | 2,354 | 3,015 |

| Trial length in days | PPE Cut off A | PPE Cut off B | PPE Cut off C | PPE Cut off D | PPE Cut off E | PPE Cut off F | PPE Cut off G | PPE Cut off H | PPE Cut off I | PPE Cut off J | PPE Cut off K |
|---|---|---|---|---|---|---|---|---|---|---|---|
| 55 | 2,406 | 2,129 | 1,694 | 2,406 | 2,308 | 1,743 | 1,743 | 1,958 | 2,275 | 2,406 | 3,068 |
| 56 | 2,459 | 2,172 | 1,710 | 2,459 | 2,346 | 1,773 | 1,773 | 1,980 | 2,313 | 2,459 | 3,121 |
| 57 | 2,512 | 2,215 | 1,727 | 2,512 | 2,384 | 1,803 | 1,803 | 2,002 | 2,351 | 2,512 | 3,175 |
| 58 | 2,564 | 2,258 | 1,744 | 2,564 | 2,422 | 1,833 | 1,833 | 2,024 | 2,389 | 2,564 | 3,228 |
| 59 | 2,617 | 2,301 | 1,760 | 2,617 | 2,459 | 1,864 | 1,864 | 2,046 | 2,427 | 2,617 | 3,281 |
| 60 | 2,669 | 2,345 | 1,777 | 2,669 | 2,497 | 1,894 | 1,894 | 2,068 | 2,465 | 2,669 | 3,335 |
| 61 | 2,722 | 2,388 | 1,794 | 2,722 | 2,535 | 1,924 | 1,924 | 2,090 | 2,503 | 2,722 | 3,388 |
| 62 | 2,775 | 2,431 | 1,811 | 2,775 | 2,572 | 1,959 | 1,959 | 2,112 | 2,542 | 2,775 | 3,442 |
| 63 | 2,827 | 2,474 | 1,827 | 2,827 | 2,610 | 2,020 | 2,020 | 2,134 | 2,580 | 2,827 | 3,495 |
| 64 | 2,880 | 2,517 | 1,844 | 2,880 | 2,648 | 2,081 | 2,081 | 2,156 | 2,618 | 2,880 | 3,549 |
| 65 | 2,933 | 2,561 | 1,861 | 2,933 | 2,686 | 2,141 | 2,141 | 2,178 | 2,656 | 2,933 | 3,602 |
| 66 | 2,985 | 2,604 | 1,877 | 2,985 | 2,723 | 2,202 | 2,202 | 2,200 | 2,694 | 2,985 | 3,656 |
| 67 | 3,038 | 2,647 | 1,894 | 3,038 | 2,761 | 2,263 | 2,263 | 2,222 | 2,776 | 3,038 | 3,709 |
| 68 | 3,091 | 2,690 | 1,911 | 3,091 | 2,799 | 2,323 | 2,323 | 2,244 | 2,865 | 3,091 | 3,763 |
| 69 | 3,144 | 2,734 | 1,927 | 3,144 | 2,836 | 2,384 | 2,384 | 2,266 | 2,954 | 3,144 | 3,816 |
| 70 | 3,196 | 2,777 | 1,944 | 3,196 | 2,874 | 2,445 | 2,445 | 2,288 | 3,043 | 3,196 | 3,870 |
| 71 | 3,249 | 2,820 | 1,961 | 3,249 | 2,912 | 2,506 | 2,506 | 2,310 | 3,132 | 3,249 | 3,923 |
| 72 | 3,302 | 2,864 | 1,978 | 3,302 | 2,950 | 2,566 | 2,566 | 2,332 | 3,221 | 3,302 | 3,977 |
| 73 | 3,355 | 2,907 | 1,994 | 3,355 | 2,987 | 2,627 | 2,627 | 2,354 | 3,310 | 3,355 | 4,031 |
| 74 | 3,407 | 2,950 | 2,016 | 3,407 | 3,025 | 2,688 | 2,688 | 2,376 | 3,399 | 3,407 | 4,084 |
| 75 | 3,460 | 2,994 | 2,040 | 3,460 | 3,063 | 2,749 | 2,749 | 2,398 | 3,488 | 3,460 | 4,138 |
| 76 | 3,513 | 3,037 | 2,064 | 3,513 | 3,101 | 2,809 | 2,809 | 2,420 | 3,577 | 3,513 | 4,192 |
| 77 | 3,566 | 3,080 | 2,089 | 3,566 | 3,138 | 2,870 | 2,870 | 2,442 | 3,666 | 3,566 | 4,245 |
| 78 | 3,619 | 3,124 | 2,113 | 3,619 | 3,176 | 2,931 | 2,931 | 2,464 | 3,755 | 3,619 | 4,299 |
| 79 | 3,672 | 3,167 | 2,137 | 3,672 | 3,214 | 2,992 | 2,992 | 2,486 | 3,844 | 3,672 | 4,353 |
| 80 | 3,724 | 3,211 | 2,161 | 3,724 | 3,251 | 3,052 | 3,052 | 2,508 | 3,933 | 3,724 | 4,406 |
| 81 | 3,777 | 3,254 | 2,185 | 3,777 | 3,289 | 3,113 | 3,113 | 2,530 | 4,023 | 3,777 | 4,460 |
| 82 | 3,830 | 3,297 | 2,210 | 3,830 | 3,327 | 3,174 | 3,174 | 2,552 | 4,112 | 3,830 | 4,514 |

| Trial length in days | PPE Cut off A | PPE Cut off B | PPE Cut off C | PPE Cut off D | PPE Cut off E | PPE Cut off F | PPE Cut off G | PPE Cut off H | PPE Cut off I | PPE Cut off J | PPE Cut off K |
|---|---|---|---|---|---|---|---|---|---|---|---|
| 83 | 3,883 | 3,341 | 2,234 | 3,883 | 3,365 | 3,235 | 3,235 | 2,575 | 4,201 | 3,883 | 4,568 |
| 84 | 3,936 | 3,384 | 2,258 | 3,936 | 3,402 | 3,295 | 3,295 | 2,597 | 4,290 | 3,936 | 4,622 |
| 85 | 3,989 | 3,428 | 2,282 | 3,989 | 3,440 | 3,356 | 3,356 | 2,619 | 4,379 | 3,989 | 4,675 |
| 86 | 4,042 | 3,471 | 2,307 | 4,042 | 3,478 | 3,417 | 3,417 | 2,641 | 4,469 | 4,042 | 4,729 |
| 87 | 4,095 | 3,515 | 2,331 | 4,095 | 3,516 | 3,478 | 3,478 | 2,663 | 4,558 | 4,095 | 4,783 |
| 88 | 4,148 | 3,558 | 2,355 | 4,148 | 3,553 | 3,539 | 3,539 | 2,685 | 4,647 | 4,148 | 4,837 |
| 89 | 4,201 | 3,602 | 2,379 | 4,201 | 3,591 | 3,599 | 3,599 | 2,707 | 4,737 | 4,201 | 4,891 |
| 90 | 4,254 | 3,645 | 2,404 | 4,254 | 3,629 | 3,660 | 3,660 | 2,729 | 4,826 | 4,254 | 4,945 |
| 91 | 4,307 | 3,689 | 2,428 | 4,307 | 3,666 | 3,721 | 3,721 | 2,751 | 4,915 | 4,307 | 4,999 |
| 92 | 4,360 | 3,733 | 2,452 | 4,360 | 3,704 | 3,782 | 3,782 | 2,774 | 5,005 | 4,360 | 5,053 |
| 93 | 4,413 | 3,776 | 2,477 | 4,413 | 3,742 | 3,843 | 3,843 | 2,796 | 5,094 | 4,413 | 5,107 |
| 94 | 4,466 | 3,820 | 2,501 | 4,466 | 3,780 | 3,903 | 3,903 | 2,818 | 5,183 | 4,466 | 5,161 |
| 95 | 4,519 | 3,863 | 2,525 | 4,519 | 3,817 | 3,964 | 3,964 | 2,840 | 5,273 | 4,519 | 5,215 |
| 96 | 4,572 | 3,907 | 2,549 | 4,572 | 3,855 | 4,025 | 4,025 | 2,862 | 5,362 | 4,572 | 5,269 |
| 97 | 4,625 | 3,951 | 2,574 | 4,625 | 3,893 | 4,086 | 4,086 | 2,884 | 5,452 | 4,625 | 5,323 |
| 98 | 4,679 | 3,994 | 2,598 | 4,679 | 3,930 | 4,147 | 4,147 | 2,906 | 5,541 | 4,679 | 5,377 |
| 99 | 4,732 | 4,038 | 2,622 | 4,732 | 3,968 | 4,207 | 4,207 | 2,929 | 5,631 | 4,732 | 5,431 |
| 100 | 4,785 | 4,082 | 2,647 | 4,785 | 4,006 | 4,268 | 4,268 | 2,951 | 5,720 | 4,785 | 5,485 |
| 101 | 4,838 | 4,125 | 2,671 | 4,838 | 4,044 | 4,329 | 4,329 | 2,973 | 5,810 | 4,838 | 5,539 |
| 102 | 4,891 | 4,169 | 2,695 | 4,891 | 4,081 | 4,390 | 4,390 | 2,995 | 5,899 | 4,891 | 5,593 |
| 103 | 4,944 | 4,213 | 2,720 | 4,944 | 4,119 | 4,451 | 4,451 | 3,032 | 5,989 | 4,944 | 5,647 |
| 104 | 4,997 | 4,257 | 2,744 | 4,997 | 4,157 | 4,512 | 4,512 | 3,073 | 6,079 | 4,997 | 5,702 |
| 105 | 5,051 | 4,300 | 2,768 | 5,051 | 4,195 | 4,573 | 4,573 | 3,114 | 6,168 | 5,051 | 5,756 |
| 106 | 5,104 | 4,344 | 2,793 | 5,104 | 4,232 | 4,633 | 4,633 | 3,155 | 6,258 | 5,104 | 5,810 |
| 107 | 5,157 | 4,388 | 2,817 | 5,157 | 4,270 | 4,694 | 4,694 | 3,196 | 6,348 | 5,157 | 5,864 |
| 108 | 5,210 | 4,432 | 2,841 | 5,210 | 4,308 | 4,755 | 4,755 | 3,237 | 6,437 | 5,210 | 5,918 |
| 109 | 5,264 | 4,475 | 2,866 | 5,264 | 4,345 | 4,816 | 4,816 | 3,278 | 6,527 | 5,264 | 5,973 |
| 110 | 5,317 | 4,519 | 2,890 | 5,317 | 4,383 | 4,877 | 4,877 | 3,319 | 6,617 | 5,317 | 6,027 |

| Trial length in days | PPE Cut off A | PPE Cut off B | PPE Cut off C | PPE Cut off D | PPE Cut off E | PPE Cut off F | PPE Cut off G | PPE Cut off H | PPE Cut off I | PPE Cut off J | PPE Cut off K |
|---|---|---|---|---|---|---|---|---|---|---|---|
| 111 | 5,370 | 4,563 | 2,914 | 5,370 | 4,421 | 4,938 | 4,938 | 3,361 | 6,706 | 5,370 | 6,081 |
| 112 | 5,423 | 4,607 | 2,939 | 5,423 | 4,459 | 4,999 | 4,999 | 3,402 | 6,796 | 5,423 | 6,135 |
| 113 | 5,477 | 4,650 | 2,963 | 5,477 | 4,496 | 5,059 | 5,059 | 3,443 | 6,886 | 5,477 | 6,189 |
| 114 | 5,530 | 4,694 | 2,987 | 5,530 | 4,534 | 5,120 | 5,120 | 3,484 | 6,976 | 5,530 | 6,244 |
| 115 | 5,583 | 4,738 | 3,012 | 5,583 | 4,572 | 5,181 | 5,181 | 3,525 | 7,066 | 5,583 | 6,298 |
| 116 | 5,637 | 4,782 | 3,036 | 5,637 | 4,610 | 5,242 | 5,242 | 3,566 | 7,155 | 5,637 | 6,352 |
| 117 | 5,690 | 4,826 | 3,060 | 5,690 | 4,647 | 5,303 | 5,303 | 3,607 | 7,245 | 5,690 | 6,406 |
| 118 | 5,743 | 4,869 | 3,085 | 5,743 | 4,685 | 5,364 | 5,364 | 3,648 | 7,335 | 5,743 | 6,460 |
| 119 | 5,797 | 4,913 | 3,109 | 5,797 | 4,723 | 5,425 | 5,425 | 3,689 | 7,425 | 5,797 | 6,514 |
| 120 | 5,850 | 4,957 | 3,133 | 5,850 | 4,760 | 5,486 | 5,486 | 3,730 | 7,515 | 5,850 | 6,569 |
| 121 | 5,904 | 5,001 | 3,158 | 5,904 | 4,798 | 5,547 | 5,547 | 3,771 | 7,605 | 5,904 | 6,623 |
| 122 | 5,956 | 5,044 | 3,182 | 5,956 | 4,836 | 5,607 | 5,607 | 3,812 | 7,693 | 5,956 | 6,677 |
| 123 | 6,009 | 5,088 | 3,206 | 6,009 | 4,874 | 5,668 | 5,668 | 3,853 | 7,782 | 6,009 | 6,731 |
| 124 | 6,061 | 5,131 | 3,230 | 6,061 | 4,911 | 5,729 | 5,729 | 3,895 | 7,871 | 6,061 | 6,785 |
| 125 | 6,114 | 5,175 | 3,254 | 6,114 | 4,949 | 5,789 | 5,789 | 3,936 | 7,959 | 6,114 | 6,839 |
| 126 | 6,167 | 5,218 | 3,278 | 6,167 | 4,987 | 5,850 | 5,850 | 3,977 | 8,048 | 6,167 | 6,892 |
| 127 | 6,219 | 5,261 | 3,302 | 6,219 | 5,025 | 5,911 | 5,911 | 4,017 | 8,137 | 6,219 | 6,945 |
| 128 | 6,272 | 5,304 | 3,326 | 6,272 | 5,062 | 5,971 | 5,971 | 4,058 | 8,225 | 6,272 | 6,999 |
| 129 | 6,324 | 5,347 | 3,350 | 6,324 | 5,100 | 6,032 | 6,032 | 4,098 | 8,314 | 6,324 | 7,052 |
| 130 | 6,377 | 5,390 | 3,374 | 6,377 | 5,138 | 6,093 | 6,093 | 4,139 | 8,403 | 6,377 | 7,106 |
| 131 | 6,430 | 5,433 | 3,398 | 6,430 | 5,175 | 6,153 | 6,153 | 4,179 | 8,491 | 6,430 | 7,159 |
| 132 | 6,482 | 5,476 | 3,422 | 6,482 | 5,213 | 6,214 | 6,214 | 4,219 | 8,580 | 6,482 | 7,212 |
| 133 | 6,535 | 5,520 | 3,446 | 6,535 | 5,251 | 6,274 | 6,274 | 4,260 | 8,669 | 6,535 | 7,266 |
| 134 | 6,588 | 5,563 | 3,470 | 6,588 | 5,289 | 6,335 | 6,335 | 4,300 | 8,757 | 6,588 | 7,319 |
| 135 | 6,640 | 5,606 | 3,494 | 6,640 | 5,326 | 6,396 | 6,396 | 4,341 | 8,846 | 6,640 | 7,373 |
| 136 | 6,693 | 5,649 | 3,518 | 6,693 | 5,364 | 6,456 | 6,456 | 4,381 | 8,935 | 6,693 | 7,426 |
| 137 | 6,745 | 5,692 | 3,542 | 6,745 | 5,402 | 6,517 | 6,517 | 4,422 | 9,023 | 6,745 | 7,479 |
| 138 | 6,798 | 5,735 | 3,566 | 6,798 | 5,439 | 6,578 | 6,578 | 4,462 | 9,112 | 6,798 | 7,533 |

| Trial length in days | PPE Cut off A | PPE Cut off B | PPE Cut off C | PPE Cut off D | PPE Cut off E | PPE Cut off F | PPE Cut off G | PPE Cut off H | PPE Cut off I | PPE Cut off J | PPE Cut off K |
|---|---|---|---|---|---|---|---|---|---|---|---|
| 139 | 6,851 | 5,778 | 3,590 | 6,851 | 5,477 | 6,638 | 6,638 | 4,503 | 9,201 | 6,851 | 7,586 |
| 140 | 6,903 | 5,821 | 3,614 | 6,903 | 5,515 | 6,699 | 6,699 | 4,543 | 9,289 | 6,903 | 7,639 |
| 141 | 6,956 | 5,864 | 3,638 | 6,956 | 5,553 | 6,760 | 6,760 | 4,584 | 9,378 | 6,956 | 7,693 |
| 142 | 7,008 | 5,908 | 3,662 | 7,008 | 5,590 | 6,820 | 6,820 | 4,624 | 9,467 | 7,008 | 7,746 |
| 143 | 7,061 | 5,951 | 3,686 | 7,061 | 5,628 | 6,881 | 6,881 | 4,664 | 9,555 | 7,061 | 7,800 |
| 144 | 7,114 | 5,994 | 3,709 | 7,114 | 5,666 | 6,942 | 6,942 | 4,705 | 9,644 | 7,114 | 7,853 |
| 145 | 7,166 | 6,037 | 3,733 | 7,166 | 5,704 | 7,002 | 7,002 | 4,745 | 9,733 | 7,166 | 7,906 |
| 146 | 7,219 | 6,080 | 3,757 | 7,219 | 5,741 | 7,063 | 7,063 | 4,786 | 9,821 | 7,219 | 7,960 |
| 147 | 7,272 | 6,123 | 3,781 | 7,272 | 5,779 | 7,124 | 7,124 | 4,826 | 9,910 | 7,272 | 8,013 |
| 148 | 7,324 | 6,166 | 3,805 | 7,324 | 5,817 | 7,184 | 7,184 | 4,867 | 9,999 | 7,324 | 8,067 |
| 149 | 7,377 | 6,209 | 3,829 | 7,377 | 5,854 | 7,245 | 7,245 | 4,907 | 10,087 | 7,377 | 8,120 |
| 150 | 7,429 | 6,252 | 3,853 | 7,429 | 5,892 | 7,305 | 7,305 | 4,948 | 10,176 | 7,429 | 8,173 |
| 151 | 7,482 | 6,296 | 3,877 | 7,482 | 5,930 | 7,366 | 7,366 | 4,988 | 10,265 | 7,482 | 8,227 |
| 152 | 7,535 | 6,339 | 3,901 | 7,535 | 5,968 | 7,427 | 7,427 | 5,029 | 10,353 | 7,535 | 8,280 |
| 153 | 7,587 | 6,382 | 3,925 | 7,587 | 6,005 | 7,487 | 7,487 | 5,069 | 10,442 | 7,587 | 8,333 |
| 154 | 7,640 | 6,425 | 3,949 | 7,640 | 6,043 | 7,548 | 7,548 | 5,110 | 10,531 | 7,640 | 8,387 |
| 155 | 7,692 | 6,468 | 3,973 | 7,692 | 6,081 | 7,609 | 7,609 | 5,150 | 10,619 | 7,692 | 8,440 |
| 156 | 7,745 | 6,511 | 3,997 | 7,745 | 6,119 | 7,669 | 7,669 | 5,190 | 10,708 | 7,745 | 8,494 |
| 157 | 7,798 | 6,554 | 4,021 | 7,798 | 6,156 | 7,730 | 7,730 | 5,231 | 10,797 | 7,798 | 8,547 |
| 158 | 7,850 | 6,597 | 4,045 | 7,850 | 6,194 | 7,791 | 7,791 | 5,271 | 10,885 | 7,850 | 8,600 |
| 159 | 7,903 | 6,641 | 4,069 | 7,903 | 6,232 | 7,851 | 7,851 | 5,312 | 10,974 | 7,903 | 8,654 |
| 160 | 7,956 | 6,684 | 4,093 | 7,956 | 6,269 | 7,912 | 7,912 | 5,352 | 11,063 | 7,956 | 8,707 |
| 161 | 8,008 | 6,727 | 4,117 | 8,008 | 6,307 | 7,973 | 7,973 | 5,393 | 11,151 | 8,008 | 8,760 |
| 162 | 8,061 | 6,770 | 4,141 | 8,061 | 6,345 | 8,033 | 8,033 | 5,433 | 11,240 | 8,061 | 8,814 |
| 163 | 8,113 | 6,813 | 4,165 | 8,113 | 6,383 | 8,094 | 8,094 | 5,474 | 11,329 | 8,113 | 8,867 |
| 164 | 8,166 | 6,856 | 4,189 | 8,166 | 6,420 | 8,155 | 8,155 | 5,514 | 11,417 | 8,166 | 8,921 |
| 165 | 8,219 | 6,899 | 4,213 | 8,219 | 6,458 | 8,215 | 8,215 | 5,555 | 11,506 | 8,219 | 8,974 |
| 166 | 8,271 | 6,942 | 4,237 | 8,271 | 6,496 | 8,276 | 8,276 | 5,595 | 11,595 | 8,271 | 9,027 |

| Trial length in days | PPE Cut off A | PPE Cut off B | PPE Cut off C | PPE Cut off D | PPE Cut off E | PPE Cut off F | PPE Cut off G | PPE Cut off H | PPE Cut off I | PPE Cut off J | PPE Cut off K |
|---|---|---|---|---|---|---|---|---|---|---|---|
| 167 | 8,324 | 6,985 | 4,261 | 8,324 | 6,534 | 8,337 | 8,337 | 5,636 | 11,683 | 8,324 | 9,081 |
| 168 | 8,376 | 7,029 | 4,285 | 8,376 | 6,571 | 8,397 | 8,397 | 5,676 | 11,772 | 8,376 | 9,134 |
| 169 | 8,429 | 7,072 | 4,309 | 8,429 | 6,609 | 8,458 | 8,458 | 5,716 | 11,861 | 8,429 | 9,188 |
| 170 | 8,482 | 7,115 | 4,333 | 8,482 | 6,647 | 8,518 | 8,518 | 5,757 | 11,949 | 8,482 | 9,241 |
| 171 | 8,534 | 7,158 | 4,357 | 8,534 | 6,684 | 8,579 | 8,579 | 5,797 | 12,038 | 8,534 | 9,294 |
| 172 | 8,587 | 7,201 | 4,380 | 8,587 | 6,722 | 8,640 | 8,640 | 5,838 | 12,127 | 8,587 | 9,348 |
| 173 | 8,639 | 7,244 | 4,404 | 8,639 | 6,760 | 8,700 | 8,700 | 5,878 | 12,215 | 8,639 | 9,401 |
| 174 | 8,692 | 7,287 | 4,428 | 8,692 | 6,798 | 8,761 | 8,761 | 5,919 | 12,304 | 8,692 | 9,454 |
| 175 | 8,745 | 7,330 | 4,452 | 8,745 | 6,835 | 8,822 | 8,822 | 5,959 | 12,393 | 8,745 | 9,508 |
| 176 | 8,797 | 7,373 | 4,476 | 8,797 | 6,873 | 8,882 | 8,882 | 6,000 | 12,481 | 8,797 | 9,561 |
| 177 | 8,850 | 7,417 | 4,500 | 8,850 | 6,911 | 8,943 | 8,943 | 6,040 | 12,570 | 8,850 | 9,615 |
| 178 | 8,903 | 7,460 | 4,524 | 8,903 | 6,948 | 9,004 | 9,004 | 6,081 | 12,659 | 8,903 | 9,668 |
| 179 | 8,955 | 7,503 | 4,548 | 8,955 | 6,986 | 9,064 | 9,064 | 6,121 | 12,747 | 8,955 | 9,721 |
| 180 | 9,008 | 7,546 | 4,572 | 9,008 | 7,024 | 9,125 | 9,125 | 6,162 | 12,836 | 9,008 | 9,775 |
| 181 | 9,060 | 7,589 | 4,596 | 9,060 | 7,062 | 9,186 | 9,186 | 6,202 | 12,925 | 9,060 | 9,828 |
| 182 | 9,113 | 7,632 | 4,620 | 9,113 | 7,099 | 9,246 | 9,246 | 6,242 | 13,013 | 9,113 | 9,881 |
| 183 | 9,166 | 7,675 | 4,644 | 9,166 | 7,137 | 9,307 | 9,307 | 6,283 | 13,102 | 9,166 | 9,935 |
| 184 | 9,218 | 7,718 | 4,668 | 9,218 | 7,174 | 9,368 | 9,368 | 6,323 | 13,191 | 9,218 | 9,988 |
| 185 | 9,271 | 7,762 | 4,692 | 9,271 | 7,211 | 9,428 | 9,428 | 6,364 | 13,279 | 9,271 | 10,042 |
| 186 | 9,323 | 7,805 | 4,716 | 9,323 | 7,248 | 9,489 | 9,489 | 6,404 | 13,368 | 9,323 | 10,095 |
| 187 | 9,376 | 7,848 | 4,740 | 9,376 | 7,285 | 9,549 | 9,549 | 6,445 | 13,457 | 9,376 | 10,148 |
| 188 | 9,429 | 7,891 | 4,764 | 9,429 | 7,322 | 9,610 | 9,610 | 6,485 | 13,545 | 9,429 | 10,202 |
| 189 | 9,481 | 7,934 | 4,788 | 9,481 | 7,360 | 9,671 | 9,671 | 6,526 | 13,634 | 9,481 | 10,255 |
| 190 | 9,534 | 7,977 | 4,812 | 9,534 | 7,397 | 9,731 | 9,731 | 6,566 | 13,723 | 9,534 | 10,309 |
| 191 | 9,587 | 8,020 | 4,836 | 9,587 | 7,434 | 9,792 | 9,792 | 6,607 | 13,811 | 9,587 | 10,362 |
| 192 | 9,639 | 8,063 | 4,860 | 9,639 | 7,471 | 9,853 | 9,853 | 6,647 | 13,900 | 9,639 | 10,415 |
| 193 | 9,692 | 8,106 | 4,884 | 9,692 | 7,508 | 9,913 | 9,913 | 6,687 | 13,988 | 9,692 | 10,469 |
| 194 | 9,744 | 8,150 | 4,908 | 9,744 | 7,545 | 9,974 | 9,974 | 6,728 | 14,077 | 9,744 | 10,522 |

| Trial length in days | PPE Cut off A | PPE Cut off B | PPE Cut off C | PPE Cut off D | PPE Cut off E | PPE Cut off F | PPE Cut off G | PPE Cut off H | PPE Cut off I | PPE Cut off J | PPE Cut off K |
|---|---|---|---|---|---|---|---|---|---|---|---|
| 195 | 9,797 | 8,193 | 4,932 | 9,797 | 7,582 | 10,035 | 10,035 | 6,768 | 14,166 | 9,797 | 10,575 |
| 196 | 9,850 | 8,236 | 4,956 | 9,850 | 7,620 | 10,095 | 10,095 | 6,809 | 14,254 | 9,850 | 10,629 |
| 197 | 9,902 | 8,279 | 4,980 | 9,902 | 7,657 | 10,156 | 10,156 | 6,849 | 14,343 | 9,902 | 10,682 |
| 198 | 9,955 | 8,322 | 5,004 | 9,955 | 7,694 | 10,217 | 10,217 | 6,890 | 14,432 | 9,955 | 10,736 |
| 199 | 10,007 | 8,365 | 5,028 | 10,007 | 7,731 | 10,277 | 10,277 | 6,930 | 14,520 | 10,007 | 10,789 |
| 200 | 10,060 | 8,408 | 5,051 | 10,060 | 7,768 | 10,338 | 10,338 | 6,971 | 14,609 | 10,060 | 10,842 |

*Cracked trial or guilty plea where the number of pages of prosecution evidence is less than or equal to the PPE
Cut-off*

6.—(1) Where in a cracked trial or guilty plea the number of pages of prosecution evidence is less    **G-71**
than or equal to the PPE Cut-off specified in the table following paragraph 5(1) as appropriate to the
Class of Offence with which the assisted person is charged, the total fee payable to the litigator is—

- (a) the basic fee, calculated in accordance with the table following sub-paragraph (2) of this
paragraph;
- (b) the defendant uplift, if any, calculated in accordance with the table following paragraph 12;
and
- (c) the adjustment for transfers and retrials, if any, calculated in accordance with paragraph
13.

(2) For the purposes of sub-paragraph (1), the basic fee appropriate to a cracked trial or a guilty
plea is specified in the table following this sub-paragraph, in accordance with the type of case and
Class of Offence with which the assisted person is charged.

BASIC FEES FOR CRACKED TRIALS AND GUILTY PLEAS (£)

| Type of case | Class of Offence | | | | | | | | | | |
|---|---|---|---|---|---|---|---|---|---|---|---|
| | A | B | C | D | E | F | G | H | I | J | K |
| Cracked trial | 904.58 | 707.32 | 524.83 | 859.35 | 233.03 | 224.23 | 224.23 | 237.00 | 253.67 | 904.58 | 773.86 |
| Guilty plea | 680.39 | 556.11 | 442.91 | 646.36 | 184.70 | 195.81 | 195.81 | 190.97 | 174.60 | 680.39 | 640.84 |

[The table following para. 6(2) is printed as substituted by the Criminal Legal Aid (Remunera-    ★
tion) (Amendment) Regulations 2014 (S.I. 2014 No. 415). The amendments made by S.I. 2014
No. 415 apply to matters in which a determination under section 13 (advice or assistance for
individuals in custody (as to which, see § 6-209 in the main work)), 15 (advice or assistance for
criminal proceedings (§ 6-211 in the main work)) or 16 (representation for criminal proceedings
(§ 6-212 in the main work)) of the LASPOA 2012 is made on or after March 20, 2014: S.I. 2014
No. 415, reg. 3.]

*Trial where the number of pages of prosecution evidence is less than or equal to the PPE Cut-off*

7.—(1) Where in a trial the number of pages of prosecution evidence is less than or equal to the    **G-71a**
PPE Cut-off specified in the table following paragraph 5(2) as appropriate to the offence for which
the assisted person is tried and the length of trial, the total fee payable to the litigator is—

- (a) the basic fee, calculated in accordance with the table following sub-paragraph (2);
- (b) the length of trial proxy, if any, calculated in accordance with the table following
subparagraph (3);
- (c) the defendant uplift, if any, calculated in accordance with the table following paragraph 12;
and
- (d) the adjustment for transfers and retrials, if any, calculated in accordance with paragraph
13.

(2) For the purposes of sub-paragraph (1), the basic fee appropriate to a trial is specified in the
table following this sub-paragraph, in accordance with the offence for which the assisted person is
tried.

BASIC FEES FOR TRIALS (£)

| Type of case | Class of Offence | | | | | | | | | | |
|---|---|---|---|---|---|---|---|---|---|---|---|
| | A | B | C | D | E | F | G | H | I | J | K |
| Trial | 1,467.58 | 1,097.66 | 739.59 | 1,394.20 | 352.72 | 357.60 | 357.60 | 357.75 | 357.44 | 1,467.58 | 1,031.82 |

(3) For the purposes of sub-paragraph (1), the length of trial proxy is specified in the table following this sub-paragraph, in accordance with the offence for which the assisted person is tried and the
length                             of                             trial.

LENGTH OF TRIAL PROXY

| Trial length in Days | Trial length proxy A | Trial length proxy B | Trial length proxy C | Trial length proxy D | Trial length proxy E | Trial length proxy F | Trial length proxy G | Trial length proxy H | Trial length proxy I | Trial length proxy J | Trial length proxy K |
|---|---|---|---|---|---|---|---|---|---|---|---|
| 1 | 0.00 | 0.00 | 0.00 | 0.00 | 0.00 | 0.00 | 0.00 | 0.00 | 0.00 | 0.00 | 0.00 |
| 2 | 0.00 | 0.00 | 0.00 | 0.00 | 0.00 | 0.00 | 0.00 | 0.00 | 0.00 | 0.00 | 0.00 |
| 3 | 252.54 | 452.88 | 432.51 | 239.92 | 716.58 | 644.94 | 644.94 | 703.69 | 862.39 | 252.54 | 574.13 |
| 4 | 769.79 | 879.65 | 843.33 | 731.30 | 1,033.65 | 898.77 | 898.77 | 1,009.83 | 1,320.93 | 769.79 | 1,140.63 |
| 5 | 1,261.16 | 1,285.08 | 1,233.61 | 1,198.10 | 1,334.86 | 1,139.90 | 1,139.90 | 1,300.64 | 1,756.54 | 1,261.16 | 1,678.81 |
| 6 | 1,761.17 | 1,695.98 | 1,621.20 | 1,673.12 | 1,617.11 | 1,386.43 | 1,386.43 | 1,589.05 | 2,200.59 | 1,761.17 | 2,181.04 |
| 7 | 2,253.87 | 2,102.22 | 2,011.03 | 2,141.18 | 1,915.45 | 1,632.83 | 1,632.83 | 1,879.51 | 2,637.65 | 2,253.87 | 2,713.26 |
| 8 | 2,746.56 | 2,508.44 | 2,400.87 | 2,609.24 | 2,213.79 | 1,875.25 | 1,875.25 | 2,169.97 | 3,074.70 | 2,746.56 | 3,245.48 |
| 9 | 3,210.92 | 2,874.04 | 2,751.71 | 3,050.38 | 2,482.29 | 2,093.45 | 2,093.45 | 2,431.38 | 3,473.43 | 3,210.92 | 3,724.49 |
| 10 | 3,675.29 | 3,239.65 | 3,102.56 | 3,491.52 | 2,750.81 | 2,311.64 | 2,311.64 | 2,692.79 | 3,872.17 | 3,675.29 | 4,203.48 |
| 11 | 4,143.10 | 3,605.74 | 3,462.93 | 3,935.94 | 3,031.66 | 2,536.06 | 2,536.06 | 2,961.38 | 4,279.02 | 4,143.10 | 4,703.99 |
| 12 | 4,607.74 | 3,971.38 | 3,823.47 | 4,377.35 | 3,312.59 | 2,760.47 | 2,760.47 | 3,229.64 | 4,686.22 | 4,607.74 | 5,204.80 |
| 13 | 5,072.39 | 4,337.02 | 4,175.80 | 4,818.77 | 3,593.15 | 2,983.98 | 2,983.98 | 3,492.07 | 5,086.28 | 5,072.39 | 5,705.63 |
| 14 | 5,537.03 | 4,702.67 | 4,528.13 | 5,260.19 | 3,865.07 | 3,203.34 | 3,203.34 | 3,754.51 | 5,486.32 | 5,537.03 | 6,206.43 |
| 15 | 6,001.68 | 5,068.31 | 4,880.46 | 5,701.59 | 4,136.15 | 3,422.69 | 3,422.69 | 4,016.95 | 5,886.37 | 6,001.68 | 6,707.21 |
| 16 | 6,466.32 | 5,433.96 | 5,232.79 | 6,143.00 | 4,407.26 | 3,642.05 | 3,642.05 | 4,279.39 | 6,286.42 | 6,466.32 | 7,207.20 |
| 17 | 6,930.96 | 5,799.60 | 5,585.12 | 6,584.42 | 4,678.35 | 3,861.41 | 3,861.41 | 4,541.82 | 6,686.47 | 6,930.96 | 7,693.86 |
| 18 | 7,395.60 | 6,165.24 | 5,937.45 | 7,025.83 | 4,949.45 | 4,080.76 | 4,080.76 | 4,804.26 | 7,086.52 | 7,395.60 | 8,180.52 |
| 19 | 7,860.25 | 6,530.88 | 6,289.77 | 7,467.24 | 5,220.54 | 4,300.12 | 4,300.12 | 5,066.69 | 7,486.57 | 7,860.25 | 8,667.17 |
| 20 | 8,324.89 | 6,896.53 | 6,642.11 | 7,908.66 | 5,491.63 | 4,519.48 | 4,519.48 | 5,329.13 | 7,886.63 | 8,324.89 | 9,153.84 |
| 21 | 8,798.40 | 7,234.27 | 6,931.61 | 8,358.47 | 5,715.66 | 4,698.94 | 4,698.94 | 5,544.96 | 8,215.37 | 8,798.40 | 9,640.50 |
| 22 | 9,271.81 | 7,571.99 | 7,221.19 | 8,808.22 | 5,939.70 | 4,878.48 | 4,878.48 | 5,760.90 | 8,544.12 | 9,271.81 | 10,127.16 |
| 23 | 9,737.21 | 7,909.69 | 7,510.79 | 9,250.36 | 6,157.06 | 5,058.02 | 5,058.02 | 5,976.83 | 8,872.90 | 9,737.21 | 10,613.82 |
| 24 | 10,202.62 | 8,239.72 | 7,800.39 | 9,692.49 | 6,374.43 | 5,237.57 | 5,237.57 | 6,192.76 | 9,198.07 | 10,202.62 | 11,100.48 |
| 25 | 10,668.04 | 8,569.74 | 8,088.48 | 10,134.63 | 6,591.80 | 5,417.10 | 5,417.10 | 6,405.21 | 9,519.15 | 10,668.04 | 11,587.14 |

| Trial length in Days | Trial length proxy A | Trial length proxy B | Trial length proxy C | Trial length proxy D | Trial length proxy E | Trial length proxy F | Trial length proxy G | Trial length proxy H | Trial length proxy I | Trial length proxy J | Trial length proxy K |
|---|---|---|---|---|---|---|---|---|---|---|---|
| 26 | 11,133.44 | 8,899.77 | 8,371.53 | 10,576.78 | 6,809.17 | 5,596.65 | 5,596.65 | 6,615.99 | 9,840.24 | 11,133.44 | 12,073.81 |
| 27 | 11,598.84 | 9,229.80 | 8,654.60 | 11,018.90 | 7,026.53 | 5,776.19 | 5,776.19 | 6,826.76 | 10,161.33 | 11,598.84 | 12,560.46 |
| 28 | 12,064.25 | 9,559.83 | 8,937.65 | 11,461.05 | 7,243.91 | 5,955.73 | 5,955.73 | 7,037.54 | 10,482.41 | 12,064.25 | 13,047.13 |
| 29 | 12,529.67 | 9,889.86 | 9,220.70 | 11,903.18 | 7,461.27 | 6,133.18 | 6,133.18 | 7,248.30 | 10,803.51 | 12,529.67 | 13,533.78 |
| 30 | 12,995.07 | 10,219.88 | 9,503.75 | 12,345.31 | 7,678.63 | 6,309.59 | 6,309.59 | 7,459.07 | 11,124.59 | 12,995.07 | 14,020.44 |
| 31 | 13,460.48 | 10,549.91 | 9,786.81 | 12,787.46 | 7,896.01 | 6,486.01 | 6,486.01 | 7,669.85 | 11,445.67 | 13,460.48 | 14,507.11 |
| 32 | 13,925.88 | 10,879.95 | 10,069.87 | 13,229.59 | 8,113.38 | 6,662.43 | 6,662.43 | 7,880.61 | 11,766.76 | 13,925.88 | 14,993.76 |
| 33 | 14,391.30 | 11,209.97 | 10,352.92 | 13,671.73 | 8,330.74 | 6,838.84 | 6,838.84 | 8,091.39 | 12,087.84 | 14,391.30 | 15,480.43 |
| 34 | 14,856.70 | 11,540.00 | 10,635.97 | 14,113.87 | 8,548.11 | 7,015.26 | 7,015.26 | 8,302.16 | 12,408.93 | 14,856.70 | 15,967.09 |
| 35 | 15,322.11 | 11,870.03 | 10,919.03 | 14,556.01 | 8,765.48 | 7,191.68 | 7,191.68 | 8,512.93 | 12,730.02 | 15,322.11 | 16,453.75 |
| 36 | 15,787.52 | 12,200.05 | 11,202.09 | 14,998.14 | 8,982.84 | 7,368.10 | 7,368.10 | 8,723.70 | 13,051.10 | 15,787.52 | 16,940.41 |
| 37 | 16,252.93 | 12,530.09 | 11,485.14 | 15,440.28 | 9,200.22 | 7,544.51 | 7,544.51 | 8,934.48 | 13,372.19 | 16,252.93 | 17,427.07 |
| 38 | 16,718.33 | 12,860.11 | 11,768.20 | 15,882.42 | 9,417.58 | 7,720.93 | 7,720.93 | 9,145.25 | 13,693.28 | 16,718.33 | 17,913.73 |
| 39 | 17,183.74 | 13,190.13 | 12,051.25 | 16,324.55 | 9,634.94 | 7,897.35 | 7,897.35 | 9,356.02 | 14,014.36 | 17,183.74 | 18,400.40 |
| 40 | 17,622.38 | 13,492.13 | 12,163.57 | 16,741.26 | 9,722.09 | 8,027.76 | 8,027.76 | 9,447.16 | 14,282.00 | 17,622.38 | 18,865.89 |
| 41 | 18,063.40 | 13,796.43 | 12,277.13 | 17,160.24 | 9,811.54 | 8,158.44 | 8,158.44 | 9,539.40 | 14,551.22 | 18,063.40 | 19,334.83 |
| 42 | 18,504.54 | 14,100.82 | 12,390.73 | 17,579.32 | 9,901.04 | 8,289.12 | 8,289.12 | 9,631.68 | 14,820.51 | 18,504.54 | 19,803.93 |
| 43 | 18,945.79 | 14,405.31 | 12,504.33 | 17,998.51 | 9,990.58 | 8,419.82 | 8,419.82 | 9,723.97 | 15,089.84 | 18,945.79 | 20,273.20 |
| 44 | 19,387.15 | 14,709.89 | 12,617.96 | 18,417.79 | 10,080.16 | 8,550.52 | 8,550.52 | 9,816.28 | 15,359.23 | 19,387.15 | 20,742.61 |
| 45 | 19,828.61 | 15,014.56 | 12,731.61 | 18,837.18 | 10,169.77 | 8,681.22 | 8,681.22 | 9,908.63 | 15,628.69 | 19,828.61 | 21,212.18 |
| 46 | 20,270.18 | 15,319.32 | 12,845.28 | 19,256.68 | 10,259.43 | 8,811.94 | 8,811.94 | 10,000.97 | 15,898.19 | 20,270.18 | 21,681.91 |
| 47 | 20,711.85 | 15,624.18 | 12,958.98 | 19,676.26 | 10,349.13 | 8,942.66 | 8,942.66 | 10,093.35 | 16,167.76 | 20,711.85 | 22,151.80 |
| 48 | 21,153.65 | 15,929.14 | 13,072.69 | 20,095.97 | 10,438.87 | 9,073.39 | 9,073.39 | 10,185.75 | 16,437.38 | 21,153.65 | 22,621.84 |
| 49 | 21,595.54 | 16,234.19 | 13,186.44 | 20,515.76 | 10,528.64 | 9,204.12 | 9,204.12 | 10,278.16 | 16,707.05 | 21,595.54 | 23,092.04 |
| 50 | 22,037.53 | 16,539.33 | 13,300.19 | 20,935.66 | 10,618.45 | 9,334.88 | 9,334.88 | 10,370.61 | 16,976.79 | 22,037.53 | 23,562.39 |
| 51 | 22,479.65 | 16,844.56 | 13,413.98 | 21,355.67 | 10,708.32 | 9,465.63 | 9,465.63 | 10,463.06 | 17,246.59 | 22,479.65 | 24,032.91 |
| 52 | 22,921.86 | 17,149.88 | 13,527.78 | 21,775.77 | 10,798.21 | 9,596.40 | 9,596.40 | 10,555.54 | 17,516.43 | 22,921.86 | 24,503.58 |

| Trial length in Days | Trial length proxy A | Trial length proxy B | Trial length proxy C | Trial length proxy D | Trial length proxy E | Trial length proxy F | Trial length proxy G | Trial length proxy H | Trial length proxy I | Trial length proxy J | Trial length proxy K |
|---|---|---|---|---|---|---|---|---|---|---|---|
| 53 | 23,364.19 | 17,455.30 | 13,641.60 | 22,195.99 | 10,888.15 | 9,727.16 | 9,727.16 | 10,648.04 | 17,786.33 | 23,364.19 | 24,974.41 |
| 54 | 23,806.62 | 17,760.82 | 13,755.44 | 22,616.29 | 10,978.13 | 9,857.94 | 9,857.94 | 10,740.56 | 18,056.29 | 23,806.62 | 25,445.40 |
| 55 | 24,249.16 | 18,066.42 | 13,869.31 | 23,036.69 | 11,068.14 | 9,988.72 | 9,988.72 | 10,833.10 | 18,326.31 | 24,249.16 | 25,916.54 |
| 56 | 24,691.80 | 18,372.13 | 13,983.20 | 23,457.22 | 11,158.20 | 10,119.52 | 10,119.52 | 10,925.66 | 18,596.39 | 24,691.80 | 26,387.85 |
| 57 | 25,134.56 | 18,677.92 | 14,097.11 | 23,877.83 | 11,248.29 | 10,250.32 | 10,250.32 | 11,018.24 | 18,866.52 | 25,134.56 | 26,859.31 |
| 58 | 25,577.42 | 18,983.81 | 14,211.04 | 24,298.55 | 11,338.39 | 10,381.13 | 10,381.13 | 11,110.84 | 19,136.71 | 25,577.42 | 27,330.92 |
| 59 | 26,020.39 | 19,289.79 | 14,325.00 | 24,719.38 | 11,428.49 | 10,511.95 | 10,511.95 | 11,203.47 | 19,406.96 | 26,020.39 | 27,802.70 |
| 60 | 26,463.47 | 19,595.86 | 14,438.97 | 25,140.29 | 11,518.59 | 10,642.77 | 10,642.77 | 11,296.10 | 19,677.26 | 26,463.47 | 28,274.63 |
| 61 | 26,906.66 | 19,902.03 | 14,552.97 | 25,561.32 | 11,608.70 | 10,773.60 | 10,773.60 | 11,388.77 | 19,947.62 | 26,906.66 | 28,746.72 |
| 62 | 27,349.94 | 20,208.30 | 14,666.99 | 25,982.45 | 11,698.80 | 10,904.44 | 10,904.44 | 11,481.46 | 20,218.04 | 27,349.94 | 29,218.96 |
| 63 | 27,793.35 | 20,514.64 | 14,781.02 | 26,403.69 | 11,788.90 | 11,035.28 | 11,035.28 | 11,574.16 | 20,488.52 | 27,793.35 | 29,691.37 |
| 64 | 28,236.86 | 20,821.10 | 14,895.09 | 26,825.02 | 11,879.00 | 11,166.14 | 11,166.14 | 11,666.89 | 20,759.04 | 28,236.86 | 30,163.93 |
| 65 | 28,680.48 | 21,127.63 | 15,009.17 | 27,246.45 | 11,969.10 | 11,297.01 | 11,297.01 | 11,759.62 | 21,029.63 | 28,680.48 | 30,636.65 |
| 66 | 29,124.20 | 21,434.28 | 15,123.28 | 27,667.99 | 12,059.20 | 11,427.88 | 11,427.88 | 11,852.39 | 21,300.28 | 29,124.20 | 31,109.52 |
| 67 | 29,568.03 | 21,741.01 | 15,237.40 | 28,089.63 | 12,149.30 | 11,558.76 | 11,558.76 | 11,945.17 | 21,570.97 | 29,568.03 | 31,582.55 |
| 68 | 30,011.97 | 22,047.83 | 15,351.55 | 28,511.37 | 12,239.40 | 11,689.65 | 11,689.65 | 12,037.98 | 21,841.73 | 30,011.97 | 32,055.74 |
| 69 | 30,456.02 | 22,354.74 | 15,465.72 | 28,933.21 | 12,329.50 | 11,820.54 | 11,820.54 | 12,130.81 | 22,112.55 | 30,456.02 | 32,529.08 |
| 70 | 30,900.17 | 22,661.76 | 15,579.91 | 29,355.16 | 12,419.60 | 11,951.45 | 11,951.45 | 12,223.66 | 22,383.42 | 30,900.17 | 33,002.60 |
| 71 | 31,344.44 | 22,968.86 | 15,694.12 | 29,777.22 | 12,509.70 | 12,082.36 | 12,082.36 | 12,316.53 | 22,654.35 | 31,344.44 | 33,476.26 |
| 72 | 31,788.81 | 23,276.06 | 15,808.35 | 30,199.37 | 12,599.80 | 12,213.28 | 12,213.28 | 12,409.42 | 22,925.33 | 31,788.81 | 33,950.08 |
| 73 | 32,233.28 | 23,583.35 | 15,922.61 | 30,621.63 | 12,689.90 | 12,344.21 | 12,344.21 | 12,502.32 | 23,196.37 | 32,233.28 | 34,424.05 |
| 74 | 32,677.87 | 23,890.74 | 16,036.89 | 31,043.98 | 12,780.00 | 12,475.14 | 12,475.14 | 12,595.26 | 23,467.47 | 32,677.87 | 34,898.19 |
| 75 | 33,122.56 | 24,198.21 | 16,151.19 | 31,466.43 | 12,870.10 | 12,606.09 | 12,606.09 | 12,688.21 | 23,738.63 | 33,122.56 | 35,372.48 |
| 76 | 33,567.36 | 24,505.78 | 16,265.50 | 31,889.00 | 12,960.20 | 12,737.03 | 12,737.03 | 12,781.18 | 24,009.84 | 33,567.36 | 35,846.92 |
| 77 | 34,012.28 | 24,813.45 | 16,379.85 | 32,311.66 | 13,050.30 | 12,867.99 | 12,867.99 | 12,874.16 | 24,281.10 | 34,012.28 | 36,321.53 |
| 78 | 34,457.29 | 25,121.21 | 16,494.21 | 32,734.43 | 13,140.40 | 12,998.95 | 12,998.95 | 12,967.17 | 24,552.43 | 34,457.29 | 36,796.30 |
| 79 | 34,902.42 | 25,429.06 | 16,608.60 | 33,157.30 | 13,230.50 | 13,129.94 | 13,129.94 | 13,060.21 | 24,823.82 | 34,902.42 | 37,271.22 |

| Trial length in Days | Trial length proxy A | Trial length proxy B | Trial length proxy C | Trial length proxy D | Trial length proxy E | Trial length proxy F | Trial length proxy G | Trial length proxy H | Trial length proxy I | Trial length proxy J | Trial length proxy K |
|---|---|---|---|---|---|---|---|---|---|---|---|
| 80 | 35,347.65 | 25,737.00 | 16,723.00 | 33,580.26 | 13,320.60 | 13,260.92 | 13,260.92 | 13,153.27 | 25,095.26 | 35,347.65 | 37,746.29 |
| 81 | 35,792.99 | 26,045.04 | 16,837.42 | 34,003.35 | 13,410.70 | 13,391.90 | 13,391.90 | 13,246.34 | 25,366.75 | 35,792.99 | 38,221.52 |
| 82 | 36,238.43 | 26,353.17 | 16,951.88 | 34,426.52 | 13,500.80 | 13,522.90 | 13,522.90 | 13,339.43 | 25,638.30 | 36,238.43 | 38,696.92 |
| 83 | 36,683.99 | 26,661.40 | 17,066.35 | 34,849.80 | 13,590.90 | 13,653.90 | 13,653.90 | 13,432.55 | 25,909.92 | 36,683.99 | 39,172.47 |
| 84 | 37,129.65 | 26,969.72 | 17,180.83 | 35,273.17 | 13,681.01 | 13,784.93 | 13,784.93 | 13,525.68 | 26,181.58 | 37,129.65 | 39,648.18 |
| 85 | 37,575.42 | 27,278.13 | 17,295.35 | 35,696.65 | 13,771.11 | 13,915.94 | 13,915.94 | 13,618.83 | 26,453.30 | 37,575.42 | 40,124.04 |
| 86 | 38,021.30 | 27,586.64 | 17,409.90 | 36,120.24 | 13,861.21 | 14,046.97 | 14,046.97 | 13,712.01 | 26,725.09 | 38,021.30 | 40,600.06 |
| 87 | 38,467.29 | 27,895.23 | 17,524.45 | 36,543.93 | 13,951.31 | 14,178.01 | 14,178.01 | 13,805.21 | 26,996.93 | 38,467.29 | 41,076.24 |
| 88 | 38,913.39 | 28,203.93 | 17,639.03 | 36,967.72 | 14,041.41 | 14,309.06 | 14,309.06 | 13,898.42 | 27,268.82 | 38,913.39 | 41,552.58 |
| 89 | 39,359.59 | 28,512.71 | 17,753.63 | 37,391.61 | 14,131.51 | 14,440.10 | 14,440.10 | 13,991.66 | 27,540.77 | 39,359.59 | 42,029.07 |
| 90 | 39,805.90 | 28,821.60 | 17,868.25 | 37,815.60 | 14,221.61 | 14,571.17 | 14,571.17 | 14,084.91 | 27,812.78 | 39,805.90 | 42,505.73 |
| 91 | 40,252.32 | 29,130.57 | 17,982.89 | 38,239.70 | 14,311.71 | 14,702.24 | 14,702.24 | 14,178.20 | 28,084.84 | 40,252.32 | 42,982.53 |
| 92 | 40,698.83 | 29,439.63 | 18,097.56 | 38,663.90 | 14,401.81 | 14,833.32 | 14,833.32 | 14,271.49 | 28,356.97 | 40,698.83 | 43,459.49 |
| 93 | 41,145.47 | 29,748.80 | 18,212.24 | 39,088.20 | 14,491.91 | 14,964.40 | 14,964.40 | 14,364.81 | 28,629.15 | 41,145.47 | 43,936.62 |
| 94 | 41,592.21 | 30,058.05 | 18,326.95 | 39,512.60 | 14,582.01 | 15,095.49 | 15,095.49 | 14,458.15 | 28,901.38 | 41,592.21 | 44,413.90 |
| 95 | 42,039.06 | 30,367.40 | 18,441.68 | 39,937.10 | 14,672.11 | 15,226.59 | 15,226.59 | 14,551.52 | 29,173.67 | 42,039.06 | 44,891.33 |
| 96 | 42,486.02 | 30,676.84 | 18,556.44 | 40,361.72 | 14,762.22 | 15,357.69 | 15,357.69 | 14,644.89 | 29,446.03 | 42,486.02 | 45,368.93 |
| 97 | 42,933.08 | 30,986.38 | 18,671.21 | 40,786.43 | 14,852.32 | 15,488.81 | 15,488.81 | 14,738.25 | 29,718.43 | 42,933.08 | 45,846.68 |
| 98 | 43,380.25 | 31,296.01 | 18,786.00 | 41,211.24 | 14,942.42 | 15,619.94 | 15,619.94 | 14,831.63 | 29,990.89 | 43,380.25 | 46,324.60 |
| 99 | 43,827.53 | 31,605.73 | 18,900.82 | 41,636.15 | 15,032.52 | 15,751.07 | 15,751.07 | 14,925.00 | 30,263.42 | 43,827.53 | 46,802.66 |
| 100 | 44,274.91 | 31,915.55 | 19,015.65 | 42,061.17 | 15,122.62 | 15,882.21 | 15,882.21 | 15,018.37 | 30,535.98 | 44,274.91 | 47,280.88 |
| 101 | 44,722.41 | 32,225.46 | 19,130.51 | 42,486.29 | 15,212.72 | 16,013.36 | 16,013.36 | 15,111.74 | 30,808.63 | 44,722.41 | 47,759.26 |
| 102 | 45,170.01 | 32,535.45 | 19,245.39 | 42,911.51 | 15,302.82 | 16,144.51 | 16,144.51 | 15,205.11 | 31,081.31 | 45,170.01 | 48,237.80 |
| 103 | 45,617.73 | 32,845.55 | 19,360.30 | 43,336.84 | 15,392.92 | 16,275.67 | 16,275.67 | 15,298.48 | 31,354.06 | 45,617.73 | 48,716.50 |
| 104 | 46,065.54 | 33,155.74 | 19,475.21 | 43,762.27 | 15,483.02 | 16,406.84 | 16,406.84 | 15,391.85 | 31,626.86 | 46,065.54 | 49,195.35 |
| 105 | 46,513.46 | 33,466.03 | 19,590.12 | 44,187.79 | 15,573.12 | 16,538.02 | 16,538.02 | 15,485.22 | 31,899.72 | 46,513.46 | 49,674.36 |
| 106 | 46,961.50 | 33,776.40 | 19,705.04 | 44,613.42 | 15,663.22 | 16,669.21 | 16,669.21 | 15,578.59 | 32,172.64 | 46,961.50 | 50,153.43 |

| Trial length in Days | Trial length proxy A | Trial length proxy B | Trial length proxy C | Trial length proxy D | Trial length proxy E | Trial length proxy F | Trial length proxy G | Trial length proxy H | Trial length proxy I | Trial length proxy J | Trial length proxy K |
|---|---|---|---|---|---|---|---|---|---|---|---|
| 107 | 47,409.64 | 34,086.84 | 19,819.95 | 45,039.15 | 15,753.32 | 16,800.40 | 16,800.40 | 15,671.96 | 32,445.62 | 47,409.64 | 50,632.48 |
| 108 | 47,857.89 | 34,397.27 | 19,934.87 | 45,465.00 | 15,843.43 | 16,931.60 | 16,931.60 | 15,765.33 | 32,718.65 | 47,857.89 | 51,111.54 |
| 109 | 48,306.24 | 34,707.71 | 20,049.78 | 45,890.93 | 15,933.53 | 17,062.82 | 17,062.82 | 15,858.70 | 32,991.74 | 48,306.24 | 51,590.60 |
| 110 | 48,754.70 | 35,018.15 | 20,164.69 | 46,316.97 | 16,023.63 | 17,194.03 | 17,194.03 | 15,952.07 | 33,264.88 | 48,754.70 | 52,069.66 |
| 111 | 49,203.28 | 35,328.59 | 20,279.60 | 46,743.12 | 16,113.73 | 17,325.26 | 17,325.26 | 16,045.44 | 33,538.08 | 49,203.28 | 52,548.71 |
| 112 | 49,651.95 | 35,639.02 | 20,394.51 | 47,169.36 | 16,203.83 | 17,456.49 | 17,456.49 | 16,138.81 | 33,811.34 | 49,651.95 | 53,027.77 |
| 113 | 50,100.74 | 35,949.45 | 20,509.43 | 47,595.72 | 16,293.93 | 17,587.73 | 17,587.73 | 16,232.18 | 34,084.66 | 50,100.74 | 53,506.84 |
| 114 | 50,549.63 | 36,259.89 | 20,624.34 | 48,022.16 | 16,384.03 | 17,718.99 | 17,718.99 | 16,325.55 | 34,358.03 | 50,549.63 | 53,985.89 |
| 115 | 50,998.64 | 36,570.33 | 20,739.25 | 48,448.70 | 16,474.13 | 17,850.24 | 17,850.24 | 16,418.92 | 34,631.46 | 50,998.64 | 54,464.95 |
| 116 | 51,447.75 | 36,880.77 | 20,854.17 | 48,875.36 | 16,564.23 | 17,981.51 | 17,981.51 | 16,512.29 | 34,904.94 | 51,447.75 | 54,944.01 |
| 117 | 51,896.97 | 37,191.20 | 20,969.08 | 49,302.12 | 16,654.33 | 18,112.78 | 18,112.78 | 16,605.66 | 35,178.49 | 51,896.97 | 55,423.07 |
| 118 | 52,346.29 | 37,501.64 | 21,083.99 | 49,728.98 | 16,744.43 | 18,244.06 | 18,244.06 | 16,699.03 | 35,452.09 | 52,346.29 | 55,902.12 |
| 119 | 52,795.73 | 37,812.07 | 21,198.91 | 50,155.94 | 16,834.53 | 18,375.35 | 18,375.35 | 16,792.40 | 35,725.74 | 52,795.73 | 56,381.19 |
| 120 | 53,245.27 | 38,122.51 | 21,313.82 | 50,583.00 | 16,924.63 | 18,506.65 | 18,506.65 | 16,885.77 | 35,999.46 | 53,245.27 | 56,860.25 |
| 121 | 53,694.91 | 38,432.95 | 21,428.73 | 51,010.17 | 17,014.73 | 18,637.95 | 18,637.95 | 16,979.14 | 36,273.23 | 53,694.91 | 57,339.30 |
| 122 | 54,137.91 | 38,743.38 | 21,543.64 | 51,431.02 | 17,104.83 | 18,768.69 | 18,768.69 | 17,072.51 | 36,543.17 | 54,137.91 | 57,818.36 |
| 123 | 54,580.90 | 39,053.82 | 21,658.55 | 51,851.87 | 17,194.93 | 18,899.43 | 18,899.43 | 17,165.88 | 36,813.11 | 54,580.90 | 58,297.42 |
| 124 | 55,023.91 | 39,360.61 | 21,771.79 | 52,272.71 | 17,285.03 | 19,030.16 | 19,030.16 | 17,259.25 | 37,083.05 | 55,023.91 | 58,775.55 |
| 125 | 55,466.90 | 39,666.39 | 21,884.98 | 52,693.55 | 17,375.13 | 19,160.90 | 19,160.90 | 17,352.62 | 37,353.00 | 55,466.90 | 59,247.42 |
| 126 | 55,909.89 | 39,972.16 | 21,998.17 | 53,114.41 | 17,465.23 | 19,291.63 | 19,291.63 | 17,445.93 | 37,622.93 | 55,909.89 | 59,719.29 |
| 127 | 56,352.90 | 40,277.95 | 22,111.36 | 53,535.25 | 17,555.33 | 19,422.37 | 19,422.37 | 17,537.91 | 37,892.88 | 56,352.90 | 60,191.17 |
| 128 | 56,795.89 | 40,583.73 | 22,224.55 | 53,956.10 | 17,645.43 | 19,553.11 | 19,553.11 | 17,629.88 | 38,162.82 | 56,795.89 | 60,663.04 |
| 129 | 57,238.88 | 40,889.51 | 22,337.74 | 54,376.94 | 17,735.53 | 19,683.85 | 19,683.85 | 17,721.85 | 38,432.76 | 57,238.88 | 61,134.92 |
| 130 | 57,681.88 | 41,195.29 | 22,450.92 | 54,797.79 | 17,825.63 | 19,814.58 | 19,814.58 | 17,813.82 | 38,702.70 | 57,681.88 | 61,606.79 |
| 131 | 58,124.87 | 41,501.07 | 22,564.12 | 55,218.63 | 17,915.74 | 19,945.32 | 19,945.32 | 17,905.79 | 38,972.65 | 58,124.87 | 62,078.65 |
| 132 | 58,567.87 | 41,806.85 | 22,677.30 | 55,639.48 | 18,005.84 | 20,076.06 | 20,076.06 | 17,997.76 | 39,242.58 | 58,567.87 | 62,550.53 |
| 133 | 59,010.87 | 42,112.63 | 22,790.49 | 56,060.32 | 18,095.94 | 20,206.79 | 20,206.79 | 18,089.73 | 39,512.53 | 59,010.87 | 63,022.41 |

| Trial length in Days | Trial length proxy A | Trial length proxy B | Trial length proxy C | Trial length proxy D | Trial length proxy E | Trial length proxy F | Trial length proxy G | Trial length proxy H | Trial length proxy I | Trial length proxy J | Trial length proxy K |
|---|---|---|---|---|---|---|---|---|---|---|---|
| 134 | 59,453.86 | 42,418.40 | 22,903.68 | 56,481.17 | 18,186.04 | 20,337.53 | 20,337.53 | 18,181.70 | 39,782.47 | 59,453.86 | 63,494.28 |
| 135 | 59,896.86 | 42,724.19 | 23,016.87 | 56,902.01 | 18,276.14 | 20,468.27 | 20,468.27 | 18,273.66 | 40,052.42 | 59,896.86 | 63,966.15 |
| 136 | 60,339.86 | 43,029.97 | 23,130.07 | 57,322.86 | 18,366.24 | 20,599.01 | 20,599.01 | 18,365.63 | 40,322.36 | 60,339.86 | 64,438.02 |
| 137 | 60,782.85 | 43,335.75 | 23,243.25 | 57,743.70 | 18,456.34 | 20,729.74 | 20,729.74 | 18,457.60 | 40,592.30 | 60,782.85 | 64,909.90 |
| 138 | 61,225.85 | 43,641.53 | 23,356.44 | 58,164.56 | 18,546.44 | 20,860.48 | 20,860.48 | 18,549.57 | 40,862.24 | 61,225.85 | 65,381.77 |
| 139 | 61,668.84 | 43,947.30 | 23,469.63 | 58,585.40 | 18,636.54 | 20,991.22 | 20,991.22 | 18,641.54 | 41,132.19 | 61,668.84 | 65,853.64 |
| 140 | 62,111.84 | 44,253.09 | 23,582.82 | 59,006.25 | 18,726.64 | 21,121.95 | 21,121.95 | 18,733.52 | 41,402.13 | 62,111.84 | 66,325.52 |
| 141 | 62,554.83 | 44,558.86 | 23,696.01 | 59,427.09 | 18,816.74 | 21,252.69 | 21,252.69 | 18,825.48 | 41,672.07 | 62,554.83 | 66,797.38 |
| 142 | 62,997.82 | 44,864.65 | 23,809.20 | 59,847.94 | 18,906.84 | 21,383.43 | 21,383.43 | 18,917.46 | 41,942.01 | 62,997.82 | 67,269.26 |
| 143 | 63,440.83 | 45,170.43 | 23,922.38 | 60,268.79 | 18,996.95 | 21,514.17 | 21,514.17 | 19,009.43 | 42,211.96 | 63,440.83 | 67,741.13 |
| 144 | 63,883.82 | 45,476.21 | 24,035.58 | 60,689.64 | 19,087.05 | 21,644.90 | 21,644.90 | 19,101.39 | 42,481.89 | 63,883.82 | 68,213.00 |
| 145 | 64,326.82 | 45,781.99 | 24,148.77 | 61,110.47 | 19,177.15 | 21,775.64 | 21,775.64 | 19,193.36 | 42,751.84 | 64,326.82 | 68,684.88 |
| 146 | 64,769.82 | 46,087.77 | 24,261.95 | 61,531.33 | 19,267.25 | 21,906.38 | 21,906.38 | 19,285.32 | 43,021.78 | 64,769.82 | 69,156.75 |
| 147 | 65,212.81 | 46,393.55 | 24,375.15 | 61,952.17 | 19,357.35 | 22,037.11 | 22,037.11 | 19,377.30 | 43,291.72 | 65,212.81 | 69,628.62 |
| 148 | 65,655.81 | 46,699.32 | 24,488.33 | 62,373.03 | 19,447.45 | 22,167.85 | 22,167.85 | 19,469.27 | 43,561.66 | 65,655.81 | 70,100.49 |
| 149 | 66,098.81 | 47,005.10 | 24,601.52 | 62,793.86 | 19,537.55 | 22,298.59 | 22,298.59 | 19,561.24 | 43,831.61 | 66,098.81 | 70,572.37 |
| 150 | 66,541.80 | 47,310.89 | 24,714.71 | 63,214.71 | 19,627.65 | 22,429.33 | 22,429.33 | 19,653.21 | 44,101.54 | 66,541.80 | 71,044.25 |
| 151 | 66,984.79 | 47,616.67 | 24,827.90 | 63,635.56 | 19,717.75 | 22,560.06 | 22,560.06 | 19,745.18 | 44,371.49 | 66,984.79 | 71,516.11 |
| 152 | 67,427.79 | 47,922.44 | 24,941.09 | 64,056.41 | 19,807.85 | 22,690.80 | 22,690.80 | 19,837.15 | 44,641.43 | 67,427.79 | 71,987.98 |
| 153 | 67,870.78 | 48,228.23 | 25,054.28 | 64,477.25 | 19,897.95 | 22,821.54 | 22,821.54 | 19,929.12 | 44,911.37 | 67,870.78 | 72,459.86 |
| 154 | 68,313.78 | 48,534.00 | 25,167.46 | 64,898.10 | 19,988.05 | 22,952.27 | 22,952.27 | 20,021.09 | 45,181.32 | 68,313.78 | 72,931.73 |
| 155 | 68,756.78 | 48,839.79 | 25,280.66 | 65,318.94 | 20,078.16 | 23,083.01 | 23,083.01 | 20,113.05 | 45,451.26 | 68,756.78 | 73,403.61 |
| 156 | 69,199.78 | 49,145.56 | 25,393.84 | 65,739.79 | 20,168.26 | 23,213.74 | 23,213.74 | 20,205.02 | 45,721.20 | 69,199.78 | 73,875.48 |
| 157 | 69,642.77 | 49,451.34 | 25,507.03 | 66,160.63 | 20,258.36 | 23,344.49 | 23,344.49 | 20,297.00 | 45,991.14 | 69,642.77 | 74,347.34 |
| 158 | 70,085.77 | 49,757.13 | 25,620.22 | 66,581.48 | 20,348.46 | 23,475.22 | 23,475.22 | 20,388.96 | 46,261.09 | 70,085.77 | 74,819.22 |
| 159 | 70,528.77 | 50,062.91 | 25,733.41 | 67,002.33 | 20,438.56 | 23,605.96 | 23,605.96 | 20,480.93 | 46,531.02 | 70,528.77 | 75,291.10 |
| 160 | 70,971.76 | 50,368.69 | 25,846.61 | 67,423.17 | 20,528.66 | 23,736.70 | 23,736.70 | 20,572.91 | 46,800.97 | 70,971.76 | 75,762.97 |

| Trial length in Days | Trial length proxy A | Trial length proxy B | Trial length proxy C | Trial length proxy D | Trial length proxy E | Trial length proxy F | Trial length proxy G | Trial length proxy H | Trial length proxy I | Trial length proxy J | Trial length proxy K |
|---|---|---|---|---|---|---|---|---|---|---|---|
| 161 | 71,414.76 | 50,674.46 | 25,959.79 | 67,844.02 | 20,618.76 | 23,867.43 | 23,867.43 | 20,664.87 | 47,070.91 | 71,414.76 | 76,234.84 |
| 162 | 71,857.75 | 50,980.24 | 26,072.98 | 68,264.86 | 20,708.86 | 23,998.17 | 23,998.17 | 20,756.85 | 47,340.85 | 71,857.75 | 76,706.71 |
| 163 | 72,300.74 | 51,286.02 | 26,186.17 | 68,685.72 | 20,798.96 | 24,128.91 | 24,128.91 | 20,848.82 | 47,610.79 | 72,300.74 | 77,178.59 |
| 164 | 72,743.74 | 51,591.80 | 26,299.36 | 69,106.56 | 20,889.06 | 24,259.64 | 24,259.64 | 20,940.78 | 47,880.74 | 72,743.74 | 77,650.46 |
| 165 | 73,186.74 | 51,897.59 | 26,412.55 | 69,527.40 | 20,979.16 | 24,390.38 | 24,390.38 | 21,032.75 | 48,150.67 | 73,186.74 | 78,122.33 |
| 166 | 73,629.73 | 52,203.37 | 26,525.74 | 69,948.25 | 21,069.26 | 24,521.12 | 24,521.12 | 21,124.72 | 48,420.62 | 73,629.73 | 78,594.21 |
| 167 | 74,072.73 | 52,509.14 | 26,638.92 | 70,369.10 | 21,159.36 | 24,651.85 | 24,651.85 | 21,216.69 | 48,690.56 | 74,072.73 | 79,066.07 |
| 168 | 74,515.73 | 52,814.93 | 26,752.12 | 70,789.95 | 21,249.46 | 24,782.59 | 24,782.59 | 21,308.66 | 48,960.50 | 74,515.73 | 79,537.95 |
| 169 | 74,958.72 | 53,120.70 | 26,865.30 | 71,210.79 | 21,339.56 | 24,913.33 | 24,913.33 | 21,400.63 | 49,230.44 | 74,958.72 | 80,009.83 |
| 170 | 75,401.72 | 53,426.48 | 26,978.49 | 71,631.63 | 21,429.66 | 25,044.06 | 25,044.06 | 21,492.60 | 49,500.39 | 75,401.72 | 80,481.69 |
| 171 | 75,844.72 | 53,732.26 | 27,091.68 | 72,052.49 | 21,519.76 | 25,174.81 | 25,174.81 | 21,584.57 | 49,770.33 | 75,844.72 | 80,953.57 |
| 172 | 76,287.71 | 54,038.04 | 27,204.87 | 72,473.33 | 21,609.86 | 25,305.54 | 25,305.54 | 21,676.54 | 50,040.28 | 76,287.71 | 81,425.44 |
| 173 | 76,730.70 | 54,343.83 | 27,318.06 | 72,894.18 | 21,699.96 | 25,436.28 | 25,436.28 | 21,768.51 | 50,310.22 | 76,730.70 | 81,897.32 |
| 174 | 77,173.70 | 54,649.60 | 27,431.25 | 73,315.02 | 21,790.06 | 25,567.02 | 25,567.02 | 21,860.48 | 50,580.16 | 77,173.70 | 82,369.19 |
| 175 | 77,616.70 | 54,955.38 | 27,544.44 | 73,735.87 | 21,880.16 | 25,697.75 | 25,697.75 | 21,952.44 | 50,850.10 | 77,616.70 | 82,841.06 |
| 176 | 78,059.69 | 55,261.16 | 27,657.63 | 74,156.71 | 21,970.26 | 25,828.49 | 25,828.49 | 22,044.41 | 51,120.05 | 78,059.69 | 83,312.94 |
| 177 | 78,502.69 | 55,566.94 | 27,770.82 | 74,577.56 | 22,060.36 | 25,959.23 | 25,959.23 | 22,136.39 | 51,389.98 | 78,502.69 | 83,784.80 |
| 178 | 78,945.69 | 55,872.72 | 27,884.00 | 74,998.40 | 22,150.47 | 26,089.96 | 26,089.96 | 22,228.35 | 51,659.93 | 78,945.69 | 84,256.68 |
| 179 | 79,388.68 | 56,178.50 | 27,997.20 | 75,419.25 | 22,240.57 | 26,220.70 | 26,220.70 | 22,320.32 | 51,929.87 | 79,388.68 | 84,728.55 |
| 180 | 79,831.68 | 56,484.28 | 28,110.38 | 75,840.09 | 22,330.67 | 26,351.44 | 26,351.44 | 22,412.30 | 52,199.81 | 79,831.68 | 85,200.42 |
| 181 | 80,274.68 | 56,790.07 | 28,223.58 | 76,260.94 | 22,420.77 | 26,482.17 | 26,482.17 | 22,504.26 | 52,469.75 | 80,274.68 | 85,672.30 |
| 182 | 80,717.67 | 57,095.84 | 28,336.77 | 76,681.78 | 22,510.87 | 26,612.91 | 26,612.91 | 22,596.24 | 52,739.70 | 80,717.67 | 86,144.17 |
| 183 | 81,160.67 | 57,401.62 | 28,449.95 | 77,102.64 | 22,599.68 | 26,743.65 | 26,743.65 | 22,688.21 | 53,009.63 | 81,160.67 | 86,616.04 |
| 184 | 81,603.66 | 57,707.40 | 28,563.15 | 77,523.48 | 22,688.43 | 26,874.38 | 26,874.38 | 22,780.17 | 53,279.58 | 81,603.66 | 87,087.91 |
| 185 | 82,046.65 | 58,013.18 | 28,676.33 | 77,944.32 | 22,777.18 | 27,005.13 | 27,005.13 | 22,872.14 | 53,549.52 | 82,046.65 | 87,559.79 |
| 186 | 82,489.66 | 58,318.96 | 28,789.52 | 78,365.17 | 22,865.93 | 27,135.86 | 27,135.86 | 22,964.11 | 53,819.46 | 82,489.66 | 88,031.67 |
| 187 | 82,932.65 | 58,624.74 | 28,902.71 | 78,786.02 | 22,954.68 | 27,266.60 | 27,266.60 | 23,056.08 | 54,089.40 | 82,932.65 | 88,503.53 |

| Trial length in Days | Trial length proxy A | Trial length proxy B | Trial length proxy C | Trial length proxy D | Trial length proxy E | Trial length proxy F | Trial length proxy G | Trial length proxy H | Trial length proxy I | Trial length proxy J | Trial length proxy K |
|---|---|---|---|---|---|---|---|---|---|---|---|
| 188 | 83,375.65 | 58,930.52 | 29,015.90 | 79,206.87 | 23,043.43 | 27,397.34 | 27,397.34 | 23,148.05 | 54,359.35 | 83,375.65 | 88,975.40 |
| 189 | 83,818.64 | 59,236.30 | 29,129.09 | 79,627.71 | 23,132.18 | 27,528.06 | 27,528.06 | 23,240.02 | 54,629.29 | 83,818.64 | 89,447.28 |
| 190 | 84,261.64 | 59,542.08 | 29,242.28 | 80,048.55 | 23,220.93 | 27,658.81 | 27,658.81 | 23,331.99 | 54,899.23 | 84,261.64 | 89,919.15 |
| 191 | 84,704.64 | 59,847.86 | 29,355.46 | 80,469.41 | 23,309.68 | 27,789.55 | 27,789.55 | 23,423.96 | 55,169.18 | 84,704.64 | 90,391.03 |
| 192 | 85,147.63 | 60,153.64 | 29,468.66 | 80,890.25 | 23,398.43 | 27,920.28 | 27,920.28 | 23,515.94 | 55,439.11 | 85,147.63 | 90,862.90 |
| 193 | 85,590.63 | 60,459.41 | 29,581.84 | 81,311.10 | 23,487.18 | 28,051.02 | 28,051.02 | 23,607.90 | 55,709.06 | 85,590.63 | 91,334.76 |
| 194 | 86,033.62 | 60,765.20 | 29,695.03 | 81,731.94 | 23,575.92 | 28,181.76 | 28,181.76 | 23,699.87 | 55,979.00 | 86,033.62 | 91,806.64 |
| 195 | 86,476.61 | 61,070.98 | 29,808.22 | 82,152.79 | 23,664.67 | 28,312.49 | 28,312.49 | 23,791.84 | 56,248.94 | 86,476.61 | 92,278.52 |
| 196 | 86,919.61 | 61,376.76 | 29,921.41 | 82,573.64 | 23,753.42 | 28,443.23 | 28,443.23 | 23,883.80 | 56,518.88 | 86,919.61 | 92,750.39 |
| 197 | 87,362.61 | 61,682.54 | 30,034.60 | 82,994.48 | 23,842.17 | 28,573.96 | 28,573.96 | 23,975.78 | 56,788.83 | 87,362.61 | 93,222.26 |
| 198 | 87,805.60 | 61,988.32 | 30,147.79 | 83,415.33 | 23,930.92 | 28,704.70 | 28,704.70 | 24,067.75 | 57,058.76 | 87,805.60 | 93,694.13 |
| 199 | 88,248.61 | 62,294.10 | 30,260.97 | 83,836.17 | 24,019.67 | 28,835.45 | 28,835.45 | 24,159.72 | 57,328.71 | 88,248.61 | 94,166.01 |
| 200 | 88,691.60 | 62,599.87 | 30,374.17 | 84,257.02 | 24,108.42 | 28,966.17 | 28,966.17 | 24,251.69 | 57,598.65 | 88,691.60 | 94,637.88 |

★ [The tables following sub-paras 7(2) and (3) are printed as substituted by the Criminal Legal Aid (Remuneration) (Amendment) Regulations 2014 (S.I. 2014 No. 415). As to their application, see *ante*, G-71.]

*Cracked trials and guilty pleas where the number of pages of prosecution evidence exceeds the PPE Cut-off*

**G-72**    8.—(1) Where in a cracked trial or guilty plea the number of pages of prosecution evidence exceeds the PPE Cut-off specified in the table following paragraph 5(1) as appropriate to the offence with which the assisted person is charged, the total fee payable to the litigator is—

    (a)  the final fee, calculated in accordance with sub-paragraph (2) of this paragraph;

    (b)  the defendant uplift, if any, calculated in accordance with the table following paragraph 12; and

    (c)  the adjustment for transfers and retrials, if any, calculated in accordance with paragraph 13.

(2) For the purposes of sub-paragraph (1), the final fee payable to a litigator in a cracked trial or guilty plea is calculated in accordance with the following formula—

$$F = I + (D \times i)$$

Where—

• **F** is the amount of the final fee;

• **I** is the initial fee specified in the tables following this paragraph, as appropriate to the type of case, the offence with which the assisted person is charged and the number of pages of prosecution evidence;

• **D** is the difference between—

    (i)  the number of pages of prosecution evidence in the case; and

    (ii)  the lower number in the PPE range as specified in the tables following this paragraph, as appropriate to the type of case, the offence with which the assisted person is charged and the number of pages of prosecution evidence in the case;

• **i** is the incremental fee per page of prosecution evidence specified in the tables following this paragraph, as appropriate to the type of case, the offence with which the assisted person is charged and the number of pages of prosecution evidence in the case.

TABLE OF FINAL FEES IN CRACKED TRIALS

| Class of Offence | PPE Range | Initial fee (£) | Incremental fee per page of prosecution evidence (£) |
|---|---|---|---|
| A and J | 0-79 | 904.58 | 0 |
| A and J | 80-249 | 904.58 | 10.70 |
| A and J | 250-999 | 2,722.89 | 6.71 |
| A and J | 1000-2799 | 7,757.90 | 3.92 |
| A and J | 2800-4599 | 14,820.75 | 3.92 |
| A and J | 4600-6399 | 21,883.61 | 3.11 |
| A and J | 6400-8199 | 27,490.35 | 3.11 |
| A and J | 8200-9999 | 33,097.09 | 3.11 |
| A and J | 10,000 | 38,700.71 | 0 |
| B | 0-69 | 709.15 | 0 |
| B | 70-249 | 709.15 | 7.83 |
| B | 250-999 | 2,117.67 | 3.66 |
| B | 1000-2799 | 4,864.56 | 2.44 |
| B | 2800-4599 | 9,255.51 | 2.44 |
| B | 4600-6399 | 13,646.46 | 2.05 |
| B | 6400-8199 | 17,338.49 | 2.05 |
| B | 8200-9999 | 21,030.50 | 2.05 |
| B | 10,000 | 24,720.46 | 0 |

| Class of Offence | PPE Range | Initial fee (£) | Incremental fee per page of prosecution evidence (£) |
|---|---|---|---|
| C | 0-39 | 524.84 | 0 |
| C | 40-249 | 524.84 | 3.92 |
| C | 250-999 | 1,348.77 | 2.25 |
| C | 1000-2799 | 3,033.06 | 1.43 |
| C | 2800-4599 | 5,607.48 | 1.43 |
| C | 4600-6399 | 8,181.89 | 1.43 |
| C | 6400-8199 | 10,756.31 | 1.43 |
| C | 8200-9999 | 13,330.74 | 1.43 |
| C | 10,000 | 15,903.73 | 0 |
| D | 0-79 | 859.35 | 0 |
| D | 80-249 | 859.35 | 10.14 |
| D | 250-999 | 2,582.50 | 6.11 |
| D | 1000-2799 | 7,163.76 | 3.61 |
| D | 2800-4599 | 13,655.74 | 3.61 |
| D | 4600-6399 | 20,147.71 | 2.96 |
| D | 6400-8199 | 25,474.79 | 2.96 |
| D | 8200-9999 | 30,801.87 | 2.96 |
| D | 10,000 | 36,125.98 | 0 |
| E | 0-39 | 233.03 | 0 |
| E | 40-249 | 233.03 | 4.60 |
| E | 250-999 | 1,199.43 | 1.46 |
| E | 1000-2799 | 2,291.54 | 0.61 |
| E | 2800-4599 | 3,390.26 | 0.61 |
| E | 4600-6399 | 4,488.97 | 0.61 |
| E | 6400-8199 | 5,587.69 | 0.61 |
| E | 8200-9999 | 6,686.41 | 0.61 |
| E | 10,000 | 7,784.51 | 0 |
| F and G | 0-49 | 224.22 | 0 |
| F and G | 50-249 | 224.22 | 4.42 |
| F and G | 250-999 | 1,107.53 | 1.79 |
| F and G | 1000-2799 | 2,450.39 | 0.70 |
| F and G | 2800-4599 | 3,704.67 | 0.70 |
| F and G | 4600-6399 | 4,958.94 | 0.70 |
| F and G | 6400-8199 | 6,213.21 | 0.70 |
| F and G | 8200-9999 | 7,467.49 | 0.70 |
| F and G | 10,000 | 8,721.06 | 0 |
| H | 0-39 | 237.00 | 0 |
| H | 40-249 | 237.00 | 4.26 |
| H | 250-999 | 1,131.61 | 1.56 |
| H | 1000-2799 | 2,298.20 | 0.70 |
| H | 2800-4599 | 3,550.79 | 0.70 |
| H | 4600-6399 | 4,803.37 | 0.70 |
| H | 6400-8199 | 6,055.96 | 0.70 |

| Class of Offence | PPE Range | Initial fee (£) | Incremental fee per page of prosecution evidence (£) |
|---|---|---|---|
| H | 8200-9999 | 7,308.55 | 0.70 |
| H | 10,000 | 8,560.44 | 0 |
| I | 0-39 | 253.68 | 0 |
| I | 40-249 | 253.68 | 5.92 |
| I | 250-999 | 1,496.80 | 2.31 |
| I | 1000-2799 | 3,231.91 | 0.90 |
| I | 2800-4599 | 4,847.36 | 0.90 |
| I | 4600-6399 | 6,462.79 | 0.90 |
| I | 6400-8199 | 8,078.23 | 0.90 |
| I | 8200-9999 | 9,693.67 | 0.90 |
| I | 10,000 | 11,308.20 | 0 |
| K | 0-119 | 773.86 | 0 |
| K | 120-249 | 773.86 | 6.55 |
| K | 250-999 | 1,624.85 | 5.02 |
| K | 1000-2799 | 5,388.98 | 4.39 |
| K | 2800-4599 | 13,299.04 | 4.39 |
| K | 4600-6399 | 21,209.12 | 3.75 |
| K | 6400-8199 | 27,954.29 | 3.75 |
| K | 8200-9999 | 34,699.46 | 3.75 |
| K | 10,000 | 41,440.89 | 0 |

TABLE OF FINAL FEES IN GUILTY PLEAS

| Class of Offence | PPE Range | Initial fee (£) | Incremental fee per page of prosecution evidence (£) |
|---|---|---|---|
| A and J | 0-79 | 680.39 | 0 |
| A and J | 80-399 | 680.39 | 5.62 |
| A and J | 400-999 | 2,478.29 | 2.96 |
| A and J | 1000-2799 | 4,256.09 | 1.89 |
| A and J | 2800-4599 | 7,666.89 | 1.89 |
| A and J | 4600-6399 | 11,077.68 | 1.12 |
| A and J | 6400-8199 | 13,090.60 | 1.12 |
| A and J | 8200-9999 | 15,103.53 | 1.12 |
| A and J | 10,000 | 17,115.33 | 0 |
| B | 0-69 | 556.11 | 0 |
| B | 70-399 | 556.11 | 4.52 |
| B | 400-999 | 2,046.59 | 2.28 |
| B | 1000-2799 | 3,411.75 | 1.45 |
| B | 2800-4599 | 6,025.92 | 1.45 |
| B | 4600-6399 | 8,640.11 | 1.06 |
| B | 6400-8199 | 10,555.35 | 1.06 |
| B | 8200-9999 | 12,470.60 | 1.06 |
| B | 10,000 | 14,384.78 | 0 |
| C | 0-39 | 442.91 | 0 |

| Class of Offence | PPE Range | Initial fee (£) | Incremental fee per page of prosecution evidence (£) |
|---|---|---|---|
| C | 40-399 | 442.91 | 2.66 |
| C | 400-999 | 1,401.88 | 1.46 |
| C | 1000-2799 | 2,276.27 | 0.79 |
| C | 2800-4599 | 3,699.93 | 0.79 |
| C | 4600-6399 | 5,123.61 | 0.79 |
| C | 6400-8199 | 6,547.28 | 0.79 |
| C | 8200-9999 | 7,970.95 | 0.79 |
| C | 10,000 | 9,393.82 | 0 |
| D | 0-79 | 646.36 | 0 |
| D | 80-399 | 646.36 | 5.23 |
| D | 400-999 | 2,320.66 | 2.75 |
| D | 1000-2799 | 3,968.37 | 1.71 |
| D | 2800-4599 | 7,046.20 | 1.71 |
| D | 4600-6399 | 10,124.03 | 1.06 |
| D | 6400-8199 | 12,036.98 | 1.06 |
| D | 8200-9999 | 13,949.91 | 1.06 |
| D | 10,000 | 15,861.79 | 0 |
| E | 0-39 | 184.70 | 0 |
| E | 40-399 | 184.70 | 2.92 |
| E | 400-999 | 1,237.24 | 1.25 |
| E | 1000-2799 | 1,989.07 | 0.46 |
| E | 2800-4599 | 2,819.70 | 0.46 |
| E | 4600-6399 | 3,650.33 | 0.46 |
| E | 6400-8199 | 4,480.96 | 0.46 |
| E | 8200-9999 | 5,311.59 | 0.46 |
| E | 10,000 | 6,141.75 | 0 |
| F and G | 0-49 | 195.81 | 0 |
| F and G | 50-399 | 195.81 | 2.83 |
| F and G | 400-999 | 1,187.73 | 0.99 |
| F and G | 1000-2799 | 1,781.21 | 0.32 |
| F and G | 2800-4599 | 2,354.07 | 0.32 |
| F and G | 4600-6399 | 2,926.93 | 0.32 |
| F and G | 6400-8199 | 3,499.78 | 0.32 |
| F and G | 8200-9999 | 4,072.64 | 0.32 |
| F and G | 10,000 | 4,645.18 | 0 |
| H | 0-39 | 190.97 | 0 |
| H | 40-399 | 190.97 | 2.79 |
| H | 400-999 | 1,196.59 | 0.99 |
| H | 1000-2799 | 1,790.74 | 0.32 |
| H | 2800-4599 | 2,359.85 | 0.32 |
| H | 4600-6399 | 2,928.98 | 0.32 |
| H | 6400-8199 | 3,498.10 | 0.32 |
| H | 8200-9999 | 4,067.22 | 0.32 |

| Class of Offence | PPE Range | Initial fee (£) | Incremental fee per page of prosecution evidence (£) |
| --- | --- | --- | --- |
| H | 10,000 | 4,636.00 | 0 |
| I | 0-39 | 174.60 | 0 |
| I | 40-399 | 174.60 | 3.12 |
| I | 400-999 | 1,298.52 | 1.36 |
| I | 1000-2799 | 2,116.29 | 0.51 |
| I | 2800-4599 | 3,033.02 | 0.51 |
| I | 4600-6399 | 3,949.75 | 0.51 |
| I | 6400-8199 | 4,866.48 | 0.51 |
| I | 8200-9999 | 5,783.22 | 0.51 |
| I | 10,000 | 6,699.45 | 0 |
| K | 0-119 | 640.84 | 0 |
| K | 120-399 | 640.84 | 5.26 |
| K | 400-999 | 2,113.13 | 2.93 |
| K | 1000-2799 | 3,869.24 | 2.73 |
| K | 2800-4599 | 8,775.55 | 2.73 |
| K | 4600-6399 | 13,681.86 | 2.08 |
| K | 6400-8199 | 17,423.28 | 2.08 |
| K | 8200-9999 | 21,164.71 | 2.08 |
| K | 10,000 | 24,904.04 | 0 |

★ [The tables in para. 8 are printed as substituted by the Criminal Legal Aid (Remuneration) (Amendment) Regulations 2014 (S.I. 2014 No. 415). As to their application, see *ante*, G-71.]

*Trials where the number of pages of prosecution evidence exceeds the PPE Cut-off*

**G-72a**     9.—(1) Where in a trial the number of pages of prosecution evidence exceeds the PPE Cut-off figure specified in the table following paragraph 5(2) as appropriate to the offence for which the assisted person is tried and the length of trial, the total fee payable to the litigator is—

(a)  the final fee, calculated in accordance with sub-paragraph (2) of this paragraph;

(b)  the defendant uplift, if any, calculated in accordance with the table following paragraph 12; and

(c)  the adjustment for transfers and retrials, if any, calculated in accordance with paragraph 13.

(2) For the purposes of sub-paragraph (1), the final fee is calculated in accordance with the following formula—

$$F = I + (D \times i)$$

Where—

•**F** is the amount of the final fee;

•**I** is the initial fee specified in the table following this paragraph as appropriate to the offence for which the assisted person is tried and the number of pages of prosecution evidence;

•**D** is the difference between—

(i)  the number of pages of prosecution evidence in the case; and

(ii)  the lower number in the PPE range as specified in the table following this paragraph, as appropriate to the offence for which the assisted person is tried and the number of pages of prosecution evidence in the case;

•**i** is the incremental fee per page of prosecution evidence specified in the table following this paragraph, as appropriate to the offence for which the assisted person is tried and the number of pages of prosecution evidence in the case.

TABLE OF FINAL FEES IN TRIALS

| Offence Class | PPE Range | Initial Fee | Incremental fee per page |
|---|---|---|---|
| A and J | 0-79 | 1,467.58 | 0 |
| A and J | 80-209 | 1,467.58 | 16.58 |
| A and J | 210-699 | 3,622.54 | 12.66 |
| A and J | 700-1049 | 9,824.91 | 10.62 |
| A and J | 1050-1999 | 13,543.42 | 9.21 |
| A and J | 2000-3599 | 22,295.42 | 8.42 |
| A and J | 3600-5199 | 35,767.03 | 8.42 |
| A and J | 5200-6799 | 49,238.64 | 8.42 |
| A and J | 6800-8399 | 62,710.26 | 8.42 |
| A and J | 8400-9999 | 76,181.87 | 8.42 |
| A and J | 10,000 | 89,645.06 | 0 |
| B | 0-69 | 1,097.66 | 0 |
| B | 70-199 | 1,097.66 | 12.81 |
| B | 200-499 | 2,762.60 | 11.44 |
| B | 500-899 | 6,195.38 | 9.63 |
| B | 900-1299 | 10,048.21 | 8.09 |
| B | 1300-1999 | 13,285.03 | 7.09 |
| B | 2000-3299 | 18,249.51 | 7.09 |
| B | 3300-4999 | 27,469.24 | 7.09 |
| B | 5000-5999 | 39,525.82 | 7.09 |
| B | 6000-7999 | 46,617.93 | 7.09 |
| B | 8000-8999 | 60,802.14 | 7.09 |
| B | 9000-9999 | 67,894.24 | 7.09 |
| B | 10,000 | 74,979.26 | 0 |
| C | 0-39 | 739.59 | 0 |
| C | 40-299 | 739.59 | 10.57 |
| C | 300-799 | 3,486.54 | 9.23 |
| C | 800-1249 | 8,101.74 | 7.73 |
| C | 1250-1999 | 11,578.09 | 6.83 |
| C | 2000-3199 | 16,700.93 | 4.72 |
| C | 3200-4559 | 22,368.79 | 4.72 |
| C | 4560-5919 | 28,792.38 | 4.72 |
| C | 5920-7279 | 35,215.96 | 4.72 |
| C | 7280-8639 | 41,639.54 | 4.72 |
| C | 8640-9999 | 48,063.12 | 4.72 |
| C | 10,000 | 54,482.00 | 0 |
| D | 0-79 | 1,394.20 | 0 |
| D | 80-209 | 1,394.20 | 15.75 |
| D | 210-699 | 3,441.41 | 12.03 |
| D | 700-1049 | 9,333.67 | 10.09 |
| D | 1050-1999 | 12,866.25 | 8.75 |
| D | 2000-3599 | 21,180.65 | 8.00 |
| D | 3600-5199 | 33,978.67 | 8.00 |
| D | 5200-6799 | 46,776.70 | 8.00 |

| Offence Class | PPE Range | Initial Fee | Incremental fee per page |
|---|---|---|---|
| D | 6800-8399 | 59,574.74 | 8.00 |
| D | 8400-9999 | 72,372.77 | 8.00 |
| D | 10,000 | 85,162.80 | 0 |
| E | 0-39 | 352.72 | 0 |
| E | 40-69 | 352.72 | 9.52 |
| E | 70-129 | 638.20 | 8.57 |
| E | 130-599 | 1,152.58 | 8.29 |
| E | 600-1349 | 5,049.74 | 5.44 |
| E | 1350-2999 | 9,131.96 | 2.39 |
| E | 3000-4749 | 13,072.77 | 2.39 |
| E | 4750-6499 | 17,252.41 | 2.39 |
| E | 6500-8249 | 21,432.04 | 2.39 |
| E | 8250-9999 | 25,611.69 | 2.39 |
| E | 10,000 | 29,788.93 | 0 |
| F and G | 0-49 | 357.60 | 0 |
| F and G | 50-229 | 357.60 | 7.31 |
| F and G | 230-699 | 1,673.21 | 6.96 |
| F and G | 700-1399 | 4,946.64 | 5.60 |
| F and G | 1400-1949 | 8,865.80 | 4.32 |
| F and G | 1950-3549 | 11,242.37 | 2.16 |
| F and G | 3550-5149 | 14,691.41 | 2.16 |
| F and G | 5150-6749 | 18,140.45 | 2.16 |
| F and G | 6750-8349 | 21,589.49 | 2.16 |
| F and G | 8350-9999 | 25,038.53 | 2.16 |
| F and G | 10,000 | 28,593.21 | 0 |
| H | 0-39 | 357.75 | 0 |
| H | 40-249 | 357.75 | 8.60 |
| H | 250-619 | 2,162.92 | 7.15 |
| H | 620-1299 | 4,807.79 | 5.31 |
| H | 1300-2999 | 8,418.74 | 4.21 |
| H | 3000-4999 | 15,583.59 | 2.27 |
| H | 5000-5999 | 20,129.84 | 2.27 |
| H | 6000-6999 | 22,402.90 | 2.27 |
| H | 7000-7999 | 24,676.03 | 2.27 |
| H | 8000-8999 | 26,949.15 | 2.27 |
| H | 9000-9999 | 29,222.28 | 2.27 |
| H | 10,000 | 31,493.13 | 0 |
| I | 0-39 | 357.44 | 0 |
| I | 40-369 | 357.44 | 9.14 |
| I | 370-799 | 3,373.66 | 9.09 |
| I | 800-1299 | 7,282.43 | 8.99 |
| I | 1300-2699 | 11,779.02 | 7.08 |
| I | 2700-4199 | 21,697.63 | 3.04 |
| I | 4200-5359 | 26,264.52 | 3.04 |
| I | 5360-6519 | 29,796.25 | 3.04 |

| Offence Class | PPE Range | Initial Fee | Incremental fee per page |
|---|---|---|---|
| I | 6520-7679 | 33,327.97 | 3.04 |
| I | 7680-8839 | 36,859.71 | 3.04 |
| I | 8840-9999 | 40,391.43 | 3.04 |
| I | 10,000 | 43,920.11 | 0 |
| K | 0-119 | 1,031.82 | 0 |
| K | 120-734 | 1,031.82 | 8.66 |
| K | 735-1289 | 6,356.06 | 8.72 |
| K | 1290-2399 | 11,193.67 | 8.87 |
| K | 2400-4499 | 21,042.53 | 8.84 |
| K | 4500-7999 | 39,605.74 | 8.84 |
| K | 8000-8399 | 70,544.40 | 8.84 |
| K | 8400-8799 | 74,080.24 | 8.84 |
| K | 8800-9199 | 77,616.08 | 8.84 |
| K | 9200-9599 | 81,151.94 | 8.84 |
| K | 9600-9999 | 84,687.78 | 8.84 |
| K | 10,000 | 88,214.79 | 0 |

[The table in para. 9 is printed as substituted by the Criminal Legal Aid (Remuneration) ★ (Amendment) Regulations 2014 (S.I. 2014 No. 415). As to its application, see *ante*, G-71.]

PART 3

FIXED FEE FOR GUILTY PLEAS AND CRACKED TRIALS

*Scope of Part 3*

10. This Part applies to a guilty plea or cracked trial in a case committed or sent for trial to the  **G-73** Crown Court on the election of a defendant where the magistrates' court has determined the case to be suitable for summary trial.

*Fixed fee for guilty pleas or cracked trials*

11. The fee payable to a litigator in relation to a guilty plea or cracked trial to which this Part applies is £330.33 per proceedings.

[Para. 11 is printed as amended by the Criminal Legal Aid (Remuneration) (Amendment) ★ Regulations 2014 (S.I. 2014 No. 415). As to the application of this amendment, see *ante*, G-71.]

PART 4

DEFENDANT UPLIFTS, RETRIALS AND TRANSFERS

*Defendant uplifts*

12.—(1) The defendant uplift payable to a litigator is calculated in accordance with the table fol-  **G-73a** lowing this paragraph.

(2) Only one defendant uplift is payable in each case.

(3) In the table following this paragraph, the total fee means—

    (a)   in a cracked trial or guilty plea where the number of pages of prosecution evidence does not exceed the PPE Cut-off specified in the table following paragraph 5(1), the basic fee specified in the table following paragraph 6(2);

    (b)   in a trial where the number of pages of prosecution evidence does not exceed the PPE Cut-off specified in the table following paragraph 5(2), the basic fee specified in the table following paragraph 7(2) plus the length of trial proxy specified in the table following paragraph 7(3);

    (c)   in a cracked trial or guilty plea where the number of pages of prosecution evidence exceeds the PPE Cut-off specified in the table following paragraph 5(1), the final fee, as calculated in accordance with paragraph 8(2); and

599

(d) in a trial where the number of pages of prosecution evidence exceeds the PPE Cut-off specified in the table following paragraph 5(2), the final fee, as calculated in accordance with paragraph 9(2);

(e) where appropriate, the fee set out in paragraph 11.

(4) In a case where the representation of one defendant would attract a fixed fee under Part 3 and the representation of one or more of the other defendants would attract a graduated fee under Part 2, the total fee is the fee falling within whichever of paragraphs (a) to (d) of sub-paragraph (3) is appropriate.

DEFENDANT UPLIFTS

| Total number of defendants represented by litigator | Percentage uplift to total fee |
|---|---|
| 2-4 | 20% |
| 5+ | 30% |

*Retrials and transfers*

**G-73b**

13.—(1) Where following a trial an order is made for a retrial and the same litigator acts for the assisted person at both trials the fee payable to that litigator is—

(a) in respect of the first trial, a fee calculated in accordance with the provisions of this Schedule; and

(b) in respect of the retrial, 25% of the fee, as appropriate to the circumstances of the retrial, in accordance with the provisions of this Schedule.

(2) Where—

(a) a case is transferred to a new litigator; or

(b) a retrial is ordered and a new litigator acts for the assisted person at the retrial,

the fee payable to the original litigator and the new litigator is a percentage of the total fee, calculated in accordance with the table following this paragraph, as appropriate to the circumstances and timing of the retrial, transfer or withdrawal of the section 16 determination.

(3) In sub-paragraph (2), "transfer" includes the making of a section 16 determination in favour of an individual who, immediately before the making of the section 16 determination—

(a) had represented themselves; or

(b) had been represented (otherwise than pursuant to a section 16 determination) by the litigator named in the order,

and for the purposes of that sub-paragraph the litigator is to be treated as a new litigator.

(4) For the purposes of sub-paragraph (2), a case is not transferred to a new litigator where—

(a) a firm of solicitors is named as litigator in the representation order and the solicitor or other appropriately qualified person with responsibility for the case moves to another firm;

(b) a firm of solicitors is named as litigator in the representation order and the firm changes (whether by merger or acquisition or in some other way), but so that the new firm remains closely related to the firm named in the order; or

(c) a solicitor or other appropriately qualified person is named as litigator in the representation order and responsibility for the case is transferred to another solicitor or appropriately qualified person in the same firm or a closely related firm.

(5) For the purposes of sub-paragraph (2), where a case which has been transferred to a new litigator is transferred again, that new litigator—

(a) must be treated as the original litigator, where the transfer takes place at any time before the trial or any retrial;

(b) must be treated as a new litigator, where the transfer takes place during the trial or any retrial; and

(c) must not receive any fee, where the transfer takes place after the trial or any retrial but before the sentencing hearing.

(6) Where a section 16 determination is withdrawn before the case ends, a litigator must receive a percentage of the total fee, in accordance with the table following this paragraph, as appropriate to the circumstances and timing of a transfer.

(7) In the table following this paragraph, the total fee means—

(a) in a cracked trial or guilty plea in a case to which Part 2 applies, where the number of pages of prosecution evidence is less than or equal to the PPE Cut-off specified in the table following paragraph 5(1), the basic fee as set out in the table following paragraph 6(2);

(b) in a trial where the number of pages of prosecution evidence is less than or equal to the PPE Cut-off specified in the table following paragraph 5(2), the basic fee specified in the table following paragraph 7(2) plus the length of trial proxy specified in the table following paragraph 7(3);

(c) in a cracked trial or guilty plea in a case to which Part 2 applies, where the number of pages of prosecution evidence exceeds the PPE Cut-off specified in the table following paragraph 5(1), the final fee as calculated in accordance with paragraph 8(2);

(d) in a trial where the number of pages of prosecution evidence exceeds the PPE Cut-off specified in the table following paragraph 5(2), the final fee, as calculated in accordance with paragraph 9(2);

(e) in a cracked trial or guilty plea in a case to which Part 3 applies, the fixed fee set out in paragraph 11.

(8) Where a case becomes a Very High Cost Case after a section 16 determination has been made and is transferred from the litigator named on the representation order to a new litigator—

(a) the original litigator must be remunerated in accordance with the individual Very High Cost Case contract entered into by that litigator; and

(b) the new litigator must be remunerated in accordance with the individual Very High Cost Case contract entered into by that litigator.

(9) Where a case becomes a Very High Cost Case after a section 16 determination has been made and the section 16 determination is withdrawn before the end of the case, the litigator must be remunerated in accordance with the table following this paragraph as appropriate to the circumstances and timing of the withdrawal.

(10) Sub-paragraph (11) applies where—

(a) the case is a case to which Part 3 would apply if it resulted in a cracked trial or guilty plea; and

(b) at the time the case is transferred to a new litigator in accordance with sub-paragraph (2) it is not known whether the case would result in a cracked trial or guilty plea or whether it would proceed to trial.

(11) Where this sub-paragraph applies—

(a) for the purpose of a claim by the original litigator at the time of the transfer of the case, "total fee" in the table following this paragraph, means the fixed fee set out in paragraph 11;

(b) the original litigator may, if the case proceeds to trial, claim the difference between the payment received at the time of transfer of the case and the payment that would have been due at that time if that payment had been based on the case proceeding to trial.

(12) A litigator may not be treated both as an original litigator and as a new litigator in a case.

RETRIALS AND TRANSFERS

| Scenario | Percentage of the total fee | Case type used to determine total fee | Claim period |
|---|---|---|---|
| Cracked trial before retrial, where there is no change of litigator | 25% | Cracked trial | — |
| Retrial, where there is no change of litigator | 25% | Trial | — |
| Up to and including plea and case management hearing transfer (original litigator) | 25% | Cracked trial | — |
| Up to and including plea and case management hearing transfer — guilty plea (new litiga-tor) | 100% | Guilty plea | — |
| Up to and including plea and case management hearing transfer — cracked trial (new litigator) | 100% | Cracked trial | — |
| Up to and including plea and case management hearing transfer — trial (new litigator) | 100% | Trial | — |
| Before trial transfer (original litigator) | 75% | Cracked trial | — |

| Scenario | Percentage of the total fee | Case type used to determine total fee | Claim period |
|---|---|---|---|
| Before trial transfer — cracked trial (new litigator) | 100% | Cracked trial | — |
| Before trial transfer — trial (new litigator) | 100% | Trial | — |
| During trial transfer (original litigator) | 100% | Trial | Claim up to and including the day before the transfer |
| During trial transfer (new litigator) | 50% | Trial | Claim for the full trial length |
| Transfer after trial or guilty plea and before sentencing hearing (original litigator) | 100% | Trial, cracked trial or guilty plea as appropriate | Claim for the full trial length, excluding the length of the sentencing hearing |
| Transfer after trial or guilty plea and before sentencing hearing (new litigator) | 10% | Trial | Claim for one day, or for the length of the sentencing hearing if longer than one day |
| Transfer before retrial (original litigator) | 25% | Cracked trial | — |
| Transfer before cracked retrial (new litigator) | 50% | Cracked trial | |
| Transfer before retrial (new litigator) | 50% | Trial | Claim for the full retrial length |
| Transfer during retrial (original litigator) | 25% | Trial | Claim up to and including the day before the transfer |
| Transfer during retrial (new litigator) | 50% | Trial | Claim for the full retrial length |
| Transfer after retrial or cracked retrial and before sentencing hearing (original litigator) | 25% | Trial or cracked trial as appropriate | Claim for the full retrial length, excluding the length of the sentencing hearing |
| Transfer after retrial or cracked retrial and before sentencing hearing (new litigator) | 10% | Trial | Claim for one day, or for the length of the sentencing hearing if longer than one day |

PART 5

FIXED FEES

*General provisions*

**G-74**    14.—(1) All work undertaken by a litigator in a case to which Part 3 applies is included within the fee set out in paragraph 11 except for a defendant uplift as provided for in paragraph 22.

(2) Except as provided under this Part, remuneration for all work undertaken by a litigator in a case to which Part 2 applies is included within the fee set out in Part 2 of this Schedule as appropriate to—

     (a)   the offence for which the assisted person is charged or tried;

     (b)   whether the case is a cracked trial, guilty plea or trial; and

     (c)   the number of pages of prosecution evidence.

*Fees for appeals and committals for sentence hearings*

**G-74a**    15. The fee payable to a litigator instructed in—

     (a)   an appeal against conviction from a magistrates' court;

(b)　an appeal against sentence from a magistrates' court; or

(c)　a sentencing hearing following a committal for sentence to the Crown Court,

is that set out in the table following paragraph 19.

*Fees for hearing subsequent to sentence*

16.—(1) The fee payable to a litigator instructed in relation to a hearing under an enactment listed **G-74b** in sub-paragraph (2) is that set out in the table following paragraph 19.

(2) The enactments are—

(a)　section 1CA of the Crime and Disorder Act 1998 (variation and discharge of orders under section 1C);

(b)　section 155 of the Powers of Criminal Courts (Sentencing) Act 2000 (alteration of Crown Court sentence);

(c)　section 74 of the Serious Organised Crime and Police Act 2005 (assistance by defendant: review of sentence).

*Fees for contempt proceedings*

17.—(1) This paragraph applies to proceedings referred to in section 14(g) of the Act in the **G-75** Crown Court.

(2) Where, in proceedings to which this paragraph applies, the contempt is alleged to have been committed by a person other than a defendant in a case to which this Schedule applies, remuneration for litigators must be at the rate set out in the table following paragraph 19.

(3) Where, in proceedings to which this paragraph applies, the contempt is alleged to have been committed by the defendant in a case to which this Schedule applies, all work undertaken by the litigator is included within—

(a)　the fee payable under Part 2 of this Schedule, or

(b)　in proceedings under paragraph 15 or paragraph 18, the fixed fee set out in the table following paragraph 19.

*Fees for alleged breaches of a Crown Court order*

18.—(1) This paragraph applies to proceedings in the Crown Court against one assisted person **G-75a** arising out of a single alleged breach of an order of the Crown Court.

(3) The fee payable to the litigator in respect of the proceedings to which this paragraph applies is that set out in the table following paragraph 19.

*Fixed Fees*

19. The table following this paragraph sets out the fixed fees payable in relation to the category of work specified in the first column of the table.

Fixed Fees

| Type of proceedings | Paragraph providing for free | Fee payable (£ per proceedings) |
| --- | --- | --- |
| Appeal against sentence from a magistrates' Court | 15 | 155.32 |
| Appeal against conviction from a magistrates' Court | 15 | 349.47 |
| Committal for sentence | 15 | 232.98 |
| Hearing subsequent to sentence | 16 | 155.32 |
| Contempt proceedings (where contempt is alleged to have been committed by a person other than the defendant) | 17(2) | 116.49 |
| Alleged breach of a Crown Court order | 18(2) | 77.66 |

[The table in para. 19 is printed as substituted by the Criminal Legal Aid (Remuneration) ★ (Amendment) Regulations 2014 (S.I. 2014 No. 415). As to its application, see *ante*, G-71.]

*Fees for special preparation*

20.—(1) This paragraph applies in any case on indictment in the Crown Court— **G-76**

(a)　where a documentary or pictorial exhibit is served by the prosecution in electronic form and—

(i)　the exhibit has never existed in paper form; and

(ii)　the appropriate officer does not consider it appropriate to include the exhibit in the pages of prosecution evidence; or

(b) in respect of which a fee is payable under Part 2 (other than paragraph 7), where the number of pages of prosecution evidence, as so defined, exceeds 10,000,

and the appropriate officer considers it reasonable to make a payment in excess of the fee payable under Part 2.

(2) Where this paragraph applies, a special preparation fee may be paid, in addition to the fee payable under Part 2.

(3) The amount of the special preparation fee must be calculated from the number of hours which the appropriate officer considers reasonable—

(a) where sub-paragraph (1)(a) applies, to view the prosecution evidence; and

(b) where sub-paragraph (1)(b) applies, to read the excess pages,

and in each case using the rates specified in the table following paragraph 27.

(4) A litigator claiming a special preparation fee must supply such information and documents as may be required by the appropriate officer in support of the claim.

(5) In determining a claim under this paragraph, the appropriate officer must take into account all the relevant circumstances of the case.

*Discontinuance or dismissal of sent or transferred proceedings*

**G-76a**

21.—(1) This paragraph applies to proceedings which are—

(a) sent for trial to the Crown Court; or

(b) transferred to the Crown Court under—

(i) section 4 of the Criminal Justice Act 1987 (transfer of serious fraud cases); or

(ii) section 53 of the Criminal Justice Act 1991 (transfer of certain cases involving children).

(2) Where proceedings to which this paragraph applies are discontinued by a notice served under section 23A of the Prosecution of Offences Act 1985 (discontinuance of proceedings after accused has been sent for trial) at any time before the prosecution serves its evidence in accordance with the Crime and Disorder Act 1998 (Service of Prosecution Evidence) Regulations 2005 the litigator must be paid 50% of the basic fee for a guilty plea, as specified in the table following paragraph 6, as appropriate to the offence for which the assisted person is charged.

(3) Where proceedings to which this paragraph applies are discontinued by a notice served under section 23A of the Prosecution of Offences Act 1985 (discontinuance of proceedings after accused has been sent for trial) at any time after the prosecution serves its evidence in accordance with the Crime and Disorder Act 1998 (Service of Prosecution Evidence) Regulations 2005, the litigator must be paid a fee calculated in accordance with paragraph 6, or, where appropriate, paragraph 8, as appropriate for representing an assisted person in a guilty plea.

(4) Where an application for dismissal is made under paragraph 2 of Schedule 3 to the Crime and Disorder Act 1998, section 6 of the Criminal Justice Act 1987 or paragraph 5 of Schedule 6 to the Criminal Justice Act 1991, and—

(a) the charge, or charges are dismissed and the assisted person is discharged; or

(b) the case is remitted to the magistrates' court in accordance with paragraph 10(3)(a), 13(2) or 15(3)(a) of Schedule 3 to the Crime and Disorder Act 1998,

the litigator instructed in the proceedings must be paid a fee calculated in accordance with paragraph 6, or where appropriate, paragraph 8, as appropriate for representing an assisted person in a guilty plea.

(5) Sub-paragraph (6) applies to—

(a) a plea and case management hearing that takes place after the prosecution serves its evidence; and

(b) any other hearing that takes place before a plea and case management hearing has taken place, but after the prosecution has served its evidence.

(6) Where, at a hearing to which this paragraph applies—

(a) the prosecution offers no evidence and the assisted person is discharged; or

(b) the case is remitted to the magistrates' court in accordance with paragraph 10(3)(a), 13(2) or 15(3)(a) of Schedule 3 to the Crime and Disorder Act 1998,

the litigator must be paid a fee calculated in accordance with paragraph 6 or where appropriate paragraph 8, as appropriate for representing an assisted person in a guilty plea.

*Defendant uplifts*

**G-77**

22.—(1) Where a litigator represents more than one assisted person in proceedings referred to in paragraph 21(2), (3), (4) or (5), a defendant uplift is payable.

(2) The defendant uplift must be calculated in accordance with the table following this paragraph.

(3) In the table following this paragraph, the total fee means—

(a) the fee specified in sub-paragraph (2) of paragraph 21 where that sub-paragraph applies;

(b) the basic fee (B) specified in the table following paragraph 6, or, where appropriate, the initial fee specified in paragraph 8, where paragraph 21(3), (4) or (5) applies, as appropriate for the circumstances set out in that sub-paragraph; or

(c) where appropriate the fee set out in paragraph 11.

(4) In a case where the representation of one defendant would attract a fixed fee under Part 3 and the representation of one or more of the other defendants would attract a graduated fee under Part 2, the total fee in the table following this paragraph means the fee falling within sub-paragraph (3)(b).

DEFENDANT UPLIFTS

| Total number of defendants represented by litigator | Percentage uplift to total fee |
|---|---|
| 2–4 | 20% |
| 5+ | 30% |

*Warrant for arrest*

23.—(1) This paragraph applies where—

(a) the assisted person fails to attend a hearing;

(b) at that hearing the court issues a warrant for the arrest of the assisted person, pursuant to section 7(1) of the Bail Act 1976 ("the warrant"); and

(c) the case does not proceed in the absence of the assisted person.

(2) Where in a case on indictment the warrant is not executed within three months of the date on which it was issued, the fee payable to the litigator is—

(a) where the warrant is issued at or before the plea and case management hearing, the fee payable for a guilty plea in accordance with paragraph 6 or where appropriate paragraph 8;

(b) where the warrant is issued after the plea and case management hearing but before the trial, the fee payable for a cracked trial in accordance with paragraph 6 or where appropriate paragraph 8, as appropriate to the Class of Offence with which the assisted person is charged; and

(c) where the warrant is issued during the trial, and the trial is aborted as a result, the fee payable for a trial as if the trial had ended on the day the warrant was issued.

(3) Where the warrant is issued during the course of proceedings referred to in paragraph 15 or 18 the fee payable to the litigator is the fee set out in the table following paragraph 19, as appropriate to the type of proceedings.

(4) Sub-paragraph (5) applies where—

(a) a fee has been paid, or is payable, to the litigator in accordance with sub-paragraph (2);

(b) the warrant is executed within 15 months of the date on which it was issued;

(c) the case proceeds after the warrant has been executed; and

(d) the litigator submits a claim for fees for the determination of the litigator's overall remuneration in the case, in accordance with regulation 5.

(5) Where this sub-paragraph applies—

(a) the appropriate officer must deduct the amount paid or payable in accordance with sub-paragraph (2) from the amount payable to the litigator on the final determination of fees in the case; and

(b) if the fee paid or payable in accordance with sub-paragraph (2) is greater than the amount payable to the litigator on the final determination of fees in the case, the appropriate officer may recover the amount of the difference by way of repayment by the litigator.

PART 6

MISCELLANEOUS

*Additional charges*

24.—(1) Where an assisted person is charged with more than one offence on one indictment, the fee payable to the litigator under this Schedule must be based on whichever of those offences the litigator selects. **G-78**

(2) Where a litigator selects one offence, in preference to another offence, under sub-paragraph (1) that selection does not affect the litigator's right to claim any of the fees provided for in Part 5 of this Schedule to which the litigator would otherwise have been entitled.

*Assisted person unfit to plead or stand trial*

**G-78a**   25. Where in any case a hearing is held to determine the question of whether the assisted person is unfit to plead or to stand trial (a "fitness hearing")—

(a)   if a trial on indictment is held, or continues, at any time thereafter, the length of the fitness hearing is included in determining the length of the trial for the calculation of the fee in accordance with Part 2;

(b)   if a trial on indictment is not held, or does not continue, thereafter by reason of the assisted person being found unfit to plead or to stand trial, the litigator must be paid—

(i)   a fee calculated in accordance with paragraph 7 or where appropriate paragraph 9, as appropriate to the combined length of—

(aa)  the fitness hearing; and

(bb)  any hearing under section 4A of the Criminal Procedure (Insanity) Act 1964 (finding that the accused did the act or made the omission charged against him); or

(ii)  a fee calculated in accordance with paragraph 6, or where appropriate paragraph 8, as appropriate, for representing an assisted person in a cracked trial,

whichever the litigator elects; and

(c)   if at any time the assisted person pleads guilty to the indictable offence, the litigator must be paid either—

(i)   a fee calculated in accordance with paragraph 7 or, where appropriate, paragraph 9, as appropriate to the length of the fitness hearing; or

(ii)  a fee calculated in accordance with paragraph 6 or, where appropriate, paragraph 8, as appropriate for representing an assisted person in a guilty plea,

whichever the litigator elects.

*Fees for confiscation proceedings*

**G-79**   26.—(1) This paragraph applies to—

(a)   proceedings under Part 2 of the Proceeds of Crime Act 2002 (confiscation: England and Wales);

(b)   proceedings under section 2 of the Drug Trafficking Act 1994 (confiscation orders); and

(c)   proceedings under section 71 of the Criminal Justice Act 1988 (confiscation orders).

(2) Where this paragraph applies, the appropriate officer may allow work done in the following classes by a litigator—

(a)   preparation, including taking instructions, interviewing witnesses, ascertaining the prosecution case, preparing and perusing documents, dealing with letters and telephone calls, instructing an advocate and expert witnesses, conferences, consultations and work done in connection with advice on appeal;

(b)   attending at court where an advocate is instructed, including conferences with the advocate at court;

(c)   travelling and waiting; and

(d)   writing routine letters and dealing with routine telephone calls.

(3) The appropriate officer must consider the claim, any further particulars, information or documents submitted by the litigator under regulation 5 and any other relevant information and must allow such work as appears to him to have been reasonably done in the proceedings.

(4) Subject to sub-paragraph (3), the appropriate officer must allow fees under this paragraph in accordance with paragraph 27.

(5) The appropriate officer must allow fees in accordance with paragraphs 27 to 29 as appropriate to such of the following grades of fee earner as the appropriate officer considers reasonable—

(a)   senior solicitor;

(b)   solicitor, legal executive or fee earner of equivalent experience; or

(c)   trainee or fee earner of equivalent experience.

*Prescribed fee rates*

**★G-80**   27. Subject to paragraphs 28 and 29, for proceedings in the Crown Court to which paragraph 26 applies the appropriate officer must allow fees for work under paragraph 26(2) at the following prescribed rates—

TABLE 1

| Class of work | Grade of fee earner | Rate | Variations |
|---|---|---|---|
| Preparation | Senior solicitor | £48.36 per hour | £50.87 per hour for a fee earner whose office is situated within the City of London or a London borough |
| | Solicitor, legal executive or fee earner of equivalent experience | £41.06 per hour | £43.12 per hour for a fee earner whose office is situated within the City of London or a London borough |
| | Trainee or fee earner of equivalent experience | £27.15 per hour | £31.03 per hour for a fee earner whose office is situated within the City of London or a London borough |
| Attendance at court where more than one representative instructed | Senior solicitor | £38.55 per hour | |
| | Solicitor, legal executive or fee earner of equivalent experience | £31.03 per hour | |
| | Trainee or fee earner of equivalent experience | £18.71 per hour | |
| Travelling and waiting | Senior solicitor | £22.58 per hour | |
| | Solicitor, legal executive or fee earner of equivalent experience | £22.58 per hour | |
| | Trainee or fee earner of equivalent experience | £11.41 per hour | |

[The table in para. 27 is printed as substituted by the Criminal Legal Aid (Remuneration) ★ (Amendment) Regulations 2014 (S.I. 2014 No. 415). As to its application, see *ante*, G-71.]

*Allowing fees at less than the prescribed rates*

**G-81**   28. In respect of any item of work, the appropriate officer may allow fees at less than the relevant prescribed rate specified in paragraph 27 where it appears to the appropriate officer reasonable to do so having regard to the competence and despatch with which the work was done.

*Allowing fees at more than the prescribed rates*

**G-81a**   29.—(1) Upon a determination the appropriate officer may, subject to the provisions of this paragraph, allow fees at more than the relevant prescribed rate specified in paragraph 27 for preparation, attendance at court where more than one representative is instructed, routine letters written and routine telephone calls, in respect of offences in Class A, B, C, D, G, I, J or K in the Table of Offences.

(2) The appropriate officer may allow fees at more than the prescribed rate where it appears to the appropriate officer, taking into account all the relevant circumstances of the case, that—

(a)   the work was done with exceptional competence, skill or expertise;

(b)   the work was done with exceptional despatch; or

(c)   the case involved exceptional complexity or other exceptional circumstances.

(3) Paragraph 3 of Schedule 1 applies to litigators in respect of proceedings in the Crown Court as it applies to advocates.

(4) Where the appropriate officer considers that any item or class of work should be allowed at more than the prescribed rate, the appropriate officer must apply to that item or class of work a percentage enhancement in accordance with the following provisions of this paragraph.

(5) In determining the percentage by which fees should be enhanced above the prescribed rate the appropriate officer must have regard to—

    (a)   the degree of responsibility accepted by the fee earner;

    (b)   the care, speed and economy with which the case was prepared; and

    (c)   the novelty, weight and complexity of the case.

(6) The percentage above the relevant prescribed rate by which fees for work may be enhanced must not exceed 100%.

(7) The appropriate officer may have regard to the generality of proceedings to which these Regulations apply in determining what is exceptional within the meaning of this paragraph.

**G-81b**    In *R. v. Farrell and Selby* [2007] Costs L.R. 495, it was held in relation to the provisions of paragraph 4 of Part 1 of Schedule 2 to the Criminal Defence Service (Funding) Order 2001 (S.I. 2001 No. 855) for paying enhanced rates to solicitors, (i) it was open to a determining officer to apply different rates of enhancement to different items of work; since a determining officer was required, in deciding on the rate of enhancement, to have regard, *inter alia*, to the "degree of responsibility accepted by the solicitor and his staff", it was permissible for a determining officer to apply a lesser rate of enhancement to work of a routine nature done by Grade B fee earners than that applied to the senior fee earners to whom they reported; (ii) when enhancement was appropriate, a determining officer should first assess what enhanced rate would have been applied if legal aid had been granted prior to October 1, 1994 (the date of commencement of the revised rules as to enhancement introduced by the Legal Aid in Criminal and Care Proceedings (Costs) (Amendment) (No. 3) Regulations 1994 (S.I. 1994 No. 2218)), *viz.* the hourly broad average direct cost rate plus an appropriate uplift for care and conduct, and then he should adjust the resulting figure upwards to allow for subsequent inflation; he should then decide on a rate of enhancement such as would match this figure; where, however, the figure exceeded the maximum enhanced rate under the 2001 order, then the determining officer should apply the maximum enhanced rate. Since the provisions under consideration corresponded to those of paragraph 6 of Schedule 2 to the Criminal Defence Service (Funding) Order 2007 (S.I. 2007 No. 1174) (prior to amendment), it could safely be taken that this decision carried across to that order (prior to amendment) with the effect—as in this case—that, wherever enhanced rates are appropriate, the rate of enhancement is always going to be 100 per cent because the 1994 hourly direct cost plus uplift for care and attention, plus uplift for inflation is always going to exceed twice the current hourly rates, which have remained unchanged for many years. This was confirmed in *R. v. Bowles* [2007] Costs L.R. 514. Whilst the provision for payment at enhanced rates under the 2013 regulations relates only to fees payable under paragraph 26, the provisions of paragraph 29 correspond to paragraph 6 of the unamended Schedule 2, and it would appear that the decision in *Farrell and Selby* will carry across to this paragraph in the same way that it carried across to paragraph 6.

Regulation 6                         SCHEDULE 3

PROCEEDINGS IN THE COURT OF APPEAL

*General provisions*

**G-82**    1.—(1) The provisions of this Schedule apply to proceedings in the Court of Appeal.

(2) In determining fees the appropriate officer must, subject to the provisions of this Schedule—

    (a)   take into account all the relevant circumstances of the case including the nature, importance, complexity or difficulty of the work and the time involved; and

    (b)   allow a reasonable amount in respect of all work actually and reasonably done.

*Claims for fees and disbursements by litigators*

2.—(1) Subject to regulation 31, no claim by a litigator for fees and disbursements in respect of work done in proceedings in the Court of Appeal pursuant to a section 16 determination must be entertained unless the litigator submits it within three months of the conclusion of the proceedings to which it relates.

(2) Subject to sub-paragraph (3), a claim for fees in proceedings in the Court of Appeal must be submitted to the appropriate officer in such form and manner as the appropriate officer may direct

and must be accompanied by the representation order and any receipts or other documents in support of any disbursement claimed.

(3) A claim must—

(a) summarise the items of work done by a fee earner in respect of which fees are claimed according to the classes specified in paragraph 3(1);

(b) state, where appropriate, the dates on which the items of work were done, the time taken, the sums claimed and whether the work was done for more than one assisted person;

(c) specify, where appropriate, the level of fee earner who undertook each of the items of work claimed;

(d) give particulars of any work done in relation to more than one indictment or a retrial; and

(e) specify any disbursements claimed, the circumstances in which they were incurred and the amounts claimed in respect of them.

(4) Where the litigator claims that paragraph 8(1) applies in relation to an item of work, the litigator must give full particulars in support of the claim.

(5) The litigator must specify any special circumstances which the litigator considers should be drawn to the attention of the appropriate officer.

(6) The litigator must supply such further information and documents as the appropriate officer may require.

(7) Where a retrospective section 16 determination has been made under regulations made under section 19 of the Act in respect of any proceedings where an appellant has been successful on appeal and granted a defendant's costs order under section 16(4) of the Prosecution of Offences Act 1985 (defence costs), the litigator must certify that no claim for fees incurred before the retrospective section 16 determination was made has been or will be made from central funds in relation to that work.

*Determination of litigators' fees*

3.—(1) The appropriate officer may allow work done in the following classes by fee earners—    **G-83**

(a) preparation, including taking instructions, interviewing witnesses, ascertaining the prosecution case, advising on plea and mode of trial, preparing and perusing documents, dealing with letters and telephone calls which are not routine, preparing for advocacy, instructing an advocate and expert witnesses, conferences, consultations, views and work done in connection with advice on appeal;

(b) advocacy, including applications for bail and other applications to the court;

(c) attending at court where an advocate is assigned, including conferences with the advocate at court;

(d) travelling and waiting; and

(e) writing routine letters and dealing with routine telephone calls.

(2) The appropriate officer must consider the claim, any further information or documents submitted by the fee earner under paragraph 2 and any other relevant information and must allow—

(a) such work as appears to the appropriate officer to have been reasonably done pursuant to the section 16 determination (including any representation or advice which is deemed to be work done pursuant to that determination) by a fee earner, classifying such work according to the classes specified in sub-paragraph (1) as the appropriate officer considers appropriate; and

(b) such time in each class of work allowed by him (other than routine letters written and routine telephone calls) as the appropriate officer considers reasonable.

(3) The fees allowed in accordance with this Schedule are those appropriate to such of the following grades of litigator as the appropriate officer considers reasonable—

(a) senior solicitor;

(b) solicitor, legal executive or fee earner of equivalent experience; or

(c) trainee or fee earner of equivalent experience.

*Determination of litigators' disbursements*

**4.** The appropriate officer must allow such disbursements claimed under paragraph 2 as appear to    **G-84**
the appropriate officer to have been reasonably incurred, provided that—

(a) if they are abnormally large by reason of the distance of the court or the assisted person's residence or both from the litigator's place of business, the appropriate officer may limit reimbursement of the disbursements to what otherwise would, having regard to all the circumstances, be a reasonable amount; and

(b) the cost of a transcript, or any part thereof, of the proceedings in the court from which the appeal lies obtained otherwise than through the registrar must not be allowed except where the appropriate officer considers that it is reasonable in all the circumstances for such disbursement to be allowed.

*Claims for fees by advocates*

5.—(1) Subject to regulation 31, a claim by an advocate for fees for work done in proceedings in the Court of Appeal pursuant to a section 16 determination must not be entertained unless the advocate submits it within three months of the conclusion of the proceedings to which the section 16 determination relates.

(2) Where the advocate claims that paragraph 9(4) applies in relation to an item of work the advocate must give full particulars in support of his claim.

(3) Subject to sub-paragraph (4), a claim for fees by an advocate in proceedings in the Court of Appeal must be submitted to the appropriate officer in such form and manner as the appropriate officer may direct.

(4) A claim must—

(a) summarise the items of work done by an advocate in respect of which fees are claimed according to the classes specified in paragraph 6(2);

(b) state, where appropriate, the dates on which the items of work were done, the time taken, the sums claimed and whether the work was done for more than one assisted person; and

(c) give particulars of any work done in relation to more than one indictment or a retrial.

(5) The advocate must specify any special circumstances which the advocate considers should be drawn to the attention of the appropriate officer.

(6) The advocate must supply such further information and documents as the appropriate officer may require.

*Determination of advocate's fees*

G-85
6.—(1) The appropriate officer must consider the claim, any further particulars and information submitted by an advocate under paragraph 5 and any other relevant information and must allow such work as appears to the appropriate officer to have been reasonably done.

(2) The appropriate officer may allow any of the following classes of fee to an advocate in respect of work allowed by him under this paragraph—

(a) a basic fee for preparation including preparation for a pre-trial review and, where appropriate, the first day's hearing including, where they took place on that day, short conferences, consultations, applications and appearances (including bail applications), views and any other preparation;

(b) a refresher fee for any day or part of a day during which a hearing continued, including, where they took place on that day, short conferences, consultations, applications and appearances (including bail applications), views at the scene of the alleged offence and any other preparation;

(c) subsidiary fees for—

(i) attendance at conferences, consultations and views at the scene of the alleged offence not covered by paragraph (a) or (b);

(ii) written advice on evidence, plea or appeal or other written work; and

(iii) attendance at pre-trial reviews, applications and appearances (including bail applications and adjournments for sentence) not covered by paragraph (a) or (b).

(3) Where a section 16 determination provides for representation by—

(a) a single advocate other than a QC; or

(b) two advocates other than QC,

and a QC agrees to appear as the single advocate or as a leading junior, that QC must be treated for all the purposes of this Schedule as having been instructed pursuant to that section 16 determination, and the remuneration of the QC must be determined as if the advocate were not a QC.

In connection with this paragraph, see *R. v. Bromige, post,* G-160.

*Litigators' fees for proceedings in the Court of Appeal*

★G-86
7.—(1) For proceedings in the Court of Appeal the appropriate officer must allow fees for work by litigators at the following prescribed rates

| Class of work | Grade of fee earner | Rate | Variations |
|---|---|---|---|
| Preparation | Senior solicitor | £48.36 per hour | £50.87 per hour for a litigator whose office is |

| Class of work | Grade of fee earner | Rate | Variations |
|---|---|---|---|
| | | | situated within the City of London or a London borough |
| | Solicitor, legal executive or fee earner of equivalent experience | £41.06 per hour | £43.12 per hour for a litigator whose office is situated within the City of London or a London borough |
| | Trainee or fee earner of equivalent experience | £26.46 per hour | £31.03 per hour for a litigator whose office is situated within the City of London or a London borough |
| Advocacy | Senior solicitor | £58.40 per hour | |
| | Solicitor | £51.10 per hour | |
| Attendance at court where more than one representative assigned | Senior solicitor | £38.55 per hour | |
| | Solicitor, legal executive or fee earner of equivalent experience | £31.03 per hour | |
| | Trainee or fee earner of equivalent experience | £18.71 per hour | |
| Travelling and waiting | Senior solicitor | £22.58 per hour | |
| | Solicitor, legal executive or fee earner of equivalent experience | £22.58 per hour | |
| | Trainee or fee earner of equivalent experience | £11.41 per hour | |
| Routine letters written and routine telephone calls | | £3.15 per item | £3.29 per item for a litigator whose office is situated within the City of London or a London borough |

(2) In respect of any item of work, the appropriate officer may allow fees at less than the relevant prescribed rate specified in the table following sub-paragraph (1) where it appears to the appropriate officer reasonable to do so having regard to the competence and despatch with which the work was done.

[The table in para. 7 is printed as substituted by the Criminal Legal Aid (Remuneration) ★ (Amendment) Regulations 2014 (S.I. 2014 No. 415). As to its application, see *ante*, G-71.]

*Allowance of litigators' fees at more than the prescribed rate*

8.—(1) Upon a determination of fees the appropriate officer may, subject to the provisions of this **G-87** paragraph, allow fees at more than the relevant prescribed rate specified in paragraph 7 for preparation, advocacy, attendance at court where more than one representative is assigned, routine letters written and routine telephone calls, in respect of offences in Class A, B, C, D, G, I, J or K in the Table of Offences in Part 7 of Schedule 1.

(2) The appropriate officer may allow fees at more than the prescribed rate where it appears to the appropriate officer, taking into account all the relevant circumstances of the case, that—

    (a)  the work was done with exceptional competence, skill or expertise;

    (b)  the work was done with exceptional despatch; or

    (c)  the case involved exceptional complexity or other exceptional circumstances.

(3) Paragraph 3 of Schedule 1 applies to litigators in respect of proceedings in the Court of Appeal as it applies to advocates.

(4) Where the appropriate officer considers that any item or class of work should be allowed at more than the prescribed rate, the appropriate officer must apply to that item or class of work a percentage enhancement in accordance with the following provisions of this paragraph.

(5) In determining the percentage by which fees should be enhanced above the prescribed rate the appropriate officer may have regard to—

    (a) the degree of responsibility accepted by the fee earner;

    (b) the care, speed and economy with which the case was prepared; and

    (c) the novelty, weight and complexity of the case.

(6) The percentage above the relevant prescribed rate by which fees for work may be enhanced must not exceed 100%.

(7) The appropriate officer may have regard to the generality of proceedings to which these Regulations apply in determining what is exceptional within the meaning of this paragraph.

*Advocates' fees for proceedings in the Court of Appeal*

**G-88**
9.—(1) Subject to sub-paragraph 9(4), for proceedings in the Court of Appeal the appropriate officer must allow fees for work by advocates at the following prescribed rates—

JUNIOR COUNSEL

| Type of proceedings | Basic fee | Full day refresher | Subsidiary fees | | |
|---|---|---|---|---|---|
| | | | *Attendance at consultation, conferences and views* | *Written work* | *Attendance at pretrial reviews, applications and other appearances* |
| All appeals | Maximum amount: £545.00 per case | Maximum amount: £178.75 per day | £33.50 per hour, minimum amount: £16.75 | Maximum amount: £58.25 per item | Maximum amount: £110 per appearance |

QC

| Type of proceedings | Basic fee | Full day refresher | Subsidiary fees | | |
|---|---|---|---|---|---|
| | | | *Attendance at consultation, conferences and views* | *Written work* | *Attendance at pretrial reviews, applications and other appearances* |
| All appeals | Maximum amount: £5,400.00 per case | Maximum amount: £330.50 per day | £62.50 per hour, minimum amount: £32.00 | Maximum amount: £119.50 per item | Maximum amount: £257.50 per appearance |

(2) Where an hourly rate is specified in the table following sub-paragraph (1), the appropriate officer must determine any fee for such work in accordance with that hourly rate, provided that the fee determined must not be less than the minimum amount specified.

(3) Where a refresher fee is claimed in respect of less than a full day, the appropriate officer must allow such fee as appears to the appropriate officer reasonable having regard to the fee which would be allowable for a full day.

(4) Where it appears to the appropriate officer, taking into account all the relevant circumstances of the case, that owing to the exceptional circumstances of the case the amount payable by way of fees in accordance with the table following sub-paragraph (1) would not provide reasonable remuneration for some or all of the work the appropriate officer has allowed, the appropriate officer may allow such amounts as appear to the appropriate officer to be reasonable remuneration for the relevant work.

**[The next paragraph is G-91.]**

*Payment of fees*

**G-91**
10.—(1) Having determined the fees payable to a representative in accordance with the terms of

this Schedule, the appropriate officer must notify the representative of the fees payable and authorise payment accordingly.

(2) Where, as a result of any redetermination or appeal made or brought pursuant to paragraph 11, the fees payable under paragraph (1) are altered—

    (a) if they are increased, the appropriate officer must authorise payment of the increase; and

    (b) if they are decreased, the representative must repay the amount of such decrease.

(3) Where the payment of any fees of the representative is ordered under regulation 29(12) or regulation 30(8), the appropriate officer must authorise payment.

*Redeterminations and appeals*

11.—(1) Where a representative is dissatisfied with—         **G-92**

    (a) the fees determined in accordance with the provisions of this Schedule; or

    (b) the decision of the appropriate officer under paragraph 3(3) of Schedule 1,

he may apply to the appropriate officer to redetermine those fees or reclassify the offence, in accordance with the provisions of regulation 28(3) to (9).

(2) Where—

    (a) a representative has made an application to the appropriate officer under sub-paragraph (1); and

    (b) the appropriate officer has given his reasons for a decision under regulation 28(7),

a representative who is dissatisfied with that decision may appeal to a costs judge, in accordance with the provisions of regulation 29(2) to (14).

(3) A representative who is dissatisfied with the decision of a costs judge on an appeal under subparagraph (2) may apply to a costs judge to certify a point of principle of general importance, and the provisions of regulation 30(2) to (8) apply.

| Regulation 8 | SCHEDULE 4 |
|---|---|

RATES PAYABLE FOR THE CLAIMS SPECIFIED IN REGULATION 8

[*Sets out the rates payable for proceedings in a magistrates' court and certain other work to which the 2010* ★**G-92a** *Standard Crime Contract applies (para. 11 was amended by the Criminal Legal Aid (Remuneration) (Amendment) Regulations 2013 (S.I. 2013 No. 2803), reg. 3(1) and (6); and paras 3 to 12 were amended by the Criminal Legal Aid (Remuneration) (Amendment) Regulations 2014 (S.I. 2014 No. 415), reg. 2(4), and Sched. 3 (as to which, see* ante, *G-71)).*]

| Regulation 16 | SCHEDULE 5 |
|---|---|

EXPERTS' FEES AND RATES

| Expert | Non-London – hourly rate unless stated to be a fixed fee | London – hourly rate unless stated to be a fixed fee | |
|---|---|---|---|
| A&E consultant | £100.80 | £108 | **G-92b** |
| Accident reconstruction | £72 | £54.40 | |
| Accountant | £64 | £64 | |
| Accountant (general staff) | £40 | £40 | |
| Accountant (manager) | £86.40 | £86.40 | |
| Accountant (partner) | £115.20 | £115.20 | |
| Anaesthetist | £108 | £72 | |
| Architect | £79.20 | £72 | |
| Back calculations | £144 fixed fee | £151.20 fixed fee | |
| Benefit expert | £72 | £72 | |
| Cardiologist | £115.20 | £72 | |
| Cell telephone site analysis | £72 | £72 | |
| Child psychiatrist | £108 | £72 | |
| Child psychologist | £100.80 | £72 | |
| Computer expert | £72 | £72 | |
| Consultant engineer | £72 | £54.40 | |
| Dentist | £93.60 | £72 | |

| Expert | Non-London – hourly rate unless stated to be a fixed fee | London – hourly rate unless stated to be a fixed fee |
| --- | --- | --- |
| Dermatologist | £86.40 | £72 |
| Disability consultant | £54.40 | £54.40 |
| DNA (testing of sample) | £252 per test | £252 per test |
| DNA (preparation of report) | £72 | £72 |
| Doctor (GP) | £79.20 | £72 |
| Drug expert | £72 | £72 |
| Employment consultant | £54.40 | £54.40 |
| Enquiry agent | £25.60 | £18.40 |
| ENT surgeon | £100.80 | £72 |
| Facial mapping | £108 | £72 |
| Fingerprint expert | £72 | £37.60 |
| Fire investigation | £72 | £54.40 |
| Firearm expert | £72 | £72 |
| Forensic scientist | £90.40 | £72 |
| General surgeon | £108 | £72 |
| Geneticist | £86.40 | £72 |
| GP (records report) | £50.40 fixed fee | £72 fixed fee |
| Gynaecologist | £108 | £72 |
| Haematologist | £97.60 | £72 |
| Handwriting expert | £72 | £72 |
| Interpreter | £28 | £25 |
| Lip reader/Signer | £57.60 | £32.80 |
| Mediator | £100.80 | £100.80 |
| Medical consultant | £108 | £72 |
| Medical microbiologist | £108 | £72 |
| Medical report | £79.20 | £72 |
| Meteorologist | £100.80 | £144 fixed fee |
| Midwife | £72 | £72 |
| Neonatologist | £108 | £72 |
| Neurologist | £122.40 | £72 |
| Neuropsychiatrist | £126.40 | £72 |
| Neuroradiologist | £136.80 | £72 |
| Neurosurgeon | £136.80 | £72 |
| Nursing expert | £64.80 | £64.80 |
| Obstetrician | £108 | £72 |
| Occupational therapist | £54.40 | £54.40 |
| Oncologist | £112 | £72 |
| Orthopaedic surgeon | £115.20 | £72 |
| Paediatrician | £108 | £72 |
| Pathologist | £122.40 | £432 fixed fee |
| Pharmacologist | £97.60 | £72 |
| Photographer | £25.60 | £18.40 |
| Physiotherapist | £64.80 | £64.80 |
| Plastic surgeon | £108 | £72 |

| Expert | Non-London – hourly rate unless stated to be a fixed fee | London – hourly rate unless stated to be a fixed fee |
|---|---|---|
| Process server | £25.60 | £18.40 |
| Psychiatrist | £108 | £72 |
| Psychologist | £93.60 | £72 |
| Radiologist | £108 | £72 |
| Rheumatologist | £108 | £72 |
| Risk assessment expert | £50.40 | £50.40 |
| Speech therapist | £79.20 | £72 |
| Surgeon | £108 | £72 |
| Surveyor | £40 | £40 |
| Telecoms expert | £72 | £72 |
| Toxicologist | £108 | £72 |
| Urologist | £108 | £72 |
| Vet | £72 | £72 |
| Voice recognition | £93.60 | £72 |

[Schedule 5 is printed as substituted by the Criminal Legal Aid (Remuneration) (Amendment) Regulations 2013 (S.I. 2013 No. 2803), reg. 3(1) and (7), and Sched. 1.]

### SCHEDULE 6

#### FEES IN VERY HIGH COST CASES

#### PART 1

#### INTERPRETATION AND APPLICATION

*Interpretation*

1.—(1) In this Schedule—      **G-92c**

  (a) a reference to a level is a reference to that level as defined in the Very High Cost Case contract;

  (b) a reference to a category is a reference to that category as defined in that contract;

  (c) the standard rates apply to work as described in the Very High Cost Case contract Guide; and

  (d) the preliminary hearing, half day and full day rates apply as described in the Very High Cost Case contract Guide.

(2) In this Part—

  (a) "Task List" has the meaning given in the Very High Cost Case contract;

  (b) "parties" means the representative who has signed the Very High Cost Case contract and the Lord Chancellor.

(3) In Table 2, a junior may be either a barrister or a solicitor-advocate.

*Application*

2.—(1) This paragraph makes provision in relation to the application of this Schedule to work  **G-92d** done in a case which is the subject of a Very High Cost Case contract signed by the parties before 2nd December 2013.

(2) Part 2 of this Schedule applies to work done pursuant to any Task List agreed between the parties before 2nd December 2013.

(3) Subject to sub-paragraph (4), Part 3 of this Schedule applies to work done pursuant to any Task List agreed between the parties on or after 2nd December 2013.

(4) Part 2 of this Schedule applies to work done in a case in which—

  (a) the court has set a trial date before 2nd December 2013; and

  (b) that trial date is on or before 31st March 2014.

(5) For the purpose of sub-paragraph (4), any adjournment or postponement of a trial which takes place after the trial date is set must be disregarded.

3. Part 3 of this Schedule applies to work done in a case which is the subject of a Very High Cost Case contract signed by the parties on or after 2nd December 2013.

PART 2

TABLE 1: PREPARATION (HOURLY RATES)

**G-92e**

|  | Category 1 (£) | Category 2 (£) | Category 3 (£) | Category 4 (£) | Standard Rates (£) |
|---|---|---|---|---|---|
| **Litigator** | | | | | |
| Level A | 145.00 | 113.00 | 91.00 | 91.00 | 55.75 |
| Level B | 127.00 | 100.00 | 79.00 | 79.00 | 47.25 |
| Level C | 84.00 | 65.00 | 51.00 | 51.00 | 34.00 |
| Pupil/junior | 45.00 | 36.00 | 30.00 | 30.00 | |
| **Barrister** | | | | | |
| QC | 145.00 | 113.00 | 91.00 | 91.00 | |
| Leading junior | 127.00 | 100.00 | 79.00 | 79.00 | |
| Led junior | 91.00 | 73.00 | 61.00 | 61.00 | |
| Junior alone | 100.00 | 82.00 | 70.00 | 70.00 | |
| 2nd Led junior | 63.00 | 50.00 | 43.00 | 43.00 | |
| **Solicitor Advocate** | | | | | |
| Leading level A | 145.00 | 113.00 | 91.00 | 91.00 | |
| Led level A | 127.00 | 100.00 | 79.00 | 79.00 | |
| Leading level B | 127.00 | 100.00 | 79.00 | 79.00 | |
| Led level B | 104.00 | 86.00 | 66.00 | 66.00 | |
| Level A alone | 131.00 | 109.00 | 88.00 | 88.00 | |
| Level B alone | 113.00 | 95.00 | 75.00 | 75.00 | |
| Second advocate | 63.00 | 50.00 | 43.00 | 43.00 | |

TABLE 2: ADVOCACY RATES

**G-92f**

|  | Preliminary hearing (£) | Half day (£) | Full day (£) |
|---|---|---|---|
| QC | 113.00 | 238.00 | 476.00 |
| Leading junior | 86.00 | 195.00 | 390.00 |
| Led junior | 58.00 | 126.00 | 252.00 |
| Junior alone | 67.00 | 143.00 | 285.00 |
| 2nd Led junior | 34.00 | 64.00 | 128.00 |
| Noting junior | 29.00 | 55.00 | 109.00 |

TABLE 3: ATTENDANCE AT COURT WITH ADVOCATE (HOURLY RATES FOR LITIGATORS)

**G-92g**

|  | £ |
|---|---|
| Level A | 42.25 |
| Level B | 34.00 |
| Level C | 20.50 |

TABLE 4: TRAVELLING, WAITING AND MILEAGE

**G-92h**

|  | £ |
|---|---|
| Travelling (hourly rates) | 25.00 (up to a maximum of 4 hours in one day) |
| Waiting (hourly rates) | 25.00 |
| Mileage | 00.45 per mile |

PART 3

TABLE 1: PREPARATION (HOURLY RATES)

|  | Category 1 (£) | Category 2 (£) | Category 3 (£) | Category 4 (£) | Standard Rates (£) |
|---|---|---|---|---|---|
| **Litigator** |  |  |  |  |  |
| Level A | 101.50 | 79.10 | 63.70 | 63.70 | 39.03 |
| Level B | 88.90 | 70.00 | 55.30 | 55.30 | 33.08 |
| Level C | 58.80 | 45.50 | 35.70 | 35.70 | 24.50 |
| Pupil/junior | 31.50 | 25.20 | 21.00 | 21.00 |  |
| **Barrister** |  |  |  |  |  |
| QC | 101.50 | 79.10 | 63.70 | 63.70 |  |
| Leading junior | 88.90 | 70.00 | 55.30 | 55.30 |  |
| Led junior | 63.70 | 51.10 | 42.70 | 42.70 |  |
| Junior alone | 70.00 | 57.40 | 49.00 | 49.00 |  |
| 2nd Led junior | 44.10 | 35.00 | 30.10 | 30.10 |  |
| **Solicitor Advocate** |  |  |  |  |  |
| Leading level A | 101.50 | 79.10 | 63.70 | 63.70 |  |
| Led level A | 88.90 | 70.00 | 55.30 | 55.30 |  |
| Leading level B | 88.90 | 70.00 | 55.30 | 55.30 |  |
| Led level B | 72.80 | 60.20 | 46.20 | 46.20 |  |
| Level A alone | 91.70 | 76.30 | 61.60 | 61.60 |  |
| Level B alone | 79.10 | 66.50 | 52.50 | 52.50 |  |
| Second advocate | 44.10 | 35.00 | 30.10 | 30.10 |  |

TABLE 2: ADVOCACY RATES

|  | Preliminary hearing (£) | Half day (£) | Full day (£) |
|---|---|---|---|
| QC | 79.10 | 166.60 | 333.20 |
| Leading junior | 60.20 | 136.50 | 273.00 |
| Led junior | 40.60 | 88.20 | 176.40 |
| Junior alone | 46.90 | 100.10 | 199.50 |
| 2nd Led junior | 23.80 | 44.80 | 89.60 |
| Noting junior | 20.30 | 38.50 | 76.30 |

TABLE 3: ATTENDANCE AT COURT WITH ADVOCATE (HOURLY RATES FOR LITIGATORS)

|  | £ |
|---|---|
| Level A | 29.58 |
| Level B | 23.80 |
| Level C | 14.35 |

TABLE 4: TRAVELLING, WAITING AND MILEAGE

|  | £ |
|---|---|
| Travelling (hourly rates) | 25.00 (up to a maximum of 4 hours in one day) |
| Waiting (hourly rates) | 25.00 |
| Mileage | 00.45 per mile |

[Schedule 6 was inserted by the Criminal Legal Aid (Remuneration) (Amendment) Regulations 2013 (S.I. 2013 No. 2803), reg. 3(1) and (8), and Sched. 2. It applies in relation to fees for work undertaken on or after December 2, 2013: *ibid.*, reg. 4.]

## C. REPRESENTATION ORDERS

G-93    Representatives are entitled to claim and be remunerated only for work done in respect of Crown Court proceedings in accordance with the provisions of the schedules to the remuneration regulations: S.I. 2013 No. 435, regs 4, 5 and 9.

### Existence of a valid representation order

G-94    Payment can only be made for work done under a representation order. There is no power under the legislation to make a payment in respect of work actually and reasonably undertaken by counsel in the genuine but mistaken belief that the appropriate order was in existence.

Solicitors are obliged to enclose a copy of the representation order with counsel's instructions, and to inform counsel of any subsequent amendments: *General Criminal Contract: Contract Specification*, Part B, para. 5.4. It is, however, incumbent upon counsel to check whether the appropriate order exists. If it is not with his instructions, then it is his duty, if he seeks to look to the legal aid fund thereafter for remuneration, to see that the appropriate authority is obtained and supplied to him: *Hunt v. East Dorset Health Authority* [1992] 1 W.L.R. 785 at 788 (Hobhouse J.); and *R. v. Welsby* [1998] 1 Cr.App.R. 197, Crown Court (Ebsworth J.) (counsel has a professional duty to ensure that he is covered by appropriate certificate).

### Determining the effective date of a representation order

G-95    The effective date of a representation order for the purposes of determining which regulations apply is the date upon which representation was first granted to counsel's instructing solicitors and not the date of the later representation order under which they instructed counsel: *R. v. Hadley* [2005] Costs L.R. 548.

### Orders made ultra vires

G-96    Representation orders assigning solicitors or counsel which are made *ultra vires* are invalid, and work done under such an order cannot be remunerated. However, where it is possible to construe an order as *intra vires*, that construction should be adopted: *R. v. O'Brien and Oliffe*, 81 Cr.App.R. 25 at 30 (Hobhouse J.). There is no power to backdate a representation order: *R. v. Welsby, ante*; *R. v. Conroy* [2004] Costs L.R. 182.

### Representation by an advocate

G-97    As to when a representation order may include representation by one or more advocates or by a Queen's Counsel, see regulations 16 to 20 of the Criminal Legal Aid (Determinations by a Court and Choice of Representative) Regulations 2013 (S.I. 2013 No. 614) (*ante*, §§ 6-263f *et seq.*).

It is submitted that a leading junior would not be entitled to any remuneration where he acts under a certificate granted for Queen's Counsel. A leading junior who acted under an unamended legal aid certificate granted to cover Queen's Counsel was not covered by the certificate and could not be remunerated under the order or by a defendant's costs order under section 16 of the Prosecution of Offences Act 1985: *R. v. Liverpool Crown Court, ex p. The Lord Chancellor, The Times*, April 22, 1993, DC. However, a Queen's Counsel must be remunerated at the appropriate rate for junior counsel where he agrees to act as a sole advocate or as a leading junior: S.I. 2013 No. 435, reg. 4(7).

### [The next paragraph is G-100.]

### Orders for Queen's Counsel acting alone

G-100    Where prior authority has been obtained to instruct a Queen's Counsel alone, the propriety of the order may not be challenged on the determination of Queen's Counsel's fees unless the solicitor knew or ought reasonably to have known that the purpose for which the authority had been given had failed or become irrelevant or unnecessary before the fees were incurred: S.I. 2013 No. 435, reg. 17(3).

### Work done under the order

The work claimed for must have been done under the order. Work done before the date of **G-101** commencement of the representation order cannot be claimed or allowed: *R. v. Clarke* (1991) Costs L.R. 496. An order cannot be backdated in respect of proceedings in the Crown Court: *R. v. North Staffordshire JJ., ex p. O'Hara* [1994] C.O.D. 248, DC; *R. v. Welsby* [1998] 1 Cr.App.R. 197, Crown Court (Ebsworth J.).

### "Topping up"

An assisted person's solicitor or advocate is prohibited from receiving or being party to the **G-102** making of any payment for work done in connection with the proceedings in respect of which the representation order was made other than payments by the Lord Chancellor or in respect of various specified disbursements: S.I. 2013 No. 435, reg. 9. These provisions are designed to prevent "topping" up of fees, rather than to prevent counsel from receiving payment for private fees incurred before the representation order was granted or *ex gratia* payments from solicitors who wrongly instructed counsel in the mistaken belief that he was covered by a representation order. However, once a representation order has been granted, the prohibition applies to all solicitors and advocates and not merely those persons acting under the representation order: *R. v. Grant* [2006] Costs L.R. 173.

### D. Reasonable Remuneration

The basic principle of remuneration under the former *ex post facto* regime was that counsel **G-103** should receive reasonable remuneration for work actually and reasonably undertaken by him. Assessment of the work undertaken and the remuneration claimed was made in each case after the event by experienced officers appointed by the Lord Chancellor's department and subject to the appellate and expert supervision of costs judges and the High Court.

Graduated fees are calculated by reference to pre-determined fixed fees. Although allowances **G-104** are made for different classes of case and for the length and size of each case, the scheme necessarily embraces a "swings and roundabouts" principle. Save in exceptional cases, graduated fees draw no distinction between straightforward and complex cases of the same length, class and size.

When they were introduced in 1997, it was intended that they would be cost neutral. The extension of fees to cover 25 to 40 day cases represented a diminution in fees for defence work, balanced by an increase in the fees of prosecution counsel who are now subject to a similar scheme. The further extension of the scheme in 2007 to all trials on indictment save for those covered by VHCC contracts was a far remove from its original ambit, and may give rise to some serious underfunding of cases or aspects of cases.

Very High Cost Cases are remunerated by an hourly preparation fee and refreshers which fall within prescribed bands. The categorisation of the class of case, rates of remuneration, refreshers and the number of hours of preparation allowed to counsel must be agreed before the work is undertaken.

### E. Interim Fees and other Pre-assessment Payments

#### (1) Staged payments for preparation in long cases

Where the period from sending to the Crown Court to the conclusion of the proceedings is **G-105** likely to exceed 12 months, a legal representative may apply for staged payments (*i.e.* interim fees for the preparation of a case) in respect of each period of preparation of 100 hours or more undertaken before trial or, in serious fraud cases, before the empanelling of a jury. Preparation in this context is widely defined and includes, *inter alia*, conferences with the defendant, written advice on evidence or plea, legal research and preparation for oral or written submissions: S.I. 2013 No. 435, reg. 20.

**[The next paragraph is G-110.]**

## (2) Interim payment of expenses

**G-110**  A litigator may make a claim for an interim payment of disbursements in accordance with the provisions of regulation 14 of S.I. 2013 No. 435.

## (3) Interim payment pending determination

### Entitlement

**G-111**  In certain circumstances, an advocate may claim an interim payment of 40 per cent of the total claim less any sum already paid: S.I. 2013 No. 435, reg. 19(1). Such payments may only be made where, (a) the basic fee claimed by counsel, or the total costs claimed by a solicitor in a related claim, or the basic fee claimed by counsel in a related claim, exceeds £4,000 (exclusive of VAT); and (b) three months have elapsed from either the date on which the bill is ready to tax or, if earlier, three months after the conclusion of the last of any related proceedings. A bill is deemed to be ready to tax on the date of receipt of the last bill in a related claim. Related claims are claims for costs of solicitors and counsel in the same proceedings acting for the same defendant or acting in related proceedings. Related proceedings are those involving the same defendant which are prepared, heard, or dealt with together, or proceedings involving more than one defendant arising out of the same incident so that the defendants are charged, tried, or disposed of together: S.I. 2013 No. 435, reg. 18.

There is no right of re-determination or appeal against the interim award: S.I. 2013 No. 435, reg. 19(2).

### Claims

**G-112**  An advocate may submit a claim for interim payment where, (a) he is entitled to such payment; (b) no payment has been made; (c) six months have elapsed since the conclusion of the proceedings against the defendant he represented; and (d) counsel has submitted a proper claim under regulation 4(3) (three-month time limit for the submission of claims): S.I. 2013 No. 435, reg. 18(2)–(6).

## (4) Hardship payments

**G-113**  A discretionary hardship payment may be made on proof of the likelihood of financial hardship. The proof required is left to the discretion of taxing officers. Counsel are advised to contact their circuit representative, before submitting a claim, to determine the form of proof likely to be acceptable. The sum paid cannot exceed the amount which is likely to be eventually paid, but payment will not be made for sums less than £5,000. Claims may only be made, (a) at least six months after the legal representative was first instructed, and (b) where final payment is unlikely to be made within the next three months by reason of which the applicant is likely to suffer financial hardship: S.I. 2013 No. 435, reg. 21.

## (5) Obligations to submit claims

**G-114**  Any person who has received a staged, interim or hardship payment must submit a claim under the appropriate regulation for final determination of his overall remuneration: S.I. 2013 No. 435, reg. 22(1). Any such payment will be set off against the overall remuneration on final determination and excess payments can be recovered: *ibid.*, reg. 22(2).

## F. GRADUATED FEES

### (1) Introduction

**G-115**  As to the introduction of the scheme for graduated fees, see *ante*, G-2.

The scheme determines the taxation and payment of fees for advocacy and preparation in something of a mechanistic or formulaic way: *Meeke and Taylor v. Secretary of State for Constitutional Affairs* [2006] Costs L.R. 1. It is a comprehensive scheme which must be applied by examining the particular wording of the legislation: *R. v. Kemp*, X15 363/99. There is no "equity" in the regulations; they have to be construed and given effect however hard the result might be: *R. v. Riddell*, X3, SCCO 319/98, even where payment is morally due: see *R. v. Dhaliwal* [2004] Costs L.R. 689. Conversely, as was pointed out in *R. v. Chubb* [2002] Costs L.R. 333:

"As has often been said, when the graduated fee system was introduced, it was on a principle which was expressed as being 'swings and roundabouts'. It is perfectly reasonable where the system operates against the Lord Chancellor's Department, that an appeal should be launched. There are many occasions, in my experience, when the graduated fee system has operated very much to the disadvantage of members of the bar and there is no reason why the bar should not take advantage when it operates in their favour."

References within this section to paragraphs are references to paragraphs in Schedule 1 to S.I. 2013 No. 435 (unless otherwise stated).

**[The next paragraph is G-118.]**

**(2) Cases on indictment**

### Scheduled offences

A "case" includes proceedings in the Crown Court against any one assisted person on one or **G-118** more counts of a single indictment: S.I. 2013 No. 435, Sched. 1, para. 1(1). Where counts or defendants are severed and dealt with separately, then each separate indictment is a separate case. Conversely, indictments which are joined should be treated as one case: GFSG: A1, A2: *R. v. Chubb* [2002] Costs L.R. 333. A "case" should not be confused with a trial; there may be two trials in one case: *R. v. Bond* [2005] Costs L.R. 533.

All cases on indictment now fall within the scheme unless specifically excluded: S.I. 2013 No. 435, Sched. 1, para. 2. As to pre-indictment hearings, see *post*, G-121a.

In *R. v. Hussain* [2011] Costs L.R. 689, after one defendant was committed for trial and a plea and case management hearing was conducted in relation to a single-count indictment, a second defendant was committed for trial, as a result of which a second indictment was preferred which included the allegation against the first defendant in the single-count indictment, and the defendants were in due course tried on the second indictment. It was held that: (i) whereas paragraph 1(1) of Schedule 2 to S.I. 2013 No. 435 (*ante*, G-69) provides that "'case' means proceedings in the Crown Court against any one assisted person—(a) on one or more counts of a single indictment ...", there were two "cases"; (ii) in respect of the second indictment, the solicitors were entitled to a graduated fee for trial, together with the appropriate uplift for representing more than one defendant; and (iii) in respect of the first indictment, they were entitled to a graduated fee for a cracked trial. The costs judge observed that whilst it might be thought that the solicitors had obtained something of a windfall for, in layman's terms, this was really only one case, the regulations must be applied mechanistically.

### Table of offences

The table of offences in Schedule 1 to S.I. 2013 No. 435 contains offences listed by statute with **G-119** a description set out only for convenience. The statutory reference includes every offence contrary to that reference, whether or not the description of the offence is apt to describe the offence actually charged: S.I. 2013 No. 435, Sched. 1, para. 3(1)(e). Cases which do not appear in the table of offences are deemed to fall within Class H: S.I. 2013 No. 435, Sched. 1, para. 3(1)(a). An advocate who is dissatisfied with that deemed classification may apply to the appropriate officer to reclassify the offence: S.I. 2013 No. 435, Sched. 1, para. 3(2).

The offences are divided into the following classes:

| | |
|---|---|
| Class A | Homicide and related grave offences |
| Class B | Offences involving serious violence or damage and serious drug offences |
| Class C | Lesser offences involving violence or damage, and less serious drug offences |
| Class D | Sexual offences and offences against children |
| Class E | Burglary and going equipped |
| Class F | Other offences of dishonesty including those where the value does not exceed £30,000 |
| Class G | Other more serious offences of dishonesty including those where the value exceeds £30,000 but does not exceed £100,000 |

| Class H | Miscellaneous lesser offences |
|---------|-------------------------------|
| Class I | Offences against public justice and similar offences |
| Class J | Serious sexual offences |
| Class K | The most serious offences of dishonesty and other offences where the value exceeds £100,000 |

★  Where counts of differing classes appear in the same indictment, the fee is based upon the class selected by the advocate: S.I. 2013 No. 435, Sched. 1, para. 27(1). Once counsel has chosen which count to use as the basis of a claim, that choice is irrevocable: *R. v. Buoniauto*, X25, SCCO 483/2000. Where an indictment is drafted in such a way that the offence charged could fall into either of two different classes in the table of offences, the advocate may choose the class to which the case is to be assigned for the purpose of calculating the fees payable: *Lord Chancellor v. Ahmed* [2014] Costs L.R. 21, QBD (Andrews J.). Where two or more advocates appear for the same defendant, the grounds of each claim must be the same: *R. v. Powell*, X8, SCTO 336/98.

The offences are summarised and listed alphabetically by statute: *post*, G-168 *et seq.*

★G-120  Conspiracy, incitement or attempt to commit an offence fall within the same class as the substantive offence: S.I. 2013 No. 435, Sched. 1, para. 3(1)(b). Conspiracy to defraud at common law does not appear in the table of offences. It will accordingly fall within Class H: S.I. 2013 No. 435, Sched. 1, para. 3(1)(a). Where the appropriate class depends upon a value, the lower value is presumed unless the claimant "proves otherwise to the satisfaction of the appropriate authority": S.I. 2013 No. 435, Sched. 1, para. 3(1)(c). This may be done by extracts from the indictment or witness statements. Values relating to offences taken into consideration should be excluded from the computation: GFSG: E10. The proof required is proof on a balance of probabilities, and the appropriate officer must take a common sense approach in deciding whether the burden has been discharged: *R. v. Garness* [2014] Costs L.R. 201.

In *R. v. O'Donnell and Fawley* [2012] Costs L.R. 431, it was held that the scheme is mechanistic and that there is no discretion for the court to say that, because the defendants may have been shown to have committed offences in a different class, which would attract a higher fee, it is permissible to reclassify the offence actually charged accordingly.

### The calculation of values

G-121  The property values of each count falling within the same class may be aggregated, provided the same property is not counted twice: S.I. 2013 No. 435, Sched. 1, para. 3(1)(d). However, offences taken into consideration are excluded from the calculation, even where it is agreed that the counts on the indictment are to be treated merely as sample counts: *R. v. Knight*, X35, SCCO 34/2003.

In *R. v. Wei* [2010] Costs L.R. 846, it was held that "value", for the purposes of paragraph 3 of Schedule 2 to S.I. 2013 No. 435 and the table of offences in Part 7 of Schedule 1 (*ante*, G-68, G-70; *post*G-168 *et seq.*), must, in the context of an offence of dishonesty, such as possession of articles for use in fraud, mean the value of the dishonest enterprise, and not the value of the particular articles. The court said that the obvious intention was to provide greater remuneration for more complex and lengthy cases within the confines of the formulaic graduated fee system.

### Preliminary hearings

G-121a  In *Lord Chancellor v. Shapiro* [2010] Costs L.R. 769, QBD (Sweeney J.), it was held that for a first hearing in the Crown Court of a case sent for trial under section 51 of the CDA 1998 (§ 1-24 in the main work) to fall within the graduated fee scheme there must be an indictment in existence at the time. It was said that since the order makes no specific provision for such hearings, it follows that they fall to be remunerated as part of the basic fee if there is an indictment in existence at the time, and, if there is not, there is no provision for payment; in particular, the order making no provision for *ex post facto* taxation (except in strictly limited circumstances), there is no power to make a payment on an *ex post facto* basis. For criticism of this decision, see the commentary in CLW/10/38/8.

### Pleas and directions hearings and pre-trial reviews

G-122  Pleas and directions hearings are not defined under the regulations. Accordingly if a matter is listed as a pleas and directions hearing, it will be so treated. There is nothing to prevent a pleas and directions hearing from being adjourned, or there being more than one or even a series of such hearings: *R. v. Beecham*, X11, QBD (Ebsworth J.). However, the listing of the case is not necessarily determinative. For example, although a case may be listed as a pleas and directions hearing, if a defendant pleads at that hearing and is sentenced, it cannot be said that a pleas and directions hearing has taken place: *R. v. Johnson*, SCCO 51/06. Pleas and directions hearings (other than those which form part of the main hearing) and pre-trial reviews are payable at a fixed rate. Any pre-trial hearings to determine, for example, the admissibility of evidence, fall outside the main hearing and are remunerated as standard appearance fees: *R. v. Rahman*, X21, SCCO 119/2000; *R. v. Carter*, X18, SCCO 384/99.

Fees are payable for preparing and filing a plea and case management questionnaire where no oral hearing takes place: S.I. 2013 No. 435, Sched. 1, para. 12(3). Fees for oral hearings which fall within the definition of a standard appearance are deemed to be included in the basic fee: see *post*, G-129. Plea and case management hearings which are not standard appearances are remunerated according to the fees set out in the table following paragraph 24: S.I. 2013 No. 435, Sched. 1, para. 12(2). As to standard appearances, see *post*, G-129.

### The start of the main hearing

In *Lord Chancellor v. Ian Henery Solicitors Ltd* [2012] Costs L.R. 205, QBD (Spencer J.), it was **G-123** held that when considering the question whether, and if so on what date, a case has proceeded to trial, the following principles apply: (i) whether or not a jury have been sworn is not conclusive; (ii) there can be no doubt that a trial will have begun if the jury have been sworn, the case has been opened, and evidence has been called; (iii) a trial will also have begun if the jury have been sworn and the case has been opened to any extent, even if only for a few minutes (*Meeke and Taylor v. Secretary of State for Constitutional Affairs* [2006] Costs L.R. 1, QBD (David Clarke J.)); (iv) a trial will not have begun, even if the jury have been sworn (and whether or not the defendant has been put in the charge of the jury), if there has been no trial in a meaningful sense, *e.g.* because, before the case can be opened, the defendant pleads guilty (*R. v. Brook* [2004] Costs L.R. 178, *R. v. Baker and Fowler* [2004] Costs L.R. 693, and *R. v. Sanghera* [2008] Costs L.R. 823); (v) a trial will have begun, even if there has been no empanelment of a jury, if submissions have begun in a continuous process resulting in the empanelling of a jury, the opening of the case, and the leading of evidence (considering *R. v. Wembo* [2011] Costs L.R. 926, *R. v. Bullingham* [2011] Costs L.R. 1078, and an unreported decision of Mitting J. in December, 2005, in the case of *R. v. Smith*); (vi) if, in accordance with modern practice in long cases, a jury have been selected but not sworn, then provided the court is dealing with substantial matters of case management it may well be that the trial has begun in a meaningful sense; and (vii) where there is likely to be any difficulty in deciding whether a trial has begun, and if so when it began, the judge should be prepared, upon request, to indicate his view on the matter for the benefit of the parties and the determining officer, in the light of these principles.

In *R. v. Budai* [2011] Costs L.R. 1073, the costs judge acknowledged the principle in (v), *ante*, but held that this did not cover a case where, on the day listed for trial, all that was done was that interpreters were sworn, a potential panel of 18 jurors was selected (prior to their being sent away until the following day to assess their availability for a lengthy trial) and there was a direction made regarding the amendment of the indictment. On the other side of the line are *R. v. Wembo*, *ante* (where, immediately prior to a jury being empanelled, counsel had attended two days of hearings that related to a witness anonymity order, those days had formed part of the trial for the purposes of calculating the graduated fee); and *R. v. Bullingham*, *ante* (where a jury had not been empanelled, but the judge directed that there should be a *voire dire* to determine the admissibility of evidence which the prosecution wanted to open to the jury, and there was such a *voire dire* at which evidence was called, the trial started with the giving of that direction even though the effect of the ruling on the *voire dire* was that the prosecution decided to accept pleas to lesser offences in consequence of which the defendant pleaded guilty and there was no requirement for a jury). The reasoning in *Bullingham* was expressly approved in *Lord Chancellor v. Ian Henery Solicitors Ltd*, *ante*, but it is submitted that the result is difficult to justify, not least for its failure to give effect to the obvious purpose of paragraph 13 of Schedule 1 (*ante*, § G-48), which the costs judge did not even refer to. Sub-paragraph (1)(d) expressly contemplates that a hearing as to the admissibility of evidence may take place before the main hearing of a case (trial or cracked trial), and if it does, it is to be remunerated in accordance with that paragraph. The decision of the costs judge effectively emasculates this by converting the admissibility hearing into the main hearing. See also the commentary in CLW/12/01/14.

The start of a preparatory hearing is the commencement of the trial for the purposes of the regulations: *R. v. Jones*, X17, SCCO 527/99: GFSG: B8, B8A.

### Calculating the length of the main hearing

G-124     Length of the main hearing means the number of days of the main hearing together with the number of days of any *Newton* hearing in relation to the assisted person whose trial is under consideration: S.I. 2013 No. 435, Sched. 1, paras 1(1) and 2(8). Thus, where counsel successfully submits that there is no case to answer, the main hearing ceases, despite the fact that the trial may continue against the co-defendants: *Secretary of State for Constitutional Affairs v. Stork*, *The Times*, October 7, 2005, QBD (Gray J.). This can lead to harsh anomalies, as where a defendant pleads guilty shortly after a jury have been sworn during an estimated three-week trial; despite preparation for a three-week trial, counsel will be remunerated as for a one day trial: *Meeke and Taylor v. Secretary of State for Constitutional Affairs*, *ante*. Non-sitting days cannot be included: *R. v. Nassir*, X13, SCCO 703/98. Where a jury are sworn, but discharged the same day for some reason other than the private or professional convenience of counsel, with a new jury sworn the following day, there may be sufficient continuity to conclude that the trial did in fact proceed, and start of the trial is the date on which the first jury were sworn: *R. v. Gussman*, X14, SCTO 40/99, but part of a day counts as a whole day: S.I. 2013 No. 435, Sched. 1, para. 4. Applications relating to abuse of process, disclosure and witness summonses are to be treated as part of the main hearing where they are heard during the main hearing: S.I. 2013 No. 435, Sched. 1, para. 13(2). The length of a fitness hearing which precedes a trial on indictment must also be included in determining the length of the trial: S.I. 2013 No. 435, Sched. 1, para. 31(a). Confiscation proceedings are excluded from the computation: S.I. 2013 No. 435, Sched. 1, para. 14(2).

Where, during the currency of a trial, there had been a day when one juror could not attend, but the judge had directed all counsel to attend in order that agreement should be reached as to how to reduce one section of the evidence, counsel was not entitled to count that day as a day of the trial; although the judge had indicated he would be available in case there was some issue on which agreement could not be reached, it had not been necessary to involve the judge and the case had not been called on in court; counsel was, however, entitled to a non-effective hearing fee for that day (under Sched. 1, para. 16 (*ante*, G-51)); the case was listed for that day, counsel had been obliged to attend, but in fact the trial did not proceed on that day: *R. v. Budai*, *ante*.

### Fees for contested trials

G-125     The calculation of any graduated fee involves arcane formulae: S.I. 2013 No. 435, Sched. 1, para. 4. To calculate the correct fee, the appropriate figures should be substituted from the tables of fees and uplifts: S.I. 2013 No. 435, Sched. 1, para. 5.

### [The next paragraph is G-129.]

### Standard appearances

G-129     Standard appearances are defined in S.I. 2013 No. 435 as appearances which do not form part of the main hearing, and constitute (i) plea and case management hearings (other than the first such hearing); (ii) pre-trial reviews; (iii) the hearing of a case listed for plea which is adjourned for trial; (iv) custody time limit, bail and other applications; (v) mentions, including applications relating to the date of trial; (vi) a sentencing hearing other than one following a committal for sentence to the Crown Court, or one where sentence has been deferred under the PCC(S)A 2000, s.1, or one where the advocate has been instructed solely for the purposes of entering a plea in mitigation under paragraph 34 of Schedule 1; (vii) a hearing, whether contested or not, relating to breach of bail, failure to surrender to bail or execution of a bench warrant; and (viii) any hearing (except a trial, plea and case management hearing, appeal against conviction or sentence, sentencing hearing following a committal for sentence to the Crown Court, or proceedings arising out of an alleged breach of an order of the Crown Court) which is listed but cannot proceed because of the failure of the assisted person or a witness to attend, the unavailability of a pre-sentence report or other good reason: Sched. 1, para. 1(1). Under S.I. 2013 No. 435, an advocate's fees payable for the first plea and case management hearing or pre-trial review and up to four standard appearances are deemed to be included in the basic fee and are not subject to separate remuneration: Sched. 1, para. 12 (*ante*, G-47). The fifth and subsequent standard appearances are remunerated as set out in the table following paragraph 24: *ibid.*, para. 12(2).

Where an advocate made three appearances at non-effective hearings, the first two of which had been listed as a plea and case management hearing and the third of which had been listed for an anticipated plea of guilty to be taken, where the third hearing was ineffective because the defendant had absconded, and where a bench warrant had been issued which remained outstanding, paragraph 12(1) did not apply as no basic fee had become payable (and thus it did not prevent payment in respect of the three appearances); payment could be made under paragraph 12(2); there was no authority in the legislation for a statement in the graduated fee scheme guidance that suggested that no fee could be paid so long as a bench warrant was outstanding: *R. v. Metcalf* [2010] Costs L.R. 646; and, to similar effect, see *R. v. Muoka* [2013] Costs L.R. 523.

### Trial of Bail Act offences

The trial of any Bail Act 1976 offence in the Crown Court entitles counsel who attends to apply  **G-130** for a new "trial" fee for the contested trial or plea: *R. v. Shaw* [2005] Costs L.R. 326; *R. v. Despres* [2005] Costs L.R. 750.

### Sendings to the Crown Court

Where cases are sent to the Crown Court under the CDA 1998, s.51, and are discontinued  **G-131** before the prosecution serve their evidence, the advocate is entitled to 50 per cent of the fee calculated on the basis of a guilty plea: S.I. 2013 No. 435, Sched. 1, para. 22(2), together with an additional 20 per cent of that fee for each additional person represented: para. 22(8)(a). Once the prosecution have served their evidence, discontinuance, the offering of no evidence at a pleas and case management hearing, or the remitting of the case to the magistrates' court at such hearing because the indictment contains no indictable offence, is treated for the purposes of calculating the relevant fee as if each was a guilty plea: *ibid.*, para. 22(3) and (5). An advocate representing more than one person in the latter circumstances is entitled to 20 per cent of the appropriate basic fee for each additional person he represents: para. 22(8)(b).

### Dismissal hearings

Where a successful application for dismissal is made under the CDA 1998, Sched. 3, para. 2,  **G-132** with the result that the case is dismissed or remitted back to the magistrates' court, the fee is calculated as if the matter had been disposed of by a guilty plea, together with an attendance fee based upon the total number of days and half days occupied by the hearing: S.I. 2013 No. 435, Sched. 1, para. 22(6) and (7). A full day's hearing is any court day which begins before and ends after the luncheon adjournment: para. 22(6)(a). An advocate representing more than one person in such circumstances is entitled to 20 per cent of the appropriate basic fee for each additional person he represents: para. 22(8)(b).

### Transfers

A case will be "transferred" to a new litigator for the purposes of paragraph 13(2)(a) of Schedule  **G-133** 2 to the Criminal Legal Aid (Remuneration) Regulations 2013 (S.I. 2013 No. 435) (*ante*, G-73b) where the representation order has been amended to substitute the new litigator and the new litigator has agreed to accept the instructions and has carried out a conflicts check; an amended representation order will not be effective to transfer a case to a new litigator who has not carried out a conflicts check because it is incumbent upon any firm of solicitors to carry out such a check before accepting instructions and, therefore, in such circumstances, it cannot be said that the new litigator has been "instructed" until that duty has been discharged: *Tuckers Solicitors v. Lord Chancellor* [2014] Costs L.R. 29, QBD (Andrews J.) (considering a corresponding provision in the Criminal Defence Service (Funding) Order 2007 (S.I. 2007 No. 1174), and observing that, in practice, it would be desirable if, when the Crown Court sends information to the putative new litigator, it were to include the indictment, witness list and, if available, the case summary, rather than leaving it to the former solicitors to do so).

In *R. v. Rayan* [2010] Costs L.R. 969, it was held that, for the purposes of paragraph 13(2) of Schedule 2 to S.I. 2013 No. 435 (*ante*, G-73b), which provides that where a case is transferred from one litigator to another, the original litigator is entitled to 25 per cent of the cracked trial fee where the transfer took place "up to and including plea and case management hearing" or a fee of 75 per cent of the cracked trial fee for a "before trial transfer", the reference to a "plea and case management hearing" must be taken to be a reference to an effective such hearing. An effective hearing, it was held, requires there to have been a plea, and for case management directions of sufficient substance to have been made such that the hearing could be described as a plea and case management hearing.

### Retrials

**G-134**    A standard graduated fee is paid for retrials, where the same advocate appears, subject to the following discounts based upon the time elapsed from the conclusion of the first trial to the start of the retrial: S.I. 2013 No. 435, para. 2(3):

| | |
|---|---|
| 30 per cent | retrial starts within one month |
| 20 per cent | retrial starts after one month |
| 40 per cent | retrial is cracked or becomes a guilty plea within one month |
| 25 per cent | retrial is cracked or becomes a guilty plea after one month. |

No discounts are applied where the advocate who conducts the retrial is not the advocate who conducted the original trial: *ibid.*, para. 2(5) and (6).

Where the case was sent to the Crown Court on the election of the defendant where the magistrates' court had determined the case to be suitable for summary trial, and the new trial becomes a cracked trial or guilty plea, the advocate will receive a graduated fee for the first trial and a fixed fee for the second trial: S.I. 2013 No. 435, Sched. 1, para. 2(4). This also applies where the trial advocate is different at the second trial: S.I. 2013 No. 435, Sched. 1, para. 2(5) and (7).

**G-134a**    Where a defence advocate was initially retained privately but, the jury at the first trial having been unable to agree on a verdict, was then instructed for the retrial under a representation order, the defendant having run out of money, and where the defendant was acquitted at the retrial with a defendant's costs order being made in his favour, no payment could be made under the defendant's costs order out of central funds in respect of work done in preparation for the retrial between the date of the first trial and the grant of the representation order; the graduated fee payable for a retrial under the Criminal Defence Service (Funding) Order 2001 (S.I. 2001 No. 855) was intended to allow for all preparation carried out for that retrial; to have authorised the payment would have resulted in a double payment out of public funds effectively in respect of the same work: *R. v. Long* [2009] Costs L.R. 151. The result would be the same under S.I. 2013 No. 435.

In *Lord Chancellor v. Purnell and McCarthy* [2010] Costs L.R. 81, QBD (Sir Christopher Holland), where a full trial had been conducted in which the jury had acquitted the defendant on the main charge of murder, but had been unable to agree on an alternative charge of manslaughter and on another count of violent disorder, where a date for a retrial had been fixed, where the prosecution eventually decided to offer no evidence, and where it was clear that counsel had not, meanwhile, been standing by awaiting a decision by the prosecution whether to proceed (it was not the case that the matter had been adjourned after trial to allow the prosecution time to decide whether they intended to proceed further) but, on the contrary, had begun preparing for the retrial, it was held that counsel were entitled to a graduated fee for a "cracked trial". They had every reason to expect and prepare for a retrial, as the case was serious and had so far featured a finding by at least three jurors that manslaughter had been proved against the defendant to the criminal standard. Under the 2001 order, there was no provision for any percentage reduction of the fee in such cases. This, however, has since been remedied: see now S.I. 2013 No. 435, Sched. 1, para. 2(2) and (3) (*ante*, G-40).

In *R. v. Seivwright* [2011] Costs L.R. 327, it was held that paragraph 13(1) of Schedule 2 to S.I.

2013 No. 435 (*ante*, G-73b) applies only where the retrial follows a trial and an order has been made for a retrial following appeal or where a jury have failed to reach a verdict, and that "retrial" for this purpose means a new trial which is not part of the same procedural and temporal matrix as the first trial. It was said that whilst this conclusion might be thought to conflict with the Litigator Graduated Fee Scheme Guidance published by the Legal Services Commission, that was merely guidance and not a source of law that was binding. On the facts, it was held that where the trial had commenced on a Monday, the jury had been discharged on the Thursday, the matter was listed for mention on the Friday when it was agreed that a new jury would be empanelled on the following Monday, and where they were so empanelled, there was but one trial.

In *R. v. Nettleton* [2014] Costs L.R. 387, it was held that where the question arises whether "an ★ order [was] made for a retrial", this is not to be confined to cases where one jury are discharged following a disagreement and an order for a new trial is made before a different jury, but it does not extend to every interruption to the trial process, even if it involves the discharge of one jury and the empanelment of a fresh jury. The question is whether the new proceeding was part of the same procedural and temporal matrix as the prior proceeding (see *Seivwright, ante*). If there is a continuous process, even a long gap will not necessarily render the second proceeding a "retrial", and the fact that additional evidence has been served by the prosecution, including from one or more new witnesses, will not *per se* render the new proceeding a retrial. In this case, it was held that it was clear that there had been a trial and a retrial where the jury at the original hearing had been discharged following the arrest of the judge, and there had then been a four-month gap before the second proceeding began with a new judge, new jury and, in the case of some defendants, new counsel.

## Guilty pleas

S.I. 2013 No. 435 defines a guilty plea as a case on indictment which is disposed of without trial   **G-135** because of the guilty plea, and is not a cracked trial: Sched. 1, para. 1(1). Cases which result in a *Newton* hearing are excluded: *ibid.*, para. 2(8)(c); and see *post*, G-147.

The graduated fee for guilty pleas is calculated by reference to the basic fee, together with the appropriate evidence uplift per page as set out in the table of fees and uplifts: S.I. 2013 No. 435, Sched. 1, paras 7 and 8 (and Table A).

Graduated fees for guilty pleas under Part 3 of Schedule 1 to S.I. 2013 No. 435 no longer apply to cases committed to the Crown Court on the election of the defendant where the magistrates' court determined that the case was suitable for summary trial: S.I. 2013 No. 435, Sched. 1, para. 6.

In *R. v. Agbobu* [2009] Costs L.R. 374, it was held that even though a case may not be a "guilty plea" within the definition in paragraph 1(1) of Schedule 2 to S.I. 2013 No. 435 (*ante*, G-69), paragraph 21(4) of Part 3 of that schedule (*ante*, G-76a) nevertheless provides that "where an application for dismissal is made ... and—(a) the charge, or charges are dismissed and the assisted person is discharged; ... the litigator instructed in the proceedings must be paid a fee calculated in accordance with paragraph 6, or where appropriate, paragraph 8, as appropriate for representing an assisted person in a guilty plea". Accordingly, the fee payable for a litigator representing a defendant against whom charges were dismissed was that payable for a guilty plea and not a cracked trial.

## Cracked trials

A cracked trial is a case on indictment in which (a) a plea and case management hearing takes   **G-136** place and (i) the case does not proceed to trial (whether by reason of pleas of guilty or for other reasons) or the prosecution offer no evidence; and (ii) either (aa) in respect of one or more counts to which the assisted person pleaded guilty, he did not so plead at the plea and case management hearing; or (bb) in respect of one or more counts which did not proceed, the prosecution did not, before or at the plea and case management hearing, declare an intention of not proceeding with them; or (b) the case is listed for trial without a plea and case management hearing taking place: S.I. 2013 No. 435, Sched. 1, para. 1(1) (the definition is defective in that in (b) there is no reference to the case not proceeding to trial (read literally it would cover cases that go to trial where no plea and case management hearing took place)). The rationale for the cracked trial fee is that it provides some element of compensation for the loss of refreshers and trial length increments which otherwise would have been payable: *R. v. Frampton* [2005] Costs L.R. 527. Graduated fees for guilty pleas under Part 3 of Schedule 1 to S.I. 2013 No. 435 no longer apply to cases committed to the Crown Court on the election of the defendant where the magistrates' court determined that the case was suitable for summary trial: S.I. 2013 No. 435, Sched. 1, para. 6.

The essence of a cracked trial is that after the conclusion of a pleas and directions hearing there are still counts on which the prosecution and defence do not agree so that a trial remains a real possibility: *R. v. Minster*, X23, SCTO 647/99; *R. v. Mohammed*, X27, SCCO 210/2000. A case listed for a plea and directions hearing is ultimately defined by what actually happens at that hearing. If a defendant pleads guilty at what is listed as a plea and directions hearing, the plea obviates the need for such a hearing. Accordingly, an advocate is entitled to a fee for a cracked trial: *R. v. Johnson* [2006] Costs L.R. 852 (*sed quaere*, as this flies in the face of the definition of a "cracked trial": see (a), *ante*). Where an indictment containing two counts was listed for trial following a plea and directions hearing, but the defendant pleaded guilty to one count, which was acceptable to the prosecution, whereupon the case was put back for sentence, and where, at the adjourned hearing, a formal not guilty verdict was entered on the other count and where the defendant was represented by different counsel on the two occasions, it was counsel who represented him on the first occasion who was entitled to the "cracked trial" fee as what happened on that occasion came within the definition of a "cracked trial" (*viz.* case was one in which a plea and directions hearing took place, the case did not proceed to trial, but the guilty plea was not entered at that hearing): *R. v. Johnson (Craig)* [2007] Costs L.R. 316. Once a meaningful trial has started, a change of plea cannot convert the trial into a cracked trial: *R. v. Maynard*, X19, SCCO 461/99; *R. v. Karra*, X19A, SCCO 375/99; and *Meeke and Taylor v. Secretary of State for Constitutional Affairs* [2006] Costs L.R. 1, QBD (David Clarke J.). Where a jury were discharged on the second day of a trial on a three count indictment, and on the following working day the prosecution added a new lesser count, and, before a new jury were sworn, the defendant offered sufficient pleas to the indictment, counsel was entitled to a fee for the first (abortive) trial, and a cracked trial fee for the later hearing at which pleas were tendered: *Frampton, ante*.

Cracked trial fees do not apply where a person pleads not guilty at a pleas and directions hearing, but later the same day changes his plea; a guilty plea fee is appropriate: *R. v. Baxter*, X22, SCCO 375/99.

The fee for a cracked trial is calculated by reference to when the case cracked, *i.e.* in the first, second or third part of a period calculated from the date when the court first fixed the date of trial or first ordered that the case should be placed into a warned list, to the date of that first fixture or the date of the start of that warned list. The fact that the fixture might later be broken, or the case moved to another warned list is immaterial and does not affect the calculation. Where the number of days in the period cannot be equally divided by three, the remainder is simply added to the last third of the period: S.I. 2013 No. 435, Sched. 1, paras 7 and 8. The fee is payable to the advocate who appeared at the hearing where pleas were entered or the last such hearing if there was more than one: *R. v. Faulkner*, X33, SCCO 201/02.

In *R. v. Carty* [2009] Costs L.R. 500, it was held that where the prosecution of one of several defendants was stayed, the case fell within the definition of a "cracked trial". The fact that the defendant's advocate had not been present on the occasion of the stay (which had been ordered at a hearing when the principal defendant, being before the court on a separate indictment, had then entered acceptable pleas to the indictment in question) did not preclude payment. Moreover, since 1996, there had been an administrative practice which permitted the prosecution to offer no evidence and an acquittal to be pronounced in open court without the legal representatives being present, and paragraph F.11 of the Graduated Fee Guidance Manual permitted a cracked trial fee to be paid in such circumstances. For this purpose, there was no reason to differentiate between a cracked trial arising from the prosecution offering no evidence and one arising from a stay.

In *R. v. Harris* [2009] Costs L.R. 507, where the defendant had pleaded guilty at a pleas and directions hearing to various offences, but where his "benefit" for the purpose of confiscation proceedings under the CJA 1988 had not yet been agreed, and where sentence and those proceedings had therefore been adjourned, the matter was held not to fall within the definition of a "cracked trial" in paragraph 9(3) of Schedule 4 to the Criminal Defence Service (Funding) Order 2001 (S.I. 2001 No. 855) (which corresponds to the current definition), and the hearing at which the confiscation order was eventually made was said not to fall within the definition of a *Newton* hearing (*R. v. Newton*, 77 Cr.App.R. 13, CA) under paragraph 1(1) (corresponding to the definition in para. 1(1) of Sched. 1 to S.I. 2013 No. 435) for the purposes of paragraph 2(6) (see now para. 2(6) of Sched. 1 to S.I. 2013 No. 435, *ante*, G-40). The prosecution had accepted the basis of the defendant's guilty plea, but in the knowledge that it would take further time, and in all likelihood another hearing, to work out the defendant's benefit. The matter, therefore, fell within the definition of "guilty plea" under paragraph 9(5).

As to the distinction between a "trial" and a "cracked trial", see also *ante*, G-123.

### Calculating the pages of prosecution evidence

Prosecution evidence includes all witness statements, documentary and pictorial exhibits and **G-137** records of interview with any defendant forming part of the committal documents or included in any notice of additional evidence, and now includes documents served in electronic form, except for a documentary or pictorial exhibit which has never existed in paper form, unless the appropriate officer decides that it would be appropriate to include it in the page count taking into account the nature of the document and any other relevant circumstances: S.I. 2013 No. 435, Sched. 1, para. 1(2) to (2C), and Sched. 2, para. 1(2) to (5). The first 50 pages must be excluded for the purposes of the calculation: S.I. 2013 No. 435, Sched. 1, para. 4. Additional documents cannot be included in the computation unless accompanied by a written notice of additional evidence: *R. v. Sturdy*, X9, December 18, 1998, SCTO 714/98; *R. v. Gkampos* [2011] Costs L.R. 142 (pages of antecedent materials relating to the defendant); and *R. v. Ward* [2012] Costs L.R. 605; but see *R. v. Qu* [2012] Costs L.R. 599 (evidence served by prosecution during trial and on which they intended to rely to be included in page count, though not accompanied by formal notice of additional evidence (see CLW/12/26/12 for the suggestion that the costs judge arrived at the correct result, but not necessarily for the right reasons)). Where one or more notices of additional evidence have been served, a page count should include the contents of all such notices, unless all sides are agreed that service of a particular notice was an administrative error; and it is irrelevant when a notice was served, or whether it was requested by the defence or prosecution: *R. v. Taylor* [2005] Costs L.R. 712 (notice served on day jury retired). A prosecution notice of intention to adduce bad character evidence does not fall within the term "any notice of additional evidence": *R. v. McCall* [2011] Costs L.R. 914 (but for a critique of the reasoning, see CLW/11/40/5). Where the Crown have exhibited and served tapes of interview, and defence counsel considers that a transcript of the interview is necessary, the pages of transcript should be included in the computation: *R. v. Brazier*, X5, SCTO 810/97. Taxing officers have been directed to include the fullest transcript produced, together with the version in the transfer bundle (if shorter), and also to include any video evidence transcripts requested by the judge: GFSG A4, A4A. Taxing officers have been directed to exclude title and separator pages: GFSG: A4A; and any additional edited versions of transcripts placed before a jury: GFSG: A5. Fax front sheets which are no more than title pages, duplicate witness statements, whether typed or hand-written, and very short lists of (*e.g.* two) exhibits should not be counted: *R. v. El Treki*, X26, SCCO 431/2000. And nor should pages comprising admissions and a jury bundle consisting of, *inter alia*, an index and details of the defendants: *R. v. Wei* [2010] Costs L.R. 846. No allowance is made for small or large typefaces or for line spacing. Unused material is also excluded.

Whereas paragraph 1(3) of Schedule 2 to S.I. 2013 No. 435 (*ante*, G-69) lists the documents that may be included when calculating the "pages of prosecution evidence" for the purposes of determining a litigator's fee under the graduated fee scheme, the list is to be taken to be exhaustive, notwithstanding that it does not include documents which will have to be read in most cases or even referred to in court (such as the indictment, custody records, correspondence, crime reports, and unused material): *R. v. Tucker* [2010] Costs L.R. 850.

The decisions of the costs judges in *R. v. O'Cuneff* [2010] Costs L.R. 476, *R. v. Burbidge* [2010] Costs L.R. 639, and *R. v. Ibefune*, unreported, June 24, 2010, evidence a conflict as between them and the Legal Services Commission as to the weight to be given to the number of pages of prosecution evidence agreed between the parties and the Crown Court at the end of the case. The commission's stance of not accepting this figure without additional objective evidence has now, however, been fully vindicated by *Criminal Practice Direction (General matters) 3B* [2013] 1 W.L.R. 3164. This inserts new requirements relating to the pagination and indexing of served evidence (as to which, see § 4-344 in the main work). It was plainly no coincidence that, in doing so, the practice direction adopted the (then) definition of "pages of prosecution evidence" contained in the Criminal Defence Service (Funding) Order 2007 (S.I. 2007 No. 1174). Compliance with the requirements of the new provisions by the prosecution will supply the commission (and costs judges) with an objective measure of the number of pages of prosecution evidence.

In *R. v. Greenwood* [2010] Costs L.R. 268, it was held that whereas paragraph 13(2) of Schedule 2 to S.I. 2013 No. 435 (*ante*, G-73b) provides that "where ...a case is transferred to a new litigator ... the fee payable to the original litigator and the new litigator is a percentage of the total fee, calculated in accordance with the table following this paragraph, as appropriate to the circumstances and timing of the ... transfer", and whereas the table provides that where a case is transferred prior to the plea and case management hearing the original litigator should receive 25 per cent of a cracked trial fee, in calculating that fee, the number of pages of prosecution evidence should be taken to be the number of such pages served on the court as at the date of transfer.

### Images and photographs

**G-138**   See now paragraphs 1(2) to (5) of Schedules 1 and 2 to S.I. 2013 No. 435. For authorities on the former provision, which will still apply where the representation order was granted before April 1, 2012, see *R. v. Rigelsford* [2006] Costs L.R. 518, and *R. v. Austin* [2006] Costs L.R. 857.

### Fees for leading and junior counsel

**G-139**   Under S.I. 2013 No. 435, fees payable to Queen's Counsel, leading juniors and led juniors are not directly related, and are calculated from the relevant tables: see, for example, the tables following paragraphs 5 and 8 of Schedule 1. Where two or more led juniors are instructed in the same case, each is paid as if they were the sole junior: Sched. 1, para. 28.

**G-140**   In *R. v. Newport* [2009] Costs L.R. 983, where two juniors appeared for the defendant when the representation order authorised instruction of junior counsel and Queen's Counsel, it was held that whilst a strict approach would lead to the conclusion that the leading junior was entitled to no payment, such an outcome would be unjust. Justice demanded that some payment should be made, especially given that the representation order had contemplated payment of two counsel. However, it was said that payment should be at the rate applicable to a leading junior. As to this case, see also *post*, G-269.

### Advocates instructed for limited purposes

**G-141**   Advocates retained for a limited purpose are remunerated according to the specific provisions of S.I. 2013 No. 435. The limited purposes are:

(a) the cross-examination of witnesses under the YJCEA 1999, s.38, which is remunerated as if for trial, save that the daily attendance fee is calculated by reference to the number of days the advocate actually attended court, instead of the number of days of the trial itself: S.I. 2013 No. 435, Sched. 1, para. 32;

(b) the provision of written or oral advice: see *post*, G-160;

(c) mitigation of sentence on indictment, which is remunerated as for a sentencing hearing together with a fee based on the fixed hourly special preparation rate according to the "reasonable number of hours" taken: S.I. 2013 No. 435, Sched. 1, para. 34(1); and an advocate who is discontented with the fee paid may seek a redetermination: para. 34(2).

### [The next paragraph is G-143.]

### Instructed and substitute advocates

**G-143**   An instructed advocate is the first advocate instructed in the case who has primary responsibility for the case, or, where a representation order provides for more than one advocate, it means both the first advocate instructed who has primary responsibility for those aspects of a case undertaken by a leading advocate and the first advocate instructed who has primary responsibility for those aspects of a case undertaken by a led advocate: S.I. 2013 No. 435, reg. 2(1).

The new scheme (RAGFS) places great emphasis on continuity of representation. It seeks to achieve this partly by identifying an "instructed advocate" who is responsible for advocacy services and partly by paying the total fee for advocacy to the instructed advocate. An instructed advocated remains an instructed advocate at all times, although provision is made for the instructed advocate to be changed, where, for example, he is unable to conduct the trial because of a clash of commitments, is dismissed by the client, or professionally embarrassed: see Sched. 1, para. 25(10). If the instructed advocate cannot attend a preliminary hearing, and sends a substitute advocate, he nevertheless remains responsible both for the conduct of the case and the ultimate payment of the substitute advocate.

Instructed advocates appointed before the pleas and directions hearing must in writing inform the court of their appointment as soon as they are appointed, otherwise the advocate who attends the pleas and directions hearing will be deemed to be the instructed advocate. If no advocate attends the plea and directions hearing, the advocate who attends the next hearing will be deemed to be and will be recorded by the court as the instructed advocate: see Sched. 1, para. 25(1)–(6). Where the representation order is amended after a plea and case management hearing to include a second advocate, each advocate must notify the court in writing whether they are the led or leading advocate. Where no additional instructed advocate is notified to the court in writing within seven days of the plea and case management hearing, the advocate to appear at the next hearing is deemed to be the instructed advocate and the court will record in writing whether he is the leading instructed advocate or the led instructed advocate, as appropriate to the circumstances of the case: *ibid.*, para. 25(7).

To give effect to the scheme, emphasise the continuity of representation, and ensure that all substitute advocates are paid for any RAGFS work they undertake, the Bar Council has introduced a *Graduated Fee Payment Protocol*. The protocol is an essential part of the mechanism by which advocates will be remunerated in future, but it falls outside the immediate scope of this work. It is available on both the Bar Council's and the Criminal Bar Association's websites.

### Sentencing hearings in cases on indictment

Any person appearing at a sentencing hearing in a case on indictment is entitled to a fixed fee   **G-144** where sentence has been deferred: S.I. 2013 No. 435, Sched. 1, para. 15.

A contested application for an anti-social behaviour order at a sentencing hearing does not attract a separate or additional fee: *R. v. Brinkworth* [2006] Costs L.R. 512.

Under S.I. 2013 No. 435, an advocate instructed solely for the purpose of mitigation shall be paid the fee payable under paragraph 15 together with a fee calculated by reference to the reasonable number of hours of preparation for that appearance multiplied by the hourly rate set out in the table following paragraph 24 which is appropriate to the category of trial advocate: Sched. 1, para. 34(1). The advocate may apply for redetermination of such fee and shall supply such information and documents as may be required by the appropriate officer as proof of the number of hours of preparation: *ibid.*, para. 34(2).

### Fitness hearings

A fitness hearing is a hearing to determine whether a defendant is fit to plead or stand trial:   **G-145** S.I. 2013 No. 435, Sched. 1, para. 31. If there is a trial on indictment at any time thereafter, the length of the fitness hearing shall be included in determining the length of the trial: *ibid.*, para. 31(a). Where a person pleads guilty at any time after a fitness hearing is held, the advocate may elect to be paid either as if the fitness hearing was a trial or for the guilty plea: *ibid.*, para. 31(c). Where a person is found to be unfit, the trial advocate may elect to treat the fitness hearing either as a trial or as a cracked trial: *ibid.*, para. 31(b).

### Cross-examination of vulnerable witnesses

Where an advocate is retained solely for the purpose of cross-examining a vulnerable witness   **G-146** under section 38 of the YJCEA 1999, the graduated fee shall be assessed as though the matter was a trial, with the length of trial uplift and refresher calculated by reference to the number of days the advocate attended court: S.I. 2013 No. 435, Sched. 1, para. 32.

### Newton hearings

Where a *Newton* hearing takes place following a trial on indictment the provisions relating to   **G-147** cracked trials, guilty pleas and sentencing hearings do not apply. The hearing is remunerated as for a contested trial. For the purposes of computation, the length of the *Newton* hearing is added to the main hearing: S.I. 2013 No. 435, Sched. 1, para. 2(8). Thus the main hearing starts on the day the plea is entered, even if this occurred during a pleas and directions hearing: *R. v. Gemeskel*, X2, SCTO 180/98. The advocate who attended the main hearing should claim the whole fee and remunerate the other advocate (if any) who attended the *Newton* hearing: GFSG: B12, 13.

Where a *Newton* hearing does not take place because the basis of plea was subsequently agreed, the case reverts to a guilty plea or cracked trial as appropriate: *R. v. Riddell*, X3, SCTO 318/98. If the hearing is aborted, the usual rules apply: see *post*, G-162, and *R. v. Ayres* [2002] Costs L.R. 330.

In *R. v. Newton*, 77 Cr.App.R. 13, the Court of Appeal clearly envisaged circumstances in which a sentencing judge could reach a conclusion without hearing evidence. However, the regulations define a *Newton* hearing as one at which evidence is heard for the purpose of determining the sentence of a convicted person in accordance with the *Newton* principles. Accordingly, a *Newton* hearing at which no evidence is called can only be remunerated by a standard appearance fee as it is not a *Newton* hearing for the purposes of the regulations: *R. v. Hunter-Brown*, X29, SCCO, 164/2001.

Where a *Newton* hearing is held on a committal for sentence, the only fee payable under Schedule 2 to S.I. 2013 No. 435 is the fixed fee payable for a committal for sentence: *R. v. Holden* [2010] Costs L.R. 851.

### Adverse judicial comment and reduction of graduated or fixed fees

G-148      Where a trial judge makes adverse observations concerning an advocate's conduct of a graduated or fixed fee case, the appropriate authority may reduce the fee by such proportion as it "considers reasonable", having first given the advocate the opportunity to make representations about the extent of the reduction: S.I. 2013 No. 435, reg. 26. See also *post*, G-220.

### (3) Additional fees

### Confiscation proceedings

G-149      Hearings under section 2 of the DTA 1994, section 71 of the CJA 1988 or Part 2 of the PCA 2002 are excluded from the length computation of the main hearing and are remunerated separately as work for which a daily or half-daily fee is payable: S.I. 2013 No. 435, Sched. 1, para. 14(1) and (2). Entitlement to the daily fee arises where the hearing begins before but ends after the luncheon adjournment; a half-daily fee is paid where the hearing ends before or begins after the luncheon adjournment: S.I. 2013 No. 435, Sched. 1, para. 14(2). The appropriate rates are set out in the table following paragraph 14(2).

### Abuse of process, disclosure and witness summonses' etc.

G-150      Applications relating to abuse of process, disclosure or witness summonses heard before the main hearing are paid at the daily rates set out in the table following paragraph 24: S.I. 2013 No. 435, Sched. 1, para. 13(2). As to remuneration for such applications where they take place as part of the main hearing, see *ante*, G-124. A hearing merely relating to the failure of the prosecution to comply with an earlier disclosure order attracts only a standard appearance fee: GFSG: 12.

In respect of representation orders granted on or after April 30, 2007, these provisions were extended to include applications relating to the admissibility of evidence, and an unsuccessful application to withdraw a guilty plea made by an advocate other than the advocate who appeared at the hearing where the plea was tendered: see now S.I. 2013 No. 435, Sched. 1, para. 13(1)(d) and (e).

### [The next paragraph is G-152.]

### Conferences and views

G-152      The first three pre-trial conferences or views are not separately remunerated; the fees are deemed to be included in the basic fee: Sched. 1, para. 19(2). Thereafter, the permitted number of further conferences or views (each not exceeding two hours) is as follows:

| 1 conference | trials of more than 20 but less than 26 days |
| 2 conferences | trials of more than 25 days but less than 36 days |
| 3 conferences | trials of more than 35 days |

The number of further conferences allowed in respect of cracked trials is similar, save that the anticipated length of trial is that accepted by the court at the plea and case management hearing (save that, on a literal reading of the legislation, three conferences will only be paid for where it was accepted that the trial would last not more than 40 days): Sched. 1, para. 19(3).

Conferences include conferences with expert witnesses: S.I. 2013 No. 435, Sched. 1, para.   **G-153** 19(1)(a). Travel expenses and the time taken in travelling, including time taken to travel to a conference with a defendant who could not reasonably be expected to attend counsel's chambers, are remunerated at the specified hourly rate: *ibid.*, para. 19(5). Where such fees are allowed, reasonable travelling expenses may also be claimed: *ibid.*, para. 19(4). The local bar rule has no application to such fees: *R. v. Carlyle* [2002] Costs L.R. 192.

**[The next paragraph is G-156.]**

## Special preparation

Special preparation is preparation substantially in excess of the amount normally done for   **G-156** cases of the type in question and undertaken because the case involves "a very unusual or novel point of law or factual issue": S.I. 2013 No. 435, Sched. 1, para. 17(1)(a). "Very" qualifies both "unusual" and "novel" and the phrase "very unusual or novel" qualifies both the expressions "point of law" and "factual issue": *Meeke and Taylor v. Secretary of State for Constitutional Affairs* [2006] Costs L.R. 1, QBD (David Clarke J.). Remuneration is calculated at an hourly rate for "the number of hours preparation in excess of the amount the appropriate officer considers reasonable for cases of the same type": S.I. 2013 No. 435, Sched. 1, para. 17(3)(a); and with no enhancement under paragraph 29 of Schedule 2: *Lord Chancellor v. McLarty & Co. Solicitors* [2012] Costs L.R. 190, QBD (Burnett J.).

What falls to be compensated is the extra work caused by the unusual or novel point by comparison with the sort of case involved without the unusual or novel point; as the term is used in relation to the quantification of fees, "type" in this context should be defined as an indication of weight; but the exercise does not include any consideration of the reasonableness of the time claimed; thus, once the determining officer has resolved that the case qualifies for a special preparation fee, he must assess the number of hours worked in excess of the norm and compensate for those hours at the prescribed hourly rate: *R. v. Goodwin* [2008] Costs L.R. 497.

*R. v. Goodwin, ante,* was considered in *R. v. Kholi* [2010] Costs L.R. 982, in which it was held that under paragraph 52(i) of the Guidance Manual for the CPS Graduated Fee Scheme (which is in materially identical terms to para. 17(1)(a) of Sched. 1 to S.I. 2013 No. 435 (*ante*, G-53)), it is only those hours of work attributable to the unusual or novel point of law or factual issue which was involved, which fall to be remunerated as special preparation; it is not the case that all time spent by the advocate in preparation over and above the norm for the type of case should be so remunerated.

The concept of "normal preparation" done for a case of the same type is wholly artificial. Other than in routine cases of burglary and theft, in virtually all other crimes in the criminal calendar, the circumstances vary infinitely: *R. v. Briers* [2005] Costs L.R. 146. The test is "What is the normal preparation for this offence?" not "What is the normal preparation for a case exhibiting these particular facts": *Briers, ante*; *R. v. Ward-Allen* [2005] Costs L.R. 745.

It is for counsel to differentiate between what he considers to be the normal preparation for a case of that type and the actual preparation that he has carried out: *Briers, ante*; *R. v. Marandola* [2006] Costs L.R. 184.

Very unusual or novel points of law have an obvious meaning, namely a point of law which either has never been raised or decided (novel) or which is outwith the usual professional experience (very unusual): *R. v. Ward-Allen, ante*. Some further assistance can be found in *Perry v. Lord Chancellor, The Times,* May 26, 1994, although it should be noted that that case was not concerned with these regulations.

Very unusual or novel factual issues have a similar meaning, namely a factual issue which either has never been raised or which is outwith the usual professional experience: *R. v. Ward-Allen, ante.* Such issues might cover extremely rare medical conditions, such as Munchausen's Syndrome by Proxy or "pubic symphysitis dysfunction", the exceptional, if not unique, nature of which was held in *R. v. Bishop* [2008] Costs L.R. 808, to justify a special preparation fee where it had contributed to prosecution material of over 600 pages (not served as part of the page count); novel issues might, for example have included DNA fingerprinting when it was introduced, but it would not qualify now. A case involving "shaken baby syndrome" does not necessarily attract a special preparation fee, unless there are additional medical complications: *R. v. Khair* [2005] Costs L.R. 542. A special preparation fee was allowed in *R. v. Thompson* [2006] Costs L.R. 668 where the defendant was accused of murdering her husband 10 years earlier. Counsel had to consider not only pathology and toxicology reports, but also a psychiatric profile on the husband prepared by a psychiatrist who had never met him, and issues arising in diabetology and physiology. Transcripts of the original coroner's inquest and the defendant's previous trials for theft and attempted murder of another husband were also served.

The novelty of the bad character provisions of the CJA 2003 did not provide grounds for claiming a special preparation fee; the criminal law is constantly changing: *R. v. Christie* [2010] 4 Costs L.R. 634.

A special preparation fee would be reasonable where counsel had to check a sample of over 33,000 original photographs of which the prosecution had only copied a representative fraction for use at trial: *R. v. Rigelsford* [2006] Costs L.R. 523; and see *ante*, G-138. But the mere fact that preparation properly undertaken for a complex three-week rape trial was "wasted" because the defendant decided to plead guilty during the prosecution opening did not justify a special preparation fee: *Meeke and Taylor v. Secretary of State for Constitutional Affairs, ante.*

A large quantity of unused material does not of itself give rise to a novel or unusual factual issue even where it is accepted that detailed examination of the material was necessary: *R. v. Lawrence* [2007] Costs L.R. 138; and even where the trial judge has extended a representation order to allow two juniors to peruse such material: *R. v. Dhaliwal* [2004] Costs L.R. 689. Such work is not remunerated under the graduated fee scheme or indeed at all: *ibid.* Nor does the mere failure of the scheme to accommodate unused material amount to a breach of the principle of equality of arms: *R. v. Marandola, ante.*

An advocate can also claim a special preparation fee where the prosecution evidence exceeds 10,000 pages and the appropriate officer considers that it is reasonable to make a payment in excess of the graduated fee which would otherwise be payable; the fee is calculated by reference to the number of hours which the appropriate officer considers reasonable to read the excess pages, using the current hourly fee rate: S.I. 2013 No. 435, Sched. 1, para. 17(1)(b), (2) and (3)(b).

An advocate's failure to keep a contemporaneous work log may result in rejection of a claim for a special preparation fee: *R. v. Dunne* [2013] Costs L.R. 1031 (considering a corresponding provision in the Criminal Defence Service (Funding) Order 2007 (S.I. 2007 No. 1174).

### Evidence served electronically

**G-157**     A special preparation fee may also be claimed where a documentary or pictorial exhibit, which has never existed in paper form, is served by the prosecution in electronic form, and the appropriate officer does not consider it appropriate to include it in the pages of prosecution evidence; and such fee may be paid if the appropriate officer considers it reasonable to make a payment in excess of the fee otherwise payable under the graduated fee scheme, with the amount of the payment depending on the number of hours which the appropriate officer considers reasonable to view the exhibit: see Sched. 1, para. 17(1)(c) and (2), and Sched. 2, para. 20(1)(a) and (2). The drafting of these provisions in the two schedules is slightly different, but it is submitted that the intent is the same. As to the drafting, this – taken at face value – gives the appropriate officer a discretion whether to make a payment even where he considers it reasonable to do so. It is submitted, however, that the legislation is unlikely to be so construed: if the appropriate officer considers it reasonable to make a payment, then it is likely to be held that he should do so. The revised wording of these provisions (introduced by the Criminal Defence Service (Funding) (Amendment) Order 2001 (S.I. 2012 No. 750)) was doubtless intended to avoid the difficulties caused by the former wording and which gave rise to a series of decisions, such as *R. v. Rigelsford* [2006] Costs L.R. 518, *R. v. Austin* [2006] Costs L.R. 857, *Lord Chancellor v. Michael J. Reed Ltd* [2010] Costs L.R. 72, QBD (Penry-Davey J.), *Lord Chancellor v. McLarty & Co. Solicitors* [2012] Costs L.R. 190, QBD (Burnett J.), and *R. v. Jones* [2010] Costs L.R. 469. For details of these authorities, which will still have application to cases in which a representation order was granted before April 1, 2012, see previous supplements.

*Lord Chancellor v. Michael J. Reed Ltd* (*ante*) was followed in *R. v. Osoteko* [2014] Costs L.R. 190, ★ but the costs judge certified a point of principle of general importance, *viz.* whether that case had created too narrow a definition of pages of prosecution evidence.

**[The next paragraph is G-159.]**

### Listening to or viewing tapes

There is now no provision for any separate payment for listening to or viewing tapes. These **G-159** are now treated as being rolled up within the whole of the graduated fee.

### Provision of written or oral advice

Any advocate instructed solely to provide written or oral advice shall be paid a fee calculated **G-160** from the reasonable number of hours of preparation for that advice using the appropriate hourly rate in the table following paragraph 24 of Schedule 1 to S.I. 2013 No. 435: see Sched. 1, para. 33(1). The advocate may apply for re-determination of such fee under regulation 28, and he shall supply such information and documents as may be required by the appropriate officer as proof of the number of hours of preparation: *ibid.*, para. 33(2).

As to whether a solicitor may properly instruct counsel other than counsel who appeared at trial to advise on the question of appeal where trial counsel has advised in the negative, see *R. v. Umezie*, § 7-165 in the main work.

*R. v. Umezie* was considered in *R. v. Bromige* [2011] Costs L.R. 145, in which it was held that where solicitors, on receipt of trial counsel's negative advice as to the prospects of a successful appeal against sentence, instructed fresh counsel to advise on the question, trial counsel's negative advice (whether written or oral) did not terminate the representation order; paragraph A1-2 of the Guide to Commencing Proceedings in the Court of Appeal (Criminal Division) (*post*, Appendix J-4) did not preclude payment of a fee for subsequent advice given by fresh counsel in relation to the appeal, because that paragraph was only concerned with the amendment of representation orders, and no amendment to the representation order granted by the magistrates' court was necessary to instruct fresh counsel to advise; however, fresh counsel's claim for a fee for his advice could only fall within paragraph 6 of Schedule 3 to S.I. 2013 No. 435 (*ante*, G-85), which provides, that upon the determination of an advocate's fees in proceedings in the Court of Appeal, "the appropriate officer must consider the claim ... and must allow such work as appears to him to have been reasonably done"; as a general principle it will not be reasonable to obtain advice on a point that has already been the subject of advice, with the obvious exceptions to this principle being if the initial advice is incompetent or ambiguous, or if there is a change in circumstances or if new evidence has come to light; the reason given in this case for seeking further advice, *viz.* that the solicitors were not convinced as to the correctness of the negative oral advice from trial counsel, was not sufficient; therefore the work done by fresh counsel was not reasonably done for the purposes of paragraph 6 because no good reason had been shown for instructing him to give advice on a point that had already been the subject of advice. For the submission that the costs judge's reliance on paragraph 6 of Schedule 3 is unsustainable, see CLW/11/08/45.

### (4) Acting for more than one defendant, or in more than one "case"

The definition of "case" in paragraph 1(1) of Schedule 2 (*ante*, G-69) could not possibly lead to **G-161** the conclusion that if a litigator represents more than one defendant charged and tried on the same indictment that litigator is then entitled to be paid on the basis that there are as many cases as there are defendants: *Lord Chancellor v. Eddowes Perry and Osbourne Ltd* [2011] Costs L.R. 498, QBD (Spencer J.). As to this case, see also *post*, G-273.

An uplift of one-fifth for each additional defendant represented may only be claimed where the regulations so provide: S.I. 2013 No. 435, Sched. 1, para. 27(2). Where an advocate acts for more than one defendant, the advocate must select the case on which remuneration is to be based (the principal case). Claims for such uplifts may be made for pleas and directions hearings, some aborted hearings, main hearings, appeals against conviction, committals for sentence, proceedings for a breach of a Crown Court order, disclosure, abuse and witness summons hearings, and confiscation proceedings: S.I. 2013 No. 435, Sched. 1, para. 27(4). But no uplifts for these hearings, with the exception of confiscation proceedings, are payable in cases that were committed to the Crown Court on the election of the defendant, where the magistrates' court had determined that the case was suitable for summary trial: *ibid.*, para. 27(3). In respect of a trial, the uplift is limited to one-fifth of the basic fee and not the basic fee enhanced by reference to the prosecution evidence, witnesses and length of trial uplift: ibid., para. 27(2)(b), *i.e.* where the main hearing in each case was heard concurrently: *R. v. Fletcher*, X6, SCTO 815/97.

The above provisions also apply where the advocate conducts two or more cases concurrently: S.I. 2013 No. 435, Sched. 1, para. 27(2). Proceedings arising out of a single notice of appeal against conviction or sentence, or single committal for sentence, constitute a separate "case": para. 1(1) of Schedule 1 to S.I. 2013 No. 435. However, a committal for sentence together with a committal for breach of a community service order constituted two separate "cases" as the latter was a committal for breach of an earlier order: *R. v. Hines*, X24, SCCO 337/2000. As a case means proceedings on one or more counts of a single indictment, it is submitted that two trials arising from a severed indictment give rise to two separate graduated fees, as the trials are not heard concurrently.

In *R. v. Fury* [2011] Costs L.R. 919, it was said that if a hearing deals with one case then another, independently of each other, it will be hearing them consecutively; hearings will be concurrent only if they are combined or conjoined or somehow interlinked; this will be so where the main hearings of a number of cases against the same defendant are listed together and the defendant either pleads guilty or is to be sentenced in all of the cases; the cases will impact on each other either as to the directions that are given for sentencing or as to the sentences that are imposed; they will not be considered independently of each other. For criticism of the actual decision in this case (cases were not heard concurrently where, as part of an agreed package, defendant pleaded guilty to one indictment and prosecution offered no evidence on the other, all counts having originally been in the same indictment), see CLW/11/40/3.

In *R. v. Sturmer and Lewis* [2009] Costs L.R. 364, it was said that the combined effect of paragraph 15 and the table in paragraph 19 of Schedule 2 to S.I. 2013 No. 435 (*ante*, G-74a, G-75a) is that where a litigator is "instructed in ... a sentencing hearing following a committal for sentence to the Crown Court", the "fee payable ... is that set out in the table" (para. 15), *i.e.* "£212.77" per proceedings (the table). "Proceedings" can involve more than one defendant and, if there is only one "proceedings", only one fee will be payable, however many defendants are represented by the litigator.

### [The next paragraph is G-163.]

### (5) Abortive hearings

**G-163**    The payment of fixed fees for abortive hearings is limited to ineffective trials: see Sched. 1, para. 16. As to this, see *R. v. Budai, ante*, G-124.

### (6) Wasted preparation

**G-164**    Wasted preparation occurs where an advocate does not represent his client because of (a) a clash of listings and the advocate has been unable to secure a change of date for either hearing; or (b) a fixture for a main hearing is altered by the court despite the advocate's objection; or (c) the advocate withdraws with leave of the court because of professional embarrassment; or (d) the advocate is dismissed by the client; or (e) the advocate is obliged to undertake judicial or other public duties: S.I. 2013 No. 435, Sched. 1, para. 18(1). A representation order replacing a single junior with Queen's Counsel acting alone does not entitle junior counsel to claim a wasted preparation fee in respect of the preparation reasonably and properly undertaken; counsel has no redress under the scheme: *R. v. Schultz*, X10, SCTO 552/98. The hourly fee may be claimed only where eight or more hours of preparation have been undertaken, and (a) the trial lasted for five days or more, or (b) in the case of a cracked trial, there are more than 150 pages of prosecution evidence: S.I. 2013 No. 435, Sched. 1, para. 18(2). The wasted preparation fee is calculated by reference to the number of hours of preparation reasonably carried out by the advocate, who must supply such information and documents in support of the claim as may be required: S.I. 2013 No. 435, Sched. 1, para. 18(3) and (5).

The requirements of paragraph 18(1) were satisfied where, following the vacation of the trial date by the trial judge and his proposal of a new date, counsel had written objecting to the new date (on the grounds that he had booked and paid for a holiday abroad that started within 10 days of the new date), but where, despite that objection, the trial had gone ahead on the proposed date, with the result that counsel had had to return the brief: *R. v. Ghaffar* [2009] Costs L.R. 980. The fact that counsel's objection was to the new date, and not to the vacation of the original fixture, was not a valid ground for refusing a wasted preparation fee in respect of the substantial preparation done by counsel prior to the vacation of the original fixture. Changing a fixture is a process and an objection to part of that process is therefore an objection to the change. There was nothing in paragraph 18(1)(b) that restricted it to counsel's professional commitments.

### (7) Appeals, pleas before venue, committals and other fees

Graduated fixed fees are also payable in respect of committals for sentence (which include plea    **G-165** before venue cases), appeals from magistrates' courts and breach of Crown Court orders: S.I. 2013 No. 435, Sched. 1, para. 20; noting briefs: *ibid.*, para. 23; bail and other applications, and mentions when not forming part of a main hearing or other hearing for which a fixed fee is provided: *ibid.*, para. 20(3). The appropriate rate is that listed in the table following paragraph 24. After the Crown Court is seized of a case, any bail applications, or executions of bench warrants made in a magistrates' court are remunerated as if made in the Crown Court: *R. v. Bailey*, X16, 378/99. As to trials of Bail Act 1976 offences, see *ante*, G-130.

### (8) Contempt proceedings

Remuneration for proceedings for contempt in the face of the court is fixed at discrete daily    **G-166** rates: S.I. 2013 No. 435, reg. 11, and Sched. 1, para. 21. The fees are fixed and there is no discretion to allow *ex post facto* payment, however regrettable and unfair the result may be: *R. v. Russell* [2006] Costs L.R. 841. Such payments do not fall within the graduated fee scheme and, therefore, such hearings do not form part of the main hearing or the sentencing hearing.

### (9) Travel expenses

Travel and hotel expenses may be claimed subject to the usual 40 kilometre local bar rule: S.I.    **G-167** 2013 No. 435, Sched. 1, para. 29 (see generally *post*, G-253). Expenses should not be paid in respect of conferences for which advocates are not entitled to be remunerated, unless the conference was abortive due to circumstances beyond the advocate's control: *R. v. Pickett*, X39.

### (10) Table of offences

The effect of the table of offences at the end of Schedule 1 to S.I. 2013 No. 435 (as amended by    **G-168** the Protection of Freedoms Act 2012 (Consequential Amendments) Order 2013 (S.I. 2013 No. 862)) is set out in the following paragraphs. Offences are divided into those below £30,000, those where the value is £30,000 or more, but less than £100,000, and those where the value involved is £100,000 or more. As to the method of calculation for the purposes of determining value, see *ante*, G-121. As to conspiracy, incitement and attempt, see *ante*, G-120. It should be noted that there are various errors in the table: for example, it refers to section 39 (rather than section 139) of the CJA 1988 (this has been corrected below) and it refers to various measures that have been repealed and replaced, including the Post Office Act 1953, the Merchant Shipping Act 1970 and the Air Navigation Order 2005 (S.I. 2005 No. 1970)).

An "armed robbery" (see the Theft Act 1968 entries) arises where the offender was armed with a firearm or imitation firearm, or was thought by the victim to have been so armed, or was armed with an offensive weapon: *R. v. Stables*, X12, SCTO 102/99.

Where a judge proposes to try an offence under the Bail Act 1976, s.6, in respect of a defendant who is first brought up before him for non-attendance, then there is a trial or guilty plea under the graduated fee scheme: *R. v. Shaw* [2005] Costs L.R. 326.

**G-169**    As several statutes are listed under more than one class, the following is a list of the statutes and orders featured in the table, with the classes in which they appear—

| | |
|---|---|
| Air Navigation Order 2005 (S.I. 2005 No. 1970) | H |
| Aviation Security Act 1982 | B |
| Bail Act 1976 | H |
| Bribery Act 2010 | I |
| Child Abduction Act 1984 | C |
| Children and Young Persons Act 1933 | B, J |
| Cremation Act 1902 | I |
| Crime and Disorder Act 1998 | B, C, H |
| Criminal Damage Act 1971 | B, C |
| Criminal Justice Act 1961 | C |
| Criminal Justice Act 1967 | I |
| Criminal Justice Act 1988 | H |
| Criminal Justice Act 1991 | B |
| Criminal Justice (International Co-operation) Act 1990 | B |
| Criminal Justice (Terrorism and Conspiracy) Act 1998 | I |
| Criminal Justice and Public Order Act 1994 | I |
| Criminal Law Act 1967 | I |
| Criminal Law Act 1977 | C |
| Customs and Excise Management Act 1979 | B, C, F, G, H, K |
| Dangerous Dogs Act 1991 | C |
| Disorderly Houses Act 1751 | H |
| Domestic Violence, Crime and Victims Act 2004 | B |
| Drug Trafficking Act 1994 | B, I |
| Drug Trafficking Offences Act 1986 | C |
| European Communities Act 1972 | I |
| Explosive Substances Act 1883 | A, B |
| Firearms Act 1968 | B, C |
| Firearms (Amendment) Act 1988 | C |
| Forgery Act 1861 | F, I |
| Forgery and Counterfeiting Act 1981 | F, G, K |
| Fraud Act 2006 | F, G, K |
| Hallmarking Act 1973 | F, G, K |
| Identity Cards Act 2006 | F |
| Immigration Act 1971 | C |
| Indecency with Children Act 1960 | J |
| Indecent Displays (Control) Act 1981 | H |
| Infant Life (Preservation) Act 1929 | A |
| Infanticide Act 1938 | A |
| Insolvency Act 1986 | G |
| Magistrates' Courts Act 1980 | I |
| Malicious Damage Act 1861 | H |
| Mental Health Act 1959 | J |

| | |
|---|---|
| Mental Health Act 1983 | D |
| Merchant Shipping Act 1970 | H |
| Misuse of Drugs Act 1971 | B, C, H |
| Nuclear Material (Offences) Act 1983 | B |
| Obscene Publications Act 1959 | H |
| Offences against the Person Act 1861 | A, B, C, H |
| Perjury Act 1911 | I |
| Post Office Act 1953 | H |
| Prevention of Corruption Act 1906 | I |
| Prevention of Crime Act 1953 | H |
| Prison Act 1952 | C |
| Prison Security Act 1992 | B |
| Proceeds of Crime Act 2002 | B |
| Prohibition of Female Circumcision Act 1985 | C |
| Protection from Eviction Act 1977 | H |
| Protection from Harassment Act 1997 | H |
| Protection of Children Act 1978 | J |
| Public Bodies Corrupt Practices Act 1889 | I |
| Public Order Act 1986 | B, C, H |
| Public Passenger Vehicles Act 1981 | H |
| Road Traffic Act 1960 | H |
| Road Traffic Act 1988 | B, H |
| Road Traffic Regulation Act 1984 | H |
| Sexual Offences Act 1956 | D, H, J |
| Sexual Offences Act 1967 | D, H |
| Sexual Offences Act 2003 | D, J |
| Sexual Offences (Amendment) Act 2000 | D |
| Stamp Duties Management Act 1891 | F, G, K |
| Submarine Telegraph Act 1885 | C |
| Suicide Act 1961 | B |
| Taking of Hostages Act 1982 | B |
| Terrorism Act 2000 | B, C |
| Theatres Act 1968 | H |
| Theft Act 1968 | B, C, E, F, G, H, K |
| Theft Act 1978 | F, G, H, K |
| Trade Descriptions Act 1968 | H, I |
| Treason Act 1842 | C |
| Value Added Tax Act 1994 | F, G, K |
| Vehicle Excise and Registration Act 1994 | H |

## Class A: homicide and related grave offences

(i) *Common law offences*
     Murder and manslaughter             **G-170**

(ii) *Offences created by primary or secondary legislation*
  Those contrary to the following provisions:
    Explosive Substances Act 1883, ss.2 and 3;
    Infant Life (Preservation) Act 1929, s.1(1);
    Infanticide Act 1938, s.1(1);
    Offences against the Person Act 1861, s.4.

## Class B: offences involving serious violence or damage, and serious drugs offences

(i) *Common law offences*
**G-171**          Kidnapping and false imprisonment

(ii) *Offences created by primary or secondary legislation*
  Those contrary to the following provisions:
    Aviation Security Act 1982, s.2(1)(b);
    Crime and Disorder Act 1998, s.30(1);
    Children and Young Persons Act 1933, s.1;
    Criminal Damage Act 1971, s.1(2) and (where the value exceeds £30,000) s.1(3);
    Criminal Justice Act 1991, s.90;
    Criminal Justice (International Co-operation) Act 1990, ss.12 and 18;
    Customs and Excise Management Act 1979, s.50 (Class A or B drugs), s.85, s.170(2)(b) or
      (c) (in relation to Class A or B drugs);
    Domestic Violence, Crime and Victims Act 2004, s.5;
    Drug Trafficking Act 1994, ss.49, 50, 51, 52 and 53;
    Explosive Substances Act 1883, s.4(1);
    Firearms Act 1968, ss.5, 16, 17 and 18;
    Misuse of Drugs Act 1971, s.4 (Class A or B drug), s.5(3) (Class A or B drug), ss.6, 8, 9, 12
      and 13;
    Nuclear Material (Offences) Act 1983, s.2;
    Offences against the Person Act 1861, ss.16, 17, 18, 21, 22, 23, 28, 29, 30, 32, 33, 34 and
      58;
    Prison Security Act 1992, s.1;
    Proceeds of Crime Act 2002, ss.327, 328, 329, 330, 331, 332, 333, 339(1A);
    Public Order Act 1986, ss.1, 2 and 38;
    Road Traffic Act 1988, ss.1, 3A and 22A;
    Suicide Act 1961, s.2;
    Taking of Hostages Act 1982, s.1;
    Terrorism Act 2000, ss.11, 12, 13, 15, 16, 17, 18, 39, 54, 56, 57, 58 and 59;
    Theft Act 1968, s.8(1) (if "armed"), s.8(2) (if "with weapon"), s.10, s.12A (if resulting in
      death) and 21.

## Class C: lesser offences involving violence or damage, and less serious drugs offences

(i) *Common law offences*
**G-172**          Permitting an escape, rescue, breach of prison and escaping from lawful custody without
          force

(ii) *Offences created by primary or secondary legislation*
  Those contrary to the following provisions:
    Child Abduction Act 1984, ss.1 and 2;
    Crime and Disorder Act 1998, ss.29(1) and 30(1);
    Criminal Damage Act 1971, s.1(1) and, where the offence does not also fall within section
      1(2) and where the value of the damage is less than £30,000, s.1(3), s.2 and s.3;
    Criminal Justice Act 1961, s.22;

Criminal Law Act 1977, s.51;

Customs and Excise Management Act 1979, s.50 (in relation to Class C drugs), s.68A(1) and (2), s.86, s.170(2)(b), (c) (in relation to Class C drugs);

Dangerous Dogs Act 1991, s.3;

Drug Trafficking Offences Act 1986, ss.26B and 26C;

Firearms Act 1968, ss.1, 2, 3, 4, 19, 20, 21(4), 21(5) and 42;

Firearms (Amendment) Act 1988, s.6(1);

Immigration Act 1971, s.25;

Misuse of Drugs Act 1971, s.4 (Class C drug), s.5(2) (Class A drug), s.5(3) (Class C drug);

Offences against the Person Act 1861, ss.20, 24, 26, 27, 31, 37, 47, 59, 60 and 64;

Prison Act 1952, s.39;

Prohibition of Female Circumcision Act 1985, s.1;

Public Order Act 1986, ss.18 to 23;

Submarine Telegraph Act 1885, s.3;

Terrorism Act 2000, s.19;

Theft Act 1968, s.8(1) (other than when "armed");

Treason Act 1842, s.2.

## Class D: sexual offences and offences against children

*Offences created by primary or secondary legislation*
Those contrary to the following provisions:  **G-173**
Criminal Law Act 1977, s.54;

Mental Health Act 1983, s.127;

Sexual Offences Act 1956, s.4, s.9, s.10 (other than by man with girl under 13), s.11, s.13 (between male aged 21 or over and male under 16), ss.14, 15, 19, 21, 23, 27, 29, 30 and 31;

Sexual Offences Act 1967, s.5;

Sexual Offences Act 2003, s.3, s.4 (without penetration), ss.11 to 13, 15 to 19, 32, 33, 36, 37, 40, 41, 52, 53, 61 to 67, 69 and 70;

Sexual Offences (Amendment) Act 2000, s.3.

## Class E: burglary, etc.

*Offences created by primary or secondary legislation*
Those contrary to the following provisions:  **G-174**
Theft Act 1968, ss.9 and 25

## Classes F, G and K: other offences of dishonesty (offences always in Class F)

*Offences created by primary or secondary legislation*
Those contrary to the following provisions:  **G-175**
Forgery Act 1861, ss.36, 37;

Identity Cards Act 2006, s.25(1), (3) and (5).

## Classes F, G and K: other offences of dishonesty (offences always in Class G)

*Offences created by primary or secondary legislation*
Those contrary to the following provisions:  **G-176**
Customs and Excise Management Act 1979, s.50 (counterfeit notes or coins), s.170(2)(b) or (c) (counterfeit notes or coins);

Forgery and Counterfeiting Act 1981, ss.14 to 17;

Insolvency Act 1986, s.360.

paragraph
numbers

**G-177**   *Archbold's Criminal Pleading—2014 ed.*

**Classes F, G and K: other offences of dishonesty (offences in Class G if value exceeds £30,000, in Class K if value exceeds £100,000 and otherwise in Class F)**

*Offences created by primary or secondary legislation*

**G-177**   Those contrary to the following provisions:

Customs and Excise Management Act 1979, s.50 (to the extent not specified elsewhere), s.168, s.170(1)(b), s.170(2)(b), (c) (to the extent not specified elsewhere);
Forgery and Counterfeiting Act 1981, ss.1 to 5;
Fraud Act 2006, ss.2, 3, 4, 6, 7, 9 and 11;
Hallmarking Act 1973, s.6;
Stamp Duties Management Act 1891, s.13;
Theft Act 1968, ss.1, 11, 13, 15, 16, 17 and 22;
Theft Act 1978, ss.1 and 2;
Value Added Tax Act 1994, s.72(1)-(8).

**Class H: miscellaneous other offences**

(i) *Common law offences*

**G-178**   Keeping a disorderly house, outraging public decency

(ii) *Offences created by primary or secondary legislation*

Those contrary to the following provisions:

Air Navigation Order 2005 (S.I. 2005 No. 1970), art. 75;
Bail Act 1976, s.9(1);
Crime and Disorder Act 1998, ss.1(10), 2(8), 31(1) and 32(1);
Criminal Justice Act 1988, s.139;
Customs and Excise Management Act 1979, ss.13 and 16;
Disorderly Houses Act 1751, s.8;
Indecent Displays (Control) Act 1981, s.1;
Malicious Damage Act 1861, s.36;
Merchant Shipping Act 1970, s.27;
Misuse of Drugs Act 1971, s.5(2) (Class B or C drug); s.11;
Obscene Publications Act 1959, ss.1 and 2;
Offences against the Person Act 1861, ss.35 and 38;
Post Office Act 1953, s.11;
Prevention of Crime Act 1953, s.1;
Protection from Eviction Act 1977, s.1;
Protection from Harassment Act 1997, ss.3(6), 4(1) and 5(5);
Public Order Act 1986, s.3;
Public Passenger Vehicles Act 1981, s.65;
Road Traffic Act 1960, s.233;
Road Traffic Act 1988, ss.2 and 173;
Road Traffic Regulation Act 1984, s.115;
Sexual Offences Act 1956, ss.2, 3, 12, 13 (other than where one participant over 21 and the other under 16), 22, 24 and 32;
Sexual Offences Act 1967, s.4;
Theatres Act 1968, s.2;
Theft Act 1968, s.12A (but not where death results);
Theft Act 1978, s.3;
Trade Descriptions Act 1968, ss.1, 8, 9, 12, 13 and 14;
Vehicle Excise and Registration Act 1994, s.44.

## Class I: offences against public justice and similar offences

(i) *Common law offences*

Embracery, fabrication of evidence with intent to mislead tribunal, perverting the course of justice and personation of jurors

(ii) *Offences created by primary or secondary legislation*

Those contrary to the following provisions:

Bribery Act 2010, ss.1, 2 and 6;
Cremation Act 1902, s.8(2);
Criminal Justice Act 1967, s.89;
Criminal Justice (Terrorism and Conspiracy) Act 1998, s.5;
Criminal Justice and Public Order Act 1994, ss.51(1) and (2), 75(1) and (2);
Criminal Law Act 1967, ss.4(1) and 5;
Drug Trafficking Act 1994, s.58(1);
European Communities Act 1972, s.11;
Forgery Act 1861, s.34;
Magistrates' Courts Act 1980, s.106;
Perjury Act 1911, ss.1 to 7(2);
Prevention of Corruption Act 1906, s.1;
Public Bodies Corrupt Practices Act 1889, s.1;
Trade Descriptions Act 1968, s.29(2).

## Class J: serious sexual offences

*Offences created by primary or secondary legislation*

Those contrary to the following provisions:

Children and Young Persons Act 1933, ss.25, 26;
Indecency with Children Act 1960, s.1(1);
Protection of Children Act 1978, s.1;
Sexual Offences Act 1956, ss.1(1), 5, 6, 7, 10, 12 (of person under 16), 16, 17, 20, 25, 26 and 28;
Sexual Offences Act 2003, ss.1, 2, 4 (activity involving penetration), 5 to 10, 14, 25, 26, 30, 31, 34, 35, 38, 39, 47 to 50 and 57 to 59A.

## G. VERY HIGH COST CASES

### Definition

For the definition of a "Very High Cost Case", see regulation 2 of S.I. 2013 No. 435 (*ante*, G-7). **G-181** Regulation 3(8) (*ante*, G-8) provides that the regulations (with the exception of reg. 12 and para. 13(8) and (9) of Schedule 2) do not apply to Very High Costs Cases.

### Background

Unlike the former scheme for the *ex post facto* taxation of fees (as to which, see Appendix G in **G-182** the supplements to the 2010 edition of this work) and the graduated fee scheme, the Very High Cost Case ("VHCC") regime is not concerned with fee assessment after the completion of a case. VHCCs operate under a contract-based system where litigators' and advocates' tasks and the time allotted for each task are agreed or determined before the work is undertaken. They are managed by the Complex Crime Unit of the Legal Aid Agency (an executive agency of the Ministry of Justice).

### Notification and classification

Litigators (referred to by the Legal Aid Agency as "organisations") are required to notify the **G-183** Legal Aid Agency of any case which is, or is likely to be, a VHCC: S.I. 2013 No. 435, reg. 12.

Notification is effected by submitting a VHCC Notification Request Form 2013, which is available on the agency's website. If a case qualifies, or if an organisation is in any doubt about this, the organisation should make the notification within five business days of the earliest hearing at which the court sets a trial estimate, or the organisation identifying that the case will be or is likely to be a VHCC, or the organisation receiving a VHCC notification request form 2013 from the agency. If the notification requirements are not met, and the agency is likely to or will suffer financial loss as a result, it may, in discharging its functions under the LASPOA 2012: (a) impose any sanction on the organisation in accordance with any other legal aid agreement or contract; (b) exclude the organisation from undertaking VHCC work or Individual Case Contract work on the case that it failed to notify; (c) where it persistently breaches this duty, exclude the organisation from undertaking future VHCC work or Individual Case Contract Work or reduce or refuse any payment to the organisation in relation to the case.

Part A of the current (2013) arrangements sets out the obligations and processes for notification and classification for all cases which may be classified as VHCCs on or after April 1, 2013. Part B applies to cases which fall to be classified on or after that date and where the trial would in the opinion of the Director of Legal Aid Casework be likely to last for more than 60 days (para. 1.4). Part C applies to cases which fall to be classified on or after that date where the case satisfies the definition of a Very High Cost Case (in reg. 2(1) of S.I. 2013 No. 435 (*ante*, G-7)) and the trial would in the opinion of the agency be likely to last for less than 61 days. Paragraph 5.4 of the arrangements states that where it is the opinion of the agency that a case will last no fewer than 25 days and no more than 40 days, it will only be classified as a Very High Cost Case if it is prosecuted by the Serious Fraud Office or it is a terrorism case.

Where a case satisfies the definition of a VHCC for organisations, the agency will issue a VHCC decision letter. If the case is one which in the director's opinion will last more than 60 days, the agency will issue a 2013 VHCC Contract (for organisations). In other cases, the agency will issue a 2013 Individual Case Contract (for organisations).

Where the case satisfies the definition of a VHCC for advocates, and a self-employed advocate has been instructed, the agency will issue a VHCC decision letter and a 2013 VHCC contract (for self-employed advocates) to the self-employed advocate. Exceptional circumstances apart, organisations and advocates must meet the eligibility criteria set out in the arrangements before they can undertake work on a Very High Cost Case.

For information as to the working of earlier arrangements, see the second supplement to the 2013 edition of this work.

Paragraph 13(9) of Schedule 2 is not to be construed literally; where, therefore, a very high cost case panel firm was instructed under the representation order prior to the case being classified as a very high cost case, where it continued to act after such classification and where, after the defendant had pleaded guilty and been put back for sentence, the representation order was withdrawn (apparently on the application of the solicitors) by order of the court, solicitors and counsel fell to be remunerated under the very high cost cases regime, not the graduated fee regime; paragraph 13(9) had no application to this situation; rather, it was intended to deal with the remuneration of a non-panel firm where a case is reclassified as a very high cost case whereupon the representation order is withdrawn (rather than being transferred to another litigator, in which case para. 13(8) is engaged): *Lord Chancellor v. Alexander Johnson & Co. Solicitors and McCarthy* [2011] Costs L.R. 987, QBD (Davis J.).

**[The next paragraph is G-187.]**

### Remuneration

G-187    Once a case is classified as a VHCC, the Legal Aid Agency will assign it to one of four categories against the criteria contained in clause 4.21 of the VHCC Specification (see also §§ 4.12 *et seq.* in the VHCC Guidance). For this purpose, the contracted organisation is required to submit a completed VHCC category assessment sheet within 15 business days of the decision letter: Arrangements, para. 8.2(c). The category to which the case is assigned determines the hourly rate payable for preparatory work undertaken by litigators. Advocacy rates are non-category specific.

Self-employed advocates are remunerated directly by the Legal Aid Agency: clause 5.21 of the VHCC Specification (for organisations). Where the VHCC has been classified both as a VHCC for organisations and for advocates, self-employed advocates must claim under their VHCC contract. Where the case is a VHCC for organisations but has not been classified as a VHCC for advocates, any self-employed advocate must claim under the advocates' graduated fee scheme. Employed advocates must claim payment through their organisation, whether under the graduated fee scheme (where the VHCC has not been classified as a VHCC for advocates) or under the VHCC scheme (where the VHCC is a VHCC in relation to both organisations and advocates).

As to rates of payments, these are now determined by regulation 12A of, and Schedule 6 (*ante*, G-18a, G-92c, *et seq.*) to the Criminal Legal Aid (Remuneration) Regulations 2013 (S.I. 2013 No. 435) for cases subject to the 2013 VHCC contract, and by the provisions of the Criminal Defence Service (Very High Cost Cases) (Funding) Order 2013 (S.I. 2013 No. 2804) for work undertaken on or after December 2, 2013 (unless the trial date was set before that date and is before April, 2014), in a "pre-commencement case" (as to which, see the Legal Aid, Sentencing and Punishment of Offenders Act 2012 (Consequential, Transitional and Saving Provisions) Regulations 2013 (S.I. 2013 No. 534), reg. 2) that was the subject of a contract made between the Legal Services Commission and members of the (now abolished) Very High Cost Case (Crime) Panel (art. 3 and Sched. 1) or was the subject of a 2010 VHCC contract (art. 4 and Sched. 2). S.I. 2013 No. 2804 also amended paragraph 25 (Very High Cost Cases) of Schedule 2 (litigators' graduated fee scheme) to the Criminal Defence Service (Funding) Order 2007 (S.I. 2007 No. 1174) (which was revoked by the Criminal Defence Service (Funding) (Amendment) Order 2011 (S.I. 2011 No. 2065) in relation to proceedings in which a representation order was granted on or after October 3, 2011) to provide for reduced fees for work done on or after December 2, 2013 (unless the trial date was set before that date and is before April, 2014), in a Very High Costs Case where a litigator instructed an advocate who was not a member of the Very High Cost Case (Crime) Panel.

**[The next paragraph is G-195.]**

### H. Preparation and Submission of Claims

#### (1) The preparation of claims

There is no mandatory graduated fee form. The use of computer-generated forms is permitted and this allows only the relevant data to be submitted. As to graduated fees generally, see *ante*, G-115 *et seq.* **G-195**

#### (2) Time limits for the submission of claims

No claim by an advocate for fees for work done shall be entertained unless submitted within three months of the conclusion of the proceedings to which it relates: S.I. 2013 No. 435, reg. 4(3). However, where a confiscation hearing under section 2 of the DTA 1994, section 71 of the CJA 1988 or Part 2 of the PCA 2002 is held more than 28 days after a person has been found or pleaded guilty, a graduated fee claim can be submitted despite the fact that the proceedings have not yet been completed: *ibid.*, reg. 4(6). The time limit may be extended for "good reason": *ibid.*, reg. 31(1); for example, where the claim is particularly complicated and difficult to prepare, where a co-defendant's case is awaiting disposal, or because there is a genuine misunderstanding about the submission of a claim. Extensions should be sought before the time limit expires. **G-196**

Where there are no good reasons, the time may be extended in "exceptional circumstances", in which case the appropriate authority shall consider whether it is reasonable to reduce the fee: S.I. 2013 No. 435, reg. 31(2). An advocate should be given a reasonable opportunity to show cause why his costs should not be reduced (*ibid.*). Any reduction may be challenged by appeal to the taxing master: *post*, G-269. As to what may constitute "good reason" or "exceptional circumstances", see *post*, G-269. **G-197**

Notwithstanding that a representation order may be expressed to cover proceedings in the Crown Court "and in the event of [the defendant] being convicted or sentenced ..., advice and assistance in regard to the making of an appeal", the legislation is clear as to the need for a claim in relation to work done in the Crown Court to be submitted within three months of the conclusion of the proceedings in that court, rather than within three months of the date on which an application for leave to appeal to the Court of Appeal was refused: *R. v. White* [2008] Costs L.R. 479.

In *R. v. Dumbaya* [2012] Costs L.R. 976, the costs judge took a different view and held that

since "representation" for the purposes of Part I of the Access to Justice Act 1999, "includes …
subject to any time limits which may be prescribed, advice and assistance as to any appeal" (the
1999 Act, s.26), proceedings should not be regarded as "concluded" until any such advice or assistance has been given. For corresponding provision in the LASPOA 2012, see section 42(1).

The Legal Services Commission disagreed with the judge in *Dumbaya*. Its November, 2012,
guidance provides that (i) the "conclusion of the proceedings" for litigators is the date on which
the defendant was acquitted or sentenced; where confiscation proceedings follow sentence, these
will be treated as separate proceedings; (ii) the "conclusion of the proceedings" for advocates is
the date on which the defendant was acquitted or sentenced or on which confiscation proceedings
are concluded; (iii) the commission is currently seeking clarification (in light of conflicting authorities) on whether the time taken, following conviction, to obtain and provide advice on appeal can
be taken into account when determining when proceedings conclude, but, pending clarification,
proposes to use the date of sentence or acquittal as the conclusion of proceedings; advocates or
litigators who risk not meeting the three-month time limit as a result of obtaining or providing
advice on appeal should contact the commission for an extension; (iv) bereavement, serious illness, burglary, and flooding in an office, are examples of what are likely to constitute "good
reason", but delay in obtaining evidence (including prosecution page counts) and administrative
errors will not; (v) those who believe that they are unlikely to meet the time limit should email
requesting an extension as soon as possible with grounds; advocates, if appropriate, should
provide the name of any firm that is refusing to provide relevant documents; (vi) while the disallowance of the entirety of a claim might constitute a disproportionate sanction and, accordingly,
an "exceptional" circumstance, as might the length of the delay and the amount of money
involved, a rigid framework for imposing financial penalties is not suitable, and claims must
instead be assessed on a case-by-case basis; (vii) accordingly, litigators and advocates who submit
claims out of time without "good reason" should provide an explanation as to the impact on them
of a total disallowance or reduction of fees for the specific case; although the amount of detail
need not be equivalent to that provided when asking for payments to be expedited on hardship
grounds, it must be sufficient to enable the determining officer to understand the impact of any
decision to disallow or reduce fees.

It is submitted that the commission's stance that proceedings conclude upon acquittal or
sentence is to be preferred to the approach of the costs judge in *Dumbaya, ante*. As there is no
provision under the 2007 order for payment for advice or assistance on appeal, there seems little
point in delaying the date on which the proceedings may be said to have concluded. Any other
view also introduces uncertainty.

### (3) Submitting an amended claim

**G-198**     Where a genuine error is made in submitting a graduated fee claim, counsel should not be
precluded for all time from submitting an amended claim where the refusal to permit him to do
so could result in his being deprived of fees to which he would have been entitled had the claim
been advanced correctly in the first place: *R. v. Hann* [2009] Costs L.R. 833. Where, therefore,
counsel, as a result of a genuine error, had submitted a claim for a cracked trial where the case
was disposed of as a guilty plea (albeit there had been a long delay between plea and sentence,
throughout which it had been on the cards that a *Newton* hearing (*R. v. Newton*, 77 Cr.App.R. 13,
CA) would eventually be required), it was held that counsel (who had been paid the appropriate
graduated fee for a guilty plea) should be granted an extension of time in which to submit an
amended claim for a guilty plea plus a special preparation fee (under what is now S.I. 2013 No.
435, Sched. 1 para. 17). See also *R. v. Lafayette* [2010] 4 Costs L.R. 650 (there is no good reason
why a lawyer who has submitted a claim should not be permitted to amend it before it has been
determined).

[The next paragraph is G-251.]

### I. DISBURSEMENTS AND EXPENSES

### (1) Disbursements

**G-251**     A barrister is not entitled to claim for disbursements or expenses other than those permitted
under S.I. 2013 No. 435.

For an example of the Legal Services Commission successfully questioning, pursuant to regulation 17 of S.I. 2013 No. 435 (*ante*, G-21), the propriety of incurring costs where the defence had sought, and obtained, prior authority to incur those costs, see *R. v. Ward* [2012] Costs L.R. 605. The costs related to the printing of a large quantity of documentation that had been contained on two computer discs and a memory stick. The solicitors had obtained authority on the ground that the files were inaccessible electronically, or that the software would corrupt their own network or that specialist software was needed to download and read the material. However, this only applied to the documents on the memory stick, and when the decision was taken not to print off the material on the memory stick, the solicitors "knew or ought reasonably to have known that the purpose for which authority had been given had failed or had become irrelevant or unnecessary before the disbursements were incurred." It had not been reasonable to incur the considerable costs when the prosecution did not intend to print the material off, and when there was no real difficulty in accessing it electronically. However, it was held that the purchase of a hard drive used by a computer expert instructed to analyse computers that had been seized was reasonable; it was inevitable that the contents would have to be copied on to a new drive, rather than a previously used drive, to avoid contamination, and such a purchase would not be part of the expert's overheads because once the drive was used, it could not be re-used for the same purpose.

### (2) Travelling and accommodation expenses

### Entitlement under the regulations

Travel and other expenses incidental to appearance at court may be claimed provided the    **G-252** court is not within 40 kilometres of the advocate's office or chambers. Unless prior approval for the expenditure has been obtained under the regulations, or unless the advocate can justify his attendance having regard to all the relevant circumstances of the case, the amount payable shall not be greater than that, if any, payable to a trial advocate from the nearest local Bar or the nearest advocate's office (whichever is the nearer): S.I. 2013 No. 435, Sched. 1, para. 29. As to interim payment of travel and accommodation expenses, see *ante*, G-107, G-108.

### Local bars

In *R. v. Comer* [2009] Costs L.R. 972, it was said that in paragraph 29 of Schedule 1 to S.I. 2013    **G-253** No. 435 (*ante*, G-62), the juxtaposition of the phrase "local Bar" with the phrase "advocate's office" suggests that a fairly modest number of practitioners can constitute a local bar. The existence of a bar mess is not a prerequisite, and whether the barristers based in an area constitute a local bar will be a question of feel. In this case, the view of the resident judge that "there is a healthy local bar" was considered to be the best evidence of such a bar. As to this case, see also *post*, G-258.

An advocate may be able to justify his attendance in a distant court which is usually serviced by a local bar where:

    (a) the instruction of local counsel might lead to suspicion of prejudice, lack of independence or lack of objectivity (*e.g.* cases of local notoriety involving public figures or officials);

    (b) there are insufficient local counsel whom instructing solicitors consider are sufficiently experienced to undertake the case in question so as to give the client a reasonable choice;

    (c) the services of an advocate who has specialised experience and knowledge of the type of case of an unusual or technical nature are required;

    (d) the advocate has previously been instructed in related matters which would assist him in the presentation or preparation of the case in question: *R. v. Conboy* (1990) Costs L.R. 493; and see *R. v. Gussman*, X14, SCTO 40/99 (counsel had represented his client seven years earlier on a charge of murder; his knowledge of his client's earlier medical condition was relevant to the current charges of rape, and this amounted to special circumstances justifying his attendance).

It is submitted that a further justification arises where an advocate is forced to follow a particular judge on circuit who is seized of his case and it was not reasonable to instruct another local advocate for that particular hearing. Where an advocate is instructed from outside a local bar for any of the above reasons it is advisable that he obtains a letter from his instructing solicitor explaining why he was instructed, and for his clerk to obtain prior approval for incurring such expenses from the court. This applies also to Queen's Counsel practising off-circuit: *post*, G-256.

**[The next paragraph is G-256.]**

### Queen's Counsel and local bars

G-256    Queen's Counsel should not be regarded as being "local" to any particular bar, even though his chambers are in one particular place. Where Queen's Counsel practises on circuit, he should as a general rule receive an amount in respect of travelling and hotel expenses actually and reasonably incurred and necessarily and exclusively attributable to his attendance at a court on the circuit on which he practises: *R. v. Thomas; R. v. Davidson; R. v. Hutton* (1985) Costs L.R. 469. Where Queen's Counsel practises outside his circuit, the "local bar" rules apply: *ante*, G-253.

### Expenses reasonably incurred

G-257    The reasonableness of an advocate's claim for travel and hotel expenses should be judged not by reference to the expenses incurred by other advocates in the same case, but in relation to the demands upon the advocate in putting forward his lay client's case and his own particular circumstances in relation to the conduct of the trial: *R. v. Plews* (1984) Costs L.R. 466; *post*, G-260.

    The regulations refer to expenditure "reasonably incurred", whereas earlier regulations referred to expenses "actually and reasonably incurred". In *R. v. Conboy* (1990) Costs L.R. 493, the taxing master observed that the current wording is wider. It is submitted that the alteration acknowledges an advocate's entitlement to recover a reasonable amount in respect of expenses necessarily and exclusively attributable to attendance at court. Thus, where the expense incurred was reasonable, an advocate should recover in full. Where the travel undertaken or accommodation used was reasonable but the cost incurred was excessive, an advocate may only claim for and recover a reasonable amount being a sum no greater than that which he would have incurred had his expenses been reasonable.

### Travel to court

G-258    In determining what is actually and reasonably incurred the relevant travel is that between court and an advocate's chambers: *R. v. Khan*, January 1989, TC C/13. Actual expenses incurred in travelling from an advocate's home to court will only be allowed if his home is nearer to court than his chambers, otherwise his journey is deemed to start from chambers: *R. v. Slessor* (1984) Costs L.R. 438. And, in such a case, he will only be entitled to travelling expenses actually incurred, *i.e.* from home to court: *R. v. Comer* [2009] Costs L.R. 972 (as to which, see also *ante*, G-253).

*(i) Public transport expenses*

G-259    Where expenses are recoverable, travel costs are generally limited to the cost of public transport actually incurred, together with the expense incurred in getting from the starting point to the railhead or coach station and the expense incurred from getting from the terminal to the court: *Slessor*, *ante*.

*(ii) Car expenses*

G-260    Where an advocate chooses to journey by car, the expenses allowed will not exceed the equivalent cost of public transport: *Slessor*, *ante*; *Conboy*, *ante*. The expenses of travel by car will be allowed where public transport is not available or is not reasonably convenient. What is "not reasonably convenient" is a matter for the discretion of the taxing officer. What may be convenient in one case may not be convenient in another. The time spent in getting from the starting point to the railhead, and from the terminus to court is always relevant: if it is considerable, the use of a car may be justified. Taxing officers have been urged to adopt a flexible and broad approach to the problem: *Slessor*, *ante*. Where the case papers are heavy and bulky, an advocate may be justified in using a car (an example given by the taxing officer in argument in *Conboy*, *ante*). In *R. v. Plews* (1984) Costs L.R. 466, counsel would have had to catch a 7.15 a.m. train from London to allow him to arrive at court in sufficient time to robe, see his client and solicitor, and to hold any pre-hearing discussions. It was therefore reasonable for counsel, bearing in mind that he had to travel from his home to the station and was faced with a full day in court, to travel by car.

*(iii)* *Expenses for reasonable travel by car*

In *Plews*, *ante*, counsel's claim, based on a mileage rate less than that prescribed for medical   **G-261**
practitioners in regulations then current, was considered reasonable, the taxing master observing
that a claim based upon the equivalent rate would have been allowed. The usual means of
estimating the expenses of travel by car is the standard mileage rate which is calculated by reference to the average cost of running a motor car, including such matters as depreciation, insurance, maintenance, *etc.*, which are referable to the running of a car of the relevant engine
capacity. Although the rate is not a precise measure of the actual cost of a particular form of
transport, it is intended to provide a mechanism for reimbursing expenses incurred when travelling by car: *Conboy*, *ante*. Where it is reasonable to incur the expense of travelling by car it must
also be reasonable to incur necessary and consequential costs of car parking (if any).

The Legal Services Commission announced an increase in its rates for civil solicitors from 36p
per mile to 45p per mile as from April 2, 2001. It is submitted that it is reasonable that similar
rates should apply to criminal advocates.

### Accommodation expenses

Hotel or accommodation expenses cannot be divorced from travelling expenses. They should   **G-262**
be paid instead of travelling expenses where an advocate reasonably chooses, or by reason of
distance is obliged, to stay near a court distant from his chambers rather than travel daily. If
travelling expenses are not payable then neither are hotel or accommodation expenses: *R. v.
Khan*, January 1989, TC C/13. Where an advocate claims expenses for overnight accommodation
and the cost equals or is less than that of the daily travel for which he would be entitled to be
reimbursed, such expenses should be allowed. Where the hotel expenses are more than the cost
of daily travel, they should be allowed if, having regard to the demands of the case on an
advocate, including the need for conferences after court and overnight preparation, the advocate
could not have returned home at a reasonable hour: *Plews*, *ante*.

### Conference travel expenses and travel time

Travel expenses reasonably incurred and necessarily and exclusively attributable to attending a   **G-263**
conference should be reimbursed where an advocate attends a conference in prison where the
authorities will only produce the client at the place of detention; the same principle applies when
the client is a patient in a psychiatric hospital: *R. v. Hindle* (1987) Costs L.R. 486.

### J. Proceedings in the Court of Appeal

### General principles

Payment for proceedings in the Court of Appeal is governed by Schedule 3 to S.I. 2013 No.   **G-264**
435 (*ante*, G-82 *et seq.*), which provides for *ex post facto* taxation, the overriding principles being
that the appropriate officer should, in determining fees, allow a "reasonable amount" in respect of
all work "actually and reasonably done".

### Advice on appeal

As to this, see, in particular, *R. v. Umezie*, § 7-165 in the main work, and *R. v. Bromige*, *ante*,   **G-265**
G-160.

### Solicitor advocates

In *R. v. Mansell* [2011] Costs L.R. 531, it was held that: (i) under S.I. 2013 No. 435, the fees of   **G-266**
a solicitor advocate in the Court of Appeal fall to be determined under Schedule 3 as if he were
an advocate, and not a litigator; (ii) a solicitor advocate is an "advocate" for all proceedings
covered by S.I. 2013 No. 435, including in the Court of Appeal (see the definition of "advocate"
in reg. 2, *ante*, G-7); and (iii) that paragraph 3 of Schedule 3 (determination of litigators' fees
(*ante*, G-83)), which permits payment of advocacy by litigators, does not mean that all advocacy by
solicitors is payable under that paragraph.

### K. DETERMINATIONS AND APPEALS

#### (1) The taxing authorities

**G-267**    Graduated fee claims are determined by Crown Court taxing officers and should usually be paid within 10 working days of receipt of the claim.

Applications for re-determination are addressed to the chief clerk of the Crown Court or the regional taxation director as appropriate. The re-determination does not have to be carried out by the original officer, although this is usually the case. Where difficult points of principle arise or large sums are in dispute the matter is referred to the regional taxing director or his assistant. Appeals from re-determinations are heard by costs judges appointed by the Lord Chancellor.

#### (2) Guide to the process of determination and appeal

**G-268**    A brief outline of the various stages of the determination of an advocate's fees is set out below. The regulations referred to are those of S.I. 2013 No. 435 (*ante*, §§ G-6 *et seq.*). The table below is merely intended as a guide to the relevant procedures.

As to the circumstances in which an advocate or a litigator may apply to the appropriate officer for a redetermination of his fees, for a review of specified decisions or for an offence to be reclassified, see regulation 28 of S.I. 2013 No. 435 (*ante*, G-34).

The references in the last column in the tables below are references to regulations of S.I. 2013 No. 435.

| Stage | Description | reg. |
|---|---|---|
| **Submission of Claim** | | 4 |
| *Time limit* | Within 3 months of conclusion of proceedings (see *ante*, G-199) | 4(3) |
| *Particulars submitted in all cases* | In the form and manner directed by the appropriate officer | 4(3) |
| **Interim payments (40% of total claim less any sum paid)** | | 19 |
| *Definition* | Payable where: | 18 |
| | (a) the basic fee claimed by any counsel in any related proceedings exceeds £4,000, and | 18(2) |
| | (b) 3 months have elapsed from the date of the conclusion of related proceedings or the date on which the bill is ready to tax, whichever is earlier. | 18(4) |
| *Related proceedings* | Proceedings involving the same defendant heard or dealt with together or proceedings involving more than one defendant arising out of the same incident so that defendants are charged, tried or disposed of together. | 18(3) |
| *When the bill is ready to tax* | Date of receipt of last bill in related proceedings. | 18(4) |
| *Entitlement* | Where counsel is entitled to an interim payment but no interim payment has been made and counsel has submitted his claim. | 18(4), (5) |
| *Time limit* | 6 months after the conclusion of proceedings against the defendant represented. | 18(5) |
| **Determination and notification of costs; authorisation of payment** | | |
| | Costs determined in accordance with Schedule 1. | 23(1) |
| | Counsel notified of costs payable and payment authorised. | 23(1) |

| Stage | Description | reg. |
|---|---|---|
| **Re-calculation of graduated fee or re-determination of decision to allow special or wasted preparation fee, or classification of offence** | | |
| *Time limit* | Within 21 days of receipt or notification of costs payable. | 28(3) |
| *Particulars to be submitted* | (a) Written notice specifying matters in respect of which application is made, grounds of objection and whether counsel wishes to appear or to be represented. | 28(3), (5) |
| | (b) Documents and information supplied with submission of claim. | 28(4) |
| | (c) Further information, particulars and documents as required by the appropriate officer. | 28(6) |
| **Re-determination of decision not to allow conference fee** (time limit and particulars as above) | | 28(1)(b) |
| **Re-determination by the appropriate officer** | | 28(7) |
| **Application for written reasons** | | 28(8) |
| *Time limit* | 21 days of notification of the decision | 28(8), (9) |
| **Appeal to costs judge** | | 29(1) |
| *Time limit* | 21 days of receipt of written reasons. | 29(2) |
| *Particulars to be submitted to costs judge and appropriate officer* | (a) Copy of written representations on application for re-determination. | 29(4) |
| | (b) Appropriate officer's written reasons. | |
| | (c) All documents supplied hereto. | |
| *Form of notice of appeal* | (a) As directed by the costs judge. | 29(5) |
| | (b) Specifying separately each item appealed against, showing amount claimed and determined for each item and the ground of objection. | |
| | (c) Stating whether appellant wishes to appear or to be represented. | |
| *Lord Chancellor's written representations* | Where the Lord Chancellor makes written representations, counsel shall have a reasonable opportunity to make representations in reply. | 29(9) |
| *Notification of hearing* | The costs judge shall inform counsel of hearing date and give directions as to conduct of appeal. | 29(10) |
| *No further evidence* | Unless costs judge otherwise directs no other evidence shall be raised at the hearing nor objection taken which was not raised at redetermination. | 29(11) |
| **Notification of costs judge's decision** | | 29(13) |
| *Costs* | Costs may be awarded where the appeal is allowed. | 29(14) |
| **Appeals to the High Court** | | 30 |
| *Right of appeal* | Right of appeal to single QBD judge from costs judge's decision on a point of principle of public importance. | 30(7) |
| *Application for costs judge's certificate* | Counsel may apply to the costs judge to certify a point of principle of general importance. | 30(1) |
| *Time limit for application* | Within 21 days of notification of costs judge's decision. | 30(2) |
| *Time limit for appeal* | Within 21 days from receipt of costs judge's certificate. | |

| Stage | Description | reg. |
|---|---|---|
| *Appeal by Lord Chancellor* | Within 21 days of notification of costs judge's decision, the Lord Chancellor may appeal the decision if counsel does not do so. | 30(5) |

### (3) The enforcement and extension of time limits

Time limits may be extended for good reason by the appropriate authority, *i.e.* the appropriate officer, costs judge, or the High Court: S.I. 2013 No. 435, reg. 31(1). Where for no good reason the time limit is not adhered to, the appropriate authority may in exceptional circumstances extend the time limit and shall consider whether it is reasonable in the circumstances to reduce the costs, subject to granting the advocate a reasonable opportunity to state either orally or in writing why the costs should not be reduced: *ibid.*, reg. 31(2). A decision not to extend time, or to reduce costs for claims out of time may be appealed by notice in writing to the senior costs judge specifying the grounds of appeal. The appeal must be instituted within 21 days of the decision being given: *ibid.*, reg. 31(3); and see *ante*, G-198. For the latest guidance from the Legal Services Commission on the submission of late claims and what may or may not be treated as "good reason" or "exceptional circumstances", see *ante*, G-197.

It was held in *R. v. Mahmood* [2008] Costs L.R. 326, that where a 10 per cent penalty was imposed following a delay of over two months in submitting a claim for costs, but where the representative had only received a notice, prior to the case being tried, stating that all late claims would be the subject of a penalty unless there was a good reason, this did not constitute notice to show cause why the claim should not be reduced. The determining officer had clearly not considered the circumstances of the particular case on its own merits.

In *R. v. Roberts* [2008] Costs L.R. 323, the oversight of two fee earners, the holiday of one of those fee-earners (even if well-deserved), and a subsequent systematic firm-wide failure did not constitute "good reason" or "exceptional circumstances" so as to justify an extension of time, following a delay of 17 months in submitting a claim for costs. Nor did previous good character constitute "exceptional circumstances", although it was said that it might amount to mitigating circumstances when considering the extent of any reduction in costs (were an extension to be granted). This was the case despite a general softening in the attitude to the delay.

A misunderstanding of the legislation cannot amount to "good reason", but could amount to "exceptional circumstances" where the evidence was that other bills that had been submitted late for like reason in the past had been accepted: *R. v. White* [2008] Costs L.R. 479. But a simple failure to follow up a case could rarely constitute "good reason" or "exceptional circumstances", and it made no difference that the firm in question had generally had a good record for submitting claims in time: *R. v. Johnson* [2008] Costs L.R. 983.

Neither "mere oversight" on the part of leading counsel nor a mistaken belief on the part of junior counsel that leading counsel's clerk was dealing with their fees could amount to "good reason" for not submitting their claims on time; but disallowance of fees *in toto* may be so disproportionate as to amount to "exceptional circumstances": see *R. v. Lafayette* [2010] 4 Costs L.R. 650.

In *R. v. Griffin* [2008] Costs L.R. 483, leading counsel had been under the mistaken impression that his junior was going to prepare a taxation note to be agreed between them before submission. However, in the event, his junior submitted his own claim independently and sent a copy of his taxation note to his leader, such note making it plain that he had submitted a claim and asserting, mistakenly, that leading counsel had already submitted his own claim. It was held that as this was already seven months out of time, and leading counsel only submitted his own claim after a further two years, neither the misunderstanding as between leader and junior, nor extreme pressure of work plus some personal pressure over the two years that followed discovery of the fact that his junior had submitted his own claim, could amount to "good reason" for the failure to submit the claim within the three-month time limit; nor could they amount to "exceptional circumstances" so as to justify an extension of time despite the absence of good reason. There had been no obligation on the determining officer to remind counsel that his claim was late and the absence, at the time, of published criteria to be applied to the submission of late claims, did not avail counsel. What was critical to the outcome was the fact that two years before his eventual submission of his claim, he had been alerted by his junior's note to the fact that he would need to submit his own claim and he had failed then to take any steps to address the situation.

In *R. v. Islami* [2009] Costs L.R. 988, following a ruling that total disallowance of a claim by    **G-270** solicitors for £58,060.13 (including disbursements and travelling expenses) due to delay (of three years and nine months) would be so disproportionate (because of the substantial effect that this would have on the firm's profits) as to amount to "exceptional circumstances" and that the claim should be re-submitted, albeit that a five per cent penalty should be applied to the sum ultimately allowed, it was held that the fact that an administrative officer at the firm had then not complied with her instructions to submit the relevant documents for taxation, and the fact that this was only discovered during her ensuing extensive sick leave, did not amount to a "good reason" for a further delay of nine months in re-submitting the claim. In these circumstances, total disallowance of the claim, and the ensuing effect on the firm's profits, was no longer a disproportionate penalty sufficient to constitute "exceptional circumstances". Had the sum been needed with the urgency suggested at the original hearing, the firm would have ensured that the claim was re-submitted immediately and carefully tracked. Instead, the administrative problems identified at the original hearing had clearly not been resolved. However, it was said that this conclusion should be applied only to the profit costs and that the claim, so far as it related to disbursements (which had long since been paid out by the firm), should still be determined (without penalty), provided that the necessary papers were lodged within 14 days.

A reduction of an out-of-time claim to zero is not automatically to be regarded as so disproportionate as to give rise to "exceptional circumstances", but the shortness of the delay, the amount of money involved and the impact on the advocate or litigator involved are capable of constituting exceptional circumstances; each case must, however, turn on its own facts; there can be no hard and fast rules or pre-set scales: *R. v. Grigoropolou* [2012] Costs L.R. 982.

In *R. v. Newport* [2009] Costs L.R. 983, it was said that, although it has often been stated that    **G-271** barristers must have suitable systems in place to ensure that claims for fees and requests for redeterminations are made within the relevant time limits, and although the delay in this particular case was significant (over three years after the determining officer had refused payment), "exceptional circumstances" for extending the time to apply for a redetermination had been made out where counsel had trusted his senior clerk to ensure that the claim and any appeal procedure was appropriately and punctually concluded, but where he had been deliberately misled by the clerk, who failed, despite counsel's regular enquiries, to inform counsel that his claim had been refused *in toto*. This was found to be a rare and regrettable situation and not akin to an argument that "pressures of work" constituted exceptional circumstances (which would not be successful).

### (4) Re-determinations and appeals

#### Graduated fees

An advocate may only seek re-determination or appeal in respect of graduated fees where, (a)    **G-272** the issue is either whether the graduated fee scheme applied to the relevant proceedings, or (b) complaint is made as to the calculation of the remuneration payable, or (c) where the advocate is dissatisfied with a refusal to allow a special preparation fee or the number of hours allowed in the calculation of such fee; or (d) where the advocate is dissatisfied with the classification of an offence which does not appear in the Table of offences: S.I. 2013 No. 435, reg. 28(3). Under S.I. 2013 No. 435 a re-determination may also be sought in respect of a decision not to allow an hourly fee in respect of attendance at conferences or views at the scene of the alleged offence, or of the number of hours allowed in the calculation of such a fee: see reg. 28(1)(b)(i).

#### Re-determination

On an application for re-determination an advocate shall specify the grounds of his objection to    **G-273** all or any part of the determination (S.I. 2013 No. 435, reg. 28(3)(b)) and may appear in person or through another to make representations: S.I. 2013 No. 435, reg. 28(5). An advocate is not obliged to provide fresh information or material to assist the determining officer in the redetermination. If no additional information is provided, the determining officer has a duty to redetermine on the basis of the information already supplied: *R. v. O'Brien* [2003] Costs L.R. 625.

Many appeals which might otherwise have succeeded have failed because the representations made to the appropriate officer have been perfunctory and inexplicit: *R. v. Davies* (1985) Costs L.R. 472.

As from January 1, 1994, the General Council of the Bar has agreed that all requests for fees to be re-determined or for written reasons to be provided should be signed by counsel personally.

Re-determination should, where possible, be carried out by the officer who determined costs. Where cases are cited in support of the re-determination, sufficient references must be given to allow an advocate to identify and look them up: *R. v. Pelepenko*, X27A, SCCO 186/2001.

Where the Legal Aid Agency makes a decision to recover an overpayment of fees pursuant to regulation 25 of S.I. 2013 No. 435 (*ante*, G-31) and the litigator requests a review, a subsequent confirmation by the commission of its decision to recoup constitutes a redetermination within the meaning of regulation 28 (*ante*, G-34), so as to allow the litigator to appeal to a costs judge pursuant to regulation 29(1) (*ante*, G-35): *Lord Chancellor v. Eddowes Perry and Osbourne Ltd* [2011] Costs L.R. 498, QBD (Spencer J.) (disapproving *R. v. Charlery; R. v. Small* [2011] Costs L.R. 331). As to this case, see also *ante*, G-161.

### Further evidence on appeal and supplemental written reasons

G-274    On appeal before a costs judge no further evidence shall be received and no ground of objection shall be valid which was not raised on the application for re-determination unless the costs judge otherwise directs: S.I. 2013 No. 435, reg. 29(11). These provisions are strictly applied. A costs judge will rarely accede to a request to adduce further evidence or allow a fresh objection to be raised. Where written reasons do not address a point raised in the claim, counsel cannot pursue the matter in the appeal. The proper method of dealing with such an omission is to seek supplemental written reasons from the appropriate officer.

### Appeals

G-275    The right of appeal to a costs judge is effectively limited in that no appeal lies against a determination unless the advocate has applied for a re-determination and, thereafter, for written reasons under S.I. 2013 No. 435, reg. 29(1).

An advocate wishing to appeal must have regard to, and be familiar with, the provisions of Part 5 of the *Practice Direction (Criminal Proceedings: Costs)* [2013] 1 W.L.R. 3255 (§§ 6-146 *et seq.* in the main work).

### Representation, costs and expenses of appeal

G-276    For the purposes of an appeal to a costs judge, an advocate is treated as the appellant and can elect to be represented at the hearing. A successful appellant may be awarded a sum in respect of part or all of any reasonable costs incurred in connection with the appeal: S.I. 2013 No. 435, reg. 29(14); and see *R. v. Boswell; R. v. Halliwell* [1987] 1 W.L.R. 705 (Leggatt J.).

A barrister without the intervention of a solicitor may accept a brief or instructions, with or without fee, directly from, and represent, another barrister on that other barrister's appeal as to his fees before a costs judge: see *Code of Conduct*, 8th ed., para. 401 (Appendix C-7, *ante*). A professional fee payable by one barrister to another for conducting the former's appeal is capable of constituting part of the costs incurred by the appellant counsel: *R. v. Boswell; R. v. Halliwell, ante*. In assessing such costs the costs judge is entitled to take account of time and skill expended by the appellant or his counsel in the drawing of grounds and preparation of the appeal, and the conduct of the hearing, and travel and subsidence costs: *ibid*. Costs incurred in instructing other counsel are clearly reasonable where there is some technical question on the applicability of some part of the regulations or other issue which legitimately deserves the attention of specialist costs counsel. Costs are not reasonably incurred if trial counsel is available, could easily have represented himself and the only real issue is the weight of the case or the value of a particular item of work undertaken: *Jackson v. Lord Chancellor* [2003] Costs L.R. 395; and *R. v. Martin* [2007] Costs L.R. 128. A successful appellant will ordinarily be entitled to the return of the fee payable in respect of the appeal.

### Appeals to the single judge

G-277    As to appeals from a costs judge to the High Court, see S.I. 2013 No. 435, reg. 30. The ambit of an appeal is strictly limited to the point of principle certified by the costs judge as being of general importance (such certificate being a pre-condition to an appeal): *Patten v. Lord Chancellor*, 151 N.L.J. 851, QBD (Leveson J.), not following *Harold v. Lord Chancellor* [1999] Costs L.R. 14. Although *Patten* was concerned with the interpretation of regulation 16 of the Legal Aid in Criminal and Care Proceedings (Costs) Regulations 1989 (S.I. 1989 No. 343), regulation 29 of S.I. 2013 No. 435 is worded in almost identical terms. A refusal of a costs judge to certify that the matter raises a point of principle of general importance is not susceptible to judicial review: *R. v. Supreme Court Taxing Office, exp. John Singh & Co* [1997] 1 Costs L.R. 49, CA (Civ. Div). As to the limited scope for a challenge, by way of judicial review, to the substantive decision of a costs judge where a certificate has been refused, see § 6-75 in the main work.

### (5) Recovery of overpayment

Where an advocate receives a sum in excess of his entitlement, the taxing authority may either **G-278** require immediate repayment of that excess, or deduct the excess from any other sum payable to the advocate under the regulations: S.I. 2013 No. 435, reg. 25. These provisions apply notwithstanding the fact that a re-determination or appeal has been or may be requested: S.I. 2013 No. 435, reg. 25(4).

### (6) Appeals under VHCCs

Under the arrangements that came into force on April 1, 2013 (*ante*, G-181 *et seq.*), both the **G-279** VHCC Specification for organisations and that for advocates provide for a right of appeal to the VHCC Appeals Panel. The details are set out in paragraph 6 of the specifications, with paragraph 6.4 listing the issues in relation to which there is a right of appeal (*e.g.* the category to which a case has been assigned) and paragraph 6.5 listing those issues in relation to which there is no right of appeal. The appeal process, including time limits, is provided for by paragraphs 6.6 to 6.30. The appeal will normally be determined by a single adjudicator but may be referred to an appeals committee. The decision of the adjudicator or committee is final (para. 6.28), but is binding only in relation to the particular appeal (para. 6.29). Anonymised versions of decisions will be published on the Legal Aid Agency's website (para. 6.30).

# APPENDIX H
## Sexual Offences (The Law as at April 30, 2004)

## A. INTRODUCTION

The history of the sexual offences legislation since 1956 is set out in detail at §§ 20-1 *et seq.* in **H-1** the main work. All the statutory provisions contained in this appendix were repealed with effect from May 1, 2004, by the SOA 2003, but, as stated in the main work, they have continuing effect in relation to conduct occurring prior to that date. It should be borne in mind that this appendix states the law as at April 30, 2004, and that, therefore, there may yet be prosecutions for offences committed prior to even earlier material changes in the law: see, in particular, the amendments effected by the SOA 1985 and the CJPOA 1994 (summarised at §§ 20-2, 20-3 in the main work).

## B. SEXUAL OFFENCES ACT 1956

### (1) Rape

#### (a) *Introduction*

Section 1 of the 1956 Act made rape an offence. Section 1(1) of the Sexual Offences (Amend- **H-2** ment) Act 1976 provided a statutory definition of rape in terms designed to give effect to the Report of the Advisory Group on the Law of Rape (Cmnd. 6352) and the views expressed by the House of Lords in *DPP v. Morgan* [1976] A.C. 182. Section 1(1) was repealed by the CJPOA 1994, which also substituted a new section 1 in the 1956 Act. The effect of this was to adopt the 1976 definition, but to extend it so as to cover anal intercourse with a woman or a man. In addition, the new provision referred simply to "sexual intercourse" whereas the 1976 Act referred to "unlawful sexual intercourse". The omission of the word "unlawful" made clear Parliament's adoption of the decision of the House of Lords in *R. v. R.* [1992] A.C. 599, that a man may rape his wife.

Section 7(2) of the 1976 Act (as amended by the CJA 1988, s.158(1) and (6)) provided that in that Act "a rape offence":

> "means any of the following, namely rape, attempted rape, aiding, abetting, counselling and procuring rape or attempted rape, incitement to commit rape, conspiracy to rape and burglary with intent to rape."

#### (b) *Statute*

**Sexual Offences Act 1956, s.1**

*Rape of woman or man*

**1.**—(1) It is an offence for a man to rape a woman or another man.     **H-3**

(2) A man commits rape if—

  (a)   he has sexual intercourse with a person (whether vaginal or anal) who at the time of the intercourse does not consent to it; and

  (b)   at the time he knows that the person does not consent to the intercourse or is reckless as to whether that person consents to it.

(3) A man also commits rape if he induces a married woman to have sexual intercourse with him by impersonating her husband.

(4) Subsection (2) applies for the purposes of any enactment.

[This section is printed as substituted (from November 3, 1994) by the CJPOA 1994, s.142.]

**Sexual Offences (Amendment) Act 1976, s.1**

**1.**—(1) [*Repealed by Criminal Justice and Public Order Act 1994, s.168(3) and Sched. 11.*]     **H-4**

(2) It is hereby declared that if at a trial for a rape offence the jury has to consider whether a man believed that a woman or man was consenting to sexual intercourse, the presence or absence of reasonable grounds for such a belief is a matter to which the jury is to have regard, in conjunction with any other relevant matters, in considering whether he so believed.

[Subs. (2) is printed as amended by the CJPOA 1994, s.168(2), and Sched. 10, para. 35(1), (2).]

As to the use of the words "man" and "woman", see *post*, H-222. As to the meaning of "a rape offence", see *ante*, H-2.

In the case of a summary trial or a trial by court-martial, the references to the jury in section 1(2) of the 1976 Act are to be construed as references to the court: *ibid.*, s.7(3).

### (c) *Anonymity*

**H-5**    See §§ 20-257 *et seq.* in the main work.

### (d) *Indictment*

#### Statement of Offence

**H-6**    *Rape, contrary to section 1(1) of the Sexual Offences Act 1956.*

#### Particulars of Offence

*A B on the ____ day of ____, 20__, had sexual intercourse with C D who at the time of the said intercourse did not consent to it, the said A B either knowing that the said C D did not so consent or being reckless as to whether she [or he] so consented.*

Where the victim is a woman, the intercourse may be vaginal or anal: s.1(1) of the 1956 Act, *ante*, H-3. It is unnecessary to specify in the indictment whether the allegation is of vaginal or anal intercourse, but there will be cases where it is of assistance to do so. This can be done by adding the words *"per vaginam"* or *"per anum"* after the words "sexual intercourse". The addition of these words will be particularly useful where it is alleged that a woman was raped both vaginally and anally; the counts will reflect this and will ensure, in the event of a conviction on one count only, that the court is aware of the basis of the jury's verdict. As to where it is unclear on the evidence whether penetration was of the vagina or the anus, see *R. v. K. (Robert)* [2009] 1 Cr.App.R. 24, CA (§ 20-20 in the main work).

Good practice does not require that, where the prosecution rely on recklessness as an alternative to knowledge, there should be separate counts (alleging respectively knowledge and recklessness): *R. v. Flitter* [2001] Crim.L.R. 328, CA.

### Allegation of joint offence

**H-7**    Where a person has been raped by more than one man on the same occasion, all the accused should be charged in one count of rape, with no mention of aiders and abettors: see the direction of the House of Lords in *DPP v. Merriman* [1973] A.C. 584. This enables the jury to be told that it matters not whether an individual accused physically committed the act of rape, or assisted or encouraged someone else to; thus, several accused may be convicted where the jury is satisfied only that each played a guilty part, but not as to who committed the physical act.

### (e) *Class of offence and mode of trial*

**H-8**    This offence and an attempt to commit it are class 2 offences (§ 2-17 in the main work), triable on indictment only: SOA 1956, s.37(2), and Sched. 2, para. 1.

### (f) *Alternative verdicts*

**H-9**    On a count of rape, the accused may be convicted of procurement of a woman by threats (s.2) or false pretences (s.3) or of administering drugs to obtain or facilitate intercourse (s.4): SOA 1956, s.37(4), and Sched. 2, para. 1.

As to alternative verdicts generally, see §§ 4-524 *et seq.* in the main work. Where the alleged victim was a girl under 16 years of age, then whether or not her age is averred in the indictment, a jury may not convict the accused under section 6(3) of the CLA 1967 (§ 4-525 in the main work) of an offence contrary to section 6 of the SOA 1956 (unlawful intercourse with a girl under 16): *R.*

*v. Fisher* [1969] 2 Q.B. 114, Assizes (Cusack J.); *R. v. Mochan*, 54 Cr.App.R. 5, Assizes (Cusack J.), approved in *R. v. Hodgson* [1973] Q.B. 565, 57 Cr.App.R. 502, CA.

As every charge of rape contains the essential ingredients of indecent assault (*viz.* an assault and indecency), it follows that where a man is acquitted of rape on the ground of the victim's consent, it is open to the jury to convict him where the victim is under 16, of indecent assault, because the consent which provided a defence to a charge of rape cannot, by virtue of the SOA 1956, ss.14(2) and 15(2), provide a defence to a charge of indecent assault. Age is not an ingredient of, nor an essential averment in the framing of a count of indecent assault: *R. v. Hodgson, ante.*

In *R. v. Timmins* [2006] 1 Cr.App.R. 18, CA, it was held that the effect of the decision in *R. v. J.* [2005] 1 A.C. 562, HL (on a true construction of the 1956 Act, it was impermissible to prosecute a charge of indecent assault under section 14(1) (*post*, H-117) in circumstances where the only conduct upon which the charge was based was an act of unlawful sexual intercourse with a girl under the age of 16 in respect of which no prosecution could be commenced under section 6(1) (*post*, H-50) by virtue of the time bar contained in section 37(2) of, and Schedule 2 to, the Act) was not such as to preclude a judge from leaving it to a jury to convict of indecent assault as an alternative to a charge of rape, under section 6(3) of the CLA 1967 (*ante*), where they were satisfied as to the act of sexual intercourse and as to the fact that the girl was under 16 at the time, and where they acquitted of rape on the ground that they were not satisfied as to lack of consent, and this was so notwithstanding that the proceedings for rape had been begun over 12 months after the alleged offence; the decision in *J.* had turned on the words of Schedule 2 to the 1956 Act, which provided that "A prosecution may not be commenced more than 12 months after the offence charged."; leaving a possible alternative verdict to a jury could not be described as a "commencement" of proceedings for the offence; but it would be an abuse of process to bring a charge of rape against a person against whom there was no evidence whatever of rape (in particular lack of consent) in order to circumvent a time limit.

In the earlier case of *R. v. Rabbitts* (2005) 149 S.J. 890, CA, it was held that, *R. v. J.* having decided that, as a matter of statutory construction, it was not open to the prosecution to bring a charge of indecent assault where the conduct on which the prosecution was based was an act of consensual sexual intercourse with a girl under 16, and where the purpose was to circumvent the statutory time limit of 12 months on prosecutions for unlawful sexual intercourse with a girl of that age, it made no difference that the count of indecent assault was included in the indictment as an alternative to a charge of rape to cater for the possibility that the jury would not be satisfied as to lack of consent.

In *R. v. Cottrell*; *R. v. Fletcher* [2008] 1 Cr.App.R. 7, CA, it was said that to the extent that *Timmins* and *Rabbitts* were inconsistent, they should be followed as they apply to the facts of the individual case. As to the flawed nature of the decision in *Timmins*, see CLW/05/43/4.

### (g) *Autrefois acquit and convict*

For the general principles, see §§ 4-183 *et seq.* in the main work. **H-10**

An acquittal upon an indictment for rape was held to be no bar to a subsequent indictment on the same facts for a common assault: *R. v. Dungey* (1864) 4 F. & F. 99 (and see now s.6(3A) of the CLA 1967 (§ 4-525 in the main work), reversing the effect of *R. v. Mearns* [1991] 1 Q.B. 82, 91 Cr.App.R. 312, CA).

An acquittal on an indictment for rape cannot be successfully pleaded as a bar to a subsequent indictment for assault with intent to commit rape: *R. v. Gisson* (1847) 2 C. & K. 781, or, in certain circumstances, to a subsequent indictment for attempted rape, see *R. v. Hearn* [1970] Crim.L.R. 175, CA (§ 4-203 in the main work).

However, it should be noted that there was (as at April 30, 2004), in all probability, no longer an offence of assault with intent to rape, contrary to common law. It did not survive the creation of an identical statutory offence in the Offences against the Person Act 1861, s.38, which was in turn abolished by virtue of section 10 of, and Schedule 3 to, the Criminal Law Act 1967: *R. v. P.* [1990] Crim.L.R. 323, Crown Court (Pill J.) (but note the commentary and reference, by Professor J. C. Smith, to the opposite view expressed by Turner J. in *R. v. J.*, unreported, June 9, 1986). *Cf.* section 16 of the 1956 Act (assault with intent to commit buggery), *post*, H-138.

### (h) *Sentence*

**Maximum**

H-11    Rape: life imprisonment—SOA 1956, s.37(3), and Sched. 2, para. 1(a).

Attempted rape: life imprisonment—SOA 1956, s.37(3), and Sched. 2, para. 1(a) (as amended by the SOA 1985, s.3).

**Guidelines**

H-12    See the guidelines of the Sentencing Guidelines Council, *post*, Appendix K-83 *et seq.*

In *R. v. H.* [2012] 2 Cr.App.R.(S.) 21, CA, it was said that in the search for principle, it is impossible to reconcile all the authorities that purport to provide guidance on sentencing for historic sexual offending; that the following considerations, derived from statute (general provisions about sentencing in the CJA 2003, Pt 12, Chap. 1 (ss.142–176), and the Coroners and Justice Act 2009, s.125 (sentencing guidelines: duty of court (§ 5-149 in the main work))) and case law, should be treated as guidance; and that reference to earlier decisions (with the exception of *R. v. Millberry*; *R. v. Morgan*; *R. v. Lackenby*, *post*, Appendix K-83) is unlikely to be helpful and is to be discouraged. First, sentence will be imposed on the basis of the legislative provisions current at the time of sentence, and by measured reference to any definitive sentencing guidelines relevant to the situation revealed by the established facts. Secondly, although sentence must be limited to the maximum permissible at the date when the offence was committed, it is wholly unrealistic to attempt an assessment of sentence by seeking to identify today what the sentence was likely to have been if the offence had come to light at or shortly after its commission. Thirdly, the particular circumstances in which the offence was committed and its seriousness must be the main focus; due allowance for the passage of time may be appropriate; the date may have a considerable bearing on the offender's culpability; for example, if he was young and immature at the time, that remains a continuing feature of the sentencing decision; similarly, if the allegations had come to light many years earlier, and the offender admitted them, but, for whatever reason, the complaint had not been drawn to the attention of, or investigated by, the police, or had been investigated but had not then been pursued to trial, these too would be relevant matters. Fourthly, careful judgment of the harm done to the victim is always a critical feature of the sentencing decision; simultaneously, equal care needs to be taken to assess the true extent of the offender's criminality by reference to what he actually did and the circumstances in which he did it. Fifthly, the passing of the years may demonstrate aggravating features if, for example, the offender has continued to commit sexual crime or he represents a continuing risk to the public; on the other hand, mitigation may be found in an unblemished life over the intervening years, particularly if accompanied by evidence of positive good character. Sixthly, early admissions and a guilty plea are of particular importance in historic cases; given that it is tempting to lie about events long ago, it is greatly to the offender's credit if he makes early admissions; even more powerful mitigation is available to the offender who, out of a sense of guilt and remorse, reports himself to the authorities. The court considered, *inter alia*, *R. v. Bowers* [1999] 2 Cr.App.R.(S.) 97, CA, *R. v. Fowler* [2002] 2 Cr.App.R.(S.) 99, CA, *Att.-Gen.'s References (Nos 37, 38, 44, 54, 51, 53, 35, 40, 43, 45, 41 and 42 of 2003)* [2004] 1 Cr.App.R.(S.) 84, CA, *R. v. McKendrick* [2005] 2 Cr.App.R.(S.) 68, CA, *R. v. Patterson* [2006] 2 Cr.App.R.(S.) 48, CA, *Att.-Gen.'s Reference (No. 39 of 2006)* (*R. v. J. (Rodney Clive)*) [2007] 1 Cr.App.R.(S.) 34, CA, *R. v. Moon* [2011] 1 Cr.App.R.(S.) 34, CA, *R. v. Hartley (Practice Note)* [2012] 1 Cr.App.R. 7, CA, and *Att.-Gen.'s Reference (No. 78 of 2010)* [2011] 2 Cr.App.R.(S.) 109, CA.

This approach to sentencing historic sexual offences has been specifically endorsed by the Sentencing Council for England and Wales: see Annex B to its definitive guideline on sexual offences (*post*, Appendix K-84).

### (i) *Ingredients of the offence*

**A "man"**

H-13    The common law presumption that a boy under the age of 14 was incapable of sexual intercourse was abolished (for both natural and unnatural intercourse) by the SOA 1993, ss.1, 2(2), (3).

A woman may be convicted as an aider and abettor: *R. v. Ram* (1893) 17 Cox 609 at 610n.

A man may be convicted of raping his wife: *R. v. R.* [1992] 1 A.C. 599, HL (confirmed by the revised definition of "rape" introduced by the CJPOA 1994, *ante*, § H-3).

## Sexual intercourse

Where it is necessary to prove sexual intercourse (whether natural or unnatural), it shall not be **H-14** necessary to prove the completion of the intercourse by the emission of seed, but it shall be deemed complete upon proof of penetration only: SOA 1956, s.44 (*post*, § H-219). "Unnatural" intercourse in section 44 means buggery (including bestiality): *R. v. Gaston*, 73 Cr.App.R. 164, CA.

The amendment of section 1 of the 1956 Act by the 1994 Act (§ 20-3 in the main work, and *ante*, H-3) did not alter the law (whereunder even the slightest penetration would be sufficient: see *R. v. R'Rue* (1838) 8 C. & P. 641; *R. v. Allen* (1839) 9 C. & P. 31) so as to make penetration of the vagina, properly so-called, an essential ingredient of "vaginal" rape; it is sufficient that there was any degree of penetration by the penis within the labia of the pudendum of the complainant; the word "vaginal" in section 1 is used in comparison with, or in addition to, "anal", and not so as to indicate that the word is being used in the medical sense, rather than the general sense of the female genitalia: *R. v. J.F.*, unreported, December 16, 2002, CA ([2002] EWCA Crim. 2936).

Sexual intercourse is a continuing act; it follows that consensual intercourse will become rape if the woman (or man) ceases to consent during the intercourse, and the man (other man), with the necessary *mens rea*, continues the act: *Kaitamaki v. R.* [1985] A.C. 147, PC (decided on the corresponding New Zealand legislation). It should be noted that these were not the facts in *Kaitamaki*; the facts were that the defendant claimed he only realised the woman was not consenting after intercourse had begun. As to this aspect of the decision, see *post*, H-20. However, the foregoing proposition appears to follow as a matter of logic from the Board's decision on the narrower point.

## Absence of consent

*General*

It must be proved that the accused had sexual intercourse with the complainant without her or **H-15** his consent: s.1(2)(a) of the 1956 Act, *ante*, H-3. This applies even where the offence is alleged to have been committed on a person under the age of 16, though sometimes in such a case the prosecution will not need to prove much more than the age of the victim: *R. v. Harling*, 26 Cr.App.R. 127, CCA. It is not, however, necessary to support a charge of rape that there is evidence that the complainant demonstrated her lack of consent or communicated it to the accused; the minimum requirement is evidence of lack of consent in fact, which might take many forms; the most obvious is the complainant's simple assertion, which may or may not be backed up by evidence of force or threats; alternatively, it may consist of evidence that by reason of drink, drugs, sleep, age or mental handicap the complainant was unaware of what was occurring and/or incapable of giving consent; or it may consist of evidence that the complainant was deceived as to the identity of the man with whom she had intercourse: *R. v. Malone* [1998] 2 Cr.App.R. 447, CA. As to intercourse with a woman known to be asleep, see *R. v. Mayers* (1872) 12 Cox 311; *R. v. Young* (1878) 14 Cox 114.

Lack of consent will have been established if the jury are satisfied that although the complainant did not dissent, her understanding and lack of knowledge were such, whether on account of age, the consumption of drink or drugs or mental handicap, that she was incapable of giving consent or of exercising any judgment on the matter: see *R. v. Howard*, 50 Cr.App.R. 56, CCA (age); *R. v. Lang*, 62 Cr.App.R. 50, CA (drink); *R. v. Fletcher* (1859) Bell 63; *R. v. Ryan* (1846) 2 Cox 115; *R. v. Fletcher* (1866) L.R. 1 C.C.R. 39; *R. v. Barratt* (1873) L.R. 2 C.C.R. 81; *R. v. Pressy* (1867) 10 Cox 635, CCR (mental handicap). To the extent that they suggest that where no force, threat or deceit was used, there must be evidence of some resistance on the part of the complainant, *Howard* and *Lang* should no longer be taken to represent the law: *Malone, ante*.

Evidence of resistance may, of course, be highly relevant to the separate issue of the defendant's knowledge or recklessness in relation to the lack of consent.

Although juries should be told that "consent" in the context of the offence of rape is a word **H-16** which must be given its ordinary meaning, it is sometimes necessary for the judge to go further.

For example, he should point out, if necessary, that there is a difference between consent and submission (as to which, see also § 20-10 in the main work). In cases where intercourse took place after threats not involving violence, or the fear of it, a jury should be directed to concentrate on the state of mind of the victim immediately before the act of intercourse. The jury should be reminded too of the wide spectrum of states of mind which consent could comprehend and that where a dividing line had to be drawn between real consent and mere submission they should apply their combined good sense, experience and knowledge of human nature and modern behaviour to all the relevant facts of the case: *R. v. Olugboja*, 73 Cr.App.R. 344, CA (*cf. R. v. McAllister* [1997] Crim.L.R. 233, CA, *post*, H-124). The word "want" should not be used in directing a jury on the issue of consent, there being a clear difference between "wanting" to have intercourse and "consenting" to it: *R. v. T. (D.)* [2000] 7 *Archbold News* 3, CA.

As to evidence about the lack of sexual experience of a complainant, see § 20-11 in the main work.

As to intercourse with a defective, see also the SOA 1956, ss.7 and 45 (*post*, H-64, H-68).

*Intercourse by false pretences*

**H-17**    The only types of fraud which vitiate consent for the purposes of the law of rape are frauds as to the nature of the act or as to the identity of the person doing the act: *R. v. Linekar* [1995] 2 Cr.App.R. 49, CA. As to frauds as to the nature of the act, see *R. v. Case* (1850) 1 Den. 580, and *R. v. Flattery* (1877) 2 Q.B.D. 410, where the consent was induced by the pretence that the act of intercourse was a form of medical treatment, and *R. v. Williams* [1923] 1 K.B. 340, 17 Cr.App.R. 56, CCA, where a choirmaster pretended to be testing a girl's breathing powers with an instrument. As to fraud as to the identity of the perpetrator of the Act, section 1(3) of the SOA 1956 (*ante*, H-3) makes express provision for the case of a man inducing a married woman to have sexual intercourse with him by impersonating her husband. This provision was first introduced by the Criminal Law Amendment Act 1885 for the purpose of reversing the decision in *R. v. Barrow* (1868) L.R. 1 C.C.R. 156. As to other instances of impersonation, it is possible that the principle in *Barrow* will still prevail; but it was dissented from in *R. v. Dee* (1884) 15 Cox C.C. 57, and doubt about the correctness of the decision was expressed in *Flattery*. What was said in *Linekar* as to fraud as to identity vitiating consent was *obiter*, the case not concerning mistake as to identity at all, but it is submitted that the view of the Court of Appeal represents the modern and better view.

See also section 3 of the SOA 1956 (*post*, H-27) in relation to false pretences of a less fundamental character; and *R. v. Tabassum* [2000] 2 Cr.App.R. 328, CA (*post*, H-124) in which it was held that a deception as to the quality of the act vitiated consent in a case of indecent assault.

*Recent complaint*

**H-18**    See § 20-12 in the main work.

*Distress of victim*

**H-19**    See § 20-13 in the main work.

**Mens rea**

*General*

**H-20**    It must be proved that at the time of the non-consensual intercourse, the defendant either knew that the victim was not consenting or that he was reckless as to whether she or he was consenting: see s.1(2)(b) of the SOA 1956, *ante*, H-3. If the tribunal of fact has to consider whether the defendant believed that a person was consenting to intercourse, the presence or absence of reasonable grounds for such a belief is a matter to which the tribunal is to have regard, in conjunction with any other relevant matters, in considering whether he so believed: Sexual Offences (Amendment) Act 1976, s.1(2), *ante*, H-4.

Sexual intercourse is a continuing act, which ends upon withdrawal. If, therefore, a man becomes aware that the other person is not consenting after intercourse has commenced and he does not desist, he will be guilty of rape from the moment that he realises that she or he is not consenting: *Kaitamaki v. R.* [1985] A.C. 147, PC. This case was decided on sections 127 and 128 of the New Zealand Crimes Act 1961, which are to the same effect as section 44 of the 1956 Act (*post*, H-219) and section 1 of the 1956 Act (*ante*, H-3). As to the situation where the victim was in fact consenting at the outset, but ceases to consent, see *ante*, H-14. This will also be rape provided that the man was aware of the change or was reckless in respect thereof.

*Restlessness*

**Substantive offences.** In *R. v. Satnam and Kewal*, 78 Cr.App.R. 149, CA, earlier confusion was    **H-21**
resolved. The authorities having been reviewed, it was held that any direction as to the definition of rape should be based upon section 1 of the Sexual Offences (Amendment) Act 1976 (see now s.1(2) of the SOA 1956, *ante*, H-3) and upon *DPP v. Morgan* [1976] A.C. 182, HL (§ 17-10 in the main work). The court suggested that a practical definition of recklessness in sexual cases had been given in *R. v. Kimber*, 77 Cr.App.R. 225, CA (a case of indecent assault), namely if the jury were sure that the defendant had been indifferent to the feelings and wishes of the victim, aptly described colloquially as "couldn't care less" then that in law was "reckless". Thus (see pp. 154-155), in summing up a case of rape which involves the issue of consent, the judge should, in dealing with the state of mind of the defendant, direct the jury that before they can convict, the Crown must have proved either that he knew the woman did not consent to sexual intercourse, or that he was reckless as to whether she consented. If the jury are sure he knew she did not consent, they will find him guilty of rape knowing there to be no consent. If they are not sure about that, they will go on to consider reckless rape. If he may genuinely have believed that she did consent, even though he was mistaken in that belief he must be acquitted: see s.1(2) of the 1976 Act, *ante*, H-4. In considering whether his belief may have been genuine, the jury should take into account all the relevant circumstances (including presence or absence of reasonable grounds: see s.1(2)). If, after considering them, the jury are sure that the defendant had no genuine belief that the woman consented to have intercourse, then they will convict. He will be guilty because that finding of fact would mean that his mental state was such that either he knew she was not consenting or he was reckless as to whether she was consenting. If the jury are sure that he could not have cared less whether she wanted to have sexual intercourse or not, but pressed on regardless, then he would have been reckless and could not have believed that she wanted to.

In *R. v. Taylor (Robert)*, 80 Cr.App.R. 327, CA, Lord Lane C.J. said (at p. 332) that in rape, the defendant is reckless if he does not believe the woman is consenting and could not care less whether she is consenting or not but presses on regardless. *Taylor* was followed and applied in *R. v. Adkins* [2000] 2 All E.R. 185, CA, where it was held to be unnecessary to give a direction as to honest belief in every case where consent is in issue; such a direction is only required when, on the evidence in the case, there is room for the possibility of a genuine mistaken belief that the victim had consented; equally, the question of honest belief does not necessarily arise where reckless rape is in issue, for the defendant might have failed to address his mind to the question whether or not there was consent, or have been indifferent as to whether or not there was consent, in circumstances where, if he had addressed his mind to the question, he could not genuinely have believed that there was consent; where, therefore, the defence case was not merely that the complainant consented but that she actively facilitated intercourse, there was no scope for a genuine, but mistaken, belief as to consent.

**Attempts.** In *R. v. Khan*, 91 Cr.App.R. 29, the Court of Appeal held that precisely the same    **H-22**
analysis can be made of the offence of attempted rape as that of the full offence, namely: (a) the intention of the offender is to have sexual intercourse with another person; (b) the offence is committed if, but only if, the circumstances are that: (i) the other person does not consent; *and* (ii) the defendant knows that he or she is not consenting or is reckless as to that fact.

*Drunkenness and mistake of fact*

It is clear from both *DPP v. Majewski* [1977] A.C. 443, HL (§ 17-107 in the main work) and *R.*    **H-23**
*v. Caldwell* [1982] A.C. 341, HL (§ 17-112 in the main work) that "recklessness" as a consequence of voluntarily induced intoxication cannot amount to a defence.

If the accused was, or may have been, genuinely mistaken as to fact (see generally, §§ 17-10 *et seq.* in the main work, and H-21, *ante*), for example, if he thought or may have thought that the complainant was consenting to sexual intercourse, and the jury are sure that that mistake was a consequence of intoxication, what then is the position? It appears to be this: implicit in such a finding is the finding that but for the voluntary consumption of drink the jury are sure that the accused would have known either that the complainant was not consenting or, at the very least, that there was a risk that she was not consenting. Whatever the true scope of the meaning of "reckless" in the context of sexual offences, it is plain (see *ante*, H-21) that to proceed knowing that there was a risk that the complainant was not consenting and not caring whether she consented or not is to act recklessly. It therefore follows that if the jury are sure that by virtue of drink (or drugs) the accused was not alerted, at the very least to the existence of that risk, that in itself constitutes the necessary recklessness for the purposes of the offence, see *Majewski* (§ 17-109 in the main work); and a genuine mistake as to fact in such circumstances constitutes no defence. This approach is borne out by the decision of the Court of Appeal in *R. v. Woods (W.)*, 74 Cr.App.R. 312. It was conceded on behalf of W that, but for section 1(2) of the Sexual Offences (Amendment) Act 1976 (*ante*, H-4), the principles in *Majewski* and *Caldwell* (as to the relevance of drink to recklessness) would apply and that accordingly a genuine mistake as to fact as a consequence of drink could found no defence. However, it was argued that section 1(2) of the 1976 Act permitted the jury to take into account a defendant's drunken state as a possible reasonable ground for his belief that a woman was consenting to intercourse. The submission was roundly rejected. "Relevant" in that subsection means "*legally* relevant". W's drunkenness was not a matter that the jury were entitled to take into consideration in deciding whether or not reasonable grounds existed for W's belief that the woman consented to intercourse.

The question was considered again in *R. v. Fotheringham*, 88 Cr.App.R. 206, CA, in which the defendant was charged with rape. His defence was that he was so drunk at the time that he believed he was having intercourse with his wife. Applying *Majewski, Caldwell, Woods, ante*, and *R. v. O'Grady* [1987] Q.B. 995, 85 Cr.App.R. 315, CA (§ 17-16 in the main work), the court held that "in rape, self-induced intoxication is no defence, whether the issue be intention, consent or, as here, mistake as to the identity of the victim" (at p. 212).

### (j) *Liability of accessories*

**H-24**     As to indicting accessories to rape, see *ante*, H-7; and as to their liability to conviction, notwithstanding the acquittal of the alleged principal, see *R. v. Cogan and Leak* [1976] Q.B. 217, 61 Cr.App.R. 217, CA (§ 20-26 in the main work).

### (k) *Attempts*

**H-25**     See § 20-27 in the main work, and, in relation to the *mens rea* of an attempt, see *ante*, H-22.

## (2) Procurement of intercourse by threats or false pretences

### (a) *Statute*

### Sexual Offences Act 1956, ss.2, 3

**H-26**     **2.**—(1) It is an offence for a person to procure a woman, by threats or intimidation, to have ... sexual intercourse in any part of the world.
     (2) [*Repealed by CJPOA 1994, s.33(1).*]

[Subs. (1) is printed as repealed in part by the CJPOA 1994, s.168(1) and (3), and Scheds 9, para. 2, and 11.]

**H-27**     **3.**—(1) It is an offence for a person to procure a woman, by false pretences or false representations, to have ... sexual intercourse in any part of the world.
     (2) [*Repealed by Criminal Justice and Public Order Act 1994, s.33(1).*]

[Subs. (1) is printed as repealed in part by the CJPOA 1994, s.168(1) and (3), and Scheds 9, para. 2, and 11.]

As to the meaning of "sexual intercourse", see *post*, H-219; as to the use of the word "woman", see *post*, H-222.

For anonymity provisions, see §§ 20-257 *et seq.* in the main work.

### (b) *Indictment*

**Statement of Offence**

*Procuration, contrary to section 3(1) of the Sexual Offences Act 1956.*

**Particulars of Offence**

*A B, on the —— day of ——, 20—, procured J N, a woman, to have sexual intercourse with himself* [or *with E F*, as the case may be] *by falsely pretending or representing to her that* [state in ordinary language the false pretence or representation].

The false pretences must be set out: *R. v. Field* (1892) 116 CCC Sess.Pap. 1891–1892, 757; but they need not be expressly negatived: *R. v. Clarke*, 59 J.P. 248.

An indictment for an offence contrary to section 2 may easily be framed from the above specimen.

### (c) *Class of offence and mode of trial*

The offence contrary to section 2 and an attempt to commit it are class 3 offences (§ 2-17 in the    **H-29** main work), triable on indictment only: SOA 1956, s.37(2), and Sched. 2, para. 7(a), (b).

The offence contrary to section 3 is a class 3 offence (§ 2-17 in the main work), triable on indictment only: SOA 1956, s.37(2), and Sched. 2, para. 8.

### (d) *Alternative verdicts*

As to the possibility of a conviction of either of these offences on a charge of rape, see *ante*, H-9.    **H-30**

### (e) *Sentence*

Either offence, or an attempt to commit the offence contrary to section 2: imprisonment not    **H-31** exceeding two years—SOA 1956, s.37(3), and Sched. 2, paras 7(a), (b), and 8.

### (f) *Ingredients of the offences*

**"Procure"**

See *post*, H-171.    **H-32**

## False pretences

Seduction by a married man of a woman under promise of marriage by false representation    **H-33** was held to be within section 3(2) of the Criminal Law Amendment Act 1885 (*rep.*), of which section 3(1) of the Act of 1956 was a replacement: *R. v. Williams*, 62 J.P. 310. It is immaterial whether the intercourse was procured with the defendant or with another: *ibid.*, and see *R. v. Jones* [1896] 1 Q.B. 4.

## (3) Administering drugs to obtain or facilitate intercourse

### (a) *Statute*

**Sexual Offences Act 1956, s.4**

**4.**—(1) It is an offence for a person to apply or administer to, or cause to be taken by, a woman    **H-34** any drug, matter or thing with intent to stupefy or overpower her so as thereby to enable any man to have unlawful sexual intercourse with her.

(2) [*Repealed by Criminal Justice and Public Order Act 1994, s.33(1).*]

As to the meaning of "sexual intercourse", see *post*, H-219; as to the use of the words "man" and "woman", see *post*, H-222.

For anonymity provisions, see *post*, §§ 20-257 *et seq.* in the main work.

### (b) *Class of offence and mode of trial*

This offence is a class 3 offence (§ 2-17 in the main work), triable only on indictment: SOA    **H-35** 1956, s.37(2), and Sched. 2, para. 9.

## (c) *Alternative verdicts*

**H-36**     As to the possibility of a conviction of this offence on a charge of rape, see *ante*, H-9.

## (d) *Sentence*

**H-37**     Imprisonment not exceeding two years: SOA 1956, s.37(3), and Sched. 2, para. 9.

## (e) *Ingredients of the offence*

**H-38**     "Unlawful" sexual intercourse means illicit sexual intercourse, *i.e.* outside the bond of marriage: *R. v. Chapman* [1959] 1 Q.B. 100, 42 Cr.App.R. 257, CCA (considering s.19 of the 1956 Act, *post*, H-148).

The essence of the offence is the administering of the drug. If there has been only one administration, there can be only one offence, even though the intention of the administration was to enable more than one man to have intercourse with the woman: *R. v. Shillingford and Vanderwall*, 52 Cr.App.R. 188, CA.

## (4) Sexual intercourse with girl under 13

### (a) *Statute*

#### Sexual Offences Act 1956, s.5

**H-39**     **5.** It is an offence for a man to have unlawful sexual intercourse with a girl under the age of thirteen.

[This section is printed as effectively amended by the CLA 1967, s.12(5)(a).]

As to the meaning of "sexual intercourse", see *post*, H-219; as to the use of the words "man" and "girl", see *post*, H-222.

For anonymity provisions, see §§ 20-257 *et seq.* in the main work.

### (b) *Indictment*

#### Statement of Offence

**H-40**     *Sexual intercourse with a girl under 13, contrary to section 5 of the Sexual Offences Act 1956.*

#### Particulars of Offence

*A B, on the —— day of ——, 20—, had sexual intercourse with J N, a girl under the age of 13 years.*

### (c) *Class of offence and mode of trial*

**H-41**     This offence and an attempt to commit it are class 2 offences (§ 2-17 in the main work), triable only on indictment: SOA 1956, s.37(2), and Sched. 2, para. 2(a), (b).

### (d) *Alternative verdicts*

**H-42**     Indecent assault, contrary to section 14(1) of the 1956 Act (*post*, H-117): *R. v. McCormack* [1969] 2 Q.B. 442, 53 Cr.App.R. 514, CA. As to alternative verdicts generally, see §§ 4-524 *et seq.* in the main work.

### (e) *Sentence*

**H-43**     The full offence: life imprisonment—SOA 1956, s.37(2), and Sched. 2, para. 2(a).

Attempt: imprisonment not exceeding seven years—*ibid.*, para. 2(b).

Custodial sentences are normally imposed, unless the offender is psychologically abnormal or of limited intelligence (see in particular *Att.-Gen.'s Reference (No. 20 of 1994)*, 16 Cr.App.R.(S.) 578, CA.). Some guidance may be obtained from the guideline of the Sentencing Guidelines Council in relation to offences under the SOA 2003 (*post*, Appendix K-83 *et seq.*); and for guidance as to how to sentence historic offences, see *R. v. H.*, *ante*, H-12.

### (f) *Ingredients of the offence*

#### Man

**H-44**     As to the abolition of the presumption that a boy under 14 is incapable of sexual intercourse, see *ante*, H-13.

### Consent immaterial

The evidence is the same as in rape, with the exception that it is immaterial whether the act   **H-45**
was done with or without the consent of the girl. If it was in fact without her consent, an indictment for rape will lie, notwithstanding the age of the child: *R. v. Dicken* (1877) 14 Cox 8; *R. v.
Harling*, 26 Cr.App.R. 127, CCA; *R. v. Howard*, 50 Cr.App.R. 56, CCA, *ante*, H-15. So, where the
defendant was indicted for an attempt to commit the offence, and the evidence was that he had
attempted to have sexual intercourse with the girl, but that she had consented to the attempt, it
was held that the fact of her consent was immaterial, and that the defendant was properly
convicted: *R. v. Beale* (1865) L.R. 1 C.C.R. 10.

### Knowledge of age immaterial

A mistake as to the age of the girl, even if based on reasonable grounds, will not avail a   **H-46**
defendant: *R. v. Prince* (1875) L.R. 2 C.C.R. 154 (*post*, H-161); *R. v. K.* [2002] 1 A.C. 462, HL; and
see the specific defence provided by section 6(3) in relation to the less serious offence of intercourse
with a girl under 16 (*post*, H-50).

(g) Evidence

### Recent complaint

See § 20-12 in the main work.      **H-47**

### Distress of victim

See § 20-13 in the main work.      **H-48**

### Age

The provisions of section 99(2) of the CYPA 1933 (§ 19-412 in the main work), as to presump-   **H-49**
tion and determination of age do not apply: see the proviso to Schedule 1 to the 1933 Act (whilst
the proviso was repealed by the SOA 2003 (see § 19-412 in the main work), its effect in relation to
any prosecution for an offence under the 1956 Act will be saved by virtue of the Interpretation
Act 1978, s.16 (*ante*, Appendix B-16)). The girl must be proved to have been under 13 years of
age when the offence was committed. The best way of doing this is to produce a duly certified
copy of the certificate of birth, coupled with evidence of identity; but the age may be proved by
any other legal means: *R. v. Cox* [1898] 1 Q.B. 179 (age could be proved by persons who had seen
the child and by a teacher at an elementary school which the child attended). Where a certificate
of birth is put in, there must be evidence of identity as well: see *R. v. Nicholls* (1867) 10 Cox 476;
*R. v. Bellis*, 6 Cr.App.R. 283, CCA; *R. v. Rogers*, 10 Cr.App.R. 276, CCA.

In the case of an adopted child, the date of birth may be proved by a certified copy of an entry
in the Adopted Children Register: Adoption and Children Act 2002, s.77(5).

(5) Sexual intercourse with a girl under 16

(a) Statute

Sexual Offences Act 1956, s.6

**6.**—(1) It is an offence, subject to the exceptions mentioned in this section, for a man to have   **H-50**
unlawful sexual intercourse with a girl ... under the age of sixteen.

(2) Where a marriage is invalid under section two of the Marriage Act 1949, or section one of the
Age of Marriage Act 1929 (the wife being a girl under the age of sixteen), the invalidity does not
make the husband guilty of an offence under this section because he has sexual intercourse with her,
if he believes her to be his wife, and has reasonable cause for the belief.

(3) A man is not guilty of an offence under this section because he has unlawful sexual intercourse
with a girl under the age of sixteen, if he is under the age of twenty-four and has not previously been
charged with a like offence, and he believes her to be of the age of sixteen or over and has reasonable
cause for the belief.

In this subsection "a like offence" means an offence under this section or an attempt to commit one, or an offence under paragraph (1) of section five of the Criminal Law Amendment Act 1885 (the provision replaced for England and Wales by this section).

[This section is printed as repealed in part by the CLA 1967, s.10(1), and Sched. 2, para. 14.]

As to the meaning of "sexual intercourse", see *post*, H-219; as to the use of the words "man" and "girl", see *post*, H-222.

As to the proof of exceptions, see the SOA 1956, s.47, *post*, H-225.

For anonymity provisions, see §§ 20-257 *et seq.* in the main work.

### Marriage Act 1949, s.2

*Marriages of persons under sixteen*

**H-51**    2. A marriage solemnized between persons either of whom is under the age of sixteen shall be void.

### (b) *Indictment*

#### Statement of Offence

**H-52**    *Sexual intercourse with a girl under 16, contrary to section 6(1) of the Sexual Offences Act 1956.*

#### Particulars of Offence

*A B, on the —— day of ——, 20—, had sexual intercourse with J N, a girl under the age of 16 years.*

### (c) *Class of offence and mode of trial*

**H-53**    This offence and an attempt to commit it are class 3 offences (§ 2-17 in the main work), triable either way: MCA 1980, s.17(1), and Sched. 1 (§ 1-130 in the main work).

### (d) *Alternative verdicts*

**H-54**    Indecent assault, contrary to section 14(1) of the 1956 Act (*post*, H-117): *R. v. McCormack* [1969] 2 Q.B. 442, 53 Cr.App.R. 514, CA. As to alternative verdicts generally, see §§ 4-524 *et seq.* in the main work.

### (e) *Time limit on prosecutions*

**H-55**    Prosecutions for an offence under section 6 or an attempt to commit such offence may not be commenced more than 12 months after the offence charged: SOA 1956, s.37(2), and Sched. 2, para. 10(a), (b).

As to what is a commencement of the prosecution, see *R. v. West* [1898] 1 Q.B. 174; *R. v. Wakely* [1920] 1 K.B. 688, 14 Cr.App.R. 121, CCA.

In appropriate circumstances, evidence of prior offences by the defendant against the same girl committed outside the 12 months' time limit will be admissible: *R. v. Shellaker* [1914] 1 K.B. 414, 9 Cr.App.R. 240, CCA; *cf. R. v. Hewitt*, 19 Cr.App.R. 64, CCA; *R. v. Adams, The Times*, April 8, 1993, CA.

As to the impropriety of bringing a prosecution for indecent assault, based on an act of consensual sexual intercourse, where a prosecution under section 6 is time barred, see *R. v. J.*, *post*, H-118.

### (f) *Sentence*

**H-56**    The full offence, or an attempt to commit it: imprisonment not exceeding two years' SOA 1956, s.37(3), and Sched. 2, para. 10(a), (b). The penalty on summary conviction is governed by section 32 of the MCA 1980 (§ 1-125 in the main work).

In *R. v. Taylor*, 64 Cr.App.R. 182, CA, the court laid down guidelines for the sentencing of persons convicted of having unlawful sexual intercourse with a girl under the age of 16. Lawton L.J. distinguished between cases where "virtuous friendship" between young people of about the same age ended in sexual intercourse, and cases where a man in a supervisory capacity set out to seduce a girl under 16 who was in his charge. In the first type of case, sentences of a punitive nature were not required; in the second, sentences near the maximum of two years should be passed.

In *R. v. Bayliss* [2000] 1 Cr.App.R.(S.) 412, CA, it was said that attitudes to teenage prostitution had changed since *Taylor*, and that there was a greater appreciation that this offence and that of taking indecent photographs of children, contrary to the Protection of Children Act 1978 (§§ 31-107 *et seq.* in the main work), had been put on the statute book for the protection of children, including against themselves.

## (g) *Ingredients of the offence*

### Man

As to the abolition of the presumption that a boy under 14 is incapable of sexual intercourse, see *ante*, H-13. **H-57**

A girl under 16 cannot be indicted for "abetting" or "inciting" a man to have unlawful sexual intercourse with herself: *R. v. Tyrrell* [1894] 1 Q.B. 710.

As to doctors who prescribe contraceptive pills to girls under 16, see *Gillick v. West Norfolk and Wisbech Area Health Authority* [1986] A.C. 112, HL, *post*, H-196.

### Consent immaterial

See *ante*, H-45, and *R. v. Ratcliffe* (1882) 10 Q.B.D. 74. **H-58**

### "Unlawful" sexual intercourse

See *R. v. Chapman, ante*, H-38. **H-59**

## (h) *Evidence*

### Recent complaint

See § 20-12 in the main work. **H-60**

### Distress of victim

See § 20-13 in the main work. **H-61**

### Age

See *ante*, H-49, the contents of which apply, *mutatis mutandis*, to the offence under section 6. **H-62**

## (i) *Defences*

In the case of a man under the age of 24, the presence of reasonable cause to believe that the girl was over the age of 16 years is a valid defence provided that the defendant has not previously been charged with a like offence: SOA 1956, s.6(3) (*ante*, H-50). As to the meaning of the expression "a like offence", see *ibid*. The defence is not incompatible with Article 6 (right to fair trial (§ 16-57 in the main work)) or 14 (prohibition on discrimination (§ 16-139 in the main work)) of the ECHR as being discriminatory on the grounds that, (a) a woman who had sexual intercourse with a boy under 16 would, if prosecuted, be charged with indecent assault, in relation to which she would have a defence, whatever her age, of genuine belief that the boy was 16 or more, and (b) it was restricted to men under the age of 24; as to (b), even though the choice of age was arbitrary, it did not introduce an element of disproportionality into the offence: *R. v. Kirk and Russell* [2002] Crim.L.R. 756, CA. **H-63**

In *R. v. Rider*, 37 Cr.App.R. 209, Assizes, Streatfeild J. had to construe the wording of the Criminal Law Amendment Act 1922. The proviso to section 2 of that Act gave a man under 24 years of age a defence to a charge of unlawful sexual intercourse with a girl under 16 years of age if at the time of the intercourse he had reasonable cause to believe that the girl was over the age of 16; but the defence was only available "on the first occasion on which he is charged with" such an offence. It was held that "charged" in this context meant "appeared before a court with jurisdiction to deal with the matter". The defendant had been committed for trial on two separate occasions in respect of like allegations relating to different girls. Both allegations were joined in the same indictment and it was held that appearance before the assize was the first occasion on which he appeared before a court with jurisdiction to deal with the matter and, therefore, the defence was available in respect of both counts. Streatfeild J. said, however, that had the magistrates refused to commit for trial in respect of the first matter, the appearance at the assize on the second matter would have been the second occasion. This result seems illogical. It should be borne in mind that at the time of *Rider*, the offence in question could be tried only on indictment. It is now triable either way and it is respectfully submitted that the defence should only be available to a person who at the time of the alleged offence has not been before a court (magistrates' court, whether or not the matter is to be tried summarily, Crown Court or service court) on a charge of such an offence. This gives due effect to the actual decision in *Rider* to the revised formulation of the defence in the 1956 Act and to the changes in the legislation relating to mode of trial. It is also consistent with the rationale underlying the restriction on the defence, *viz.* that once the serious nature of such conduct has been brought to the attention of a man, he can legitimately be expected to be more careful about a girl's age.

To constitute a defence under this proviso, where it applies, the defendant must have reasonable cause to believe, and, in fact, must have believed that the girl was over the age of 16 years: *R. v. Banks* [1916] 2 K.B. 621, 12 Cr.App.R. 74, CCA; *R. v. Harrison*, 26 Cr.App.R. 166, CCA. The question of the existence of reasonable cause to believe is one for the jury: *R. v. Forde* [1923] 2 K.B. 400, 17 Cr.App.R. 99, CCA.

The defence is available not only where intercourse has taken place, but also where it has been merely attempted: *R. v. Collier* [1960] Crim.L.R. 204, Assizes (Streatfeild J.).

As to the burden of proof of the "exceptions" (defences) in subsections (2) and (3) of section 6, see section 47 of the 1956 Act, *post*, H-225.

### (6) Intercourse with defectives

#### (a) *Statute*

**Sexual Offences Act 1956, ss.7, 9**

*Intercourse with defective*

**H-64**      **7.**—(1) It is an offence, subject to the exception mentioned in this section, for a man to have unlawful sexual intercourse with a woman who is a defective.

(2) A man is not guilty of an offence under this section because he has unlawful sexual intercourse with a woman if he does not know and has no reason to suspect her to be a defective.

[This section is printed as substituted by the MHA 1959, s.127(1)(a).]

*Procurement of defective*

**H-65**      **9.**—(1) It is an offence, subject to the exception mentioned in this section, for a person to procure a woman who is a defective to have unlawful sexual intercourse in any part of the world.

(2) A person is not guilty of an offence under this section because he procures a defective to have unlawful sexual intercourse, if he does not know and has no reason to suspect her to be a defective.

As to the meaning of "sexual intercourse", see *post*, H-219 as to the use of the words "man" and "woman", see *post*, H-222; as to the meaning of "defective", see *post*, H-68.

For anonymity provisions, see §§ 20-257 *et seq.* in the main work.

As to the burden of proof in relation to the exception in subsection (2) of both sections, see section 47 of the Act, *post*, H-225.

#### (b) *Class of offence and mode of trial*

**H-66**      Offences against sections 7 and 9, and attempts to commit them, are class 3 offences (§ 2-17 in the main work), triable only on indictment: SOA 1956, s.37(2), and Sched. 2, paras 11(a), (b), and 13(a), (b).

#### (c) *Sentence*

**H-67**      Offences against sections 7 and 9, and attempts to commit them: imprisonment not exceeding two years—SOA 1956, s.37(3), and Sched. 2, paras 11(a), (b), and 13(a), (b). For an illustrative example, see *R. v. Adcock* [2000] 1 Cr.App.R.(S.) 563, CA.

## (d) *Ingredients of the offences*

## "Defective"

### Sexual Offences Act 1956, s.45

*Meaning of defective*

**45.** In this Act "defective" means a person suffering from a state of arrested or incomplete develop- **H-68** ment of mind which includes severe impairment of intelligence and social functioning.

[This section is printed as substituted by the MHA 1959, s.127(1); and as amended by the Mental Health (Amendment) Act 1982, Sched. 3.]

The words "severe impairment of intelligence and social functioning" are ordinary English words and not words of art; they were inserted in the definition to protect women, if defectives, from exploitation. Severe impairment is to be measured against the standards of normal persons: *R. v. Hall (J.H.)*, 86 Cr.App.R. 159, CA. The trial judge's direction that it was for them to decide on all the evidence whether the victim was severely impaired within the ordinary meaning of those words was correct.

## "Unlawful" sexual intercourse

See *R. v. Chapman, ante*, H-38.     **H-69**

## "Procure"

See *post*, H-171.     **H-70**

## (7) Incest by a man

### (a) *Statute*

### Sexual Offences Act 1956, s.10

**10.**—(1) It is an offence for a man to have sexual intercourse with a woman whom he knows to be **H-71** his grand-daughter, daughter, sister or mother.

(2) In the foregoing subsection "sister" includes half-sister and for the purposes of that subsection any expression importing a relationship between two people shall be taken to apply notwithstanding that the relationship is not traced through lawful wedlock.

As to the meaning of "sexual intercourse", see *post*, H-219; as to the use of the words "man" and "woman", see *post*, § H-222.

For anonymity provisions, see §§ 20-257 *et seq.* in the main work.

### (b) *Indictment*

### Statement of Offence

*Incest, contrary to section 10(1) of the Sexual Offences Act 1956.*     **H-72**

### Particulars of Offence

*A B, being a male person, on the —— day of ——, 20—, had sexual intercourse with J N, whom he knew to be his daughter* [if under the age of 13, add her age].

An indictment which charged the offence as having been committed "on divers days" between two specified dates was held to be bad for duplicity: *R. v. Thompson* [1914] 2 K.B. 99, 9 Cr.App.R. 252, CCA.

Where a brother and sister were charged in separate counts of the same indictment with committing incest and were tried separately, with the result that the brother was convicted and the sister acquitted, it was held that the acquittal of the sister did not make the conviction of the brother bad: *R. v. Gordon*, 19 Cr.App.R. 20, CCA. As to inconsistent verdicts generally, see §§ 7-70 *et seq.* in the main work.

### (c) *Class of offence and mode of trial*

This offence, and an attempt to commit it, are class 3 offences (unless with a girl under 13, in **H-73** which case they are class 2 offences) (§ 2-17 in the main work), triable only on indictment: SOA 1956, s.37(2), and Sched. 2, para. 14(a), (b).

### (d) *Alternative verdicts*

**H-74**    On a charge of the full offence, unlawful sexual intercourse with a girl under 13 (s.5) or with a girl under 16 (s.6): SOA 1956, s.37(4), and Sched. 2, para. 14(a). Where the girl is under 16, indecent assault (whether or not the indictment avers her age): *R. v. Regina*, 64 Cr.App.R. 79, CA. This possibility arises by virtue of the combination of section 37(5) (*post*, H-226) and the specific provision in Schedule 2 for a conviction of an offence under either section 5 or 6 (indecent assault being an alternative on an indictment charging either of those offences, *ante*, H-42, H-54).

### (e) *Restriction on prosecution*

**H-75**    A prosecution for this offence, or an attempt to commit it, may not be commenced except by or with the consent of the DPP: SOA 1956, s.37(2), and Sched. 2, para. 14(a), (b).

### (f) *Sentence*

**Maximum**

**H-76**    The full offence and an attempt to commit it: if with a girl under 13, and so charged in the indictment, life imprisonment, otherwise imprisonment not exceeding seven years— SOA 1956, s.37(3), and Sched. 2, para. 14(a), (b).

**Basis of sentence**

**H-77**    See *R. v. Huchison*, 56 Cr.App.R. 307, CA.

**Guidelines**

**H-78**    In *Att.-Gen.'s Reference (No. 1 of 1989)*, 90 Cr.App.R. 141, the Court of Appeal laid down guidelines for sentencing in cases of incest by a father against a daughter. The court made the following suggestions "as a broad guide" to the level of sentence for various categories of the crime of incest. All were on the assumption that there had been no plea of guilty. They should be read subject to *Practice Statement (Crime: Sentencing)* [1992] 1 W.L.R. 948. See, in particular, paragraph 10 thereof.

(i) *Girl aged over 16 years*

**H-79**    A range from three years' imprisonment down to a nominal penalty would be appropriate depending in particular on the one hand whether force was used and the degree of harm if any, to the girl, and, on the other, the desirability where it existed of keeping family disruption to a minimum. The older the girl the greater the possibility that she might have been willing or even the instigating party, a factor which would be reflected in the sentence.

(ii) *Girl aged from 13 to 16 years*

**H-80**    A sentence between about five years' and three years' imprisonment would be appropriate. Much the same principles would apply as in the case of the girl over 16 years, though the likelihood of corruption increased in inverse proportion to the age of the girl.

(iii) *Girl aged under 13 years*

**H-81**    It was here that the widest range of sentences was likely to be found. If any case of incest could properly be described as the "ordinary" type of case, it would be one where the sexual relationship between husband and wife had broken down; the father had probably resorted to excessive drinking and the eldest daughter was gradually, by way of familiarities, indecent acts and suggestions made the object of the father's frustrated inclinations. If the girl was not far short of her thirteenth birthday and there were no particularly adverse or favourable features, a term of about six years' imprisonment would seem to be appropriate. The younger the girl when the sexual approach was started, the more likely it would be that the girl's will was overborne and, accordingly, the more serious would be the crime.

(iv) *Aggravating factors*

Whatever the age of the girl, the following, *inter alia*, would aggravate the offence:   **H-82**
  (a) physical or psychological suffering from the offence;
  (b) the incest taking place at frequent intervals or over a long period;
  (c) the use of threats or violence, or the girl being otherwise terrified of her father;
  (d) the incest being accompanied by perversions abhorrent to the girl, such as buggery or *fellatio*;
  (e) the girl becoming pregnant; and
  (f) the commission of similar offences against more than one girl.

(v) *Mitigating features*

Possible mitigating features were, *inter alia*:   **H-83**
  (a) a plea of guilty;
  (b) genuine affection on the defendant's part rather than the intention to use the girl simply as an outlet for his sexual inclinations;
  (c) previous sexual experience by the girl; and
  (d) deliberate attempts at seduction by the girl.

In relation to a plea of guilty, the court said that such a plea was seldom not entered and it should be met by an appropriate discount, depending on the usual considerations, that is, how promptly the defendant confessed, the degree of contrition and so on. The court also said that occasionally a shorter term of imprisonment than would otherwise be imposed might be justified as being of benefit to the victim and the family.

For cases illustrating the application of these guidelines, see CSP B4–2. For cases of incest by a brother with a sister, see *ibid.*, B4–2.3D; for a case of incest by a mother with her young son, see *ibid.*, B4–2.3E.

### (g) *Effect of adoption*

The prohibition contained in section 10(1) applies notwithstanding the adoption of one of the   **H-84** parties: Adoption and Children Act 2002, s.74(1)(b) (whilst this provision was amended to substitute a reference to sections 64 and 65 of the SOA 2003 for the references to sections 10 and 11 of the 1956 Act, its previous operation will be saved by virtue of section 16 of the Interpretation Act 1978 (*ante*, Appendix B-16)).

### (h) *Ingredients of the offence*

If a man makes a genuine mistake as to the identity of the person with whom he has intercourse,   **H-85** he will not commit the offence: *R. v. Baillie-Smith*, 64 Cr.App.R. 76, CA (intercourse with daughter, thinking her to be his wife).

As to the abolition of the common law presumption that a boy under 14 is incapable of sexual intercourse, see *ante*, H-13.

### (i) *Evidence*

The relationship between the parties may be proved by oral evidence or by certificates of mar-   **H-86** riage and birth, coupled with identification. An admission by the defendant that the person with whom the offence had been committed was his daughter may be sufficient evidence of the relationship: *R. v. Jones (Evan)*, 24 Cr.App.R. 55, CCA.

Evidence tending to show pre-existent sexual passion between the parties is admissible: *R. v. Ball* [1911] A.C. 47, HL.

The defendant was charged with incest with S, who was alleged to be his daughter. His defence was that he had no knowledge that S *was* his daughter. He desired to give evidence:
  (a) that he had been told by his first wife (the mother of S) that S had been begotten by another man and that he believed that statement to be true;
  (b) that he had told his second wife that he was not the father of S;
  (c) explaining statements which he had made on certain occasions acknowledging S to be his daughter.

It was held (on appeal) that this evidence was relevant to the issue whether the defendant *knew* that S was his daughter and that he was entitled to give any evidence relevant to that issue, including evidence of an admission by his first wife: *R. v. Carmichael* [1940] 1 K.B. 630, 27 Cr.App.R. 183, CCA.

## (8) Incitement to incest of girls under 16

**H-87**     See the CLA 1977, s.54, *post*, H-239.

## (9) Incest by a woman

### (a) *Statute*

#### Sexual Offences Act 1956, s.11

**H-88**     **11.**—(1) It is an offence for a woman of the age of sixteen or over to permit a man whom she knows to be her grandfather, father, brother or son to have sexual intercourse with her by her consent.

(2) In the foregoing subsection "brother" includes half-brother, and for the purposes of that subsection any expression importing a relationship between two people shall be taken to apply notwithstanding that the relationship is not traced through lawful wedlock.

As to the meaning of "sexual intercourse", see *post*, H-219; as to the use of the words "woman" and "man", see *post*, H-222.

For anonymity provisions, see §§ 20-257 *et seq.* in the main work.

### (b) *Indictment*

#### Statement of Offence

**H-89**     *Incest, contrary to section 11(1) of the Sexual Offences Act 1956.*

#### Particulars of Offence

*A B, being a female person of the age of 18, on the _____ day of _____, 20___, with her consent permitted J N, whom she knew to be her father, to have sexual intercourse with her.*

As to the form of the indictment, see also *R. v. Thompson, ante*, H-72.

### (c) *Class of offence and mode of trial*

**H-90**     This offence, and an attempt to commit it, are class 3 offences (§ 2-17 in the main work), triable only on indictment: SOA 1956, s.37(2), and Sched. 2, para. 15(a), (b).

### (d) *Restriction on prosecution*

**H-91**     A prosecution for this offence or an attempt to commit it may not be commenced except by or with the consent of the DPP: SOA 1956, s.37(2), and Sched. 2, para. 15(a), (b).

### (e) *Sentence*

**H-92**     The full offence: imprisonment not exceeding seven years—SOA 1956, s.37(3), and Sched. 2, para. 15(a).

Attempt: imprisonment not exceeding two years—*ibid.*, para. 15(b).

### (f) *Effect of adoption*

**H-93**     The prohibition contained in section 11(1) applies notwithstanding the adoption of one of the parties: Adoption and Children Act 2002, s.74(1)(b) (as to which, see *ante*, H-84).

### (g) *Ingredients of offence*

**H-94**     The common law presumption as to incapacity in relation to boys under 14 years of age (*ante*, H-13) had no application where a woman was charged with committing incest with such a boy: *R. v. Pickford* [1995] 1 Cr.App.R. 420, CA.

## (10) Buggery

### (a) *Introduction*

The SOA 1956 contains two "unnatural offences", namely buggery (with a person or with an **H-95**
animal) and gross indecency between men. There are time limits and requirements as to the
consent of the DPP in respect of both offences in certain circumstances.

The SOA 1967 amended the law by providing, in particular, that consenting men over the age
of 21 (reduced to 18 by the CJPOA 1994, and to 16 by the Sexual Offences (Amendment) Act
2000) who commit buggery or gross indecency in private, do not commit an offence (s.1, *post*,
H-97). There are different rules regarding the lawfulness of procuration of buggery and gross
indecency (s.4, *post*, H-236). Section 11(3) provides that section 46 of the 1956 Act (use of words
"man", "boy" and other expressions) shall apply for the purposes of the provisions of the 1967
Act as it applies for the purposes of that Act. For section 46, see *post*, H-222.

The CJPOA 1994 effected further changes in the law. Apart from reducing the age of consent
for homosexual acts to 18 (*ante*), it redefined the offence of rape to include non-consensual anal
intercourse with a man or a woman (*ante*, H-3). Non-consensual buggery should, therefore, be
charged as rape. Consensual buggery between two people will not be an offence if the act takes
place in private and both parties have achieved the age of 16.

As to the offences of indecent assault on a man and assault with intent to commit buggery,
which may be on a man or a woman (categorised in the 1956 Act as "assault" offences rather than
as "unnatural offences"), see sections 15, *post*, H-127, and 16, *post*, H-138.

### (b) *Statute*

#### Sexual Offences Act 1956, s.12

**12.**—(1) It is an offence for a person to commit buggery with another person otherwise than in the **H-96**
circumstances first described in subsection (1A) or (1AA) below or with an animal.

(1A) The circumstances referred to in subsection (1) are that the act of buggery takes place in
private and both parties have attained the age of sixteen.

(1AA) The other circumstances so referred to are that the person is under the age of sixteen and
the other person has attained that age.

(1B) An act of buggery by one man with another shall not be treated as taking place in private if it
takes place—

    (a)   when more than two persons take part or are present; or

    (b)   in a lavatory to which the public have or are permitted to have access, whether on payment
         or otherwise.

(1C) In any proceedings against a person for buggery with another person it shall be for the
prosecutor to prove that the act of buggery took place otherwise than in private or that one of the
parties to it had not attained the age of sixteen.

(2), (3) [*Repealed by Police and Criminal Evidence Act 1984, Sched. 7.*]

[Subs. (1) is printed as amended by the CLA 1967, s.12(5)(a); the CJPOA 1994, s.143(1), (2);
and the Sexual Offences (Amendment) Act 2000, s.2(1)(a) and (b); subss. (1A), (1B) and (1C) were
inserted by the 1994 Act, s.143(1), (3); and are printed as amended by the 2000 Act, s.1(1); subs.
(1AA) was inserted by the 2000 Act, s.2(1)(c).]

For anonymity provisions, see §§ 20-257 *et seq.* in the main work.

As to conspiracy or incitement to commit this offence, see *R. v. Boulton* (1871) 12 Cox 87.

#### Sexual Offences Act 1967, s.1

*Amendment of law relating to homosexual acts in private*

**1.**—(1) Notwithstanding any statutory or common law provision, ... **H-97**

    (a)   a homosexual act in private shall not be an offence provided that the parties consent
         thereto and have attained the age of sixteen years; and

    (b)   a homosexual act by any person shall not be an offence if he is under the age of sixteen
         and the other party has attained that age.

(2) An act which would otherwise be treated for the purposes of this Act as being done in private
shall not be so treated if done—

    (a) when more than two persons take part or are present; or

    (b) in a lavatory to which the public have or are permitted to have access, whether on payment or otherwise.

    (3) A man who is suffering from severe mental handicap cannot in law give any consent which, by virtue of subsection (1) of this section, would prevent a homosexual act from being an offence, but a person shall not be convicted, on account of the incapacity of such a man to consent, of an offence consisting of such an act if he proves that he did not know and had no reason to suspect that man to be suffering from severe mental handicap.

    (3A) In subsection (3) of this section "severe mental handicap" means a state of arrested or incomplete development of mind which includes severe impairment of intelligence and social functioning.

    (4) Section 128 of the Mental Health Act 1959 (prohibition on men on the staff of a hospital, or otherwise having responsibility for mental patients, having sexual intercourse with women patients) shall have effect as if any reference therein to having unlawful sexual intercourse with a woman included a reference to committing buggery or an act of gross indecency with another man.

    (5) [*Repealed by CJPOA 1994, s.168(3) and Sched. 11*].

    (6) It is hereby declared that where in any proceedings it is charged that a homosexual act is an offence the prosecutor shall have the burden of proving that the act was done otherwise than in private or otherwise than with the consent of the parties or that any of the parties had not attained the age of sixteen years.

    (7) For the purposes of this section a man shall be treated as doing a homosexual act if, and only if, he commits buggery with another man or commits an act of gross indecency with another man or is a party to the commission by a man of such an act.

[This section is printed as amended and repealed in part by the Mental Health (Amendment) Act 1982, s.65(1), (2), and Scheds 3, para. 34, and 4; the CJPOA 1994, ss.146(1) and 168(3), and Sched. 11; and the Sexual Offences (Amendment) Act 2000, ss.1(2)(a) and 2(3)(a) and (b).]

As to the use of the word "man", see *post*, H-222.

For section 128 of the MHA 1959, see *post*, H-228.

### (c) *Indictment for buggery with a person*

#### Statement of Offence

*Buggery, contrary to section 12(1) of the Sexual Offences Act 1956.*

#### Particulars of Offence

*A B, a person of [or over] the age of 21 years, on the _____ day of _____, 20___, committed buggery with J N, a person under the age of 18 years.*

Because the penalty provisions have the effect of creating a number of separate offences (see *post*, H-103), the particulars should be clear as to which offence is alleged; in the specimen set out above, it is a five year offence that is alleged. Alternative counts may be laid, where appropriate: see *R. v. Reakes* [1974] Crim.L.R. 615, CA.

As to the correct practice where old offences are charged, see *R. v. R.* [1993] Crim.L.R. 541, CA; *R. v. B.*, *ibid.* As to the need for special caution where extremely old offences are alleged, *i.e.* dating back to the period prior to the passing of the SOA 1967 (July 27, 1967), see *R. v. D.* [1993] Crim.L.R. 542, CA.

As to the particulars which need to be averred on a charge of attempted buggery, see *R. v. D.*, *ante*. The principles are the same as for the full offence.

### (d) *Indictment for buggery with an animal (bestiality)*

#### Statement of Offence

**H-99**

*Buggery, contrary to section 12(1) of the Sexual Offences Act 1956.*

#### Particulars of Offence

*A B, a person of [or over] the age of 21 years, on the _____ day of _____, 20___, committed buggery with a cow [or as the case may be].*

### (e) *Class of offence and mode of trial*

**H-100**    This offence, and an attempt to commit it, are class 3 offences (§ 2-17 in the main work), triable only on indictment: SOA 1956, s.37(2), and Sched. 2, para. 3(a), (b).

## (f) *Time limits*

**Sexual Offences Act 1967, s.7**

**7.**—(1) No proceedings for an offence to which this section applies shall be commenced after the **H-101**
expiration of twelve months from the date on which that offence was committed.
(2) This section applies to—
   (a) any offence under section 13 of the Act of 1956 (gross indecency between men);
   (b) [*repealed by Criminal Law Act 1977, Sched. 13*];
   (c) any offence of buggery by a man with another man not amounting to an assault on that
       other man and not being an offence by a man with a boy under the age of 16.

For section 13 of the 1956 Act, see *post*, H-107.

Where it was unclear upon the evidence given at the trial whether the offence charged had
been committed within the 12 month period prior to the commencement of proceedings for the
offence, the court quashed the conviction: *R. v. Lewis*, 68 Cr.App.R. 310, CA. A judge need not in
every case to which section 7(1) applies direct the jury that they must be sure the offence was
committed within the prescribed period. However, he must do so where an issue under the
subsection is raised by the defence, or where it clearly arises on the evidence given at the trial:
*ibid.*

## (g) *Restriction on prosecutions*

**Sexual Offences Act 1967, s.8**

**8.** No proceedings shall be instituted except by or with the consent of the Director of Public **H-102**
Prosecutions against any man for the offence of buggery with, or gross indecency with, another man
... or for aiding, abetting, counselling, procuring or commanding its commission where either of
those men was at the time of its commission under the age of sixteen.

[This section is printed as amended by the Sexual Offences (Amendment) Act 2000, s.1(2)(b);
and as repealed in part by the Criminal Jurisdiction Act 1975, s.14(5), and Sched. 6, Pt I; and the
Criminal Attempts Act 1981, s.10, and Sched., Pt I.]

Failure to obtain the consent of the DPP will lead to the quashing of the conviction: *R. v. Angel*,
52 Cr.App.R. 280, CA; *Secretary of State for Defence v. Warn* [1970] A.C. 394, HL (proceedings
before court-martial).

Section 8 does not apply to proceedings under the Indecency with Children Act 1960 (*post*,
H-230): CJA 1972, s.48.

## (h) *Sentence*

### Maximum

The full offence, or an attempt to commit it: if with a person under the age of 16 or with an **H-103**
animal, life imprisonment; if the accused is of or over the age of 21 and the other person is under
the age of 18, imprisonment not exceeding five years; otherwise, imprisonment not exceeding two
years—SOA 1956, s.37(3), and Sched. 2, para. 3(a), (b) (as substituted by the CJPOA 1994,
s.144(1), (2)). (For an offence of non-consensual buggery with a male over 15 committed before
the commencement of the amendments effected by the 1994 Act (November 3, 1994), the
maximum remains at 10 years: *Att.-Gen.'s Reference (No. 48 of 1994) (R. v. Jeffrey)*, 16 Cr.App.R.(S.)
980, CA.)

The effect of the different penalty provisions is to create distinct offences: see *R. v. Courtie*
[1984] A.C. 463, HL.

Absence of consent not being an ingredient of the offence, it is not open to a judge to sentence
on the basis that there was lack of consent; if lack of consent is alleged, there should be a charge
of rape: *R. v. Davies* [1998] 1 Cr.App.R.(S.) 380, CA; *R. v. D. (Anthony)* [2000] 1 Cr.App.R.(S.) 120,
CA.

### Guidelines

The bracket of sentencing in cases of homosexual offences against boys with neither aggravat- **H-104** ing nor mitigating factors was set out in *R. v. Willis*, 60 Cr.App.R. 146, CA, as being from three to five years. The court in that case also identified the principal aggravating and mitigating features. In *R. v. A. and W.* [2001] 2 Cr.App.R. 18, CA, the court specifically said that the guidelines in *Willis* remained the starting point. In *R. v. Patterson* [2006] 2 Cr.App.R.(S.) 48, however, the Court of Appeal said that sentences in historic cases of buggery should now be determined as if the offence were one of rape in accordance with the guidelines in *R. v. Millberry*; *R. v. Morgan*; *R. v. Lackenby* [2003] 1 Cr.App.R. 25, CA, instead of by reference to the *Willis* guidelines. The court said that it is important that the sentence should reflect the gravity of the offence rather than the particular label attached to it, and since there is no distinction in principle or in essential gravity made in the *Millberry* guidelines between rape of a male and rape of a female, it would be wrong for a sentence of buggery to be imposed on any other basis. This approach was taken further in *R. v. Kearns* [2009] 1 Cr.App.R.(S.) 107, CA, where it was applied to what was apparently a case of consensual buggery of a 15-year-old boy. For criticism of the *Patterson/Kearns* approach, see the commentaries at CLW/06/34/24 and CLW/09/16/8. Whilst this criticism remains valid, sentencers dealing with historic offending should now be guided, as to general principles, by the judgment of the Court of Appeal in *R. v. H.*, *ante*, H-12.

### (i) *Ingredients of the offence*

**H-105**   The definition of the offence derives from the common law. It consists of sexual intercourse (*per anum*—*R. v. Jacobs* (1817) R. & R. 331) by man with man or, in the same manner, by man with woman (*R. v. Wiseman* (1718) Fortescue K.B. 91; Fost. 91), or by man or woman in any manner (*R. v. Bourne*, 36 Cr.App.R. 125, CCA) with beast (also referred to as bestiality): see 1 Hale 669; 1 Hawk. c. 4; 1 East P.C. 480; 1 Russ. Cr., 12th ed., 735. Once penetration is proved, both parties (if consenting) are equally guilty.

Penetration, without emission, is sufficient: *R. v. Reekspear* (1832) 1 Mood. 342.

As to the abolition of the common law presumption that a boy under 14 is incapable of sexual intercourse, see *ante*, H-13.

The offence of bestiality does not depend on consent but on the commission of a particular act: *R. v. Bourne*, *ante* (defendant convicted of aiding and abetting his wife to commit buggery with a dog, it being assumed that she would have been entitled to an acquittal on the ground of duress).

The following direction on the question of privacy (1967 Act, s.1, *ante*) has been approved by the Court of Appeal: "you look at all the circumstances, the time of night, the nature of the place including such matters as lighting and you consider further the likelihood of a third person coming upon the scene": *R. v. Reakes* [1974] Crim.L.R. 615.

In relation to subsection (3A) of section 1 of the 1967 Act, it is open to the prosecution to prove severe mental handicap without calling medical evidence but by inviting the jury to observe the behaviour and reactions of the complainant and to draw what they consider to be an appropriate inference: *R. v. Robbins* [1988] Crim.L.R. 744, CA.

### (j) *Evidence*

**H-106**   The rule as to the admissibility of recent complaints was held to apply in the case of buggery with a youth of 19: *R. v. Wannell*, 17 Cr.App.R. 53, CCA.

### (11) Gross indecency

#### (a) *Statute*

#### Sexual Offences Act 1956, s.13

**H-107**    **13.** It is an offence for a man to commit an act of gross indecency with another man otherwise than in the circumstances described below, whether in public or private, or to be a party to the commission by a man of an act of gross indecency with another man, or to procure the commission by a man of an act of gross indecency with another man.

The circumstances referred to above are that the man is under the age of sixteen and the other man has attained that age.

[This section is printed as amended by the Sexual Offences (Amendment) Act 2000, s.2(2)(a) and (b).]

Gross indecency is no longer an offence where the act takes place in private and both parties consent thereto and both have attained the age of 16: see SOA 1967, s.1 (as amended by the Sexual Offences (Amendment) Act 2000, s.1(2)(a)), *ante*, H-97.

Furthermore, it is not an offence under this section for a man to procure the commission by another man of an act of gross indecency with himself which by reason of section 1 of the 1967 Act is not an offence under this section: see section 4(3) of the 1967 Act, *post*, H-236. As to procuration of gross indecency, see further H-113, *post*.

As to the use of the word "man", see *post*, H-222.

### (b) *Indictment*

#### Statement of Offence

*Gross indecency, contrary to section 13 of the Sexual Offences Act 1956.*

#### Particulars of Offence

*A B, on the _____ day of _____, 20___, being a male person, committed an act of gross indecency with J N, a male person otherwise than in private* [or *with J N, a male person under the age of 18 years, namely, of the age of _____ years*].

### (c) *Class of offence and mode of trial*

Offences contrary to section 13, and an attempt to procure the commission by a man of an act of gross indecency with another man, are class 3 offences (§ 2-17 in the main work), triable either way: MCA 1980, s.17(1), and Sched. 1 (§ 1-130 in the main work).

### (d) *Time limits and restrictions on prosecutions*

See *ante*, H-101, H-102.

### (e) *Sentence*

Offences contrary to section 13: if by a man of or over the age of 21 with a man under the age of 16, imprisonment not exceeding five years, otherwise two years—SOA 1956, s.37(3), and Sched. 2, para. 16(a) (as amended by the CJPOA 1994, s.144(1), (3), and the Sexual Offences (Amendment) Act 2000, s.1(1)).

An attempt to procure the commission by a man of an act of gross indecency with another man: as for the full offences—SOA 1956, s.37(3), and Sched. 2, para. 16(b) (as amended by the CJPOA 1994, s.144(1), (3), and the Sexual Offences (Amendment) Act 2000, s.1(1)).

Penalties on summary conviction are provided for by the MCA 1980, s.32 (§ 1-125 in the main work).

An attempt to commit any other offence than the one specifically provided for by the 1956 Act will be punishable in accordance with the Criminal Attempts Act 1981, ss.1 and 4 (§§ 33-128 *et seq.* in the main work).

### (f) *Ingredients of the offences*

## Gross indecency

If there is an agreement whereby two male persons act in concert to behave in a grossly indecent manner, as, for example, to make a grossly indecent exhibition, the offence is committed even though there has been no actual physical contact: *R. v. Hunt*, 34 Cr.App.R. 135, CCA.

An offence of indecency between men is not committed unless both men participate in the indecency. "With another man" in section 13 cannot be construed as meaning "against" or "directed towards" a person who did not consent: *R. v. Preece and Howells* [1977] Q.B. 370, 63 Cr.App.R. 28, CA, and see *R. v. Hornby and Peaple*, 32 Cr.App.R. 1, CCA, and *R. v. Hunt, ante*.

Where two persons are jointly indicted for an offence under the section, one may be convicted and the other acquitted: *R. v. Jones* [1896] 1 Q.B. 4; *R. v. Pearce*, 35 Cr.App.R. 17, CCA; but see *R. v. Batten, The Times*, March 16, 1990, CA, where two men were charged with committing an act of gross indecency with each other. The jury convicted one defendant, but failed to agree in respect of the other and were discharged. The Court of Appeal quashed the conviction: the issue was the same in the case of both men and it was not a case where there was some evidence such as a confession, implicating one man but not the other. If both are to be convicted, it is important that the jury should be directed that, to establish the offence, it must be proved that there was an act of gross indecency by the one defendant with the other and that the two defendants were acting in concert: *R. v. Hornby and Peaple, ante.*

A conviction for attempting to commit an act of gross indecency may be maintained where one of the persons implicated alone has been charged and the other has not been charged but has been called as a witness for the prosecution and swears that he did not consent to any act of indecency: *R. v. Pearce, ante.*

### Procuring gross indecency

**H-113**    It is an offence within section 13 for a male person to procure the commission with himself of an act of gross indecency by another male person: *R. v. Jones, ante*; *R. v. Cope*, 16 Cr.App.R. 77, CCA. But, if the act itself is not an offence by virtue of section 1 of the SOA 1967, the procuration thereof will not be an offence either: *ibid.*, s.4(3). See *ante*, H-97, and *post*, H-236.

If a male person persuades, or attempts to persuade, a boy to handle him indecently, such person alone may be charged and convicted under this section. In a case where indecent assault may be difficult or impossible to prove, because no threat or hostile act by the defendant towards the boy can easily be established, the proper charge is that of procuring or attempting to procure (as the case may be) an act of gross indecency with the defendant himself: *R. v. Burrows*, 35 Cr.App.R. 180, CCA.

On a charge of incitement to procure an act of gross indecency, it is not necessary that there should be, at the time of the incitement, an ascertained person with whom the act was to be committed: *R. v. Bentley* [1923] 1 K.B. 403, CCA.

As to the meaning of "procure", see also *post*, H-171.

### Attempting to procure an act of gross indecency

**H-114**    Procuring the commission of an act of gross indecency under section 13 of the 1956 Act is itself a substantive offence. Section 1(4)(b) of the Criminal Attempts Act 1981 (§ 33-128 in the main work) does not preclude the charging of an attempt to procure an act of gross indecency under section 1(1) of the 1981 Act because section 1(4)(b) applies in circumstances when the alleged procurement is additional to and not part of the substantive offence: *Chief Constable of Hampshire v. Mace*, 84 Cr.App.R. 40, DC. (The penalty for such attempt is specifically provided for by the 1956 Act: see *ante*, H-111.)

What conduct will be sufficient to constitute an attempt will depend on the application of the formula in section 1(1) of the 1981 Act: was what was done "more than merely preparatory to the commission of the offence"?

Authorities decided prior to the 1981 Act can be no more than illustrative: see *R. v. Cope, ante*; *R. v. Woods*, 22 Cr.App.R. 41, CCA; *R. v. Miskell*, 37 Cr.App.R. 214, Ct-MAC.

### (g) *Evidence*

### Guilty plea by one defendant

**H-115**    See *R. v. Mattison* [1990] Crim.L.R. 117, CA (§ 9-90 in the main work).

### Recent complaint

**H-116**    The rule as to admissibility of recent complaints was held not to apply to this offence on the ground that consent of the other male person is immaterial: *R. v. Hoodless*, 64 J.P. 282.

### (12) Indecent assault on a woman

#### (a) *Statute*

**Sexual Offences Act 1956, s.14**

*Indecent assault on a woman*

**H-117**    **14.**—(1) It is an offence, subject to the exception mentioned in subsection (3) of this section, for a person to make an indecent assault on a woman.

(2) A girl under the age of sixteen cannot in law give any consent which would prevent an act be-ing an assault for the purposes of this section.

(3) Where a marriage is invalid under section two of the Marriage Act 1949, or section one of the Age of Marriage Act 1929 (the wife being a girl under the age of sixteen), the invalidity does not make the husband guilty of any offence under this section by reason of her incapacity to consent while under that age, if he believes her to be his wife and has reasonable cause for the belief.

(4) A woman who is a defective cannot in law give any consent which would prevent an act being an assault for the purposes of this section, but a person is only to be treated as guilty of an indecent assault on a defective by reason of that incapacity to consent, if that person knew or had reason to suspect her to be a defective.

As to the use of the words "woman" and "girl", see *post*, H-222.

As to the meaning of "defective", see *ante*, H-68.

For the Marriage Act 1949, s.2, see *ante*, H-51.

For the burden of proof of exceptions, see section 47 of the 1956 Act, *post*, H-225.

For anonymity provisions, see *post*, §§ 20-257 *et seq.* in the main work.

### (b) *Indictment*

**Statement of Offence**

*Indecent assault, contrary to section 14(1) of the Sexual Offences Act 1956.*     **H-118**

**Particulars of Offence**

*A B, on the _____ day of _____, 20___, indecently assaulted J N, a woman.*

Age is not an essential ingredient of, nor an essential averment in, the framing of a count under section 14(1): *R. v. Hodgson* [1973] Q.B. 565, 57 Cr.App.R. 502, CA. As to the need, however, to specify the age of the girl in certain old cases, see *post*, H-120.

Where the prosecution case leaves it open to the jury to convict on either of two distinct factual bases, it will be necessary for the judge to direct them as to the need for unanimity as to the basis of any verdict of guilty: see *R. v. Turner* [2000] Crim.L.R. 325, CA, and *R. v. D.* [2001] 1 Cr.App.R. 13, CA.

In *R. v. J.* [2005] 1 A.C. 562, HL, it was held that, on a true construction of the SOA 1956, it is impermissible to prosecute a charge of indecent assault under section 14(1) in circumstances where the only conduct upon which that charge was based was an act of unlawful sexual intercourse with a girl under the age of 16 in respect of which no prosecution might be com-menced under section 6(1) (*ante*, H-50) by virtue of the time bar of 12 months contained in sec-tion 37(2) of, and Schedule 2, para. 10, to, the Act (as to which, see *ante*, H-55). Their Lordships held that the court was under a duty to give effect to a statute which was plain and unambiguous; it must have been intended that the prohibition in paragraph 10 would have some meaningful ef-fect, otherwise there would have been no possible purpose in prohibiting prosecution under sec-tion 6 after a lapse of 12 months if exactly the same conduct could thereafter be prosecuted, with exposure to the same penalty (at the time of enactment), under section 14; but this did not prevent a prosecution being properly founded on independent acts other than sexual intercourse itself or conduct inherent in or forming part of it. As to the effect of this decision in relation to indecent assault as a possible alternative verdict on a charge of rape, see the cases cited at H-9, *ante*.

### (c) *Class of offence and mode of trial*

This offence is a class 3 offence (§ 2-17 in the main work), triable either way: MCA 1980,     **H-119**
s.17(1), and Sched. 1 (§ 1-130 in the main work).

### (d) *Sentence*

Imprisonment, not exceeding 10 years: SOA 1956, s.37, and Sched. 2, para. 17 (as amended by     **H-120**
the SOA 1985, s.3(3)). The 1985 amendment took effect on September 16, 1985: prior to that, the maximum penalty was two years' imprisonment, save where the girl was under 13 and was so stated in the indictment, in which case the maximum was five years' imprisonment. In relation to cases where the facts date back beyond September 16, 1985, see *R. v. R.* [1993] Crim.L.R. 541, CA; *R. v. B.*, *ibid.*

Where a defendant charged with rape of a girl under 16 is acquitted of rape, but convicted of indecent assault on the basis that consent is no defence, the sentence should not exceed the maximum for an offence of unlawful sexual intercourse with a girl under 16 (as to which, see *ante*, H-56): *R. v. Iles* [1998] 2 Cr.App.R.(S.) 63, CA.

The fact that the victim had been abused on a previous occasion does not reduce, but might increase, the gravity of further offending by an adult thereafter. If, however, by reason of being corrupted or precocious, or both, the victim instigated offences against herself, that was an aspect which the judge was entitled to take into account. But it was mitigation only in a negative sense, namely that the child was not being treated in a way which she was personally resisting or found repugnant: *Att.-Gen.'s Reference (No. 36 of 1995) (R. v. Dawson)* [1996] 2 Cr.App.R.(S.) 50, CA.

There is no sentencing principle which precludes the imposition of a custodial sentence on a first conviction of a persistent indecent assault (on a female on an underground train): *R. v. Townsend*, 16 Cr.App.R.(S.) 553, CA, *R. v. Tanyildiz* [1998] 1 Cr.App.R.(S.) 362, CA, and *R. v. Diallo* [2000] 1 Cr.App.R.(S.) 426, CA (not following *R. v. Neem*, 14 Cr.App.R.(S.) 18, CA).

Cases decided prior to the increase in the statutory maximum effected by the SOA 1985 could not be regarded as authoritative in relation to the tariff after the increase; the conclusion in *R. v. Demel* [1997] 2 Cr.App.R.(S.) 5, CA, that the upper end of the tariff for a single incident involving a breach of trust following a trial was in the range of 13 to 18 months' imprisonment should not be followed as the authorities relied on were decided in relation to a different statutory framework or had been decided without apparent appreciation of the effect of the 1985 Act: *R. v. L.* [1999] 1 Cr.App.R. 117, CA (two years' imprisonment following trial for "grave" breach of trust by 52-year-old man on nine-year-old girl upheld; declining to issue guidelines, but observing that in most cases the personal circumstances of the offender would have to take second place to the duty of the court to protect victims). See also *R. v. Wellman* [1999] 2 Cr.App.R.(S.) 162, CA.

For cases of indecent assault, see CSP B4–6.

As to the non-applicability of the Sentencing Guidelines Council's guideline on sexual offences (*post*, Appendix K-83 *et seq.*) to offences under the 1956 Act, see *Att.-Gen.'s Reference (No. 78 of 2010)* [2011] 2 Cr.App.R.(S.) 109, CA (pointing out that offences under the SOA 2003 are differently defined and have different (more severe) maximum penalties); but see *R. v. H.*, *ante*, H-12, as to the approach to sentencing for historic offences generally.

(e) *Ingredients of the offence*

**General**

H-121     For a full exposition of the elements of the offence, see *R. v. Court* [1989] A.C. 28, HL.

 (a) Most indecent assaults will be clearly of a sexual nature. Some may have only sexual undertones. The jury must decide whether "right-minded persons would consider the conduct indecent or not". The test is whether what occurred was so offensive to contemporary standards of modesty and privacy as to be indecent.

 (b) If the circumstances of the assault are *incapable* of being regarded as indecent, then the undisclosed intention of the accused could not make the assault an indecent one: see *R. v. George* [1956] Crim.L.R. 52, Assizes (Streatfeild J.).

 (c) The victim need not be aware of the circumstances of indecency or apprehended indecency.

 (d) Cases which ordinarily present no problem are those in which the facts, *devoid of explanation*, will give rise to the irresistible inference that the defendant intended to assault his victim in a manner which right-minded persons would clearly think was indecent. Where the circumstances are such as only to be *capable* of constituting an indecent assault, in order to determine whether or not right-minded persons might think that the assault was indecent the following factors are relevant:

 (i)  the relationship of the defendant to the victim (relative, friend, stranger);

 (ii)  how the defendant had come to embark on this conduct and why he was so behaving. Such information helps a jury to answer the vital question: are we sure that the defendant not only intended to commit an assault but an assault which was indecent? Any evidence which tends to explain the reason for the defendant's conduct is relevant to establish whether or not he intended to commit not only an assault but an indecent one.

(e) The prosecution must prove: (i) that the accused intentionally assaulted the victim; (ii) that the assault, or the assault and the circumstances accompanying it, are capable of being considered by right-minded persons as indecent; and (iii) that the accused intended to commit such an assault as is referred to in (ii) above.

The above propositions are founded upon Lord Ackner's speech (at p.36), with which the other members of the House concurred, except Lord Goff, who dissented from the decision. It follows that no offence will be committed where the man believes that the woman is consenting to his conduct, whether his belief is based on reasonable grounds or not: this was the effect of the earlier Court of Appeal decision in *R. v. Kimber*, 77 Cr.App.R. 225.

*R. v. Court* was considered in *R. v. C.* [1992] Crim.L.R. 642, CA, in which it was held that where an assault was indecent in itself, it was unnecessary to establish a specific indecent intent. In *Court*, the issue of whether or not what had occurred amounted to an indecent assault turned on motive and, therefore, specific intent had been necessary to the verdict. Where there was no question whether what had occurred was indecent or not, the basic intent of assault was sufficient. The law before *Court* remained the law and indecent assault remained an offence of basic intent; self-induced voluntary intoxication is not a defence. See also *DPP v. H.* [1992] C.O.D. 266, an earlier decision of the Divisional Court to the same effect.

*Court* and *George, ante*, were referred to in *R. v. Price* [2004] 1 Cr.App.R. 12, CA, in which it was held that stroking a woman's legs over trousers and below the knee was capable of amounting to an indecent assault.

In *R. v. Kumar* (2006) 150 S.J. 1053, CA, it was said that whilst *Court* was authority for the proposition that a doctor who obtained sexual satisfaction from a necessary medical examination properly conducted was not guilty of indecent assault where the prosecution case was limited to an allegation that he had carried out a medical examination in appropriate circumstances but in an inappropriate way and as a cloak for his own sexual gratification, where the issue had been as to the manner in which the defendant had carried out the examination (*i.e.* in an appropriate way in the presence of a chaperon or in an inappropriate way in the absence of a chaperon), there had been no need to direct the jury as to the remote theoretical possibility suggested in *Court*.

## Person

A woman may be guilty of an offence under this section: *R. v. Hare* [1934] 1 K.B. 354, 24 **H-122** Cr.App.R. 108, CCA.

## Assault

As to this, see generally, §§ 19-221 *et seq.* in the main work. **H-123**

In *Fairclough v. Whipp*, 35 Cr.App.R. 138, DC, the respondent exposed himself in the presence of a girl aged nine and invited her to touch his exposed person, which she did. *Held*, an invitation to another person to touch the invitor could not amount to an assault on the invitee, and that therefore there had been no assault and consequently no indecent assault by the respondent: applied in *DPP v. Rogers*, 37 Cr.App.R. 137, DC; but *cf. Beal v. Kelley*, 35 Cr.App.R. 128, DC, and *R. v. Sargeant*, 161 J.P. 127, CA, *post*, H-133. See also *R. v. Sutton*, 66 Cr.App.R. 21, CA, *post*, H-134, and the Indecency with Children Act 1960, *post*, H-230 *et seq.*

If a man inserts his finger into the vagina of a girl under 16, this is an indecent assault, however willing or co-operative the girl may be: *R. v. McCormack* [1969] 2 Q.B. 442, 53 Cr.App.R. 514, CA.

## Consent

If the person assaulted is under 16, her consent is no defence: SOA 1956, s.14(2) (*ante*, H-117). **H-124**

Where the woman's consent was procured by fraud as to the nature (*R. v. Case* (1850) 4 Cox 220) or quality (*R. v. Tabassum* [2000] 2 Cr.App.R. 328, CA) of the act, such consent constitutes no defence. See also § 19-233 in the main work, and *ante*, H-17.

Where a jury asked for the difference between consent and submission to be defined, it was not incumbent on the judge to direct the jury that reluctant acquiescence amounted to consent; it was for the jury to decide whether there was consent and their good sense and experience should lead them to the right conclusion: *R. v. McAllister* [1997] Crim.L.R. 233, CA (*cf. R. v. Olugboja*, 73 Cr.App.R. 344, CA, *ante*, H-16).

Consent cannot be a defence where the indecent assault consists in the infliction of blows intended or likely to cause bodily harm: *R. v. Donovan* [1934] 2 K.B. 498, 25 Cr.App.R. 1, CCA; approved and applied by the House of Lords in *R. v. Brown (Anthony)* [1994] 1 A.C. 212. (As to *Brown*, see also § 19-233 in the main work.) *Donovan* was also referred to in *R. v. Boyea* [1992] Crim.L.R. 574, CA, in which it was held that an assault which was intended or likely to cause bodily harm, and which was accompanied by indecency, constituted the offence of indecent assault regardless of consent, provided that the injury was not "transient or trifling". However, the tribunal of fact must take account of changing social attitudes, particularly in the field of sexual relations between adults. As a generality, the level of vigour in sexual congress which was generally acceptable, and therefore the voluntarily accepted risk of incurring some injury was probably higher now than in 1934, when *Donovan* was decided. It followed that the phrase "transient or trifling" must be understood in the light of current conditions. *Boyea* was approved in *Brown (Anthony)*, *ante*. (See also *R. v. Wilson (A.)* [1996] 2 Cr.App.R. 241, CA (§ 19-235 in the main work).)

### Bona fide belief as to age of girl

**H-125**    Where the complainant was under the age of 16 at the time of the alleged offence, the defendant's genuine belief that she was in fact 16 or over at the time will negative criminal liability if the complainant in fact consented or the defendant genuinely believed that she was consenting: *R. v. K.* [2002] 1 A.C. 462, HL.

### Indecent assault within marriage

**H-126**    A man may be guilty of indecent assault upon his wife: *R. v. Kowalski*, 86 Cr.App.R. 339, CA.

### (13) Indecent assault on a man

#### (a) *Statute*

**Sexual Offences Act 1956, s.15**

**H-127**    **15.**—(1) It is an offence for a person to make an indecent assault on a man.

(2) A boy under the age of sixteen cannot in law give any consent which would prevent an act being an assault for the purposes of this section.

(3) A man who is a defective cannot in law give any consent which would prevent an act being an assault for the purposes of this section, but a person is only to be treated as guilty of an indecent assault on a defective by reason of that incapacity to consent, if that person knew or had reason to suspect him to be a defective.

(4), (5) [*Repealed by Police and Criminal Evidence Act 1984, Sched. 7.*]

As to the use of the words "man" and "boy", see *post*, H-222.

As to the meaning of "defective", see *ante*, H-68.

For anonymity provisions, see §§ 20-257 *et seq.* in the main work.

#### (b) *Indictment*

**Statement of Offence**

**H-128**        *Indecent assault on male person, contrary to section 15(1) of the Sexual Offences Act 1956.*

**Particulars of Offence**

*A B, on the _____ day of _____, 20___, indecently assaulted J N, a male person.*

In practice, the age of the alleged victim, if he was under the age of 16, was usually averred.

#### (c) *Class of offence and mode of trial*

**H-129**    This offence is a class 3 offence (§ 2-17 in the main work), triable either way: MCA 1980, s.17(1), and Sched. 1 (§ 1-130 in the main work).

#### (d) *Sentence*

**H-130**    Imprisonment not exceeding 10 years: SOA 1956, s.37(3), and Sched. 2, para. 18.

As to the approach to sentencing for historic offences, see *R. v. H.*, *ante*, H-12.

### (e) *Ingredients of the offence*

#### General

See *R. v. Court* and *R. v. C.*, *ante*, H-121, which, it is submitted, apply equally to this offence. **H-131**

#### Person

A woman may be guilty of this offence: *R. v. Hare*, *ante*, H-122. **H-132**

#### Assault

As to assaults generally, see §§ 19-221 *et seq.* in the main work. **H-133**

An offence under section 15 is committed when a woman immediately prior to having sexual intercourse with a 14-year-old boy holds his penis. The act alleged to constitute the assault is an indecent act, consent is therefore no defence (s.15(2)—see *R. v. Sutton*, 66 Cr.App.R. 21, CA): *Faulkner v. Talbot*, 74 Cr.App.R. 1, DC.

*Semble*, an allegation of sexual intercourse by a woman with a boy under 16, *per se* connotes an allegation of indecent assault: see *R. v. McCormack* [1969] 2 Q.B. 442, 53 Cr.App.R. 514, CA; *Faulkner v. Talbot*, *ante*.

If there is an assault committed in circumstances of indecency, then there need not be an indecent touching: see *Beal v. Kelly*, 35 Cr.App.R. 128, DC (when boy refused to touch defendant's penis when asked to do so, defendant pulled boy towards him, but let him go); and *R. v. Sargeant*, 161 J.P. 127, CA (grabbed boy, then used threat of further force to compel boy to masturbate himself). *Cf. Fairclough v. Whipp*, *ante*, H-123.

In order to constitute an assault against a child under 16, the act complained of either must **H-134** itself be inherently indecent or it must be one that is hostile or threatening or an act which the child is demonstrably reluctant to accept (see *DPP v. Rogers*, 37 Cr.App.R. 137, DC, and *Williams v. Gibbs* [1958] Crim.L.R. 127, DC). Although sections 14(2) and 15(2) of the 1956 Act bar the child's consent from preventing an act being an indecent assault, consent does avail to prevent the act being an assault if the act is not inherently indecent. The proper course where there is an act which could not conceivably be called an assault but which takes place in an indecent situation, is to prosecute under the Indecency with Children Act 1960 (*post*, H-230 *et seq.*): *R. v. Sutton*, 66 Cr.App.R. 21, CA. The defendant photographed partially clothed and unclothed boys, intending to sell the photographs to magazines. In order to arrange poses, he touched the boys on the hands, legs and torso; the actions were not threatening or hostile and the boys consented to them. His convictions under section 15(1) were quashed: touching merely to indicate a pose was not of itself indecent and was consented to. Consent did therefore avail to prevent the acts having been assaults and the question of indecency did not arise.

#### Consent

Consent is a defence as it negatives the assault: see *R. v. Wollaston* (1872) 12 Cox 180, CCR. See **H-135** also *ante*, H-124.

A boy under the age of 16 cannot in law give any consent which would prevent an act being an assault for the purposes of the section: s.15(2), *ante*, H-127; but see the cases cited in the previous paragraph.

#### Bona fide belief as to age of boy

See *R. v. K.* [2002] 1 A.C. 462, HL, *ante*, H-125; and *R. v. Fernandez*, *The Times*, June 26, 2002, **H-136** CA (confirming that the decision of the House of Lords applies equally to this offence).

### (f) *Evidence*

The rule as to the admissibility of recent complaints (§§ 8-207 *et seq.* in the main work) was held **H-137** to apply in the case of an indecent assault upon a boy of 15: *R. v. Camelleri* [1922] 2 K.B. 122, 16 Cr.App.R. 162, CCA.

## (14) Assault with intent to commit buggery

### (a) *Statute*

#### Sexual Offences Act 1956, s.16

**H-138**    **16.**—(1) It is an offence for a person to assault another person with intent to commit buggery.
(2)–(3) [*Repealed by Police and Criminal Evidence Act 1984, Sched. 7.*]

As to the offence of buggery, see *ante*, H-96 *et seq.*
As to assault, see generally, §§ 19-221 *et seq.* in the main work.
For anonymity provisions, see §§ 20-257 *et seq.* in the main work.

### (b) *Indictment*

#### Statement of Offence

**H-139**    *Assault with intent to commit buggery, contrary to section 16(1) of the Sexual Offences Act 1956.*

#### Particulars of Offence

*A B, on the _____ day of _____, 20___, assaulted J N with intent to commit buggery with the said J N.*

### (c) *Class of offence*

**H-140**    This offence is a class 3 offence (§ 2-17 in the main work), triable only on indictment: SOA 1956, s.37(2), and Sched. 2, para. 19.

### (d) *Sentence*

**H-141**    Imprisonment not exceeding 10 years: SOA 1956, s.37(3), and Sched. 2, para. 19.

### (e) *Effect of Criminal Justice and Public Order Act 1994*

**H-142**    It seems that no thought could have been given to the effect on this offence of the redefinition of rape to include non-consensual anal intercourse. The logical solution would have been to substitute "rape" for "buggery" at the end of subsection (1). The offence consisting of an assault allied to a specific intent suggests non-consensual buggery, but because of the bizarre nature of the amendments to section 12, not all nonconsensual buggery (*e.g.* both parties over 18 and the act takes place in private) constitutes the *offence* of buggery, although it will always be rape. It is submitted that the proper interpretation is that an offence under section 16 is committed where there is an assault accompanied by the requisite intent regardless of whether or not the act itself, if completed, would constitute the offence of buggery. This does, of course, lead to anomalous results; it would be an offence contrary to this provision to assault a woman intending to have anal intercourse with her but it would not be an offence to do so intending to have vaginal intercourse, although both acts, if completed, would constitute rape. The alternative interpretation would be to confine the offence to the commission of an assault with intent to commit buggery in circumstances which would make the act, if completed, an offence contrary to section 12. Because of the assault ingredient, this would effectively confine the offence to assaults on persons under 18. This seems to be an unwarranted restriction of the scope of the offence; Parliament having, if anything, deemed non-consensual buggery to be a more serious offence than it was previously, it would be an extremely curious result of the legislation if someone who committed an assault with the intention of committing that more serious offence should no longer be guilty of an offence under section 16.

As to whether there was a common law offence of assault with intent to rape, see *ante*, H-10.

## (15) Abduction of woman by force or for the sake of her property

### (a) *Statute*

#### Sexual Offences Act 1956, s.17

**H-143**    **17.**—(1) It is an offence for a person to take away or detain a woman against her will with the intention that she shall marry or have unlawful sexual intercourse with that or any other person, if she is so taken away or detained either by force or for the sake of her property or expectations of property.

(2) In the foregoing subsection, the reference to a woman's expectations of property relates only to property of a person to whom she is next of kin or one of the next of kin, and "property" includes any interest in property.

[This section is printed as effectively amended by the CLA 1967, s.12(5)(a).]

As to the meaning of "sexual intercourse", see *post*, H-219; as to the use of the word "woman", see *post*, H-222.

### (b) *Indictment*

#### Statement of Offence

*Abduction, contrary to section 17(1) of the Sexual Offences Act 1956.* **H-144**

#### Particulars of Offence

*A B, on the _____ day of _____, 20___, took away* [or *detained*] *J N against her will and by force* [or *for the sake of her property or expectations of property*] *with the intention that she should have unlawful sexual intercourse with him the said A B or with another* [or *with the intention that she should marry him the said A B or another*].

### (c) *Class of offence and mode of trial*

This offence is a class 3 offence (§ 2-17 in the main work), triable on indictment only: SOA **H-145** 1956, s.37(2), and Sched. 2, para. 4.

### (d) *Sentence*

Imprisonment not exceeding 14 years: SOA 1956, s.37(3), and Sched. 2, para. 4. **H-146**

### (e) *Ingredients of the offence*

As to the meaning of "unlawful" sexual intercourse, see *ante*, H-38. **H-147**

If the woman is taken away with her own consent, but afterwards refuses to continue further with the offender, and is forcibly detained by him, this is within the statute: see 1 Hawk. c.41 (*Forcible Marriage*), s.7.

## (16) Abduction of unmarried girl under 18 from parent or guardian

### (a) *Statute*

#### Sexual Offences Act 1956, s.19

**19.**—(1) It is an offence, subject to the exception mentioned in this section, for a person to take an **H-148** unmarried girl under the age of eighteen out of the possession of her parent or guardian against his will, if she is taken with the intention that she shall have unlawful sexual intercourse with men or with a particular man.

(2) A person is not guilty of an offence under this section because he takes such a girl out of the possession of her parent or guardian as mentioned above, if he believes her to be of the age of eighteen or over and has reasonable cause for the belief.

(3) In this section "guardian" means any person having the parental responsibility for or care of the girl.

[This section is printed as amended by the Children Act 1989, s.108(4), and Sched. 12, para. 11.]

As to the meaning of "sexual intercourse", see *post*, H-219; as to the use of the words "girl" and "man", see *post*, H-222; as to the meaning of "parental responsibility", see *post*, H-224.

For the burden of proof of exceptions, see section 47 of the 1956 Act, *post*, H-225.

689

### (b) *Indictment*

#### Statement of Offence

**H-149**          *Abduction of girl, contrary to section 19(1) of the Sexual Offences Act 1956.*

#### Particulars of Offence

*A B, on the _____ day of _____, 20___, unlawfully took or caused to be taken J N, an unmarried girl under the age of 18, out of the possession and against the will of her father [or mother or of C D then having parental responsibility for or care of her] with an intent unlawfully to have sexual intercourse with her [or that she should have unlawful sexual intercourse with E F or generally].*

### (c) *Class of offence and mode of trial*

**H-150**     This offence is a class 3 offence (§ 2-17 in the main work), triable on indictment only: SOA 1956, s.37(2), and Sched. 2, para. 20.

### (d) *Sentence*

**H-151**     Imprisonment not exceeding two years: SOA 1956, s.37(3), and Sched. 2, para. 20.

### (e) *Ingredients of the offence*

**H-152**     For the evidence necessary to support this indictment, see *post*, H-157 *et seq.*, *mutatis mutandis.* As to the meaning of "unlawful" sexual intercourse, see *ante*, H-38.

Upon an indictment under this section for taking a girl out of the possession of her father, it was proved that at the time of the commission of the alleged offence she was employed by another person as barmaid at a distance from her father's home. It was held that she was under the lawful charge of her employer and not in the possession of her father, and that therefore the defendant could not be convicted of the offence with which he was charged: *R. v. Henkers* (1886) 16 Cox 257. The age of the girl must be proved by the prosecution, as *ante*, H-49. The presumption of the CYPA 1933, s.99, does not apply to this offence: see the proviso to Schedule 1 to the 1933 Act (as to which see *ante*, H-49).

## (17) Abduction of unmarried girl under 16 from parent or guardian

### (a) *Statute*

#### Sexual Offences Act 1956, s.20

**H-153**          **20.**—(1) It is an offence for a person acting without lawful authority or excuse to take an unmarried girl under the age of sixteen out of the possession of her parent or guardian against his will.

(2) In the foregoing subsection "guardian" means any person having parental responsibility for or care of the girl.

[This section is printed as amended by the Children Act 1989, s.108(4), and Sched. 12, para. 12.]

As to the use of the word "girl", see *post*, H-222; as to the meaning of "parental responsibility", see *post*, H-224.

See now section 2 of the Child Abduction Act 1984 (§ 19-397 in the main work) which covers much the same ground and is not limited to the abduction of girls.

### (b) *Indictment*

#### Statement of Offence

**H-154**          *Abduction of a girl, contrary to section 20(1) of the Sexual Offences Act 1956.*

#### Particulars of Offence

*A B, on the _____ day of _____, 20___, unlawfully took or caused to be taken J N, an unmarried girl aged 14, out of the possession and against the will of her father [or mother or of E F then having parental responsibility for or care of her].*

### (c) *Class of offence and mode of trial*

**H-155**     This offence is a class 3 offence (§ 2-17 in the main work), triable on indictment only: SOA 1956, s.37(2), and Sched. 2, para. 21.

### (d) *Sentence*

Imprisonment not exceeding two years: SOA 1956, s.37(3), and Sched. 2, para. 21. **H-156**

### (e) *Ingredients of the offence*

### That the girl was in the possession of her father, etc.

This is a question for the jury: *R. v. Mace*, 50 J.P. 776. A girl will still be in the possession of her **H-157** parent/guardian even while she is away from home if she intends to return; and if, when so out of the house, the defendant induces her to run away with him, he is guilty: *R. v. Mycock* (1871) 12 Cox 28. See also *R. v. Baillie* (1859) 8 Cox 238; *R. v. Green* (1862) 3 F. & F. 274; and *R. v. Miller* (1876) 13 Cox 179.

### The taking

The taking need not be by force, either actual or constructive, and it is immaterial whether the **H-158** girl consents or not: *R. v. Manktelow* (1853) 6 Cox 143, and see *R. v. Kipps* (1850) 4 Cox 167; *R. v. Booth* (1872) 12 Cox 231; and *R. v. Robins* (1844) 1 C. & K. 456 (where the girl positively encouraged the defendant).

The words "taking out of the possession and against the will" of the parent mean some conduct amounting to a substantial interference with the possessory relationship of parent and child: *R. v. Jones (J.W.)* [1973] Crim.L.R. 621 (Swanwick J.)—attempt to take girls (aged 10) for a walk with a view to indecently assaulting them held not to constitute an attempt to commit the offence. (*Cf. R. v. Leather*, 98 Cr.App.R. 179, CA, decided on the Child Abduction Act 1984 (§ 19-399 in the main work).)

It is no defence that the defendant acted in concert with the girl and had no intention of keeping her away from her home permanently: *R. v. Timmins* (1860) 8 Cox 401; *R. v. Frazer and Norman*, *ibid.* at 446. See also *R. v. Baillie*, *ibid.* at 238.

Instead of a taking, it can be shown that a girl left her parent or guardian, in consequence of some persuasion, inducement or blandishment held out to her by the defendant: *R. v. Henkers* (1886) 16 Cox 257, following *R. v. Olifier* (1866) 10 Cox 402.

Where a man induces a girl, by promise of what he will do for her, to leave her father's house **H-159** and live with him, he may be convicted, although he is not actually present or assisting her at the time when she leaves her father's roof: *R. v. Robb* (1864) 4 F. & F. 59. If the girl leaves her father, without any persuasion, inducement or blandishment held out to her by the defendant, so that she has got fairly away from home, and then goes to him, although it may be his moral duty to return her to her father's custody, yet his not doing so is no infringement of this statute, for the statute does not say he shall restore, but only that he shall not take her away: *R. v. Olifier, ante*, and this is so even though it be proved that before she so left he had taken her about to places of amusement and had intercourse with her: *R. v. Kauffman*, 68 J.P. 189. If the suggestion to go away with the defendant comes from the girl only, and he takes merely the passive part of yielding to her suggestion, he is entitled to an acquittal: *R. v. Jarvis* (1903) 20 Cox 249. It is submitted that the ruling to the contrary in *R. v. Biswell* (1847) 2 Cox 279 is not law. For a discussion of the authorities, see *R. v. Mackney* (1903) 29 Vict.L.R. 22, where the English cases are considered.

### Against the will, etc.

If the defendant induced the parents, by false and fraudulent representations, to allow him to **H-160** take the child away, this is an abduction: *R. v. Hopkins* (1842) C. & Mar. 254.

Where the girl's mother had encouraged her in a lax course of life, by permitting her to go out alone at night and dance at public-houses, from one of which she went away with the defendant, Cockburn C.J. ruled that she could not be said to be taken away against her mother's will: *R. v. Primelt* (1858) 1 F. & F. 50.

To prove this element of the offence, it has been said that the parent or guardian must be called: *R. v. Nash, The Times*, July 2, 1903. *Sed quaere*.

### Under 16, etc.

Prove that she was under the age of 16 years and unmarried. As to the power of a court to **H-161** presume her age from her appearance, see the CYPA 1933, s.99(2) (§ 19-412 in the main work) and Sched. 1 (§ 19-408 in the main work (prior to its repeal by the SOA 2003, the proviso to Sched. 1 stipulated that s.99(2) did apply to offences under s.20)). It is no defence that the defendant did not know her to be under 16, or might suppose from her appearance that she was older: *R. v. Olifier, ante*; *R. v. Mycock, ante*; *R. v. Booth, ante*; or even that the defendant bona fide believed and had reasonable grounds for believing that she was over 16: *R. v. Prince* (1875) L.R. 2 C.C.R. 154. Doubts about *Prince* were expressed by the House of Lords in *B. (a Minor) v. DPP* [2000] 2 A.C. 428 (*post*, H-235) and *R. v. K.* [2002] 1 A.C. 462 (*ante*, H-125), but its correctness did not fall to be decided upon. Those expressions of doubt are likely to found a challenge to *Prince*, but it is submitted that the express provision of a defence based on mistake as to age in relation to the offence contrary to section 19 (*ante*, H-148) makes it abundantly clear that Parliament intended that there should be no corresponding defence in relation to the abduction of a girl under 16.

### Mens rea

**H-162**    The act of abduction is positively prohibited, and therefore the absence of a corrupt motive is no answer to the charge: see *R. v. Booth, ante*.

If the defendant, at the time he took the girl away, did not know, and had no reason to know, that she was subject to the parental responsibility and care of her father, mother or some other person, he is not guilty of this offence: *R. v. Hibbert* (1869) L.R. 1 C.C.R. 184.

### Without lawful authority or excuse

**H-163**    The defendant must show that he had either lawful authority or a lawful excuse; motive is irrelevant: *R. v. Tegerdine*, 75 Cr.App.R. 298, CA (statutory history reviewed). It is submitted that the burden on the defendant is merely an evidential one, which is discharged if there is sufficient evidence to raise an issue on the matter: *cf.* the specific provision in section 47 (*post*, H-225) in relation to "exceptions" under the Act. And see generally, §§ 4-444 *et seq.* in the main work.

### (18) Abduction of defective from parent or guardian

#### (a) *Statute*

**Sexual Offences Act 1956, s.21**

**H-164**    **21.**—(1) It is an offence, subject to the exception mentioned in this section, for a person to take a woman who is a defective out of the possession of her parent or guardian against his will, if she is so taken with the intention that she shall have unlawful sexual intercourse with men or with a particular man.

(2) A person is not guilty of an offence under this section because he takes such a woman out of the possession of her parent or guardian as mentioned above, if he does not know and has no reason to suspect her to be a defective.

(3) In this section "guardian" means any person having parental responsibility for or care of the woman.

[This section is printed as amended by the Children Act 1989, s.108(4), and Sched. 12, para. 13.]

As to the meaning of "sexual intercourse", see *post*, H-219; as to the meaning of "unlawful" sexual intercourse, see *ante*, H-38; as to the use of the words "man" and "woman", see *post*, H-222; as to the meaning of "defective", see *ante*, H-68; as to the meaning of "parental responsibility", see *post*, H-224.

For the burden of proof of exceptions, see section 47 of the 1956 Act, *post*, H-225.

#### (b) *Class of offence and mode of trial*

**H-165**    This offence is a class 3 offence (§ 2-17 in the main work), triable on indictment only: SOA 1956, s.37(2), and Sched. 2, para. 22.

#### (c) *Sentence*

**H-166**    Imprisonment not exceeding two years: SOA 1956, s.37(3), and Sched. 2, para. 22.

## (19) Causing prostitution of women

### (a) *Statute*

**Sexual Offences Act 1956, s.22**

**22.**—(1) It is an offence for a person— **H-167**
- (a) to procure a woman to become, in any part of the world, a common prostitute; or
- (b) to procure a woman to leave the United Kingdom, intending her to become an inmate of or frequent a brothel elsewhere; or
- (c) to procure a woman to leave her usual place of abode in the United Kingdom, intending her to become an inmate of or frequent a brothel in any part of the world for the purposes of prostitution.

(2) [*Repealed by Criminal Justice and Public Order Act 1994, s.33(1).*]

As to the use of the word "woman", see *post*, H-222.

### (b) *Indictment*

**Statement of Offence**

*Procuring a woman to become a common prostitute, contrary to section 22(1)(a) of the Sexual Offences Act 1956.* **H-168**

**Particulars of Offence**

*A B, on or about the _____ day of _____, 20___, at _____ procured C D, a woman, to become a common prostitute.*

### (c) *Class of offence and mode of trial*

This offence, and an attempt to commit it, are class 3 offences (§ 2-17 in the main work), triable **H-169** on indictment only: SOA 1956, s.37(2), and Sched. 2, para. 23(a), (b).

### (d) *Sentence*

The full offence, and an attempt to commit it: imprisonment not exceeding two years: SOA **H-170** 1956, s.37(3), and Sched. 2, para. 23(a), (b).

### (e) *Ingredients of the offence*

**"Procure"**

As to the meaning of the word "procure" in general, see §§ 18-22, 18-23 in the main work, and **H-171** see *Att.-Gen.'s Reference (No. 1 of 1975)* [1975] Q.B. 773, 61 Cr.App.R. 118, CA; *Re Royal Victoria Pavilion, Ramsgate* [1961] Ch. 581, Ch D, and *Blakely v. DPP* [1991] R.T.R. 405, DC. In the first of these authorities, Lord Widgery C.J. said that to procure, "means to produce by endeavour. You procure a thing by setting out to see that it happens and taking the appropriate steps to produce that happening" (at pp.779, 121). In *Re Royal Victoria Pavilion, Ramsgate*, Pennycuick J. (at p.587) defined "to procure" as "to obtain by care and effort" or "to see to it".

In *R. v. Broadfoot*, 64 Cr.App.R. 71, CA, the court described *Att.-Gen's Reference (No. 1 of 1975)*, *ante*, as a useful guide. Whilst saying that the interpretation of the word was a matter of common sense for the jury to determine in the light of the particular facts, the court appears to have approved (see p.74) the suggestion of Shaw L.J., during argument, that it could be regarded as bringing about a course of conduct which the woman in question would not have embarked upon of her own volition. *R. v. Christian* (1913) 23 Cox 541, was distinguished. It was there held that procuration could be negatived by evidence showing the girl was not really procured, because she needed no procuring, and acted of her own free will.

If a woman is already a common prostitute she cannot become one and accordingly cannot be procured to become one. It follows that if there is evidence of procuration but "the woman" is a police officer it is a good defence to a charge of attempting to procure a woman to become a prostitute contrary to section 1(1) of the Criminal Attempts Act 1981, that the defendant thought that "the woman" he was attempting to procure was already a prostitute. If he believed (or might

693

have believed) that, it could not be said that he was trying to procure her to become that which he believed she already was. Section 1(3) of the 1981 Act (§ 33-128 in the main work) is concerned with the converse case where the woman is a common prostitute but the defendant believes she is not. In such circumstances, he may be convicted of an attempt even though the commission of the offence is impossible: *R. v. Brown (R.A.)*, 80 Cr.App.R. 36, CA.

As to "attempting to do the impossible", see also § 33-137 in the main work.

### "Common prostitute"

**H-172**    This includes a woman who offers her body commonly for acts of lewdness for payment although there is no act or offer of an act of ordinary sexual intercourse: *R. v. De Munck* [1918] 1 K.B. 635, 13 Cr.App.R. 113, CCA. The word "common" in the term "common prostitute" is not mere surplusage—a common prostitute is any woman who offers herself commonly for lewdness for reward. Whether or not the performance by a woman of a single act of lewdness with a man on one occasion for reward constitutes the woman a prostitute, it plainly does not make her a woman who offers herself commonly for lewdness. That must be someone who is prepared for reward to engage in acts of lewdness with all and sundry or with anyone who may hire her for that purpose: *R. v. Morris-Lowe*, 80 Cr.App.R. 114, CA, applying *R. v. De Munck, ante*.

It is not necessary that she should have submitted to acts of lewdness in a passive way. Active acts of indecency by the woman herself, *e.g.* masturbation by her of clients when acting as a masseuse will fall within the section: *R. v. Webb* [1964] 1 Q.B. 357, 47 Cr.App.R. 265, CCA.

In *R. v. McFarlane* [1994] Q.B. 419, 99 Cr.App.R. 8, CA, it was held in relation to a prosecution under section 30 of the 1956 Act (*post*, H-197) that the essence of prostitution is the making of an offer of sexual services for reward, and that it is immaterial that the person making the offer does not intend to perform them and does not do so. It is obviously desirable that "prostitution" is given the same meaning wherever it appears in a statute; accordingly, this decision is likely to be applied to section 22. For a criticism of this decision, see the 1996 edition of this work.

### (20) Procuration of girl under 21

#### (a) *Statute*

#### Sexual Offences Act 1956, s.23

**H-173**    **23.**—(1) It is an offence for a person to procure a girl under the age of twenty-one to have unlawful sexual intercourse in any part of the world with a third person.

(2) [*Repealed by Criminal Justice and Public Order Act 1994, s.33(1).*]

As to the meaning of "sexual intercourse", see *post*, H-219; as to the use of the word "girl", see *post*, H-222.

#### (b) *Class of offence and mode of trial*

**H-174**    This offence, and an attempt to commit it, are class 3 offences (§ 2-17 in the main work), triable on indictment only: SOA 1956, s.37(2), and Sched. 2, para. 24(a), (b).

#### (c) *Sentence*

**H-175**    The full offence, and an attempt to commit it: imprisonment not exceeding two years; SOA 1956, s.37(3), and Sched. 2, para. 24(a), (b).

#### (d) *Ingredients of the offence*

**H-176**    As to the meaning of "procure", see *ante*, H-171. As to the meaning of "unlawful" sexual intercourse, see *ante*, H-38.

Before the defendant can be found guilty of an offence contrary to this section, it is necessary to prove that unlawful sexual intercourse did take place; if intercourse is not proved to have taken place but procurement with the intention that it should take place is proved, there may be a conviction of an attempt to commit the full offence: *R. v. Johnson* [1964] 2 Q.B. 404, 48 Cr.App.R. 25, CCA. As to the difference between an attempt and an intention, see *R. v. Landow*, 8 Cr.App.R. 218, CCA. As to conspiracy with the procurer, see *R. v. Mackenzie and Higginson*, 6 Cr.App.R. 64, CCA.

## (21) Detention of a woman in brothel or other premises

### (a) *Statute*

#### Sexual Offences Act 1956, s.24

**24.**—(1) It is an offence for a person to detain a woman against her will on any premises with the   **H-177**
intention that she shall have unlawful sexual intercourse with men or with a particular man, or to
detain a woman against her will in a brothel.

(2) Where a woman is on any premises for the purpose of having unlawful sexual intercourse or is
in a brothel, a person shall be deemed for the purpose of the foregoing subsection to detain her
there if, with the intention of compelling or inducing her to remain there, he either withholds from
her her clothes or any other property belonging to her or threatens her with legal proceedings in the
event of her taking away clothes provided for her by him or on his directions.

(3) A woman shall not be liable to any legal proceedings, whether civil or criminal, for taking away
or being found in possession of any clothes she needed to enable her to leave premises on which she
was for the purpose of having unlawful sexual intercourse or to leave a brothel.

As to the meaning of "sexual intercourse", see *post*, H-219; as to the use of the words "man"
and "woman", see *post*, H-222.

### (b) *Indictment*

#### Statement of Offence

*Detaining a woman against her will for unlawful sexual intercourse* [or *in a brothel*], *contrary to section 24(1) of*   **H-178**
*the Sexual Offences Act 1956.*

#### Particulars of Offence

*A B, on or about the* _____ *day of* _____, *20____, detained C D, a woman, against her will at* _____
*intending her to have unlawful sexual intercourse with men* [or *with E F, a man*] [or *detained C D, a woman,*
*against her will at* _____, *a brothel*].

### (c) *Class of offence and mode of trial*

This offence is a class 3 offence (§ 2-17 in the main work), triable on indictment only: SOA   **H-179**
1956, s.37(2), and Sched. 2, para. 25.

### (d) *Sentence*

Imprisonment not exceeding two years: SOA 1956, s.37(3), and Sched. 2, para. 25.   **H-180**

### (e) *Ingredients of offence*

## Unlawful sexual intercourse

See *ante*, H-38.   **H-181**

## "Brothel"

See §§ 20-233 *et seq.* in the main work.   **H-182**

### (f) *Evidence*

See § 20-235 in the main work.   **H-183**

## (22) Allowing premises to be used for intercourse

### (a) *Statute*

#### Sexual Offences Act 1956, ss.25, 26, 27

*Permitting girl under thirteen to use premises for intercourse*

**25.** It is an offence for a person who is the owner or occupier of any premises, or who has, or acts   **H-184**
or assists in, the management or control of any premises, to induce or knowingly suffer a girl under

the age of thirteen to resort to or be on those premises for the purpose of having unlawful sexual intercourse with men or with a particular man.

[This section is printed as effectively amended by the CLA 1967, s.12(5)(a).]

*Permitting girl between thirteen and sixteen to use premises for intercourse*

**H-185**      **26.** It is an offence for a person who is the owner or occupier of any premises, or who has, or acts or assists in, the management or control of any premises, to induce or knowingly suffer a girl … under the age of sixteen, to resort to or be on those premises for the purpose of having unlawful sexual intercourse with men or with a particular man.

[The words omitted were repealed by the CLA 1967, s.10(1), and Sched. 2, para. 14. This repeal renders the marginal note misleading.]

*Permitting defective to use premises for intercourse*

**H-186**      **27.**—(1) It is an offence, subject to the exception mentioned in this section, for a person who is the owner or occupier of any premises, or who has, or acts or assists in, the management or control of any premises, to induce or knowingly suffer a woman who is a defective to resort to or be on those premises for the purpose of having unlawful sexual intercourse with men or with a particular man.

(2) A person is not guilty of an offence under this section because he induces or knowingly suffers a defective to resort to or be on any premises for the purpose mentioned, if he does not know and has no reason to suspect her to be a defective.

As to the meaning of "sexual intercourse", see *post*, H-219; as to the use of the words "man", "woman" and "girl", see *post*, H-222; as to the meaning of "defective", see *ante*, H-68.

For the burden of proof of exceptions, see section 47 of the 1956 Act, *post*, H-225.

### (b) *Class of offence and mode of trial*

**H-187**      Section 25— this offence is a class 3 offence (§ 2-17 in the main work), triable only on indictment: SOA 1956, s.37(2), and Sched. 2, para. 6.

Section 26—this offence is a class 3 offence (§ 2-17 in the main work), triable either way: MCA 1980, s.17(1), and Sched. 1 (§ 1-130 in the main work).

Section 27—this offence is a class 3 offence (§ 2-17 in the main work), triable only on indictment: SOA 1956, s.37(2), and Sched. 2, para. 27.

### (c) *Sentence*

**H-188**      Section 25—life imprisonment: SOA 1956, s.37(3), and Sched. 2, para. 6.

Section 26—imprisonment not exceeding two years: SOA 1956, s.37(3), and Sched. 2, para. 26. The penalty on summary conviction is provided for by the MCA 1980, s.32 (§ 1-125 in the main work).

Section 27—imprisonment not exceeding two years: SOA 1956, s.37(3), and Sched. 2, para. 27.

### (d) *Ingredients of the offences*

### "Management", "assists in the management"

**H-189**      See the following cases, decided in relation to section 33 of the 1956 Act ("assisting in the management of a brothel"): *Abbott v. Smith* [1965] 2 Q.B. 662, DC (meaning of "management"); *Gorman v. Standen; Palace-Clark v. Standen* [1964] 1 Q.B. 294, 48 Cr.App.R. 30, DC; *Jones and Wood v. DPP*, 96 Cr.App.R. 130, DC; and *Elliott v. DPP; Dublides v. DPP, The Times*, January 19, 1989, DC ("assisting in the management"). In the last of these cases, the court appears to have accepted a distinction between assisting in the management of premises and assisting the management of premises.

### "Unlawful" sexual intercourse

**H-190**      See *ante*, H-38.

### "Knowingly suffer"

**H-191**      In *R. v. Webster* (1885) 16 Q.B.D. 134, it was held that the words "knowingly suffer" mean that the defendant knew of the girl's purpose in being on the premises and did not prevent the unlawful sexual intercourse from occurring when it was in his power to do so. The girl was the defendant's daughter, and the premises were her home, where she resided with the defendant. But see *R. v. Merthyr Tydfil JJ.* (1894) 10 T.L.R. 375, where a mother was held not within the section, who for the purposes of obtaining conclusive evidence against a man who had seduced her daughter, permitted him to come to her house to repeat his unlawful intercourse.

## (23) Causing or encouraging prostitution, etc.

### (a) *Statute*

#### Sexual Offences Act 1956, ss.28, 29

*Causing or encouraging prostitution of, intercourse with, or indecent assault on, girl under sixteen*

**28.**—(1) It is an offence for a person to cause or encourage the prostitution of, or the commission **H-192** of unlawful sexual intercourse with, or of an indecent assault on, a girl under the age of sixteen for whom he is responsible.

(2) Where a girl has become a prostitute, or has had unlawful sexual intercourse, or has been indecently assaulted, a person shall be deemed for the purposes of this section to have caused or encouraged it, if he knowingly allowed her to consort with, or to enter or continue in the employment of, any prostitute or person of known immoral character.

(3) The persons who are to be treated for the purposes of this section as responsible for a girl are (subject to subsection (4) of this section)—

(a) her parents;

(b) any person who is not a parent of hers but who has parental responsibility for her; and

(c) any person who has care of her.

(4) An individual falling within subsection (3)(a) or (b) of this section is not to be treated as responsible for a girl if—

(a) a residence order under the Children Act 1989 is in force with respect to her and he is not named in the order as the person with whom she is to live; *or*

(aa) a special guardianship order under that Act is in force with respect to her and he is not her special guardian; or

(b) a care order under that Act is in force with respect to her.

(5) If, on a charge of an offence against a girl under this section, the girl appears to the court to have been under the age of sixteen at the time of the offence charged, she shall be presumed for the purposes of this section to have been so, unless the contrary is proved.

[This section is printed as amended by the Children Act 1989, s.108(4), and Sched. 12, para. 14; and the Adoption and Children Act 2002, s.139(1), and Sched. 3, para. 8.]

*Causing or encouraging prostitution of defective*

**29.**—(1) It is an offence, subject to the exception mentioned in this section, for a person to cause **H-193** or encourage the prostitution in any part of the world of a woman who is a defective.

(2) A person is not guilty of an offence under this section because he causes or encourages the prostitution of such a woman, if he does not know and has no reason to suspect her to be a defective.

As to the meaning of "sexual intercourse", see *post*, H-219; as to the use of the words "woman" and "girl", see *post*, H-222; as to the meaning of "parental responsibility", see *post*, H-224; as to the meaning of "defective", see *ante*, H-68.

For the burden of proof of exceptions, see section 47 of the 1956 Act, *post*, § H-225.

### (b) *Class of offence and mode of trial*

These offences are class 3 offences (§ 2-17 in the main work), triable only on indictment: SOA **H-194** 1956, s.37(2), and Sched. 2, paras 28 and 29.

### (c) *Sentence*

Sections 28 and 29—imprisonment not exceeding two years: SOA 1956, s.37(3), and Sched. 2, **H-195** paras 28 and 29.

### (d) *Ingredients of the offences*

As to what constitutes "causing" or "encouraging", see *R. v. Ralphs*, 9 Cr.App.R. 86, CCA; *R. v.* **H-196** *Chainey* [1914] 1 K.B. 137, 9 Cr.App.R. 175, CCA.

In *R. v. Drury*, 60 Cr.App.R. 195, CA, it was held that there was evidence on which it could be held that a girl (aged 14) was in the care of the defendant where, at the time of the assault by a friend of the defendant, she was babysitting for him. The case was decided on the original wording of section 28(3)(c), *viz.* "any other person who has the custody, charge or care of her". The 1989 amendment (*ante*) would not appear to affect this point. As to encouragement, the court said that there must be encouragement in fact and an intention to encourage.

A doctor who in the exercise of his clinical judgment gives contraceptive advice and treatment to a girl under 16 without her parents' consent does not commit an offence under section 6 or 28 of the 1956 Act, because the bona fide exercise by the doctor of his clinical judgment negates the *mens rea* which is an essential ingredient of those offences: *Gillick v. West Norfolk and Wisbech Area Health Authority* [1986] A.C. 112, HL.

As to the meaning of "unlawful" sexual intercourse, see *ante*, H-38.

### (24) Man living on earnings of prostitution

#### (a) *Statute*

**Sexual Offences Act 1956, s.30**

**H-197**      **30.**—(1) It is an offence for a man knowingly to live wholly or in part on the earnings of prostitution.

(2) For the purposes of this section a man who lives with or is habitually in the company of a prostitute, or who exercises control, direction or influence over a prostitute's movements in a way which shows he is aiding, abetting or compelling her prostitution with others, shall be presumed to be knowingly living on the earnings of prostitution, unless he proves the contrary.

As to the use of the word "man", see *post*, H-222.

#### (b) *Indictment*

**Statement of Offence**

**H-198**      *Living on prostitution, contrary to section 30(1) of the Sexual Offences Act 1956.*

**Particulars of Offence**

*A B, being a man, on the _____ day of _____, 20___, and on other days between that date and the _____ day of _____, 20___, knowingly lived wholly or in part on the earnings of the prostitution of J N.*

In an indictment for this offence a person may be charged with having committed the offence on one specified day only: *R. v. Hill*, 10 Cr.App.R. 56, CCA. Evidence is admissible to show what the defendant's relations with the woman in question had been either before or after the day specified in the indictment: *ibid.*

As to the application of the alibi notice provisions to this offence, see *R. v. Hassan*, 54 Cr.App.R. 56, CA (§ 12-57a in the main work).

#### (c) *Class of offence and mode of trial*

**H-199**      This offence is a class 3 offence (§ 2-17 in the main work), triable either way: SOA 1956, s.37(2), and Sched. 2, para. 30.

#### (d) *Sentence*

### Maximum

**H-200**      On conviction on indictment, imprisonment not exceeding seven years; on summary conviction, six months, or a fine not exceeding £5,000: SOA 1956, s.37(3), and Sched. 2, para. 30 (as amended by the Street Offences Act 1959, s.4), and the MCA 1980, ss.32, 34(3)(a).

### Guidelines

**H-201**      A sentence exceeding two years should be reserved for cases where there is some evidence of physical or mental coercion of the prostitutes involved, or of corruption. The existence of such coercion or corruption is the crucial sentencing factor: *R. v. Farrugia*, 69 Cr.App.R. 108, CA. See also *R. v. Thomas*, 5 Cr.App.R.(S.) 138, CA; *R. v. El-Gazzar*, 8 Cr.App.R.(S.) 182, CA; *R. v. Malik* [1998] 1 Cr.App.R.(S.) 115, CA; and CSP B5–1.

### (e) *Ingredients of the offence*

#### "Man"

In *R. v. Tan* [1983] Q.B. 1053, 76 Cr.App.R. 300, CA, it was held that a person who was born a **H-202** man and who remained biologically a man was a man for all purposes although he had undergone hormone treatment and surgical treatment consisting of sex-change operations and had become philosophically or psychologically female (applying *Corbett v. Corbett* [1971] P. 83).

#### Prostitution

As to what constitutes "prostitution", see *ante*, H-172. As to proving that at the material time **H-203** the woman was a prostitute, see § 20-235 in the main work, and *R. v. Wilson (D.T.)*, 78 Cr.App.R. 247, CA, in which *Woodhouse v. Hall*, 72 Cr.App.R. 39, DC, was applied in the context of a prosecution under section 30.

#### Knowingly living on earnings of prostitution

There are three distinct foundations upon which the prosecution can rely in order to raise a **H-204** presumption that an offence has been committed under section 30(2) (*ante*, H-197):

    (a) proof that the accused was at the material time living with the prostitute;

    (b) proof that he was habitually at the material time in her company;

    (c) proof that he exercised control, direction or influence over her movements in a way which showed him to be aiding or abetting her prostitution.

Once evidence giving rise to the presumption has been led, it then has two facets: (a) it is presumed that he is living on immoral earnings; and (b) it is presumed that he is doing so knowingly: *R. v. Clarke*, 63 Cr.App.R. 16, CA. It is not necessary to prove that he was living with or habitually in the company of such a prostitute in a way which showed that he was aiding, abetting or compelling her prostitution with others: *ibid*. See also *R. v. Lawrence, post,* H-206.

In *R. v. Stewart*, 83 Cr.App.R. 327, CA, the court was referred to *R. v. Silver*, 40 Cr.App.R. 32, **H-205** CCC (Judge Maude); *R. v. Thomas*, 41 Cr.App.R. 121, CCA; *Shaw v. DPP* [1962] A.C. 220, HL; *R. v. Calderhead and Bidney*, 68 Cr.App.R. 37, CA; and *R. v. Wilson (D.T.), ante*. Mustill L.J. said, in giving the court's judgment:

> "What we collect from them is as follows: according to the literal meaning of the section any person who supplies goods or services to a prostitute is in one sense living off the earnings of prostitution: for in part he earns his livelihood from payments which the woman would not be able to make but for her trade. This cannot be the right view. There has to be a closer connection between the receipt of money and the trade before the recipient commits an offence. We doubt whether it is possible to devise a definition of the type and closeness of the necessary connection which will deal with all the circumstances which may arise; and, indeed, it is dangerous to treat words or phrases from judgments delivered in relation to one set of facts, as if they provided a statutory gloss which can be reliably applied to facts of a quite different nature ... .
>
> Subject to this reservation, we believe that an approach which will often be useful is to identify for the jury the flavour of the words 'living off', and then to express this general concept in the shape of guidance more directly referable to the case in hand. In our judgment, the word 'parasite' (to be found in the speech of Lord Reid in *Shaw v. DPP* ...), or some expanded equivalent, provides a useful starting point for this exercise, and does express a concept which accounts for all the reported cases except for *Silver*.
>
> Adopting this general approach, and dealing specifically with a defendant who supplies goods or services to a prostitute, a good working test, sufficient to deal with many cases, is whether the fact of supply means that the supplier and the prostitute were engaged in the business of prostitution together: and 'the fact of supply' will include the scale of supply, the price charged and the nature of the goods or services. It will be impossible to say in advance that certain categories of supplies must necessarily fall outside the section, any more than that other categories must be within it, but the idea of participation in the prostitute's business will enable the jury to distinguish readily between (say) the supplier of groceries on the one hand and the publisher of prostitutes'

advertisements on the other. There will remain a residue of more difficult cases, and these include the situation where premises are let at a market rent with knowledge of the purpose to which they are to be put. We see no room here for any rule of thumb distinction between premises which are or are not let at abnormally high rates. Certainly, the jury will find it easier to infer in the former case that the lessor participates in the woman's earnings. ... We can, however, see no logic in the suggestion that the lessor cannot be convicted unless the rent is exorbitant and indeed the judgment of Ashworth J. in *Shaw v. DPP* (at p.230) and the speech of Lord Simonds in the same case (at p.265 ... see the words 'whatever the rent') are authority for the view that the presence or absence of this factor is not conclusive. Nor in our opinion is the question whether the premises are occupied or capable of occupation as residential premises to be taken as the touchstone.

Instead, the judge must bear in mind when framing his direction the distinction between the offence under section 30(1), and the offences under sections 34, 35 and 36, and must not allow the jury to believe that knowledge of use to which the premises are put will be sufficient in itself to found a conviction. He must draw the attention of the jury to whatever factors are material to the individual case. These will often include, but not be limited to, the nature and location of the premises, the involvement of the lessor in adapting, furnishing or outfitting the premises for prostitution, the duration of the letting, the hours during which the premises are occupied, the rent at which they are let, the method of payment of rent, the fact that the prostitute does or does not live as well as work at the premises, the presence or absence of a personal relationship between the lessor and the lessee, the steps taken by the lessor to remove the prostitutes from his premises, and the steps taken by the lessor to disguise his relationship with the premises and the persons working there. Having presented the facts to the jury, the judge will invite them to consider whether they are sure that the lessor was involved together with the prostitute in the business of prostitution" (at pp.332–333).

**H-206**    Mustill L.J. then said that in the opinion of the court, the judge's direction, that where a letting was referable to prostitution and nothing else it was immaterial whether the letting was at a higher than normal rent, was correct, and to the extent that *Silver, ante*, is a decision to the contrary, it should not be followed.

It is essential that a jury should receive a clear and careful direction with regard to this offence and the burden of proof in relation to it. In particular, where the prosecution rely on subsection (2) (*ante*, H-197), the jury's attention should be directed to the various alternatives contained in the subsection, and to any evidence relating to any of those alternatives: *R. v. Lawrence*, 47 Cr.App.R. 72, CCA.

In *R. v. Howard*, 94 Cr.App.R. 89, CA, Lord Lane C.J. said that what is required is a simple direction based primarily on what was said in *Shaw v. DPP, ante*, and *Stewart, ante*, adjusted to the facts of the particular case.

### (f) Evidence

**H-207**    That the defendant knowingly lived wholly or in part on the earnings of prostitution is usually proved by evidence that the prostitute paid the rent of rooms where both were living together, or paid for his food, or supplied him with money, or paid for drink consumed by him in public-houses, or the like. Whether conversation and association with a prostitute amounts to proof that the defendant was habitually in her company is a question of fact for the jury: *R. v. Ptohopoulos*, 52 Cr.App.R. 47, CA.

There need not be proof that the prostitute handed money to the defendant if the evidence establishes that what the defendant received was earned by the prostitute (see *Calvert v. Mayes* [1954] 1 Q.B. 242, approved in *Shaw*). Nor, as was held in *R. v. Ansell* [1975] Q.B. 215, 60 Cr.App.R. 45, CA, if the money comes from the men with whom the prostitutes are dealing and not from the prostitutes themselves, does that fact in law prevent the money being the earnings of prostitution: see, for example, *R. v. Farrugia*, 69 Cr.App.R. 108, CA.

### (25) Woman exercising control over prostitute

#### (a) Statute

**Sexual Offences Act 1956, s.31**

**H-208**    **31.** It is an offence for a woman for purposes of gain to exercise control, direction or influence over a prostitute's movements in a way which shows she is aiding, abetting or compelling her prostitution.

As to the use of the word "woman", see *post*, H-222. As to the meaning of "prostitution", see *ante*, H-172.

### (b) *Class of offence and mode of trial*

This offence is a class 3 offence (§ 2-17 in the main work), triable either way: SOA 1956, s.37(2), and Sched. 2, para. 31.     **H-209**

### (c) *Sentence*

On conviction on indictment, imprisonment not exceeding seven years; on summary conviction, six months, or a fine not exceeding £5,000: SOA 1956, s.37(3), and Sched. 2, para. 31 (as amended by the Street Offences Act 1959, s.4), and the MCA 1980, ss.32, 34(3)(a).     **H-210**

## (26) Solicitation for immoral purposes

### (a) *Statute*

#### Sexual Offences Act 1956, s.32

**32.** It is an offence for a man persistently to solicit or importune in a public place for immoral purposes.     **H-211**

As to the use of the word "man", see *post*, H-222.

### (b) *Class of offence and mode of trial*

This offence is a class 3 offence (§ 2-17 in the main work), triable either way: SOA 1956, s.37(2), and Sched. 2, para. 32.     **H-212**

### (c) *Sentence*

On conviction on indictment, imprisonment not exceeding two years; on summary conviction, six months, or a fine not exceeding £5,000: SOA 1956, s.37(3), and Sched. 2, para. 32, and the MCA 1980, ss.32, 34(3)(a).     **H-213**

### (d) *Ingredients of the offence*

#### "persistently"

Two separate acts of importuning within the period named in the information or indictment are sufficient to render the importuning persistent: *Dale v. Smith* [1967] 1 W.L.R. 700, DC (justices entitled to treat the use of the word "Hello" by the defendant to a youth in a public lavatory as an act of importuning, in view of the fact that the same word had been used by the defendant to another youth on the previous evening and had been followed by an undoubted act of importuning, *viz.* an invitation to look at indecent photographs).     **H-214**

#### "solicit"

In *Behrendt v. Burridge*, 63 Cr.App.R. 202, DC, the defendant was observed for about 50 minutes sitting on a high stool in the bay window of a house. She sat silent and motionless, dressed in a low cut top and mini-skirt. The bay window was illuminated by a red light. She was charged with soliciting for the purpose of prostitution, contrary to section 1 of the Street Offences Act 1959. The Divisional Court said that the fact that her behaviour could be described as an explicit form of advertising was not decisive in her favour: advertising and soliciting are not mutually exclusive. It was clear that she was soliciting in the sense of tempting or allowing prospective customers to come in for the purposes of prostitution.     **H-215**

See also *Horton v. Mead* [1913] 1 K.B. 154, DC, and *Burge v. DPP* [1962] 1 W.L.R. 265, DC.

Archbold
paragraph
numbers

### "importune"

**H-216**    See *Dale v. Smith, ante,* H-214.

### "public place"

**H-217**    No definition appears in the 1956 Act, but it is a frequently used expression in legislation: see, for example, the Public Order Act 1936, s.9 (§ 25-329 in the main work), the Prevention of Crime Act 1953, s.1(4) (§ 24-106a in the main work) and the Firearms Act 1968, s.57(4) (§ 24-85 in the main work).

### "for immoral purposes"

**H-218**    An immoral purpose within section 32 has to be some kind of sexual activity: *Crook v. Edmondson* [1966] 2 Q.B. 81, DC; *R. v. Kirkup,* 96 Cr.App.R. 352, CA.

Section 32 applies both to heterosexual and homosexual behaviour: *R. v. Goddard,* 92 Cr.App.R. 185, CA.

Although section 1 of the SOA 1967 (*ante,* H-97) prevents homosexual practices in private between consenting parties who have attained the age of 16 from being a criminal offence, the 1967 Act did not change the law to the extent of preventing approaches for such purposes from being the offence of persistently importuning for "immoral purposes": *R. v. Ford,* 66 Cr.App.R. 46, CA. The judge correctly ruled that the conduct complained of could amount to an offence and correctly left the jury to decide whether the conduct was or was not immoral.

Similarly, in *R. v. Goddard, ante,* the unchallenged evidence of two young women was that they had had explicit sexual invitations made to them by G. It was held: (a) that it did not matter that the proposed sexual activity may be within the law; and (b) that it was a matter for the jury to decide, whether the invitations were for sexually immoral purposes, considering the circumstances in which the overtures were made and the nature of the overtures. This decision effectively over-ruled that part of the majority decision in *Crook v. Edmondson, ante,* which had held that "immoral purposes" was to be confined to purposes declared to be offences under other provisions of the 1956 Act.

The correct procedure is for the trial judge to rule whether the acts complained of could amount to an offence and, provided they are so capable, to leave it to the jury to decide whether the conduct, in fact, involved an immoral purpose, applying contemporary standards of morality: *R. v. Goddard, ante.*

### (27) Interpretation

#### (a) *Meaning of "sexual intercourse"*

#### Sexual Offences Act 1956, s.44

**H-219**    **44.** Where, on the trial of any offence under this Act, it is necessary to prove sexual intercourse (whether natural or unnatural), it shall not be necessary to prove the completion of the intercourse by the emission of seed, but the intercourse shall be deemed complete upon proof of penetration only.

See further, *ante,* H-14.

### Boys under the age of 14

**H-220**    As to the abolition of the common law presumption that a boy under the age of 14 is incapable of sexual intercourse, see *ante,* H-13. The presumption did not apply to a charge of aiding and abetting the commission of an offence: 1 Hale 630; *R. v. Williams* [1893] 1 Q.B. 320. Nor would it apply where the boy was not the defendant: see *R. v. Pickford* [1995] 1 Cr.App.R. 420, CA (*ante,* H-94).

#### (b) *Meaning of "defective"*

**H-221**    See section 45 of the SOA 1956, *ante,* H-68.

(c) *Use of words "man", "boy", "woman" and "girl"*

**Sexual Offences Act 1956, s.46**

**46.** The use in any provision of this Act of the word "man" without the addition of the word "boy",  **H-222**
or *vice versa*, shall not prevent the provision applying to any person to whom it would have applied if
both words had been used, and similarly with the words "woman" and "girl".

As to the use of the word "man", see *R. v. Tan* [1983] Q.B. 1053, 76 Cr.App.R. 300, CA, *ante*,
H-202.

Section 46 applies for the purposes of the provisions of the SOA 1967 as it applies for the
purposes of the provisions of the 1956 Act: SOA 1967, s.11(3). It also has effect as if the reference
to the 1956 Act included a reference to the Sexual Offences (Amendment) Act 1976: Sexual Offences (Amendment) Act 1976, s.7(2).

(d) *Meaning of "parental responsibility"*

**Sexual Offences Act 1956, s.46A**

**46A.** In this Act "parental responsibility" has the same meaning as in the Children Act 1989.  **H-223**

[This section was inserted by the Children Act 1989, s.108(4), and Sched. 12, para. 17.]

Section 105(1) of the Act of 1989 provides that in that Act "parental responsibility" has the
meaning given by section 3.

**Children Act 1989, s.3**

**3.**—(1) In this Act "parental responsibility" means all the rights, duties, powers, responsibilities  **H-224**
and authority which by law a parent of a child has in relation to the child and his property.

(2) It also includes the rights, powers and duties which a guardian of the child's estate (appointed,
before the commencement of section 5, to act generally) would have had in relation to the child and
his property.

(3) The rights referred to in subsection (2) include, in particular, the right of the guardian to
receive or recover in his own name, for the benefit of the child, property of whatever description and
wherever situated which the child is entitled to receive or recover.

(4) The fact that a person has, or does not have, parental responsibility for a child shall not affect—

    (a)  any obligation which he may have in relation to the child (such as a statutory duty to
        maintain the child); or

    (b)  any rights which, in the event of the child's death, he (or any other person) may have in
        relation to the child's property.

(5) A person who—

    (a)  does not have parental responsibility for a particular child; but

    (b)  has care of the child,

    may (subject to the provisions of this Act) do what is reasonable in all the circumstances of the case
for the purpose of safeguarding or promoting the child's welfare.

Further reference may need to be made to sections 2 (parental responsibility for children) and
12 (residence orders and parental responsibility) of the 1989 Act.

## (28) Proof of exceptions

**Sexual Offences Act 1956, s.47**

**47.** Where in any of the foregoing sections the description of an offence is expressed to be subject  **H-225**
to exceptions mentioned in the section, proof of the exception is to lie on the person relying on it.

## (29) Powers and procedure for dealing with offenders

**Sexual Offences Act 1956, s.37**

*Prosecution and punishment of offences*

**37.**—(1) The Second Schedule to this Act shall have effect, subject to and in accordance with the  **H-226**

following provisions of this section, with respect to the prosecution and punishment of the offences listed in the first column of the Schedule, being the offences under this Act and attempts to commit certain of those offences.

(2) The second column in the Schedule shows, for any offence, if it may be prosecuted on indictment or summarily, or either ... and what special restrictions (if any) there are on the commencement of a prosecution.

(3) The third column in the Schedule shows, for any offence, the punishments which may be imposed on conviction on indictment or on summary conviction, a reference to a period giving the maximum term of imprisonment and a reference to a sum of money the maximum fine.

(4) The fourth column in the Schedule contains provisions which are either supplementary to those in the second or third column or enable a person charged on indictment with the offence specified in the first column to be found guilty of another offence if the jury are not satisfied that he is guilty of the offence charged or of an attempt to commit it, but are satisfied that he is guilty of the other offence.

(5) A provision in the fourth column of the Schedule enabling the jury to find the accused guilty of an offence specified in that provision authorises them, if not satisfied that he is guilty of the offence so specified, to find him guilty of any other offence of which they could find him guilty if he had been indicted for the offence so specified.

(6) Where in the Schedule there is used a phrase descriptive of an offence or group of offences followed by a reference to a section by its number only, the reference is to a section of this Act, and the phrase shall be taken as referring to any offence under the section mentioned.

(7) Nothing in this section or in the Second Schedule to this Act shall exclude the application to any of the offences referred to in the first column of the Schedule—

(a) of section 24 of the Magistrates' Courts Act 1980 (which relates to the summary trial of young offenders for indictable offences); or

(b) of subsection (5) of section 121 of the Magistrates' Courts Act 1980 (which limits the punishment which may be imposed by a magistrates' court sitting in an occasional courthouse); or

(c) of any enactment or rule of law restricting a court's power to imprison; or

(d) of any enactment or rule of law authorising an offender to be dealt with in a way not authorised by the enactments specially relating to his offence; or

(e) of any enactment or rule of law authorising a jury to find a person guilty of an offence other than that with which he is charged.

[This section is printed as amended by the MCA 1980, Sched. 7, para. 17; and as repealed in part by the Courts Act 1971, s.56(4), and Sched. 11, Pt IV.]

Subsection (5) was considered in *R. v. Regina*, 64 Cr.App.R. 79, CA, *ante*, H-74.

**Attempts**

**H-227**    Schedule 2 to the 1956 Act is not set out in this appendix. All relevant provisions thereof are referred to in the context of the individual offences, *ante*. Some of the paragraphs in the Schedule specifically refer to an attempt to commit a particular offence (sometimes with a different penalty to the full offence, sometimes with the same penalty). Wherever there is specific reference to an attempt in the schedule, this is referred to in the text in relation to the offence in question; where there is no such reference in the text, this is because there is no separate reference to an attempt in the schedule. In such cases, the Criminal Attempts Act 1981 will exclusively determine liability to prosecution and punishment for an attempt: for the 1981 Act, see §§ 33-128 *et seq.* in the main work.

# C. Mental Health Act 1959

### Mental Health Act 1959, s.128

*Sexual intercourse with patients*

**H-228**    **128.**—(1) Without prejudice to section seven of the Sexual Offences Act 1956, it shall be an offence, subject to the exception mentioned in this section,—

(a) for a man who is an officer on the staff of or is otherwise employed in, or is one of the managers of, a hospital independent hospital or care home to have unlawful sexual intercourse with a woman who is for the time being receiving treatment for mental disorder in that hospital or home, or to have such intercourse on the premises of which the hospital or home forms part with a woman who is for the time being receiving such treatment there as an outpatient;

(b) for a man to have unlawful sexual intercourse with a woman who is a mentally disordered patient and who is subject to his guardianship under the Mental Health Act 1983 or is otherwise in his custody or care under the Mental Health Act 1983 or in pursuance of arrangements under ... Part III of the National Assistance Act 1948 ... or the National Health Service Act 1977, or as a resident in a care home.

(2) It shall not be an offence under this section for a man to have sexual intercourse with a woman if he does not know and has no reason to suspect her to be a mentally disordered patient.

(3) Any person guilty of an offence under this section shall be liable on conviction on indictment to imprisonment for a term not exceeding two years.

(4) No proceedings shall be instituted for an offence under this section except by or with the consent of the Director of Public Prosecutions.

(5) This section shall be construed as one with the Sexual Offences Act 1956; and section 47 of that Act (which relates to the proof of exceptions) shall apply to the exception mentioned in this section.

(6) In this section "independent hospital" and "care home" have the same meaning as in the Care Standards Act 2000.

[This section is printed as amended by the National Health Service Act 1977, s.129, Sched. 15, para. 29, and Sched. 16; the MHA 1983, s.148, and Sched. 3, para. 15; the Registered Homes Act 1984, s.57, and Sched. 1, para. 2; and the Care Standards Act 2000, s.116, and Sched. 4, para. 2.]

As to the meaning of "sexual intercourse", see *ante*, H-219; as to the meaning of "unlawful"    **H-229** sexual intercourse, see *R. v. Chapman*, *ante*, H-38; as to the use of the words "man" and "woman", see *ante*, H-222.

For anonymity provisions, see §§ 20-257 *et seq.* in the main work.

For section 47 of the 1956 Act (burden of proof of exceptions), see *ante*, H-225.

By section 1(4) of the Sexual Offences Act 1967, section 128 is to have effect as if any reference therein to having unlawful sexual intercourse with a woman included a reference to committing buggery or an act of gross indecency with another man.

In connection with the offences created by this section, see *R. v. Davies and Poolton* [2000] Crim.L.R. 297, CA (§ 19-363 in the main work), decided in relation to the similarly worded section 127 of the 1959 Act.

# D. INDECENCY WITH CHILDREN ACT 1960

## (1) Statute

### Indecency with Children Act 1960, s.1(1)

**1.**—(1) Any person who commits an act of gross indecency with or towards a child under the age    **H-230** of sixteen, or who incites a child under that age to such an act with him or another, shall be liable on conviction on indictment to imprisonment for a term not exceeding ten years, or on summary conviction to imprisonment for a term not exceeding six months, to a fine not exceeding the prescribed sum, or to both.

(2) [*Repealed by Police and Criminal Evidence Act 1984, Sched. 7.*]

(3) References in the Children and Young Persons Act 1933 ... to the offences mentioned in the First Schedule to that Act shall include offences under this section.

(4) offences under this section shall be deemed to be offences against the person for the purpose of section three of the Visiting Forces Act 1952 (which restricts the trial by United Kingdom courts of offenders connected with visiting forces).

[Subs. (1) is printed as amended by the C(S)A 1997, s.52 (substitution of "ten" for "two"); and the CJCSA 2000, s.39 (substitution of "sixteen" for "fourteen"). The first of these amendments took effect on October 1, 1997, but does not apply to offences committed before that date: Crime (Sentences) Act (Commencement No. 2 and Transitional Provisions) Order 1997 (S.I. 1997 No. 2200). The second amendment took effect on January 11, 2001: Criminal Justice and Court Services Act 2000 (Commencement No. 1) Order 2000 (S.I. 2000 No. 3302).]

As to Schedule 1 to the CYPA 1933, see § 19-408 in the main work.

For anonymity provisions, see §§ 20-257 *et seq.* in the main work.

## (2) Indictment

### Statement of Offence

*Indecency with a child, contrary to section 1(1) of the Indecency with Children Act 1960.*

### Particulars of offence

*A B, on the ———— day of ————, 20——, committed an act of gross indecency with [or towards] J N, a child of the age of 10 years [or incited J N, a child of the age of 10 years to commit an act of gross indecency with him the said A B (or with Y Z)].*

It is a prerequisite of a conviction contrary to section 1 that the child was under the age of 16 at the time of the act or incitement: the child's age is an ingredient of the offence about which the jury must be satisfied and, unless age is admitted, calls for an appropriate direction from the judge: see *R. v. Goss and Goss*, 90 Cr.App.R. 400, CA, and *R. v. Radcliffe* [1990] Crim.L.R. 524, CA.

As to the propriety of preferring a charge of outraging public decency although the facts are covered by section 1(1), see *R. v. May (J.)*, 91 Cr.App.R. 157, CA (§ 20-238 in the main work).

## (3) Class of offence and mode of trial

This offence is a class 3 offence (§ 2-17 in the main work), triable either way: s.1(1), *ante*.

## (4) Sentence

See section 1(1), *ante*. As to "the prescribed sum", see section 32 of the MCA 1980 (§ 1-125 in the main work).

## (5) Consent of Director of Public Prosecutions

Section 8 of the SOA 1967 (no proceedings shall be instituted except by or with the consent of the Director against any man for gross indecency or certain other offences where any person involved is under 21) shall not apply to proceedings under the Indecency with Children Act 1960: CJA 1972, s.48.

## (6) Ingredients of the offence

In *R. v. Speck*, 65 Cr.App.R. 161, CA, it was held that section 1 was contravened where S passively permitted a child to keep her hand on his penis for so long (in this case about five minutes) that his inactivity amounted to an invitation to her to continue the activity. If such an invitation could properly be inferred, it would constitute an "act" within section 1(1). Apart from allowing the child's hand to remain where she had placed it, S did nothing to encourage the child. A proper direction to the jury in such circumstances would be that the defendant's conduct might constitute an offence under section 1(1) if it amounted to an invitation from the defendant to the child to continue the activity in question. If they took that view (*i.e.* that there had been an "act") then they should go on to determine whether the act was an act of gross indecency. See also *R. v. B.* [1999] Crim.L.R. 594, CA.

Section 1(1) creates one offence of gross indecency, namely, the committing of an act of gross indecency involving a child; that is, "with or towards a child" is to be read as a phrase: *DPP v. Burgess* [1971] Q.B. 432, DC; *R. v. Francis*, 88 Cr.App.R. 127, CA. In *Francis*, the court considered the circumstances in which a man contravened section 1(1) if he masturbated in the presence of a child: the act had to be directed towards the child, the offender at the very least deriving satisfaction from the knowledge that the child was watching what he was doing.

As to the age of the victim being an essential ingredient of the offence, see *ante*, H-220; and it is necessary for the prosecution to prove the absence of a genuine belief on the part of the defendant that the victim was 16 years or above: *B. (a Minor) v. DPP* [2000] 2 A.C. 428, HL. The presence or absence of reasonable grounds for such belief goes only to whether such belief was genuinely held: *ibid.*

## E. Sexual Offences Act 1967

### (1) Procuring others to commit homosexual acts

#### Sexual Offences Act 1967, s.4

4.—(1) A man who procures another man to commit with a third man an act of buggery which by reason of section 1 of this Act is not an offence shall be liable on conviction on indictment to imprisonment for a term not exceeding two years.

(2) [*Repealed by Criminal Law Act 1977, Sched. 13.*]

(3) It shall not be an offence under section 13 of the Act of 1956 for a man to procure the commission by another man of an act of gross indecency with the first-mentioned man which by reason of section 1 of this Act is not an offence under the said section 13.

The offence under subsection (1) is triable either way: MCA 1980, s.17(1), and Sched. 1 (§ 1-125 in the main work).

As to the use of the word "man", see *ante*, H-222.

As to the offence of buggery, see *ante*, H-95 *et seq.*

For section 13 of the 1956 Act, see *ante*, H-107.

As to "procures", see *ante*, H-171.

## (2) Living on earnings of male prostitution

### Sexual Offences Act 1967, s.5

**5.**—(1) A man or woman who knowingly lives wholly or in part on the earnings of prostitution of **H-237** another man shall be liable—

    (a)  on summary conviction to imprisonment for a term not exceeding six months, or

    (b)  on conviction on indictment to imprisonment for a term not exceeding seven years.

(2) [*Repealed by Criminal Law Act 1977, Sched. 13.*]

(3) Anyone may arrest without a warrant a person found committing an offence under this section.

As to the use of the words "man" and "woman", see *ante*, H-222 and—in relation to "man"— **H-238** see *R. v. Tan* [1983] Q.B. 1053, 76 Cr.App.R. 300, CA, *ante*, H-202.

The offence is a class 3 offence (§ 2-17 in the main work).

Subsection (3) has ceased to have effect by virtue of the PACE Act 1984, s.26(1) (§ 15-133 in the main work).

## F. CRIMINAL LAW ACT 1977

### Criminal Law Act 1977, s.54

*Incitement of girls under 16*

**54.**—(1) It is an offence for a man to incite to have sexual intercourse with him a girl under the **H-239** age of sixteen whom he knows to be his grand-daughter, daughter or sister.

(2) In the preceding subsection "man" includes boy, "sister" includes half-sister, and for the purposes of that subsection any expression importing a relationship between two people shall be taken to apply notwithstanding that the relationship is not traced through lawful wedlock.

(3) The following provisions of section 1 of the Indecency with Children Act 1960, namely—

...

    subsection (3) (references in Children and Young Persons Act 1933 to the offences mentioned in Schedule 1 to that Act to include offences under that section);

    subsection (4) (offences under that section to be deemed offences against the person for the purpose of section 3 of the Visiting Forces Act 1952),

shall apply in relation to offences under this section.

(4) A person guilty of an offence under this section shall be liable—

    (a)  on summary conviction, to imprisonment for a term not exceeding six months or to a fine not exceeding the prescribed sum or both;

    (b)  on conviction on indictment to imprisonment for a term not exceeding two years.

[This section is printed as effectively amended by the MCA 1980, s.32(2) (substitution of reference to "the prescribed sum"); and as repealed in part by the PACE Act 1984, Sched. 7.]

As to Schedule 1 to the CYPA 1933, see § 19-408 in the main work. **H-240**

As to "the prescribed sum", see the MCA 1980, s.32(2) and (9) (§ 1-125 in the main work).

For anonymity provisions, see §§ 20-257 *et seq.* in the main work.

Section 54 filled a *lacuna* in the law, identified in *R. v. Whitehouse* [1977] Q.B. 868, 65 Cr.App.R. 33, CA.

As to incitement at common law, see *ante*, §§ 33-74 *et seq.*

## G. Sexual Offences (Amendment) Act 2000

### (1) Statute

#### Sexual Offences (Amendment) Act 2000, ss.3, 4

*Abuse of position of trust*

**H-241**   **3.**—(1) Subject to subsections (2) and (3) below, it shall be an offence for a person aged 18 or over—

> (a)   to have sexual intercourse (whether vaginal or anal) with a person under that age; or
>
> (b)   to engage in any other sexual activity with or directed towards such a person,

if (in either case) he is in a position of trust in relation to that person.

(2) Where a person ("A") is charged with an offence under this section of having sexual intercourse with, or engaging in any other sexual activity with or directed towards, another person ("B"), it shall be a defence for A to prove that, at the time of the intercourse or activity—

> (a)   he did not know, and could not reasonably have been expected to know, that B was under 18;
>
> (b)   he did not know, and could not reasonably have been expected to know, that B was a person in relation to whom he was in a position of trust; or
>
> (c)   he was lawfully married to B.

(3) It shall not be an offence under this section for a person ("A") to have sexual intercourse with, or engage in any other sexual activity with or directed towards, another person ("B") if immediately before the commencement of this Act—

> (a)   A was in a position of trust in relation to B; and
>
> (b)   a sexual relationship existed between them.

(4) A person guilty of an offence under this section shall be liable—

> (a)   on summary conviction, to imprisonment for a term not exceeding six months, or to a fine not exceeding the statutory maximum, or to both;
>
> (b)   on conviction on indictment, to imprisonment for a term not exceeding five years, or to a fine, or to both.

(5) In this section, "sexual activity"—

> (a)   does not include any activity which a reasonable person would regard as sexual only with knowledge of the intentions, motives or feelings of the parties; but
>
> (b)   subject to that, means any activity which such a person would regard as sexual in all the circumstances.

As to "the commencement of this Act", see the Sexual Offences (Amendment) Act 2000 (Commencement No. 1) Order 2000 (S.I. 2000 No. 3303), which brought the Act into force on January 8, 2001.

*Meaning of "position of trust"*

**H-242**   **4.**—(1) For the purposes of section 3 above, a person aged 18 or over ("A") is in a position of trust in relation to a person under that age ("B") if any of the four conditions set out below, or any condition specified in an order made by the Secretary of State by statutory instrument, is fulfilled.

(2) The first condition is that A looks after persons under 18 who are detained in an institution by virtue of an order of a court or under an enactment, and B is so detained in that institution.

(3) The second condition is that A looks after persons under 18 who are resident in a home or other place in which—

> (a)   accommodation and maintenance are provided by an authority under section 23(2) of the Children Act 1989 or Article 27(2) of the Children (Northern Ireland) Order 1995;
>
> (b)   accommodation is provided by a voluntary organisation under section 59(1) of that Act or Article 75(1) of that Order; or
>
> (c)   accommodation is provided by an authority under section 26(1) of the Children (Scotland) Act 1995,

and B is resident, and is so provided with accommodation and maintenance or accommodation, in that place.

(4) The third condition is that A looks after persons under 18 who are accommodated and cared for in an institution which is—

> (a)   a hospital;
>
> (b)   a residential care home, nursing home, mental nursing home or private hospital;
>
> (c)   a community home, voluntary home, children's home or residential establishment; or

(d)  a home provided under section 82(5) of the Children Act 1989,

and B is accommodated and cared for in that institution.

(5) The fourth condition is that A looks after persons under 18 who are receiving full-time education at an educational institution, and B is receiving such education at that institution.

(6) No order shall be made under subsection (1) above unless a draft of the order has been laid before and approved by a resolution of each House of Parliament.

(7) A person looks after persons under 18 for the purposes of this section if he is regularly involved in caring for, training, supervising or being in sole charge of such persons.

(8) For the purposes of this section a person receives full-time education at an educational institution if—

(a)  he is registered or otherwise enrolled as a full-time pupil or student at the institution; or

(b)  he receives education at the institution under arrangements with another educational institution at which he is so registered or otherwise enrolled.

(9) In this section, except where the context otherwise requires—

"authority" means—

(a)  in relation to Great Britain, a local authority; and

(b)  [*Northern Ireland*];

"children's home" has—

(a)  in relation to England and Wales, the meaning which would be given by subsection (3) of section 63 of the Children Act 1989 if the reference in paragraph (a) of that subsection to more than three children were a reference to one or more children; and

(b)  [*Northern Ireland*];

"community home" has the meaning given by section 53(1) of the Children Act 1989;

"hospital" has—

(a)  in relation to England and Wales, the meaning given by section 128(1) of the National Health Service Act 1977;

(b)  [*Scotland*]; and

(c)  [*Northern Ireland*];

"mental nursing home" has, in relation to England and Wales, the meaning given by section 22(1) of the Registered Homes Act 1984

"nursing home"—

(a)  in relation to England and Wales, has the meaning given by section 21(1) of the Registered Homes Act 1984;

(b)  [*Scotland*];

(c)  [*Northern Ireland*];

"private hospital" has—

(a)  [*Scotland*]; and

(b)  [*Northern Ireland*];

"residential care home"—

(a)  in relation to England and Wales, has the meaning given by section 1(2) of the Registered Homes Act 1984;

(b)  [*Scotland*]; and

(c)  [*Northern Ireland*];

"residential establishment" has the meaning given by section 93(1) of the Children (Scotland) Act 1995 as the meaning of that expression in Scotland;

"voluntary home" has—

(a)  in relation to England and Wales, the meaning given by section 60(3) of the Children Act 1989; and

(b)  [*Northern Ireland*].

## (2) Indictment

### Statement of Offence

**H-243**    *Abuse of a position of trust, contrary to section 3(1)(a) of the Sexual Offences (Amendment) Act 2000.*

### Particulars of Offence

*A B, on the _____ day of _____, 20___, being a person of the age of at least 18 years, had sexual intercourse with J N, being a person under the age of 18 years, and being at the time in a position of trust in relation to J N, in that at the time he looked after persons under the age of 18 years who were receiving full-time education at _____ school, and J N was at the time in receipt of such education at the aforesaid school.*

## (3) Class of offence and mode of trial

**H-244**    This offence is a class 3 offence (§ 2-17 in the main work), triable either way: s.3(4), *ante*.

## (4) Sentence

**H-245**    See s.3(4), *ante*.

The setting out of the various positions of trust in section 4(2) to (5) is not to be taken as indicative of descending seriousness: *R. v. Hubbard* [2002] 2 Cr.App.R.(S.) 101, CA.

# APPENDIX J
# A Guide to Commencing Proceedings in the Court of Appeal (Criminal Division)

*NOTE:* the text of the guide that follows has been subjected to some editorial revision (in relation to such matters as punctuation, use of upper and lower case, abbreviations, manner of citation of legislative references and authorities, and in order to correct a small number of obvious, minor errors). None of these revisions has any effect on the sense of the guide.

## A GUIDE TO COMMENCING PROCEEDINGS IN THE COURT OF APPEAL (CRIMINAL DIVISION)

### Foreword by the Lord Chief Justice of England and Wales

In recent years the Court of Appeal Criminal Division has faced increased complexity in appeals, not only against conviction but also against sentence, particularly in the light of the plethora of recent sentencing legislation. Additionally, the jurisdiction of the court has expanded to encompass a variety of diverse applications and appeals by the defence, the Crown and other interested parties. **J-1**

This guide provides invaluable advice as to the initial steps for commencing proceedings in the Court of Appeal Criminal Division generally and in relation to perhaps unfamiliar provisions.

The first and most important step is, of course, the preparation of the grounds of appeal. The rules prescribe the form and content of the Notice and Grounds of Appeal. Practitioners are also required to summarise the facts and outline their arguments concisely. Well drafted grounds of appeal assist the single judge when considering leave and serve to shorten any hearing before the full court. Ill-prepared and prolix documents necessarily lead to wasted time spent on preparation and unnecessarily protracted hearings.

It is important that we all take seriously our responsibility to ensure the effective progression of cases and keep delay to a minimum. Once an application or appeal is commenced, the responsible officer at the Criminal Appeal Office will be available to assist with any queries on practice or procedure.

The court could not deal with this volume of work efficiently without the support of the Registrar and his staff in the Criminal Appeal Office. Their experience and expertise is invaluable and can always be relied on by those who use the court, not least those who are unfamiliar with its practice and procedures.

Judge C.J.
October 2008

### Introduction

Since the publication of the last Guide to Proceedings in the Court of Appeal (Criminal Division), the court's jurisdiction has increased. It hears appeals not only against conviction and sentence, but also against various interlocutory rulings, as well as other appeals and applications. **J-2**

This guide provides practical information about how to commence and conduct proceedings before the court. Once proceedings are commenced, an application will have its own unique reference number and a case progression officer who can help with any difficulties or queries about procedure.

The guide is set out as follows:

    A. General principles of practice and procedure when applying for leave to appeal conviction and sentence.

    B. Guidance on appeals against rulings made in preparatory hearings.

    C. Guidance on prosecution appeals against 'terminating' rulings.

    D. Brief guidance on other appeals in bullet point form showing:

- the type of appeal,
- the relevant section of the statute
- the relevant Criminal Procedure Rules
- who can apply
- the forms to be used and time limits
- respondents' notices,
- whether representation orders are available
- whether leave to appeal is required

    E. Guidance on applications for a retrial for a serious offence.

A list of all up to date forms referred to in this guide may be accessed from the HMCS website at www.hmcourts-service.gov.uk or the Criminal Procedure Rules Committee website at www.justice.gov.uk/criminal/procrules. Where the Criminal Procedure Rules do not provide for a specific form, this guide indicates the appropriate form to be used.

This guide was prepared under my direction by the staff of the Criminal Appeal Office, but principally by Ms Alix Beldam and Ms Susan Holdham. It describes the law and practice of the Court as at 1st October 2008.

Master Venne

Registrar of Criminal Appeals

### Terminology

**J-3**      The Criminal Appeal Act 1968 refers to "leave to appeal". This is now referred to as "permission to appeal" in the Criminal Procedure Rules 2007. This guide keeps to the terminology used by the Act.

Also consistently with the Act, an "appellant" is referred to without distinction, but it should be borne in mind that it is the accepted practice of the Criminal Appeal Office (CAO) to refer to a person who has served notice of appeal but not been granted leave to appeal as an "applicant" and use the term "appellant" to refer to a person who has been granted leave to appeal.

Any reference to counsel should be read as including a solicitor advocate as appropriate.

A. GENERAL PRINCIPLES OF PRACTICE AND PROCEDURE WHEN APPLYING FOR LEAVE TO APPEAL CONVICTION AND SENTENCE

### A1 Advice and assistance

**J-4**      A1-1 Provision for advice or assistance on appeal is included in the trial representation order issued by the Crown Court. Solicitors should not wait to be asked for advice by the defendant. Immediately following the conclusion of the case, the legal representatives should see the defendant and counsel should express orally his final view as to the prospects of a successful appeal (whether against conviction or sentence or both). If there are no reasonable grounds of appeal, that should be confirmed in writing and a copy provided then, or as soon as practicable thereafter, to the defendant by the solicitor. If there are reasonable grounds, grounds of appeal should be drafted, signed and sent to instructing solicitors as soon as possible. Solicitors should immediately send a copy of the documents received from counsel to the defendant.

A1-2 Prior to the lodging of the notice and grounds of appeal by service of Form NG, the Registrar has no power to grant a representation order. Also, the Crown Court can only amend a representation order in favour of fresh legal representatives if advice on appeal has not been given by trial legal representatives and it is necessary and reasonable for another legal representative to be instructed. Where advice on appeal has been given by trial legal representatives, application for funding may only be made to the Legal Services Commission (LSC).

A1-3 Once the Form NG has been lodged, the Registrar is the authority for decisions about representation orders, in accordance with the principle that the court before which there are proceedings is the court with power to grant a right to representation (Access to Justice Act 1999, Sched. 3, affirmed by regulation 10 of the Criminal Defence Service (General) (No. 2) Regulations 2001 (S.I. 2001 No. 1437)).

A1-4 Where, in order to settle grounds of appeal, work of an exceptional nature is contemplated or where the expense will be great, legal representatives should submit a Form NG with provisional grounds of appeal and with a note to the Registrar requesting a representation order to cover the specific work considered necessary to enable proper grounds of appeal to be settled.

### A2 Form NG and grounds of appeal

**J-5**      A2-1 Where counsel has advised an appeal, solicitors should forward the signed grounds of appeal to the Crown Court accompanied by Form NG and such other forms as may be appropriate. It should be noted that Form NG and grounds of appeal are required to be served within the relevant time limit in all cases, whether or not leave to appeal is required (*e.g.* where a trial judge's certificate has been granted). However, on a reference by the Criminal Cases Review Commission (CCRC), if no Form NG and grounds are served within the required period, then the reference shall be treated as the appeal notice: rule 68.5(2).

A2-2 Grounds must be settled with sufficient particularity to enable the Registrar, and subsequently the court, to identify clearly the matters relied upon. A mere formula such as "the conviction is unsafe" or "the sentence is in all the circumstances too severe" will be ineffective as grounds and time will continue to run against the defendant.

A2-3 Rule 68.3(1) sets out the information that must be contained in the appeal notice. The notice must ... [*see § 7-382 in the main work*].

**A2-4** There is now a requirement for the grounds of appeal to set out the relevant facts and nature of the proceedings concisely in one all encompassing document, not separate grounds and advice. The intended readership of this document is the court and not the lay or professional client. Its purpose is to enable the single judge to grasp quickly the facts and issues in the case. In appropriate cases, draft grounds of appeal may be perfected before submission to the single judge *(see further below para. A5)*.

**A2-5** Any document mentioned in the grounds should be identified clearly, by exhibit number or otherwise. Similarly, if counsel requires an original exhibit or shorthand writer's tape recording, he should say so well in advance of any determination or hearing.

**A2-6** Counsel should not settle or sign grounds unless they are reasonable, have some real prospect of success and are such that he is prepared to argue them before the court. Counsel should not settle grounds he cannot support because he is "instructed" to do so by a defendant.

**A2-7** Procedure in relation to particular grounds of appeal

**A2-7.1** *Applications to call fresh evidence*

A Form W and a statement from the witness in the form prescribed by section 9 of the CJA 1967 should be lodged in respect of each witness it is proposed to call. The Form W should indicate whether there is an application for a witness order. The Registrar or the single judge may direct the issue of a witness order, but only the court hearing the appeal may give leave for a witness to be called.

The court will require a cogent explanation for the failure to adduce the evidence at trial. A supporting witness statement or affidavit from the appellant's solicitor should be lodged in this regard (*R. v. Gogana, The Times,* July 12, 1999).

If there is to be an application to adduce hearsay and/or evidence of bad character or for special measures, then the appropriate forms should be lodged: rule 68.7(1).

**A2-7.2** *Complaints against trial counsel as a ground of appeal*

Where a ground of appeal explicitly criticises trial counsel and/or trial solicitors, the Registrar will institute the "waiver of privilege" procedure. The appellant will be asked to "waive privilege" in respect of instructions to and advice at trial from legal representatives. If he does waive privilege, the grounds of appeal are sent to the appropriate trial representative(s) and they are invited to respond. Any response will be sent to the appellant or his fresh legal representatives for comment. All these documents will be sent to the single judge when considering the application for leave. The single judge may draw inferences from any failure to participate in the process. "Waiver of privilege" is a procedure that should be instigated by the Registrar and not by fresh legal representatives, who should go no further than obtaining a waiver of privilege from the appellant: *R. v. Doherty and McGregor* [1997] 2 Cr.App.R. 218.

**A2-7.3** *Insufficient weight given to assistance to prosecution authorities*

Where a ground of appeal against sentence is that the judge has given insufficient weight to the assistance given to the prosecution authorities, the "text" which had been prepared for the sentencing judge is obtained by the Registrar. Grounds of appeal should be drafted in an anodyne form with a note to the Registrar alerting him to the existence of a "text". The single judge will have seen the "text" when considering leave as will the full court before the appeal hearing and it need not be alluded to in open court.

## A3 Time limits

**A3-1** Notice and grounds should reach the Crown Court within 28 days from the date of the conviction in the case of an application for leave to appeal against conviction and within 28 days from the date of sentence in the case of an application for leave to appeal against sentence [CAA 1968, s.18 and rule 68.2(1)]. On a reference by the CCRC, Form NG and grounds should be served on the Registrar not more than 56 days after the Registrar has served notice that the CCRC has referred a conviction and not more than 28 days in the case of a sentence referral: rule 68.2(2). **J-6**

**A3-2** A confiscation order (whether made under the CJA 1988, the DTA 1994 or the PCA 2002) is a sentence [CAA 1968, s.50]. Where sentences are passed in separate proceedings on different dates there may be two appeals against sentence. Thus, there may be an appeal against the custodial part of a sentence and an appeal against a confiscation order (*R. v. Neal* [1999] 2 Cr.App.R.(S.) 352).

**A3-3** An application for extension of the 28 day period in which to give notice of application for leave to appeal or notice of appeal must always be supported by reasons why the application for leave was not submitted in time. It is not enough merely to tick the relevant box on Form NG.

**A3-4** Such an application should be submitted when the application for leave to appeal against either conviction or sentence is made and not in advance. Notwithstanding the terms of section 18(3) of the CAA 1968, it has long been the practice of the Registrar to require the extension of time application to be made at the time of service of the notice and grounds of appeal. This practice is now reflected by Criminal Procedure Rule 65.4.

## A4 Transcript and notes of evidence

A4-1 In conviction cases, transcripts of the summing up and proceedings up to and including verdict are obtained as a matter of course. Similarly, the transcript of the prosecution opening of facts on a guilty plea and the judge's observations on passing sentence are usually obtained in sentence cases. There is now an obligation under rule 68.3(2) for counsel to identify any further transcript which counsel considers the court will need and to provide a note of names, dates and times to enable an order to be placed with the shorthand writers. Whether or not any further transcript is required is a matter for the judgment of the Registrar or his staff.

A4-2 Transcript should only be requested if it is essential for the proper conduct of the appeal in the light of the grounds. If the Registrar and counsel are unable to agree the extent of the transcript to be obtained, the Registrar may refer that matter to a judge. In some cases the Registrar may propose that counsel agree a note in place of transcript.

A4-3 In certain circumstances the costs of unnecessary transcript could be ordered to be paid by the appellant. Where transcript is obtained otherwise than through the Registrar, he may disallow the cost on taxation of public funding.

## A5 Perfection of grounds of appeal

A5-1 The purpose of perfection is (a) to save valuable judicial time by enabling the court to identify at once the relevant parts of the transcript and (b) to give counsel the opportunity to reconsider his original grounds in the light of the transcript. Perfected grounds should consist of a fresh document which supersedes the original grounds of appeal and contains *inter alia* references by page number and letter (or paragraph number) to all relevant passages in the transcript.

A5-2 In conviction or confiscation cases, the Registrar will almost certainly invite counsel to perfect grounds in the light of the transcript obtained, to assist the single judge or full court. Where counsel indicates a wish to perfect grounds of appeal against sentence, the Registrar will consider the request and will only invite perfection where he considers it necessary for the assistance of the single judge or full court.

A5-3 If perfection is appropriate, counsel will be sent a copy of the transcript and asked to perfect his grounds within 14 days. In the absence of any response from counsel, the existing notice and grounds of appeal will be placed before the single judge or the court without further notice. If counsel does not wish to perfect his grounds, the transcript should be returned with a note to that effect.

A5-4 If, having considered the transcript, counsel is of opinion that there are no valid grounds, he should set out his reasons in a further advice and send it to his instructing solicitors. He should inform the Registrar that he has done so, but should not send him a copy of that advice. Solicitors should send a copy to the appellant and obtain instructions, at the same time explaining that if the appellant persists with his application the court may consider whether to make a loss of time order (*see further below A-13*).

## A6 Respondent's notice

A6-1 The Criminal Procedure Rules 2005 provide for the service of a respondent's notice. Under rule 68.6(1) the Registrar may serve the appeal notice on any party directly affected by the appeal (usually the prosecution) and must do so in a CCRC case. That party may then serve a respondent's notice if it wishes to make representations and must do so if the Registrar so directs: rule 68.6(2). The respondent's notice should be served within 14 days (rule 68.6(4)) on the appellant, the Registrar and any other party on whom the Registrar served the appeal notice (rule 68.6(3)). The respondent's notice must be in the specified form [Form RN], in which a respondent should set out the grounds of opposition (rule 68.6(5)) and which must include the information set out in rule 68.6(6).

A6-2 In practice, this procedure primarily applies prior to consideration of leave by the single judge in both conviction and sentence cases. The Attorney General and the Registrar, following consultation with representatives from the Crown Prosecution Service (CPS) and the Revenue and Customs Prosecution Office (RCPO), have agreed guidance on types of cases and/or issues where the Registrar should consider whether to serve an appeal notice and direct or invite a party to serve a respondent's notice before the consideration of leave by the single judge. Examples of when the Registrar might **direct** a respondent's notice include where the grounds concern matters which were the subject of public interest immunity (PII), allegations of jury irregularity, criticism of the conduct of the judge and complex frauds. Cases where it might be appropriate for the Registrar to **invite** a respondent's notice include, for example, homicide offences, serious sexual offences, cases with national profile or high media interest, cases of violence or domestic violence.

A6-3 In conviction cases where leave has been granted or where the application for leave has been referred to the full court, the Crown is briefed to attend the hearing and required to submit a respondent's notice/skeleton argument. In relation to sentence cases where leave has been granted, referred or an appellant is represented on a renewed application, the sentence protocol set out in paragraph II.1 of the consolidated criminal practice direction [see now *Criminal Practice Direction (Appeal) 68A* [2013] 1 W.L.R. 3164 (§ 7-203 in the main work)] will apply. In those cases, a respondent's notice/skeleton argument will have to be served when the Crown indicates a wish to attend or when the Registrar invites or directs the Crown to attend.

### A7 Referral by the Registrar

A7-1 Leave to appeal is required in all cases except where the trial judge or sentencing judge has **J-10** certified that the case is fit for appeal (CAA 1968, ss.1(2) and 11(1A)) or where the case has been referred by the CCRC. The appellant must obtain leave to pursue grounds not related to the Commission's reasons for referral: CAA 1995, s.14(4B).

A7-2 Where leave to appeal is required and the Registrar has obtained the necessary documents, he will refer the application(s) either (a) to a single judge for decision under section 31 of the CAA 1968 or (b) directly to the full court, in which case a representation order is usually granted for the hearing. However, the Registrar will not grant a representation order when the presence of counsel is not required, *e.g.* where the application refers solely to an amendment of the number of days to be credited as "remand time" and the figure is agreed by the parties. Where an application is referred to the full court by the Registrar because an unlawful sentence has been passed or other procedural error identified, a representation order will ordinarily be granted, but counsel should be aware that the court may make observations for the attention of the determining officer that a full fee should not be allowed on taxation.

A7-3 Where leave to appeal is not required, *e.g.* on appeal by certificate of the trial judge, the Registrar will usually grant a representation order for the hearing. On a reference from the CCRC, it is the Registrar's usual practice to grant a representation order in the first instance, to solicitors for them to nominate and instruct counsel to settle grounds of appeal. Once counsel's details are known, a further representation order will be granted to cover the preparation (including settling grounds) and presentation of the appeal by counsel and further work by solicitors, as necessary in light of the grounds.

### A8 Bail pending appeal

A8-1 Bail may be granted (a) by a single judge or the full court or (b) by a trial or sentencing **J-11** judge who has certified the case fit for appeal. In the latter case, bail can only be granted within 28 days of the conviction or sentence which is the subject of the appeal and may not be granted if an application for bail has already been made to the Court of Appeal.

A8-2 An application to the Court of Appeal for bail must be supported by a completed Form B, whether or not the application is made at the same time as the notice and grounds are served. The completed Form B must be served on the Registrar and the prosecution at least 24 hours before any application is made to enable the Crown to make representations (either written or oral) about the application and any conditions.

A8-3 An application for bail will not be considered by a single judge or the court until notice of application for leave to appeal or notice of appeal has first been given. In practice, judges will also require the relevant transcripts to be available so they may take a view as to the merits of the substantive application.

A8-4 It is the practice of the court, if bail is granted, to require a condition of residence. An application for variation of conditions of bail may be determined by the Registrar (if unopposed) or a single judge.

### A9 Consideration of the applications by single judge

A9-1 Normally a single judge will consider the application for leave to appeal together with any **J-12** ancillary applications, *e.g.* for bail or representation order, without hearing oral argument. Counsel may request an oral hearing, but it is only in very rare circumstances that the Registrar would consider it appropriate to grant a representation order for the proceedings before a single judge at an oral hearing, but counsel may appear to argue the applications before the single judge where instructed to do so, usually appearing either *pro bono* or privately funded. Oral applications for leave and bail are usually heard at 9.30 a.m. before the normal court sittings. Counsel appears unrobed. If counsel considers that an application may take longer than 20 minutes, the Registrar must be informed.

### A10 Powers of the single judge

A10-1 The single judge may grant the application for leave, refuse it or refer it to the full court. In **J-13** conviction cases and in sentence cases where appropriate, the single judge may grant limited leave, *i.e.* leave to argue some grounds but not others. If the grounds upon which leave has been refused are to be renewed before the full court, counsel must notify the Registrar within 14 days. In the absence of any notification of renewal, it will be assumed that the grounds upon which leave was refused will not be pursued.

The single judge may also grant, refuse or refer any ancillary application.

### A11  Grant of leave or reference to full court

**J-14**

A11-1 Where the single judge grants leave or refers an application to the court, it is usual to grant a representation order for the preparation and presentation of the appeal. This is usually limited to the services of counsel only, in which event counsel will be assigned by the Registrar. In such a case the Registrar will provide a brief but does not act as an appellant's solicitor. Counsel who settled grounds of appeal will usually be assigned. However, the Registrar may assign one counsel to represent more than one appellant if appropriate. If it is considered that a representation order for two counsel and/or solicitors is required, counsel should notify the Registrar and provide written justification in accordance with the Criminal Defence Service (General) (No. 2) Regulations 2001.

A11-2 If solicitors are assigned, it should be noted that by virtue of regulation 13 of the Criminal Defence Service (General) (No. 2) Regulations 2001, a representation order can only be issued to a solicitor if he holds a General Criminal Contract (Crime Franchise) with the LSC. A solicitor not holding such a franchise may apply to the LSC for an individual case contract (by virtue of which the solicitor is employed on behalf of the LSC to represent an appellant in a given case). Such a contract is sufficient for the purposes of regulation 13.

A11-3 In some circumstances, the Registrar may refer an application to the full court. This may be because there is a novel point of law or because in a sentence case, the sentence passed is unlawful and regardless of the merits, the sentence should be amended. A representation order for counsel is usually granted. Counsel for the prosecution usually attends a Registrar's referral.

### A12  Refusal by the single judge

**J-15**

A12-1 Where the single judge refuses leave to appeal, the Registrar sends a notification of the refusal, including any observations which the judge may have made, to the appellant, who is informed that he may require the application to be considered by the court by serving a renewal notice [Form SJ-Renewal] upon the Registrar within 14 days from the date on which the notice of refusal was served on him.

A12-2 A refused application which is not renewed within 14 days lapses. An appellant may apply for an extension of time in which to renew his application for leave: CAA 1968, s.31, and rule 65.5(2). The Registrar will normally refer such an application to the court to be considered at the same time as the renewed application for leave to appeal. An application for extension for time in which to renew must be supported by cogent reasons.

A12-3 If it is intended that counsel should represent the appellant at the hearing of the renewed application for leave to appeal, whether privately instructed or on a *pro bono* basis, such intention must be communicated to the CAO in writing as soon as that decision has been made. Whilst a representation order is not granted by the Registrar in respect of a renewed application for leave, counsel may apply at the hearing to the court for a representation order to cover that appearance. In practice, this is only granted where the application for leave is successful.

### A13  Directions for loss of time

**J-16**

A13-1 The CAA 1968, s. 29, empowers the court to direct that time spent in custody as an appellant shall not count as part of the term of any sentence to which the appellant is for the time being subject. The court will do so where it considers that an application is wholly without merit. Such an order may not be made where leave to appeal or a trial judge's certificate has been granted, on a reference by the CCRC or where an appeal has been abandoned.

A13-2 The mere fact that counsel has advised that there are grounds of appeal will not be a sufficient answer to the question as to whether or not an application has indeed been brought which was wholly without merit: *R. v. Hart*; *R. v. George*; *R. v. Clarke*; *R. v. Brown* [2007] 1 Cr.App.R. 31.

A13-3 The Form SJ, on which the single judge records his decisions, and the reverse of which is used by appellants to indicate their wish to renew, includes:

- a box for the single judge to initial to indicate that that the full court should consider loss of time if the application is renewed and
- a box for the applicant to give reasons why such an order should not be made, whether or not an indication has been given by a single judge.

### A14  Abandonment

**J-17**

A14-1 An appeal or application may be abandoned at any time before the hearing without leave by completing and lodging Form A. An oral instruction or letter indicating a wish to abandon is insufficient.

A14-2 At the hearing, an application or appeal can only be abandoned with the permission of the court: rule 65.13(2). An appeal or application which is abandoned is treated as having been dismissed or refused by the full court, as the case may be: rule 65.13(4)(c).

A14-3 A notice of abandonment cannot be withdrawn nor can it be conditional. A person who wants to reinstate an application or appeal after abandonment must apply in writing with reasons: rule 65.13(5). The court has power to allow reinstatement only where the purported abandonment can be treated as a nullity (see *R. v. Medway*, 62 Cr.App.R. 85; *R. v. Burt, The Independent,* December 3, 2004; *R. v Grant* (2005) 149 S.J. 1186).

### A15  Case management duties

A15-1 Rule 65.2 gives the court and parties the same powers and duties of case management as in Part 3 of the rules. In accordance with those duties, for each application received, the Registrar nominates a case progression officer (the "responsible officer"). There is also a duty on the parties actively to assist the court to progress cases. Close contact between counsel and solicitors and the responsible officer is encouraged in order to facilitate the efficient preparation and listing of appeals, especially in complex cases and those involving witnesses.    **J-18**

A15-2 Powers exercisable by the single judge and the Registrar are contained in the CAA 1968, s.31. These powers include the power to make procedural directions for the efficient and effective preparation of an application or appeal and the power to make an order under section 23(1)(a) of the 1968 Act for the production of evidence etc. necessary for the determination of the case.

A15-3 Procedural directions given by the Registrar may be appealed to a single judge. Those given by a single judge, including a single Lord Justice, are final.

B. Interlocutory Appeals against Rulings in Preparatory Hearings

*Appeal against a ruling under section 9 of the Criminal Justice Act 1987 or a decision under section 35 of the Criminal Procedure and Investigations Act 1996 [Part 66 Criminal Procedure Rules 2007]*

B1 Where a judge has ordered a preparatory hearing, he may make a ruling as to the admissibility of evidence; any other question of law relating to the case or any question as to the severance or joinder of charges. (s.9(3)(b), (c) and (d) of the 1987 Act/s.31(3)(a), (b) and (c) of the 1996 Act)    **J-19**

B2 Under section 9(11) of the 1987 Act/section 35(1) of the 1996 Act the defence or the prosecution may appeal to the CACD (and ultimately to the House of Lords) against such a ruling, but only with the leave of the trial judge, single judge or the full court. As to the scope of a judge's powers in relation to a preparatory hearing and thus the extent of appeal rights, see *R. v. H* (§ 7-310 in the main work).

B3 If the trial date is imminent and the application is urgent, the Registrar should be notified so that he may consider referring the application directly to the full court and make arrangements for listing.

B4 If an application for leave to appeal is made to the trial judge, it should be made orally immediately after the ruling, or within two business days by serving a notice of an application on the appropriate officer of the Crown Court and all parties directly affected: rule 66.4. Notice of appeal or application for leave to appeal [Form NG (Prep)] is to be served on the Registrar, the Crown Court and the parties within five business days of the ruling or the trial judge's decision whether to grant leave: rule 66.2.

B5 The notice and grounds of appeal having been served on the other parties, grounds of opposition should be served in a respondent's notice [Form RN (Prep)] within five business days of service of the appeal notice: rule 66.5.

B6 Defence representatives are usually covered by the Crown Court representation order if one is in force (Access to Justice Act 1999, Sched. 3, para. 2(2)).

B7 If the relevant time limits are not complied with, the court has power to grant an extension of time, but cogent grounds in support of the application will be required. Where a single judge refuses leave to appeal or an extension of time within which to serve a notice, the application may be renewed for determination by the full court by serving the notice of refusal, appropriately completed, upon the Registrar within five business days of the refusal being served (rule 66.7).

C. Appeals by a Prosecutor Against a "Terminating" Ruling

*Criminal Justice Act 2003, s.58 [Part 67 Criminal Procedure Rules 2007]*

C1 Section 58 of the 2003 Act gives the prosecution a right of appeal in relation to a "terminating"    **J-20** ruling: in effect where the prosecution agrees to the defendant's acquittal if the appeal against the ruling is not successful (*R. v. Y.* [2008] 1 Cr.App.R. 34). This is wide enough to encompass a case management decision (*R. v. Clarke* [2008] 1 Cr.App.R. 33).

C2 There is no right of appeal in respect of a ruling that the jury be discharged or a ruling in respect of which there is a right of appeal to the Court of Appeal by virtue of another enactment (s.57(2)). The prosecution should therefore consider whether there is a right of appeal under section 9 of the CJA 1987 or section 35 of the CPIA 1996.

C3 The prosecution must inform the court that it intends to appeal or request an adjournment to consider whether to appeal (s.58(4)), which will be until the next business day (rule 67.2(2)). The judge has a discretion to adjourn for longer if there is a real reason for doing so (*R. v. H.* [2008] EWCA Crim 483). The prosecution can then ask the trial judge to grant leave to appeal (rule 67.5), although leave to appeal can be granted by the trial judge, the single judge or the full court. The Crown must give the undertaking (as to the defendant's acquittal if the appeal is abandoned or leave to appeal is not obtained) at the time when it informs the court of its intention to appeal. The failure to give it then is fatal to an application to the Court of Appeal for leave: s.58(8); *R. v. Arnold* [2008] R.T.R. 25.

C4 Whether or not leave is granted, the trial judge must then decide if the appeal is to be expedited and if so, adjourn the case. If he decides that the appeal should not be expedited, then he can adjourn the case or discharge the jury (s.59). Leave should be granted only where the trial judge considers there is a real prospect of success and not in an attempt to speed up the hearing of the appeal (*R. v. J.G.* [2006] EWCA Crim 3276).

C5 Whether the appeal is expedited or not affects the time limits for service of the notice of appeal [Form NG (Pros)] and respondent's notice [Form RN (Pros)]. If expedited, the appeal notice must be served the next business day after the decision, if not expedited, it must be served within five business days. Similar time limits apply to the service of the respondent's notice. Defence representatives are usually covered by the Crown Court representation order if one is in force (such proceedings being considered incidental within the Access to Justice Act 1999, Sched. 3, para. 2(2)). If the relevant time limits are not complied with, the court has power to grant an extension of time.

C6 Expedition does not impose time limits on the Registrar or Court of Appeal. However, if leave has not been granted by the trial judge, the application may be referred to the full court by the Registrar to enable the application and appeal to be heard together to ensure that the matter is dealt with quickly.

C7 The Registrar endeavours to list prosecution appeals where a jury has not been discharged as quickly as possible. He is unlikely to be able to list an appeal in less than a week from the ruling because it is necessary for the prosecution to obtain transcripts, papers to be copied and the judges to read their papers. It is of great assistance if it is anticipated that there is to be an appeal against a ruling where the jury has not been discharged, that a telephone call is made to the Registrar or CAO general office (020 7947 6011) notifying the office even before the appeal notice is sent, so that the list office may be put on notice. The listing of an urgent appeal invariably means that other cases have to be removed from the list.

## D. OTHER APPEALS

### D1 Prosecution appeal against the making of a confiscation order or where the court declines to make one (save on reconsideration of benefit)

J-21
- S.31 of the PCA 2002.
- Parts 71 and 72 of the Criminal Procedure Rules.
- From April 1, 2008 only the prosecution can appeal
- Proceedings are commenced by serving a Form PoCA 1 on the defendant and the Crown Court within 28 days of the decision appealed against. [Proceeds of Crime Act (Appeals under Part 2) Order 2003, art. 3(2)(a).]
- A respondent's notice PoCA 2 is to be served on the Registrar of Criminal Appeals and the appellant not later than 14 days after receiving PoCA 1.
- An undischarged Crown Court representation order will cover advice and assistance on the merits of opposing the appeal and drafting the respondent's notice, otherwise an application for a representation order can be made to the Registrar [Access to Justice Act 1999, ss.12(2)(b), 26]. In any event, where an application for a representation order is made on PoCA 2, the Registrar will consider a representation order for the hearing.
- Leave to appeal can be granted by a single judge or the full court.

### D2 Appeal in relation to a restraint order

J-22
- S.43 of the PCA 2002.

- Parts 71 and 73 of the Criminal Procedure Rules.
- The prosecution or an accredited financial investigator can appeal a refusal to make a restraint order. A person who applied for an order or who is affected by the order can apply to the Crown Court to vary or discharge the order and then appeal that decision to the Court of Appeal.
- Proceedings are commenced by serving a form PoCA 3 on the Crown Court within 14 days of the decision being appealed. PoCA 3 must then be served on any respondent, and on any person who holds realisable property to which the appeal relates, or is affected by the appeal, not later than seven days after the form is lodged at the Crown Court. The documents which are to be served with PoCA 3 are set out in rule 73.2(3).
- A respondent's notice PoCA 4 is to be served on the Registrar not later than 14 days after the respondent is notified that the appellant has leave to appeal or notified that the application for leave and any appeal are to be heard together. PoCA 4 is then to be served on the appellant and any other respondent as soon as is practicable and not later than seven days after it was served on the Registrar.
- An application for a restraint order can be made as soon as a criminal investigation has begun. The proposed defendant may not have been charged: PCA 2002, s.40. This affects the type of public funding.
- If a defendant has been charged with a criminal offence connected to the restraint order then the restraint proceedings are regarded as incidental to the criminal proceedings and are treated as criminal proceedings for funding purposes [Criminal Defence Service (General) (No. 2) Regulations 2001, reg.3(3)(c)] and the Registrar can grant a representation order if a defendant appeals a decision on an application to vary or discharge the restraint order.
- If the prosecution apply for a restraint order in the Crown Court before the subject of the restraint order has been charged with a criminal offence and the subject of that order wishes to appeal a decision on an application to vary or discharge the restraint order then civil legal aid may be available as these proceedings fall within the Access to Justice Act 1999, Sched. 2, para. 3. The Legal Services Commission should be contacted for funding within the Community Legal Service scheme.
- Similarly, a person affected by the order who wishes to appeal a decision on an application to vary or discharge the restraint order should apply to the Legal Services Commission for funding within the Community Legal Service scheme.
- Leave to appeal can be granted by a single judge or full court.

### D3 Appeal in relation to a receivership order

- S.65 of the PCA 2002. **J-23**
- Parts 71 and 73 of the Criminal Procedure Rules.
- An appeal can be brought by:
  (a) the person who applied for the order,
  (b) a person who is affected by the order or,
  (c) the receiver.
  The orders against which an appeal will lie are:
  (1) the appointment or non-appointment of a receiver,
  (2) the powers of a receiver,
  (3) an order giving a direction to a receiver, and
  (4) the variation or discharge of a receivership order.
- Proceedings are commenced by serving a Form PoCA 3 on the Crown Court within 14 days of the decision being appealed. PoCA 3 must then be served on any respondent and on any person who holds realisable property to which the appeal relates, or is affected by the appeal, not later than seven days after the form is lodged at the Crown Court. The documents which are to be served with PoCA 3 are set out in rule 73.2(3).
- A respondent's notice PoCA 4 is to be served on the Registrar not later than 14 days after the respondent is notified that the appellant has leave to appeal or is notified that the application for leave and any appeal are to be heard together. PoCA 4 is then to be served on the appellant and any other respondent as soon as is practicable and not later than seven days after it was served on the Registrar.
- If a defendant has been charged with a criminal offence connected to a receivership order then the receivership proceedings are regarded as incidental to the criminal proceedings and are treated as criminal proceedings for funding purposes [Criminal

Defence Service (General) (No. 2) Regulations 2001, reg.3(3)(c)] and the Registrar can grant a representation order if a defendant appeals a decision relating to a receivership order.
- If a management receivership order or an application for such an order is made in the Crown Court before a criminal offence has been charged and a person affected by the order (including the proposed defendant) wishes to appeal a decision then civil legal aid may be available as these proceedings fall within Access to Justice Act 1999, Sched. 2, para. 3. The Legal Services Commission should be contacted for funding within the Community Legal Service scheme.
- Leave to appeal can be granted by a single judge or the full court.

**D4 Appeal against an order of the Crown Court in the exercise of its jurisdiction to punish for contempt – usually a finding of contempt or sentence for contempt**

J-24
- S.13 of the Administration of Justice Act 1960.
- Part 68 of the Criminal Procedure Rules.
- Anyone dealt with by the Crown Court for contempt may appeal.
- Proceedings are commenced by lodging a Form NG at the Crown Court not more than 28 days after the order to be appealed.
- The Registrar may direct a respondent's notice Form RN or the Crown may serve one if they wish to make representations to the court.
- An undischarged Crown Court representation order will cover advice and assistance on appeal. The Registrar will usually grant a representation order for the hearing: Access to Justice Act 1999, s.12(2)(b).
- No leave to appeal is required. The appeal is as of right.
- Appeals occur most frequently when an appellant wishes to appeal a sentence for failing to appear at the Crown Court as the failing to appear is dealt with as if it were contempt.

**D5 Appeal against a minimum term set or reviewed by a High Court judge**

J-25
- Para. 14 of Schedule 22 to the CJA 2003
- Part 68 of the Criminal Procedure Rules
- A defendant with a mandatory life sentence imposed before December 18, 2003 who has had his minimum term set or reviewed by a High Court judge can appeal.
- Proceedings are commenced by service of Form NG (MT) on the Registrar not more than 28 days after the decision.
- The Registrar may direct a respondent's notice Form RN or the Crown may serve one if they wish to make representations to the court.
- An application for a representation order can be made to the Registrar [Access to Justice Act 1999, s.12(2)(b)].
- Leave to appeal is required and can be granted by the full court or a single judge: Criminal Justice Act 2003 (Mandatory Life Sentences: Appeals in Transitional Cases) Order 2005 (S.I. 2005 No. 2798), art. 8.

**D6 Attorney General's reference of an unduly lenient sentence**

J-26
- S.36 of the CJA 1988.
- Part 70 of the Criminal Procedure Rules.
- The Attorney General can refer sentences only in relation to specific offences or sentences [CJA 1988, ss.35, 36, and Criminal Justice Act 1988 (Reviews of Sentencing) Order 2006] including a minimum term, set or reviewed by a High Court judge [CJA 2003, Sched. 22, para. 15].
- Although rule 70.3(1) implies there is a specific form to commence proceedings, in practice a standard letter with supporting documents is sent by the Attorney General's office no more than 28 days after sentence.
- If the defendant wishes to make representations to the court he must serve a respondent's notice within 14 days of the Registrar serving the application upon him. Again, there is no specific form designated.
- Representation orders are not issued to respond to an Attorney General's reference but a defendant who appears by counsel is entitled to his reasonable costs from central funds. The cost of instructing leading counsel in addition to or instead of junior counsel is generally not considered reasonable unless there is a compelling reason. It is advisable to consult with the Registrar before leading counsel is instructed.

- The leave of the Court of Appeal is required.

### D7 Attorney General's reference of a point of law on an acquittal

- S.36 of the CJA 1972.
- Part 70 of the Criminal Procedure Rules.
- The Attorney General can refer a point of law to the Court of Appeal for an opinion on the acquittal on indictment of the defendant.
- Although rule 70.3(1) implies there is a specific form to commence proceedings, there is no such form and rule 70.3 sets out what should be included in the reference. The defendant should not be identified.
- There is no time limit.
- If the defendant wishes to make representations to the court he must serve a respondent's notice within 28 days of the Registrar serving the application upon him. Again there is no specific form.
- Representation orders are not issued to respond to an Attorney General's reference but a defendant who appears by counsel is entitled to his reasonable costs from central funds.
- Leave is not required.

### D8 Appeal against a finding of unfitness to plead or a finding that the accused did the act or made the omission charged

- S.15 of the CAA 1968.
- Part 68 of the Criminal Procedure Rules.
- The accused can appeal (by the person appointed to represent the accused) against
  — a finding of unfitness to plead (but not fitness to plead as the defendant can appeal any subsequent conviction in the usual way on the basis he was not fit to plead) or
  — that he did the act or made the omission charged or
  — both findings.
  The appeal does not lie until both findings have been made.
- Proceedings are commenced by the service of Form NG on the Crown Court not more than 28 days after the finding made which the accused wishes to appeal.
- The Crown should serve a respondent's notice Form RN if directed by the Registrar or if they wish to make representations to the court.
- There does not appear to be any statutory provision empowering the grant of a representation order. The Prosecution of Offences Act 1985, s.19, refers to costs from central funds being available to cover the fees of a person appointed by the Crown Court under section 4A of the Criminal Procedure (Insanity) Act 1964. In *R. v. Antoine* ([1999] 2 Cr.App.R 225, CA) this was interpreted to include the costs of an appeal. The Prosecution of Offences Act 1985, s.16(4) provides that where the Court of Appeal <u>allows an appeal</u> under Part 1 of the CAA 1968 against a finding under the Criminal Procedure (Insanity) Act 1964 that the appellant is under a disability, or that he did the act or made the omission charged against him the court may make a defendant's costs order in favour of the accused.
- Leave to appeal may be granted by the Crown Court judge, a single judge or the full court.

### D9 Appeal against a verdict of not guilty by reason of insanity

- S.12 of the CAA 1968.
- Part 68 of the Criminal Procedure Rules.
- The defendant can appeal a verdict of not guilty by reason of insanity.
- Proceedings are commenced by the service of Form NG on the Crown Court not more than 28 days after the verdict.
- The Crown should serve a respondent's notice Form RN if directed by the Registrar or if they wish to make representations to the court.
- There does not appear to be any statutory provision empowering the grant of a representation order. The Prosecution of Offences Act 1985, s.16(4), provides that where the Court of Appeal <u>allows an appeal</u> then the court may make a defendant's costs order. If the appeal is not allowed costs from central funds should be available on the same basis as was allowed in *Antoine* (*ante*) in the absence of any statutory provision.
- Leave to appeal may be granted by the Crown Court judge, a single judge or the full court.

### D10 Appeal against the order following a verdict of not guilty by reason of insanity or a finding of unfitness to plead

**J-30**
- S.16A of the CAA 1968.
- Part 68 of the Criminal Procedure Rules.
- An accused who, as a result of a verdict of not guilty by reason of insanity or a finding of fitness to plead has a hospital order, interim hospital order or supervision order made against him may appeal against the order.
- Proceedings are commenced by the service of Form NG on the Crown Court not more than 28 days after the order.
- [As D9, *ante*.]
- [As D9, *ante*.]
- [As D9, *ante*.]

### D11 Appeal against review of sentence

**J-31**
- S.74(8) of the SOCPA 2005.
- Part 68 of the Criminal Procedure Rules.
- A defendant or specified prosecutor may appeal.
- Proceedings are commenced by serving a Form NG (RD) on the Crown Court not more than 28 days after the review.
- A respondent's notice Form RN should be served if directed by the Registrar or if the respondent wishes to make representations to the Court.
- An application for a representation order can be made to the Registrar: Access to Justice Act 1999, s.12(2)(b).
- Leave to appeal can be granted by the single judge or full court [Serious Organised Crime and Police Act 2005 (Appeals under section 74) Order 2006 (S.I. 2006 No. 2135)].

### D12 Appeal against an order for trial by jury of sample counts

**J-32**
- S.18 of the Domestic Violence, Crime and Victims Act 2004.
- Part 66 of the Criminal Procedure Rules.
- The defendant can appeal.
- An application for the jury to try some counts as sample counts and the judge to try the remainder if the jury convict, must be determined at a preparatory hearing and section 18 confers rights of interlocutory appeal. A Form NG (Prep) must be served on the Crown Court, the Registrar and any party directly affected not more than five business days after the order or the Crown Court judge granting or refusing leave. (*For applications to the Crown Court judge, see Part B above.*)
- A respondent's notice Form RN (Prep) should be served if the court directs or the Crown (or any party affected) wants to make representations to the court.
- Defence representatives are usually covered by the Crown Court representation order if one is in force [Access to Justice Act 1999, Sched. 3, para. 2(2)].
- The Crown Court Judge, single judge or full court can grant leave to appeal.

### D13 Appeal against an order relating to a trial to be conducted without a jury where there is a danger of jury tampering

**J-33**
- S.9(11) of the CJA 1987 and s.35(1) of the CPIA 1996.
- Part 66 of the Criminal Procedure Rules.
- The prosecution can appeal the refusal to make an order; the defence can appeal the making of an order.
- A Form NG (Prep) must be served on the Crown Court, the Registrar and any party directly affected not more than five business days after the order or the Crown Court judge grants or refuses leave. (*For applications to the Crown Court judge, see Part B above.*)
- A respondent's notice Form RN (Prep) should be served if the court directs or the Crown (or any party affected) wants to make representations to the court.
- Defence representatives are usually covered by the Crown Court representation order if one is in force [Access to Justice Act 1999, Sched. 3, para.2 (2)].
- Leave is required. The Crown Court judge, single judge or full court can grant leave to appeal.

### D14 Appeal against an order that a trial should continue without a jury or a new trial take place without a jury after jury tampering

**J-34**
- S.47 of the CJA 2003.

- Part 66 of the Criminal Procedure Rules (relating to appeals against an order made in a preparatory hearing notwithstanding the ruling will not have been in the context of a preparatory hearing).
- The defendant can appeal.
- As D13, *ante*
- As D13, *ante*
- As D13, *ante*
- As D13, *ante*

### D15 Appeal against orders restricting or preventing reports or restricting public access

- S.159 of the CJA 1988    **J-35**
- Part 69 of the Criminal Procedure Rules
- A person aggrieved may appeal.
- Applications against orders <u>restricting reporting</u> shall be made within 10 business days after the date on which the order was made by serving Form NG (159) on the Registrar, the Crown Court, the prosecutor and defendant and any other affected person. Applications against orders to <u>restrict public access</u> must be made the next business day after the order was made. If advance notice of an order restricting public access is given, then advance notice of an intention to appeal may be made not more than five business days after the advance notice is displayed.
- A person on whom an appeal notice is served should serve a respondent's notice Form RN (159) within three business days if he wishes to make representations to the court or the court so directs.
- The court may make such order as to costs as it thinks fit (CJA 1988, s.159(5)(c)), but not out of central funds - *Holden v. CPS (No. 2)* [1994] 1 A.C. 22, HL.
- A single judge or the full court can grant leave to appeal: CAA 1968, s.31(2B).
- Applications for leave to appeal and appeals in relation to reporting restrictions <u>may</u> be heard in private (rule 65.6 (1)). Applications for leave to appeal and appeals relating to restricting public access must be determined <u>without</u> a hearing (rule 65.6(3)).

### D16 Appeal against a wasted costs order and appeal against a third party costs order

- Regulation 3C (costs wasted) and 3E (third party costs) of the Costs in Criminal Cases   **J-36** (General) Regulations 1986.
- A legal or other representative against whom a wasted costs order has been made in the Crown Court or a third party against whom a third party costs order has been made may appeal.
- Notice of appeal should be served on the Crown Court within 21 days of the order being made. There is no specific form. The notice should be served on any interested party (including, if appropriate, the Ministry of Justice).
- Any interested party can make representations orally or in writing.
- There is no power to grant a representation order or to order costs out of central funds as these proceedings are civil in nature.
- Leave to appeal is not required.

### D17 Appeal relating to serious crime prevention orders

- S.24 of the SCA 2007.    **J-37**
- Part 68 of the Criminal Procedure Rules.
- A person subject to the order, an applicant authority or anyone given the opportunity to make representations at the Crown Court about the making, refusal to make, variation or non-variation of an order may appeal.
- Proceedings are commenced by the service of Form NG (SCPO) on the Crown Court not more than 28 days after the order.
- A respondent's notice Form RN (SCPO) should be served if directed by the Registrar or if the respondent wishes to make representations to the court.
- Proceedings before the Crown Court or the Court of Appeal relating to serious crime prevention orders and arising by virtue of section 19, 20, 21 or 24 of the SCA 2007 are criminal proceedings for the purposes of section 12(2)(g) of the Access to Justice Act 1999 [see the Criminal Defence Service (General) (No. 2) (Amendment) Regulations (S.I. 2008 No. 725)]. Accordingly, the Registrar may grant a representation order to a person

subject to the order. A person who made representations at the Crown Court can apply to the LSC for funding. The court has discretion to order costs as it thinks fit [Serious Crime Act 2007 (Appeals under section 24) Order 2008 (S.I. 2008 No. 1863), Pt 3].
- Leave to appeal can be granted by the Crown Court judge, full court or single judge [S.I. 2008 No. 1863, art. 9].

### D18 Appeal against the non-making of a football banning order

**J-38**
- S.14A(5A) of the Football Spectators Act 1989.
- Part 68 of the Criminal Procedure Rules.
- The prosecution can appeal.
- The appeal notice should be served on the Crown Court within 28 days of the decision not to make an order. However, there is no designated form.
- A respondent's notice should be served if directed by the Registrar or if the respondent wishes to make representations to the court. However, again there is no designated form.
- An application for a representation order may be made to the Registrar - Access to Justice Act 1999, s.12(2)(b).
- Currently, the Court of Appeal has been given no powers to deal with these appeals.

### E. Application for a Retrial for a Serious Offence

#### E1 Application by a prosecutor to quash an acquittal and seek a retrial for a qualifying offence

*S.76(1) of the Criminal Justice Act 2003 [Part 41 of the Criminal Procedure Rules]*

**J-39**
E1-1 There must be new and compelling evidence and it must be in the interests of justice for the acquitted person to be retried for a qualifying offence as listed in the CJA 2003, Sched. 5, Pt 1 (CJA 2003, ss.78, 79: see *R. v. Dunlop* [2007] 1 Cr.App.R. 8, and *R. v. Miell* [2008] 1 Cr.App.R. 23).

E1-2 Proceedings can begin in one of two ways.
(1) By serving notice of the application under section 76 on the Court of Appeal and within two days serving the notice on the acquitted person (s.80). This notice charges him with the offence. It requires the personal written consent of the Director of Public Prosecutions (DPP) (s.76(3)). If the acquitted person is not in custody the prosecution can ask the Crown Court to issue:
(i) a summons for the acquitted person to appear before the Court of Appeal for the hearing of the application or
(ii) a warrant for his arrest (s.89(3)).
Once arrested on the warrant the acquitted person must be brought before the Crown Court within 48 hours (s.89(6)).
(2) An acquitted person may be charged with the offence before an application under section 76 has been made. This may be after an arrest in an investigation authorised by the DPP (s.85(2)) or where no authorisation has been given, after arrest under a warrant issued by a justice of the peace (s.87(1)). Having been charged, the acquitted person must be brought before the Crown Court to consider bail within 24 hours (s.88(2)). He can then be remanded in custody or on bail for 42 days whilst an application under s.76 is prepared: s.88(6) unless an extension is granted under subsection (8). Once a notice of application under section 76 has been served, stating that the acquitted person has previously been charged with the offence, the acquitted person must be brought before the Crown Court to consider bail within 48 hours of the notice being given to the Registrar, if the acquitted person is already in custody under secton 88 (*ante*) (s.89(2)).

E1-3 Thus in either case, bail is dealt with largely by the Crown Court. The Court of Appeal only considers bail on the adjournment of the hearing of the application under section 76 (s.90(1)).

E1-4 The notice ["Notice of a s.76 application required by s.80(1) Criminal Justice Act 2003"] should where practicable be accompanied by the witness statements which are relied on as the new and compelling evidence, the original witness statements, unused statements, indictment, paper exhibits from the original trial, any relevant transcripts from the original trial and any other documents relied on: rule 41.2(2).

E1-5 An acquitted person who wants to oppose a section 76 application must serve a response ["Response of the acquitted person under s.80 Criminal Justice Act 2003"] not more than 28 days after receiving the notice: rule 41.3(2).

#### E2 Application by a prosecutor for a determination whether a foreign acquittal is a bar to a trial and if so, an order that it not be a bar

*S.76(2) of the Criminal Justice Act 2003 [Part 41 of the Criminal Procedure Rules]*

**J-40**
E2-1 The prosecution can apply, with the personal written consent of the DPP (s.76(3)) for a

determination whether an acquittal outside the UK is a bar to the acquitted person being tried in England and Wales and if it is found to be so, an order that the acquittal not be a bar. Proceedings can begin in the same way as for an application under section 76(1).

### E3 Application for restrictions on publication relating to an application under section 76

*S.82 of the Criminal Justice Act 2003 [Part 41 of the Criminal Procedure Rules]*

E3-1 An application can be made by the DPP for reporting restrictions. This can be made after a **J-41** notice of an application for a retrial has been made and may also be made by the court of its own motion (s.82(5)). An application can also be made by the DPP for reporting restrictions *before* a notice of an application for a retrial if an investigation has been commenced: s.82(6). The application for reporting restrictions must be served on the Registrar ["Application for restrictions on publication under s.82 Criminal Justice Act 2003"] and (usually) the acquitted person (rule 41.8(1)).

E3-2 A party who wants to vary or revoke an order for restrictions on publication under section 82(7) may apply to the Court of Appeal in writing at any time after the order was made (rule 41.9(1)).

### E4 Representation orders

E4-1 The Registrar will usually grant a representation order to the acquitted person for solicitors **J-42** and counsel to respond to any of the above applications.

# APPENDIX K
## Guidelines issued by the Sentencing Guidelines Council and by the Sentencing Council for England and Wales

# I. GUIDELINES

## A. REDUCTION IN SENTENCE FOR A GUILTY PLEA

### GUIDELINE

CONTENTS

FOREWORD

**K-2**    One of the first guidelines to be issued by the Sentencing Guidelines Council related to the statutory obligation to take account of any guilty plea when determining sentence. As set out in the foreword to that guideline,[3] the intention was "to promonelsonte consistency in sentencing by providing clarity for courts, court users and victims so that everyone knows exactly what to expect". Prior to that guideline there had been different understandings of the purpose of the reduction and the extent of any reduction given.

Since the guideline was issued, there has been much greater clarity but there still remain concerns about some of the content of the guideline and about the extent to which the guideline has been consistently applied. Accordingly the council has undertaken a review of the guideline (in accordance with the statutory obligation placed upon it to do so from time to time[4]); it has also requested that the Judicial Studies Board consider further ways in which judicial training can incorporate the guideline.

The council is extremely grateful to the Sentencing Advisory Panel for the speed and thoroughness with which it has prepared its advice following extensive consultation. The council has accepted almost all the recommendations of the panel; the issues and arguments are set out fully in the panel's advice (see www.sentencing-guidelines.gov.uk). This revised guideline applies to all cases sentenced on or after 23 July 2007.

The council has agreed with the panel that the general approach of the guideline is correct in setting out clearly the purpose of the reduction for a guilty plea, in settling for a reduction no greater than one third (with lower levels of reduction where a plea is entered other than at the first reasonable opportunity) and in continuing to provide for a special approach when fixing the minimum term for a life sentence imposed following conviction for murder.

The council has agreed with the panel that some discretion should be introduced to the approach where the prosecution case is "overwhelming".

The council has not accepted the panel's recommendation in relation to circumstances where a magistrates' court is sentencing an offender for a number of offences where the overall maximum imprisonment is six months. The council continues to consider that there must be some incentive to plead guilty in such circumstances; this is consistent with other aspects of the guideline.

The council has not accepted the panel's recommendation in relation to the "capping" of the effect of reduction on very large fines. The number of such fines is very low and the council was not convinced that the arguments were strong enough to justify a departure from the general approach in the guideline not to "cap" the effect of the reduction. In addition, the revised guideline provides guidance as to when the "first reasonable opportunity" is likely to occur in relation to indictable only offences; emphasises that remorse and material assistance provided to prosecuting authorities are

---

[3] Published December 2004.
[4] Criminal Justice Act 2003, s.170(4).

separate issues from those to which the guideline applies and makes clear that the approach to calculation of the reduction where an indeterminate sentence is imposed (other than that following conviction for murder) should be the same as that for determinate sentences.

Since the guideline was issued in 2004, there have been changes in the statutory provisions governing the reduction for guilty plea and in those relating to sentences for public protection. The review has provided an opportunity to bring the guideline up to date and those changes have been incorporated.

The council published a draft guideline in accordance with section 170(8) of the Criminal Justice Act 2003 inviting responses by 14 March 2007. A response has been received from the Home Affairs Committee, a response has been received from the Attorney General and seven other responses have been received. A summary of the responses and the decisions of the council has been published separately.

**Chairman of the Council**
**July 2007**

### A. Statutory Provisions

Section 144 Criminal Justice Act 2003 provides [the guideline here sets out the text of section 144 **K-3** of the 2003 Act, set out in the main work at § 5-107].

Section 174(2) Criminal Justice Act 2003 provides [the guideline here sets out the text of section 174(2)(d) of the 2003 Act, set out in the main work at § 5-165].

1.1 This guideline applies whether a case is dealt with in a magistrates' court or in the Crown Court and whenever practicable in the youth court (taking into account legislative restrictions such as those relevant to the length of detention and training orders).

1.2 The application of this guideline to sentencers when arriving at the appropriate minimum term for the offence of murder is set out in Section F.

1.3 This guideline can also be found at www.sentencing-guidelines.gov.uk or can be obtained from the Council's Secretariat at 4th Floor, 8–10 Great George Street, London SW1P 3AE.

### B. Statement of Purpose

2.1 When imposing a custodial sentence, statute requires that a court must impose the shortest **K-4** term that is commensurate with the seriousness of the offence(s)[3]. Similarly, when imposing a community order, the restrictions on liberty must be commensurate with the seriousness of the offence(s)[4]. Once that decision is made, a court is required to give consideration to the reduction for any guilty plea. As a result, the final sentence after the reduction for a guilty plea will be less than the seriousness of the offence requires.

2.2 A reduction in sentence is appropriate because a guilty plea avoids the need for a trial (thus enabling other cases to be disposed of more expeditiously), shortens the gap between charge and sentence, saves considerable cost, and, in the case of an early plea, saves victims and witnesses from the concern about having to give evidence. The reduction principle derives from the need for the effective administration of justice and not as an aspect of mitigation.

2.3 Where a sentencer is in doubt as to whether a custodial sentence is appropriate, the reduction attributable to a guilty plea will be a relevant consideration. Where this is amongst the factors leading to the imposition of a non-custodial sentence, there will be no need to apply a further reduction on account of the guilty plea. A similar approach is appropriate where the reduction for a guilty plea is amongst the factors leading to the imposition of a financial penalty or discharge instead of a community order.

2.4 When deciding the most appropriate length of sentence, the sentencer should address separately the issue of remorse, together with any other mitigating features, before calculating the reduction for the guilty plea. Similarly, assistance to the prosecuting or enforcement authorities is a separate issue which may attract a reduction in sentence under other procedures; care will need to be taken to ensure that there is no "double counting".

2.5 The implications of other offences that an offender has asked to be taken into consideration should be reflected in the sentence before the reduction for guilty plea has been applied.

2.6 A reduction in sentence should only be applied to the punitive elements of a penalty[5]. The guilty plea reduction has no impact on sentencing decisions in relation to ancillary orders, including orders of disqualification from driving.

---

[3] Criminal Justice Act 2003, s.153(2).
[4] Criminal Justice Act 2003, s.148(2).
[5] Where a court imposes an indeterminate sentence for public protection, the reduction principle applies in the normal way to the determination of the minimum term (see para. 5.1, footnote and para. 7 below) but release from custody requires the authorisation of the Parole Board once that minimum term has been served.

C. APPLICATION OF THE REDUCTION PRINCIPLE

**K-5**    3.1 Recommended approach

The court decides sentence for the offence(s) taking into account aggravating and mitigating factors and any other offences that have been formally admitted (TICs)

⇩

The court selects the amount of the reduction by reference to the sliding scale

⇩

The court applies the reduction

⇩

When pronouncing sentence the court should usually state what the sentence would have been if there had been no reduction as a result of the guilty plea.

D. DETERMINING THE LEVEL OF REDUCTION

**K-6**    4.1 The level of reduction should be *a proportion of the total sentence* imposed, with the proportion calculated by reference to the circumstances in which the guilty plea was indicated, in particular the stage in the proceedings. The greatest reduction will be given where the plea was indicated at the "first reasonable opportunity".

4.2 Save where section 144(2) of the 2003 Act applies[6], the level of the reduction will be gauged on a *sliding scale* ranging from a recommended *one third* (where the guilty plea was entered at the first reasonable opportunity in relation to the offence for which sentence is being imposed), reducing to a recommended *one quarter* (where a trial date has been set) and to a recommended *one tenth* (for a guilty plea entered at the 'door of the court' or after the trial has begun). *See diagram below.*

4.3 The level of reduction should reflect the stage at which the offender indicated a *willingness to admit guilt* to the offence for which he is eventually sentenced:

   (i) the largest recommended reduction will not normally be given unless the offender indicated willingness to admit guilt at the first reasonable opportunity; when this occurs will vary from case to case (see *Annex 1 for illustrative examples*);

   (ii) where the admission of guilt comes later than the first reasonable opportunity, the reduction for guilty plea will normally be less than one third;

   (iii) where the plea of guilty comes very late, it is still appropriate to give some reduction;

   (iv) if after pleading guilty there is a *Newton* hearing and the offender's version of the circumstances of the offence is rejected, this should be taken into account in determining the level of reduction;

   (v) if the not guilty plea was entered and maintained for tactical reasons (such as to retain privileges whilst on remand), a late guilty plea should attract very little, if any, discount.

[6] See section A above.

In each category, there is a presumption that the recommended reduction will be given unless there are good reasons for a lower amount.

| First reasonable opportunity | After a trial date is set | Door of the court/ after trial has begun |
|---|---|---|

======= | ============ | ============ |

recommended 1/3     recommended 1/4     recommended 1/10

### E. Witholding a Reduction

**On the basis of dangerousness**

5.1   Where a sentence for a "dangerous offender" is imposed under the provisions in the Criminal **K-7** Justice Act 2003, whether the sentence requires the calculation of a minimum term or is an extended sentence, the approach will be the same as for any other determinate sentence (see also section G below)[7].

**Where the prosecution case is overwhelming**

5.2   The purpose of giving credit is to encourage those who are guilty to plead at the earliest opportunity. Any defendant is entitled to put the prosecution to proof and so every defendant who is guilty should be encouraged to indicate that guilt at the first reasonable opportunity.

5.3   Where the prosecution case is overwhelming, it may not be appropriate to give the full reduction that would otherwise be given. Whilst there is a presumption in favour of the full reduction being given where a plea has been indicated at the first reasonable opportunity, the fact that the prosecution case is overwhelming without relying on admissions from the defendant may be a reason justifying departure from the guideline.

5.4   Where a court is satisfied that a lower reduction should be given for this reason, a recommended reduction of 20% is likely to be appropriate where the guilty plea was indicated at the first reasonable opportunity.

5.5   A court departing from a guideline must state the reasons for doing so[8].

**Where the maximum penalty for the offence is thought to be too low**

5.6   The sentencer is bound to sentence for the offence with which the offender has been charged, and to which he has pleaded guilty. The sentencer cannot remedy perceived defects (for example an inadequate charge or maximum penalty) by refusal of the appropriate discount.

**Where jurisdictional issues arise**

*(i) Where sentencing powers are limited to six months' imprisonment despite multiple offences*

5.7   When the total sentence for both or all of the offences is six months' imprisonment, a court may determine to impose consecutive sentences which, even allowing for a reduction for a guilty plea where appropriate on each offence, would still result in the imposition of the maximum sentence available. In such circumstances, in order to achieve the purpose for which the reduction principle has been established[9], some modest allowance should normally be given against the total sentence for the entry of a guilty plea.

*(ii) Where a maximum sentence might still be imposed*

5.8   Despite a guilty plea being entered which would normally attract a reduction in sentence, a magistrates' court may impose a sentence of imprisonment of 6 months for a single either-way offence where, but for the plea, that offence would have been committed to the Crown Court for sentence.

[7] There will be some cases arising from offences committed before the commencement of the relevant provisions of the Criminal Justice Act 2003 in which a court will determine that a longer than commensurate, extended, or indeterminate sentence is required for the protection of the public. In such a case, the minimum custodial term (but not the protection of public element of the sentence) should be reduced to reflect the plea.
[8] Criminal Justice Act 2003, s.174(2)(a).
[9] See section B above.

5.9 Similarly, a detention and training order of 24 months may be imposed on an offender aged under 18 if the offence is one which would but for the plea have attracted a sentence of long-term detention in excess of 24 months under the Powers of Criminal Courts (Sentencing) Act 2000, s.91.

F. APPLICATION TO SENTENCING FOR MURDER

**K-8**

6.1 Murder has always been regarded as the most serious criminal offence and the sentence prescribed is different from other sentences. By law, the sentence for murder is imprisonment (detention) for life and an offender will remain subject to the sentence for the rest of his/her life.

6.2 The decision whether to release the offender from custody during this sentence will be taken by the Parole Board which will consider whether it is safe to release the offender on licence. The court that imposes the sentence is required by law to set a minimum term that has to be served before the Parole Board may start to consider whether to authorise release on licence. If an offender is released, the licence continues for the rest of the offender's life and recall to prison is possible at any time.

6.3 Uniquely, Parliament has set starting points[10] (based on the circumstances of the killing) which a court will apply when it fixes the minimum term. Parliament has further prescribed that, having identified the appropriate starting point, the court must then consider whether to increase or reduce it in the light of aggravating or mitigating factors, some of which are listed in statute. Finally, Parliament specifically provides[11] that the obligation to have regard to any guilty plea applies to the fixing of the minimum term, by making the same statutory provisions that apply to other offences apply to murder without limiting the court's discretion (as it did with other sentences under the Powers of Criminal Courts (Sentencing) Act 2000).

6.4 There are important differences between the usual fixed term sentence and the minimum term set following the imposition of the mandatory life sentence for murder. The most significant of these, from the sentencer's point of view, is that a reduction for a plea of guilty in the case of murder will have double the effect on time served in custody when compared with a determinate sentence. This is because a determinate sentence will provide (in most circumstances) for the release of the offender[12] on licence half way through the total sentence whereas in the case of murder a minimum term is the period in custody before consideration is given by the Parole Board to whether release is appropriate.

6.5 Given this difference, the special characteristic of the offence of murder and the unique statutory provision of starting points, careful consideration will need to be given to the extent of any reduction and to the need to ensure that the minimum term properly reflects the seriousness of the offence. Whilst the general principles continue to apply (both that a guilty plea should be encouraged and that the extent of any reduction should reduce if the indication of plea is later than the first reasonable opportunity), the process of determining the level of reduction will be different.

**6.6 Approach**

**K-9**

1. Where a court determines that there should be a whole life minimum term, there will be no reduction for a guilty plea.

2. In other circumstances,

    (a) the court will weigh carefully the overall length of the minimum term taking into account other reductions for which the offender may be eligible so as to avoid a combination leading to an inappropriately short sentence;

    (b) where it is appropriate to reduce the minimum term having regard to a plea of guilty, the reduction will not exceed one sixth and will never exceed five years;

    (c) the sliding scale will apply so that, where it is appropriate to reduce the minimum term on account of a guilty plea, the maximum reduction (one sixth or five years whichever is the less) is only available where there has been an indication of willingness to plead guilty at the first reasonable opportunity, with a recommended 5% for a late guilty plea;

    (d) the court should then review the sentence to ensure that the minimum term accurately reflects the seriousness of the offence taking account of the statutory starting point, all aggravating and mitigating factors and any guilty plea entered.

---

[10] Criminal Justice Act 2003, Schedule 21.
[11] Criminal Justice Act 2003, Schedule 1, para 12(c).
[12] In accordance with the provisions of the Criminal Justice Act 2003.

G. Application to other Indeterminate Sentences

7.1 There are other circumstances in which an indeterminate sentence will be imposed. This may **K-10** be a discretionary life sentence or imprisonment for public protection.

7.2 As with the mandatory life sentence imposed following conviction for murder, the court will be obliged to fix a minimum term to be served before the Parole Board is able to consider whether the offender can be safely released.

7.3 However, the process by which that minimum term is fixed is different from that followed in relation to the mandatory life sentence and requires the court first to determine what the equivalent determinate sentence would have been. Accordingly, the approach to the calculation of the reduction for any guilty plea should follow the process and scale adopted in relation to determinate sentences, as set out in section D above.

**ANNEX 1**

**First reasonable opportunity**

1. The critical time for determining the maximum reduction for a guilty plea is the first reason- **K-11** able opportunity for the defendant to have indicated a willingness to plead guilty. This opportunity will vary with a wide range of factors and the court will need to make a judgement on the particular facts of the case before it.

2. The key principle is that the purpose of giving a reduction is to recognise the benefits that come from a guilty plea not only for those directly involved in the case in question but also in enabling courts more quickly to deal with other outstanding cases.

3. This Annex seeks to help courts to adopt a consistent approach by giving examples of circumstances where a determination will have to be made:

(a) the first reasonable opportunity may be the first time that a defendant appears before the court and has the opportunity to plead guilty;

(b) but the court may consider that it would be reasonable to have expected an indication of willingness even earlier, perhaps whilst under interview;

*Note: For (a) and (b) to apply, the court will need to be satisfied that the defendant (and any legal adviser) would have had sufficient information about the allegations*

(c) where an offence triable either way is committed to the Crown Court for trial and the defendant pleads guilty at the first hearing in that court, the reduction will be less than if there had been an indication of a guilty plea given to the magistrates' court (recommended reduction of one third) but more than if the plea had been entered after a trial date had been set (recommended reduction of one quarter), and is likely to be in the region of 30%;

(d) where an offence is triable only on indictment, it may well be that the first reasonable opportunity would have been during the police station stage; where that is not the case, the first reasonable opportunity is likely to be at the first hearing in the Crown Court;

(e) where a defendant is convicted after pleading guilty to an alternative (lesser) charge to that to which he/she had originally pleaded not guilty, the extent of any reduction will be determined by the stage at which the defendant first formally indicated to the court willingness to plead guilty to the lesser charge and the reason why that lesser charge was proceeded with in preference to the original charge.

**[The next paragraph is K-13.]**

B. Overarching Principles: Seriousness

**GUIDELINE**

Contents

737

          (ii) Mitigating factors

          (iii) Personal mitigation

          (iv) Reduction for a guilty plea

E     The sentencing thresholds

       The custody threshold

       The threshold for community sentences

F     Prevalence

### FOREWORD

**K-14**    In accordance with the provisions of section 170(9) Criminal Justice Act 2003, the Sentencing Guidelines Council issues this guideline as a definitive guideline. By virtue of section 172 of the Act, every court must have regard to a relevant guideline.

    The Council was created in 2004 in order to frame Guidelines to assist Courts as they deal with criminal cases across the whole of England and Wales.

    The Council has stated that it intends to follow a principled approach to the formulation of guidelines to assist sentencers which will include consideration of overarching and general principles relating to the sentencing of offenders. Following the planned implementation of many of the sentencing provisions in the 2003 Act in April 2005, this guideline deals with the general concept of seriousness in the light of those provisions and considers how sentencers should determine when the respective sentencing thresholds have been crossed when applying the provisions of the Act.

    **This guideline applies only to sentences passed under the sentencing framework applicable to those aged 18 or over although there are some aspects that will assist courts assessing the seriousness of offences committed by those under 18. The Council has commissioned separate advice from the Sentencing Advisory Panel on the sentencing of young offenders.**

    This is the first time that it has been possible to produce definitive guidelines not only before new provisions come into force but also before much of the training of judiciary and practitioners.

    The Council has appreciated greatly the work of the Sentencing Advisory Panel in preparing the advice on which this guideline has been based and for the many organisations and individuals who have responded so thoughtfully to the consultation of both the Panel and the Council. The advice and this guideline are available on www.sentencing-guidelines.gov.uk or from the Sentencing Guidelines Secretariat. A summary of the responses to the Council's consultation also appears on the website.

Chairman of the Council

December 2004

### SERIOUSNESS

#### A. STATUTORY PROVISION

**K-15**    1.1 In every case where the offender is aged 18 or over at the time of conviction, the court must have regard to the five purposes of sentencing contained in section 142(1) Criminal Justice Act 2003:

        (a) the punishment of offenders

        (b) the reduction of crime (including its reduction by deterrence)

        (c) the reform and rehabilitation of offenders

        (d) the protection of the public

        (e) the making of reparation by offenders to persons affected by their offence

    1.2 The Act does not indicate that any one purpose should be more important than any other and in practice they may all be relevant to a greater or lesser degree in any individual case—the sentencer has the task of determining the manner in which they apply.

    1.3 The sentencer must start by considering the seriousness of the offence, the assessment of which will:

        • determine which of the sentencing thresholds has been crossed;

        • indicate whether a custodial, community or other sentence is the most appropriate;

        • be the key factor in deciding the length of a custodial sentence, the onerousness of requirements to be incorporated in a community sentence and the amount of any fine imposed.

    1.4 A court is required to pass a sentence that is commensurate with the seriousness of the offence. The seriousness of an offence is determined by two main parameters; the **culpability** of the offender and the **harm** caused or risked being caused by the offence

1.5 Section 143(1) Criminal Justice Act 2003 provides [see § 5-67 in the main work].

B. Culpability

1.6 Four levels of criminal culpability can be identified for sentencing purposes:  **K-16**

1.7 Where the offender;

    (i) has the **intention** to cause harm, with the highest culpability when an offence is planned. The worse the harm intended, the greater the seriousness.

    (ii) is **reckless** as to whether harm is caused, that is, where the offender appreciates at least some harm would be caused but proceeds giving no thought to the consequences even though the extent of the risk would be obvious to most people.

    (iii) has **knowledge** of the specific risks entailed by his actions even though he does not intend to cause the harm that results.

    (iv) is guilty of **negligence**.

**Note:** *There are offences where liability is strict and no culpability need be proved for the purposes of obtaining a conviction, but the degree of culpability is still important when deciding sentence. The extent to which reckless-ness, knowledge or negligence are involved in a particular offence will vary.*

C. Harm

1.8 The relevant provision is widely drafted so that it encompasses those offences where harm is  **K-17** caused but also those where neither individuals nor the community suffer harm but a risk of harm is present.

**To individual victims**

1.9   The types of harm caused or risked by different types of criminal activity are diverse and victims may suffer physical injury, sexual violation, financial loss, damage to health or psychological distress. There are gradations of harm within all of these categories.

1.10   The nature of harm will depend on personal characteristics and circumstances of the victim and the court's assessment of harm will be an effective and important way of taking into considera-tion the impact of a particular crime on the victim.

1.11   In some cases no actual harm may have resulted and the court will be concerned with as-sessing the relative dangerousness of the offender's conduct; it will consider the likelihood of harm occurring and the gravity of the harm that could have resulted.

**To the community**

1.12   Some offences cause harm to the community at large (instead of or as well as to an individual victim) and may include economic loss, harm to public health, or interference with the administra-tion of justice.

**Other types of harm**

1.13   There are other types of harm that are more difficult to define or categorise. For example, cruelty to animals certainly causes significant harm to the animal but there may also be a human victim who also suffers psychological distress and/or financial loss.

1.14   Some conduct is criminalised purely by reference to public feeling or social mores. In addi-tion, public concern about the damage caused by some behaviour, both to individuals and to society as a whole, can influence public perception of the harm caused, for example, by the supply of prohibited drugs.

D. The Assessment of Culpability and Harm

1.15 Section 143(1) makes clear that the assessment of the seriousness of any individual offence  **K-18** must take account not only of any harm actually caused by the offence, but also of any harm that was intended to be caused or might foreseeably be caused by the offence.

1.16 Assessing seriousness is a difficult task, particularly where there is an imbalance between culpability and harm:

    • sometimes the harm that actually results is greater than the harm intended by the of-fender;

    • in other circumstances, the offender's culpability may be at a higher level than the harm resulting from the offence

1.17 Harm must always be judged in the light of culpability. The precise level of culpability will be

739

determined by such factors as motivation, whether the offence was planned or spontaneous or whether the offender was in a position of trust.

**Culpability will be greater if:**
- an offender deliberately causes more harm than is necessary for the commission of the offence, or
- where an offender targets a vulnerable victim (because of their old age or youth, disability or by virtue of the job they do).

1.18 Where unusually serious harm results and was unintended and beyond the control of the offender, culpability will be significantly influenced by the extent to which the harm could have been foreseen.

1.19 If much **more** harm, or much **less** harm has been caused by the offence than the offender intended or foresaw, the culpability of the offender, depending on the circumstances, may be regarded as carrying greater or lesser weight as appropriate.

**The culpability of the offender in the particular circumstances of an individual case should be the initial factor in determining the seriousness of an offence.**

**(i) Aggravating factors**

**K-19**

1.20 Sentencing guidelines for a particular offence will normally include a list of aggravating features which, if present in an individual instance of the offence, would indicate *either* a higher than usual level of culpability on the part of the offender, *or* a greater than usual degree of harm caused by the offence (or sometimes both).

1.21 The lists below bring together the most important aggravating features with potential application to more than one offence or class of offences. They include some factors (such as the vulnerability of victims or abuse of trust) which are integral features of certain offences; in such cases, the presence of the aggravating factor is already reflected in the penalty for the offence and **cannot be used as justification for increasing the sentence further**. The lists are not intended to be comprehensive and the aggravating factors are not listed in any particular order of priority. On occasions, two or more of the factors listed will describe the same feature of the offence and care needs to be taken to avoid "double counting". Those factors starred with an asterisk are statutory aggravating factors where the statutory provisions are in force. Those marked with a hash are yet to be brought into force but as factors in an individual case are still relevant and should be taken into account.

1.22 **Factors indicating higher culpability:**
- Offence committed whilst on bail for other offences
- Failure to respond to previous sentences
- Offence was racially or religiously aggravated
- Offence motivated by, or demonstrating, hostility to the victim based on his or her sexual orientation (or presumed sexual orientation)
- Offence motivated by, or demonstrating, hostility based on the victim's disability (or presumed disability)
- Previous conviction(s), particularly where a pattern of repeat offending is disclosed
- Planning of an offence
- An intention to commit more serious harm than actually resulted from the offence
- Offenders operating in groups or gangs
- "Professional" offending
- Commission of the offence for financial gain (where this is not inherent in the offence itself)
- High level of profit from the offence
- An attempt to conceal or dispose of evidence
- Failure to respond to warnings or concerns expressed by others about the offender's behaviour
- Offence committed whilst on licence
- Offence motivated by hostility towards a minority group, or a member or members of it
- Deliberate targeting of vulnerable victim(s)
- Commission of an offence while under the influence of alcohol or drugs
- Use of a weapon to frighten or injure victim
- Deliberate and gratuitous violence or damage to property, over and above what is needed to carry out the offence
- Abuse of power

- Abuse of a position of trust

1.23 **Factors indicating a more than usually serious degree of harm:**
- Multiple victims
- An especially serious physical or psychological effect on the victim, even if unintended
- A sustained assault or repeated assaults on the same victim
- Victim is particularly vulnerable
- Location of the offence (for example, in an isolated place)
- Offence is committed against those working in the public sector or providing a service to the public
- Presence of others *e.g.* relatives, especially children or partner of the victim
- Additional degradation of the victim (*e.g.* taking photographs of a victim as part of a sexual offence)
- In property offences, high value (including sentimental value) of property to the victim, or substantial consequential loss (*e.g.* where the theft of equipment causes serious disruption to a victim's life or business)

### (ii) Mitigating factors

1.24 Some factors may indicate that an offender's culpability is **unusually** low, or that the harm caused by an offence is less than usually serious. **K-20**

1.25 **Factors indicating significantly lower culpability:**
- A greater degree of provocation than normally expected
- Mental illness or disability
- Youth or age, where it affects the responsibility of the individual defendant
- The fact that the offender played only a minor role in the offence

### (iii) Personal mitigation

1.26 Section 166(1) Criminal Justice Act 2003 makes provision for a sentencer to take account of any matters that "in the opinion of the court, are relevant in mitigation of sentence". **K-21**

1.27 When the court has formed an initial assessment of the seriousness of the offence, then it should consider any offender mitigation. The issue of remorse should be taken into account at this point along with other mitigating features such as admissions to the police in interview.

### (iv) Reduction for a guilty plea

1.28 Sentencers will normally reduce the severity of a sentence to reflect an early guilty plea. This subject is covered by a separate guideline and provides a sliding scale reduction with a normal maximum one-third reduction being given to offenders who enter a guilty plea at the first reasonable opportunity. **K-22**

1.29 Credit may also be given for ready co-operation with the authorities. This will depend on the particular circumstances of the individual case.

E. The Sentencing Thresholds

1.30 Assessing the seriousness of an offence is only the first step in the process of determining the appropriate sentence in an individual case. Matching the offence to a type and level of sentence is a separate and complex exercise assisted by the application of the respective threshold tests for custodial and community sentences. **K-23**

### The custody threshold

1.31 Section 152(2) Criminal Justice Act 2003 provides [see § 5-458 in the main work]. **K-24**

1.32 In applying the threshold test, sentencers should note: the clear intention of the threshold test is to reserve prison as a punishment for the most serious offences;
- it is impossible to determine definitively which features of a particular offence make it serious enough to merit a custodial sentence;
- passing the custody threshold does not mean that a custodial sentence should be deemed inevitable, and custody can still be avoided in the light of personal mitigation or where there is a suitable intervention in the community which provides sufficient restriction (by way of punishment) while addressing the rehabilitation of the offender to prevent future crime. For example, a prolific offender who currently could expect a short custodial sentence (which, in advance of custody plus, would have no provision for supervision on release) might more appropriately receive a suitable community sentence.

1.33   The approach to the imposition of a custodial sentence under the new framework should be as follows:

(a)   has the custody threshold been passed?

(b)   if so, is it unavoidable that a custodial sentence be imposed?

(c)   if so, can that sentence be suspended? (sentencers should be clear that they would have imposed a custodial sentence if the power to suspend had not been available)

(d)   if not, can the sentence be served intermittently?

(e)   if not, impose a sentence which takes immediate effect for the term commensurate with the seriousness of the offence.

**The threshold for community sentences**

K-25        1.34   Section 148(1) Criminal Justice Act 2003 provides [see § 5-248 in the main work].

1.35   In addition, the threshold for a community sentence can be crossed even though the seriousness criterion is not met. Section 151 Criminal Justice Act 2003 provides that, in relation to an offender aged 16 or over on whom, on three or more previous occasions, sentences had been passed consisting only of a fine, a community sentence may be imposed (if it is in the interests of justice) despite the fact that the seriousness of the current offence (and others associated with it) might not warrant such a sentence.

1.36   Sentencers should consider all of the disposals available (within or below the threshold passed) at the time of sentence before reaching the provisional decision to make a community sentence, so that, even where the threshold for a community sentence has been passed, a financial penalty or discharge may still be an appropriate penalty.

**Summary**

K-26        1.37   It would not be feasible to provide a form of words or to devise any formula that would provide a general solution to the problem of where the custody threshold lies. Factors vary too widely between offences for this to be done. It is the task of guidelines for individual offences to provide more detailed guidance on what features within that offence point to a custodial sentence, and also to deal with issues such as sentence length, the appropriate requirements for a community sentence or the use of appropriate ancillary orders.

**Having assessed the seriousness of an individual offence, sentencers must consult the sentencing guidelines for an offence of that type for guidance on the factors that are likely to indicate whether a custodial sentence or other disposal is most likely to be appropriate.**

F. PREVALENCE

K-27        1.38   The seriousness of an individual case should be judged on its own dimensions of harm and culpability rather than as part of a collective social harm. It is legitimate for the overall approach to sentencing levels for particular offences to be guided by their cumulative effect. However, it would be wrong to further penalise individual offenders by increasing sentence length for committing an individual offence of that type.

1.39   There may be exceptional local circumstances that arise which may lead a court to decide that prevalence should influence sentencing levels. The pivotal issue in such cases will be the harm being caused to the community. It is essential that sentencers both have supporting evidence from an external source (for example the local Criminal Justice Board) to justify claims that a particular crime is prevalent in their area and are satisfied that there is a compelling need to treat the offence more seriously than elsewhere.

**The key factor in determining whether sentencing levels should be enhanced in response to prevalence will be the level of harm being caused in the locality. Enhanced sentences should be exceptional and in response to exceptional circumstances. Sentencers must sentence within the sentencing guidelines once the prevalence has been addressed. Having assessed the seriousness of an individual offence, sentencers must consult the sentencing guidelines for an offence of that type for guidance on the factors that are likely to indicate whether a custodial sentence or other disposal is most likely to be appropriate.**

## C. New Sentences: Criminal Justice Act 2003

### GUIDELINE

#### Foreword

In accordance with the provisions of section 170(9) Criminal Justice Act 2003, the Sentencing   **K-28**
Guidelines Council issues this guideline as a definitive guideline. By virtue of section 172 of the Act,
every court must have regard to a relevant guideline.

The Council was created in 2004 in order to frame Guidelines to assist Courts as they deal with
criminal cases across the whole of England and Wales.

This guideline relates to the new sentencing framework introduced by the Criminal Justice Act
2003, which affects the nature of community and custodial sentences. Only those sentences and
related provisions which are expected to come into force by April 2005 are dealt with in this guideline.
It will be followed by further guidelines in due course. This is an unusual guideline since it covers a
range of sentences outside the context of individual offences and does so in readiness for the coming
into force of the statutory provisions creating the sentences. It is designed with the object of ensuring
a consistent approach when the sentences become available.

**This guideline applies only to sentences passed under the sentencing framework applicable to
those aged 18 or over.**

The guideline is divided into two sections:

- Sections 1 covers the practical aspects of implementing the non-custodial powers namely
  the new community sentence and the new form of deferred sentence;
- Section 2 deals with the new custodial sentence provisions relating to suspended
  sentences, prison sentences of 12 months or more, and intermittent custody.[13]

The Act also contains an extensive range of provisions to protect the public from dangerous
offenders. These will be dealt with separately.

The Advice of the Sentencing Advisory Panel to the Council (published on 20th September 2004)
has been broadly accepted by the Council and forms the basis of this guideline. Further information
on the issues covered in this guideline can be found in that Advice or in the discussion document
that preceded it. All these documents are available on www.sentencing-guidelines.gov.uk or from the
Sentencing Guidelines Secretariat.

Chairman of the Council

December 2004

#### Contents

---

[13] References to the Probation Service reflect current roles and responsibilities. By the time these provisions come into
force, some or all of those roles and responsibilities may be those of the National Offender Management Service
(NOMS).

SECTION 1 PART 1—COMMUNITY SENTENCES

### A. Statutory Provisions

*(i) The thresholds for community sentence*

**K-30**    1.1.1  Seriousness—Section 148 Criminal Justice Act 2003 [sets out subsection (1), as to which, see § 5-248 in the main work].

    1.1.2  Persistent offenders—Section 151 Criminal Justice Act 2003 [sets out subsections (1) and (2), as to which, see § 5-252 in the main work].

*(ii) The sentences available*

**K-31**    1.1.3  Meaning of community sentence—Section 147 Criminal Justice Act 2003 [sets out subsection (1), as to which, see § 5-247 in the main work].

    1.1.4  Offenders aged 16 or over—Section 177 Criminal Justice Act 2003 [sets out subsections (1) to (4), as to which, see § 5-253 in the main work].

*(iii) Determining which orders to make & requirements to include*

**K-32**    1.1.5  Suitability—Section 148 Criminal Justice Act 2003 [sets out subsection (2), as to which see § 5-248 in the main work].

    1.1.6  Restrictions on liberty—Section 148 Criminal Justice Act 2003 [sets out subsection (1), as to which see § 5-248 in the main work].

    1.1.7  Compatibility—Section 177 Criminal Justice Act 2003 [sets out subsection (6), as to which see § 5-253 in the main work].

*(iv) Electronic monitoring*

**K-33**    1.1.8  Section 177 Criminal Justice Act 2003 [sets out subsections (3) and (4), as to which see § 5-253 in the main work].

### B. Imposing a Community Sentence—The Approach

**K-34**    1.1.9 On pages 8 and 9 of the seriousness guideline the two thresholds for the imposition of a community sentence are considered. Sentencers must consider all of the disposals available (within or below the threshold passed) at the time of sentence, and reject them before reaching the provisional decision to make a community sentence, so that even where the threshold for a community sentence has been passed a financial penalty or discharge may still be an appropriate penalty. Where an offender has a low risk of reoffending, particular care needs to be taken in the light of evidence that indicates that there are circumstances where inappropriate intervention can increase the risk of re-offending rather than decrease it. In addition, recent improvements in enforcement of financial penalties make them a more viable sentence in a wider range of cases.

    1.1.10 Where an offender is being sentenced for a non-imprisonable offence or offences, great care will be needed in assessing whether a community sentence is appropriate since failure to comply could result in a custodial sentence.

    1.1.11 Having decided (in consultation with the Probation Service where appropriate) that a community sentence is justified, the court must decide which requirements should be included in the community order. The requirements or orders imposed will have the effect of restricting the offender's liberty, whilst providing punishment in the community, rehabilitation for the offender, and/or ensuring that the offender engages in reparative activities.

**The key issues arising are:**
- **(i) which requirements to impose;**
- **(ii) how to make allowance for time spent on remand; and**
- **(iii) how to deal with breaches.**

### (i) Requirements

1.1.12   When deciding which requirements to include, the court must be satisfied on three matters—     **K-35**
- (i) that the **restriction on liberty is commensurate with the seriousness** of the offence(s);[14]
- (ii) that the **requirements are the most suitable** for the offender;[15] and
- (iii) that, where there are two or more requirements included, they are **compatible with each other.**[16]

1.1.13   Sentencers should have the possibility of breach firmly in mind when passing sentence for the original offence. If a court is to reflect the seriousness of an offence, there is little value in setting requirements as part of a community sentence that are not demanding enough for an offender. on the other hand, there is equally little value in imposing requirements that would "set an offender up to fail" and almost inevitably lead to sanctions for a breach.

**In community sentences, the guiding principles are proportionality and suitability. Once a court has decided that the offence has crossed the community sentence threshold and that a community sentence is justified, the initial factor in defining which requirements to include in a community sentence should be the seriousness of the offence committed.**

1.1.14   This means that "seriousness" is an important factor in deciding whether the court chooses the low, medium or high range (see below) but, having taken that decision, selection of the content of the order within the range will be determined by a much wider range of factors.
- **Sentencing ranges must remain flexible enough to take account of the suitability of the offender, his or her ability to comply with particular requirements and their availability in the local area.**
- **The justification for imposing a community sentence in response to persistent petty offending is the persistence of the offending behaviour rather than the seriousness of the offences being committed. The requirements imposed should ensure that the restriction on liberty is proportionate to the seriousness of the offending, to reflect the fact that the offences, of themselves, are not sufficiently serious to merit a community sentence.**

### (a) Information for sentencers

1.1.15   In many cases, a pre-sentence report[17] will be pivotal in helping a sentencer decide     **K-36** whether to impose a custodial sentence or whether to impose a community sentence and, if so, whether particular requirements, or combinations of requirements, are suitable for an individual offender. The court must always ensure (especially where there are multiple requirements) that the restriction on liberty placed on the offender is proportionate to the seriousness of the offence committed.[18] The court must also consider the likely effect of one requirement on another, and that they do not place conflicting demands upon the offender.[19]

1.1.16   The council supports the approach proposed by the panel at paragraph 78 of its advice that, having reached the provisional view that a community sentence is the most appropriate disposal, the sentencer should request a pre-sentence report, indicating which of the three sentencing ranges is relevant and the purpose(s) of sentencing that the package of requirements is required to fulfil. Usually the most helpful way for the court to do this would be to produce a written note for the report writer, copied on the court file. If it is known that the same tribunal and defence advocate will be present at the sentencing hearing and a probation officer is present in court when the request for

---

[14] Criminal Justice Act 2003 section 148(2)(b).
[15] *ibid.*, section 148(2)(a).
[16] *ibid.*, section 177(6).
[17] Under the Act, a pre-sentence report includes a full report following adjournment, a specific sentence report, a short format report or an oral report. The type of report supplied will depend on the level of information requested. Wherever it appears, the term "pre-sentence report" includes all these types of report.
[18] Criminal Justice Act 2003 section 148(2).
[19] *ibid.*, section 177(6).

a report is made, it may not be necessary to commit details of the request to writing. However, events may change during the period of an adjournment and it is good practice to ensure that there is a clear record of the request for the court. These two factors will guide the Probation Service in determining the nature and combination of requirements that may be appropriate and the onerousness and intensity of those requirements. A similar procedure should apply when ordering a pre-sentence report when a custodial sentence is being considered.

1.1.17   There will be occasions when any type of report may be unnecessary despite the intention to pass a community sentence though this is likely to be infrequent. A court could consider dispensing with the need to obtain a pre-sentence report for adult offenders—

- where the offence falls within the LOW range of seriousness (see pp.9-10); and
- where the sentencer was minded to impose a single requirement, such as an exclusion requirement (where the circumstances of the case mean that this would be an appropriate disposal without electronic monitoring); and
- where the sentence will not require the involvement of the Probation Service, for example an electronically monitored curfew (subject to the court being satisfied that there is an appropriate address at which the curfew can operate).

**(b)  Ranges of sentence within the community sentence band**

**K-37**     1.1.18   To enable the court to benefit from the flexibility that community sentences provide and also to meet its statutory obligations, any structure governing the use of community requirements must allow the courts to choose the most appropriate sentence for each individual offender.

1.1.19   Sentencers have a statutory obligation to pass sentences that are commensurate with the seriousness of an offence. However, within the range of sentence justified by the seriousness of the offence(s), courts will quite properly consider those factors that heighten the risk of the offender committing further offences or causing further harm with a view to lessening that risk. The extent to which requirements are imposed must be capable of being varied to ensure that the restriction on liberty is commensurate with the seriousness of the offence.

1.1.20   The council recognises that it would be helpful for sentencers to have a framework to help them decide on the most appropriate use of the new community sentence. While there is no single guiding principle, the seriousness of the offence that has been committed is an important factor. Three sentencing ranges (low, medium and high) within the community sentence band can be identified. It is not possible to position particular types of offence at firm points within the three ranges because the seriousness level of an offence is largely dependent upon the culpability of the offender and this is uniquely variable. The difficulty is particularly acute in relation to the medium range where it is clear that requirements will need to be tailored across a relatively wide range of offending behaviour.

1.1.21   In general terms, the lowest range of community sentence would be for those offenders whose offence was relatively minor within the community sentence band and would include persistent petty offenders whose offences only merit a community sentence by virtue of failing to respond to the previous imposition of fines. Such offenders would merit a 'light touch' approach, for example, normally a single requirement such as a short period of unpaid work, or a curfew, or a prohibited activity requirement or an exclusion requirement (where the circumstances of the case mean that this would be an appropriate disposal without electronic monitoring).

1.1.22   The top range would be for those offenders who have only just fallen short of a custodial sentence and for those who have passed the threshold but for whom a community sentence is deemed appropriate.

1.1.23   In all three ranges there must be sufficient flexibility to allow the sentence to be varied to take account of the suitability of particular requirements for the individual offender and whether a particular requirement or package of requirements might be more effective at reducing any identified risk of re-offending. It will fall to the sentencer to ensure that the sentence strikes the right balance between proportionality and suitability.

**There should be three sentencing ranges (low, medium and high) within the community sentence band based upon seriousness.**

**It is not intended that an offender necessarily progress from one range to the next on each sentencing occasion. The decision as to the appropriate range each time is based upon the seriousness of the new offence(s).**

**The decision on the nature and severity of the requirements to be included in a community sentence should be guided by:**

   **(i) the assessment of offence seriousness (low, medium or high);**
   **(ii) the purpose(s) of sentencing the court wishes to achieve;**
   **(iii) the risk of re-offending;**

**(iv) the ability of the offender to comply, and**

**(v) the availability of requirements in the local area.**

**The resulting restriction on liberty must be a proportionate response to the offence that was committed.**

1.1.24   Below we set out a non-exhaustive description of examples of requirements that might be appropriate in the three sentencing ranges. These examples focus on punishment in the community, although it is recognised that not all packages will necessarily need to include a punitive requirement. There will clearly be other requirements of a rehabilitative nature, such as a treatment requirement or an accredited programme, which may be appropriate depending on the specific needs of the offender and assessment of suitability. Given the intensity of such interventions, it is expected that these would normally only be appropriate at medium and high levels of seriousness, and where assessed as having a medium or high risk of re-offending. In addition, when passing sentence in any one of the three ranges, the court should consider whether a rehabilitative intervention such as a programme requirement, or a restorative justice intervention might be suitable as an additional or alternative part of the sentence.

*Low*

1.1.25   For offences only just crossing the community sentence threshold (such as persistent petty   **K-38**
offending, some public order offences, some thefts from shops, or interference with a motor vehicle, where the seriousness of the offence or the nature of the offender's record means that a discharge or fine is inappropriate).

1.1.26   Suitable requirements might include:

- 40 to 80 hours of unpaid work; or
- a curfew requirement within the lowest range (*e.g.* up to 12 hours per day for a few weeks); or
- an exclusion requirement (where the circumstances of the case mean that this would be an appropriate disposal without electronic monitoring) lasting a few months; or
- a prohibited activity requirement; or
- an attendance centre requirement (where available).

1.1.27   Since the restriction on liberty must be commensurate with the seriousness of the offence, particular care needs to be taken with this band to ensure that this obligation is complied with. In most cases, only one requirement will be appropriate and the length may be curtailed if additional requirements are necessary.

*Medium*

1.1.28   For offences that obviously fall within the community sentence band such as handling   **K-39**
stolen goods worth less than £1000 acquired for resale or somewhat more valuable goods acquired for the handler's own use, some cases of burglary in commercial premises, some cases of taking a motor vehicle without consent, or some cases of obtaining property by deception.

1.1.29   Suitable requirements might include:

- a greater number (*e.g.* 80 to 150) of hours of unpaid work; or
- an activity requirement in the middle range (20 to 30 days); or
- a curfew requirement within the middle range (*e.g.* up to 12 hours for 2-3 months); or
- an exclusion requirement lasting in the region of six months or
- a prohibited activity requirement.

1.1.30   Since the restriction on liberty must be commensurate with the seriousness of the offence, particular care needs to be taken with this band to ensure that this obligation is complied with.

*High*

1.1.31   For offences that only just fall below the custody threshold or where the custody threshold   **K-40**
is crossed but a community sentence is more appropriate in all the circumstances, for example some cases displaying the features of a standard domestic burglary committed by a first-time offender.

1.1.32   More intensive sentences which combine two or more requirements may be appropriate at this level. Suitable requirements might include an unpaid work order of between 150 and 300 hours; an activity requirement up to the maximum 60 days; an exclusion order lasting in the region of 12 months; a curfew requirement of up to 12 hours a day for 4-6 months.

### (c) Electronic monitoring

**K-41**

1.1.33   The court must also consider whether an electronic monitoring requirement[20] should be imposed which is mandatory[21] in some circumstances.

**Electronic monitoring should be used with the primary purpose of promoting and monitoring compliance with other requirements, in circumstances where the punishment of the offender and/or the need to safeguard the public and prevent re-offending are the most important concerns.**

### (d) Recording the sentence imposed

**K-42**

1.1.34   Under the new framework there is only one (generic) community sentence provided by statute. This does not mean that offenders who have completed a community sentence and have then re-offended should be regarded as ineligible for a second community sentence on the basis that this has been tried and failed. Further community sentences, perhaps with different requirements, may well be justified.

1.1.35   Those imposing sentence will wish to be clear about the 'purposes' that the community sentence is designed to achieve when setting the requirements. Sharing those purposes with the offender and Probation Service will enable them to be clear about the goals that are to be achieved.

1.1.36   Any future sentencer must have full information about the requirements that were inserted by the court into the previous community sentence imposed on the offender (including whether it was a low/medium/high level order) and also about the offender's response. This will enable the court to consider the merits of imposing the same or different requirements as part of another community sentence. The requirements should be recorded in such a way as to ensure that they can be made available to another court if another offence is committed.

**When an offender is required to serve a community sentence, the court records should be clearly annotated to show which particular requirements have been imposed.**

#### (ii) Time spent on remand

**K-43**

1.1.37   The court will need to consider whether to give any credit for time spent in custody on remand.[22] (For further detail from the Panel's Advice, see Annex A.)

**The court should seek to give credit for time spent on remand (in custody or equivalent status) in all cases. It should make clear, when announcing sentence, whether or not credit for time on remand has been given (bearing in mind that there will be no automatic reduction in sentence once section 67 of the Criminal Justice Act 1967 is repealed) and should explain its reasons for not giving credit when it considers either that this is not justified, would not be practical, or would not be in the best interests of the offender.**

1.1.38   Where an offender has spent a period of time in custody on remand, there will be occasions where a custodial sentence is warranted but the length of the sentence justified by the seriousness of the offence would mean that the offender would be released immediately. Under the present framework, it may be more appropriate to pass a community sentence since that will ensure supervision on release.

1.1.39   However, given the changes in the content of the second part of a custodial sentence of 12 months or longer, a court in this situation where the custodial sentence would be 12 months or more should, under the new framework, pass a custodial sentence in the knowledge that licence requirements will be imposed on release from custody. This will ensure that the sentence imposed properly reflects the seriousness of the offence.

1.1.40   Recommendations made by the court at the point of sentence will be of particular importance in influencing the content of the licence. This will properly reflect the gravity of the offence(s) committed.

#### (iii) Breaches

**K-44**

1.1.41   Where an offender fails, without reasonable excuse, to comply with one or more requirements, the 'responsible officer'[23] can either give a warning or initiate breach proceedings. Where the offender fails to comply without reasonable excuse for the second time within a 12-month period, the 'responsible officer' must initiate proceedings.

---

[20] *ibid.*, section 177(3) and (4).
[21] Unless the necessary facilities are not available or, in the particular circumstances of the case, the court considers it inappropriate.
[22] Criminal Justice Act 2003 section 149.
[23] Criminal Justice Act 2003 Schedule 8, paragraphs 5-6.

1.1.42   In such proceedings the court must[24] either **increase the severity of the existing sentence** (i.e. impose more onerous conditions including requirements aimed at enforcement, such as a curfew or supervision requirement) or **revoke the existing sentence and proceed as though sentencing for the original offence**. The court is required to take account of the circumstances of the breach,[25] which will inevitably have an impact on its response.

1.1.43   In certain circumstances (where an offender has wilfully and persistently failed to comply with an order made in respect of an offence that is not itself punishable by imprisonment), the court can **impose a maximum of 51 weeks custody**.[26]

1.1.44   When increasing the onerousness of requirements, the court must consider the impact on the offender's ability to comply and the possibility of precipitating a custodial sentence for further breach. For that reason, and particularly where the breach occurs towards the end of the sentence, the court should take account of compliance to date and may consider that extending the supervision or operational periods will be more sensible; in other cases it might choose to add punitive or rehabilitative requirements instead. In making these changes the court must be mindful of the legislative restrictions on the overall length of community sentences and on the supervision and operational periods allowed for each type of requirement.

1.1.45   The court dealing with breach of a community sentence should have as its primary objective ensuring that the requirements of the sentence are finished, and this is important if the court is to have regard to the statutory purposes of sentencing. A court that imposes a custodial sentence for breach without giving adequate consideration to alternatives is in danger of imposing a sentence that is not commensurate with the seriousness of the original offence and is solely a punishment for breach. This risks undermining the purposes it has identified as being important. Nonetheless, courts will need to be vigilant to ensure that there is a realistic prospect of the purposes of the order being achieved.

**Having decided that a community sentence is commensurate with the seriousness of the offence, the primary objective when sentencing for breach of requirements is to ensure that those requirements are completed.**

1.1.46   A court sentencing for breach must take account of the extent to which the offender has complied with the requirements of the community order, the reasons for breach and the point at which the breach has occurred. Where a breach takes place towards the end of the operational period and the court is satisfied that the offender's appearance before the court is likely to be sufficient in itself to ensure future compliance, then given that it is not open to the court to make no order, an approach that the court might wish to adopt could be to re-sentence in a way that enables the original order to be completed properly—for example, a differently constructed community sentence that aims to secure compliance with the purposes of the original sentence.

1.1.47   If the court decides to increase the onerousness of an order, it must give careful consideration, with advice from the Probation Service, to the offender's ability to comply. A custodial sentence should be the last resort, where all reasonable efforts to ensure that an offender completes a community sentence have failed.

- **The Act allows for a custodial sentence to be imposed in response to breach of a community sentence. Custody should be the last resort, reserved for those cases of deliberate and repeated breach where all reasonable efforts to ensure that the offender complies have failed.**

- **Before increasing the onerousness of requirements, sentencers should take account of the offender's ability to comply and should avoid precipitating further breach by overloading the offender with too many or conflicting requirements.**

- **There may be cases where the court will need to consider re-sentencing to a differently constructed community sentence in order to secure compliance with the purposes of the original sentence, perhaps where there has already been partial compliance or where events since the sentence was imposed have shown that a different course of action is likely to be effective.**

---

[24] *ibid.*, paragraphs 9-10.
[25] *ibid.*, paragraph 9(2).
[26] *ibid.*, paragraph 9(1)(c).

### A. Statutory Provisions

**K-45**   1.2.1 Under the existing legislation,[27] a court can defer a sentence for up to six months, provided the offender consents and the court considers that deferring the sentence is in the interests of justice.

1.2.2 The new provisions[28] continue to require the consent of the offender and that the court be satisfied that the making of such a decision is in the interests of justice. However, it is also stated that the power to defer sentence can only be exercised where:

> "the offender undertakes to comply with any requirements as to his conduct during the period of the deferment that the court considers it appropriate to impose;".[29]

1.2.3 This enables the court to impose a wide variety of conditions (including a residence requirement).[30] The Act allows the court to appoint the probation service or other responsible person to oversee the offender's conduct during this period and prepare a report for the court at the point of sentence i.e. the end of the deferment period.

1.2.4 As under the existing legislation, if the offender commits another offence during the deferment period the court may have the power to sentence for both the original and the new offence at once. Sentence cannot be deferred for more than six months and, in most circumstances, no more than one period of deferment can be granted.[31]

1.2.5 A significant change is the provision enabling a court to deal with an offender before the end of the period of deferment.[32] For example if the court is satisfied that the offender has failed to comply with one or more requirements imposed in connection with the deferment, the offender can be brought back before the court and the court can proceed to sentence.

### B. Use of Deferred Sentences

**K-46**   1.2.6 Under the new framework, there is a wider range of sentencing options open to the courts, including the increased availability of suspended sentences, and deferred sentences are likely to be used in very limited circumstances. A deferred sentence enables the court to review the conduct of the defendant before passing sentence, having first prescribed certain requirements. It also provides several opportunities for an offender to have some influence as to the sentence passed—

(a) it tests the commitment of the offender not to re-offend;

(b) it gives the offender an opportunity to do something where progress can be shown within a short period;

(c) it provides the offender with an opportunity to behave or refrain from behaving in a particular way that will be relevant to sentence.

1.2.7 Given the new power to require undertakings and the ability to enforce those undertakings before the end of the period of deferral, the decision to defer sentence should be predominantly for a small group of cases at either the custody threshold or the community sentence threshold where the sentencer feels that there would be particular value in giving the offender the opportunities listed because, if the offender complies with the requirements, a different sentence will be justified at the end of the deferment period. This could be a community sentence instead of a custodial sentence or a fine or discharge instead of a community sentence. It may, rarely, enable a custodial sentence to be suspended rather than imposed immediately.

> **The use of deferred sentences should be predominantly for a small group of cases close to a significant threshold where, should the defendant be prepared to adapt his behaviour in a way clearly specified by the sentencer, the court may be prepared to impose a lesser sentence.**

1.2.8 A court may impose any conditions during the period of deferment that it considers appropriate.[33] These could be specific requirements as set out in the provisions for community sentences,[34] or requirements that are drawn more widely. These should be specific, measurable conditions so that the offender knows exactly what is required and the court can assess compliance; the restriction on liberty should be limited to ensure that the offender has a reasonable expectation of being able to comply whilst maintaining his or her social responsibilities.

---

[27] Powers of Criminal Courts (Sentencing) Act 2000 sections 1 and 2.
[28] Criminal Justice Act 2003 schedule 23 repealing and replacing sections 1 and 2 of the 2000 Act.
[29] *ibid.*, new section 1(3)(b) as inserted by Schedule 23 to the Criminal Justice Act 2003.
[30] *ibid.*, new section 1A(1).
[31] *ibid.*, new section 1(4).
[32] *ibid.*, new section 1B.
[33] *ibid.*, new section 1 (3)(b) as inserted by Schedule 23 to the Criminal Justice Act 2003.
[34] Criminal Justice Act 2003 section 177.

1.2.9 Given the need for clarity in the mind of the offender and the possibility of sentence by another court, the court should give a clear indication (and make a written record) of the type of sentence it would be minded to impose if it had not decided to defer and ensure that the offender understands the consequences of failure to comply with the court's wishes during the deferral period.

**When deferring sentence, the sentencer must make clear the consequence of not complying with any requirements and should indicate the type of sentence it would be minded to impose. Sentencers should impose specific, measurable conditions that do not involve a serious restriction on liberty.**

SECTION 2—CUSTODIAL SENTENCES PART 1—CUSTODIAL SENTENCES OF 12 MONTHS OR MORE

### A. Statutory Provisions

2.1.1 Under existing legislation:    **K-47**

- an adult offender receiving a custodial sentence of at least 12 months and below 4 years will automatically be released at the halfway point and will then be supervised under licence until the three-quarter point of the sentence. [For some, the actual release date may be earlier as a result of release on home detention curfew (HDC).]
- an adult offender receiving a determinate sentence of 4 years or above will be eligible for release from the halfway point and, if not released before, will automatically be released at the two-thirds point. After release, the offender will be supervised under licence until the three-quarter point of the sentence.

2.1.2 Under the new framework, the impact of a custodial sentence will be more severe since the period in custody and under supervision will be for the whole of the sentence term set by the court. Additionally, separate provisions for the protection of the public will be introduced for those offenders designated as "dangerous" under the Act which are designed to ensure that release only occurs when it is considered safe to do so.

2.1.3 Where a prison sentence of 12 months or more is imposed on an offender who is not classified as "dangerous", that offender will be entitled to be released from custody after completing half of the sentence. The whole of the second half of the sentence will be subject to licence requirements. These requirements will be set shortly before release by the Secretary of State (with advice from the Governor responsible for authorising the prisoner's release in consultation with the Probation Service) but a court will be able to make recommendations at the sentencing stage on the content of those requirements.[35] The conditions that the Secretary of State may attach to a licence are to be prescribed by order.[36]

2.1.4 The Act requires that a custodial sentence for a fixed term should be for the shortest term that is commensurate with the seriousness of the offence.[37]

### B. Imposition of Custodial Sentences of 12 Months or More

*(i) Length of sentence*

2.1.5 The requirement that the second half of a prison sentence will be served in the community    **K-48**
subject to conditions imposed prior to release is a major new development and will require offenders to be under supervision for the full duration of the sentence prescribed by the court. The Probation Service will be able to impose a number of complementary requirements on the offender during the second half of a custodial sentence and these are expected to be more demanding and involve a greater restriction on liberty than current licence conditions.

2.1.6 As well as restricting liberty to a greater extent, the new requirements will last until the very end of the sentence, rather than to the three-quarter point as at present, potentially making a custodial sentence significantly more demanding than under existing legislation. Breach of these requirements at any stage is likely to result in the offender being returned to custody and this risk continues, therefore, for longer under the new framework than under the existing legislation.

**Transitional arrangements**

2.1.7 In general, a fixed term custodial sentence of 12 months or more under the new framework    **K-49**
will increase the sentence actually served (whether in custody or in the community) since it continues to the end of the term imposed. Existing guidelines issued since 1991 have been based on a different

---

[35] Criminal Justice Act 2003 section 238(1).
[36] *ibid.*, section 250.
[37] *ibid.*, section 153(2).

framework and so, in order to maintain consistency between the lengths of sentence under the current and the new framework, there will need to be some adjustment to the starting points for custodial sentences contained in those guidelines (subject to the special sentences under the 2003 Act where the offender is a "dangerous" offender).

2.1.8   This aspect of the guideline will be temporary to overcome the short-term situation where sentencing guidelines (issued since implementation of the reforms to custodial sentences introduced by the Criminal Justice Act 1991) are based on a different framework and the new framework has made those sentences more demanding. As new guidelines are issued they will take into account the new framework in providing starting points and ranges of appropriate sentence lengths for offences and an adjustment will not be necessary.

2.1.9   Since there are so many factors that will vary, it is difficult to calculate precisely how much more demanding a sentence under the new framework will be. The council's conclusion is that the sentencer should seek to achieve the best match between a sentence under the new framework and its equivalent under the old framework so as to maintain the same level of punishment. As a guide, the Council suggests the sentence length should be reduced by in the region of 15%.

2.1.10   The changes in the nature of a custodial sentence will require changes in the way the sentence is announced. Sentencers will need to continue[38] to spell out the practical implications of the sentence being imposed so that offenders, victims and the public alike all understand that the sentence does not end when the offender is released from custody. The fact that a breach of the requirements imposed in the second half of the sentence is likely to result in a return to custody should also be made very clear at the point of sentence.

- **When imposing a fixed term custodial sentence of 12 months or more under the new provisions, courts should consider reducing the overall length of the sentence that would have been imposed under the current provisions by in the region of 15%.**
- **When announcing sentence, sentencers should explain the way in which the sentence has been calculated, how it will be served and the implications of non-compliance with licence requirements. In particular, it needs to be stated clearly that the sentence is in two parts, one in custody and one under supervision in the community.**
- **This proposal does not apply to sentences for dangerous offenders, for which separate provision has been made in the Act.**

*(ii)  Licence conditions*

K-50

2.1.11   Under the Act, a court imposing a prison sentence of 12 months or more may recommend conditions that should be imposed by the Secretary of State (with advice from the governor responsible for authorising the prisoner's release in consultation with the Probation Service) on release from custody.[39] Recommendations do not form part of the sentence and they are not binding on the Secretary of State.[40]

2.1.12   When passing such a sentence, the court will not know with any certainty to what extent the offender's behaviour may have been addressed in custody or what the offender's health and other personal circumstances might be on release and so it will be extremely difficult, especially in the case of longer custodial sentences, for sentencers to make an informed judgement about the most appropriate licence conditions to be imposed on release. However, in most cases, it would be extremely helpful for sentencers to indicate areas of an offender's behaviour about which they have the most concern and to make suggestions about the types of intervention whether this, in practice, takes place in prison or in the community.

2.1.13   The involvement of the Probation Service at the pre-sentence stage will clearly be pivotal. A recommendation on the likely post-release requirements included in a presentence report will assist the court with the decision on overall sentence length, although any recommendation would still have to be open to review when release is being considered. A curfew, exclusion requirement or prohibited activity requirement might be suitable conditions to recommend for the licence period. A court might also wish to suggest that the offender should complete a rehabilitation programme, for example for drug abuse, anger management, or improving skills such as literacy and could recommend that this should be considered as a licence requirement if the programme has not been undertaken or completed in custody.

2.1.14   The governor responsible for authorising the prisoner's release, in consultation with the Probation Service, is best placed to make recommendations at the point of release; this is the case at present and continues to be provided for in the Act. Specific court recommendations will only generally be appropriate in the context of relatively short sentences, where it would not be unreasonable

---

[38] Having reference to the *Consolidated Criminal Practice Direction* [2002] 2 Cr App R 533, Annex C, as suitably amended.
[39] Criminal Justice Act 2003 section 238(1).
[40] *ibid.*, section 250.

for the sentencer to anticipate the relevance of particular requirements at the point of release. Making recommendations in relation to longer sentences (other than suggestions about the types of intervention that might be appropriate at some point during the sentence) would be unrealistic. The governor and Probation Service should have due regard to any recommendations made by the sentencing court and the final recommendation to the Secretary of State on licence conditions will need to build upon any interventions during the custodial period and any other changes in the offender's circumstances.

- **A court may sensibly suggest interventions that could be useful when passing sentence, but should only make specific recommendations about the requirements to be imposed on licence when announcing short sentences and where it is reasonable to anticipate their relevance at the point of release. The governor and Probation Service should have due regard to any recommendations made by the sentencing court but its decision should be contingent upon any changed circumstances during the custodial period.**
- **The court should make it clear, at the point of sentence, that the requirements to be imposed on licence will ultimately be the responsibility of the Governor and Probation Service and that they are entitled to review any recommendations made by the court in the light of any changed circumstances.**

SECTION 2 PART 2—SUSPENDED SENTENCES OF IMPRISONMENT

### A. Statutory Provisions

2.2.1 Section 189 Criminal Justice Act 2003 [sets out full text of section 189, as to which, see § 5-547 in the main work]. **K-51**

2.2.2 Imposition of requirements—Section 190 Criminal Justice Act 2003 [sets out full text of section 190, as to which, see § 5-556 in the main work]. **K-52**

2.2.3 Power to provide for review—Section 191 Criminal Justice Act 2003 [sets out full text of section 191, as to which, see § 5-551 in the main work]. **K-53**

2.2.4 Periodic reviews—Section 192 Criminal Justice Act 2003 [sets out full text of section 192, as to which, see § 5-552 in the main work]. **K-54**

2.2.5 Breach, revocation or amendment of orders, and effect of further conviction—Section 193 Criminal Justice Act 2003 [sets out full text of section 193, as to which, see § 5-554 in the main work]. **K-55**

### B. Imposing A Suspended Sentence

2.2.6 A suspended sentence is a sentence of imprisonment. it is subject to the same criteria as a sentence of imprisonment which is to commence immediately. in particular, this requires a court to be satisfied that the custody threshold has been passed and that the length of the term is the shortest term commensurate with the seriousness of the offence. **K-56**

2.2.7 A court which passes a prison sentence of less than 12 months may suspend it for between six months and two years (the operational period).[41] During that period, the court can impose one or more requirements for the offender to undertake in the community. The requirements are identical to those available for the new community sentence.

2.2.8 The period during which the offender undertakes community requirements is "the supervision period" when the offender will be under the supervision of a "responsible officer"; this period may be shorter than the operational period. The court may periodically review the progress of the offender in complying with the requirements and the reviews will be informed by a report from the responsible officer.

2.2.9 If the offender fails to comply with a requirement during the supervision period, or commits a further offence during the operational period, the suspended sentence can be activated in full or in part or the terms of the supervision made more onerous. There is a presumption that the suspended sentence will be activated either in full or in part.

#### (i) The decision to suspend

2.2.10 There are many similarities between the suspended sentence and the community sentence. in both cases, requirements can be imposed during the supervision period and the court can respond to breach by sending the offender to custody. The crucial difference is that the suspended sentence is a prison sentence and is appropriate only for an offence that passes the custody threshold and for which imprisonment is the only option. A community sentence may also be imposed for an offence that passes the custody threshold where the court considers that to be appropriate. **K-57**

---

[41] The power to suspend a sentence is expected to come into force earlier than the provisions implementing "custody plus" and transitional provisions are expected to enable any sentence of imprisonment of under 12 months to be suspended. This guideline therefore is written in the language of the expected transitional provisions.

2.2.11    The full decision making process for imposition of custodial sentences under the new framework (including the custody threshold test) is set out in paragraphs 1.31-1.33 of the seriousness guideline. For the purposes of suspended sentences the relevant steps are:

    (a) has the custody threshold been passed?

    (b) if so, is it unavoidable that a custodial sentence be imposed?

    (c) if so, can that sentence be suspended? (sentencers should be clear that they would have imposed a custodial sentence if the power to suspend had not been available)

    (d) if not, can the sentence be served intermittently?

    (e) if not, impose a sentence which takes immediate effect for the term commensurate with the seriousness of the offence.

*(ii) Length of sentence*

**K-58**

2.2.12    Before making the decision to suspend sentence, the court must already have decided that a prison sentence is justified and should also have decided the length of sentence that would be the shortest term commensurate with the seriousness of the offence if it were to be imposed immediately. The decision to suspend the sentence should not lead to a longer term being imposed than if the sentence were to take effect immediately.

**A prison sentence that is suspended should be for the same term that would have applied if the offender were being sentenced to immediate custody.**

2.2.13    When assessing the length of the operational period of a suspended sentence, the court should have in mind the relatively short length of the sentence being suspended and the advantages to be gained by retaining the opportunity to extend the operational period at a later stage (see below).

**The operational period of a suspended sentence should reflect the length of the sentence being suspended. As an approximate guide, an operational period of up to 12 months might normally be appropriate for a suspended sentence of up to 6 months and an operational period of up to 18 months might normally be appropriate for a suspended sentence of up to 12 months.**

*(iii) Requirements*

**K-59**

2.2.14    The court will set the requirements to be complied with during the supervision period. Whilst the offence for which a suspended sentence is imposed is generally likely to be more serious than one for which a community sentence is imposed, the imposition of the custodial sentence is a clear punishment and deterrent. In order to ensure that the overall terms of the sentence are commensurate with the seriousness of the offence, it is likely that the requirements to be undertaken during the supervision period would be less onerous than if a community sentence had been imposed. These requirements will need to ensure that they properly address those factors that are most likely to reduce the risk of re-offending.

**Because of the very clear deterrent threat involved in a suspended sentence, requirements imposed as part of that sentence should generally be less onerous than those imposed as part of a community sentence. A court wishing to impose onerous or intensive requirements on an offender should reconsider its decision to suspend sentence and consider whether a community sentence might be more appropriate.**

**C. Breaches**

**K-60**

2.2.15  The essence of a suspended sentence is to make it abundantly clear to an offender that failure to comply with the requirements of the order or commission of another offence will almost certainly result in a custodial sentence. Where an offender has breached any of the requirements without reasonable excuse for the first time, the responsible officer must either give a warning or initiate breach proceedings.[42] Where there is a further breach within a twelve-month period, breach proceedings must be initiated.[43]

2.2.16  Where proceedings are brought the court has several options, including extending the operational period. However, the presumption (which also applies where breach is by virtue of the commission of a further offence) is that the suspended prison sentence will be activated (either with its original custodial term or a lesser term) unless the court takes the view that this would, in all the

---

[42] Criminal Justice Act 2003 schedule 12, para. 4.
[43] *ibid.*, para. 5.

circumstances, be unjust. In reaching that decision, the court may take into account both the extent to which the offender has complied with the requirements and the facts of the new offence.[44]

2.2.17 Where a court considers that the sentence needs to be activated, it may activate it in full or with a reduced term. Again, the extent to which the requirements have been complied with will be very relevant to this decision.

2.2.18 If a court amends the order rather than activating the suspended prison sentence, it must either make the requirements more onerous, or extend the supervision or operational periods (provided that these remain within the limits defined by the Act).[45] In such cases, the court must state its reasons for not activating the prison sentence,[46] which could include the extent to which the offender has complied with requirements or the facts of the subsequent offence.

2.2.19 If an offender near the end of an operational period (having complied with the requirements imposed) commits another offence, it may be more appropriate to amend the order rather than activate it.

2.2.20 If a new offence committed is of a less serious nature than the offence for which the suspended sentence was passed, it may justify activating the sentence with a reduced term or amending the terms of the order.

2.2.21 It is expected that any activated suspended sentence will be consecutive to the sentence imposed for the new offence.

2.2.22 If the new offence is non-imprisonable, the sentencer should consider whether it is appropriate to activate the suspended sentence at all.

**Where the court decides to amend a suspended sentence order rather than activate the custodial sentence, it should give serious consideration to extending the supervision or operational periods (within statutory limits) rather than making the requirements more onerous.**

## ANNEX A

### Time spent on remand—Sentencing Advisory Panel's advice

The Act makes provision for a sentencer to give credit for time spent on remand in custody where **K-70** a custodial sentence is passed.[47] It also empowers the court to have regard to time spent on remand in custody when determining the restrictions on liberty to be imposed by a community order or youth community order.[48] Where an offender has spent several weeks in custody, this may affect the nature of the offence that is passed. For example, where the court decides that a custodial sentence is justified some sentencers may decide to pass a community sentence instead, on the basis that the offender has already completed the equivalent of a punitive element in a sentence. The Panel takes the view that, given the changes in the content of the second part of a custodial sentence, in such cases it will be more appropriate to pass a custodial sentence knowing that licence requirements will be imposed on release from custody (which may be immediate). Recommendations made by the court at the point of sentence will then be of particular importance in influencing the content of the licence. This will help to ensure that the record clearly shows the assessment of seriousness of the offending behaviour.

Whereas the Act clearly states that time spent on remand is to be regarded as part of a custodial sentence unless the Court considers it unjust,[49] it states that sentencers passing a community sentence may have regard to time spent on remand, but no further information is given on how this discretion should be exercised. The Panel recognises that giving credit for time spent on remand is likely to be easier to apply in relation to punitive requirements rather than the rehabilitative elements of a community sentence. For example, reducing the number of unpaid work hours could be fairly easy, whereas reducing the length of a rehabilitation programme might not be appropriate as it could undermine its effectiveness. Where an offender has been kept on remand, one could take the view that this action was justified by the bail provisions and that the sentencer should not, therefore, feel obliged to adjust the terms of the community sentence. However, in principle, the Panel recommends that the court should seek to give credit for time spent on remand in all cases and should explain its reasons for not doing so when it considers either that this is not justified, would not be practical, or would not be in the best interests of the offender.

*The court should seek to give credit for time spent on remand in all cases. It should make clear, when announc-*

[44] *ibid.*, para. 8(4).
[45] *ibid.*, section 189(3) and (4).
[46] *ibid.*, schedule 12, para. 8(3).
[47] Criminal Justice Act 2003 section 240.
[48] *ibid.*, section 149.
[49] *ibid.*, section 240 (which will, at a future date, replace Criminal Justice Act 1967, section 67, by which such period is now deducted automatically).

*ing sentence, whether or not credit for time on remand has been given and should explain its reasons for not giving credit when it considers either that this is not justified, would not be practical, or would not be in the best interests of the offender.*

**Where, following a period of time spent in custody on remand, the court decides that a custodial sentence is justified then, given the changes in the content of the second part of a custodial sentence, the court should pass a custodial sentence in the knowledge that licence requirements will be imposed on release from custody. Recommendations made by the court at the point of sentence will be of particular importance in influencing the content of the licence.**[50]

## D. Manslaughter by Reason of Provocation

### GUIDELINE

#### Foreword

**K-71**   In accordance with section 170(9) of the Criminal Justice Act 2003, the Sentencing Guidelines Council issues this guideline as a definitive guideline. By virtue of section 172 of the Act, every court must have regard to a relevant guideline. This guideline applies to offenders convicted of manslaughter by reason of provocation who are sentenced after 28 November 2005.

This guideline stems from a reference from the Home Secretary for consideration of the issue of sentencing where provocation is argued in cases of homicide, and, in particular, domestic violence homicides. For the purpose of describing "domestic violence", the Home Secretary adopted the Crown Prosecution Service definition.[51] The guideline applies to sentencing of an adult offender for this offence in whatever circumstances it occurs. it identifies the widely varying features of both the provocation and the act of retaliation and sets out the approach to be adopted in deciding both the sentencing range and the starting point within that range.

**This guideline is for use where the conviction for manslaughter is clearly founded on provocation alone. There will be additional, different and more complicated matters to be taken into account where the other main partial defence, diminished responsibility, is a factor.**

The Council's Guideline *New Sentences: Criminal Justice Act 2003* recognised the potentially more demanding nature of custodial sentences of 12 months or longer imposed under the new framework introduced by the Criminal Justice Act 2003. Consequently the sentencing ranges and starting points in this guideline take that principle into account.

Guidelines are created following extensive consultation. The Sentencing Advisory Panel first consults widely on the basis of a thoroughly researched consultation paper, then provides the Council with advice. Having considered the advice, the Council prepares a draft guideline on which there is further consultation with Parliament, with the Home Secretary and with Ministers of other relevant Government Departments. This guideline is the culmination of that process.

The Council has appreciated greatly the work of the Sentencing Advisory Panel in preparing the advice on which this guideline has been based and for those who have responded so thoughtfully to the consultation of both the Panel and the Council.

The advice and this guideline are available on www.sentencing-guidelines.gov.uk or from the Sentencing Guidelines Secretariat at 85 Buckingham Gate, London SW1E 6PD. A summary of the responses to the Council's consultation also appears on the website.

Chairman of the Council

November 2005

#### Contents

**K-72**   Foreword

---

[50] This recommendation only applies to sentences of 12 months and above pending the implementation of 'custody plus'.

[51] "Any criminal offence arising out of physical, sexual, psychological, emotional or financial abuse by one person against a current or former partner in a close relationship, or against a current or former family member." A new definition of domestic violence was agreed in 2004 (and appears in the CPS Policy on Prosecuting cases of Domestic Violence, 2005) "any incident of threatening behaviour, violence or abuse [psychological, physical, sexual, financial or emotional] between adults who are or have been intimate partners or family members, regardless of gender or sexuality".

The extent and timing of the retaliation
Post-offence behaviour
Use of a weapon
D   Sentence Ranges and Starting Points
Identifying sentence ranges
Factors to take into consideration
Guideline

MANSLAUGHTER BY REASON OF PROVOCATION

### A. Statutory Provision

1.1 Murder and manslaughter are common law offences and there is no complete statutory defini-   **K-73**
tion of either. 'Provocation' is one of the partial defences by which an offence that would otherwise
be murder may be reduced to manslaughter.

1.2 Before the issue of provocation can be considered, the Crown must have proved beyond
reasonable doubt that all the elements of murder were present, including the necessary intent (*i.e.*
the offender must have intended either to kill the victim or to cause grievous bodily harm). The
court must then consider section 3 of the Homicide Act 1957, which provides:

> *Where on a charge of murder there is evidence on which the jury can find that the person charged was
> provoked (whether by things done or by things said or by both together) to lose his self-control, the question
> whether the provocation was enough to make a reasonable man do as he did shall be left to be determined by the
> jury; and in determining that question the jury shall take into account everything both done and said according
> to the effect which, in their opinion, it would have on a reasonable man.*

**Although both murder and manslaughter result in death, the difference in the
level of culpability creates offences of a distinctively different character.
Therefore the approach to sentencing in each should start from a different
basis.**

### B. Establishing the Basis for Sentencing

2.1 The Court of Appeal in *Attorney General's References (Nos. 74, 95 and 118 of 2002) (Suratan and*   **K-74**
*others)*,[52] set out a number of assumptions that a judge must make in favour of an offender found not
guilty of murder but guilty of manslaughter by reason of provocation. The assumptions are required
in order to be faithful to the verdict and should be applied equally in all cases whether conviction follows a trial or whether the Crown has accepted a plea of guilty to manslaughter by reason of
provocation:

- first, that the offender had, at the time of the killing, lost self-control; mere loss of temper
  or jealous rage is not sufficient
- second, that the offender was caused to lose self-control by things said or done, normally
  by the person killed
- third, that the offender's loss of control was reasonable in all the circumstances, even
  bearing in mind that people are expected to exercise reasonable control over their emotions and that, as society advances, it ought to call for a higher measure of self-control
- fourth, that the circumstances were such as to make the loss of self-control sufficiently
  excusable to reduce the gravity of the offence from murder to manslaughter.

[52] [2003] 2 Cr.App.R.(S.) 42.

> Bearing in mind the loss of life caused by manslaughter by reason of
> provocation, the starting point for sentencing should be a custodial sentence.
> Only in a very small number of cases involving very exceptional mitigating
> factors should a judge consider that a on-custodial sentence is justified.
>
> The same general sentencing principles should apply in all cases of
> manslaughter by reason of provocation irrespective of whether or not the
> killing takes place in a domestic context.

### C. Factors Influencing Sentence

**K-75**     3.1 A number of elements must be considered and balanced by the sentencer. Some of these are common to all types of manslaughter by reason of provocation; others have a particular relevance in cases of manslaughter in a domestic context.

3.2 **The degree of provocation as shown by its nature and duration**—An assessment of the *degree* of the provocation as shown by its nature and duration is the critical factor in the sentencing decision.

   (a) In assessing the *degree* of provocation, account should be taken of the following factors:
- if the provocation (which does not have to be a wrongful act) involves gross and extreme conduct on the part of the victim, it is a more significant mitigating factor than conduct which, although significant, is not as extreme
- the fact that the victim presented a threat not only to the offender, but also to children in his or her care
- the offender's previous experiences of abuse and/or domestic violence either by the victim or by other people
- any mental condition which may affect the offender's perception of what amounts to provocation
- the nature of the conduct, the period of time over which it took place and its cumulative effect
- discovery or knowledge of the fact of infidelity on the part of a partner does not necessarily amount to *high* provocation. The gravity of such provocation depends entirely on all attendant circumstances.

   (b) Whether the provocation was suffered over a *long or short* period is important to the assessment of gravity. The following factors should be considered:
- the impact of provocative behaviour on an offender can build up over a period of time
- consideration should not be limited to acts of provocation that occurred immediately before the victim was killed. For example, in domestic violence cases, cumulative provocation may eventually become intolerable, the latest incident seeming all the worse because of what went before.

   (c) When looking at the *nature* of the provocation the court should consider both the type of provocation and whether, in the particular case, the actions of the victim would have had a particularly marked effect on the offender:
- actual (or anticipated) violence from the victim will <u>generally</u> be regarded as involving a higher degree of provocation than provocation arising from abuse, infidelity or offensive words unless that amounts to psychological bullying
- in cases involving actual or anticipated violence, the culpability of the offender will therefore <u>generally</u> be less than in cases involving verbal provocation
- where the offender's actions were motivated by fear or desperation, rather than by anger, frustration, resentment or a desire for revenge, the offender's culpability will <u>generally</u> be lower.

3.3 **The extent and timing of the retaliation**—It is implicit in the verdict of manslaughter by reason of provocation that the killing was the result of a loss of self-control because of things said and/or done. The intensity, extent and nature of that loss of control must be assessed in the context of the provocation that preceded it.

3.4 The *circumstances of the killing* itself will be relevant to the offender's culpability, and hence to the appropriate sentence:

- in general, the offender's violent response to provocation is likely to be less culpable the shorter the time gap between the provocation (or the last provocation) and the killing—as evidenced, for example, by the use of a weapon that happened to be available rather than by one that was carried for that purpose or prepared for use in advance
- conversely, it is not necessarily the case that greater culpability will be found where there has been a significant lapse of time between the provocation (or the last provocation) and the killing. Where the provocation is cumulative, and particularly in those circumstances where the offender is found to have suffered domestic violence from the victim over a significant period of time, the required loss of self-control may not be sudden as some experience a "slow-burn" reaction and appear calm
- choosing or taking advantage of favourable circumstances for carrying out the killing (so that the victim was unable to resist, such as where the victim was not on guard, or was asleep) may well be an aggravating factor—unless this is mitigated by the circumstances of the offender, resulting in the offender being the weaker or vulnerable party.

3.5 The *context of the relationship* between the offender and the victim must be borne in mind when **K-76** assessing the nature and degree of the provocation offered by the victim before the crime and the length of time over which the provocation existed. In cases where the parties were still in a relationship at the time of the killing, it will be necessary to examine the balance of power between one party and the other and to consider other family members who may have been drawn into, or been victims of, the provocative behaviour.

Although there will usually be less culpability when the retaliation to provocation is sudden, it is not always the case that greater culpability will be found where there has been a significant lapse of time between the provocation and the killing.

It is for the sentencer to consider the impact on an offender of provocative behaviour that has built up over a period of time.

An offence should be regarded as aggravated where it is committed in the presence of a child or children or other vulnerable family member, whether or not the offence takes place in a domestic setting.

3.6 **Post-offence behaviour**—The behaviour of the offender after the killing can be relevant to sentence:

- immediate and genuine remorse may be demonstrated by the summoning of medical assistance, remaining at the scene, and co-operation with the authorities
- concealment or attempts to dispose of evidence or dismemberment of the body may aggravate the offence.

Post-offence behaviour is relevant to the sentence. It may be an aggravating or mitigating factor. When sentencing, the judge should consider the motivation behind the offender's actions.

3.7 **Use of a weapon**

(a) In relation to this offence, as in relation to many different types of offence, the carrying and use of a weapon is an aggravating factor. Courts must consider the type of weapon used and, importantly, whether it was to hand or carried to the scene and who introduced it to the incident.

(b) The use or not of a weapon is a factor heavily influenced by the gender of the offender. Whereas men can and do kill using physical strength alone, women often cannot and thus resort to using a weapon. The issue of key importance is whether the weapon was to hand or carried deliberately to the scene, although the circumstances in which the weapon was brought to the scene will need to be considered carefully.

## D. Sentence Ranges and Starting Points

**K-77**    **4.1 Manslaughter is a "serious offence" for the purposes of the provisions in the Criminal Justice Act 2003**[53] **for dealing with dangerous offenders. It is possible that a court will be required to use the sentences for public protection prescribed in the Act when sentencing an offender convicted of the offence of manslaughter by reason of provocation. An alternative is a discretionary life sentence. In accordance with normal practice, when setting the minimum term to be served within an indeterminate sentence under these provisions, that term will usually be half the equivalent determinate sentence.**

4.1 **Identifying sentence ranges**—The key factor that will be relevant in every case is the nature and the duration of the provocation.

(a) The process to be followed by the court will be:

identify the sentence range by reference to the degree of provocation

adjust the starting point within the range by reference to the length of **time** over which the provocation took place

take into consideration the circumstances of the killing (e.g. the length of time that had elapsed between the provocation and the retaliation and the circumstances in which any weapon was used)

(b) This guideline establishes that:
- there are three sentencing ranges defined by the **degree of provocation**—low, substantial and high
- within the three ranges, the starting point is based on provocation taking place over **a short period of time**.
- the court will move from the starting point (based upon the degree of provocation) by considering the length of time over which the provocation has taken place, and by reference to any **aggravating and mitigating factors**

MANSLAUGHTER BY REASON OF PROVOCATION

### Factors to take into consideration

**K-78**    1. The sentences for public protection <u>must</u> be considered in all cases of manslaughter.

2. The presence of any of the general aggravating factors identified in the Council's Guideline *Overarching Principles: Seriousness* or any of the additional factors identified in this Guideline will indicate a sentence above the normal starting point.

3. This offence will not be an initial charge but will arise following a charge of murder. The Council Guideline *Reduction in Sentence for a Guilty Plea* will need to be applied with this in mind. In particular, consideration will need to be given to the time at which it was indicated that the defendant would plead guilty to manslaughter by reason of provocation.

4. An assessment of the *degree* of the provocation as shown by its nature and duration is the critical factor in the sentencing decision.

5. The intensity, extent and nature of the loss of control must be assessed in the context of the provocation that preceded it.

6. Although there will usually be less culpability when the retaliation to provocation is sudden, it is not always the case that greater culpability will be found where there has been a significant lapse of time between the provocation and the killing.

7. It is for the sentencer to consider the impact on an offender of provocative behaviour that has built up over a period of time.

8. The use of a weapon should not necessarily move a case into another sentencing bracket.

9. Use of a weapon may reflect the imbalance in strength between the offender and the victim and how that weapon came to hand is likely to be far more important than the use of the weapon itself.

---

[53] Sections 224-230.

10. It will be an aggravating factor where the weapon is brought to the scene in contemplation of use *before* the loss of self-control (which may occur some time before the fatal incident).

11. Post-offence behaviour is relevant to the sentence. It may be an aggravating or mitigating factor. When sentencing, the judge should consider the motivation behind the offender's actions.

### Manslaughter by Reason of Provocation

This is a serious offence for the purposes of section 224 of the Criminal Justice Act 2003
Maximum penalty: **Life imprisonment**

K-79

| Type/Nature of Activity | Sentence Ranges & Starting Points |
|---|---|
| **Low degree of provocation:**<br>A low degree of provocation occurring over a short period | Sentence Range: 10 years – life<br>Starting Point – 12 years custody |
| **Substantial degree of provocation:**<br>A substantial degree of provocation occurring over a short period | Sentence Range: 4 – 9 years<br>Starting Point – 8 years custody |
| **High degree of provocation:**<br>A high degree of provocation occurring over a short period | Sentence Range: if custody is necessary, up to 4 years<br>Starting Point – 3 years custody |

| Additional aggravating factors | Additional mitigating factors |
|---|---|
| 1. Concealment or attempts to dispose of evidence*<br>2. Dismemberment or mutilation of the body*<br>3. Offence committed in the presence of a child/children or other vulnerable family member<br><br>*subject to para 3.6 above. | 1. The offender was acting to protect another<br>2. Spontaneity and lack of premeditation<br>3. Previous experiences of abuse and/or domestic violence<br>4. Evidence that the victim presented an ongoing danger to the offender or another<br>5. Actual (or reasonably anticipated) violence from the victim |

*The Council Guideline New Sentences: Criminal Justice Act 2003 recognised the potentially more demanding nature of custodial sentences of 12 months or longer imposed under the new framework introduced by the Criminal Justice Act 2003. The sentencing ranges and starting points in the above guideline take account of this.*

## E. Robbery

The Sentencing Guidelines Council has issued a definitive guideline on robbery (Theft Act 1968, s.8(1) (§ 21-84 in the main work)). It deals with offenders sentenced on or after August 1, 2006. The drafting of the guideline is inconsistent and repetitious. It lacks a coherent structure, and consists, in large part, of a series of lists and bullet points. Accordingly, it is not set out in full here. The following is a summary of its essential contents, but for those wishing to refer to the original, it may be located at www.sentencingguidelines.gov.uk.

K-80

The foreword states that robbery will usually merit a custodial sentence, but that exceptional circumstances may justify a non-custodial penalty for an adult and, more frequently, for a young offender; that the guideline is not, therefore, intended to mark a significant shift in sentencing practice; and that the sentencing ranges and starting points in the guideline take into account the more demanding nature of custodial sentences of 12 months or more under the CJA 2003. The guideline only provides guidance in relation to street robberies, robberies of small businesses, and less sophisticated commercial robberies. No guidance is provided in relation to violent personal robberies in the home and professionally planned commercial robberies.

The sentences suggested by the guideline are determined by the identification of one of three levels of seriousness. These are themselves determined by reference to the type of activity which characterises the offence, and the degree of force or threat present. Level 1 involves a threat and/or minimal use of force. Level 2 involves use of a weapon to threaten and/or use of significant force. Level 3 involves use of a weapon and/or significant force, and the causing of serious injury. Where the offence will fall within a particular level is determined by the presence of one or more aggravating features. However, exceptionally serious aggravating features may have the effect of moving the case to the next level. Aggravating factors which are particularly relevant to the assessment of seriousness are:

   (a) the nature and degree of any force or violence used or threatened;

   (b) the nature of any weapon carried or used, or the use of which is threatened;

   (c) the vulnerability of the victim;

   (d) the number of offenders involved and their roles;

   (e) the value of the property taken;

   (f) the fact that the offence was committed at night or in the hours of darkness; and

   (g) the wearing of a disguise.

Mitigating factors which are particularly relevant are:

   (a) an unplanned or opportunistic offence;

   (b) a peripheral involvement in the offence; and

   (c) the voluntary return of the property taken.

Where an offence is committed by a young offender, sentencers should additionally take into account age and immaturity and any group pressure under which the offender may have been acting. Further, in relation to such an offender, the guideline requires that where there is evidence that the offence was committed to fund a drug habit and that treatment might help tackle offending behaviour, the court should consider a drug treatment requirement as part of a supervision order or action plan. In all cases, the court should consider making a restitution or compensation order; in cases where a non-custodial order is made, the court may consider making an anti-social behaviour order.

Starting points and sentencing ranges are prescribed depending on whether the offender is an adult or a young offender. In each case, the starting point is based upon a first time offender who has pleaded not guilty, and who has not been assessed as being dangerous for the purposes of the dangerous offender provisions under the CJA 2003, Pt 12, Chap. 5 (ss.224 *et seq.*) (§§ 5-495 *et seq.* in the main work). In the case of young offenders, the starting points are based on a 17-year-old. Sentencers are required to consider whether a lower starting point is justified on account of the offender's age or immaturity. In the case of an adult offender, the starting point for a level 1 offence is 12 months' custody and the sentence range is from a community order (in exceptional circumstances, as stated in the foreword) to three years' custody. The starting point for a level 2 offence is four years' custody and the sentence range is two to seven years. The starting point for a level 3 offence is eight years' custody and the sentence range is seven to 12 years. In the case of the notional young offender, the starting point for a level 1 offence is a community order and the sentence range is from a community order to a 12-month detention and training order. The starting point for a level 2 offence is three years' detention and the sentence range is one to six years' detention. The starting point for a level 3 offence is seven years' detention and the sentence range is six to 10 years' detention.

## F. Breach of a Protective Order

**K-81**    The Sentencing Guidelines Council has issued a definitive guideline relating to the sentencing of offenders who have breached either a restraining order under the Protection from Harassment Act 1997, s.5 (§ 19-350 in the main work), or a non-molestation order imposed under section 42 of the Family Law Act 1996 (breach being made an offence by section 42A, which is inserted, as from a day to be appointed, by the Domestic Violence, Crime and Victims Act 2004, s.1). It deals with offenders sentenced on or after December 18, 2006.

Paragraph 2 points out that the facts constituting the breach may amount to a substantive offence in their own right. It advises that in such cases it is desirable that there should be separate counts, and, where necessary, there should be consecutive sentences to reflect the seriousness of the counts and to achieve the appropriate totality. It continues, however, by saying that where there is only the one count, the overall sentence should not generally be affected. If the sole count is the breach, the sentence should reflect the nature of the breach; and if the substantive offence alone has been charged, the fact that it constituted a breach of a court order should be regarded as a matter of aggravation. Where no substantive offence was involved, the sentence should reflect the circumstances of the breach, including whether it was an isolated breach, or part of a course of conduct in breach of the order; whether it was planned or spontaneous; and any consequences of the breach, including psychiatric injury or distress to the person protected by the order.

Paragraph 3 is headed "Factors influencing sentencing". It says that since the order will have been made for the purpose of protecting an individual from harm, the main aim of the sentencer should be to achieve future compliance with the order where that is realistic. The nature of the original conduct or offence is relevant in so far as it allows a judgment to be made on the level of harm caused to the victim by the breach and the extent to which that harm was intended by the offender (para. 3.5). However, sentence following a breach is for the breach alone and must avoid punishing the offender again for the offence or conduct as a result of which the order was made (para. 3.7).

When dealing with a breach, a court will need to consider the extent to which the conduct amounting to the breach put the victim at risk of harm (para. 3.8). Where the order is breached by the use of physical violence, the starting point should normally be a custodial sentence (para. 3.9). Non-violent behaviour and/or indirect contact can also cause (or be intended to cause) a high degree of harm and anxiety. In such circumstances, it is likely that the custody threshold will have been crossed (para. 3.10). Where an order was made in civil proceedings, its purpose may have been to cause the subject of the order to modify behaviour rather than to imply that the conduct was especially serious. If so, it is likely to be disproportionate to impose a custodial sentence for a breach of the order if the breach did not involve threats or violence (para. 3.11). In some cases where a breach might result in a short custodial sentence but the court is satisfied that the offender genuinely intends to reform his behaviour and there is a real prospect of rehabilitation, the court may consider it appropriate to impose a sentence that will allow this. This may mean imposing a suspended sentence order or a community order (where appropriate with a requirement to attend an accredited domestic violence programme) (para. 3.12).

Paragraph 4 deals with matters of aggravation and mitigation. The matters of aggravation mirror those in the guideline on domestic violence (*post*, Appendix K-82), but there is added the fact that the breach was a further breach following previous breach proceedings or that it was committed shortly after the order was made. The matters of mitigation that are listed are that the breach followed a long period of compliance, or that the victim initiated contact.

At the end of the guideline there is a table with suggested starting points. The premise is that the "activity has either been prosecuted separately as an offence or is not of a character sufficient to justify prosecution of it as an offence in its own right". The first column is headed "Nature of activity" and the second column is headed "Starting points". There are five entries in the first column, "Breach (whether one or more) involving significant physical violence and significant physical or psychological harm to the victim", "More than one breach involving some violence and/or significant physical or psychological harm to the victim", "Single breach involving some violence and/or significant physical or psychological harm to the victim", "More than one breach involving no/ minimal contact or some direct contact" and "Single breach involving no/ minimal direct contact". The corresponding entries in the second column are, "More than 12 months. The length of the ... sentence will depend on the nature and seriousness of the breaches.", "26-39 weeks' custody [Medium/High Custody Plus order] (when the relevant provisions of the CJA 2003 are in force)", "13-26 weeks' custody [Low/Medium Custody Plus order] (when the relevant provisions of the CJA 2003 are in force)", "Medium range community order" and "Low range community order".

### G. DOMESTIC VIOLENCE

The Sentencing Guidelines Council has issued a definitive guideline for use in all cases that fall **K-82** within the Crown Prosecution Service definition of "domestic violence", *viz.* "Any incident of threatening behaviour, violence or abuse [psychological, physical, sexual, financial or emotional] between adults who are or have been intimate partners or family members, regardless of gender or sexuality." It deals with offenders sentenced on or after December 18, 2006. The guideline makes clear that offences committed in a domestic context should be regarded as being no less serious than offences committed in a non-domestic context. Indeed, because an offence has been committed in a domestic context, there are likely to be aggravating factors present that make it more serious. The foreword, signed by Lord Phillips C.J., as chairman of the council, states that in many situations of domestic violence, the circumstances require the sentence to demonstrate clearly that the conduct is unacceptable, but that there will be cases where all parties genuinely and realistically wish the relationship to continue as long as the violence stops. In such cases, and where the violence is towards the lower end of the scale of seriousness, it is likely to be appropriate for the court to impose a sentence that provides the necessary support.

Paragraph 1 defines "domestic violence" for the purposes of the guideline (*ante*). Paragraph 2 relates to the assessment of seriousness and says nothing new. Paragraph 3 is concerned with matters of aggravation and mitigation. By way of preamble it is stated that the history of the relationship will be relevant to the assessment of seriousness. There follows a non-exhaustive list of aggravating matters, *viz.* abuse of trust or power, that the victim is particularly vulnerable, the exposure of children to an offence (directly or indirectly), using contact arrangements with a child to instigate an offence, a proven history of violence or threats by the offender in a domestic setting, a history of disobedience to court orders and conduct which has forced the victim to leave home. The two matters of mitigation that are listed are positive good character and provocation, but, as to the former, the point is made that the perpetrator of domestic violence may have two personae, and that good character in relation to conduct outside the home should generally be of no relevance where there is a proven pattern of behaviour.

Paragraph 4 deals with the relevance of the wishes of the victim to the sentence. As a matter of general principle, the sentence should be determined by the seriousness of the offence, not by the expressed wishes of the victim. The guideline states that it is particularly important that this principle should be observed in this context, as (a) it is undesirable that a victim should feel a responsibility for the sentence imposed; (b) there is a risk that a plea for mercy made by a victim will be induced by threats made by, or by a fear of, the offender; and (c) the risk of such threats will be increased if it is generally believed that the severity of the sentence may be affected by the wishes of the victim. However, there may be cases in which the court can properly mitigate a sentence to give effect to the expressed wish of the victim that the relationship should be permitted to continue. The court must, however, be confident that such a wish is genuine, and that giving effect to it will not expose the victim to a real risk of further violence. Up-to-date information in a pre-sentence report and victim personal statement will be of vital importance. Either the offender or the victim (or both) may ask the court to take into consideration the interests of any children and to impose a less severe sentence. The court will wish to have regard not only to the effect on the children if the relationship is disrupted but also to the likely effect on the children of any further incidents of domestic violence.

The final section of the guideline is headed "Factors to Take into Consideration". It contains nothing new, save that it advises that where "the custody threshold is only just crossed, so that if a custodial sentence is imposed it will be a short sentence, the court will wish to consider whether the better option is a suspended sentence order or a community order, including in either case a requirement to attend an accredited domestic violence programme. Such an option will only be appropriate where the court is satisfied that the offender genuinely intends to reform his ... behaviour and that there is a real prospect of rehabilitation being successful. Such a situation is unlikely to arise where there has been a pattern of abuse."

## H. Sexual Offences

### (1) Sentencing Guidelines Council

**K-83**   The Sentencing Guidelines Council issued a definitive guideline on sexual offences, which applied to offenders sentenced on or after May 14, 2007. For the great majority of sexual offences, this will be overtaken, in relation to offenders sentenced on or after April 1, 2014, by the definitive guideline issued by the Sentencing Council for England and Wales (*post*, K-84 *et seq.*). Those wishing to consult the full detail of the former guideline should refer to the first supplement to this edition.

The new guideline does not cover three offences that were covered by the former guideline, and, since the new guideline does not purport to "revoke" its predecessor, it would appear that the former guideline will still hold sway in relation to those three offences.

*Intercourse with an animal (s.69 of the SOA 2003)*

**K-83a**   For a basic offence assuming no aggravating or mitigating factors, the recommended starting point was a community order and the range was an "appropriate non-custodial sentence". The one specified aggravating feature was "recording activity and circulating pictures/video", and the one specified mitigating factor was "symptom of isolation rather than depravity".

*Sexual penetration of a corpse (s.70 of the SOA 2003)*

**K-83b**   For a basic offence assuming no aggravating or mitigating factors, the recommended starting point was a community order and the range was an "appropriate non-custodial sentence". For a case of repeat offending or one accompanied by aggravating factors, the range was four weeks' to 18 months' custody, with a starting point of 26 weeks' custody. There were four aggravating factors that were specifically identified, *viz.* distress caused to relatives or friends of the deceased, physical damage caused to the body of the deceased, corpse was that of a child, and offence was committed in a funeral home or a mortuary.

*Sexual activity in a public lavatory (s.71 of the SOA 2003)*

For a basic offence assuming no aggravating or mitigaging factors, the recommended starting **K-83c** point was a fine, and the range was an "appropriate non-custodial sentence". For a case of repeat offending or one accompanied by aggravating factors, the range was the same but the starting point was a community order. The one aggravating factor specifically identified was "intimidating behaviour/threats of violence to member(s) of the public".

## (2) Sentencing Council for England and Wales

The Sentencing Council for England and Wales has issued a definitive guideline covering the **K-84** sexual offences set out at I to XXXIII, *post*, applying to all offenders aged 18 or over who are sentenced on or after April 1, 2014.

The guideline sets out nine steps to be followed (in order) when sentencing for these offences, which correspond broadly to the steps set out in the guideline on offences against the person (*post*, K-113 *et seq.*). The offence in XVIII, *post*, only has eight steps (missing out the step requiring the court to consider whether an offender meets the dangerousness criteria).

In particular, step one requires the court to determine the offence category, based on harm and culpability. In determining the harm and culpability, the court should refer only to the indicators set out for each offence (*post*) (although this is not specified for XVI, *post*). Step two requires the court to use the starting point identified for the relevant category to reach a sentence within the category range (*post*). The starting point applies to all offenders irrespective of plea or previous convictions. The court should then consider adjustment within the category range for aggravating or mitigating features set out for each offence, *post*, which contain a non-exhaustive list of additional factual elements providing the context of the offence and factors relating to the offender. A case of particular gravity, reflected by multiple features of culpability or harm in step one, could merit upward adjustment of the starting point before further adjustment for aggravating or mitigating features. Having considered all factors, it might be appropriate to move outside the identified category range.

Annex A contains further information about ancillary orders and provisions that apply automatically by operation of law, Annex B describes the approach to sentencing for historic sexual offences (see *R. v. H.*, *ante*, Appendix H-12), Annex C lists the various historic offences and Annex D sets out fine bands, and a non-exhaustive description of examples of requirements that might be appropriate for low, medium and high level community orders, corresponding to those in the guideline on offences against the person (*ante*).

## Key to factors indicating varying levels of harm and culpability (step one)

*Harm factors*

1. Severe psychological or physical harm **K-84a**
2. Pregnancy or STI as a consequence of offence
3. Additional degradation/humiliation
4. Abduction
5. Prolonged detention/sustained incident
6. Violence or threats of violence (beyond what is inherent in the offence, where relevant)
7. Forced/uninvited entry into victim's home or residence

8. Victim is particularly vulnerable due to personal circumstances and/or (offences against victims under 13) extreme youth

9. Penetration using large or dangerous object(s)

10. Touching of naked genitalia or naked breasts

11. Penetration of vagina or anus (using body or object) by, or of, the victim

12. Penile penetration of mouth by, or of, the victim

13. Touching, or exposure, of naked genitalia or naked breasts by, or of, the victim

14. Other sexual activity

15. Touching of naked genitalia or naked breasts by, or of, the victim

16. Causing victim to view extreme pornography

17. Causing victim to view indecent/prohibited images of children

18. Engaging in, or causing a victim to view live, sexual activity involving sadism/violence/ sexual activity with an animal/child

19. Engaging in, or causing a victim to view images of or view live, sexual activity involving penetration of vagina or anus (using body or object) or penile penetration of the mouth or masturbation

20. Continued contact despite victim's attempts to terminate contact

21. Sexual images exchanged

22. Victim exposed to extreme sexual content (*e.g.* extreme pornography)

23. Abduction/detention

24. Sustained and systematic psychological abuse

25. Individual(s)/those working in brothel forced or coerced to participate in unsafe/ degrading sexual activity

26. Individual(s)/those working in brothel forced or coerced into seeing many "customers"

27. Individual(s)/ those working in brothel forced/coerced/deceived into prostitution

28. Under 18-year-olds working in brothel

29. Established evidence of community impact

30. Victims involved in penetrative activity

31. Victim(s) participated in unsafe/ degrading sexual activity beyond that which is inherent in the offence

32. Victim(s) passed around by the offender to other "customers" and/or moved to other brothels

33. Victim subjected to unsafe/degrading sexual activity (beyond that which is inherent in the offence)

34. Victim(s) under 18

35. Victim(s) forced/coerced into prostitution

36. Victim(s) tricked/deceived as to purpose of visit

37. Victim followed/pursued

38. Offender masturbated

39. Image(s) available to be viewed by others

40. Victim observed or recorded in their own home or residence

41. Child conceived

42. Offence committed in victim's home

*Culpability factors*

43. Significant degree of planning
44. Acting with others to commit offence
45. Use of alcohol/drugs on victim to facilitate the offence
46. Abuse of trust
47. Previous violence against victim
48. Offence committed in course of burglary
49. Recording of the offence
50. Commercial exploitation and/or motivation
51. Offence racially or religiously aggravated
52. Offence motivated by, or demonstrating, hostility to the victim based on his sexual orientation (or presumed sexual orientation) or transgender identity (or presumed transgender identity)
53. Offence motivated by, or demonstrating, hostility to the victim based on his disability (or presumed disability)
54. Grooming behaviour used against victim
55. Sexual images of victim recorded, retained, solicited or shared
56. Deliberate isolation of victim
57. Use of threats (including blackmail)
58. Specific targeting of a particularly vulnerable child/victim
59. Offender lied about age
60. Significant disparity in age
61. Communication indicates penetrative sexual activity is intended
62. Offender lied about persona
63. Use of gifts, bribes
64. Abduction/detention
65. Causing, inciting or controlling prostitution/ keeping brothel/ directing or organising child prostitution or pornography/ directing or organising trafficking on significant commercial basis
66. Expectation of significant financial or other gain
67. Exploitation of those known to be trafficked
68. Significant involvement in limiting the freedom of prostitute(s)/ those working in brothel/ victims of child prostitution or pornography/ significant influence over others in trafficking organisation/ hierarchy
69. Grooming of individual(s) to enter prostitution/ child pornography/ work in brothel, including through cultivation of a dependency on drugs or alcohol
70. Close involvement with prostitute(s)/ those working in brothel, *e.g.* control of finances, choice of clients, working conditions, *etc.*, or with inciting, controlling, arranging or facilitating child prostitution or pornography (where offender's involvement is not as a result of coercion)
71. Performs limited function under direction
72. Close involvement but engaged by coercion/intimidation/ exploitation
73. Involvement in keeping a number of brothels
74. Keeping/ managing premises
75. Use of alcohol/ drugs on victim
76. Blackmail or other threats made

77.   Offender aware that he has a sexually transmitted disease

78.   Offender aware victim has been trafficked

79.   Significant influence over others in trafficking organisation/ hierarchy

80.   Operational or management function within hierarchy

81.   Involves others in operation whether by coercion/ intimidation/ exploitation or reward (and offender's involvement is not as a result of coercion)

82.   Specific or previous targeting of a particularly vulnerable victim

83.   Image(s) recorded

84.   Intended sexual offence carries a statutory maximum of life imprisonment

85.   Possession of weapon or other item to frighten or injure

## Key to aggravating and mitigating factors (step two)

*Statutory aggravating factors*

86.   Previous convictions (CJA 2003, s.143(2) (§ 5-67 in the main work))

87.   Offence committed whilst on bail (*ibid.*, s.143(3))

*Other aggravating factors*

88.   Specific targeting of a particularly vulnerable victim

89.   Ejaculation (where not taken into account at step one)

90.   Blackmail or other threats made (where not taken into account at step one)

91.   Location of offence

92.   Timing of offence

93.   Use of weapon or other item to frighten or injure

94.   Victim compelled to leave their home, institution, school, *etc.*

95.   Failure to comply with current court orders

96.   Offence committed whilst on licence

97.   Exploiting contact arrangements with a child to commit an offence

98.   Presence of others, especially children

99.   Any steps taken to prevent the reporting of an incident, obtaining assistance and/ or from assisting or supporting the prosecution

100.   Attempts to dispose of or conceal evidence

101.   Commission of offence whilst under the influence of alcohol or drugs

102.   Victim encouraged to recruit others

103.   Pregnancy or STI as a consequence of offence

104.   Failure of offender to respond to previous warnings

105.   Period over which offence committed/ operation has been run

106.   Severe psychological or physical harm

107.   Age and/ or vulnerability of the child depicted (this should be given significant weight; in cases where the actual age is difficult to determine, sentencers should consider the development of the child – infant, pre-pubescent, post-pubescent)

108.   Discernible pain or distress suffered by child depicted

109.   High volume of images possessed, distributed or produced

110.   Placing images where there is the potential for a high volume of viewers

111.   Collection includes moving images

112. Abuse of trust
113. Child depicted known to offender
114. Active involvement in a network or process that facilitates or commissions the creation or sharing of indecent images of children
115. Commercial exploitation and/ or motivation
116. Deliberate or systematic searching for images portraying young children, category A images or the portrayal of familial sexual abuse
117. Large number of different victims
118. Child depicted intoxicated or drugged
119. Deliberate isolation of victim(s)/ prostitute(s)/ those working in brothel
120. Threats made to expose victim(s)/ prostitute(s)/ those working in brothel to the authorities (*e.g.* immigration or police), family/ friends or others
121. Harm threatened against the family/ friends of victim(s)/ prostitute(s)/ those working in brothel
122. Passport/ identity documents removed
123. Victim(s)/ prostitute(s)/ those working in brothel prevented from seeking medical treatment
124. Food withheld
125. Earnings withheld/ kept by offender or evidence of excessive wage reduction or debt bondage, inflated travel or living expenses or unreasonable interest rates
126. Prostitute/ those working in brothel forced or coerced into pornography
127. Those working in brothel passed around by offender and moved to other brothels
128. Vulnerability of victim(s)
129. Victim prevented from attending school
130. Children of victim(s) left in home country due to trafficking
131. Exploitation of victim(s) from particularly vulnerable backgrounds
132. Victim(s) previously trafficked/ sold/ passed around
133. Use of drugs/ alcohol or other substance to secure victim's compliance
134. Distribution of images, whether or not for gain
135. Placing images where there is the potential for a high volume of viewers
136. Period over which victim observed
137. Period over which images were made or distributed

*Mitigating factors*

138. No previous convictions or no relevant/recent convictions                    **K-84e**
139. Remorse
140. Previous good character and/ or exemplary conduct (but the more serious the offence the less weight should be attributed to this factor, particularly where it has been used to facilitate the offence, when it may well be an aggravating factor; where this number is followed by a *, the factor should not normally be given any significant weight or justify a reduction in what would otherwise be the appropriate sentence)
141. Age and/ or lack of maturity where it affects the responsibility of the offender
142. Mental disorder or learning disability, particularly where linked to the commission of the offence
143. Demonstration of steps taken to address offending behaviour

144. Sexual activity was incited but no activity took place because the offender voluntarily desisted or intervened to prevent it

*Consideration of custody threshold*

**K-84f** In the following sections, where there is a sufficient prospect of rehabilitation, a community order with a sex offender treatment programme requirement can be a proper alternative to a short or moderate custodial sentence: II to IV, VII, IX to XI, XIV, and XV to XXX.

When sentencing for some or all of the categories within the various offences, it is sometimes indicated that the court should consider whether the custody threshold has been passed, if so, whether it is unavoidable that a custodial sentence be imposed, and, if so, whether that sentence can be suspended, or whether the community order threshold has been passed. The categories for which these should be considered, if at all, are indicated at the end of step two for each section, *e.g.*, as follows:

Consideration of custody threshold: category 2 or 3
Consideration of community order threshold: category 3

## I. Rape (SOA 2003, s.1 (§ 20-19 in the main work))

**K-85** Offences here may be of such severity, for example including a campaign of rape, that sentences of 20 years and above may be appropriate.

*Factors indicating harm and culpability (step one)*

*Harm*

Category 1: The extreme nature of one or more category 2 factors or the extreme impact caused by a combination of category 2 factors **may** elevate to category 1

Category 2: Factors 1–8

Category 3: Factor(s) in categories 1 and 2 not present

*Culpability*

Category A: Factors 43–53

Category B: Factor(s) in category A not present

*Starting point and category range (step two)*

|  | **A** | **B** |
|---|---|---|
| **Category 1** | **Starting point** 15 years <br> **Range** 13 – 19 years | **Starting point** 12 years <br> **Range** 10 – 15 years |
| **Category 2** | **Starting point** 10 years <br> **Range** 9 – 13 years | **Starting point** 8 years <br> **Range** 7 – 9 years |
| **Category 3** | **Starting point** 7 years <br> **Range** 6 – 9 years | **Starting point** 5 years <br> **Range** 4 – 7 years |

*Aggravating and mitigating factors*

Aggravating factors: Factors 86-101

Mitigating factors: Factors 138, 139, 140*, 141, 142

## II. Assault by penetration (2003 Act, s.2 (ibid., § 20-28))

*Factors indicating harm and culpability (step one)*

Harm **K-85b**

Category 1: The extreme nature of one or more category 2 factors or the extreme impact caused by a combination of category 2 factors **may** elevate to category 1

Category 2: Factors 1, 3–9

Category 3: Factor(s) in categories 1 and 2 not present

*Culpability*

Same as I (*ante*)

*Starting point and category range (step two)*

|  | A | B |
|---|---|---|
| **Category 1** | **Starting point** 15 years<br>**Range** 13 – 19 years | **Starting point** 12 years<br>**Range** 10 – 15 years |
| **Category 2** | **Starting point** 8 years<br>**Range** 5 – 13 years | **Starting point** 6 years<br>**Range** 4 – 9 years |
| **Category 3** | **Starting point** 4 years<br>**Range** 2 – 6 years | **Starting point** 2 years<br>**Range** high level community order – 4 years |

Consideration of custody threshold: category 3

*Aggravating and mitigating factors*

Aggravating factors: Factors 86-88, 90-101

Mitigating factors: Factors 138, 139, 140*, 141, 142

## III. Sexual assault (2003 Act, s.3 (ibid., § 20-29))

*Factors indicating harm and culpability (step one)*

Harm **K-85c**

Category 1: Factors 1, 4, 6, 7

Category 2: Factors 3, 5, 8, 10

Category 3: Factor(s) in categories 1 and 2 not present

*Culpability*

Same as I (*ante*)

*Starting point and category range (step two)*

|  | A | B |
|---|---|---|
| **Category 1** | **Starting point** 4 years<br>**Range** 3 – 7 years | **Starting point** 2.5 years<br>**Range** 2 – 4 years |
| **Category 2** | **Starting point** 2 years<br>**Range** 1 – 4 years | **Starting point** 1 year<br>**Range** high level community order – 2 years |

| Category 3 | **Starting point** 26 weeks **Range** high level community order – 1 year | **Starting point** high level community order **Range** medium level community order – 26 weeks |
|---|---|---|

Consideration of custody threshold: category 2 or 3

*Aggravating and mitigating factors*

Aggravating factors:           Factors 86-88, 90-101

Mitigating factors:            Factors 138-143

## IV. Causing a person to engage in sexual activity without consent (2003 Act, s.4 (ibid., § 20-40))

*Factors indicating harm and culpability (step one)*

**K-86**    *Harm*

Category 1:    The extreme nature of one or more category 2 factors or the extreme impact caused by a combination of category 2 factors **may** elevate to category 1

Category 2:    Factors 1–9

Category 3:    Factor(s) in categories 1 and 2 not present

*Culpability*
Same as I (*ante*)

*Starting point and category range (step two)*

Where offence involved penetration: same as II (*ante*)
Where offence did not involve penetration: same as III (*ante*)

Consideration of custody threshold: category 2 or 3

*Aggravating and mitigating factors*

Same as I (*ante*)

## V. Rape of a child under 13 (2003 Act, s.5 (ibid., § 20-49))

**K-87**    Offences here may be of such severity, for example including a campaign of rape, that sentences of 20 years and above may be appropriate. Sentencers should have particular regard to the fact that these offences are not only committed through force or fear of force but may include exploitative behaviour towards a child, that should be considered to indicate high culpability. This guideline is designed to deal with the majority of offending behaviour but there may be exceptional cases where a lengthy community order with a requirement to participate in a sex offender treatment programme may be the best way of changing the offender's behaviour and of protecting the public by preventing any repetition of the offence.

This guideline may not be appropriate where the sentencer is satisfied that on the available evidence, and in the absence of exploitation, a young or particularly immature defendant genuinely believed, on reasonable grounds, that the victim was aged 16 or over and that they were engaging in lawful sexual activity.

*Factors indicating harm and culpability (step one)*

*Harm*

Same as I (*ante*)

*Culpability*

Category A: Factors 43–48, 50–56

Category B: Factor(s) in category A not present

*Starting point and category range (step two)*

|  | **A** | **B** |
|---|---|---|
| **Category 1** | **Starting point** 16 years<br>**Range** 13 – 19 years | **Starting point** 13 years<br>**Range** 11 – 17 years |
| **Category 2** | **Starting point** 13 years<br>**Range** 11 – 17 years | **Starting point** 10 years<br>**Range** 8 – 13 years |
| **Category 3** | **Starting point** 10 years<br>**Range** 8 – 13 years | **Starting point** 8 years<br>**Range** 6 – 11 years |

*Aggravating and mitigating factors*

Aggravating factors: Factors 86-102

Mitigating factors: Factors 138, 139, 140*, 141, 142

## VI. Assault of a child under 13 by penetration (2003 Act, s.6 (ibid., § 20-50))

*Factors indicating harm and culpability (step one)*

*Harm* **K-87a**

Same as II (*ante*)

*Culpability*

Same as V (*ante*)

*Starting point and category range (step two)*

|  | **A** | **B** |
|---|---|---|
| **Category 1** | **Starting point** 16 years<br>**Range** 13 – 19 years | **Starting point** 13 years<br>**Range** 11 – 17 years |
| **Category 2** | **Starting point** 11 years<br>**Range** 7 – 15 years | **Starting point** 8 years<br>**Range** 5 – 13 years |
| **Category 3** | **Starting point** 6 years<br>**Range** 4 – 9 years | **Starting point** 4 years<br>**Range** 2 – 6 years |

*Aggravating and mitigating factors*

Aggravating factors: Factors 86-88, 90-102

Mitigating factors: Factors 138, 139, 140*, 141, 142

## VII. Sexual assault of a child under 13 (2003 Act, s.7 (ibid., § 20-51))

*Factors indicating harm and culpability (step one)*

**K-87b**     *Harm*

Same as III (*ante*)


*Culpability*

Same as V (*ante*)


*Starting point and category range (step two)*

|            | A | B |
|------------|---|---|
| **Category 1** | **Starting point** 6 years<br>**Range** 4 – 9 years | **Starting point** 4 years<br>**Range** 3 – 7 years |
| **Category 2** | **Starting point** 4 years<br>**Range** 3 – 7 years | **Starting point** 2 years<br>**Range** 1 – 4 years |
| **Category 3** | **Starting point** 1 year<br>**Range** 26 weeks – 2 years | **Starting point** 26 weeks<br>**Range** high level community order – 1 year |

*Aggravating and mitigating factors*

Same as VI (*ante*)


## VIII. Causing or inciting a child under 13 to engage in sexual activity (2003 Act, s.8 (ibid., § 20-52))

*Factors indicating harm and culpability (step one)*

**K-87c**     *Harm*

Category 1:     The extreme nature of one or more category 2 factors or the extreme impact caused by a combination of category 2 factors **may** elevate to category 1

Category 2:     Factors 1, 3–8, 11, 12

Category 3:     Factor(s) in categories 1 and 2 not present


*Culpability*

Same as V (*ante*)


*Starting point and category range (step two)*

|            | A | B |
|------------|---|---|
| **Category 1** | **Starting point** 13 years<br>**Range** 11 – 17 years | **Starting point** 11 years<br>**Range** 10 – 15 years |
| **Category 2** | **Starting point** 8 years<br>**Range** 5 – 10 years | **Starting point** 6 years<br>**Range** 3 – 9 years |
| **Category 3** | **Starting point** 5 years<br>**Range** 3 – 8 years | **Starting point** 2 years<br>**Range** 1 – 4 years |

*Aggravating and mitigating factors*

| | |
|---|---|
| Aggravating factors: | Factors 86-103 |
| Mitigating factors: | Factors 138, 139, 140*, 141, 142, 144 |

## IX. Sexual activity with a child (2003 Act, s.9 (ibid., § 20-58)); causing or inciting a child to engage in sexual activity (2003 Act, s.10 (ibid., § 20-64))

*Factors indicating harm and culpability (step one)*

*Harm*                                                                                                    **K-88**

| | |
|---|---|
| Category 1: | Factors 11, 12 |
| Category 2: | Factor 13 |
| Category 3: | Factor 14 |

*Culpability*

| | |
|---|---|
| Category A: | Factors 43–46, 50–55, 57–60 |
| Category B: | Factor(s) in category A not present |

*Starting point and category range (step two)*

| | A | B |
|---|---|---|
| **Category 1** | **Starting point** 5 years <br> **Range** 4 – 10 years | **Starting point** 1 year <br> **Range** high level community order – 2 years |
| **Category 2** | **Starting point** 3 years <br> **Range** 2 – 6 years | **Starting point** 26 weeks <br> **Range** high level community order – 1 year |
| **Category 3** | **Starting point** 26 weeks <br> **Range** high level community order – 3 years | **Starting point** medium level community order <br> **Range** low level – high level community order |

Consideration of custody threshold: category 2 or 3

*Aggravating and mitigating factors*

| | |
|---|---|
| Aggravating factors: | Factors 86, 87, 89, 91, 92, 94-106 |
| Mitigating factors: | Factors 138, 139, 140*, 141, 142, 144 |

## X. Sexual activity with a child family member (2003 Act, s.25 (ibid., § 20-110)); inciting a child family member to engage in sexual activity (2003 Act, s.26 (ibid., § 20-111))

It should be assumed that the greater the trust, the more serious the offence.          **K-89**

*Factors indicating harm and culpability (step one)*

*Harm*

| | |
|---|---|
| Category 1: | Factors 11, 12 |
| Category 2: | Factor 15 |
| Category 3: | Factor 14 |

*Culpability*

| | |
|---|---|
| Category A: | Factors 43–45, 50–55, 57, 58, 60 |
| Category B: | Factor(s) in category A not present |

*Starting point and category range (step two)*

| | A | B |
|---|---|---|
| **Category 1** | **Starting point** 6 years<br>**Range** 4 – 10 years | **Starting point** 3.5 years<br>**Range** 2.5 – 5 years |
| **Category 2** | **Starting point** 4 years<br>**Range** 2 – 6 years | **Starting point** 18 months<br>**Range** 26 weeks – 2.5 years |
| **Category 3** | **Starting point** 1 year<br>**Range** high level community order – 3 years | **Starting point** medium level community order<br>**Range** low level – high level community order |

Consideration of custody threshold: category 3

*Aggravating and mitigating factors*

Same as IX (*ante*)

## XI. Engaging in sexual activity in the presence of a child (2003 Act, s.11 (ibid., § 20-69)); causing a child to watch a sexual act (2003 Act, s.12 (ibid., § 20-74))

*Factors indicating harm and culpability (step one)*

**K-90**   *Harm*

| | |
|---|---|
| Category 1: | Factors 16–18 |
| Category 2: | Factor 19 |
| Category 3: | Factor(s) in categories 1 and 2 not present |

*Culpability*

| | |
|---|---|
| Category A: | Factors 43–46, 50–54, 57, 58, 60 |
| Category B: | Factor(s) in category A not present |

*Starting point and category range (step two)*

| | A | B |
|---|---|---|
| **Category 1** | **Starting point** 4 years<br>**Range** 3 – 6 years | **Starting point** 2 years<br>**Range** 1 – 3 years |
| **Category 2** | **Starting point** 2 years<br>**Range** 1 – 3 years | **Starting point** 1 year<br>**Range** high level community order – 18 months |
| **Category 3** | **Starting point** 26 weeks<br>**Range** high level community order – 1 year | **Starting point** medium level community order<br>**Range** low level – high level community order |

Consideration of custody threshold: category 2 or 3

*Aggravating and mitigating factors*

| | |
|---|---|
| Aggravating factors: | Factors 86, 87, 91, 92, 94–102, 104 |
| Mitigating factors: | Factors 138–143 |

## XII. Arranging or facilitating the commission of a child sex offence (2003 Act, s.14 (ibid., § 20-84))

Sentencers should refer to the guideline for the applicable, substantive offences under sections **K-90a** IX and XI. The level of harm should be determined by reference to the type of activity arranged or facilitated. For offences involving significant commercial exploitation and/ or an international element, it may, in the interests of justice, be appropriate to increase a sentence to a point above the category range. In exceptional cases, such as where a vulnerable offender performed a limited role, having been coerced or exploited by others, sentences below the starting point and range may be appropriate.

## XIII. Meeting a child following sexual grooming (2003 Act, s.15 (ibid., § 20-91))

*Factors indicating harm and culpability (step one)*

| | | |
|---|---|---|
| Category 1: | Raised harm **and** raised culpability | **K-90b** |
| Category 2: | Raised harm **or** raised culpability | |
| Category 3: | Grooming **without** raised harm or culpability factors present | |

Where an offence does not fall squarely into a category, individual factors may require a degree of weighting before making an overall assessment and determining the appropriate offence category.

*Indicators of raised harm*
Factors 8, 20–22

*Indicators of raised culpability*
Factors 44, 46, 50–53, 57–59, 61–64

*Starting point and category range (step two)*

| Category 1 | **Starting point** 4 years<br>**Range** 3 – 7 years |
|---|---|
| Category 2 | **Starting point** 2 years<br>**Range** 1 – 4 years |
| Category 3 | **Starting point** 18 months<br>**Range** 1 – 2.5 years |

*Aggravating and mitigating factors*

| | |
|---|---|
| Aggravating factors: | Factors 86, 87, 95, 96, 99, 100, 102 |
| Mitigating factors: | Factors 138-143 |

### XIV. Abuse of position of trust: sexual activity with a child (2003 Act, s.16 (ibid., § 20-96)); abuse of position of trust: causing a child to engage in sexual activity (2003 Act, s.17 (ibid., § 20-97))

*Factors indicating harm and culpability (step one)*

**K-90c**  *Harm*

| | |
|---|---|
| Category 1: | Factors 11, 12 |
| Category 2: | Factor 13 |
| Category 3: | Factor(s) in categories 1 and 2 not present |

*Culpability*

| | |
|---|---|
| Category A: | Factors 43–45, 50–55, 57, 58 |
| Category B: | Factor(s) in category A not present |

*Starting point and category range (step two)*

| | A | B |
|---|---|---|
| **Category 1** | **Starting point** 18 months<br>**Range** 1 – 2 years | **Starting point** 1 year<br>**Range** 26 weeks – 18 months |
| **Category 2** | **Starting point** 1 year<br>**Range** 26 weeks – 18 months | **Starting point** 26 weeks<br>**Range** high level community order – 1 year |
| **Category 3** | **Starting point** 26 weeks<br>**Range** high level community order – 1 year | **Starting point** medium level community order<br>**Range** low level – high level community order |

Consideration of custody threshold: category 2 or 3

*Aggravating and mitigating factors*

| | |
|---|---|
| Aggravating factors: | Factors 86, 87, 89, 91, 92, 94-96, 98-104 |
| Mitigating factors: | Factors 138-144 |

### XV. Abuse of position of trust: sexual activity in the presence of a child (2003 Act, s.18 (ibid., § 20-98)); abuse of position of trust: causing a child to watch a sexual act (2003 Act, s.19 (ibid., § 20-99))

*Factors indicating harm and culpability (step one)*

**K-90d**  *Harm*

Same as XI (*ante*)

*Culpability*

| | |
|---|---|
| Category A: | Factors 43–45, 50–54, 57, 58 |
| Category B: | Factor(s) in category A not present |

*Starting point and category range (step two)*

Same as XIV (*ante*)

Consideration of custody threshold: category 2 or 3

*Aggravating and mitigating factors*

| | |
|---|---|
| Aggravating factors: | Factors 86, 87, 91, 92, 94-96, 98-102, 104 |
| Mitigating factors: | Factors 138-143 |

## XVI. Possession of indecent photograph of child (CJA 1988, s.160 (ibid., § 31-115)); indecent photographs of children (Protection of Children Act 1978, s.1 (ibid., § 31-107))

*Factors indicating harm and culpability (step one)*

| | Possession | Distribution | Production |
|---|---|---|---|
| **Category A** | Of images involving penetrative sexual activity | Sharing such images | Creating such images |
| | Of images involving sexual activity with an animal or sadism | Sharing such images | Creating such images |
| **Category B** | Of images involving non-penetrative sexual activity | Sharing such images | Creating such images |
| **Category C** | Of other indecent images not falling within categories A or B | Sharing such images | Creating such images |

Distribution includes possession with a view to distributing or sharing images. Production includes the taking or making of any image at source, for instance the original image. Making an image by simple downloading should be treated as possession for the purposes of sentencing.

In most cases the intrinsic character of the most serious of the offending images will initially determine the appropriate category. If, however, the most serious images are unrepresentative of the offender's conduct, a lower category may be appropriate. A lower category will not, however, be appropriate if the offender has produced or taken (*e.g.* photographed) images of a higher category.

*Starting point and category range (step two)*

| | Possession | Distribution | Production |
|---|---|---|---|
| **Category A** | **Starting point** 1 year **Range** 26 weeks – 3 years | **Starting point** 3 years **Range** 2 – 5 years | **Starting point** 6 years **Range** 4 – 9 years |
| **Category B** | **Starting point** 26 weeks **Range** high level community order – 18 months | **Starting point** 1 year **Range** 26 weeks – 2 years | **Starting point** 2 years **Range** 1 – 4 years |
| **Category C** | **Starting point** high level community order **Range** medium level community order – 26 weeks | **Starting point** 13 weeks **Range** high level community order – 26 weeks | **Starting point** 18 months **Range** 1 – 3 years |

Consideration of custody threshold: category 2 or 3

*Aggravating and mitigating factors*

| | |
|---|---|
| Aggravating factors: | Factors 86, 87, 95, 96, 100, 105, 107–118 |
| Mitigating factors: | Factors 138–143 |

## XVII. Causing or inciting prostitution for gain (2003 Act, s.52 (ibid., § 20–172)); controlling prostitution for gain (2003 Act, s.53 (ibid., § 20–173))

*Factors indicating harm and culpability (step one)*

**K-92**      *Harm*

| | |
|---|---|
| Category 1: | Factors 6, 23–27 |
| Category 2: | Factor(s) in category 1 not present |

*Culpability*

| | |
|---|---|
| Category A: | Factors 46, 65–69 |
| Category B: | Factor 70 |
| Category C: | Factors 71, 72 |

*Starting point and category range (step two)*

| | A | B | C |
|---|---|---|---|
| **Category 1** | **Starting point** 4 years<br>**Range** 3 – 6 years | **Starting point** 2.5 years<br>**Range** 2 – 4 years | **Starting point** 1 year<br>**Range** 26 weeks – 2 years |
| **Category 2** | **Starting point** 2.5 years<br>**Range** 2 – 5 years | **Starting point** 1 year<br>**Range** high level community order – 2 years | **Starting point** medium level community order<br>**Range** low level – high level community order |

Consideration of custody threshold: category 2 or 3

*Aggravating and mitigating factors*

| | |
|---|---|
| Aggravating factors: | Factors 86, 87, 95, 96, 99, 100, 105, 119-126 |
| Mitigating factors: | Factors 138-143 |

## XVIII. Keeping a brothel used for prostitution (SOA 1956, s.33A (ibid., § 20-229))

*Factors indicating harm and culpability (step one)*

**K-92a**      *Harm*

| | |
|---|---|
| Category 1: | Factors 6, 23–29 |
| Category 2: | Factor(s) in category 1 not present |

*Culpability*

| | |
|---|---|
| Category A: | Factors 46, 65–69, 73 |
| Category B: | Factors 70, 74 |
| Category C: | Factors 71, 72 |

*Starting point and category range (step two)*

|  | A | B | C |
|---|---|---|---|
| **Category 1** | **Starting point** 5 years<br>**Range** 3 – 6 years | **Starting point** 3.5 years<br>**Range** 2 – 5 years | **Starting point** 1 year<br>**Range** high level community order – 18 months |
| **Category 2** | **Starting point** 3 years<br>**Range** 2 – 5 years | **Starting point** 1 year<br>**Range** 26 weeks – 2 years | **Starting point** medium level community order<br>**Range** low level – high level community order |

Consideration of custody threshold: category 1

*Aggravating and mitigating factors*

Aggravating factors:      Factors 86, 87, 95, 96, 99, 100, 105, 119-127

Mitigating factors:      Factors 138-143

## XIX. Causing or inciting child prostitution or pornography (2003 Act, s.48 (ibid., § 20-160)); controlling a child prostitute or child involved in pornography (2003 Act, s.49 (ibid., § 20-167)); arranging or facilitating child prostitution or pornography (2003 Act, s.50 (ibid., § 20-161))

*Factors indicating harm and culpability (step one)*

*Harm*                                                                                                    **K-92b**

Category 1:      Factors 6, 23, 24, 30–32

Category 2:      Factor(s) in category 1 not present

*Culpability*

Same as XVII (*ante*)

*Starting point and category range (step two)*

|  | Age of victim | A | B | C |
|---|---|---|---|---|
| **Category 1** | U13 | **Starting point** 10 years<br>**Range** 8 – 13 years | **Starting point** 8 years<br>**Range** 6 – 11 years | **Starting point** 5 years<br>**Range** 2 – 6 years |
|  | 13–15 | **Starting point** 8 years<br>**Range** 6 – 11 years | **Starting point** 5 years<br>**Range** 4 – 8 years | **Starting point** 2.5 years<br>**Range** 1 – 4 years |
|  | 16–17 | **Starting point** 4 years<br>**Range** 3 – 7 years | **Starting point** 2 years<br>**Range** 1 – 4 years | **Starting point** 1 year<br>**Range** 26 weeks – 2 years |
| **Category 2** | U13 | **Starting point** 8 years<br>**Range** 6 – 11 years | **Starting point** 6 years<br>**Range** 4 – 9 years | **Starting point** 2 years<br>**Range** 1 – 4 years |

| | | | | |
|---|---|---|---|---|
| | 13–15 | **Starting point** 6 years<br>**Range** 4 – 9 years | **Starting point** 3 years<br>**Range** 2 – 5 years | **Starting point** 1 year<br>**Range** 26 weeks – 2 years |
| | 16–17 | **Starting point** 3 years<br>**Range** 2 – 5 years | **Starting point** 1 year<br>**Range** 26 weeks – 2 years | **Starting point** 26 weeks<br>**Range** high level community order – 1 year |

Consideration of custody threshold: category 2

*Aggravating and mitigating factors*

Aggravating factors:          Factors 86, 87, 95, 96, 99, 100, 105, 119-125, 128, 129

Mitigating factors:           Factors 138, 139, 140*, 141, 142

**XX. Paying for the sexual services of a child (2003 Act, s.47 (ibid., § 20-155))**

**K-92c**    This guideline should only be used where the victim was aged 16 or 17.

*Factors indicating harm and culpability (step one)*

*Harm*

> Category 1:      Factors 6, 11, 12, 33
>
> Category 2:      Factor 15
>
> Category 3:      Factor 14

*Culpability*

> Category A:      Factors 44, 46, 47, 55, 64, 75–78
>
> Category B:      Factor(s) in category A not present

*Starting point and category range (step two)*

| | A | B |
|---|---|---|
| **Category 1** | **Starting point** 4 years<br>**Range** 2 – 5 years | **Starting point** 2 years<br>**Range** 1 – 4 years |
| **Category 2** | **Starting point** 3 years<br>**Range** 1 – 4 years | **Starting point** 1 year<br>**Range** 26 weeks – 2 years |
| **Category 3** | **Starting point** 1 year<br>**Range** 26 weeks – 2 years | **Starting point** 26 weeks<br>**Range** high level community order – 1 year |

Consideration of custody threshold: category 3

*Aggravating and mitigating factors*

Aggravating factors:          Factors 86, 87, 89, 95, 96, 99, 100

Mitigating factors:           Factors 138-143

**XXI. Trafficking people for sexual exploitation (2003 Act, s.59A (ibid., § 20-155)) (and also ss.57-59 before their replacement by s.59A)**

*Factors indicating harm and culpability (step one)*

*Harm*　　　　　　　　　　　　　　　　　　　　　　　　　　　　**K-93**

| | |
|---|---|
| Category 1: | Factors 6, 23–25, 34–36 |
| Category 2: | Factor(s) in category 1 not present |

*Culpability*

| | |
|---|---|
| Category A: | Factors 46, 65, 66, 68 |
| Category B: | Factors 80, 81 |
| Category C: | Factors 71, 72 |

*Starting point and category range (step two)*

| | A | B | C |
|---|---|---|---|
| **Category 1** | **Starting point** 8 years<br>**Range** 6 – 12 years | **Starting point** 6 years<br>**Range** 4 – 8 years | **Starting point** 18 months<br>**Range** 26 weeks – 2 years |
| **Category 2** | **Starting point** 6 years<br>**Range** 4 – 8 years | **Starting point** 4 years<br>**Range** 2 – 6 years | **Starting point** 26 weeks<br>**Range** high level community order – 18 months |

Consideration of custody threshold: category 2

*Aggravating and mitigating factors*

| | |
|---|---|
| Aggravating factors: | Factors 86, 87, 95, 96, 99, 100, 105, 119-125, 131-133 |
| Mitigating factors: | Factors 138, 139, 140*, 141, 142 |

**XXII. Sexual activity with a person with a mental disorder impeding choice (2003 Act, s.30 (ibid., § 20-125)); causing or inciting such a person to engage in a sexual activity (2003 Act, s.30 (ibid., § 20-126))**

*Factors indicating harm and culpability (step one)*

*Harm*　　　　　　　　　　　　　　　　　　　　　　　　　　　　**K-94**

| | |
|---|---|
| Category 1: | The extreme nature of one or more category 2 factors or the extreme impact caused by a combination of category 2 factors **may** elevate to category 1 |
| Category 2: | Factors 1–7 |
| Category 3: | Factor(s) in categories 1 and 2 not present |

*Culpability*

| | |
|---|---|
| Category A: | Factors 43–48, 50–56 |
| Category B: | Factor(s) in category A not present |

*Starting point and category range (step two)*

> Where offence involved penetration: same as V (*ante*)
>
> Where offence did not involve penetration: same as VII (*ante*)

Consideration of custody threshold: when appropriate

*Aggravating and mitigating factors*

| | |
|---|---|
| Aggravating factors: | Factors 86, 87, 89, 90-96, 98-101 |
| Mitigating factors: | Factors 138, 139, 140*, 141, 142, 144 |

**XXIII. Engaging in sexual activity in the presence of a person with a mental disorder impeding choice (2003 Act, s.32 (ibid., § 20-127)); causing such a person to watch a sexual act (2003 Act, s.33 (ibid., § 20-128))**

*Factors indicating harm and culpability (step one)*

**K-95** *Harm*

> Same as XI (*ante*)

*Culpability*

| | |
|---|---|
| Category A: | Factors 43–46, 50–54, 57 |
| Category B: | Factor(s) in category A not present |

*Starting point and category range (step two)*

> Same as XI (*ante*)

Consideration of custody threshold: category 2 or 3

*Aggravating and mitigating factors*

| | |
|---|---|
| Aggravating factors: | Factors 86, 87, 91, 92, 95, 96, 99-101 |
| Mitigating factors: | Factors 138-143 |

**XXIV. Inducement, threat or deception to procure sexual activity with a person with a mental disorder (2003 Act, s.34 (ibid., § 20-134)); causing such a person to engage in or agree to engage in sexual activity by inducement, threat or deception (2003 Act, s.35 (ibid., § 20-135))**

*Factors indicating harm and culpability (step one)*

**K-96** *Harm*

> Same as IX (*ante*)

*Culpability*

| | |
|---|---|
| Category A: | Factors 43–46, 50–53, 55 |
| Category B: | Factor(s) in category A not present |

*Starting point and category range (step two)*

> Same as IX (*ante*)

Consideration of custody threshold: category 2 or 3

*Aggravating and mitigating factors*

| | |
|---|---|
| Aggravating factors: | Factors 86, 87, 89, 91, 92, 94-96, 99-101, 103, 106 |
| Mitigating factors: | Factors 138, 139, 140*, 141, 142 |

## XXV. Engaging in sexual activity in the presence, procured by inducement, threat or deception, of a person with a mental disorder (2003 Act, s.36 (ibid., § 20-136)); causing such a person to watch a sexual act by inducement, threat or deception (2003 Act, s.37 (ibid., § 20-137))

*Factors indicating harm and culpability (step one)*

*Harm*                                                                                        **K-97**

Same as XI (*ante*)

*Culpability*

| | |
|---|---|
| Category A: | Factors 43–46, 50–53 |
| Category B: | Factor(s) in category A not present |

*Starting point and category range (step two)*

Same as XI (*ante*)

Consideration of custody threshold: category 2 or 3

*Aggravating and mitigating factors*

| | |
|---|---|
| Aggravating factors: | Factors 86, 87, 91, 92, 95, 96, 99-101 |
| Mitigating factors: | Factors 138-143 |

## XXVI. Care workers: sexual activity with a person with a mental disorder (2003 Act, s.38 (ibid., § 20-144)); care workers: causing or inciting sexual activity (2003 Act, s.39 (ibid., § 20-145))

*Factors indicating harm and culpability (step one)*

*Harm*                                                                                        **K-98**

Same as XIV (*ante*)

*Culpability*

| | |
|---|---|
| Category A: | Factors 43–45, 50–55, 57 |
| Category B: | Factor(s) in category A not present |

*Starting point and category range (step two)*

| | A | B |
|---|---|---|
| **Category 1** | **Starting point** 5 years<br>**Range** 4 – 10 years | **Starting point** 18 months<br>**Range** 1 – 2 years |
| **Category 2** | **Starting point** 3 years<br>**Range** 2 – 6 years | **Starting point** 26 weeks<br>**Range** medium level community order – 1 year |

| Category 3 | **Starting point** 26 weeks<br>**Range** high level community order – 3 years | **Starting point** medium level community order<br>**Range** low level – high level community order |
|---|---|---|

Consideration of custody threshold: category 2 or 3

*Aggravating and mitigating factors*

Aggravating factors:          Factors 86, 87, 89, 91, 92, 94-96, 99-101, 103, 104

Mitigating factors:          Factors 138, 139, 140*, 141, 142, 144

**XXVII. Care workers: sexual activity in the presence of a person with a mental disorder (2003 Act, s.40 (ibid., § 20-145)); care workers: causing such a person to watch a sexual act (2003 Act, s.41 (ibid., § 20-146))**

*Factors indicating harm and culpability (step one)*

*Harm*

Same as XI (*ante*)

*Culpability*

Category A:     Factors 43–45, 50–54, 57

Category B:     Factor(s) in category A not present

*Starting point and category range (step two)*

Same as XIV (*ante*)

Consideration of custody threshold: category 2 or 3

*Aggravating and mitigating factors*

Aggravating factors:          Factors 86, 87, 91, 92, 95, 96, 99-101, 104

Mitigating factors:          Factors 138-143

**XXVIII. Exposure (2003 Act, s.66 (ibid., § 20-208))**

*Factors indicating harm and culpability (step one)*

Category 1:     Raised harm **and** raised culpability

Category 2:     Raised harm **or** raised culpability

Category 3:     Exposure **without** raised harm or culpability factors present

Where an offence does not fall squarely into a category, individual factors may require a degree of weighting before making an overall assessment and determining the appropriate offence category.

*Indicators of raised harm*

Factors 37, 38

*Indicators of raised culpability*

Factors 46, 51–53, 57, 82

*Starting point and category range (step two)*

| Category 1 | **Starting point** 26 weeks<br>**Range** 12 weeks – 1 year |
| Category 2 | **Starting point** high level community order<br>**Range** medium level community order – 26 weeks |
| Category 3 | **Starting point** medium level community order<br>**Range** band A fine – high level community order |

Consideration of custody threshold: category 2
Consideration of community order threshold: category 3

*Aggravating and mitigating factors*

Aggravating factors:      Factors 86, 87, 91, 92, 95, 96, 98, 99, 101
Mitigating factors:      Factors 138-143

## XXIX. Voyeurism (2003 Act, s.67 (ibid., § 20-212))

*Factors indicating harm and culpability (step one)*

Category 1:      Raised harm **and** raised culpability      **K-101**
Category 2:      Raised harm **or** raised culpability
Category 3:      Voyeurism **without** raised harm or culpability factors present

Where an offence does not fall squarely into a category, individual factors may require a degree of weighting before making an overall assessment and determining the appropriate offence category.

*Indicators of raised harm*
Factors 39, 40

*Indicators of raised culpability*
Factors 43, 46, 50–53, 82, 83

*Starting point and category range (step two)*

| Category 1 | **Starting point** 26 weeks<br>**Range** 12 weeks – 18 months |
| Category 2 | **Starting point** high level community order<br>**Range** medium level community order – 26 weeks |
| Category 3 | **Starting point** medium level community order<br>**Range** band A fine – high level community order |

Consideration of custody threshold: category 2
Consideration of community order threshold: category 3

*Aggravating and mitigating factors*

Aggravating factors:      Factors 86, 87, 91, 92, 95, 96, 99, 100, 134-137
Mitigating factors:      Factors 138-143

### XXX. Sex with an adult relative: penetration (2003 Act, s.64 (ibid., § 20-202)); sex with an adult relative: consenting to penetration (2003 Act, s.65 (ibid., § 20-203))

*Factors indicating harm and culpability (step one)*

**K-102**       Category 1:     Raised harm **and** raised culpability

                Category 2:     Raised harm **or** raised culpability

                Category 3:     Sex with an adult relative **without** raised harm or culpability factors present

Where an offence does not fall squarely into a category, individual factors may require a degree of weighting before making an overall assessment and determining the appropriate offence category.

*Indicators of raised harm*

Factors 8, 41

*Indicators of raised culpability*

Factors 54, 57

*Starting point and category range (step two)*

| Category 1 | **Starting point** 1 year<br>**Range** 26 weeks – 2 years |
|---|---|
| Category 2 | **Starting point** high level community order<br>**Range** medium level community order – 1 year |
| Category 3 | **Starting point** medium level community order<br>**Range** band A fine – high level community order |

Consideration of custody threshold: category 2
Consideration of community order threshold: category 3

*Aggravating and mitigating factors*

Aggravating factors:          Factors 86, 87, 95, 96, 99, 100, 104

Mitigating factors:           Factors 138-143

### XXXI. Administering a substance with intent (2003 Act, s.61 (ibid., § 20-187))

*Factors indicating harm and culpability (step one)*

**K-103**       Category 1:     Raised harm **and** raised culpability

                Category 2:     Raised harm **or** raised culpability

                Category 3:     Administering a substance with intent **without** raised harm or culpability factors present

Where an offence does not fall squarely into a category, individual factors may require a degree of weighting before making an overall assessment and determining the appropriate offence category. Where no substantive sexual offence has been committed the main consideration for the court will be the offender's conduct as a whole including, but not exclusively, the offender's intention.

*Indicators of raised harm*

Factors 1, 3, 5

*Indicators of raised culpability*

> Factors 43, 44, 46, 49–53, 58, 84

*Starting point and category range (step two)*

| Category 1 | **Starting point** 6 years<br>**Range** 4 – 9 years |
|---|---|
| Category 2 | **Starting point** 4 years<br>**Range** 3 – 7 years |
| Category 3 | **Starting point** 2 years<br>**Range** 1 – 5 years |

*Aggravating and mitigating factors*

> Aggravating factors:  Factors 86, 87, 91, 92, 95, 96, 99, 100
>
> Mitigating factors:  Factors 138-143

### XXXII. Committing an offence with intent to commit a sexual offence (2003 Act, s.62 (ibid., § 20-192))

The starting point and range should be commensurate with that for the preliminary offence **K-104** actually committed, but with an enhancement to reflect the intention to commit a sexual offence. This will vary depending on the nature and seriousness of the intended sexual offence, but two years is suggested as a suitable enhancement where the intent was to commit rape or assault by penetration.

### XXXIII. Trespass with intent to commit a sexual offence (2003 Act, s.63 (ibid., § 20-197))

*Factors indicating harm and culpability (step one)*

> Category 1:  Raised harm **and** raised culpability **K-105**
>
> Category 2:  Raised harm **or** raised culpability
>
> Category 3:  Trespass with intent to commit a sexual offence **without** raised harm or culpability factors present

Where an offence does not fall squarely into a category, individual factors may require a degree of weighting before making an overall assessment and determining the appropriate offence category. Where no substantive sexual offence has been committed the main consideration for the court will be the offender's conduct as a whole including, but not exclusively, the offender's intention.

*Indicators of raised harm*

> Factors 3, 5, 42

*Indicators of raised culpability*

> Factors 43, 44, 46, 50–53, 58, 84, 85

*Starting point and category range (step two)*

> Same as XXXI (*ante*)

*Aggravating and mitigating factors*

>    Same as XXXI (*ante*)

### Errors

**K-106**    In XXVII, the starting point for a category 1A offence is given as 18 years' custody. It has been assumed that this should be 18 months. In XI, XXIII and XXV, the top of the range for a category 3B offence is given as a medium level community order (the same as the starting point), and thus it has been assumed that the top of the range should be a high level community order.

## I. FAILING TO SURRENDER TO BAIL

**K-107**    The Sentencing Guidelines Council has issued a definitive guideline on failing to surrender to bail (Bail Act 1976, s.6(1) and (2) (§ 3-31 in the main work)). It deals with offenders sentenced on or after December 10, 2007, and only relates to the sentencing of those aged 18 or over.

### Assessment of seriousness

**K-108**    The seriousness of an offence is to be determined by: (a) the offender's culpability (in particular, whether the failure to surrender was intended to cause harm and, if so, what level of harm), and (b) any harm which the offence caused, was intended to cause or might foreseeably have caused (in particular, to what extent the failure to surrender impeded the course of justice), and "harm" includes not only harm caused to victims and witnesses but also the consequential drain on the police and the courts and the wider negative impact on public confidence in the criminal justice system. The same approach to sentencing should be adopted for offences under both section 6(1) and (2), though the seriousness is likely to be less for an offence under subsection (2). The assessment of culpability requires consideration of the immediate reason why the defendant failed to appear, which can range from forgetfulness or fear of the outcome of the hearing to a deliberate act, and where the failure to surrender was deliberate, it will be relevant whether it was designed to disrupt the system to the defendant's advantage or whether the defendant simply gave no thought at all to the consequences. Failure to surrender will always cause some degree of harm, will inevitably delay justice, and will almost always waste public money. The circumstances of an offence, and the harm likely to be caused, will range from failure to appear for a first hearing but attending shortly afterwards (where the only harm caused is likely to be financial and procedural), to failure to appear for trial or sentence, especially where the trial does not proceed in the defendant's absence (where the harm caused may extend to the prevention of justice). Generally, the same approach should be taken whether the failure to surrender is to a court or to a police station, but the harm caused is likely to be less in the case of a police station, and there are also circumstances where the culpability may be less. Where sentence is passed in advance of the offence in respect of which bail was granted, the seriousness of that offence should not affect the assessment of seriousness, but the nature of that offence may affect the degree or likelihood of harm caused, such as where it is a violent or sexual offence, and an acquittal for that offence will not affect the seriousness of the failure to surrender.

   Aggravating factors that are particularly relevant to the assessment of seriousness are: (a) repeated offences under section 6; (b) the absence of the offender causing a lengthy delay to the administration of justice; and (c) a determined effort to avoid the jurisdiction of the court or to undermine the course of justice. Mitigating factors that are particularly relevant are: (a) prompt voluntary surrender (if initiated by the offender); (b) misunderstanding (which must be differentiated from a mistake on the part of the offender); (c) a failure to comprehend the requirements or significance of bail; and (d) caring responsibilities (where these are the cause of the failure to surrender). The fact that the offender has a disorganised or chaotic lifestyle (which may be due to dependence on drugs or alcohol) does not mitigate the seriousness of the offence (though it may amount to personal mitigation).

### Procedural issues

**K-109**    *As to when to sentence*, the key principle is stated to be that a court should deal with a defendant who fails to surrender as soon as it is practicable, even if the trial or other hearing for the offence in respect of which bail was granted is adjourned. Relevant factors when deciding what is practicable include: (a) when the proceedings in respect of which bail was granted are expected to conclude; (b) the seriousness of that offence; and (c) the type of penalty that might be imposed for that offence and for the failure to surrender. Liability for the section 6 offence should be determined as soon as possible, since it will be central to the issue of whether bail should be renewed; accordingly, a trial should be held on the first appearance after arrest or surrender, unless an adjournment is necessary. Occasions on which it may be more appropriate to sentence both offences together include circumstances where the totality of sentence may affect sentence type and where the harm caused cannot be assessed at an earlier stage.

*As to sentencing*, the alternatives to immediate custody are a community order, including an **K-110** electronically monitored curfew requirement and, perhaps, a supervision or activity requirement, and, in more serious cases, a suspended sentence. Where custodial sentences are imposed both for the section 6 offence and for the substantive offence, they should normally be consecutive, but should be concurrent where otherwise the overall sentence would be disproportionate to the combined seriousness of the offences.

*As to trial in the defendant's absence*, where it has proved possible to proceed to trial or conclude **K-111** proceedings in the absence of the defendant, this should have no bearing on culpability, but may be relevant to the assessment of harm, if the harm caused by the failure to attend has been reduced or avoided by such a course.

### Sentencing ranges and starting points

The sentencing ranges and starting points relate to persons convicted following a plea of not **K-112** guilty, and who do not have a conviction which, by virtue of the CJA 2003, s.143(2) (§ 5-67 in the main work), must be treated as an aggravating factor. A court should identify the description that most nearly matches the facts of the offence and this will identify a starting point, from which a provisional sentence can be reached. The sentencing range is the bracket into which the provisional sentence will fall after consideration of aggravating or mitigating factors (although particular circumstances, particular matters of aggravation or mitigation or the reduction for a guilty plea may require a sentence outside of that range). A court should give reasons for imposing a sentence of a different kind or outside the range provided in the guideline.

For a deliberate failure to attend causing delay and/or interference with the administration of justice, the starting point is 14 days' custody, and the range, in a magistrates' court, should be from a community order (low) to 10 weeks' custody, and in the Crown Court, should be from a community order (medium) to 40 weeks' custody, with the type and degree of harm actually caused affecting where in the range the case falls. For a negligent or non-deliberate failure to attend causing delay and/or interference with the administration of justice, the starting point should be a fine, and the range (regardless of court) should be from a fine to a community order (medium). Where the defendant surrenders late, but the case proceeds as planned, the starting point and the range should be a fine.

### J. Assault and Other Offences Against the Person

The Sentencing Council for England and Wales has issued a definitive guideline on non-fatal **K-113** offences against the person, applying to all offenders aged 18 or over who are sentenced on or after June 13, 2011, regardless of the date of their offence. The offences covered are: (A) causing grievous bodily harm, or wounding, with intent to do grievous bodily harm (Offences against the Person Act 1861, s.18 (§ 19-251 in the main work)), (B) inflicting grievous bodily harm or unlawful wounding (1861 Act, s.20 (*ibid.*, § 19-252)) and racially or religiously aggravated grievous bodily harm or unlawful wounding (CDA 1998, s.29 (*ibid.*, § 19-266)), (C) assault occasioning actual bodily harm (1861 Act, s.47 (*ibid.*, § 19-242)) and racially or religiously aggravated actual bodily harm (1998 Act, s.29), (D) assault with intent to resist arrest (1861 Act, s.38 (*ibid.*, § 19-316)), (E) assault on a police constable in execution of his duty (Police Act 1996, s.89), and (F) common assault (CJA 1988, s.39) and racially or religiously aggravated common assault (1998 Act, s.29).

The guideline sets out eight to nine steps to be followed (in order) when sentencing for these **K-114** offences, which are as follows, subject to any modifications set out in the specific sections relating to each group (*post*).

Step one requires the court to determine within which of three categories reflecting various degrees of seriousness the offence falls. Category 1 requires greater harm and higher culpability, category 2 requires either greater harm and lower culpability or lesser harm and higher culpability, and category 3 requires lesser harm and lower culpability. In determining the offender's culpability and the harm caused (or intended), the court should refer only to the factors indicating harm and culpability set out in the specific sections relating to A to F, *post*, which comprise the principal factual elements of the offence.

Step two requires the court to use the starting point identified for the relevant category (as to which, see also the specific sections relating to A-F, *post*) to reach a sentence within the category range (*post*). The starting point applies to all offenders irrespective of plea or previous convictions. A case of particular gravity, reflected by multiple features of culpability in step one, could merit upward adjustment from the starting point before further adjustment is made for the aggravating or mitigating factors increasing or reducing seriousness or reflecting personal mitigation set out in the specific sections relating to A to F, post, which contain a non-exhaustive list of additional factual elements providing the context of the offence and factors relating to the offender. Having considered all these, and other relevant factors, it might be appropriate to move outside the identified category range.

At step three, the court should take into account sections 73 and 74 of the SOCPA 2005 (assistance by defendants: reduction or review of sentence (*ibid.*, §§ 5-132, 5-133)), and any other rule of law by virtue of which an offender may receive a discounted sentence in consequence of assistance given (or offered) to the prosecutor or investigator.

At step four, the court should take account of any potential reduction for a guilty plea in accordance with section 144 of the CJA 2003 (*ibid.*, § 5-107) and the revised guideline on reductions in sentence for guilty pleas (*ante*, Appendix K-1 *et seq.*).

At step five, which does not apply to the offence in E (assault on a police constable in execution of his duty), the court will consider whether the offender meets the dangerousness criteria for a life sentence or imprisonment for public protection (in respect of those offences which are serious offences within the meaning of the 2003 Act, Ch. 5 (*ibid.*, §§ 5-495 *et seq.*), in which case the notional determinate sentence should be used as the basis for setting the minimum term) or an extended sentence (in respect of those offences which are specified offences within the meaning of the 2003 Act, Ch. 5).

At step six (or five), the court should apply the totality principle, step seven (or six), consider whether to make compensation or other ancillary orders or both, step eight (or seven), give its reasons for, and explain the effect of, the sentence (2003 Act, s.174 (*ibid.*, § 5-165)), and step nine (or eight) take into account any time spent on remand in custody or on bail (2003 Act, ss.240 and 240A (*ibid.*, §§ 5-640, 5-645)).

For offences under the 1998 Act, s.29, only, the court should determine the appropriate sentence for the offence without taking account of the element of aggravation, and then make an addition to the sentence, considering the level of aggravation involved. It may be appropriate to move outside the identified category range, taking into account the increased statutory maximum.

### Key to factors indicating greater harm and higher or lower culpability (step one)

*Factors indicating greater harm*

**K-115**     a. Injury (which includes disease transmission and/ or psychological harm) which is serious in the context of the offence (must normally be present).
　　b. Victim is particularly vulnerable because of personal circumstances.
　　c. Sustained or repeated assault on the same victim.
　　d. Injury or fear of injury which is serious in the context of the offence (must normally be present).

*Factors indicating higher culpability*

**K-116**     Statutory aggravating factors:
　　e. offence racially or religiously aggravated.
　　f. offence motivated by, or demonstrating, hostility to the victim based on his or her sexual orientation (or presumed sexual orientation).

g. offence motivated by, or demonstrating, hostility to the victim based on the victim's disability (or presumed disability).

Other aggravating factors:

h. A significant degree of premeditation.

i. Use of weapon or weapon equivalent (*e.g.* shod foot, headbutting, use of acid, use of animal).

j. Threatened use of weapon or weapon equivalent.

k. Intention to commit more serious harm than actually resulted from the offence.

l. Deliberately causes more harm than is necessary for commission of offence.

m. Deliberate targeting of vulnerable victim.

n. Leading role in group or gang.

o. Offence motivated by, or demonstrating, hostility based on the victim's age, sex, gender identity (or presumed gender identity).

*Factors indicating lower culpability*

p. Subordinate role in group or gang.                                          **K-117**

q. A greater degree of provocation than normally expected.

r. Lack of premeditation.

s. Mental disorder or learning disability, where linked to commission of the offence.

t. Excessive self defence.

## Key to factors increasing or reducing seriousness or reflecting personal mitigation (step 2)

*Factors increasing seriousness*

Statutory aggravating factors:                                                 **K-118**

u. Previous convictions (in accordance with the 2003 Act, s.143(2) (§ 5-67 in the main work)).

v. Offence committed whilst on bail (2003 Act, s.143(3)).

Other aggravating factors include:

w. Location of the offence.

x. Timing of the offence.

y. Continuing effect upon the victim.

z. Offence committed against those working in the public sector or providing a service to the public.

aa. Presence of others including relatives, especially children or partner of the victim.

bb. Gratuitous degradation of victim.

cc. In domestic violence cases, victim forced to leave home.

dd. Failure to comply with current court orders.

ee. Offence committed whilst on licence.

ff. An attempt to conceal or dispose of evidence.

gg. Failure to respond to warnings or concerns expressed by others about the offender's behaviour.

hh. Commission of offence whilst under the influence of alcohol or drugs.

ii. Abuse of power and/ or position of trust.

jj. Exploiting contact arrangements with a child to commit an offence.

kk. Any steps taken to prevent the victim reporting an incident, obtaining assistance and/ or from assisting or supporting the prosecution.

ll. Offences taken into consideration.

*Factors reducing seriousness or reflecting personal mitigation*

mm. No previous convictions or no relevant/ recent convictions.                **K-119**

nn. Single blow.

oo. Remorse.

pp. Good character and/ or exemplary conduct.

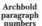
qq. Determination and/ or demonstration of steps taken to address addiction or offending behaviour.

rr. serious medical conditions requiring urgent, intensive or long-term treatment.

ss. isolated incident.

tt. Age and/ or lack of maturity where it affects the responsibility of the offender.

uu. Lapse of time since the offence where this is not the fault of the offender.

vv. Mental disorder or learning disability, where not linked to the commission of the offence.

ww. Sole or primary carer for dependent relatives.

### Fine bands

**K-120**

| Fine band | Starting point (applicable to all offenders) | Category range (applicable to all offenders) |
|---|---|---|
| band A | 50% of relevant weekly income | 25 – 75% of relevant weekly income |
| band B | 100% of relevant weekly income | 75 – 125% of relevant weekly income |
| band C | 150% of relevant weekly income | 125 – 175% of relevant weekly income |

### Community orders

**K-121**      The following table sets out a non-exhaustive description of examples of requirements that might be appropriate for low, medium and high level community orders (respectively). Where two or more requirements are ordered, they must be compatible with each other.

| Low | Medium | High |
|---|---|---|
| In general, only one requirement will be appropriate and the length may be curtailed if additional requirements are necessary | | More intensive sentences which combine two or more requirements may be appropriate |
| Suitable requirements might include:<br>• 40 – 80 hours unpaid work<br>• curfew requirement within the lowest range (*e.g.* up to 12 hours per day for a few weeks)<br>• exclusion requirement, without electronic monitoring, for a few months<br>• prohibited activity requirement<br>• attendance centre requirement (where available) | Suitable requirements might include:<br>• greater number of hours of unpaid work (*e.g.* 80 – 150 hours)<br>• an activity requirement in the middle range (20 – 30 days)<br>• curfew requirement within the middle range (*e.g.* up to 12 hours for two – three months)<br>• exclusion requirement, lasting in the region of six months<br>• prohibited activity requirement | Suitable requirements might include:<br>• 150 – 300 hours unpaid work<br>• activity requirement up to the maximum of 60 days<br>• curfew requirement up to 12 hours per day for four – six months<br>• exclusion order lasting in the region of 12 months |

## A. Causing grievous bodily harm, or wounding, with intent to do grievous bodily harm

In assessing whether there has been greater harm for the purposes of determining the offence **K-122** category in respect of these offences, serious injury must normally be present.

*Factors indicating harm and culpability (step one)*

      Greater harm: a–c
      Lesser harm: injury which is less serious in the context of the offence
      Higher culpability: e–i, k–o
      Lower culpability: p–t

*Starting point and category range (step two)*

| Offence category | | Starting point (applicable to all offenders) | Category range (applicable to all offenders) |
| --- | --- | --- | --- |
| category 1 | | 12 years' custody | nine – 16 years' custody |
| category 2 | | six years' custody | five – nine years' custody |
| category 3 | | four years' custody | three – five years' custody |

*Factors increasing or reducing seriousness or reflecting personal mitigation*

      Factors increasing seriousness: u–z, aa–ll
      Factors reducing seriousness or reflecting personal mitigation: mm–ww

## B. Inflicting grievous bodily harm or unlawful wounding and racially or religiously aggravated grievous bodily harm or unlawful wounding

In assessing whether there has been greater harm for the purposes of determining the offence **K-123** category in respect of these offences, serious injury must normally be present.

*Factors indicating harm and culpability (step one)*

      Greater harm: a–c
      Lesser harm: injury which is less serious in the context of the offence
      Higher culpability: f–i, k–o
      Lower culpability: p–t

*Starting point and category range (step two)*

| Offence category | Starting point (applicable to all offenders) | Category range (applicable to all offenders) |
| --- | --- | --- |
| category 1 | three years' custody | 30 months' — four years' custody |
| category 2 | 18 months' custody | one –three years' custody |
| category 3 | high level community order | low level community order — 51 weeks' custody |

When sentencing for category three offences, the court should consider whether the custody threshold has been passed, if so, whether it is unavoidable that a custodial sentence be imposed and, if so, whether that sentence can be suspended.

*Factors increasing or reducing seriousness or reflecting personal mitigation*

      Same as for A, *ante*.

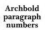

### C. Assault occasioning actual bodily harm and racially or religiously aggravated actual bodily harm

**K-124**    In assessing whether there has been "greater harm" for the purposes of determining the offence category in respect of these offences, serious injury must normally be present.

*Factors indicating harm and culpability (step one)*
Same as for B, *ante*.

*Starting point and category range (step two)*

| Offence category | Starting point (applicable to all offenders) | Category range (applicable to all offenders) |
|---|---|---|
| category 1 | 18 months' custody | one – three years' custody |
| category 2 | 26 weeks' custody | low level community order – 51 weeks' custody |
| category 3 | medium level community order | band A fine – high level community order |

When sentencing for category two offences, the court should consider whether the custody threshold has been passed, if so, whether it is unavoidable that a custodial sentence be imposed and, if so, whether that sentence can be suspended; and in sentencing for category three offences, the court should also consider whether the community order threshold has been passed.

*Factors increasing or reducing seriousness or reflecting personal mitigation*
Same as for A and B, *ante*.

### D. Assault with intent to resist arrest

*Factors indicating harm and culpability (step one)*
**K-125**    Greater harm: c
Lesser harm: injury which is less serious in the context of the offence
Higher culpability: e–i, k–l, n, o
Lower culpability: p, r, s

*Starting point and category range (step two)*

| Offence category | Starting point (applicable to all offenders) | Category range (applicable to all offenders) |
|---|---|---|
| category 1 | 26 weeks' custody | 12 – 51 weeks' custody |
| category 2 | medium level community order | low level community order – high level community order |
| category 3 | band B fine | band A fine – band C fine |

When sentencing for category one offences, the court should consider whether the sentence can be suspended.

*Factors increasing or reducing seriousness or reflecting personal mitigation*
Factors increasing seriousness: u–y, bb, dd–hh, kk, ll
Factors reducing seriousness or reflecting personal mitigation: mm–tt, vv, ww

### E. Assault on a police constable in execution of his duty

*Factors indicating harm and culpability (step one)*
**K-126**    Same as for D, *ante*.

796

*Starting point and category range (step two)*

| Offence category | Starting point (applicable to all offenders) | Category range (applicable to all offenders) |
| --- | --- | --- |
| category 1 | 12 weeks' custody | low level community order – 26 weeks' custody |
| category 2 | medium level community order | low level community order – high level community order |
| category 3 | band B fine | band A fine – band C fine |

When sentencing for category one offences, the court should consider whether the custody threshold has been passed, if so, whether it is unavoidable that a custodial sentence be imposed and, if so, whether that sentence can be suspended.

*Factors increasing or reducing seriousness or reflecting personal mitigation*
  Factors increasing seriousness: u–y, bb, dd–hh, kk, ll
  Factors reducing seriousness or reflecting personal mitigation: mm–ww

## F. Common assault and racially or religiously aggravated common assault

In assessing whether there has been "greater harm" for the purposes of determining the of- **K-127** fence category in respect of these offences, injury or fear of injury must normally be present.

*Factors indicating harm and culpability (step one)*
  Greater harm: b–d
  Lesser harm: injury which is less serious in the context of the offence
  Higher culpability: f–o
  Lower culpability: p–t

*Starting point and category range (step two)*

| Offence category | Starting point (applicable to all offenders) | Category range (applicable to all offenders) |
| --- | --- | --- |
| category 1 | high level community order | low level community order – 26 weeks' custody |
| category 2 | medium level community order | band A fine – high level community order |
| category 3 | band A fine | discharge – band C fine |

When sentencing for category one offences, the court should consider whether the custody threshold has been passed, if so, whether it is unavoidable that a custodial sentence be imposed and, if so, whether that sentence can be suspended. When sentencing for category two offences, the court should consider whether the community order threshold has been crossed.

*Factors increasing or reducing seriousness or reflecting personal mitigation*
  Same as for A, B and C, *ante*.

**[The next paragraph is K-131.]**

### K. Assaults on Children and Cruelty to a Child

The Sentencing Guidelines Council has issued a definitive guideline (i) supplementing the **K-131** guideline on assaults and other offences against the person (*ante*, K-113 *et seq.*) by detailing additional principles which apply where the victim of the offence was aged 15 or under and (ii) on the offence of cruelty to a child (CYPA 1933, s.1(1)). It deals with offenders sentenced on or after March 3, 2008, and only relates to the sentencing of those aged 18 or over.

## Part 1: Assaults on children: general principles

**Assessing seriousness**

K-132    The seriousness of an offence is to be determined by (a) the culpability of the offender and (b) the harm caused, intended or reasonably foreseeable, and guidance on whether sentencing thresholds have been reached is provided by the guideline on seriousness. Where an offender has previous convictions, the court must consider whether it should treat any of them as an aggravating factor, having regard to the nature and relevance of each offence and the time that has elapsed since the conviction. The fact that the victim is a child is likely to aggravate the seriousness of the offence where the offender is an adult.

*Aggravation*

K-133    The fact that the victim of an assault is a child will often mean that the offence involves a particularly vulnerable victim. The most relevant aggravating factors are: (i) the victim is particularly vulnerable; (ii) an abuse of power; (iii) an abuse of a position of trust; (iv) an especially serious physical or psychological effect on the victim, even if unintended; (v) the presence of others, *e.g.* relatives, especially other children; and (vi) additional degradation of the victim. Additional aggravating factors are: (i) sadistic behaviour; (ii) the making of threats to prevent the victim reporting the offence; (iii) the deliberate concealment of the victim from the authorities; and (iv) a failure to seek medical help. The location and particular circumstances of the offence may also be relevant aggravating factors.

*Mitigation*

K-134    The defence of lawful chastisement is only available on a charge of common assault, and where that defence is not available or is not made out, sentencing for the offence should normally be approached in the same way as for any other assault, even where an offender held a genuine belief that his actions amounted to no more than a legitimate form of physical punishment. However, if an offender has been charged with assault occasioning actual bodily harm and the court has found that he only intended to administer lawful chastisement to the child, and that the injury that was inflicted was neither intended nor foreseen by him, there should be a substantial reduction in sentence and a custodial sentence should not normally be imposed. Where the injury was neither intended nor foreseen, and was not even reasonably foreseeable, then a discharge might be appropriate.

**Other factors relevant to sentencing**

*Adverse effect of the sentence on the victim*

K-135    Imposition of a custodial sentence will often protect a victim from further harm and anguish, and some children will be less traumatised once they are no longer living with an abusive carer, but where imprisonment of the offender deprives a child victim of his sole or main carer (and may result in the child being taken into care), it may punish and re-victimise the child. Imposing a custodial sentence on the offender may be the only option, but where other sentencing options remain open, the court should take into account the impact that a custodial sentence for the offender might have on the victim. The court also needs to be aware of the progress of any concurrent family proceedings.

*Offenders who have primary care responsibilities*

K-136    Where the offender is the sole or primary carer of the victim or other dependants, this should potentially be taken into account for sentencing purposes, regardless of whether the offender is male or female. In such cases, an immediate custodial sentence may not be appropriate and, subject to a risk assessment, the offender may be able to resume care of or have contact with the victim.

## Part 2: Cruelty to a child

**Assessing seriousness**

K-137    One category of child cruelty is not automatically more serious than another and, in order properly to assess the seriousness of an offence, its precise nature must be established before consideration is given to a range of contingent factors, including the defendant's intent, the length of time over which the cruelty took place, and the degree of physical and psychological harm suffered by the victim.

*Culpability*

Culpability should be the initial factor in determining the seriousness of an offence. An offence **K-138** may be the consequence of a wide range of factors including: (i) sadism; (ii) violence resulting from any number of causes; (iii) a reduced ability to protect a child in the face of aggression from an overbearing partner; (iv) indifference or apathy resulting from low intelligence or induced by alcohol or drug dependence; (v) immaturity or social deprivation resulting in an inability to cope with the pressures of caring for children; and (vi) psychiatric illness. It might also arise as the result of a momentary lack of control by an otherwise responsible and loving carer. The extent to which any of these factors might have contributed to the commission of an offence will be important in determining the culpability of the offender. A court must strike a balance between the need to reflect the serious view which society takes of the ill-treatment of young children and the need to protect those children, and also the pressures upon immature and inadequate parents attempting to cope with the problems of infancy, and the extent to which remorse should influence sentence will always have to be judged in the light of all the circumstances. The normal starting point should be a custodial sentence, the length of which should be influenced by the circumstances surrounding the offence.

*Harm*

It is helpful if the indictment clearly states the nature of the offender's conduct, but even where **K-139** this is clear, difficulties arise in determining the relative seriousness of the different forms of child cruelty. There is, however, a significant distinction between cases of wilful ill-treatment which usually involve positive acts of abuse and physical violence, and cases of neglect which are typified by the absence of actions. There is also a distinction between cases involving physical injury, whether resulting directly from an assault or ill-treatment or resulting from a period of abandonment or neglect, and cases where the harm occasioned is exposure to the risk of harm or lack of proper care, attention or supervision. In addition, whether one form of cruelty is worse than another will depend not only on the degree to which the victim suffers as a result but also on the motivation and culpability of the offender.

*Aggravating and mitigating factors*

The guideline refers to the guideline on seriousness for general aggravating and mitigating **K-140** factors. In particular, care should be taken to avoid "double-counting" when an essential element of an offence might, in other circumstances, be an aggravating factor, and the abuse of trust or abuse of power inherent in the offence have been built into the guideline and should not be treated as aggravating factors. Relevant aggravating factors are targeting one particular child from the family and the four additional aggravating factors listed under "Assaults on children: general principles" (*ante*). The sole relevant mitigating factor is seeking medical help or bringing the situation to the notice of the authorities.

## Other factors relevant to sentencing

*Long-term psychological harm*

The starting points have been calculated to reflect the likelihood of psychological harm and this **K-141** cannot be treated as an aggravating factor. Where there is an especially serious physical or psychological effect on the victim, even if unintended, this should result in an increased sentence.

*Adverse effect of the sentence on the victim*

As in Part 1, *ante*. **K-142**

*Offenders who have primary care responsibilities*

As in Part 1, *ante*. **K-143**

*Personal mitigation*

The most relevant areas of personal mitigation are likely to be: (i) mental illness/ depression; **K-144**

(ii) inability to cope with the pressures of parenthood; (iii) lack of support; (iv) sleep deprivation; (v) domination of the offender by an abusive or stronger partner; (vi) extreme behavioural difficulties in the child, often coupled with a lack of support; and (vii) inability to secure assistance or support services in spite of every effort having been made by the offender. However, some of these factors could be regarded as an inherent part of caring for children, especially with young children, and so before they are accepted in mitigation, there must be evidence that these factors were present to a high degree and had an identifiable and significant impact on the offender's behaviour.

### Factors to take into consideration

**K-145**     *Dangerous offenders*: the offence is a "specified offence" within the CJA 2003, s.224, and so a court must consider the imposition of a sentence for public protection. The guideline only applies to offenders who have not been classed as dangerous.

*Categories of offence*: the same starting point applies regardless of which of the various ways in which the offence can be committed is in point, and it already assumes an abuse of trust or power and the likelihood of psychological harm, and is designed to reflect the seriousness with which society as a whole regards these offences.

*Additional factors*: only additional aggravating and mitigating factors specifically relevant to this offence are included in the guideline, and a court must always take into account the full list of factors in the guideline on seriousness.

### Sentencing ranges and starting points

**K-146**     The sentencing ranges and starting points relate to persons convicted following a plea of not guilty, and who do not have a conviction which, by virtue of the 2003 Act, s.143(2) (§ 5-67 in the main work), must be treated as an aggravating factor. A court should identify the description that most nearly matches the facts of the offence and this will identify a starting point, from which a provisional sentence can be reached. The sentencing range is the bracket into which the provisional sentence will fall after consideration of aggravating or mitigating factors (although particular circumstances, particular matters of aggravation or mitigation, or the reduction for a guilty plea may require a sentence outside of that range). The provisional sentence may then be reduced by matters of personal mitigation, which may also take it outside the appropriate sentencing range. A court should give reasons for imposing a sentence of a different kind or outside the range provided in the guideline.

Where there has been (i) serious cruelty over a period of time, (ii) serious long-term neglect, or (iii) a failure to protect a child from either of these, the starting point is six years' custody and the sentencing range is five to nine years' custody.

Where there has been (i) a series of assaults (the more serious the individual assaults and the longer the period over which they are perpetrated, the more serious the offence), (ii) protracted neglect or ill-treatment (the longer the period of ill-treatment or neglect and the longer the period over which it takes place, the more serious the offence), or (iii) a failure to protect a child from either of these, the starting point is three years' custody and the sentencing range is two to five years' custody.

Where there has been (i) an assault resulting in injuries consistent with assault occasioning actual bodily harm, (ii) more than one incident of neglect or ill-treatment (but not amounting to long-term behaviour), (iii) a single incident of long-term abandonment or regular incidents of short-term abandonment (the longer the period of long-term abandonment or the greater the number of incidents of short-term abandonment, the more serious the offence), or (iv) a failure to protect a child from any of these, the starting point is 36 weeks' custody and the sentencing range is 26 weeks' to two years' custody.

Where there has been (i) short-term neglect or ill-treatment, (ii) a single incident of shortterm abandonment, or (iii) a failure to protect a child from any of these, the starting point is 12 weeks' custody and the sentencing range is a community order (low) to 26 weeks' custody.

### L. SENTENCING IN MAGISTRATES' COURTS

### Introduction

**K-147**     The Sentencing Guidelines Council has issued a guideline on offences for which sentence is frequently imposed in magistrates' courts when dealing with adult offenders, which replaces the guidelines which were effective from January 1, 2004. The foreword and introduction state that they are to apply to all relevant cases appearing for allocation (mode of trial) or for sentence on or after August 4, 2008, not only in magistrates' courts, but also in the Crown Court when dealing with appeals against sentence and when sentencing for summary only offences. The guideline should be consulted when dealing with an either-way offence for which there is no plea or an indication of a not guilty plea, since they will be relevant to the mode of trial decision, and where an offence is included in this guideline, it supersedes the equivalent part of the mode of trial guidelines in Part V.51 of the consolidated criminal practice direction (§ 1-119 in the main work). The guideline will also be relevant to decisions as to committal for sentence.

There have been 12 updates to these guidelines. An update that took effect on January 5, 2009, made changes to Parts 1 (indices), 3 (offence guidelines) and 5 (explanatory material). The effect of the changes to Part 3 was (i) to include extracts from the guideline on breach of an anti-social behaviour order (*post*, K-196 *et seq.*) and the guideline on theft and burglary in a building other than a dwelling (*post*, K-209 *et seq.*) in these guidelines in the appropriate places, and (ii) to make a clarificatory amendment to the existing guideline for burglary in a dwelling. Consequential amendments were made to the section in Part 5 that relates to ancillary orders, in respect of anti-social behaviour orders, and an amendment was also made to that section in respect of orders disqualifying an offender from driving, to reflect recent case law.

An update implemented on August 4, 2008, made equivalent changes to Part 3 in relation to the guideline on causing death by driving (*post*, K-185 *et seq.*) and modified Part 5 in respect of explanatory material relating to dangerous offenders (to take account of changes made by the CJIA 2008).

The third update was published on October 13, 2009. This included new guidelines for statutory offences of fraud (reflective of the guideline for such offences (*post*, K-228 *et seq.*). In addition, supplementary guidance was provided in relation to sentencing for health and safety offences following changes to the maximum penalty for certain offences effected by the Health and Safety (Offences) Act 2008 and which came into effect on January 16, 2009.

As from June 13, 2011, a fourth update will apply to all offenders aged 18 or over who are sentenced on or after that date, regardless of the date of their offence, with the effect that the new guideline on offences against the person (as to which, see *ante*, K-113 *et seq.*) is imported, except for those parts dealing with indictable-only offences, with the imposition of sentences which magistrates are not entitled to impose, and with sections 73 and 74 of the SOCPA 2005 (§§ 5-132, 5-133 in the main work), since they apply only in the Crown Court.

A fifth update was issued on October 13, 2011, and applies to all offenders aged 18 or over who are sentenced on or after January 16, 2012, regardless of the date of their offence. The effect is to import the guidelines on domestic and non-domestic burglary (but not aggravated burglary, which is an indictable-only offence) (as to which, see *post*, K-259 *et seq.*), except that, at step three, there is no mention of sections 73 and 74 of the SOCPA 2005 (§§ 5-132, 5-133 in the main work), since they apply only in the Crown Court. The starting points and category ranges apply to all offenders in all cases, irrespective of plea or previous convictions.

A sixth update was issued on January 24, 2012. This applies to all offenders aged 18 or over who are sentenced on or after February 27, 2012, regardless of the date of their offence. The effect is to import the guidelines on drug offences (*post*, K-271 *et seq.*).

As from June 11, 2012, a seventh update applies to all offenders aged 18 or over who are sentenced on or after that date, regardless of the date of their offence, with the effect that a new definitive guideline on the allocation of offences (see *ante*, § 1-97) and a guideline on offences taken into consideration (*ante*, §§ 5-160 *et seq.*) and totality (*post*, K-280 *et seq.*) are imported. It also corrects an error in one of the drug offence guidelines (importation) issued in the sixth update (this correction has been incorporated into the supplement at K-275, *post*).

As from August 20, 2012, an eighth update applies to all offenders aged 18 or over who are sentenced on or after that date, regardless of the date of their offence, with the effect that a new definitive guideline on dangerous dog offences (*post*, K-291 *et seq.*) is imported into the guideline.

A ninth update makes alterations to Part 5 (explanatory material) to reflect changes made to the victim surcharge by the Criminal Justice Act 2003 (Surcharge) Order 2012 (S.I. 2012 No. 1696) (see §§ 5-1300 *et seq.* in the main work) and amendments (not yet in force) to sentencing legislation effected by the LASPOA 2012. As to the latter, the new material deals, in particular, with the new requirements (foreign travel prohibition and alcohol abstinence and monitoring) that may be attached to a community sentence or a suspended sentence, the new law relating to suspended sentences (their length and the necessity or otherwise to attach community requirements) and the making of hostility based on transgender identity a statutory aggravating factor.

The Sentencing Council issued a tenth update, applying to all offenders aged 18 or over who are sentenced on or after April 1, 2014. The principal effect was to replace the incorporation of the previous Sentencing Guideline's Council guideline on sexual offences with the new Sentencing Council's guideline on sexual offences (*ante*, K-84 *et seq.*), save for such parts thereof as can only have any application in the Crown Court. The starting points apply in all cases, irrespective of previous convictions or plea.

The update also revised the explanatory material in Part 5 relating to road traffic offences. The starting point when considering disqualification from driving in a defendant's absence is now that disqualification should be imposed in an offender's absence if there is no reason to believe that the defendant is unaware of the proceedings and where the statutory notice has been served pursuant to the MCA 1980, s.11(4). It should not be imposed in the absence of the offender where there is evidence that there is an acceptable reason for the defendant's absence or where there are reasons to believe it would be contrary to the interests of justice.

★    As from July 1, 2014, an eleventh update to the sentencing guidelines for magistrates' courts applies to all offenders aged 18 or over who are sentenced on or after that date, the principal effect of which was to incorporate the Sentencing Council's guideline on environmental offences (as to which, see *ante*, § 5-147), and to expand the explanatory material relating to health and safety offences to include environmental offences. The update also corrects an error in the section of the tenth update (*ante*) relating to indecent photographs of children.

★    As from October 1, 2014, a twelfth update to the sentencing guidelines for magistrates' courts applies to all offenders aged 18 or over who are sentenced on or after that date. The principal effect is to incorporate the Sentencing Council's guideline on fraud, money laundering and bribery offences (*post*, Appendix K-297 *et seq.*), but the opportunity has also been taken to bring up to date the table of offences for which fixed penalty notices are available and the amount of such penalties in Annex B to the explanatory material.

### Recommendations

K-148    The following recommendations are sentence recommendations where the starting points are based on a first time offender who has pleaded not guilty. However, the guideline makes plain that they are to be used by magistrates in making decisions as to whether or not an offender should be tried or sentenced in the magistrates' court or the Crown Court. What is set out below is confined to that which is material to the latter decision. It follows, therefore, that the full range of recommendations is not necessarily set out. For example, in the case of burglary of a dwelling, for a case involving an unforced entry with property of low value being stolen and no aggravating features, the top end of the recommended range is 12 weeks' custody, which is well within the maximum available to a magistrates' court. Any description of offence which is of a less serious nature than the descriptions set out below may, therefore, be taken to be suitable for summary trial.

Whilst the guideline itself lists aggravating and mitigating features for all the offences, these are only set out below where the presence or absence of such features is relevant to the decision as to the appropriate court for trial or sentence.

### Burglary in a dwelling

K-149    The guideline recommends—
(i) a starting point of 12 weeks' custody and a range of sentence from a high level community order to sentence in the Crown Court for a case of forced entry where the goods stolen were not of high value and without aggravating features;
(ii) sentence in the Crown Court where the goods stolen were of high value and any aggravating feature was present.

K-150    Particular aggravating features mentioned are: (*as indicating higher culpability*) ransacking, professionalism, a victim deliberately targeted, *e.g.* out of spite, the carrying of housebreaking implements or weapons; (*as indicating greater degree of harm*) occupier at home or returning home during burglary, goods stolen being of sentimental value.

As to aggravating features, see *R. v. Saw, post*, § K-441.

For offences for which sentence is passed on or after January 16, 2012, see now the guideline issued by the Sentencing Council for England and Wales, *post*, K-259 *et seq.*

## Handling stolen goods

The guideline recommends—     **K-151**
 (i) a starting point of 12 weeks' custody and a range of sentence from six weeks' custody to sentence in the Crown Court for sophisticated offending or the presence of at least two aggravating features;
 (ii) sentence in the Crown Court where the offence was committed in the context of a business, the offender acts as an organiser/ distributor of the proceeds of crime, the offender makes himself available to other criminals as willing to handle the proceeds of thefts or burglaries, the offending was highly organised or professional, or the original offence was particularly serious, *e.g.* armed robbery.

Particular aggravating features mentioned are: (*as indicating higher culpability*) closeness of offender to primary offence, which may be geographical (arising from presence at or near the primary offence) or temporal (where offender instigated primary offence or, soon after, provided safe haven or route for disposal), high level of profit made or expected; (*as indicating greater degree of harm*) seriousness of the primary offence, including domestic burglary, high (including sentimental) value of goods; threats of violence or abuse of power by offender over others, such as an adult commissioning criminal activity by children or a drug dealer pressurising addicts to steal to fund their habit.     **K-152**

## Going equipped for theft

The guideline recommends a starting point of a high level community order and a range of a medium level community order to sentence in the Crown Court in the case of possession of items for burglary or robbery.     **K-153**

## False statements/representations to obtain social security benefits

For offences under the Social Security Administration Act 1992, s.111A, see the fraud guideline, *post*, K-228 *et seq.*     **K-154**

## Vehicle licence/registration fraud (Vehicle Excise and Registration Act 1994, s.44)

The guideline recommends sentence in the Crown Court in the case of (a) use of number plates from another vehicle, or (b) the forging or altering of licence/ number plates for sale to another.     **K-155**

## Assault occasioning actual bodily harm and racially/religiously aggravated versions

The guideline recommends—     **K-156**
 (i) a starting point of 24 weeks' custody and a range of 12 weeks' custody to sentence in the Crown Court for a pre-meditated assault resulting in minor, non-permanent injury;
 (ii) sentence in the Crown Court for a pre-meditated assault either resulting in relatively serious injury or involving the use of a weapon.

## Inflicting grievous bodily harm/wounding and racially/religiously aggravated versions

The guideline recommends—     **K-157**
 (i) a starting point of 24 weeks' custody and a range of a high level community order to sentence in the Crown Court for "other assault" where no weapon has been used;
 (ii) a starting point of sentence in the Crown Court and a range of 24 weeks' custody to sentence in the Crown Court for a pre-meditated assault where no weapon has been used;

(iii) sentence in the Crown Court for a pre-meditated assault where a weapon has been used or for any other assault where particularly grave injury results or a weapon has been used.

### Assault with intent to resist arrest

**K-158** The guideline recommends a starting point of sentence in the Crown Court and a range from 24 weeks' custody to sentence in the Crown Court.

### Threats to kill

**K-159** The guideline recommends sentence in the Crown Court for repeated threats or a threat accompanied by a visible weapon.

### Firearm, carrying in public place (Firearms Act 1968, s.19)

**K-160** The guideline recommends (but note that certain offences under this section are triable only on indictment (not mentioned in the guideline) and certain offences are triable only summarily, as to which, see § 24-57 in the main work)—
(i) a starting point of a high level community order and a range of a medium level community order to sentence in the Crown Court for the carrying of an imitation firearm or an unloaded shot gun without ammunition;
(ii) sentence in the Crown Court for the carrying of a loaded shot gun or for the carrying of a shot gun or any other firearm together with ammunition for it.

### Bladed article/offensive weapon (possession of)

**K-161** The guideline recommends—
(i) a starting point of six weeks' custody and a range of a high level community order to sentence in the Crown Court where the weapon was not used to threaten or cause fear but the offence was committed in dangerous circumstances;
(ii) sentence in the Crown Court where the weapon was used to threaten or cause fear and the offence was committed in dangerous circumstances.

### Cruelty to a child

**K-162** The guideline recommends—
(i) a starting point of sentence in the Crown Court and a range of 26 weeks' custody to sentence in the Crown Court for an assault (assaults) resulting in injuries consistent with actual bodily harm, more than one incident of neglect or ill-treatment (but not amounting to long-term behaviour), a single incident of long-term abandonment or regular incidents of short-term abandonment (the longer the period of abandonment or the greater the number of incidents of short-term abandonment, the more serious the offence) or failure to protect a child from any of the foregoing;
(ii) sentence in the Crown Court for a series of assaults, protracted neglect or ill- treatment, serious cruelty over a period of time or failure to protect a child from any of the foregoing.

### Affray

**K-163** The guideline recommends 18 weeks' custody as a starting point and a range of 12 weeks' custody to sentence in the Crown Court in the case of a fight involving a weapon or the throwing of objects or conduct causing risk of serious injury.

### Harassment (putting people in fear of violence) (Protection from Harassment Act 1997, s.4), and the racially/religiously aggravated version

**K-164** The guideline recommends—
(i) a starting point of 18 weeks' custody and a range of 12 weeks' custody to sentence in the Crown Court for a case involving deliberate threats or persistent action over a longer period or an intention to cause a fear of violence;
(ii) sentence in the Crown Court for "sexual threats, vulnerable person targeted".

### Breach of a protective order (other than in a domestic context)

The guideline recommends—  **K-165**
  (i) a starting point of sentence in the Crown Court and a range of 26 weeks' custody to
sentence in the Crown Court for more than one breach involving some violence and/or
significant physical or psychological harm to the victim;
  (ii) sentence in the Crown Court for a breach (one or more) involving significant physical
violence and significant physical or psychological harm to the victim.

### Witness intimidation

The guideline recommends—  **K-166**
  (i) a starting point of 18 weeks' custody and a range of 12 weeks' custody to sentence in the
Crown Court for conduct amounting to a threat, staring at, approaching or following witnesses, talking about the case, trying to alter or stop evidence;
  (ii) sentence in the Crown Court for threats of violence to witnesses and/or their families or
for deliberately seeking out witnesses.

### Sexual assault (SOA 2003, ss.3, 7)

See Sections III and VII of the sexual offences guideline, *ante*, K-85c, K-87b.  **K-167**

### Child prostitution and pornography

The guideline recommends that these offences should normally be dealt with in the Crown  **K-168**
Court but that there may be rare cases of non-penetrative activity involving a victim aged 16 or
17 where the offender's involvement is minimal and not for gain in which a custodial sentence
within the power of a magistrates' court may be appropriate.

### Exploitation of prostitution (SOA 2003, ss.52, 53)

See Section XVII of the sexual offences guideline, *ante*, K-92.  **K-169**

### Exposure (SOA 2003, s.66)

See Section XXVIII of the sexual offences guideline, *ante*, K-100.  **K-170**

### Voyeurism (SOA 2003, s.67)

See Section XXIX of the sexual offences guideline, *ante*, K-101.  **K-171**

### Keeping a brothel used for prostitution (SOA 1956, s.33A)

See Section XVIII of the sexual offences guideline, *ante*, K-92a.  **K-172**

### Indecent photographs of children

See Section XVI of the sexual offences guideline, *ante*, K-91.  **K-173**

### Failure to comply with the notification requirements applicable to sex offenders

The guideline recommends a starting point of 18 weeks' custody and a range of six weeks'  **K-174**
custody to sentence in the Crown Court for a deliberate failure to comply or the supply of
information known to be false accompanied by long-period of non-compliance or attempts to
avoid detection.

### Drugs

See *ante*, K-147; and *post*, K-271 *et seq.*  **K-175**

**[The next paragraph is K-179.]**

### Dangerous driving

The guideline recommends sentence in the Crown Court for (a) prolonged bad driving involv-  **K-179**
ing deliberate disregard for the safety of others, (b) incidents involving excessive speed or show-

ing off, especially on busy roads or in a built up area, by a disqualified driver, or while driver was being pursued by the police.

### Aggravated vehicle-taking (damage to property other than the vehicle taken in accident or to the vehicle)

**K-180**  The guideline recommends sentence in the Crown Court if the vehicle was taken as part of a burglary or from private premises and the damage caused was valued at in excess of £5,000.

### Aggravated vehicle-taking (dangerous driving or accident causing injury)

**K-181**  The guideline recommends sentence in the Crown Court if there was a course of prolonged bad driving involving deliberate disregard for the safety of others.

### Arson

**K-182**  The guideline recommends sentence in the Crown Court in the case of "significant" damage.

### Criminal damage (not arson) and racially/religiously aggravated version of offence

**K-183**  The guideline recommends sentence in the Crown Court if the value of the damage done was in excess of £10,000.

### Identity documents (possession of false or of another's improperly obtained) (Identity Cards Act 2006, s.25(5))

**K-184**  The guideline recommends—

(i) a starting point of 12 weeks' custody and a range of a six weeks' custody to sentence in the Crown Court for a small number of documents where there is no evidence of dealing;

(ii) sentence in the Crown Court for "considerable number of documents possessed, evidence of involvement in larger operation".

## M. Causing Death by Driving

**K-185**  The Sentencing Guidelines Council has issued a guideline on the offences of causing death by dangerous driving (RTA 1988, s.1), causing death by careless driving when under the influence of drink or drugs or having failed without reasonable excuse either to provide a specimen for analysis or to permit the analysis of a blood sample (*ibid.*, s.3A), causing death by careless or inconsiderate driving (*ibid.*, s.2B) and causing death by driving while unlicensed, disqualified or uninsured (*ibid.*, s.3ZB). The guideline applies to offenders aged 18 or over who are sentenced on or after August 4, 2008, and is based on first-time offenders convicted after trial.

The guideline has an introduction and four parts. Part A sets out factors relating to the assessment of seriousness, Part B relates to ancillary orders, Part C contains explanatory material relating to sentencing ranges and starting points, and a description of the decision making process, and Part D contains the offence guidelines. The introduction also refers to Annex A which sets out the statutory definitions of dangerous driving, careless driving and inconsiderate driving, and gives examples.

The introduction makes plain that since the causing of death is common to all offences covered by the guideline, the factor that is going to have the greatest weight in determining a starting point for any particular offence will be the culpability of the offender and, accordingly, the primary task for the court (apart from s.3ZB cases) will be an evaluation of the quality of the driving involved and the degree of danger that it foreseeably created. The degree of intoxication must also be considered where this is an element of the offence. The introduction further points out that the guideline draws a distinction between those factors of an offence that are intrinsic to the quality of the driving ("determinants of seriousness") and those which, while they aggravate the offence (*e.g.* more than one death), are not.

### Part A: Assessing seriousness

*Determinants of seriousness*

**K-186**  There are five determinants of seriousness, for each of which the guideline sets out examples:

(i) the offender's awareness of risk (*e.g.* typified by a prolonged, persistent and deliberate course of bad driving), (ii) where the presence of alcohol or drugs is not an element of the offence, the effect of consumption of any alcohol or drugs (which includes a failure to supply a specimen for analysis (unless inherent in the offence or charged separately) and the consumption of legal drugs where this impaired the offender's ability to drive and the offender knew or should have known about the likelihood of impairment), (iii) whether the offender was driving at an inappropriate speed, (iv) whether the offender behaved in a seriously culpable manner, and (v) the identity of the victim (*e.g.* failing to have regard to, and to take extra care when driving near, vulnerable road users such as cyclists, motorcyclists, horse riders, pedestrians and those working in the road).

Examples of (iv), *ante*, are aggressive driving, driving whilst using a hand-held mobile telephone, driving whilst the driver's attention is avoidably distracted (*e.g.* reading or adjusting the controls of electronic equipment), driving when knowingly suffering from a medical or physical condition that significantly impairs the offender's driving skills (including failure to take prescribed medication), driving when knowingly deprived of adequate sleep or rest, particularly where this is caused by commercial concerns, and driving a poorly maintained or dangerously loaded vehicle, again, particularly where this is caused by commercial concerns. A distinction is drawn between ordinary avoidable distractions and gross avoidable distractions (*e.g.* reading or composing a text message over a period of time), but where the degree of impairment is so serious that it is used to determine whether the offence is based on dangerous or careless driving, care must be taken to avoid double counting.

*Aggravating and mitigating factors*

Once the court has considered the determinants of seriousness, it must then consider whether **K-187** any aggravating or mitigating factors affect culpability so as to increase or decrease the starting point, or move the offence into a different sentencing range. When assessing seriousness, the court should have regard to the full list of aggravating and mitigating factors set out in the guideline on seriousness (*ante*, § K-13) and the particular aggravating and mitigating factors applicable to each offence, a key to which is set out, *post*:

*Key to aggravating factors:*

| | | |
|---|---|---|
| 1 | Previous convictions for motoring offences, particularly offences that involve bad driving or the consumption of excessive alcohol or drugs before driving. | **K-188** |
| 2 | Previous convictions for motoring offences, particularly offences that involve bad driving. | |
| 3 | Previous convictions for motoring offences, whether involving bad driving or an offence of the same kind that forms part of the present conviction. | |
| 4 | More than one person killed as a result of the offence. Where the number of deaths is high and that was reasonably foreseeable, this is likely to provide sufficient justification for moving an offence into the next highest sentencing range. | |
| 5 | Serious injury to one or more victims, in addition to the death(s). | |
| 6 | Disregard of warnings. | |
| 7 | Other offences committed at the same time, such as driving other than in accordance with the terms of a valid licence, driving while disqualified, *etc.* | |
| 8 | Irresponsible behaviour such as failing to stop, falsely claiming that one of the victims was responsible, or trying to throw the victim off the car by swerving in order to escape. | |
| 9 | Irresponsible behaviour such as failing to stop or falsely claiming that one of the victims was responsible for the collision. | |
| 10 | Driving off in an attempt to avoid detection or apprehension. | |

*Key to mitigating factors:*

| | | |
|---|---|---|
| 11 | Alcohol or drugs consumed unwittingly. | **K-189** |

12    Offender was seriously injured in the collision, but the greater the driver's fault, the less effect this factor should have on mitigation.

13    The victim was a close friend or relative, but the greater the driver's fault, the less effect this factor should have on mitigation.

14    Actions of the victim or a third party contributed significantly to the likelihood of a collision occurring and/ or death resulting.

15    Actions of the victim or a third party contributed to the commission of the offence.

16    The offender's lack of driving experience contributed significantly to the likelihood of a collision occurring and/ or death resulting.

17    The offender's lack of driving experience contributed to the commission of the offence.

18    The driving was in response to a proven and genuine emergency falling short of a defence.

19    The offender genuinely believed that he or she was insured or licensed to drive.

*Personal mitigation*

**K-190**    If the offender can show that he previously had a good driving record, or can demonstrate remorse or that he provided direct and positive assistance to a victim at the scene of the accident, this may justify a reduction in sentence.

### Part B: Ancillary orders

**K-191**    An order disqualifying an offender from driving is usually a mandatory requirement when sentencing for these offences. In principle, the minimum period of disqualification should either equate to the length of the custodial sentence imposed or the relevant statutory minimum disqualification period, whichever results in the longer period of disqualification.

    The court may also consider whether to impose an order depriving the offender of property, *e.g.*, a vehicle.

### Part D: Offence guidelines

*Causing death by dangerous driving*

**K-192**    There are three levels of seriousness which relate predominantly to the standard of driving.

    **Level 1** (starting point 8 years, sentencing range of 7-14 years): driving that involved a deliberate decision to ignore (or a flagrant disregard for) the rules of the road and an apparent disregard for the great danger being caused to others. Determinants of seriousness (as identified *ante*) that will fix a case at this level include (a) a prolonged, persistent and deliberate course of bad driving, (b) consumption of substantial amounts of alcohol or drugs leading to gross impairment, and/or (c) a group of determinants of seriousness which in isolation or smaller number would place the offence in level 2. The presence of both (a) and (b), particularly if accompanied by aggravating factors will move the offence towards the top of the sentencing range.

    **Level 2** (starting point 5 years, sentencing range of 4-7 years): driving that created a *substantial* risk of danger. Determinants of seriousness that will fix a case at this level include greatly excessive speed, racing or competitive driving, gross avoidable distraction, driving whilst ability to drive is impaired as a result of consumption of alcohol or drugs, failing to take prescribed medication or a known medical condition, or a group of determinants of seriousness which in isolation or smaller number would place the offence in level 3.

    **Level 3** (starting point 3 years, sentencing range of 2-5 years): driving that created a *significant* risk of danger. Relevant determinants of seriousness include driving above the speed limit or at a speed that is inappropriate for the prevailing conditions, driving when knowingly deprived of adequate sleep or rest or knowing that the vehicle has a dangerous defect or is poorly maintained or is dangerously loaded, a brief but obvious danger arising from a seriously dangerous manoeuvre, driving whilst avoidably distracted, or failing to have proper regard to vulnerable road users. Where the driving is markedly less serious than this level, reference should be made to the starting point for the most serious level of causing death by careless driving.

Additional aggravating and mitigating factors applicable to sentencing for this offence: 1, 4-8, 10-13, 16, 17 (as to which, see the key, *ante*).

*Causing death by careless driving when under the influuence of drink or drugs etc.*

K-193

| The legal limit of alcohol is 35µg breath (80mg in blood and 107mg in urine) | Careless/ inconsiderate driving arising from momentary inattention with no aggravating factors | Other cases of careless/ inconsiderate driving | Careless/ inconsiderate driving falling not far short of dangerousness |
|---|---|---|---|
| **Level 1** 71µg or above of alcohol/ high quantity of drugs OR deliberate non-provision of specimen where evidence of serious impairment | Starting point 6 years Sentencing range 5–10 years | Starting point 7 years Sentencing range 6–12 years | Starting point 8 years Sentencing range 7–14 years |
| **Level 2** 51–70µg of alcohol/ moderate quantity of drugs OR deliberate non-provision of specimen | Starting point 4 years Sentencing range 3–7 years | Starting point 5 years Sentencing range 4–8 years | Starting point 6 years Sentencing range 5–9 years |
| **Level 3** 35–50µg of alcohol/ minimum quantity of drugs OR test refused because of honestly held but unreasonable belief | Starting point 18 months Sentencing range 26 weeks–4 years | Starting point 3 years Sentencing range 2–5 years | Starting point 4 years Sentencing range 3–6 years |

Additional aggravating and mitigating factors applicable to sentencing for this offence: 1, 4, 5, 7, 9, 11-14, 18 (as to which, see the key, *ante*).

*Causing death by careless or inconsiderate driving*

K-194

There are three levels of seriousness defined by the degree of carelessness involved in the standard of driving. A fine is unlikely to be an appropriate sentence for this offence. The most likely requirements to be included in a community order are unpaid work requirements, activity requirements, programme requirements and curfew requirements.

**Level 1** (starting point 15 months, sentencing range of 36 weeks-3 years): careless or inconsiderate driving falling not far short of dangerous driving.

**Level 2** (starting point 36 weeks, sentencing range of community order (high)-2 years): other cases of careless or inconsiderate driving.

**Level 3** (starting point community order (medium), sentencing range of community order (low)-community order (high)): careless or inconsiderate driving arising from momentary inattention with no aggravating features. Examples include misjudging the speed of a vehicle or turning without seeing an oncoming vehicle because of restricted visibility.

Additional aggravating and mitigating factors applicable to sentencing for this offence: 2, 4, 5, 7, 9, 11, 12, 14, 15, 17 (as to which, see the key, *ante*).

*Causing death by driving while unlicensed, disqualified or uninsured*

A fine is unlikely to be an appropriate sentence for this offence.

K-195

**Level 1** (starting point 12 months, sentencing range of 36 weeks-2 years): (i) the offender was disqualified from driving or (ii) the offender was unlicensed or uninsured and there are two or more aggravating features from the list, *post*.

**Level 2** (starting point 26 weeks, sentencing range of community order (high)-36 weeks): the offender was unlicensed or uninsured and there was at least one aggravating factor from the list, *post*.

**Level 3** (starting point community order (medium), sentencing range of community order (low)-community order (high)): the offender was unlicensed or uninsured, with no aggravating factors.

Additional aggravating and mitigating factors applicable to sentencing for this offence: 3, 4, 5, 9, 11, 12, 17, 19 (as to which, see the key, *ante*).

## N. Breach of an Anti-Social Behaviour Order

### Summary

**K-196**     The Sentencing Guidelines Council has issued a guideline on the sentencing of offenders convicted of breaching an anti-social behaviour order. It applies to the sentencing of adult and young offenders, who are sentenced on or after January 5, 2009, and is based on first-time offenders (*i.e.* in respect of adult offenders, those who do not have a previous conviction for breach of an anti-social behaviour order and, in respect of young offenders, to have its usual meaning) convicted after trial. Since the sentencing framework for offenders under 18 is significantly different from that for older offenders, the guidance for young offenders is in the form of principles (see Part E, *post*). It is noted that regard should also be had to the approach to sentencing for breaches of orders set out in the guideline on new sentences (*ante*, K-28 *et seq.*) and the guideline on breach of a protective order (*ante*, K-81).

The guideline is in five parts. Part A sets out section 1(10), and summarises the effect of section 1(11), of the CDA 1998 (§ 5-1199 in the main work), Part B is an introduction, Part C sets out factors relating to the assessment of seriousness, Part D contains explanatory material relating to sentencing ranges and starting points, a description of the decision making process, and the sentencing guideline for adult offenders, and Part E sets out sentencing principles in relation to young offenders.

### Part B: introduction

**K-197**     The main aim of sentencing for breach of an order is to achieve the purpose of the order.When sentencing, the primary consideration should therefore be to reflect the harassment, alarm or distress involved, with the fact that it constituted a breach of a court order (and the consequent harm caused by the undermining of public confidence in the effective administration of justice) being a secondary consideration.

### Part C: assessing seriousness

**K-198**     This must be assessed by considering the offender's culpability in committing the offence and the harm which the offence caused, was intended to cause, or might foreseeably have caused. In order properly to assess the seriousness of a breach, a court needs to be aware of the purpose of the order and the context in which it was made. To this end, Annex A summarises the key principles and considerations applicable when making an order. Whereas a breach may be of one or more prohibitions in an order, the approach to sentencing should be based on an assessment of the seriousness of the harm arising from the breach (or intended by the offender) rather than the number of prohibitions not complied with.

*Culpability and harm*

**K-199**     When determining the seriousness of a breach, the court will need to consider (a) the degree to which the offender intended to breach the order, and (b) the degree to which the offender intended to cause the harm that resulted (or could have resulted).

*Relevance of the originating conduct*

**K-200**     As stated in previous guidelines, the original conduct that led to the making of an order is relevant in so far as it indicates the level of harm caused and whether this was intended. High culpability and/ or harm may be indicated if the breach continues a pattern of behaviour against an identifiable victim, but the offence may be less serious if there is little connection between the breach and the behaviour that the order was aimed at. The court should examine the prohibitions of the order itself (particularly those in older orders made without the benefit of the guidance set out in Annex A), and their necessity and reasonableness in the circumstances.

### *Breach of an interim order*

Breach of such an order is as serious as breach of a final order, and the same approach to sentencing should be taken. If the hearing regarding the final order can be brought forward, this should be done so that the two issues can be considered together, but sentencing for the interim breach should not be delayed for this purpose and should take place as soon as possible. The court should also consider the extent to which an urgent need for specific interim prohibitions was originally demonstrated, or if the interim order was sought principally in order to obtain additional time to prepare a case for the full hearing.

**K-201**

### *Breach that also constitutes another criminal offence*

If the substantive offence only has been charged, the fact that it also constitutes breach of an anti-social behaviour order should be treated as an aggravating factor.

**K-202**

If breach of the order only has been charged, the sentence should reflect the full circumstances of the breach, which will include the conduct that could have been charged as a substantive offence.

Where breach of the order also constitutes another offence with a lower maximum penalty, that penalty is an element to be considered in the interests of proportionality, although the court will not be limited by it.

### *Aggravating and mitigating factors*

For ease of reference, Annex B sets out the aggravating and mitigating factors in the guideline on seriousness (*ante*, K-13 *et seq.*) that might increase or mitigate the seriousness of an offence. Additional aggravating and mitigating factors are identified in the guideline (*post*).

**K-203**

### *Personal mitigation*

This is particularly relevant to breach of an anti-social behaviour order, since compliance depends on an ability to understand its terms and make rational decisions. Sentence may be mitigated where the offender has a lower level of understanding due to mental health issues or learning difficulties, was acting under the influence of an older or more experienced offender or has complied with an individual support order or intervention order imposed at the same time as the anti-social behaviour order.

**K-204**

## Part D: sentencing guideline—adult offenders

There are three levels of seriousness:

**K-205**

(i) *serious harm caused or intended*: examples may involve the use of violence, significant threats or intimidation, or the targeting of individuals or groups of people in a manner that leads to a fear of violence;

(ii) *lesser degree of harm intended or likely*: examples may include lesser degrees of threats or intimidation, the use of seriously abusive language or causing more than minor damage to property;

(iii) *no harm caused or intended*: examples may involve being drunk or begging, the prohibited use of public transport, or entry into a prohibited area, provided there is no evidence that harassment, alarm or distress was caused or intended.

The suggested starting points, *post*, are based on the assumption that the offender had the highest level of culpability (*i.e.* he intended the breach). Care needs to be taken to ensure that there is no double counting when an element of the breach determines the level of seriousness where it might in other circumstances be an aggravating factor. In the most serious cases involving repeat offending and a breach causing serious harassment, together with the presence of several aggravating factors such as the use of violence, a sentence beyond the highest range will be justified.

**K-206**

A conditional discharge is not available as a sentence for this offence.

| Nature of failure and harm | Starting point | Sentencing range |
|---|---|---|
| **Serious** harassment, alarm or distress has been caused or where such harm was intended | 26 weeks' custody | Custody threshold–2 years' custody |
| **Lesser degree** of harassment, alarm or distress, where such harm was intended, or where it would have been likely if the offender had not been apprehended | 6 weeks' custody | Community order (medium)–26 weeks' custody |
| **No** harassment, alarm or distress was actually caused by the breach and none was intended by the offender | Community order (low) | Fine (Band B)–community order (medium) |

**K-207**     Additional aggravating factors:
  (i) offender has a history of disobedience to court orders;
  (ii) breach was committed immediately or shortly after the order was made;
  (iii) breach was committed subsequent to earlier breach proceedings arising from the same order;
  (iv) targeting of a person the order was made to protect or a witness in the original proceedings.
  Additional mitigating factors:
  (i) breach occurred after a long period of compliance;
  (ii) the prohibition(s) breached was/were not fully understood, especially where an interim order was made without notice.

### Part E: sentencing guideline—young offenders

**K-208**     It is noted that the principles covered in Part C apply equally to young offenders.

Apart from those cases where the court is bound to make a referral order, in less serious cases, such as where the breach has not involved any harassment, alarm or distress, a fine may be appropriate if it will be paid by the offender; otherwise a reparation order. In most cases, however, the appropriate sentence will be a community sentence. The custody threshold should be set at a significantly higher level than for adults, and will usually not be crossed unless the breach involves serious harassment alarm or distress (as to which, see the levels of seriousness, *ante*). Exceptionally, the custody threshold may also be crossed where a youth is being sentenced for more than one offence of breach (committed on separate occasions within a short period) involving a lesser but substantial degree of harassment, alarm or distress. Even where the custody threshold is crossed, the court should normally impose a community sentence in preference to a detention and training order and custody should be used only as a last resort. Where custody is unavoidable, the starting point for sentencing should be four months' detention, with a range of up to 12 months. Where the youth is being sentenced for more than one breach involving serious harassment, alarm or distress, however, the sentence may go beyond that range.

Factors likely to aggravate or mitigate a breach are the same as the additional factors listed in the guideline for adult offenders (*ante*) and the principles relating to personal mitigation (*ante*) also apply. In addition, peer pressure and lack of parental support may justify mitigation of sentence.

When imposing a community sentence, a court must consider what requirements will best prevent further offending and the individual circumstances of the offender, including his particular stage of intellectual or emotional maturity. Any requirements imposed must be compatible both with each other and with the prohibitions of the anti-social behaviour order, if it remains in force, and the combination of both must not be so onerous as to make further breaches likely.

## O. Theft and Burglary in a Building Other Than a Dwelling

### Summary

The Sentencing Guidelines Council has issued a guideline on these offences. The guideline ap-     **K-209**
plies only to the sentencing of offenders aged 18 and over, who are sentenced on or after January
5, 2009, and is based on first-time offenders convicted after trial (but as to offences of burglary for
which sentence is to be passed on or after January 16, 2012, see *post*, K-259 *et seq.*).

The guideline is in five parts. Part A sets out the statutory provisions relating to the offences,
Part B sets out factors relating to the assessment of seriousness, Part C relates to ancillary orders,
Part D contains explanatory material relating to sentencing ranges and starting points, and a
description of the decision making process, and Part E contains the offence guidelines.

### Part A: statutory provisions

In addition to setting out the relevant statutory provisions, the mode of trial and the maximum     **K-210**
penalties, Part A states that (i) in relation to burglary, the guideline relates solely to cases in which
an offender enters a building other than a dwelling as a trespasser with intent to steal or, having
entered a building as a trespasser, actually goes on to steal, and (ii) the forms of theft covered by
the guideline are theft in breach of trust, theft in a dwelling, theft from persons, and theft from
shops; but that (iii) the principles in Parts B and C are of general application and likely to be of
assistance where a court is sentencing for any other form of theft.

### Part B: assessing seriousness

This must be assessed by considering the offender's culpability in committing the offence and     **K-211**
the harm which the offence caused, was intended to cause, or might foreseeably have caused.
When assessing the harm caused, the starting point should be the loss suffered by the victim.
However, the monetary value might not reflect the full extent of the harm and the court should
take into account the impact of the offence on the particular victim (*e.g.* where the value of the
loss is high in proportion to the victim's financial circumstances), any harm to a person other than
the immediate victim, and any harm in the form of public concern or erosion of public confidence.

Aggravating and mitigating factors which may affect the seriousness of the offence must be
considered, including those identified in the guideline on seriousness (*ante*, K-13 *et seq.*) (and set
out in Annex A) and the additional factors identified in each offence guideline. Since the suggested starting points and sentencing ranges are based on the assumption that the offender was
motivated by greed or a desire to live beyond his means, in order to avoid double counting, such
a motivation should not be treated as a factor that increases culpability. The aggravating factors
from the seriousness guideline most relevant to these offences are planning, offenders operating
in groups or gangs and deliberate targeting of vulnerable victims, and the most relevant aggravating factors indicating a more than usually serious degree of harm are particularly vulnerable
victims, high levels of gain and the high value (including sentimental value) of property to the
victim or substantial consequential loss.

The court must also consider the following matters of personal mitigation: return of stolen
property (depending on voluntariness and timeliness of return), whether the offender has been
motivated by addiction (in which case, while seriousness will not be mitigated, it may be appropriate to impose a drug rehabilitation requirement, alcohol treatment requirement or activity or
supervision requirement, as part of a community or suspended sentence order), and whether the
offender has been motivated by desperation or need (which may count as personal mitigation in
exceptional circumstances).

### Part C: ancillary orders

The ancillary orders which a court must consider are restitution (PCC(S)A 2000, s.148 (§ 5-711     **K-212**
in the main work)), compensation (*ibid.*, s.130 (§ 5-691 in the main work)), deprivation (*ibid.*, s.143
(§ 5-726 in the main work)) and confiscation (PCA 2002, s.6 (§ 5-805 in the main work)). Neither
restitution nor compensation orders should normally impact or influence the choice of sentence.
However, where an offender has acted (as opposed to offered) to free assets in order to pay
compensation, this is akin to making voluntary restitution and may be regarded as personal

mitigation. In making compensation orders, consideration should be given to the wishes of the victim and, where it is difficult to ascertain the full amount of the loss suffered, the making of an order for an amount representing the agreed or likely loss.

## Part D: offence guidelines

*Theft in breach of trust*

**K-213**    While the seriousness of the offence will generally increase in line with the level of trust breached, the extent to which the nature and degree of trust placed in an offender should be regarded as increasing seriousness will depend on a careful assessment of the circumstances of each individual case, including the type and terms of the relationship between the offender and victim. A court should also consider whether a suspended sentence would be appropriate, particularly where this may allow reparation to be made either to the victim or to the community at large.

| Type/ nature of activity | Starting point | Sentencing range |
|---|---|---|
| Theft of £125,000 or more **or** theft of £20,000 or more in breach of a high degree of trust | 3 years' custody | 2–6 years' custody |
| Theft of £20,000 or more but less than £125,000 **or** theft of £2,000 or more but less than £20,000 in breach of a high degree of trust | 2 years' custody | 12 months–3 years' custody |
| Theft of £2,000 or more but less than £20,000 **or** theft of less than £2,000 in breach of a high degree of trust | 18 weeks' custody | Community order (high)–12 months' custody |
| Theft of less than £2,000 | Community order (medium) | Fine–26 weeks' custody |

**K-214**    Additional aggravating factors:
   (i) long course of offending;
   (ii) suspicion deliberately thrown on others;
   (iii) offender motivated by intention to cause harm or out of revenge.
Additional mitigating factors:
   (i) offender has been given inappropriate degree of trust or responsibility;
   (ii) genuine cessation of offending before discovery (particularly where evidence of remorse);
   (iii) offender reports undiscovered offending;
   (iv) other than in the most exceptional of circumstances, loss of employment and any consequential hardship should *not* constitute personal mitigation.

*Theft in a dwelling*

**K-215**    It is noted that the guideline does not apply where the offender has been convicted of a burglary (for which the authorities on sentencing are discussed at § 21-113 *et seq.* in the main work).

    For the purposes of the table, post, property should generally be regarded as having a high monetary value if it is worth more than £2,000 and a victim is vulnerable if he is targeted by the offender because it is anticipated that he will be unlikely or unable to resist the theft.

| Type/ nature of activity | Starting point | Sentencing range |
|---|---|---|
| **Where the effect on the victim is particularly severe, the stolen property is of high value (see ante), or substantial consequential loss (e.g. serious disruption to victim's life or busi-** | | |

| Type/ nature of activity | Starting point | Sentencing range |
|---|---|---|
| **ness) results, a sentence higher than the range into which the offence otherwise would fall may be appropriate** | | |
| Theft from a vulnerable victim (see *ante*) involving intimidation or the use or threat of force (falling short of robbery) or the use of deception | 18 months' custody | 12 months–3 years' custody |
| Theft from a vulnerable victim | 18 weeks' custody | Community order (high)–12 months' custody |
| Theft not involving vulnerable victim | Community order (medium) | Fine–18 weeks' custody |

Additional aggravating factors:                                              **K-216**
  (i) offender motivated by intention to cause harm or out of revenge;
  (ii) intimidation or face-to-face confrontation with victim (except where this takes the offence into a higher sentencing range);
  (iii) use of force, or threat of force, against victim (not amounting to robbery) (except where this takes the offence into a higher sentencing range);
  (iv) use of deception (except where this takes the offence into a higher sentencing range);
  (v) offender takes steps to prevent the victim from reporting the crime or seeking help.

*Theft from the person*

It is noted that the guideline does not apply where the offender has been convicted of robbery   **K-216a** (the guideline for which is set out *ante*, K-80 *et seq.*). As to the approach, to issues of local prevalence, see the seriousness guideline (*ante*, K-27). Issues of national prevalence should *not* be used by sentencers to justify including a deterrent element as this is already taken into account in these and other guidelines.

For the purposes of the table, post, property should generally be regarded as having a high monetary value if it is worth more than £2,000 and a victim is vulnerable if he is targeted by the offender because it is anticipated that he will be unlikely or unable to resist the theft (*e.g.* because of youth or age or disability).

| Type/ nature of activity | Starting point | Sentencing range |
|---|---|---|
| **Where the effect on the victim is particularly severe, the stolen property is of high value (see ante), or substantial consequential loss (e.g. serious disruption to victim's life or business) results, a sentence higher than the range into which the offence otherwise would fall may be appropriate** | | |
| Theft from a vulnerable victim (see *ante*) involving intimidation or the use or threat of force (falling short of robbery) | 18 months' custody | 12 months–3 years' custody |
| Theft from a vulnerable victim | 18 weeks' custody | Community order (high)–12 months' custody |
| Theft not involving vulnerable victim | Community order (medium) | Fine–18 weeks' custody |

Additional aggravating factors:                                              **K-216b**
  (i) offender motivated by intention to cause harm or out of revenge;
  (ii) intimidation or face-to-face confrontation with victim (except where this takes the offence into a higher sentencing range);
  (iii) use of force, or threat of force, against victim (not amounting to robbery) (except where this takes the offence into a higher sentencing range);

(iv) high level of inconvenience caused to victim, *e.g.* replacing house keys, credit cards, *etc.*, or where the victim is a tourist.

*Theft from a shop*

**K-217**     When assessing the level of harm, the circumstances of the retailer (*e.g.* size) are a proper consideration. However, the seriousness of an individual case must be judged on its own dimension of harm and culpability and the sentence on an individual offender should not be increased to reflect the harm caused to retailers in general by the totality of this type of offending (*e.g.* higher insurance premiums, cost of preventative security measures). Whereas the seriousness guideline requires the value of goods to be taken into account in property offences, where this is associated with other aggravating factors such as the degree of planning and/or operating in a group, care will need to be taken to avoid double counting.

When taking previous convictions into account, if the offender demonstrates a level of persistent or seriously persistent offending, the community and custody thresholds may be crossed even though the other characteristics of the offence would otherwise warrant a lesser sentence.

| Type/ nature of activity | Starting point | Sentencing range |
|---|---|---|
| Organised gang/ group **and** intimidation or the use or threat of force (short of robbery) | 12 months' custody | 36 weeks–4 years' custody |
| Significant intimidation or threats **or** use of force resulting in slight injury **or** very high level of planning **or** significant related damage | 6 weeks' custody | Community order (high)–36 weeks' custody |
| Low level intimidation or threats **or** some planning, *e.g.* a session of stealing on the same day or going equipped **or** some related damage | Community order (low) | Fine–community order (medium) |
| Little or no planning or sophistication **and** goods stolen of low value | Fine | Conditional discharge–community order (low) |

**K-218**     Additional aggravating factors:
  (i) child accompanying offender where child is involved or aware of theft;
  (ii) offender is subject to a banning order that includes the store targeted (care to be taken to avoid double counting where offender also being sentenced for breach of order);
  (iii) offender motivated by intention to cause harm or out of revenge;
  (iv) professional offending;
  (v) victim particularly vulnerable (*e.g.* small, independent shop);
  (vi) offender targeted high value goods;
  (vii) intimidation, threat or use of force (falling short of robbery) and additional damage to property.

**[The next paragraph is K-221.]**

### P. ATTEMPTED MURDER

**K-221**     The Sentencing Guidelines Council has issued a guideline which applies only to the sentencing of offenders aged 18 and over, who are sentenced on or after July 27, 2009, and is based on first-time offenders convicted after trial. The guideline is not intended to provide for an offence found to be based on a genuine belief that murder would be an act of mercy, although the approach to assessing the seriousness in such cases might be similar.

### Part A: Assessing seriousness

**K-222**     This must be assessed, first, by considering the offender's culpability in committing the offence.

While an offender convicted of an offence of attempted murder will have already demonstrated a high level of culpability (intention to kill), the precise level of culpability will vary in line with the circumstances of the offence (*e.g.* whether a weapon was used) and whether it was planned or spontaneous.

Next, the court must consider the harm caused. Since there is a potential imbalance between culpability and harm, the degree of (or lack of) physical or psychological harm suffered by a victim may generally influence sentence, in particular where the degree of harm actually caused to the victim is negligible.

Aggravating and mitigating factors will also affect the seriousness of the offence. The court should consider (i) the specific factors identified in Part D (*post*), which follow those set out in the CJA 2003, Sched. 21 (§ 5-425 in the main work), (ii) the factors identified in the guideline on seriousness (*ante*, K-13 *et seq.*), although, here, care needs to be taken to ensure that there is no double counting where an essential element of the offence charged might, in other circumstances, be an aggravating factor, and (iii) the additional statutory aggravating factor introduced by the Counter-Terrorism Act 2008, s.30 (§ 25-213 in the main work) and Sched. 2 (offence having a terrorist connection).

## Part B: ancillary orders

A court must consider making a compensation order.     **K-223**

## Part C: sentencing ranges and starting points

Part C contains explanatory material relating to sentencing ranges and starting points, and a  **K-224** description of the decision making process. This is largely repetitive of material that appears in previous guidelines (see, in particular, the guideline on the assessment of seriousness, *ante*, K-13 *et seq.*, and, in relation to sexual offences, *ante*, K-85).

## Part D: offence guidelines

| Nature of offence | Starting point | Sentencing range |
|---|---|---|
| **Level 1** | | |
| *The most serious offences including those which (if the charge had been murder) would come within the 2003 Act, Sched. 21, paras 4 and 5* | | |
| Serious and long term physical or psychological harm | 30 years' custody | 27–35 years' custody |
| Some physical or psychological harm | 20 years" custody | 17–25 years' custody |
| Little or no physical or psychological harm | 15 years' custody | 12–20 years' custody |
| **Level 2** | | |
| *Other planned attempt to kill* | | |
| Serious and long term physical or psychological harm | 20 years' custody | 17–25 years' custody |
| Some physical or psychological harm | 15 years' custody | 12–20 years' custody |
| Little or no physical or psychological harm | 10 years' custody | 7–15 years' custody |
| **Level 3** | | |
| *Other spontaneous attempt to kill* | | |
| Serious and long term physical or psychological harm | 15 years' custody | 12–20 years' custody |
| Some physical or psychological harm | 12 years' custody | 9–17 years' custody |
| Little or no physical or psychological harm | 9 years' custody | 6–14 years' custody |

**K-225**

Specific aggravating factors:     **K-226**

(i) the fact that the victim was particularly vulnerable, *e.g.*, because of age or disability;

(ii) mental or physical suffering inflicted on the victim;

(iii) the abuse of a position of trust;

(iv) the use of duress or threats against another person to facilitate the commission of the offence;

(v) the fact that the victim was providing a public service or performing a public duty.

**K-227**  Specific mitigating factors:

(i) the fact that the offender suffered from any mental disorder or mental disability which lowered his degree of culpability;

(ii) the fact that the offender was provoked (for example, by prolonged stress);

(iii) the fact that the offender acted to any extent in self-defence;

(iv) the age of the offender.

## Q. Fraud — Statutory Offences

★**K-228**  The Sentencing Guidelines Council issued a guideline on statutory offences of fraud (*viz.* Fraud Act 2006, ss.1, 6 and 7 (§§ 21-356, 21-390, 21-391 in the main work), Theft Act 1968, s.17 (*ibid.*, § 21-226), Tax Credits Act 2002, s.35, Social Security Administration Act 1992, s.111A, Value Added Tax Act 1994 s.72 (*ibid.*, § 25-532), and CEMA 1979, ss.50, 170 and 170B (*ibid.*, §§ 25-430, 25-474, 25-505)). It applied only to offenders aged 18 and over, who fell to be sentenced on or after October 26, 2009, and was based on first-time offenders convicted after trial. For offenders falling to be sentenced on or after October 1, 2014, it is superseded by the Sentencing Council's guideline on fraud, bribery and money laundering offences (*post*, K-297 *et seq.*).

The guideline is in six parts and there are two annexes. Annex A contains statutory definitions and the maximum penalties for fraud offences included in the guideline. Annex B sets out in full the aggravating and mitigating factors identified in the guideline on overarching principles and the assessment of seriousness (*ante*, K-13 *et seq.*).

### Part A: statutory provisions and introduction

**K-229**  In addition to listing the offences covered, Part A states that: (i) the guideline aims to produce a coherent and consistent approach to sentencing all forms of fraudulent behaviour; as such it supersedes previous guideline (and other significant) cases; (ii) the guidelines focus on the type of fraud, rather than the specific offence of which the offender has been convicted; (iii) the types of offence covered are confidence fraud, possessing, making or supplying articles for use in fraud, banking and insurance fraud, and the obtaining of credit through fraud, benefit fraud and revenue fraud; (iv) as the offence of obtaining services dishonestly (Fraud Act 2006, s.11 (§ 21-403 in the main work)) may be committed in circumstances that otherwise could be charged as an offence of fraud or may be more akin to making off without payment, it has not been included specifically within any of the guidelines, the guideline to be applied being determined by the nature of the conduct forming the basis of the conviction; and (v) the primary consideration in sentencing is the seriousness of the offending behaviour.

### Part B: assessing seriousness

**K-230**  This must be assessed by considering the offender's culpability in committing the offence and the harm which the offence caused, was intended to cause, or might foreseeably have caused. When assessing the harm caused, the primary consideration is the loss to the victim or to the community at large. In some cases, the harm that results may be greater than the harm intended by the offender. In others, the offender may have intended more harm than actually results. In these situations, the harm caused by the offence should be judged in light of the offender's culpability. In general terms, the greater the loss, the more serious the offence. However, the financial value of the loss may not reflect the full extent of the harm caused by the offence, and the court should take into account the impact of the offence on the victim (including relative harm and sentimental value), any harm to persons other than the direct victim, any erosion of public confidence, any physical harm or risk of physical harm to the direct victim or any other person, any difference between the loss intended and the actual result, and any legitimate entitlement to part or all of the amount obtained.

Aggravating and mitigating factors which may affect the seriousness of the offence must be considered, including those identified in the guideline on seriousness. The aggravating factors most likely to be present in offences of fraud are planning, an intention to commit more serious harm than actually resulted, operating in groups or gangs, "professional offending", a high level of profit, any attempt to conceal or dispose of evidence, the deliberate targeting of the vulnerable, abuse of a position of trust, multiple victims and high value (including sentimental value) of property to the victim, or subsequent consequential loss. Factors that are particularly relevant when sentencing for fraud are the number of persons involved and the role of the offender, the period of time over which the offending was carried out, the use of another person's identity, and the offence having a lasting effect on the victim.

Mitigating factors most likely to be present are mental illness or disability, youth or age where it affects responsibility, the fact that the offender played only a minor role, the offender's behaviour not being fraudulent from the outset, and the offender having been given misleading or incomplete advice. Personal mitigation that may be peculiarly relevant includes a voluntary cessation of offending (depending on the reasons and the time elapsed since the last offence), a complete and unprompted disclosure of the extent of the fraud (having regard to the point at which the disclosure is made and the degree of assistance to the authorities), voluntary restitution, and, in exceptional circumstances, financial pressure on the offender, where that pressure is not of the offender's own making.

## Part C: other sentencing matters

In light of the extensive powers available to the court relating to confiscation and to seizure of **K-231** assets or the proceeds of crime, and of the general powers relating to compensation, forfeiture and confiscation, a court normally should not impose a fine alongside a custodial sentence. Exceptionally, it may be appropriate to do so where: (i) a confiscation order is not being contemplated; (ii) there is no obvious victim in whose favour a compensation order can be made; and (iii) the offender has, or will have, resources from which a fine can be paid. A court must ensure that the overall sentence remains commensurate with the seriousness of the offence and that the size of the fine does not allow wealthier offenders to "buy themselves out of custody".

## Part D: ancillary orders

The ancillary orders which a court must consider or which are most likely to be imposed are **K-232** compensation (PCC(S)A 2000, s.148 (§ 5-691 in the main work)), confiscation (PCA 2002, s.6 (*ibid.*, § 5-805)), deprivation (2000 Act, s.143 (*ibid.*, § 5-726)), restitution (2000 Act, s.148 (*ibid.*, § 5-711)), disqualification from acting as a company director (CDDA 1986, s.2 (*ibid.*, § 5-1117)), disqualification from driving (2000 Act, ss.146, 147 (*ibid.*, §§ 5-1106 *et seq.*)), financial reporting (SOCPA 2005, s.76 (*ibid.*, § 5-1212)) and serious crime prevention (SCA 2007, ss.1 and 19 (*ibid.*, §§ 5-1151, 5-1168). Neither restitution nor compensation orders should normally impact or influence the choice of sentence. However, where an offender has acted (as opposed to offered) to free assets in order to pay compensation, this is akin to making voluntary restitution and may be regarded as personal mitigation. In making compensation orders, consideration should be given (i) to the wishes of the victim, and (ii) where it is difficult to ascertain the full amount of the loss suffered, to the making of an order for an amount representing the agreed or likely loss. Disqualification from driving is a punitive sanction and should be taken into account in ensuring that the overall sentence is commensurate with the seriousness of the offence.

## Part E: sentencing ranges and starting points

See *ante*, K-224. **K-233**

## Part F: offence guidelines

The maximum penalty for most of the offences covered by this guideline is seven years' **K-234** imprisonment. Where fraud under the 2006 Act is charged, the maximum penalty is 10 years; and the proposed sentencing ranges leave headroom for offences involving the most serious frauds to be sentenced outside the range and up to that maximum. In all cases where the value of property or consequential loss involved is one of the determinants of seriousness, if the amount the offender intended to obtain cannot be established, the appropriate measure will be the amount that was likely to be achieved in all the circumstances.

*Confidence fraud*

**K-235**    This type of offending involves a victim transferring money and/or property as a result of being deceived or misled by the offender. It includes advance fee frauds, such as lottery/ prize draw and foreign money-making scams and the fraudulent sale of goods (non-existent or worthless) or services (unnecessary, overpriced or never performed).

| Nature of offence | **Value of property or consequential loss** | | | |
|---|---|---|---|---|
| | **£500,000 or more**<br><br>Starting point based on:<br>£750,000* | **£100,000 or more and less than £500,000**<br><br>Starting point based on:<br>£300,000* | **£20,000 or more and less than £100,000**<br><br>Starting point based on:<br>£60,000* | **Less than £20,000**<br><br>Starting point based on:<br>£10,000* |
| Large scale advance fee fraud **or** other confidence fraud involving the deliberate targeting of a large number of vulnerable victims | **Starting point:**<br>6 years' custody<br>**Range:**<br>5–8 years' custody | **Starting point:**<br>5 years' custody<br>**Range:**<br>4–7 years' custody | **Starting point:**<br>4 years' custody<br>**Range:**<br>3–6 years' custody | **Starting point:**<br>3 years' custody<br>**Range:**<br>2–5 years' custody |
| Lower scale advance fee fraud **or** other confidence fraud characterised by a degree of planning and/or multiple transactions | **Starting point:**<br>5 years' custody<br><br>**Range:**<br>4–7 years' custody | **Starting point:**<br>4 years' custody<br><br>**Range:**<br>3–6 years' custody | **Starting point:**<br>3 years' custody<br><br>**Range:**<br>2–5 years' custody | **Starting point:**<br>18 months' custody<br><br>**Range:**<br>26 weeks–3 years' custody |
| Single fraudulent transaction confidence fraud involving targeting of a vulnerable victim | | | **Starting point:**<br>26 weeks' custody<br>**Range:**<br>community order (high)–18 months' custody | **Starting point:**<br>6 weeks' custody<br>**Range:**<br>community order (medium) –26 weeks' custody |
| Single fraudulent transaction confidence fraud not targeting a vulnerable victim, and involving no or limited planning | | | **Starting point:**<br>12 weeks' custody<br>**Range:**<br>community order (medium) – 3–6 weeks' custody | **Starting point:**<br>community order (medium)<br>**Range:**<br>fine–6 weeks' custody |

    * Where the actual amount is smaller than the figure on which the starting point is based, that is likely to be one of the factors that will move the sentence within the range.

*Possessing, making or supplying articles for use in fraud*

The sentencing range for the most serious category of this type of offence is deliberately wide; **K-236** most offences will be at the lower end of the range but there are likely to be some offences, possibly but not exclusively those with an international dimension, that will justify a sentence at the top of the range or even higher.

| Type of offence | | |
|---|---|---|
| **Nature of offence** | Making, adapting, supplying or offering to supply (s.7) | Possessing (s.6) |
| Article(s) intended for use in an extensive and skilfully planned fraud | *Starting point:*<br>4 years' custody<br>*Range:*<br>2–7 years' custody | *Starting point:*<br>36 weeks' custody<br>*Range:*<br>6 weeks – 2 years' custody |
| Article(s) intended for use in a less extensive and less skilfully planned fraud | *Starting point:*<br>26 weeks' custody<br><br>*Range:*<br>community order (high) – 2 years' custody | *Starting point:*<br>community order (medium)<br><br>*Range:*<br>community order (low) – 26 weeks' custody |

*Banking and insurance fraud, and obtaining credit through fraud*

Use of another person's identity is a feature of nearly all payment card and bank account **K-237** frauds. Courts should therefore depart from the suggested starting points in all cases of payment card and bank account fraud (and any other case in which it arises) to reflect the presence of this matter of aggravation.

| Nature of Offence | Amount obtained or intended to be obtained | | | | |
|---|---|---|---|---|---|
| | £500,000 or more<br><br>starting point based on: £750,000* | £100,000 or more and less than £500,000<br>starting point based on: £300,000* | £20,000 or more and less than £100,000<br>starting point based on: £60,000* | £5,000 or more and less than £20,000<br>starting point based on: £12,500* | Less than £5,000<br><br>starting point based on: £2,500* |
| Fraudulent from the outset, professionally planned **and either** fraud carried out over a significant period of time **or** multiple frauds | **Starting point:**<br>5 years' Custody<br>**Range:**<br>4–7 years' custody | **Starting point:**<br>4 years' Custody<br>**Range:**<br>3–5 years' custody | **Starting point:**<br>2 years' Custody<br>**Range:**<br>18 months–3 years' custody | | |

| | | | | | |
|---|---|---|---|---|---|
| Fraudulent from the outset **and either** fraud carried out over a significant period of time **or** multiple frauds | **Starting point:** 4 years' custody <br><br> **Range:** 3–7 years' custody | **Starting point:** 3 years' custody <br><br> **Range:** 2–4 years' custody | **Starting point:** 15 months' custody <br><br> **Range:** 18 weeks-30 months' custody | **Starting point:** 12 weeks' custody <br><br> **Range:** community order (high)-12 months' custody | **Starting point:** community order (high) <br><br> **Range:** community order (low)-6 weeks' custody |
| Not fraudulent from the outset **and either** fraud carried out over a significant period of time **or** multiple frauds | **Starting point:** 3 years' custody <br><br> **Range:** 2–6 years' custody | **Starting point:** 2 years' custody <br><br> **Range:** 12 months-3 years' custody | **Starting point:** 36 weeks' custody <br><br> **Range:** 12 weeks–18 months' custody | **Starting point:** 6 weeks custody <br><br> **Range:** community order (medium)- 26 weeks' custody | **Starting point:** community order (medium) <br><br> **Range:** fine-community order (high) |
| Single fraudulent transaction, fraudulent from the outset | | | **Starting point:** 26 weeks' custody <br><br> **Range:** 6 weeks–12 months' custody | **Starting point:** community order (high) <br><br> **Range:** fine-18 weeks' custody | **Starting point:** community order (low) <br><br> **Range:** fine-community order (medium) |
| Single fraudulent transaction, not fraudulent from the outset | | | **Starting point:** 12 weeks' custody <br><br> **Range:** community order (medium)-36 weeks' custody | **Starting point:** community order (medium) <br><br> **Range:** fine-6 weeks' custody | **Starting point:** fine <br><br> **Range:** fine-community order (low) |

\* Where the actual amount is greater or smaller than the figure on which the starting point is based, that is likely to be one of the factors that will move the sentence within the range.

*Benefit fraud*

**K-238**    The fact that sums obtained fraudulently may have been, or are in the process of being, recovered is not relevant to the choice of the type of sentence to be imposed. The guidelines themselves are in identical terms to those for banking and insurance fraud, and obtaining credit through fraud (*ante*).

*Revenue fraud*

The guidelines (in identical terms to those for banking and insurance fraud, and obtaining **K-239** credit through fraud (*ante*)) take as a starting point an offender who acts intentionally. Where the offender acts recklessly courts should adjust the assessment of seriousness to take account of the offender's reduced culpability (this being relevant only to offences under the Value Added Tax Act 1994).

## R. Sentencing Youths

The Sentencing Guidelines Council has now issued a definitive guideline in relation to the **K-240** sentencing of offenders who are under 18 years of age. It applies to any sentence imposed on or after November 30, 2009. The foreword states that the offence-specific guidelines for youths convicted of offences under the SOA 2003 which have a lower maximum penalty when committed by a person under the age of 18 (*ante*, K-83 *et seq.*), and of robbery (*ante*, K-80), continue to apply and are not superseded by these guidelines. As with other guidelines issued by the council, there is a great deal of repetition both within the guideline itself and of material from other guidelines.

## General approach

*Statutory provisions*

As well as summarising key statutory provisions, this section reminds sentencers that they must **K-241** be aware of a range of international conventions which emphasise the importance of avoiding "criminalisation" of young people while ensuring that they are held responsible for their actions and, where possible, take part in repairing the damage that they have caused, the intention being to establish responsibility and to promote re-integration rather than to impose retribution.

*Sentencing principles*

The approach will be individualistic, with the response varying significantly according to the **K-242** actual age and maturity of the offender. Sentences must remain proportionate (except in the case of dangerous offenders), with particular care needing to be taken where a young person has committed a relatively less serious offence but there is a high risk of re-offending. Whilst a court is sometimes required to treat the seriousness of an offence as aggravated where there are previous convictions (CJA 2003, s.143(2) (§ 5-67 in the main work)), a sentence that follows re-offending does not need to be more severe than a previous sentence solely because of the previous conviction.

As to the CDA 1998, s.37 (principal aim of the youth justice system is to prevent offending by children and young people (§ 5-63 in the main work)), the guideline points out that, in relation to the offender, this incorporates the need to demonstrate that his conduct is not acceptable in a way that makes an impact on him whilst also identifying and seeking to address any other factors that make offending more likely; and that, for any victim and society as a whole, it incorporates the need to demonstrate that the law is being effectively enforced and to sustain confidence in the rule of law. Overall, the emphasis should be on approaches that seem most likely to be effective in realising the aim set out in section 37.

As to the duty to have regard to the welfare of the offender (CYPA 1933, s.44 (§ 5-64 in the main work)), a court should ensure that it is alert to—

   (i) the high incidence of mental health problems and learning difficulties or disabilities amongst young people in the criminal justice system;

  (ii) the effect that speech and language difficulties might have on the ability of the young person (or any adult with them) to communicate with the court, to understand the sanction imposed or to fulfil the obligations resulting from that sanction;

 (iii) the extent to which young people anticipate that they will be discriminated against by those in authority and the effect that it has on the way that they conduct themselves during court proceedings;

  (iv) the vulnerability of young people to self harm, particularly within a custodial environment;

  (v) the extent to which the changes which take place during adolescence can lead to experimentation; and

(vi) the effect on young people of experiences of loss or abuse.

*Effect on sentence of the offender being a young person*

**K-243**    There is an expectation that, generally, a youth will be dealt with less severely than an adult, although the distinction diminishes as the offender approaches the age of 18. Factors which govern the approach to the sentencing of young people who offend (compared with the approach for adult offenders), and which will affect the sentence imposed in individual cases, include:

(i) offending by a young person is frequently a phase which passes fairly rapidly and therefore the reaction to it needs to be kept well balanced in order to avoid alienating the young person from society;

(ii) a criminal conviction at this stage of a person's life may have a disproportionate impact on the ability of the offender to gain meaningful employment and play a worthwhile role in society;

(iii) the impact of punishment is felt more heavily by young people in the sense that any sentence will seem far longer in comparison with their relative age than a like sentence imposed on an adult;

(iv) young people may be receptive to changing the way they conduct themselves and should be able to respond more quickly to interventions;

(v) young people should be given greater opportunity to learn from their mistakes; and

(vi) young people will be no less vulnerable than adults to the contaminating influences that can be expected within a custodial context and probably more so.

Having taken account of all relevant considerations, the court should, within a disposal that is no more restrictive of liberty than is proportionate to the seriousness of the offence(s), impose a sentence which:

(i) confronts the young offender with the consequences of the offending (either for the offender himself, his family, the victim(s) or the community), and helps him to develop a sense of personal responsibility;

(ii) tackles the particular factors (personal, family, social, educational or health) that put the young person at risk of offending;

(iii) strengthens those factors that reduce the risk that the young person will continue to offend;

(iv) encourages reparation; and

(v) defines, agrees and reinforces the responsibilities of the parents.

*Crossing a significant age threshold between commission of an offence and sentence*

**K-244**    Where an increase in the age of an offender results in the maximum sentence on the date of conviction being greater than that available on the date on which the offence was committed, a court should take as its starting point the sentence likely to have been imposed on the date on which the offence was committed. It would be rare for a court to have to consider passing a sentence more severe than the maximum it would have had jurisdiction to pass at the time the offence was committed even where the offender has subsequently attained the age of 18. However, a sentence at or close to the maximum may be appropriate, especially where a serious offence was committed by an offender close to the age threshold.

*Persistent offenders*

**K-245**    Whereas certain sentences are available only where the offender is a "persistent offender", in determining whether a young person is a persistent offender for these purposes a court should consider simply whether he is someone who persists in offending. A finding of persistence may be derived from previous convictions but may also arise from other orders or disposals which require an admission or finding of guilt. A finding of persistence is likely where an offender has been convicted of, or made subject of a pre-court disposal that involved an admission or finding of guilt in relation to, imprisonable offences on at least three occasions in a 12-month period.

*Enforcing the responsibilities of parents and guardians*

**K-246**    In considering whether to make a parenting order under the CDA 1998, s.8(6) (§ 5-1282 in the main work), a court must consider the strength of familial relationships and any diversity issues,

in particular relating to sexual orientation or race, which might impact on the achievement of the
purpose of the order.

## Particular sentences and orders

*Referral orders*

A court should be prepared to use the full range of periods allowed; in general, orders of 10 to **K-247**
12 months should be made only for more serious offences. Typically, the length of an order
should be three to five months, five to seven months or seven to nine months according to
whether the court assesses the seriousness of the offending to be relatively low, of medium
seriousness or relatively high.

*Financial orders*

It will rarely be appropriate to take an education maintenance allowance or a similar means- **K-248**
related provision into account as a resource from which a young person may pay a financial
penalty, especially where the recipient is a young person who is living independently or as part of
a household primarily dependent on state benefit.

*Youth rehabilitation orders*

From the commencement (on November 30, 2009) of section 1 of the CJIA 2008 (§ 5-314 in **K-249**
the main work), youth rehabilitation orders have been the sole available community sentence for
young offenders. Where a court is considering sentence for an offence for which a custodial
sentence is justified, a guilty plea may be one of the factors that persuades a court that it can
properly impose a youth rehabilitation order instead, and in those circumstances no further
adjustment to that sentence would need to be made in order to fulfil the obligation to give credit
for the plea. Where, however, the provisional sentence is already a youth rehabilitation order, the
necessary reduction for a guilty plea should apply to those requirements within the order that are
primarily punitive rather than those which are primarily rehabilitative.

**Determining the requirements and the length of an order:** where a court concludes that a **K-249a**
youth rehabilitation order is appropriate, taking account of the assessment in the presentence
report, the court should consider (i) the requirements that are most suitable for the offender, (ii)
what period is necessary to ensure that all requirements may be satisfactorily completed, and (iii)
whether the restrictions on liberty that result from those requirements are commensurate with
the seriousness of the offence.

**Orders with intensive supervision and surveillance:** when imposing a youth rehabilitation **K-249b**
order with intensive supervision and surveillance a court must ensure that the requirements are
not so onerous as to make the likelihood of a breach almost inevitable.

**Orders with a fostering requirement:** it is unlikely that the statutory criteria, contained in **K-249c**
Schedule 1, para. 4, to the 2008 Act (§ 5-318 in the main work), will be met in many cases; where
they are met and the court is considering making an order, care should be taken to ensure that
there is a well developed plan for the care and support of the young person throughout the
period of the order and following conclusion of the order.

**Breaches:** the primary objective when dealing with a breach of an order is to ensure that the **K-249d**
young person completes the requirements imposed by the court. Where the failure arises primarily from non-compliance with reporting or other similar obligations, if a sanction is necessary, the
most appropriate one is likely to be the inclusion of, or increase in, a primarily punitive
requirement. A court must ensure that it has sufficient information to enable it to understand why
the order has been breached and that all steps have been taken by relevant authorities to give the
young person appropriate opportunity and support. This will be particularly important if the
court is considering imposing a custodial sentence as a result of the breach. Where a court is
considering whether a young person has "wilfully and persistently" breached an order, it should
apply the same approach as when determining whether an offender is a "persistent offender" (as
to which, see *ante*). In particular, a young person almost certainly will have "persistently" breached
an order where there have been three breaches (each resulting in an appearance before the
court) demonstrating a lack of willingness to comply with the order.

*Custodial sentences*

**Threshold and approach:** a pre-sentence report must be considered in all cases before a **K-250**

custodial sentence is imposed. Even where the custody threshold (*viz.* that the youth cannot properly be dealt with by a fine alone or by a youth rehabilitation order) has been crossed, a court is not required to impose a custodial sentence. This is likely only to be the case where a custodial sentence will be more effective in preventing offending by children and young persons. The obligation to have regard to the welfare of the offender will require the court to take account of a wide range of issues including those relating to mental health, capability and maturity.

**K-250a**    **Length of sentence (offenders aged 15, 16 or 17):** where the offender is aged 15, 16 or 17, the court will need to consider the maturity of the offender as well as age. Where there is no offence-specific guideline it may be appropriate, depending on maturity, to consider a starting point from half to three-quarters of that which would have been identified for an adult offender. The closer the offender was to being 18 when the offence was committed, and the greater the maturity of the offender, or the sophistication of the offence, the closer the starting point is likely to be to that appropriate for an adult. For younger offenders, greater flexibility is required to reflect the potentially wider range of culpability. Where an offence shows considerable planning or sophistication, a court may need to adjust this approach upwards; conversely, where an offender is particularly immature, the approach may need to be adjusted downwards. It will be particularly important to consider maturity when the court has to sentence multiple offenders. When the offenders are of different ages, including when one or more is over 18, the court will also need to have proper regard to parity between their sentences.

**K-250b**    **Length of sentence (offenders aged under 15):** where the offender is under 15, sentence should normally be imposed in a youth court, and the length of sentence will normally be shorter than for an older offender convicted of the same offence. An offender should be sentenced to detention under the PCC(S)A 2000, s.91 (§ 5-610 in the main work), only where necessary for the protection of the public, either because of the risk of harm from future offending or the persistence of the offending behaviour, or, exceptionally, because the seriousness of the offence alone warrants such a disposal.

**K-250c**    **Length of sentence (detention and training orders):** in determining the term of a detention and training order the proper approach to taking account of any period for which the offender has been remanded in custody or on bail subject to a qualifying curfew condition and electronic monitoring (see s.101(8) of the Act of 2000 (*ibid.*, § 5-598)) is to reduce, if possible, the length of the part of the sentence that is to be served in custody from what would otherwise have been appropriate, in order to reflect that period.

### Trial and sentencing of cases in the Crown Court

**K-251**    A youth will appear for trial and sentence in the Crown Court only when charged with homicide, when subject to a statutory minimum sentence, when charged with a "grave crime" and a youth court has determined that, if convicted, its powers of sentence would be insufficient, or when charged together with an adult offender who has been sent to the Crown Court and it has been determined that the cases should be kept together. Where a sentence under the "dangerous offender" provisions is likely to be needed the youth may be committed for trial or for sentence.

*"Grave crimes"*

**K-251a**    The power of a youth court to commit a young person charged with a "grave crime" for trial (MCA 1980, s.24 (§ 1-110 in the main work)) should be exercised sparingly, since (i) it is the general policy of Parliament that those under 18 should be tried in a youth court wherever possible, (ii) trial in the Crown Court should be reserved for the most serious cases, recognising the greater formality of the proceedings and the greatly increased number of people involved, and (iii) offenders aged under 15 will rarely attract a period of detention under the "grave crimes" provision, and those under 12 even more rarely. A child aged 10 or 11 (or aged 12 to 14 but not a persistent offender) should be committed to the Crown Court only when charged with an offence of such gravity that, despite the normal prohibition on a custodial sentence for a person of that age, a sentence exceeding two years is a realistic possibility. A young person aged 12 to 17 (for whom a detention and training order could have been imposed) should be committed to the Crown Court only when charged with an offence of such gravity that a sentence substantially beyond the two year maximum for a detention and training order is a realistic possibility.

*Dangerous offenders*

**K-251b**    A sentence under the dangerous offender provisions of the CJA 2003 (§§ 5-497, 5-499 in the main work) may be imposed only where an equivalent determinate sentence of at least four years would have been imposed. Criteria relating to future offending and the risk of serious harm must be assessed in light of the maturity of the offender, the possibility of change in a much shorter time than would apply for an adult, and the wider circumstances of a young person. Where a young person charged with a specified offence would not otherwise be committed or sent to the Crown Court for trial, it is generally preferable for the decision whether to commit under these provisions to be taken after conviction.

## *Remittal from the Crown Court*

Where a child or young person is convicted before the Crown Court of an offence other than **K-251c** homicide there is an obligation to remit to a youth court for sentence unless it would be undesirable to do so. In considering whether remittal is undesirable, a court should balance the need for expertise in the sentencing of young offenders with the benefits of sentence being imposed by the court which has determined guilt. Particular attention should be given to the obligation to remit where a young person appears before the Crown Court only because he was jointly charged with an adult.

For the full text of the guidelines, see www.sentencing-guidelines.gov.uk/guidelines/council/final.html.

## S. Corporate Manslaughter and Health and Safety Offences Causing Death

The Sentencing Guidelines Council has issued a definitive guideline in relation to corporate **K-252** manslaughter and health and safety offences causing death. It applies to the sentencing of organisations on or after February 15, 2010.

The guidelines are in nine parts (elements of the offences; factors likely to affect seriousness; **K-253** financial information — size and nature of the organisation; level of fines; compensation; costs; publicity orders; remedial orders; summary of approach to sentence) and there is an annex (financial information expected to be provided to the court). Part B emphasises that the guideline only applies to corporate manslaughter and to those health and safety offences where the offence is shown to have been a significant cause of the death. The approach to the assessment of seriousness requires the court to consider the foreseeability of serious injury, how far short of the applicable standard the defendant fell, how common the kind of breach in the organisation was, and at what level the organisation was at fault. There is a non-exhaustive list of aggravating factors (more than one death/ grave injury in addition to death/ failure to heed warnings or advice/ cost-cutting/ deliberate failure to obtain or comply with relevant licences/ injury to vulnerable persons), and a similar list of mitigating factors (prompt acceptance of responsibility/ high level of co-operation with investigation beyond that which will always be expected/ genuine efforts to remedy defect/ good record/ responsible attitude). Paragraph 9 states that it is unlikely, in relation to an offence of corporate manslaughter (having regard to the definition of the offence), that the unauthorised act of an employee will significantly reduce the culpability of the defendant, whereas paragraph 10 advises that, where a health and safety offence is established solely by reference to the unauthorised act of an employee, an assessment of the culpability of the organisation itself must be undertaken.

Part C states that there is no direct correlation between size and culpability. Size is, however, **K-254** relevant, as the means of any defendant are relevant to the fine (which is the principal available penalty for organisations) that is to be imposed in any case. Paragraph 14 states that the court should require information about the financial circumstances of the defendant, and that the best practice in such circumstances would be to call for the relevant information for a three year period including the year of the offence, so as to avoid any risk of atypical figures in a single year. The financial information ordinarily expected to be provided to the court is set out in Annex A. A fixed correlation between turnover and fine is not appropriate (para. 15). Paragraph 19 sets out a non-exhaustive list of factors which may or may not be relevant when the court is assessing the financial consequences of a fine. The effect on the employment of the innocent may be relevant; the effect on shareholders, directors or prices will not normally be relevant, save in the case of the prices of a monopoly supplier of public services; the effect on the provision of services to the public will be relevant; liability to pay civil compensation and the cost of meeting any remedial work will ordinarily be irrelevant; whether the fine will have the effect of putting the defendant out of business will be relevant, although in bad cases, this may be an acceptable consequence.

Although in the case of a large organisation payment of any fine should be required within 28 days, it is permissible, in the case of a smaller or financially stretched organisation, to require payment to be spread over a much longer period. Where commission of the offence resulted in a broadly quantifiable saving, it will be appropriate to ensure that the fine is such as to remove the profit and impose an additional penalty.

**K-255**     Part D states that the level of fine will vary considerably, but that any fine must be punitive and sufficient to have an impact on the defendant. For an offence of corporate manslaughter the appropriate fine will seldom be less than £500,000 and may be measured in millions of pounds. For health and safety offences, the range of seriousness is greater, but the appropriate fine will seldom be less than £100,000 and may be measured in hundreds of thousands of pounds or more. Part E states that, in the great majority of cases, the court should conclude that compensation should be dealt with in a civil court, and should say that no order is made for that reason. Part F provides that the defendant ought ordinarily (subject to means) to be ordered to pay the properly incurred costs of the prosecution.

**K-256**     Part G concerns publicity orders, which are available under the Corporate Manslaughter and Corporate Homicide Act 2007, s.10 (§ 19-149 in the main work), and which should ordinarily be imposed in such cases. The order should particularise the matters to be published, the place where the public announcement is to be made, the size of any notice and the number of insertions (if to be made in a newspaper). The prosecution should serve a draft order on the court and the defendant and the judge should personally endorse the final form of the order. The order may stipulate that any comment placed by the defendant alongside the required announcement should be separated from it and clearly identified as such. Since a publicity order is part of the penalty, the cost of compliance should be kept in mind when fixing the fine.

**K-257**     Part H concerns remedial orders under section 9 of the 2007 Act (§ 19-148 in the main work) and section 42 of the Health and Safety at Work etc. Act 1974. Where appropriate remedial action has not already been taken, such an order should be imposed, provided that it can be made sufficiently specific to be enforceable.

**K-258**     Annex A says that for companies, partnerships and "third sector" organisations, audited accounts should be produced. In the case of the first two, particular attention should be paid to turnover, profit before tax, directors' remuneration (partners' drawings), loan accounts and pension provision, and assets, as disclosed by the balance sheet. Where such information is not produced, an inference may properly be made that the defendant can afford any appropriate fine. For local authorities, police and fire authorities and similar public bodies, it is said that reference should be made to their annual revenue budget. For health trusts, reference should be made to the quarterly reports and annual figures as to their financial strength and stability published by Monitor, their regulator. This will reveal their annual income.

## T. Aggravated Burglary and Burglary

**K-259**     On October 13, 2011, the Sentencing Council for England and Wales issued a definitive guideline on burglary, applying to all offenders aged 18 or over who are sentenced on or after January 16, 2012, regardless of the date of their offence. The offences covered are: (A) aggravated burglary (Theft Act 1968, s.10 (§ 21-129 in the main work)), (B) domestic burglary (1968 Act, s.9 (*ibid.*, § 21-108)) and (C) non-domestic burglary (1968 Act, s.9).

The guideline sets out nine steps to be followed (in order) when sentencing for these offences, which correspond to the steps set out in the guideline on assault and other offences against the person (*ante*, K-114), subject to the modifications set out in the specific sections A to C relating to each offence (*post*).

In particular, step one requires the court to determine within which of three categories reflecting various degrees of seriousness the offence falls. Category 1 requires greater harm and higher culpability, category 2 requires either greater harm and lower culpability or lesser harm and higher culpability, and category 3 requires lesser harm and lower culpability. In determining the offender's culpability and the harm caused or intended, the court should refer only to the factors indicating harm and culpability set out in the specific sections relating to A to C, *post*, which comprise the principal factual elements of the offence. Where an offence does not fall squarely into a category, individual factors may require a degree of weighting before making an overall assessment and determining the appropriate offence category.

Step two requires the court to use the starting point identified for the relevant category (as to which, see also the specific sections relating to A-C, *post*) to reach a sentence within the category range (*post*). The starting point applies to all offenders irrespective of plea or previous convictions. A case of particular gravity, reflected by multiple features of culpability in step one, could merit upward adjustment from the starting point before further adjustment is made for the aggravating or mitigating factors increasing or reducing seriousness or reflecting personal mitigation set out in the specific sections A to C, *post*, which contain a non-exhaustive list of additional factual elements providing the context of the offence and factors relating to the offender. In particular, relevant recent convictions are likely to result in an upward adjustment. Having considered all these, and other relevant factors, it might be appropriate to move outside the identified category range.

Fine bands, and a non-exhaustive description of examples of requirements that might be appropriate for low, medium and high level community orders, correspond to those set out in the guideline on assaults and other offences against the person (*ante*), and are set out in the annex to the guideline.

## Key to factors indicating greater or lesser harm and higher or lower culpability (step one)

A number of the following factors may apply when determining the offence category for aggravated burglary, and domestic and non-domestic burglary. As to which factors may apply to each type of offence, see the specific sections A–C, *post*.   **K-260**

(a) *Factors indicating greater harm*

   i. Theft of/damage to property causing a significant degree of loss to the victim (whether   **K-261**
economic, sentimental or personal).

   ii. Soiling, ransacking or vandalism of property.

   iii. Occupier and/or victim at home or on the premises (or returns) while offender present.

   iv. Significant physical or psychological injury or other significant trauma to the victim.

   v. Violence used or threatened against victim (particularly, in relation to offences of aggravated burglary, involving a weapon).

   vi. Context of general public disorder.

   vii. Trauma to the victim, beyond the normal inevitable consequence of intrusion and theft.

(b) *Factors indicating lesser harm*

   i. No physical or psychological injury or other significant trauma to the victim.   **K-262**

   ii. No violence used or threatened and a weapon is not produced.

   iii. Nothing stolen or only property of very low value to the victim (whether economic, sentimental or personal).

   iv. Limited damage or disturbance to property.

(c) *Factors indicating higher culpability*

   i. Victim or premises deliberately targeted (for example, due to vulnerability or hostility   **K-263**
based on disability, race, sexual orientation, and, in relation to offences of non-domestic burglary, to include a pharmacy or doctor's surgery).

   ii. A significant degree of planning or organisation.

   iii. Equipped for burglary (for example, implements carried and/or use of vehicle).

   iv. Weapon present on entry.

   v. Member of a group or gang.

   vi. Knife or other weapon carried (where not charged separately).

(d) *Factors indicating lower culpability*

   i. Offender exploited by others.   **K-264**

   ii. Mental disorder or learning disability, where linked to the commission of the offence.

   iii. Offence committed on impulse, with limited intrusion into property.

## Key to factors increasing or reducing seriousness or reflecting personal mitigation (step 2)

A number of the following factors may apply when determining the sentence within the   **K-265** category range for offences of aggravated burglary, and domestic and non-domestic burglary. As to which factors may apply to each type of offence, see the specific sections A-C, *post.*

(e) *Factors increasing seriousness*

Statutory aggravating factors:

**K-266**
    i. Previous convictions (in accordance with the Criminal Justice Act 2003, s.143(2) (*ibid.*, § 5-54)).
    ii. Offence committed whilst on bail (2003 Act, s.143(3)).

Other aggravating factors include:

    iii. Child at home (or returns home) when offence committed.
    iv. Offence committed at night (particularly, in relation to offences of non-domestic burglary, where staff are, or are likely to be, present).
    v. Abuse of power and/or position of trust.
    vi. Gratuitous degradation of victim.
    vii. Any steps taken to prevent the victim reporting the incident or obtaining assistance and/or from assisting or supporting the prosecution.
    viii. Victim compelled to leave home (in particular victims of domestic violence).
    ix. Established evidence of community impact.
    x. Commission of offence whilst under the influence of alcohol or drugs.
    xi. Failure to comply with current court orders.
    xii. Offence committed whilst on licence.
    viii. Offences taken into consideration.

(f) *Factors reducing seriousness or reflecting personal mitigation*

**K-267**
    i. Subordinate role in a group or gang.
    ii. Injuries caused recklessly.
    iii. Nothing stolen or only property of low value to the victim (whether economic, commercial, sentimental or personal).
    iv. Offender has made voluntary reparation to the victim.
    v. No previous convictions or no relevant/recent convictions.
    vi. Remorse.
    vii. Good character and/or exemplary conduct.
    viii. Determination, and/or demonstration of steps taken to address addiction or offending behaviour.
    ix. Serious medical condition requiring urgent, intensive or long-term treatment.
    x. Age and/or lack of maturity where it affects the responsibility of the offender.
    xi. Lapse of time since the offence where this is not the fault of the offender.
    xii. Mental disorder or learning disability, where not linked to the commission of the offence.
    xiii Sole or primary carer for dependent relatives.

## A. Aggravated burglary

*Factors indicating harm and culpability (step one)*

**K-268**

| | |
|---|---|
| Greater harm<br>*list (a)* | i–vi |
| Lesser harm<br>*list (b)* | i, ii |
| Higher culpability<br>*list (c)* | i–iii, v, vi |
| Lower culpability<br>*list (d)* | i–iii |

*Starting point and category range (step two)*

| Offence category | Starting point (applicable to all offenders) | Category range (applicable to all offenders) |
| --- | --- | --- |
| category 1 | 10 years' custody | nine –13 years' custody |
| category 2 | six years' custody | four –nine years' custody |
| category 3 | two years' custody | one –four years' custody |

*Factors increasing or reducing seriousness or reflecting personal mitigation*

| Factors increasing seriousness *list (e)* | i–xiii |
| --- | --- |
| Factors reducing seriousness or reflecting personal mitigation *list (f)* | i–xiii |

## B. Domestic burglary

*Factors indicating harm and culpability (step one)*

**K-269**

| Greater harm *list (a)* | i–iii, v–vii |
| --- | --- |
| Lesser harm *list (b)* | iii, iv |
| Higher culpability *list (c)* | i–iii, v, vi |
| Lower culpability *list (d)* | i–iii |

*Starting point and category range (step two)*

| Offence category | Starting point (applicable to all offenders) | Category range (applicable to all offenders) |
| --- | --- | --- |
| category 1 | three years' custody | two –six years' custody |
| category 2 | one year's custody | high level community order –two years' custody |
| category 3 | high level community order | low level community order –26 weeks' custody |

Where the defendant is dependent on, or has a propensity to misuse, drugs and there is sufficient prospect of success, a community order with a drug rehabilitation requirement under section 209 of the 2003 Act (*ibid.*, § 5-145) may be a proper alternative to a short or moderate custodial sentence.

When sentencing for category 2 or 3 offences, the court should consider whether the custody threshold has been passed, if so, whether it is unavoidable that a custodial sentence be imposed and, if so, whether that sentence can be suspended.

*Factors increasing or reducing seriousness or reflecting personal mitigation*

| Factors increasing seriousness *list (e)* | i–iv, vi–xiii |
| --- | --- |

| Factors reducing seriousness or reflecting personal mitigation *list (f)* | i, iv–xiii |
| --- | --- |

## C. Non-domestic burglary

*Factors indicating harm and culpability (step one)*

**K-270**     As for B, *ante.*

*Starting point and category range (step two)*

| Offence category | Starting point (applicable to all offenders) | Category range (applicable to all offenders) |
| --- | --- | --- |
| category 1 | two years' custody | one –five years' custody |
| category 2 | 18 weeks' custody | low level community order –51 weeks' custody |
| category 3 | medium level community order | band B fine –18 weeks' custody |

Where the defendant is dependent on, or has a propensity to misuse, drugs and there is sufficient prospect of success, a community order with a drug rehabilitation requirement under section 209 of the 2003 Act may be a proper alternative to a short or moderate custodial sentence.

When sentencing for category 2 or 3 offences, the court should consider whether the custody threshold has been passed, if so, whether it is unavoidable that a custodial sentence be imposed and, if so, whether that sentence can be suspended; and in sentencing for category three offences, the court should also consider whether the community order threshold has been passed.

*Factors increasing or reducing seriousness or reflecting personal mitigation*

| Factors increasing seriousness *list (e)* | i, ii, iv–vii, ix–xiii |
| --- | --- |
| Factors reducing seriousness or reflecting personal mitigation *list (f)* | i, iv–xiii |

## U. DRUG OFFENCES

**K-271**     On January 24, 2012, the Sentencing Council for England and Wales issued a definitive guideline, applying to all offenders aged 18 or over who are sentenced on or after February 27, 2012, regardless of the date of their offence. The offences covered are:

    I. fraudulent evasion of a prohibition on the importation or exportation of a controlled drug (CEMA 1979, s.170(2) (§ 25-474 in the main work));

    II. supplying or offering to supply such a drug (Misuse of Drugs Act 1971, s.4(3) (*ibid.*, § 27-28)) and possession of such a drug with intent to supply it to another (1971 Act, s.5(3) (*ibid.*, § 27-50));

    III. production of such a drug (1971 Act, s.4(2)(a) or (b)) and cultivation of a cannabis plant (1971 Act, s.6(2) (*ibid.*, § 27-79));

    IV. permitting premises to be used (1971 Act, s.8 (*ibid.*, § 27-84)); and

    V. possession of a controlled drug (1971 Act, s.5(2)).

The guideline sets out eight steps to be followed (in order), which broadly correspond to the steps set out in the guideline on offences against the person (*ante*, Appendix K-113 *et seq.*), except that there is no step requiring the court to consider whether an offender meets the dangerousness criteria.

Step one requires the court to determine the offence category based on varying factors set out in the specific sections I to V (*post*).

Step two requires the court to use the starting point identified for the relevant category (as to which, see also the specific sections relating to I-V, *post*) to reach a sentence within the category range (*post*) dependent on whether the offence in question relates to a Class A, B or C drug. The starting point applies to all offenders. The court should then consider adjustment within the category range for aggravating or mitigating features set out in the specific sections I to V, *post*, which contain a non-exhaustive list of additional factual elements providing the context of the offence and factors relating to the offender. Having considered all these, and other relevant factors, it might be appropriate to move outside the identified category range. In cases where the offender is regarded as being at the very top of a "leading role" (which does not apply to section IV and V offences), it may be justifiable for the court to depart from the guideline. Where the defendant is dependent on, or has a propensity to misuse, drugs and there is a sufficient prospect of success, a community order with a drug rehabilitation requirement under the CJA 2003, s.209 (§ 5-275 in the main work), can be a proper alternative to a short or moderate length custodial sentence. As with previous guidelines, the council emphasises that, where appropriate, courts should consider whether community or custodial thresholds have been passed and, if the latter threshold has been passed, whether it is unavoidable that a custodial sentence be imposed and, if so, whether that sentence can be suspended. The guidelines are subject to section 110 of the PC-C(S)A 2000 (minimum sentences for third drug trafficking offence (*ibid.*, § 5-443)).

In addition to considering whether to make ancillary orders, step six also requires the court, except for section V offences, to consider confiscation where the Crown invokes the process or where it considers it appropriate.

Fine bands, and a non-exhaustive description of examples of requirements that might be appropriate for low, medium and high level community orders, correspond to those in the guideline on offences against the person (*ante*), and are set out in the annex to the guideline.

## Key to factors increasing or reducing seriousness or reflecting personal mitigation (step two)

A number of the following factors may apply when determining the sentence within the **K-272** category range. As to which factors may apply to each type of offence, see the specific sections I to V, *post*.

(a) *Factors increasing seriousness*

Statutory aggravating factors:

  (i) Previous convictions (CJA 2003, s.143(2) (§ 5-67 in the main work)).     **K-273**
  (ii) using or permitting a person under 18 to deliver a controlled drug to a third person (1971 Act, s.4A (*ibid.*, § 27-28a)).
  (iii) Supplying or offering to supply a drug on, or in the vicinity of, school premises (1971 Act, s.4A).
  (iv) Offence committed on bail (2003 Act, s.143(3)).

Other aggravating factors include:

  (v) Targeting of any premises to locate vulnerable individuals or supply to such individuals and/ or supply to those under 18.
  (vi) Nature of any likely supply.
  (vii) Level of any profit element.
  (viii) Use of premises accompanied by unlawful access to electricity/ other utility supply.
  (ix) Continuing/ large scale operation as evidenced by presence and nature of specialist equipment.
  (x) Exposure of others to more than usual danger, *e.g.* drugs cut with harmful substances.
  (xi) Length of time over which premises used for drug activity.
  (xii) Volume of drug activity permitted.
  (xiii) Premises adapted to facilitate drug activity.
  (xiv) Location of premises, *e.g.* proximity to school.
  (xv) Attempts to conceal or dispose of evidence, where not charged separately.
  (xvi) Possession of drug in prison or in a school or licensed premises.
  (xvii) Presence of others, especially children and/ or non-users.

(xviii) Presence of weapon(s), where not charged separately.

(xix) Charged as importation of a very small amount.

(xx) High purity or high potential yield.

(xxi) Failure to comply with current court orders or offence committed on licence.

(xxii) Established evidence of community impact.

(b) *Factors reducing seriousness or reflecting personal mitigation*

**K-274**    (i) Involvement due to pressure, intimidation or coercion, except where already taken into account at step one.

(ii) Supply only of drug to which offender addicted.

(iii) Mistaken belief as to type of drug, taking into account the reasonableness of such belief.

(iv) Isolated incident.

(v) Low purity.

(vi) No previous convictions or no relevant or recent convictions.

(vii) Offender's vulnerability was exploited.

(viii) Remorse.

(ix) Good character and/ or exemplary conduct.

(x) Offender is using cannabis to help with a diagnosed medical condition.

(xi) Determination and/ or demonstration of steps having been taken to address addiction or offending behaviour.

(xii) Serious medical conditions requiring urgent, intensive or long-term treatment.

(xiii) Age and/ or lack of maturity where it affects the responsibility of the offender.

(xiv) Mental disorder or learning disability.

(xv) Sole or primary carer for dependent relatives.

## I. Fraudulent evasion of a prohibition on importation or exportation

*Determining the offence category (step one)*

**K-275**    The court should determine the weight of the drugs involved and the offender's culpability demonstrated by his role, by reference to the tables below. Where there are characteristics present that fall under different role categories, the court should balance them to reach a fair assessment of the offender's culpability.

| **Culpability demonstrated by offender's role** |
| --- |
| One or more of these characteristics may demonstrate the offender's role. These lists are not exhaustive. |
| **LEADING role:** <br>• directing or organising buying and selling on a commercial scale; <br>• substantial links to, and influence on, others in a chain; <br>• close links to original source; <br>• expectation of substantial financial gain; <br>• use of business as cover; <br>• abuse of a position of trust or responsibility. |
| **SIGNIFICANT role:** <br>• operational or management function within a chain; <br>• involvement of others whether by pressure, influence, intimidation or reward; <br>• motivated by financial or other advantage, whether or not operating alone; <br>• some awareness and understanding of scale of operation. |
| **LESSER role:** <br>• performance of limited function under direction; |

- engaged by pressure, coercion, intimidation;
- involvement through naïvety/ exploitation;
- no influence on those above in a chain;
- little, if any, awareness or understanding of the scale of operation;
- if own operation, solely for own use (considering reasonableness of account).

| Category of harm |
|---|
| Indicative quantity of drug concerned (upon which the starting point is based): |
| **Category 1** - heroin, cocaine - 5 kg; Ecstasy - 10,000 tablets; LSD - 250,000 squares; amphetamine - 20 kg; cannabis - 200 kg; ketamine - 5 kg. |
| **Category 2** - heroin, cocaine - 1 kg; Ecstasy - 2,000 tablets; LSD - 25,000 squares; amphetamine - 4 kg; cannabis - 40 kg; ketamine - 1 kg. |
| **Category 3** - heroin, cocaine - 150g; Ecstasy - 300 tablets; LSD - 2,500 squares; amphetamine - 750g; cannabis - 6 kg; ketamine - 150g. |
| **Category 4** - heroin, cocaine - 5g; Ecstasy - 20 tablets; LSD - 170 squares; amphetamine - 20g; cannabis - 100g; ketamine - 5g. |

Where the operation is on the most serious and commercial scale, involving a quantity of drugs significantly higher than category 1, sentences of 20 years and above may be appropriate, depending on the role of the offender.

*Starting point and category range (step two)*

| Class A | Leading role | Significant role | Lesser role |
|---|---|---|---|
| *Category 1* | *Starting point* 14 years *Category range* 12 –16 years | *Starting point* 10 years *Category range* 9 –12 years | *Starting point* 8 years *Category range* 6 –9 years |
| *Category 2* | *Starting point* 11 years *Category range* 9 –13 years | *Starting point* 8 years *Category range* 6.5 –10 years | *Starting point* 6 years *Category range* 5 –7 years |
| *Category 3* | *Starting point* 8.5 years *Category range* 6.5 –10 years | *Starting point* 6 years *Category range* 5 –7 years | *Starting point* 4.5 years *Category range* 3.5 –5 years |
| *Category 4* | Where the quantity falls below the indicative amount set out for category 4 in the "category of harm" table (*ante*), first identify the role for the importation offence, then refer to the starting point and ranges for possession or supply offences, depending on intent. Where the quantity is significantly larger than the indicative amounts for category 4 but below category 3 amounts, refer to the category 3 ranges above. | | |

| Class B | Leading role | Significant role | Lesser role |
|---|---|---|---|
| *Category 1* | *Starting point* 8 years *Category range* 7 –10 years | *Starting point* 5.5 years *Category range* 5 –7 years | *Starting point* 4 years *Category range* 2.5 –5 years |

| Category 2 | *Starting point* 6 years *Category range* 4.5 –8 years | *Starting point* 4 years *Category range* 2.5 –5 years | *Starting point* 2 years *Category range* 1.5 –3 years |
| Category 3 | *Starting point* 4 years *Category range* 2.5 –5 years | *Starting point* 2 years *Category range* 1.5 –3 years | *Starting point* 1 year *Category range* 12 weeks –18 months |
| Category 4 | As for "Category 4" Class A offences, *ante*. | | |

| Class C | Leading role | Significant role | Lesser role |
|---|---|---|---|
| *Category 1* | *Starting point* 5 years *Category range* 4 –8 years | *Starting point* 3 years *Category range* 2 –5 years | *Starting point* 1.5 years *Category range* 1 –3 years |
| *Category 2* | *Starting point* 3.5 years *Category range* 2 –5 years | *Starting point* 1.5 years *Category range* 1 –3 years | *Starting point* 26 weeks *Category range* 12 weeks –18 months |
| *Category 3* | *Starting point* 1.5 years *Category range* 1 –3 years | *Starting point* 26 weeks *Category range* 12 weeks – 18 months | *Starting point* high level community order *Category range* medium level community order – 12 weeks |
| *Category 4* | As for "Category 4" class A offences, *ante*. | | |

*Factors increasing or reducing seriousness or reflecting personal mitigation*

| Factors increasing seriousness | i, iv, xi–xv, xvii, xviii, xx–xxii |
|---|---|
| Factors reducing seriousness or reflecting personal mitigation | i, iv–ix, xi–xv |

## II. Supplying, offering to supply, possession with intent to supply

*Determining the offence category (step one)*

K-276    The court should determine the weight of the drugs and the offender's culpability demonstrated by his role, by reference to the tables below. Where there are characteristics present that fall under different role categories, the court should balance them to reach a fair assessment of the offender's culpability.

| **Culpability demonstrated by offender's role** |
|---|
| One or more of these characteristics may demonstrate the offender's role. These lists are not exhaustive. |
| **LEADING role:** |
| As for "Leading role" in section I, *ante*. |

**SIGNIFICANT role:**

As for "Significant role" in section I, *ante*, but also:

supply, other than by a person in a position of responsibility, to a prisoner for gain without coercion.

**LESSER role:**

As for "Lesser role" in section I, *ante*, save that:

if own operation, absence of any financial gain, *e.g.* joint purchase for no profit, or sharing minimal quantity between peers on non-commercial basis.

**Category of harm**

Indicative quantity of drug concerned (upon which the starting point is based):

**Category 1**

As for "Category 1" in section I, *ante*.

**Category 2**

As for "Category 2" in section I, *ante*.

**Category 3**

As for "Category 3" in section I, *ante*.

OR

supplying drugs in prison by a prison employee or "street dealing", *i.e.* selling directly to users (including test purchase officers).

**Category 4**

As for "Category 4" in section I, *ante*,

Where the operation is on the most serious and commercial scale, involving a quantity of drugs significantly higher than category 1, sentences of 20 years and above may be appropriate, depending on the role of the offender.

*Starting point and category range (step two)*

| Class A | Leading role | Significant role | Lesser role |
|---|---|---|---|
| *Category 1* | *Starting point* 14 years *Category range* 12 – 16 years | *Starting point* 10 years *Category range* 9 – 12 years | *Starting point* 7 years Category range 6 – 9 years |
| *Category 2* | *Starting point* 11 years *Category range* 9 – 13 years | *Starting point* 8 years *Category range* 6.5 – 10 years | *Starting point* 5 years *Category range* 3.5 – 7 years |
| *Category 3* | *Starting point* 8.5 years *Category range* 6.5 – 10 years | *Starting point* 4.5 years *Category range* 3.5 – 7 years | *Starting point* 3 years *Category range* 2 – 4.5 years |
| *Category 4* | *Starting point* 5.5 years *Category range* 4.5 – 7.5 years | *Starting point* 3.5 years *Category range* 2 – 5 years | *Starting point* 1.5 years *Category range* high level community order – 3 years |

| Class B | Leading role | Significant role | Lesser role |
|---|---|---|---|
| **Category 1** | *Starting point* 8 years | *Starting point* 5.5 years | *Starting point* 3 years |

| | Leading role | Significant role | Lesser role |
|---|---|---|---|
| | *Category range*<br>7 – 10 years | *Category range*<br>5 – 7 years | Category range<br>2.5 – 5 years |
| *Category 2* | *Starting point*<br>6 years<br>*Category range*<br>4.5 – 8 years | *Starting point*<br>4 years<br>*Category range*<br>2.5 – 5 years | *Starting point*<br>1 year<br>*Category range*<br>26 weeks – 3 years |
| *Category 3* | *Starting point*<br>4 years<br>*Category range*<br>2.5 – 5 years | *Starting point*<br>1 year<br>*Category range*<br>26 weeks – 3 years | *Starting point*<br>high level community order<br>*Category range*<br>low level community order – 26 weeks |
| *Category 4* | *Starting point*<br>1.5 years<br>*Category range*<br>26 weeks – 3 years | *Starting point*<br>high level community order<br>*Category range*<br>medium level community order – 26 weeks | *Starting point*<br>low level community order<br>*Category range*<br>band B fine – medium level community order |

| **Class C** | **Leading role** | **Significant role** | **Lesser role** |
|---|---|---|---|
| *Category 1* | *Starting point*<br>5 years<br>*Category range*<br>4 – 8 years | *Starting point*<br>3 years<br>*Category range*<br>2 – 5 years | *Starting point*<br>1.5 years<br>Category range<br>1 – 3 years |
| *Category 2* | *Starting point*<br>3.5 years<br>*Category range*<br>2 – 5 years | *Starting point*<br>1.5 years<br>*Category range*<br>1 – 3 years | *Starting point*<br>26 years<br>*Category range*<br>12 weeks – 1.5 years |
| *Category 3* | *Starting point*<br>1.5 years<br>*Category range*<br>1 – 3 years | *Starting point*<br>26 years<br>*Category range*<br>12 weeks – 1.5 years | *Starting point*<br>high level community order<br>*Category range*<br>low level community order – 12 weeks |
| *Category 4* | *Starting point*<br>26 years<br>*Category range*<br>high level community order – 1.5 years | *Starting point*<br>high level community order<br>*Category range*<br>low level community order – 12 weeks | *Starting point*<br>low level community order<br>*Category range*<br>band A fine – medium level community order |

*Factors increasing or reducing seriousness or reflecting personal mitigation*

| | |
|---|---|
| Factors increasing seriousness | i–v, x, xv, xvii–xxii |
| Factors reducing seriousness or reflecting personal mitigation | i–ix, xi–xv |

## III. Production of a controlled drug OR cultivation of a cannabis plant

*Determining the offence category (step one)*

The court should determine the offender's culpability demonstrated by his role and the output **K-277** or potential output based on the weight of the product or number of plants/ scale of operation, by reference to the tables below. Where there are characteristics present that fall under different role categories, the court should balance them to reach a fair assessment of the offender's culpability.

| Culpability demonstrated by offender's role |
|---|
| One or more of these characteristics may demonstrate the offender's role. These lists are not exhaustive. |
| **LEADING role:** |
| As for "Leading role" in section I, *ante*, save that there is no reference here to closeness to the original source. |
| **SIGNIFICANT role:** |
| As for "Significant role" in section I, *ante*. |
| **LESSER role:** |
| As for "Lesser role" in section I, *ante*. |
| **Category of harm**<br>Indicative quantity of drug concerned (upon which the starting point is based): |
| **Category 1**<br>As for "Category 1" in section I, *ante*, except that the quantity specified for cannabis is an operation capable of producing industrial quantities for commercial use. |
| **Category 2**<br>As for "Category 2" in section I, *ante*, except that the quantity specified for cannabis is an operation capable of producing significant quantities for commercial use. |
| **Category 3**<br>As for "Category 3" in section I, *ante*, except that the quantity specified for cannabis is 28 plants (with an assumed yield of 40g per plant). |
| **Category 4**<br>As for "Category 4" in section I, *ante*, except that the quantity specified for cannabis is nine plants (with an assumed yield of 40g per plant) (domestic operation). |

Where the operation is on the most serious and commercial scale, involving a quantity of drugs significantly higher than category 1, sentences of 20 years and above may be appropriate, depending on the role of the offender.

*Starting point and category range (step two)*

For Class A offences, as for "Class A" in section II, *ante*, except for category 3:

| Class A | Leading role | Significant role | Lesser role |
|---|---|---|---|
| *Category 3* | *Starting point*<br>8.5 years<br>*Category range*<br>6.5 – 10 years | *Starting point*<br>5 years<br>*Category range*<br>3.5 – 7 years | *Starting point*<br>3.5 years<br>*Category range*<br>2 – 5 years |

For Class B offences, as for "Class B" in section II, *ante*, except for category 4:

| Class B | Leading role | Significant role | Lesser role |
|---|---|---|---|
| *Category 4* | *Starting point*<br>1 year<br>*Category range* | *Starting point*<br>high level community order<br>*Category range* | *Starting point*<br>band C fine<br>*Category range* |

|  |  | high level community order – 3 years | medium level community order – 26 weeks | discharge – medium level community order |

| Class C | Leading role | Significant role | Lesser role |
|---|---|---|---|
| *Category 1* | *Starting point*<br>5 years<br>*Category range*<br>4 – 8 years | *Starting point*<br>3 years<br>*Category range*<br>2 – 5 years | *Starting point*<br>1.5 years<br>*Category range*<br>1 – 3 years |
| *Category 2* | *Starting point*<br>3.5 years<br>*Category range*<br>2 – 5 years | *Starting point*<br>1.5 years<br>*Category range*<br>1 – 3 years | *Starting point*<br>26 weeks<br>*Category range*<br>high level community order – 1.5 years |
| *Category 3* | *Starting point*<br>1.5 years<br>*Category range*<br>1 – 3 years | *Starting point*<br>26 weeks<br>*Category range*<br>high level community order – 1.5 years | *Starting point*<br>high level community order<br>*Category range*<br>low level community order – 12 weeks |
| *Category 4* | *Starting point*<br>26 weeks<br>*Category range*<br>high level community order – 1.5 years | *Starting point*<br>high level community order<br>*Category range*<br>low level community order – 12 weeks | *Starting point*<br>band C fine<br>*Category range*<br>discharge – medium level community order |

*Factors increasing or reducing seriousness or reflecting personal mitigation*

| Factors increasing seriousness | i, iv, vi–x, xv, xvii, xviii, xx–xxii |
|---|---|
| Factors reducing seriousness or reflecting personal mitigation | i, iv–ix, xi–xv |

## IV. Permitting premises to be used

*Determining the offence category (step one)*

**K-278**   The court should determine into which of three categories the offence falls by reference to the offender's culpability and the harm caused (which will be based on the extent of the activity and/ or the quantity of drugs). Category 1 requires greater harm and higher culpability, category 2 requires either greater harm and lower culpability or lesser harm and higher culpability, and category 3 requires lesser harm and lower culpability.

Factors indicating higher culpability (non-exhaustive):
- Premises used primarily for drug activity, *e.g.* crack house.
- Expectation of substantial financial gain.
- Use of legitimate business premises to aid and/ or conceal illegal activity, *e.g.* public house or club.

Factors indicating lower culpability (non-exhaustive):
- Limited or no financial gain.
- No active role in any supply taking place.
- Involvement through naivety.

Factors indicating greater harm (non-exhaustive):
- Regular drug-related activity.
- Higher quantity of drugs, *e.g.* more than 5g of heroin or cocaine or more than 50g of cannabis.

Factors indicating lesser harm (non-exhaustive):
- Infrequent drug-related activity.
- Lower quantity of drugs.

*Starting point and category range (step two)*

| Class A | Starting point | Category range |
|---|---|---|
| Category 1 | 2.5 years | 1.5 – 4 year |
| Category 2 | 36 weeks | high level community order – 1.5 years |
| Category 3 | medium level community order | low level community order – high level community order |

| Class B | Starting point | Category range |
|---|---|---|
| Category 1 | 1 year | 26 weeks – 1.5 years |
| Category 2 | high level community order | low level community order – 26 weeks |
| Category 3 | band C fine | band A fine – low level community order |

| Class C | Starting point | Category range |
|---|---|---|
| Category 1 | 12 weeks | high level community order – 26 weeks (3 months if tried summarily) |
| Category 2 | low level community order | band C fine – high level community order |
| Category 3 | band A fine | discharge – band C fine |

*Factors increasing or reducing seriousness or reflecting personal mitigation*

| Factors increasing seriousness | i, iv, xi–xv, xvii, xviii, xx–xxii |
|---|---|
| Factors reducing seriousness or reflecting personal mitigation | i, iv–ix, xi–xv |

## V. Possession of a controlled drug

*Determining the offence category (step one)*
The court should determine the offence category based on the class of drug involved.     **K-279**

*Starting point and category range (step two)*

| Offence category | Starting point | Category range |
|---|---|---|
| Category 1 (Class A) | band C fine | band A fine – 51 weeks |
| Category 2 (Class B) | band B fine | discharge – 26 weeks |
| Category 3 (Class C) | band A fine | discharge – medium level community order |

*Factors increasing or reducing seriousness or reflecting personal mitigation*

| Factors increasing seriousness | i, iv, xv–xvii, xix, xxi, xxii |
|---|---|
| Factors reducing seriousness or reflecting personal mitigation | iv, vi, viii–xv |

## V. Offences Taken into Consideration and Totality

**K-280**    The Sentencing Council has issued a guideline on the related topics of taking offences into consideration (TICs) and totality, applying to all offenders whose cases are dealt with on or after June 11, 2012. In addition to setting out the applicable principles to be gleaned from legislation and case-law, the guideline covers the following.

### A. Offences taken into consideration

**K-281**    See *ante*, §§ 5-160 *et seq.*

### B. Totality

**K-282**    This part of the guideline applies to the sentencing of an offender for multiple offences or when he is serving an existing sentence. The principle of totality comprises two elements: (i) all courts when sentencing for more than a single offence should pass a just and proportionate total sentence that reflects all the offending behaviour, whether the sentences are structured as concurrent or consecutive (in respect of which there is no inflexible rule); (ii) it is usually impossible to arrive at a just and proportionate total sentence simply by adding together notional single sentences - it is necessary to address the offending behaviour, together with the factors personal to the offender, as a whole.

The general approach (as applied to determinate custodial sentences) consists of four steps:
  (i) consider the sentence for each individual offence;
  (ii) determine whether the case calls for concurrent or consecutive sentences;
  (iii) test the overall sentence against the requirement that it should be just and proportionate; and
  (iv) consider whether the sentence is structured in a way that will be best understood by all concerned with it.

As to (ii), concurrent sentences will ordinarily be appropriate where the offences arise out of the same incident or facts or where there is a series of offences of the same or similar kind, especially when committed against the same person, with examples of both being set out in the guideline. Consecutive offences will be appropriate where the offences arise out of unrelated facts or incidents, where the offences are of the same or similar kind, but where the overall criminality will not sufficiently be reflected by concurrent sentences, or where one or more offence qualifies for a statutory minimum sentence and concurrent sentences would improperly undermine that minimum. Examples are again set out, including ways in which the court can reach a just and proportionate sentence where this is not achieved by simply aggregating the consecutive sentences (*e.g.* with offences of a similar level of severity, by reducing all of the sentences proportionately or by identifying the most serious principal offence and reducing the remainder proportionately; with offences of differing levels of seriousness, by recording lesser offences as "no separate penalty" or by ordering the lesser sentences to run concurrently).

Tables follow the guideline, setting out the approach to be taken when applying the totality principle in specified circumstances (this is in large part based on existing legislation and case-law).

*Determinate custodial sentence to be passed*

**K-283**    a. where the offender is serving an existing custodial determinate sentence: if the new offence was committed before the imposition of that sentence, the court should consider what sentence would have been imposed if the court had dealt with the offences at the same time; if it was committed after that sentence, then generally the sentence will be consecutive;

   b. where the offender is serving a custodial determinate sentence, but had been released from custody prior to being recalled, the court should follow *R. v. Costello* [2010] 2 Cr.App.R.(S.) 94, CA (§ 5-669 in the main work);

   c. where the offender is liable to be returned to custody under the PCC(S)A 2000, s.116 (*ante*, § 5-633), see subsection (6)(c);

d. where the offender is in breach of a suspended sentence, the additional sentence will
generally be consecutive to the activated suspended sentence;

*Extended sentences*

e. when using multiple offences to calculate the requisite determinate term (in accordance   **K-284**
with *R. v. Joyce; R. v. Pinnell* [2011] 2 Cr.App.R.(S.) 30, CA (§ 5-523 in the main work)), the
custodial period must be adjusted for totality in the same way as determinate sentences
would be;

*Indeterminate sentences*

f. when imposing multiple indeterminate sentences and using multiple offences to calculate   **K-285**
the minimum term for an indeterminate sentence, assess the notional determinate term
for all offences (serious, specified or otherwise) in the usual way, adjusting for totality, and
then, normally, impose the indeterminate sentence on all serious specified offences concurrently;

g. where the offender is already serving an existing determinate sentence, the court should
order the sentence to run concurrently but adjust the minimum term to reflect half of any
period still remaining to be served under the existing sentence; where the offender is
already serving an existing indeterminate sentence, the court may order the sentence to
run consecutively to the existing sentence (*R. v. Hills* [2009] 1 Cr.App.R.(S.) 75, CA (§
5-523 in the main work)), but the aggregate minimum terms should be adjusted if this is
not just and proportionate;

h. when ordering a determinate sentence to run consecutively to an indeterminate sentence,
the court should consider the total sentence that the offender will serve before becoming
eligible for consideration for release, achieving justice and proportionality, if necessary, by
reducing the length of the determinate sentence or, alternatively, ordering the second
sentence to be served concurrently;

*Multiple fines for non-imprisonable offences*

i. where the offender has been convicted of more than one offence where a fine is appropri-   **K-286**
ate, there are various ways in which the court can achieve a just and proportionate fine if
this is not achieved by simply totting up the fines; the court should also consider *R. v. John
Pointon & Sons Ltd* [2008] 2 Cr.App.R.(S.) 82, CA (as to the need to avoid double counting);

*Fines in combination with other sentences*

j. a fine may be imposed in addition to any other sentence (subject to statutory exceptions),   **K-287**
but combining a fine with an immediate custodial sentence is only likely to be justifiable if
a confiscation order is not contemplated, there is no obvious victim to receive compensation and the offender has the means to pay;

*Community orders*

k. multiple offences that do not individually cross the custody threshold may do so when   **K-288**
taken in combination;

l. where there is more than one offence, with one meriting immediate custody and one
meriting a community order, the custodial sentence should be enhanced by virtue of the
associated offence or no separate penalty should be imposed for the lesser offence;

m. where the offender has been convicted of more than one offence where a community
order is appropriate, the court should generally impose a single community order that
reflects the overall criminality of the offending behaviour; where it is necessary to impose
more than one community order, these should be ordered to run concurrently and, for
ease of administration, each of the orders should be identical;

n. where the offender is convicted of an offence while serving a community order, the court
should consider if the overall seriousness of the offending behaviour justifies a custodial
sentence; if not, it should impose a single community order reflecting the overall totality of
criminality; and it should take into account the extent to which the offender complied with
the requirements of the previous order;

*Disqualifications from driving*

o. where the offender has been convicted of two or more obligatory disqualification offences,   **K-289** the court should take into account all offences when determining the disqualification periods and should generally impose like periods for each offence (which have to be concurrent);

p. where the offender has been convicted of two or more offences and is liable to disqualification under the "totting up" provisions of the RTOA 1988, s.35 (§ 32-192 in the main work), the guideline simply sets out the effect of subsection (3);

q. where the offender has otherwise been convicted of two or more offences involving discretionary disqualification, it is generally desirable for the court to impose a single disqualification order that reflects the overall criminality of the offending behaviour;

*Compensation orders*

**K-290**       r. a global compensation order should not be made unless the offences were committed against the same victim; where there are competing claims for limited funds, the amount available should normally be apportioned on a *pro rata* basis;

s. compensation may be combined with a fine (with priority to compensation), a confiscation order, a community order, a suspended sentence or an immediate custodial sentence (where the offender is clearly able to pay or has good prospects of employment on release).

## W. Dangerous Dog Offences

**K-291**    The Sentencing Council for England and Wales issued a definitive guideline, applying to all offenders aged 18 or over who were sentenced on or after August 20, 2012, regardless of the date of the offence. The offences covered are: (A) owning or being in charge of a dog that injures a person whilst dangerously out of control in a public place (Dangerous Dogs Act 1991, s.3(1) (§ 31-35 in the main work)), and allowing a dog to enter a private place where the dog is not permitted to be, where it then injures any person (1991 Act, s.3(3)(a)), (B) owning or being in charge of a dog dangerously out of control in a public place (1991 Act, s.3(1)), and allowing a dog to enter a private place where the dog is not permitted to be, and, while it is there, there are grounds for reasonable apprehension that it will injure any person (1991 Act, s.3(3)(b)), and (C) possession of a prohibited dog (1991 Act, s.1(3)), and breeding, selling, exchanging or advertising a prohibited dog (1991 Act, s.1(2)).

★    In view of the legislative changes made to the 1991 Act by the Anti-social Behaviour, Crime and Policing Act 2014, including by way of abolishing the offences under section 3(3), extending the offence under section 3(1) to private places as well as public places, and increasing the penalties for aggravated offences under section 3(1), the guideline now needs to be approached with considerable caution. For the details of the legislative amendments, see *ante*, §§ 31-35 *et seq.*

The guideline sets out eight steps to be followed (in order), which broadly correspond to the steps set out in the guideline on offences against the person (*ante*, K-113 *et seq.*), except that there is no step requiring the court to consider whether an offender meets the dangerousness criteria, and consideration of compensation and/ or ancillary orders is step five (as to which, see the specific sections relating to A to C, *post*), preceding consideration of the totality principle (now step six).

Step one requires the court to determine within which of three categories reflecting various degrees of seriousness the offence falls. In determining the offender's culpability and the harm caused (or intended), the court should refer only to the factors indicating harm and culpability set out in the specific sections relating to A to C, *post*, which comprise the principal factual elements of the offence.

Step two requires the court to use the starting point identified for the relevant category (as to which, see also the specific sections relating to A to C, *post*) to reach a sentence within the category range. The starting point applies to all offenders irrespective of plea or previous convictions. The court should then consider adjustment within the category range for aggravating or mitigating features set out in the specific sections A to C, *post*, which contain a non-exhaustive list of additional factual elements providing the context of the offence and factors relating to the offender. Having considered all these, and other relevant factors, it might be appropriate to move outside the identified category range. As with previous guidelines, the council emphasises that, where appropriate, courts should consider whether community or custodial thresholds have been passed and, if the latter threshold has been passed, whether it is unavoidable that a custodial sentence be imposed and, if so, whether that sentence can be suspended.

Fine bands, and a non-exhaustive description of examples of requirements that might be appropriate for low, medium and high level community orders, correspond to those in the guideline on offences against the person (*ante*), and are set out in the annex to the guideline.

## Key to factors increasing or reducing seriousness or reflecting personal mitigation (step two)

A number of the following factors may apply when determining the sentence within the **K-292** category range. As to which factors may apply to each type of offence, see the specific sections A to C, *post*.

(a) *Factors increasing seriousness*

Statutory aggravating factors:

   i. Previous convictions.

   ii. Offence committed on bail.

Other aggravating factors include:

   iii. Injury to other animal(s).

   iv. Location of offence.

   v. Continuing effect upon victim and/ or others.

   vi. Failure to take adequate precautions to prevent dog escaping.

   vii. Allowing insufficiently experienced or trained person to be in charge of dog.

   viii. Presence of children or others who are vulnerable because of personal circumstances.

   ix. Ill-treatment or failure to ensure welfare needs of dog, where not charged separately.

   x. Dog known to be prohibited.

   xi. Lack or loss of control of dog due to influence of alcohol or drugs.

   xii. Offence committed against those working in the public sector or providing a service to the public.

   xiii. Established evidence of community impact.

   xiv. Failure to comply with current court orders or offence committed on licence.

(b) *Factors reducing seriousness or reflecting personal mitigation*

   i. No previous convictions or no relevant/ recent convictions.

   ii. Isolated incident.

   iii. No previous complaints against, or incidents involving, the dog.

   iv. Unaware that dog was prohibited type despite reasonable efforts to identify type.

   v. Evidence of safety or control measures having been taken by owner.

   vi. Prosecution results from owner notification.

   vii. Remorse.

   viii. Good character and/ or exemplary conduct.

   ix. Evidence of responsible ownership.

   x. Determination, and/ or demonstration of steps taken, to address addiction or offending behaviour.

   xi. Serious medical condition requiring urgent, intensive or long-term treatment.

   xii. Age and/ or lack of maturity where it affects the responsibility of the offender.

   xiii. Lapse of time since the offence where this was not the fault of the offender.

   xiv. Mental disorder or learning disability (for offences in sections A and B only, where not linked to commission of the offence).

   xv. Sole or primary carer for dependent relatives.

## A. Dog dangerously out of control in a public place, injuring any person, or allowing a dog to enter a private place where the dog is not permitted to be, where it then injures any person

*Determining the offence category (step one)*

Category 1 requires greater harm and higher culpability, category 2 requires either greater **K-293** harm and lower culpability or lesser harm and higher culpability, and category 3 requires lesser harm and lower culpability.

*Factors indicating greater harm*
- Serious injury (including disease transmission and/ or psychological harm)
- Sustained or repeated attack
- Victim is a child or otherwise vulnerable because of personal circumstances

*Factors indicating lesser harm*
- Minor injury

*Factors indicating higher culpability*
Statutory aggravating factors:
- Offence racially or religiously aggravated
- Offence motivated by, or demonstrating, hostility to the victim based on sexual orientation or disability (or presumed sexual orientation or disability)
Other aggravating factors:
- Failure to respond to others' warnings or concerns about dog's behaviour
- Goading, or allowing goading, of dog
- Dog used as weapon to intimidate victim
- Offence motivated by, or demonstrating, hostility to the victim based on age, sex, or (presumed) gender identity

*Factors indicating lower culpability*
- Attempts made to regain control of dog and/ or intervene
- Provocation of dog without fault of offender
- Evidence of safety or control measures taken
- Mental disorder or disability, where linked to the commission of the offence

*Starting point and category range (step two)*

| Offence category | Starting point (applicable to all offenders) | Category range (applicable to all offenders) |
|---|---|---|
| category 1 | six months' custody | medium level community order - 18 months' custody |
| category 2 | medium level community order | band B fine - six months' custody |
| category 3 | band B fine | discharge - band C fine |

*Factors increasing or reducing seriousness or reflecting personal mitigation*
Factors increasing seriousness: i-vii, ix-xiv
Factors reducing seriousness or reflecting personal mitigation: i-iii, vii-xii, xiv, xv

*Compensation and ancillary orders (step five)*
The court should consider whether to make a compensation order and/ or other ancillary orders. The court may disqualify the offender from having custody of a dog, the test being whether the offender is a fit and proper person to have custody of a dog. The court shall make a destruction order (after giving the owner, where not the offender, an opportunity to be present and make representations) unless satisfied that the dog would not constitute a danger to public safety. In reaching a decision, the court should consider the relevant circumstances, which include (i) the incident — what degree of harm was caused by the dog's behaviour, (ii) past behaviour of the dog — whether this was an isolated incident or whether there have been previous warnings or incidents, and (iii) the owner's character — whether the owner is a fit and proper person to own the particular dog. If satisfied that the dog would not constitute a danger to public safety, the court shall make a contingent destruction order imposing certain conditions. Where the court makes a destruction order, it may order the offender to pay reasonable expenses.

## B. Dog dangerously out of control in a public place, or allowing a dog to enter a private place where the dog is not permitted to be, where there are grounds for reasonable apprehension that it will injure any person

*Determining the offence category (step one)*
Same categories as for A, *ante*.

**K-294**

*Factors indicating greater harm*
- Presence of children or others who are vulnerable because of personal circumstances
- Injury to another animal(s)

*Factors indicating lesser harm*
- Low risk to the public

*Factors indicating higher culpability*
- Same as for A, *ante*

*Factors indicating lower culpability*
- Same as for A, *ante*

*Starting point and category range (step two)*

| Offence category | Starting point (applicable to all offenders) | Category range (applicable to all offenders) |
|---|---|---|
| category 1 | medium level community order | band C fine - six months' custody |
| category 2 | band B fine | band A fine - low level community order |
| category 3 | band A fine | discharge - band B fine |

*Factors increasing or reducing seriousness or reflecting personal mitigation*
Factors increasing seriousness: i, ii, iv-vii, ix-xiv
Factors reducing seriousness or reflecting personal mitigation: i-iii, vii-xii, xiv, xv

*Compensation and ancillary orders (step five)*
Same as for A, *ante*, except the court is permitted (rather than required) to make a destruction order or contingent destruction order. In reaching a decision, the court should consider the relevant circumstances, which include those set out in section A, *ante*.

## C. Possession of a prohibited dog, or breeding, selling, exchanging or advertising a prohibited dog

*Determining the offence category (step one)*
Category 1 requires greater harm and higher culpability, category 2 requires either greater **K-295** harm or higher culpability, and category 3 requires that there be neither greater harm nor higher culpability.

*Factors indicating greater harm*
- Injury to person
- Injury to another animal(s)

*Factors indicating higher culpability*
- Dog known to be prohibited
- Offence committed for gain
- Dog used to threaten or intimidate

- Permitting fighting
- Training and/ or possession of paraphernalia for dog fighting

*Starting point and category range (step two)*

| Offence category | Starting point (applicable to all offenders) | Category range (applicable to all offenders) |
|---|---|---|
| category 1 | medium level community order | band C fine - six months' custody |
| category 2 | band C fine | band A fine - medium level community order |
| category 3 | band A fine | discharge - band B fine |

*Factors increasing or reducing seriousness or reflecting personal mitigation*

Factors increasing seriousness: i, ii, viii, ix, xiii, xiv

Factors reducing seriousness or reflecting personal mitigation: i, iv-xv.

*Ancillary orders (step five)*

**K-296**     The court may disqualify the offender from having custody of a dog, the test being whether the offender is a fit and proper person to have custody of a dog. The court shall make a destruction order unless satisfied that the dog would not constitute a danger to public safety. In reaching a decision, the court should consider the relevant circumstances, which include those set out in section A, *ante*. If the court does not make a destruction order, the court shall make a contingent destruction order providing that unless the dog is exempted from the prohibition within two months it shall be destroyed. Where the offender is the owner of the dog, it would not normally be appropriate to make a contingent destruction order in conjunction with a disqualification order. Further, the court must not transfer ownership of the dog to another. Where the court makes a destruction order, it may order the offender to pay reasonable expenses.

## X. FRAUD, BRIBERY AND MONEY LAUNDERING

★**K-297**     The Sentencing Council for England and Wales has issued a definitive guideline for offences of fraud, money laundering and bribery falling to be sentenced on or after October 1, 2014. The guideline is in seven sections, the seventh of which relates to corporate offenders and incorporates an earlier guideline issued by the Sentencing Council.

Each section (apart from Section VII, which is dealt with separately, *post*) describes eight steps to be gone through.

## Step 1 (determining the offence category)

★**K-298**     This involves determination of the offence category by reference to the tables in each section. In order to do this, the court should make an assessment of culpability and harm. The level of culpability is determined by weighing up all the factors of the case to determine the offender's role and the extent to which the offending was planned and the sophistication with which it was carried out.

The following indicators of culpability are used throughout the guideline (apart from Section VII, which is dealt with separately (*post*)).

*Higher culpability (A)*

HC1:     A leading role where offending is part of a group activity

HC2:     Involvement of others through pressure, influence

HC3:     Abuse of position of power, trust or responsibility

HC4:     Sophisticated nature of offence/ significant planning

HC5:     Fraudulent activity conducted over sustained period of time

HC6:     Large number of victims

HC7:     Deliberate targeting of victim on basis of vulnerability

HC8:     Articles deliberately designed to target victims on basis of vulnerability

HC9:     Criminal activity/ offending conducted over sustained period of time

HC10:    Intended corruption (directly or indirectly) of a senior official performing a public
         function or of a law enforcement officer

HC11:    Motivated by expectation of substantial financial, commercial or political gain

*Medium culpability (B)*

MC1:     Other cases where characteristics for categories A or C are not present

MC2:     A significant role where offending is part of a group activity

MC3:     Claim not fraudulent from outset

*Lesser culpability (C)*

LC1:     Involved through coercion, intimidation or exploitation

LC2:     Not motivated by personal gain

LC3:     Peripheral role in organised fraud

LC4:     Opportunistic "one-off" offence

LC5:     Limited awareness or understanding of the extent of the fraudulent activity

LC6:     Performed limited function under direction

   Where there are characteristics present that fall under different levels of culpability, the court
should balance them to reach a fair assessment of the offender's culpability.

   As to the assessment of harm, see the individual sections.

## Step 2 (starting point and category range)

   Having determined the category, the court should use the appropriate starting point to reach a ★**K-299**
sentence within the category range in the tables. The starting points apply to all offenders irrespective of plea and previous convictions. Where the starting point is based on a particular
value (as in Sections I, III, IV and V), this should be adjusted upwards or downwards according
to the actual value involved. Where the value greatly exceeds the amount of the starting point for
a category 1 case, it may be appropriate to move outside the identified range.

   The tables of starting points and category ranges in each section are followed by a "non-
exhaustive list of additional factual elements providing the context of the offence and factors
relating to the offender." The court is then to identify whether any combination of these or other
relevant factors should result in an upward or downward adjustment from the sentence arrived at
based on culpability and harm alone. In each section, it is also stated that consecutive sentences
for multiple offences may be appropriate where large sums are involved.

   The following aggravating and mitigating factors are used throughout the guideline (apart
from Section VII, which is dealt with separately (*post*)).

*Aggravating factors*

A1:      Previous convictions, having regard to (a) the nature of the offence to which the
         conviction relates and its relevance to the current offence; and (b) the time that
         has elapsed since the conviction

A2:      Offence committed whilst on bail

A3:      Steps taken to prevent the victim reporting or obtaining assistance and/ or from
         assisting or supporting the prosecution

A4:      Attempts to conceal/ dispose of evidence

A5:          Established evidence of community/ wider impact

A6:          Failure to comply with current court orders

A7:          Offence committed on licence

A8:          Offences taken into consideration

A9:          Failure to respond to warnings about behaviour

A10:        Offences committed across borders

A11:        Blame wrongly placed on others

A12:        Involves multiple frauds

A13:        Number of false declarations

A14:        Damage to third party (*e.g.* as a result of identity theft, or loss of employment to legitimate employees)

A15:        Dealing with goods with an additional health risk

A16:        Disposing of goods to under age purchasers

A17:        Claim fraudulent from outset

A18:        Proceeds of fraud funded lavish lifestyle

A19:        Length of time over which offending was committed

A20:        Pressure exerted on another party

A21:        Offence committed to facilitate other criminal activity

*Mitigating factors*

M1:          No previous convictions or no relevant/ recent convictions

M2:          Remorse

M3:          Good character and/ or exemplary conduct

M4:          Little or no prospect of success

M5:          Serious medical conditions requiring urgent, intensive or long-term treatment

M6:          Age and/ or lack of maturity where it affects the responsibility of the offender

M7:          Lapse of time since apprehension where this does not arise from the conduct of the offender

M8:          Mental disorder or learning disability

M9:          Sole or primary carer for dependent relatives

M10:       Offender co-operated with investigation, made early admissions and/ or voluntarily reported offending

M11:       Determination and/ or demonstration of steps having been taken to address addiction or offending behaviour

M12:       Activity originally legitimate

M13:       Legitimate entitlement to benefits not claimed

M14:       Offender experiencing significant financial hardship or pressure at time fraud was committed due to exceptional circumstances

### Steps 3-8

★**K-300**    These are standard steps in guidelines issued by the Sentencing Council. They require the court to consider the SOCPA 2005, ss.73 and 74 (assistance by defendants; reduction or review of sentence (§§ 5-132, 5-133 in the main work)), credit for a guilty plea, the totality principle, the question of confiscation, compensation and any appropriate ancillary orders, the need to give reasons and to make any appropriate allowance for time spent on bail (CJA 2003, s.240A (5-645 in the main work)).

## I. Fraud

This section covers fraud (Fraud Act 2006, s.1, (§ 21-356 in the main work)), conspiracy to       ★**K-301**
defraud (§§ 33-37 *et seq.* in the main work) and false accounting (Theft Act 1968, s.17 (§ 21-226 in
the main work)), but none of these if the fraud is a revenue or benefit fraud (as to which, see Sections III and IV, *post*).

*Step 1: determine the level of culpability and the harm category (and see generally, ante)*
  *Culpability*

| High culpability (HC) | Medium culpability (MC) | Lesser culpability (LC) |
|---|---|---|
| HC1–HC7 | MC1, MC2 | LC1–LC5 |

  *Harm*

This is initially assessed by the actual, intended or risked loss that may arise from the offence.
The values in the table below are to be used for actual or intended loss only. Intended loss relates
to offences where circumstances prevent the actual loss that is intended to be caused by the
fraudulent activity. Risk of loss (*e.g.* in mortgage frauds) involves consideration of the likelihood
of harm occurring and its extent if it does, and is less serious than actual or intended loss. Where
the offence has caused risk of loss but no (or much less) actual loss, the normal approach is to
move down to the corresponding point in the next category. This may be inappropriate if the
likelihood or extent of risked loss is particularly high.

| **Category 1** | £500k or more | Starting point based on £1m |
|---|---|---|
| **Category 2** | £100k–£500k or risk of category 1 harm | Starting point based on £300k |
| **Category 3** | £20k–£100k or risk of category 2 harm | Starting point based on £50k |
| **Category 4** | £5k–20k or risk of category 3 harm | Starting point based on £12.5k |
| **Category 5** | Less than £5k or risk of category 4 harm | Starting point based on £2.5k |

If there is risk of category 5 harm, the court should move further down the range within the
category.

  *Harm B — Victim impact*

The court should then take into account the level of harm caused to the victim or others to
determine whether it warrants the sentence being moved up to the corresponding point in the
next category or further up the range of the initial category.

---

**High impact** — move up a category; if in category 1 move up the range
  • Serious detrimental effect on the victim whether financial or otherwise, *e.g.* substantial
    damage to credit rating.
  • Victim particularly vulnerable (due to factors including, but not limited to, age, financial
    circumstances and mental capacity).

**Medium impact** — move upwards within the category range
  • Considerable detrimental effect on the victim, financial or otherwise.

**Lesser impact** — no adjustment
  • Some detrimental impact on victim, financial or otherwise.

---

*Step 2: use the following tables to reach a provisional sentence (and see generally, ante)*
  *Table 1 (fraud and conspiracy to defraud)*

| Harm | Culpability (A) | Culpability (B) | Culpability (C) |
|---|---|---|---|
| **Category 1** | *Starting points and ranges*<br>7 years<br>5–8 years | *Starting points and ranges*<br>5 years<br>3–6 years | *Starting points and ranges*<br>3 years<br>1.5–4 years |
| **Category 2** | 5 years<br>3–6 years | 3 years<br>1.5–4 years | 1.5 years<br>26 weeks–3 years |
| **Category 3** | 3 years<br>1.5–4 years | 1.5 years<br>26 weeks–3 years | 26 weeks<br>Medium level community order–12 months |
| **Category 4** | 1.5 years<br>26 weeks–3 years | 26 weeks<br>Medium level community order–12 months | Medium level community order<br>Band B fine–high level community order |
| **Category 5** | 36 weeks' custody<br>High level community order–12 months | Medium level community order<br>Band B fine–26 weeks | Band B fine<br>Discharge–medium level community order |

*Table 2 (false accounting)*

| Harm | Culpability (A) | Culpability (B) | Culpability (C) |
|---|---|---|---|
| **Category 1** | *Starting points and ranges*<br>5.5 years<br>4–6.5 years | *Starting points and ranges*<br>4 years<br>2.5–5 years | *Starting points and ranges*<br>2.5 years<br>15 months–3.5 years |
| **Category 2** | 4 years<br>2.5–5 years | 2.5 years<br>15 months–3.5 years | 15 months<br>26 weeks–2.5 years |
| **Category 3** | 2.5 years<br>15 months–3.5 years | 15 months<br>High level community order–2.5 years | High level community order<br>Low level community order–36 weeks |
| **Category 4** | 15 months<br>High level community order–2.5 years | High level community order<br>Low level community order–36 weeks | Low level community order<br>Band B fine–medium level community order |
| **Category 5** | 26 weeks<br>Medium level community order–36 weeks | Low level community order<br>Band B fine–medium level community order | Band B fine<br>Discharge–low level community order |

Adjust the provisional sentence according to the presence of the following factors:

| Factors increasing seriousness | Factors reducing seriousness or reflecting personal mitigation |
|---|---|
| A1–A11 | M1–M12 |

Steps 3–8: see *ante*

## II. Possessing, making or supplying articles for use in fraud

★**K-302**   This section covers the offences contrary to sections 6 and 7 of the Fraud Act 2006 (§§ 21-390, 21-391 in the main work)).

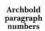

*Step 1: determine the level of culpability and the harm category (and see generally, ante).*
Culpability

| High culpability (A) | Medium culpability (B) | Lesser culpability (C) |
|---|---|---|
| HC1–HC5, HC8 | MC1, MC2 | LC1, LC2, LC4–LC6 |

*Harm*

The level of harm is determined by weighing up all the factors to determine the harm that would be caused if the article(s) was (were) used to commit a substantive offence.

**Greater harm**
- Large number of articles created/ supplied/ in possession.
- Article has potential to facilitate fraudulent acts affecting large number of victims.
- Article has potential to facilitate fraudulent acts involving significant sums.
- Use of third party identities.
- Offender making considerable gain as result of the offence.

**Lesser harm**
- All other offences.

*Step 2: use the following tables to reach a provisional sentence (and see generally, ante).*
*Table 1 (possessing articles for use in fraud (2006 Act, s.6))*

| Harm | Culpability (A) | Culpability (B) | Culpability (C) |
|---|---|---|---|
| **Greater** | *Starting points and ranges*<br>1.5 years<br>36 weeks–3 years | *Starting points and ranges*<br>36 weeks<br>High level community order–2 years | *Starting points and ranges*<br>High level community order<br>Medium level community order–26 weeks |
| **Lesser** | 26 weeks<br>High level community order–1.5 years | Medium level community order<br>Low level community order–26 weeks | Band B fine<br>Band A fine–medium level community order |

*Table 2 (making, adapting or supplying articles for use in fraud (2006 Act, s.7))*

| Harm | Culpability (A) | Culpability (B) | Culpability (C) |
|---|---|---|---|
| **Greater** | *Starting points and ranges*<br>4.5 years<br>3–7 years | *Starting points and ranges*<br>2.5 years<br>1.5–5 years | *Starting points and ranges*<br>12 months<br>High level community order–3 years |
| **Lesser** | 2 years<br>26 weeks–4 years | 36 weeks<br>Low level community order–2 years | Medium level community order<br>Band C fine–26 weeks |

The table of additional factual elements providing the context of the offence and factors relating to the offender is the same as in Section I (*ante*).

Steps 3–8: see *ante*.

## III. Revenue fraud

This section covers the same offences as in Section I, plus cheating the public revenue and offences under the Taxes Management Act 1970, s.106A (fraudulent evasion of income tax), the  ★K-303

CEMA 1979, ss.50, 170 and 170B (fraudulent evasion of duty; improper importation of goods (§§ 25-430, 25-474, 25-505 in the main work)), and the Value Added Tax Act 1994, s.72 (§ 25-532 in the main work).

*Step 1: determine the level of culpability and the harm category (and see generally, ante).*
  *Culpability*

| High culpability (A) | Medium culpability (B) | Lesser culpability (C) |
|---|---|---|
| HC1–HC5 | MC1, MC2 | LC1, LC2, LC4–LC6 |

*Harm*
Gain or intended gain, or loss or intended loss.

| | | |
|---|---|---|
| **Category 1** | £50m or more | Starting point based on £80m |
| **Category 2** | £10m–£50m | Starting point based on £30m |
| **Category 3** | £2m–£10m | Starting point based on £5m |
| **Category 4** | £500k–£2m | Starting point based on £1m |
| **Category 5** | £100k–£500k | Starting point based on £300k |
| **Category 6** | £20k–100k | Starting point based on £50k |
| **Category 7** | Less than £20k | Starting point based on £12.5k |

*Step 2: use the following tables to reach a provisional sentence (and see generally, ante).*
  *Table 1 (2006 Act, s.1, conspiracy to defraud)*
  Where the value of the fraud is over £2 million, the court should refer to the corresponding category in Table 3, subject to the maximum sentence of 10 years for these offences.

| Harm | Culpability (A) | Culpability (B) | Culpability (C) |
|---|---|---|---|
| | *Starting points and ranges* | *Starting points and ranges* | *Starting points and ranges* |
| **Category 4** | 7 years<br>5–8 years | 5 years<br>3–6 years | 3 years<br>1.5–4 years |
| **Category 5** | 5 years<br>3–6 years | 3 years<br>1.5–4 years | 1.5 years<br>26 weeks–3 years |
| **Category 6** | 3 years<br>1.5–4 years | 1.5 years<br>26 weeks–3 years | 26 weeks<br>Medium level community order–12 months |
| **Category 7** | 1.5 years<br>36 weeks–3 years | 36 weeks<br>Medium level community order–18 months | Medium level community order<br>Low–high level community order |

  *Table 2 (1968 Act, s.17, 1970 Act, s.106(a), 1979 Act, ss.50(1)(a) and (2), 170(1)(a)(i) and (ii), (1)(b), and (2)(a), and 170B, and 1994 Act, s.72(1), (3) and (8))*

| Harm | Culpability (A) | Culpability (B) | Culpability (C) |
|---|---|---|---|
| | *Starting points and ranges* | *Starting points and ranges* | *Starting points and ranges* |
| **Category 4** | 5.5 years<br>4–6.5 years | 4 years<br>2.5–5 years | 2.5 years<br>15 months–3.5 years |
| **Category 5** | 4 years<br>2.5–5 years | 2.5 years<br>15 months–3.5 years | 15 months<br>26 weeks–2.5 years |

| Harm | Culpability (A) | Culpability (B) | Culpability (C) |
|---|---|---|---|
| | *Starting points and ranges* | *Starting points and ranges* | *Starting points and ranges* |
| **Category 6** | 2.5 years | 15 months | High level community order |
| | 15 months–3.5 years | High level community order–2.5 years | Low level community order–36 weeks |
| **Category 7** | 15 months | 26 weeks | Medium level community order |
| | 26 weeks–2.5 years | Medium level community order–15 months | Band C fine–high level community order |

*Table 3 (cheating the revenue)*

Where the offending is on the most serious scale, involving sums significantly higher than the starting point in category 1, sentences of 15 years and above may be appropriate. In cases involving sums below £2 million, the court should refer to Table 1.

| Harm | Culpability (A) | Culpability (B) | Culpability (C) |
|---|---|---|---|
| | *Starting points and ranges* | *Starting points and ranges* | *Starting points and ranges* |
| **Category 1** | 12 years | 8 years | 6 years |
| | 10–17 years | 7–12 years | 4–8 years |
| **Category 2** | 10 years | 7 years | 5 years |
| | 8–13 years | 5–9 years | 3–6 years |
| **Category 3** | 8 years | 6 years | 4 years |
| | 6–10 years | 4–7 years | 3–5 years |

Adjust the provisional sentence according to the presence of the following factors:

| Factors increasing seriousness | Factors reducing seriousness or reflecting personal mitigation |
|---|---|
| A1, A2, A4, A6–A9, A11–A16 | M1–M12 |

Steps 3–8: see *ante*.

## IV. Benefit fraud

This section covers the offences in Section I, plus offences under the Social Security Administra-   ★**K-304**
tion Act 1992, ss.111A (dishonest representations for obtaining benefit, *etc.*) and 112 (false representations for obtaining benefit, *etc.*), and the Tax Credits Act 2002, s.35 (tax credit fraud).

*Step 1: determine the level of culpability and the harm category (and see generally, ante).*
Culpability

| High culpability (A) | Medium culpability (B) | Lesser culpability (C) |
|---|---|---|
| HC1-HC4 | MC1-MC3 | LC1, LC6 |

*Harm*
Amount obtained or intended to be obtained:

| Category 1 | £500k–£2m [*sic*] | Starting point based on £1m |
|---|---|---|
| **Category 1** | £500k–£2m [*sic*] | Starting point based on £1m |
| **Category 2** | £100k–£500k | Starting point based on £300k |
| **Category 3** | £50k–£100k | Starting point based on £75k |
| **Category 4** | £10k–£50k | Starting point based on £30k |
| **Category 5** | £2.5k–£10k | Starting point based on £5k |
| **Category 6** | Less than £2.5k | Starting point based on £1k |

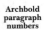

*Step 2: use the following tables to reach a provisional sentence (and see generally, ante).*

*Table 1 (1968 Act, s.17, 1992 Act, s.111A, 2002 Act, s.35)*

| Harm | Culpability (A) | Culpability (B) | Culpability (C) |
|---|---|---|---|
| | *Starting points and ranges* | *Starting points and ranges* | *Starting points and ranges* |
| **Category 1**<br>£500k or more<br>[*sic*] | 5.5 years<br>4–6.5 years | 4 years<br>2.5–5 years | 2.5 years<br>15 months–3.5 years |
| **Category 2** | 4 years<br>2.5–5 years | 2.5 years<br>15 months–3.5 years | 12 months<br>26 weeks–2.5 years |
| **Category 3** | 2.5 years<br>2–3.5 years | 12 months<br>26 weeks–2.5 years | 26 weeks<br>High level community order–36 weeks |
| **Category 4** | 1.5 years<br>36 weeks–2.5 years | 36 weeks<br>Medium level community order–21 months | Medium level community order<br>Low level community order–26 weeks |
| **Category 5** | 36 weeks<br>Medium level community order–1.5 years | Medium level community order<br>Low level community order–26 weeks | Low level community order<br>Band B fine–medium level community order |
| **Category 6** | Medium level community order<br>Low level community order–26 weeks | Low level community order<br>Band A fine–medium level community order | Band A fine<br>Discharge–band B fine |

*Table 2 (1992 Act, s.112)*

| Harm | Culpability (A) | Culpability (B) | Culpability (C) |
|---|---|---|---|
| | *Starting points and ranges* | *Starting points and ranges* | *Starting points and ranges* |
| **Category 5**<br>Above £2.5k | High level community order | Medium level community order | Low level community order |
| Starting point based on £5k | Medium level community order–12 weeks | Band B fine–high level community order | Band A fine–medium level community order |
| **Category 6**<br>Less than £2.5k | Medium level community order | Band B fine | Band A fine |
| Starting point based on £1k | Low–high level community order | Band A–band C fine | Discharge–band B fine |

*Table 3 (2006 Act, s.1, conspiracy to defraud)*

| Harm | Culpability (A) | Culpability (B) | Culpability (C) |
|---|---|---|---|
| | *Starting points and ranges* | *Starting points and ranges* | *Starting points and ranges* |
| **Category 1**<br>£500k or more<br>[*sic*] | 7 years | 5 years | 3 years |
| Starting point based on £1m | 5–8 years | 3–6 years | 1.5–4 years |

| Harm | Culpability (A) | Culpability (B) | Culpability (C) |
|---|---|---|---|
| **Category 2** | *Starting points and ranges*<br>5 years<br>3–6 years | *Starting points and ranges*<br>3 years<br>1.5–4 years | *Starting points and ranges*<br>15 months<br>26 weeks–3 years |
| **Category 3** | 3 years<br>2.5–4 years | 15 months<br>36 weeks–3 years | 36 weeks<br>26 weeks–12 months |
| **Category 4** | 21 months<br>12 months–3 years | 12 months<br>High level community order–2 years | High level community order<br>Low level community order–26 weeks |
| **Category 5** | 12 months<br>High level community order–2 years | High level community order<br>Low level community order–26 weeks | Medium level community order<br>Band C fine–high level community order |
| **Category 6** | High level community order<br>Low level community order–26 weeks | Low level community order<br>Band B fine–medium level community order | Band B fine<br>Discharge–band C fine |

Adjust the provisional sentence according to the presence of the following factors:

| Factors increasing seriousness | Factors reducing seriousness or reflecting personal mitigation |
|---|---|
| A1, A2, A4, A6–A9, A11, A13, A14, A17–A19 | M1–M11, M13, M14 |

Steps 3–8: see *ante.*

## V. Money laundering

This section covers offences contrary to the PCA 2002, ss.327–329 (§§ 26-11 *et seq.* in the main work).    ★**K-305**

*Step 1: determine the level of culpability and the harm category (and see generally, ante).*
*Culpability*

| High culpability (A) | Medium culpability (B) | Lesser culpability (C) |
|---|---|---|
| HC1–HC4, HC9 | MC1, MC2 | LC1, LC2, LC4–LC6 |

*Harm A*
Harm is initially assessed by the value of the money laundered.

| | | |
|---|---|---|
| **Category 1** | £10m or more | Starting point based on £30m |
| **Category 2** | £2m–£10m | Starting point based on £5m |
| **Category 3** | £500k–£2m | Starting point based on £1m |
| **Category 4** | £100k–£500k | Starting point based on £300k |
| **Category 5** | £10k–£100k | Starting point based on £50k |
| **Category 6** | Less than £10k | Starting point based on £5k |

*Harm B*
To complete the assessment of harm, the court should take into account the level of harm associated with the underlying offence to determine whether it warrants upward adjustment of the starting point within the range, or in appropriate cases, outside the range. Where it is possible to identify the underlying offence, the court should have regard to the relevant sentencing levels for that offence.

*Step 2: use the following table to reach a provisional sentence (and see generally, ante).*

| Harm | Culpability (A) | Culpability (B) | Culpability (C) |
|---|---|---|---|
| | *Starting points and ranges* | *Starting points and ranges* | *Starting points and ranges* |
| **Category 1** | 10 years<br>8–13 years | 7 years<br>5–10 years | 4 years<br>3–6 years |
| **Category 2** | 8 years<br>6–9 years | 5 years<br>3.5–7 years | 3.5 years<br>2–5 years |
| **Category 3** | 7 years<br>5–8 years | 5 years<br>3–6 years | 3 years<br>1.5–4 years |
| **Category 4** | 5 years<br>3–6 years | 3 years<br>1.5–4 years | 1.5 years<br>26 weeks–3 years |
| **Category 5** | 3 years<br>1.5–4 years | 1.5 years<br>26 weeks–3 years | 26 weeks<br>Medium level community order–12 months |
| **Category 6** | 12 months<br>26 weeks–2 years | High level community order<br>Low level community order–12 months | Low level community order<br>Band B fine–medium level community order |

Adjust the provisional sentence according to the presence of the following factors:

| Factors increasing seriousness | Factors reducing seriousness or reflecting personal mitigation |
|---|---|
| A1, A2, A4–A11, A14. | M1–M12 |

Steps 3–8: see *ante*.

## VI. Bribery

★K-306    This section covers offences under sections 1, 2 and 6 of the Bribery Act 2010 (§§ 31-171, 31-172, 31-176 in the main work).

*Step 1: determine the level of culpability and the harm category (and see generally, ante).*
*Culpability*

| High culpability (A) | Medium culpability (B) | Lesser culpability (C) |
|---|---|---|
| HC1–HC4, HC9–HC11 | MC1, MC2 | LC1–LC5 |

Harm is to be assessed in relation to any impact caused by the offending (whether to identifiable victims or in a wider context) and the actual or intended gain to the offender, and it is demonstrated by one or more of the following factors:

| **Category 1** | • Serious detrimental effect on individuals (*e.g.* by provision of sub-standard goods or services resulting from the corrupt behaviour).<br>• Serious environmental impact.<br>• Serious undermining of the proper function of local or national government, business or public services.<br>• Substantial actual or intended financial gain to offender or another or loss caused to others. |
|---|---|
| **Category 2** | • Significant detrimental effect on individuals. |

|  | |
|---|---|
|  | • As 2–4 in Category 1, but with substitution of "Significant" for "Serious" (2 & 3) and "Substantial" (4)<br>• Risk of category 1 harm. |
| **Category 3** | • Limited detrimental impact on individuals, the environment, government, business or public services.<br>• Risk of category 2 harm. |
| **Category 4** | • Risk of category 3 harm. |

*Step 2: use the following table to reach a provisional sentence (and see generally, ante).*

| Harm | Culpability (A) | Culpability (B) | Culpability (C) |
|---|---|---|---|
| **Category 1** | *Starting points and ranges*<br>7 years<br>5–8 years | *Starting points and ranges*<br>5 years<br>3–6 years | *Starting points and ranges*<br>3 years<br>1.5–4 years |
| **Category 2** | 5 years<br>3–6 years | 3 years<br>1.5–4 years | 1.5 years<br>26 weeks–3 years |
| **Category 3** | 3 years<br>1.5–4 years | 1.5 years<br>26 weeks–3 years | 26 weeks<br>Medium level community order–12 months |
| **Category 4** | 1.5 years<br>26 weeks–3 years | 26 weeks<br>Medium level community order–12 months | Medium level community order<br>Band B fine–high level community order |

Adjust the provisional sentence according to the presence of the following factors:

| *Factors increasing seriousness* | *Factors reducing seriousness or reflecting personal mitigation* |
|---|---|
| A1, A2, A3–A11, A20, A21 | M1–M10 |

Steps 3–8: see *ante*.

## VII. Corporate offenders

This section applies to corporate offenders and covers the offences in Sections I, II, V and VI ★**K-307** plus cheating the public revenue, fraudulent evasion of value added tax (Value Added Tax Act 1994, s.72 (§ 25–532 in the main work)), fraudulent evasion of duty (CEMA 1979, s.170 (§ 25–474 in the main work)), and failure of commercial organisations to prevent bribery (Bribery Act 2010, s.7 (§ 31–177 in the main work)).

The guideline sets out 10 steps to be followed when sentencing for these offences. Step one **K-308** requires the court to consider making a compensation order. Step two requires the court to consider confiscation. Step three requires the court to determine the level of culpability and the harm caused or intended. Where there are characteristics present that fall under different categories, the court should balance them to reach a fair assessment of the offender's culpability. The culpability attaching to the offender's role and motivation may be demonstrated by one or more of the following non-exhaustive characteristics:

| High culpability (A) | Medium culpability (B) | Lesser culpability (C) |
|---|---|---|
| Plays a leading role in organised, planned activity (whether acting alone or with others).<br>Wilful obstruction of detection (*e.g.* destruction of evidence, misleading investigators, suborning employees). | Plays a significant role in activity organised by others. Activity not unlawful from the outset.<br>Recklessness in making false statement (1994 Act, s.72). | Plays a minor, peripheral role in activity organised by others.<br>Some effort made to put bribery prevention measures in place but insufficient to amount to a defence (2010 Act, s.7). |
| Involving others through pressure or coercion (*e.g.* employees or suppliers).<br>Targeting of vulnerable victims or large number of victims.<br>Corruption of local or national government officials or ministers, or of law enforcement officials.<br>Abuse of dominant market position or position of trust or responsibility.<br>Offending committed over a sustained period of time.<br>Culture of wilful disregard of offences by employees or agents with no effort to put effective systems in place (2010 Act, s.7, only). | All other cases where characteristics for categories A or C are not present. | Involvement through coercion, intimidation or exploitation. |

**K-309**    Harm is represented by a financial sum calculated by reference to the table below:

| Fraud | For fraud, conspiracy to defraud, cheating the Revenue and fraudulent evasion of duty or value added tax, harm will normally be the actual or intended gross gain to the offender. |
|---|---|
| Bribery | The appropriate figure will normally be the gross profit from the contract obtained, retained or sought as a result of the offending. An alternative measure for offences under s.7 may be the likely cost avoided by failing to put in place appropriate measures to prevent bribery. |
| Money laundering | The appropriate figure will normally be the amount laundered or, alternatively, the likely cost avoided by failing to put in place an effective anti-money laundering programme if this is higher. |
| General | Where the actual or intended gain cannot be established, the appropriate measure will be the amount that the court considers was likely to be achieved in all the circumstances.<br>In the absence of sufficient evidence of the amount that was likely to be obtained, 10–20 per cent of the relevant revenue (*e.g.* 10–20 per cent of the worldwide revenue derived from the product or business area to which the offence relates for the period of the offending) may be an appropriate measure. |

| | There may be large cases in which the true harm is to commerce or markets generally. That may justify adopting a harm figure beyond the normal measures here set out. |
|---|---|

Having determined the culpability level, step four requires the court to determine the starting point within the category range using the table below. The harm figure from step three is multiplied by the relevant percentage figure representing culpability. **K-310**

| | A (high) | B (medium) | C (low) |
|---|---|---|---|
| Harm figure multiplier | Starting point 300% Category range 250% to 400% | Starting point 200% Category range 100% to 300% | Starting point 100% Category range 20% to 150% |

After determining the appropriate starting point, the court should then consider adjustment within the category range for aggravating or mitigating features. In some cases it may be appropriate to move outside the identified category range. The following is a non-exhaustive list of aggravating and mitigating factors: **K-311**

| Increasing seriousness | Reducing seriousness or reflecting mitigation |
|---|---|
| Previous relevant convictions or subject to previous relevant civil or regulatory enforcement action. | No previous relevant convictions or previous relevant civil or regulatory enforcement action. |
| Corporation or subsidiary set up to commit fraudulent activity. | Victims voluntarily reimbursed/compensated. No actual loss to victims. |
| Fraudulent activity endemic within corporation. | Corporation co-operated with investigation, made early admissions and/or voluntarily reported offending. |
| Attempts made to conceal misconduct. | |
| Substantial harm (whether financial or otherwise) suffered by victims of offending or by third parties affected by offending. | Offending committed under previous director(s)/manager(s). |
| Risk of harm greater than actual or intended harm (*e.g.* in banking/credit fraud). | Little or no actual gain to corporation from offending. |
| Substantial harm to integrity or confidence of markets. | |
| Substantial harm to integrity of local or national governments. | |
| Serious nature of underlying criminal activity (money laundering offences). | |
| Offence committed across borders or jurisdictions. | |

The court should determine the appropriate level of fine in accordance with the CJA 2003, s.164 (§ 5-674 in the main work). Where the offender fails to provide comprehensive accounts for the last three years, or where the court is not satisfied that it has been given sufficiently reliable information, the court will be entitled to draw reasonable inferences as to the offender's means from evidence it has heard and from all the circumstances of the case. The information that should be examined in relation to different companies and bodies is then set out (this coincides with the guidance in the Sentencing Guidelines Council's guideline on corporate manslaughter and health and safety offences causing death (*ante*, K-258)). **K-312**

Under step five, the court should consider the overall effect of its orders and whether there are any further factors that require an adjustment in the level of the fine. The combination of orders ought to achieve the removal of all gain, appropriate additional punishment and deterrence. The court may adjust the fine to ensure that these objectives are met in a fair way, and should consider any further factors relevant to the setting of the fine to ensure that it is proportionate, with regard to the seriousness of the offence and the size and financial position of the organisation. The fine must be substantial enough to have a real economic impact. Whether the fine will put **K-313** the offender out of business will be relevant, and in some bad cases this may be an acceptable consequence. The court should consider whether the level of fine would cause unacceptable harm to third parties (bearing in mind that the payment of any compensation should take priority over any fine). Below is a non-exhaustive list of additional factual elements to consider in adjusting the level of fine:

- whether it fulfils the objectives of punishment, deterrence and removal of gain;
- the offender's value, worth or available means;
- whether the fine impairs the offender's ability to make restitution to the victims;
- the fine's impact on the offender's ability to implement effective compliance programmes;
- the fine's impact on the employment of staff, service users, customers and the local economy (but not shareholders);
- the fine's impact on the performance of public or charitable functions.

**K-314**     At step six, the court should take into account the SOCPA 2005, ss.73 (assistance by defendant: reduction of sentence (§ 5-132 in the main work)) and 74 (assistance by defendant: review of sentence (*ibid.*, § 5-133)), and any other rule of law by virtue of which an offender may receive a discounted sentence in consequence of assistance given (or offered) to the prosecutor or investigator. At step seven, the court should take into account any potential reduction for a guilty plea. At step eight, the court must consider whether to make any ancillary orders, and at step nine, if sentencing the offender for more than one offence, it must consider the totality principle. At step 10, the court must give reasons for and explain the effect of the sentence.

**[The next paragraph is K-350.]**

*II. AUTHORITIES ON OFFICIAL GUIDELINES*

A. REDUCTION IN SENTENCE FOR GUILTY PLEA

**Introduction**

**K-350**     The purpose of this section of this appendix is to give details of authorities considering particular aspects of final guidelines issued by the Sentencing Guidelines Council and which are set out in full or summarised in the previous section of this appendix. There is, however, a fine line that divides cases specifically on some aspect of a guideline from those considering a statutory provision or some more general aspect of sentencing. Accordingly, practitioners looking for authorities on sentencing in relation to one of the guideline subjects should also make reference to the relevant paragraphs of the main work.

**Relevant main work references**

**K-351**     For sentencing guidelines generally, see section 125 of the Coroners and Justice Act 2009 (§ 5-149 in the main work); and for the reduction in sentence for a guilty plea, see section 144 of that Act (*ibid.*, § 5-107), and the authorities set out at §§ 5-109 *et seq.*, and, in particular, §§ 5-115, 5-118.

**First reasonable opportunity**

**K-351a**     See *R. v. Caley, ante,* § 5-114.

**Credit in overwhelming cases**

**K-352**     Even in overwhelming cases, a plea of guilty was a distinct public benefit and the earlier it was put forward the better it was for everyone; where, therefore, the judge had given no credit for a plea of guilty on the basis that the evidence was such that the offender had had no option but to plead guilty, and where no specific feature of the case required the Sentencing Guidelines Council's guidance on credit for pleas of guilty (*ante,* K-7) to be disapplied, it was appropriate to vary the sentence to allow limited credit; it would be productive ultimately of chaos, and would undermine consistency in sentencing and the value of a guilty plea to the criminal justice system, if an existing guideline could be disregarded, unless it was possible to find that the interests of justice required its disapplication; it was important to underline that part of the advice that would

862

be given to a defendant was that a guilty plea, even in an extreme case, would attract some discount: *R. v. Wilson* [2012] 2 Cr.App.R.(S.) 77, CA.

*Wilson, ante,* was considered in *R. v. Caley, ante,* § 5-115.

**[The next paragraph is K-360.]**

## B. Overarching Principles: Seriousness

### Introduction

As to the purpose of this section of this appendix, see *ante*, K-350.  **K-360**

### Relevant main work references

For sentencing guidelines generally, see section 125 of the Coroners and Justice Act 2009 (§  **K-361**
5-149 in the main work); and for the determination of the seriousness of an offence, see section 143 of that Act (*ibid.*, § 5-67).

### Vulnerability of victim

It had not been open to the Crown Court to sentence on the basis that the victim of a domestic  **K-362**
assault was particularly vulnerable where none of the features of vulnerability mentioned in paragraph 1.17 of the guideline on overarching principles (*ante*, K-18) or in paragraph 3 of the domestic violence guideline (*ante*, K-82 *et seq.*) were present, with the finding instead being based on the complainant's timid demeanour when giving evidence: *Barnard v. DPP* [2011] A.C.D. 108, DC.

## C. New Sentences: Criminal Justice Act 2003

### Introduction

As to the purpose of this section of this appendix, see *ante*, K-350.  **K-370**

### Relevant main work references

For sentencing guidelines generally, see section 125 of the Coroners and Justice Act 2009 (§  **K-371**
5-149 in the main work). As to community sentences generally, see § 5-185 *et seq.* in the main work; as to the restrictions on the imposition of such sentences, see *ibid.*, § 5-248; as to community orders generally, see *ibid.*, §§ 5-253 *et seq.*; as to the requirements that may be included in a community order, see *ibid.*, §§ 5-265 *et seq.*; as to the misleading terminology adopted in this guideline, see *ibid.*, § 5-288.

### Transitional arrangements

In *R. v. Whittle* (2007) 151 S.J. 398, CA, it was said that whereas paragraph 2.1.9 suggests that  **K-372**
any sentence of 12 months or more should be reduced by in the region of 15 per cent to reflect the more onerous nature of the release on licence regime under the CJA 2003, where an offender is sentenced to a term of four years or more, the sentencer may be entitled not to reduce the sentence to the full extent or at all; in relation to such sentences, the increased onerousness of the licence conditions would be more or less in balance with the fact that the offender would be entitled to release at the half way point under the new regime instead of at the two-thirds point under the pre-existing regime.

## D. Manslaughter by Reason of Provocation

### Introduction

As to the purpose of this section of this appendix, see *ante*, K-350.  **K-380**

### Relevant main work references

For sentencing guidelines generally, see section 125 of the Coroners and Justice Act 2009 (§  **K-381**
5-149 in the main work); and for provocation as a defence to a charge of murder generally, see

*ante*, §§ 19-65 *et seq.* For "loss of control" as a defence to murder, see §§ 19-54 *et seq.* in the main work. It is submitted that pending the issuing of any new guideline, the existing guideline may be applied to the new defence, with appropriate caution to take account of the differing ingredients of the two defences.

### Approach to guideline

**K-382**    Referring to heightened and justifiable public concern about cases involving the stabbing of one teenager by another, the court in *R. v. Daley* [2008] 2 Cr.App.R.(S.) 95, CA, said that the guideline had not been intended to lay down fixed or rigid boundaries.

In *Att.-Gen.'s Reference (No. 8 of 2011) (R. v. Edwards)* [2012] 1 Cr.App.R.(S.) 53, CA, the court emphasised that the guideline on manslaughter by reason of provocation should be approached with caution. It did not reflect the impact on sentencing for murder of Schedule 21 to the CJA 2003 (§§ 5-425 *et seq.* in the main work); and, in a series of cases, it had now been recognised that the upward shift in sentencing for murder required a corresponding upward shift in sentencing for manslaughter (see, in particular, *R. v. Thornley, post*, K-383). The court commented that the apparently higher threshold for the loss of control defence under the Coroners and Justice Act 2009 (§§ 19-55, 19-56 in the main work), as compared with the common law defence of provocation, may impact on sentencing both for murder and for manslaughter.

For a case considering *Att.-Gen.'s Reference (No. 8 of 2011) (R. v. Edwards)*, and its significance for manslaughter by reason of loss of control, see *R. v. Ward* (§ 19-64 in the main work).

### Use of a knife

**K-383**    Just as sentencing guidelines are not tramlines, nor are they ring-fenced; the interests of justice require that consideration be given to any subsequent thinking of the Court of Appeal and the legislature on sentencing issues which may impact on any definitive guideline; since the guideline on manslaughter by reason of provocation was issued, there had been at least four developments relevant to the sentencing of manslaughter by provocation using a knife (*viz.* (a) the Court of Appeal had, in *R. v. Povey* (§ 24-109 in the main work), addressed the issue of knife crime generally, and the need for the courts to be alert on appropriate occasions to impose deterrent sentences on those who carry knives, (b) the court had come to appreciate the impact of Schedule 21 to the CJA 2003 (*ibid.*, §§ 5-425 *et seq.*) on cases of manslaughter because of the need for there to be a proportionate relationship with sentences for murder, (c) a specific provision relating to the use of a knife as a murder weapon had been introduced into Schedule 21, and (d) the entire law on provocation had been changed by legislation); as to (a) and (b), the weight to be attached to decisions of the Court of Appeal on sentencing issues or policy was undiminished by the issue of guidelines; as to (c) and (d), these changes could not be ignored on the basis of a guideline issued in 2005; accordingly, the use of a knife should now be regarded as a more significant feature of aggravation than it was when the guideline was published: *R. v. Thornley* [2011] 2 Cr.App.R.(S.) 62, CA.

### E. Robbery

### Introduction

**K-390**    As to the purpose of this section of this appendix, see *ante*, K-350.

### Relevant main work references

**K-391**    For sentencing guidelines generally, see section 125 of the Coroners and Justice Act 2009 (§ 5-149 in the main work)). As to this guideline, see, in particular, § 21-93 in the main work; as to sentencing for armed robbery, for robbery in the course of burglary and for the hijacking of cars, see *ibid.*, §§ 21-91, 21-92 and 21-94 respectively. For examples of the application of the dangerous offender provisions of the 2003 Act to cases of robbery, see *ibid.*, § 5-520.

### Dangerous offenders

**K-391a**    The guideline is unequivocal (see para. G.1) about its non-applicability to offenders who have been assessed as dangerous. However, since section 227(3) of the CJA 2003 (§ 5-498 in the main work) requires the custodial element of an extended sentence to be fixed by reference to the term that would have been passed had the offender not been found to be dangerous, it would seem that the sentencer is bound to have regard to the guideline where an extended sentence is to be imposed: see, for example, *R. v. Greaves* [2009] 2 Cr.App.R.(S.) 88, CA.

### "less sophisticated commercial robbery"

In *Att.-Gen.'s References (Nos 32, 33 and 34 of 2007) (R. v. Bate)* [2007] Crim.L.R. 815, CA, it was **K-392** held that for the purposes of the guideline on robbery, (i) the boundary between a "less sophisticated commercial robbery" falling within the guideline and a "professionally planned commercial robbery" falling without the guideline is not a hard and fast one (to like effect, see *R. v. Lafferty* [2012] 2 Cr.App.R.(S.) 93, CA, and *R. v. O'Bryan* [2013] 2 Cr.App.R.(S.) 16, CA (a case which fell on or just over the borderline)) and many cases would properly be regarded as falling on either side of the line; and a judge had been entitled to regard as falling within the guideline (and to regard the case as a level 1 case) two robberies during normal working hours (involving prior reconnaissance or information and the use of a stolen car) in which the three unarmed defendants, wearing masks and using a stolen car, had intercepted unaccompanied lorry drivers making deliveries of cigarettes to shops; and (ii) whereas "vulnerability of the victim" as an aggravating factor is expressly stated to be "targeting the elderly, the young, those with disabilities and persons performing a service to the public, especially outside normal working hours", there was nonetheless a low level of vulnerability (and hence aggravation) where the targets of the robberies were delivery drivers working alone, albeit delivering to shops where there were people to receive them.

Whilst the CJA 2003, s.172, required a court to have regard to a relevant sentencing guideline (see now the Coroners and Justice Act 2009, s.125 (§ 5-149 in the main work)), a guideline is only a guideline and the guideline on robbery cannot cover each and every category because of the immense variety of circumstances in which offences of robbery are committed, and as such there is a wide spectrum of offences that fall between "less sophisticated commercial robberies" and "professionally-planned commercial robberies", as described in the guideline; where, therefore, four men had "swiftly" robbed the driver of a delivery van in a robbery that was "cynically and callously planned" with one of the men persuading him to drive with them to a secluded place whilst wearing a mask and rubber gloves and being armed with a knife, the case did not fall neatly and cleanly within the category of the "less sophisticated commercial robbery" (which has an indicated starting point of four years' custody) and instead fell within a range of six to 10 years (possibly more for a ring leader); and, in the case of the respondent (40), who acted as the driver of the robbers' vehicle, three years' imprisonment on conviction was unduly lenient given that, although he was not a prime mover and did not wield the knife, it must have been within his contemplation that some degree of threat or force would be used on the victim; taking account, however, of the fact that he suffered from Asperger's syndrome, which made him vulnerable to being manipulated by more sophisticated offenders, the appropriate bracket was six to eight years' imprisonment: *Att.-Gen.'s Reference (No. 147 of 2006) (R. v. Gunner)* [2008] 1 Cr.App.R.(S.) 9(2), CA (substituting six years).

As to there being a category of case that falls between the "less sophisticated commercial robbery" and the "professionally planned commercial robbery", see also *R. v. Eccleston* [2008] 2 Cr.App.R.(S.) 56, CA.

In *R. v. Yarboi* [2010] 2 Cr.App.R.(S.) 40, CA, one of the defendants snatched a cash box containing £11,530 from a security guard who was attempting to deliver it to a cash machine. He ran to a car (the number plates of which had been removed) being driven by another of the defendants and, after half a mile, they abandoned the car and got into a third vehicle driven by a further defendant. The Court of Appeal found that the case did not fit easily within any of the categories within the Sentencing Guidelines Council's guideline (see *ante*, K-80), being close to the border between "less sophisticated commercial robberies" and "professionally planned robberies". The most aggravating feature was that the robbery had been pre-planned, although cases could come within the least serious category even where there had been some pre-planning. The removal of the first car's number plates, and the use of a second "clean" getaway car, however, made the case rather more unusual, and showed a significant degree of planning. On the other hand, the force used was minimal, being only that which was necessary in order to snatch the container from the security guard, there was only a single robber involved at that stage, and there was no intimidation from a group, no weapon, no threat of force, and no disguises were used. The court said that whilst the planning, therefore, might have taken the case out of the least serious category, it was difficult to conclude that it was of such sophistication as to justify a starting point of double the maximum for that category. In all the circumstances, it was decided that the proper starting point was four-and-a-half years.

### "vulnerability of the victim"

K-393     See *Att.-Gen.'s References (Nos 32, 33 and 34 of 2007) (R. v. Bate)*, *ante*, § K-392.

### Ranges

K-394     For an example of a sentence that was significantly above the recommended range being upheld on account of "additional aggravating features", albeit that most of them are foreshadowed in the guideline, see *R. v. Sheller* [2010] 1 Cr.App.R.(S.) 107, CA.

In *R. v. Taylor (Shaun)* [2012] 2 Cr.App.R.(S.) 98, CA, it was held that the judge had been wrong to sentence on the basis that the guideline sentences were out of date and that it had been "almost a different world when they came into force"; when appropriate, the court added, it is of course open to a judge to sentence outside guidelines and to support such a course by giving reasons for doing so; but personal disagreement with a guideline will not furnish a good reason for departing from them; and the guideline was not out of date.

### F. Breach of a Protective Order

### Introduction

K-400     As to the purpose of this section of this appendix, see *ante*, K-350.

### Relevant main work references

K-401     For sentencing guidelines generally, see section 125 of the Coroners and Justice Act 2009 (§ 5-149 in the main work); for breach of a restraining order under the Protection from Harassment Act 1997, see *ibid.*, § 19-357; and for breach of a sexual offences prevention order, see *ibid.*, § 20-334. As to breach of an anti-social behaviour order, see *ante*, K-196 *et seq.*

### Taking the original offence into account

K-401a     As to the importance of avoiding sentencing again for the original offence when sentencing for a breach, and as to the need to reserve the maximum sentence for the most serious of breaches, see *R. v. McDonald* [2013] 1 Cr.App.R.(S.) 3, CA.

### Repeated breaches

K-402     For a case in which a sentence substantially outside the guidelines was upheld where there had been repeated (low-level) breaches of a restraining order over a long period, see *R. v. Todd* [2013] 1 Cr.App.R.(S.) 89, CA.

### G. Domestic Violence

### Introduction

K-410     As to the purpose of this section of this appendix, see *ante*, K-350.

### Relevant main work references

K-411     For sentencing guidelines generally, see section 125 of the Coroners and Justice Act 2009 (§ 5-149 in the main work); and for breach of a restraining order under the Protection from Harassment Act 1997, see § 19-357 in the main work.

### Attitude of victim

K-412     In *R. v. Fazli*, unreported, April 24, 2009, CA ([2009] EWCA Crim. 939), the court emphasised that the principle (see para. 4 of the guideline) that a sentence should not be determined by the expressed wishes of the victim, was of particular importance in cases of domestic violence. The court said that, in the case with which it was concerned, the victim (the defendant's wife) had been made to feel responsible for his incarceration, and that such feelings on the part of the victim were a familiar consequence of controlling and intimidating behaviour such as that of the offender. The responsibility for what had happened to him lay entirely with him.

### Vulnerability of victim

See *Barnard v. DPP, ante*, K-362.     **K-413**

### Aggravating factors

In *R. v. Caceres* [2014] 1 Cr.App.R.(S.) 23, CA, it was said that whilst the guideline stressed that     **★K-414** violence in the home was no less serious than violence elsewhere simply because it was committed in the home, and whilst this was correct in so far as it went, where someone is put in constant peril and fear in their own home as a result of repetitive domestic abuse, that was potentially a substantial aggravating factor. The court said that the aggravation is compounded where the perpetrator is in reality controlling the victim and abusing his position in the home, and the victim is, in the domestic context, vulnerable; and a further aggravating feature is where the victim is effectively forced to leave home as a consequence of the abuse.

## H. Sexual Offences

### Introduction

As to the purpose of this section of this appendix, see *ante*, K-350.     **K-420**

### Relevant main work references

For sentencing guidelines generally, see section 125 of the Coroners and Justice Act 2009 (§     **K-421** 5-149 in the main work).

### Historic offences

See *R. v. H., ante*, H-12 *et seq.*     **K-421a**

### Age of offence/offender

In *Att.-Gen.'s Reference (No. 70 of 2008) (R. v. W.)* [2009] 2 Cr.App.R.(S.) 64, CA, it was said,     **K-422** without making any reference to the guideline, that in cases of serious sexual assault, the age of the offender or the age of the offence could be mitigation although, in many cases, they would not receive much weight, especially if the offender had pressurised his victims into silence; but they did not cease to be factors which could form part of the mitigation, and they were not always of comparatively little weight.

In *R. v. S.* [2011] 1 Cr.App.R.(S.) 9, CA, the offender (18) went, in 1991, to the 45-year-old victim's home asking if he could use the lavatory. The victim suffered from cerebral palsy, had significant communication problems, and used a wheelchair at home. After using the lavatory, the offender forced the victim onto her bed and raped her, causing heavy bleeding from the vagina, which required an operation and a blood transfusion. The victim also suffered bruising and cuts around her vagina and anus compatible with being caused by a fist or knee. It was not until 2008 that a DNA sample taken from the victim was matched to a sample provided by the offender in 2005. A sentence of 16-and-a-half years' imprisonment on a late plea of guilty was quashed and a sentence of nine years' imprisonment substituted. Among the reasons for reducing the sentence was that the offender was young at the time, and it was said that although the passage of time was not in itself a reason for imposing a lesser sentence, the fact that the offender had not been in trouble since the offence was committed suggested that he was no longer a danger to women.

In the case of a young offender who fell to be sentenced, following guilty pleas, for five counts of rape and one count of assault on a child under 13 by penetration, where the charges arose out of conduct that occurred over a three-year period and which began when the offender was aged 12, and the victim, his half-sister, was five, the court emphasised the importance of not losing sight of the need for flexibility and sensitivity to the particular facts when looking at guidelines that were geared to adults: *R. v. B.* [2011] 2 Cr.App.R.(S.) 57, CA.

In *R. v. Record* [2011] 2 Cr.App.R.(S.) 83, CA, an 18-year-old had unprotected consensual sexual intercourse with a friend's sister (11 days short of her 15th birthday) when staying the night at his friend's house. The court held that the parties' ages were important and drew particular attention to the fact that the guideline (*ante*, K-87) emphasised that youth and immaturity of the offender were important in the context of sexual offences. It also held that, given that the offender was aged just over 18, the judge should have had regard to the fact that the maximum sentence for an offender under 18 is only five years' detention (2003 Act, s.13(2)(b) (§ 20-79 in the main work)) (compared to 14 years' custody if aged 18 or over: 2003 Act, s.9 (§ 20-58 in the main work)), and that, in such cases, the guideline recommends a starting point of a detention and training order of 12 months, and a range of six to 24 months (compared to a starting point of four years' custody and a range of three to seven years for an offender aged 18 or over); furthermore, it is a mitigating factor if the difference in age between complainant and offender is small. To similar effect, see *R. v. Hoare* [2011] 2 Cr.App.R.(S.) 1, CA.

When considering an offence of sexual activity with a child, contrary to section 9 of the SOA 2003 (§ 20-58 in the main work), the nearer the offender is to the age of the victim, and the nearer the victim is to the age of consent, the more the starting point and range in the guideline must be adjusted: *R. v. Hines-Randle* [2012] 1 Cr.App.R.(S.) 65, CA.

### Gender of victim/offender

**K-422a**     Sentencing guidelines were put forward on the basis that they should apply irrespective of the gender of the victim or of the offender (see *ante*, K-84), except in specified circumstances where a distinction is justified by the nature of the offence; Parliament did not seek to distinguish between the genders in the legislation and neither should the courts: *Att.-Gen.'s Reference (No. 67 of 2008) (R. v. Edwards)* [2009] 2 Cr.App.R.(S.) 60, CA.

### Ranges

**K-423**     For an illustration of the need for a non-literal approach to the categories provided for in the guidelines, see *R. v. Elliott* [2010] 2 Cr.App.R.(S.) 55, CA.

In *Att.-Gen.'s Reference (No. 79 of 2010) (R. v. Sidaway)* [2011] 2 Cr.App.R.(S.) 56, CA, the court stressed that the ranges set out in the guideline are not rigid, and the presence of aggravating factors can make an offence significantly more serious than the nature of the sexual activity alone might suggest so as to render a sentence unduly lenient, notwithstanding that, on a literal reading of the guideline, the sentence would be in accord with it (15 months' imprisonment on plea of guilty to sexual assault increased to four years where the suggested range was 26 weeks to two years).

In *R. v. Frew* [2009] 1 Cr.App.R.(S.) 17, CA, the court said that the recommended range for the offence in question was three to seven years' imprisonment and that, in terms of gravity, the particular offence was not at the bottom of the range, yet it substituted a sentence that equated to 27 months after a trial. Whilst the court said that the guideline emphasised the need for flexibility and variability, the result suggests that the ranges are considerably wider than those recommended in the guideline. To similar effect, see *R. v. P. (John James)* [2009] 1 Cr.App.R.(S.) 45, CA (assault by penetration of child under 13 came within most serious category, with range of 11 to 17 years; appropriate penalty before discount for plea was seven-and-a-half years). For a case in which the court went above the relevant range without giving reasons, see *R. v. Olawo, post,* K-434b.

For two cases in which the Court of Appeal held the appropriate sentences to be lower than the minimum recommended in the Sentencing Guidelines Council's definitive guideline, see *R. v. Johnson* [2011] 1 Cr.App.R.(S.) 97 (where, on conviction for sexual activity with a person with a mental disorder impeding choice, contrary to section 30 of the SOA 2003 (§ 20-125 in the main work), the sentence imposed on appeal was five years' imprisonment, falling outside the 11 to 17 years recommended in the guideline (*ante*, K-96) for this offence), and *R. v. F.B.* [2011] 1 Cr.App.R.(S.) 99 (where, on conviction for sexual assault on a child under 13 by penetration, contrary to section 6 of the SOA 2003 (§ 20-50 in the main work), the sentence imposed on appeal was nine years' imprisonment, falling outside the 11 to 17 years recommended in the guideline (*ante*, K-94) for this offence).

For an example of a suspended sentence of six months' imprisonment (on an early plea of guilty) being adjudged lenient, but not unduly so, where the recommended range was three to seven years' custody, see *Att.-Gen.'s Reference (No. 72 of 2009) (R. v. Kent)* [2010] 2 Cr.App.R.(S.) 10, CA (observing that it was unfortunate that the judge had failed to refer to the guideline).

In *R. v. Ayeva* [2010] 2 Cr.App.R.(S.) 22, CA, a 33-year-old approached his 19-year-old victim outside a public library, where she was waiting for her father to collect her, and engaged her in conversation. He asked personal questions and told her he loved her, after which she made excuses and left, but when she returned he reappeared. She went into the library with the offender, hoping her father would have arrived by the time they came back outside. However, he had not, and the offender put his arm around the victim's waist. She went down an alleyway to escape, but the offender followed her and grabbed her from behind, at which point he bent her arm behind her back and forced her to take hold of his erect penis, and, holding his hand around hers, forced her to masturbate him to ejaculation. The Court of Appeal found there to be a number of aggravating features which took this offence outside the correct sentencing guideline for an offence of causing a person to engage in sexual activity without consent (contact between the naked genitalia of the offender and another part of the victim's body (as to which, *see ante*, Appendix K-94)), which has a range of 26 weeks to two years, with a starting point of 12 months. These were that the unwelcome conduct was persisted in over a significant period of time, the victim had made it clear that the offender's attentions were unwelcome, the offender had first grabbed the victim's breasts, there was not a brief, isolated, touching of the penis, but rather the victim was held so that she could not escape, the offender ejaculated (which was a significant aggravating feature), the conduct replicated behaviour which had previously led to him being cautioned, and he had been less than frank with the police and had effectively denied the offence in an interview with a probation officer conducted for the purpose of preparing a pre-sentence report. Thus, it was considered that the appropriate sentence after a trial would have been 30 months' imprisonment. The Court of Appeal, in its judgment, reiterated the need for the sentencing process for sexual offences, more than for many others, to allow for flexibility and variability.

## Multiple offences

Where the offender fell to be dealt with for two offences and the recommended starting point **K-423a** was 10 years' imprisonment for a single offence, the judge's starting point of 12 years was said to be unimpeachable in *R. v. Clements* [2009] 2 Cr.App.R.(S.) 97, CA.

## Rape

As a matter of principle, a court should approach rape within a relationship, including mar- **K-424** riage, as being no less serious than rape by a stranger, although the aggravating features will be different in the sense that rape within a relationship constitutes a betrayal of trust: *Att.-Gen.'s Reference (No. 1 of 2011) (R. v. A.)* [2011] 2 Cr.App.R.(S.) 112, CA.

The appropriate category (*ante*, K-94) was that of "repeated rape of same victim over a course of time", rather than rape accompanied by a "sustained attack", where the offender, over a period of four hours, slapped the victim around the face, dragged her across the floor, inserted his fingers into her vagina twice, forcefully inserted a vibrator into her vagina four times and into her anus, rammed his penis into her mouth three times, penetrated her anus with his fingers and twice with his penis, and inserted his penis into her vagina: *R. v. S. (Charles Derek)* [2011] 1 Cr.App.R.(S.) 83, CA.

For an example of a case in which a planned attack in which the offender used sexual violence to punish, degrade and humiliate the victim, was considered to have constituted a "sustained attack" so as to place the offence in the intermediate category (range of six to 11 years) in the guideline (*ante*, K-94), see *R. v. Cadogan* [2011] 1 Cr.App.R.(S.) 53, CA.

The rape of a victim in her own home is a pitiless, life-scarring crime; given that culpability will be at its highest and the harm done to the victim at its most grave, such offences should be approached as if they are among the most serious offences of their kind; whilst they are not dealt with directly in the current sentencing guideline, it would, for example, be wrong in principle for an offence of rape in such circumstances to be treated as a "single offence of rape by [a] single offender"; dealing with the matter very generally, in a case where rape has been committed after, or in the course of, burglary in the victim's home, even if there are no additional features beyond the rape and the burglary, the starting point should rarely be less than 12 years' imprisonment;

and, where there are (as will usually be the case) aggravating features, the starting point will increase to 15 years' imprisonment and beyond; the pernicious new habit of criminals taking photographs of their victims, often just to show off to their friends, often just to add something to the humiliation which the victim is already suffering, and sometimes as a form of pressure to discourage any complaint (in that sense a form of blackmail), but also possibly for the purposes of blackmail, should always be treated as an aggravating feature of any case and, in particular, of any sexual case, where it will usually constitute a seriously aggravating feature: *Att.-Gen.'s References (Nos 73, 75 of 2010, and 03 of 2011) (R. v. Anigbugu)* [2011] 2 Cr.App.R.(S.) 100, CA. As to this case, see also §§ 5-144, 5-514 in the main work.

*R. v. Donoghue* [2011] 1 Cr.App.R.(S.) 46, CA, was a case of vaginal and oral rape, where the offences were committed in the victim's own home, where the offender was armed with a knife which he repeatedly held against the victim's throat, where he ejaculated into the victim's mouth and he took, or pretended to take, photographs of what he was doing. In upholding a sentence of life imprisonment, the court said that there could be few worse cases of rape.

A case of trespass with intent to commit rape, contrary to the SOA 2003, s.63 (§ 20-197 in the main work), followed by an offence of rape or attempted rape inside the premises entered as a trespasser with such intent, will fall within the general guidance in *Att.-Gen.'s References (Nos 73, 75 of 2010, and 03 of 2011) (R. v. Anigbugu)*, *ante*, relating to rape and burglary: *R. v. Taylor* [2013] 1 Cr.App.R.(S.) 55, CA.

### Rape of a child under 13

K-424a      Actual consent is capable of being a mitigating factor, but careful consideration has to be given in all cases, and particularly where there is a significant difference in age, to the extent to which ostensible consent had been obtained opportunistically, or by means of coercion, which might be subtle, or exploitation, which could be particularly relevant where there may have been an element of grooming; in such cases, ostensible consent might well have little value as mitigation, and in all cases the age difference would be of great significance; as to a reasonable belief that the victim was aged 16 or over, this was capable of being mitigation (even where the offender was aged 18 or over (though the guideline only lists such a mistaken belief as mitigation where the offender is under 18), but the older the offender, the less relevant a mistake as to age would be; in determining the extent to which mitigation relating to consent or a mistaken belief as to age can justify departing from the sentencing bracket (of eight to 13 years), it may be helpful to consider the guideline on penetrative sexual activity with a person under the age of 16, where the offender does not reasonably believe that the other person is 16 or over (contrary to section 9 of the 2003 Act), *viz.* a starting point of four years and a sentencing range of three to seven years; bearing this, and the legislative purpose of creating the absolute offence under section 5 for victims under the age of 13, in mind, four years should be the minimum for an offence under section 5, subject to plea and personal mitigation, in the case of a young adult where there is ostensible consent and a reasonable belief that the victim was 16 or over: *Att.-Gen.'s References (Nos 74 and 83 of 2007) (R. v. Fenn; R. v. Foster)* [2008] 1 Cr.App.R.(S.) 110, CA.

*Att.-Gen.'s References (Nos 74 and 83 of 2007) (R. v. Fenn; R. v. Foster)* was considered in *Att.-Gen.'s References (Nos 11 and 12 of 2012) (R. v. Channer and Monteiro)* [2013] 1 Cr.App.R.(S.) 43, CA. It was said that section 5 embraces a wide range of seriousness; and the guideline provides valuable assistance as to the correct approach to the assessment of seriousness. First, careful analysis of the circumstances is always required and a *Newton* hearing (§ 5-99 in the main work) may be necessary when a claim is made that the victim was consenting in fact and/or that the offender believed the victim to be significantly older than her chronological age; the prosecution bear a burden of responsibility for ensuring that factual concessions are made only when justified and that, if made, the precise import of the concession is understood by the offender and the court; secondly, there is a strong element of deterrence, whether the victims are sexually experienced and "willing" or not; they are, by reason of their age, vulnerable to exploitation and require protection, sometimes from themselves; it can be assumed that, whatever the circumstances, there is likely to be considerable long-term harm; thirdly, exploitative sexual behaviour towards a child under 13 without consideration of the vulnerability of the child may be just as serious as submission obtained by the use or threat of force; "ostensible consent" and "willingness" are terms which, in the context of offences against the young in particular, are susceptible to misunderstanding and, even if accurately used, are liable to obscure the true nature of the encounter; and fourthly, the culpability of the offender is measured in part by his own understanding of the harm he was causing or was likely to cause; the guideline does not, however, recognise as a mitigating factor a belief by the offender that the victim was aged 13 to 15 years; nevertheless, the younger the victim, the more serious is the harm likely to result and the greater is likely to be the culpability of the offender; the difference in age between the parties is an important factor (considering *R. v. Corran* [2005] 2 Cr.App.R.(S.) 73, CA).

In *R. v. Charles* [2012] 1 Cr.App.R.(S.) 74, CA, it was said that the guideline for this offence was not suitable where young men have consensual sexual activity with girls whom they believe to be over 16; and that the correct approach was set out in the pre-guideline case of *R. v. Corran, ante,* where it was said that a short period of custody is likely to suffice for a teenager where the other party consents; and that, in exceptional cases, a non-custodial sentence may be appropriate for a young defendant.

For a case which did not fit readily within the guideline in relation to rape at all, and where the sentence imposed on appeal (a 12-month detention and training order) fell far below the range in the guideline (eight to 13 years), see *R. v. Mooney* [2010] 2 Cr.App.R.(S.) 97, CA.

### Causing or inciting a child under 13 to engage in sexual activity

In *Att.-Gen.'s Reference (No. 28 of 2010) (R. v. Charnley)* [2011] 1 Cr.App.R.(S.) 58, CA, the 55- **K-424b** year-old offender had, on 35 occasions, over a period of 10 weeks, contacted adults in the Philippines via the internet and agreed to pay them to abuse children (including by penetration) aged between two and 17, according to his instructions, while he watched the events in real time and then downloaded the images. Increasing the original sentence to a total sentence of 12 years' imprisonment on pleas of guilty to various offences, including five counts under section 8 of the SOA 2003 (one of which involved penetration) and 19 counts of making indecent photographs, the court said that the gravity and cruelty of the offences went beyond anything contained in the guidelines or in the previous authority of the court.

### Sexual activity with a child

In *R. v. Micklewright* [2013] 1 Cr.App.R.(S.) 41, CA, it was said that the guideline was of limited **K-425** value where the relationship between the offender and the victim was a genuinely affectionate one. In the particular case, the age difference was 10 years and sexual activity began when the complainant was aged 14 and it continued for approximately two years.

In *Att.-Gen.'s Reference (No. 53 of 2013) (R. v. Wilson)*, unreported, October 8, 2013, CA, it was said that the fact that the complainant had initiated the activity was an aggravating rather than mitigating factor; it has long been clear that Parliament's purpose in passing legislation making it a crime to have sexual relations with those under 16 was to protect those under 16; to reduce the punishment on the basis that the person needing protection encouraged the offence is simply wrong; an under-age person who encourages sexual relations with herself needs more not less protection.

### Sexual assault

In *Att.-Gen.'s Reference (No. 26 of 2009) (R. v. Heeney)* [2010] 1 Cr.App.R.(S.) 41, CA, where the **K-426** offence took place in the victim's home in the early hours of the morning, it was said that one of the difficulties in applying the guideline (*ante*, K-94) is that individual cases may not slot easily into any particular category. This case was more akin to an offence under section 63 of the 2003 Act (trespass with intent to commit a sexual offence (*ibid.*, § 20-197)) than a straightforward sexual assault.

### Exposure

In *R. v. Lam-Callinan* [2010] 1 Cr.App.R.(S.) 49, CA, it was held that, for the purposes of the **K-427** guideline (*ante*, K-100), an offender may be a "repeat offender" though he does not have previous convictions (doubting *R. v. Bell* [2008] 2 Cr.App.R.(S.) 55, CA).

In *R. v. Jones* [2013] 2 Cr.App.R.(S.) 66, CA, a sentence of 12 months' imprisonment (with another 12 months consecutive in respect of a previous like offence for which a community sentence had been imposed in the first instance) was upheld for "an exceptionally serious persistent sex offender"; it was unsurprising that the judge considered that the standard range in the guideline for a repeat offender was not intended to restrict, and could not properly restrict, the court's powers in this instance.

### Trafficking

**K-428**      In *R. v. Pacan* [2010] 2 Cr.App.R.(S.) 2, CA, the court pointed out that there is a degree of ambiguity in the guideline relating to offences under sections 57 to 59 of the SOA 2003 (*ante*, K-103, K-104), in that the bracket for the more serious of the two forms of trafficking (range of four to nine years' custody) assumes coercion, but coercion is further listed as a potentially aggravating factor.

## I. Failing to Surrender to Bail

### Introduction

**K-430**      As to the purpose of this section of this appendix, see *ante*, K-350.

### Relevant main work references

**K-431**      For sentencing guidelines generally, see section 125 of the Coroners and Justice Act 2009 (§ 5-149 in the main work); for paragraph I.13 of the consolidated criminal practice direction (which touches on the same issues), see §§ 3-35 *et seq.* in the main work.

### Sentencing outside recommended range

**★K-432**      For a case where the imposition of the maximum sentence, outside the recommended range in the guideline, was upheld on appeal, see *R. v. Chowdhury* [2014] 1 Cr.App.R.(S.) 27, CA (defendant had been at large for 13 years; trial of the substantive offence had become impossible as a result of the delay).

## J. Assault and Other Offences Against the Person

### Introduction

**K-433**      As to the purpose of this section of this appendix, see *ante*, K-350.

### Relevant main work references

**K-434**      For sentencing guidelines generally, see section 125 of the Coroners and Justice Act 2009 (§ 5-149 in the main work).

### Use in case of young offenders

**K-434a**      In *R. v. Bowley* [2009] 1 Cr.App.R.(S.) 79, CA, where a 17-year-old pleaded guilty to causing grievous bodily harm with intent after stabbing a rival gang member, the court said (i) that the judge had been entitled to look to this guideline for assistance, even though it does not apply to offenders under 18 and (ii) in making use of it, the judge need not have been unduly constrained by the particular sentencing brackets set out therein, because the case was one where an element of deterrence was an essential ingredient of the sentencing decision.

### Ranges

**K-434b**      In *R. v. Olawo* [2008] 2 Cr.App.R.(S.) 113, a sentence of 12 months' imprisonment was imposed by the Court of Appeal for an offence contrary to section 20 of the Offences against the Person Act 1861, for which the recommended range was up to 36 weeks' imprisonment. The court said that the fact that the victim was a certified enforcement officer was a seriously aggravating factor, but this is a factor specifically mentioned in the guideline on seriousness (see K-19, *ante*) and is presumptively allowed for in the range. No reason was given by the court for going outside the range. For a case in which the court went below the relevant range without giving reasons, see *R. v. Frew*, *ante*, K-423; and for an exceptional case of wounding with intent which the guidelines did not address and in which a suspended sentence was justified, see *Att.-Gen.'s Reference (No. 95 of 2009) (R. v. Blight)* [2010] 2 Cr.App.R.(S.) 83, CA.

As to whether deterrence is a legitimate reason for going outside the recommended bracket, see *R. v. Bowley*, *ante*, K-434a.

As to the need, when sentencing for an offence of violence to have regard to foreseeable harm, as well as actual or intended harm, when assessing the seriousness of any given case, see *R. v. Abbas* [2010] 1 Cr.App.R.(S.) 47, CA.

Where an offence of assault occasioning actual bodily harm fell within category 2 as being one of lesser harm and greater culpability, the judge had been entitled to go outside the category range where there were present six factors from the non-exhaustive list of 18 factors that are capable of increasing the seriousness of the offence and there was just one factor reducing its seriousness: *R. v. Nelson, The Times*, October 27, 2011, CA.

As to departure from the guidelines when sentencing those convicted of an offence committed during the widespread public disorder of the kind seen in the riots that occurred around the country in August, 2011, and as to the appropriateness of sentences beyond the range set out in those guidelines, see *R. v. Blackshaw*, *ante*, § 29-9.

## Section 18

*Use of a knife*

In *R. v. Osman* [2008] 2 Cr.App.R.(S.) 89, CA, it was said that the need for the courts to take **K-434c** account of legitimate public concern and to deter the premeditated carrying and use of a knife to inflict an intentional wound by the imposition of condign and/or deterrent sentences was all too obvious; and was reflected in the guideline.

In *R. v. Fadairo* [2013] 1 Cr.App.R.(S.) 66, CA, a case of "wounding" (not "causing grievous bodily harm") in which "lesser harm" was caused but with higher culpability, the court said that a starting point above the category two range was justified because of the use of a knife. Parliament had dictated, the court said, in enacting section 18 of the 1861 Act, that assaults with a knife or other bladed weapon should be regarded and punished more seriously than assaults without a weapon or with another kind of weapon; and there was a need for deterrence. For critical consideration of this approach to the guideline, see CLW/12/27/3.

*Revenge attacks*

As to a case where, despite the fact that the purpose of an attack was revenge, the circumstances **K-434d** of the case were exceptional and fell outside the scope of the guideline, see *R. v. Hussain (Tokeer) and Hussain (Munir)* [2010] 2 Cr.App.R.(S.) 60, CA. For a more conventional view as to the seriousness of revenge attacks, see *Att.-Gen.'s Reference (No. 102 of 2009) (R. v. Martin)* [2010] 2 Cr.App.R.(S.) 80, CA.

## Section 20

In *R. v. Abdille* [2010] 1 Cr.App.R.(S.) 18, CA, the court commented on the difficulty of apply- **K-434e** ing the guideline for offences contrary to section 20 of the Offences against the Person Act 1861. The case concerned a serious, unprovoked attack on a young girl as she tried to get away from the offender, who was in a drunken, aggressive state. The Court of Appeal found that the punch which he inflicted upon her had not itself been premeditated, but it had caused a serious injury, albeit not one, in the words of the guideline, which was "particularly grave". It was said that, on a literal reading of the guideline, the offence would be in the very bottom range, with a starting point of 24 weeks' custody and a sentencing range of a community order to 36 weeks' custody. However, the court considered that the case had features which took it well outside that range and that, after a trial, it would have merited a sentence of 24 to 30 months' imprisonment. As to this case, see also § 5-584 in the main work.

In *R. v. Williamson* [2010] 1 Cr.App.R.(S.) 16, CA, the offender punched and kicked his girlfriend to the extent that she suffered a broken nose, loose teeth and a fractured cheekbone.

On a plea of guilty entered at the earliest opportunity, four years' imprisonment was held to be wrong in principle and manifestly excessive. The court explained that whilst this was a grave offence, and the offender was fortunate not to have been charged with a more serious offence, it would be quite wrong to sentence on the basis that he had been under-charged.

### Sections 18 and 20 ("particularly grave injury")

**K-434f**    In *R. v. Collins* [2010] 2 Cr.App.R.(S.) 3, CA, it was said that, whilst the guideline (*ante*, K-113 *et seq.*) throws no particular light on what is meant by "particularly grave injury" (bearing in mind that "grievous" bodily harm is by definition serious), bullet wounds to two vital parts of the body, one of which perforated the colon in several places and led to two major operations (a colostomy and a reversal of that colostomy), were on any view particularly grave injuries, and the fact that the victim had made a good recovery did not show otherwise. A non-permanent injury may be particularly grave, and a permanent injury (such as a scar) may not be particularly grave. The Court of Appeal said that where one of the shots had been potentially fatal, since it had been aimed close to both the liver and the kidney, this was also relevant to the overall view of the gravamen of the matter.

In *R. v. Howard* [2010] 1 Cr.App.R.(S.) 88, CA, it was said that a broken hip could not be said to be a "particularly grave injury".

## K. Assaults on Children and Cruelty to a Child

### Introduction

**K-436**    As to the purpose of this section of this appendix, see *ante*, K-350.

### Relevant main work references

**K-437**    For sentencing guidelines generally, see section 125 of the Coroners and Justice Act 2009 (§ 5-149 in the main work).

### The four categories of seriousness

**K-438**    In *R. v. S. (Will)* [2009] 1 Cr.App.R.(S.) 40, CA, the offender (30/good character/no previous parenting experience) subjected a "challenging" five-year-old, one of the four children of his (now ex-)partner, to a particularly harsh regime of discipline. She was shouted at, made to feel unwanted, and sent to her room for long periods (sometimes day after day). No violence was used except on one occasion, when the offender put masking tape over her mouth (for which he later expressed regret). At school, it was noticed that the child, from being a relatively happy child, became tearful and unsettled. On pleas of guilty to two counts of "causing cruelty to a child", 30 months' imprisonment was held to be manifestly and grossly excessive. The court found that it was clear that the offender's actions were not those of a gratuitous bully, but of an inexperienced parent, at the end of his tether, who, together with the mother, was doing what he mistakenly believed to be the right thing in respect of what he saw as an ill-behaved child. In particular, it was said that the judge had wrongly identified the case as falling within the second of the four categories of seriousness in the guideline, which, the court noted, should properly be reserved for cases of actual abuse, either through physical violence or deprivation of food, clothing, shelter or attendance. A community order with a supervision requirement (to include a parenting course) was substituted.

It had been open to a judge to place the offender's intense neglect of her child into the category of "protracted" neglect (*ante*, Appendix K-146), where it took place over a period that adults might regard as a relatively short period (a few days): *R. v. Sutherland* [2011] 1 Cr.App.R.(S.) 90, CA.

## L. Sentencing in Magistrates' Courts

### Introduction

**K-439**    As to the purpose of this section of this appendix, see *ante*, K-350.

### Relevant main work references

**K-440**    For sentencing guidelines generally, see section 125 of the Coroners and Justice Act 2009 (§

5-149 in the main work); for general mode of trial considerations, see *Criminal Practice Direction (Preliminary proceedings) 9A* [2013] 1 W.L.R. 3165 (§ 1-119 in the main work).

### Burglary in a dwelling

In *R. v. Saw* [2009] 2 Cr.App.R.(S.) 54, the Court of Appeal observed that when applying the provisions of the guideline relating to dwelling house burglaries, regard should always be had to all the matters of aggravation and mitigation listed in the judgment (as to which, see § 21-114 in the main work). **K-441**

For offences for which sentence is passed on or after January 16, 2012, see now the guideline issued by the Sentencing Council for England and Wales, *ante*, K-259 *et seq.*

## M.  Causing Death by Driving

### Introduction

As to the purpose of this section of this appendix, see *ante*, K-350. **K-442**

### Relevant main work references

For sentencing guidelines generally, see section 125 of the Coroners and Justice Act 2009 (§ 5-149 in the main work). For the penalty provisions relating to the offences covered by this guideline, see § 32-6 (causing death by dangerous driving); § 32-47e (causing death by careless or inconsiderate driving); § 32-59 (causing death by careless driving when under the influence of drink or drugs or having failed without reasonable excuse either to provide a specimen for analysis or to permit the analysis of a blood sample) and § 32-63e (causing death by driving while unlicensed, disqualified or uninsured). As to disqualification and endorsement, see §§ 32-167 *et seq.* **K-443**

### Aggravating and mitigating factors

As to the importance of taking care to ensure that factors which put an offence into a particular category are not then double-counted as matters of aggravation, see *R. v. Watson* [2010] 1 Cr.App.R.(S.) 29, CA. **K-444**

In *R. v. Lawes* [2010] 2 Cr.App.R.(S.) 43, CA, it was held that the potentially aggravating feature, identified in the guideline, of more than one death was not intended to apply to the case of a pregnant mother and her unborn child.

### Borderline between careless and dangerous driving

For a case of dangerous driving that was close to the borderline with careless driving, see *R. v. Foster* [2010] 1 Cr.App.R.(S.) 36, CA. A 64-year-old man had been driving his wife, who suffered from motor neurone disease, home from the hospital, where she had been told that her condition had deteriorated to the point that her treatment should no longer be continued, when he crossed onto the wrong side of the road and collided with a motorcyclist. The central issue at trial had been whether the defendant had crossed onto the wrong side of the road because he had "blacked out"; in passing sentence, the judge proceeded on the basis that the defendant had convinced himself that that was what had happened. On appeal, the court reduced a sentence of 18 months' imprisonment to 12 months' imprisonment suspended for two years, on the basis that the appellant was distracted for a "matter of seconds at most" and, importantly, when his emotions as a result of the hospital visit must have made him susceptible to distraction. The court pointed out that the guideline on causing death by driving states (see *ante*, K-192) that where the driving is markedly less culpable than for the lowest of the three categories for the offence of causing death by dangerous driving, reference should be made to the starting point for the most serious level of causing death by careless driving (starting point 15 months' imprisonment, range of 36 weeks to three years) and that, having regard to this, and to the other mitigation, in particular the appellant's character and his deep and genuine remorse, that starting point could be reduced. The court concluded that if it be a merciful sentence to suspend the term of imprisonment, this was a proper case for mercy. **K-445**

In *R. v. Crew* [2010] 2 Cr.App.R.(S.) 23, CA, a 52-year-old, the day after an overnight flight from the United States (where he lived), fell asleep momentarily at the wheel of his car while travelling along a long straight road in daylight hours. It was likely that, on waking, he instinctively over-corrected the car's direction of travel as he was used to driving on the opposite side of the road, and in so doing he collided with an oncoming car. A sentence of 14 months' imprisonment on a plea of guilty, entered at the earliest opportunity, was upheld by the Court of Appeal. It was said that the case fell into the most serious category identified in the Sentencing Guidelines Council's guideline (*ante*, Appendix K-194), and that the carelessness had bordered on dangerous driving. The offender had had no more than five hours' sleep in the previous 24 hours, during which he had twice been disturbed to take his young son to the lavatory, and, as an experienced traveller, he must have known the risk he was taking, so his culpability was accordingly high.

### Causing death by careless or inconsiderate driving

**K-446**    In *R. v. Campbell (Karl)* [2010] 2 Cr.App.R.(S.) 28, CA, the court said that whereas the guideline (*ante*, K-194) identified three categories of case, the most serious being cases where the driving was not far short of dangerous driving and the least serious comprising cases of momentary inattention with no aggravating features, the guideline provided no assistance as to the intermediate category of "other cases", but this could include cases of single misjudgments, such as a failure to see a vehicle approaching from the right when emerging from a minor road and when the visibility permitted the vehicle to have been seen in good time.

*Campbell (Karl)* was considered in *R. v. Odedara* [2010] 2 Cr.App.R.(S.) 51, CA, in which the court said of a case of momentary inattention with no aggravating features and some mitigating features, that it did not pass the custody threshold on a plea of guilty and probably would not have done so on conviction.

### Ranges

**K-447**    In *R. v. Shepherd* [2010] 2 Cr.App.R.(S.) 54, CA, it was pointed out that since the recommended range for the most serious of the three categories of cases of causing death by careless driving stops short (at four years' custody) of the statutory maximum (five years), there must be cases in which a judge will be entitled to go above the recommended range.

Where the offender, despite being aware that the braking system of the coach he was driving was not operating satisfactorily, drove the coach in terrain where there were regular hills, the driving created a "substantial risk of danger" such that the case fell within level 2, rather than a "significant risk of danger" such that the case would fall within level 3, of the guideline relating to causing death by dangerous driving (*ante*, K-192): *R. v. Oughton* [2011] 1 Cr.App.R.(S.) 62, CA.

## N.  BREACH OF AN ANTI-SOCIAL BEHAVIOUR ORDER

### Introduction

**K-450**    As to the purpose of this section of this appendix, see *ante*, K-350.

### Relevant main work references

**K-451**    For sentencing guidelines generally, see section 125 of the Coroners and Justice Act 2009 (§ 5-149 in the main work). For the power to make an anti-social behaviour order on conviction, see section 1C of the CDA 1998 (§ 5-1198 in the main work). For authorities considering the imposition of an anti-social behaviour order, see § 5-1202 in the main work.

### Ranges

**K-452**    In *R. v. Fagan* [2011] 1 Cr.App.R.(S.) 105, CA, the court upheld a sentence that was above the upper bracket for the most serious category in the guideline (*ante*, K-206), even though it was accepted that the case fell within the intermediate category. Referring to the maximum permissible sentence of five years' imprisonment, the court said that it followed that the guideline (which recommended a maximum of two years for a single offence) was not appropriate in the case of a persistent offender such as the appellant.

## O. Theft and Burglary in a Building Other Than a Dwelling

### Introduction

As to the purpose of this section of this appendix, see *ante*, K-350.   **K-475**

### Relevant main work references

For sentencing guidelines generally, see section 125 of the Coroners and Justice Act 2009 (§   **K-476**
5-149 in the main work). For previous guidelines in relation to various types of theft, see §§ 21-4c
*et seq.* in the main work.

### Theft in breach of trust

In *R. v. Hakimzadeh* [2010] 1 Cr.App.R.(S.) 8, CA, the appellant was a 61-year-old American of   **K-477**
Iranian origin, who was an expert on cultural relations between Iran and the western world. He
owned an extensive collection of materials relating to that topic and considered his library to be
the fourth most significant in the world. Over a substantial period, in order to improve his
personal library, he stole maps and illustrations from books and some books themselves from the
British and Bodleian libraries. The court said that whilst the guideline did not specifically address
such cases, the section on theft in breach of trust provided some relevant basis of comparison; the
offender was able to access the books in the manner that he did partly because of his reputation
and partly because he was trusted to treat them in the way that scholars should treat such
important resources. See also § 5-1267 in the main work.

*R. v. Hakimzadeh*, *ante*, was considered in *R. v. Jacques* [2011] 2 Cr.App.R.(S.) 39, CA, a case that
involved the theft of a set of 13 rare books from The Linley, the public library of the Royal
Horticultural Society, which were valued at £40,000 for insurance purposes (but could have been
sold for £27,000). The offender had gained access using a reader's card under an assumed name
and was found to be in possession of a list of 70 other books and their valuations. The court held
that the case was wholly different to *R. v. Hakimzadeh*, *ante*, because none of what was regarded as
exceptional mitigation in that case applied here. As to the guideline, it was said that this provided
an inadequate foundation for identifying the appropriate level of sentence in a case such as this;
to categorise this case as a breach of trust was a poor guide to the gravity of this type of offending,
which constituted a deliberate attack undermining the importance of libraries.

### Pickpocketing

In *R. v. De Weever* [2010] 1 Cr.App.R.(S.) 3, CA, the appellant had pushed a woman as she   **K-478**
boarded a tube train and stolen a purse from her shoulder bag. The Court of Appeal found that
the offence fell into the bottom level of seriousness identified in the Sentencing Guidelines
Council's guidelines on theft from the person (see *ante*, K-215). However, they considered that
there were a number of grave aggravating factors (*viz.* the offence was clearly planned and was
carried out in a highly professional manner, it involved the use of force (a push) short of robbery
and resulted in a high level of inconvenience to the victim, the offender had a number of like
convictions, albeit from many years ago, and he had failed to respond to his most recent sentences)
which took the offence out of the lowest level in the guideline, and to the top of the level above it,
where the starting point would be 12 months' imprisonment.

### Offences occurring in the context of widespread public disorder

As to departure from the guidelines when sentencing those convicted of theft and burglary in   **K-479**
the context of widespread public disorder of the kind seen in the riots that occurred around the
country in August, 2011, and as to the appropriateness of sentences beyond the range set out in
those guidelines, see *R. v. Blackshaw*, *ante*, § 29-9.

## P. Attempted Murder

### Introduction

As to the purpose of this section of this appendix, see *ante*, § K-350.   **K-500**

### Relevant main work references

For sentencing guidelines generally, see section 125 of the Coroners and Justice Act 2009 (§   **K-501**

5-149 in the main work). For the statutory guidelines on fixing the minimum term in a case of murder, see Schedule 21 to the CJA 2003 (§§ 5-425 *et seq.* in the main work).

### Conspiracy to murder

**K-502**   It was correct for the judge to have considered the Sentencing Guidelines Council's guideline on attempted murder in a case charged as a conspiracy to murder but in which the facts would have supported a charge of attempted murder: *R. v. Jolie* [2011] 1 Cr.App.R.(S.) 87, CA.

### Ranges

**K-503**   The Sentencing Guidelines Council's guideline had no application to the scale of criminality involved in a "hideous" case where the offender woke the lone female victim at night, stole from her and subjected her to rape, beatings, stabbings and set fire to her clothes and her home after tying her up, see *Att.-Gen.'s Reference (No. 37 of 2011) (R. v. Parsons)* [2012] 1 Cr.App.R.(S.) 84, CA.

An indeterminate sentence with a minimum term which reflected a notional determinate term that was way above the top of the recommended range for a determinate sentence was justified where the term was intended to reflect a course of violent offending (including a second attempted murder and two offences of wounding with intent to cause grievous bodily harm): *R. v. Onyenaychi* [2013] 1 Cr.App.R.(S.) 59, CA.

### Use of a knife or other weapon

**K-504**   Although the guideline was published prior to the insertion of paragraph 5A (taking a knife or other weapon to the scene/25-year starting point) in Schedule 21 to the 2003 Act (*ante*), given the way the guideline was constructed with direct reference to Schedule 21, it was incumbent on a judge to take account of the amendment of the law in relation to knives in a case involving the use of a knife: *R. v. Barnaby* [2013] 1 Cr.App.R.(S.) 53, CA; and, to similar effect, see *R. v. Gayzer-Tomlinson* [2013] 1 Cr.App.R.(S.) 98, CA.

### Q. FRAUD—STATUTORY OFFENCES

### Introduction

**K-525**   As to the purpose of this section of this appendix, see *ante*, K-350.

### Relevant main work references

**K-526**   For sentencing guidelines generally, see section 125 of the Coroners and Justice Act 2009 (§ 5-149 in the main work). For the Theft Act 1968, s.17 (false accounting), see § 21-226; for the Fraud Act 2006, s.1 (offence of fraud), see § 21-356; for sections 6 (possession of articles for use in fraud) and 7 (making or supplying articles for use in fraud) of the 2006 Act, see §§ 21-390, 21-391; for the CEMA 1979, ss.50 (improper importation of goods), 170 (fraudulent evasion of duty) and 170B (taking preparatory steps for evasion of duty), see §§ 25-430, 25-474, 25-505; and for the Value Added Tax Act 1994, s.72, see § 25-532.

### Confidence fraud

**K-527**   For a case in which the confidence fraud guideline was applied where the conduct of the offender was arguably more akin to theft in breach of trust (*ante*, K-213), see *R. v. Lawson* [2010] 2 Cr.App.R.(S.) 71, CA.

### Assessing seriousness

**K-528**   In *R. v. Chaytor* [2011] 2 Cr.App.R.(S.) 114, CA, it was held that whereas paragraph 21 of the guideline (*ante*, K-230) provides that, where an offender may have been entitled to all or part of the money obtained (*e.g.* where claims have been exaggerated), the starting point should be based on the amount to which the offender was not legitimately entitled, it does not follow that, in a case of making fraudulent expenses claims, the calculation of the losses consequent on the dishonesty actually perpetrated falls to be reduced because the defendant might, operating honestly and within the relevant rules, have been able to make legitimate claims for some or all of the amounts claimed.

## Conspiracies

As to whether the guideline applies to conspiracy to defraud, see *Att.-Gen.'s References (Nos 7 and 8 of 2013) (R. v. Kallakis and Williams); R. v. Levene* (§ 33-40 in the main work), and now reported at [2013] Lloyd's Rep. F.C. 417, *sub nom.R. v. Kallakis; R. v. Levene.*
**K-529**

Although the guideline was not specifically directed to conspiracies, it provided a helpful ★ indication of the appropriate level of sentence for cases of conspiracy fraudulently to evade excise duty: *R. v. Hareem and Salih* [2014] 1 Cr.App.R.(S.) 50, CA. As to this case, see also *ante*, § 25-507.

## R. Sentencing Youths

### Introduction

As to the purpose of this section of this appendix, see *ante*, K-350.
**K-550**

### Relevant main work references

As to the aim of the youth justice system, see section 37 of the CDA 1998 (§ 5-63 in the main work); as to the requirement for a court to have regard to the welfare of a child or young person, see section 44 of the CYPA 1933 (*ibid.*, § 5-64); as to the purposes of sentencing when dealing with young offenders, see section 142A of the CJA 2003 (*ibid.*, § 5-66) (not in force as at October 12, 2011); as to youth rehabilitation orders, see §§ *5-314 et seq.* in the main work; as to the enforcement of such orders, see §§ 5-380 *et seq.* in the main work; as to detention and training orders, see sections 100 to 107 of the PCC(S)A 2000 (§§ 5-597 *et seq.* in the main work); and as to the detention of young offenders convicted of certain grave crimes, see section 91 of the 2000 Act (*ibid.*, § 5-610).
**K-551**

For sentencing guidelines generally, see section 125 of the Coroners and Justice Act 2009 (§ 5-149 in the main work).

## S. Corporate Manslaughter and Health and Safety Offences Causing Death

### Introduction

As to the purpose of this section of this appendix, see *ante*, K-350.
**K-575**

### Relevant main work references

For sentencing guidelines generally, see section 125 of the Coroners and Justice Act 2009 (§ 5-149 in the main work). As to the offence of corporate manslaughter, see §§ 19-138 *et seq.* in the main work. For the maximum sentence, for the power to order the taking of remedial action and for the power to order a conviction to be publicised, see sections 1(2), 9 and 10 of the Corporate Manslaughter and Corporate Homicide Act 2007 respectively (§§ 19-138, 19-148, 19-149 in the main work). For decisions of the Court of Appeal considering the proper approach to determining the amount of a fine, see § 5-688 in the main work.
**K-576**

## T. Aggravated Burglary and Burglary

### Introduction

As to the purpose of this section of this appendix, see *ante*, K-350.
**K-600**

### Relevant main work references

For sentencing guidelines generally, see section 125 of the Coroners and Justice Act 2009 (§ 5-149 in the main work). For previous guidelines in relation to burglary of a dwelling, see § 21-114 in the main work (and for previous guidelines in relation to burglary otherwise than in a dwelling, see *ante*, K-209 *et seq.*). For section 9 of the Theft Act 1968 (burglary), see § 21-108 in the main work; and for section 10 of the 1968 Act (aggravated burglary, see § 21-129 in the main work).
**K-601**

## Harm

**K-602**     Whereas one of the factors indicative of greater harm is "theft of/damage to property causing a significant degree of loss to the victim (whether economic, sentimental or personal value)", this is primarily addressing the position at the time of the theft or damage; subsequent recovery of the property, particularly if it is through voluntary reparation, may be a mitigating factor, but it does not change the character of the offence: *R. v. Franks* [2013] 1 Cr.App.R.(S.) 65, CA.

## Distraction burglaries

**★K-603**     In *R. v. Dance* [2014] 1 Cr.App.R.(S.) 51, CA, the court held that while courts must apply the guideline when passing sentence for distraction burglaries, judges are entitled to have regard to previous decisions of the Court of Appeal, provided that they bear in mind that those cases were decided before the guideline came into force. The earlier authorities provided a useful reminder that distraction burglaries targeted at vulnerable victims are a very serious crime, despite the fact that they may involve no violence to person or property. Such offences may well merit a sentence higher than the top of the range in the guidelines, particularly if there is a pattern of repeat offending of this kind.

## U. DRUG OFFENCES

## Introduction

**K-625**     As to the purpose of this section of this appendix, see *ante*, K-350.

## Relevant main work references

**K-626**     For sentencing guidelines generally, see section 125 of the Coroners and Justice Act 2009 (§ 5-149). For section 170 of the CEMA 1979, see § 25-474; and for the penalty provisions in Schedule 1 to that Act, see § 25-508; for section 4 of the Misuse of Drugs Act 1971 (restriction of production and supply of controlled drugs), see § 27-28; for section 4A of the 1971 Act (aggravation of offence of supply of controlled drug), see § 27-28a; for section 5 of the 1971 Act (restriction of possession of controlled drug), see § 27-50; for section 6 of the 1971 Act (restriction of cultivation of cannabis plant), see § 27-79; for section 8 of the 1971 Act (occupiers of premises), see § 27-84; for section 25 of the 1971 Act (prosecution and punishment of offences), see § 27-105; for the sentencing guidelines of the Court of Appeal, see §§ 27-107 *et seq.*; and for the table of maximum penalties under the 1971 Act (and mode of trial provisions), see § 27-130.

## Scope of the guideline

**K-626a**     The Sentencing Council's guideline on drug offences does not cover the offence of taking a prohibited article into prison, contrary to the Prison Act 1952, s.40B (§ 28-194 in the main work), where the article in question is a controlled drug and it is supplied to, or intended for supply to, a prisoner: *R. v. Simmons* [2013] 1 Cr.App.R.(S.) 109, CA. For critical consideration of this approach, see CLW/13/20/4.

The guideline applies to an offence of conspiracy to supply a controlled drug, but it should be approached with a degree of common sense and flexibility; whilst a judge should reflect the individual's culpability in the sentence passed, perhaps by adjusting the category to one better reflecting the reality, the fact of involvement in a conspiracy is an aggravating feature, since each conspirator playing his part gives comfort and assistance to others knowing that he is doing so, and the greater his awareness of the scale of the enterprise in which he is assisting, the greater his culpability: *R. v. Khan (Kazim Ali), Khan (Umar), Khan (Mohammed Arfan) and Khan (Mohammed Ahsan)* [2014] 1 Cr.App.R.(S.) 10, CA. The court also held that a judge was not confined to category 3 of the guideline because the end point activity of a conspiracy was street dealing; the words in the guideline "Where the offence is street dealing ... the quantity of the product is less indicative of the harm caused and therefore the starting point is not based on quantity." were plainly intended to move what would otherwise be category 4 offending into category 3; and it did not follow that those involved in street dealing of quantities which in aggregate went far beyond the amounts shown in category 4 can limit themselves to category 3 no matter what the scale of their dealing. As to street dealing, see also *R. v. Dyer, post,* § K-629.

## Prospective or retrospective

The guideline is not retrospective: *R. v. Boakye and other cases* [2013] 1 Cr.App.R.(S.) 2, CA.    **K-627**

## Categorisation of role

In *Att.-Gen.'s References (Nos 15, 16 and 17 of 2012) (R. v. Lewis)* [2013] 1 Cr.App.R.(S.) 52, CA, it   **K-628**
was said that there may be a misunderstanding as to how to categorise the role of an offender; the
essential nature of a drugs hierarchy remains the same even if the terminology in the guideline
("leading", "significant" and "lesser" roles) has changed; the guideline provides a list of
characteristics to guide the judge in his task, but the list is not exhaustive, and it is not necessary
for an offender to possess every characteristic before he can be described as fulfilling any particular
role; there may be a tendency to focus on the "non-exhaustive" list of characteristics provided and
to give them far too strict a meaning; the words chosen have a broad meaning and judges should
be astute not to place offenders in a lower category than is appropriate; the judge should declare
his conclusions on step one in his sentencing remarks, for the benefit of the offender, those advising the offender, and the Court of Appeal; at step two, having determined the offender's role and
the category of harm, the judge should "use the corresponding starting point to reach a sentence
within the category ranges" which follow, and then factor in any aggravating or mitigating
features.

It is not the case that a "leading role" should be reserved for cases where there is an operational
hierarchy and a chain of employees, and that a "significant role" should apply to an organiser
where there is no such chain: *R. v. Descombre and Thomas* [2013] 2 Cr.App.R.(S.) 51, CA (considering *R. v. Healey, post*, K-630).

## Categorisation of harm

For a case applying the principle that the quantities of drug listed in the categories of harm in   **★K-628a**
the drugs guideline are not thresholds but indicative quantities, see *R. v. Henry* [2014] 1
Cr.App.R.(S.) 55, CA.

## Community impact

Where the offender, having installed a sophisticated cannabis cultivation set-up at his home, fell   **★K-628b**
to be sentenced for an offence of production of a controlled drug, the judge had been entitled to
take the case to the top of the relevant bracket having regard to the evidence provided by a community impact statement of a detective inspector, which dealt with the effect of drugs in the South
Yorkshire area, and which noted that there was a significant risk of harm to communities from associated crime, namely, violence directed at cannabis producers in order to "tax" them ("taxing"
being the street term used to describe the taking of drugs and other assets from those engaged in
crime), and that innocent victims were also sometimes the target of "taxing" due to mistaken
identity: *R. v. Wicks* [2014] 1 Cr.App.R.(S.) 57, CA.

## Supply

In *R. v. Dyer* [2014] 1 *Archbold Review* 3, CA, it was held: (i) against the background of the   **K-629**
Sentencing Council's definitive guideline, earlier authorities have limited, if any, relevance, and
further reliance on *R. v. Afonso; R. v. Sajid; R. v. Andrews* [2005] 1 Cr.App.R.(S.) 99, CA (sentencing of unemployed drug addicts), is inappropriate; (ii) in relation to selling directly to users
("street dealing"), harm is not categorised by quantity in the guideline; the fact of street dealing is
sufficient to put the offending into Category 3 irrespective of the quantity involved; street dealing
will inevitably be in quantities far smaller than those listed in the guideline (but see *R. v. Khan
(Kazim Ali), Khan (Umar), Khan (Mohammed Arfan) and Khan (Mohammed Ahsan), ante*, K-626a); (iii)
the fact that drugs have been supplied to a test purchase or undercover officer is not a reason to
reduce the category; (iv) whereas "lesser role" in the guideline includes "if own operation,
absence of any financial gain, for example joint purchase for no profit, or sharing minimal
quantity between peers on non-commercial basis", street dealers funding their own habit, or
perhaps an extremely meagre living, are motivated by financial and other advantage and are not
the same as those who, for example, are funded by friends to buy drugs for the group without

any question of financial or other reward; and (v) as street dealing is always likely to be at a low level and the category is fixed, the descriptors "some awareness and understanding of the scale of the operation" in relation to "significant role", and "very little, if any, awareness or understanding of the scale of the operation" in relation to "lesser role", are of far greater relevance to those being sentenced on the basis of the quantity of the drug concerned (*e.g.* a courier or low-level participant in a substantial drug dealing operation). As to this case, see also *ante*, §§ 5-141, 5-159.

*Att.-Gen.'s References (Nos 82-96 and 104-109 of 2011) (R. v. Page)* [2012] 2 Cr.App.R.(S.) 56, CA, was a pre-guideline case. However, the court's general observations as to the assessment of roles would seem to carry over to sentencing under the guideline (*Dyer*, *ante*, notwithstanding). The court said that all dealers are not the same; on the whole, the greater the quantity, the longer the period over which supplies were made, and the greater the profit, the more serious the offence is likely to be, with wholesale supply likely to be more serious than retail supply because of the quantity involved; and just as dealers vary, so do transporters or "couriers"; some people fulfilling the role of transporting drugs may in fact be very close to the central organisers of the trade, the "entrepreneurs"; other couriers, however, are little more than hired hands, operating under the direction of the entrepreneurs, and are likely to be paid per task; when sentencing, therefore, it is necessary to ensure that couriers or other handlers of drugs are placed in the right relationship with the entrepreneurs, especially the principals (those responsible for large scale purchase and sale), but also the entrepreneurs who are dealers, wholesale or retail.

In *R. v. Sanchez-Canadas* [2013] 1 Cr.App.R.(S.) 114, CA, it was said that the judge had been wrong to elevate a case from category 4 to category 3 on the ground that the supply was to a prisoner; as to culpability, however, the court said that the supply of drugs into a prison ought normally to be regarded as best fitting the description of "significant role"; and it will ordinarily demand a prison sentence, even when there is no commercial motive, and even where the supplier has come under some moral pressure.

★    Where the person supplied dies as a result of taking the drug supplied, this had to be treated as a substantial aggravating feature notwithstanding that it was not intended, it was not anticipated, it was greatly regretted, and there was no reason for the offender to consider that it would result, except for the fact that any supply of Class A drugs carries risks: *R. v. Harrod* [2014] 1 Cr.App.R.(S.) 76, CA.

★    In *R. v. Bush* [2014] 1 Cr.App.R.(S.) 40, CA, the court held that anyone involved in selling drugs at summer music festivals, even on a relatively low level basis, must expect an immediate custodial sentence; such festivals are an increasingly important part of the popular culture and teenagers, who are often away from direct parental control for the first time, attend them in groups and are thus particularly vulnerable to those trying to sell them drugs.

★    Where the drug being sold turns out to be Class A, not Class B, as the seller believed, this should not lead to the seller being sentenced as if he were selling a Class B drug; however, a genuine misunderstanding as to the nature of a drug was relevant, because it is more culpable to sell a Class A drug, knowing it to be Class A, than to sell a Class A drug, reasonably believing it to be Class B: *R. v. Bird* [2014] 1 Cr.App.R.(S.) 77, CA.

### Cultivation and production

**K-630**    In *R. v. Healey* [2013] 1 Cr.App.R.(S.) 33, CA, it was said that whereas the guideline uses pictorial boxes to describe the broad categories of offence, adjacent boxes are not mutually exclusive; there is an inevitable overlap between the scenarios described; the guideline sets out to describe such sliding scales and graduations as occur in real-life offending; the quantities which appear in the boxes as broad indicators of harm are neither fixed points nor thresholds; they are "indicative" quantities designed to enable the experienced judge to put the case into the right context on the sliding scale. In production cases, the court continued, it is the output or the potential output that counts, and the number of plants is to be considered only as a route to the more fundamental question of output or potential output; there may be evidence that the yield per plant is higher than the assumption used in the guideline, in which case the application of the guideline must be adjusted accordingly. It was held that those who create a purpose-built room in their loft, cellar or garage, or who dedicate a bedroom to cultivating cannabis, having invested substantially in professional equipment for watering, for lighting and/or for electronically controlled timing, can perfectly properly be described as being at the next level up (*viz.* having a "significant role") from

Archbold
paragraph
numbers

those who are at the lowest level; and where there is a real likelihood of additional wider circulation, in other words supply, whether for money or not, they are to be positioned higher up in the "significant role" category; as the quantity of cannabis increases, the likelihood of it being intended for the sole consumption of the defendant reduces; and a judge faced with a defendant who asserts that an improbably large quantity of cannabis is entirely for his own use should indicate that he is not presently inclined to accept that assertion, and give the defendant and his counsel the opportunity to give evidence about it if he wishes; what a judge is not entitled to do is to say that he accepts the assertion that the drug cultivation was all for the defendant's own use and yet sentence on the basis that there is likely to be a supply to somebody else. As to this case, and what was said about guidelines generally, see also §§ 5-152, 5-153 in the main work. *Healey* (which was considered in *R. v. Descombre and Thomas, ante,* K-628) may be contrasted with *R. v. Bamford* [2012] Crim.L.R. 633, CA, which was decided a month earlier, where the defendant had converted a bedroom into a professionally-equipped small cannabis farm. The court said that, as it was accepted that it was all for his own use, he was properly to be described as having a "lesser role".

## Importation

In *R. v. Jaramillo* [2013] 1 Cr.App.R.(S.) 110, CA, the court considered what is said in the guideline about a starting point of 20 years (*ante,* K-275), but said that such a starting point is likely to be reserved for cases of commercial importation where the amount of drugs involved is enormous, the offender is an organiser, he has taken part in more than one importation, or he has a record of serious drug dealing.

**K-631**

## MDPV

In determining the category of harm into which an offence falls, the harm associated with the synthetic Class B drug methylenedioxypyrovalerone (or "MDPV"), a derivative of cathinone, is to be treated as commensurate to the harm associated with amphetamine, and the potential of a particular quantity of MDPV for causing harm is to be taken to be the same as the potential for the same quantity of amphetamine; the purity of any given quantity was to be taken into account at step 2, that is when determining where in the range the sentence should be positioned: *R. v. Brown* [2014] 1 Cr.App.R.(S.) 84, CA.

**★K-632**

## V. Offences Taken into Consideration and Totality

### Introduction

As to the purpose of this section of this appendix, see *ante,* K-350.

**K-650**

### Relevant main work references

For sentencing guidelines generally, see section 125 of the Coroners and Justice Act 2009 (§ 5-149).

**K-651**

As to offences taken into consideration, see §§ 5-160 *et seq.*

As to "totality" and consecutive or concurrent sentences, see the CJA 2003, ss.166(3)(b) (§ 5-126) and 265 (§ 5-668); and for the existing case law, see §§ 5-585 *et seq.*

## W. Dangerous Dog Offences

### Introduction

As to the purpose of this section of this appendix, see *ante,* K-350.

**K-675**

### Relevant main work references

For sentencing guidelines generally, see section 125 of the Coroners and Justice Act 2009 (§ 5-149). For sections 3, 4 and 4A of the Dangerous Dogs Act 1991, see §§ 31-35, 31-38 and 31-38a respectively (and *ante*).

**K-676**

## X. Fraud, Bribery and Money Laundering

### Introduction

As to the purpose of this section of this appendix, see *ante,* K-350.

**K-700**

Supplement No. 3—July, 2014

883

### Relevant main work references

★K-701    For sentencing guidelines generally, see section 125 of the Coroners and Justice Act 2009 (§ 5-149). For conspiracy to defraud, see §§ 33-37 *et seq.*; for false accounting (Theft Act 1968, s.17), see § 21-226; for possession, *etc.*, of articles for use in fraud (2006 Act, s.6), see § 21-390; for making or supplying articles for use in fraud (2006 Act, s.7), see § 21-391; for fraudulent evasion of value added tax (Value Added Tax Act 1994, s.72), see § 25-532, for improper importation of goods (CEMA 1979, s.50), see § 25-430; for fraudulent evasion of duty (CEMA 1979, s.170), see § 25-474; for taking steps to evade duty (CEMA 1979, s.170B), see § 25-505; for cheating the public revenue, see §§ 25-409 *et seq.*; for money laundering (PCA 2002, ss.327 to 329), see §§ 26-11 *et seq*; for bribery (Bribery Act 2010, ss.1, 2 and 6), see §§ 31-171, 31-172, 31-176; and for failure of commercial organisations to prevent bribery (2010 Act, s.7), see § 31-177.

### III. COMPENDIUM OF GUIDELINE CASES

K-1000    The Sentencing Guidelines Council has published a compendium of those cases that it regards as constituting considered guidance and issued over the past 30 years. The list is in two parts, "Generic sentencing principles" and "Offences". It has been updated five times, with some cases having been removed from the original list.

In the first list are: *R. v. Martin (Selina)* [2007] 1 Cr.App.R.(S.) 3 (**approach to sentencing**); *Att.-Gen.'s Reference (No. 4 of 1989) (R. v. Brunt)*, 11 Cr.App.R.(S.) 517 (**Attorney-General's references**); *R. v. Montgomery*, 16 Cr.App.R.(S.) 274 (**contempt**); *R. v. Bernard* [1997] 1 Cr.App.R.(S.) 135 (**health of the offender**); *R. v. Goodyear* [2005] 3 All E.R. 117; *R. v. Kulah* [2008] 1 Cr.App.R.(S.) 85 (**indication of sentence**); *R. v. Buckland* [2000] 1 W.L.R. 1262 (**automatic life sentences**); *R. v. Hodgson*, 52 Cr.App.R. 113; *R. v. Chapman* [2000] 1 Cr.App.R. 77; *R. v. McNee, Gunn and Russell* [2008] 1 Cr.App.R.(S.) 24; *R. v. Kehoe* [2009] 1 Cr.App.R.(S.) 9; *R. v. Davies* [2009] 1 Cr.App.R.(S.) 15 (**discretionary life sentences**); *R. v. M. (Discretionary Life Sentence); R. v. L.* [1999] 1 W.L.R. 485; *R. v. Szczerba* [2002] 2 Cr.App.R.(S.) 86 (**life sentence—specified period**); *R. v. McLean*, 6 Cr.App.R. 26; *R. v. Simons*, 37 Cr.App.R. 120; *R. v. Walsh*, unreported, March 8, 1973 (**taking offences into consideration**); *Att.-Gen.'s Reference (No. 52 of 2003) (R. v. Webb)* [2004] Crim.L.R. 306 (**prosecution duty**); *R. v. Kelly and Donnelly* [2001] 2 Cr.App.R.(S.) 73; *R. v. McGillivray* [2005] 2 Cr.App.R.(S.) 60; *R. v. O'Callaghan* [2005] 2 Cr.App.R.(S.) 83 (**racially aggravated offences**); *R. v. A. and B.* [1999] 1 Cr.App.R.(S.) 52; *R. v. Guy* [1999] 2 Cr.App.R.(S.) 24; *R. v. X. (No. 2)* [1999] 2 Cr.App.R.(S.) 294; *R. v. R. (Informer: Reduction in sentence), The Times*, February 18, 2002; *R. v. P.; R. v. Blackburn* [2008] 2 Cr.App.R.(S.) 5 (**discount on account of assistance given to the police**); *R. v. Bird*, 9 Cr.App.R.(S.) 77; *R. v. Tiso*, 12 Cr.App.R.(S.) 122 (**discount on account of lapse of time since offence**); *R. v. Bibi* [1980] 1 W.L.R. 1193; *R. v. Ollerenshaw* [1999] 1 Cr.App.R.(S.) 65; *R. v. Kefford* [2002] 2 Cr.App.R.(S.) 106 (**length of custodial sentences**); *R. v. Nelson* [2002] 1 Cr.App.R.(S.) 134; *R. v. Cornelius* [2002] 2 Cr.App.R.(S.) 69; *R. v. Pepper* [2006] 1 Cr.App.R.(S.) 20 (**length of extended sentences**); *R. v. Lang* [2006] 2 Cr.App.R.(S.) 3; *R. v. S.; R. v. Burt* [2006] 2 Cr.App.R.(S.) 35; *CPS v. South East Surrey Youth Court* [2006] 2 Cr.App.R.(S.) 26 (**dangerousness**); *R. v. Reynolds* [2007] 2 Cr.App.R.(S.) 87; *R. v. Johnson* [2007] 1 Cr.App.R.(S.) 112; *R. v. O'Brien* [2007] 1 Cr.App.R.(S.) 75; *R. v. O'Halloran*, unreported, November 14, 2006 ([2006] EWCA Crim. 3148) (**dangerousness: imprisonment for public protection**); *R. v. Brown and Butterworth* [2007] 1 Cr.App.R.(S.) 77; *R. v. Lay* [2007] 2 Cr.App.R.(S.) 4; *R. v. C.; R. v. Bartley* [2007] 2 Cr.App.R.(S.) 98 (**dangerousness: extended sentences**); *Att.-Gen.'s Reference (No. 101 of 2006) (R. v. P.)*, unreported, December 8, 2006 ([2006] EWCA Crim. 3335) (**deferment of sentence**); *R. v. Cain* [2007] 2 Cr.App.R.(S.) 25 (**prosecution and defence duty to assist at sentencing**); *R. v. Seed; R. v. Stark* [2007] 2 Cr.App.R.(S.) 69 (**sentence length: custodial sentences**); *R. (Stellato) v. Secretary of State for the Home Department* [2007] 2 A.C. 70 (**sentence length: licence period**); *Att.-Gen.'s Reference (No. 6 of 2006) (R. v. Farish)* [2007] 1 Cr.App.R.(S.) 12 (**sentence length: minimum sentences**); *R. v. Gordon* [2007] 2 All E.R. 768 (**sentence length: time spent in custody on remand**); *R. v. Tyre*, 6 Cr.App.R.(S.) 247 (**sentence length: joint conviction with a juvenile offender**); *R. v. Davies* [2009] 1 Cr.App.R.(S.) 15 (**sentence length: standard of proof**); *R. v. Raza* [2010] 1 Cr.App.R.(S.) 56, CA (**sentence length: discounts; totality and mandatory minimum sentences**); *R. v. Round; R. v. Dunn* [2010] 2 Cr.App.R.(S.) 45, CA (**sentence length: early release provisions**); *Att.- Gen.'s Reference (No. 55 of 2008) (R. v. C.)* [2009] 2 Cr.App.R.(S.) 22, CA (**sentence length: imprison-**

ment for public protection); *R. v. Costello* [2010] 2 Cr.App.R.(S.) 94, CA (**sentence length: offence committed whilst on licence**); *R. v. McGrath* [2005] 2 Cr.App.R.(S.). 85; *R. v. Morrison* [2006] 1 Cr.App.R.(S.) 85; *R. v. Lamb* [2006] 2 Cr.App.R.(S.) 11 (**anti-social behaviour orders**); *R. v. P. (Shane Tony)* [2004] 2 Cr.App.R.(S.) 63 (**anti-social behaviour order imposed with custody**); *R. v. Sullivan* [2003] EWCA Crim. 1736 (**compensation with custody**); *R. v. Robinson* [2002] 2 Cr.App.R.(S.) 95; *Att.-Gen.'s Reference (No. 64 of 2003)* [2004] 2 Cr.App.R.(S.) 22; *R. v. Woods and Collins* [2006] 1 Cr.App.R.(S.) 83 (**drug treatment and testing orders**); *R. v. Richards* [2007] 1 Cr.App.R.(S.) 120 (**sexual offences prevention orders**); *R. v. Kidd; R. v. Canavan; R. v. Shaw (Dennis)* [1998] 1 W.L.R. 604; *R. v. Tovey; R. v. Smith* [2005] 2 Cr.App.R.(S.) 100 (**specimen offences**); *R. v. Perks* [2001] 1 Cr.App.R.(S.) 66; *R. v. Ismail* [2005] 2 Cr.App.R.(S.) 88 (**victim's wishes**); *R. v. Danga*, 13 Cr.App.R.(S.) 408 (**age for purpose of sentencing**); *R. (W.) v. Southampton Youth Court; R. (K.) v. Wirral Borough Magistrates' Court* [2003] 1 Cr.App.R.(S.) 87 (**venue for trial**); *R. v. Sharma* [2006] 2 Cr.App.R.(S.) 63 (**confiscation orders**); *R. v. Oshungbure and Odewale* [2005] 2 Cr.App.R.(S.) 102 (**confiscation proceedings following sentence**); *R. v. Richards (Michael)* [2005] 2 Cr.App.R.(S.) 97 (**confiscation order: obtaining social security benefits by false representations**); *R. v. Debnath* [2006] 2 Cr.App.R.(S.) 25 (**restraining orders**); *R. v. Lees-Wolfenden* [2007] 1 Cr.App.R.(S.) 119 (**suspended sentence orders**); *R. v. Sheppard* [2008] 2 Cr.App.R.(S.) 93, CA; *R. v. Chalmers*, unreported, August 7, 2009, CA ([2009] EWCA Crim. 1814) (**activation of suspended sentences**).

In the second list are:—

**affray**—*R. v. Fox and Hicks* [2006] 1 Cr.App.R.(S.) 17;

**breach of licence**—*R. v. Pick and Dillon* [2006] 1 Cr.App.R.(S.) 61;

**burglary (domestic)**—*R. v. McInerney; R. v. Keating* [2003] 1 All E.R. 1089; *R. v. Saw* [2009] 2 Cr.App.R.(S.) 54, CA [but see now *R. v. Dance, ante,* K-603];

**counterfeiting and forgery**—*R. v. Howard*, 7 Cr.App.R.(S.) 320 (dealing in counterfeit currency); *R. v. Crick*, 3 Cr.App.R.(S.) 275 (counterfeiting coins); *R. v. Kolawole* [2005] 2 Cr.App.R.(S.) 14; *R. v. Mutede* [2006] 2 Cr.App.R.(S.) 22; *Att.-Gen.'s Reference (Nos 1 and 6 of 2008) (R. v. Dziruni and Laby)* [2008] 2 Cr.App.R.(S.) 99; *R. v. Mabengo, Lomoka, Salang and Birindwa, The Times,* July 17, 2008, CA; and *R. v. Ovieriakhi* [2009] 2 Cr.App.R.(S.) 91, CA (false passports);

**drugs**—[for a listing of the cases included in the compendium, see the first supplement to this edition; they have not been included here in light of the observations of the Court of Appeal in *R. v. Dyer, ante,* K-629 about the citation of pre-guideline authorities];

**explosive offences**—*R. v. Martin* [1999] 1 Cr.App.R.(S.) 477;

**firearms offences**—*R. v. Avis; R. v. Barton; R. v. Thomas; R. v. Torrington; R. v. Marquez; R. v. Goldsmith* [1998] 1 Cr.App.R. 420; *Att.-Gen.'s Reference (No. 43 of 2009) (R. v. Bennett); R. v. Wilkinson* [2010] 1 Cr.App.R.(S.) 100; *R. v. Rehman; R. v. Wood* [2006] 1 Cr.App.R.(S.) 77 (exceptional circumstances);

**fraud**—*R. v. Feld* [1999] 1 Cr.App.R.(S.) 1 (company management); *R. v. Palk and Smith* [1997] 2 Cr.App.R.(S.) 167 (fraudulent trading); *R. v. Roach* [2002] 1 Cr.App.R.(S.) 12 (obtaining money transfer by deception);

**handling stolen goods**—*R. v. Webbe* [2002] 1 Cr.App.R.(S.) 22;

**health and safety offences**—*R. v. F. Howe and Son (Engineers) Ltd* [1999] 2 All E.R. 249; *R. v. Rollco Screw and Rivet Co Ltd* [1999] 2 Cr.App.R.(S.) 436; *R. v. Balfour Beatty Infrastructure Ltd* [2007] 1 Cr.App.R.(S.) 65;

**immigration**—R. v. Le and Stark [1999] 1 Cr.App.R.(S.) 422; R. v. Ai (Lu Zhu) [2006] 1 Cr.App.R.(S.) 5 (failing to produce an immigration document);

**incest**—*Att.-Gen.'s Reference (No. 1 of 1989)*, 11 Cr.App.R.(S.) 409;

**indecent assault**—*Att.-Gen.'s References (Nos 120, 91 and 119 of 2002)* [2003] 2 All E.R. 955 (general); *R. v. Lennon* [1999] 1 Cr.App.R. 117 (on male);

**insider dealing**—*R. v. McQuoid* [2010] 1 Cr.App.R.(S.) 43, CA;

**intimidation of witness**—*R. v. Williams* [1997] 2 Cr.App.R.(S.) 221; *R. v. Chinery* [2002] 2 Cr.App.R.(S.) 244(55);

**kidnapping**—*R. v. Spence and Thomas*, 5 Cr.App.R.(S.) 413;

**manslaughter**—*R. v. Chambers*, 5 Cr.App.R.(S.) 190 (diminished responsibility); *R. v. Furby*

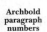
[2006] 2 Cr.App.R.(S.) 8; *Att.-Gen.'s Reference (No. 60 of 2009) (R. v. Appleby)* [2010] 2 Cr.App.R.(S.) 46, CA ("single punch"); *Att.-Gen.'s Reference (No. 111 of 2006) (R. v. Hussain)* [2007] 2 Cr.App.R.(S.) 26 ("motor"); *R. v. Wood* [2010] 1 Cr.App.R.(S.) 2, CA (diminished responsibility);

**money laundering**—*R. v. Basra* [2002] 2 Cr.App.R.(S.) 100; *R. v. Gonzalez and Sarmineto* [2003] 2 Cr.App.R.(S.) 9 (general); *R. v. El-Delbi* [2003] 7 *Archbold News* 1 (proceeds of drug trafficking);

**murder**—*R. v. Jones* [2006] 2 Cr.App.R.(S.) 19; *R. v. Barot* [2008] 1 Cr.App.R.(S.) 31; *R. v. McNee, Gunn and Russell* [2008] 1 Cr.App.R.(S.) 24 (conspiracy); *R. v. Davies* [2009] 1 Cr.App.R.(S.) 15 (minimum term); *R. v. Javed* [2008] 2 Cr.App.R.(S.) 12 (soliciting); *R. v. M.; R. v. A.M.; R. v. Kika* [2010] 2 Cr.App.R.(S.) 19, CA (with a knife);

**offensive weapons**—*R. v. Poulton; R. v. Celaire* [2003] 4 All E.R. 869; *R. v. Povey* [2009] 1 Cr.App.R.(S.) 42;

**perjury**—*R. v. Archer* [2003] 1 Cr.App.R.(S.) 86;

**perverting the course of justice**—*R. v. Walsh and Nightingale*, 14 Cr.App.R.(S.) 671; *R. v. Tunney* [2007] 1 Cr.App.R.(S.) 91, CA;

**pornography**—*R. v. Holloway*, 4 Cr.App.R.(S.) 128 (having obscene articles for publication for gain); *R. v. Nooy and Schyff*, 4 Cr.App.R.(S.) 308 (importation of indecent or obscene publications);

**prison breaking (escape)**—*R. v. Coughtrey* [1997] 2 Cr.App.R.(S.) 269;

**public nuisance**—*R. v. Kavanagh* [2008] 2 Cr.App.R.(S.) 86;

**riot**—*R. v. Najeeb* [2003] 2 Cr.App.R.(S.) 69;

**robbery**—*R. v. Snowden, The Times,* November 11, 2002 (hijacking of cars);

**sex offenders' register**—*Att.-Gen.'s Reference (No. 50 of 1997) (R. v. V.)* [1998] 2 Cr.App.R.(S.) 155;

**theft**—*R. v. Evans* [1996] 1 Cr.App.R.(S.) 105 ("ringing" stolen cars);

**trafficking women for prostitution**—*Att.-Gen.'s Reference (No. 6 of 2004) (R. v. Plakici)* [2005] 1 Cr.App.R.(S.) 19;

**violent disorder**—*R. v. Chapman* (2002) 146 S.J. (LB 242);

**K-1001**    In addition to the compendium of cases (*ante*), the Sentencing Guidelines Council issued a "guide" for practitioners and sentencers concerning the dangerous offender provisions of the CJA 2003 in September, 2007. It has now been updated to take account of the amendments effected by the CJIA 2008 which apply to everyone sentenced on or after July 14, 2008. The introduction expressly states that the "guide" is not a "guideline" for the purposes of section 172 of the 2003 Act (§ 5-144 in the main work). Its purpose is to set out clearly the statutory requirements that determine whether one (or more) of the new sentences is available, and to summarise the Court of Appeal (and High Court) guidance regarding the application of those requirements. The guide does not apply to protective sentences under the pre-2003 Act regimes.

Parts 2 and 3 of the guide respectively set out the criteria for imposing sentences under the dangerous offender provisions in respect of offenders aged 18 or over and offenders aged under 18. Part 4 sets out matters in connection with the determination of venue where an offender is under the age of 18. Part 5 deals with the giving of a *Goodyear* indication (*R. v. Goodyear (Practice note)* [2005] 2 Cr.App.R. 20, CA (§ 5-110 in the main work)) in relation to offenders charged with serious or specified offences. Part 6 deals with the assessment of dangerousness. Part 7 sets out matters in connection with the imposition of imprisonment (or custody or detention) for life. Part 8 deals with the choice of whether an extended sentence or a sentence for public protection should be imposed in respect of an offender aged under 18. Part 9 deals with the fixing of "minimum terms", and "custodial terms" and "extension periods". Part 10 deals with questions arising where an offender falls to be sentenced for more than one offence and/or is serving an existing custodial sentence. Part 11 deals with the correction of errors and omissions. Part 12 is a glossary.

There are six annexes. Annex A sets out simple flow charts. Annexes B and C purport to list all serious and specified violent offences; and Annexes D and E purport to do the same in respect of sexual offences. Annex F reproduces sections 225 to 229 of the 2003 Act in amended form, including the new Schedule 15A.

# APPENDIX  N
## Protocols

## A. Control and Management of Heavy Fraud and other Complex Criminal Cases

A protocol issued by the Lord Chief Justice of England and Wales **N-1**

22 March 2005

Introduction

The investigation

The role of the prosecuting authority and the judge

Interviews

The prosecution and defence teams

Initial consideration of the length of a case

Notification of cases likely to last more than 8 weeks

Notification of cases likely to last more than 8 weeks

Venue

Designation of the trial judge

The assignment of a judge

Case management

Objectives

The assignment of a judge

Case management

Objectives

Fixing the trial date

The first hearing for the giving of initial directions

The first Case Management Hearing

Further Case Management Hearings

Consideration of the length of the trial

The exercise of the powers

Fixing the trial date

The first hearing for the giving of initial directions

The first Case Management Hearing

Further Case Management Hearings

Consideration of the length of the trial

The exercise of the powers

Expert Evidence

Surveillance Evidence

Disclosure

Abuse of process

The trial

The particular hazard of heavy fraud trials

Judicial mastery of the case

The order of the evidence

Case management sessions

## Introduction

N-2      There is a broad consensus that the length of fraud and trials of other complex crimes must be controlled within proper bounds in order:

(i) To enable the jury to retain and assess the evidence which they have heard. If the trial is so long that the jury cannot do this, then the trial is not fair either to the prosecution or the defence.

(ii) To make proper use of limited public resources: see *Jisl* [2004] EWCA Crim 696 at [113]-[121].

There is also a consensus that no trial should be permitted to exceed a given period, save in exceptional circumstances; some favour 3 months, others an outer limit of 6 months. Whatever view is taken, it is essential that the current length of trials is brought back to an acceptable and proper duration.

This Protocol supplements the Criminal Procedure Rules and summarises good practice which experience has shown may assist in bringing about some reduction in the length of trials of fraud and other crimes that result in complex trials. Flexibility of application of this Protocol according to the needs of each case is essential; it is designed to inform but not to proscribe.

This Protocol is primarily directed towards cases which are likely to last eight weeks or longer. It should also be followed, however, in all cases estimated to last more than four weeks. This Protocol applies to trials by jury, but many of the principles will be applicable if trials without a jury are permitted under s.43 of the Criminal Justice Act 2003.

The best handling technique for a long case is continuous management by an experienced Judge nominated for the purpose.

It is intended that this Protocol be kept up to date; any further practices or techniques found to be successful in the management of complex cases should be notified to the office of the Lord Chief Justice.

## 1. The investigation

### (i) The role of the prosecuting authority and the judge

N-3      (a) Unlike other European countries, a judge in England and Wales does not directly control the investigation process; that is the responsibility of the Investigating Authority, and in turn the Prosecuting Authority and the prosecution advocate. Experience has shown that a prosecution lawyer (who must be of sufficient experience and who will be a member of the team at trial) and the prosecution advocate, if different, should be involved in the investigation as soon as it appears that a heavy fraud trial or other complex criminal trial is likely to ensue. The costs that this early preparation will incur will be saved many times over in the long run.

(b) The judge can and should exert a substantial and beneficial influence by making it clear that, generally speaking, trials should be kept within manageable limits. In most cases 3 months should be the target outer limit, but there will be cases where a duration of 6 months, or in exceptional circumstances, even longer may be inevitable.

### (ii) Interviews

(a) At present many interviews are too long and too unstructured. This has a knock-on effect **N-4** on the length of trials. Interviews should provide an opportunity for suspects to respond to the allegations against them. They should not be an occasion to discuss every document in the case. It should become clear from judicial rulings that interviews of this kind are a waste of resources.

(b) The suspect must be given sufficient information before or at the interview to enable them to meet the questions fairly and answer them honestly; the information is not provided to give him the opportunity to manufacture a false story which fits undisputable facts.

(c) It is often helpful if the principal documents are provided either in advance of the interview or shown as the interview progresses; asking detailed questions about events a considerable period in the past without reference to the documents is often not very helpful.

### (iii) The prosecution and defence teams

(a) **The Prosecution Team**

While instructed it is for the lead advocate for the prosecution to take all necessary deci- **N-5** sions in the presentation and general conduct of the prosecution case. The prosecution lead advocate will be treated by the court as having that responsibility.

However, in relation to policy decisions the lead advocate for the prosecution must not give an indication or undertaking which binds the prosecution without first discussing the issue with Director of the Prosecuting authority or other senior officer.

"Policy" decisions should be understood as referring to non-evidential decisions on: the acceptance of pleas of guilty to lesser counts or groups of counts or available alternatives: offering no evidence on particular counts; consideration of a re-trial; whether to lodge an appeal; certification of a point of law; and the withdrawal of the prosecution as a whole (for further information see the "Farquharson Guidelines" on the role and responsibilities of the prosecution advocate).

(b) **The Defence Team**

In each case, the lead advocate for the defence will be treated by the court as having responsibility to the court for the presentation and general conduct of the defence case.

(c) In each case, a case progression officer must be assigned by the court, prosecution and defence from the time of the first hearing when directions are given (as referred to in paragraph 3(iii)) until the conclusion of the trial.

(d) In each case where there are multiple defendants, the LSC will need to consider carefully the extent and level of representation necessary.

### (iv) Initial consideration of the length of a case

If the prosecutor in charge of the case from the Prosecuting Authority or the lead advocate for the **N-6** prosecution consider that the case as formulated is likely to last more than 8 weeks, the case should be referred in accordance with arrangements made by the Prosecuting Authority to a more senior prosecutor. The senior prosecutor will consider whether it is desirable for the case to be prosecuted in that way or whether some steps might be taken to reduce its likely length, whilst at the same time ensuring that the public interest is served.

Any case likely to last 6 months or more must be referred to the Director of the Prosecuting Authority so that similar considerations can take place.

### (v) Notification of cases likely to last more than 8 weeks

Special arrangements will be put in place for the early notification by the CPS and other Prosecut- **N-7** ing Authorities, to the LSC and to a single designated officer of the Court in each Region (Circuit) of any case which the CPS or other Prosecuting Authority consider likely to last over 8 weeks.

### (vi) Venue

The court will allocate such cases and other complex cases likely to last 4 weeks or more to a **N-8** specific venue suitable for the trial in question, taking into account the convenience to witnesses, the parties, the availability of time at that location, and all other relevant considerations.

## 2. Designation of the trial judge

### *The assignment of a judge*

(a) In any complex case which is expected to last more than four weeks, the trial judge will be assigned under the direction of the Presiding Judges at the earliest possible moment.

(b) Thereafter the assigned judge should manage that case "from cradle to grave"; it is essential that the same judge manages the case from the time of his assignment and that arrangements are made for him to be able to do so. It is recognised that in certain court centres with a large turnover of heavy cases (*e.g.* Southwark) this objective is more difficult to achieve. But in those court centres there are teams of specialist judges, who are more readily able to handle cases which the assigned judge cannot continue with because of unexpected events; even at such courts, there must be no exception to the principle that one judge must handle all the pre-trial hearings until the case is assigned to another judge.

## 3. Case management

### *(i) Objectives*

(a) The number, length and organisation of case management hearings will, of course, depend critically on the circumstances and complexity of the individual case. However, thorough, well-prepared and extended case management hearings will save court time and costs overall.

(b) Effective case management of heavy fraud and other complex criminal cases requires the judge to have a much more detailed grasp of the case than may be necessary for many other Plea and Case Management Hearings (PCMHs). Though it is for the judge in each case to decide how much pre-reading time he needs so that the judge is on top of the case, it is not always a sensible use of judicial time to allocate a series of reading days, during which the judge sits alone in his room, working through numerous boxes of ring binders.

See paragraph 3(iv)(e) below

### *(ii) Fixing the trial date*

Although it is important that the trial date should be fixed as early as possible, this may not always be the right course. There are two principal alternatives:

(a) The trial date should be fixed at the first opportunity—*i.e.* at the first (and usually short) directions hearing referred to in The first hearing for the giving of initial directions. From then on everyone must work to that date. All orders and pre-trial steps should be timetabled to fit in with that date. All advocates and the judge should take note of this date, in the expectation that the trial will proceed on the date determined.

(b) The trial date should not be fixed until the issues have been explored at a full case management hearing (referred to in The first Case Management Hearing), after the advocates on both sides have done some serious work on the case. Only then can the length of the trial be estimated.

Which is apposite must depend on the circumstances of each case, but the earlier it is possible to fix a trial date, by reference to a proper estimate and a timetable set by reference to the trial date, the better.

It is generally to be expected that once a trial is fixed on the basis of the estimate provided, that it will not be **increased** if, and only if, the party seeking to extend the time justifies why the original estimate is no longer appropriate.

### *(iii) The first hearing for the giving of initial directions*

At the first opportunity the assigned judge should hold a short hearing to give initial directions. The directions on this occasion might well include:

(a) That there should be a full case management hearing on, or commencing on, a specified future date by which time the parties will be properly prepared for a meaningful hearing and the defence will have full instructions.

(b) That the prosecution should provide an outline written statement of the prosecution case at least one week in advance of that case management hearing, outlining in simple terms:

(i) the key facts on which it relies;

(ii) the key evidence by which the prosecution seeks to prove the facts.

The statement must be sufficient to permit the judge to understand the case and for the defence to appreciate the basic elements of its case against each defendant. The prosecution may be invited to highlight the key points of the case orally at the case management hearing by way of a short mini-opening. The outline statement should not be considered binding, but it will serve the essential purpose in telling the judge, and everyone else, what the case is really about and identifying the key issues.

(c) That a core reading list and core bundle for the case management hearing should be delivered at least one week in advance.

(d) Preliminary directions about disclosure: see paragraph 4.

*(iv) The first case management hearing*

(a) At the first case management hearing: **N-13**

(1) the prosecution advocate should be given the opportunity to highlight any points from the prosecution outline statement of case (which will have been delivered at least a week in advance;

(2) each defence advocate should be asked to outline the defence.

If the defence advocate is not in a position to say what is in issue and what is not in issue, then the case management hearing can be adjourned for a short and limited time and to a fixed date to enable the advocate to take instructions; such an adjournment should only be necessary in exceptional circumstances, as the defence advocate should be properly instructed by the time of the first case management hearing and in any event is under an obligation to take sufficient instructions to fulfil the obligations contained in sections 33–39 of Criminal Justice Act 2003.

(b) There should then be a real dialogue between the judge and all advocates for the purpose of identifying:

(i) the focus of the prosecution case;

(ii) the common ground;

(iii) the real issues in the case. (Rule 3.2 of the Criminal Procedure Rules.)

(c) The judge will try to generate a spirit of co-operation between the court and the advocates on all sides. The expeditious conduct of the trial and a focussing on the real issues must be in the interests of **all** parties. It cannot be in the interests of any defendant for his good points to become lost in a welter of uncontroversial or irrelevant evidence.

(d) In many fraud cases the primary facts are not seriously disputed. The real issue is what each defendant knew and whether that defendant was dishonest. Once the judge has identified what is in dispute and what is not in dispute, the judge can then discuss with the advocate how the trial should be structured, what can be dealt with by admissions or agreed facts, what uncontroversial matters should be proved by concise oral evidence, what timetabling can be required under Rule 3.10 Criminal Procedure Rules, and other directions.

(e) In particularly heavy fraud or complex cases the judge may possibly consider it necessary to allocate a whole week for a case management hearing. If that week is used wisely, many further weeks of trial time can be saved. In the gaps which will inevitably arise during that week (for example while the advocates are exploring matters raised by the judge) the judge can do a substantial amount of informed reading. The case has come "alive" at this stage. Indeed, in a really heavy fraud case, if the judge fixes one or more case management hearings on this scale, there will be need for fewer formal reading days. Moreover a huge amount can be achieved in the pre-trial stage, if all trial advocates are gathered in the same place, focussing on the case **at the same time**, for several days consecutively.

(f) Requiring the defence to serve proper case statements may enable the court to identify

(i) what is common ground and

(ii) the real issues.

It is therefore important that proper defence case statements be provided as required by the Criminal Procedure Rules; judges will use the powers contained in ss.28–34 of the Criminal Proceedings and Evidence Act 1996 [*sic*] (and the corresponding provisions of the CJA 1987, ss.33 and following of the Criminal Justice Act 2003) and the Criminal Procedure Rules to ensure that realistic defence case statements are provided.

(g) Likewise this objective may be achieved by requiring the prosecution to serve draft admissions by a specified date and by requiring the defence to respond within a specified number of weeks.

*(v) Further case management hearings*

(a) The date of the next case management hearing should be fixed at the conclusion of the **N-14** hearing so that there is no delay in having to fix the date through listing offices, clerks and others.

(b) If one is looking at a trial which threatens to run for months, pre-trial case management on an intensive scale is essential.

*(vi) Consideration of the length of the trial*

**N-15**

(a) Case management on the above lines, the procedure set out in paragraph 1(iv), may still be insufficient to reduce the trial to a manageable length; generally a trial of 3 months should be the target, but there will be cases where a duration of 6 months or, in exceptional circumstances, even longer may be inevitable.

(b) If the trial is not estimated to be within a manageable length, it will be necessary for the judge to consider what steps should be taken to reduce the length of the trial, whilst still ensuring that the prosecution has the opportunity of placing the full criminality before the court.

(c) To assist the judge in this task,

(i) the lead advocate for the prosecution should be asked to explain why the prosecution have rejected a shorter way of proceeding; they may also be asked to divide the case into sections of evidence and explain the scope of each section and the need for each section;

(ii) the lead advocates for the prosecution and for the defence should be prepared to put forward in writing, if requested, ways in which a case estimated to last more than three months can be shortened, including possible severance of counts or defendants, exclusions of sections of the case or of evidence or areas of the case where admissions can be made.

(d) One course the judge may consider is pruning the indictment by omitting certain charges and/or by omitting certain defendants. The judge must not usurp the function of the prosecution in this regard, and he must bear in mind that he will, at the outset, know less about the case than the advocates. The aim is achieve [*sic*] fairness to all parties

(e) Nevertheless, the judge does have two methods of pruning available for use in appropriate circumstances:

(i) persuading the prosecution that it is not worthwhile pursuing certain charges and/or certain defendants;

(ii) severing the indictment. Severance for reasons of case management alone is perfectly proper, although judges should have regard to any representations made by the prosecution that severance would weaken their case. Indeed the judge's hand will be strengthened in this regard by rule 1.1(2)(g) of the Criminal Procedure Rules. However, before using what may be seen as a blunt instrument, the judge should insist on seeing full defence statements of all affected defendants. Severance may be unfair to the prosecution if, for example, there is a cut-throat defence in prospect. For example, the defence of the principal defendant may be that the defendant relied on the advice of his accountant or solicitor that what was happening was acceptable. The defence of the professional may be that he gave no such advice. Against that background, it might be unfair to the prosecution to order separate trials of the two defendants.

*(vii) The exercise of the powers*

**N-16**

(a) The Criminal Procedure Rules require the court to take a more active part in case management. These are salutary provisions which should bring to an end interminable criminal trials of the kind which the Court of Appeal criticised in *Jisl* [2004] EWCA 696 at [113]-[121].

(b) Nevertheless these salutary provisions do not have to be used on every occasion. Where the advocates have done their job properly, by narrowing the issues, pruning the evidence and so forth, it may be quite inappropriate for the judge to "weigh in" and start cutting out more evidence or more charges of his own volition. It behoves the judge to make a careful assessment of the degree of judicial intervention which is warranted in each case.

(c) The note of caution in the previous paragraph is supported by certain experience which has been gained of the Civil Procedure Rules (on which the Criminal Procedure Rules are based). The CPR contain valuable and efficacious provisions for case management by the judge on his own initiative which have led to huge savings of court time and costs. Surveys by the Law Society have shown that the CPR have been generally welcomed by court users and the profession, but there have been reported to have been isolated instances in which the parties to civil litigation have faithfully complied with both the letter and the spirit of the CPR, and have then been aggrieved by what was perceived to be unnecessary intermeddling by the court.

### (viii) Expert evidence

(a) Early identification of the subject matter of expert evidence to be adduced by the prosecution and the defence should be made as early as possible, preferably at the directions hearing. **N-17**

(b) Following the exchange of expert evidence, any areas of disagreement should be identified and a direction should generally be made requiring the experts to meet and prepare, after discussion, a joint statement identifying points of agreement and contention and areas where the prosecution is put to proof on matters of which a positive case to the contrary is not advanced by the defence. After the statement has been prepared it should be served on the court, the prosecution and the defence. In some cases, it might be appropriate to provide that to the jury.

### (ix) Surveillance evidence

(a) Where a prosecution is based upon many months' observation or surveillance evidence and it appears that it is capable of effective presentation based on a shorter period, the advocate should be required to justify the evidence of such observations before it is permitted to be adduced, either substantially or in its entirety. **N-18**

(b) Schedules should be provided to cover as much of the evidence as possible and admissions sought.

### 4. Disclosure

[*Replaced by the 2013 judicial protocol on disclosure: see* post, *N-52* et seq.] **N-19**

### 5. Abuse of process

(i) Applications to stay or dismiss for abuse of process have become a normal feature of heavy and complex cases. Such applications may be based upon delay and the health of defendants. **N-20**

(ii) Applications in relation to absent special circumstances [*sic*] tend to be unsuccessful and not to be pursued on appeal. For this reason there is comparatively little Court of Appeal guidance: but see: *Harris and Howells* [2003] EWCA Crim 486. It should be noted that abuse of process is not there to discipline the prosecution or the police.

(iii) The arguments on both sides must be reduced to writing. Oral evidence is seldom relevant.

(iv) The judge should direct full written submissions (rather than "skeleton arguments") on any abuse application in accordance with a timetable set by him; these should identify any element of prejudice the defendant is alleged to have suffered.

(v) The judge should normally aim to conclude the hearing within an absolute maximum limit of one day, if necessary in accordance with a timetable. The parties should therefore prepare their papers on this basis and not expect the judge to allow the oral hearing to be anything more than an occasion to highlight concisely their arguments and answer any questions the court may have of them; applications will not be allowed drag on.

### 6. The trial

#### (i) The particular hazard of heavy fraud trials

A heavy fraud or other complex trial has the potential to lose direction and focus. This is a disaster for three reasons: **N-21**

(a) the jury will lose track of the evidence, thereby prejudicing both prosecution and defence;

(b) the burden on the defendants, the judge and indeed all involved will become intolerable;

(c) scarce public resources are wasted. Other prosecutions are delayed or—worse—may never happen. Fraud which is detected but not prosecuted (for resource reasons) undermines confidence.

#### (ii) Judicial mastery of the case

(a) It is necessary for the judge to exercise firm control over the conduct of the trial at all stages. **N-22**

(b) In order to do this the judge must read the witness statements and the documents, so that the judge can discuss case management issues with the advocates on—almost—an equal footing.

(c) To this end, the judge should not set aside weeks or even days for pre-reading (see paragraph 3(i)(b)). Hopefully the judge will have gained a good grasp of the evidence during the case management hearings. Nevertheless, realistic reading time must be provided for the judge in advance of trial.

(d) The role of the judge in a heavy fraud or other complex criminal trial is different from his/ her role in a "conventional" criminal trial. So far as possible, the judge should be freed from other duties and burdens, so that he/she can give the high degree of commitment which a heavy fraud trial requires. This will pay dividends in terms of saving weeks or months of court time.

*(iii) The order of the evidence*

**N-23**

(a) By the outset of the trial at the latest (and in most cases very much earlier) the judge must be provided with a schedule, showing the sequence of prosecution (and in an appropriate case defence) witnesses and the dates upon which they are expected to be called. This can only be prepared by discussion between prosecution and defence which the judge should expect, and say he/she expects, to take place: See: Criminal Procedure Rule 3.10. The schedule should, in so far as it relates to prosecution witnesses, be developed in consultation with the witnesses, via the witness care units, and with consideration given to their personal needs. Copies of the schedule should be provided for the Witness Service.

(b) The schedule should be kept under review by the trial judge and by the parties. If a case is running behind or ahead of schedule, each witness affected must be advised by the party who is calling that witness at the earliest opportunity.

(c) If an excessive amount of time is allowed for any witness, the judge can ask why. The judge may probe with the advocates whether the time envisaged for the evidence-in-chief or cross-examination (as the case may be) of a particular witness is really necessary.

*(iv) Case management sessions*

**N-24**

(a) The order of the evidence may have legitimately to be departed from. It will, however, be a useful tool for monitoring the progress of the case. There should be periodic case management sessions, during which the judge engages the advocates upon a stock-taking exercise: asking, amongst other questions, "where are we going?" and "what is the relevance of the next three witnesses?". This will be a valuable means of keeping the case on track. Rule 3.10 of the Criminal Procedure Rules will again assist the judge.

(b) The judge may wish to consider issuing the occasional use of "case management notes" to the advocates, in order to set out the judge's tentative views on where the trial may be going off track, which areas of future evidence are relevant and which may have become irrelevant (*e.g.* because of concessions, admissions in cross-examination and so forth). Such notes from the judge plus written responses from the advocates can, cautiously used, provide a valuable focus for debate during the periodic case management reviews held during the course of the trial.

*(v) Controlling prolix cross-examination*

**N-25**

(a) Setting **rigid** time limits in advance for cross-examination is rarely appropriate—as experience has shown in civil cases; but a timetable is essential so that the judge can exercise control and so that there is a clear target to aim at for the completion of the evidence of each witness. Moreover the judge can and should indicate when cross-examination is irrelevant, unnecessary or time wasting. The judge may limit the time for further cross-examination of a particular witness.

*(vi) Electronic presentation of evidence*

**N-26**

(a) Electronic presentation of evidence (EPE) has the potential to save huge amounts of time in fraud and other complex criminal trials and should be used more widely.

(b) HMCS is providing facilities for the easier use of EPE with a standard audio visual facility. Effectively managed, the savings in court time achieved by EPE more than justify the cost.

(c) There should still be a core bundle of those documents to which frequent reference will be made during the trial. The jury may wish to mark that bundle or to refer back to particular pages as the evidence progresses. EPE can be used for presenting all documents not contained in the core bundle.

(d) Greater use of other modern forms of graphical presentations should be made wherever possible.

### (vii) *Use of interviews*

The judge should consider extensive editing of self serving interviews, even when the defence **N-27** want the jury to hear them in their entirety; such interviews are not evidence of the truth of their contents but merely of the defendant's reaction to the allegation.

### (viii) *Jury management*

(a) The jury should be informed as early as possible in the case as to what the issues are in a **N-28** manner directed by the Judge.

(b) The jury must be regularly updated as to the trial timetable and the progress of the trial, subject to warnings as to the predictability of the trial process.

(c) Legal argument should be heard at times that causes the least inconvenience to jurors.

(d) It is useful to consider with the advocates whether written directions should be given to the jury and, if so, in what form.

### (ix) *Maxwell hours*

(a) Maxwell hours should only be permitted after careful consideration and consultation with **N-29** the Presiding Judge.

(b) Considerations in favour include:

   (i) legal argument can be accommodated without disturbing the jury;

   (ii) there is a better chance of a representative jury;

   (iii) time is made available to the judge, advocates and experts to do useful work in the afternoons

(c) Considerations against include:

   (i) the lengthening of trials and the consequent waste of court time;

   (ii) the desirability of making full use of the jury once they have arrived at court;

   (iii) shorter trials tend to diminish the need for special provisions *e.g.* there are fewer difficulties in empanelling more representative juries;

   (iv) they are unavailable if any defendant is in custody.

(d) It may often be the case that a maximum of one day of Maxwell hours a week is sufficient; if so, it should be timetabled in advance to enable all submissions by advocates, supported by skeleton arguments served in advance, to be dealt with in the period after 1:30 pm on that day.

### (x) *Livenote*

If Livenote is used, it is important that all users continue to take a note of the evidence, otherwise **N-30** considerable time is wasted in detailed reading of the entire daily transcript.

### 7. Other issues

#### (i) *Defence representation and defence costs*

(a) Applications for change in representation in complex trials need special consideration; **N-31** the ruling of HH Judge Wakerley QC (as he then was) in *Asghar Ali* has been circulated by the JSB.

(b) Problems have arisen when the Legal Services Commission have declined to allow advocates or solicitors to do certain work; on occasions the matter has been raised with the judge managing or trying the case.

(c) The Legal Services Commission has provided guidance to judges on how they can obtain information from the LSC as to the reasons for their decisions; further information in relation to this can be obtained from *Nigel Field, Head of the Complex Crime Unit, Legal Services Commission, 29-37 Red Lion Street, London, WC1R 4PP.*

#### (ii) *Assistance to the judge*

Experience has shown that in some very heavy cases, the judge's burden can be substantially offset **N-32** with the provision of a judicial assistant or other support and assistance.

## B. Management of Terrorism Cases

A protocol issued by Sir Igor Judge P.

January 30, 2007

### Terrorism cases

1. This protocol applies to "terrorism cases". For the purposes of this protocol a case is a "terrorism case" where:

   (a) one of the offences charged against any of the defendants is indictable only and it is alleged by the prosecution that there is evidence that it took place during an act of terrorism or for the purposes of terrorism as defined in section 1 of the Terrorist Act 2000 [*sic*]; this may include, but is not limited to:

      i. murder;

      ii. manslaughter;

      iii. an offence under section 18 of the Offences against the Person Act 1861 (wounding with intent);

      iv. an offence under section 23 or 24 of that Act (administering poison *etc*);

      v. an offence under section 28 or 29 of that Act (explosives);

      vi. an offence under section 2, 3 or 5 of the Explosive Substances Act 1883 (causing explosions);

      vii. an offence under section 1(2) of the Criminal Damage Act 1971 (endangering life by damaging property);

      viii. an offence under section 1 of the Biological Weapons Act 1974 (biological weapons);

      ix. an offence under section 2 of the Chemical Weapons Act 1996 (chemical weapons);

      x. an offence under section 56 of the Terrorism Act 2000 (directing a terrorist organisation);

      xi. an offence under section 59 of that Act (inciting terrorism overseas);

      xii. offences under (v), (vii) and (viii) above given jurisdiction by virtue of section 62 of that Act (terrorist bombing overseas);

      xiii. an offence under section 5 of the Terrorism Act 2006 (preparation of terrorism acts);

   (b) one of the offences so charged includes an allegation by the prosecution of serious fraud that took place during an act of terrorism or for the purposes of terrorism as defined in section 1 of the Terrorist Act 2000 [*sic*] and meets the test to be transferred to the Crown Court under section 4 of the Criminal Justice Act 1987;

   (c) one of the offences charged is indictable only includes [*sic*] an allegation that a defendant conspired, incited or attempted to commit an offence under sub-paragraphs (1)(a) or (b) above;

   (d) it is a case (which can be indictable only or triable either way) that a judge of the terrorism cases list (see paragraph 2(a) below) considers should be a terrorism case. In deciding whether a case not covered by sub-paragraphs (1)(a), (b) or (c) above should be a terrorism case, the judge may hear representations from the Crown Prosecution Service.

### The terrorism cases list

2. (a) All terrorism cases, wherever they originate in England and Wales, will be managed in a list known as the "terrorism cases list" by the Presiding Judges of the South Eastern Circuit and such other judges of the High Court as are nominated by the President of the Queen's Bench Division.

   (b) Such cases will be tried, unless otherwise directed by the President of the Queen's Bench Division, by a judge of the High Court as nominated by the President of the Queen's Bench Division.

3. The judges managing the terrorism cases referred to in paragraph 2 will be supported by the London and South Eastern Regional Co-ordinator's Office (the "Regional Co-ordinator's Office"). An official of that office or nominated by that office will act as the case progression officer for cases in that list for the purposes of part 3.4 of the Criminal Procedure Rules.

### Procedure after charge

4. Immediately after a person has been charged in a terrorism case, anywhere in England and Wales, a representative of the Crown Prosecution Service will notify the person on the 24 hour rota for special jurisdiction matters at Westminster Magistrates' Court of the following information:

(a) the full name of each defendant and the name of his solicitor of [*sic*] other legal representative, if known;

(b) the charges laid;

(c) the name and contact details of the crown prosecutor with responsibility for the case, if known;

(d) confirmation that the case is a terrorism case.

5. The person on the 24-hour rota will then ensure that all terrorism cases wherever they are **N-38** charged in England and Wales are listed before the Chief Magistrate or other District Judge designated under the Terrorism Act 2000. Unless the Chief Magistrate or other District Judge designated under the Terrorism Act 2000 directs otherwise the first appearance of all defendants accused of terrorism offences will be listed at Westminster Magistrates' Court.

6. In order to comply with section 46 of the Police and Criminal Evidence Act 1984, if a defendant **N-39** in a terrorism case is charged at a police station within the local justice area in which Westminster Magistrates' Court is situated the defendant must be brought before Westminster Magistrates' Court as soon as is practicable and in any event not later than the first sitting after he is charged with the offence. If a defendant in a terrorism case is charged in a police station outside the local justice area in which Westminster Magistrates' Court is situated, unless the Chief Magistrate or other designated judge directs otherwise, the defendant must be removed to that area as soon as is practicable. He must then be brought before Westminster Magistrates' Court as soon as is practicable after his arrival in the area and in any event not later than the first sitting of Westminster Magistrates' Court after his arrival in that area.

7. As soon as is practicable after charge a representative of the Crown Prosecution Service will also **N-40** provide the Regional Listing Co-ordinator's Office with the information listed in paragraph 4 above.

8. The Regional Co-ordinator's Office will then ensure that the Chief Magistrate and the Legal **N-41** Services Commission have the same information.

### Cases to be sent to the Crown Court under section 51 of the Crime and Disorder Act 1998

9. A preliminary hearing should normally be ordered by the magistrates' court in a terrorism case. **N-42** The court should ordinarily direct that the preliminary hearing should take place about 14 days after charge.

10. The sending magistrates' court should contact the Regional Listing Co-ordinator's Office who **N-43** will be responsible for notifying the magistrates' court as to the relevant Crown Court to which to send the case.

11. In all terrorism cases, the magistrates' court case progression form for cases sent to the Crown **N-44** Court under section 51 of the Crime and Disorder Act 1998 should not be used. Instead of the automatic directions set out in that form, the magistrates' court shall make the following directions to facilitate the preliminary hearing at the Crown Court:

(a) three days prior to the preliminary hearing in the terrorism cases list, the prosecution must serve upon each defendant and the Regional Listing co-ordinator:

  i. a preliminary summary of the case;

  ii. the names of those who are to represent the prosecution, if known;

  iii. an estimate of the length of the trial;

  iv. a suggested provisional timetable which should generally include:

   • the general nature of further enquiries being made by the prosecution;

   • the time needed for the completion of such enquiries;

   • the time required by the prosecution to review the case;

   • a timetable for the phased service of the evidence;

   • the time for the provision by the Attorney General for his consent if necessary;

   • the time for service of the detailed defence case statement;

   • the date for the case management hearing;

   • estimated trial date;

  v. a preliminary statement of the possible disclosure issues setting out the nature and scale of the problem including the amount of unused material, the manner in which the prosecution seeks to deal with these matters and a suggested timetable for discharging their statutory duty;

  vi. any information relating to bail and custody time limits;

(b) one day prior to the preliminary hearing in the terrorist cases list, each defendant must serve in writing on the Regional Listing Co-ordinator and the prosecution:

  i. the proposed representation;

ii. observations on the timetable;

iii. an indication of plea and the general nature of the defence.

### Cases to be transferred to the Crown Court under section 4(1) of the Criminal Justice Act 1987

**N-45**    13. If a terrorism case is to be transferred to the Crown Court the magistrates' court should proceed as if it is being sent to the Crown Court, as in paragraphs 10-12 above.

**N-46**    14. When a terrorism case is so sent or transferred the case will go into the terrorism list and be managed by a judge as described in paragraph 2 above.

### The preliminary hearing at the Crown Court

**N-47**    15. At the preliminary hearing, the judge will determine whether the case is one to remain in the terrorism list and if so give directions setting the provisional timetable.

**N-48**    16. The Legal Services Commission must attend the hearing by an authorised officer to assist the court.

### Use of video link

**N-49**    17. Unless a judge otherwise directs, all Crown Court hearings prior to the trial will be conducted by video link for all defendants in custody.

### Security

**N-50**    18. The police service and the prison service will provide the Regional Listing Co-ordinator's office with an initial joint assessment of the security risks associated with any court appearance by the defendants within 14 days of charge. Any subsequent changes in circumstances or the assessment of risk which have the potential to impact upon the choice of trial venue will be notified to the Regional Listing Co-ordinator's Office immediately.

**N-51**    The following "protocol" was published on February 20, 2006. The protocol appeared to have the authority of the Court of Appeal (it had the royal coat of arms with the words "Court of Appeal" underneath at the top of the first page), but it was unsigned, and a reading of the text of the protocol itself gives no indication whatsoever as to its authorship. An "outline note" (similarly headed) recited that it was drafted by a team led by Fulford and Openshaw JJ. (the latter's name being misspelt), and "which included representatives from the CPS, SFO and CEPO" (presumably this should have read the Revenue and Customs Prosecutions Office). The note was itself unsigned, but it concluded by referring the reader to the "Judicial Communications Office" for further information. The judicial communications office is part of the Judicial Office for England and Wales. The head of this office (described in *The Times* (October 18, 2005) as a "new mini-ministry") is a civil servant. The outline note had all the appearances of a Whitehall briefing note, and would appear to have been the product of the judicial communications office itself. The note did nothing to answer the question as to the status of the protocol. On the contrary, it left it even more uncertain. First, the Court of Appeal did not appear to have contributed to it in any way. It is true that the two named puisne judges both regularly sat in the Court of Appeal, but they were not (and are not) judges of the Court of Appeal. Secondly, the note refers to the team having "included" representatives of various organisations. Who else was included? And, if it was only those cited, what authority does a protocol drafted by two judges and the representatives of three prosecution agencies have? According to a "news release" issued by the judicial communications office on February 20, 2006, the protocol was "drawn up" by "the judiciary", which is then elaborated as the two named judges "and a working group representative of all involved in the criminal justice system". It does not go on to reveal who was on the working group to represent those in independent practice or those who have a defence practice.

For the Court of Appeal's endorsement of the protocol, see *R. v. K. (Note)* (§ 12-45 in the main work).

As to the status of protocols generally, see the preface to the 2007 edition of this work.

### C. DISCLOSURE OF UNUSED MATERIAL IN CRIMINAL CASES

#### Foreword

**N-52**    *[Identical to the foreword to the Attorney-General's guidelines: ante, § A-242a.]*

## Introduction

This protocol is prescribed for use by CPD IV Disclosure 22A: Disclosure of Unused Material. It is **N-53**
applicable in all the criminal courts of England and Wales, including the Crown Court, the Court
Martial[1] and the magistrates' courts. It replaces the previous judicial document 'Disclosure: a
Protocol for the Control and Management of Unused Material in the Crown Court'[2] and it also
replaces section 4 'Disclosure' of the Lord Chief Justice's Protocol on the Control and Management
of Heavy Fraud and Other Complex Criminal Cases, dated 22 March 2005.[3]

This protocol is intended to provide a central source of guidance for the judiciary, although
that produced by the Attorney General also requires attention.

In summary, this judicial protocol sets out the principles to be applied to, and the importance
of, disclosure; the expectations of the court and its role in disclosure, in particular in relation to
case management; and the consequences if there is a failure by the prosecution or defence to
comply with their obligations.

Readers should note that a review of disclosure in the magistrates' courts is currently being
undertaken by H.H.J. Kinch Q.C. and the Chief Magistrate, on behalf of Lord Justice Gross,
the Senior Presiding Judge. Amendments may therefore be made following the recommendations of that review, and in accordance with other forthcoming changes to the criminal justice
system.

### The importance of disclosure for fair trials

1. Disclosure remains one of the most important – as well as one of the most misunderstood and **N-54**
abused – of the procedures relating to criminal trials. Lord Justice Gross' review has reemphasised
the need for all those involved to understand the statutory requirements and to undertake their roles
with rigour, in a timely manner.

2. The House of Lords stated in *R. v. H.* [2004] UKHL 3; [2004] 2 A.C. 134; [2004] 2 Cr.App.R.
10:

> "Fairness ordinarily requires that any material held by the prosecution which weakens its case or
> strengthens that of the defendant, if not relied on as part of its formal case against the defendant,
> should be disclosed to the defence. Bitter experience has shown that miscarriages of justice may
> occur where such material is withheld from disclosure. The golden rule is that full disclosure of
> such material should be made" ([2004] 2 A.C. 134, at 147).

The Criminal Cases Review Commission has recently noted that failure to disclose material to the
defence to which they were entitled remains the biggest single cause of miscarriages of justice.

3. However, it is also essential that the trial process is not overburdened or diverted by erroneous
and inappropriate disclosure of unused prosecution material or by misconceived applications.
Although the drafters of the Criminal Procedure and Investigations Act 1996 ('CPIA 1996') cannot
have anticipated the vast increase in the amount of electronic material that has been generated in
recent years, nevertheless the principles of that Act still hold true. Applications by the parties or decisions by judges based on misconceptions of the law or a general laxity of approach (however well-
intentioned) which result in an improper application of the disclosure regime have, time and again,
proved unnecessarily costly and have obstructed justice. As Lord Justice Gross noted, the burden of
disclosure must not be allowed to render the prosecution of cases impracticable.

4. The overarching principle is that unused prosecution material will fall to be disclosed if, and
only if, it satisfies the test for disclosure applicable to the proceedings in question, subject to any overriding public interest considerations. The test for disclosure will depend on the date the criminal
investigation in question commenced, as this will determine whether the common law disclosure
regime applies, or either of the two disclosure regimes under the CPIA 1996.

5. The test for disclosure under section 3 of the CPIA 1996 as amended will be applicable in
nearly every case and all those involved in the process will need to be familiar with it. Material fulfils
the test if – but only if – it "might reasonably be considered capable of undermining the case for the
prosecution ... or of assisting the case for the accused."

---

[1] The timetables given here may vary in the Court Martial and reference should be made to the Criminal Procedure
and Investigations Act 1996 (Application to the Armed Forces) Order 2009 and to any practice note issued by the
Judge Advocate General.
[2] The previous judicial protocol was endorsed by the Court of Appeal in *R. v. K.* [2006] EWCA Crim 724; [2006] 2 All
ER 552 (Note).
[3] This protocol also replaces the Protocol for the Provision of Advance Information, Prosecution Evidence and
Disclosure of Unused Material in the Magistrates' Courts, dated 12 May 2006, which was adopted as part of the Stop
Delaying Justice initiative.

6. The disclosure process must be led by the prosecution so as to trigger comprehensive defence engagement, supported by robust judicial case management. Active participation by the court in the disclosure process is a critical means of ensuring that delays and adjournments are avoided, given failures by the parties to comply with their obligations may disrupt and (in some cases) frustrate the course of justice.

### Disclosure of unused material in criminal cases

7. The court should keep the timetable for prosecution and defence disclosure under review from the first hearing. Judges should as a matter of course ask the parties to identify the issues in the case, and invite the parties to indicate whether further disclosure is sought, and on what topics. For example, it is not enough for the judge to rely on the content of the PCMH form. Proper completion of the disclosure process is a vital part of case preparation, and it may well affect the progress of the case. The court will expect disclosure to have been considered from the outset; the prosecution and defence advocates need to be aware of any potential problems and substantive difficulties should be explained to the judge; and the parties should propose a sensible timetable. Realism is preferable to optimistic but unachievable deadlines which may dislocate the court schedule and imperil the date of trial. It follows that judges should not impose deadlines for service of the case papers or disclosure until they are confident that the prosecution advocate has taken instructions from the individuals who are best placed to evaluate the work to be undertaken.

8. The advocates – both prosecution and defence – must be kept fully informed throughout the course of the proceedings as to any difficulties which may prevent them from complying with their disclosure obligations. When problems arise or come to light after directions have been given, the advocates should notify the court and the other party (or parties) immediately rather than waiting until the date set by the court for the service of the material is imminent or has passed, and they must provide the court with a suggested timetable in order to resolve the problem. The progress of the disclosure process should be reviewed at every hearing. There remains no basis in practice or law for counsel to counsel disclosure.

9. If there is a preliminary hearing the judge should seize the opportunity to impose an early timetable for disclosure and to identify any likely problems including as regards third party material and material that will require an application to the Family Court. In an appropriate case the court should consider holding a joint criminal/care directions hearing. See "Material held by Third Parties", from paragraph 44 below.

10. For the PCMH to be effective, the defence must have a proper opportunity to review the case papers and consider initial disclosure, with a view to preparing a properly completed defence statement which will inform the judge's conduct of the PCMH, and inform the prosecution of the matters required by sections 5, 6A and 6C of the CPIA. As the Court of Appeal noted in *R. v. Newell* [2012] EWCA Crim. 650; [2012] 2 Cr.App.R. 10, "a typed defence statement must be provided before the PCMH. If there is no defence statement by the time of the PCMH, then a judge will usually require the trial advocate to see that such a statement is provided and not proceed with the PCMH until that is done. In the ordinary case the trial advocate will be required to do that at the court and the PCMH resumed later in the day to avoid delay". There may be some instances when there will be a well-founded defence application to extend the 28-day time limit for serving a proper defence statement. In a proper case (but never routinely), it may be appropriate to put the PCMH back by a week or more, to enable an appropriate defence statement to be filed.

11. The defence statement can be admitted into evidence under section 6E(4) of the CPIA 1996. However, information included on the PCMH form (which is primarily an administrative form) will not usually be admitted in evidence when the defence advocate has complied with the letter and the spirit of the Criminal Procedure Rules.[4] Introducing the PCMH form (or part of it) during the trial is likely to be an exceptional event. The status of the trial preparation form in the magistrates' court is somewhat different, as discussed below.

12. The court should not extend time lightly or as a matter of course. If an extension is sought, it ought to be accompanied by an appropriate explanation. For instance, it is not sufficient for the prosecutor merely to say that the investigator has delivered the papers late: the underlying reasons are to be provided to the court. The same applies if the defence statement is delayed. Whichever party is at fault, realistic proposals for service are to be set out.

13. Judges should not allow the prosecution to avoid their statutory responsibility for reviewing the unused material by the expedient of permitting the defence to have access to (or providing the defence with copies of) the material listed in the schedules of non-sensitive unused prosecution material irrespective of whether it satisfies, wholly or in part, the relevant test for disclosure. Additionally, it is for the prosecutor to decide on the manner of disclosure, and it does not have to mirror the

---

[4] *R. v. Newell* [2012] EWCA Crim. 650; [2012] 2 Cr.App.R. 10.

form in which the information was originally recorded. Rose L.J. gave guidance on case management issues in this context in *R. v. CPS (Interlocutory Application under sections 35/36 CPIA)* [2005] EWCA Crim. 2342. Allowing the defence to inspect items that fulfil the disclosure test is also a valid means of providing disclosure.

14. The larger and more complex the case, the more important it is for the prosecution to adhere to the overarching principle and ensure that sufficient prosecution attention and resources are allocated to the task. Handing the defendant the "keys to the warehouse" has been the cause of many gross abuses in the past, resulting in considerable expenditure by the defence without any material benefit to the course of justice. The circumstances relating to large and complex cases are outlined below.

15. The court will require the defence to engage and assist in the early identification of the real issues in the case and, particularly in the larger and more complex cases, to contribute to the search terms to be used for, and the parameters of, the review of any electronically held material (which can be very considerable). Any defence criticisms of the prosecution approach to disclosure should be timely and reasoned; there is no place for disclosure "ambushes" or for late or uninformative defence statements. Admissions should be used so far as possible to narrow the real issues in dispute.

16. A constructive approach to disclosure is a necessary part of professional best practice, for the defence and prosecution. This does not undermine the defendant's legitimate interests, it accords with his or her obligations under the rules and it ensures that all the relevant material is provided. Delays and failures by the prosecution and the defence are equally damaging to a timely, fair and efficient trial, and judges should be vigilant in preventing and addressing abuses. Accordingly, whenever there are potential failings by either the defence or the prosecution, judges, in exercising appropriate oversight of disclosure, should carefully investigate the suggested default and give timely directions.

17. In the Crown Court, the defence statement is to be served within 28 days of the date when the prosecution complies with its duty of initial disclosure (or purports to do so) and whenever section 5(5) of the CPIA applies to the proceedings, and the defence statement must comply with section 6A of the CPIA. Service of the defence statement is a most important stage in the disclosure process, and timely service is necessary to facilitate proper consideration of the disclosure issues well in advance of the trial date. Judges expect a defence statement to contain a clear and detailed exposition of the issues of fact and law. Defence statements that merely rehearse the suggestion that the defendant is innocent do not comply with the requirements of the CPIA.

18. The prosecutor should consider the defence statement carefully and promptly provide a copy to the disclosure officer, to assist the prosecution in its continuing disclosure obligations. The court expects the Crown to identify any suggested deficiencies in the defence statement, and to draw these to the attention of the defence and the court; in particular in large and complex cases, it will assist the court if this is in writing. Although the prosecution's ability to request, and the court's jurisdiction to give, an adverse inference direction under section 11 of CPIA is not contingent on the prosecution having earlier identified any suggested deficiencies, nevertheless the prosecutor must provide a timely written explanation of its position.

19. Judges should examine the defence statement with care to ensure that it complies with the formalities required by the CPIA. As stated in *R. v. H.* (*supra*) (para. 35):

> "If material does not weaken the prosecution case or strengthen that of the defendant, there is no requirement to disclose it. For this purpose the parties' respective cases should not be restrictively analysed. But they must be carefully analysed, to ascertain the specific facts the prosecution seek to establish and the specific grounds on which the charges are resisted. The trial process is not well served if the defence are permitted to make general and unspecified allegations and then seek far-reaching disclosure in the hope that material may turn up to make them good. Neutral material or material damaging to the defendant need not be disclosed and should not be brought to the attention of the court."

20. If no defence statement – or an inadequate defence statement – is served within the relevant time limits, the judge should investigate the position. At every PCMH where there is no defence statement, including those where an extension has been given, or the time for filing has not yet expired, the defence should be warned in appropriate terms that pursuant to section 6E(2) of the CPIA an adverse inference may be drawn during the trial, and this result is likely if there is no justification for the deficiency. The fact that a warning has been given should be noted.

21. An adverse inference may be drawn under section 11 of the CPIA if the accused fails to discharge his or her disclosure obligations. Whenever the amended CPIA regime applies, the prosecution may comment on any failure in defence disclosure (except where the failure relates to a point of law) without leave of the court, but counsel should use a measure of judgment as to whether

it is wise to embark on cross-examination about such a failure.[5] If the accused is cross-examined about discrepancies between his evidence and his defence statement, or if adverse comment is made, the judge must give appropriate guidance to the jury.[6]

22. In order to secure a fair trial, it is vital that the prosecution is mindful of its continuing duty of disclosure. Once the defence statement has been received, the Crown must review disclosure in the light of the issues identified in the defence statement. In cases of complexity, the following steps are then likely to be necessary:

    i. service by the prosecution of any further material due to the defence following receipt of the defence statement;

    ii. any defence request to the prosecution for service of additional specific items; as discussed below, these requests must be justified by reference to the defence statement and they should be submitted on the section 8 form;

    iii. prosecution response to the defence request;

    iv. if the defence considers that disclosable items are still outstanding, a section 8 application should be made using the appropriate form.

23. It follows that all requests by the defence to the prosecution for disclosure should be made on the section 8 application form, even if no hearing is sought in the first instance. Discussion and co-operation between the parties outside of court is encouraged in order to ensure that the court is only asked to issue a ruling when strictly necessary. However, use of the section 8 form will ensure that focussed requests are clearly set out in one place.

24. The judge should set a date as part of the timetabling exercise by which any application under section 8 is to be made, if this appears to be a likely eventuality.

25. The court will require the section 8 application to be served on the prosecution well in advance of the hearing – indeed, prior to requesting the hearing – to enable the Crown to identify and serve any items that meet the test for disclosure.

26. Service of a defence statement is an essential precondition for an application under section 8, and applications should not be heard or directions for disclosure issued in the absence of a properly completed statement (see Part 22 of the Criminal Procedure Rules). In particular, blanket orders in this context are inconsistent with the statutory framework for disclosure laid down by the CPIA and the decision of the House of Lords in *R. v. H.* (*supra*). It follows that defence requests for disclosure of particular pieces of unused prosecution material which are not referable to any issue in the case identified in the defence statement should be rejected.

27. Judges must ensure that defendants are not prejudiced on account of the failures of their lawyers, and, when necessary, the professions should be reminded that if justice is to be done, and if disclosure is to be dealt with fairly in accordance with the law, a full and careful defence statement and a reasoned approach to section 8 applications are essential. In exploring the adequacy of the defence statement, a judge should always ask what the issues are and upon what matters of fact the defendant intends to rely[7] and on what matters of fact the defendant takes issue.

### Listing

N-56

28. Sufficient time is necessary for the judge properly to undertake the PCMH, and this is a paramount consideration when listing cases. Unless the court is able to sit early, judges who are part heard on trials are probably not best placed to conduct PCMHs.

29. Cases that raise particularly difficult issues of disclosure should be referred to the resident judge for directions (unless a trial judge has been allocated) and, for trials of real complexity, the trial judge should be identified at an early stage, prior to the PCMH if possible. Listing officers, working in consultation with the resident judge and, if allocated, the trial judge, should ensure that sufficient time is allowed for judges to prepare and deal with prosecution and defence applications relating to disclosure, particularly in the more complex cases.

### Magistrates' courts (including the youth court)

N-57

30. The principles relating to disclosure apply equally in the magistrates' courts. It follows that whilst disclosure of unused material in compliance with the statutory test is undoubtedly essential in order to achieve justice, it is critical that summary trials are not delayed or made over-complicated by misconceived applications for, or inappropriate disclosure of, prosecution material.

31. Magistrates will rely on their legal advisers for guidance, and the latter should draw the attention of the parties and the court to the statutory provisions and the applicable case law. Cases raising

---

[5] *R. v. Essa* [2009] EWCA Crim. 43, para. 22.
[6] *R. v. Hanyes* [2011] EWCA Crim. 3281.
[7] *R. v. Rochford* [2010] EWCA Crim. 1928; [2011] 1 Cr.App.R. 11.

disclosure issues of particular complexity should be referred to a District Judge (Magistrates' Courts), if available.

32. Although service of a defence statement is voluntary for summary trials (s.6 CPIA), the defendant cannot make an application for specific disclosure under section 8 CPIA, and the court cannot make any orders in this regard, unless a proper defence statement has been provided. It follows that although providing a defence statement is not mandatory, it remains a critical stage in the disclosure process. If disclosure issues are to be raised by the defence, a defence statement must be served well in advance of the trial date. Any section 8 application must be made in strict compliance with the rules.

33. The case-management forms used in the magistrates' courts fulfil some of the functions of a defence statement, and the prosecution must take into account the information provided as to the defence case when conducting its on-going review of unused material. As the Court of Appeal noted in *R. v. Newell* (*supra*), admissions can be made in the trial preparation form and the defence is able to identify the matters that are not in issue. Admissions made in these circumstances may be admissible during the trial. However, other information on the form that does not come within the section relating to admissions should be treated in the same way as the contents of a PCMH form in the Crown Court and it should not generally be introduced as part of the evidence at trial. However, the contents of the trial preparation form do not replace the need to serve a defence statement if the defendant seeks to apply for disclosure under section 8 CPIA.

34. The standard directions require that any defence statement is to be served within 14 days of the date upon which the prosecution has complied with, or purported to comply with, the duty to provide initial disclosure. There may be some instances when there will be a wellfounded defence application to extend the 14-day time limit for serving the defence statement. These applications must be made in accordance with the Criminal Procedure Rules, in writing and before the time limit expires.

35. Although CCTV footage frequently causes difficulties, it is to be treated as any other category of unused material and it should only be disclosed if the material meets the appropriate test for disclosure under the CPIA. The defence should either be provided with copies of the sections of the CCTV or afforded an opportunity to view them. If the prosecution refuses to disclose CCTV material that the defence considers to be discloseable, the courts should not make standard or general directions requiring the prosecutor to disclose material of this kind in the absence of an application under section 8. When potentially relevant CCTV footage is not in the possession of the police, the guidance in relation to third party material will apply, although the police remain under a duty to pursue all reasonable lines of inquiry, including those leading away from a suspect, whether or not defence requests are made.

36. The previous convictions of witnesses and any disciplinary findings against officers in the case are frequently discloseable and care should be taken to disclose them as appropriate. Documents such as crime reports or records of emergency calls should not be provided on a routine basis, for instance as part of a bundle of disclosed documents, irrespective of whether the material satisfies the appropriate test for disclosure. Defence advocates should not request this material in standard or routine correspondence, and instead focussed consideration should be given to the circumstances of the particular case. Unjustified requests for disclosure of material of this kind are routinely made, frequently leading to unnecessary delays and adjournments. The prosecution should always consider whether the request is properly made out.

37. The supervisory role of the courts is critical in this context, and magistrates must guard against granting unnecessary adjournments and issuing unjustified directions.

### Large and complex cases in the Crown Court

38. Disclosure is a particular problem with the larger and more complex cases, which require a scrupulous approach by the parties and robust case management by the judiciary. If possible, the trial judge should be identified at the outset. **N-58**

39. The legal representatives need to fulfil their duties in this context with care and efficiency; they should co-operate with the other party (or parties) and the court; and the judge and the other party (or parties) are to be informed of any difficulties, as soon as they arise. The court should be provided with an up-to-date timetable for disclosure whenever there are material changes in this regard. A disclosure-management document, or similar, prepared by the prosecution will be of particular assistance to the court in large and complex cases.

40. Judges should be prepared to give early guidance as to the prosecution's approach to disclosure, thereby ensuring early engagement by the defence.

41. Cases of this nature frequently include large volumes of digitally stored material. The Attorney General's 2011 guidance (now included as an annex to the Attorney General's Guidelines on Disclosure 2013) is of particular relevance and assistance in this context.

42. Applications for witness anonymity orders require particular attention; as the Court of Appeal noted in *R. v. Mayers* [2008] EWCA Crim. 2989; [2009] 1 Cr.App.R. 30, in making such an application, the prosecution's obligations of disclosure "go much further than the ordinary duties of disclosure".

43. If the judge considers that there are reasonable grounds to doubt the good faith of the investigation, he or she will be concerned to see that there has been independent and effective appraisal of the documents contained in the disclosure schedule and that its contents are adequate. In appropriate cases where this issue has arisen and there are grounds which show there is a real issue, consideration should be given to receiving evidence on oath from the senior investigating officer at an early case management hearing.

### Material held by third parties

**N-59**    44. Where material is held by a third party such as a local authority, a social services department, hospital or business, the investigators and the prosecution may need to make enquiries of the third party, with a view to inspecting the material and assessing whether the relevant test for disclosure is met and determining whether any or all of the material should be retained, recorded and, in due course, disclosed to the accused. If access by the prosecution is granted, the investigators and the prosecution will need to establish whether the custodian of the material intends to raise PII issues, as a result of which the material may have to be placed before the court for a decision. This does not obviate the need for the defence to conduct its own enquiries as appropriate. Speculative enquiries without any proper basis in relation to third party material – whether by the prosecution or the defence – are to be discouraged, and, in appropriate cases, the court will consider making an order for costs where an application is clearly unmeritorious and misconceived.

45. The 2013 Protocol and Good Practice Model on Disclosure of Information in Cases of Alleged Child Abuse and Linked Criminal and Care Directions Hearings has recently been published. It provides a framework and timetable for the police and CPS to obtain discloseable material from local authorities, and for applications to be made to the Family Court. It is applicable to all cases of alleged child abuse where the child is aged 17 years or under. It is not binding on local authorities, but it does represent best practice and therefore should be consulted in all such cases. Delays in obtaining this type of material have led to unacceptable delays to trials involving particularly vulnerable witnesses and every effort must be made to ensure that all discloseable material is identified at an early stage so that any necessary applications can be made and the defence receive material to which they are entitled in good time.

46. There is no specific procedure for disclosure of material held by third parties in criminal proceedings, although the procedure established under section 2 of the Criminal Procedure (Attendance of Witnesses) Act 1965 or section 97 of the Magistrates' Courts Act 1980 is often used for this purpose. Where the third party in question declines to allow inspection of the material, or requires the prosecution to obtain an order before providing copies, the prosecutor will need to consider whether it is appropriate to obtain a witness summons under either section 2 of the Criminal Procedure (Attendance of Witnesses) Act 1965 or section 97 of the Magistrates' Courts Act 1980. Part 28 of the Criminal Procedure Rules and paragraphs 3.5 and 3.6 of the Code of Practice under the CPIA 1996 should be followed.

47. Applications for third party disclosure must identify the documents that are sought and provide full details of why they are discloseable. This is particularly relevant when access is sought to the medical records of those who allege they are victims of crime. It should be appreciated that a duty to assert confidentiality may arise when a third party receives a request for disclosure, or the right to privacy may be claimed under Article 8 of the ECHR (see in particular Crim. P.R., Pt 28.6). Victims do not waive the confidentiality of their medical records, or their right to privacy under Article 8 of the ECHR, by making a complaint against the accused. The court, as a public authority, must ensure that any interference with the right to privacy under Article 8 is in accordance with the law, and is necessary in pursuit of a legitimate public interest. General and unspecified requests to trawl through such records should be refused. Confidentiality rests with the subject of the material, not with the authority holding it. The subject is entitled to service of the application and has the right to make representations: Criminal Procedure Rule 22.3 and *R. (B.) v. Stafford Combined Court* [2006] EWHC 1645 (Admin.); [2006] 2 Cr.App.R. 34. The 2013 Protocol and Good Practice Model at paragraph 13 should be followed. It is likely that the judge will need to issue directions when issues of this kind are raised (*e.g.* whether enquiries with the third party are likely to be appropriate; who is to make the request; what material is to be sought, and from whom; and a timetable should be set).

48. The judge should consider whether to take any steps if a third party fails, or refuses, to comply with a request for disclosure, including suggesting that either of the parties pursue the request and, if necessary, make an application for a witness summons. In these circumstances, the court will need to set an appropriate timetable for compliance with Part 28 of the rules. Any failure to comply with

the timetable must immediately be referred back to the court for further directions, although a hearing will not always be necessary. Generally, it may be appropriate for the defence to pursue requests of this kind when the prosecution, for good reason, decline to do so and the court will need to ensure that this procedure does not delay the trial.

49. There are very limited circumstances in which information relating to Family Court proceedings (*e.g.* where there have been care proceedings in relation to a child who has complained to the police of mistreatment) may be communicated without a court order: see the Family Procedure Rules 12.73. Reference should be made to the 2013 Protocol and Good Practice Model. In most circumstances, a court order will be required and paragraph 11 of the Protocol which sets out how an application should be made should be followed.

### Other government departments

50. Material held by other government departments or other Crown agencies will not be prosecution material for the purposes of section 3(2) or section 8(4) of the CPIA if it has not been inspected, recorded and retained during the course of the relevant criminal investigation. The *CPIA Code of Practice and the Attorney General's Guidelines on Disclosure*, however, impose a duty upon the investigators and the prosecution to pursue all reasonable lines of inquiry and that may involve seeking disclosure from the relevant body. **N-60**

### International matters

51. The obligations of the Crown in relation to relevant third-party material held overseas are as set out in *R. v. Flook* [2009] EWCA Crim. 682; [2010] 1 Cr.App.R. 30: the Crown must pursue reasonable lines of enquiry and if it appears there is relevant material, all reasonable steps must be taken to obtain it, whether formally or otherwise. To a great extent, the success of these enquiries will depend on the laws of the country where the material is held and the facts of the individual case. It needs to be recognised that when the material is held in a country outside of the European Union, the power of the Crown and the courts of England and Wales to obtain third-party material may well be limited. If informal requests are unsuccessful, the avenues are limited to the Crime (International Co-operation) Act 2003 and any applicable international conventions. It cannot, in any sense, be guaranteed that a request to a foreign government, court or body will produce the material sought. Additionally, some foreign authorities may be prepared to show the material in question to the investigating officers, whilst refusing to allow the material to be copied or otherwise made available. **N-61**

52. As the Court of Appeal observed in *R. v. Khyam* [2008] EWCA Crim. 1612; [2009] 1 Cr.App.R.(S.) 77:

"The prosecuting authorities in this jurisdiction simply cannot compel authorities in a foreign country to acknowledge, let alone comply with, our disclosure principles" (at [37]).

The obligation is therefore to take reasonable steps. Whether the Crown has complied with that obligation is for the courts to judge in each case.

53. It is, therefore, important that the prosecution sets out the position clearly in writing, including any inability to inspect or retrieve any material that potentially ought to be disclosed, along with the steps that have been taken.

### Applications for non-disclosure in the public interest

54. Applications in this context, whenever possible, should be considered by the trial judge. The House of Lords in *R. v. H.* (*supra*) has provided useful guidance as to the proper approach to be applied (para. [36]): **N-62**

"When any issue of derogation from the golden rule of full disclosure comes before it, the court must address a series of questions:
    (1) What is the material which the prosecution seek to withhold? This must be considered by the court in detail.
    (2) Is the material such as may weaken the prosecution case or strengthen that of the defence? If No, disclosure should not be ordered. If Yes, full disclosure should (subject to (3), (4) and (5) below) be ordered.
    (3) Is there a real risk of serious prejudice to an important public interest (and, if so, what) if full disclosure of the material is ordered? If No, full disclosure should be ordered.
    (4) If the answer to (2) and (3) is Yes, can the defendant's interest be protected without disclosure or disclosure be ordered to an extent or in a way which will give adequate protection to the public interest in question and also afford adequate protection to the interests of the defence?

This question requires the court to consider, with specific reference to the material which the prosecution seek to withhold and the facts of the case and the defence as disclosed, whether the prosecution should formally admit what the defence seek to establish or whether disclosure short of full disclosure may be ordered. This may be done in appropriate cases by the preparation of summaries or extracts of evidence, or the provision of documents in an edited or anonymised form, provided the documents supplied are in each instance approved by the judge. In appropriate cases the appointment of special counsel may be a necessary step to ensure that the contentions of the prosecution are tested and the interests of the defendant protected (see para. [22] above). In cases of exceptional difficulty the court may require the appointment of special counsel to ensure a correct answer to questions (2) and (3) as well as (4).

(5) Do the measures proposed in answer to (4) represent the minimum derogation necessary to protect the public interest in question? If No, the court should order such greater disclosure as will represent the minimum derogation from the golden rule of full disclosure.

(6) If limited disclosure is ordered pursuant to (4) or (5), may the effect be to render the trial process, viewed as a whole, unfair to the defendant? If Yes, then fuller disclosure should be ordered even if this leads or may lead the prosecution to discontinue the proceedings so as to avoid having to make disclosure.

(7) If the answer to (6) when first given is No, does that remain the correct answer as the trial unfolds, evidence is adduced and the defence advanced?

It is important that the answer to (6) should not be treated as a final, once-and-for-all, answer but as a provisional answer which the court must keep under review."

55. In this context, the following matters are to be emphasised:

a. the procedure for making applications to the court is set out in the Criminal Procedure Rules, Pt 22;

b. when the PII application is a Type 1 or Type 2 application, proper notice to the defence is necessary to enable the accused to make focused submissions to the court and the notice should be as specific as the nature of the material allows; it is appreciated that in some cases only the generic nature of the material can be identified; in some wholly exceptional cases (Type 3 cases) it may be justified to give no notice at all; the judge should always ask the prosecution to justify the form of notice (or the decision to give no notice at all);

c. the prosecution should be alert to the possibility of disclosing a statement in a redacted form by, for example, simply removing personal details; this may obviate the need for a PII application, unless the redacted material satisfies the test for disclosure;

d. except when the material is very short (for instance only a few sheets), or for reasons of sensitivity, the prosecution should supply securely sealed copies to the judge in advance, together with a short statement explaining the relevance of each document, how it satisfies the disclosure test and why it is suggested that disclosure would result in a real risk of serious prejudice to an important public interest; in undertaking this task, the use of merely formulaic expressions is to be discouraged; in any case of complexity a schedule of the material should be provided, identifying the particular objection to disclosure in relation to each item, and leaving a space for the judge's decision;

e. the application, even if held in private or in secret, should be recorded; the judge should give some short statement of reasons; this is often best done document by document as the hearing proceeds;

f. the recording, copies of the judge's orders (and any copies of the material retained by the court) should be clearly identified, securely sealed and kept in the court building in a safe or locked cabinet consistent with its security classification, and there should be a proper register of the contents; arrangements should be made for the return of the material to the prosecution once the case is concluded and the time for an appeal has elapsed.

### Conclusion

**N-63**    56. Historically, disclosure was viewed essentially as being a matter to be resolved between the parties, and the court only became engaged if a particular issue or complaint was raised. That perception is now wholly out of date. The regime established under the Criminal Justice Act 2003 and the Criminal Procedure Rules gives judges the power – indeed, it imposes a duty on the judiciary – actively to manage disclosure in every case. The efficient, effective and timely resolution of these issues is a critical element in meeting the overriding objective of the Criminal Procedure Rules of dealing with cases justly.

# ALMANAC

*TABLE OF CONTENTS*

## 2010

### JANUARY

| M | T | W | Th | F | Sa | Su |
|---|---|---|----|---|----|----|
|   |   |   |    | 1 | 2  | 3  |
| 4 | 5 | 6 | 7  | 8 | 9  | 10 |
| 11| 12| 13| 14 | 15| 16 | 17 |
| 18| 19| 20| 21 | 22| 23 | 24 |
| 25| 26| 27| 28 | 29| 30 | 31 |

### FEBRUARY

| M | T | W | Th | F | Sa | Su |
|---|---|---|----|---|----|----|
| 1 | 2 | 3 | 4  | 5 | 6  | 7  |
| 8 | 9 | 10| 11 | 12| 13 | 14 |
| 15| 16| 17| 18 | 19| 20 | 21 |
| 22| 23| 24| 25 | 26| 27 | 28 |

### MARCH

| M | T | W | Th | F | Sa | Su |
|---|---|---|----|---|----|----|
| 1 | 2 | 3 | 4  | 5 | 6  | 7  |
| 8 | 9 | 10| 11 | 12| 13 | 14 |
| 15| 16| 17| 18 | 19| 20 | 21 |
| 22| 23| 24| 25 | 26| 27 | 28 |
| 29| 30| 31|    |   |    |    |

### APRIL

| M | T | W | Th | F | Sa | Su |
|---|---|---|----|---|----|----|
|   |   |   | 1  | 2 | 3  | 4  |
| 5 | 6 | 7 | 8  | 9 | 10 | 11 |
| 12| 13| 14| 15 | 16| 17 | 18 |
| 19| 20| 21| 22 | 23| 24 | 25 |
| 26| 27| 28| 29 | 30|    |    |

### MAY

| M | T | W | Th | F | Sa | Su |
|---|---|---|----|---|----|----|
|   |   |   |    |   | 1  | 2  |
| 3 | 4 | 5 | 6  | 7 | 8  | 9  |
| 10| 11| 12| 13 | 14| 15 | 16 |
| 17| 18| 19| 20 | 21| 22 | 23 |
| 24| 25| 26| 27 | 28| 29 | 30 |
| 31|   |   |    |   |    |    |

### JUNE

| M | T | W | Th | F | Sa | Su |
|---|---|---|----|---|----|----|
|   | 1 | 2 | 3  | 4 | 5  | 6  |
| 7 | 8 | 9 | 10 | 11| 12 | 13 |
| 14| 15| 16| 17 | 18| 19 | 20 |
| 21| 22| 23| 24 | 25| 26 | 27 |
| 28| 29| 30|    |   |    |    |

### JULY

| M | T | W | Th | F | Sa | Su |
|---|---|---|----|---|----|----|
|   |   |   | 1  | 2 | 3  | 4  |
| 5 | 6 | 7 | 8  | 9 | 10 | 11 |
| 12| 13| 14| 15 | 16| 17 | 18 |
| 19| 20| 21| 22 | 23| 24 | 25 |
| 26| 27| 28| 29 | 30| 31 |    |

### AUGUST

| M | T | W | Th | F | Sa | Su |
|---|---|---|----|---|----|----|
|   |   |   |    |   |    | 1  |
| 2 | 3 | 4 | 5  | 6 | 7  | 8  |
| 9 | 10| 11| 12 | 13| 14 | 15 |
| 16| 17| 18| 19 | 20| 21 | 22 |
| 23| 24| 25| 26 | 27| 28 | 29 |
| 30| 31|   |    |   |    |    |

### SEPTEMBER

| M | T | W | Th | F | Sa | Su |
|---|---|---|----|---|----|----|
|   |   | 1 | 2  | 3 | 4  | 5  |
| 6 | 7 | 8 | 9  | 10| 11 | 12 |
| 13| 14| 15| 16 | 17| 18 | 19 |
| 20| 21| 22| 23 | 24| 25 | 26 |
| 27| 28| 29| 30 |   |    |    |

### OCTOBER

| M | T | W | Th | F | Sa | Su |
|---|---|---|----|---|----|----|
|   |   |   |    | 1 | 2  | 3  |
| 4 | 5 | 6 | 7  | 8 | 9  | 10 |
| 11| 12| 13| 14 | 15| 16 | 17 |
| 18| 19| 20| 21 | 22| 23 | 24 |
| 25| 26| 27| 28 | 29| 30 | 31 |

### NOVEMBER

| M | T | W | Th | F | Sa | Su |
|---|---|---|----|---|----|----|
| 1 | 2 | 3 | 4  | 5 | 6  | 7  |
| 8 | 9 | 10| 11 | 12| 13 | 14 |
| 15| 16| 17| 18 | 19| 20 | 21 |
| 22| 23| 24| 25 | 26| 27 | 28 |
| 29| 30|   |    |   |    |    |

### DECEMBER

| M | T | W | Th | F | Sa | Su |
|---|---|---|----|---|----|----|
|   |   | 1 | 2  | 3 | 4  | 5  |
| 6 | 7 | 8 | 9  | 10| 11 | 12 |
| 13| 14| 15| 16 | 17| 18 | 19 |
| 20| 21| 22| 23 | 24| 25 | 26 |
| 27| 28| 29| 30 | 31|    |    |

# 2011

### JANUARY

| M | T | W | Th | F | Sa | Su |
|---|---|---|----|---|----|----|
|   |   |   |   |   | 1 | 2 |
| 3 | 4 | 5 | 6 | 7 | 8 | 9 |
| 10 | 11 | 12 | 13 | 14 | 15 | 16 |
| 17 | 18 | 19 | 20 | 21 | 22 | 23 |
| 24 | 25 | 26 | 27 | 28 | 29 | 30 |
| 31 |   |   |   |   |   |   |

### FEBRUARY

| M | T | W | Th | F | Sa | Su |
|---|---|---|----|---|----|----|
|   | 1 | 2 | 3 | 4 | 5 | 6 |
| 7 | 8 | 9 | 10 | 11 | 12 | 13 |
| 14 | 15 | 16 | 17 | 18 | 19 | 20 |
| 21 | 22 | 23 | 24 | 25 | 26 | 27 |
| 28 |   |   |   |   |   |   |

### MARCH

| M | T | W | Th | F | Sa | Su |
|---|---|---|----|---|----|----|
|   | 1 | 2 | 3 | 4 | 5 | 6 |
| 7 | 8 | 9 | 10 | 11 | 12 | 13 |
| 14 | 15 | 16 | 17 | 18 | 19 | 20 |
| 21 | 22 | 23 | 24 | 25 | 26 | 27 |
| 28 | 29 | 30 | 31 |   |   |   |

### APRIL

| M | T | W | Th | F | Sa | Su |
|---|---|---|----|---|----|----|
|   |   |   |   | 1 | 2 | 3 |
| 4 | 5 | 6 | 7 | 8 | 9 | 10 |
| 11 | 12 | 13 | 14 | 15 | 16 | 17 |
| 18 | 19 | 20 | 21 | 22 | 23 | 24 |
| 25 | 26 | 27 | 28 | 29 | 30 |   |

### MAY

| M | T | W | Th | F | Sa | Su |
|---|---|---|----|---|----|----|
| 2 | 3 | 4 | 5 | 6 | 7 | 1 |
|   |   |   |   |   |   | 8 |
| 9 | 10 | 11 | 12 | 13 | 14 | 15 |
| 16 | 17 | 18 | 19 | 20 | 21 | 22 |
| 23 | 24 | 25 | 26 | 27 | 28 | 29 |
| 30 | 31 |   |   |   |   |   |

### JUNE

| M | T | W | Th | F | Sa | Su |
|---|---|---|----|---|----|----|
|   |   | 1 | 2 | 3 | 4 | 5 |
| 6 | 7 | 8 | 9 | 10 | 11 | 12 |
| 13 | 14 | 15 | 16 | 17 | 18 | 19 |
| 20 | 21 | 22 | 23 | 24 | 25 | 26 |
| 27 | 28 | 29 | 30 |   |   |   |

### JULY

| M | T | W | Th | F | Sa | Su |
|---|---|---|----|---|----|----|
|   |   |   |   | 1 | 2 | 3 |
| 4 | 5 | 6 | 7 | 8 | 9 | 10 |
| 11 | 12 | 13 | 14 | 15 | 16 | 17 |
| 18 | 19 | 20 | 21 | 22 | 23 | 24 |
| 25 | 26 | 27 | 28 | 29 | 30 | 31 |

### AUGUST

| M | T | W | Th | F | Sa | Su |
|---|---|---|----|---|----|----|
| 1 | 2 | 3 | 4 | 5 | 6 | 7 |
| 8 | 9 | 10 | 11 | 12 | 13 | 14 |
| 15 | 16 | 17 | 18 | 19 | 20 | 21 |
| 22 | 23 | 24 | 25 | 26 | 27 | 28 |
| 29 | 30 | 31 |   |   |   |   |

### SEPTEMBER

| M | T | W | Th | F | Sa | Su |
|---|---|---|----|---|----|----|
|   |   |   | 1 | 2 | 3 | 4 |
| 5 | 6 | 7 | 8 | 9 | 10 | 11 |
| 12 | 13 | 14 | 15 | 16 | 17 | 18 |
| 19 | 20 | 21 | 22 | 23 | 24 | 25 |
| 26 | 27 | 28 | 29 | 30 |   |   |

### OCTOBER

| M | T | W | Th | F | Sa | Su |
|---|---|---|----|---|----|----|
|   |   |   |   |   | 1 | 2 |
| 3 | 4 | 5 | 6 | 7 | 8 | 9 |
| 10 | 11 | 12 | 13 | 14 | 15 | 16 |
| 17 | 18 | 19 | 20 | 21 | 22 | 23 |
| 24 | 25 | 26 | 27 | 28 | 29 | 30 |
| 31 |   |   |   |   |   |   |

### NOVEMBER

| M | T | W | Th | F | Sa | Su |
|---|---|---|----|---|----|----|
|   | 1 | 2 | 3 | 4 | 5 | 6 |
| 7 | 8 | 9 | 10 | 11 | 12 | 13 |
| 14 | 15 | 16 | 17 | 18 | 19 | 20 |
| 21 | 22 | 23 | 24 | 25 | 26 | 27 |
| 28 | 29 | 30 |   |   |   |   |

### DECEMBER

| M | T | W | Th | F | Sa | Su |
|---|---|---|----|---|----|----|
|   |   |   | 1 | 2 | 3 | 4 |
| 5 | 6 | 7 | 8 | 9 | 10 | 11 |
| 12 | 13 | 14 | 15 | 16 | 17 | 18 |
| 19 | 20 | 21 | 22 | 23 | 24 | 25 |
| 26 | 27 | 28 | 29 | 30 | 31 |   |

## 2012

### JANUARY

| M | T | W | Th | F | Sa | Su |
|---|---|---|----|---|----|----|
| 2 | 3 | 4 | 5 | 6 | 7 | 8 |
| 9 | 10 | 11 | 12 | 13 | 14 | 15 |
| 16 | 17 | 18 | 19 | 20 | 21 | 22 |
| 23 | 24 | 25 | 26 | 27 | 28 | 29 |
| 30 | 31 | | | | | |

### FEBRUARY

| M | T | W | Th | F | Sa | Su |
|---|---|---|----|---|----|----|
| 6 | 7 | 1 | 2 | 3 | 4 | 5 |
| 13 | 14 | 8 | 9 | 10 | 11 | 12 |
| 20 | 21 | 15 | 16 | 17 | 18 | 19 |
| 27 | 28 | 22 | 23 | 24 | 25 | 26 |
| | | 29 | | | | |

### MARCH

| M | T | W | Th | F | Sa | Su |
|---|---|---|----|---|----|----|
| 5 | 6 | 7 | 1 | 2 | 3 | 4 |
| 12 | 13 | 14 | 8 | 9 | 10 | 11 |
| 19 | 20 | 21 | 15 | 16 | 17 | 18 |
| 26 | 27 | 28 | 22 | 23 | 24 | 25 |
| | | | 29 | 30 | 31 | |

### APRIL

| M | T | W | Th | F | Sa | Su |
|---|---|---|----|---|----|----|
| 2 | 3 | 4 | 5 | 6 | 7 | 1 |
| 9 | 10 | 11 | 12 | 13 | 14 | 8 |
| 16 | 17 | 18 | 19 | 20 | 21 | 15 |
| 23 | 24 | 25 | 26 | 27 | 28 | 22 |
| 30 | | | | | | 29 |

### MAY

| M | T | W | Th | F | Sa | Su |
|---|---|---|----|---|----|----|
| 7 | 1 | 2 | 3 | 4 | 5 | 6 |
| 14 | 8 | 9 | 10 | 11 | 12 | 13 |
| 21 | 15 | 16 | 17 | 18 | 19 | 20 |
| 28 | 22 | 23 | 24 | 25 | 26 | 27 |
| | 29 | 30 | 31 | | | |

### JUNE

| M | T | W | Th | F | Sa | Su |
|---|---|---|----|---|----|----|
| 4 | 5 | 6 | 7 | 1 | 2 | 3 |
| 11 | 12 | 13 | 14 | 8 | 9 | 10 |
| 18 | 19 | 20 | 21 | 15 | 16 | 17 |
| 25 | 26 | 27 | 28 | 22 | 23 | 24 |
| | | | | 29 | 30 | |

### JULY

| M | T | W | Th | F | Sa | Su |
|---|---|---|----|---|----|----|
| 2 | 3 | 4 | 5 | 6 | 7 | 1 |
| 9 | 10 | 11 | 12 | 13 | 14 | 8 |
| 16 | 17 | 18 | 19 | 20 | 21 | 15 |
| 23 | 24 | 25 | 26 | 27 | 28 | 22 |
| 30 | 31 | | | | | 29 |

### AUGUST

| M | T | W | Th | F | Sa | Su |
|---|---|---|----|---|----|----|
| 6 | 7 | 1 | 2 | 3 | 4 | 5 |
| 13 | 14 | 8 | 9 | 10 | 11 | 12 |
| 20 | 21 | 15 | 16 | 17 | 18 | 19 |
| 27 | 28 | 22 | 23 | 24 | 25 | 26 |
| | | 29 | 30 | 31 | | |

### SEPTEMBER

| M | T | W | Th | F | Sa | Su |
|---|---|---|----|---|----|----|
| 3 | 4 | 5 | 6 | 7 | 1 | 2 |
| 10 | 11 | 12 | 13 | 14 | 8 | 9 |
| 17 | 18 | 19 | 20 | 21 | 15 | 16 |
| 24 | 25 | 26 | 27 | 28 | 22 | 23 |
| | | | | | 29 | 30 |

### OCTOBER

| M | T | W | Th | F | Sa | Su |
|---|---|---|----|---|----|----|
| 1 | 2 | 3 | 4 | 5 | 6 | 7 |
| 8 | 9 | 10 | 11 | 12 | 13 | 14 |
| 15 | 16 | 17 | 18 | 19 | 20 | 21 |
| 22 | 23 | 24 | 25 | 26 | 27 | 28 |
| 29 | 30 | 31 | | | | |

### NOVEMBER

| M | T | W | Th | F | Sa | Su |
|---|---|---|----|---|----|----|
| 5 | 6 | 7 | 1 | 2 | 3 | 4 |
| 12 | 13 | 14 | 8 | 9 | 10 | 11 |
| 19 | 20 | 21 | 15 | 16 | 17 | 18 |
| 26 | 27 | 28 | 22 | 23 | 24 | 25 |
| | | | 29 | 30 | | |

### DECEMBER

| M | T | W | Th | F | Sa | Su |
|---|---|---|----|---|----|----|
| 3 | 4 | 5 | 6 | 7 | 1 | 2 |
| 10 | 11 | 12 | 13 | 14 | 8 | 9 |
| 17 | 18 | 19 | 20 | 21 | 15 | 16 |
| 24 | 25 | 26 | 27 | 28 | 22 | 23 |
| 31 | | | | | 29 | 30 |

# 2013

### JANUARY

| M | T | W | Th | F | Sa | Su |
|---|---|---|----|---|----|----|
|   | 1 | 2 | 3  | 4 | 5  | 6  |
| 7 | 8 | 9 | 10 | 11 | 12 | 13 |
| 14 | 15 | 16 | 17 | 18 | 19 | 20 |
| 21 | 22 | 23 | 24 | 25 | 26 | 27 |
| 28 | 29 | 30 | 31 |   |   |   |

### FEBRUARY

| M | T | W | Th | F | Sa | Su |
|---|---|---|----|---|----|----|
|   |   |   |   | 1 | 2 | 3 |
| 4 | 5 | 6 | 7 | 8 | 9 | 10 |
| 11 | 12 | 13 | 14 | 15 | 16 | 17 |
| 18 | 19 | 20 | 21 | 22 | 23 | 24 |
| 25 | 26 | 27 | 28 |   |   |   |

### MARCH

| M | T | W | Th | F | Sa | Su |
|---|---|---|----|---|----|----|
|   |   |   |   | 1 | 2 | 3 |
| 4 | 5 | 6 | 7 | 8 | 9 | 10 |
| 11 | 12 | 13 | 14 | 15 | 16 | 17 |
| 18 | 19 | 20 | 21 | 22 | 23 | 24 |
| 25 | 26 | 27 | 28 | 29 | 30 | 31 |

### APRIL

| M | T | W | Th | F | Sa | Su |
|---|---|---|----|---|----|----|
| 1 | 2 | 3 | 4 | 5 | 6 | 7 |
| 8 | 9 | 10 | 11 | 12 | 13 | 14 |
| 15 | 16 | 17 | 18 | 19 | 20 | 21 |
| 22 | 23 | 24 | 25 | 26 | 27 | 28 |
| 29 | 30 |   |   |   |   |   |

### MAY

| M | T | W | Th | F | Sa | Su |
|---|---|---|----|---|----|----|
|   |   | 1 | 2 | 3 | 4 | 5 |
| 6 | 7 | 8 | 9 | 10 | 11 | 12 |
| 13 | 14 | 15 | 16 | 17 | 18 | 19 |
| 20 | 21 | 22 | 23 | 24 | 25 | 26 |
| 27 | 28 | 29 | 30 | 31 |   |   |

### JUNE

| M | T | W | Th | F | Sa | Su |
|---|---|---|----|---|----|----|
|   |   |   |   |   | 1 | 2 |
| 3 | 4 | 5 | 6 | 7 | 8 | 9 |
| 10 | 11 | 12 | 13 | 14 | 15 | 16 |
| 17 | 18 | 19 | 20 | 21 | 22 | 23 |
| 24 | 25 | 26 | 27 | 28 | 29 | 30 |

### JULY

| M | T | W | Th | F | Sa | Su |
|---|---|---|----|---|----|----|
| 1 | 2 | 3 | 4 | 5 | 6 | 7 |
| 8 | 9 | 10 | 11 | 12 | 13 | 14 |
| 15 | 16 | 17 | 18 | 19 | 20 | 21 |
| 22 | 23 | 24 | 25 | 26 | 27 | 28 |
| 29 | 30 | 31 |   |   |   |   |

### AUGUST

| M | T | W | Th | F | Sa | Su |
|---|---|---|----|---|----|----|
|   |   |   | 1 | 2 | 3 | 4 |
| 5 | 6 | 7 | 8 | 9 | 10 | 11 |
| 12 | 13 | 14 | 15 | 16 | 17 | 18 |
| 19 | 20 | 21 | 22 | 23 | 24 | 25 |
| 26 | 27 | 28 | 29 | 30 | 31 |   |

### SEPTEMBER

| M | T | W | Th | F | Sa | Su |
|---|---|---|----|---|----|----|
|   |   |   |   |   |   | 1 |
| 2 | 3 | 4 | 5 | 6 | 7 | 8 |
| 9 | 10 | 11 | 12 | 13 | 14 | 15 |
| 16 | 17 | 18 | 19 | 20 | 21 | 22 |
| 23 | 24 | 25 | 26 | 27 | 28 | 29 |
| 30 |   |   |   |   |   |   |

### OCTOBER

| M | T | W | Th | F | Sa | Su |
|---|---|---|----|---|----|----|
|   | 1 | 2 | 3 | 4 | 5 | 6 |
| 7 | 8 | 9 | 10 | 11 | 12 | 13 |
| 14 | 15 | 16 | 17 | 18 | 19 | 20 |
| 21 | 22 | 23 | 24 | 25 | 26 | 27 |
| 28 | 29 | 30 | 31 |   |   |   |

### NOVEMBER

| M | T | W | Th | F | Sa | Su |
|---|---|---|----|---|----|----|
|   |   |   |   | 1 | 2 | 3 |
| 4 | 5 | 6 | 7 | 8 | 9 | 10 |
| 11 | 12 | 13 | 14 | 15 | 16 | 17 |
| 18 | 19 | 20 | 21 | 22 | 23 | 24 |
| 25 | 26 | 27 | 28 | 29 | 30 |   |

### DECEMBER

| M | T | W | Th | F | Sa | Su |
|---|---|---|----|---|----|----|
|   |   |   |   |   |   | 1 |
| 2 | 3 | 4 | 5 | 6 | 7 | 8 |
| 9 | 10 | 11 | 12 | 13 | 14 | 15 |
| 16 | 17 | 18 | 19 | 20 | 21 | 22 |
| 23 | 24 | 25 | 26 | 27 | 28 | 29 |
| 30 | 31 |   |   |   |   |   |

# 2014

## JANUARY

| M | T | W | Th | F | Sa | Su |
|---|---|---|---|---|---|---|
| 6 | 7 | 1 | 2 | 3 | 4 | 5 |
| 13 | 14 | 8 | 9 | 10 | 11 | 12 |
| 20 | 21 | 15 | 16 | 17 | 18 | 19 |
| 27 | 28 | 22 | 23 | 24 | 25 | 26 |
| | | 29 | 30 | 31 | | |

## FEBRUARY

| M | T | W | Th | F | Sa | Su |
|---|---|---|---|---|---|---|
| 3 | 4 | 5 | 6 | 7 | 1 | 2 |
| 10 | 11 | 12 | 13 | 14 | 8 | 9 |
| 17 | 18 | 19 | 20 | 21 | 15 | 16 |
| 24 | 25 | 26 | 27 | 28 | 22 | 23 |

## MARCH

| M | T | W | Th | F | Sa | Su |
|---|---|---|---|---|---|---|
| 3 | 4 | 5 | 6 | 7 | 1 | 2 |
| 10 | 11 | 12 | 13 | 14 | 8 | 9 |
| 17 | 18 | 19 | 20 | 21 | 15 | 16 |
| 24 | 25 | 26 | 27 | 28 | 22 | 23 |
| 31 | | | | | 29 | 30 |

## APRIL

| M | T | W | Th | F | Sa | Su |
|---|---|---|---|---|---|---|
| 7 | 1 | 2 | 3 | 4 | 5 | 6 |
| 14 | 8 | 9 | 10 | 11 | 12 | 13 |
| 21 | 15 | 16 | 17 | 18 | 19 | 20 |
| 28 | 22 | 23 | 24 | 25 | 26 | 27 |
| | 29 | 30 | | | | |

## MAY

| M | T | W | Th | F | Sa | Su |
|---|---|---|---|---|---|---|
| 5 | 6 | 7 | 1 | 2 | 3 | 4 |
| 12 | 13 | 14 | 8 | 9 | 10 | 11 |
| 19 | 20 | 21 | 15 | 16 | 17 | 18 |
| 26 | 27 | 28 | 22 | 23 | 24 | 25 |
| | | | 29 | 30 | 31 | |

## JUNE

| M | T | W | Th | F | Sa | Su |
|---|---|---|---|---|---|---|
| 2 | 3 | 4 | 5 | 6 | 7 | 1 |
| 9 | 10 | 11 | 12 | 13 | 14 | 8 |
| 16 | 17 | 18 | 19 | 20 | 21 | 15 |
| 23 | 24 | 25 | 26 | 27 | 28 | 22 |
| 30 | | | | | | 29 |

## JULY

| M | T | W | Th | F | Sa | Su |
|---|---|---|---|---|---|---|
| 7 | 1 | 2 | 3 | 4 | 5 | 6 |
| 14 | 8 | 9 | 10 | 11 | 12 | 13 |
| 21 | 15 | 16 | 17 | 18 | 19 | 20 |
| 28 | 22 | 23 | 24 | 25 | 26 | 27 |
| | 29 | 30 | 31 | | | |

## AUGUST

| M | T | W | Th | F | Sa | Su |
|---|---|---|---|---|---|---|
| 4 | 5 | 6 | 7 | 1 | 2 | 3 |
| 11 | 12 | 13 | 14 | 8 | 9 | 10 |
| 18 | 19 | 20 | 21 | 15 | 16 | 17 |
| 25 | 26 | 27 | 28 | 22 | 23 | 24 |
| | | | | 29 | 30 | 31 |

## SEPTEMBER

| M | T | W | Th | F | Sa | Su |
|---|---|---|---|---|---|---|
| 1 | 2 | 3 | 4 | 5 | 6 | 7 |
| 8 | 9 | 10 | 11 | 12 | 13 | 14 |
| 15 | 16 | 17 | 18 | 19 | 20 | 21 |
| 22 | 23 | 24 | 25 | 26 | 27 | 28 |
| 29 | 30 | | | | | |

## OCTOBER

| M | T | W | Th | F | Sa | Su |
|---|---|---|---|---|---|---|
| 6 | 7 | 1 | 2 | 3 | 4 | 5 |
| 13 | 14 | 8 | 9 | 10 | 11 | 12 |
| 20 | 21 | 15 | 16 | 17 | 18 | 19 |
| 27 | 28 | 22 | 23 | 24 | 25 | 26 |
| | | 29 | 30 | 31 | | |

## NOVEMBER

| M | T | W | Th | F | Sa | Su |
|---|---|---|---|---|---|---|
| 3 | 4 | 5 | 6 | 7 | 1 | 2 |
| 10 | 11 | 12 | 13 | 14 | 8 | 9 |
| 17 | 18 | 19 | 20 | 21 | 15 | 16 |
| 24 | 25 | 26 | 27 | 28 | 22 | 23 |
| | | | | | 29 | 30 |

## DECEMBER

| M | T | W | Th | F | Sa | Su |
|---|---|---|---|---|---|---|
| 1 | 2 | 3 | 4 | 5 | 6 | 7 |
| 8 | 9 | 10 | 11 | 12 | 13 | 14 |
| 15 | 16 | 17 | 18 | 19 | 20 | 21 |
| 22 | 23 | 24 | 25 | 26 | 27 | 28 |
| 29 | 30 | 31 | | | | |

Archbold paragraph numbers

# 2015

## JANUARY

| M | T | W | Th | F | Sa | Su |
|---|---|---|----|---|----|----|
| 5 | 6 | 7 | 1 | 2 | 3 | 4 |
| 12 | 13 | 14 | 8 | 9 | 10 | 11 |
| 19 | 20 | 21 | 15 | 16 | 17 | 18 |
| 26 | 27 | 28 | 22 | 23 | 24 | 25 |
|  |  |  | 29 | 30 | 31 |  |

## FEBRUARY

| M | T | W | Th | F | Sa | Su |
|---|---|---|----|---|----|----|
| 2 | 3 | 4 | 5 | 6 | 7 | 1 |
| 9 | 10 | 11 | 12 | 13 | 14 | 8 |
| 16 | 17 | 18 | 19 | 20 | 21 | 15 |
| 23 | 24 | 25 | 26 | 27 | 28 | 22 |

## MARCH

| M | T | W | Th | F | Sa | Su |
|---|---|---|----|---|----|----|
| 2 | 3 | 4 | 5 | 6 | 7 | 1 |
| 9 | 10 | 11 | 12 | 13 | 14 | 8 |
| 16 | 17 | 18 | 19 | 20 | 21 | 15 |
| 23 | 24 | 25 | 26 | 27 | 28 | 22 |
| 30 | 31 |  |  |  |  | 29 |

## APRIL

| M | T | W | Th | F | Sa | Su |
|---|---|---|----|---|----|----|
| | | 1 | 2 | 3 | 4 | 5 |
| 6 | 7 | 8 | 9 | 10 | 11 | 12 |
| 13 | 14 | 15 | 16 | 17 | 18 | 19 |
| 20 | 21 | 22 | 23 | 24 | 25 | 26 |
| 27 | 28 | 29 | 30 |  |  |  |

## MAY

| M | T | W | Th | F | Sa | Su |
|---|---|---|----|---|----|----|
| 4 | 5 | 6 | 7 | 1 | 2 | 3 |
| 11 | 12 | 13 | 14 | 8 | 9 | 10 |
| 18 | 19 | 20 | 21 | 15 | 16 | 17 |
| 25 | 26 | 27 | 28 | 22 | 23 | 24 |
|  |  |  |  | 29 | 30 | 31 |

## JUNE

| M | T | W | Th | F | Sa | Su |
|---|---|---|----|---|----|----|
| 1 | 2 | 3 | 4 | 5 | 6 | 7 |
| 8 | 9 | 10 | 11 | 12 | 13 | 14 |
| 15 | 16 | 17 | 18 | 19 | 20 | 21 |
| 22 | 23 | 24 | 25 | 26 | 27 | 28 |
| 29 | 30 |  |  |  |  |  |

## JULY

| M | T | W | Th | F | Sa | Su |
|---|---|---|----|---|----|----|
| | | 1 | 2 | 3 | 4 | 5 |
| 6 | 7 | 8 | 9 | 10 | 11 | 12 |
| 13 | 14 | 15 | 16 | 17 | 18 | 19 |
| 20 | 21 | 22 | 23 | 24 | 25 | 26 |
| 27 | 28 | 29 | 30 | 31 |  |  |

## AUGUST

| M | T | W | Th | F | Sa | Su |
|---|---|---|----|---|----|----|
| | | | | | 1 | 2 |
| 3 | 4 | 5 | 6 | 7 | 8 | 9 |
| 10 | 11 | 12 | 13 | 14 | 15 | 16 |
| 17 | 18 | 19 | 20 | 21 | 22 | 23 |
| 24 | 25 | 26 | 27 | 28 | 29 | 30 |
| 31 |  |  |  |  |  |  |

## SEPTEMBER

| M | T | W | Th | F | Sa | Su |
|---|---|---|----|---|----|----|
| 7 | 1 | 2 | 3 | 4 | 5 | 6 |
| 14 | 8 | 9 | 10 | 11 | 12 | 13 |
| 21 | 15 | 16 | 17 | 18 | 19 | 20 |
| 28 | 22 | 23 | 24 | 25 | 26 | 27 |
|  | 29 | 30 |  |  |  |  |

## OCTOBER

| M | T | W | Th | F | Sa | Su |
|---|---|---|----|---|----|----|
| 5 | 6 | 7 | 1 | 2 | 3 | 4 |
| 12 | 13 | 14 | 8 | 9 | 10 | 11 |
| 19 | 20 | 21 | 15 | 16 | 17 | 18 |
| 26 | 27 | 28 | 22 | 23 | 24 | 25 |
|  |  |  | 29 | 30 | 31 |  |

## NOVEMBER

| M | T | W | Th | F | Sa | Su |
|---|---|---|----|---|----|----|
| 2 | 3 | 4 | 5 | 6 | 7 | 1 |
| 9 | 10 | 11 | 12 | 13 | 14 | 8 |
| 16 | 17 | 18 | 19 | 20 | 21 | 15 |
| 23 | 24 | 25 | 26 | 27 | 28 | 22 |
| 30 |  |  |  |  |  | 29 |

## DECEMBER

| M | T | W | Th | F | Sa | Su |
|---|---|---|----|---|----|----|
| 7 | 1 | 2 | 3 | 4 | 5 | 6 |
| 14 | 8 | 9 | 10 | 11 | 12 | 13 |
| 21 | 15 | 16 | 17 | 18 | 19 | 20 |
| 28 | 22 | 23 | 24 | 25 | 26 | 27 |
|  | 29 | 30 | 31 |  |  |  |

# 2016

## JANUARY

| M | T | W | Th | F | Sa | Su |
|---|---|---|---|---|---|---|
|  |  |  |  | 1 | 2 | 3 |
| 4 | 5 | 6 | 7 | 8 | 9 | 10 |
| 11 | 12 | 13 | 14 | 15 | 16 | 17 |
| 18 | 19 | 20 | 21 | 22 | 23 | 24 |
| 25 | 26 | 27 | 28 | 29 | 30 | 31 |

## FEBRUARY

| M | T | W | Th | F | Sa | Su |
|---|---|---|---|---|---|---|
| 1 | 2 | 3 | 4 | 5 | 6 | 7 |
| 8 | 9 | 10 | 11 | 12 | 13 | 14 |
| 15 | 16 | 17 | 18 | 19 | 20 | 21 |
| 22 | 23 | 24 | 25 | 26 | 27 | 28 |
| 29 |  |  |  |  |  |  |

## MARCH

| M | T | W | Th | F | Sa | Su |
|---|---|---|---|---|---|---|
|  | 1 | 2 | 3 | 4 | 5 | 6 |
| 7 | 8 | 9 | 10 | 11 | 12 | 13 |
| 14 | 15 | 16 | 17 | 18 | 19 | 20 |
| 21 | 22 | 23 | 24 | 25 | 26 | 27 |
| 28 | 29 | 30 | 31 |  |  |  |

## APRIL

| M | T | W | Th | F | Sa | Su |
|---|---|---|---|---|---|---|
|  |  |  |  | 1 | 2 | 3 |
| 4 | 5 | 6 | 7 | 8 | 9 | 10 |
| 11 | 12 | 13 | 14 | 15 | 16 | 17 |
| 18 | 19 | 20 | 21 | 22 | 23 | 24 |
| 25 | 26 | 27 | 28 | 29 | 30 |  |

## MAY

| M | T | W | Th | F | Sa | Su |
|---|---|---|---|---|---|---|
|  |  |  |  |  |  | 1 |
| 2 | 3 | 4 | 5 | 6 | 7 | 8 |
| 9 | 10 | 11 | 12 | 13 | 14 | 15 |
| 16 | 17 | 18 | 19 | 20 | 21 | 22 |
| 23 | 24 | 25 | 26 | 27 | 28 | 29 |
| 30 | 31 |  |  |  |  |  |

## JUNE

| M | T | W | Th | F | Sa | Su |
|---|---|---|---|---|---|---|
|  |  | 1 | 2 | 3 | 4 | 5 |
| 6 | 7 | 8 | 9 | 10 | 11 | 12 |
| 13 | 14 | 15 | 16 | 17 | 18 | 19 |
| 20 | 21 | 22 | 23 | 24 | 25 | 26 |
| 27 | 28 | 29 | 30 |  |  |  |

## JULY

| M | T | W | Th | F | Sa | Su |
|---|---|---|---|---|---|---|
|  |  |  |  | 1 | 2 | 3 |
| 4 | 5 | 6 | 7 | 8 | 9 | 10 |
| 11 | 12 | 13 | 14 | 15 | 16 | 17 |
| 18 | 19 | 20 | 21 | 22 | 23 | 24 |
| 25 | 26 | 27 | 28 | 29 | 30 | 31 |

## AUGUST

| M | T | W | Th | F | Sa | Su |
|---|---|---|---|---|---|---|
| 1 | 2 | 3 | 4 | 5 | 6 | 7 |
| 8 | 9 | 10 | 11 | 12 | 13 | 14 |
| 15 | 16 | 17 | 18 | 19 | 20 | 21 |
| 22 | 23 | 24 | 25 | 26 | 27 | 28 |
| 29 | 30 | 31 |  |  |  |  |

## SEPTEMBER

| M | T | W | Th | F | Sa | Su |
|---|---|---|---|---|---|---|
|  |  |  | 1 | 2 | 3 | 4 |
| 5 | 6 | 7 | 8 | 9 | 10 | 11 |
| 12 | 13 | 14 | 15 | 16 | 17 | 18 |
| 19 | 20 | 21 | 22 | 23 | 24 | 25 |
| 26 | 27 | 28 | 29 | 30 |  |  |

## OCTOBER

| M | T | W | Th | F | Sa | Su |
|---|---|---|---|---|---|---|
|  |  |  |  |  | 1 | 2 |
| 3 | 4 | 5 | 6 | 7 | 8 | 9 |
| 10 | 11 | 12 | 13 | 14 | 15 | 16 |
| 17 | 18 | 19 | 20 | 21 | 22 | 23 |
| 24 | 25 | 26 | 27 | 28 | 29 | 30 |
| 31 |  |  |  |  |  |  |

## NOVEMBER

| M | T | W | Th | F | Sa | Su |
|---|---|---|---|---|---|---|
|  | 1 | 2 | 3 | 4 | 5 | 6 |
| 7 | 8 | 9 | 10 | 11 | 12 | 13 |
| 14 | 15 | 16 | 17 | 18 | 19 | 20 |
| 21 | 22 | 23 | 24 | 25 | 26 | 27 |
| 28 | 29 | 30 |  |  |  |  |

## DECEMBER

| M | T | W | Th | F | Sa | Su |
|---|---|---|---|---|---|---|
|  |  |  | 1 | 2 | 3 | 4 |
| 5 | 6 | 7 | 8 | 9 | 10 | 11 |
| 12 | 13 | 14 | 15 | 16 | 17 | 18 |
| 19 | 20 | 21 | 22 | 23 | 24 | 25 |
| 26 | 27 | 28 | 29 | 30 | 31 |  |

# 2017

### JANUARY

| M | T | W | Th | F | Sa | Su |
|---|---|---|----|---|----|----|
| 2 | 3 | 4 | 5 | 6 | 7 | 1 |
| 9 | 10 | 11 | 12 | 13 | 14 | 8 |
| 16 | 17 | 18 | 19 | 20 | 21 | 15 |
| 23 | 24 | 25 | 26 | 27 | 28 | 22 |
| 30 | 31 | | | | | 29 |

### FEBRUARY

| M | T | W | Th | F | Sa | Su |
|---|---|---|----|---|----|----|
| 6 | 7 | 1 | 2 | 3 | 4 | 5 |
| 13 | 14 | 8 | 9 | 10 | 11 | 12 |
| 20 | 21 | 15 | 16 | 17 | 18 | 19 |
| 27 | 28 | 22 | 23 | 24 | 25 | 26 |

### MARCH

| M | T | W | Th | F | Sa | Su |
|---|---|---|----|---|----|----|
| 6 | 7 | 1 | 2 | 3 | 4 | 5 |
| 13 | 14 | 8 | 9 | 10 | 11 | 12 |
| 20 | 21 | 15 | 16 | 17 | 18 | 19 |
| 27 | 28 | 22 | 23 | 24 | 25 | 26 |
| | | 29 | 30 | 31 | | |

### APRIL

| M | T | W | Th | F | Sa | Su |
|---|---|---|----|---|----|----|
| 3 | 4 | 5 | 6 | 7 | 1 | 2 |
| 10 | 11 | 12 | 13 | 14 | 8 | 9 |
| 17 | 18 | 19 | 20 | 21 | 15 | 16 |
| 24 | 25 | 26 | 27 | 28 | 22 | 23 |
| | | | | | 29 | 30 |

### MAY

| M | T | W | Th | F | Sa | Su |
|---|---|---|----|---|----|----|
| 1 | 2 | 3 | 4 | 5 | 6 | 7 |
| 8 | 9 | 10 | 11 | 12 | 13 | 14 |
| 15 | 16 | 17 | 18 | 19 | 20 | 21 |
| 22 | 23 | 24 | 25 | 26 | 27 | 28 |
| 29 | 30 | 31 | | | | |

### JUNE

| M | T | W | Th | F | Sa | Su |
|---|---|---|----|---|----|----|
| 5 | 6 | 7 | 1 | 2 | 3 | 4 |
| 12 | 13 | 14 | 8 | 9 | 10 | 11 |
| 19 | 20 | 21 | 15 | 16 | 17 | 18 |
| 26 | 27 | 28 | 22 | 23 | 24 | 25 |
| | | | 29 | 30 | | |

### JULY

| M | T | W | Th | F | Sa | Su |
|---|---|---|----|---|----|----|
| 3 | 4 | 5 | 6 | 7 | 1 | 2 |
| 10 | 11 | 12 | 13 | 14 | 8 | 9 |
| 17 | 18 | 19 | 20 | 21 | 15 | 16 |
| 24 | 25 | 26 | 27 | 28 | 22 | 23 |
| 31 | | | | | 29 | 30 |

### AUGUST

| M | T | W | Th | F | Sa | Su |
|---|---|---|----|---|----|----|
| 7 | 1 | 2 | 3 | 4 | 5 | 6 |
| 14 | 8 | 9 | 10 | 11 | 12 | 13 |
| 21 | 15 | 16 | 17 | 18 | 19 | 20 |
| 28 | 22 | 23 | 24 | 25 | 26 | 27 |
| | 29 | 30 | 31 | | | |

### SEPTEMBER

| M | T | W | Th | F | Sa | Su |
|---|---|---|----|---|----|----|
| 4 | 5 | 6 | 7 | 1 | 2 | 3 |
| 11 | 12 | 13 | 14 | 8 | 9 | 10 |
| 18 | 19 | 20 | 21 | 15 | 16 | 17 |
| 25 | 26 | 27 | 28 | 22 | 23 | 24 |
| | | | | 29 | 30 | |

### OCTOBER

| M | T | W | Th | F | Sa | Su |
|---|---|---|----|---|----|----|
| 2 | 3 | 4 | 5 | 6 | 7 | 1 |
| 9 | 10 | 11 | 12 | 13 | 14 | 8 |
| 16 | 17 | 18 | 19 | 20 | 21 | 15 |
| 23 | 24 | 25 | 26 | 27 | 28 | 22 |
| 30 | 31 | | | | | 29 |

### NOVEMBER

| M | T | W | Th | F | Sa | Su |
|---|---|---|----|---|----|----|
| 6 | 7 | 1 | 2 | 3 | 4 | 5 |
| 13 | 14 | 8 | 9 | 10 | 11 | 12 |
| 20 | 21 | 15 | 16 | 17 | 18 | 19 |
| 27 | 28 | 22 | 23 | 24 | 25 | 26 |
| | | 29 | 30 | | | |

### DECEMBER

| M | T | W | Th | F | Sa | Su |
|---|---|---|----|---|----|----|
| 4 | 5 | 6 | 7 | 1 | 2 | 3 |
| 11 | 12 | 13 | 14 | 8 | 9 | 10 |
| 18 | 19 | 20 | 21 | 15 | 16 | 17 |
| 25 | 26 | 27 | 28 | 22 | 23 | 24 |
| | | | | 29 | 30 | 31 |

## Holidays and Notable Dates

| Holiday, etc. | 2010 | 2011 | 2012 | 2013 | 2014 | 2015 | 2016 | 2017 |
|---|---|---|---|---|---|---|---|---|
| New Year's Day | Jan. 1 | Jan. 1 | Jan. 1 | Jan. 1 | Jan. 1 | Jan. 1 | Jan. 1 | Jan. 1 |
| New Year Holiday (England) | — | Jan. 3 | Jan. 2 | — | — | — | — | — |
| New Year Holiday (Scotland) | Jan. 4 | Jan. 4 | Jan. 3 | Jan. 2 | Jan. 2 | Jan. 2 | Jan. 2 | Jan. 2 |
| St David's Day (Wales) | Mar. 1 | Mar. 1 | Mar. 1 | Mar. 1 | Mar. 1 | Mar. 1 | Mar. 1 | Mar. 1 |
| St Patrick's Day (Ireland) | Mar. 17 | Mar. 17 | Mar. 17 | Mar. 17 | Mar. 17 | Mar. 17 | Mar. 17 | Mar. 17 |
| Good Friday | Apr. 2 | Apr. 22 | Apr. 6 | Apr.29 | Apr. 18 | Mar. 3 | Apr. 25 | Mar. 14 |
| Easter Monday | Apr. 5 | Apr. 25 | Apr. 9 | Apr.1 | Apr. 21 | Apr. 6 | Apr. 28 | Mar. 17 |
| St George's Day (England) | Apr. 23 | Apr. 23 | Apr. 23 | Apr. 23 | Apr. 23 | Apr. 23 | Apr. 23 | Apr. 23 |
| May Day Holiday | May 3 | May 2 | May 7 | May 6 | May 5 | May 4 | May 2 | May 1 |
| Queen's Diamond Jubilee | — | — | Jun.4 | — | — | — | — | — |
| Spring Bank Holiday | May 31 | May 30 | Jun.5 | May 27 | May 26 | May 25 | May 30 | May 29 |
| August Bank Holiday | Aug. 30 | Aug. 29 | Aug. 27 | Aug. 26 | Aug. 25 | Aug. 24 | Aug. 29 | Aug. 28 |
| St Andrew's Day (Scotland) | Nov. 30 | Nov. 30 | Nov. 30 | Nov. 30 | Nov. 30 | Nov. 30 | Nov. 30 | Nov. 30 |
| Christmas Day | Dec. 25 | Dec. 25 | Dec. 25 | Dec. 25 | Dec. 25 | Dec. 25 | Dec. 25 | Dec. 25 |
| Boxing Day | Dec. 26 | Dec. 26 | Dec. 26 | Dec. 26 | Dec. 26 | Dec. 26 | Dec. 26 | Dec. 26 |
| Christmas Holiday(s) | — | — | — | — | — | — | Dec. 27 | — |

## Measurement Conversion Tables

The measurements set out below are based upon the following standards set by the Weights and Measures Act 1985, Sched. 1, Pts I to V:

YARD = 0.9144 metre; GALLON = 4.546 09 cubic decimetres or litres; POUND = 0.453 592 37 kilograms

**Measurements of Length**

| Imperial Units of Length | | Metric Equivalents |
|---|---|---|
| Mil | 1/1000 inch | 0.0254 millimetres |
| Inch | 1000 mils | 2.54 centimetres |
| Link | 7.92 inches | 20.1168 centimetres |
| Foot | 12 inches | 0.3048 metres |
| Yard | 3 feet | 0.9144 metres |
| Fathom | 6 feet | 1.8288 metres |
| Cable | 60 feet or 10 fathoms | 18.288 metres |
| Chain | 22 yards (100 links) | 20.1168 metres |
| Furlong | 220 yards | 201.168 metres |
| Mile | 1,760 yards (8 furlongs) | 1.609344 kilometres |
| Nautical mile | 6080 feet | 1.853184 kilometres |

| Metric Units of Length | | Imperial Equivalents |
|---|---|---|
| Micron | 1/1000 millimetre | 0.03937007 mils |
| Millimetre | 1/1000 metre | 0.03937007 inches |
| Centimetre | 1/100 metre | 0.3937 inches |
| Decimetre | 1/10 metre | 3.937 inches |
| Metre | Metre | 1.09361329 yards |
| Kilometre | 1000 metres | 0.62137712 miles or 0.53961 nautical miles |

# Measurements of Area

| *Imperial Units of Area* | *Metric Equivalents* |
|---|---|
| Square inch | 6,4516 square centimetres |
| Square foot | 929.0304 square centimetres |
| Square yard | 0.83613 square metres |
| Square chain | 404.685642 square metres |
| Rood | 1011.714 square metres |
| Acre | 4046.85642 sq. ms or 40.4685642 acres |
| Square mile | 258.998811 hectares |

| | |
|---|---|
| 1/144 square feet | |
| 1/9 square yard | |
| Square yard | |
| 484 square yards | |
| 1,210 square yards | |
| 4 roods or 4840 square yards | |
| 640 acres | |

| *Metric Units of Area* | *Imperial Equivalents* |
|---|---|
| Square millimetre | 0.00155 square inches |
| Square centimetre | 0.155 square inches |
| Square decimetre | 15.5 square inches |
| Square metre | 1.1959 sq. yards or 10.7639 sq. ft |
| Are | 119.599 sq. yds or 0.09884 roods |
| Dekare | 0.2471 acres |
| Hectare | 2.47105 acres |
| Square kilometre | 247.105 acres or 0.3861 square miles |

| | |
|---|---|
| 1/100 square centimetre | |
| 1/100 square decimetre | |
| 1/100 metre | |
| Square metre | |
| 100 square metres | |
| 10 ares | |
| 100 ares (1,000 square metres) | |
| 100 hectares | |

**AL-12**

## Measurements of Volume

| Imperial Units of Volume | | Metric Equivalents |
|---|---|---|
| Cubic inch | | 16.387064 cubic centimetres |
| Cubic foot | 1,728 cubic inches | 28.3168465 decimetres |
| Cubic yard | 27 cubic feet | 0.76455485 cubic metres |

| Metric Units of Volume | | Imperial Equivalents |
|---|---|---|
| Cubic centimetre | 1,000 cubic millimetres | 0.06102374 cubic inches |
| Cubic decimetre | 1,000 cubic centimetres | 0.0353466 cubic feet |
| Cubic metre | 1,000 cubic decimetres | 1.30795061 cubic yards or 35.3147 cu. ft. |

# Measurements of Capacity

| *Imperial, Apothecaries and US Units of Capacity* | | *Metric Equivalents* |
|---|---|---|
| Minim | Minim | 0.0591938 millilitres |
| Fluid Drachm | 60 minims | 0.35516328 centilitres |
| Fluid ounce | 8 fluid drachms | 2.84130625 centilitres |
| US fluid ounce | 1.0408 UK fluid ounces | 29.573522656 millilitres |
| Gill | 5 fluid ounces | 1.42065312 decilitres |
| Pint | 4 gills or 20 fluid ounces | 0.56826125 litres |
| US pint | 0.8327 UK pints or 16 US fluid ounces | 0.47317636 litres |
| Quart | 2 pints or 8 gills | 1.1365225 litres |
| Gallon | 4 quarts.or 1.20095 US gallons | 4.54609 litres |
| US gallon | 0.08327 UK gallons | 3.7854109 litres |
| Peck | 2 gallons or 16 pints | 9.09218 litres |
| Bushel | 4 pecks or 8 gallons | 36.36872 litres |
| Quarter | 8 bushels or 36 pecks | 2.909976 hectolitres |
| Chaldron | 36 bushels or 4 ½ quarters | 13.0927392 hectolitres |

| *Metric Units of Capacity* | | *Imperial Equivalents* |
|---|---|---|
| Millilitre | Millilitre | 0.28156064 fluid drachms |
| Centilitre | 10 millilitres | 0.35195080 fluid ounces |
| Decilitre | 10 centilitres | 0.70390160 gills |
| Litre | 10 decilitres | 1.75975398 pints or 0.21996924 UK gallons |
| Dekalitre | 10 litres | 2.1996924 UK gallons |
| Hectolitre | 10 dekalitres or 100 litres | 21.996824 UK gallons |

Archbold
paragraph
numbers

**AL-13**

*Archbold's Criminal Pleading—2014 ed.*

**AL-14**

## Measurements of Weight

| Imperial and Apothecaries Units of Weight | | Metric Equivalents |
|---|---|---|
| Grain | Grain | 64.79891 milligrams |
| Scruple | 20 grains | 1.2959782 grams |
| Pennyweight | 24 grains | 1.55517384 grams |
| Drachm | 3 scruples or 60 grains | 3.8879346 grams |
| Troy ounce | 8 drachms or 480 grains | 31.1034768 grams |
| Dram | 1/16 ounce | 1.77184519 grams |
| Ounce | 16 drams or 437.5 grains | 28.3495231 gram |
| Troy pound (US) | 12 troy ounces or 5,760 grains | 373.241721 grams |
| Pound | 16 ounces or 7,000 grains | 453.59237 grams or 0.45359237 kilograms |
| Stone | 14 pounds | 6.35029318 kilograms |
| Quarter | 28 pounds or 2 stone | 12.7005863 kilograms |
| Cental | 100 pounds | 45.359237 kilograms |
| Hundredweight | 4 quarters or 112 pounds | 50.8023454 kilograms |
| Short hundredweight (US) | 100 pounds | 45.359237 kilograms |
| Ton (UK or long ton) | 20 cwt or 2,240 pounds | 1.0160469 metric tonnes (tonne) |
| Ton (US or short ton) | 2,000 pounds | 0.90718474 metric tonnes |

| *Metric Units of Weight* | | *Imperial Equivalents* |
|---|---|---|
| Milligram | .001 grams | 0.012432 grains |
| Centigram | .01 grams | 0.15432 grains |
| Decigram | .1 grams | 1.5432 grains |
| Gram | 1 gram | 0.03527396 ounces or 0.03215 troy ounces |
| Dekagram | 10 grams | 0.35273961 ounces |
| Hectogram | 100 grams | 3.52739619 ounces |
| Kilogram | 1,000 grams | 2.20462262 pounds |
| Myriagram | 10 kilograms | 22.0462 pounds |
| Quintal | 100 kilograms | 1.9684 hundredweight |
| Tonne | 1,000 kilograms | 0.984207 UK tons or 1.10231 US tons |

## Measurements of Velocity

| *Per Hour* | *Per Minute* | *Per Second* |
|---|---|---|
| Mile | 88 feet | 17.6 inches per second |
| 1.609344 kph | 26.8224 metres | 44.704 centimetres per second |
| Kilometres | 16.6667 metres | 27.7778 centimetres |
| 0.62137 mph | 54.6806 feet | 10.9361 inches |

## Système Internationale D'unites or SI Units

**AL-16**    1. SI units are increasingly being used to report laboratory results. They have largely replaced earlier systems such as c.g.s. units (centimetre, gram, second), m.k.s. or Giorgi units (metre, kilogram, second), and Imperial units (yard, pound, second).

2. S.I. Units comprise 7 base units and 2 supplementary units. Other units are derived from these. 18 derived units are currently widely accepted.

### Base SI Units

**AL-17**

| Physical Quantity | Unit | Symbol |
|---|---|---|
| Length | metre | m |
| Mass | kilogram | kg |
| Time | second | s |
| Electric current | ampere | A |
| Temperature | kelvin | K |
| Luminosity | candela | cd |
| Amount of substance | mole | mol |
| Plane angle* | radian* | rad |
| Solid angle* | steradian* | sr |

*Supplementary Units

### Derived SI Units

**AL-18**

| Physical Quantity | Unit | Symbol |
|---|---|---|
| Frequency | hertz | Hz |
| Energy | joule | J |
| Force | newton | N |
| Power | watt | W |
| Pressure | pascal | Pa |
| Electric charge | coulomb | C |
| Electric potential difference | volt | V |
| Electrical resistance | ohm | $\Omega$ |
| Electric conductance | siemens | S |
| Electric capacitance | farad | F |
| Magnetic flux | weber | Wb |
| Inductance | henry | H |
| Magnetic flux density | tesla | T |
| Luminous flux | lumen | lm |
| Illuminance | lux | lx |
| Absorbed dose | gray | Gy |
| Activity | becquerel | Bq |
| Dose Equivalence | sievert | Sv |

### Multiples and Subdivisions of SI Units

**AL-19**

| Prefix | Symbol | Power | Value |
|---|---|---|---|
| exa | E | $10^{18}$ | 1,000,000,000,000,000,000 |

| Prefix | Symbol | Power | Value |
| --- | --- | --- | --- |
| peta | P | $10^{15}$ | 1,000,000,000,000,000 |
| tera | T | $10^{12}$ | 1,000,000,000,000 |
| giga | G | $10^{9}$ | 1,000,000,000 |
| mega | M | $10^{6}$ | 1,000,000 |
| kilo | k | $10^{3}$ | 1,000 |
| hecto | h | $10^{2}$ | 100 |
| deca | da | $10$ | 10 |
| - | | | 1 |
| deci | d | $10^{-1}$ | 1/10 |
| centi | c | $10^{-2}$ | 1/100 |
| milli | m | $10^{-3}$ | 1/1,000 |
| micro | μ | $10^{-6}$ | 1/1,000,000 |
| nano | n | $10^{-9}$ | 1/1,000,000,000 |
| pico | p | $10^{-12}$ | 1/1,000,000,000,000 |
| femto | f | $10^{-15}$ | 1/1,000,000,000,000,000 |
| atto | a | $10^{-18}$ | 1/1,000,000,000,000,000,000 |

## International Time Differences

The following time differences are based upon Greenwich Mean Time (GMT).     **AL-20**
British Summer Time (BST) is one hour in advance of GMT.

| Country | | Hours +/- |
|---|---|---|
| Algeria | | +1 hour |
| Argentina | | -3 hours |
| Australia | South Australia | +9½ hours |
| | New South Wales | +10 hours |
| | Tasmania | +10 hours |
| | Victoria | +10 hours |
| Austria | | +1 hour |
| Belgium | | +1 hour |
| Bolivia | | -4 hours |
| Brazil | | -3 hours |
| Bulgaria | | +2 hours |
| Canada | Newfoundland | -3½ hours |
| | Atlantic | -4 hours |
| | Eastern | -5 hours |
| | Central | -6 hours |
| | Mountain | -7 hours |
| | Pacific | -8 hours |
| | Yukon | -9 hours |
| Chile | | -4 hours |
| China | | +8 hours |
| Columbia | | -5 hours |
| Czech Lands | | +1 hour |
| Denmark | | +1 hour |
| Egypt | | +2 hours |
| Finland | | +2 hours |

| Country | Hours +/- |
|---|---|
| France | +1 hour |
| Germany | +1 hour |
| Ghana | |
| Greece | +2 hours |
| Holland | +1 hour |
| Hong Kong | +8 hours |
| Hungary | +1 hour |
| India | +5½ hours |
| Iraq | +3 hours |
| Ireland | |
| Israel | +2 hours |
| Italy | +1 hour |
| Jamaica | -5 hours |
| Japan | +9 hours |
| Kenya | +3 hours |

| Country | Hours +/- |
|---|---|
| Luxembourg | +1 hour |
| Malaysia | +8 hours |
| Malta | +1 hour |
| Morocco | |
| New Zealand | +12 hours |
| Nigeria | +1 hour |
| Norway | +1 hour |
| Peru | -5 hours |
| Philippines | +8 hours |
| Poland | +1 hour |
| Portugal | |
| Romania | +2 hours |
| Russia | |
|   Moscow | +3 hours |
|   Vladivostock | +10 hours |
| Saudi Arabia | +3 hours |
| Serbia | +1 hours |
| Singapore | +8 hours |
| South Africa | +2 hours |
| Spain | +1 hour |
| Sri Lanka | +5½ hours |
| Sweden | +1 hour |
| Switzerland | +1 hour |
| Taiwan | +8 hours |
| Thailand | +7 hours |
| Tunisia | +1 hour |
| Turkey | +2 hours |

| Country | | Hours +/- |
|---|---|---|
| Ukraine | | +3 hours |
| United Arab Emirates | | +4 hours |
| United States | Eastern | -5 hours |
| | Central | -6 hours |
| | Mountain | -7 hours |
| | Pacific | -8 hours |
| Zambia | | +2 hours |
| Zimbabwe | | +2 hours |

## Stopping Distances

| Speed (m.p.h.) | Stopping distance (feet) |
|---|---|
| 20 | 40 |
| 30 | 75 |
| 40 | 120 |
| 50 | 175 |
| 60 | 240 |
| 70 | 315 |

## Useful Contact Details

|  | Telephone | Email |
|---|---|---|
| *Courts, etc.* | | |
| House of Lords, Judicial Office | (020) 7219 3111 | |
| Royal Courts of Justice | (020) 7947 6000 | |
| Registrar, Criminal Appeals | (020) 7947 6103 | |
| Criminal Appeal Office | (020) 7947 6011 | Criminalappealoffice.generaloffice@hmcourts-service.x.gsi.gov.uk |
| Administrative Court Office | (020) 7947 6205 | |
| *Official Bodies* | | |
| Home Office | (020) 7035 4848 | public.enquiries@homeoffice.gsi.gov.uk |
| Serious Fraud Office | (020) 7239 7272 | public.enquiries@sfo.gsi.gov.uk |
| H.M. Revenue and Customs | 0845 010 9000 | Enquiries.estn@hmrc.gsi.gov.uk This address handles all enquiries related to VAT, Excise and other duties formerly administered by HM Customs and Excise (with the exception of International Trade) |
| New Scotland Yard | (020) 7230 1212 | new.scotland.yard@met.police.uk |
| City of London Police | (020) 7601 2222 | postmaster@cityoflondon.police.uk |
| British Transport Police | 0800 40 50 40 | |
| *Others* | | |
| Justice | (020) 7329 5100 | admin@justice.org.uk |
| Liberty | (020) 7403 3888 | |
| Bar Council | (020) 7242 0082 | |
| Bar Council Ethical Enquiries Line | (020) 7611 1307 | |
| Bar Standards Board | (020) 7611 1444 | |

|  | *Telephone* | *Email* |
|---|---|---|
| Law Society — Lawyerline | 0870 606 2588 | |
| Law Society — Practice Advice Service | 0870 606 2522 | |

# INDEX

## LEGAL TAXONOMY
### FROM SWEET & MAXWELL

This index has been prepared using Sweet and Maxwell's Legal Taxonomy. Main index entries conform to keywords provided by the Legal Taxonomy except where references to specific documents or non-standard terms (denoted by quotation marks) have been included. These keywords provide a means of identifying similar concepts in other Sweet & Maxwell publications and online services to which keywords from the Legal Taxonomy have been applied. Readers may find some minor differences between terms used in the text and those which appear in the index. Suggestions to *sweetandmaxwell.taxonomy@thomson.com*.

All references are to paragraph numbers.